MATTHEW

MATTHEW

A Commentary on His Literary and Theological Art

by

Robert H. Gundry

WILLIAM B. EERDMANS PUBLISHING COMPANY
GRAND RAPIDS, MICHIGAN

Copyright © 1982 by Wm. B. Eerdmans Publishing Company
255 Jefferson Ave., S.E., Grand Rapids, MI 49503

Library of Congress Cataloging in Publication Data

Gundry, Robert Horton.
Matthew, a commentary on his literary
and theological art.

Bibliography, p. xii.
Includes indexes.
1. Bible. N.T. Matthew—Commentaries.   I. Bible.
N.T. Matthew.   II. Title.
BS2575.3.G85   226'.206   81-12448
ISBN 0-8028-3549-X   AACR2

Contents

v

CONTENTS

CONTENTS

vii

CONTENTS

CONTENTS

CONTENTS

Preface

My first word is one of thanks to Mr. Marlin VanElderen and those associated with him at Wm. B. Eerdmans Publishing Company for taking on the publication of this commentary and carrying it out with characteristic expertise. Thanks also go to my typist, Mrs. Betty Bouslough, and to my longsuffering family: to Lois for wifely encouragement, to Judy and Connie for their understanding, and to Mark for good humor in tolerating my habit of calling him "Matthew" while the commentary was being written.

I hope that the commentary will not only shed light on the text of Matthew, but also contribute to solving the synoptic problem, which has come under renewed discussion. In particular, the commentary should, I believe, confirm Matthew's use of Mark and Matthew's and Luke's use of non-Markan tradition, but broaden our concept of that tradition considerably beyond the limits usually imposed on Q and favor Luke's using Matthew as a secondary source in addition to his primary sources Mark and a broadened Q.

It is unfortunate from my standpoint that the comments on the nativity story must come first. Those comments had to be completely rewritten once I saw how freely and creatively Matthew edited his sources in the rest of his gospel. I can only urge the reader to withhold negative judgment against my advocating that Matthew used haggadic and midrashic techniques on the very tradition later appearing in the early chapters of Luke—and to reread the sections on Matthew 1–2 after perusing the rest of the commentary for the way Matthew treats his sources.

ROBERT H. GUNDRY

Westmont College
Santa Barbara, California

xi

Select Bibliography

This bibliography is only representative of the vast amount of material published on Matthew as a whole, on particular passages and topics within Matthew, and on larger matters related to Matthew or incorporating it. Interested readers can easily supplement the bibliography by going to standard introductions to the NT, other commentaries on Matthew, monographs on Matthean and synoptic passages and themes, general works on the gospels and the NT, and the bibliographical aids mentioned in the introduction to this commentary. It needs emphasis, however, that illumination of Matthew's text often comes from unexpected sources never mentioned in the places usually mined for bibliographical information; so there is no substitute for wide reading in New Testament and cognate studies. The following selections are based variously on scholarly quality, breadth of implication for Matthean studies, recency of publication, and attainment of recognition as a standard.

Abel, E. L. "Who Wrote Matthew?" *NTS* 17 (1970-71) 138-52.

Albright, W. F., and Mann, C. S. *Matthew.* AB 26. New York: Doubleday, 1971.

Allen, W. C. *A Critical and Exegetical Commentary on the Gospel according to S. Matthew.* ICC. 3rd ed. Edinburgh: T. & T. Clark, 1912.

Bacon, B. W. "The 'Five Books' of Matthew against the Jews," *Expositor* 15, 8th series (1918) 56-66.

_____. *Studies in Matthew.* New York: Holt, 1930.

Banks, R. *Jesus and the Law in the Synoptic Tradition.* SNTSMS 28. New York: Cambridge, 1975.

Benoit, P., and Boismard, M-É. *Synopse des quatres évangiles en francais.* Vol. 2. *Commentaire* (by Boismard). Paris: Cerf, 1972.

Blair, E. P. *Jesus in the Gospel of Matthew.* Nashville: Abingdon, 1960.

Bonnard, P. *L'Évangile selon saint Matthieu.* CNT 1. 2nd ed. Neuchâtel: Delachaux et Niestlé, 1970.

Bornkamm, G., Barth, G., and Held, H. J. *Tradition and Interpretation in Matthew.* NTL. Philadelphia: Westminster, 1963.

Broadus, J. A. *Commentary on the Gospel of Matthew.* Philadelphia: American Baptist Publication Society, 1886.

Brown, R. E. *The Birth of the Messiah*. Garden City, N.Y.: Doubleday, 1977.

Carlston, C. E. *The Parables in the Triple Tradition*. Philadelphia: Fortress, 1975.

Christian, P. *Jesus und seine Geringsten Brüder*. Erfurter Theologische Schriften 12. Leipzig: St. Benno, 1975.

Clark, K. W. "The Gentile Bias in Matthew," *JBL* 66 (1947) 165-72.

Cope, O. Lamar. *Matthew: A Scribe Trained for the Kingdom of Heaven*. CBQMS 5. Washington: Catholic Biblical Association, 1976.

Dahl, N. A. "Die Passiongeschichte bei Matthäus," *NTS* 2 (1955-56) 17-32.

Davies, W. D. *The Setting of the Sermon on the Mount*. Cambridge: University Press, 1964.

Davis, C. T. "Tradition and Redaction in Matthew 1:18-2:23," *JBL* 90 (1971) 404-21.

Derrett, J. D. M. *Jesus's Audience*. New York: Seabury, 1974.

————. *Law in the New Testament*. London: Darton, Longman & Todd, 1970.

————. *Studies in the New Testament*. 2 vols. Leiden: Brill, 1977-1978.

Descamps, A. "Le Christianisme comme justice dans le Premier Évangile," *ETL* 22 (1946) 5-33.

Didier, M., ed. *L'Évangile selon Matthieu. Rédaction et théologie*. Journées bibliques de Louvain, 1970. BETL 29. Gembloux: Duculot, 1972.

Dobschütz, E. von. "Matthäus als Rabbi und Katechet," *ZNW* 27 (1928) 338-48.

Dodd, C. H. *New Testament Studies*. New York: Scribner's, 1954. Pp. 53-66 on "Matthew and Paul."

Doeve, J. W. *Jewish Hermeneutics in the Synoptic Gospels and Acts*. Assen: Van Gorcum, 1954.

Ellis, P. F. *Matthew: His Mind and His Message*. Collegeville, Minn.: Liturgical Press, 1974.

Farrer, A. *St. Matthew and St. Mark*. 2nd ed. Westminster: Dacre, 1966.

Fenton, J. C. "Inclusio and Chiasmus in Matthew," *SE I*. TU 73. Berlin: Akademie, 1959. Pp. 174-79.

Fenton, J. C. *The Gospel of St. Matthew*. Pelican Gospel Commentaries. Baltimore: Penguin, 1964.

Fiedler, P. *Die Formel "und siehe" im Neuen Testament*. SANT 20. Munich: Kösel, 1969.

Frankemölle, H. "Amtskritik im Matthäusevangelium?" *Bib* 54 (1973) 247-62.

————. *Jahwebund und Kirche Christi*. NTAbh 10. Münster: Aschendorff, 1974.

Fuchs, A. *Sprachliche Untersuchungen zu Matthäus und Lukas*. AnBib 49. Rome: Biblical Institute, 1971.

Gaechter, P. *Die literarische Kunst im Matthäus-Evangelium*. SBS 7. Stuttgart: KBW, 1966.

————. *Das Matthäus-Evangelium*. Innsbruck: Tyrolia, 1964.

Gaston, L. "The Messiah of Israel as Teacher of the Gentiles," *Int* 29 (1975) 24-40.

Gerhardsson, B. *The Testing of God's Son*. ConBNT 2/1. Lund: Gleerup, 1966.

————. "Gottes Sohn als Diener Gottes. Messias, Agape, und Himmelsherrschaft nach dem Matthäusevangelium," *ST* 27 (1973) 73-106.

Gibbs, J. M. "Purpose and Pattern in Matthew's Use of the Title 'Son of David,'" *NTS* 10 (1963-64) 446-64.

————. "The Son of God as the Torah Incarnate in Matthew," *SE IV*. TU 102. Berlin: Akademie, 1968. Pp. 38-46.

Glasson, T. F. "Anti-Pharisaism in St. Matthew," *JQR* 51 (1960-61) 316-20.

Gnilka, J. "Die Kirche des Matthäus und die Gemeinde von Qumran," *BZ* ns 7 (1963) 43-63.

Goodspeed, E. J. *Matthew, Apostle and Evangelist*. Philadelphia: Winston, 1959.

Goulder, M. D. *Midrash and Lection in Matthew*. London: SPCK, 1974.

Green, H. B. *The Gospel according to Matthew*. New Clarendon Bible. New York: Oxford, 1975.

Grundmann, W. *Das Evangelium nach Matthäus*. THKNT 1. 3rd ed. Berlin: Evangelische Verlagsanstalt, 1972.

Gundry, R. H. *The Use of the Old Testament in St. Matthew's Gospel*. NovTSup 18. Leiden: Brill, 1967.

Hare, D. R. A. *The Theme of the Jewish Persecution of Christians in the Gospel according to St. Matthew*. SNTSMS 6. Cambridge: University Press, 1967.

Harrington, D. J. "Matthean Studies since Joachim Rohde," *HeyJ* 16 (1975) 375-88.

Hill, D. *The Gospel of Matthew*. NCB. London: Marshall, Morgan & Scott, 1972.

Hoffman, P., Brox, N., and Pesch, W., eds. *Orientierung an Jesus. Zur Theologie der Synoptiker. Für Josef Schmid*. Freiburg: Herder, 1973.

Hummel, R. *Die Auseinandersetzung zwischen Kirche und Judentum im Matthäusevangelium*. BEvT 33. 2nd ed. Munich: Kaiser, 1966.

Jeremias, J. *Abba*. Göttingen: Vandenhoeck & Ruprecht, 1966.

Kilpatrick, G. D. *The Origins of the Gospel according to St. Matthew*. Oxford: Clarendon, 1946.

Kingsbury, J. D. *The Parables of Jesus in Matthew 13*. Richmond: John Knox, 1969.

————. *Matthew: Structure, Christology, Kingdom*. Philadelphia: Fortress, 1975.

————. "The Title 'Son of David' in Matthew's Gospel," *JBL* 95 (1976) 591-602.

————. "The Verb *Akolouthein* ('To Follow') as an Index of Matthew's View of his Community," *JBL* 97 (1978) 56-73.

Klostermann, E. *Das Matthäusevangelium*. HNT 4. 4th ed. Tübingen: Mohr (Siebeck), 1971.

Knox, W. L. *The Sources of the Synoptic Gospels*. Vol. 2. *St. Luke and St. Matthew*. Ed. H. Chadwick. Cambridge: University Press, 1957.

Kratz, R. *Auferweckung als Befreiung*. SBS 65. Stuttgart: KBW, 1973.

Krentz, E. "The Extent of Matthew's Prologue: Towards the Structure of the First Gospel," *JBL* 83 (1964) 409-14.

Kretzer, A. *Die Herrschaft der Himmel und die Söhne des Reiches*. SBM 10. Stuttgart: KBW, 1971.

Kruijf, T. De. *Der Sohn des lebendigen Gottes*. AnBib 16. Rome: Pontifical Biblical Institute, 1962.

Künzel, G. *Studien zum Gemeindeverständnis des Matthäus-Evangeliums*. Calwer Theologische Monographien, Reihe A: Bibelwissenschaft 10. Stuttgart: Calwer, 1978.

Lagrange, M.-J. *Évangile selon Saint Matthieu*. EBib. 8th ed. Paris: Gabalda, 1948.

Lange, J. *Das Erscheinen des Auferstandenen im Evangelium nach Mattäus*. Forschung zur Bibel 11. Würzburg: Echter, 1973.

Lohmeyer, E. *Das Evangelium des Matthäus*. Ed. W. Schmauch. MeyerK, Sonderband. 4th ed. Göttingen: Vandenhoeck & Ruprecht, 1967.

Lohr, C. H. "Oral Techniques in the Gospel of Matthew," *CBQ* 23 (1961) 403-35.

Luz, U. "Die Jünger im Matthäusevangelium," *ZNW* 62 (1971) 141-71.

McConnell, R. S. *Law and Prophecy in Matthew's Gospel*. Basel: Reinhardt, 1969.

McKenzie, J. L. "The Gospel according to Matthew," *Jerome Biblical Commentary II*. Eds. R. E. Brown et al. Englewood Cliffs, N. J.: Prentice-Hall, 1968. Pp. 62-114.

McNeile, A. H. *The Gospel according to St. Matthew*. London: Macmillan, 1915.

Massaux, É. *Influence de l'évangile de saint Matthieu sur la littérature chrétienne avant saint Irénée*. Louvain: Publications Universitaires, 1950.

Meier, J. P. *Law and History in Matthew's Gospel*. AnBib 71. Rome: Biblical Institute, 1976.

————. *Matthew*. NT Message 3. Wilmington, Del.: Glazier, 1980.

————. *The Vision of Matthew*. Theological Inquiries. New York: Paulist, 1979.

Michaelis, W. *Das Evangelium nach Matthäus*. 2 vols. Zürich: Zwingli, 1948-49.

Neirynck, F. "La rédaction matthéenne et la structure du premier évangile," *ETL* 43 (1967) 41-73.

Nellessen, E. *Das Kind und seine Mutter*. SBS 39. Stuttgart: KBW, 1970.

Nepper-Christensen, P. *Das Matthäusevangelium. Ein judenchristliches Evangelium?* Acta Theologica Danica 1. Aarhus: Universitetsforlaget, 1958.

Nolan, B. M. *The Royal Son of God*. OBO 23. Fribourg: Editions Universitaires, 1979.

Paul, A. *L'Évangile de l'Enfance selon saint Matthieu*. Lire la Bible 17. Paris: Cerf, 1968.

Pesch, R. "Eine alttestamentliche Ausführungsformel im Matthäus-Evangelium," *BZ* 10 (1966) 220-45; 11 (1967) 79-95.

————. "Der Gottessohn im matthäischen Evangelienprolog (Mt 1-2)," *Bib* 48 (1967) 395-420.

Pesch, W., ed. *Jesus in den Evangelien*. SBS 45. Stuttgart: KBW, 1970.

Plummer, A. *An Exegetical Commentary on the Gospel according to S. Matthew*. 5th ed. London: E. Stock, 1920.

Pregeant, R. *Christology Beyond Dogma: Matthew's Christ in Process Hermeneutic*. Semeia Supplements 7. Philadelphia: Fortress, 1978.

Radermakers, J. *Au fil de l'évangile selon saint Matthieu*. 2 vols. Heverlee-Louvain: Institut d'Etudes Théologiques, 1972.

Rigaux, B. *The Testimony of St. Matthew*. Chicago: Franciscan Herald, 1968.

Rohde, J. *Rediscovering the Teaching of the Evangelists*. NTL. Philadelphia: Westminster, 1968.

Rothfuchs, W. *Die Erfüllungszitate des Matthäus-Evangeliums*. BWANT 88. Stuttgart: Kohlhammer, 1969.

Schille, G. "Das Evangelium des Matthäus als Katechismus," *NTS* 4 (1957-58) 101-14.

Schlatter, A. *Der Evangelist Matthäus*. 6th ed. Stuttgart: Calwer, 1963.

_____. *Die Kirche des Matthäus*. BFCT 33/1. Gütersloh: Bertelsmann, 1929.

Schmid, J. *Das Evangelium nach Mätthaus*. RNT 1. 5th ed. Regensburg: Pustet, 1965.

Schniewind, J. *Das Evangelium nach Matthäus*. NTD 2. 12th ed. Göttingen: Vandenhoeck & Ruprecht, 1968.

Schweizer, E. "Christianity of the Circumcised and Judaism of the Uncircumcised," *Jews, Greeks and Christians*. Essays in Honor of W. D. Davies. Ed. R. Hammerton-Kelly and R. Scroggs. SJLA 21. Leiden: Brill, 1976. Pp. 245-60.

_____. "Observance of the Law and Charismatic Activity in Matthew," *NTS* 16 (1969-70) 213-30.

_____. *The Good News according to Matthew*. Atlanta: John Knox, 1975.

_____. *Matthäus und seine Gemeinde*. SBS 71. Stuttgart: KBW, 1974.

Senior, D. *The Passion Narrative according to Matthew*. BETL 39. Gembloux: Duculot, 1975.

Soares Prabhu, G. M. *The Formula Quotations in the Infancy Narrative of Matthew*. AnBib 63. Rome: Biblical Institute, 1976.

Stendahl, K. "Matthew," *Peake's Commentary on the Bible*. Ed. M. Black and H. H. Rowley. New York: Nelson, 1962. Pp. 769-98.

_____. "Quis et Unde? An Analysis of Mt. 1-2," *Judentum, Urchristentum, Kirche. Festschrift für Joachim Jeremias*. Ed. W. Eltester. BZNW 26. 2nd ed. Berlin: Töpelmann, 1964. Pp. 94-105.

_____. *The School of St. Matthew and Its Use of the Old Testament*. ASNU 20. 2nd ed. Lund: Gleerup, 1968.

Stonehouse, N. B. *Origins of the Synoptic Gospels*. Grand Rapids: Eerdmans, 1963.

Strecker, G. *Der Weg der Gerechtigkeit*. FRLANT 82. 3rd ed. Göttingen: Vandenhoeck & Ruprecht, 1971.

Suggs, M. J. *Wisdom, Christology, and Law in Matthew's Gospel*. Cambridge, Mass.: Harvard, 1970.

Tagawa, K. "People and Community in the Gospel of Matthew," *NTS* 16 (1969-70) 149-62.

Thieme, K. "Matthäus, der schriftgelehrte Evangelist," *Judaica* 5 (1949) 130-52.

Thompson, W. G. *Matthew's Advice to a Divided Community*. AnBib 44. Rome: Pontifical Biblical Institute, 1970.

_____. "An Historical Perspective in the Gospel of Matthew," *JBL* 93 (1974) 243-62.

Thysman, R. *Communauté et directives éthiques. La catéchèse de Matthieu*. Recherches et Synthèses: Section d'exégèse 1. Gembloux: Duculot, 1974.

Trilling, W. *Das wahre Israel*. SANT 10. 3rd ed. Munich: Kösel, 1964.

Van Tilborg, S. *The Jewish Leaders in Matthew*. Leiden: Brill, 1972.

Vögtle, A. *Messias und Gottessohn*. Theologische Perspektiven. Düsseldorf: Patmos, 1971.

Walker, R. *Die Heilsgeschichte im ersten Evangelium*. FRLANT 91. Göttingen: Vandenhoeck & Ruprecht, 1967.

Zahn, T. *Das Evangelium des Matthäus*. Kommentar zum Neuen Testament 1. 4th ed. Leipzig: Deichert, 1922.

Zinniker, F. *Probleme der sogenannten Kindheitsgeschichte bei Matthäus*. Fribourg: Paulusverlag, 1972.

Zumstein, J. *La condition du croyant dans l'évangile selon Matthieu*. OBO 16. Fribourg: Editions Universitaires, 1977.

Abbreviations

Abbreviations are those standardized in the *Journal of Biblical Literature* 95 (1976) 335-46, plus the ones listed below:

Aland = *Synopsis Quattuor Evangeliorum* (ed. K. Aland; Stuttgart: Württembergische Bibelanstalt, 1964)

Black, *Aramaic Approach* = M. Black, *An Aramaic Approach to the Gospels and Acts* (3rd ed.; Oxford: Clarendon, 1967)

Derrett, *Law in the NT* = J. D. M. Derrett, *Law in the New Testament* (London: Darton, Longman & Todd, 1970)

Gundry, "Recent Investigations" = R. H. Gundry, "Recent Investigations into the Literary Genre 'Gospel,' " *New Dimensions in New Testament Study* (ed. R. N. Longenecker and M. C. Tenney; Grand Rapids: Zondervan, 1974) 97-114.

Gundry, *Use of the OT* = R. H. Gundry, *The Use of the Old Testament in St. Matthew's Gospel* (NovTSup 18; Leiden: Brill, 1967)

Hatch and Redpath = E. Hatch and H. Redpath, *A Concordance to the Septuagint* (3rd ed.; Graz: Akademische Druck- u. Verlagsanstalt, 1954)

Jeremias, *Eucharistic Words* = J. Jeremias, *The Eucharistic Words of Jesus* (London: SCM, 1966)

Jeremias, *NT Theology* = J. Jeremias, *New Testament Theology* (New York: Scribners, 1971)

Jeremias, *Parables* = J. Jeremias, *The Parables of Jesus* (2nd ed.; New York: Scribners, 1963)

JETS = *Journal of the Evangelical Theological Society*

KBW = Katholisches Bibelwerk

Metzger, *Textual Commentary* = Bruce M. Metzger, *A Textual Commentary on the Greek New Testament* (New York: United Bible Societies, 1971)

UBS = *The Greek New Testament* (ed. K. Aland, M. Black, C. M. Martini, Bruce M. Metzger, and A. Wikgren; 3rd ed.; New York: United Bible Societies, 1975)

v.l. = varia lectio, variant reading

Note: other commentaries on Matthew are referred to by the last names of their authors; and unless otherwise indicated, OT references conform to the chapter and verse divisions in Kittel-Kahle, *Biblica Hebraica*, followed by those of the English Bible (and sometimes of the LXX), where different.

Introduction

SOME CHARACTERISTICS OF THE
PRESENT COMMENTARY
INCLUDING THE USE OF WORD-STATISTICS

From one standpoint, commentaries fall into two classes: (1) heavily documented commentaries that include a great deal of interplay with views expressed in other works of modern scholarship, and (2) commentaries in which the author fully develops his own line of interpretation. The volume of publications devoted to study of the gospels has increased immensely in recent years. Consequently, a commentary of manageable and publishable size cannot carry both heavily documented interplay and full development of the favored line. Furthermore, heavily documented commentaries give only the appearance of thoroughness. Limitations of space inevitably cause worthy possibilities of interpretation to go unconsidered.

On the other hand, the ready availability of comprehensive and up-to-date bibliographical aids and the abundance of monographs and articles devoted to discussion of opposing views make heavy documentation a doubtful use of space (see esp. *NTA*; Bruce M. Metzger, *Index to Periodical Literature on Christ and the Gospels* [NTTS 6; Leiden: Brill, 1966]; idem, *Index of Articles on the New Testament and the Early Church Published in Festschriften* [SBLMS 5; Philadelphia: Society of Biblical Literature, 1951, supplemented in 1955]; P.-E. Langevin, *Bibliographie biblique* [2 vols.; Quebec: Laval, 1972-78]; *Elenchus Bibliographicus Biblicus; Internationale Zeitschriftenschau für Bibelwissenschaft und Grenzgebiete*; and Günther Wagner's *New Testament Exegetical Bibliographical Aids*). Better to do justice to the favored line of interpretation, then, and let readers make critical comparisons of their own. For this reason, the present commentary gives a fairly complete account of Matthew's literary and theological art. Even small peculiarities gain attention. Often their significance surpasses expectation and fits into a larger picture. References to Gundry, *Use of the OT*, have saved some duplication of textual comparisons; but where such comparisons affect our understanding of Matthew's theological message, the commentary includes them.

Similarly, we already have a good supply of comparative materials in the history of religions. Outstanding examples come to mind in the commentaries of P. Billerbeck (in association with H. L. Strack), A. Schlatter,

1

and E. Klostermann, and in H. Braun's *Qumran und das Neue Testament* (Tübingen: Mohr, 1966) and the writings of J. Jeremias. The present commentary therefore carries only the most germane references of this sort. Nevertheless, the debt here owed to both primary and secondary sources defies calculation. My own translations of ancient texts tend toward literalism for closer examination of the original languages.

Disregard of the Gospel of Thomas reflects the belief that that gospel depends almost entirely on the canonical gospels rather than on other dominical traditions. This commentary does not provide a suitable arena for arguing in favor of that belief, but at least the demonstration of Matthew's redaction in those features of his text shared only with the Gospel of Thomas will partly substantiate it. On this topic and the whole question of gospels as a literary genre and the relationship of various answers to modern theological currents, see Gundry, "Recent Investigations" 97-114.

Parallels in John to features of Matthew not shared with Mark or Luke are here presumed to stem from direct or indirect influence of Matthew on John. As before, this commentary does not provide a suitable arena to argue in favor of that presumption. But again, the demonstration of redaction by Matthew in those features shared only with John will offer partial substantiation.

Limitations of space, theological commitment to the canonical text (not to antecedent traditions or to supposedly brute facts of history) as divine revelation, and scepticism about the scientific validity of form criticism (see the above-mentioned "Recent Investigations") have led to an emphasis on the meaning of Matthew's text. This meaning best comes to light through the enterprise of so-called redaction criticism, i.e., study of the way the evangelist edits the dominical tradition and editorializes on it. Such study demands attention to the text of Matthew in its own right. But the intent of the first evangelist appears even more clearly in a comparison of his gospel with the other synoptics. The comparison undertaken here will show that the peculiarities of Matthew derive almost wholly from his own revisions of and additions to Mark and the materials shared only with Luke (i.e., the materials usually designated Q). For Matthew, in other words, the need to attempt form-critical extrapolation back to oral tradition reduces nearly to the vanishing point. This reduction has obvious and important implications for the historical reconstruction of Jesus' life and for the development of NT theology.

In examining the way Matthew uses Mark and the materials shared only with Luke, we discover the outstanding features of his style. These, in turn, help us identify the outstanding features of his theology. We will quickly learn that he delights in conforming phraseology to the OT, as well as in quoting the OT explicitly, and that he likes to put his materials in parallelistic form, often by tightening the parallelism that already characterizes the tradition. Normally, the traditional parallelism has a looseness typical of extemporaneous speech, and Matthew's parallelism a closeness that characterizes careful writing. See the Topical Index for a number of other stylistic and theological traits.

Matthew's choice of words also betrays his editorial hand. Here statistics concerning word frequency come under consideration. In large measure the way we appraise their significance will depend on our view of the synoptic problem. If Matthew wrote first, we might assign words appearing with special frequency in his gospel to the tradition that came to him. But if Mark wrote first and Matthew and Luke used Mark and shared another tradition, such words signal Matthew's editorial work. As already implied, this commentary rests on the latter hypothesis, mainly because it provides the framework for what seem to be the most cogent explanations of the similarities and differences of detail among the synoptics and partly because Matthew's specially frequent words appear in obviously editorial passages as well as in traditional materials (though conceivably we might explain this phenomenon as due to an influence of the tradition on Matthew's own diction). The order of materials has not played a major role; for often considerations of this kind can be reversed to harmonize with another theory.

Insertions of words in paralleled materials show with utmost clarity Matthew's fondness for the words inserted. Occurrences of words in unparalleled passages occupy a place of secondary importance; for though they might come from an unshared tradition, these passages often turn out to be constructs of the first evangelist himself. If he inserts his pet expressions in the tradition, he would naturally use them when writing creatively. Thus we may feel free to attribute unparalleled passages either to unshared but edited tradition or—given enough evidence of his favorite diction, style, and theology—to the first evangelist himself.

Theoretically, in material shared only with Luke the peculiar wording of Matthew might be regarded as belonging to the tradition, and Luke's as resulting from redaction by Luke. Statistics occasionally point in this direction. Usually, however, Matthew also inserts his words and expressions in Mark's material and includes them in unique passages as well. This practice favors insertion by Matthew in material shared only with Luke.

That another synoptist uses a word or phrase more often than Matthew uses it does not necessarily imply its falling outside the category of a Mattheanism, i.e., outside Matthew's favorite diction. For, on the one hand, considerations besides diction may lead Matthew to omit even his favorite expressions now and then. On the other hand, another evangelist may like these expressions even more and may therefore insert them in the tradition more often. We need to hold open the latter possibility especially for words that appear in Luke more often than in Matthew. *Overall statistical comparisons among the synoptics do not count for very much, then; but Matthew's insertions in common tradition and inclusions in passages peculiar to his gospel stand out as significant. Accordingly, the body of the commentary contains these two statistics in that order. Full statistics are usually reserved for the Greek Index, which readers are urged to consult.*

The divisions in Aland's synopsis provide the standard by which words are classified as insertions or as part of distinctive material. That is to say, when Matthew alone writes words in a division of that synopsis where Mark or Luke or both of them offer at least some parallel material, these words count as insertions. If the passage as defined by Aland lacks any parallels, all its words belong to the class of words in distinctive material. Though we might disagree with Aland's divisions occasionally, and do so in a way that would necessitate a slight revision of the statistics, nothing essential rides on such disagreements.

By choosing to make whole passages rather than individual sentences our standard of judgment, we get a higher number of insertions and a lower number of occurrences in unparalleled material. This choice reflects an openness to Matthean creativity, as opposed to form critics' assigning unparalleled sentences to earlier traditions of a piecemeal sort; and it is justified by Matthew's many insertions in shared sentences of the very same words that often make up unshared sentences. Contrast L. Gaston, *Horae Synopticae Electronicae* (SBLSBS 3; Missoula, Montana: Society of Biblical Literature, 1973).

Words in sayings repeated by Matthew but occurring only once in the other synoptics count once as paralleled. Beyond that they count for one or the other kind of unparalleled occurrences, because the repetitions show Matthew's special interest in the terminology and meaning of the saying. Very occasionally a word is counted as unparalleled even though it occurs in a parallel. But this happens only when the parallel listed by Aland seems extremely distant or subtle. Though it is lacking in his synopsis, Jas 5:12 parallels Matt 5:33-37. The statistics reflect this parallel.

If comparison shows only a difference between simple and compound forms of a word, the occurrence in Matthew falls into the unimportant class of paralleled occurrences. Words in OT quotations absent from the other synoptics count as unparalleled, however, because they sometimes represent Matthew's own translation. Even when they do not (as in quotations of the LXX), those words may have helped attract the evangelist to the OT passage. Now and then a word does not appear in an exactly parallel statement written by Mark or Luke, but does occur in the immediate vicinity. It becomes a matter of judgment whether the uses are different enough to warrant counting the Matthean occurrence as unparalleled. Uncertain text-critical judgments lead to a hyphen, meaning "or," in the statistics. All of this results in a few (but very few) differences from the figures found in R. Morgenthaler's *Statistik des neutestamentlichen Wortschatzes* (Zürich: Gotthelf, 1958), and *Vollständige Konkordanz zum Griechischen Neuen Testament. Band II. Specialübersichten* (ed. K. Aland; New York: Walter de Gruyter, 1978) 1-305. Seldom, if ever, do these differences seriously affect the evidence for and against Mattheanisms. To set up a numerical rule regarding what does and does not constitute a Mattheanism would be to overlook differences among words. Because of their meanings some words are more likely to be used, others less likely. Each word and each set of words has to be treated individually. It is even possible for an author to have a penchant for certain words that are used quite commonly. That a word is common should not keep it from being recognized as a Mattheanism, then, if Matthew habitually inserts it and uses it in unique passages.

Observations made throughout the commentary will lead to the following conclusions. Both Matthew and Luke used Mark and non-Markan tradition in common. The shared non-Markan tradition included not only the material usually designated Q, but also the nativity story and some of the materials usually regarded as peculiar to Matthew (M) and Luke (L). Q included more than is usually thought, in other words; but at times Matthew redacted it so freely that his drawing on Q has gone unrecognized and separate traditions have wrongly been posited. For example, the parable of the two sons (21:28-32) does not come from a separate tradition, but from the tradition represented by the parable of the prodigal son and his elder brother (Luke 15:11-32). Close similarities between Matthew and Luke in the non-Markan tradition require that they used that tradition in an already existing Greek form. Whether small or large, differences between Matthew and Luke in their use of the non-Markan tradition are better explained as redactions of its Greek form than as different translations of a Semitic original. Luke appears not to have edited this tradition so radically as Matthew did, for the differences on Matthew's side usually turn out to be the same kinds of differences that characterize Matthew in comparison with Mark (cf. G. B. Caird in *ExpTim* 87 [1976] 169-70).

Because Mattheanisms occasionally appear as foreign bodies in Luke, we also have to think of Luke's using Matthew as an overlay on his primary sources. That Matthew's gospel did not provide one of those sources is shown by the disarrangement of Matthean material we would otherwise have to suppose. But that the Matthean foreign bodies come from our present Gospel of Matthew, not from an earlier source, is shown by their conforming to Matthew's distinctive diction, style, and theology as evident elsewhere and by their frequently depending for their point on Matthew's context (often stemming from Mark), whereas in Luke they lack contextual point. Therefore we need not fret over the numerous minor agreements of Matthew and Luke against Mark that do not fall into the category of Mattheanisms (see F. Neirynck, *The Minor Agreements of Matthew and Luke against Mark* [BETL 37; Leuven: Leuven University Press, 1974]). They, too, may represent Matthean overlay in Luke, though apart from the Matthean foreign bodies we would not have known so with any confidence.

THE THEOLOGY OF MATTHEW

By noting Matthew's emphases we can infer the situation in which he wrote and the purposes for which he wrote. This will also reveal the theology characteristic of his gospel. Here we can mention only the main themes with representative and usually distinctive references. The concatenation of these themes will prepare for the detailed discussions scattered throughout the commentary proper.

Matthew shows great concern over the problem of a mixed church. The church has grown large through the influx of converts from all nations (28:18-20). But these converts include false as well as true disciples (13:24-30, 36-43, 47-50; 22:11-14; 25:1-13). The distinction between them is coming to light through persecution of the church (5:10-12). This persecution does not have its source in the Roman government, but among the Jewish leaders in Jerusalem. Matthew constantly exposes and heightens

5

their guilt (27:62-66; 28:11-15). Their getting Jesus killed climaxes a pattern starting in the OT period and continuing into the age of the church (23:27-39).

True disciples are suffering with endurance. Some of them have had to flee for their lives (10:23). In doing so, they have become itinerant missionaries who depend on the hospitality of other true disciples willing to risk their own necks by harboring these fugitive preachers, by giving them food and drink, by supplying them with clothes, by ministering to them in illness, and by going so far as to visit them in prison (10:40-42; 25:31-46). Together, then, they dare to live openly as Jesus' disciples and to preach the gospel publicly—despite the persecution that comes on them from Jewish authorities (5:13-16).

False disciples, on the other hand, are making public disclaimers of Jesus in order to avoid persecution (10:32-33; 26:70). Some are even betraying true disciples in hope of pleasing the persecuting authorities and in an attempt to prove their own dissociation from those who follow Jesus closely and openly (24:10; cf. 27:3-10). All the false disciples have stopped living according to the high standards of Jesus' teaching (24:12). That would mark them out as easy targets for persecution.

At their head, the false disciples have false prophets, who appear to be settled ecclesiastics, i.e., church officials whose easygoing attitudes and policies of accommodation have preserved them from the hardships of an itinerant ministry (7:21-23). These false prophets seem to have come into the church from the Pharisaical sect and the scribal occupation (23:1-36). They teach secret discipleship. Their public speech and conduct do not conform to Jesus' standards. In short, to avoid persecution they teach and practice antinomianism, and the natural desire to avoid persecution has led a great many people in the church to be duped by them.

To lend themselves authority the false prophets talk about having met with Jesus at hideouts in the city and desert (24:23-28). Thus they justify their neglect of his teaching as preserved in the tradition. After all, they have seen and heard him more recently! This antinomianism does not stand over against Jewish legalism, for according to Matthew Jewish legalism is itself antinomian in its failure to require true righteousness (5:19-20). Rather, it contrasts with the law of Christ, who made far higher demands on his disciples by carrying the OT law to its true ends (5:21-48). The contrast with Christ's law and the condemnation of Jewish legalism as antinomian make it very doubtful that the Gospel of Matthew arises out of a Judaizing reaction to the Pauline doctrine, or even a corrupted form of the Pauline doctrine, of justification by faith.

The widespread fear of persecution leads Matthew to emphasize the danger of little faith, or doubt, among Jesus' disciples (6:30; 8:26; 14:31; 16:8; 28:17). For the same reason, he stresses the necessity of confessing Jesus in public and the eternal danger of denying him in public (10:32-33; 26:70). Since the courage to do the one and avoid the other can come only through prayer accompanied by fasting and prolonged at the expense of sleeping, the evangelist stresses this kind of praying (4:2; 6:16-18; 9:14-15; 26:31-46 with 69-75). Above all, Matthew emphasizes the doing of good works before men (5:13-16). These good works constitute the righteousness surpassing that of the scribes and Pharisees.

Without this surpassing righteousness as evidence of genuine discipleship, no one will enter the kingdom of heaven (5:19-20). Though it has to show, such righteousness must grow out of the heart (5:8, 28; 11:29; 13:15; 18:35). Neither hypocrisy (i.e., pretense) nor ostentation (i.e., pretentiousness) has any place in it (6:1-18; 23:13-36). Nor does any feeling of merit (20:1-16). Therefore, ecclesiastical leaders must reject honorific titles (23:8-10); they must humble themselves (18:4; 23:12). Through service, as opposed to self-seeking, they must adopt the position of little people in the church (18:3; 23:11). In other words, they must be meek, like Jesus, the persecuted teacher of righteousness who gave himself for others (5:5; 11:29; 20:20-28; 21:5).

As a teacher of righteousness, Jesus resembles John the Baptist, who also came "in the way of righteousness" and lost his life for doing so (21:32). And as a teacher of righteousness, Jesus legislates the law that his disciples are to obey (5:21-48; 7:24-28; 28:20). Thus emphasis falls on his words (7:28; 11:1; 13:53; 19:1; 26:1). Not only do these words gravitate together in five lengthy discourses (chaps. 5–7, 10, 13, 18, 23–25), but even in the narrative sections the description of what Jesus does shrinks for the sake of greater attention to what he says. This makes him look like a new legislator greater than Moses. In fact, he affirms that he did not come to destroy the law—or prophets—but to fulfill them (5:17-18).

The law changes, however. The change does not come about through Jesus' denying the law, but through his perfecting it. He carries out the tendencies of the OT law to their radical ends (5:21-48; 19:10-12). The commandment to love your neighbor as yourself takes on special importance (19:19; 22:39), theologically because only by loving your neighbor in that way can love for God be worked out, and practically because loving your neighbor as yourself will forestall Christians' betraying one another (24:10-12). It will cause them to minister to their persecuted fellow disciples even though such ministry jeopardizes their own safety (10:40-42; 25:31-46). Mutual love will encourage Christians to endure persecution and will show itself in deeds of mercy (5:7).

Obviously, the law of Christ needs to be learned. So Matthew emphasizes discipleship, which by definition is "learning" (13:52; 27:57; 28:19). But learning includes both the theoretical and the practical. So also, Matthew emphasizes hearing and understanding Jesus' words (13:13-15, 19, 23, 51) and obeying them (21:6, 28-32; 28:20). The figure of following Jesus symbolizes this obedience (4:22; 8:1, 22-23; 10:38; etc.). Lack of knowledge makes obedience impossible. But to those who understand the law of Christ so far as they have had opportunity to hear and obey it, further teaching of that law is given (13:12). There results growth in knowledge and progress in obedience toward the ideal of perfection (5:48; 17:13).

To accentuate the authority of Christ's law Matthew paints an awe-inspiring portrait of Jesus. Even in the nativity story, the primary stress rests on Jesus as "Immanuel . . . God with us" (1:23), and on Jesus as the Son of God (2:15). This stress continues to be heard throughout the gospel (see, e.g., 16:16). The climax is reached in Jesus' claim to have been given "all authority in heaven and on earth"—and this in connection with making the baptized from all nations learn and obey all his commandments, without exception (28:18-20). Not only is Jesus "Immanuel" and "the Son of God." He belongs to the Trinity (28:20). He constantly receives the designation "Lord" (see 8:6, 21, 25 for a few of the many unparalleled examples). Repeatedly, people worship him (2:2, 11; 8:2; 9:18; 14:33; 15:25; 20:20; 28:9, 17). He has angels (13:41; 16:27; 24:31). Even the kingdom belongs to him as the Son of man (13:41; 16:28). All these represent special and sometimes exclusive emphases of Matthew.

The kingdom that belongs to Jesus also belongs to the Father (6:10, 33 v.1.; 13:43; 26:29). The association of Jesus with the Father further enhances Jesus' dignity as the authoritative teacher of the law (7:21; 10:32-33; 12:50; 16:17; 18:10, 19, 35). Furthermore, Matthew gives the kingdom the designation "of heaven"—unique among the gospels—to stress the universality of the dominion exercised by Jesus and his Father. In the same vein, emphasis falls on the transcendence of God. He is not just the Father. He is the Father "in heaven," the "heavenly" Father (see 6:10 for one of many distinctive examples). Through all of this we see not only a warning against violation of the law governing members of the kingdom, but also comfort in the midst of persecution. In his fatherly role God cares for his suffering children. This care is proved by the vindication of Jesus the Son and martyr par excellence. God raised him from the dead and gave him all authority—everywhere (28:18). In the Father's care, in the paradigm of Jesus, and in the majestic transcendence of both the Father and the Son the persecuted disciples have a heavenly anchor.

To his disciples Jesus gives authority to replicate his ministry in word and deed. They are to teach by word and example the righteousness which surpasses that of the scribes and Pharisees and to heal the sick and cast out demons. Thus Matthew pictures the disciples as Christian scribes (i.e., teachers of Christ's law—13:52; 23:34; 28:20) and as Christian healers and exorcists (10:1).

Till the Son of man comes, they must carry on the mission to the Jewish masses (10:23; cf. 10:5-6; 15:23-24; 17:24-27). Matthew himself participates in this Jewish mission by portraying Jesus as the Son of David (1:1; 9:27; 12:23; etc.) and long-promised Messiah (1:1, 16, 17, 18; 2:4; 11:2; etc.), who has fulfilled the predictions concerning him in the OT (1:22-23; 2:15, 17-18, 23; 4:14-16; 8:17; 12:17-21; 13:14-15, 35; 21:4-5; 27:9-10). Though blame for Jesus' death is heaped on the Jewish leaders (27:15-26), the crowds they deceived (27:20, 62-66; 28:11-15) remain proper subjects for evangelism (10:23).

Moreover, in their numbers and in their following Jesus during his earthly ministry, the Jewish crowds symbolize the international church, including the many Gentiles who were later to become disciples (4:25–5:1 with 7:28–8:1; 21:8-9, 11). The evangelistic enterprise encompasses all nations (28:19) and makes a new nation of Jesus' people, who take the place of Israel (21:43; cf. 1:21; 8:11-12; 16:18). Just as he enlarges the role of the Jewish leaders in Jesus' crucifixion, so also Matthew diminishes the

Roman role and even puts Pontius Pilate and his wife in a good light in order to win Gentiles (27:15-26). In the first gospel, then, we have Jewish Christianity breaking out into the wide world of the Gentiles. Perhaps here lies the reason behind Matthew's interest in cities, the centers of population (see πόλις in the Greek Index).

Out of the effort to make disciples of all nations there has resulted the church, large and mixed. (At this point our consideration of Matthew's theology and its setting has come full circle.) Matthew likes to portray the church as a brotherhood (5:21-26, 47; 18:15-17, 35; 23:8; 25:40; 28:10). Its little ones—the poor and persecuted outcasts, the itinerant preachers fleeing persecution, the young people, the blind and crippled—need care (18:1-20; 21:14-16). They, rather than comfortable and well-off antinomians, are Jesus' true disciples. But they stand in danger of deception by antinomian false prophets. The little ones who do stray from Christ's law in order to avoid persecution need reclaiming (18:10-14). Their eternal destiny lies in the balance, because apostasy will bring eternal punishment. Therefore private judgments of excommunication are prohibited in favor of private attempts to correct backsliding (5:21-26; 7:1-5; 18:15-16). If these attempts fail, the church must impose collective discipline (18:17). On the other hand, repentance by the backslider needs to be met with a forgiveness by the church on earth that matches divine forgiveness in heaven (16:19; 18:18-35).

The figure of Peter stands out, not as an ecclesiastical overlord, but as a representative disciple (10:2; 17:24). He typifies disciples both in their understanding and confession of Jesus as the Christ and Son of God (16:16-19), and in their prayerlessness (26:36-46), little faith (14:28-31), and denials of Jesus in time of persecution (26:69-75). Such disciples make up the professing church, the present sphere of God's rule—or "the kingdom of heaven," as Matthew likes to call it. This kingdom is headed for a future consummation, one in which false disciples—the antinomians—will be rooted out and given over to eternal punishment along with those who do not even profess Christian discipleship, indeed, along with the Devil himself and his angels (13:36-42, 47-50; 22:11-14; 25:41). Thus a loud warning of eschatological judgment sounds. A complementary emphasis falls on the reward of the righteous (5:12; 10:40-42; 13:48).

All in all, Matthew writes his gospel to keep persecution of the church from stymieing evangelism. He reminds true disciples of their duty to obey Christ's law and make it known despite persecution. He warns false disciples and those tempted to follow their antinomian course of least resistance that everlasting torment awaits the disobedient. These emphases pose the danger of legalism and need balancing by the doctrine of the indwelling Spirit, through whose life and power alone Jesus' disciples can fulfill the righteous requirement of the law (Rom 8:1-4). But it is good to have Matthew's emphases without that balance; for in some situations to introduce the doctrine of the Spirit quickly is to dull the edge of the demands made on Jesus' disciples. They might fail to feel the pain caused by the sharp edge of those demands. Only when that pain is felt will the Spirit's enablement amount to more than a comfortable sanctification open to the incursion of antinomianism. Wherever the church has grown large and mixed, wherever the church is polarized between the extremes of latitudinarianism and sectarianism, wherever the church feels drawn to accommodation with forces that oppose the gospel, wherever the church loses its vision of worldwide evangelism, wherever the church lapses into smug religiosity with its attendant vices of ostentation, hypocrisy, and haughty disdain for its underprivileged and correspondingly zealous members— there the Gospel of Matthew speaks with power and pertinence.

THE STRUCTURE OF MATTHEW

We should avoid imposing an outline on Matthew. It is doubtful that the first evangelist thought in terms of one, for his favorite points keep reappearing. The chronology of Jesus' life determined his ordering of some of the materials, e.g., the story of the nativity and the account of Jesus' death and resurrection. The latter had already come at the close of Mark's gospel, which provided a pattern for the ordering of previous materials as well. At first Matthew freely rearranged his Markan materials in addition to inserting other materials (often shared with Luke). But editorial fatigue set in, so that in the latter half of his gospel he stuck close to Mark's order even when continuing to insert other materials.

In 4:17 we read, "From then on Jesus began [ἀπὸ τότε ἤρξατο ὁ Ἰησοῦς] to preach and say, 'Repent, for the kingdom of heaven is near.'" The reappearance of ἀπὸ τότε ἤρξατο ὁ Ἰησοῦς in 16:21 suggests a threefold division of the first gospel: (1) the book of Jesus' origin, beginning with 1:1; (2) Jesus' public proclamation of repentance and the kingdom, accompanied by healings and exorcisms and beginning at 4:17; and (3) the private predictions of Jesus concerning his death and resurrection, beginning in 16:21 and fulfilled in chaps. 26–28. But this division of the gospel hardly tells the whole story. For not only do themes such as Jesus' Davidic messiahship and divine sonship, begun in the first section, continue to be emphasized in the second and third sections; but also Jesus carries on his public ministry of preaching, teaching, healing, and exorcism in the third section. The private predictions of his passion and resurrection are simply added. Furthermore, the book of Jesus' origin is probably limited to the genealogy in 1:2-17; and 4:17 and 16:21 seem to mark turning points in Jesus' life, not in Matthew's gospel. Finally, the threefold division does not take into account the formula that closes each of Jesus' five discourses (7:28-29; 11:1; 13:53; 19:1-2; 26:1-2).

This formula highlights the discourse on righteousness as a requirement for entrance into the kingdom (5:1–7:27); the discourse on persecution in the preaching of the kingdom (10:1-42); the discourse on understanding the kingdom as a requirement of discipleship (13:1-52); the discourse on the necessity of humility and forgiveness in the brotherhood of the kingdom (18:1-35); and the discourse on the danger of hypocrisy, which will result in expulsion from the kingdom (23:1–25:46). The fivefoldness of the Pentateuch, the Book of Psalms, the Megilloth, the Mac-

10

cabean history written by Jason of Cyrene (see 2 Macc 2:23), *1 Enoch*, the original Perekim that make up *Pirke Aboth*, and Papias's "Expositions of the Lord's Oracles" (perhaps patterned after the five discourses in Matthew) supports the fivefold arrangement in Matthew. Such an arrangement had become customary because of the great authority of the Pentateuch.

But we look in vain for similarities in the contents of Moses' five books and Jesus' five discourses. And narrative sections begin and end the first gospel and separate the five discourses from one another. This separation is unlike the analogous literature. The number of the six narrative sections does not allow a pairing with the discourses. And neither the number six nor the contents of the narrative sections correspond to the Pentateuch, which is a compound of both narrative and legislation. Finally, even outside the five discourses, Matthew emphasizes the words of Jesus (see esp. chap. 11). We conclude that the Gospel of Matthew is structurally mixed.

The Commentary Proper

THE ORIGIN OF JESUS CHRIST
1:1 (Mark 1:1; Luke 1:1-4)

1:1 (Mark 1:1; Luke 1:1-4) Matthew's "a record of the origin" replaces Mark's "the beginning of the gospel" and reflects OT phraseology, such as that in Gen 2:4; 5:1 LXX. The immediate mention of Jesus Christ matches Mark, however. Matthew's record of Jesus Christ's origin is a genealogy (vv 2-17). In Genesis the first entry gives a genealogy its name. But Matthew names his after its final entry, Jesus Christ. This reversal and the borrowing of the OT phrase make the genealogy portray Jesus as the goal and fulfillment of the OT.

To reinforce the point, Matthew describes Jesus as "son of David son of Abraham" (cf. *T. Levi* 8:14-15). This description shows that the record of origin is limited to the genealogy, which starts with Abraham, gives prominence to David, and climaxes in a gematria on David's name (see v 17 with comments). "Son of David son of Abraham" also substitutes for the probably original phrase in Mark, "Son of God." Jesus' divine sonship will be introduced by God himself in Matt 2:15 (cf. 3:17) and emphasized throughout the gospel (see υἱὸς θεοῦ in the Greek Index). For now, Matthew's substitute leads nicely to the genealogy, which appeals to Jewish readers, fathered as a nation by Abraham. The substitute may also imply that Jesus is Abraham's seed, a blessing to all nations in fulfillment of God's promise (Gen 12:1-3; 18:18; 22:15-18; cf. "Universality" in the Topical Index and esp. Matt 28:18-20). Since elsewhere Matthew will show little interest in Abraham, however, he may have intended his readers to understand David rather than Jesus as the son of Abraham. Certainly the emphasis falls here and later on Jesus as the king who fulfills God's promise to David (2 Samuel 7), a promise reiterated and expanded in many messianic prophecies (see, e.g., Isa 9:5-6[6-7]; 11:1ff.) and in Jewish expectation (see esp. *Psalms of Solomon* 17–18 and, for Matthew's emphasis, υἱὸς Δαυίδ in the Greek Index; cf. Rom 1:3). Matthew found this Davidic Christology already in the tradition of Jesus' nativity (see Luke 1:32-33).

13

A MESSIANIC GENEALOGY OF JESUS
1:2-17 (Luke 3:23-38)

Matthew now inserts a body of materials (1:2–2:23) lacking in Mark but appearing with fewer revisions in Luke. These materials portray Jesus as fulfilling OT messianic expectations from the very beginning of his life. The genealogy has a counterpart in Luke. There, the genealogy goes back from Jesus to Adam and finally to God himself. In order to conform to 1 Chronicles 1–3 Matthew reverses the order. The reversal makes the genealogy build up to a climax in Jesus. Furthermore, in contrast with Luke and 1 Chronicles the omission of all names prior to Abraham leads to the identification of Jesus as "the King of the Jews" (see esp. 2:2).

1:2-6a (Luke 3:31-34) The statement that Abraham begat Isaac comes from 1 Chr 1:34a. The verb ἐγέννησεν occurs irregularly in 1 Chronicles 1–3, but for the sake of parallelism Matthew will continue to use it. The names of Jacob, Judah, Perez, Zerah, Tamar, Hezron, Aram, Amminadab, Nahshon, Salmon, Boaz, Obed, Jesse, and David come from 1 Chr 1:34b LXX (so also Luke 3:34 against "Israel" in the MT); 2:1, 4, 5, 9 LXX (against "Ram" in the MT), 10, 11 LXX (against "Salma" in the MT), 12, 15. From Perez through David, Ruth 4:18-22 offers a parallel genealogy; but Matthew's "Zerah," "Tamar," "Aram," and "Salmon" agree only with the Septuagint of 1 Chronicles. To the name of Judah, progenitor of the tribe to which the Davidic dynasty belonged (see Gen 49:8-12), Matthew adds a reference to Judah's brothers. This reference, unnecessary to the genealogy proper, may have been suggested by the list of Judah's brothers in 1 Chr 2:1-2. But it grows primarily out of Matthew's interest in portraying the people of God as a brotherhood (see ἀδελφός in the Greek Index); i.e., Judah and his brothers prefigure the brotherhood of the church.

The mention of Zerah in addition to Perez and of Tamar their mother differs from Luke, conforms to 1 Chr 2:4, and calls attention to Tamar as a prototype of the Gentiles whose evangelization Matthew champions. For she was probably a Canaanite (see Genesis 38) and was certainly thought to be so by many Jews in the NT era (see M. D. Johnson, *The Purpose of the Biblical Genealogies* [NTSMS 8; London: Cambridge, 1969] 270-72). Her being "more righteous" than Judah (Gen 38:26) may have contributed to her mention by Matthew, who repeatedly stresses righteousness (see δικ- in the Greek Index and esp. 5:20).

For the names Arni and Admin in the probably correct text of Luke 3:33, Matthew puts Aram to conform to 1 Chr 2:9 LXX. So also he puts Salmon in place of Sala (Luke 3:32) to conform to 1 Chr 2:11 LXX. His assimilations to the OT bring the ancient Scriptures and the gospel into a unity of promise and fulfillment. The name of Rahab, spelled according to the Hebrew rather than the LXX (see Josh 2:1, 3; 6:17, 23, 25; Heb 11:31; Jas 2:25), enters without parallel in Luke or 1 Chronicles and, so far as her mothering Boaz is concerned, without support anywhere in the OT. A Canaanite who was often celebrated by Jewish rabbis as a Gentile proselyte, Rahab joins Tamar in prefiguring the influx of Gentiles into the church. Mention of Ruth as the mother of Obed has no counterpart in Luke or

14

1 Chronicles. But in Ruth 4:9-22, where a parallel genealogy appears, we discover an association of Ruth with Tamar. So Matthew, having mentioned Tamar already, inserts Ruth in order to conform to that association and to portray Ruth, too, as a prototype of Gentiles coming into the church. For Ruth was a Moabitess and, like Rahab, a Gentile proselyte celebrated by Jewish rabbis (see Johnson, *The Purpose of the Biblical Genealogies* 153-79).

The designation of David as "the king" does not occur in Luke or 1 Chronicles 1-3, but appears often with his name elsewhere in the OT. By adopting the OT designation Matthew puts him forward as a prototype of Jesus and brings to a close the first section of the genealogy (cf. v 17).

1:6b-11 (Luke 3:28-31) The names in vv 6b-11 come from 1 Chr 3:5, 10-16. Differing in every instance from the corresponding names in Luke, they represent those descendants of David who succeeded him in rulership up to the Babylonian Exile. Thus by his usual practice of assimilation to the OT text Matthew forsakes a genealogy of physical descent for Joseph, Jesus' foster father (so Luke 3:23); instead, he lists royal prototypes of Jesus the King of the Jews. The genealogy has become a large figure of speech for Jesus' messianic kingship.

For the fourth time a woman appears. She comes from 1 Chr 3:5, where we read of "Bathshua" (βηρσαβεέ in the LXX) as Solomon's mother. But Matthew omits her name and switches from the Chronicler's descriptive phrase, "the daughter of Ammiel," to "the [wife] of Uriah" (so 2 Sam 11:26; 12:10, 15). The change calls attention to her taking on the status of a Gentile through marriage to Uriah, repeatedly designated a Hittite. In fact, the stress falls not so much on Uriah's wife—for in contrast with 2 Samuel Matthew leaves out "wife"—as on Uriah himself. Thus again the genealogy foreshadows the place of Gentiles in the church.

It has been suggested that Tamar, Rahab, Ruth, and the wife of Uriah prefigure Mary. But they make odd choices for such a role! Surely Matthew would have chosen famous mothers of Israel such as Sarah, Rebekah, Rachel, and Leah. Others have thought that he had in mind the adulteries of Tamar and Uriah's wife and the harlotry of Rahab and wanted to undermine Jewish slander concerning Jesus' birth, as though to say, "People in glass houses shouldn't throw stones—look at your own history!" But why the inclusion of Ruth? And such a counterattack would have deepened suspicions concerning the legitimacy of Jesus' birth. Besides, the fault lay with Judah and David, not with Tamar and Bathshua (Bathsheba; see Genesis 38; 2 Samuel 11; cf. Ruth 4:12); and the Jews extolled Rahab for helping the Israelites—they did not criticize her for harlotry (cf. Josh 2:1ff.; 6:1ff.; Heb 11:31; Jas 2:25; 1 Clement 12). Johnson (*The Purpose of the Biblical Genealogies* 176-79) suggests that Matthew mentions these women, all linked with the tribe of Judah and subject to controversy among the rabbis, to support a Davidic royal messianism against an Aaronic priestly messianism related to the tribe of Levi. But the evidence for controversy over Rahab is admittedly weak.

Matthew's addition of φ to Asa's name (1 Chr 3:10) produces a secondary allusion to the psalmist Asaph, who, according to very early tradition in the title, wrote Psalm 78. In 13:35 Matthew will quote part of that psalm as fulfilled. Thus a note of prophecy comes into the genealogy. To help get fourteen generations prior to the Babylonian Exile (cf. v 17), Matthew omits the three successive kings Ahaziah, Joash, and Amaziah (cf. 1 Chr 3:11-12 and the omission of six successive generations in Ezra 7:3 compared with 1 Chr 5:33-36[6:7-10]). Each omitted king suffered a violent death because of his wickedness (2 Chr 22:1-9; 24:20-27; 25:14-28). The first, Ahaziah, had Athaliah, daughter of the infamous King Ahab, as his mother. In agreement with Matthew's practice of conforming to the OT, then, the omission of Ahaziah, Joash, and Amaziah reflects the Lord's visiting the iniquity of Ahab on the third and fourth generations of his children, here even through his daughter's line (Exod 20:5; Num 14:18; cf. 1 Kgs 21:21; 2 Kgs 10:30).

Some have thought that Matthew omitted Joash, Amaziah, and Azariah (also called Uzziah) rather than Ahaziah, Joash, and Amaziah—this because the short form of Ahaziah in 1 Chr 3:11 LXX^{A,B,V} ('Οζ[ε]ία[ς]) elsewhere stands for Uzziah and thus may have caused Matthew to skip to Uzziah's successor. But Matthew's desire to achieve the number fourteen favors design over such an extremely fortunate accident. In 1 Chr 3:12 LXX Uzziah appears under his other, less easily confused name 'Αζαρία(ς). So it is probable that Matthew deliberately took 'Οζ[ε]ία[ς] from the LXX, intended there for Ahaziah (usually 'Οχοζ[ε]ίας in the LXX), but made it apply to Uzziah-Azariah according to its usual reference in the LXX. This correction of the LXX resulted in an omission of Ahaziah, Joash, and Amaziah that made for the number fourteen.

Matthew writes "Amos" instead of "Amon" (1 Chr 3:14). Orthographical variation or simple confusion of names (with possible influence from Matthew) in the textual tradition of the LXX suggests we have nothing more than that here. But Matthew may have chosen or coined the spelling "Amos" for a secondary allusion to the prophet Amos, just as he spelled Asa's name like that of Asaph to introduce a prophetic note. In support of this possibility, Matthew's version of Jesus' saying recorded in 10:29 and worded differently in Luke 12:6 conforms to Amos 3:5. Jehoiakim (1 Chr 3:15) drops out in order that the second section of the genealogy may end with the Babylonian Exile and still have only fourteen generations.

Again Matthew mentions brothers—those of Jeconiah, also called Jehoiachin in the OT. But 1 Chr 3:16 does not indicate that Jeconiah had more than one brother. Matthew's mentioning brothers in the plural has led to the supposition of an early scribal mistake: a copyist wrote Jeconiah's name where Matthew had originally written that of Jehoiakim, whose brothers appear in 1 Chr 3:15 (cf. the use of Jehoiakim's name for Jehoiachin in 4 Kingdoms 24–25 LXX). Additionally, the supposition allows us to count Jeconiah in the third set of fourteen generations (v 17) so as to get the number fourteen more easily.

Conjectural emendations always suffer from doubt, however; and the doubtfulness of this one increases when we note that Matthew links Jeconiah with the deportation to Babylon, an apparent reference to the Chronicler's description of Jeconiah, not Jehoiakim, as "the captive" (1 Chr 3:17 MT). Furthermore, 1 Chr 3:16-17 did not offer Matthew the name Jehoiachin, but Jeconiah, which was not easily confused with Jehoiakim.

Probably, then, Matthew deliberately skips Jehoiakim and means his readers to understand the brothers of Jeconiah not as members of his immediate family, but as his fellow Jews. Their being led away with him into the Babylonian Exile is prominently mentioned in 2 Kgs 24:10-16, which in the LXX contains the word μετοικεσία, used by Matthew for the deportation. Just as Judah's brothers made up the people of God in their time (v 2), so also Jeconiah and his brothers the Jews made up the people of God who went into exile. Throughout Matthew we encounter brotherhood in a wide theological sense (cf. ἀδελφός in the Greek Index). Indeed, the old brotherhood, which began with Jacob's twelve sons and landed in exile, contrasts with the new brotherhood of Jesus' disciples, who are to go make disciples of all nations (28:19). Matthew's reference to the deportation marks the end of the second section of the genealogy just as "the king" added to David's name marked the end of the first section (v 6a).

1:12-16 (Luke 3:23-27) Matthew does not intend "after the deportation to Babylon" to be construed with Jeconiah's fathering Salathiel (that would be obviously untrue), but with the third section as a whole. The Lord's disqualifying Jeconiah's offspring (Jer 22:24-30) had to do only with immediate offspring, i.e., the sons of Jeconiah; for the Lord called his grandson Zerubbabel a chosen "signet" (Hag 2:23), the very figure used in the disqualification of the sons. Matthew writes that Jeconiah fathered Salathiel (Shealtiel), but Luke that Neri fathered Salathiel (Luke 3:27). Unless we are to think of textual corruption, namesakes, levirate marriage, adoptions, or the like, the possibility suggests itself that already in the OT the curse on the immediate offspring of Jeconiah led to replacement of his son Pedaiah with Salathiel, who came from another branch of David's family (cf. 1 Chr 3:19 MT with 1 Chr 3:19 LXX; Ezra 3:2, 8; 5:2; Neh 12:1; Hag 1:1, 12, 14; 2:2, 23). Thus Luke gives Salathiel's physical father Neri, and Matthew gives Salathiel's legal, dynastic father Jeconiah. In Zerubbabel, Jeconiah's grandson, the physical and legal lines reunite.

Matthew comes back into agreement with Luke in Salathiel and Zerubbabel. Both evangelists agree with 1 Chr 3:17-19 LXX against the MT in making Salathiel instead of Pedaiah the father of Zerubbabel. Since 1 Chr 3:19-20 offers the names of seven sons (and one daughter) of Zerubbabel and further names from several generations following, the agreement of Matthew with Luke in now leaving 1 Chronicles favors that Matthew has been working and continues to work with a genealogy like the one recorded in Luke. But his substitution of reigning kings has shown that he does not mean to give a line of physical descent. So also in this last section Matthew substitutes freely. It looks as though "Eliezer" in the corresponding region of the genealogy recorded in Luke (see Luke 3:29) reminded Matthew of the well-known high priest Eleazar. As a result, the evangelist's thoughts turned to the priestly genealogy in 1 Chr 5:29ff.(6:3ff.), for all along he has been drawing on the early chapters of 1 Chronicles for his revisions. From the priestly genealogy there first comes "Abiud" (so the LXX for Abihu), listed just before Eleazar. Matthew has no interest in priestly Christology. But he has great interest in the royal Christology associated with the tribe of Judah, and so he takes "Abiud" as meaning "My father is Judah" and as pointing to the royal heritage of Jesus the King of the Jews.

With "Eliezer" still in the back of his mind, Matthew now notices "Eliakim" in the genealogy of Joseph (see Luke 3:30), for the two names begin alike. Eliakim was also the name given to Jehoiakim (2 Chr 36:4), whom Matthew omitted in v 11. Furthermore, this name belongs to the man who will receive the key of David according to Isa 22:20-24, a passage that Matthew will draw on in 16:19. To offset his omission of Jehoiakim and inject a bit of Davidic Christology, then, Matthew writes "Eliakim."

Matthew has recently listed the kings of Judah, one of whom had Azariah as an alternate name (see vv 8-9 with comments). Consequently, the name "Azariah" in the priestly genealogy (1 Chr 5:35-36[6:9-10]) catches his eye. But Matthew shortens it to "Azor" after the pattern of Neh 10:18(17); Jer 28:1(35:1 LXX); Ezek 11:1. This revision should not surprise us in view of his changing the spellings of Asa and Amon in vv 7-8 and 10. The obscuring of his priestly source protects Davidic Christology. His interest in this Christology leads to the name "Zadok," an outstanding high priest during David's reign (1 Chr 5:34[6:8]). The Chronicler mentions Zadok in the verse preceding the one containing the name Azariah, just shortened by Matthew. The evangelist then goes quite naturally to Zadok's son Ahimaaz (Ἀχιμάας in the LXX; 1 Chr 5:34-35[6:8-9]), but shortens that name to Ἀχίμ (cf. 1 Chr 24:17 LXX^B) with the same purpose he had in Azor. Still concerned to cover the traces of his priestly source, Matthew again introduces a reference to the royal tribe of Judah, this time with "Eliud" (cf. 1 Chr 12:21 LXX^A), which he presents as meaning "God of Judah" (cf. the comments on "Abiud"). Finally there surfaces the name that pointed Matthew to the priestly genealogy in the first place—viz., "Eliezer" (Luke 3:29), but changed in spelling to "Eleazar" to conform to 1 Chr 5:29-30(6:3-4).

His eye back on the genealogy of Joseph, Matthew leaves 1 Chronicles to take up the name of Joseph's grandfather "Matthat" (Luke 3:24), which becomes "Matthan" for exact conformity to the Hebrew מַתָּן (cf. 2 Chr 23:17; Jer 38:1[45:1 LXX] and the change in Matt 9:9 of "Levi" [Mark 2:14; Luke 5:27] to "Matthew," based on מַתָּי). "Jacob" replaces "Heli" (Luke 3:23) to conform to the fathering of the patriarch Joseph by the patriarch Jacob (cf. the changing of Joses [Mark 6:3] to Joseph in 13:55). The names of Joseph and Jesus stay (cf. Luke 3:23). But Matthew adds that Joseph was "the husband of Mary" to show that Jesus, though not fathered by Joseph, belonged to David's line; for legal rights came through the father even though he was only a foster father, and Joseph took Mary to wife before Jesus' birth (vv 20-25).

A further addition appears in the description of Mary as the one "from whom was born Jesus, who is called Christ." The feminine gender of ἧς prepares for the virgin birth by shifting attention from Joseph to Mary (see Metzger, *Textual Commentary* ad loc.; R. E. Brown, *The Birth of the Messiah* [Garden City, N.Y.: Doubleday, 1977] 61-64 on the textual variants in 1:16). The passive voice of ἐγεννήθη—the only passive among the forty occurrences of this verb in the genealogy—prepares for divine action

18

in the conception and birth of Jesus. Matthew likes to use λέγω, especially in a participial form, to introduce Semitic names. Here the participle introduces "Christ," a favorite of his (8,5). This designation identifies Jesus as the anointed one of Jewish expectation.

1:17 1 Chr 1:34; 2:1-15 provided fourteen generations from Abraham through David. But why does Matthew divide the rest of the genealogy into two more sets of fourteen generations each, even at the cost of making several omissions? Apparently he wants to say that in Jesus the Davidic Messiah has come; for the numerical values of the Hebrew letters in the name David add up to fourteen: ד (4) + ו (6) + ד (4). (Before the introduction of Arabic numerals, letters of the alphabet stood for numbers.) Readers limited to Greek may not have caught the point, but Matthew himself probably intended it and might well have expected Jewish addressees to understand. Otherwise the correspondence between the repetitious genealogical fourteen and David's name seems too unlikely.

The first section ended with royal power ("David," called "the king" in v 6a), the second with loss of royal power ("the deportation to Babylon"). The third climaxes with the revival of royal power in Jesus, whose designation "Christ" has the force of a title because of the definite article modifying it (cf. the periodization of history in Dan 9:24-27 and extrabiblical Jewish literature cited in Str-B 1. 43-45). To get his third fourteen Matthew probably counts Mary as well as Joseph; i.e., the one chronological generation carries two other kinds of generations within it, a legal (Joseph's) and a physical (Mary's). Otherwise we have only thirteen, since Jeconiah belongs to the second fourteen just as David belonged to the first. The counting of Mary harmonizes with Matthew's distinction between the royal lineage of Jesus through Joseph (cf. Joseph's being addressed as "son of David" in v 20) and the divine generation of Jesus through Mary.

It is forced to count "Jesus" and "Christ" separately in order to gain fourteen generations in the third section. For genealogies among lay Jews, see J. Jeremias, *Jerusalem in the Time of Jesus* (London: SCM, 1967) 269-302, who favors public written records more or less accurate, and Johnson, *The Purpose of the Biblical Genealogies* 99-108, who favors oral or only private written records more or less fanciful. See R. R. Wilson, *Genealogy and History in the Biblical World* (New Haven: Yale, 1977), on genealogical fluidity. In view of this fluidity, Matthew's free revisions should hardly surprise us.

THE BIRTH OF JESUS CHRIST
AS THE SON OF DAVID AND GOD WITH US
1:18-25 (Luke 1:5–2:7)

On the one hand, this paragraph shows how Jesus came to have the legal status of a son of David even though Joseph did not father him: "Joseph son of David" (v 20) made Jesus his son by taking Mary to wife prior to Jesus' birth and by naming the infant on his birth (cf. *m. B. Bat.* 8:6). Without this explanation the preceding genealogy of Joseph is pointless (see esp. v 16). On the other hand, this paragraph highlights Jesus' deity by noting that Mary became pregnant after her betrothal to Joseph but before her marriage to and cohabitation with him. Therefore we ought to think neither of Joseph nor of another man as Jesus' father. Rather, Mary bore a divine child as a result of generation by the Holy Spirit.

1:18 By coming first, the phrase "of Jesus Christ" ties the following to 1:1-17, which began and ended with references to Jesus Christ, and emphasizes both the name Jesus, about to be explained (v 21), and the messiahship—i.e., Christhood—of Jesus in virtue of his Davidic status. The Latin and early Syriac textual traditions omit "Jesus." Does the difficulty of the definite article with "Jesus Christ" favor omission of "Jesus" so as to produce an easier "the Christ" (cf. v 17)? Or does it favor retention of "Jesus" as the more difficult reading so as to produce the sense, "the 'Jesus Christ' mentioned in vv 1 and 16"? The weight of external evidence tips the scales in favor of the latter (see Metzger, *Textual Commentary* ad loc.). ἡ γένεσις echoes 1:1, but because of what follows it carries the narrower connotation of birth rather than origin (cf. Luke 1:14). Since birth is one kind of origin, readers of the Greek text would hardly have noticed the narrowing. οὕτως is a Mattheanism (18,5).

The massive transformation of a physical genealogy into a Christological statement has prepared us for the similar change of a historical report (cf. Luke 1:1-4) into a theological tale (see the Theological Postscript on the question of scriptural inspiration in this kind of writing). We only have to suppose that Matthew had the traditions that later went into Luke 1–2 to see what happens under his artistry. He fuses the stories about the births of John the Baptist and Jesus just as he will assimilate their messages to each other in 4:17 and just as he will conflate the separate deliverances of two demoniacs (8:28-34) and the separate healings of two blind men (9:27-31; 20:29-34; see the comments on these passages and "John the Baptist parallel Jesus" and "Conflation" in the Topical Index for a host of similar assimilations).

First, after the pattern of the annunciation to Zechariah (Luke 1:5-20) Matthew turns the annunciation to Mary before her conceiving Jesus (Luke 1:26-38) into an annunciation to Joseph after her conceiving Jesus. Behind this change lie the purposes of portraying Joseph as a model of righteousness, mercy, and obedience to God and of emphasizing the Davidic messiahship of Jesus as a result of Joseph's obedience. The genitive absolute construction in μνηστευθείσης τῆς μητρὸς αὐτοῦ Μαρίας τῷ Ἰωσήφ typifies Matthew's style. The annunciation to Mary provided the reference to betrothal (see Luke 1:27; cf. Luke 2:5). The designation of Mary as the mother of Jesus without a corresponding designation of Joseph as his father prepares for the virgin birth and, consequently, for the identification of Jesus as "God with us" (v 23; cf. v 16; Luke 1:43; 2:33-34). Matthew is fond of μήτηρ (3,6). The phrase "before they came together" rules out Joseph's fatherhood (cf. Luke 2:26 for πρὶν ἤ in the nativity story, though with another referent).

Mary's finding (εὗρες) favor with God (Luke 1:30; cf. Luke 2:12) becomes her being found (εὑρέθη) pregnant through the Holy Spirit. Matthew likes to use this verb (7,8). Here its passive voice lets the emphasis fall on the agency of the Holy Spirit. In anticipation of his quoting Isa 7:14 in v 23 Matthew uses ἐν γαστρὶ ἔχουσα rather than συλλήμψῃ ἐν γαστρί (Luke 1:31) for Mary's pregnancy. Again we detect his habit of conforming phraseology to the OT. The agency of the Holy Spirit comes from the annunciation to Mary (Luke 1:35), but Matthew's preposition ἐκ echoes its use in vv 3, 5 (bis), 6, and 16. The lack of the definite article with "Holy Spirit" agrees with Luke 1:35. In his own composition Matthew uses the definite article (see 28:19; contrast 3:11; 12:32, where he follows the tradition, as here and in v 20).

1:19 The designation of Joseph as Mary's husband again comes from the annunciation to Mary (see Luke 1:27) and both militates against any thought that another man fathered Jesus and emphasizes that Jesus was born into a Davidic family (cf. v 16). Full betrothal was so binding that its breaking required a certificate of divorce, and the death of one party made the other a widow or widower (*m. Ketub.* 1:2; *m. Soṭa* 1:5; *m. Giṭ.* passim; *EncJud* 11. 1032, 1045-48; *IDB* 3. 284). Hence, Joseph is called Mary's "husband" before marriage. In describing him as "righteous" Matthew draws on the description of Zechariah and Elizabeth as "righteous," which occurs in the story of the annunciation of John's birth (Luke 1:6; cf. Luke 1:75; 2:25; Gen 6:9). Joseph is not only righteous in his care to do the right thing; he is also merciful in his not wanting to disgrace Mary. By exhibiting righteousness and mercy Joseph becomes a prototype of Jesus and his disciples, for Matthew repeatedly stresses these virtues (see δικ- and ἐλεε- in the Greek Index). Matthew's love of parallelism shows in the participles ὤν and μὴ θέλων and in the infinitive phrases αὐτὴν δειγματίσαι and ἀπολῦσαι αὐτήν. The latter infinitive appears more often in Matthew (5,2) than in the other synoptics. θέλων is a Mattheanism (18,8), and λάθρᾳ occurs elsewhere in the synoptics only in Matt 2:7.

According to common opinion, in ignorance or unbelief Joseph supposed that Mary's pregnancy had come about through fornication with another man after she was betrothed to Joseph (cf. the aorist tense of μνηστευθείσης and Luke 1:26ff.). Because he wanted to keep the Mosaic law, Joseph considered himself obligated at least to divorce Mary (Deut 22:23-24). Some rabbinic evidence suggests relaxation of the prescribed stoning (Str-B 1. 50-53), and an offending male is absent here in Matthew. Cf. Deut 24:1-4; and *m. Soṭa* 4:1, where the public ordeal of drinking bitter water (Num 5:11-31) is ruled out. Yet Joseph was magnanimous and possibly retained affection for Mary; so he planned to spare her disgrace by handing her the bill of divorce in the presence of only two or three signing witnesses. If the pregnancy had not yet made itself obvious, they might not even know the reason for the divorce.

To the contrary, the presence and participation of two or three witnesses doubtfully meets the demands of Matthew's "secretly" (cf. 2:7, where all but the principals stay out of the picture), for two or three witnesses were *normally* involved (see DJD 2. 104-9; *m. Giṭ.* passim). Furthermore, the later words of the angel to Joseph, ". . . do not fear to take Mary as your wife" (v 20), suggest reverential hesitation to intrude rather than suspicion of unfaithfulness; i.e., Matthew portrays Joseph not as fearing to break the law through failure to divorce Mary, but as fearing to do wrong by taking Mary to wife when she was pregnant by divine causation. Then the statement in v 18, "she was found to be pregnant through the Holy Spirit," does not come as a piece of advance information to the reader, but bears its more natural sense that Joseph found out the reason for, as well as the fact of, Mary's pregnancy early in the episode (and presumably from Mary; cf. Luke 1:26-45). *That*, not a wrong deduction, left Joseph in a quandary. In deference to the Holy Spirit he decided to divorce Mary. In consideration of Mary he planned to hand her the certificate of divorce without any witnesses at all. The Mosaic law did not require them, anyway. They had become customary to protect a man from a divorced wife's false denial of divorce. But, according to Matthew, Joseph intended to waive that precaution. The angel will repeat what Joseph already believed both to assure him of its truth and to provide a basis for the command to marry. Meanwhile, readers of Matthew have no reason to suspect Mary of what not even Joseph suspected her.

1:20-21 Again Matthew starts with a genitive absolute. Joseph's thinking right and merciful thoughts contrasts with the scribes' evil and merciless thoughts about the healing of a paralytic on the Sabbath (9:4, where Matthew's ἐνθυμήσεις . . . ἐνθυμεῖσθε rather than forms of the stem διαλογιζ-, as in Mark 2:6-8; Luke 5:21-22, echoes 1:20). It also contrasts with the Pharisees' thinking evil of "the son of David" who heals the sick and delivers demoniacs (12:25, with ἐνθυμήσεις, lacking in Mark 3:23; Luke 11:17).

The Mattheanism ἰδού (34,9) calls attention to Jesus' Davidic status and deity in the following message of the angel of the Lord. The annunciations to Zechariah and Mary provide the angel (see Luke 1:11ff., 26ff.; cf. Luke 2:9ff.), but divested of the name Gabriel for conformity to the OT, where he is nameless. After further appearances in 2:13, 19, the angel of the Lord reappears only once, at the empty tomb to announce Jesus' resurrection (28:2-7; contrast the phraseology of Mark 16:5; Luke 24:4). As there, intervention by no less a figure than the angel of the Lord serves to accentuate Jesus' deity. The conveying of the message through a dream yet further emphasizes divine intervention. The phrase κατ᾽ ὄναρ occurs in 1:20; 2:12, 13, 19, 22; 27:19 and nowhere else in the NT. The famous dreams of the patriarch Joseph (Gen 37:5-11) influenced Matthew to conform the traditional vision of Zechariah and visitation to Mary in the daytime (Luke 1:11, 22, 26-28, 38) to the OT pattern of Joseph's dreams in the nighttime (see vv 15-16 for an assimilation of the genealogy of Joseph in the NT to that of the patriarch Joseph). ἐφάνη and λέγων belong to Matthew's favorite diction (5,8; 61,23).

The annunciation to Mary is the source of the angel's addressing Joseph as a "son of David" (see Luke 1:27: "Joseph from the house of David"; cf. Luke 2:4). But for emphasis on Davidic Christology Matthew models his phrase after the designation of Jesus in 1:1. The command not to fear—a Mattheanism (4,1; see φοβέομαι with μή in the Greek Index)—comes from the annunciations to Zechariah and Mary (Luke 1:13, 30; cf. Luke 2:10). παραλαβεῖν and γυναῖκα are further favorites of Matthew (4,6;

10,3). "Your wife" complements "her husband" in v 19 (cf. v 16) and renews the emphasis of Jesus' belonging to a Davidic family. The angel's explanation of Jesus' generation, prediction of the birth of a son, and command to call his name Jesus all stem from the annunciation to Mary (Luke 1:31-32; cf. Luke 2:6, 7, 11, 21; and Gen 16:11; 17:19; Judg 13:3, 5, 7; Isa 7:14; Matt 1:23). γάρ is a Mattheanism (62-63,15), but occurs here in the tradition (Luke 1:30). So also "what has been begotten" and the agency of the Holy Spirit come from the annunciation to Mary (Luke 1:35; cf. the comments on the passive voice in v 16, and v 18 for Matthew's use of ἐκ).

At the start of v 21, δέ shifts attention from generation through the Holy Spirit to the giving birth by Mary and the naming by Joseph, which constitute the reason Joseph should not fear. Generation through the Holy Spirit might well frighten Joseph away. But the Lord's purpose that Joseph himself should name the son gives assurance. "And you shall call his name Jesus" exactly matches Luke 1:31c in the annunciation to Mary. But Matthew's change of address to Joseph not only conforms to the naming of John by his father Zechariah (Luke 1:13, 62-63), but also underscores the adoption of Jesus by Joseph as his legal, though not physical, offspring. Joseph must bring Jesus into David's line in order that Jesus may become the messianic king. Naming by Mary will not avail. Matthew has a predilection for καλέω (8,8) and ὄνομα (9,5) and especially for Ἰησοῦς (80,12), which appears almost twice as often in his gospel as in Mark and Luke each. See *TDNT* 3. 285-87 on the commonness of that name.

But to *be* a king one must *act* like a king by saving his people from oppression (cf. 1 Sam 10:25-27, esp. v 27a, with 1 Sam 11:1-11; 2 Sam 5:1-3). The Davidic kingship of Jesus therefore implies that "he will save his people," as indicated in the personal name to be given him. For "Jesus," Greek form of the Hebrew name "Joshua," means "Yahweh is salvation" according to popular etymology (see M. Noth, *Die israelitischen Personennamen* [BWANT 3/10; Stuttgart: Kohlhammer, 1978] 106-7). To draw out the meaning, Matthew quotes Ps 130:8 (cf. Titus 2:14), but replaces the psalmist's "will redeem" with "will save" (cf. Judg 13:5) for a closer link with the meaning of "Jesus." Several times Matthew will insert the verb "save" to show fulfillment of that meaning. "His people" replaces "Israel"; and despite Matthew's liking πᾶς (63,25-26) and ἀνομία (3,1), "from their sins" replaces "from all his iniquities ['lawlessnesses' in the LXX]." These replacements betray Matthew's source, viz., the tradition behind Luke 1:77: "to give knowledge of *salvation* to *his people* in the forgiveness of *their sins*" (cf. Luke 1:10, 17, 21, 47, 68, 69, 71; 2:10, 11, 30, 32). As often, Matthew has assimilated the tradition to OT phraseology in order to show fulfillment.

In Luke 1:77 "his" refers to God. Here it refers to Jesus. This shift ties in with Matthew's distinctive references to Jesus' church (16:18) and to the kingdom of Jesus the Son of man (13:41; 16:28; 20:21). Who are Jesus' people? The genealogy in 1:2-17 might suggest their identification with Israel. But the replacement of "Israel" in the quotation of Ps 130:8, the correspondence between Jesus' people, church, and kingdom, the transferal of the kingdom to a new nation (see 21:43, an insertion), and Matthew's shifting the remission of sins from John's baptism of repentance to the Words of Institution (cf. 3:2; 26:28; Mark 1:4; 14:24; Luke 3:3; 22:20) show that the disciples of Jesus make up his people, saved from their sins and now including Gentiles (see "Universality" in the Topical Index and esp. 28:19). Contrast the reference to Israel in Luke 1:77 and the preceding context. In typical messianic expectation among the Jews, salvation from sins took second place to deliverance from political oppression by Gentiles (so, e.g., *Psalms of Solomon* 17).

1:22-23 But only God can forgive sins (Mark 2:7c; Luke 5:21c, omitted in Matt 9:3 to avoid any implication that Jesus is not God and therefore cannot forgive sins). Indeed, in Ps 130:8 it is Yahweh who will act as redeemer from sins. And so Jesus is "God with us" (v 23), not in static presence but in saving activity (see W. C. van Unnik in *New Testament Essays* [Studies in Memory of T. W. Manson; ed. A. J. B. Higgins; Manchester: Manchester University Press, 1959] 270-305). Matthew will continue to stress the presence of Jesus as God with his people (see "Immanuel" in the Topical Index).

The quotation of Isa 7:14 is the first of the eleven "fulfillment-quotations" distinctive of Matthew (1:22-23; 2:15, 17-18, 23; 4:14-16; 8:17; 12:17-21; 13:14-15, 35; 21:4-5; 27:9-10). The introductory formula reflects the tradition behind Luke 1:20, 70, conformed as usual to OT phraseology (cf. 1 Kgs 2:27; 8:15; 2 Chr 6:4; 36:21-22; Ezra 1:1). Matthew likes ὅλος (7,3) and the particular form γέγονεν (3,2; cf. Luke 2:15). Unless it is aoristic, the perfect tense of γέγονεν indicates abiding significance (cf. 21:4; 26:56, both peculiar to Matthew). The statement "And this whole thing happened" reappears in 26:56 as an insertion. Here as there, ὅλον, which appears in none of the other introductions to fulfillment-quotations, points to all the items in the preceding context. And as in 21:4 (where ὅλον does not occur); 26:56, the clause as a whole looks forward to a fulfillment guaranteed by the preceding. ἵνα indicates divine purpose. πληρωθῇ (9,6), ῥηθέν (18,9), προφήτου (19,6), and λέγοντος (61,23) are Mattheanisms. Elsewhere Matthew names Isaiah when quoting him explicitly (3:3; 4:14; 8:17; 12:17; 13:14; cf. 13:35 v.l.). Here, "by the Lord" replaces Isaiah's name with the result that the son in the quotation is brought into association with the Lord. This association emphasizes Jesus' divine sonship, a prominent theme in Matthew (see υἱὸς θεοῦ in the Greek Index and the comments on 2:15 for the same phenomenon in the only other fulfillment-quotation containing a reference to Jesus as "a son"; cf. 22:31 in contrast with Mark 12:26; Luke 20:37). Divine sonship links up, then, with deity ("God with us").

The designation of Mary as "a virgin" in the tradition concerning the annunciation to her (Luke 1:27) turned Matthew to Isa 7:14 LXX, a prediction addressed—significantly for Matthew and his Davidic Christology—to the "house of David" (Isa 7:13). "Virgin" clears the way not only for a miraculous conception and birth, but also for the incarnation of God himself.

From the LXX Matthew adopts παρθένος, the Greek word for "virgin," as a translation of עַלְמָה, a Hebrew word meaning "young maiden" with the implication of virginity. Since Isaiah goes on to speak of the near future, we are to think of his prophecy as having come to pass partly during the youth of Mahershalalhashbaz (see Isa 7:15–8:22). But the part of his prophecy having to do with the virginal conception and birth of a divine child awaited fulfillment till Jesus' nativity. The NT distinction between two advents of Christ similarly rests on the phenomenon of partial fulfillment followed at some distance by a completion. Examples abound if we do not deny predictive prophecy out of hand. Sometimes in pagan mythology gods impregnated women carnally. Therefore we can hardly call the resultant births "virgin" or draw a good parallel with the creative work of the Holy Spirit in Mary. Notably, the Jews did not expect the Messiah to be born of a virgin. See Justin Martyr *Dial*. 49 and, for an evaluation of suggested pagan parallels, E. Nellessen, *Das Kind und seine Mutter* (SBS 39; Stuttgart: KBW, 1969) 97-109.

The verb ἕξει agrees with LXX[A,Q] against the rest of the Septuagintal tradition. Its future tense, agreeing with all the Septuagintal tradition against the Hebrew adjective (or participle) הָרָה, brings out Isaiah's predictive intent and thus contributes to Matthew's notation of fulfillment. Matthew goes against all known textual traditions in using the third person plural καλέσουσιν (see Gundry, *Use of the OT* 89-90, for a variety of other readings). This revision turns the quotation into a prediction of the church's confession. Just as "you [Joseph son of David] shall call his name Jesus, for he will save his people from their sins," so also "they [the people of Jesus] will call his name Immanuel." "They" are the church, the people he saves. And he saves them because they acknowledge him as Immanuel. The transliteration Ἐμμανουήλ (so also the LXX) enables Matthew to draw out the meaning of the title with a translation ("God with us") that stresses the deity of Jesus. He is with his people to save them from their sins, not merely in behalf of God, but as God.

1:24-25 The Mattheanism ἐγερθείς (2-3,5) marks Joseph as a good example of immediate obedience. The reference to his sleep stems from the earlier reference to his dreaming, another Mattheanism (see v 20). ἐποίησεν (19,19) typifies Matthew's diction, especially when he wants to emphasize works of obedience. "As the angel of the Lord commanded him" comes close to the distinctive wording in 21:6 (also 26:19; 28:15-16). These expressions rest on OT phraseology (see, e.g., Lev 8:4; Num 20:27; Job 42:9). ὡς is another favorite of Matthew (23,8).

Joseph's taking his wife—i.e., taking her home in wedlock—echoes v 20 and assures Jesus' place in the Davidic line. According to the tradition of the annunciation to Mary, she said, "I do not know [meaning, 'have not had sexual intercourse with'] a man" (Luke 1:34). Matthew turns this into a statement that Joseph did not know her till she had given birth to a son. By itself ἕως οὗ, which belongs to Matthew's preferred diction (4,2), does not necessarily imply that Joseph and Mary entered into normal sexual relations after Jesus' birth. From the redaction-critical standpoint, however, later references to Jesus' brothers (12:46, 47; 13:55) and sisters (13:56) do favor such an implication. The delay in sexual union suits Joseph's original hesitation and preserves the virginity of the birth. The rest of v 25 echoes the tradition recorded also in Luke 2:21. But love of parallelism leads Matthew to conform its phraseology to v 21ab (cf. v 23a). See the com-

25

ments on that verse. The naming of the infant by Joseph amounts to formal acknowledgment of the infant as his legal son and clinches Jesus' place in the Davidic line.

THE WORSHIP OF JESUS
BY A VANGUARD OF GENTILES
2:1-12 (Luke 2:1-20)

2:1-2 Matthew is unconcerned to rehearse the details of Jesus' birth; so he mentions it only in a characteristic genitive absolute (contrast the detailed report in Luke 2:1-7). The name of Jesus picks up the last word in chap. 1. The definite article with the name here in 2:1 carries the force of "the aforementioned Jesus" and thus reminds us of the salvific meaning of his name (see 1:21). The passive voice of "was born" harks back to 1:16, 20 (see earlier comments for interpretation). "In Bethlehem of Judea" comes from the tradition of Jesus' birth (Luke 2:4). Matthew omits the earlier residence in Nazareth and leaves the impression that everything has been happening in Bethlehem (see also the comments on 2:22-23). The stress on Bethlehem serves his interest in Davidic Christology. The birth of Jesus takes place, then, in David's hometown five miles south of Jerusalem. We might think that the added phrases "of Judea" (vv 1 and 5) and "land of Judah" (v 6) are meant to distinguish this Bethlehem from another Bethlehem seven miles northwest of Nazareth (Josh 19:15). But that purpose would have required only a single reference to Judea or the land of Judah. The tripling of the reference emphasizes the royal status of Jesus; he came from the tribe and territory that produced the Davidic kings (cf. 1:2; Gen 49:10). "In the days of Herod the king" matches Luke 1:5. There, too, we read "of Judea." Apparently tradition triggered Matthew's Judean references. The seemingly otiose tripling of Herod's designation as the king (see also vv 3 and 9) throws into contrast the designation of Jesus as "the king of the Jews" (v 2) and sets the stage for a struggle over royal power.

Herod was born in 73 B.C., became governor of Galilee in 47 B.C., was named "King of Judea" by the Roman Senate in 40 B.C., gained control of Judea in 37 B.C., and died in 4 or 1 B.C. (for the latter, see E. L. Martin, *The Birth of Christ Recalculated* [Pasadena: Foundation for Biblical Research, 1978]). Herod ruled cleverly but cruelly under Roman sponsorship.

Matthew now turns the visit of the local Jewish shepherds (Luke 2:8-20) into the adoration by Gentile magi from foreign parts. Just as the four women (besides Mary) in the genealogy pointed forward to the bringing of Gentiles into the church, so also the coming of the magi previews the entrance of disciples from all nations into the circle of those who acknowledge Jesus as the king of the Jews and worship him as God. The Mattheanism ἰδού (34,9) accentuates this role of the magi.

Characteristically, Matthew gets the magi from the OT—in particular, from Dan 2:2, 10 LXX Theod, a passage concerning a dream and therefore easily associated with this dream-laden account (see 1:20; 2:12, 13, 19, 22; cf. also the Theodotionic version of Dan 1:20; 2:27; 4:4; 5:7, 11, 15). The magi were astrologers. Matthew selects them as his substitute for the shepherds in order to lead up to the star, which replaces the angel and heavenly host in the tradition (Luke 2:8-15a). In the Benedictus of Zechariah we read of ἀνατολὴ ἐξ ὕψους, "the rising from on high" (Luke 1:78); the magi announce that they have seen a star ἐν τῇ ἀνατολῇ, "at its rising" (not "in the east," since Matthew would probably have used the plural, as in 2:1; 8:11; 24:27, for that meaning). The definite article has the force of a weak possessive. See also v 9; Num 24:17; Isa 60:1-3 (cf. the allusion to Isa 60:6 in Matt 2:11); Mic 5:3(4). Like the Gentile prophet Balaam they have come "from the east" (Num 23:7 LXX; cf. Matt 8:11 and Philo's calling Balaam a magus in *Mos.* 1. 50 §276). The star they have seen at its rising corresponds to and derives from the royal star seen to rise by Balaam (Num 24:17-19 LXX) and interpreted messianically in late Judaism (see further Gundry, *Use of the OT* 128-29, and cf. Bar Cochba, "son of a star," acclaimed as the Messiah by some Jews during the Second Jewish War of A.D. 132-135). Obviously, then, heavy emphasis falls on Jesus as the star of David, the royal Messiah.

It would be a mistake to think that because Matthew fails to quote Num 23:7; 24:17-19 explicitly he has little or no interest in them. Throughout his gospel he subtly conforms phraseology to the OT. Since Jesus has already been introduced as David's son, Matthew expects his readers to catch such allusions; or he takes private delight in them. Contrary to the opinion of some, the rising of the star represents the coming of a king in both Numbers and Matthew. Therefore the association proves easy. See Nellessen, *Das Kind und seine Mutter* 75-76, for an evaluation of the story concerning King Tiridates' visit to Nero, a story sometimes put forward as a source for Matthew.

The verb παρεγένοντο will occur again in 3:1, 13, both times as an insertion. Matthew brings in Jerusalem as the center of antagonism toward Jesus. The question introduced with a typical λέγοντες (61,23) points toward Bethlehem as part of Matthew's Davidic Christology. τεχθείς links this episode with the preceding (see 1:21, 23, 25). "The king of the Jews" anticipates 27:11, 29, 37 and shows Matthew's partiality to βασιλεύς (6,9). Jesus' kingship contrasts with Herod's. The addition "of the Jews" contrasts with the bare title of King Herod and may suggest the legitimacy of Jesus' kingship over against the illegitimacy of Herod's rule. Herod was not a Davidic king, not even a Jew, but an Idumean. Only the magi and Gentiles in the passion account call Jesus the king of the Jews. Thus Matthew notes recognition of Jesus' messiahship by Gentiles just as Luke notes the acknowledgment of Jesus by Jewish shepherds, Simeon, and Anna. The magi's coming (ἤλθομεν) corresponds to the shepherds' coming (διέλθωμεν . . . ἦλθον—Luke 2:15-16). προσκυνῆσαι (6,5) finds no match in the tradition concerning the shepherds. Matthew adds the worship of Jesus to emphasize his deity. Other peculiarly Matthean combinations of ἔρχομαι and προσκυνέω will occur in v 8; 15:25 (cf. the distinctive combinations of προσέρχομαι and προσκυνέω in 8:2; 9:18; 20:20; 28:9).

J. Finegan (*Handbook of Biblical Chronology* [Princeton: Princeton University Press, 1964] 238-48) discusses suggested identifications of the star. If the star is simply literary and theological, however, such identifications—and also discussions concerning the movement of the star—lose their meaning.

2:3-4 In its first position the aorist nominative participle ἀκούσας typifies Matthew's style (10,3). According to the tradition both Zechariah and Mary were "troubled" (Luke 1:12, 29). In a passage that gave Matthew his magi, King Nebuchadnezzar is troubled (Dan 2:1-2 LXX); so Matthew switches the troubling from Zechariah and Mary to King Herod. As is well known, Herod harbored psychopathic suspicions that others were trying to seize his throne (see Book 17 in Josephus's *Antiquities*). In addition, Matthew writes that "all Jerusalem" was troubled "with him," i.e., with Herod at the prospect of another king, not at the prospect of a Herodian reprisal against them. Matthew often uses πᾶσα for emphasis (63,25-26). Here it shows the strength of his desire to range Jerusalem alongside Herod as the center of antagonism toward Jesus and of later persecution against the church (see chaps. 21ff., and cf. 14:26 for an insertion of ἐταράχθησαν).

Though the troubling of all Jerusalem with Herod portends Jesus' final rejection, the blame for that rejection does not rest equally on all Jews. For Matthew will regularly make the Jewish crowds prefigure the church; and he will do so at the same time he traces the rejection of the Jewish people as a nation (see esp. 27:15-26). The blame rests most heavily on their leaders, whom Herod now gathers for cooperation in his attempt to destroy Jesus. To punctuate the point, Matthew puts "all" with "the chief priests and scribes of the people" just as he added "all" to "Jerusalem." The leading priests, including past high priests and the current high priest, made up the chief priests, most of whom were Sadducees from the theological standpoint. Scribes came primarily from the Pharisaical sect. With the elders these select groups formed the Great Sanhedrin, or Jewish supreme court (see esp. 16:21). Matthew mentions the chief priests because their position entailed working with King Herod, and the scribes because their expertise in the OT made them knowledgeable to answer the question of the Messiah's birthplace. For lack of function in the context, the elders go unmentioned. Therefore the phrase "of the people," which Matthew alone will attach to the elders in 21:23; 26:3, 47; 27:1, goes over to the scribes. Thus he points to the scribes' role in leading the Jewish people astray. Matthew likes to use γραμματεύς (10,2) and λαός (8,4).

The participle συναγαγών (10,10) is cognate to συναγωγή (2,2) and slyly alludes to the unbelieving synagogue, dominated by the chief priests and scribes. They know the data of messianic prophecy, but not the Messiah himself. ποῦ and γεννᾶται echo v 2, but ὁ Χριστός (8,5) substitutes for the earlier ὁ τεχθεὶς βασιλεὺς τῶν Ἰουδαίων. The new designation reflects the tradition of the nativity (Luke 2:11; cf. Luke 2:26), echoes 1:1, 16-17, and stresses Jesus' messiahship. Besides, King Herod would hardly have referred to anyone except himself as king of the Jews.

2:5-6 "In Bethlehem of Judea" echoes v 1 and comes from the tradition (Luke 2:4). The introduction to the quotation of Mic 5:1(2) contains favorite words of Matthew in γάρ (62-63,15) and οὕτως (18,5). The standard "it is written," used throughout the NT to introduce OT quotations, appears instead of the formula of fulfillment beloved by Matthew (see the comments on 1:22). His placement of the quotation on the tongues of the chief priests and scribes makes the formula inappropriate. Nevertheless, the phrase "through the prophet" does make its way from the formula into the present introduction (cf. προφη- in the Greek Index).

Matthew edits the quotation so as to bring out Jesus' Davidic messiahship. "Land of Judah" both contemporizes the archaic "Ephrathah" and conforms to vv 1 and 5—but not wholly, for those verses read "Judea" rather than "land of Judah." γῆ is a favorite word (21,6) and betrays Matthew's typically Jewish land-consciousness (cf. vv 20-21; 1[3] Kg[dm]s 19:3 LXX with MT). But why "Judah" instead of "Judea," as in the context? The reason is not the common designation "Bethlehem-Judah" in the OT, for then we would expect exactly that instead of "Bethlehem, *land of* Judah." Rather, Matthew wants an allusion to Judah, progenitor of the royal tribe (1:2-3), in order to heighten the stress on Jesus' kingship (cf. Gen 49:10).

Now Matthew inserts "by no means." As a result he denies Bethlehem's leastness, which the present Hebrew consonantal text in Micah affirms, or at least questions (see Gundry, *Use of the OT* 91-93). Many have offered conjectural emendations of Micah's text in order to assimilate it to Matthew's; but the difficulty of the present text stands in its favor, and Matthew's penchant for interpretation in quoting the OT militates against assimilation of Micah to Matthew. For Matthew the birth of Jesus has transformed Bethlehem from the unimportant village it was at the time of Micah's prediction into the supremely important birthplace of the messianic king from David's line (cf. Matthew's distinctive uses of ἐλάχιστος, "least," in 5:19 [bis]; 25:40, 45, in both of which passages we read about the *importance* of the least). Cf. the insertion of "not" in *Tg. Ps.-J.* and *Frg. Tg.* Gen 37:33 and, for other examples of targumic reversals of the OT text, M. L. Klein in *Bib* 57 (1976) 515-37.

By supplying different vowels to the Hebrew consonantal text, Matthew reads "rulers" instead of "thousands" or "clans" (MT, LXX). Thus he personifies the clans, just as Bethlehem has already been personified ("and you, Bethlehem"), in order to affirm the superiority of Jesus over his predecessors in the Davidic dynasty (1:6-11). Later, in his account of Jesus' passion and resurrection, Matthew will interject the designation of Pilate as ἡγεμών eight times. By using the same word in his quotation of Mic 5:1, the evangelist makes Jesus Pilate's superior, too, the true governor of Judah.

The Mattheanism γάρ (62-63,15) is not in the MT or LXX. It makes what follows a reason for Bethlehem's importance. The switch from leastness to importance demanded justification. Matthew drops the phrase "to me [the Lord]" (MT, LXX) in order to bring together "governor" and its modifying clause. The pronoun "my" in that clause makes the phrase "to me" unnecessary, anyway. The reappearance of "governor" (this time as an anarthrous substantive participle) reinforces the connotations noted above. The LXX has a different word.

The last clause of the quotation replaces Micah's "one who is to be ruler in Israel" and comes from the Lord's promise in 2 Sam 5:2; 1 Chr 11:2 to make David the shepherd-king over Israel. ὅστις appears often in Matthew (23,5) and emphasizes the governorship rather than the personal identity of Jesus. This governorship takes the form of shepherding God's people Israel (cf. the motif of Israel in Luke 1:16, 54, 68, 80; 2:25, 32, 34). Shepherding was David's youthful activity. Matthew will enlarge the portrait of Jesus as the new shepherd-king by inserting "Israel" in his account of Jesus' ministry (5,4) and by portraying Jesus as a shepherd (9:36; 25:31-46; 26:31). His turning to the Davidic covenant in 2 Sam 5:2; 1 Chr 11:2 shows that he has in mind the Davidic association of Bethlehem even though he does not include the traditional description of Bethlehem as "the city of David" (Luke 2:4).

For Jewish expectation of the Messiah's origin, see John 7:41-42 and *Tg. Neb.* Mic 5:1. Some think that Micah used Bethlehem only as a figure for the Davidic dynasty, not as a genuine place-name. But if so, why did Micah emphasize the smallness of Bethlehem? Jerusalem had long been the home of David's dynasty. Nevertheless, Matthew would have found no fault with a fulfillment more literal than Micah had envisioned. Like Matthew, the OT Peshitta and the concordance of Rabbi Nathan lack the phrase "to me" in Mic 5:1; but it is doubtful that Matthew's text of Mic 5:1 lacked the phrase, for Matthew had reason to omit it.

2:7-8 The Mattheanism τότε (66,17) helps make a story line. "Secretly" describes a meeting between Herod and the magi at night, for according to v 9 the magi set out for Bethlehem under starlight after they heard what the king had to say. Matthew is not so historically concerned as to imply that Herod needed secrecy in order to forestall a spiriting away of his dangerous rival by parents and revolutionaries. Rather, he wants to make out of Herod's malevolence, which lies behind the secrecy, a dramatic foil to the gentleness of Jesus the shepherd-king (see 11:28-29; 21:4-5, both unique to Matthew) and especially to Joseph's plan to divorce Mary secretly (see 1:19, the only other place where λάθρα occurs in the synoptics). Here we have a preview of the Sanhedrin's plot to arrest Jesus stealthily and kill him (26:3-5). The aorist nominative participle καλέσας is a Mattheanism (8,8).

The verb ἠκρίβωσεν, "ascertained," occurs in the NT only here and in v 16. It depicts the care with which Herod went about his cruel purpose. We meet a series of Mattheanisms in φαινομένου (5,8), πέμψας (3,1), and πορευθέντες (8,4). ἐξετάσατε appears in the synoptics only here and, as an insertion, in 10:11. ἀκριβῶς plays on the cognate ἠκρίβωσεν. Thus Matthew reemphasizes Herod's malevolence, which foreshadows not only the passion of Jesus but also the persecution of the church in Matthew's own day.

τοῦ παιδίου occurs throughout this chapter and stems from the tradition (Luke 1:59, 66, 76, 80; and esp. 2:17). Matthew takes εὕρητε from the tradition (Luke 2:12), partly because of his independent liking of the verb (7,8). He also likes ἀπαγγείλατε (3,2). Except for αὐτῷ, every word in the last clause of Herod's command, ὅπως κἀγὼ ἐλθὼν προσκυνήσω αὐτῷ, stems from Matthew's favorite diction (8,7; 5,3; 10,10; 6,5). The last three of these words echo v 2. That Herod's statement consists almost entirely of Mattheanisms supports our understanding Matthew himself to be forming this episode out of the shepherds' visit, with use of collateral materials.

2:9 The aorist nominative participle ἀκούσαντες echoes v 3 and typifies Matthew's style and diction (10,3). Similarly, τοῦ βασιλέως (6,9) comes down from vv 1 and 3. The redesignation of Herod as king and the reappearance of the star again set the legitimacy of Jesus' kingship and the illegitimacy of Herod's in opposition to each other. The favorite ἐπορεύθησαν (13,10) reflects v 8. Yet another favorite, ἰδού (34,9), highlights the star as symbolic of Jesus the Davidic king. The description of the star derives from v 2. The shepherds' coming at night lies behind the starry journey of the magi. προῆγεν will occur without parallel also in 21:31. Since according to v 8 the magi already knew to go to Bethlehem, the star does not guide them to Bethlehem so much as it confirms their direction and then identifies in Bethlehem the particular place where they will find Jesus. The town was easy enough to find, but not the house. We meet another string of Mattheanisms in ἕως (13,14), ἐλθών (10,10), and ἐπάνω (7,1), and perhaps in οὗ (0,3).

2:10 The magi's seeing the star echoes vv 2 and 9, and ἰδόντες characterizes Matthew's style (10-11,7). Here the participle introduces a typically Matthean parallel of five clauses linked by καί's. Each begins with an aorist participial phrase and ends with an aorist verbal phrase. The "great joy" of the magi derives from the "great joy" of the shepherds (Luke 2:10; cf. Jonah 4:6; 1 Chr 29:9). Matthew likes both χαράν (3,2) and μεγάλην (11,1). Two further Mattheanisms, ἐχάρησαν (2,1; cf. Luke 1:14, 28) and σφόδρα (5,2), add strength to an already strong expression. Matthew can hardly restrain his joy in contemplating the messianic salvation (cf. his multiplication of beatitudes in 5:4, 5, 7, 8, 9, 10; 16:17, all found only in this gospel).

2:11-12 Again we meet a Mattheanism in ἐλθόντες (10,10), which corresponds to Luke 2:15-16. In Matthew "the house" means Jesus' house (see the comments on 9:10; 13:1; cf. Luke 1:40). Here it replaces the traditional manger, hardly a fit place for distinguished magi to offer expensive gifts to a king. The seeing of the child with Mary his mother reflects the tradition behind Luke 2:16-17. But Joseph has dropped out, the child has come forward in order of mention, and Mary has gained the designation "his mother," as in 1:18—all to emphasize Jesus' virgin birth and deity.

His deity receives further emphasis in the added, untraditional clause "and falling down, they worshipped him." This means that they knelt down before him with heads to the ground. Matthew inserts the same combination of falling down and worshipping in 4:9 and uses it in unique material at 18:26. Individually, too, πεσόντες (5,3) and προσεκύνησαν (6,5) typify his diction (see esp. vv 2 and 8; cf. Dan 3:5; also Ps 72:9, 11, a passage about to be used for the gifts of the magi). In particular, πεσόντες sharpens Matthew's point, for in 4:9 falling down will accompany worship in the alternatives of worshipping God and worshipping Satan, and without parallel it describes the response of the disciples who witnessed the transfiguration (17:6).

Yet further emphasis accrues to Jesus' deity and kingship from the magi's offering expensive gifts. Mattheanisms abound in ἀνοίξαντες (5,2), θησαυρούς (1,4), προσήνεγκαν (9,2), δῶρα (7,1), and χρυσόν (4,1). προσήνεγκαν very often has to do with offerings to God (see 8:4 and a host of references in the LXX). Elsewhere in Matthew δῶρον is used exclusively and fairly often for offerings to God. The magi stand, then, as prototypes of Jesus' disciples, who give up earthly treasures for heavenly treasures (see 6:19-21; 19:21).

Typically, Matthew draws on the OT to specify the gifts of the magi. Like the Gentile kings in Ps 72:10-11, 15, they bring gifts of gold to a superior king in Israel. So also in Isa 60:2-3, 6, Gentile kings bring gold and frankincense. The ancient ascription of Psalm 72 to Solomon, David's son, suits the Davidic Christology of Matthew and leads him to Cant 3:6; 4:6, where King Solomon is described as perfumed with myrrh and frankincense. Cf. 1 Kgs 10:2; 2 Kgs 20:13; Isa 39:2; *1 Enoch* 53:1; *Pss. Sol.* 17:31(34).

χρηματισθέντες compares with ἦν . . . κεχρηματισμένον in Luke 2:26. Perhaps Matthew has turned the traditional revelation to Simeon into a warning to the magi. "In a dream" echoes 1:20 (see earlier comments on its Matthean character). All three words in the statement ἄλλης ὁδοῦ ἀνεχώρησαν represent favorite diction (14,4; 9,2; 4,5). χώραν comes from the tradition concerning the shepherds (Luke 2:8) and with ἀνεχώρησαν makes a wordplay. In v 12 as a whole, then, Matthew has transformed the praiseful return of the shepherds (Luke 2:20) into the magi's flight from persecution. This flight offers an example for persecuted Christians to follow (see "Flight from persecution" in the Topical Index and esp. 10:23).

THE PRESERVATION OF JESUS AS A SIGN OF HIS DIVINE SONSHIP
2:13-15 (Luke 2:22)

2:13 To carry on the motif of flight from persecution Matthew changes the going up to Jerusalem by the Holy Family (Luke 2:22) into a flight to Egypt. Another use of ἀναχωρέω links this paragraph with the preceding (cf. v 12 with comments). Then, to emphasize a new divine intervention, Matthew repeats the phraseology of 1:20 (see earlier comments on the distinctive character of every expression, and cf. 1QapGen 19:14-24). Both here and there a typically Matthean genitive absolute comes first, and ἰδού, a favorite Matthean device for getting attention, introduces the appearance of the angel. Here, however, Matthew uses the historical present, "appears," in order to heighten emphasis on the divine intervention that signifies Jesus' status as Son of God.

The angel commands Joseph to get up, take his family, and flee to Egypt. The aorist nominative participle ἐγερθείς echoes 1:24, παράλαβε harks back to 1:20 again, and both expressions betray Matthew's hand

(2-3,5; 4,6). The reference to the child and his mother recalls v 11 and, like v 11, echoes 1:18 in a further reminder of Jesus' virgin birth and deity. Matthew will insert φεῦγε twice (10:23; 23:33). Just as Joseph's father Jacob and Joseph's dreams came from the story of the patriarch Joseph (see the comments on 1:15-16, 20), so also the going to Egypt comes from that story. Matthew will shortly pick up a typological thread in Moses, whose story deals with Egypt and follows Joseph's in the OT. The Egyptian sojourn of the NT Joseph and his family thus corresponds to the Egyptian sojourn of the patriarch Joseph and his family. The location of Bethlehem in southern Palestine and the tradition of southwesterly escape to Egypt (see 1 Kgs 11:40; Jer 26:20-23; 41:16-18; 43:5-7; Josephus *Ant.* 14.2.1 §21; 15.3.2 §46; *J.W.* 7.10.1 §§409-19) made it easy for Matthew to bend the dominical material in this direction. See 5:25 for an insertion of ἴσθι. Here the verb is followed by two specially Matthean words, ἐκεῖ (16,6) and ἕως (13,14).

Again we meet favorite words of Matthew in γάρ (62-63,15) and μέλλει (5-6,1). Composition by him gains confirmation also from characteristic borrowing of OT phraseology. This is seen in the reference to Herod's seeking to destroy the child, which reflects Pharaoh's seeking to slay Moses in Exod 2:15. Though Jesus' divine sonship will predominate (see v 15), Matthew is making Jesus the greater Moses just as he has already made him the greater David (see the comments on vv 20-21, and "Moses parallel Jesus" in the Topical Index). "The child" substitutes for Moses' name. τοῦ ἀπολέσαι is a genitive articular infinitive. This construction is distinctive of Matthew in 2:13; 3:13; 11:1; 21:32 and has parallels only in 13:3; 24:45. Here the expression translates לַהֲרֹג. The LXX has ἀνελεῖν. Matthew's word is a favorite (8,1) and relates to 27:20, where we read of the chief priests' and elders' persuading the crowd to have Jesus destroyed (ἀπολέσωσιν) instead of Barabbas released (ἀπολύσῃ—so Mark 15:11). In other words, the choice of the verb in these two passages derives from the motif of the Jewish leaders' opposition to Jesus: what Herod failed to do with their help they succeeded in doing at a later time without his help (cf. the comments on vv 3-4).

2:14-15 The phraseology of vv 14-15a closely resembles that of v 13bcd (see earlier comments). The resemblance points up the exactitude of Joseph's obedience as a model for Christian discipleship (cf. 1:24). The addition "during the night" shows immediacy of obedience, another exemplary point, and recalls "from his sleep" in 1:24. Nighttime fits flight from persecution better than sleep would. Matthew likes νυκτός (4,3) and ἀνεχώρησεν (4,5). The latter both revives the allusion to Exod 2:15 (see the LXX) and echoes vv 12 and 13a. Though τελευτῆς occurs only here in the gospels, words with the stem τελ- belong to Matthew's favorite vocabulary (16,7), and the noun corresponds to ἐτελεύτησεν in Exod 4:19 LXX.

The formula of fulfillment introducing the quotation from Hos 11:1 reads exactly as 1:22b (see earlier comments). The preceding mention of Egypt has united with "Son of God" and "Son of the Highest" in the tradition of Jesus' nativity (Luke 1:32, 35) and with Matthew's own interest in Jesus' divine sonship (see υἱὸς θεοῦ in the Greek Index) to suggest the statement in Hos 11:1. There, the Lord addresses the nation of Israel as his son. The multiplicity of parallels drawn between the history of Israel and the life of Jesus suggests that Matthew saw that history as both recapitulated and anticipated in the "king of the Jews"; like Israel in the messianic age Jesus receives homage from the Gentiles (2:11); as a son he, like Israel, receives God's fatherly protection in Egypt (2:15); his oppression brings sorrow as the oppression of Israel brought sorrow (2:17-18); like Israel he is tempted in the wilderness (4:1-10). The messianic reference preceding the statement "God brought him [the Messiah] out of Egypt" in Num 24:7-8 LXX may also have facilitated quotation of the similar statement in Hos 11:1. For Matthew has recently used Numbers 24 (see the comments on vv 1-12).

Though Egypt provides the background for Matthew's use of Hos 11:1, emphasis falls on Jesus' divine sonship, not on the geography of Jesus' travels. The quotation comes before the return from Egypt to Palestine. Matthew's fulfillment-quotations regularly refer backward to what has already happened in the narrative. The clause immediately preceding the present quotation stresses residence in Egypt till Herod's death, not departure from Egypt after Herod's death. Therefore Matthew is not highlighting Jesus' later departure from Egypt as a new Exodus, but God's preservation of Jesus in Egypt as a sign of his divine sonship: God cares for Jesus as a father cares for his son. Confirmation comes from the introduction to the quotation. As in 1:22-23, Matthew inserts a reference to the Lord's speaking and suppresses the name of the prophet. Why? Because here as there—and only in these two fulfillment-quotations—Jesus appears as "son" in the quoted words. Hence, Matthew makes sure "the Lord" is speaking, with the result that the son belongs to God (cf. "Deity of Jesus" in the Topical Index and 4QpsDan A^a [= 4Q 243], discussed by J. A. Fitzmyer, *A Wandering Aramean* [SBLMS 25; Missoula: Scholars Press, 1979] 90-93, 102-7).

Matthew does not portray Jesus as God's Son merely in the sense that Jesus acted in God's behalf and submitted perfectly to God's authority. His emphasis on the virgin birth, on Jesus as being always with his people, on the worship of Jesus and the bringing of offerings to him, and on the title κύριος ("Lord") and his putting Jesus as the Son alongside the Father and Holy Spirit in a baptismal formula (28:19) all point to essential as well as functional deity. That Matthew does not use Greek philosophical terms to describe this deity hardly spoils the point.

A PREVIEW OF JEWISH CALAMITIES
RESULTING FROM THE REJECTION OF JESUS
2:16-18 (Luke 2:22-38)

2:16 Matthew pursues Mosaic typology farther with an episode corresponding to Pharaoh's slaughtering the male babies of the Israelites at the time of Moses' birth (Exod 1:15-22; cf. the comments on vv 13-14 and 20-21). To do so, he changes the sacrificial slaying of "a pair of turtledoves or two young pigeons," which took place at the presentation of the baby Jesus in the Temple (Luke 2:24; cf. Lev 12:6-8), into Herod's slaughtering the babies in Bethlehem (cf. *As. Mos.* 6:2-6). The sorrow of the babies' mothers corresponds to the sword that was going to pierce the heart of Mary, according to Simeon's prediction at the presentation in the Temple (Luke 1:35; cf. Matt 2:18). Herod's massive crimes made it easy for Matthew to manipulate the dominical tradition in this way. Since the Slaughter of the Innocents resulted from the cooperation of the chief priests and scribes with Herod, this episode previews calamities to befall the Jewish nation for their, and especially their leaders', rejection of Jesus (cf. 23:33-39; 27:20-25).

Matthew's favorite τότε (66,17) carries on the story line. The aorist nominative participle ἰδών represents his style and diction (10-11,7). ἐνεπαίχθη will occur as an insertion in 27:29. There, Jesus the true king of the Jews is mocked; here, Herod the illegitimate king. The verb also makes a wordplay with its cognate παῖδας. λίαν, which Matthew will insert in 4:8; 8:28; 27:14, accentuates Herod's rage and warns of similar calamities to come. The aorist participial form of ἀποστείλας reflects Matthew's style. ἀνεῖλεν comes from Exod 2:15 LXX and compensates for its displacement in v 13. Matthew habitually compensates in this manner (see "Compensation" in the Topical Index). πάντας and πᾶσι come from Exod 1:22, typify Matthew's diction (63,25-26), and intensify the slaughter so as to heighten the warning that calamities will fall on the Jewish nation for their rejecting Christ. The double use of this adjective implicates the whole nation, just as in vv 3-4. Matthew will insert ὁρίοις in 4:13; 15:39.

Pharaoh had the male babies of the Israelites killed immediately at birth. The circumstances that Jesus has already been born and that the magi have used up considerable time in their travels force Matthew to identify a reasonable age limit. But an infant would have been considered two years old immediately on entering his second year. Therefore we should express the thought with the phrase "one year old and under" despite Matthew's reference to two years (διετοῦς; see the Greek Index for Matthew's liking δια-compounds—6,6). The last line of v 16, beginning "according to the time," echoes v 7 (see earlier comments).

2:17-18 Again τότε carries on the story line. But it also provides a clue to Matthew's intent, since in quotations concerning fulfillment this conjunction replaces ἵνα and ὅπως in only one other place. That is 27:9-10, where the very same formula will introduce another statement of Jeremiah in reference to the penalty paid for an act hostile to Jesus. Other fulfillments have their origin in the work of God through Jesus (or through those who act on his behalf during his infancy)—hence the purposive ἵνα and ὅπως. These two fulfillments come about because of the rejection of Jesus— hence the temporal τότε, which allows a limitation of the fulfillment to God's permissive will (cf. the avoidance of ἵνα in 13:13, against Mark 4:12). The dropping of "by the Lord" and insertion of "Jeremiah" also distance God from the event (contrast 1:22b; 2:15b). Concerning the rest of the introductory formula see the comments on 1:22b.

The quotation comes from Jer 31(38):15. In it, Matthew might have avoided the difference between Bethlehem and Ramah (located a little farther north of Jerusalem than Bethlehem lay to the south) by translating בְּרָמָה as a common noun, "in the height" (so LXX^A). His suppressing "Ephrath(ah)" in the quotation of Mic 5:1(2) in v 6 militates against his associating Rachel's sepulchre in Ramah with Bethlehem-Ephrath. (Besides, according to Gen 35:16, 19; 48:7 [cf. 1 Sam 10:2] Jacob buried Rachel on his *way* from Bethel to Bethlehem-Ephrath and at some *distance* from the latter.) Therefore, the meaning Matthew sees in the slaughter does not have its center of gravity in the geographical locale, as though he was trying to explain the Messiah's seemingly inappropriate departure from Davidic Bethlehem on a journey that would eventually take him to that oddity for a messianic hometown—Nazareth in Galilee. To do that, Matthew needed only a direct transfer from Bethlehem to Nazareth with supporting Scripture. Rather, the stress here lies on the dreadful consequences of rejecting Jesus.

Though Matthew agrees with the LXX against our Hebrew text by inserting "and" between "weeping" and "great mourning," he makes the latter two expressions somewhat more emphatic by treating them as appositives to "voice" (so also the Hebrew, whereas the weaker genitives in the LXX lead to the translation, "a voice . . . *of* lament and weeping and mourning"). Then Matthew, by lopping off θρῆνου from the LXX, makes κλαυθμός and ὀδυρμός refer to different Hebrew nouns in reverse order. The result is an a-b-a-b parallel in which κλαίουσα, "weeping," answers to κλαυθμός, "weeping"; and οὐκ ἤθελεν παρακληθῆναι, ὅτι οὐκ εἰσίν, "she refused to be comforted, because they were no more," answers to ὀδυρμός, "mourning." Matthew then turns תַמְרוּרִים, "bitterness," into his favorite πολύς (23,1) for modification of ὀδυρμός. Thus he avoids breaking up the parallelism and wins a huge emphasis on the motif of sorrow. This emphasis relates to 27:25: "And answering, all the people said, 'Let his [Jesus'] blood be on us and on our children.' " By taking Herod's side and forcing Pilate's hand in their rejection of Jesus, the Jewish leaders will bring sorrowful consequences on the innocent children of the people they influence. To prepare for this correspondence, Matthew here replaces "sons" (so the MT and LXX) with "children" (as in 27:25). For further textual comparisons, see Gundry, *Use of the OT* 94-97.

In Jer 31:15 the prophet portrays Rachel as weeping in her grave for Israelites whom the Assyrians were taking into captivity. Though she did not mother Judah (to whose tribal territory Bethlehem belonged), neither did she mother a number of the northern tribes. Jeremiah makes her the nation's representative mother because she was Jacob's favorite wife and died giving birth to Benjamin, whom she called Ben-oni, "The son of my sorrow" (Gen 35:18). Matthew simply takes over this portrait. The infamous cruelties of Herod the Great serve equally well to support, by analogy, the historicity of the Slaughter of the Innocents and to provide the impetus for a literary creation of that slaughter. Therefore Matthew's treatment of traditions acknowledgedly parallel decides the issue here (see the rest of this commentary and, for a good example of the creative use of tradition, 26:14-16; 27:3-10 with comments).

Though they are not always so insuperable as sometimes alleged, problems of harmonizing the stories in Matthew and Luke support creativity on Matthew's part. For example, Luke says that the Holy Family went back to Nazareth when (ὡς) they finished the ceremonies in the Temple

(Luke 2:39), i.e., forty days after Jesus' birth (Leviticus 12). This statement leaves no room for the Slaughter of the Innocents, the flight to Egypt, and the residence there till the death of Herod. In its other fifty-nine occurrences throughout Luke-Acts, ὡς does not allow for gaps like that. On the contrary, it draws temporal connections so close that we often need to translate it "while, as." Luke's and Josephus's failure to mention the slaughter pose a further difficulty in view of Matthew's statement that all Jerusalem was troubled along with Herod. See the discussion in Nellessen, *Das Kind und seine Mutter* 113-25.

It may be asked how Matthew can put forward his embellishments of tradition as fulfillments of the OT. But this phenomenon should surprise us no more than his transforming historical statements in the OT—those concerning the Exodus and the Babylonian Exile—into messianic prophecies. We will have to broaden our understanding of "happened" as well as of "fulfilled" when reading that such-and-such happened in order that so-and-so's prophecy might be fulfilled. Two features of Matthew's practice save him from fantasy: (1) his embellishments rest on historical data, which he hardly means to deny by embellishing them; (2) the embellishments foreshadow genuinely historical events such as the vindications of Jesus as God's Son in the resurrection and in the calamities befalling the Jewish nation after Jesus' lifetime. Sadly, it needs emphasis that Matthew does not write out of anti-Semitism. Himself a Jew, he is trying to save Jews from calamity, not contribute to their pain.

THE RETURN OF THE GREATER MOSES TO BECOME THE BRANCH OF DAVID
2:19-23 (Luke 2:39)

2:19-21 The going of the Holy Family to Nazareth comes back in line with the traditional return to Nazareth (Luke 2:39-40). The construction of the genitive absolute τελευτήσαντος δὲ τοῦ Ἡρῴδου typifies Matthew's style and echoes v 15 (see earlier comments). Except for the understandable insertion "in Egypt," the words from "behold" through "his mother" match v 13 exactly. There, too, a genitive absolute preceded them, a command to travel followed them, next a γάρ-clause with forms of ζητέω and τὸ παιδίον, then identical statements concerning Joseph's getting up and taking the child and his mother (except that here "during the night" drops out because they are no longer making a hasty getaway), and finally a statement with εἰς regarding travel. For Mattheanisms and a further reference to 1:20, see the comments on v 13.

Because the persecution has passed, the Mattheanism πορεύου (13,10) replaces φεῦγε (v 13). Of course, Egypt needs replacement as the destination. But we read "land of Israel" instead of "land of Judah" (Matthew's insertion in the quotation from Mic 5:1 in v 6). The reason is that Matthew needs a term broad enough to cover Galilee, the unplanned but eventual destination, as well as Judea, the planned destination. Only here in the NT do we read "the land of Israel." Yet Matthew exhibits fondness for both

37

words individually (21,6; 5,4), rabbis used the phrase for Palestine almost exclusively (see Str-B 1. 90-91), and Matthew tends to use rabbinic language (see "Rabbinic language" in the Topical Index). The phrase matches "to the land of Egypt" in Exod 4:19-20, which he has begun to quote for further parallels between Jesus and Moses (cf. vv 13 and 16). There, the Lord told Moses in Midian, " 'Go return to Egypt, for all those who were seeking your life are dead.' And Moses took his wife and his sons . . . and returned to the land of Egypt." The destinations differ, to be sure, but the similarities of phraseology are remarkable.

Whether or not Israel has ironically become a new Egypt because of the Jewish leaders' cooperation with that new baby-killing Pharaoh, Herod, the parallel between Moses and Jesus comes out even more clearly than before. πορεύου translates לֵךְ, differs from βαδίζε in the LXX, and echoes vv 8-9. Matthew omits the verb of returning (cf. Exodus), because Joseph will not settle with Jesus and Mary in the part of Israel where Jesus spent his first days. Matthew's first reference to the land of Israel has no counterpart in Exodus, but he inserts it to balance the second reference, which does have a counterpart in the MT of Exodus (where the LXX drops the phrase for the sake of consistency in omission). Matthew has mentioned the death of Herod alone (vv 15 and 19). Yet the influence of Exodus strikingly leads to the plural number in Matthew's statement that those who had been seeking the child's life (literally "soul") were dead. The "all" in Exodus drops out because of Matthew's limiting the plural to Herod. To seek somebody's soul means to try to take somebody's life. This Semitic expression makes another striking example of influence from the narrative concerning Moses, as does, finally, the verb of taking (see further textual comparisons in Gundry, *Use of the OT* 130-31). But the reference to Jesus' mother rather than to a wife and the mention of the child ahead of her, both in contrast with Exodus, do not let us forget that the virgin-born Immanuel surpasses Moses in importance. "He entered" replaces the verb of returning in Exodus because there is a change of destination within the land of Israel. Once again Joseph's obedience to a divine command makes a good example (cf. 1:24-25; 2:14-15).

2:22-23 The typically Matthean participle ἀκούσας (10,3) introduces Archelaus. To him Herod had bequeathed the title "king" and the territories of Judea, Samaria, and Idumea. But Caesar Augustus withheld the title till Archelaus should prove his worth. Archelaus did not. Misruling from 4 B.C. to A.D. 6, he was finally banished (Josephus *Ant.* 17.8.1-17.13.5 §§188-355; *J.W.* 2.1.1-2.7.4 §§1-116). The ruthless massacre ordered by Archelaus right after his father's funeral (Josephus *Ant.* 17.9.3 §§213-18; *J.W.* 2.1.1-3 §§1-13; 2.6.2 §89) joined the tradition of Jesus' growing up in Nazareth (Luke 2:39-40) in giving Matthew good reason to make Joseph avoid settling in Judea. Theologically, the use of βασιλεύει despite Augustus's refusal to confirm the kingly title, the specification of Judea the place of former rejection (cf. vv 1, 5), and the preposition ἀντί, "in place of," with "his father" all imply that Archelaus is another illegitimate rival with whom the Jewish leaders would cooperate in plotting the death of Jesus the true king of the Jews. πατρός is a Mattheanism (22,13).

38

The words ἐφοβήθη ἐκεῖ ἀπελθεῖν also come from Matthew's preferred vocabulary (8,2; 16,6; 14,11). Furthermore, ἀπελθεῖν reflects Exod 4:19-20 LXX. The word did not come over in the earlier quotation of that passage (vv 20-21). The evangelist makes up for the omission here (see "Compensation" in the Topical Index). The warning in a dream and the departure recall vv 12-14 and again connote flight from persecution (see earlier comments). The warning in a dream also replaces the traditional completion of the law as the antecedent to the journey northward (Luke 2:39). Instead of "they returned" we read "he withdrew" because Matthew's Joseph has not lived in Nazareth before. ἀνεχώρησεν is a favorite of Matthew (4,5), and elsewhere he will insert μέρη twice (see 15:21; 16:13). The mention of Galilee both suits his taste (3,2) and rests on tradition (Luke 2:39; cf. 1:26).

The nominative aorist participle ἐλθών is a Mattheanism (10,10), and κατῴκησεν will come twice as an insertion (4:13; 23:21). As here, 4:13 has these same words in an unparalleled combination followed by εἰς and the name of a city. In both passages the expression means going to settle rather than coming home, in contrast with the tradition behind Luke 2:39. πόλιν derives from the tradition (Luke 2:39) and conforms to Matthew's diction (18,3). As often, λεγομένην introduces a Semitic name (10,2). Because in Matthew's story Joseph and Mary have not lived in Nazareth before, λεγομένην, "called," stands where Luke writes ἑαυτῶν, "their own." Though "Nazareth" here rests on the tradition, Matthew will insert it in 4:13; 21:11 to stress Jesus' coming from Nazareth in a continuing fulfillment of the prophecy about to be cited.

Matthew likes ὅπως (8,7), a conjunction that in introductions to fulfilled prophecies Matthew reserves for citations climaxing a series of items (see also 8:17; 13:35). For the rest of the introductory formula, see the comments on 1:22b. The parallel between the calling of Jesus by the name "Jesus" and his being called "Nazarene" (1:25; 2:23) indicates that the present quotation climaxes the intervening events of chap. 2.

But where does the quotation come from? As such the quoted words appear nowhere in the OT, and κληθήσεται—the verb in the quotation—is a Mattheanism (8,8). The plural of "the prophets" in the introductory formula suggests, therefore, a quotation of substance (as in Ezra 9:10-12 and rabbinic literature—see Str-B 1. 92-93) instead of exact words. This agrees with the absence of λέγοντος, which occurs in the other introductions to direct quotations preceded by a formula of fulfillment. ὅτι needs, then, to be understood as introducing an indirect quotation and accordingly translated "that." Confirmation comes from the absence of ὅτι in all other introductory formulas to Matthew's fulfillment-quotations, all of which are direct, and in the indirect use of ὅτι concerning the fulfillment of the Scriptures in 26:54, which only Matthew has. Cf. his habit of omitting the recitative ὅτι (see F. Neirynck, *The Minor Agreements of Matthew and Luke against Mark* [BETL 37; Leuven: Leuven University Press, 1974] 213-16). The plural "prophets" then means that we are to look for the substance of more than one OT passage. Confirmation of this further inference comes from 26:56, where the plural term "the prophets" in the statement, "But this whole thing happened in order that the scriptures [note this plural, too] of the prophets might be fulfilled," represents a surplus over the wording in Mark 14:49.

We need now more than one OT passage that relates to the Messiah as a "Nazarene," i.e., an inhabitant of Nazareth. But since Nazareth does not appear in the OT, we must look for a subtle connection between the NT place-name and an OT messianic title. Isaiah's prediction of a נֵצֶר, "branch, shoot," from the roots of Jesse, David's father, provides a start (Isa 11:1). From both Isaiah and other prophets come additional passages that use the synonym צֶמַח for the Davidic Messiah (Isa 4:2; and Jer 23:5; 33:15, where "the righteous Branch" must have appealed to Matthew because of his interest in righteousness [18-19,10-9; see δικ- in the Greek Index]; Zech 3:8, where "my servant the Branch" may have appealed to Matthew because of his interest in Jesus as the Lord's Servant [see the quotation of Isa 42:1-4 in Matt 12:18-21]; and Zech 6:12).

Of course, צֶמַח bears no phonetic similarity to Nazareth or Nazarene; and נֵצֶר does so only as a Hebrew word, whereas Matthew writes in Greek. But undeterred by his Greek medium, Matthew has already treated us to Hebrew wordplays on the numerical value of the name "David" and on the name "Jesus" (1:17, 21). In the latter, the use of Ps 130:8 depended on an association of פָּדָה, "redeem," with a word of similar meaning, viz., יָשַׁע, "save" in the hiphil. Furthermore, not only do the righteousness and servanthood of the messianic Branch cater to Matthew's interests. So also does its sprouting like a shoot out of the stump of David's dynasty (see υἱὸς Δαυίδ in the Greek Index for the Davidic Christology of Matthew). Its easy rejection (cf. Isa 14:19: "like a rejected branch"—though not messianic) agrees with the obscurity of Nazareth and the theme of Jesus' rejection in Matthew. See 26:56, where in the story of Jesus' arrest Matthew inserts the plural "the prophets" expressly as a reference back to the prophets who according to 2:23 predicted the rejection of Jesus the נֵצֶר. See also the contemptuous statement in 26:71: "This fellow [Peter] was with Jesus the Nazarene." The Davidic origin of the Branch provides a fitting capstone to Matthew's version of Jesus' nativity, which began with a reference to "Jesus Christ the son of David" (1:1; cf. Rev 22:16). Thus Matthew marries phonetics with Christology.

The "he" who goes to settle in Nazareth is Joseph. The "he" who is taken along so as to be called a "Nazarene" is Jesus. In the QL, targums, and rabbinic literature the Branch receives a messianic interpretation with special reference to despised lowliness (see Str-B 1. 94; Gundry, *Use of the OT* 104). Other views, such as interpretation in terms of Judg 13:5, 7; 16:17, are less likely because of phonetic difficulties, lack of attention to the plural "the prophets," and failure to tie in with Matthean motifs so well as passages concerning the messianic Branch of David do (see ibid. 97-104, with special attention to p. 102 on the difference between ω and α in Ναζωραῖος and Ναζαρέτ.

Cf. the midrashic and haggadic Jewish literature discussed in relation to Matthew 1–2 by M. M. Bourke ("The Literary Genus of Matthew 1–2," *CBQ* 22 [1960]

160-75) and E. Nellessen (*Das Kind und seine Mutter* 58-80, 89-91) among others. But see ibid. and Gundry (*Use of the OT* 196 n. 1) against a link with the haggadah concerning Laban's attempt to destroy Jacob's children. As in such literature, Matthew plays especially on the stories of the patriarchs and Moses. But the Jewish literature rests on the ancient and sacred text of the OT. Matthew practices his art on tradition concerning a recent historical figure, Jesus. How quickly that tradition attained a kind of canonical status worthy of embroidery, with the OT now a means rather than an object of embroidery! This turnabout gives eloquent testimony to the impact Jesus made. Cf. Gundry, "Recent Investigations" 97-114, for an extended discussion of the literary phenomenon. The recency of Jesus' lifetime may account for a certain reserve in Matthew's version of the nativity, for we should have expected a description of the star as bright, of the baby's face as shining, etc., as in comparable Jewish literature.

JESUS' BAPTISM BY JOHN AS A MODEL OF RIGHTEOUSNESS
3:1-17 (Mark 1:2-11; Luke 3:1-18, 21-22; cf. John 1:19-34)

3:1-2 (Mark 1:4; Luke 3:1-3) Matthew returns to Mark for the first time since 1:1, but delays the OT quotation in Mark 1:2-3 in order to gain a narrative transition and introduce the preaching of John the Baptist before rather than after the OT quotation concerning it. Luke agrees with Matthew, and a number of immediately following agreements against Mark do not lend themselves to easy explanation by Luke's use of Matthew or vice versa. Therefore we need to suppose that the first and third evangelists are conflating Mark and another, overlapping source as well as that Luke uses Matthew as an overlay (see also pp. 4-5).

"And in those days" comes forward from Mark 1:9 and for that reason is later omitted (see v 13). This advance and the later omission weld together John's ministry and Jesus' baptism in a single episode. The unique expansion in vv 14-15 puts the primary stress on Jesus' baptism as the model for Christian baptism. Luke agrees with Matthew in drawing up the temporal phrase and omitting it later, but he transforms it into a dating by means of world and local history. Because of its OT flavor, Matthew retains Mark's wording (cf. Gen 6:4; Exod 2:11; Deut 17:9, 12 LXX; 19:17; 26:3; Judg 18:1; Jer 3:16, 18; 31:29; 50:4, 20[27:4, 20]; Dan 10:2; Joel 4:1[3:1]; Zech 8:23). Since the phrase occurs in noneschatological as well as eschatological contexts and since the demonstrative pronoun necessarily points to the context, it is wrong to think that in and of itself "in those days" connotes eschatological time. Here it refers to the time of Jesus' residence in Nazareth, just mentioned.

Mark and Luke have ἐγένετο, but Matthew writes παραγίνεται, which repeats the opening main verb in chap. 2 and again recalls OT terminology (see Hatch and Redpath, s.v. παραγίγνεσθαι, παραγίνεσθαι; and v 13 for the same change by Matthew). Against Mark and Luke and his own 2:1, Matthew puts the verb in the present tense to emphasize that John's preaching starts the proclamation of the gospel of the kingdom that will continue to the end (see 4:23; 9:35; 24:14; 26:13; and esp. 11:12 in comparison with

Luke 16:16). Indeed, just as Matthew made Joseph prototypical of disciples in practicing righteousness (see the comments on 1:19), so he makes John the Baptist prototypical of disciples in preaching—and even prototypical of Jesus himself, for John "comes" (παραγίνεται) just as Jesus "comes" (παραγίνεται, v 13).

Matthew designates John as ὁ βαπτιστής, "the Baptist," rather than [ὁ] βαπτίζων, "[the one] baptizing" (so Mark). This transformation of the activity of baptizing into a mere identification diverts attention from that activity to the accompanying activity of preaching (so consistently in 3:1; 11:11, 12; 14:2, 8; 16:14; 17:13—usually or always against the parallels, depending on text-critical decisions in them). Thus Matthew clears the baptism of repentance out of the way to prepare for his later, distinctive introduction of baptism in the name of the Father, Son, and Holy Spirit (28:19). Furthermore, "preaching," the activity John shares with Jesus (4:17, 23; 9:35; 11:1) and with the apostles (10:7, 27) and other disciples (24:14; 26:13), gains emphasis by appearing ahead of "in the desert" (contrast the Greek order of words in Mark 1:4; Luke 3:3). Consequently, it is not so much the baptizing as the preaching that takes place in the desert. Historically, of course, "in the desert" applies equally to John's preaching and baptizing. But the emphasis on preaching instead of baptism enables Matthew to display the parallel between John and Jesus and, as an added benefit, make a better connection with the quotation of Isa 40:3 in v 3, where "a voice" comes from "one *calling* in the desert," not from one who is baptizing there. Thus the narrative corresponds more closely to the quotation than it does in Mark. Luke's similarity to Matthew in the geographical phrase looks like Matthean overlay rather than use of the source common to Matthew and Luke, for Luke retains Mark's emphasis on John's baptism.

"Of Judea" (not in Mark or Luke) comes from 2:1, 5, 22. Thus John the Baptist prepares the Davidic territory for the Davidic Messiah. The ill-defined territory of Judea might easily be thought to extend as far as the Jordan River (so Josephus *J.W.* 3.3.5 §51), but John ministered in Transjordan within the territory governed by Herod Antipas (Mark 6:14-29; Matt 14:1-12; Luke 9:7-9; John 1:28; Josephus *Ant.* 18.5.2 §§116-19—cf. John 3:23 and the probable location of Aenon on the West Bank, however). Therefore Matthew's stretching Judea to include Transjordan belongs to the paralleling of John and Jesus in the first gospel: both men now make their initial appearance in Judea. For the same stretching of Judea see also 19:1.

Mark and Luke lack the typically Matthean participle λέγων (61,23). It puts emphasis on the following proclamation by John; indeed, it introduces his actual words where (here at least) Mark and Luke do not have them. For Matthew, John is primarily a man of words, as Jesus is (7:28a; 11:1; 13:53; 19:1a; 26:1a; cf. 28:20a, all but the first peculiar to this gospel). Thus the proclamation of repentance displaces the baptism of repentance to counteract an antinomianism in which evidence of repentance fails to follow baptism (cf. ἀνομία in the Greek Index and pp. 6-7, 9 in the Introduction). John's proclamation exactly matches—in fact, derives from—that of Jesus: "Repent, for the kingdom [or 'reign'] of heaven is near" (cf. 4:17).

And Matthew introduces the proclamation with the same compound expression, "preaching . . . and saying" (cf. the corresponding infinitives in 4:17). According to 10:7, Jesus tells the twelve to go "preach, saying, 'The kingdom of heaven is near.' " John the prototype, Jesus the teacher, the twelve disciples—all preach the same message.

Mark's and Luke's "baptism" drops out. "Of repentance" becomes the imperative "Repent," after the pattern of Mark 1:15, here anticipated. The Mattheanism γάρ (62-63,15) provides a reason for repentance and displaces the καί of Mark 1:15. Matthew takes the rest of John's proclamation from that of Jesus in the later Markan verse. But the already used reference to repentance causes Matthew to jump over "The time is fulfilled" at the beginning and lop off "Repent and believe in the gospel" at the end. The supporting statement that the kingdom is near crowds out "for the forgiveness of sins" (so Mark and Luke), which Matthew saves for association with Jesus' blood of the covenant (see 26:28, where the phrase is lacking in all parallel accounts of the Words of Institution). Ultimately, not John's baptism of repentance but Jesus' covenantal blood effects the forgiveness of sins. Cf. 1:21: "you shall call his name Jesus, because *he* [intensive αὐτός] will save his people from their sins."

John's preaching the nearness of the kingdom rather than the forgiveness of sins as the reason for repentance marks the beginning of a major theme in Matthew's theology, the kingdom of heaven (see βασιλεία τῶν οὐρανῶν in the Greek Index). βασιλεία may denote a sphere of rule or, as here, the rule itself. Heaven does not indicate the sphere of rule, but its source. In particular, heaven stands for God. Since among the evangelists only Matthew has "heaven" for "God" in the expression, and that nearly always, we may presume Jesus ordinarily spoke of the kingdom of God and Matthew paraphrased with τῶν οὐρανῶν. It seems unlikely that all the other evangelists paraphrased in the opposite direction with absolute consistency.

Because he was writing for Jews, Matthew may have wished to defer to the increasingly common Jewish practice of avoiding the divine names by substituting other terms, such as "heaven" (cf. Luke 15:18, 21; Dan 4:23[26]; 1 Macc 3:50, 60; 4:55; see Str-B 1. 172-84, 862-65 for rabbinic materials). But "God" occurs no fewer than fifty-eight times in the first gospel, including four or five combinations with the kingdom (6:33 v.1.; 12:28; 19:24; 21:31, 43). Therefore the Jewish practice only gave Matthew a means of stressing another of his favorite motifs, the majesty of God's universal dominion (see οὐράνιος with πατήρ and οὐρανός with πατήρ in the Greek Index). "Heaven" has the ring of such sovereignty, and Dan 3:31—4:34 (4:1-37) provided Matthew with the seed-plot for this use of the term. Furthermore, since Jesus is Immanuel (1:23) and the Son of God who has all authority in heaven as well as on earth (28:18), Matthew prefers heaven to God so as to keep his readers from inferring that God the Father rules to the exclusion of Jesus. Rather, Jesus rules as God, as God's Son, and also as the Son of man (see 13:41; 16:28; 20:21; 25:31, all unique to the first gospel).

The verb ἤγγικεν indicates nearness right up to, but not including, the point of arrival (cf. 21:1, 34; 26:45, 46). "The kingdom of heaven is near" means, then, that God's sovereign, universal rule verges on arrival. This does not have to do with his general control over creation, but with his special activity of overcoming evil and bringing final salvation in the last stage of human history.

3:3 (Mark 1:2-3; Luke 3:4-6) Verse 3 contains an OT quotation. See the comments on v 1 concerning its placement. The Mattheanism γάρ (62-63,15) replaces Mark's "just as" in the introduction. This replacement strengthens the correspondence between the narrative and the quotation and makes the prophecy to be quoted the very reason for John's preaching in the desert. Matthew next puts "this is he who was spoken about *through* Isaiah" in place of Mark's "it is written *in* Isaiah." This substitution points toward God as the ultimate source of the prophecy. "This is" anticipates 11:10, where it is traditional (Luke 7:27). With or without the prophet's name, the phrase "through the prophet, saying" characterizes Matthew's formulas leading into OT quotations, especially those cited as fulfilled (see the comments on 1:22b—also for ὁ ῥηθείς, which corresponds to τὸ ῥηθέν in all the introductions to fulfillment-quotations). Despite his mentioning John before the quotation, as though Isaiah's words found fulfillment in John, and despite his conforming the introduction largely to the introductory formulas of fulfillment, Matthew does not import the crucial verb "fulfill." Rather, he keeps that verb for the story of Jesus. In this respect John the preacher does not compare with Jesus, who is the great fulfiller as well as a preacher. For the same phenomenon, see the comments on 11:10a. All in all, Matthew's changes in the present introductory formula result in an emphasis on John as a prototypical Christian preacher, for the stress has shifted from the writtenness of Scripture (so Mark and Luke) to the identity of John as the one whose voice cries in the wilderness.

Matthew's decision to exclude Mark's initial, composite quotation of Exod 23:20 and Mal 3:1 causes the weight to fall entirely on the voice and what it says. Of course, the later use of this quotation in 11:10 and Luke's agreement with Matthew in the present omission and later use (Luke 7:27) suggest that these evangelists are following a source different from Mark (see also vv 7-10). It is enough to note that for his emphasis on John as a preacher Matthew chooses to follow that source.

Omission of Exod 23:20 and Mal 3:1 eliminates the embarrassment of having Isaiah's name immediately followed by a non-Isaianic quotation. But in view of Matthew's quoting Zechariah under Jeremiah's name in 27:9-10, we should not think that he would have been embarrassed to follow Mark here. As in Mark and Luke, the quotation of Isa 40:3 follows the LXX for the most part. Notably, ἐν τῇ ἐρήμῳ goes with φωνὴ βοῶντος (as in the LXX, Targum, and OT Peshitta) rather than with ἑτοιμάσατε τὴν ὁδὸν κυρίου (as in the MT). Though Matthew's syntax makes for better correspondence with preaching in the desert (v 1), the same syntax appears in Mark, where stress falls on baptizing in the desert; and the MT is probably unoriginal (see Albright and Mann, 25; Gundry, *Use of the OT* 9-10). Besides, Matthew emphasizes what John said, not the place where he said it.

Originally, Isaiah was predicting the return of Jewish exiles from Babylonia. Here the passage applies to the beginnings of a greater deliverance, but with an emphasis on the straightness of the paths which make up the way of the Lord, i.e., the way of righteousness, on which he will save his people from their sins (cf. 1:21; 21:32, both peculiar to Matthew). At the end of the quotation "his" replaces Isaiah's reference to God, because that reference might cause readers to think of God in contradistinction to Jesus. "His" naturally refers back to the Lord, and the genitive case of αὐτοῦ reflects the LXX in contrast with "for our God" in the MT. Readers will easily identify the Lord with Jesus, whose way John prepares. This feature of the quotation is shared with the other synoptics.

3:4 (Mark 1:6) Where Mark goes into the baptizing activity of John and Luke extends the quotation of Isaiah and then switches to John's preaching, with a unique emphasis on its social aspects, Matthew brings forward Mark's description of John in terms of Elijah. The resultant delay of the people's coming to be baptized makes a good lead into vv 7-10, missing in Mark but not in Luke, and further accentuates John's role as a prototype of Christian preachers. In the description of John, the distinctive and intensive αὐτός (a Mattheanism—7,1) emphasizes this role yet further. So also does the position of John's name in front of the verb instead of behind it (as in Mark).

The comparison between John and Elijah has to do with John's clothing, made of camel's hair, and Elijah's description as (literally) "a possessor of hair" (2 Kgs 1:8), which may mean "a hairy man" (so the LXX) or a man who wore a shaggy coat of skin or haircloth (cf. Zech 13:4). The immediate mention of a girdle in 2 Kgs 1:8 favors the latter meaning, which provides a basis for the present comparison with John. Since Elijah was to prepare the way of the Lord (Mal 3:1, 23[4:5]), the likeness of John to Elijah puts John in subordination to Jesus the Lord (cf. 17:11-12).

"He had his clothing from hair" replaces Mark's "was clothed with hair." The replacement prepares for parallelism (a characteristic of Matthew's style) between "clothing" and "food." Even in his diet John portrays true discipleship. For that diet, Matthew uses "food" rather than Mark's "eating" and so makes John exemplary in his unconcern for food (see 6:25; 10:10; 24:45 for Matthew's special interest in the "food" of Jesus' disciples). Locusts and wild honey not only indicate a sparse diet appropriate to the desert, but also a specially holy one devoid of flesh from which blood has had to be drained (hence locusts) and devoid of wine (hence honey).

3:5-6 (Mark 1:5) The Mattheanism τότε (66,17) replaces Mark's καί for establishment of the story line. "Jerusalem" takes the place of Mark's "all the Jerusalemites" for conformity to 2:3. Matthew has emphasized Jerusalem as a place full of persecutors by using "all" with "Jerusalem" in 2:3. But he will not admit to a Jerusalem full of penitents; therefore he omits "all" here. The name of Jerusalem comes forward to make a natural progression from Jerusalem eastward through surrounding Judea to the region around the Jordan River, including Transjordan (contrast Mark and see also 4:25 against Mark 3:7–8; Luke 6:17). Mark's χώρα drops out as awkward after the noun Ἰουδαία. But Matthew immediately takes up χώρα into περίχωρος (suggested perhaps by Mark 1:28), adds πᾶσα ἡ in front of it for a parallel with πᾶσα ἡ 'Ιουδαία, and tacks on τοῦ 'Ιορδάνου as a lead into John's baptizing people in the Jordan. The reference to all the surrounding region of the Jordan corresponds to Luke 3:3, where because of it John appears as an itinerant. But since we can easily see how Matthew developed the phrase from Mark, Luke seems to have borrowed it from Matthew and transferred it slightly (and not altogether appropriately in view of the necessity of staying at the river to baptize people). ἐν τῷ 'Ιορδάνῃ comes forward by attraction to the preceding reference to the Jordan, just inserted.

3:7-10 (Luke 3:7-15) In vv 7-10 the decision of Matthew to follow his source different from Mark further emphasizes John as a preacher. Luke follows that source, too, even though he has retained Mark's statement (replaced by Matthew) that John preached the baptism of repentance. ἰδών is not in Luke. As often, Matthew inserts it (10-11,7). Here it sets up the following condemnation. The Pharisees and Sadducees seen by John differ from the crowds in Luke, who repentantly ask what they should do. Thus a further parallel between John and Jesus starts to develop; contrary to the other synoptics Matthew will also pit the Pharisees and Sadducees against Jesus in 16:1-12. In both passages we read about the failure of the Pharisees and Sadducees to take account of the eschatological time. Matthew wants to carry on the theme of opposition by these Jewish leaders (who made up the two leading sects in Judaism)—a theme begun in his account of the nativity. Therefore they become the particular objects of John's rebuke. Matthew inserts πολλούς (23,1) both to compensate for his omission of the crowds and to emphasize the role of the Pharisees and Sadducees as antagonists. Because of ἐξεπορεύετο in v 5, Matthew has only ἐρχομένους in the present text, where Luke, who omitted the earlier statement, has ἐκπορευομένοις. According to Luke, the crowds were going "to be baptized by him [John]." But Matthew would hardly let the Pharisees and Sadducees come to show repentance by submitting themselves to baptism; hence, they simply come "to the baptism," presumably for critical observation.

Now Matthew adopts from the non-Markan tradition he shares with Luke a new element in his description of the opponents—viz., hypocrisy, which becomes an important theme in its own right (see ὑπόκρισις and ὑποκριτής in the Greek Index). John calls the opponents a brood of vipers, just as Jesus will talk about the brood of vipers who try to speak good things out of evil hearts (12:33-38a; cf. 23:3, unique to Matthew) and about the brood of vipers who hypocritically build and decorate the tombs of the prophets while they plot the crucifixion of the greatest of the prophets (23:29-36). In Luke the question "Who warned you to flee from the coming wrath?" (cf. Matt 23:33) suggests that the crowds had come out of sincerity. But because of the shift in address to the Pharisees and Sadducees, John asks the question with bitter sarcasm in Matthew. The command to produce fruit in keeping with repentance—an insinuating command when addressed to them rather than the crowds—calls attention to misplaced pride in Abrahamic descent at the expense of genuine righteousness.

By contrast, genuine righteousness characterizes—indeed, *is*—Isaiah's "way of the Lord": "For John came to you in the way of righteousness"

(21:32, not in Mark or Luke). The genuineness of this righteousness consists in the correspondence of a disciple's thoughts with the goodness of his words and works. Therefore in the exhortation not to say within themselves that they have Abraham as their father, Matthew writes "do not think" in place of the Semitic, otiose, and original "do not begin" (so Luke). There results an emphasis on inner thoughts (cf. 5:27-32, esp. the unparalleled v 27). For this emphasis Matthew will insert ἐν ἑαυτοῖς four times in shared materials (16:7, 8; 21:25, 38). He likes δόξητε (6,3); and in association with the works to which thoughts should correspond, ποιήσατε occurs often in Matthew alone (19,19). The figure of fruit and the adjectives "good" and "worthy" describe people and their conduct. We can hardly overestimate Matthew's emphasis on the contrast between the righteousness which springs from within and the facade of righteousness better termed "hypocrisy" (cf. 1QS 3:4-12). For parallelism, the singular "fruit," where Luke 3:8 has the plural, conforms to the singular in v 10, where Luke 3:9, too, has the singular. Here, Luke's plural looks original because of the reference to particular good works as showing repentance. The number then changes to the singular because of the figure of a single tree, which naturally produces only one kind of fruit.

Failure to produce genuine righteousness will bring down the coming wrath (cf. Eph 5:6; Col 3:6; 1 Thess 1:10). This threatening note sounds loudly here and throughout the rest of Matthew. The readiness of the axe to cut down bad trees extends the figure of fruit bearing and leads to a description of final punishment as being thrown into fire. Matthew cannot include the further tradition behind Luke 3:10-15, because the Pharisees and Sadducees, substituted by him for the crowds, would hardly respond in the repentant way indicated.

We should not underestimate the vigor of John's preaching by thinking that this thunderer would not have addressed a general audience under the figure of snakes fleeing a grass fire. History has known more than one Savonarola. For misplaced confidence in physical descent from Abraham, see John 8:33; Rom 9:6-9; 2 Cor 11:22; cf. Romans 4. In v 9 we probably have a play on the Hebrew words for "children" (בָּנִים) and "stones" (אֲבָנִים). As a Semitic expression, "to raise up from" can mean "to cause to be born from," and with the figure of stones may additionally connote the building of a house, itself a figure for a family (as in "the house of David"). Jews of the NT era sometimes thought that God would judge only the heathen, or exempt from judgment at least pious Jews like themselves. Because of the preceding reference to coming wrath, we should understand the present tense of ἐκκόπτεται and βάλλεται as futuristic. The ἤδη with κεῖται then indicates the imminence of future judgment.

3:11-12 (Mark 1:7-8; Luke 3:16-18) Omission of Mark's "And he was preaching, saying" makes the preceding and the following a continuous discourse, for in Matthew alone John is already speaking (see "Omissions of narrative interruptions" in the Topical Index). The reference to John's baptizing with water comes forward, as it does in Luke, for a comparison between John and Jesus instead of a comparison between their baptisms. The construction μέν . . . δέ, also shared by Luke but inserted into common material fifteen times by Matthew, highlights the comparison between John and Jesus. The coming forward of ὑμᾶς, in contrast with Mark and Luke, further de-emphasizes the comparison between baptisms.

The present tense in "I baptize" contrasts with the aorist in Mark and arises out of Matthew's desire to conform to the present tense of "is" in the next line of the couplet. Luke's present tense in "I baptize" arises by way of parallelism with "comes." Mark's aorist contrasts what John has been doing and the future baptism by Jesus. Matthew adds "in" before "water" to locate the element of baptism more clearly. His further addition "for repentance" (not in the other synoptics) compensates for the replacement in v 2 of Mark's "baptism of repentance for the forgiveness of sins" (cf. "Compensation" in the Topical Index). This further addition, along with retention of the confession of sins (v 6, as in Mark), makes it a mistake to think that earlier Matthew dropped the forgiveness of sins because he was embarrassed about Jesus' baptism by John. He would have dropped the related repentance and confession of sins, too. "For repentance" implies that baptism enabled people to actualize their repentance by carrying it out in symbolic action.

Matthew changes the verb "comes" (so Mark and Luke) to "he who . . . comes." He also advances "after me" to an attributive position, adds "is," turns "the one stronger than I" into a predicate adjective phrase by omitting the definite article, and puts that phrase before the verb. All these revisions have the purpose and result of shifting emphasis from the coming of the stronger one after John to the fact that the coming one is stronger— i.e., more authoritative—than John. We see now why Matthew wanted to compare the two men themselves rather than their baptisms. Since Luke shared the comparison between the men rather than the baptisms but does *not* share the present stress on the greater strength of Jesus rather than on Jesus' coming later, his earlier agreement with Matthew betrays either piecemeal influence from Matthew or—if Luke depends with Matthew on a common source at this point—piecemeal influence of Mark on Luke. With the latter possibility, cf. the non-Markan material shared in Matt 3:7-10, 12; 4:2b-11 and Luke 3:7-15, 17-18; 4:2b-13.

τὰ ὑποδήματα, "the sandals," replaces Mark's τὸν ἱμάντα τῶν ὑποδημάτων αὐτοῦ, "the strap of his sandals" (awkward after οὗ, "whose"), and comes forward for greater proximity to οὗ. Then βαστάσαι, "to remove" (see BAG s.v. βαστάζω for this meaning), replaces Mark's κύψας λῦσαι, "stooping to loosen," because prior elimination of the strap leaves nothing to loosen, but only the sandals to remove. We may still ask why Matthew did not simply eliminate Mark's αὐτοῦ to get rid of awkwardness. The more extensive revision prepares for the unique quotation of Isa 53:4 in 8:17: "he removed [ἐβάστησεν] our diseases." Jesus removed our diseases; John was unfit even to remove Jesus' sandals. That is how much stronger Jesus is.

Because emphasis no longer attaches to the contrast between baptisms, Mark's adversative δέ drops out (so also Luke). Again ὑμᾶς comes forward to de-emphasize the contrast, again Matthew adds "in," and Luke agrees with Matthew against Mark in both respects. But since Luke did not agree with Matthew before, he once more betrays piecemeal influence from Matthew if Mark is his main source, or from Mark if he is depending mainly on another source shared with Matthew. Like Luke, but unlike Mark, Matthew includes fire along with the Holy Spirit in the baptism Jesus will administer. The inclusion leads to the following figure of fiery judgment, lacking in Mark. The loosening of the parallel between John's and Jesus' baptisms and the putting of judgmental fire both before and after the baptismal fire (cf. v 10) militate against interpreting it as a purification of the righteous. Jesus will administer only one baptism in the Holy Spirit and fire, but its effect will differ according to good fruit or bad (cf. 13:24-30, 36-43, 47-50; 25:31-46, all peculiar to Matthew; and Isa 41:15-16). Those producing good fruit will receive the gift of the Holy Spirit. Those producing bad fruit will suffer unending punishment. The weight of emphasis falls heavily on the aspect of punishment. Nevertheless, Jesus' wheat enjoy a better prospect (cf. the figure of wheat for sons of the kingdom in 13:25, 29, 30—so Matthew alone). In Luke the third αὐτοῦ in the statement about winnowing goes with ἀποθήκην. In Matthew it goes with σῖτον. (The αὐτοῦ with ἀποθήκην is text-critically uncertain [see Metzger, *Textual Commentary* ad loc.].) Matthew connects αὐτοῦ with σῖτον in order to win a correspondence between "his wheat" and "his people," the people whom Jesus "will save . . . from their sins" (1:21), i.e., "gather . . . into the barn."

Since Matthew has avoided saying that the Pharisees and Sadducees came to be baptized, ὑμᾶς has to be understood in his text as a general "you" despite the uninterrupted addressing of the Pharisees and Sadducees from v 7 onward. This inconcinnity favors that the crowds in Luke were the original addressees. Concerning the gift of the Spirit, sometimes linked with water, cf. Isa 32:15; 44:3; Ezek 36:25-27; 39:29; Joel 3:1-2 (2:28-29); 1QS 4:20-21. For one of many examples of messianic judgment, see 1QH 3:27-32.

3:13 (Mark 1:9; Luke 3:21) Again Matthew comes into parallel with Mark. For enhancement of the story line τότε substitutes for καί. Mark's ἐγένετο and ἦλθεν give way to παραγίνεται for a parallel between Jesus and John (see v 1). The present tense of Matthew's verb suggests that Jesus' coming for baptism belongs to the current practice of the church and makes an example to be followed (cf. 28:19). Mark's "in those days" drops out on account of its use already in v 1. Matthew's interest in Nazareth (see Ναζαρέτ and Ναζωραῖος in the Greek Index) might lead us to think it strange that Mark's reference to Nazareth disappears here. But Matthew is saving it for 4:13-16, where it has to do with Jesus' shifting his residence from Nazareth to Capernaum in order to fulfill Isa 8:23–9:1. Meanwhile, Matthew does not want to leave the misimpression that Jesus is now pulling up stakes. The phrase "in those days"—i.e., during the time Jesus had a residence in Nazareth—still applies (see v 1).

"To the Jordan" comes forward to complement "from Galilee." ἐπί takes the place of Mark's εἰς, because the change of position makes the Jordan refer to the destination of a journey, not to the element of baptism (as in Mark). Matthew's quick introduction of the Jordan identifies baptism as the purpose of the journey and again makes Jesus' coming for baptism

49

an example to be followed. By inserting "to John" Matthew prepares for the conversation he is going to insert in vv 14-15. The replacement of Mark's "and he was baptized" with "in order to be baptized" not only indicates Jesus' exemplary purpose—indeed, determination (as it turns out)—but also prepares for the following conversation (see the comments on 2:13 concerning Matthew's fondness for the genitive articular infinitive). Matthew takes his telic expression from the tradition behind Luke 3:7, which he revised earlier because of his changing the crowds to the Pharisees and Sadducees (v 7). Thus the purpose, "to be baptized," having been disallowed to those hypocrites, shifts to Jesus.

3:14-15 Verses 14-15 have no parallel and appear to come from Matthew himself. They display his stylistic and theological traits in central as well as peripheral matters. Though διεκώλυεν occurs only here in the NT, Matthew brings into his gospel eight other compound words beginning with δια- (see δια- in the Greek Index). Since none of these words occurs even once in the other synoptics, we seem to be dealing with his favorite diction. λέγων and ἐγώ are Mattheanisms (61,23; 12-13,3). Though frequent, the combination χρείαν ἔχω appears as an insertion also in 6:8 and 14:16. ὑπὸ σοῦ βαπτισθῆναι echoes v 13 with a reversal in word order to emphasize the figure of Jesus. Matthew likes the nominative pronoun σύ (6,4) and uses it here as an antithetic parallel to ἐγώ. He delights in such parallelism. ἔρχῃ stems from ἦλθεν in Mark 1:9 and compensates for its earlier replacement (see "Compensation" in the Topical Index). πρὸς μέ echoes v 13 with a necessary substitution of the pronoun for John's name.

The combination ἀποκριθείς . . . εἶπεν comes as an insertion no fewer than twenty-nine times, besides six instances in passages peculiar to the first gospel and only eleven common occurrences. Matthew specifies the name Jesus far more often (150 times) than Mark (81 times) or Luke (89 times). Almost every remaining word in these verses shares the same characteristic of occurring often, usually very often, as an insertion and as part of unique materials: ἀφίημι (12,5), ἄρτι (7,0), οὕτως (18,5), γάρ (62-63,15), πληρόω (9,6), πᾶς (63,25-26), δικαιοσύνη (5,2; and 18-19,10-9 including cognates), and τότε (66,17).

As distinct from its synonym νῦν, ἄρτι implies instantaneousness. That, in turn, emphasizes the significance of Jesus' baptism as a model for Christian baptism: converts are not to delay this first step on the way of righteousness (see 28:19). οὕτως means "just as I ask you to do." πληρόω is usually passive for fulfillment of prophecy, but here Matthew writes the active πληρῶσαι for doing the right thing (cf. 6:1, not found elsewhere, and the phrase "to be filled after the Lord" for obedience to him—Num 14:24; 32:11-12; Deut 1:36; Josh 14:8-9, 14; 1 Kgs 11:6). "All righteousness" implies a quantitative concept of righteousness that fits 5:20, another of Matthew's compositions. Since the baptismal voice will allude to a passage from Isaiah concerning the Servant of the Lord (cf. v 17 with Isa 42:1) and since Matthew will interject quotations of two such passages (cf. 8:17 with Isa 53:4; and 12:17-21 with Isa 42:1-4) and one allusion (cf. 27:57 with Isa 53:9), the description of the Lord's Servant as righteous probably influences Matthew here. And in accord with his paralleling John the Baptist and

Jesus, "us" brings together these two men—and by implication Jesus' disciples—for the fulfilling of all righteousness. Only πρέπον, "proper," remains a significant word unaccounted for. It occurs only here in the gospels; nevertheless, it belongs to a family of words that Matthew often inserts because of their similar meanings: ἀνάγκη, "necessity" (18:7), ἀρκετόν, "sufficient" (6:34; 10:25), δεῖ, "it is necessary" (18:33; 25:27; 26:54), and συμφερεῖ, "it is advantageous" (5:29, 30; 18:6; 19:10).

The insistence of Jesus on this seemingly inappropriate humiliation illustrates his lowliness, a characteristically Matthean motif (cf. 2:23; 11:29; 21:5, all unique to this gospel), and offers an example to would-be converts. On the other hand, both the attempt of John to deter Jesus and his capitulation to Jesus' insistence exemplify the disciplelike qualities of humility and obedience, both of which exalt the superiority of Jesus. But does Matthew intend us to understand John's attempt to deter him as arising out of a belief that the stronger one should not subordinate himself to the mere baptizer in water? Or out of an assumption that the baptizer in the Holy Spirit and fire does not need the inferior baptism in water? Or out of a hope that the time has come for replacing baptism in water with baptism in the Holy Spirit and fire? Or out of a conviction that the sinlessness of Jesus rules out baptism with water "for repentance" (v 11)? All the possibilities fit the context well, and they do not conflict with one another. The statement of John, "I need to be baptized by you," supports the view that according to Matthew he expected Jesus now to baptize him and others in the Holy Spirit and fire. An emphasis on the sinlessness of Jesus is possibly seen in Matthew's making him get out of the water immediately (see the comments on v 16).

The notion that the fulfillment of all righteousness refers to procurement of all righteousness for Jesus' followers illegitimately imposes the Pauline connotation of justification by faith on a word that in Matthew denotes right conduct (usually on the part of people, occasionally on the part of God in his exercising justice). Though Isaiah's description of the Lord's Servant as righteous may have influenced Matthew, then, the Servant's activity of justifying many did not.

3:16 (Mark 1:10; Luke 3:21-22) "And Jesus, having been baptized" takes up Mark 1:9 again (cf. v 13) and provides a transition back to Markan material. Initial participles in the aorist tense and nominative case, like βαπτισθείς, characterize Matthew's style. Now he makes Jesus go up from the water immediately after the baptism, i.e., clamber up on the riverbank without first confessing sins (cf. v 6; also Acts 8:39, where the baptizer as well as the baptized comes out of the water). This differs from Mark, whose ἐκ might be mistaken for the final movement in the rite proper and whose εὐθύς probably goes with εἶδεν, "he saw," rather than with ἀναβαίνων, "going up." Matthew's ἀπό does not negate the thought of emergence contained in Mark's ἐκ, but it indicates more clearly Jesus' complete departure from the waters of the Jordan. The differences suggest, then, that Matthew did not want anybody to think Jesus stayed in the river to confess his sins. He had none. He was fulfilling all righteousness. That Matthew rarely retains εὐθύς (Mark has it often) lends further support to this understanding.

51

The typical addition of "and behold" highlights Jesus' reception of the Spirit (cf. the comments on v 17a and the Greek Index for ἰδού—34,9). Matthew delays Mark's "he saw" and changes "being split" (cf. Isa 63:11, 14, 19) to "were opened" for agreement with Ezekiel's inaugural vision (Ezek 1:1). Also, he is fond of ἀνοίγω (5,2; cf. Luke 3:21). Unless we are to omit αὐτῷ with ℵ* B /²¹¹ᵐ,¹⁰⁴³ᵐ,¹⁶²⁷ᵐ syrᶜ·ˢ copˢᵃ geoᴮ Irenaeus Hilary Vigilius, its addition contributes to Matthew's approaching emphasis on the Trinity. Finally, "he saw" comes from Mark to parallel "were opened," as in Ezek 1:1.

By adding "of God" to "Spirit" Matthew signals a trinitarian emphasis, as also in 12:28, where he will make the same addition. He wants to establish continuity between Jesus' baptism and later Christian baptism "in the name of the Father and of the Son and of the Holy Spirit" (28:19). Such continuity gives the story more exemplary force. Matthew usually prefers "Holy" as a modifier of "Spirit" (see 1:18, 20; 3:11; 12:32; 28:19). Therefore his adding "of God" here makes for a clearer allusion to the Trinity: God, Jesus his beloved Son, and the Spirit of God. Matthew also advances the participle καταβαῖνον to a position before ὡσεὶ περιστεράν in order to allow the addition of another participle, ἐρχόμενον (not in Mark or Luke). There results a trinitarian correspondence between the Spirit as coming and Jesus as the one who is coming (cf. v 11, where only Matthew has the participle ἐρχόμενος). There also results a shift from the Spirit himself as dovelike (so Mark and Luke) to the Spirit's descent as dovelike. Matthew has already scaled down the comparison between the Spirit and a dove by putting ὡσεί, "as if," in place of Mark's and Luke's ὡς, "as" (see 9:36 for the same change and the present parallel in Luke for the opposite tendency). Mark's εἰς yields to ἐπ' in anticipation of 12:18 (an interpolation by Matthew). Luke agrees with Matthew in ἐπ', but has a different reason, viz., that the bodily form of the Spirit (so Luke alone) allows only a perching on top of Jesus. The Spirit's descent on Jesus makes him an example of baptism in the Spirit as well as of baptism in water.

Some have compared Gen 1:2 (but no dove appears there) and Gen 8:8-12 (but the Spirit does not appear there). The lack of OT precedent and the failure of the comparison to appear in known Jewish literature of the NT era favor historical tradition over ecclesiastical invention.

3:17 (Mark 1:11; Luke 3:22) The addition of another ἰδού accentuates God's owning Jesus and parallels the same addition in v 16. This twofold emphasis on the reception of the Spirit by Jesus and on his divine sonship highlights the trinitarian contours of Matthew's account. Omission of Mark's ἐγένετο (if it is original) adds to the exclamatory effect of ἰδού. And the typical insertion of λέγουσα (61,23) points up the words expressing Jesus' sonship.

Matthew alone reports the Father as saying, "This is . . . in whom," instead of, "You are . . . in you." The change from second person to third conforms both to Matthew's diction (οὗτός ἐστιν—12,0) and to the Father's declaration at the transfiguration (17:5; Mark 9:7; Luke 9:35). It also transforms the statement from an assurance to Jesus into a proclamation of Jesus' divine sonship for the benefit of Matthew's readers (not John, since in Matthew's version John has already shown awareness of Jesus' identity). Matthew sees in the Father's declaration a combination of the divine sonship of the royal Messiah and the endowment of the Servant of the Lord with God's Spirit. Cf. Matthew's allusion in 22:34 to Psalm 2, from which the baptismal words concerning sonship come, and quotation in 12:18-21 of Isa 42:1-4, from which the words concerning the Father's delight in Jesus come. The connection between the baptismal statement and the later quotation from Isaiah is confirmed by Matthew's importing ἀγαπητός, "beloved," into the later quotation, where it is a very unusual translation, or substitute, for the Hebrew בָּחִיר, "chosen" (ἐκλεκτός in the LXX). The emphases on the opening of heaven and the proclamatory character of the Father's declaration serve to exalt Jesus over John.

Matthew's unique reference to Jesus' baptism as the fulfillment of all righteousness (v 15) changes the verb εὐδόκησα from a timeless aorist based on the Hebrew stative perfect in Isa 42:1 (and translated properly by the present tense in English) into a historical aorist referring to God's pleasure in the baptism of Jesus, a pleasure would-be disciples might also come to enjoy by following his example.

In rabbinic literature the so-called בַּת־קוֹל, "daughter of a voice" or distant echo of God's voice, was thought to replace prophetic revelation. We have little indication of that notion here. The declaration of Jesus' divine sonship cannot refer to baptismal adoption in Matthew, for Jesus has already appeared as God's son (2:15). The rabbis generally treated Psalm 2 as messianic (Str-B 3. 675ff.). Despite the change of wording in *Tg. Ket.* Ps 2:7, that paraphrase seems to provide a better source for "beloved" (not in the MT or LXX) than Gen 22:2, 12, 16 LXX provides; for a typology of Isaac vis-à-vis Jesus plays little or no role elsewhere in the gospels. Against attempts to eliminate the allusions to Ps 2:7 and Isa 42:1, see I. H. Marshall in *NTS* 15 (1969) 326-36; Gundry, *Use of the OT* 29-32.

JESUS AS A MODEL OF OBEDIENCE TO DIVINE LAW
4:1-11 (Mark 1:12-13; Luke 4:1-13)

The story of Jesus' resistance to Satanic temptation could show that Jesus did not get his miraculous power from the Devil. But Matthew does not make the story serve that point. Unlike Adam in the Garden of Eden, Jesus refuses to sin even under the trying conditions of a wilderness. Mark goes so far as to note the presence of wild animals (1:13b). But in omitting the reference to wild animals Matthew pays no attention to the comparison between Jesus and Adam. Instead, he sticks to the non-Markan source he shares with Luke. In that source Jesus' answers to Satan, all drawn from passages concerning the testing of Israel in the wilderness, imply a parallel between Jesus and Israel. Where Israel failed, Jesus passed the test. Matthew may have appreciated the parallel; he himself drew a similar one in

2:15. But here the parallel comes from the non-Markan source; for Luke has it, too, and Matthew carries it no further.

Matthew shows a special interest, rather, in a comparison between Jesus and Moses, a comparison already introduced in 2:13, 16, 20-21. Moses stands for law. Therefore a portrayal of Jesus in the colors of Moses combats antinomianism in the church. Matthew has been leading up to this attack since the outset of his comparison of these two figures (see "Moses parallel Jesus" in the Topical Index).

4:1 (Mark 1:12-13; Luke 4:1-2) The substitution of τότε for Mark's καί tightens up the narrative. As usual, Mark's εὐθύς drops out. The specification of Jesus, unnamed in Mark, suits Matthew's style (80,12), but Luke's agreement may point to the non-Markan source. With the change in the voice of the verb emphasis now falls on Jesus rather than on the Spirit. ἀνήχθη, "was led up," disagrees with Mark's ἐκβάλλει, "drives out," and—presumably through dependence on the non-Markan source—agrees basically with Luke's ἤγετο, "was being led." But the agreement suffers two qualifications. First, the imperfect tense in Luke describes a leading that lasted forty days in the wilderness, whereas Matthew's aorist indicates a journey into the wilderness at the start of the forty days. Second, the prefix ἀν- shows that Matthew has drawn from the temptation concerning the kingdoms of the world, where Luke 4:5 has the compound form of the verb. But why this advance of that verb? Matthew wants to display Jesus as a new and greater Moses who goes up into the mountainous part of the wilderness just as Moses went up Mount Sinai in the wilderness (see Deut 9:9, a passage located in the very section of Deuteronomy about to supply Jesus' replies to Satan; cf. also Exod 34:1ff. LXX).

The reference to temptation comes forward in Matthew and takes the form of a telic infinitive rather than a participle (as in Mark and Luke). The testing of Jesus' obedience as God's Son becomes, then, the very purpose of the Spirit's leading him up into the wilderness (cf. Deut 8:1-2); i.e., the Spirit descended on Jesus at his baptism in order to lead him on the way of righteousness, a way of obedience to the law, which he will quote in parrying the Devil. Thus, to attack antinomianism, Matthew makes the postbaptismal obedience of Jesus to the law of Moses a paradigm of postbaptismal obedience of Christians to the law of Christ (cf. 1 Cor 9:21; Gal 6:2; Jas 1:25; 2:12; 2 Pet 3:2; and above all the uniquely Matthean passage in 28:19-20 of our gospel). Probably relying on their non-Markan source, both Matthew and Luke write "Devil" rather than Mark's transliterated Hebrew, "Satan." Both mean "accuser" but have the force of a name here, since no accusations come into view.

4:2 (Mark 1:13; Luke 4:2) In common dependence on their non-Markan source, Matthew and Luke detail three temptations. Characteristically, Matthew's account begins with an aorist nominative participle (νηστεύσας, "having fasted"). Matthew has delayed the forty days till now in order to associate them with Jesus' fasting (contrast their association with Jesus' being in the wilderness in Mark and Luke). Next, Matthew adds forty nights to the forty days in order to conform to Moses' fasting forty days and forty nights according to Deut 9:9-18, set again in the section of

Deuteronomy that will provide Jesus' answers to the Devil (cf. Exod 34:28). For the sake of comparison with another OT figure—viz., Jonah—Matthew will also add three nights to Jesus' stay in the heart of the earth (cf. 12:40 with Jonah 2:1[1:17]).

Like Moses, then, Jesus fasted forty days and forty nights. Mark says nothing about this, and Luke simply notes that Jesus ate nothing during those days. Only Matthew uses the word for fasting. He alone follows it with instructions concerning the way Jesus' disciples ought to fast (6:16-18). In the one other passage where fasting appears (9:14-15; Mark 2:18-20; Luke 5:33-35) Matthew modifies the saying that the guests of the bridegroom cannot fast while the bridegroom is with them (so Mark and Luke) to read that they cannot "mourn"; and he drops the phrase "on that day" (so Mark and, similarly, Luke). In other words, Matthew takes away the grounds for any appeal to nonfasting during Jesus' lifetime—there is no excuse for failure to fast now—and insures that Christians do not misunderstand fasting as limited to the time just after Jesus the bridegroom was taken away. Rather, Christians are to practice fasting during the *whole* period of his absence. Jesus' own fasting therefore provides an example to be followed. ὕστερον has a Matthean ring (3,3), but ἐπείνασεν matches Luke. For the number forty, especially as a number of testing, but also of punishment and oppression, see Gen 7:4, 12, 17; Exod 24:18; Deut 9:11, 25; 10:10; Judg 13:1; 1 Kgs 19:8; Ps 95:10.

4:3 (Luke 4:3) As often, Matthew inserts προσελθών (38,6). It connotes the divine dignity of Jesus, who is to be approached only with reverence (cf. *TDNT* 2. 683-84). Instead of "the Devil" (so Luke) Matthew has "the tempter." The result is clearer parallels with the Pharisees and Sadducees and with the disciples of the Pharisees and the Herodians, all of whom tempt Jesus later in the gospel (16:1; 19:3; 22:18, 35). Notably, in 16:1 Matthew will introduce, against Mark and Luke, the same combination of προσέρχομαι and πειράζω for the Pharisees and Sadducees that he alone has here for the Devil (cf. 19:3 along with Mark 10:2; and the proximity of the two verbs in 22:18, 23, 35). πειράζω refers to testing when God stands in the forefront, to temptation when an evil force such as the Devil stands in the forefront. The leading of the Spirit and the enticements of the Devil give the verb a double connotation here.

"If you are the Son of God" flashes back to 3:17 (so also v 6 here). εἰ means "if" in the sense of "since." The Devil does not tempt Jesus to doubt his divine sonship, just pronounced at his baptism, but to rely on that sonship in self-serving ways that would lead him disobediently from the path to the cross. This comes out clearly in the last temptation.

Matthew uses the plurals "these stones" and "loaves of bread." Luke reads the singular, and as a lone individual Jesus would have needed but one loaf. Matthew's first plural conforms to "these stones" in 3:9, where John the Baptist was addressing the Pharisees and Sadducees. Outside these two passages Matthew always puts λίθος in the singular, and ἄρτος will occur in the singular in Jesus' reply to Satan (v 4). Furthermore, in the first half of chap. 16 Matthew will add references to loaves of bread (vv 10, 11, 12) in a passage already loaded with such references having synoptic parallels (vv 5, 7, 8, 9); and he will cap the passage with a unique warning against "the teaching of the Pharisees and Sadducees" (v 12). Apparently, then, the plural of "these stones" and "loaves of bread" indicates that he is portraying the Devil as a type of the Jewish leaders who opposed Jesus, just as in his use of "the tempter."

4:4 (Luke 4:4) Matthew extends the quotation of Deut 8:3, which makes up Jesus' first reply to the Devil, beyond its Lukan form to include "but on every word coming out through the mouth of God." This extension presents Jesus as an example of obedience to the word of divine law. He was no antinomian! And since Matthew has already identified Jesus as "God with us" (1:23), the word of divine law necessary for Christians to obey will refer particularly to the teaching of Jesus (cf. 5:2; 28:20). ῥήματι, "word," suits this point well. It is lacking in the MT, but comes from the LXX and agrees with the targums (see Gundry, *Use of the OT* 66-67—also for an uncertain argument for the short Western reading, which does not affect the sense).

4:5-6 (Luke 4:9-11) Luke has a special interest in Jerusalem (see esp. Luke 9:51; 19:28; Acts 1:4, 8). For the sake of climax, therefore, he probably delayed till last the temptation located there. If so, Matthew preserves the original order. This view agrees with the distinctive "then" and "again" at the beginning of the second and third temptations, respectively (vv 5 and 8), and with the greater naturalness of having first the two subtle temptations beginning "If you are the Son of God" and only then the blatant temptation to worship Satan. That Matthew's order of temptations produces the inverse order Deut 8:3; 6:16, 13 in Jesus' replies speaks in its favor, as may also the possible correspondence between Matthew's order and the command in Deut 6:5 to love God with one's heart (thus the refusal to make bread in self-interest), soul (understood as "life" and thus the refusal to jump off the pinnacle of the Temple to capitalize on divine protection of life and limb), and might (understood as "possessions" and thus the refusal to worship Satan for possession of the whole world; see B. Gerhardsson in *NTS* 14 [1968] 165-93).

Matthew has a characteristic παραλαμβάνει (4,6) instead of Luke's ἤγαγεν. "The Devil," absent at this point in Luke, comes in to specify the subject and compensate for the replacement of that designation in v 3. Instead of Luke's "Jerusalem" we read "the holy city." This expression will occur also in the passage about the resurrection of "holy people" and their appearance to many in "the holy city" after Jesus' resurrection (27:51b-53, peculiar to Matthew). It is the only other passage in the gospels to have the expression. Hence, the episode it describes will offer the demonstration of deity that the Devil here tempts Jesus to give. "The pinnacle of the Temple" may refer to the southeast corner of the outer court, which dropped off into the Kidron Valley, to the lintel of the gateway into the Temple, or to the pinnacle of the sanctuary proper (see *TDNT* 3. 236). Since the wilderness would have provided many precipices for private capitalization on divine providence, the selection of the Temple implies the public display of a messianic sign.

The historical present λέγει differs from Luke's aorist, typifies Mat-

56

thew's style (47,11), and accentuates Jesus' divine sonship in the opening
clause of the temptation. Luke's ἐντεῦθεν does not appear in Matthew and
probably originates with the third evangelist himself, since it appears without parallel also in Luke 13:31. The Devil takes his quotation from Ps
91(90):11-12, but omits the phrase "in all your ways" because the deliberate
throwing of oneself from a high perch does not correspond to accidental
stumbling over a stone on one's path (as in the psalm). Luke's τοῦ
διαφυλάξαι σε does not appear in Matthew, but may stem from Luke in
view of his fondness for the cognates φυλακή, φυλακίζω, φύλαξ and φυλάσσω.

4:7 (Luke 4:12) In place of Luke's καὶ ἀποκριθεὶς εἶπεν αὐτῷ, we read
ἔφη αὐτῷ. The asyndeton stresses the scriptural word of Jesus' reply.
Matthew likes Luke's expression (29,6), but sometimes he prefers the present one (6,1). He often omits πάλιν, but at other times it is unique to his
text (8,4). Here he inserts it to underscore the written law and Jesus'
obedience to it. This emphasis makes a thrust against antinomianism. "It
is written" in v 4 provides the referent for πάλιν, "again," which now requires Matthew to switch from a verb of speaking ("it is said"—so Luke)
to another "it is written." With yet another "it is written" in v 10 (so also
Luke), Matthew gains a threefold parallel. Had "it is written" formed part
of the tradition here, Luke would almost surely have kept it as he usually
does (see the concordance and cf. Acts 2:16; 13:40 for apparently traditional occurrences of "what was spoken"). The singular of "you shall not
test" (so also Luke) agrees with the LXX against the MT and suits well the
individual context here.

4:8-9 (Luke 4:5-7) Yet another πάλιν substitutes for καί (so Luke)
and harks back to v 5, which then supplies the words παραλαμβάνει αὐτὸν
ὁ διάβολος εἰς in place of ἀναγαγών (so Luke), already used by Matthew in
v 1 (see the comments on v 5 for Matthew's diction). To be the object of
εἰς, the evangelist adds ὄρος ὑψηλὸν λίαν, "an exceedingly high mountain,"
i.e., higher yet, since according to Matthew's version Jesus has already been
led up (v 1). ὑψηλόν anticipates the description of the Mount of Transfiguration (17:1), and ὄρος and λίαν belong to Matthew's favorite vocabulary
(6,1; 3,1). Above all, the added phrase carries forward the parallel between
Jesus and Moses: Jesus views all the kingdoms of the world from a mountain
just as Moses viewed not only all the land of Canaan (Deut 34:1-4), but
also "the west and north and south and east" (Deut 3:27), from Mount
Pisgah, or Nebo. Again the portrayal of Jesus in terms of that man of law,
Moses, strikes against antinomianism in the church. The present tense of
"shows" veers from Luke's aorist to match the present tense of "takes along"
in the preceding clause. κόσμου is a Mattheanism (5,2), just as Luke's
οἰκουμένης is typical of Luke-Acts. "And their glory" belongs to what the
Devil shows Jesus rather than to what the Devil said he could give him (as
in Luke). But "their" has no antecedent in the Devil's preceding words
according to Luke; so Luke may have displaced the phrase. Matthew will
assign "glory" to Jesus in 16:27; 19:28 (as an interpolation); 24:30; 25:31
(bis and unparalleled).

Internal considerations do not decide the issue concerning the textual
variants λέγει and εἶπεν, for λέγει may have arisen out of influence from v 6

and εἶπεν may have arisen out of influence from Luke. Therefore we should follow the better attested εἶπεν. Besides, it seems unlikely that Matthew would want to stress the Devil's offer with a vivid historical present (though he did so stress the Devil's reference to the divine sonship of Jesus in v 6). For emphasis, the Mattheanism ταῦτα . . . πάντα (7,1) stands at the beginning of the offer. These words replace τὴν ἐξουσίαν ταύτην ἄπασαν (so Luke) to avoid the implication that the Devil has "all this authority." That implication would contradict the possession of divine authority by Jesus already during his earthly ministry (9:6; cf. 9:8, distinctive in its use of "authority") and his claim after the resurrection to have received all authority in heaven and on earth (28:18). In fact, Matthew may have transferred "all authority" from the tradition of the temptation to 28:18. Cf. 7:29; 8:9; 10:1; 11:27; 21:23, 24, 27.

For the same purpose of denuding the Devil of authority Matthew, we might think, omits the statement, "because to me [the Devil] it has been given over and I give it to whomever I want." But probably that statement is the result of composition by Luke, since he introduces similar causal explanations in 6:19b; 8:37; 9:38; 11:18. Likewise, "you therefore," lacking in Matthew and dependent on the causal explanation, probably comes from Luke rather than the tradition. But Matthew adds a distinctive and characteristic πεσών (5,3) in order to leave no doubt concerning the issue: worship of Jesus as divine (as in 2:11, where the same combination of falling down and worshipping occurs) versus worship of Satan as divine. "Before" and "all will be yours" do not appear in Matthew. Both are attributable to Luke.

4:10 (Luke 4:8) As often, τότε substitutes for καί. Even though Matthew is fond of ἀποκριθείς . . . εἶπεν (29,6), here it yields to another Mattheanism, the historical present λέγει (47,11), which along with αὐτῷ comes forward to emphasize Jesus' word. Only in Matthew does Jesus rid himself of Satan with a sovereign command. That command, "Go, Satan!" derives by anticipation from Jesus' later rebuke of Peter (16:23). In the rebuke, "behind me" reflects the expectation that a disciple follow his teacher (quite literally) rather than take him aside. Here, the phrase drops out as inappropriate to Satan, hardly a disciple. ὕπαγε is a favorite of Matthew (5,6).

Typically, Matthew adds γάρ to γέγραπται to make Scripture the reason for refusing the temptation (cf. v 6). Scriptural commands form the bulwark against antinomianism. In "you shall worship" (so also Luke) we see an assimilation of the verb of fearing in Deut 6:13 to the Satanic temptation concerning worship. The agreement of LXX[A,Pap.963] comes by way of influence from the NT (see Gundry, *Use of the OT* 68-69). Matthew's and Luke's "only" may reflect 1 Sam 7:3 MT; it does not appear in Deut 6:13 except for Septuagintal tradition influenced by the NT.

4:11 (Mark 1:13; Luke 4:13) Apart from the simple statement concerning the Devil's departure from Jesus, Luke's version looks highly redactional (see the concordance). Matthew's τότε substitutes as usual for an original καί. ἀφίησιν represents Matthew's diction (12,5) and differs from Luke's synonymous ἀπέστη in taking the present tense and a forward position for emphasis on the dramatic effect of Jesus' authoritative command.

Matthew returns to Mark for a statement absent from the non-Markan source but open to use for emphasis on Jesus' deity. He characteristically inserts ἰδού (34,9) and προσῆλθον (38,6) for such an emphasis (cf. the comments on v 3). The ministering of angels to Jesus includes the serving of food, but in Matthew it also becomes an example for the ministry of "the sheep" to Jesus, through their kindnesses to the least of his brothers (25:44, unique to Matthew), and for the ministry to Jesus of "many women" who followed him as disciples (27:55). Cf. 1 Kgs 19:5-8.

GOING INTO GENTILE TERRITORY BECAUSE OF PERSECUTION
4:12-16 (Mark 1:14, 21; Luke 4:14, 31; John 4:1-3)

4:12 (Mark 1:14; Luke 4:14; John 4:1-3) This paragraph begins with the typically Matthean ἀκούσας (10,3). Absent in the parallels, the participle makes John's arrest the reason for Jesus' departure to Galilee (cf. John 4:1-3). ἀνεχώρησεν belongs to Matthew's special vocabulary (4,5). It replaces Mark's ἦλθεν and connotes avoidance of persecution by withdrawal from the area where John had suffered arrest. παρεδόθη, which indicates John's arrest, comes from Mark and occurs often in the gospels; but Matthew will insert it in 24:9; 26:2, 25 and use it in distinctive material at 27:3, 4 for Jesus' and his disciples' being given over to maltreatment. Thus in the first gospel Jesus exemplifies his command to flee persecution (10:23; cf. 2:22 and "Flight from persecution" in the Topical Index), and the sufferings of John prefigure the sufferings of Jesus and his disciples. Mark's specification of Jesus' name drops out because Matthew has mentioned the name more recently than Mark has.

4:13-16 (Mark 1:21; Luke 4:31) According to vv 13-16 Jesus leaves Nazareth to settle in Capernaum, which will become his base of operations throughout the whole of Galilee. The passage is largely distinctive; Matthew wants it to symbolize the going of Christian preachers to Gentiles as well as Jews (see "Universality" in the Topical Index). Jesus' later entrance into Capernaum—a mere visit—planted the thought in Matthew's mind (cf. Mark 1:21). But the evangelist goes much further.

In the first place, the material comes forward to produce a prefiguring of worldwide evangelism from the very start of the Galilean ministry. Mark does not write about the entrance into Capernaum till after a summary of Jesus' preaching and the call of the four fishermen (1:14-21a), and Luke not till after a similar summary and the rejection of Jesus at Nazareth (4:13-31a). Moreover, only Matthew writes that Jesus "left" (καταλιπών)— i.e., forsook Nazareth as his permanent address—and settled in Capernaum (κατῴκησεν, "set up house," in contrast with Mark's εἰσπορεύονται, "go into," and Luke's κατῆλθεν, "went down"; cf. John 2:12 and the possible absence from Nazareth of all Jesus' family, except for his presumably married sisters, according to Mark 6:3; Matt 13:55-56). The words ἐλθὼν κατῴκησεν (not in Mark or Luke) echo 2:23 exactly (see earlier comments on their Matthean character).

59

The mention of Jesus' settling in Capernaum stems from Matthew's desire to prefigure worldwide evangelization of Gentiles. Cf. οἱ κατοικοῦντες in Isa 9:1(2) LXX, which may have reminded Matthew of his own κατῴκησεν in 2:23. Of course he knows that Nazareth lies in Galilee (see 2:22-23; 3:13). He simply means that Jesus abandoned his hometown in order to save his people who, living elsewhere in Galilee, had not yet seen his light (cf. λαός in v 16). The form Ναζαρά occurs elsewhere in the NT only at the start of Luke's version of the rejection in Nazareth (Luke 4:16-30), just before the mention of Jesus' going down to Capernaum (Luke 4:31). Here in Matthew Ναζαρά may reflect pre-Lukan tradition and against that background imply a connotation of abandonment in Matthew's distinctive καταλιπών (3,0).

Only Matthew describes Capernaum as a city beside the sea in the borders of Zebulun and Naphtali. The description comes from the following quotation of Isa 8:23-9:1(9:1-2), most obviously in the pairing of Zebulun's tribal territory with Naphtali's, since Capernaum belonged to the latter. Matthew shapes the text this way to strengthen the thought of fulfillment. For two other distinctive occurrences of ὅριον, see 2:16; 15:39; and concerning the formula of fulfillment, see the comments on 1:22b.

The quotation itself begins a series of several from Isaiah (see further 8:17; 12:17-21; 13:14-15). All but the last carry salvific content; and because the last does not, its introductory formula lacks the note of purpose. Here, first blessings in the messianic times were promised through Isaiah to Israelites in the far north of Palestine, for they went into exile first. So now Jesus begins his ministry in that region.

To begin the quotation with a list of geographical terms relevant to his purpose, Matthew tears those terms from their grammatical associations in Isaiah and drops the statement "and later he will make [the land] glorious" from the middle of the list. Properly, ὁδὸν θαλάσσης should mean the western part of Galilee facing, so to speak, "toward the sea," i.e., toward the Mediterranean Sea. But παραθαλασσίαν, "beside the sea," has modified Capernaum in anticipation of θαλάσσης in the quotation and must refer to the Sea of Galilee because of Capernaum's location. We conclude that Matthew wants his readers to take ὁδὸν θαλάσσης as meaning that same part, viewed as facing toward the Sea of Galilee.

The description of Galilee as "of the Gentiles" provides the key point in the quotation. Though Jesus will minister in Galilee mainly to Jews, this description makes that ministry prefigure his disciples' wider mission to Gentiles, as shown by Matthew's seven insertions of ἔθνος and two uses of the term in unshared material, besides six paralleled occurrences. "In the region and shadow of death" is a hendiadys meaning "in the region of death's shadow." Matthew puts "has risen" in place of Isaiah's reference to shining in order to make the dawn of Jesus' ministry fulfill the promise contained in the rising of the messianic star (2:2, 9; cf. Isa 58:10). The double meaning of ἀνατέλλω, "rise, shine," helped link the present quotation with the earlier allusion to Num 24:17. See Gundry, *Use of the OT* 105-8; G. M. Soares Prabhu, *The Formula Quotations in the Infancy Narrative of Matthew* (AnBib 63; Rome: Biblical Institute Press, 1976) 86-104, for further textual comparisons and especially for divergences from, as well as some agreements with, the LXX. Matthew's liking γῆ (21,6), ὁδός (9,2), and κάθημαι (8,0) supplies further help in understanding the textual peculiarities of this quotation.

JESUS AS A MODEL DISCIPLER
4:17-25 (Mark 1:14-20, 28, 32, 34, 39; 3:7-13a; 6:6b; Luke 4:14, 40-41, 44; 6:17-20a; 8:1; cf. Luke 5:1-11; John 1:35-51)

In order to set the stage for the details of Jesus' words and works—especially the words—Matthew here gives a programmatic introduction to the Galilean ministry. Jesus appears as a model for those he will send to make disciples of all the nations (28:19).

4:17 (Mark 1:14-15; Luke 4:15) As in 16:20, where it occurs again as an insertion, ἀπὸ τότε ἤρξατο followed by an infinitive marks a shift. The move to Capernaum has signalled the start of Jesus' exemplary activities in public, the proclamation of repentance and of the kingdom with accompanying healings. At 16:21 Jesus will begin to tell his disciples privately that he is going to die and be raised from the dead. His present activities take place in Galilee (4:12-16); his passion predictions look to what will happen in Jerusalem (mentioned distinctively in 16:21). Mark's "the gospel of God" drops out because of the following substitute concerning repentance and the nearness of the kingdom (see the comments on 3:1-2).

Some think that Matthew drops Mark's reference to fulfillment in order to keep the kingdom in the future even though it is near (cf. the insertion of "before the time" in 8:29). But even in the present parallel, Mark 1:15, the kingdom has only .drawn near. The fulfillment of the time implies that the kingdom verges on coming. With his ministry well under way, Jesus will say that the kingdom has arrived (Matt 12:28; Luke 11:20). Matthew drops Mark's reference to fulfillment for the parallel between John and Jesus, not for futurist eschatology.

4:18 (Mark 1:16) Matthew substitutes περιπατῶν, "walking [around]," for Mark's παράγων, "going along," because for him παράγω means "depart" (see 9:9, 27; 20:30). The substitute hints at the itinerant nature of Jesus' exemplary ministry (cf. the comments on v 23; 10:23; 24:14; 28:19). The addition of "two brothers" before the names of Simon and Andrew and despite the paralleled description of Andrew as Simon's brother means that in this physical brotherhood we are to catch an intimation of the churchly brotherhood. This intimation is confirmed by Matthew's general preoccupation with ἀδελφός (11,8), especially in its religious sense. δύο is also a Mattheanism (19,4). To the Semitic name "Simon" Matthew typically adds τὸν λεγόμενον (10,2) and the Greek name "Peter" (i.e., "Rock"—8,1). He does so to put Peter forward as representative (but not superior—see the comments on passages listed under Πέτρος in the concordance). The replacement of "Simon's" (so Mark) with "his" lets the emphasis stay on Peter, the representational name.

4:19-20 (Mark 1:17-18) The historical present λέγει (47,11) replaces Mark's εἶπεν and emphasizes Jesus' following words as a call to discipleship and to the activity of making more disciples. Mark's "Jesus" disappears because Matthew added the name in v 17. "After me" refers quite literally to a position behind Jesus as he walks about. His initiative in calling disciples, the literalness of their following, and their role of bringing others to discipleship contrast with the rabbinic paradigm, in which the would-be disciple took the initiative, lived the sedentary life of a student, and aspired to become a rabbi himself, greater if possible than his master. The proclamation of the kingdom and the analogy of the prophetic call in the OT contribute to the differences in discipleship to Jesus. With "fishers of men," a figure of speech that connotes persuasion and grows out of the first disciples' occupation, cf. 13:47-50; Luke 5:1-11; John 21:4-8; Ezek 47:10; 1QH 5:8; and especially Jer 16:16, where fishing for men probably refers to the restoration of God's people in accord with the preceding two verses, not to their judgment in accord with the following two verses. See John 1:19-51 for previous acquaintance with Jesus, which might explain the willingness of the two pairs of brothers to follow him here. Mark's vulgar εὐθύς comes over in its refined form εὐθέως. Since Matthew usually omits it, the present retention puts stress on the immediate leaving of the nets to follow Jesus.

4:21 (Mark 1:19) Mark's ὀλίγον gives way to the Mattheanism ἐκεῖθεν (8,1). Again despite a following "his brother," Matthew typically inserts δύο ἀδελφούς (19,4; 11,8), this time preceded by ἄλλους, another favorite of his (14,4). This overuse of ἀδελφός carries on the theme of churchly brotherhood, symbolized by the family relationship of James and John. Matthew takes καὶ αὐτούς in Mark as a reference to the hired hands mentioned in the next Markan verse. He will omit them, and so omits the present phrase in anticipation. The mention of Zebedee moves up to prepare for the sacrifice of leaving a father in order to follow Jesus (cf. 8:21-22; 10:35-37; 19:29). The positioning of "their father" after Zebedee's name, in contrast with Mark's order of words, and the addition of "their" to "nets" produce a parallel between the two final occurrences of "their." In addition, the second "their" implies a sacrifice of their own fishing gear, not just their father's, for the sake of discipleship (cf. v 20).

4:22 (Mark 1:20) Again Mark's vulgar εὐθύς comes over in its refined form εὐθέως. But it shifts from "he called" (so Mark) to "leaving." The shift produces a typically Matthean parallel with v 20, which also begins, "And they, immediately leaving. . . ." Along with the unusual retention of the adverb the shift results in heavy emphasis on leaving to follow Jesus, i.e., on the immediacy of the brothers' obedience rather than the immediacy of Jesus' call. Such obedience leaves no room for antinomianism. The reference to the boat advances to match the order of boat before father in v 21 (so Matthew alone). Furthermore, the changing of the prepositional phrase "in the boat," which in Mark tells where the father was left, to the accusative "the boat" makes the boat as well as the father an object of leaving to follow Jesus (cf. the leaving of the nets in v 20). The previous advance of Zebedee's name results in its omission here. Since the hired hands do not

62

make suitable objects of leaving for the sake of discipleship, Matthew omits "with the hired hands." Despite his fondness for ἀπέρχομαι (14,11), Mark's "they went after him" yields to an expression that more obviously connotes discipleship: "they followed him." Seven other times, too, Matthew will insert ἀκολουθέω.

4:23 (Mark 1:34, 39; 6:6b; Luke 4:40-41, 44; 8:1) Mark 1:21 has already been used in v 13. Mark 1:22 will come over in 7:28-29, Mark 1:23-28 in 8:28-34, and Mark 1:29-31 in 8:14-15. Matthew partly reserves Mark 1:32-39 for use in 8:16-17, but partly uses it—plus some other material—now. His characteristic conflation of scattered Markan phrases (see "Conflation" in the Topical Index) produces a summary that will influence the writing of 9:35 and that describes the activities of Jesus. This summary will allow Matthew to move immediately to Jesus' teaching of the law (chaps. 5–7)—the evangelist's chief goal in view of the antinomian threat— before taking up in detail Jesus' miracles.

"He was going around" comes from Mark 6:6b and portrays Jesus' ministry as exemplary of itinerant evangelism. Cf. the use of this verb in 9:35, which comes at the beginning of Jesus' sending the twelve, and 23:15, a distinctive verse, where the verb has to do with winning a convert. The itineration of Jesus distinguishes him from other Jewish prophets and teachers. The reference to the whole of Galilee comes from Mark 1:39. Advancing this reference revives the prefiguration of the church's worldwide mission (cf. the comments on vv 13-16).

"Teaching" comes from Mark 6:6b and starts a series of three participial phrases in the parallelistic style typical of Matthew. He puts this participle in first place to stress Jesus' teaching, which is about to appear in chaps. 5–7, as an antidote to lawlessness. The reference to the Galileans' synagogues and the participle "proclaiming" both come from Mark 1:39. Introduction of "the gospel of the kingdom" (so Matthew alone) compensates for the replacement of "the gospel of God" in v 17 (cf. Mark 1:14). Substitution of "the kingdom" for "God" links with Jesus' preaching the nearness of the kingdom. Cf. 24:14 as well as 9:35. Matthew's emphasis on the kingdom—i.e., God's rule—as the subject matter of the gospel scores another point against antinomianism.

The phrase that starts with "healing" derives from Mark 1:34. Mark's finite verb changes to a participle for the sake of parallelism. πᾶσαν comes from Matthew's favorite diction (63,25-26) and replaces Mark's ποικίλαις, which will go into v 24. νόσον comes from Mark with a change of case and number. But Matthew reserves κακῶς ἔχοντας for use in v 24. He compensates here by adding the phrase καὶ πᾶσαν μαλακίαν. We have just noted his fondness for πᾶσαν. μαλακία occurs three times as an insertion in Matthew and nowhere else in the NT. "Among the people" (not in Mark or Luke) links with 4:16, also unique, in suggesting that the Galilean beneficiaries of Jesus' healing represent the churchly people of Jesus, whom he will save from sins (1:21). For the healing of physical ailments symbolizes and forms part of such salvation (cf. Matthew's use of Isa 53:4 in 8:17 for Jesus' healings, and of Isa 53:9 in 27:57 for an aspect of Jesus' death for the remission of sins). All in all, v 23 presents Jesus as the model of an itinerant teacher, preacher, and healer.

4:24 (Mark 1:28, 32, 34; Luke 4:37, 40-41) The first clause of v 24 comes from Mark 1:28. Mark's ἐξῆλθεν gives way to ἀπῆλθεν, a synonymous favorite of Matthew (14,11). The replacement compensates for his rejecting ἀπῆλθον in v 22 (cf. Mark 1:20). As usual, Mark's εὐθύς vanishes. Matthew also omits "everywhere" as unneeded, even redundant, with "the whole of." "Syria" replaces Mark's "the surrounding region of Galilee," because in v 23 Matthew already had Jesus going around in the whole of Galilee. The report concerning Jesus needs to go farther away. The reference to Tyre and Sidon in Mark 3:8, soon to be used by Matthew in v 25, suggests Syria, the country of their location. The expansion of Tyre (Mark 7:24) to Tyre and Sidon in 15:21 will make up for the replacement of Tyre and Sidon here; and "Syrophoenician" (Mark 7:26) will drop out at least partly because of the present importation of Syria. Therefore, Matthew is now bringing in Syria as an anticipation of Jesus' ministry to a Gentile woman who lived in the Phoenician part of Syria (15:21-28; Mark 7:24-30) and for the purpose of giving Jesus' ministry among Galilean Jews overtones of later evangelization of Gentiles.

The second clause in v 24 comes mainly from Mark 1:32 (cf. Matt 8:16 and esp. 14:35). For Mark's ἔφερον πρὸς αὐτόν Matthew writes the synonymous προσήνεγκαν αὐτῷ, which may carry connotations of an offering to God and thus of Jesus' deity (see the comments on 2:11). To be sure, the sick and demon possessed make a strange offering. But that may only highlight divine mercy.

Since Matthew has just mentioned Syria as the region the report concerning Jesus went to, those who brought the afflicted to Jesus must at least include Syrians. Thus he expands Jesus' Galilean ministry to include Gentiles from foreign lands. Again we see a prefigurement of the disciples' ministry to Gentiles throughout the world (24:14; 28:19). "With various diseases" comes from Mark 1:34. βασάνοις represents Matthew's special diction (2,1 for βασαν-). "Demon possessed" derives from Mark 1:32. Its mate "epileptics" will be inserted for demon possession also in 17:15. And in 8:6 Matthew will associate a paralytic with torment in a fashion similar to his adding "paralytics" to the present list of those who are afflicted with torments.

Throughout Matthew's gospel the statement "and he healed them" sounds like a refrain, never fully matched though always occurring in parallel passages (4:24; 12:15, 22 [with "him"]; 14:14 [with "their sick people"]; 15:30; 19:2; 21:14). Here, the verb stems from Mark 1:34. Matthew presents exorcism as a kind of healing. The length of the list of afflictions adds emphasis to the healings performed by Jesus. The juxtaposition of his words and healings in vv 23 and 24 corresponds to the same juxtaposition in chaps. 5–7 and 8–9, though we will see that even in his accounts of healings Matthew accentuates Jesus' words.

4:25 (Mark 3:7-8; Luke 6:17-18) To gain geographical terms, the evangelist now skips to Mark 3:7-8, a summary very much like the one he is here constructing. "Followed" comes forward and "him [Jesus]" is added for emphasis on discipleship (cf. v 22). "Crowds" replaces Mark's "multitude." Matthew regularly uses the crowds (usually in the plural) to represent the masses in the church, professing disciples both true and false— the result of extensive evangelism among the Gentiles. Here, their following Jesus lends itself to this representation.

"From Galilee" originates in Mark 3:7 and reminds Matthew of the association between Galilee and the Gentiles in 4:15. This reminder and the movement of his thoughts southward lead him to insert "Decapolis." This region of ten cities was located southeast of the Sea of Galilee, had a largely Gentile population, and further serves Matthew's portrayal of Jesus as an exemplary evangelist to Gentiles. (In 8:34 and 15:29 Decapolis will drop out for reasons unrelated to the present emphasis.) Matthew reverses Mark's order of Judea and Jerusalem to conform to his distinctive order in 3:5 (see earlier comments for explanation). Mark's references to Idumea and Tyre and Sidon (the latter already taken up by Syria in v 24) drop out, again for conformity to 3:5. But "Transjordan" remains because of its correspondence to "the region around the Jordan" in 3:5. Matthew wants to match 3:5 in order to parallel so far as possible the ministries of John and Jesus. Notably, the geographical designations cover all parts of Palestine except Samaria: the northwest (Galilee), the northeast (Decapolis), the southwest (Jerusalem and Judea), and the southeast (Transjordan).

THE ENCOURAGING WORD OF GOD AS TAUGHT BY THE GREATER MOSES TO HIS PERSECUTED DISCIPLES
5:1-10 (Mark 3:13a; Luke 6:20-25)

Chapter 5 begins the first of the five great discourses in Matthew. Jesus has just appeared as teacher, preacher, and healer (4:23). Matthew has already indicated the content of his preaching (4:17). Now he details Jesus' teaching (chaps. 5–7) and healing (chaps. 8–9) in the order of their mention in the preceding summary (4:23). This order leads him to delay some of the narratives that now make their appearance in Mark and Luke. In the first discourse Matthew will interpolate a number of dominical sayings which also appear in other contexts. These interpolations show his intention to provide a summarizing pattern for discipleship.

5:1-2 (Mark 3:13a; Luke 6:20a) Matthew reserves the rest of Mark 3:7-12, used partly in 4:24-25, for treatment in 12:15-21. The reservation enables him to skip to Mark 3:13a for a parallel between Jesus and Moses. But first he inserts "and seeing the crowds" in order to make Jesus' teaching the law apply to the universal church (see the comments on 4:25 for this representative role of the crowds). ἰδών is a Mattheanism (10-11,7), and we will find two more insertions of Jesus' seeing the crowds in 8:18; 9:36.

"He went up a mountain [or 'into mountainous country']" comes from Mark with a change of the historical present to the aorist tense. According to Luke 6:12-20a, Jesus went out to a mountain, prayed all night, called his disciples, chose twelve of them, went down with them, stood on a level place (or plain), healed a great number of other people who had come from a distance, and finally spoke a sermon to a large crowd of his disciples. Matthew has already written about the healing of the sick in 4:23-24, and he holds the twelve for later listing in 10:1-4. The delay in their listing results in a loss of the original framework, viz., their being summoned along with a larger crowd of disciples and chosen from among them. After mentioning Jesus' ascent up the mountain in accord with Mark 3:13a, therefore, Matthew goes immediately to the sermon. Otherwise the ascent (5:1) and descent (8:1) would appear purposeless. Just as he will telescope the chronologies of the triumphal entry and cleansing of the Temple, and of the cursing and withering of the fig tree (see 21:1-22; cf. 8:5-13), so here he brings forward Jesus' sermon.

Luke's level place, or plain, hardly means a level place on the mountainside. That would not agree with the prior statement that Jesus went down the mountain. There is also the improbability that large numbers of diseased people ascended a mountainside to hear Jesus and receive healing (see Luke 6:12 with 17-19).

Because it falls between the ascent of Jesus up the mountain and his descent, the sermon gains the connotation of law, related to the Mosaic law, which was also issued from a mountain. Indeed, ἀνέβη occurs frequently in the LXX for Moses' going up Mount Sinai to receive the law for promulgation. So also does the phrase εἰς τὸ ὄρος. See Hatch and Redpath, s.v. ἀναβαίνω and ὄρος, and cf. Matthew's continuing references to Jesus' going up a mountain in 14:23, where ἀνέβη lacks a parallel, and 15:29b, where the entire statement that Jesus went up a mountain and sat down there is unique to the first gospel and is followed by the approach of great crowds, as here in 5:1.

With help only from the traditional reference to Jesus' disciples (see Luke 6:20), Matthew composes the second clause of v 1 in order to stress the divine authority of Jesus as the supreme teacher of the law. The construction of the genitive absolute καθίσαντος αὐτοῦ typifies Matthew's style. More importantly, the sitting contrasts with the standing in Luke 6:17 and appears again—without parallel—in 19:28; 25:31 for the sitting of the Son of man on his glorious throne and, more significantly for the present passage, in 23:2: "the scribes and the Pharisees sit on Moses' seat." In Matthew Jesus replaces the scribes and the Pharisees, then, by taking the seated position normal for teachers (cf. 13:1-2; 24:3; 26:55; Luke 4:20; 5:3; *m. 'Abot* 1:4; 3:2, 6). The distinctive προσῆλθαν further accentuates Jesus' authority by connoting reverential approach (see the comments on 4:3 for this Mattheanism—38,6).

Matthew uses "the crowds" and "his disciples" interchangeably. We are not to think that the disciples came to Jesus from among the crowds. They *were* the crowds (cf. Luke 6:17), for Matthew has written in 4:25 that large crowds *followed* him—an indication of discipleship—and he will yet write that the crowds responded with amazement to this sermon, which he had been teaching them (7:28). Therefore the disciples about to be taught at the beginning of the sermon must be none other than the crowds that have been taught at the close.

In Matthew Jesus begins by opening his mouth instead of lifting up his eyes (as in Luke). Matthew's phrase reflects Semitic idiom (see Job 3:1; 33:2; Dan 10:16; Acts 8:35; 10:34). It will occur in the distinctive quotation of Ps 78:2 for Jesus' parabolic teaching (13:35). Here it echoes 4:4: "every word that comes out through the mouth of God" (so Matthew alone). Jesus is "God with us" in the first gospel (1:23). When he opens his mouth, therefore, his disciples hear nothing less than the Word of God. To make the point clear, Matthew will repeatedly conform Jesus' phraseology to the OT Word of God. Both ἀνοίγω and στόμα come from his preferred diction (5,2; 8,1).

By definition disciples are "learners." Therefore Matthew writes ἐδίδασκεν (to be taken as an inceptive imperfect, "he began to teach"). The verb harks back to Mark 1:21, recently used in 4:13 without adoption of the verb. Its present adoption compensates for the former omission. Now Matthew will add the content of Jesus' teaching, which does not appear after Mark 1:21. Only in Matthew does the sermon fall under the rubric of teaching. According to Luke Jesus merely speaks (ἔλεγεν, subordinated into the participle λέγων by Matthew). In 23:8 Matthew will insert Jesus' self-identification as the sole person properly bearing the title "Teacher" (even though disciples are to teach according to 5:19 and 28:20). This insertion shows that Matthew's placement of the term as an address to Jesus in the mouths of opponents does not represent a denigration of the title, but a use of those opponents to express an aspect of Matthew's own Christology.

5:3 (Luke 6:20b) We come now to the beatitudes. In the first, Jesus pronounces a blessing on "the poor." That term had come to refer to those whose deprivations led them to cry out for deliverance from oppression (see, e.g., Pss 37:14; 40:18[17]; 69:29-30[28-29], 33-34[32-33]; Isa 61:1; *Pss. Sol.* 10:7). Matthew adds "in spirit" from Isa 66:2, where the Lord speaks assuringly "to him who is poor and contrite of spirit." In that verse Isaiah himself interprets the meaning of the poor who appeared earlier in his prophecy at 61:1. This earlier verse, which figures in several subsequent beatitudes, provided the source of the first beatitude as well as a sermonic text for Jesus ("he has anointed me to preach good news to the poor," Luke 4:16-21; cf. Matt 11:5; Luke 7:22); and, as here, Isa 61:1 and 66:2 are combined in 1QH 18:14-15 (cf. Ps 34:19[18]; Prov 16:19; 29:23; Isa 57:15; 1QH 14:3; 1QM 11:10; 14:7; 1QS 4:3; *m. 'Abot* 4:4, 7, 10; Gundry, *Use of the OT* 69-71). The originally bare term stressed the humiliation of poverty. Matthew's addition emphasizes relying on God within the spirit, as opposed to depending on visible means of support, such as wealth and the power it brings (cf. Acts 18:25; 1 Cor 7:34 for similar uses of "in spirit," and Josh 2:11; 5:1; Pss 77:4[3]; 142:4[3]; 143:4 for "spirit" as "courage," which would imply that poverty of spirit connotes a sense of personal inadequacy).

In addition, Matthew changes this beatitude and the following (except for vv 11-12, which do not belong to the present group) from the second person plural, "you" (so Luke where parallel), to the third person plural, "they" and "theirs." He made a similar change earlier: the baptismal voice

"You are . . ." became "This is . . ." (3:17). Here, the change transforms a personal assurance into a didactic statement that makes the characteristics of the blessed an implied criticism of antinomianism. But there is more. In OT beatitudes the third person predominates over the second person (see E. Schweizer in *NTS* 19 [1973] 123-24). Hence, Matthew's going to the third person amounts to an assimilation of Jesus' style to the Word of God in the OT. Similarly, the changing of "the kingdom of God" (so Luke) to "the kingdom of heaven" harks back to Daniel 4 (esp. v 23[26]; see the comments on Matt 3:2).

"Blessed" means "to be congratulated" in a deeply religious sense and with more emphasis on divine approval than on human happiness. Such blessedness points to a turning of the tables for Jesus' poor, persecuted disciples when God consummates his kingdom on earth (cf. 6:10). "Theirs" probably means that the kingdom will belong to them in compensation for their present poverty. The present tense of "is" (see also v 10) needs to be taken futuristically, since we read the future tense in the second halves of the following beatitudes and since in v 12 the phrase "in heaven" almost demands a futuristic understanding. In Aramaic and Hebrew "is" would have been left to be supplied. It is possible, but not agreed, that the addition of "in spirit" (and of the references to righteousness in vv 6 and 10) spoils a poetic rhythm of three beats in the Aramaic form of the beatitude. The greater likelihood of a change from the difficult to the easy, rather than vice versa, supports the originality of the somewhat awkward transition from third person to second in Luke 6:20b-21. Obviously, we are meant to surmount the awkwardness by understanding "Blessed are you the poor," and so forth. The revisions of Mark's third person to second in Luke 5:30, 34; 6:2; 21:16, 19 entail a complete shift of referent or arise by way of minor assimilation to the prevalence of second persons in the surrounding context. Here, however, we have a whole body of material—and one in which "you" and "they" would refer to the same people without distinction. The supposed parallels break down, then, and do not establish a Lukan habit of changing third persons to second.

5:4 (Luke 6:21b, 24b, 25b) The second beatitude in Matthew, "Blessed are they who mourn, because they will be comforted," corresponds distantly to the third beatitude in Luke: "Blessed are you who weep now, because you will laugh" (6:21b). Matthew has drawn his substitute "they who mourn" from the third of the four woes that match the four beatitudes in the tradition: "Woe to you who laugh now, because you will mourn [πενθήσετε] and weep" (Luke 6:25b). The clause "because they will be comforted [παρακληθήσονται]" derives from the first woe: "But woe to you rich people, because you are receiving in full your comfort [τὴν παράκλησιν ὑμῶν—i.e., all the comfort you are going to get]" (Luke 6:24). Why does Matthew revise the beatitude by means of the woes? He wants conformity to the Servant of the Lord's happy mission "to comfort all who mourn" (Isa 61:2; cf. Matthew's unique substitution of mourning for fasting in 9:15). We can now see why he draws up this beatitude from later material in the tradition: the correspondence to Isa 61:2 makes natural its placement after a beatitude alluding to Isa 61:1. Mourning refers to the abject condition of persecuted disciples, not to mourning in repentance from sins or in sorrow over the dead. The intensive and typically Matthean αὐτοί (14,3), lacking here and below in Luke, implies "these and not their persecutors." The passive voice of "they will be comforted" implies that God will comfort them. So also the passives in vv 6, 7, and 9.

Here and there we may detect the hand of Luke in his version of the beatitudes and woes. But none of Matthew's dependencies has to do with likely Lukanisms. Against the authenticity of the woes—or at least against the originality of their association with the beatitudes—it is said that they do not agree with Jesus' addressing the disciples. But the crowd was large, and we have in Jas 4:14–5:6 something very similar right in the middle of material addressed by the author to his "brethren."

5:5 The assimilation of the woes into the beatitudes suits the address of Matthew to a persecuted church and the portrayal of Jesus as the teacher gentle to his disciples. After all, Jesus is addressing his disciples here (see 11:28-30; 12:19; 21:5—all unique to the first gospel). Furthermore, Matthew wants to save Jesus' pronouncement of woes for an attack on the scribes and Pharisees in chap. 23. Thus the first discourse features beatitudes favoring the righteous disciples of Jesus; the fifth and last discourse will feature woes condemning his hypocritical enemies. Yet Matthew desires fidelity to the eightfold scheme still apparent in Luke, where four woes follow four beatitudes. To recapture the original eightfoldness, therefore, he constructs four new beatitudes. Here in the third we see the first of these newcomers.

Matthew starts by taking advantage of the interplay between the Hebrew words עָנִי, "poor," and עָנָו, "meek." In fact, we may regard these words as largely synonymous. In Isa 61:1 the Servant of the Lord preaches the good news to the meek according to the MT, to the poor according to the LXX. Matthew has already alluded to the poor in Isa 61:1 (v 3). Now he alludes to the meek, as Isaiah's text was also understood. This third beatitude grows out of the one regarding the poor and rests on the double meaning of Isa 61:1, then, but its overall wording conforms more nearly to Ps. 37:11: "But the meek will inherit the earth [or 'land']" (cf. 4QpPs 37; Deut 28:8). In Matthew Jesus himself provides an example of meekness that corresponds to Moses, who was "very meek, more than any man who was on the face of the earth" (Num 12:3). Again see 11:29; 12:19; 21:5; cf. "Moses parallel Jesus" in the Topical Index. Matthew likes γῆ (21,6), and in 19:29 he will insert κληρονομέω in a reference to eschatological reward, as here (so also 25:34, peculiar to this gospel). Thus his habit of borrowing OT phraseology unites with his favorite diction and theological interests to confirm his composition of this beatitude.

"Meekness" implies acceptance of the lowly position that "poor" indicates. The words so coalesced, however, that their vowels were sometimes interchanged. In the Hebrew consonantal text the words differ only in the letters ו and י. The close similarity of these letters makes the words impossible to distinguish in some ancient manuscripts. γῆν, like the Hebrew אֶרֶץ, may mean "land" (of Palestine, for example) or "earth." Here it refers to the earthly locale of God's kingdom (cf. 6:10). See

Metzger, *Textual Commentary* ad loc., and G. Barth in *Tradition and Interpretation in Matthew* (Philadelphia: Westminster, 1963) 123 n. 2, on the originality of this verse in Matthew's text and on its placement in the order of the beatitudes.

5:6 (Luke 6:21a) "And thirst for righteousness" has no counterpart in Luke. Since "they will be filled" (both Matthew and Luke) answers to hunger but not to thirst and since hunger and thirst occur in combination several times without parallel in Matt 25:35, 37, 42, 44, we may safely say that Matthew has added "and thirst." In doing so he conforms Jesus' words to Isa 49:10: "they shall not hunger or thirst." (Isaiah is talking about the salvation of those who *do* hunger and thirst at the present time; cf. Ps 107:9; Isa 55:1-2; 65:13; Jer 31:25; John 6:35; Rev 7:16.)

Because Matthew likes δικαιοσύνη and its cognates (18-19,10-9) and because an accusative object (such as δικαιοσύνην) is unusual after διψῶντες and especially after πεινῶντες, we may also regard "righteousness" as an addition by Matthew. It is natural to his theology, but unnatural to the original locution. No evidence would lead us to think that in a Pauline manner he means a sentence of justification when he uses the term. Ordinarily in his gospel "righteousness" refers to right conduct on the human side. But evidence has already accumulated in the description of the disciples as poor and mourning and meek, and will appear even more clearly in vv 10-12, that Matthew plays up the element of persecution. Therefore it is likely that "righteousness" here refers to right conduct on God's side, i.e., to the exercise of divine justice that finally results in the vindication longed for by the persecuted. This likelihood is strengthened by the parallelism of the causal clauses in the other beatitudes. They almost undeniably contain eschatological references (see esp. vv 5, 8, 12). The likelihood turns into near certainty when we bring the Lord's promise in Isaiah 61— the basic text of the first three beatitudes in Matthew—into view. According to that promise, in the day of vengeance the oppressed poor will be called "oaks of righteousness," i.e., will be vindicated as "the planting of the Lord" (v 3). Shortly afterward we read about "eating the wealth of the nations" (v 6), which Matthew may have related to the second part of the beatitude ("they will be filled"), and about righteousness as justice resulting in vindication: "he [my God] has wrapped me with a robe of righteousness . . . the Lord Yahweh will cause righteousness and praise to spring up before all nations" (vv 10-11; see the context for the note of vindication and cf. M. P. Miller in *JBL* 88 [1969] 467-69 on Isa 61:1-2 as the unifying element in 11QMelch). The filling refers, then, not to fulfilled desire to live godly in the present time, but to vindication at the last day—and this under the well-known figure of the messianic banquet. See 8:11-12; 22:1-10; 26:29; Mark 14:25; Luke 13:28-29; 14:15-24; 22:18, 29-30; Rev 2:17; 19:9; Isa 25:6; 1QSa; 4QpPs 37; *1 Enoch* 62:14; *2 Apoc. Bar.* 29:4-8. Thus Matthew makes the righteousness of divine justice compensate for persecution because of righteousness in conduct (cf. v 10), and once again he conforms Jesus' words to God's Word in the OT.

5:7 The fifth beatitude has no parallel. Matthew has constructed it out of Jesus' teaching on mercy—a very prominent theme in the first gospel (see the cognates listed under ἐλεε- in the Greek Index—7,5)—in particular, out of Jesus' command, "Be merciful [Luke has the variant οἰκτίρμονες] as also your Father is merciful" (Luke 6:36). The present borrowing of the motif will lead to a substitution in 5:48, the proper parallel to Luke 6:36. As before, Matthew conforms the beatitude to an OT text, here to Ps 18:26(25): "With the merciful (חָסִיד) you will show yourself merciful" (the LXX differs, but in 9:13; 12:7 Matthew uses ἔλεος for חֶסֶד in Hos 6:6; see also Hatch and Redpath, s.v.). Among the gospels, only Matthew attributes any of the cognates concerning mercy to disciples as well as to Jesus. Cf. Prov 21:13.

There are a number of specially Matthean passages where the ethic of mercy is prominent even though terms for mercy do not occur: Joseph shows mercy in not wanting to put Mary to open shame (1:19); a husband is to show mercy to his wife by not divorcing her (5:31-32 with comments); the parable of the debtors describes forgiveness as an act of mercy (18:23-35); paying a full day's wage to laborers who have worked only one hour is also such an act (20:1-16); Jesus' attention to "the little ones" (chap. 18), to the children, the blind, and the lame in the Temple (21:14-16), and to publicans and prostitutes (21:28-32) exhibits mercy; and acts of mercy distinguish the sheep from the goats at the last judgment (25:31-46).

5:8 The sixth beatitude also lacks a parallel. Matthew is still filling the vacuum left by his omission of the four woes; so he constructs this beatitude from Jesus' emphasis on the inwardness of true piety (see esp. Luke 6:45 and, because of the word "heart," Matt 12:33-35; but cf. also Matt 5:21-22, 27-28; 6:1-6, 16-18; 15:8; 23:25-28). The beatitude is modelled after Ps 24:3-6: "Who shall ascend the hill of the Lord? And who shall stand in his holy place? He who has clean hands and a pure heart. . . . He will receive blessing from the Lord and righteousness. . . . Such is the generation of those who seek your face. . . ." Besides the obvious similarity between Matthew and the psalm so far as purity of heart is concerned, we may also note that Matthew's "blessed" corresponds to "blessing from the Lord" in the psalm and that the promise, "they will see God," corresponds to seeking the "face" of God, who comes into view later in the psalm by entering through the gates as the King of glory (cf. Ps 17:15; Rev 22:4; 2 Esdr 7:98). Since Matthew has identified Jesus as "God with us" (1:23), he may intend his readers to understand the blessed vision of God in the future as the sight of Jesus returning in glory (24:30; 26:64; cf. 28:7, 10). Naturally, the psalmist's reference to righteousness in the sense of divine justice leading to vindication would have caught Matthew's eye. And the inwardness of the purity required for blessedness provides ammunition to fight against hypocritical antinomians. See 27:59 for another insertion of καθαρός, and 10:8; 23:26 for insertions of καθαρίζω. καρδία is a Mattheanism (5,2). Again, characteristic borrowing from OT phraseology, favorite diction, and a special theological interest unite to substantiate Matthew's construction of the beatitude.

τῇ καρδίᾳ corresponds to τῷ πνεύματι, Matthew's addition in v 3. M. Black suggests that because of closeness in spelling, the Aramaic behind "pure in heart" relates to the "brokenhearted" in Isa 61:1 (*Aramaic Approach*, 158 n. 2). If so, we should probably think, not of an inadvertent mistranslation, but of a deliberate wordplay in which Matthew milks Isaiah 61 once again.

5:9 (Luke 6:22) Matthew extracts material for his seventh and eighth beatitudes from the fourth and final beatitude in the tradition, but keeps his ninth beatitude, the proper counterpart to the fourth beatitude in the tradition, outside his series of eight. The ninth falls into a threefold description of the relation of Jesus' disciples to the world. The peacemakers in the seventh beatitude stand over against the men who hate the disciples in the final beatitude of the tradition (Luke 6:22). Matthew has turned haters into peacemakers in accord with the requirement of constructing another beatitude, in accord with Jesus' nearby command to love even one's enemies (5:38-47; the command is even closer to the beatitudes in Luke 6:27-35), and especially in accord with Jesus' teaching in Mark 9:50c: "be at peace with one another." Because Matthew uses this teaching here, he will omit it when taking over the material in Mark 9:42-50 (see Matt 18:6-9).

As usual, there is assimilation to the OT, in particular, to Ps 34:15b(14b): "Seek peace, and pursue it" (cf. the beatitude in v 8 of the psalm, and in vv 15 and 18 the references to "the righteous," "the brokenhearted" [cf. Isa 61:1], and the "crushed in spirit" [cf. Matt 5:3], all of which would appeal to Matthew). See also Prov 10:10 LXX; Jas 3:18, where peacemaking means making one's own peace with others, not making peace between others; and cf. *1 Enoch* 52:11; *m. 'Abot* 1:12 (but the latter meaning obtains in *m. Pe'a* 1:1 and other rabbinic literature cited by Str-B 1. 215-18). The promise that peacemakers will be called sons of God—i.e., acknowledged by God as his sons at the last judgment—suits Matthew's special interests in the last judgment, in καλέω (8,8), in Jesus as υἱὸς θεοῦ (4,2), and in the corresponding sonship of the disciples to God the Father (esp. in the Sermon on the Mount: 5:16, 45, 48; 6:1, 4, 6, 8, 9, 14, 15, 18, 26, 32; 7:11; see also 10:20, 29; 13:43; 18:14; 23:9, all unique in this respect except for 5:45, 48; 6:9, 14; 7:11). Since Matthew has already quoted Hos 11:1 in 2:15 and has been conforming the beatitudes to OT phraseology all along, here he may be alluding to Hos 2:1(1:10): "it will be said to them, 'You are the sons of the living God' " (cf. Deut 14:1; Rom 9:25-26; Sir 4:1-10; Wis 2:18; *Jub.* 1:23-25; *Pss. Sol.* 17:30).

5:10 (Luke 6:22) In the eighth beatitude δεδιωγμένοι is typical of Matthew's diction (5,0). The word does not necessarily refer to killing, but means hounding (see 10:23; 23:34) and here corresponds to ἀφορίσωσιν, "exclude," in the final beatitude of the tradition (Luke 6:22). As in v 6, Matthew adds a reference to righteousness. But there the term echoed several verses in Isaiah 61 and meant divine justice. Here it takes its usual meaning, the disciples' right conduct, in a twofold allusion to Ps 15:1, "O Lord, . . . who shall dwell on your holy hill [cf. Ps 24:3-4, used by Matthew in 5:8]? He who . . . does righteousness," and Isa 51:7a, "Listen to me, you who know righteousness, a people in whose heart is my law." The rest of the verse in Isaiah forms the basis of Jesus' original wording (see the comments on v 11). Matthew recognized the allusion and reached into the immediately preceding part of Isaiah to gain greater conformity to the OT.

The promise of the kingdom of heaven repeats the conclusion to the first beatitude in Matthew's version (see earlier comments). By means of this inclusio, Matthew marks the close of his series of eight beatitudes. The first four have emphasized the persecuted condition of Jesus' disciples. The latter four have emphasized the ethical qualities which led to their persecution. Accordingly, the first four end on the note of righteousness as divine justice, the second four on the note of righteousness as good conduct. Within each quartet the first and third are roughly synonymous. The first four exhibit an alliteration with π after μακάριοι οἱ. And each of the quartets has thirty-six words, a perfect balance. We do not have in these beatitudes a gospel for the unevangelized, but a word of encouragement to the suffering church.

The Hebrew text of Isa 66:5 may stand behind the thoughts of hating and excluding in the tradition (see Luke 6:22). Matthew has ἀφορίζω elsewhere, but only in the context of the last judgment (13:49; 25:32). He avoids it here in the context of persecution. The perfect tense of δεδιωγμένοι may suggest some recent experience of persecution. Since for Matthew a Christian is righteous by definition (otherwise he is a hypocrite), we have no reason to distinguish between righteousness as the occasion of persecution and righteousness as the cause of persecution.

THE DISCIPLES' PERSECUTION AND MISSION IN THE WORLD
5:11-16 (Mark 4:21; 9:49-50; Luke 6:22-23, 26; 8:16; 11:33; 14:34-35; cf. John 8:12)

5:11-12 (Luke 6:22-23, 26) The pronouncement of blessing with which vv 11-12 begin recalls the pronouncements of blessing in the eight preceding beatitudes. But these verses do not form a ninth beatitude belonging to the first eight. For Matthew has already included a beatitude on the persecuted; in fact, he extracted it from the tradition behind the ninth (see the comments on v 10). His ninth stands apart from the series of eight beatitudes and within a series of statements concerning the disciples' witness to the world. Gone is the third person ("they" and "theirs") of the eight beatitudes. Now we read the second person ("you") in three successive clusters of statements: "Blessed are you . . ." (vv 11-12), "You are . . ." (v 13), "you are . . ." (vv 14-16). The first cluster has to do with the persecution of disciples for their witness to Christ and closes with an encouragement to rejoice. The second and third clusters deal with the witness itself—in the form of good works—and close, respectively, with a warning of judgment for failure to do good works and with a positive exhortation to do them.

In his ninth beatitude Matthew changes the tradition, as we can tell from a comparison with Luke 6:22-23. The changes serve his emphasis on persecution. In v 11 ὀνειδίσωσιν matches Luke. But Matthew omits excommunication (so Luke), and adds his preferred διώξωσιν (5,0; cf. v 10). In εἴπωσιν we see adaptation of a word that appears in the fourth woe (Luke 6:26). πονηρόν appears in the last beatitude of the tradition (see Luke 6:22) and makes a counterpart to καλῶς in the fourth woe. Typically, Matthew adds πᾶν (63,25-26) to πονηρόν for added emphasis and as a counterpart to πάντες in the fourth woe (where it modifies οἱ ἄνθρωποι). καθ᾽ ὑμῶν, "against you," corresponds to ἐκβάλωσιν τὸ ὄνομα ὑμῶν, "throw out your name" (cf. Luke 6:22), and reflects his fondness for κατά with the genitive (10,1). With ψευδόμενοι he picks up the notion of falsity from the fourth woe; there we read about "the false prophets." Matthew likes words with the stem ψευδ- (6,0). By changing false prophesying to false reports against the disciples he seeks to insure that persecution comes for good works rather than bad (cf. 1 Pet 2:12). ἕνεκεν ἐμοῦ corresponds to ἕνεκα τοῦ υἱοῦ τοῦ ἀνθρώπου (cf. Luke 6:22). It seems unlikely that a clear first person pronoun would have been changed to the mysterious Son of man. Probably, then, Matthew has substituted the first person pronoun to interpret the Son of man as Jesus in conformity to 10:18, 39; 16:25 (cf. 19:29) and parallels (cf. also 16:21 with Mark 8:31; Luke 9:22). The verbal persecution described here need not imply formal charges in court, but only informal abuse through face-to-face insults and slanderous reports to others.

Rejoicing appears also in Luke. But because of the phrase "in that day" Luke puts the verb in a punctiliar aorist (χάρητε). Matthew lacks the temporal phrase and puts the verb in a linear present (χαίρετε), which generalizes in a way similar to his use of the third person in vv 3-10. We read ἀγαλλιᾶσθε where Luke has σκιρτήσατε (cf. 1 Pet 1:6, 8; Rev 19:7). Perhaps Isa 61:10 LXX has influenced Matthew. But since Luke assimilates the praise of the crowds at the triumphal entry to the praise of the angels at the nativity (cf. Mark 11:10; Matt 21:9; Luke 2:14; 19:38), we have reason to think that here he assimilates an original exultation to a leaping for joy in accord with Luke 1:41, 44. The association of leaping with exultation in Luke 1:44 may have suggested and facilitated the assimilation. The special character of Luke's usage (see *TDNT* 7. 401-2) supports this judgment over against theories of a wrongly or differently translated Aramaic verb or of a confusion of Aramaic verbs (Black, *Aramaic Approach* 193).

ὅτι looks more original than the Lukanism ἰδοὺ γάρ. The promise of great reward in heaven comes from the tradition behind Luke. As might be expected in a gospel emphasizing works of righteousness, μισθός, "reward," appears relatively often (2,5). οὕτως differs from Luke's κατὰ τὰ αὐτά and represents Matthew's diction (18,5). Though Luke's ἐποίουν appears very often in Matthew where corresponding passages in Mark and Luke do not have it (19,19), here ἐδίωξαν is inserted for the third time in three successive verses. These insertions show how much Matthew emphasizes persecution as the present fate of the righteous. He changes the treatment of the prophets by the fathers (so Luke) to "the prophets who were before you" in order to imply that Jesus' disciples are now prophets (cf. Gal 1:17: "those who were apostles before I was"). See the comments on 7:15-23;

10:41 concerning Christian prophets, and Gen 15:1; Isa 51:7; 66:5 for passages from which Jesus drew some of his phraseology (cf. Gundry, *Use of the OT* 71-72).

The indefinite third person plural that we find in several of the verbs here and in v 15 appears often in Aramaic. Since excommunication of one kind or another marked disciplinary practice in Judaism even prior to the Benediction against Heretics (usually dated ca. A.D. 85), Luke's reference to excommunication need not presuppose late redaction rather than early dominical tradition. See especially the QL.

5:13 (Mark 9:49-50; Luke 14:34-35) The sayings concerning salt reintroduce the reason for the persecution of disciples: the witness of their good works in an evil world. Mark has similar material in another context and Luke in yet another. Nevertheless, all three synoptists relate the salt to discipleship. As an agent of seasoning, purification, preservation, and even fertilization, salt lent itself easily to metaphorical use. In Mark 9:50, it represents peace among disciples. Since Matthew has taken over the element of peace in his seventh beatitude (v 9), he omits it here but takes over the element of salt as a figurative repetition of the beatitude on peacemakers. In fact, the entirety of 5:13-16 consists of figurative statements about the ethical qualities which appear in the preceding beatitudes.

The use of salt as a figure of judgment (Mark 9:49 with preceding verses) does not suit Matthew's purpose. He therefore omits the comparison and then changes the further statement "Salt is good" (so Mark and Luke) to read "You are the salt of the earth." In Mark's and Luke's statement salt represents a quality of discipleship. Matthew makes salt represent the disciples themselves. "Of the earth" comes from the statement "It is useful neither for the earth" (Luke 14:35a). But Matthew makes a positive statement: "You *are* the salt of the earth." Cf. his putting elements of the woes in beatitudes. "Of the earth" modifies "the salt" because salt was used in small amounts as fertilizer (cf. Luke's "useful . . . for the earth" and see E. P. Deatrick in *BA* 25 [1962] 44-45). γῆς means "earth" in the sense of "soil," then, and stands for the world of people (see the parallel statement in v 14 and the explanation in v 16; cf. 9:26, 31; 10:15, 34; 11:24). Thus Matthew makes the metaphor of salt serve the motif of worldwide evangelism (cf. 28:19-20).

The rest of v 13 agrees largely with Luke's wording rather than Mark's. Mark and Matthew-Luke differ because of variant possibilities of translation from Aramaic (or Hebrew) into Greek. Matthew does not have Luke's καί. But it is textually questionable in Luke; and on the assumption of its genuineness, Luke probably added it for emphasis and clarity. We read ἁλισθήσεται in place of Luke's ἀρτυθήσεται (cf. ἀρτύσετε in Mark 9:50). Matthew has brought in ἁλισθήσεται from the quite different saying in Mark 9:49, "For everyone will be salted with fire," a saying which otherwise does not appear in his gospel.

The losing of saltiness may refer to fraudulent adulteration of salt for gaining greater profits in its sale, to the dissolving away of sodium chloride from impure salt, to masking the taste of salt with gypsum, or to all of these (Deatrick, op. cit. 41-48). Matthew has already referred to the earth; so he summarizes the saying, "It is useful neither for the earth [as fertilizer] nor for the manure pile [as a retardant to fermentation]" (cf. Luke 14:35a), with the words, "It is good for nothing any more." This summary shows that he is switching from Mark to a tradition recorded also in Luke. We might wonder whether in 17:16 οὐκ ἠδυνήθησαν replaces the synonymous οὐκ ἴσχυσαν (Mark 9:18), concerning the disciples' inability to cast out a demon, because the latter verb has already appeared in 5:13 in order to anticipate that example of losing saltiness. Matthew often anticipates a word or expression and then replaces it. The short statement "They throw it out" (so Luke) grows into the long phrase "except to be trampled by men after being thrown out." The street was the place where people threw refuse, though flat rooftops, where people also walked, are another possibility. The Mattheanism τῶν ἀνθρώπων (35,17) defines the indefinite third person plural in the tradition (cf. Luke 14:35 and see Luke 6:22 for the same definition). For καταπατεῖσθαι, see 7:6. The last part of v 13 warns against failure to persevere in good works. Such failure will falsify a profession of discipleship and put one under an irrevocable sentence of judgment. The question how spoiled salt can be made salty again ends in hopelessness. Cf. especially 7:15-20, 21-23; 13:36-43; 22:11-13; 24:45-51 and the frequent use of βάλλω and ἐκβάλλω for judgment (3:10; 5:13, 25, 29; 7:19; 8:12; 13:42, 48 [with ἔξω as here in 5:13]; 18:8, 9; 22:13; 25:30).

"With what will it [the salt] be salted?" poses an ironic question. μωρανθῇ literally means "becomes foolish," but gets the metaphorical sense "loses its saltiness" from the Hebrew-Aramaic verb תָּפֵל, which carries both meanings. To call μωρανθῇ a mistranslation is to overlook the possibility of an accepted carry-over from the Semitic verb to the Greek verb. The utter nonsense of "the salt becomes foolish" makes a mistake unlikely. The welding together of Matt 5:13 and Luke 14:35 into two couplets (so Black, *Aramaic Approach* 166-67) rests on an overlooking of Matthew's redaction and requires the tacking of a clause from Matthew on the end of Luke's couplet.

5:14-16 (Mark 4:21; Luke 8:16; 11:33; cf. John 8:12) The metaphor of light comes from the saying about the lamp put on a lampstand in order that people who enter may see the light (see esp. Luke 8:16; 11:33). For emphasis on discipleship and a parallel with v 13, Matthew again draws an equation with the disciples themselves. As Jesus is the light (4:16), so also are they. The addition τοῦ κόσμου (not in Mark or Luke) exhibits one of Matthew's favorite nouns (5,2). Other favorites are πόλις (18,3), κρυβῆναι (4,2—suggested by κρυπτόν in Mark's next verse), ἐπάνω (7,1), and ὄρους (6,1). Though it does not occur so often as in the other synoptics, δύναται comes as an insertion thirteen times in Matthew, and κειμένη twice. We may therefore deduce that Matthew has composed the saying in v 14 around the figure of light, which comes from the tradition, and that he has done so for expansive reemphasis on the motif of worldwide evangelism (cf. v 13).

The city situated on a mountain may mean not just any city—though cities commonly stood on hills for the purpose of easier defense—but the new Jerusalem, shedding the light of divine glory throughout the world during the messianic kingdom. This would accord with Isa 2:2-4; 4:5-6; 60:1-22 (see G. von Rad, *The Problem of the Hexateuch and Other Essays* [New York: McGraw-Hill, 1966] 232-42). It would also fit composition by Matthew, who loves to introduce OT phraseology. He would see in the good works of disciples, future residents of that city, a foretaste of its glory. And in the evangelizing effect of their good works he would see an anticipation of the flowing of Gentiles to the city to worship God. Nevertheless, the lack of a definite article with "city" and the coordination of "city" and "lamp"— any lamp, it seems—cause doubt.

In v 15 Matthew along with Luke interprets the coming (i.e., bringing in) of a lamp (Mark 4:21) as the lighting of a lamp; but the two later evangelists use different verbs, καίουσιν and ἄψας, to express the thought. Mark refers both to a "peck measure" and to a "bed." Matthew takes over only the peck measure. Then, in a way familiar to us from his treatment of the beatitudes, he coordinates the clauses for the sake of parallelism:

Neither do people light a lamp
And put it under a peck measure.
Rather, they put it on a lampstand
And it gives light to everyone in the house.

Only Luke gives a parallel to the last line. Therefore it looks as though Matthew and Luke had access to another form of the saying besides the one in Mark (cf. esp. the differing contexts of Mark 4:21 and Luke 11:33). But Luke refers to "those who come in," whereas Matthew writes of "all those in the house" to produce a characteristic pairing of city and house (cf. Matt 10:14 with Mark 6:11; Luke 9:5, and Matt 12:25 with Mark 3:24-25; Luke 11:17). πᾶσιν, an emphatic addition typical of Matthew (63,25-26), yet again carries forward the motif of worldwide evangelism. Luke's φῶς drops out because of its prior use (v 14). In its place appears λάμπει, which Matthew inserts three times (see also the next verse and 17:2, against no occurrences in Mark and only one in Luke).

The generic use of the definite articles with μόδιον and λυχνίαν reflects the Aramaic original. Matthew has in mind a one-room house with a single lamp.

As in v 14, we see expansion in v 16, which begins with the Mattheanism οὕτως (18,5). According to the contexts in Mark and Luke, the unhidden lamp represents Jesus' preceding revelation of the mystery of the kingdom to insiders (disciples) rather than to outsiders (nondisciples), with a consequent warning to "take care how you hear" in order that judgmental obscuration of the mystery may be avoided and further revelation may be gained (Mark 4:24-25; Luke 8:18). Matthew transforms this warning into a command to do good works. For him, proper hearing of the mysteries revealed *then* entails the public witness of good works *now*. τὸ φῶς, anticipated in v 14 and omitted in v 15, makes a second appearance in order to be interpreted. For the same purpose λάμπει (v 15) reappears in the imperative form λαμψάτω. ἔμπροσθεν τῶν ἀνθρώπων echoes ὑπὸ τῶν ἀνθρώπων in v 13 (cf. 6:1; 10:32; 23:14). Matthew shows special fondness for ἔμπροσθεν (9,4), and indeed for the whole present phrase (3,1). He is also fond of καλά (1,6) and ἔργα (4,1), which in combination show his liking of rabbinic expressions (see *TDNT* 3. 545-48). In 3:10; 7:17, 18, 19; 12:33 the adjective describes fruits and trees in language figurative of good works. By comparing Luke 8:16; 11:33 we can tell that ἴδωσιν comes from the traditional saying recorded in v 15, compensates for its replacement there, and differs from Luke's βλέπωσιν only as a matter of style. Further Mattheanisms appear possibly in δοξάσωσιν (2,1) and certainly in πατέρα (22,13), especially as modified by ἐν τοῖς οὐρανοῖς (10,2). In other words, the vocabulary of v 16 leads to the conclusion that Matthew constructed the exhortation in order to accentuate evangelism through "good works." In view of his stress on mercy and neighborly love (see, e.g., 9:13; 12:7; 19:19; 22:39) he means works of charity especially, though not exclusively.

THE AFFIRMATION OF THE OLD TESTAMENT IN JESUS' TEACHING OF THE LAW AND FULFILLMENT OF THE PROPHETS
5:17-20 (Luke 16:16-17)

5:17-18 (Luke 16:17) In 5:17 and 7:12 references to the law and the prophets bracket Jesus' teaching of the law, which makes up the main body of the Sermon on the Mount. Here the portrayal of Jesus as the greater Moses attains its greatest clarity. Indeed, the desire to gain such a portrayal causes Matthew to introduce and expand the dominical saying recorded also in Luke 16:17: "But it is easier for heaven and earth to pass away than for one tittle of the law to fall." He takes over the references to heaven and earth, their passing away, and one tittle of the law. We miss "But it is easier" and "to fall," but discover the following additions: "Do not think that I have come to abolish," "or the prophets," "I have not come to abolish, but to fulfill," "For truly I say to you," "one jot," "will not pass away from the law till all things have happened," and the entirety of the further statements in vv 19-20. When Matthew later adopts the tradition behind the preceding verse in Luke (see Matt 11:12-13; Luke 16:16), he omits the tradition behind Luke 16:17. This omission shows that like Luke he draws from a tradition in which the two sayings occurred side by side and that here in 5:17-18 he is inserting and enlarging the second of the two sayings rather than following a fuller tradition concerning it.

We see evidence of Matthew's hand in μὴ νομίσητε ὅτι ἦλθον followed by an infinitive phrase and οὐκ ἦλθον plus ἀλλά and another infinitive; for the same phraseology appears again in 10:34, where the corresponding passage in Luke 12:51 reads differently (see also 20:10 for another distinctive occurrence of νομίζω). καταλῦσαι comes in as a contrast with πληρῶσαι. The latter word belongs to Matthew's favorite diction (9,6). In the synoptics outside Matt 11:13; Luke 16:16 (cf. Luke 24:44), only Matthew

78

pairs the law and the prophets, as here and in 7:12; 22:40. The pairing is always an insertion in shared tradition. Cf. insertions of νόμος by itself in 12:5; 22:36; 23:23 and Matthew's great fondness for προφήτης (19,6). The combination of the two terms was suggested by its occurrence in the saying immediately preceding the one here taken over by Matthew: "The law and the prophets were until John" (Luke 16:16; cf. Matt 11:13; also 2 Macc 15:9; 4 Macc 18:11). ἤ comes from his favorite vocabulary (32,12). And the obvious parallelisms confirm his hand, for he loves to write in this style (though, of course, he is not the only one to use it).

"The law and the prophets" made up only the first two sections of the Hebrew OT, but could imply the third, "the writings," as a matter of course. Cf. Matthew's using "prophet" in the introduction to a quotation from the writings (13:35). See also Luke 24:27 with 44, and the quotation of a psalm as part of the law in John 10:34.

In v 18 we first meet a favorite clause of Matthew, "For truly I say to you" (15,8). It occurs thirty-one times in the first gospel, but only thirteen in Mark and six in Luke. Nine further times Luke omits the Semitic ἀμήν, or makes a substitution for it, and takes over the rest. In the triple tradition Luke lacks the entire clause only twice, and both times Mark shares that lack over against Matthew's inclusion (cf. Luke 18:24 with Mark 10:23; Matt 19:23, and Luke 21:6 with Mark 13:2; Matt 24:2). Therefore, though Jesus doubtless used the expression, in Matt 5:18 its originality to him would probably have resulted in Luke's having it, too, but without the ἀμήν. That the expression as a whole here comes from Matthew gains further support from the fact that only he ever uses the conjunction γάρ with the other words in it (see also 10:23; 13:17; 17:20).

Matthew models his expansion in v 18 after the saying he will take over in 24:34.

5:18	24:34
For truly I say to you,	Truly I say to you,
till heaven and earth pass away,	
not one jot or one tittle	that this generation
will pass away from the law	will not pass away
till all things have	till all these things have
happened.	happened.

Furthermore, the next verse in chap. 24 reads, "Heaven and earth will pass away, but my words will not pass away." The similarities to 5:18 are evident. Characteristically, Matthew strives for parallelism in the central part of his expansion:

A: ἕως ἂν παρέλθῃ	B: ὁ οὐρανὸς καὶ ἡ γῆ
B': ἰῶτα ἓν ἢ μία κεραία	A': οὐ μὴ παρέλθῃ

The parallelism is chiastic.

The appended phrase "from the law" reflects the original "of the law"

(Luke 16:17). Matthew escalates "But it is easier" (Luke 16:17) to the emphatic negative οὐ μή, "by no means." Luke, who was very Hellenistic, would hardly have omitted "one iota," for iota was the smallest letter of the Greek alphabet. Matthew's adding it to "one tittle" not only produces a parallel with "heaven and earth," but also strengthens the denial of opposition to the law and the prophets and provides something understandable to Greek readers who might not know the Hebraic meaning of "tittle." We ourselves have no certainty concerning that meaning. The term may refer to the small projections that alone distinguish certain pairs of Hebrew and Aramaic letters (ב and כ, ד and ר, ה and ח), to the letter ו (waw), to the letter י (yodh, sometimes indistinguishable from ו in ancient manuscripts), to the hook at the top of the ancient י, or to scribal ornamentation of certain letters. As an editorial insertion aimed at Greek readers, "iota" probably does not refer to the yodh or to any other Hebrew feature of the OT.

Emphasis falls on the authority of Scripture down to the details of its wording. Matthew's second "pass away," a replacement of "to fall" (Luke 16:17), again contributes both to the parallelism and to the strengthening of Jesus' denial that he opposes the law and the prophets. We would have to overlook the emphasis on Jesus as the greater Moses who teaches the law to say that Matthew neutralizes the affirmation of the law by inserting the fulfillment of the prophets. Rather, he heightens the affirmation of the law at the same time he interjects the fulfillment of the prophets for the sake of a holistic view of the OT.

As noted, "till all things have happened" anticipates a similar clause in 24:34, but with the omission of "these" because Jesus has yet to give his teaching about the future. In 24:34 ἕως cannot mean "in order that" (a disputable sense for ἕως, anyway). Therefore we should hardly think of a telic meaning here. And since "all these things" in 24:34 refers to things spoken by Jesus concerning the great tribulation, introduction of the clause in 5:18d means that Matthew presents Jesus' teaching as of a piece with the law and the prophets. Along with Jesus' teaching, furthermore, the law and the prophets stand valid till the consummation. Hence, we are not to think of this clause as redundant of the earlier "till heaven and earth pass away" (5:18b). Without the reference to "all things" in 5:18d the inclusion of Jesus' teaching alongside the law and the prophets would not have come into view. Besides, the two clauses beginning with ἕως make an inclusio similar to "theirs is the kingdom of heaven" at the beginning and end of the beatitudes (vv 3b, 10b). Since Matthew wants to stress only Jesus' fulfillment of the law and the prophets, the question whether or not they will pass away when heaven and earth pass away is not appropriate.

But how are we to understand the fulfilling of the law and the prophets? Is it Jesus' obedience to the law in contrast with abolishment by disobedience? That receives support from the putting of the law before the prophets (contrast 11:13, where fulfillment through historical events stands in the forefront, so that the prophets come before the law). It also seems to get support from the use of πληρόω in 3:15 for Jesus' obedience in baptism. But in 3:15 πληρῶσαι πᾶσαν δικαιοσύνην occurred instead of ποιέω plus a verb of the Lord's commanding (cf. typically Matthean expressions of this sort in 1:24; 21:6; 26:19; 28:15, 16) because Jesus' insistence on being baptized did not represent obedience to any of the Lord's commandments in the OT. Furthermore, throughout Matthew πληρόω regularly refers to fulfillment of prophecies through historical events; and the contrastive καταλῦσαι, "to abolish," seems too strong for disobedience. If Matthew had in mind only obedience versus disobedience to the law, why did he include the prophets along with the verb that refers to prophetic fulfillment?

We might regard fulfillment as teaching in support of the law, in contrast with abolishing the law by teaching against it. This view would allow the most natural meaning for the contrastive καταλῦσαι, and it suits well the putting of the law before the prophets and the portrayal of Jesus as the greater Moses. Again we wonder, however, why Matthew included the prophets along with the verb of fulfillment. And elsewhere he does not use πληρόω for the teaching activity of Jesus.

Fulfillment might then refer to the accomplishment of prophecies, in contrast with abolishment by failure to fulfill them. This view would fit the regular use of πληρόω, explain the importation of the prophets from the preceding saying in the tradition (cf. Luke 16:16), and harmonize with the anticipation of 24:34. But καταλῦσαι requires something more deliberate than failure of prophecies to come to pass (they might yet find fulfillment in someone else!). And under this view why did not Matthew put the prophets ahead of the law, as in 11:13? Besides, throughout the Sermon on the Mount emphasis falls on Jesus as the greater Moses who teaches the law.

καταλῦσαι and πληρῶσαι do not make a good match, then. But this disparity holds the clue to a proper understanding. καταλῦσαι refers to a kind of teaching Jesus did not come to do and heightens the original denial of antinomianism. πληρῶσαι refers to the accomplishment of prophecies Jesus did come to accomplish and makes the parallel inexact because Matthew wants to weld Jesus' fulfilling prophecies to his teaching the law. The two are united so closely that in v 18 the law remains (as in the original form of the saying—cf. Luke 16:17) even in association with an immediately added clause concerning the fulfillment of prophecies. There results an affirmation of the OT together with the life and teaching of Jesus himself.

5:19-20 Verses 19-20 were suggested by "the Pharisees . . . who justify yourselves" and by people's forcing "into it [the kingdom]" in the tradition immediately preceding what Matthew has just taken over (Luke 16:14-16). The verses have no parallel and exhibit Matthew's favorite diction and distinctive theology.

ὅς (ἐ)άν and οὖν are Mattheanisms (14,1; 35,11). λύσῃ derives from καταλῦσαι in v 17 and occurs in Matthew five times as a theological metaphor, but never as a theological metaphor in Mark or Luke. All five occurrences are insertions (5:19; 16:19 [bis]; 18:18 [bis]). μίαν echoes the traditional saying taken over in v 18 and comes from Matthew's favorite diction (24,7). ἐντολή, "commandment," links with his interest in the law and occurs as an insertion also in 22:38. We may simply list ἐλαχίστων/-ος (2,3), διδάξῃ (3,3), οὕτως (18,5), ἀνθρώπους (35,17), κληθήσεται (8,8), βασιλείᾳ τῶν οὐρανῶν (25,7), ποιήσῃ (19,19), οὗτος in a resumptive usage (5,0), μέγας (11,1), γάρ (62-63,15), λέγω ὑμῖν (27,7), περισσεύσῃ (3,0), δικαιοσύνη (5,2), πλεῖον (3,1), γραμματέων καὶ Φαρισαίων (9,0), and εἰσέλθητε εἰς τὴν βασιλείαν τῶν οὐρανῶν with a negative (5,0).

Matthew shows a greater or lesser tendency to interject all these expressions in shared traditions and to use them in unique passages. Often the total number of times he uses them exceeds that in Mark and Luke. Furthermore, the careful parallelism in v 19 typifies his style, and the combination ἐὰν μή . . . οὐ μή in v 20 turns up again in 18:3 against the other synoptics. Therefore we may fairly judge that in vv 19-20 he continues to expand the traditional saying lying at the core of v 18. The state of Matthew's church demanded this forceful attack on antinomianism.

In v 19, "Whoever annuls [λύσῃ] one of the least of these commandments and teaches men thus" defines the abolishing (καταλῦσαι) that Jesus did not come to do and makes him an example for teachers in the church. Because of the adjective "least," the demonstrative pronoun "these" identifies the commandments with the jot and tittle mentioned in v 18. No careless inattention to the details of the law here! No easy resting in the spirit of the law or even in the pervasive principle of love (cf. esp. 23:2-3; 28:20, also peculiar to Matthew)! In fact, with poetic justice those guilty of antinomianism in any of the least commandments will be called least in the kingdom. And why is that so? The reason is that even to enter the kingdom requires more righteousness than the scribes and Pharisees have. If mere entrance requires so much, greatness requires even more, i.e., obedience to all the least commandments, too. The following part of the sermon tells how to surpass the righteousness of the scribes and Pharisees.

Not all scribes belonged to the Pharisaical sect and not all Pharisees took the scribal role of teaching the law. The associating of the scribes with the Pharisees arises out of the dominance of the Pharisees among the scribes, out of the Pharisaical scribes' providing the main source of opposition to Jesus, and out of Matthew's desire to distinguish Christians as scribes from the Pharisaical scribes (cf. 8:19; 13:52; 23:34 with comments). The evangelist uses the latter to represent ecclesiastical leaders who make a show of righteousness but live lawlessly. The true righteousness Matthew writes about gives evidence of genuine discipleship, but does not deserve salvation. In reference to teachers, greatness makes a play on the literal meaning of "Rabbi," viz., "my great one." Because of the three insertions of ῥαββί in 23:7, 8; 26:25, this play substantiates Matthew's composition of vv 19-20.

THE RIGHTEOUSNESS THAT SURPASSES THAT OF THE SCRIBES AND PHARISEES
5:21-48 (Mark 9:43-48; 10:4, 11-12; 11:25; Luke 6:27-36; 12:57-59; 16:18; cf. Matt 18:8-9; 19:7, 9; 23:22)

Detailed indications of ways in which the righteousness of Jesus' disciples is to surpass that of the scribes and Pharisees appear in this section. These indications take the form of six antitheses, so called because of the repeated formula "You have heard that it was said. . . . But I say to you . . ." (vv 21-22, 27-28, 31-32, 33-34, 38-39, 43-44). Unfortunately, the term "antitheses" designates the material incorrectly. As we shall see, Jesus contradicts neither the law nor current rabbinic interpretations of it. Rather, he carries out its tendencies to their divinely intended ends. Nevertheless, we shall continue to use the term "antitheses" because it has become traditional in discussions of this passage.

The expression "I say to you" (with and without conjunctions, ἐγώ, and adverbs such as ἀμήν) occurs often in the synoptics. Matthew has it fifty-eight times, Mark sixteen, and Luke forty-five. But it occurs in conjunction with the statement "You have heard that it was said" only in this section of Matthew. ἀκούω appears often in its own right for authoritative teaching, however, and a number of times Matthew alone uses it this way (see 5:21, 27, 33, 38; 11:15; 13:14, 15 [bis], 16, 18; 21:33 for insertions, and 13:43 for an occurrence in a distinctive passage, besides eighteen shared examples). Also, Matthew uses forms of εἴρω (here, ἐρρέθη) significantly more often (thirty times) than Mark (twice) or Luke (nineteen times) and almost always uniquely (18,9). The following passages, all peculiar to his gospel, contain supportive references to the OT: 1:22; 2:15, 17, 23; 3:3; 4:14; 8:17; 12:17; 13:35; 21:4; 22:31; 24:15; 27:9. In addition, "it was said" offers the most frequent introduction to citations of Scripture in rabbinic literature. Therefore we have reason to believe that in 5:21-48 the OT appears in a positive light and quite apart from any misinterpretation charged against the rabbis. Matthew's fondness for ἀκούω (26,6) and forms of εἴρω (18,9), combined with the frequency of λέγω ὑμῖν apart from as well as within the antithetic structure (27,7), leads to the conclusion that he himself has constructed the antitheses out of expressions that appeared differently and often independently in the dominical tradition.

The last clause in v 18 arose by anticipation of 24:34. The very next verse in chap. 24 reads, "Heaven and earth will pass away, but my words will not pass away" (cf. Mark 13:31; Luke 21:33). "But my words" apparently led Matthew to think of the tradition behind Luke 6:27, "But I say to you who hear," which now provides the raw material for some literary and theological artistry (cf. v 44). He expands "who hear" into the full-blown first member of the antitheses, "You have heard that it was said to the ancients." Then he keeps "But I say to you"—with δέ, as in 24:35, instead of ἀλλά—to introduce the second member. Thus the single statement in the tradition becomes two statements on the order of 24:35, which triggered this all. The adversative conjunction between them ceases to contrast love of enemies and the coming judgment of persecutors (so Luke). Also, the hearing ceases to have Jesus' teaching as its object. Rather, Matthew's adversative conjunction ties together the two parts of each antithesis, but not in a wholly negative fashion—hence a weak δέ instead of a strong ἀλλά. And just as he has filled out the beatitudes with the OT in order to identify the words of Jesus with the Word of God—because Jesus is "God with us" (1:23)—so here he fills out "You have heard . . ." with the OT as a lead into Jesus' own teaching, which comes from the dominical tradition.

We will see below that the last clauses of vv 21 and 43 represent the

OT rather than misinterpretation charged against the rabbis. The false teachers mentioned in v 19 belong to the professing church; the Jewish scribes and Pharisees came in for a slurring comment only because of their wrong *practices* (v 20; cf. 6:1-18; 23:1-36, esp. 23:3). Criticism of rabbinic traditions appears only in material shared with the other synoptics (see 15:1-20). It is not Matthew's distinctive emphasis. Thus we ought not to say that 5:21-48 originally applied to scribal interpretations and 6:1-18 to Pharisaical practices (against Jeremias, *NT Theology* 1. 144-45). Matthew arranges the whole section 5:21-48 with an eye on the OT, not on rabbinic traditions of interpretation.

Attention to Mattheanisms forestalls appeal to rabbinic usage as standing behind "You have heard that it was said. . . . But I say to you. . . ." Besides, comparable expressions either do not stand paired in rabbinic literature, or they lack an essential element of Matthew's expression, e.g., the emphatic ἐγώ by which Jesus claims an authority the scribes did not claim. See J. Suggs, *Wisdom, Christology, and Law in Matthew's Gospel* (Cambridge, Mass.: Harvard, 1970) 111-12. We are to take ἀρχαίοις as an indirect object ("to the ancients"), not as an indication of speakers ("by the ancients"). Elsewhere in Matthew passive forms of the verb of speaking always take διά or ὑπό for the speaker. In the one place where both speaker and those addressed appear together, ὑπό introduces the speaker and, as here, the addressed are put in the simple dative (see 22:31 in contrast with Mark 12:26; Luke 20:37). The hearing of what was said to the ancients refers to hearing the OT read in the synagogues.

MURDER AND ANGER
5:21-26 (Mark 11:25; Luke 12:57-59)

5:21-22 In a quotation from the decalogue Jesus will begin with the prohibition against murder (19:18; Mark 10:19). Matthew takes a cue and starts his first antithesis the same way (cf. Exod 20:13; Deut 5:17). Both the anticipating of later dominical tradition and the quoting of the OT characterize his style. "And anyone who murders will be subject to the judgment" does not come from rabbinic tradition, but represents Matthew's own summary of the OT penalty for murder. The judgment has to do with judicial proceedings in human society, not with eternal punishment at the hands of God. See Num 35:12, ". . . the manslayer may not die till he stands before the congregation for judgment" (cf. Deut 17:8-13; *Tgs. Ps.-J.* and *Onq.* Gen 9:6; and "Judgment" in the Topical Index).

Matthew goes on to write that anger against a brother—i.e., against a fellow disciple—deserves the same punishment. ὀργιζόμενος denotes the inward feeling of anger. But the feeling may issue in the saying of ῥακά, an epithet probably brought over from רֵיקָא or רֵיקָה, Aramaic for "empty one." And that epithet may graduate to the even more serious epithet μωρέ, "fool." Elsewhere in Matthew this term applies to those who do not belong to the kingdom of heaven (7:26; 23:17; 25:2, 3, 8, all distinctive, for the other evangelists never use μωρός). Presumably it carries the same connotation here. If so, we have no need to see confusion with the Hebrew word מָרָה, "stubborn, rebellious." Rather, the Greek word has to do with expressing a negative judgment, private and premature, against a brother's membership in the kingdom (see also 7:1-5 and, peculiar to Matthew, 13:24-30, 36-43, 47-50).

Similarly, the prescribed penalties move from bad to worse: "the judgment"—punishment by a local court; "the Sanhedrin"—more frightening punishment by the supreme court; "the hell of fire"—eternal punishment by God himself. The progressive heightening of the crimes and their penalties powerfully emphasizes the seriousness of disruption in the fellowship of Christian brothers (cf. 1QS 6:24-27). The final warning implies that offenders may find themselves eternally doomed as the very kind of false disciples they had accused others of being. We do not have a principle of legal justice for the whole body politic; Matthew's Jesus does not proscribe anger because it might lead to murder in society at large. Rather, within the brotherhood of disciples he makes anger and its offspring offenses just as grave as murder is in the outside world (cf. 18:15-20 on the local church as a court in such cases).

Matthew likes to use πᾶς (63,25-26). ὁ ὀργιζόμενος occurs without parallel also in 18:34. The repeated τῷ ἀδελφῷ αὐτοῦ (11,8) carries on the theme of Christian brotherhood. And the following words also typify Matthew's diction: κρίσει (8,0), ὅς . . . ἄν (14,1), μωρέ (3,3-4), γέενναν (3,0), and πυρός (2,4). See especially 18:9, where Matthew takes the word for fire out of the next verse in Mark's parallel—i.e., out of Mark 9:48, otherwise omitted by him—and attaches it to the word for hell, just as here. Besides all this, the parallelism evident in the present saying characterizes his literary style. We may justly conclude that Matthew composed this antithesis.

γέεννα referred at first to the Valley of Hinnom, a ravine on the south side of Jerusalem, where fire-worship of Moloch took place and where refuse was burned. Out of that use developed a metaphorical use for hell, the place of punishment for the wicked in an afterlife.

5:23-24 (Mark 11:25) Commands to brotherly reconciliation (vv 23-24 and 25-26) naturally follow the warnings against anger and verbal abuse. Cf. the beatitude on peacemakers (v 9). Verses 23-24 abound in Mattheanisms: ἐὰν οὖν (4,0), προσφέρῃς/-ε (9,2), δῶρον (7,1), θυσιαστήριον/-ου (5,0), κἀκεῖ (3,0), ἀδελφός/-ῷ (11,8), ἄφες (12,5), ἐκεῖ (16,6), ἔμπροσθεν (9,4), ὕπαγε (5,6), πρῶτον (3,1), τότε (66,17), and ἐλθών (10,10). μνησθῇς will occur again without parallel in 27:63. διαλλάγηθι anticipates ἀπηλλάχθαι in the tradition represented by Luke 12:57-59 and coming up next in Matt 5:25-26, where because of the present anticipation another expression substitutes. Only the task of accounting for ἔχει τι κατὰ σοῦ is left.

Now in 21:20-22, to which Mark 11:20-25 corresponds, Matthew will not use the material in Mark's v 25. But in 6:5-7 he will use the part of that material that concerns praying and in 6:14-15 the part that concerns forgiveness. The rest Matthew takes over here in 5:23-24. In order to avoid duplication of Jesus' criticism of standing and praying to be seen by men (6:5-7), the standing and praying has become the bringing of a gift to the altar. And your having something against someone else (εἴ τι ἔχετε κατά τινος, so Mark) becomes a brother's having something against you (ἔχει τι κατὰ σοῦ). This latter change avoids duplication of Jesus' instructions concerning a brother's sinning against you (18:21-22) and also leads nicely into the next two verses, where an adversary is taking you to court through having something against you (5:25-26). By means of this arrangement and revision Matthew gains from Jesus' teaching back-to-back instructions against brotherly anger and for brotherly reconciliation. If one's own anger is wrong, so also is that of a brother. Therefore (οὖν, v 23) the prohibition of murder requires not only avoidance of anger against a brother, but also appeasement of a brother's anger.

5:25-26 (Luke 12:57-59) To illustrate the necessity of reconciliation between disciples at odds with each other, Matthew now brings in Jesus' portrayal of an insolvent debtor whose only hope lies in coming to an agreement with his creditor before landing in a debtor's prison. The introduction to that portrayal—"But why do you not judge on your own initiative what is right [τὸ δίκαιον]?" (Luke 12:57)—contains in τὸ δίκαιον a term that helped attract Matthew to the material. But the reproachful tone ill suits Jesus' kind instruction to the disciples in Matthew. Therefore the question drops out.

Comparison with the rest of Luke's parallel reveals the intent of Matthew. He draws "make an effort to be released from him [i.e., to settle with him]" from its original later position (so Luke) up to the very beginning and, having anticipated ἀπηλλάχθαι with his own διαλλάγηθι in v 24, changes the wording to a more positive ἴσθι εὐνοῶν, "Make friends with" (cf. 2:13 for another distinctive use of ἴσθι). These revisions put reconciliation in the forefront. The insertion of "quickly" lends further emphasis to reconciliation (cf. the insertions of ταχύ also in 28:7, 8). Matthew's diction appears in ἕως ὅτου (4,2), where Luke has ὡς, for the meaning "while." The use of "go" in the preceding verse results in its rejection here in favor of a simple "you are." This shift away from a verb of motion leads, in turn, to the dropping of "to the magistrate" and the attachment of "on the road" to "you are" rather than to "make friends with." Matthew also advances "will give over" to substitute for the vivid "drag." This revision satisfies his liking for παραδίδωμι (6,3), which in the next clause he leaves to be supplied. It also avoids the appearance of a distinction between going and being dragged (so Luke might be misunderstood) and makes a good contrast with ἀποδῷς, "give back," in the last clause of v 26. An early papyrus distinguishes the ὑπηρέτης as a servant of the court and the πράκτωρ as the constable in charge of the debtor's prison (see BAG s.v. πράκτωρ). The throwing of the debtor in prison by the πράκτωρ agrees with this distinction (so Luke). But in Matthew the judge gives the debtor to the ὑπηρέτης and it is left uncertain who throws the debtor in prison. Matthew eliminates the second mention of the officer, changes the verb of throwing from active to passive, and puts it last—all in contrast with Luke's version but in agreement with his own emphasis on the last judgment, in which βάλλω figures prominently, often in the passive and without parallel (2,4). Now we can see that the elimination of "to the magistrate" not only relates to loss of the verb of motion and keeps readers from wrongly distinguishing between the magistrate and the judge; it also makes the judgmental activity of the magistrate stand out in unrelenting fashion.

For the un-Greek and un-Roman but Palestinian judgeship presupposed here, see A. N. Sherwin-White, *Roman Society and Roman Law in the New Testament* (Oxford: Clarendon, 1963) 133-34. In a Jewish setting, reference to the Gentiles' cruel practice of throwing debtors in prison, where they had no way of earning money to pay their debts, was sure to grab attention and put a warning stress on the judgment portrayed.

Matthew's ἀμήν belongs to Jesus. As in other passages, Luke has avoided this transliteration of a Semitic word (see the comments on 5:21-48). The κοδράντην (1/4¢) in Matthew has twice the value of the λεπτόν (1/8¢) in Luke (see Mark 12:42). Luke's coin, along with the ascensive καί and the putting of the direct object ahead of its verb, highlights the smallness of the amount. Matthew, having already made his emphases, probably follows the phraseology of the tradition.

Like anger, then, failure to make things right with a brother in the church falsifies profession of discipleship and lands a person in hell, the prison of eternally hopeless debtors, i.e., of sinners (cf. the comments on 6:12). The wording and setting in Luke show that Jesus originally spoke concerning the need to recognize the critical character of the time: "I have come to throw fire on the earth. . . . How is it that you do not know how to analyze the time?" (Luke 12:49-56, excerpts). The shifts in setting and phraseology make Matthew's version a parable of reconciliation rather than of eschatology.

ADULTERY AND LUST
5:27-30 (Mark 9:43-48; cf. Matt 18:8-9)

5:27-28 Matthew shortens his introduction to the second so-called antithesis by omitting "to the ancients." He wants his readers to supply it mentally. Once again the dominical tradition in 19:18; Mark 10:19 forms a pattern, for there Jesus goes from the prohibition against murder to the next in the decalogue, the prohibition against adultery (cf. the comments on vv 21-22 and see Exod 20:14; Deut 5:18). After the quotation Matthew might have appended a statement concerning the OT penalty for adultery just as he appended a summary of the OT penalty for murder in v 21b. Instead, he switches immediately to Jesus' teaching. The parallel between "that everyone who looks" and "that everyone who is angry" (v 22a) typifies his style. His diction is evident in πᾶς (63,25-26), γυναῖκα (10,3), πρός plus an articular infinitive (3,2), and καρδία (5,2). In 13:17 he will again insert ἐπιθυμῆσαι; and though ἤδη appears more often in the other synoptics, he inserts it three times elsewhere. "Has committed adultery" characteristically stems from the OT quotation. Thus the evidence for composition by Matthew is overwhelming. He is saying that disciples are to regard lustful looking at a woman as an offense no less serious than an act of adultery:

such is the import of having "already committed adultery with her in his heart."

On the one hand, there is no condemning the natural desire of a man for a woman. On the other hand, we do read a condemnation of that desire escalated to lust—the leering look (cf. Job 31:1; Sir 23:4-6; 26:9-11; *T. Iss.* 7:2; *Pss. Sol.* 4:4-5; and rabbinic literature cited in Str-B 1. 298-301). The phrase "in his heart" precludes a toning down of Jesus' statement by limiting it to lust that has begun to take steps toward its satisfaction. Adultery implies that the woman is another man's wife. Against sexual intercourse with any woman at all unless one is married to her, see especially 1 Cor 7:1-2.

5:29-30 (Mark 9:43, 47; cf. Matt 18:8-9) From Mark 9:43, 47 (cf. Matt 18:8-9) Matthew now brings in Jesus' sayings about getting rid of one's eye and hand, if necessary, in order to keep from going to hell. In Mark and 18:8-9 the sayings occur in association with causing "little ones" to sin. The reference to the eye provides Matthew with a link by which he brings together these sayings and the lustful look, which in the present passage becomes one way the eye may cause sin. There is deep irony here; for σκανδαλίζει means "trap" or "cause to stumble," yet eyesight is supposed to keep one from falling into a trap or stumbling! Gouging out an eye, cutting off a hand, throwing them away—these expressions teach radical self-discipline. Alongside the death penalty, the loss of a hand or an eye seemed humane. Comparison with Josephus *Life* 34 §§169-78; *J.W.* 2.21.10 §§642-44; *m. Nid.* 2:1; *b. Nid.* 13:6; Aelianus *Varia Historia* 13.24; Valerius Maximus 6.5.3 suggests that Jesus was not speaking hyperbolically.

In giving us a preview of these sayings, which he will later record in their original context, Matthew makes some changes. Twice he inserts "right" (not in Mark or 18:8-9), which he will insert also in v 39 and 27:29 (see also 6:3; 25:33, 34 for occurrences in distinctive passages). Since most people are right-handed, the insertion sharpens the point. The shift from Mark's subjunctive mood to the indicative also sharpens the point. It suggests the actuality of stumbling blocks at the time Matthew writes (so also 18:8-9). And in both of his passages Matthew expands "throw it out" (Mark 9:47) and "cut it off" (Mark 9:43) to the compound statements, "gouge it out and throw it from you" and "cut it off and throw it from you." The greater vividness of the separation between gouging and cutting, on the one hand, and throwing, on the other hand, adds emphasis to the demand for self-discipline. In the gospels ἔξελε, "gouge out," occurs only here and in 18:9. Mark's prefix ἐκ- has moved over to the added -ελε. Similarly, Mark's prefix ἀπο- has become the prepositional phrase ἀπὸ σοῦ (bis), and its place has been taken by the prefix ἐκ- for a parallel between ἔξελε and ἔκκοψον. The simple βάλε (bis) belongs to Matthew's favorite vocabulary (12,8) and here sets up an antithetic parallel between throwing away a physical member that causes one to sin and being thrown, whole-bodied, into hell.

In the latter half of each of the two sayings, Matthew paraphrases the thought in the corresponding part of Mark and 18:8-9. As often, he inserts γάρ (62-63,15). συμφέρει twice replaces καλόν ἐστιν (see 18:6; 19:10 for further insertions of συμφέρει). As here, Matthew often interjects ἀπόληται (8,1) and ἕν (24,7). This is the only place in the gospels where μελῶν appears. Probably the traditional "one-eyed" (so Mark and 18:9) inspired Matthew's reference to "one of your members." ὅλον (7,3) and σῶμα (5,0) round out the list of Mattheanisms.

The omission of entrance into the kingdom (so Mark) and into life (so 18:8-9) makes all the stress fall on the warning against being thrown into hell. In the last clause of v 30 Matthew takes "go away into hell" from Mark 9:43. His doing so will cause in 18:8 the substitution of "to be thrown," the dropping of the reference to hell (but see 18:9), and the retention of Mark's additional reference to fire. These phenomena show that Matthew is indeed anticipating the later passage and is taking care to preserve the expressions for judgment, the one expression here and the other expression there. In fact, his desire to emphasize the gravity of adultery in the heart is so overpowering that he reverses the original order, hand—foot—eye, in order to bring the eye next to adultery. He also omits the foot, but carries along the saying about the hand even though that saying does not suit adultery in the heart. It ends with judgment, and that is reason enough for retaining it. Despite the reshaping of the text, the first halves of vv 29-30 match each other perfectly. So also do the second halves. Matthew has lost none of the original parallelism.

The physical connotations of eye and hand and of the contrast between one part of the body and the whole body falsify a nonphysical definition of σῶμα as person or personality. Rather, Jesus assumes a physical resurrection of the wicked as well as of the righteous (cf. R. H. Gundry, Sōma *in Biblical Theology* [SNTSMS 29; Cambridge: Cambridge University Press, 1976] 24).

DIVORCE AND COMPASSION

5:31-32 (Mark 10:4, 11-12; Luke 16:18; Matt 19:7, 9)

5:31 (Mark 10:4; Matt 19:7) The first and second antitheses came by anticipation from Mark 10:19. The second dealt with adultery. Adultery naturally leads to divorce, a topic discussed a little earlier in Mark 10:2-12 and now taken up by Matthew. Because this third antithesis forms an appendix to the second, the presentation of another kind of adultery alongside the lustful look, Matthew shortens the introduction to a mere "it has been said" and attaches it to the foregoing with δέ. But the center of attention has shifted from adultery per se to divorce. Therefore Matthew wants to bring in Jesus' saying on divorce recorded also in Luke 16:18. To do so, and to adhere to the structure of the antitheses throughout 5:21-48, he first sets up the teaching of the OT in Deut 24:1 with a preview of material that will appear more fully in 19:7, 9 and context.

"Whoever divorces his wife" summarizes the situation envisioned in Deuteronomy, echoes the first antithesis, represents Matthew's diction in ὃς ἄν (14,1—cf. vv 19, 21), and reappears word for word in 19:9. A closer quotation of Deut 24:1 appears in the clause "let him give her a divorcement." Matthew feels less bound by Mark than he will in 19:7; so he omits "certificate" and the phrase "and to divorce [her]."

5:32 (Mark 10:11-12; Luke 16:18; Matt 19:9) In 19:9 we will read, as here, the typically Matthean "But I say to you" (27,7) instead of Mark's "and he says to them." This assimilation to 5:32 shows that Matthew associates the two passages with each other and anticipates his later material in the present passage. The same conclusion follows from the occurrence of the exceptive phrase in 19:9 as well as in the present saying, paralleled primarily in Luke 16:18. The saying in Luke comes right after Jesus' statement, "It is easier for heaven and earth to pass away than for one tittle of the law to fall" (Luke 16:17; cf. Matt 5:18). In Matthew's present conflation of Mark's later material with the tradition behind Luke 16:18, "everyone who divorces his wife" coincides exactly with the wording preserved by Luke. Matthew now inserts "apart from the matter of immorality." This represents עֶרְוַת דָּבָר, "nakedness of a matter," in Deut 24:1. Matthew reverses the order of words to read "a matter of nakedness" and get the meaning of unchastity, immorality (cf. Str-B 1. 312-15). The exceptive phrase is not present in the other synoptics or reflected elsewhere in the NT. It comes from Matthew, not from Jesus, as an editorial insertion to conform Jesus' words to God's Word in the OT.

Matthew stresses the responsibility of the husband to have compassion on his wife. In contrast with all the other passages, the husband's remarrying drops out. Matthew substitutes a unique reference to making the wife commit adultery (cf. his liking ποιέω [19,19]). Special emphasis falls, then, on the demand that a husband not contribute to the adultery of his wife, as would happen if she remarried because he had divorced her. A warning follows that whoever marries a divorced woman is committing adultery (so also Luke, but not Mark or Matt 19:9). ὃς ἐάν again typifies Matthew's style (14,1), and it makes an inclusio with ὃς ἄν in v 31. This warning provides the basis of the preceding insertion: Matthew has deduced that if a man makes himself an adulterer by marrying a divorced woman (so the dominical tradition adopted by both Matthew and Luke), the divorced woman herself also commits adultery by remarrying—and her first husband ought to prevent it by not freeing her and giving her economic reason to marry another man (so Matthew alone). Throughout, it is assumed that a second marriage is adulterous.

If the wife proves unchaste prior to divorce, her husband may divorce her. *He* will not have made her an adulteress. Here Matthew writes nothing about the question of remarriage by the husband who has divorced his wife for unchastity. Luke gives an unambiguously negative answer. Matthew's concern lies elsewhere, i.e., on husbandly compassion as a deterrent to divorce. But it would be a mistake to think that Matthew allows the husband to remarry. To the contrary, his dropping "and marries another woman" (so Mark and Luke) favors that in 19:9 (where remarriage of the husband does appear) the exceptive phrase applies only to divorce. In the word order of 19:9 the exceptive phrase immediately follows the mention of divorce but precedes the mention of remarriage by the husband. Had Matthew been concerned to establish the right of the husband to remarry under the exception, he would hardly have omitted remarriage here in 5:32 and then put the exception only after the matter of divorce in 19:9. To be sure, the Jews took the right of remarriage after divorce as a matter of course. But it is not for nothing that Matthew's Jesus demands a surpassing sort of righteousness (vv 19-20; cf. 1 Cor 7:10-11).

In Palestinian Jewish society, women did not have the right to divorce. Here that question does not even arise. But see Mark 10:12, where some take the woman's initiative in divorce as Mark's assimilation to Greco-Roman culture, and others take that initiative as an authentically dominical allusion to Herodias's divorcing Philip in order to marry Antipas (Josephus *Ant.* 18.5.1, 4 §§110-11, 136).

During NT times the followers of Rabbi Hillel interpreted Deut 24:1 loosely, the followers of Rabbi Shammai strictly of unchastity alone (*m. Giṭ.* 9:10). Matthew agrees with the Shammaites. But we have already seen that he has not forsaken Jesus' prohibition of a second marriage for the husband, not even though the wife is guilty of unchastity. This stricture outdoes even the Shammaites. Because Matthew depends on Deuteronomy in accord with the Shammaites' understanding, we have no need to adopt obscure definitions of πορνείας, such as marriage within the forbidden degrees (cf. Lev 18:6-18 and possibly, but not probably, Acts 15:20, 29), mixed marriage with an unbeliever (cf. 1 Cor 7:39), and continued immorality which the husband fails to stop. The specific word for adultery, μοιχεία, does not appear in the exceptive phrase simply because a general expression occurs in Deuteronomy. Cf. Sir 23:23; Hos 2:4 LXX for associations of πορνεία with adultery.

The Semitic character of παρεκτὸς λόγου πορνείας, "apart from the matter of immorality," does not signal pre-Matthean tradition; it only shows Matthew's characteristic dependence on the text of Deut 24:1 (cf. esp. λόγου with דָּבָר). The shift to μὴ ἐπὶ πορνείᾳ, "except on the basis of immorality," in 19:9 shows Matthew's Hellenistic side. Addition of the exceptive phrase allows for the Jewish requirement that a man divorce his wife if she falls into immorality. Matthew reasons that an act of immorality by the wife has already made her an adulteress; hence, the husband who divorces her does not bear the responsibility of making her an adulteress by pushing her into an illicit marriage to another man. Did Jesus assume this exception when he prohibited divorce? At least Matthew's not granting the right of remarriage means that he does not blunt the point of Jesus' teaching. Technically, "she alone shall be with him all the days of her life" in 11QTemple 57:17-19 implies a prohibition of divorce. But the topic under discussion is polygamy (and royal polygamy at that). It is uncertain, therefore, whether we should draw inferences for the question of divorce, which the author may not have had in mind.

OATHS AND DIVINE MAJESTY
5:33-37 (Jas 5:12; cf. Matt 23:16-22)

5:33 The reference to Deut 24:1-4 in the third antithesis leads Matthew backward to Deut 23:22-24(21-23), where vows are discussed. He does not quote the passage, but it reminds him of other passages so suitable that he does quote them. These quotations of the OT combine with his characteristic diction and parallelistic style to confirm a large amount of editing on his part. This includes the expansion of a dominical saying preserved with little or no editing (it would appear) in Jas 5:12. Furthermore, the OT quotations display a mixture of Septuagintal and non-Septuagintal traits that is typical of Matthew (see Gundry, *Use of the OT* 108-9).

The introductions to the first three antitheses have progressively shrunk. Now Matthew makes a new beginning by inserting πάλιν, a favorite word of his (8,4), and by returning to the full form, "you have heard that it was said to the ancients." Then he imports the OT as a lead into Jesus' teaching. "You shall not break your oath" goes back to Lev 19:12. "But you shall pay to the Lord your oaths" comes from Ps 50:14 with a change of "the Most High" to the preferred τῷ κυρίῳ (34,15; cf. also Matthew's special fondness for ἀποδίδωμι—5,11). Both the Hebrew and the Septuagintal texts of Ps 50:14 read "vows" (cf. Deut 23:22-24[21-23]). Thus the two OT passages deal with the related practices of oath taking and making vows. By substituting oaths for vows in the quotation of Ps 50:14, Matthew assimilates the passage to the topic of oaths. The ensuing prohibition of swearing confirms this shift in terminology, and the association of vowing and swearing in Num 30:3 shows how easy Matthew found the shift.

5:34-37 From now on, with the partial exception of v 44, the second halves of the antitheses will feature μή plus infinitives and commands rather than πᾶς ὁ plus participles and commands. Here, the negative comes from the tradition, but the traditional "swear" changes to the infinitive "to swear" (cf. Jas 5:12). Matthew adds an intensifying ὅλως, "at all," to the prohibition of swearing. This adverb occurs only at this point in the gospels, but its cognate ὅλος is a Mattheanism (7,3). To Jesus' reference to heaven (so James) Matthew adds "because it is the throne of God" (cf. 23:22), and to Jesus' reference to earth (so James) he adds "because it is the footstool of his feet." Characteristically, both additions come from the OT, in particular, from Isa 66:1. Doubtless Matthew's interest in the topic of swearing (ὀμνύω—1,10), his habit of pairing heaven and earth (6,0—see οὐρανός . . . γῆ in the Greek Index), and his liking θρόνος (2,2) and πούς (4,1) helped draw him to the dominical saying.

Jesus seems to have closed the prohibitive part of his saying with the generalizing phrase "neither with any other oath" (cf. James). But Matthew produces another couplet that exhibits his interests, parallelistic style, and practice of borrowing from the OT. The designation of Jerusalem as "the city of the great King" goes back to Ps 48:3(2). Matthew's preoccupation with Jerusalem shows up elsewhere, too (see pp. 602-3). Mattheanisms occur in πόλις (18,3), μεγάλου (11,1), βασιλέως (6,9), and perhaps in κεφαλῇ (2,1). ὀμόσῃς echoes the dominical ὀμόσαι in v 34, and its insertion here agrees with ten distinctive occurrences in 23:16-22. δύνασαι (13,0), μίαν (24,7), ποιῆσαι (19,19), and ἤ (32,12) all stem from Matthew's favorite vocabulary. Cf. 10:30; Luke 12:7 for a combination of hair and head that may have helped composition of the present phrase.

For the commonplace of swearing by heaven and earth, see examples in Philo *Spec.* 2.1 §5; *m. Šebu.* 4:13. For swearing by Jerusalem and by one's head, see *m. Ned.* 1:3 and *m. Sanh.* 3:2.

Back in close parallel with the dominical tradition, Matthew characteristically inserts λόγος (16,2—not in Jas 5:12). The definite article with λόγος replaces the definite article with the first ναί (cf. James). This replacement favors a change of meaning from "let your yes be yes and [your] no [be] no" (so James; cf. Philo *Spec.* 2.1 §4) to "let your word be 'yes, yes, no, no'" (cf. 2 Cor 1:17-20, where the point contrasts with vacillation, however). Matthew's dropping καί between the double affirmative and the double negative confirms the change of meaning, for the asyndeton combined with ellipsis becomes very awkward if we try to translate Matthew's text as "But let your word 'yes' be yes, 'no' [be] no." On the other hand, because of the wholesale condemnation of oaths (cf. esp. the addition of ὅλως in v 34), we should hardly think that Matthew softens Jesus' absolute prohibition by putting forward the double affirmative and the double negative as legitimate forms of oath (cf. *2 Enoch* 49:1-2; *b. Šebu.* 36a). He wants to emphasize the strength of Jesus' demands, not weaken them by conformity to rabbinic teaching. Furthermore, in his account of Jesus' trial Matthew alone will make Caiaphas charge Jesus under oath to tell whether he is the Christ, the Son of God; and then, to keep from leaving the impression that Jesus accepted the oath in violation of his own teaching, Matthew will change Jesus' answer from "I am" (Mark 14:62) to *"You* said it" (Matt 26:64). Therefore we should say that in the first gospel the double affirmative and the double negative are merely emphatic (or perhaps distributive, meaning "each time, on each occasion"). Against the opinion of other rabbis, R. Eleazar (ca. A.D. 270) regarded a *single* yes or no as an oath (*b. Šebu.* 36a). Thus it appears that we are dealing with a development beginning with the requirement that oaths be taken in the name of someone or something (against which Jesus puts a simple yes or no and Matthew puts a doubled yes or no), going to the interpretation of a doubled yes or no as also an oath because of its emphatic nature, and ending in the interpretation of a single yes or no as also an oath. But no unanimity of opinion or usage existed. Though Matthew likes κρίσιν (8,0) and πέσητε (5,3), his treatment of the second ναί and the second οὔ as doublings rather than predicate nominatives leads him to replace "lest you fall under judgment" (so James) with the quantitative statement, "but more than these is from the evil one." He inserts περισσόν twice in his gospel, the cognate περισσεύω three times, and πονηροῦ ten times (plus four occurrences in unique passages).

All in all, Matthew's putting the prohibition of oaths into an antithesis makes the prohibition an extrapolation from the strictures put on oaths in the OT. And the causal statements make it not just a matter of the disciples' establishing a reputation for always telling the truth, as in the unadorned tradition of what Jesus said. To that Matthew adds the rationale that oaths detract from the majesty of God. Even substitutions for his name stand in association with him, since his authority is universal. The related passage 23:16-22 shows that scribal casuistry concerning oaths lies behind their total abolishment.

The Essenes had an aversion to oaths in general, but took an oath on admission into the sect (see CD 15:5; 1QS 5:7-11; Josephus *J.W.* 2.8.6-7 §§135, 139-42). In other sectors of Judaism and in daily speech oaths played a large part (see the mishnaic tractate *Šebu'ot*).

RETALIATION, MEEKNESS, AND HELPFULNESS
5:38-42 (Luke 6:29-30)

5:38 Matthew's thoughts are now moving in the sphere of OT legislation; so they easily jump to the lex talionis, which provides the starting point of the fifth antithesis. His liking ὀφθαλμός (8,1) gives further impetus in this direction. As in v 27, the introduction takes a short form. "An eye for an eye, and a tooth for a tooth" comes from Exod 21:24; Lev 24:20; Deut 19:21. Not only did this principle work for justice by demanding that wrongdoers be punished (see esp. Deut 19:15-21). It also worked against vindictiveness and cruelty by demanding that punishments suit rather than exceed crimes (contrast, e.g., Gen 4:23-24). Matthew's Jesus regards this latter demand as the more fundamental tendency and commands his disciples to be so meek and helpful that this tendency will be carried to the point of a surpassing righteousness (cf. v 20).

The accusative case of ὀφθαλμόν and ὀδόντα derives from their being objects of the verb "give" in Exod 21:23-24. The accusative became frozen in the extraction and proverbial use of the phrases.

5:39-42 (Luke 6:29-30) Luke's parallel lacks the command "not to resist an evil person." The command grammatically depends on "But I say to you." Therefore the work of composition includes not only the first half of the antithesis and the introduction to the second half, but also this initial, summarizing command. Matthew draws ἀντιστῆναι from Isa 50:8 (see esp. the LXX), where the expression has to do with verbal resistance in a court of law: the Lord himself will vindicate his Servant; thus the vindication will not be the Servant's own doing. Jesus' allusion to Isa 50:6 in the following part of v 39 gives rise to Matthew's present allusion to Isa 50:8 (cf. the comments on Matt 26:67). The Mattheanism τῷ πονηρῷ (10,4) echoes v 37. As there, it may refer to Satan as the instigator of oppression, to evil as a principle, or to an evil human being.

Matthew now shapes Jesus' statements very artistically in order to gain symmetry and parallelism. "And whoever will requisition you one mile, go with him two" (v 41) balances "But whoever strikes you on your right cheek, turn to him the other also" (v 39). "To the one who asks you, give" (v 42) balances "And to the one who wants to sue you and take your tunic, allow to him your cloak, also" (v 40). The concluding "And do not turn away from the one who wants to borrow from you" (v 42) corresponds to the introductory "But I say to you not to resist an evil person" (v 39).

Luke has two pairs of parallel sayings. But since Matthew has made the last one correspond to his introductory "But I say to you not to resist an evil person," he composes v 41 ("And whoever will requisition you one mile, go with him two") in order to maintain symmetry and parallelism. ὅστις represents his favorite diction (23,5). ἀγγαρεύσει probably anticipates the story of Simon of Cyrene, whom Roman soldiers requisitioned to carry Jesus' cross (27:32). ἕν is another Mattheanism (24,7). It must have been on Matthew's mind because of its recent and distinctive appearances in vv 18, 19, 29, 30, 36. ὕπαγε and δύο instance two further Mattheanisms (5,6; 19,4). The diction in v 41 favors, then, that Matthew composed this saying as an extension of Jesus' teaching (contrast the view that Luke omitted a dominical saying because he disliked the barbarisms ἀγγαρεύσει and μίλιον—cf. H. J. Cadbury, *The Style and Literary Method of Luke* [Harvard Theological Studies 6; Cambridge, Mass.: Harvard, 1920] 154-58). But this extension does not merely enable Matthew to satisfy his literary taste for parallelism. It also fulfills his theological purpose to emphasize that disciples must learn from him who is meek and lowly in heart (11:29).

Matthew wants meekness to stand out in its own right; so he takes these sayings out of their traditional setting, that of loving one's enemies (see Luke 6:27-36), and puts them into an independent antithesis. ὅστις (not in Luke) derives from his special vocabulary (23,5). To conform Jesus' words to the OT and draw on his example of meekness as Isaiah's Servant of the Lord (cf. 8:17; 12:18-21; and 25:57—all unique in this identification), Matthew replaces τύπτοντι (so Luke) with its synonym ῥαπίζει, and πάρεχε (so Luke) with στρέψον (3,2). These changes accord with 1QIsaᵃ and the LXX of Isa 50:6, where the word "cheek" also occurs. The phraseology of Isa 50:6 will later affect Matt 26:67 (see Gundry, *Use of the OT* 61, 72-73). To intensify the command, Matthew inserts δεξιάν (4,3), which implies a backhanded slap on the right cheek by a right-handed person. According to *m. B. Qam.* 8:6, such a slap was doubly insulting and merited twice the fine imposed for a slap with the open palm. But surpassing righteousness requires meekness even in the face of the worst insult.

The beginning of v 40, "And to the one who wants to sue you," has no counterpart in Luke; Matthew composes it. He loves θέλοντι (18,8). κριθῆναι, "to sue," comes from Isa 50:8 LXX, where it appears twice in this sense. As in v 39, Matthew creates his text partly out of Isaiah, again with an eye on the exemplary meekness of Jesus the Lord's Servant. Luke does not have λαβεῖν, and ἄφες stands where Luke has μὴ κωλύσῃς. Statistics on λαβεῖν (21,16) and ἄφες (12,5) confirm a high degree of editorial activity by Matthew. This activity spoils the poetic rhythm of the Aramaic reconstructed from Luke's version (see C. H. Talbert and E. V. McKnight in *JBL* 91 [1972] 357-59).

The allusion to Isa 50:8 has a repercussion. In the original form of the saying concerning tunic and cloak, a highway robbery is in view. The robber naturally takes the cloak, or outer garment, first; then the disciple is to offer his tunic, or inner garment, as well (so Luke). Matthew's allusion to Isa 50:8 shifts the setting to a courtroom. This shift results in a changing of the robber to a suer and in a switching of the garments. For the suer can hardly demand the outer garment, used as a blanket at night. According to the law, it belonged to a man as his inalienable possession and could be taken by someone else only till sunset (Exod 22:25-26[26-27]; Deut 24:12-13). Therefore the suer demands the inner garment. But—and here Matthew's intensification shows up—surpassing righteousness in a disciple of Jesus includes relinquishing even the outer garment!

Luke's parallel to the saying about giving to borrowers has παντί with αἰτοῦντί σε. Matthew often adds this modifier (63,25-26), but does not have it here. Hence, either Luke has added it or, more probably, Matthew has omitted it in order to avoid an indiscriminate giving that would include people not in need, i.e., the merely rapacious. This purpose seems to lie behind Matthew's aorist imperative δός, "give," which contrasts with Luke's present imperative δίδου, "keep on giving." δανίσασθαι substitutes for αἴροντος (so Luke) and comes from another set of sayings that soon follow in the tradition (Luke 6:34-35). As a result of their present representation by δανίσασθαι, Matthew will omit them when he comes to his section on loving enemies, which provides their setting in the tradition. But the substitution of borrowing for taking seems again to interpret the command in a way that avoids succumbing to the rapacity of people not in need. It also results in a switch from "do not demand [it] back" (so Luke) to "do not turn away" and in the insertion of "who wants." θέλω occurs often in Matthew (18,8). See 26:52 for another insertion of ἀποστρέφω, which never occurs in Mark and appears only once in Luke. Cf. Deut 15:7-11.

The shifts from the second person plural (vv 38-39a; Luke 6:27-28) to the second person singular (vv 39b-42; Luke 6:29-30) and back to the second person plural (vv 43ff.; Luke 6:31ff.) do not necessarily signal a composite tradition behind Matthew and Luke. The second person singular derives from the individuality of having your cheek struck and your things asked for and taken. The generality of the surrounding instructions makes the plural appropriate. Therefore the shifts may reflect Jesus' sensitivity to the varying content of his teaching on a single occasion. Cf. the frequent changes of this sort in *Tg. Neofiti*.

PERFECT LOVE
5:43-48 (Luke 6:27-28, 32-36)

5:43-44 (Luke 6:27-28) Since he has brought the tradition behind Luke 6:29-30 into the fifth antithesis, Matthew naturally goes to the associated matter of loving your enemies (Luke 6:27-28, 32-36). The sixth antithesis begins with another introduction shortened by omitting "to the ancients" (cf. vv 27, 38). As in the preceding antitheses, Matthew draws "you have heard" from "you who hear" in the tradition behind Luke 6:27 and consequently omits the reference to hearing in the traditional statement "But I say to you who hear." The command to love your neighbor comes from Lev 19:18 and supplies part of the OT lead into Jesus' teaching. Matthew will interpolate this same OT command in 19:19 (cf. 22:39).

Under the erroneous presumption that Matthew sets Jesus' true interpretation of the OT opposite Jewish misinterpretation, search is usually made in the extracanonical literature of late Judaism for the command to hate your enemy (see esp. 1QS 1:4, 9-10). But Matthew has not been attacking Jewish misinterpretation of the law, nor does he attack it now. Just as in the first antithesis the statement that anyone who murders will be subject to judgment summarized the OT penalty for murder in Num 35:12 and related passages, so here in the final antithesis the command to hate your enemy summarizes the OT attitude toward persecutors of God's people as voiced in Ps 139(138):21-22: "Do I not hate those who hate you,

O Lord? . . . I hate them with perfect [τέλειον in the LXX—cf. τέλειοι/-ος in Matt 5:48!] hatred; I count them my enemies" (cf. Deut 30:7; Ps 26:5). Though hatred of enemies in Ps 139:21-22 does not take the form of a command, Matthew entertains no doubt that God inspired the psalmist, and such inspiration implies a command. Thus Matthew has taken "you shall hate" from the tradition behind Luke 6:27, "do good to those who hate you," and "enemy" from "love your enemies" in the same tradition, and put them together in reminiscence of the OT. The OT allusions and the reference to "those who persecute you" (v 44) show that in this passage "your enemy" means "your persecutor" and "your neighbor" means "your fellow disciple."

But Jesus extends the law of love to include enemies, i.e., persecutors. Thus righteous hate fades into oblivion along with those other features of the OT that let anger and lust go unpunished and allow divorce-with-remarriage, oaths, and standing up for your rights. These did not have their origin in God's will so much as in people's hardheartedness (cf. Matt 19:8). The center of gravity in the OT lies in more basic tendencies that Jesus carries out fully for the new time of the kingdom.

In v 44 Matthew drops the command to do good to those who hate you (Luke 6:27c) because he has already used the element of hate in the first half of his antithesis. The omission leaves three lines out of the original quartet (cf. Luke 6:27b-28). In order to gain a couplet, therefore, Matthew also drops the command to bless those who curse you. And so, whereas in Luke's two couplets loving your enemies parallels doing good to those who hate you and blessing those who curse you parallels praying for those who mistreat you, in Matthew's single remaining couplet loving your enemies parallels praying for those who persecute you (cf. 1QapGen 20:28-29). As in vv 10-12, Matthew uses a favorite word of his, διωκόντων, "persecute" (5,0), instead of Luke's ἐπηρεαζόντων, "mistreat." Perhaps he is conforming Jesus' words to Deut 30:7, where "your enemies," "those who hate you," and "those who persecuted you" parallel one another and relate to "these curses." The emphatic ἐγώ leads to a placement of ὑμῖν last in its clause. In Luke ὑμῖν has an emphatic first position before λέγω. Matthew does not want to emphasize the disciples as hearers, but Jesus as the greater Moses who authoritatively teaches the law.

It is gratuitous to think that ἀλλά in Luke 6:27a implies a truncated antithesis of Matthew's kind. The contrast deals rather with the preceding woes. See Black, *Aramaic Approach* 179-81, for Aramaic wordplay. In view of the OT origin of hating persecutors with righteous indignation, we need not reduce the meaning of "hate" to "need not love" or "love less." Outside the introductory formulas in vv 43-44, Matthew still has two couplets, as Luke 6:27b-28 has. But unlike Luke, one couplet belongs to "You have heard that it was said," the other to "But I say to you." The first couplet has antithetic parallelism; the second, synonymous parallelism. Both of Luke's couplets follow "But I say to you" and have synonymous parallelism. Though the love-commandment here climaxes the antitheses, it would be an exaggeration to say that this commandment encompasses them all. "Love" means "do good to," not merely "feel good toward" (see esp. Luke).

5:45 (Luke 6:35) In v 45, "in order that you may be sons of your Father in heaven" derives from "and you will be sons of the Most High" in the tradition (Luke 6:35e). Matthew has reached down to a saying near the end of this complex and brought it up to a prominent position in order to emphasize the necessity that disciples demonstrate sonship to the heavenly Father by a meek and loving manner of life. ὅπως replaces καί and represents Matthew's diction (8,7). γένησθε, where the tradition has ἔσεσθε, may come from another clause in the tradition, viz., γίνεσθε οἰκτίρμονες κτλ. (Luke 6:36). It means "be [now]" instead of "become [in the future]." Otherwise Jesus' disciples could afford to delay their emulation of God the Father. Substitution of the Father in heaven for the Most High not only satisfies Matthew's taste for the former expression (10,2), but also makes an inclusio with the heavenly Father at the close of this paragraph (v 48).

The second half of v 45 begins with ὅτι, which comes from the traditional line ὅτι αὐτὸς χρηστός ἐστιν ἐπὶ τοὺς ἀχαρίστους καὶ πονηρούς (Luke 6:35f.). But Matthew artfully rewrites the rest of the line. ἐπί and πονηρούς stay; but against evil people Matthew arrays good people. The latter stem from the entirely different saying "For even if you do good to those who do good to you . . ." (Luke 6:33a, also 35b). The contrast between evil and good typifies the first gospel (4,1). Matthew now retains the alpha-privative in ἀχαρίστους (so Luke) and builds a second contrasting pair, δικαίους καὶ ἀδίκους. Words with the stem δικ- enjoy his special favor (16-17,10-9). Notably, where Jesus spoke only of the ungrateful and evil, Matthew has added their positive counterparts, the good and righteous. But this is only part of an overall expansion directed against antinomianism. The Father's causing the sun to rise and the rain to fall forms the rest of Matthew's expansive interpretation of the single statement that the Most High is kind (Luke 6:35f.). Matthew alone will write that Jesus' face shone like the sun at the transfiguration (17:2). He has already used ἀνατέλλω in his unique application of Isa 8:23–9:1(9:1-2) to Jesus (4:14-16). And in his version of the nativity story he used the cognate ἀνατολή concerning the star of the Messiah (2:2, 9). The vocabulary is Matthean, then, and may carry a hint that the Father's sun is the Father's Son.

"Sends rain" comes from the later saying about the raining of fire and brimstone from heaven on Sodom (Luke 17:28-29). Because he uses the verb here, Matthew will omit it when he comes to take over the surrounding material there (24:37-39). In this way he avoids even the appearance of a contradiction, for here the rain from the Father in heaven represents providence. For Sodom it would have represented divine judgment (as in Luke).

5:46-47 (Luke 6:32-34) In the clause concerning loving those who love you, Matthew brings up γάρ (lacking in Luke 6:32a) and ἐάν with the subjunctive (in place of εἰ with the indicative, as in Luke) from the later saying which begins καὶ γὰρ ἐὰν ἀγαθοποιῆτε (Luke 6:33a). This change makes a better parallel with v 47a, καὶ ἐὰν ἀσπάσησθε. For the word μισθόν Matthew reaches down to a saying that he otherwise omits, "your reward will be great" (Luke 6:35d). This word replaces χάρις (Luke 6:32b). The exchange occurs in the question where Matthew has τίνα instead of Luke's ποία, and ἔχετε instead of Luke's ἐστιν with the possessive dative ὑμῖν. μισθόν and the doctrine of rewards that it represents characterize Matthew's interests (2,5). This fact and the special meaning "credit," instead of the usual "grace, favor," support our attributing χάρις to the tradition rather than to Luke's editing (as is usually done because of word-statistics).

The declaration that even sinners love those who love them becomes a question in v 46c: "Are not even tax collectors doing the same thing?" Matthew wants a parallel with the interrogative form of the preceding line: "what reward will you have?" Also, Luke's sinners have become tax collectors in agreement with Matthew's special attention to tax collectors, whom he interpolates three times and writes about twice in unique passages (for a description, see Jeremias, *NT Theology* 1. 110-11). "Do the same thing" replaces "love those who love them" (so Luke) and again makes a closer parallel with v 47c, where "do the same thing" appears also in the tradition (cf. Luke 6:33c). In v 47c Matthew once more turns the original declaration into a question for a parallel with the preceding line.

At the beginning of v 47 γάρ (so Luke) drops out because of its anticipation in v 46a. Matthew has already drawn "good" in v 45 from the verb for doing good in the tradition behind Luke 6:33; so here he substitutes "you greet" (see 10:12 for a similar insertion). But he will drop greetings *to Jesus* in 17:14 (contrast Mark 9:15) and 27:29 (contrast Mark 15:18) because Immanuel deserves worship, not mere greetings—hence the substitution of kneeling in both of those passages. The evangelist will also drop Jesus' prohibition that the disciples not greet others along the road during their mission (10:10; contrast Luke 10:4) lest that seem to contradict the command to give greetings on entering a house (10:12). Greetings were more than a simple "Hello." They consisted in expressions of desire for the other person's welfare. Such greetings characterize the fellowship of disciples. Therefore, in the present verse Matthew adds "your brothers," which represents a favorite theme of his (11,8). The insertion of μόνον confirms his editorial work. It occurs seven times in his gospel, always as an insertion. Mark has it only twice, Luke only once.

As a second substitute for χάρις (Luke 6:33b), περισσόν echoes v 20, where περισσεύσῃ appeared. Matthew likes these cognates (5,0). In line with v 46b, τί takes the place of ποία, and ποιεῖτε (a favorite of his—19,19) substitutes for ὑμῖν . . . ἐστιν (so Luke). Consequently, "What extra are you doing?" makes a neat parallel with "What reward do you have?" and by recalling v 20 it reemphasizes the need for a surpassing righteousness. In the last line of v 47 ἐθνικοί replaces ἁμαρτωλοί (so Luke). The latter term might refer to religiously careless Jews or to Gentiles or to both. Because of his interest in Gentiles, Matthew eliminates the ambiguity. Cf. the similar insertions in 6:7; 18:17 (in the latter passage paired with tax collectors, as here; see further the comments on 18:17). Because he anticipated lending in v 42 and wants to save it for a full parable in 18:23-35, Matthew skips the tradition about lending (Luke 6:34).

5:48 (Luke 6:36) As often, Matthew inserts οὖν (35,11). He wants a substitute for γίνεσθε in the tradition (Luke 6:36a) because he has already used that verb in a saying with a reference to "your Father" (v 45a). Therefore ἔσεσθε comes from the tradition behind Luke 6:35e, a saying already borrowed from. More importantly, Matthew replaces the original οἰκτίρμονες/-ων (Luke 6:36) with the key word τέλειοι/-ος. His doing so is evident from his insertion of the same word in 19:21, again in association with the love-commandment, which he also inserts in the tradition (19:19). Statistics give confirmation: words with the stem τελ- are among his favorites (16,7). The present substitution has the purpose of conforming Jesus' words to Deut 18:13: "You shall be perfect before the Lord your God" (see further Lev 19:2 and *Tg. Ps.-J.* Lev 22:27-28). Characteristically, Matthew adds οὐράνιος (6,1) to ὁ πατήρ.

This perfection of love brings to a climax the description of surpassing righteousness in the six antitheses. In all of them Matthew has shown that Jesus carried out the tendencies of the OT law to their true ends: OT prohibitions of murder and adultery escalate to prohibitions of anger and lust; OT limitations on divorce and oaths escalate to demands for marital compassion and simple truthfulness; and the guard against revenge and commands to love neighbors and hate enemies in the OT escalate to the requirements of meekness and love even for enemies.

Some have thought that a wordplay between the Aramaic words for "greet" (שְׁלָם) and "perfect" (שְׁלִים) favors the originality of Matthew's "perfect" over Luke's "merciful." But we have seen that the element of greeting comes from the hand of Matthew himself. If there is wordplay, then, it takes place first in the Semitic part of his mind.

THE TEACHING OF JESUS THE SAGE
6:1–7:27 (12:33-35; Mark 11:25; Luke 6:31, 37-38, 41-44, 46-49; 11:1-4, 9-13, 34-36; 12:22-34; 13:23-27; 16:13)

Just as the expression "your righteousness" stands at the head of the legislative part of the Sermon on the Mount (see 5:20 with 5:21-48), so that same expression here marks a new beginning. In this new and final section, 6:1–7:27, we read no quotations from the OT law with Jesus' teaching attached. Their absence contrasts sharply with 5:21-48. Now Jesus appears as the supreme sage, who teaches the wisdom of righteousness (see esp. 7:24-27). His instructions take on the tone of OT wisdom literature.

The section 6:1–7:27 consists mainly of prohibitions. These start with a general prohibition of showiness in religious practices (6:1). Particular prohibitions of showiness in almsgiving (6:2-4), praying (6:5-15), and fasting (6:16-18) follow. Each of these prohibitions mentions the ironic results of showiness and indicates the proper way to practice righteousness. Next we read a prohibition of hoarding earthly wealth (6:19-21), with related references to greed (6:22-23) and anxiety (6:24-34), and a prohibition of judging (7:1-12). The sermon ends with a command to practice righteousness despite the fewness of the righteous (7:13-14), in contrast with the false prophets (7:15-23), and like a wise man (7:24-27).

AGAINST OSTENTATION
6:1-18 (Mark 11:25; Luke 11:1-4)

Matthew has finished the antitheses explaining the righteousness required of Jesus' disciples (5:21-48). Now he thinks back to the beatitude on those who suffer persecution on account of righteousness (5:10) and to the tradition behind it (cf. Luke 6:22-23). In that tradition Jesus' woe against the rich follows immediately (cf. Luke 6:24). Matthew has not used this woe; so now he takes up the theme of its latter half, viz., already receiving in full what is desired and thus losing the prospect of any future reward. Around this theme he builds 6:1-18 with the help of further dominical materials found in Mark 11:25 and Luke 11:1-4. The three main pillars of Jewish piety—prayer, fasting, and almsgiving (see, e.g., Tob 12:8)—provide the framework for his building. But because Jesus' woe against the rich gives the initial impulse for writing this passage, Matthew first takes up almsgiving (the sharing of one's riches) and then steps back for prayer and fasting.

6:1 The leading statements in v 1 highlight the following criticism of religious ostentation. The similar insertion at 23:5 shows that Matthew himself composes v 1. With the single exception of the common verb "have," every significant expression belongs to his favorite diction. Even the exception, along with its object "reward," echoes his insertion in 5:46. "Your righteousness" recalls the insertion at 5:20 and carries on the attack against antinomianism. "Before men" echoes the insertion at 5:16, and the reference to God as Father continues a theme found in 5:16, 43-48.

The Mattheanisms are προσέχετε (3,3), δικαιοσύνην (5,2), ποιεῖν (19,19), ἔμπροσθεν (9,4), ἀνθρώπων (35,17), ἔμπροσθεν τῶν ἀνθρώπων (3,1), πρός + an articular infinitive (3,2), θεαθῆναι (2,1), μισθόν (2,5), παρά + dative (2,2), πατρί (22,13), οὐρανοῖς (46,11), and the description of the Father as being in heaven (10,2).

"Your righteousness" might refer solely to the almsgiving described in vv 2-4. But the echo of 5:20, where the phrase obviously has a general sense, and the repetition of the themes of vv 2-4 in vv 5-18, where other practices come into view, militate against such a restriction. Therefore the phrase stands as a heading over the whole of vv 1-18. The criticism of religious ostentation does not contradict the command in 5:13-16 to do good works before men. For there Matthew was concerned with the temptation to hide one's discipleship in order to escape persecution (cf. 5:10-12), and he takes care to aim the doing of good works at the glory of the Father in heaven (5:16b). Here he strikes against the doing of good works for one's own glory.

6:2-18 The next three subsections (vv 2-4, 5-15, 16-18) have numerous parallels among themselves. Each begins with "whenever," followed by a subjunctive verb. Each contains the phrase "as the hypocrites" and the dreary refrain "Truly I say to you, they receive their reward in full." Each has the contrastive "but you." The "you" is singular and marks a shift from the plural of public hypocrisy to the singular of individual piety. Each subsection has at least one clause beginning "so that." And each offers the happy refrain that the disciple's Father, who sees in secret, will reward him. This parallelistic style characterizes Matthew's writing.

6:2-4 Verses 2-4 have no parallel and abound in Mattheanisms, which again point to composition by the evangelist himself. His Jesus does not forbid almsgiving, an important part of Jewish piety. Rather, it is the publicizing of almsgiving with the fanfare of a trumpet that is prohibited. We have no evidence that any Jews had a trumpet blown ahead of them as they went to dispense charity. Therefore the prohibition probably carries a bitingly sarcastic hyperbole: it is *as though* the hypocrites had trumpets blown ahead of them. ὑποκριταί, usually translated "hypocrites," means "actors" and here refers to acting in pretense of concern for the needy when the real concern is for admiration from other men. It makes no difference whether or not hypocrites have an awareness of their motive. They have received their reward in full when they get what they wanted in the first place, i.e., other men's admiration. But they will get no reward from God, for ἀπέχουσιν appears in commercial language and on receipts for completion of payment (see MM, s.v.).

Jesus' disciples are not to let their left hand know what their right hand is doing when the right hand is stretched out with a gift in its palm. The general sense is plain. But does the left hand stand for a man's best friend (as still in modern Arabic), so that not even he is supposed to know? Or do we have a figurative command that a disciple should not let himself think about his deeds of charity? Probably the expression is to be understood literally: a gift should be slipped unobtrusively to the receiver with the right hand alone, not offered with both hands in a fashion designed to attract the attention of others nearby. Then we can more easily understand how the giving can take place secretly even in public places haunted by beggars (cf. the public setting implied in v 18).

We can see Matthew's diction somewhat in ὅταν (5,5), though for contextual reasons it occurs less often than in Mark or Luke, and very clearly in οὖν (35,11), ποιῇς (19,19), and ἐλεημοσύνην (0,3 plus 7,2 of cognates). σαλπίσῃς appears only here in the gospels, but Matthew will insert its cognate noun (also hapax in the gospels) in 24:31. We come on a string of Mattheanisms in ἔμπροσθεν (9,4), ὥσπερ (6,3), ὑποκριταί (8,3), ποιοῦσιν (19,19), συναγωγαῖς (2,2; cf. συνάγω—10,10), ὅπως (8,7), and ἀνθρώπων (35,17). ῥύμαις occurs only here and at Luke 14:21 in the gospels, but its making a pair with the synagogues answers to Matthew's parallelistic style. Though it occurs more often in Luke (but only once in Mark), δοξασθῶσιν occurs twice as an insertion (cf. δόξα—1,2). The statistics for ἀμὴν λέγω ὑμῖν are 15,8, besides 8 shared instances (see further the comments on 5:18). ἀπέχουσιν comes from the tradition behind Luke 6:24, but a Matthean favorite, μισθόν (2,5), substitutes for the traditional παράκλησιν.

In vv 3-4 the opening genitive absolute typifies the style of Matthew. We have already seen his interest in ἐλεημοσύνην. He likes γνώτω (8,2), δεξιά (4,3—for which ἀριστερά comes in as a match), ὅπως (8,7), the identification of God as Father, κρυπτῷ (with its cognate κρύπτω—4,6), βλέπων (9,3), and ἀποδώσει (5,11).

For God's ability to see in secret, see the many references to ancient Jewish literature cited by G. F. Moore, *Judaism* (Cambridge, Mass.: Harvard, 1927-30; reprinted 1966) 1. 368-74. Hypocrisy as acting derives from Greek culture. But

Matthew shows many Hellenistic as well as Jewish traits. And since Hellenization had long affected Palestine, we should have little difficulty in thinking that Jesus, too, utilized the idea. Contexts favor this traditional understanding. Therefore no need exists to redefine hypocrisy as Jewish legalistic casuistry rather than pretense. But, of course, such casuistry may well have contributed to and grown out of pretense.

6:5 (Mark 11:25) "And whenever you pray" comes from Mark 11:25 (already alluded to in Matt 5:23) with a delay of the element of standing and a consequent change of Mark's participle to a finite verb. The next clause comes from Matthew himself. The imperatival "you shall be," here with "not," echoes 5:48. ὡς and ὑποκριταί belong to his favorite diction (23,8; 8,3). The latter echoes v 2. He keeps on composing in the "because"-clause with use of φιλοῦσιν (2,1) and συναγωγαῖς (2,2), another echo of v 2. "The corners of the streets" does not appear elsewhere in the NT, but its addition to the synagogues makes a pair agreeable to Matthew's parallelistic style, again just as in v 2. Cf. the mention of streets in the distinctive quotation of Isa 42:1-4 (Matt 12:17-21). The reference to standing while praying harks back to Mark 11:25 once more. But there it indicates the posture of the disciples, here that of the hypocrites. Except for φανῶσιν (a Mattheanism—5,8), the rest of v 5 echoes vv 1-2 (see earlier comments for further Mattheanisms).

6:6 Verse 6 opens with yet another allusion to Mark 11:25, but the second person shifts to the singular because of the coming reference to private prayer. After that reference, the number will naturally go back to the plural. The emphatic σύ (6,4) sets Jesus' disciples against the hypocrites, who act as though they are praying to God when they are really seeking the admiration of their fellows. Characteristically, Matthew borrows phraseology from the OT in the command to enter one's storeroom and close the door (see Isa 26:20 and Gundry, *Use of the OT* 134; cf. 2 Kgs 4:33). In most homes only the storeroom had a door. Thus privacy demanded the use of that room. See 25:10 for another distinctive combination of κλείω and θύρα. The references to God as Father agree with Mark 11:25 and, along with the rest of v 6, echo v 4 with its Mattheanisms. To avoid an overloading of v 6, "your Father in secret" contains an ellipsis. "Who sees" needs to be inserted from v 4. Then the full expression recurs.

For prayer, Jews regularly stood. Neither Jesus nor Matthew condemns that posture. The condemnation goes against the love of being noticed at prayer in public places. The command to secret prayer does not imply that praying with others is wrong. But private prayer ought to be secret prayer, uncorrupted by the desire for recognition. Perhaps Matthew alludes to a practice of going to the streets in order to stand in public view at the hour of prayer, three o'clock in the afternoon.

6:7-8 Finally "praying" comes over from Mark 11:25. Attention shifts from Jewish ostentation to Gentile babbling (cf. Sir 7:14). Within βατταλογήσητε we see a stem of Matthew's liking. It is -λογ- (see λόγος and λέγω in the Greek Index). But the definition of the verb stands in some doubt. The verb may denote meaningless or repetitive speech, as in the extensive listing of divine names by pagans. They hoped that at least one of the names might prove effective for an answer. (It was thought that knowing the name of a god and pronouncing it correctly gave a certain power to manipulate the god.) Possibly, however, this practice, or wordiness in general, appears only in the expression "many words." Then βατταλογήσητε might mean "Do not pray ineffectually," for among the Dead Sea Scrolls an Aramaic papyrus has the verb בְּטֵל, like the first part of the Greek verb here, in the sense of ineffectuality (see DJD 2. 135; cf. the Hebrew of Ezra 4:24). The Father's foreknowledge of the disciples' needs makes wordiness unnecessary.

Verse 7 comes to a close with further Mattheanisms in ἐθνικοί (3,0—an echo of 5:47), δοκοῦσιν (6,3), and γάρ (62-63,15). The evangelist likes πολύς (23,1) and λόγος (16,2), which combine to make πολυλογία. In the gospels εἰσακουσθήσονται appears only here and at Luke 1:13, but the simple ἀκούω enjoys his favor (26,6). μή with the subjunctive of prohibition echoes vv 2 and 3. The resultant parallelism characterizes composition by Matthew. οὖν (35,11), ὁμοιωθῆτε (2,3), οἶδεν (7,2), πατήρ (22,13), χρείαν ἔχετε (3,0), and αἰτῆσαι (2,1) belong to his special diction. πρός + an articular infinitive recalls the similar Mattheanism in v 1.

     M. Black (*Aramaic Approach*, 176-78) notes that Luke 11:2 D reads like Matthew 6:7, except that in place of οἱ ἐθνικοί we read οἱ λοιποί, "the rest" of mankind including Jews and Gentiles alike. Cf. Luke 18:9, 11; Eph 2:3; 1 Thess 4:13; 5:6; Rev 9:20. Black then translates οἱ λοιποί back into Aramaic and suggests that in Luke 11:2 D we have a literal and correct translation of the Aramaic, but in Matt 6:7 an incorrect Jewish restriction of the expression to Gentiles. All of this arises out of the doubtful supposition that Jews would not need to be warned against praying in a pagan manner. But that is to miss the "bite" in the damning juxtaposition of Jewish ostentation and Gentile wordiness. Besides, the statement as a whole describes the praying of Gentiles far better than the praying of Jews. The similarities of the Aramaic words to which Black appeals seem somewhat accidental rather than deliberate, and he has to resort to one admittedly rare Aramaic word. It would seem, then, that the expunging of the slurring reference to the Gentiles in Luke 11:2 D does not go back to an Aramaic original, but represents a pro-Gentile counterpart to anti-Judaism in the D-text (pointed out in Acts by E. J. Epp, *The Theological Tendency of Codex Bezae Cantabrigiensis in Acts* [SNTSMS 3; Cambridge: Cambridge University Press, 1966]). Therefore Luke 11:2 D does not give good evidence for dominical tradition as opposed to Matthew's composition. See further the comments on 18:17.

     6:9a (Luke 11:1-2a) The Pater Noster ("Our Father"), or Lord's Prayer, now follows (vv 9-13). The Kaddish, an Aramaic prayer used in the liturgy of the synagogue, probably provided Jesus a seed-plot for the Lord's Prayer. The Kaddish reads in part, "Exalted and *hallowed be his* great *name* in the world which he created according to *his will. May he let his kingdom rule*" (italics for parallels with the Lord's Prayer; see Jeremias, *NT Theology* 1. 197-99). Jesus taught the Lord's Prayer in response to a request that he teach his disciples to pray as John the Baptist had taught his disciples to pray (Luke 11:1-4). Matthew drops the narrative introduction, removes the prayer from its original context, and inserts it here to teach that Jesus' disciples ought to pray with an economy of words. The opening instruction in Luke, "When you pray, say," makes the prayer a recitation. The liturgical style of the prayer in Matthew's version probably implies that the revised

introduction also indicates recitation (see *Did.* 8:2-3). Two Mattheanisms—
οὖν (35,11) and οὕτως (18,5)—replace Luke's ὅταν. The first forges a link
with the preceding context; the second emphasizes a manner of prayer that
contrasts with wordiness. In this respect the insertion of ὑμεῖς (15,3) emphasizes the contrast between pagans and Jesus' disciples. The tradition did
not have such a contrast (cf. Luke). The imperative mood comes over to
the verb of praying, and Luke's λέγετε drops out.

6:9b-15 *(Mark 11:25; Luke 11:2b-4)* In Matthew the prayer itself
consists of an address and seven petitions (vv 9b-13). One of the petitions
gets a didactic expansion (vv 14-15). Luke's version lacks "Our" and "who
are in heaven" with "Father" and has only five petitions. Matthew's third
petition, "your will come to pass on earth as also [it comes to pass] in
heaven," and seventh petition, "but deliver us from the evil one," do not
appear in Luke. Neither does the expansion on the topic of forgiveness. In
accord with his stress on God's being the Father of the disciples, Matthew
takes the first petition, "hallowed be your name," with the address; i.e.,
"Father" is the name to be hallowed. For better balance between the first
two lines, "Father" gains both the pronoun "Our" (in accord with "your"
in v 8) and the phrase "who are in heaven" (in accord with Matthew's habit
elsewhere—10,2). Matthew then adds the two petitions not in Luke in
order to gain three couplets in the main body of the prayer:

1) *Our* Father *who are in heaven*, hallowed be your name.
⌈2) Your kingdom come,
⌊3) *your will come to pass on earth as also [it comes to pass] in heaven*.
⌈4) Give us the coming day's bread today,
⌊5) and forgive us our debts as we also have forgiven our debtors.
⌈6) And bring us not into temptation,
⌊7) *but deliver us from the evil one* [italics for Matthew's additions].

6:9b *(Luke 11:2b)* "Father" goes back to the Aramaic אַבָּא (cf. Mark
14:36; Rom 8:15-16; Gal 4:6), a word learned in infancy, perhaps like
"Dadda" or "Daddy." But unlike its possible English equivalents, אַבָּא remained in use during adulthood for addressing one's father. The retention
of usage in adulthood casts doubt on the hypothesis that Jesus innovated
by addressing God with אַבָּא in an intimately childlike manner (instead of
using the corresponding Hebrew word אָב) and by teaching his disciples to
use אַבָּא. Furthermore, we may well question whether Jews felt a marked
difference between the Hebrew and Aramaic words. The use of the traditional Hebrew word in prayers that have survived from late Judaism may
rest on habit rather than fear of irreverence in the Aramaic word. And
whatever individualism may characterize the use of אַבָּא in those NT passages where it is transliterated, the plural of the first person pronoun
throughout the Lord's Prayer makes "Father" a communal address (even
when unaccompanied by "Our," as in Luke). The Aramaic word may be
transliterated in other passages simply because Jesus prayed and taught the
Lord's Prayer in Aramaic. There is no need to see a theological difference
between the Aramaic word and its Hebrew equivalent. For the designation

of God as Father in late Judaism, see Sir 23:1, 4; Wis 2:16; 14:3; Tob 13:4; 3 Macc 5:7; 6:3, 8; *Jub.* 1:24. The Hellenization of Palestine keeps us from ruling out any of these references as irrelevant because of the Hellenistic tone of the books where they occur.

In anticipation of the later first person plural pronouns, Matthew's addition of "Our" immediately brings into focus the communal nature of the prayer. The addition of "who are in heaven" does not merely distinguish God from earthly fathers; it points to divine majesty as a complement to divine fatherhood. Cf. Mark 11:25, reflected by Matthew also in vv 5, 7, and 14; and see Moore, *Judaism* 2. 201-11, for rabbinic usage. "Hallowed be your name" parallels Luke exactly. But Matthew's pairing the following couplets and adding the honorific "who are in heaven" to "Father" imply that "your name" matches "Father." *That* name is to be hallowed, i.e., reverenced as a revelation of God's relation to Jesus' disciples.

6:10 (Luke 11:2c) It is left indeterminate who will hold in reverence the name; but in his additions Matthew is lashing out against antinomians, whose lawless conduct grows out of failure to reverence the Father. The immediately following request for the coming of the kingdom might suggest a prayer that the whole world regard God as Father when he imposes his rule over all the earth in the future. On the other hand, Jesus taught a present coming of God's rule (see esp. 12:28; Luke 11:20), and Matthew equates God's name with "Father" in relation to disciples (cf. 5:9, 45-46). These counter-considerations suggest a prayer that at the present time more people become children of God through taking on themselves the yoke of discipleship and so do the will of God on earth as it is done in heaven.

Probably, then, Jesus let the emphasis fall on God's action in making his rule finally complete at the end of the age. But in order to stress obedience to the law as expounded by Jesus in the Sermon on the Mount, Matthew magnifies the element of realized eschatology. θέλημα is among his favorites (3,1; cf. θέλω—18,8). In each of its occurrences the will of God as Father lies in view (parabolically in 21:31). And except for the Father's will that none of "the little ones" perish (18:14), all the other passages deal with that will of the Father which is to be done now (see esp. 7:21). Therefore we are to understand 6:10b in the same way. Jesus himself provides the example of obedience. Indeed, "your will come to pass" corresponds verbatim to Matthew's version of Jesus' prayer in Gethsemane (26:42d). There, the subject matter comes from dominical tradition (cf. Luke 22:42). The wording, however, comes from Matthew, in agreement with 6:10. Elsewhere, too, he interpolates the particular form γενηθήτω several times (8:13; 9:29; 15:28). Thus, in wording typical of his style and interests, he constructs 6:10b and conforms 26:42d to it in order to draw a parallel between Jesus and the disciples in their obedience to the heavenly Father's will.

The pairing of heaven and earth characterizes Matthew's style (6,0), and ὡς his diction (23,8). At first the phrases seem otiose here. But he has added them to round off the first couplet: "As also [it comes to pass] in heaven" makes an inclusio with his earlier addition "who are in heaven." There we read an idiomatic plural for "heaven," but here a singular that matches the singular for "earth." The reference to heaven also fits his regular designation of the kingdom as "the kingdom of heaven." The giving to Jesus of all authority in heaven and on earth and his commissioning the disciples to go make more disciples of all nations by baptizing and teaching them all his commandments (28:18-20, a heavily redacted passage) interpret Matthew's additions to the first part of the Lord's Prayer.

Do the appended phrases concerning heaven and earth qualify all three preceding petitions? Probably not, for the kingdom does not "come" in heaven. Therefore the phrases round off the first couplet of petitions (the second and third), but qualify only the last stated petition, "your will come to pass."

6:11 (Luke 11:3) Jesus has instructed his disciples to pray for the future consummation (cf. 1 Cor 16:22). Matthew has made the doing of God's will in the present time an anticipation of the consummated rule of heaven. Now Jesus turns attention to the daily needs of his disciples for food and forgiveness. Luke puts the verb of giving into the iterative present (δίδου) and has τὸ καθ' ἡμέραν. This phraseology indicates a succession of daily provisions. It is often thought that the delay of Jesus' parousia caused Luke (or his source) to substitute an extension of history for waning eschatological hope. But we might expect that in speaking to "the poor," Jesus would tell them to pray for daily provisions (see E. M. Yamauchi in *WTJ* 28 [1966] 145-56). Probably Matthew has assimilated the wording to the context into which he has imported the Lord's Prayer. The shifts from the present tense of giving to the aorist (δός) and from "each day" to "today" take away emphasis on the repetition of giving. In Matthew's form the petition now agrees with the passage coming in vv 25-34, especially with v 34: "therefore do not worry about tomorrow, for tomorrow will worry about itself. . . ." σήμερον is a Mattheanism (4,3). Just as Matthew has shifted emphasis from the future coming of God's rule to its present coming in the obedience of disciples, so also he shifts emphasis from the future succession of daily provisions to the provisions for this day alone. No room remains for anxiety over tomorrow.

There exists a fair amount of agreement among modern scholars that the difficult word ἐπιούσιον most easily derives from ἐπιέναι, "to come," and probably means bread for the coming day. But we still have no need to take an eschatological view, as though Jesus' disciples should pray to eat bread soon in the kingdom of God, on the day of the Lord. That would disagree both with Luke's succession of days and with Matthew's opposing today against tomorrow in the matter of anxiety over present physical needs. Rather, the meaning "for the coming day" implies an evening and morning prayer that God will supply the next day's bread, and will supply it repeatedly, just as the prayer is repeated each evening and morning prior to the coming day. We do not read τὸν ἄρτον . . . τὸν αὔριον, "tomorrow's bread," because that would not suit a morning prayer for that very day. But ἐπιούσιον, "coming," suits a prayer in the morning for the day just beginning as well as an evening prayer for the following day. The harshness of Matthew's σήμερον with ἐπιούσιον—"Give us the *coming* day's bread *today*"—confirms the originality of Luke's text and demonstrates the strength of

107

Matthew's urge to conform this petition to its new context, where we read warnings against anxiety about tomorrow. In fact, Matthew's version of the petition makes sense only in the larger context of those warnings. For the literature on ἐπιούσιον, see J. Carmignac, *Recherches sur le "Notre Père"* (Paris: Letouzey & Ané, 1969) 121-43, 214-20. Cf. Prov 30:8 and the giving of manna in the wilderness (esp. Exod 16:4).

6:12 (Luke 11:4ab) The petition for bread has its counterpart in the petition for forgiveness. Matthew reads "debts," and Luke reads "sins." Behind both readings lies the Aramaic חוּבָא, which had the literal meaning of monetary debt and the figurative meaning of sin as a moral debt. Luke gives the figurative meaning first and then reverts to the literal in "everyone who is in debt," just as Jesus, in his wordplay, referred first to divine forgiveness of sins and then to human forgiveness of financial debts (see Deut 15:1-2). If Luke represents the Greek tradition used by Matthew (as usually seems to be so), Matthew changes sins to debts in order to match the debtors in the last part of the petition. The change would exemplify his striving for close parallelism.

Also for the sake of parallelism, Matthew changes Luke's participle ὀφείλοντι to the noun ὀφειλέταις (cf. the corresponding noun ὀφειλήματα). For the same reason he switches from the singular of debtor to the plural and drops "everyone." Even the change from αὐτοί to ἡμεῖς represents conformity to ἡμῖν in the first part of the petition. Yet again for the sake of a more exact parallelism, he shifts from the present tense ἀφίομεν to the aorist tense ἀφήκαμεν (cf. the corresponding aorist tense ἄφες). In these ways he not only satisfies his taste for parallelism, but also takes away the iterative emphasis apparent in Luke ("we repeatedly forgive every time anyone goes in debt to us"). Just as the succession of days for bread giving reduces to the present day in Matthew, so the succession of forgivenesses reduces to the particular forgiveness of others that immediately precedes a request for forgiveness from God. "Each day has enough trouble of its own" (v 34c, peculiar to this gospel).

Matthew conforms the two clauses in this petition to each other in a wholesale fashion. Such conformation makes it unnecessary to suppose translational variants of an Aramaic perfectum praesens in Matthew's ἀφήκαμεν and Luke's ἀφίομεν. Matthew has simply assimilated the verb to its aorist tense in the first clause. At most, the Aramaic perfectum praesens is a happy coincidence.

As a finishing touch Matthew added "on earth as also [it comes to pass] in heaven" to the first couplet. He also thinks of Jesus' reference to forgiveness of debtors as a finishing touch to the second couplet of petitions and therefore changes "for" to "as" in correspondence with v 10b and his general liking of ὡς (23,8). Stylistically, this change produces the combination "as also," which appears three times in the first gospel (6:12; 18:33; 20:14), but never in the other synoptics—a confirmation of his editing. Theologically, the change produces an interpretation of the original "for" as indicating a paradigm of forgiveness rather than a reason for forgiveness; i.e., forgiveness of others presents God with an example of the forgiveness sought from him, not with a meritorious act by which God's forgiveness might be earned. Forgiveness of others demonstrates sincerity in asking forgiveness from God (see 18:23-35).

6:13 (Luke 11:4c) In the last couplet of petitions, "And bring us not into temptation" does not mean that the Father should keep the disciples from meeting temptation. Rather, it means "Do not let us succumb to temptation." See 26:41; Mark 14:38, where Jesus tells them, "Watch and pray lest you enter into temptation," even though temptation has already confronted them—they have fallen asleep! Also see 11QPs^a 24:10; *b. Ber.* 60b; and cf. Jas 1:13. But what is the temptation? πειρασμόν can connote either enticement to sin or testing of faith. But it would be a mistake to distinguish the connotations sharply; for every enticement to sin tests faith, and every test of faith holds an enticement to sin.

A more important question arises: does the temptation refer to the great tribulation just before Christ's return (24:3-28; Mark 13:3-23; Luke 21:7-24; cf. Rev 3:10) or to present temptation? In 26:41; Mark 14:38, the command to watch as well as pray probably lends an eschatological overtone to the temptation not to be entered. Jesus' agony in Gethsemane seems to preview the agony of his disciples in the coming tribulation. The disciples need fortification against pressure to apostatize. But just as Matthew shifted the emphasis from future to present in the coming of the kingdom and in the giving of bread, so here his addition "but deliver us from the evil one" shifts the reference of the temptation from the coming great tribulation to the current plight of Jesus' disciples. For the evil one has recently appeared in the Sermon on the Mount in connection with present trials and temptations (5:37, 39; see also 13:19, 38). Matthew has imported the Lord's Prayer from another context. Now he adds the petition for deliverance from the evil one and not only gains a couplet, but also ties the prayer to its new context, which deals with the present evil age. πονηρός is a Mattheanism (10,4).

6:14 (Mark 11:25) Most Jewish prayers ended with a doxology, and later Christians added a doxology to the Lord's Prayer ("for yours is the kingdom and the power and the glory forever. Amen"—so some late MSS; cf. an earlier, shorter doxology in *Did.* 8:2). Originally, however, Jesus left the prayer open-ended. Matthew takes advantage of this. He has rounded off the first couplet of petitions with the addition "on earth as also [it comes to pass] in heaven" and has considered the basically traditional "as we also have forgiven our debtors" a rounding off of the second couplet. Now he rounds off the last couplet by bringing in yet again the saying of Jesus recorded in Mark 11:25 (cf. vv 5 and 7 above).

Here, the saying interprets our debtors (v 12b) as men who have trespassed against us, not as men who owe us money (see the comment on v 12 referring to Deut 15:1-2). Matthew omits Jesus' words concerning standing and praying (Mark 11:25). He has already used them in v 5. They would not have yielded a smooth transition from the Lord's Prayer, and they would have made the disciples look like the hypocrites in v 5. As a result of the omission, "in order that" turns into a conditional "for if" (cf. Matthew's fondness for γάρ—62-63,15). This makes forgiveness of others a condition of the divine forgiveness sought in the fifth petition. The in-

serted τοῖς ἀνθρώποις is a Mattheanism (35,17). Because of prior use in
5:23, having something against someone drops out. The Father "who is in
heaven" becomes "the heavenly" Father, because the former expression has
just been used at the beginning of the Lord's Prayer.

6:15 Matthew is not content with the positive statement alone (v 14);
so he constructs a negative parallel (v 15). Though the negative thought
comes close to 18:35, the phraseology derives from v 14 here. Besides the
negation, Matthew takes away the just-used "heavenly" from "your Father"
and moves the trespasses from the first clause to the second. As a result,
the emphasis shifts from *"their* trespasses" in v 14 to *"your* trespasses" in
v 15. Matthew designs the importation of the saying, the changes in wording, and the negative expansion to highlight the necessity that disciples
forgive others in obedience to the law of Christ.

6:16-18 The last criticism of religious ostentation deals with fasting
(vv 16-18, unparalleled). Fasting often accompanied prayer as an indication
of the sorrow out of which the prayer grew and the seriousness with which
the prayer was offered (see 2 Chr 20:1-12; Tob 12:8). Matthew finds it
natural, then, to introduce some instructions concerning fasting. He builds
these instructions around the dominical theme of full receipt in the present
time (cf. Luke 6:24 and the comments on 6:1-18) and the teaching of Jesus
that his disciples will fast (9:14-15; Mark 2:18-20; Luke 5:33-35).

In the style characteristic of Matthew's composition, v 16 and vv 17-18
run along parallel lines. They both begin with references to fasting introduced by δέ (to be translated "and" in v 16, "but" in v 17). From there on,
the parallels are antithetic: hypocrites versus disciples, sullenness versus
putting oil on the head, disfiguring faces versus washing the face, display
in fasting versus hiding one's fasting, and full receipt of reward in the
present versus future repayment by the Father.

Other evidences of composition by Matthew abound in vv 16-18. The very topic
of fasting betrays a special interest of his, as we can see from the insertion of fasting
in 4:2 and from the editing in 9:14-15. As in vv 5 and 6, "whenever" reflects Mark
11:25. The combination γίνεσθε ὡς, occurring once in Luke but never in Mark, is
a Mattheanism (3,1). Further Mattheanisms are ὡς by itself (23,8), ὑποκριταί (8,3),
and γάρ (62-63,15). ἀφανίζουσιν occurs in the gospels only here and twice as an
insertion in vv 19, 20. Furthermore, this verb is cognate to φαίνω (5,8), a clear
favorite of Matthew's that appears in the next clause for contrastive wordplay. Three
times elsewhere he will insert πρόσωπα. The rest of v 16—from ὅπως φανῶσιν
through τὸν μισθὸν αὐτῶν—parallels the last parts of vv 2 and 5 (see earlier comments on the Matthean character of the diction).

In v 17, "but you" starts a parallel with vv 3 and 6, and the two commands
balance each other chiastically in a manner characteristic of Matthew. κεφαλήν (2,1)
and πρόσωπον (3,2) reveal his hand. The entirety of v 18 harks back to vv 4, 6cd,
and 16d in a parallelistic manner (again see earlier comments for Matthew's diction).
κρυφαίῳ replaces κρυπτῷ as a synonym. Only σκυθρωποί, ἄλειψαι, and νίψαι remain
unaccounted for in vv 16-18. But it seems doubtful that they point to a dominical
tradition standing behind vv 16-18 and known only to Matthew, for their number
is too few and the surrounding subject matter provides ample reason for their use.
The phraseology of Rom 2:28-29, sometimes cited as evidence for the traditional
character of this passage, does not come close enough to sustain dominical origin.

There the question has to do with circumcision, which does not enter the picture here.

The somber look of the hypocrites was designed to earn admiration for fasting; it was not true expression of sorrow showing God the seriousness with which prayers were offered. The hypocrites disfigured their faces by pouring ashes on their head. The ashes settled on their cheeks and made them look wan. ἀφανίζουσιν literally means "they cause to vanish," and usually connotes destruction, but here, unrecognizability. Ironically, the hypocrites made themselves unrecognizable (ἀφανίζουσιν) in trying to be recognized (φανῶσιν).

For Jesus' disciples, putting oil on the head and washing the face are to replace putting ashes on the head and adoption of a pale, somber look. The resultant glistening of the hair and brightness of countenance keep others from knowing about their fasting and thus protect its Godward address. Ancient Jews did not wash their faces and put oil on their heads daily for hygienic and cosmetic reasons. They reserved those practices for joyous occasions. But our passage does not teach a hypocrisy of joy. Others would hardly look on oiled heads and washed faces as signs of religiosity. Rather, unusual religious sorrow within is to be compensated for, and thus kept from corruption, by unusual outward signs of an opposite sort. The Jews observed several national fasts, such as the one on the Day of Atonement. But Matthew refers to fasts by individuals who wanted attention from the nonfasting public. Such special fasting took place on Mondays and Thursdays (see *Did.* 8:1; *m. Taʻan.* 1:4-7; 2:9).

AGAINST HOARDING EARTHLY WEALTH
6:19-34 (Luke 12:22-36; 16:13)

6:19-21 (Luke 12:33-34) The mention of reward in the preceding paragraph leads to a prohibition of hoarding earthly wealth because of greed and anxiety. In Luke's parallel, disciples of Jesus are to gain heavenly treasure by selling their possessions and giving alms. But Matthew has already written about almsgiving (vv 2-4) and will yet put "sell your possessions" (19:21) where Mark and Luke have "sell" with another object (Mark 10:21; Luke 18:22). Therefore he omits those matters here. The omissions and the attachment of the remainder to prohibitions of greed and anxiety give the negative side of the originally positive commands to sell and give. In Matthew, that is, the disciples of Jesus are to exchange earthly treasures for heavenly treasures by avoiding greed and anxiety.

Typically, Matthew recasts the sayings on treasure for closer parallelism and a purer, more prominent emphasis on treasures. For the saying in v 20, he draws "treasures in heaven" from "treasure in the heavens" (so Luke). The singular "treasure" changes to the plural "treasures" to correspond with the compound reference to moth and rust in the second clause and with the plural reference to thieves in the third clause. The original, Semitic plural for heaven (cf. 1 Pet 1:4) becomes a singular to match the singular of "earth" in the preceding, parallel v 19. Matthew's ὑμῖν and Luke's ἑαυτοῖς are stylistic variants meaning "for yourselves." Matthew does not take over the command to provide purses that do not grow old (so Luke), because for him the old treasures are good (see 13:52, peculiar to his gospel), and he does not want his readers to think there is a contradiction between the desirability of old treasures that do not pass away and the inferiority of earthly treasures, which do pass away with age. Cf. the omission of a purse also in in 10:9 (contrast Luke 10:4).

In place of "provide" Matthew chooses "treasure up" in order to match "treasures" with a cognate and thus heap all possible emphasis on the motif of treasures. He then seizes on the idea in διαφθείρει, "destroys" (so Luke; cf. 1 Pet 1:4), but switches to the synonym ἀφανίζει in assimilation to and wordplay with the same verb in v 16: moth and rust destroy earthly treasures just as the hypocrites "destroy" (i.e., disfigure) their faces. The assimilation ties this saying to the sermonic context into which Matthew has imported it.

In Luke we read of destruction only by moths, and the destruction consists in the eating of holes in a purse. As a result, the coins fall out and are lost. But Matthew does not refer to purses, and moths do not eat coins. Furthermore, in his gospel treasures are not at all limited to coins: in 2:11 they are gold, incense, and myrrh; in 12:35, good things and evil things; in 13:44, something hidden in a field (possibly coins); in 13:52, new things and old things (apparently a wardrobe); and in 19:21, possessions which have yet to be turned into money by being sold. Yet further, βρῶσις seems not to mean "rust" or "corrosion," but "eating" (see the Greek lexicons, where references outside the present passage are lacking for the meaning "rust, corrosion"). In other words, the omission of purses with coins leads Matthew to write of treasures in a wider sense, especially treasures of expensive clothing characteristic of the wealthy. The moth that eats holes in purses (so Luke) now eats holes in garments—except that the heavenly locale of the treasures prevents it from doing so. By the addition of "eating" to "moth" Matthew shows that he does not think of coins in a purse.

Some have thought of mice and vermin eating stores of grain. But the association with moths favors clothing, as probably in 13:52. Besides the influence of v 16 and the evidence of 1 Pet 1:4, the paronomasia in Luke's form of the saying when translated back into Aramaic with the use of קְרֵב, "comes near," and רְקַב, "destroys," favors the originality of that wording and the editing of this saying by Matthew (see Black, *Aramaic Approach* 178).

The making of the compound expression "neither moth nor eating" leads in the next clause to the expansion of "comes near" (so Luke). The result is another compound expression, "do not break in and steal." διορύσσουσιν literally means "dig through" and refers to a thief's digging through the mud-brick wall of a house. Matthew imports the verb from the tradition behind 24:43; Luke 12:39. The singular "thief" (so Luke) becomes the plural "thieves" to match the compound reference to a moth and eating. Together, these expansions result in two clauses beginning with "where."

Originally there was only one (in this saying by itself—so Luke). In the tradition the drawing near of a thief preceded the destruction of purses by a moth; because after the coins had fallen through the holes during the owner's goings and comings, there would have been no money for a thief to steal (see Luke). In Matthew the thief actually steals; therefore the effect is equivalent to that of destruction. But Matthew reverses the order by putting destruction before theft because he has written only about the destruction of clothes by moths that eat them. Thus even after the moths have spoiled the wardrobe, there remain treasures of money and other valuables for a thief to take.

We have been considering the revisions in v 20. But before making those revisions of the positive command found also in Luke 12:33, Matthew composes an exactly matching negative form of the saying (v 19), just as he composed the negative saying about forgiveness from a positive saying (vv 14-15). The results are a favorite phrase of his, "on the earth" (8,2), and his beloved contrast between heaven and earth (6,0). He also gains twice as much emphasis on treasures and a parallel with the prohibitive form of the leading commands throughout this part of the Sermon on the Mount (see vv 2, 3, 5, 7, 8, 16, 25, 31, 34). On laying up treasures in heaven, cf. Col 3:1-2; Sir 29:11; *Pss. Sol.* 9:9; *T. Levi* 13:5; *m. Pe'a* 1:1.

"For where your treasure is, there your heart will be also" (v 21) parallels Luke 12:34 almost exactly. But despite the previous plurals, Matthew changes ὑμῶν (so Luke) to σου for closer agreement with the singular references to treasure and heart. In the last clause ἔσται comes forward to give ἡ καρδία σου the last position, in line with ὁ θησαυρός σου. The final accent falls, then, on the importance of treasure as the determinant of the heart.

6:22-23 (Luke 11:34-36) Mention of the heart induces Matthew to bring in a set of sayings concerning the body and the eye. Their context in Luke 11:29ff. is distant from the sayings on treasure. Good and bad eyes have to do with recognizing the messianic time. A good eye is ἁπλοῦς, "single," in the sense that it does not see a double image, but allows the light of visible events outside to fill the inside of the body in a meaningful way. So also discernment of messianic events allows reception of messianic salvation. Conversely, eyesight that is bad (πονηρός—literally "evil") prevents perception. Originally, then, Jesus spoke the sayings as an eschatological parable of clear vision versus astigmatism.

But Matthew notes that ἁπλοῦς and its cognates often connote generosity (see Prov 11:24-26 LXX; 1 Chr 29:17 LXX; *T. Iss.* 3:4; Rom 12:8; 2 Cor 8:2; 9:11, 13; Jas 1:5) and that an evil eye often connotes stinginess and greed (see esp. 20:15, where an evil eye is attributed to those who wanted more than they had contracted for; also Deut 15:9 LXX; 28:54-56; Prov 23:6; 28:22; Tob 4:7; Sir 14:10; *m. 'Abot* 5:16). Because of the "commercial" connotations of these expressions, Matthew brings the sayings in which they occur out of their eschatological context into association with treasures (vv 19-21) and money (vv 24ff.). Now the parable teaches generosity as opposed to greediness and goes against antinomians, whose evil lack of love makes them niggardly.

With giving, ἁπλοῦς means "generous" in that "single" conveys the notion of simple, uncalculated, and therefore generous giving. In and of itself the adjective does not mean "healthy" (see *TDNT* 6. 556), but in the Lukan context keen perception of the signs of the times leads to that meaning. The antonym πονηρός may easily mean "diseased, ill" (see Plato *Hp. Mi.* 374D).

Now we read a leading statement (v 22a), two couplets with synthetic parallelism within each and with antithetic parallelism between the couplets (vv 22bc and 23ab), and a concluding couplet with synthetic parallelism (v 23cd). In v 22a Matthew omits σου (so Luke). It is unnecessary here, it will appear soon enough in the next clause, and its omission leaves ὀφθαλμός at the end of the line in assonance with ἁπλοῦς at the end of the next line. In v 22b Matthew writes ἐὰν οὖν instead of ὅταν (so Luke) for a parallel with ἐὰν δέ in v 23a and with εἰ οὖν in v 23c. He likes ἐὰν οὖν both together (4,0) and separately (28,3; 35,11). ᾖ, "is," advances toward the front of the clause. The advance allows ἁπλοῦς to stand at the end in assonance with ὀφθαλμός at the end of the first line. In v 22c Matthew drops καί (so Luke) as somewhat interruptive of the parallelism. And he changes the present tense ἐστιν to the future tense ἔσται in order to match the same form in v 23b. The particular form ἔσται is a favorite of his (16,5).

In v 23a ἐπάν turns into the Mattheanism ἐάν (28,3) for a parallel with vv 22b and 23c. And the evangelist fills the ellipsis in the tradition behind Luke with "your eye." In v 23b καί changes to ὅλον, another Mattheanism (7,3); and the ellipsis of the verb is eliminated with ἔσται, which Matthew draws from the clause represented in Luke 11:36c and which compensates for his omitting that clause in other respects.

In v 23cd Matthew condenses the tradition in order to maintain parallelism, which Jesus forsakes according to Luke 11:35-36. (Even in Luke 11:34 several ellipses obscure the parallelism; the unevenness of parallelistic style stems from the extemporariness of Jesus' speech.) "If therefore" comes from the tradition behind Luke 11:36a, otherwise omitted by Matthew. "The light in you is darkness" comes from the tradition behind Luke 11:36b, the first part of which Matthew omits. "How great is that darkness!" draws its emphatic tone from the omitted phrase behind Luke 11:36b ("not having any part dark"). But with his exclamation Matthew turns the negative thought around to the positive implication of having *every* part dark. The warning tone stems from the omitted command to see to it that the light within is not darkness (Luke 11:35). We will find two more insertions of πόσον in 10:25; 12:12.

6:24 (Luke 16:13) In Luke 16:13 the saying about the impossibility of serving the two masters God and Money follows the parable of the shrewd manager. Matthew puts the saying after the comments about the single eye in order to gain a contrast between "single" and "two." The parallel texts agree word for word except that Matthew omits, or Luke adds, οἰκέτης, "servant" (usually a domestic slave). δουλεύειν means "to serve *as a slave.*" As a matter of fact, we know that slaves did sometimes serve more than one master. For a scriptural example, see Acts 16:16; cf. *TDNT* 2. 270; Str-B 1. 433. Therefore Jesus is saying either that no one can serve these two particular masters *God* and *Money* at the same time (v 24d then defines rather than applies v 24a) or that no one can serve *well* any two masters (v 24d then gives an application of the general principle in v 24a). Under either interpretation the reason for the impossibility lies in the resistance of human nature to divided loyalties. Because of the chiastic and synonymous parallelism, "he will love" matches "he will be devoted to." Both expressions refer to a slave's faithful labor more than to affection. Similarly, "he will hate" and "he will despise" refer primarily to slackness in labor. For the comparative use of love and hate, see especially Gen 29:30, 33, where hating one wife means not loving her as much as another wife. "Money" is kept in its Semitic form μαμωνᾳ probably because of the personification.

6:25-34 *(Luke 12:22-32)* Verses 25-34 deal with the other main reason, besides greed, for hoarding earthly wealth—anxiety. The subsection begins with a prohibition of anxiety about food, drink, and clothing (v 25a-f), continues with expansions of the topics of food (vv 25g-27) and clothing (vv 28-30), offers reasons against anxiety in its heathenism and in God's fatherly knowledge of disciples' needs (vv 31-32), contains a positive command in replacement of anxiety (v 33), and closes with a recapitulation of the prohibition of anxiety (v 34). The parallel passage in Luke 12:22-32 does not appear in Luke's version of this sermon. Rather, it comes at the close of the parable concerning the rich fool, which ends with a reference to "the one who lays up treasure for himself and is not rich toward God" (Luke 12:21), and just before the command to lay up treasure in heaven (Luke 12:33-34), which Matthew has already used (vv 19-21). Therefore Matthew is stepping back slightly in the tradition recently taken up and is continuing to put into the Sermon on the Mount sayings spoken on other occasions. This procedure makes it possible for him to capitalize on the topical similarities of dominical sayings having different origins.

6:25 *(Luke 6:22-23)* "On account of this" refers in Matthew to the impossibility of serving God and Money, in Luke to the folly of the rich fool. But both preceding contexts carry the same antagonism to hoarding earthly wealth. The translation "life" goes back to ψυχῇ, which also means "soul" and "self." Here it refers to the soul as the animus of physical existence. This existence requires the nourishment of food and drink and the warmth of clothing. Matthew adds "your" (not in Luke) for clarification and perhaps for a kind of parallel with "to you" at the end of the preceding line. "Or what you will drink" is missing in Luke's version. Some ancient texts lack it in Matthew as well (see the UBS and Metzger, *Textual Commentary* ad loc.). But Matthew has probably brought up the clause from v 31c (where Luke has it, too) for a parallel with "what you will eat" and for the resultant emphasis. Addition of "your" (probably not in Luke) to "body" produces a parallel with "your soul." "Is not the soul [i.e., life] more than food and the body than clothing?" corresponds to Luke's "For the soul is more than food and the body more than clothing." Matthew changes the declaration offering a reason ("For . . .") into a question demanding reflection ("Is not . . . ?"). This is the first of three such questions beginning with

115

the negative. None of them occurs as a question in Luke's version. See vv 26, 30.

Some have thought that the prohibition of anxiety not only deals with mental anxiety, but also entails a prohibition of working to earn money for physical needs (cf. anxiety and work in Exod 5:9 LXX; Bar 3:18; Luke 10:41). If so, Jesus addressed his remarks to disciples who were commissioned to preach constantly and therefore had to depend on the Father's provision of food and clothing through those they ministered to (see 1 Cor 9:14). But μεριμνάω normally refers to mental anxiety alone, as in 10:19, its only other occurrence in Matthew. Even in the other passages cited, anxiety is only associated with work, not identified with it. And the meaning "work" for "anxiety" does not fit the question "Who of you by being anxious can add a single hour to his life?" (v 27). Besides, the task of preaching does not appear in this passage. Commentators usually go out of their way to deny that Jesus endorses idleness in prohibiting anxiety. Though the qualification has truth, mention of it at this point tends to dull the edge of his words. Cf. Rom 14:17.

6:26 (Luke 12:24) In v 26 Matthew puts ἐμβλέψατε, "look at," where Luke has κατανοήσατε, "consider." The switch assimilates the passage to its new surroundings in the Sermon on the Mount, where βλέπω occurs a number of times (5:28; 6:4, 6, 18; 7:3). Throughout the first gospel Matthew shows a liking of this verb (9,3). The prefixing of ἐμ- may intensify its meaning and correspond to the prefix κατα- in the tradition and in Matthew's parallel verb καταμάθετε ("learn from," v 28). Matthew generalizes the ravens (so Luke) into the birds of the heaven (i.e., of the sky). The birds come from the tradition behind Luke 12:24f., otherwise omitted by Matthew. The addition of τοῦ οὐρανοῦ makes a parallel with τοῦ ἀγροῦ in vv 28 and 30 (cf. Matthew's distinctive use of the word for heaven in 16:2, 3; 24:30 [bis] and many times with "the kingdom"). Moreover, "birds of the heaven" occurs often in the OT, so that Matthew gains an assimilation of Jesus' words to God's Word there. Parallelism and conformity to the OT offer the most likely reasons for his revision, then; but it remains possible that he also wanted to avoid offending Jews with a positive portrayal of the unclean raven. See Black, *Aramaic Approach* 179, for the paronomasia between "ravens" and "feed" in Palestinian Syriac. The paronomasia favors the originality of Luke's version.

"They do not have a storeroom or a barn" (so Luke) becomes "nor do they gather into barns." The inserted and typically Matthean οὐδέ (17,3) makes a parallel with the two preceding clauses: "they do not [οὐ] sow, nor [οὐδέ] do they reap." Because he has already used ταμεῖον in v 6, Matthew can afford to omit it here. The change from the mere possession of facilities (which might stand empty) to the verb of gathering insures that readers will take the statement as referring to actual storage. In the next clause the putting of "your heavenly Father" in place of "God" (so Luke) arises out of Matthew's characteristic desire to emphasize God's fatherhood (6,1). In the last clause a declaration once again becomes a question for reflection. Matthew has used the traditional πόσῳ as recently as v 23; so he makes another exchange, this time by substituting an interrogative "not" to match the negatives in the parallel questions in vv 25 and 30 (cf. 7:16).

6:27 (Luke 12:26) Yet another question appears. Matthew advances προσθεῖναι to a position right after δύναται. This makes for an easier connection. The addition of "one" (not in Luke) to "cubit" compensates for the omission of the whole next clause, "If then you are not able to do even a very little thing" (so the tradition as represented by Luke). "One" corresponds specially to the omitted "a very little thing" and belongs to Matthew's preferred vocabulary (εἷς—24,7). ἡλικίαν may mean "life span" or "stature." "Stature" would agree with the more usual meaning "cubit" (approximately eighteen inches) of πῆχυν, also translated "hour" (in the sense of an indefinitely short period of time). But the addition of a whole cubit to a man's stature would hardly be "a very little thing"! And in both Matthew and Luke Jesus discusses food for survival, not for growth. Therefore the translation "one hour to his life" stands firm.

6:28-29 (Luke 12:26-27) Without the reference to "even a very little thing," the further reference to "the remaining things" does not make easy sense. Therefore Matthew drops that, too, and characteristically substitutes ἐνδύματος (6,0) as a lead into the following subsection on clothing. As in v 26, Luke's κατανοήσατε disappears. Here in v 28, however, Matthew substitutes καταμάθετε in order to carry out his emphasis on discipleship, which is learning. The simple form of the verb occurs as an insertion in 9:13, as part of unique material in 11:29, and in parallel only at 24:32. The cognates μαθητεύω and μαθητής carry a huge emphasis in Matthew (1,2; 31,5). The prefix κατα- in the present verse merely shows that the evangelist is revising a tradition containing another verb beginning with κατα-.

To the lilies Matthew typically adds τοῦ ἀγροῦ, "of the field" (3,10). The addition produces a parallel with the birds of the heaven (v 26) and the grass of the field (v 30). As a second benefit, it results in a correspondence between Jesus' words and Ps 103:15: "As a flower of the field. . . ." Perhaps the word translated "lilies" (κρίνα) needs to be translated generally as "flowers." Alternatively, it refers to anemones, which had a purple color possibly comparable to that of King Solomon's clothing, mentioned in the next verse. Laboring and spinning allude to men's work in the field and women's work at home. Matthew has used οὐδέ as a substitute in v 26; so he drops it from v 29b in the reference to Solomon's clothing. ὅτι stands in its stead, perhaps for a parallel with ὅτι in v 26.

6:30 (Luke 12:28) "In a field" changes to "of the field," which Matthew then delays till after "the grass" (contrast the word order in the Greek text of Luke). These revisions make a parallel with the birds of the air (v 26) and the lilies of the field (v 28; cf. the weeds of the field in 13:36). Also in the interest of parallelism, Matthew puts ὄντα after σήμερον to correspond with the position of its fellow participle βαλλόμενον. The grass of the field refers specially to the lilies of the field, which rapidly become dried up fuel for the oven. In the second half of v 30 the traditional declaration turns into a question (cf. the comments on vv 25 and 26).

6:31 (Luke 12:29) "Do not seek" becomes "Do not be anxious." Thus Matthew conforms the tradition behind Luke to the prohibition of anxiety in v 25 (cf. v 34). He does so in order to unify the passage around that prohibition. "What shall we wear?" replaces "and do not worry" (so Luke) to round out the rehearsal of questions discussed in the preceding passage. Cf. v 25 with v 31, and the insertion of clothing in v 28. The doubled substitution of ἤ for καί betrays Matthew's hand (32,12).

6:32 (Luke 12:30) In v 32 Matthew brings πάντα to the head of the sentence in order that no one may associate the adjective with τὰ ἔθνη—as the *RSV* does in Luke—instead of with ταῦτα. "All these things" comfortingly emphasizes God's omniscience. As much as possible Matthew wants to avoid slurring Gentiles (cf. "Universality" in the Topical Index). Therefore his version also lacks "of the world" (so Luke). Though he likes κόσμος (5,2), its omission helps subdue the slur on Gentiles. Alternatively, we might think that Luke adds the reference to the world in order to distinguish unbelieving Gentiles, who belong to it, from believing Gentiles, who belong to the church. But the distancing of πάντα from the Gentiles favors that Matthew is unloading the reference in order to make the slur as inconspicuous as possible. In v 32b the Mattheanism γάρ (62-63,15) replaces δέ and makes the Father's knowledge a second reason not to have anxiety. The first reason—that anxiety is pagan—was also introduced by γάρ. Typically, Matthew adds "heavenly" to "your Father" in order to make a parallel with the same expression, unique to him, in v 26 and thus to reemphasize the majesty of God's fatherhood (6,1). By connoting power, that majesty offers solace to disciples in need. In the next clause "all" is added to "these things" for an emphatic parallel with "all these things" preceding (v 32a; cf. v 33 and the special frequency of πᾶς in the first gospel—63,25-26). Matthew puts his additions at the ends of both the second and the third clauses; this placement requires a change of word order in the second.

6:33 (Luke 12:31) We discover a favorite of Matthew in πρῶτον (3,1) and might think at first that it softens the command to seek the kingdom, as though after seeking the kingdom Jesus' disciples might legitimately seek earthly security. But the adversative δέ, the provision of "these things" by the *Father*, and the command *not* to have anxiety about tomorrow negate a softening interpretation. Hence, the adverb is emphatic rather than permissive. To "the kingdom" Matthew characteristically adds "and his righteousness" (5,2). Yet again the addition ties the passage to its new context, the Sermon on the Mount, where the theme of righteousness prevails. But what connotation attaches to δικαιοσύνην, the right conduct of disciples at the present time (so 5:10, 20; 6:1 earlier in the sermon) or the right conduct of the Father when he finally imposes his kingdom with full force—i.e., divine justice with consequent vindication of Jesus' disciples (so 5:6 earlier in the sermon)? We should say the latter because in writing about the right conduct of the disciples Matthew uses "your" (see 5:20; 6:1, both distinctive of his gospel; cf. the absence in Zeph 2:3 of "his"—despite a preceding command to seek the Lord—in a command to seek righteousness, and the same absence in the similar phraseology of 1 Macc 2:29). But here we read "his" in reference to God the Father. Because of their persecution, the disciples seek justice from him (see 5:6). Furthermore, their persecutions bring on them the very economic hardship Jesus has been telling them not to be anxious about (cf. the use of μεριμνάω in association with persecution also in 10:19; Luke 12:11). Again Matthew adds πάντα for an emphatic parallel with v 32a and c in the promise "and all these things will be added to you." Since "his righteousness" looks forward to future vindication, this promise is not fulfilled in the present life of disciples, but in their coming life, when they will have obtained justice against their persecutors (cf. 19:27-29, where Matthew omits "in this present age" in contrast with Mark 10:30; Luke 18:30). By the same token, seeking the kingdom of the Father means desiring the final coming of his rule on earth.

If we are to believe an impressive array of textual witnesses favoring the modification of τὴν βασιλείαν by τοῦ θεοῦ ("of God"; see the UBS and cf. Metzger, *Textual Commentary* ad loc.), Matthew here compensates for his omission of God's name in v 26. But the lack of this modification in ℵ B it[(k),l] arm cop[sa,bo] Aphraates Tertullian Eusebius, the unusualness of God's name with references to the kingdom in Matthew, scribal familiarity with the frequency of God's name in such references elsewhere, and the temptation to fill out the somewhat jarring absolute construction (esp. to get a closer antecedent for αὐτοῦ) favor omission.

6:34 (Luke 12:32) The command that the little flock not be afraid (so Luke) changes to a prohibition of anxiety about tomorrow. The substitution of "do not be anxious" recalls vv 25 and 31 and results in a threefold prohibition of anxiety. οὖν (not in Luke) characterizes Matthew's diction (35,11). "For tomorrow" echoes "tomorrow" in v 30a. Now Matthew constructs a clause beginning with his beloved γάρ (62-63,15) in order to give a reason for the prohibition of anxiety and make a parallel with vv 31 and 32, where the second prohibition of anxiety is followed by reasons also introduced with γάρ. Here in v 34, he draws the reason straight out of the main words of the preceding prohibition, "tomorrow" and "be anxious." Thus, "for tomorrow will be anxious for itself" takes the place of "because your Father has been pleased to give you the kingdom" (so Luke). Despite his interest in the kingdom, Matthew wants the emphasis to stay on the prohibition of anxiety (cf. *b. Sanh.* 100b; *b. Ber.* 9b; Prov 27:1; Jas 4:13-14).

The final clause of v 34, "Each day has enough trouble of its own," is unmatched in Luke. Evidently Matthew composes it as a concluding remark, for he inserts ἡμέρα fifteen times and includes the word in unique materials nine times, besides twenty-one shared occurrences. Furthermore, in 10:25 he will insert ἀρκετόν (unused elsewhere in the gospels), and in a distinctive passage he will write its cognate verb (25:9). Thus the section ends with an emphasis on the present day, an emphasis reminiscent of the Lord's Prayer in Matthew's version (see esp. v 11).

AGAINST JUDGING
7:1-12 (Mark 7:24; Luke 6:31, 37-38, 41-42; 11:9-13)

This section opens with a prohibition of judgment against fellow disciples (vv 1-5). The prohibition is balanced by a precautionary note that nondisciples ought to be barred from the fellowship of the church (v 6). The section then closes on the positive note of doing good to others, as God does, in contrast with judging (vv 7-12).

7:1-2 (Mark 4:24; Luke 6:37-38) In chap. 6 Matthew drew nothing from the sermonic tradition lying behind Luke 6:29-49 and used by him in chap. 5. But now, to finish up his series of prohibitions, he returns to that tradition at the point where he left off in 5:48. The initial καί in the original prohibition of judging connects the prohibition with the preceding command to mercifulness (see Luke 6:36-37). Since he covered that ground long ago, Matthew drops καί and makes a fresh start. Also, he replaces καὶ οὐ μή, "and not" (so Luke), with ἵνα μή, "lest"; i.e., the danger of incurring judgment becomes a deterrent to passing judgment. The shift to a hypotactic construction makes patent the meaning latent in the paratactic construction, which goes back to a Semitic original.

The present tense of μὴ κρίνετε does not merely prohibit *habitual* judging, as though *occasional* judging meets no disapproval, but carries the force "Stop judging" or "Don't ever judge." The later command to exercise church discipline (18:15-18) shows that private rather than communal judgments are in view here (cf. 5:21-26).

Earlier insertions of material about giving (6:1-4) and forgiveness (6:14-15) lead to omission of sayings on those topics that now appear in the tradition (Luke 6:37c-38a). Matthew retains only the prohibition of condemnation, but exchanges the verb of condemning (καταδικάζετε/-σθῆτε) for terms of judgment (κρίματι κρίνετε κριθήσεσθε). This exchange is an assimilation to v 1. Along with the omission of other topics, it keeps attention fixed on the motif of judgment.

Matthew also changes the form of the statement from a prohibition followed by a strong denial concerning the future ("do not condemn, and you will not be condemned," so Luke) to an affirmation that the future will correspond to the past ("for with the judgment by which you judge, you will be judged"). This revision produces a typically Matthean parallel with the next saying about the measure. The parallel shows itself in the connective καί, inserted at the start of v 2b. The displaced γάρ advances to v 2a (contrast Luke). But Matthew's ἐν (with ᾧ, bis) and lack of the prefix ἀντι- (so Luke, with μετρηθήσεται) agree with Mark's form of the saying on the measure (Mark 4:24) rather than with Luke's slightly Hellenized form. Mark has the saying in a passage about hearing the Word, with the result that man's measuring refers to the way hearers respond to the Word. Despite affinities with the diction in Mark, Matthew's version agrees with Luke's in referring the figure to judgment of another person, in particular a fellow disciple (cf. "brother" in vv 3-5; also Jas 4:11-12, a likely allusion to these dominical sayings).

What kind of judgment comes back on the one who judges? Probably not judgment in the present from other people, but final judgment from God (so the predominant meaning of judgment in the synoptics; cf. Jas 2:12-13; 4:12). Thus the future tense in "you will be judged" and "it will be measured to you" refers to the last day, and the passive voice represents God's action (cf. Jeremias, *NT Theology* 1. 9-14 [corrected to a significant degree by E. M. Sidebottom in *ExpTim* 87 (1976) 200-4], and the Palestinian targumic texts of Gen 38:26, cited by M. McNamara, *The New Testament and the Palestinian Targum to the Pentateuch* [AnBib 27; Rome: Pontifical Biblical Institute, 1966] 138-42). God's judgment on those who refuse forgiveness to others comes close to the present passage (see 6:14-15; 18:23-35). In Luke we read about the possibility of an overflowingly good measure from God; but in Matthew the omission of forgiveness and of giving leaves only a negative judgment from God for the sin of judging. With v 2, cf. *m. Soṭa* 1:7; *b. Roš Haš.* 16b.

7:3-5 *(Luke 6:41-42)* But what kind of judging by a professing disciple falsifies his profession and draws eternal punishment from God? It is judging a fellow disciple out of self-righteousness, i.e., in a way that shows failure to surpass the ostentatious righteousness of the scribes and Pharisees. The sayings about the speck and the plank (vv 3-5) specify and describe this kind of judging. In Luke the "parable" of the blind leading the blind (6:39) and the saying about the similarity of a disciple to his teacher (6:40) come between the sayings on judgment and measurement and the sayings about a speck and a plank. But Matthew saves parables till chap. 13, and he will later write concerning the blind leading the blind (15:14) and the similarity of a disciple to his teacher (10:24-25). He omits those matters here, then, and goes straight from judgment and measurement to speck and plank. The omissions enable him to pursue the theme without interruption.

In v 3 σῷ differs from ἰδίῳ in Luke 6:41 (cf. *b. 'Arak.* 16b) only as a stylistic variant, and the slightly different word orders are insignificant. Matthew likes forms of εἴρω (18,9) and therefore writes ἐρεῖς in v 4a instead of δύνασαι λέγειν (so Luke 6:42). The dropping of δύνασαι makes his version more forceful in that now the stress falls on actuality rather than potentiality.

It has been suggested that the future of ἐρεῖς represents the Semitic imperfect tense, which may mean "can . . . ," as here in Luke. But Matthew's penchant for forms of εἴρω makes this explanation unnecessary.

The tradition behind v 4b begins with ἀδελφέ (see Luke). Brotherhood figures prominently throughout the first gospel (11,8), but the kind of statement which the traditional ἀδελφέ introduces destroys brotherhood. Therefore Matthew drops the address. He also changes "in your eye," construed with "the speck" in Luke, to "out of your eye," now construed with "let me take." He does so twice again in v 5 to maintain the parallelism and increase emphasis on *taking* the speck or plank out of the eye rather than on the *presence* of the speck or plank in the eye. The only exception occurs in v 4c, where the absence of the verb for taking leads Matthew to retain "in" with "your eye" (so also Luke).

As an alternative to Matthew's dropping ἀδελφέ in order to protect the concept of brotherhood from a statement destructive of it, we might think that Luke added the address after the pattern of Acts 9:17; 21:20; 22:13 and other passages in which it occurs in the plural. Luke usually sticks closer to his sources than Matthew does, however; and, as we have seen, Matthew had reason to drop the address.

In the tradition behind v 4c (Luke 6:42c), αὐτός is doubly difficult because of its distance from the verbal ending -σαι, which it modifies (see Luke 6:42a), and because of the distance of βλέπων, which modifies αὐτός but does not come till the end of the question. The clearing up of this difficulty gives Matthew opportunity to throw in a favorite of his, the emphatic ἰδού (34,9).

In v 5 Matthew moves "to take out" to a position right after "you will see clearly." The shift contributes to his emphasis on taking the speck out of the eye, for which the presence of the speck in the eye is a mere precondition. According to his interpretation, then, Jesus does not teach the wrongness of taking a speck out of a brother's eye, i.e., of rebuking a fellow disciple for a sin (see 18:15-18). Rather, Jesus teaches the wrongness of doing so with the larger sin of self-righteousness on one's own part (cf. 6:1-18 and contrast 5:3-10). Self-righteousness makes the rebuke a hypocritical "act" of showiness instead of a genuine attempt to ensure the well-being of the sinning brother. On the other hand, absence of self-righteousness will not only make the rebuke more suitable, but also make the one who rebukes better able ("you will see clearly") to restore his brother; and it will keep the one who rebukes from reading his fellow disciple out of the kingdom. To do the latter would violate 13:24-30, 36-43, 47-50 (cf. 22:11-14)—all uniquely Matthean.

"Then you will see clearly to remove the speck out of your brother's eye" may seem to contradict the absolute prohibition of judging in v 1. For this reason, indeed, some take it as pure irony: you will never see clearly enough to judge. But to do so is to miss the distinction between judging self-righteously, which is prohibited, and helping a brother overcome sin, which is not merely allowed, but commanded (cf. Luke 17:3; Gal 6:1; 1 Tim 5:20; 2 Tim 4:2; Titus 1:13; 2:15).

7:6 Avoiding judgment of fellow disciples and awaiting God's final separation of true and false disciples might well lead to a church dominated by the false—unless care is taken not to allow into fellowship those who are recognizably undiscipled. The prohibition of giving dogs what is sacred and of throwing pearls to pigs (v 6) warns against easy conditions of entrance into the church. Such conditions result in the influx of those who not only contaminate the fellowship (cf. *Did.* 9:5), but also turn against other disciples by informing on them in times of persecution (see Matt 24:10, 49).

Matthew composes this distinctive saying out of concern about the mixed church and with use of his favorite diction, an OT allusion, and parallelism. These are what we should expect from him. μή, μηδέ, and μήποτε signal the parallelism of lines. Mattheanisms include δῶτε (8-9,10), ἅγιον (4,4), μηδέ (7,1), βάλητε (12,8), μαργαρίτας (0,3), ἔμπροσθεν (9,4), μήποτε (2,4), ποσίν (4,1), and στραφέντες (3,2). Matthew inserted καταπατήσουσιν in 5:13. "Dogs" and "pigs" are the only important words unaccounted for. But these stem from the typically Jewish vocabulary of derogation. Jewish-minded Matthew finds it easy to use them. In fact, he probably draws the figure of dogs from Ps 22:17(16), where it stands for those among God's people who turn on the righteous in persecution—

exactly the implication here (cf. Phil 3:2; Rev 22:15). The figure of dogs naturally leads to that of pigs for the sake of parallelism. Only ῥήξωσιν remains, and it is hardly enough to establish pre-Matthean tradition. Perhaps Matthew's present use of the verb will help lead to its omission in 17:15 (cf. Mark 9:18).

In chiastic fashion, the trampling refers to the pigs, the turning and tearing to pieces to the dogs. Among the Jews, "dogs" and "pigs" stood for Gentiles (see *TDNT* 3. 1101-3; Str-B 1. 449-50). But among Jesus' disciples, who are the new people of God, "Gentiles" can lose the meaning "non-Jews" and take the meaning "nondisciples" (see 5:47; 6:7, 32; 18:17; Luke 12:30). By the same token "dogs" and "pigs" can shift from non-Jews to nondisciples, including falsely professing disciples.

"What is holy" represents sacrificial offerings, often called "holy" in the OT (see Exod 29:33-34; Lev 2:3; 22:10-16; Num 18:8-19; cf. *b. Ber.* 15a). One would no more toss dogs a piece of sacred meat from an animal sacrificed to God than he would throw valuable but inedible pearls in front of pigs. Not only did Jews abhor pigs (cf. Lev 11:7; Luke 15:15-16), but also dogs were generally detested. They roamed the streets scavenging for food and rarely became objects of affection in the ancient Middle East (see *TDNT* 3. 1101-3, and cf. 2 Pet 2:22).

See 1QS 9:17, 22; cf. 8:12. Because of a supposed incongruity in the parallel between "what is holy" and "your pearls," some think that τὸ ἅγιον came about through a translation of קְדָשָׁא, "ring," as though it was קַדְשָׁא, "holy." Originally, then, throwing pearls before pigs was hanging a string of pearls around a pig's snout (cf. Prov 11:22), just as a ring (presumably of expensive gold) is put in a dog's nose. But the parallel between pigs trampling pearls in the mire and dogs devouring the sacred flesh of sacrifices may have more congruity than a mistranslation of Aramaic has likelihood. In itself, of course, each figure in Matthew's text portrays a startling incongruity. But the force of the saying depends on a parallelism of incongruities, not on a parallel between a ring and pearls. Nothing in the context would lead us to suppose that the saying prohibits evangelism of Gentiles as "pigs" and "dogs."

7:7-8 (Luke 11:9-10) Matthew will insert οὖν at the beginning of the Golden Rule (v 12; cf. Luke 6:31). The insertion will imply that because God gives good gifts to those who ask him (vv 7-11), Jesus' disciples should do good to others. We deduce that Matthew does not bring in Jesus' teaching on prayer (vv 7-11), which belongs to an entirely different context in the tradition (see Luke 11:9-13), in order to teach about prayer himself. He has already treated that topic in 6:5-15. Rather, he imports these sayings to buttress the Golden Rule. Thus the center of gravity lies in the heavenly Father's giving, not in the disciples' asking; and the Golden Rule demands a Father-like graciousness which forestalls the judging prohibited at the start of this section (vv 1-5). The keeping of the Golden Rule shows true discipleship, in contrast with the actions of those false disciples—"pigs" and "dogs"—who turn on their fellow disciples by betraying them to persecutors (v 6; again cf. 24:10 [a distinctive saying], 49). In v 7 Matthew drops the introductory "and I say to you" (so Luke) in order to work the following importation more smoothly into his passage. Otherwise, vv 7-8 match Luke exactly and reflect the wisdom of beggars, who know that tenacity in asking brings favorable results.

7:9-11 (Luke 11:11-13) The maze of variants facing the textual critic of Luke 11:11 witnesses to the difficulty of the grammatical construction in the tradition behind Matt 7:9. In working out the wrinkles, Matthew begins by putting ἤ, a favorite of his (32,12), where the tradition had δέ. Cf. his twice putting ἤ for καί in 6:31 (cf. Luke 12:29). Luke's accusative τίνα, "which?" is awkward because of its initial position, which distances it from its noun πατέρα; so Matthew writes a nominative τίς, "who?" which stands on its own two feet. To keep τίς from modifying a noun (despite modern translations to the contrary), he delays the son's asking till later and inserts ἐστιν instead. This makes τίς the subject and ἄνθρωπος (a Mattheanism—35,17) the predicate nominative. ἄνθρωπος replaces πατέρα, which Matthew saves for God in agreement with his emphasizing divine Fatherhood. Now the phrase αἰτήσει ὁ υἱὸς αὐτοῦ ἄρτον comes in, introduced by ὅν. A simple question results—with an anacoluthon, to be sure, but easily understood: "Or who is (the) man from among you whom his son will ask for bread—he will not give him a stone, will he?"

But the tradition lacks references to bread and a stone (see Luke). Jesus spoke rather of a fish and a snake, of an egg and a scorpion. Matthew himself inserts bread and a stone in order to assimilate this passage to the Lord's Prayer, which stands close by in the tradition (see Luke 11:1-4). There God appears as the heavenly Father who gives bread to his children (6:11). So also in v 11b Matthew adds "your" to "Father" and puts "in heaven" where the tradition lacks the possessive and has "from heaven" (cf. his fondness for the heavenly Fatherhood of God [10,2], and the contrast between stones and bread in the narrative of Jesus' temptation—4:3). Because of the insertion of bread and a stone, Matthew stops with a fish and a snake (cf. the association of bread and fish in the feedings of the five thousand and four thousand). Omission of an egg and a scorpion leaves a couplet. All these sayings depend on a rough similarity in appearance between round, flat breadcakes and stones, between a fish and a snake, and (in the tradition) between an egg and the body of a scorpion.

Remaining differences between vv 9-11 and Luke's parallel are stylistic for the most part. Matthew lacks the unnecessary phrase "instead of a fish" and consistently puts the direct objects before the verbs and the indirect objects after the verbs. In Luke both kinds of objects occur bunched together, now before the verb, now after the verb. Similarly, Matthew's ὄντες differs only stylistically from Luke's ὑπάρχοντες (used by Matthew only three times, by Luke fifteen times).

More importantly, where Luke reads "the Holy Spirit" Matthew reads "good," with "gifts" understood from the preceding clause. Luke is usually suspected of substituting the Holy Spirit because he often stresses the gift of the Spirit in answer to prayer (see Acts 1:14; 2:1-4; 8:15; 9:11, 17). That emphasis may grow out of the tradition, however. Since the gift of the Spirit was prominent in the preaching of John the Baptist, a reference to it by Jesus should not prove surprising. Matthew has been revising the tradition heavily, and Luke usually sticks closer to his sources. It would be just like Matthew to assimilate the Holy Spirit to the good gifts in v 11a. He then satisfies his desire for close parallelism, generalizes the saying, and ties it to the goodness of God the Father as described in the latter parts of both chaps. 5 and 6.

That πονηροί usually describes nondisciples has led to the supposition that originally Jesus addressed the group of sayings in vv 9-11 to nondisciples. But the supposition has a weak base. Here πονηροί modifies the disciples *considered as human beings*. After all, giving good gifts to one's children represents a human quality, not a quality distinctive of Jesus' disciples.

7:12 (Luke 6:31) In v 12 Matthew reverts once again to the tradition of Jesus' sermon, where the Golden Rule follows commands to give to those who ask and not to refuse those who take (Luke 6:31). In the tradition, therefore, the Golden Rule has to do with charity and nonresistance. But Matthew relates it to the Father's giving good gifts as a pattern for Jesus' disciples to follow. καί is replaced by the typically Matthean οὖν (35,11). The replacement hardly refers to all the preceding parts of the sermon as they appear in the first gospel; for many of those parts, including all of chap. 6, do not deal with doing to others what a person wants done to himself. Rather, οὖν makes the Father's giving good gifts a reason for Jesus' disciples to treat others well. More particularly, in Matthew the Golden Rule requires giving good gifts to fellow disciples (vv 7-11) instead of judging them false (vv 1-5), let alone betraying them to persecution (v 6; see 8:27; 9:8; 13:44, 45, 52; 27:57 for other instances of ἄνθρωπος for disciples). Characteristically, Matthew adds πάντα . . . ὅσα (2,3) and ὑμεῖς (15,3). Neither is in Luke, both add emphasis, and ὑμεῖς makes a parallel with οἱ ἄνθρωποι. οὕτως καί and Luke's ὁμοίως are stylistic variants. Matthew has οὕτως thirty-two times, Luke twenty-one times; Matthew has ὁμοιώς only three times, Luke eleven times.

To the Golden Rule Matthew adds "For this is the law and the prophets" (not in Luke). His favorite diction comes forward in every word except the definite articles: γάρ (62-63,15), οὗτος . . . ἐστιν (12,0), νόμος (6,0), and προφῆται (19,6). This statement relates to another, later insertion that contains the imperatives of loving God and your neighbor: "On these two commandments hang the whole law and the prophets" (22:40). But since the Golden Rule covers only love toward other human beings, not love toward God, here Matthew does not use "whole." The interrelating of these passages through similar insertions shows that the positive form of the Golden Rule demands acts of love, not mere avoidance of harming others, as in a negative form ("Do not do to others what you would not have them do to you"). The reference to the law and the prophets indicates that the extended definition of surpassing righteousness, which began with Jesus' coming to fulfill the law and the prophets (5:17), has drawn to a close.

See *b. Šabb.* 31a for Rabbi Hillel's statement of the Golden Rule in a negative form almost a hundred years earlier than Jesus' positive statement of it. As in Matthew, Hillel made it a summation of the law. Did Matthew have Hillel's statement in mind, and add a reference to the prophets because of messianic fulfillment? For a convenient summary of the other main parallels, see V. P. Furnish, *The Love Command in the New Testament* (Nashville: Abingdon, 1972) 63. An earlier but non-Palestinian statement of the Golden Rule in positive as well as negative form appears in *Ep. Arist.* 207. Despite modern misunderstandings, the treatment of others just as one would like to be treated by them does not rest on egoism. It rests on a readiness to deny oneself in order to serve others in a way one would otherwise like to be served.

EXHORTATIONS TO OBEDIENCE
IN HEEDLESSNESS OF ANTINOMIAN FALSE PROPHETS
7:13-27 (3:10; 12:33-35; Luke 6:43-44, 46-49; 13:23-27)

The Sermon on the Mount concludes with a series of exhortations set in the framework of a contrast between the two ways of righteousness and lawlessness. For an expansive emphasis on this contrast, Matthew inserts material found elsewhere in the tradition. The narrow gate and constricted road contrast with the wide gate and broad road (vv 13-14). Hearing and doing Jesus' words contrast with hearing and not doing them and define the narrow way as hearing and doing, the broad way as hearing and not doing (vv 24-27). In between lies a warning not to heed the siren call to lawlessness of those false prophets whose use of the title "Lord" for Jesus contrasts with their disobedience to his teaching concerning the heavenly Father's will (vv 15-23). And the contrast between entrance into life and consignment to destruction at the last judgment overarches the whole.

7:13-14 (Luke 13:23-24) The expressions—"enter/-ing," "through the narrow gate," "many," and "few"—come with some revision from the tradition behind Luke. The thought of Matthew's statement concerning the broadness of the road leading to destruction is the converse of the need for effort to enter the narrow door in the tradition (so Luke). And though "will seek" in the tradition refers to a futile attempt, in conjunction with vv 7-8 it probably suggested the Mattheanism οἱ εὐρίσκοντες, "they who find" (7,8). Matthew's leading statement, "Enter through the narrow gate," corresponds to Luke fairly closely. In the rest of vv 13-14 Matthew writes freely in accord with his parallelistic style. The remaining clauses of v 13 match in order the clauses of v 14.

In the tradition, someone asks Jesus whether few will be saved. He responds that people should "strive to enter through the narrow door." Inside the door lies the banquet hall for the messianic feast of salvation. Many will try to enter but fail, initially not because the door is already closed, but because the door is too narrow for vast throngs to crowd through. In other words, few will be saved. Therefore make sure you are one of them, for after the few have entered and filled the hall to capacity the Lord will shut the door (see Luke). Matthew drops "strive" because in his version there are no throngs trying to crowd through a narrow door before the banquet hall fills up. And the door into a banquet hall becomes a gate into a city, presumably the city of God, since entrance implies salvation (cf. Isa 4:2-6; Rev 3:12; 21:1–22:5). But Matthew's gate is as narrow as the door in the tradition; and apparently it refers to a small, doorlike gate set within or beside the large city gate in order that known citizens might be allowed into the closed city at night and in times of danger (see E. F. F. Bishop, *Jesus of Palestine* [London: Lutterworth, 1955] 83-84). The big gates are shut! Hurry into the city of salvation by the one available way.

The narrowness of the small gate prevents the entrance of more than one person at a time and represents the strictures of the surpassing righteousness just taught by Jesus as a requirement for entering the kingdom. In the tradition the narrowness of the door has to do only with the fewness of the saved. In Matthew the broadness of the gate leading into the city of destruction (cf. "the gates of Hades" in 16:18, peculiar to this gospel) represents the easy way of lawlessness. According to the tradition, Jesus referred only to a door too narrow, as all doors are, for vast crowds to press through at once. The distinction between the large gate and the small gate set within or beside the large enables Matthew to draw a contrast between them. The contrast suits his importing the well-known doctrine of the two ways (see, e.g., Deut 11:26-28; 30:15-20; Ps 1:6; 119:29-30; 139:24; Jer 21:8; Wis 5:6-7; *Testament of Asher* 1-6; 1QS cols. 3-4: 2 Esdras 7; *Testament of Abraham* 11-13; *Didache* 1-6; *Barnabas* 18-20). Indeed, the very change from the original door to gates is due to the importation of this doctrine, for gates rather than doors relate to roadways. Matthew has an interest in ὁδός (9,2); cf. especially his inserting "the way of righteousness" in 21:32 (also 3:3; 22:16). Here the way of righteousness is the way of persecution, for τεθλιμμένη, "constricted, narrow," and its cognate θλῖψις, "tribulation," connote persecution (see 13:21; 24:9, 21, 29, and many passages elsewhere in the NT). Cf. persecution for the sake of righteousness in 5:10-12. Conversely, the broad way represents the antinomian course of least resistance. That one does not enter through a road, but through a gate, and that one would find a small gate less easily than a roadway confirm Matthew's insertion of the roadways in these sayings. They also confirm the originality of the single door, which has become two gates in Matthew.

By setting the two roadways alongside the two gates, Matthew shows that entrance into life at the last day requires travelling the narrow way—living the life of surpassing righteousness—in the present time. What is more, he implies that travelling the narrow road already constitutes an entering through the narrow gate; for after adopting the traditional aorist tense in the command to enter, he switches to the linear present in his descriptions of those who are entering and finding. In other words, we are to think not only of travelling a roadway *to* one or the other gate at the final judgment (with the result that the order gate–road makes a hysteron proteron due to Matthew's importation of roadways), but also of travelling a road and entering through a gate as independent figures, both of which stand for the present life of discipleship. Cf. Matthew's putting the present aspect of the kingdom alongside the future in 6:10-11, 13.

See *TDNT* 6. 923 for the use of πύλη in eschatological passages. Relatively flat country allowed broad roads easy to travel. But mountainous terrain constricted roads and made them hard to travel. Should we catch a hint of a steep ascent to the city of God, set on a mountain? On the textual question of the gate in vv 13 and 14, see the UBS and Metzger, *Textual Commentary* ad loc. "The gate" should probably be retained in both places. If not, the descriptions apply to the roadways. And since the one roadway parallels the narrow gate (textually unquestioned), the essential meaning stays the same. At the beginning of v 14, the UBS reads τί, "how!" instead of ὅτι, "because." Metzger argues in favor of τί that a scribe did not understand the unusual Semitic use of τί for מָה in the sense "how!" and therefore switched to ὅτι in the preceding verse. But such parallelism characterizes the style of Matthew himself, and in other respects vv 13bcd and 14 parallel each other exactly. Though τί has more textual support, the original texts of the great codices Sinaiticus and Vaticanus read ὅτι. And it can be argued the ὅτι is more difficult, and therefore more probably original, than τί. For ὅτι demands an unusually long sustaining of the governing clause "Enter . . ." (v 13a), whereas an exclamatory τί enables the reader to catch his breath and make a fresh start. If we are to read ὅτι, "because" relates to the command to enter the narrow gate, not to the immediately preceding statement that many enter through the wide gate.

7:15-23 (3:10; 12:33-35; Luke 6:43-44, 46; 13:25-27) Verses 15-23 concern false prophets whose confession of Jesus as Lord and whose use of that powerful name in exorcising demons and working miracles might deceive disciples into accepting their antinomian teaching and aping their antinomian behavior. Again Matthew revises the tradition freely in order to counteract those who would keep people from entering the narrow gate and taking the narrow way. The subsection opens with a leading statement that offers the key for explaining the following figure as a reference to false prophets (v 15). Verses 16-20 deal with the figure of fruits. Verses 21-23 portray the Lord's rejection of the false prophets at the last judgment as a pattern to be followed by disciples in the present.

In the sayings about fruits, v 16a introduces the figure. Verse 16b contains a negative couplet beginning with μήτι. Verse 17 has a positive couplet beginning οὕτως πᾶν δένδρον. Verse 18 has another negative couplet beginning with οὐ and matching the preceding positive couplet. Verse 19 contains another positive couplet beginning πᾶν δένδρον. For inclusio, v 20 repeats the statement that introduced the figure of fruit in v 16a. In the prediction of judgment against the false prophets, the mere confession of Jesus as Lord in the present (v 21a) stands in antithetic parallelism with doing the will of Jesus' heavenly Father (v 21b), and the mere appeal to Jesus as Lord at the future judgment (v 22) stands in antithetic parallelism with Jesus' rejection of those who work lawlessness (v 23). The parallels are designed to stress the warning against false prophets.

7:15 The opening warning comes from Matthew himself as a leading statement for what follows. The diction is of his liking. We may begin with προσέχετε (3,3), usually accompanied by ἀπό (3,2). The verb has appeared in another leading statement composed by Matthew earlier in the sermon (see 6:1). For "false prophets" see 24:11, 24, where Matthew doubles the single reference to such men in Mark 13:22. ἐνδύμασι occurs seven times in Matthew, six times as an insertion, but elsewhere in the NT only in Luke 12:23. Matthew also likes προβάτων (6,2). Sheep stand for the people of God. Here the donning of sheep's clothing represents the claim to follow

Jesus (cf. vv 21-22; 13:24-25, 38-39). At least sometimes prophets in Israel had worn a hairy mantle as a sign of their prophetic office (2 Kgs 1:8; Zech 13:4; cf. Matt 3:4). (We need not infer that Christian prophets followed the practice.) The falsity of the prophets here in view appears in their having the inward nature of ravenous wolves. Matthew will insert ἔσωθεν also in 23:27, 28 and ἁρπάζω, which is cognate to ἅρπαγες, in 11:12; 12:29; 13:19. The ravenousness of the wolves in sheep's clothing refers to the luxurious living of the false prophets at the expense of their followers and to other undue exercises of authority (Ezek 22:27; Zeph 3:3; John 10:12; Acts 20:28-30; *Didache* 11–13). Cf. 10:16 for sheep as disciples who preach and for wolves as nondisciples.

7:16-20 (3:10; 12:33-35; Luke 6:43-44) "By their fruits you will recognize them" goes back to the tradition of Jesus' sermon (Luke 6:44a; cf. Matt 12:33c). The traditional version, "For each tree is known by its own fruit," refers to the generality of professing disciples. It follows on the heels of the passage regarding a speck and a plank, with which it is linked by γάρ twice in succession. In Matt 12:33c, "For a tree is known by its fruit" relates to the Pharisees' unpardonable sin of speaking against the Holy Spirit. Here in 7:16a, Matthew applies the principle to false prophets in the church. Unlike both parallels, Matthew puts ἀπό in place of ἐκ for "by," a stylistic variation for the sake of distinguishing between his two uses of the saying. The singular of fruit becomes the plural, and "its own" (so Luke) becomes "their." The parallel in 12:33c lacks a possessive. "Them" is added because here the saying applies to the false prophets just mentioned. In the parallels the saying speaks only of a tree; the application of the figure requires a second step. The verb changes from a gnomic present, regarding the way a tree is known, to the future tense; for Matthew has in mind the entrance of false prophets into the church at a time future to Jesus. The simple verb of knowing, γινώσκεται, changes to the stronger verb ἐπιγνώσεσθε because of the need for personally recognizing the false prophets so as to steer clear of them. See also 7:20; 11:27 (bis); 14:35; 17:12, always of personal recognition and, with the sole exception of 14:35, by way of insertion. Matthew drops γάρ (so Luke and 12:33c) because he is not giving a reason for wariness of false prophets, but a way of recognizing them.

The rest of v 16 has a parallel only in Luke 6:44b. Matthew changes the original declarative statement into a question inviting reflection (as in 6:25-26, 30) and demanding a negative answer. Hence, the negative changes from οὐδέ to μήτι. συλλέγουσιν stays, but Matthew draws it forward in order that readers may supply it in the next clause as a replacement for τρυγῶσιν (so Luke). For a second and third time in the verse Matthew puts ἀπό for ἐξ/ἐκ. Thus the verse attains a tightly knit unity. After ἀκανθῶν, "thornbushes," Matthew puts τριβόλων, "thistles." Luke has βάτου, "a briarbush." Perhaps Matthew wants parallelism in the -ων endings or conformity to the OT (see Gen 3:18, quoted in Heb 6:8; cf. Hos 10:8). In opposition to Luke, grapes come first and figs second, perhaps because Matthew thinks of the thornbushes as a figure for wild grapevines and of the thistles as standing for fig trees of poor quality. Cf. Jas 3:12. In συλλέγουσιν the impersonal third plural is an Aramaism.

129

Since v 19 will come straight out of 3:10b, Matthew begins to construct v 17—a parallel to v 19—by putting 3:10b, "every tree that does not produce good fruit," in the positive form, "every good tree bears good fruits." The change to the plural "fruits" occurs also in the second clause and conforms to v 16. οὕτως typifies Matthew's diction (18,5). The addition of ἀγαθόν, "good," to "tree" stresses the nature of the tree as the reason for the quality of fruits yielded. The synonymous καλούς describes the fruits and agrees with 3:10b (and 7:19) except for its plural number.

Now Matthew leaves 3:10b and constructs v 17b as an opposite to v 17a: the generic article τό replaces πᾶν; a bad tree replaces the good tree; bearing bad fruits replaces bearing good fruits. σαπρόν describes the tree as "bad." πονηρούς describes the fruits as "bad" (contrast 12:33; Luke 6:43). Thus Matthew uses synonyms for the sake of a parallel with the synonyms describing the same nouns as "good" in the first part of the verse.

Verse 18 has its parallel in Luke 6:43. The couplets in both begin οὐ . . . οὐδέ, and the thoughts expressed match. But Matthew changes the diction so as to make the saying an antithetic parallel to the preceding saying in v 17. "Good tree" and "bad tree," "bad fruit" and "good fruit," and ποιεῖν, "to bear" (bis), all come from v 17. As will happen in 12:34, the insertion of δύναται (13,0) underscores the evil nature of antinomian teachers: they have lost the capacity to do good.

See the UBS and Metzger, *Textual Commentary* ad loc., against the reading ἐνεγκεῖν (bis). Cf. Black, *Aramaic Approach* 138, for ποιεῖν in the horticultural sense "yield, bear."

The warning that every tree not bearing fruit is cut down and thrown in the fire (v 19) comes from the preaching of John the Baptist (3:10b; cf. Luke 3:9b) and carries on Matthew's attack against antinomianism and assimilation of the messages of John the Baptist and Jesus to each other (see "John the Baptist parallel Jesus" in the Topical Index). Here the saying applies to the eternal judgment of false prophets. Temporarily, Matthew reverts to the original singular in the metaphor of good fruit lest he mar the correspondence between the messages of John and Jesus. Only the οὖν of 3:10b drops out, for here it has lost its former reference to the lying of the axe at the root of the trees. See further the comments on 3:10b.

Matthew concludes the little discussion of fruits by repeating the statement in v 16a. Cf. 5:3b with 5:10b; 19:30 with 20:16; 24:42 with 25:13. ἄρα γε introduces this concluding repetition (cf. 17:26), and the repetition itself not only reinforces the point, but also sustains the motif of false prophets, whose fruits make them recognizable. ἄρα is distinctive several times in this gospel (4,1).

7:21 *(Luke 6:46)* Matthew starts the prediction of the false prophets' final judgment with a paraphrase of the sermonic saying behind Luke 6:46 ("And why do you call me, 'Lord, Lord,' and do not do the things that I say?"). In the tradition, Jesus addresses the question to professing disciples in general, and the parable of the two foundations follows immediately. Matthew transforms the question into a flat denial of entrance into the kingdom, applies the statement to the false prophets in particular, and puts it in the framework of the last judgment, described in vv 22-23. These verses lie between "Lord, Lord . . ." and the parable of the two foundations and have their parallel back in Luke 13:25-27 (cf. Matt 7:15-23).

In v 21, "everyone" comes up from material paralleled later in Luke 13:27, where we read of "all" the evildoers. The Mattheanism λέγων (61,23) displaces καλεῖτε for a contrast between saying and doing. The same distinctive contrast will appear again in 23:3. Cf. the contrast between teaching and doing in 5:19, also peculiar to Matthew. "Lord, Lord" matches Luke's parallel (cf. 25:11; Pss 109[108]:21; 141[140]:8). Since this address to Jesus is spoken at the last judgment here and in the next verse, κύριε carries a stronger implication of deity than in Luke, where the term may be taken as a respectful address (like "Sir") to a teacher. "Will enter" echoes v 13, where it occurred twice. "Kingdom of heaven" is a well-known Mattheanism (25,7). The whole expression "will enter the kingdom of heaven" is inserted also in 5:20; 18:3; 23:13 (bis). It has a synoptic parallel only in 19:23, 24. Matthew builds the contrastive "but he who does the will of my Father who is in heaven" out of ποιεῖτε (so Luke), which has appeared five times in the immediately preceding verses about fruit bearing and occurs without parallel often in the first gospel (19,19), and out of two favorite expressions, "will of (the Father)" (3,1) and "the Father in heaven" (10,2). The latter correspond to Luke's "the things that I say." For Matthew, then, the will of the heavenly Father appears in the things Jesus says. For the first time in Matthew "my," referring to Jesus, modifies the Father in heaven, perhaps because in the next two verses Jesus will appear as the Father's authorized representative at the judgment (cf. Matthew's Christology of Jesus as υἱὸς θεοῦ—4,2).

Matthew's desire to contrast saying and doing eliminates the need for explaining λέγων as an overly literal translation of an original אמר, for which Luke has an idiomatic καλεῖτε. Of course, the Semitic use of "say" for "call, name" may explain how Matthew was able to change from the verb of calling in the Greek tradition. For doing the will of the Father in heaven, cf. m. 'Abot 5:22.

7:22-23 (Luke 13:25-27) Matthew now returns to the continuation of the parable concerning the narrow door. The intervening verses obscure the connection with what became the narrow gate. The characteristic addition of πολλοί (23,1) at the beginning of v 22 shows the seriousness of the threat posed by false prophets in the church. ἐροῦσιν corresponds to ἐρεῖ a little later in the tradition (Luke 13:27) and suits Matthew's liking for forms of εἴρω (18,9). "On that day," like "in those days," gets its referent from the context (see 3:1; 13:1; 22:23; 24:19, 38). Here it refers to the day of judgment, as often in eschatological passages (see TDNT 2. 945ff.). "Lord" appears in the tradition, but Matthew doubles it for a parallel with his preceding verse and for emphasis—even in the mouth of false prophets—on Jesus' deity. The eating and drinking with Jesus the houseowner by people in general and his teaching in their streets (so the tradition behind Luke) become in Matthew the false prophets' prophesying, exorcising demons, and doing miracles in Jesus' name "Lord" (cf. 24:24). In other words, Matthew retains the tripartness of the action but makes changes to fit the false prophets. ὄνομα occurs with distinctive frequency in his gospel (9,5). Since elsewhere the expression "in the name of" regularly takes a preposition in Greek and always does so elsewhere in Matthew (see 10:41 [bis], 42; 18:5, 20; 21:9; 23:39; 24:5; 28:19), the simple dative of ὀνόματι shows that Matthew here conforms Jesus' words to God's Word concerning false prophets in Jer 14:14; 27:15(34:12) LXX. Matthew will insert references to driving out demons also in 10:8; 17:18, and will insert δυνάμεις also in 11:23. πολλάς is a favorite of his (23,1).

At the beginning of v 23 Matthew inserts his beloved τότε (66,17). ὁμολογήσω then substitutes for ἐρεῖ (so Luke). Matthew has just used ἐρουσιν at the start of v 22 and wants a counterpart to 10:32, where ὁμολογήσω will occur for Jesus' acknowledging true disciples at the last judgment (cf. the insertion of this verb in 14:7). λέγων drops out because of its insertion in v 21. "To you" becomes "to them" because of Matthew's focus on false prophets. Addition of a recitative ὅτι before direct quotation of the judgmental sentence makes up for the omission of λέγων. "I do not know" becomes "I never knew" because emphasis falls on falsity of ministry in the past rather than on strangeness to Christ at the last judgment. That emphasis, in turn, derives from Matthew's purpose of persuading Christians to reject the false prophets now just as Christ will do then. Here, "knowing" means regarding as one's own as, e.g., in 25:12; Amos 3:2; 1 Cor 8:3; Gal 4:9; 2 Tim 2:19. Matthew is fond of οὐδέποτε (5,0) and γινώσκω (8,2). He drops πόθεν, "from where," because for him the point does not lie in unknown origin, but in the lawless teaching and conduct of the false prophets.

"Depart from me, you who produce lawlessness" comes from Ps 6:9a(8a). But Matthew omits "all" (so Luke in accord with the psalm), because he has already drawn it up to the head of the paragraph (v 21, in the singular, "everyone"). His text of the address reads in agreement with the LXX: οἱ ἐργαζόμενοι τὴν ἀνομίαν. (Luke hellenizes with ἐργάται ἀδικίας, "you workers of unrighteousness.") But Matthew does *not* follow the LXX in the command ἀποχωρεῖτε ἀπ' ἐμοῦ; the LXX, followed by Luke, has ἀπόστητε ἀπ' ἐμοῦ πάντες. Therefore Matthew's agreement with the LXX in the final phrase, particularly in ἀνομίαν, has significance. The word appears four times in Matthew (7:23; 13:41; 23:28; 24:12), never in the other gospels. The first evangelist is striking against antinomians, here against their leaders the false prophets. The law which the false prophets disregard is the will of the heavenly Father as taught by Jesus (5:17–7:12).

Cf. Jer 14:14-15; 27:14-15; Mark 9:38-40; Acts 19:13-17; Phil 1:15, 17; Jas 5:14-15. The ease with which Mark 9:38-40; Luke 9:49-50 can be taken to contradict the present passage and encourage laxity toward false prophets may have led Matthew to omit it. In fact, however, the present passage deals with those who use Jesus' name "Lord" both in exorcisms and miracle working *and also in their confession of faith*, whereas in Mark 9:38-40 Jesus talks about the impossibility of using his name in exorcisms and miracle working *while otherwise denying him* (cf. Acts 19:13-17). The question of bad conduct and erroneous teaching does not arise in Mark.

The identification of the false prophets in Matthew with Hellenistic libertines seems doubtful. The argument from their appeal to charismatic activities as a substitute for good works fails to carry conviction. Acts supplies evidence for charismatic activity by relatively un-Hellenistic Jewish Christians, too (cf. 1 Cor 1:22). And we have no indication in Matthew that at the time the false prophets point to their charismatic activities they yet know the charge of lawlessness. Therefore it is not a matter of attempted substitution.

Also, the antinomianism of the false prophets is not to be identified with Paul's denial of the Mosaic law as a way of salvation. Rather, the antinomianism contrasts with strictures in Jesus' teaching of the law (5:17–7:12). Like Matthew, Paul writes about "the law of Christ" (1 Cor 9:21; Gal 6:2), the fulfillment of "the righteous requirement of the law" (Rom 8:4), and the centrality of the command to love (Gal 5:13-14; cf. Matt 24:12). And like Paul, Matthew shows that undeserved grace lies at the base of salvation (20:1-16, unique to his gospel).

Since the false prophets seem to be associated with the scribes and Pharisees, who are also characterized as antinomian because their teaching and conduct fall short of Christ's law (5:19-20), we might identify the false prophets as Jews or Gentiles who Judaized their Christianity in order to escape persecution. From Matthew's standpoint, Jewish legalism in the church amounts to antinomianism. It would be going too far to think that Matthew puts staid Christian scribes in place of prophets who work miracles and exorcise demons, for elsewhere he portrays Jesus as a model both for working miracles and for exorcising demons (see 4:23-24 and chaps. 8–10).

7:24-25 (Luke 6:47-48) The Sermon on the Mount now closes with the parable of the two foundations (though Matthew does not call it a parable). Cf. the parabolic ending of the discourse in chap. 18. In closing with this parable, Matthew comes back to the tradition of Jesus' sermon, where it immediately follows the question "And why do you call me, 'Lord, Lord,' and do not practice the things that I say?" (Luke 6:46). He characteristically inserts οὖν (35,11) in order to make the lesson of the parable flow logically from the preceding description of the judgment of false prophets. The false prophets *say* "Lord, Lord" but do not practice the will of Jesus' Father in heaven. As a result, they will not stand in the judgment. The disciples of Jesus should therefore avoid the corresponding sin of *hearing* but not doing his words concerning the Father's will. Otherwise they, too, will fall under judgment. The linkage by means of οὖν makes clear that the collapse of the house built on sand refers to condemnation at the last judgment.

Matthew omits "he who comes to me" because he regards ὁ ἐρχόμενος as a sacrosanct title for the Messiah (see 3:11; 11:3; 21:9; 23:39 with comments). With the coming to Jesus out of the picture, stress falls entirely on hearing and doing his words. The omission also enables Matthew to avoid the anacoluthon of a nominative absolute (so Luke) in favor of a smoother sentence with a dependent clause introduced by ὅστις, a Mattheanism (23,5). This form of the relative pronoun stresses type rather than individual identity. Here it refers to types characterized by hearing and doing and by hearing but not doing. The escalation of the participles "hearing" and "doing" to the verbs "hears" and "does" increases emphasis on hearing and doing. In both Matthew and Luke μου has an emphatic position ahead of λόγους. Thus a stress falls on Jesus' words as the standard of final judgment. Matthew intensifies the stress by adding τούτους, "these." A particular reference to the Sermon on the Mount results (cf. 19:1; 26:1).

Luke's "I will show you what he is like" represents rabbinic style: "I will relate a parable to you. . . . It is like . . ." (see Jeremias, *Parables* 100-2, who prefers the translation, "It is the case with . . . as with . . ."). Matthew's characteristic change to ὁμοιωθήσεται, "will be like" (2,3), is also rabbinic in style and helps smooth out the original anacoluthon. Furthermore, it sharpens the reference to the last judgment, for now the future tense does not refer to Jesus' teaching ("I will show you in this parable"), but to the person in the parable ("At the last judgment everyone . . . will be like"). So also v 26 and 25:1.

Matthew adds φρονίμῳ. It connotes prudence of action and typifies his diction (2,4). ἀνθρώπῳ changes to ἀνδρί, "man" in contrast with "woman," because the additions of "wise" and "foolish" anticipate the parable of the ten virgins, five "wise" and five "foolish" (25:1-13, the only other passage with the future of ὁμοιόω). The wise man corresponds to the five wise virgins, the foolish man to the five foolish virgins. On the greater suitability of ἀνδρί for the male as a counterpart to the female, see especially 14:21; 15:38.

In referring to the building of a house Matthew does not begin a new sentence, as Luke does, but continues with another ὅστις-clause. Doing so typifies his parallelistic style and special diction (23,5). Insertion of αὐτοῦ in an emphatic position before τὴν οἰκίαν makes for a clearer contrast with the fool's house and anticipates μου in the later, unique reference to Jesus' church, which he will "build on this rock" (16:18). Indeed, Matthew skips over references to digging, going deep, and laying a foundation and goes immediately to "on the rock." He will then repeat the phrase for emphasis (v 25, different from Luke). The foundational rock represents Jesus' teaching of the law, then, and the wise man's building on it represents true disciples' obedience to that teaching. Cf. Sir 22:16-18.

Matthew inserts καταβαίνω five times. Some have thought that Luke's reference to excavation represents adaptation to a Hellenistic technique of building unusual in Palestine, and that the flooding river in Luke represents an adaptation of flash floods in Palestinian wadis to extra-Palestinian topography and weather. But in Palestine the Jordan River flooded, and the infrequency of excavation enabled Jesus to make a point of emphasis out of the technique. We have already noted reasons for changes by Matthew. The reference to excavation in a rabbinic parable recorded in *Yal.* 1. 766 (Num 23:9) shows that Luke's version need not represent a Hellenistic alteration. Cf. Prov 1:33.

Verse 25 shows that though Matthew does not have very much interest in the process of building (he has just omitted the particulars of that), he has great interest in the impregnability of the house on the rock. This corresponds to the impregnability of the church on the rock (see 16:18 again). To dramatize that impregnability, he details a storm instead of contenting himself with a passing reference to a flooding river (so the tradition, reflected by Luke). Just as in Luke the three details of digging, going deep, and laying a foundation follow a general statement about building, Matthew works up to a general statement about the testing of the house with the three details of rain, rivers, and winds. There is no rain or winds in Luke, but only an overflowing river near the house. In Matthew a cloud bursts, flash floods race down the usually dry ravines—hence the plural of rivers in place of Luke's singular—and winds blow fiercely during the storm. A statement that the house did not fall climaxes Matthew's impressive list of parallel statements beginning with καί. "Could not shake it" (so Luke) becomes "it did not fall" for an antithetic parallel with the fall of the next house. The use of ἔπεσεν (a Mattheanism—5,3) leads to changing the preceding verb from προσέρηξεν, "burst on," to προσέπεσαν, "fell on." This produces wordplay and fits Matthew's picture of flash floods tumbling down steep ravines instead of a single river bursting its banks.

The reason for the resistance of the house to the storm escalates from a mere prepositional phrase (διά + an articular infinitive in Luke) to a full-scale clause beginning with γάρ, a favorite of Matthew (62-63,15). Furthermore, the general reference to being well built is replaced by a specific, second reference to being founded on a rock (cf. 16:18 again). Finally the matter of the foundation has come into view, but Matthew transmutes θεμέλιον (so Luke) to its verbal form and puts that in the pluperfect tense (τεθεμελίωτο) for a final emphasis on impregnability. And no longer is the foundation *put* on a rock (so Luke). Being founded on a rock means that the foundation *is* a rock, as in 16:18. Thus the obedient disciple will be as impregnable in the day of judgment as the whole church will be to the gates of Hades.

7:26-27 (Luke 6:49) For a parallel with the preceding, the second half of the parable opens with a yielding of δέ, which is usually adversative in Matthew, to καί and with a typical addition of πᾶς (63,25-26; cf. v 24). But not as in the preceding, where he escalated participles to verbs, Matthew here retains the participles of hearing and not doing. Emphasis must not fall on *that* kind of response to Jesus' teaching! On the other hand, he repeats the earlier references to Jesus' words (not in Luke here), including τούτους, which he inserted before. Repetition of the distinctive "will be like a man" once again intimates the last judgment. A typical insertion of μωρῷ (3,3-4) makes a contrast with φρονίμῳ and completes the anticipation of the wise and foolish virgins.

For the sake of full parallelism, Matthew continues according to the form of the first half of the parable. "Ground" gives way to "sand." Matthew has switched from a flooding river to a cloudburst and here has in mind loose soil washed down by previous flash floods into a concourse of steep ravines. The stupidity of building there exceeds even the stupidity of building without a foundation on a riverbank. And the alluvial sand makes an even more striking picture of instability, contrasting with the impregnability of the house on the rock. Since the rock *was* the foundation in Matthew's version of the wise man's house, mere mention of the sand makes unnecessary, and even inappropriate, the traditional phrase "without a foundation" (so Luke). It therefore drops out. But in agreement with the first half of the parable and against Luke's short statement, Matthew fully describes the storm that results in a flash flood. The fullness and doubling of the description underscore the warning of judgment to come.

We read "beat on" instead of "fell on." The verbs parallel each other in that they both begin with προσ-. But the second differs in its main part, probably in anticipation of a different result. "And immediately it fell together [i.e., collapsed]" gives way to "and it fell," as in the first half of the parable except for the omission of "not." Cf. Prov 14:11. In the last clause of v 27 Matthew stops rewriting the second half to match the first: "and its fall was great" hardly corresponds to "for it was founded on the rock." Earlier he omitted that the second house had no foundation at all, not even a foundation on easily eroded soil (so Luke). But as in the tradition, his refusal to say that the second house was founded on sand (cf. vv 25-26) shows that sand hardly qualifies to be a foundation.

Instead of giving a reason for the fall of the second house (as v 25 gives the reason why the first house did not fall), Matthew emphasizes the disaster (so also Luke). But because he has just referred to "that house," he omits the expression here (contrast Luke); and because he has avoided references to the bursting of banks by a flooding river, he switches from ῥῆγμα, "bursting," to πτῶσις, "fall." The greatness of the fall consists in the completeness of the destruction. Thus the parable ends with a sober warning. The presently secure antinomians, whose careless conduct keeps them from persecution, are headed for final doom. This contrasts with the ultimate security of true disciples, who are persecuted because of their obedience to the law of Christ.

A TRANSITIONAL FORMULA
CONCLUDING THE FIRST "BOOK" OF JESUS' LAW
7:28-29

7:28-29 (Mark 1:21-22; Luke 4:32; 7:1) Verses 28-29 consist of a closing comment about the Sermon on the Mount. This comment forms a bridge from the sermon to the following narrative. Cf. 11:1; 13:53; 19:1; 26:1, all at the conclusions of the five great discourses in Matthew (cf. concluding formulas in Num 16:31; Deut 32:45; Jer 26:8). At first, Luke 7:1a provides a parallel: "when he completed all his words in the hearing of the people." Matthew rewords the statement. He draws καὶ ἐγένετο, a Semitism occurring in Matthew only in these concluding formulas, from the last clause in the tradition of the preceding parable, where he omitted it in his revision (v 27; cf. Luke 6:49b). Instead of ἐπειδή, which is probably a Lukanism, we read the more usual ὅτε. ἐπλήρωσεν becomes ἐτέλεσεν (5,2) in order that πληρόω might be reserved for the notion of fulfillment (with the understandable exception of literal filling in 13:48; 23:32). Characteristically, Matthew inserts the name of Jesus to clarify the subject (80,12). And instead of "all his words" we read "these words," which echoes vv 24 and 26.

Now Matthew goes back to Mark's narrative at the point where he left it in 4:22. He takes over the statement regarding the people's amazement at Jesus' teaching (Mark 1:21-22; Luke 4:31-32). As often, he inserts "the crowds" (17,1). The insertion identifies the disciples who went up the mountain to Jesus and heard his teaching there (5:1b-2) with the crowds mentioned previously (4:25–5:1a). And in order to identify the crowds as those who listened to the Sermon on the Mount rather than as the audience at the synagogue in Capernaum, Matthew omits Mark's references to Jesus' entering Capernaum and the synagogue. Cf. Mark 11:18.

The formula closes with a reference to Jesus' teaching "as one who had authority, and not as their scribes," i.e., not as the trained rabbis, who constantly quoted past scribal authorities. The contrast does not lie between Jesus and mere village teachers, but between Jesus and all other rabbis, including the greatest of them. He taught in his own name (in 5:21-48 "but *I* say to you . . ." follows quotations, not of mere rabbinic tradition, but of the OT itself) and performed miracles as an accompaniment to his teaching (chaps. 8–9). Because Matthew is interested in Jesus' teaching and authority, he takes over Mark's statement about those topics with only one change. "Scribes" gains the modifier "their" in order to distinguish Jewish scribes from the Christian scribes mentioned in 8:19 (with 8:21); 13:52; 23:34. Cf. the addition of "their" to "cities" in 11:1 and to "synagogues" in 9:35; 10:17; 12:9; 13:54, and of "your," referring to the scribes and Pharisees, to "synagogues" in 23:34. Only 4:23 has a synoptic parallel in this respect.

THE AUTHORITY OF JESUS
8:1–9:34

In 8:1–9:34 Matthew gathers together narrative material that is scattered in Mark and Luke. It demonstrates the authority of Jesus in his deeds in addition to the authority evident in his words. The theme grows out of the conclusion to the Sermon on the Mount (7:28-29). Most of the material deals with miracles. Yet Matthew regularly abbreviates the narrative in order to let Jesus' authoritative words stand out in bold relief. The accounts tend to reduce to didactic conversations, then, with the result that didactic conversations lacking the framework of a miracle (8:18-22; 9:9-17) seem not to intrude.

The number of miracles gathered by Matthew into these chapters comes to ten if we count only those that are particularized: (1) the healing of the leper (8:1-4); (2) the healing of a centurion's paralyzed servant (8:5-13); (3) the healing of Peter's mother-in-law (8:14-15); (4) the stilling of the storm (8:23-27); (5) the deliverance of the two Gadarene demoniacs (8:28-34); (6) the healing of a paralytic carried by four (9:1-8); (7) the healing of the woman with a flow of blood (9:20-22); (8) the raising of the daughter of a synagogue ruler (9:18-19, 23-26); (9) the healing of two blind men (9:27-31); and (10) the healing of a dumb man (9:32-34). The probability that Matthew has combined two exorcisms into one and two healings of blind men into one may lend significance to the number ten. We have seen that he portrays Jesus as the greater Moses in the Sermon on the Mount. The very first statement in chap. 8 alludes to Moses again, and the first miracle climaxes on a note concerning Mosaic legislation. It is possible, then, that Matthew constructs these chapters as a counterpart to the narrative in Exodus concerning Moses' ten miracles in Egypt. If so, we may note that in Exodus Moses' legislation followed the deliverance of God's people and that by reversing the order in his gospel Matthew shows he is interested mainly in Jesus' authoritative words. The emphasis on them even in accounts of miracles agrees with this interest and with the Mosaically colored portrait in general, for—despite all his miracles—Moses appears in the OT primarily as a man of words.

On the other hand, a number of considerations cast doubt on the hypothesis that Matthew intended a parallel between the miracles in chaps. 8–9 and Moses' miracles in Egypt. His emphasizing Jesus' words rather than the miracles themselves and his including purely didactic materials of some length (8:18-22; 9:9-17) point away from the hypothesis. The many miracles mentioned in 8:16 but not particularized in chaps. 8–9 suggest that Matthew had no interest in the number of miracles individually described. Furthermore, the judgmental nature of Moses' miracles, called "plagues," does not correspond to the kinds of miracles (mainly healings and exorcisms) Jesus performed. Neither are there convincing individual correspondences. Therefore we must remain skeptical of the interpretation.

In 8:16-22 a summary, a quotation of Isa 53:4, and an account of two conversations about discipleship divide the first three miracles from the second three. In 9:9-17 the story of Matthew's becoming a disciple and instructions on fasting divide the second three miracles from the last four. Together, these interruptions point up Matthew's interlacing the dominant motif of Jesus' authority with other motifs. This interlacing is evident also within the accounts of the miracles. Attempts to assign different themes to the several groupings of miracles break down. Since the healing of the woman with a flow of blood and the raising of a synagogue ruler's daughter together form a single story, the last group of miracles is made up of three stories just as each of the first two groups has three stories.

JESUS' AUTHORITY
IN FULFILLING THE LAW OF LEPROSY
8:1-4 (Mark 1:40-45; Luke 5:12-16)

Matthew omits the exorcism of a demon in the synagogue at Capernaum— the first of Jesus' powerful acts recorded in the other two synoptics (Mark 1:21-28; Luke 4:31-37)—and skips over the healing of Peter's mother-in-law, second in the gospels of Mark and Luke. The healing of Peter's mother-in-law will yet appear in Matthew, and exorcisms will follow. Matthew wants a healing that shows Jesus' fulfilling the law immediately after the Sermon on the Mount, which carries that theme. Therefore the story of the leper comes first.

8:1 The story starts with a statement lacking in Mark and Luke but reminiscent of repeated statements concerning Moses' descent from Mount Sinai: "And when he came down from the mountain" (cf. Exod 19:14; 32:1, 15; 34:29). The next statement, also lacking in Mark and Luke, echoes

138

4:25 and again casts the crowds in the role of Jesus' disciples: "large crowds followed him." This repeated, peculiar, and deliberately unrealistic portrayal of the crowds as disciples implies that Matthew sees in them a foretaste of the disciples who will come from all nations (28:19). Elsewhere, too, he shows special fondness for καταβάντος (5,0), ὄρους (6,1), ἠκολούθησαν (8,0), ὄχλοι (17,1), and πολλοί (23,1).

8:2 (Mark 1:40; Luke 5:12) The emphatic ἰδού (not in Mark) typifies Matthew's style (34,9). Yet Luke has it, too. In conjunction with other agreements between Matthew and Luke against Mark—agreements that sometimes are typical of Matthew but not Luke—this one suggests that Luke knew Matthew as well as Mark. In place of Mark's ἔρχεται πρός for the leper's approaching Jesus, Matthew puts προσελθών (38,6). And where Mark has "beseeching him and falling on his knees," Matthew uses his favorite προσεκύνει, "was worshipping" (6,5). As a result, "him" (i.e., Jesus) becomes the object of worship rather than the object of "saying" (as in Mark). Thus Matthew stresses that Jesus is worthy of worship. Lest his readers fail to notice this, he characteristically inserts "Lord" (34,15) at the beginning of the leper's appeal to Jesus. In having this address, Luke agrees with Matthew again.

"Leprosy" may mean, not Hansen's disease, but other skin diseases (see J. Wilkinson in *SJT* 31 [1978] 153-66 and E. V. Hulse in *PEQ* 107 [1975] 87-105). "Lepers" suffered ostracism from the rest of society (Leviticus 13–14).

8:3 (Mark 1:41-43; Luke 5:13) Mark's reference to Jesus' compassion drops out, somewhat surprisingly since elsewhere Matthew retains such references and writes σπλαγχνίζομαι, "have compassion," five times. Yet he often omits other emotions of Jesus. Perhaps his text of Mark contained a reference to anger (ὀργισθείς, so some representatives of the Western family), which he found easier to omit than a reference to compassion would have been. Whatever word he read in Mark, Matthew strips it away in order to keep attention solely on Jesus' authority (cf. the omission of the angry warning in the next verse). The description of Jesus' stretching out his hand and touching the leper stays. But αὐτοῦ moves to a position after ἥψατο, where it becomes the object of the verb ("he touched him") rather than a modifier of χεῖρα ("his hand"). This change emphasizes that it is a leper whom Jesus touched. Consonant with this emphasis, Mark's "and he says to him" becomes the participle λέγων (a Mattheanism—61,23). Thus the center of gravity is located in Jesus' touching the leper, to which stretching out the hand and speaking to the leper are subordinated. In all of this Luke again agrees with Matthew.

As Jesus taught by his own authority, "not as the scribes" (7:29), so he does not even ascribe the miracle to God his Father, but performs it by his own authority: "I will; be cleansed." Matthew omits the immediate going away of the leprosy (so Mark and Luke) and retains only the cleansing. In Matthew it is not the leper who is cleansed (as in Mark); rather, the leprosy is cleansed. To keep the emphasis on this cleansing, Matthew (seconded by Luke) omits the leper's being sent away with a severe warning (so Mark). As a result, the following prohibition of publicity lacks emphasis.

139

8:4 (Mark 1:44-45; Luke 5:14-16) The distinctive naming of Jesus avoids confusion between him and the leper (cf. 7:28). The dropping of Mark's μηδέν at the same time μηδενί is retained avoids two forms of the same word in succession (so also Luke). "The gift" is inserted (cf. distinctive occurrences of the phrase "offer the gift[s]" also in 2:11; 5:23, 24 [bis]). Mark's and Luke's "for your cleansing" is omitted because in Matthew Jesus cleansed the leprosy immediately. The other synoptists write only that the leprosy "went away"; i.e., in Mark and Luke the cleansing takes place in two steps, the physical departure of the leprosy and the ceremonial cleansing of a priestly pronouncement followed by the prescribed offering (see Leviticus 14). But in Matthew the authoritative word of Jesus "Be clean!" leaves no more cleansing to be done. The offering of the gift no longer arises out of a need for further cleansing by a priest in the Temple, but solely from Jesus' command, which agrees with the Mosaic law (cf. 5:17).

Previously we have seen that Jesus' fulfilling the law through teaching does not mean mere repetition. Rather, it consists in carrying out the tendencies of the law to their divinely appointed ends (see the comments on 5:21-48). So here Jesus' touching the leper and cleansing his leprosy seem at first to contradict the Mosaic prohibition against touching a leper (see Lev 5:3; 13:1ff.). In fact, the healing touch carries out the intention in the law to provide cleansing for lepers. The offering of the gift is not needed, then, except to bear witness to Jesus' miracle as a fulfillment of that intention. Since "priest" is singular, the "them" to whom witness is borne are people in general. By omitting the following proclamation and its results (cf. Mark and Luke), Matthew ends the story on the point of Jesus' authority in fulfilling the law. The omission also avoids any semblance of a discrepancy between Jesus' staying in lonely places, yet entering Capernaum.

The command to secrecy does not fit well the seeming presence of large crowds (v 1). But the large crowds are lacking in Mark, and Matthew imports the story without attention to the command. The difficulty is artificial in that his point lies elsewhere. The command that the leper show himself to a priest may imply the nearness of the Temple (cf. Luke 4:44). We should probably take the phrase "as a testimony to them" with the whole of the preceding command rather than with any of the particular expressions "show yourself," "offer the gift," or "Moses commanded." The ex-leper's act of obedience was supposed to be the testimony in lieu of a spoken report. αὐτοῖς might be translated "against them," as in Mark 6:11; Luke 9:5 (see also Jas 5:3). But the present context does not give good indication of a negative connotation, and elsewhere in Matthew the phrase εἰς μαρτύριον αὐτοῖς, "for a witness to them," seems to carry a good connotation (see 10:18; 24:14).

JESUS' AUTHORITY IN PRONOUNCING BELIEVING GENTILES ACCEPTED AND UNBELIEVING ISRAELITES REJECTED
8:5-13 (Mark 2:1; Luke 7:1-10; John 4:46b-54)

8:5-6 (Mark 2:1; Luke 7:1-5) In Mark, right after healing the leper Jesus enters Capernaum, forgives and heals a paralytic carried by four other men, and then calls Levi (Mark 2:1-17). Matthew mentions Jesus' entry into Capernaum right after the healing of the leper, but delays the healing of the paralytic carried by four and the call of Levi, named Matthew, till chap. 9. The healing of the centurion's servant, which has no counterpart in Mark, and several other pieces of material intervene. Nevertheless, Matthew compensates for his delaying the story of the paralytic. He does so by describing the centurion's servant as paralyzed (8:6). Luke's version, representing the tradition, lacks this description (cf. Luke 7:1-10).

But why does Matthew interrupt Mark's sequence with the healing of the centurion's servant? The reason is the motif of Jesus' authority in the story. This motif dominates chaps. 8–9. In Luke the entry into Capernaum and the healing of the centurion's servant follow the Sermon on the Mount, but neither the healing of the leper nor material parallel to Matthew's subsequent material intervenes. More importantly, at the end of Jesus' sermon Luke does not mention the amazement of the listeners at Jesus' authority, which in Matthew links up with Jesus' authority in the story of the centurion's servant. So far as order is concerned, then, we see more evidence of arrangement by Matthew than of influence from a source common to Matthew and Luke.

Matthew reduces the independent clause concerning Jesus' entering Capernaum (so Luke) to a genitive absolute and makes the centurion rather than his servant the subject of the sentence. In harmony with the latter change, the description of the servant as one "who was highly regarded by him [the centurion]" drops out. Thus attention centers on the centurion more than on the servant. But because the centurion is prototypical of Gentile Christian believers, Matthew does not care to have Jewish elders glorify him for loving their nation and building their synagogue (Luke 7:3-5). In Matthew, God has transferred the kingdom of heaven to another "nation" (21:43), and the synagogue is designated "*their* synagogue" in opposition to the church (5,0). Therefore Matthew omits the part of the story concerning the delegation of Jewish elders. The centurion now appears to approach Jesus directly. Consequently, Matthew also omits the further delegation of the centurion's friends, though he retains almost all the conversation between Jesus and the centurion as represented by his friends (Luke 7:6-8).

In v 5 προσῆλθεν replaces ἀπέστειλεν (so Luke). This substitution accords with the dropping of the delegation and with Matthew's fondness for his verb, which connotes Jesus' dignity (38,6). παρακαλῶν and λέγων come from the account of the Jewish elders' plea to Jesus (see Luke 6:4).

A centurion might naturally live in Capernaum, a garrison city and post for customs. In the Roman army a centurion commanded one hundred soldiers. But we may have here a loose usage for a military official in the service of Herod Antipas, tetrarch of the region. The centurion may have come from nearby Syria. Cf. Josephus *Ant.* 18.5.1 §§109-15. On Matthew's dropping the intermediaries between the centurion and Jesus, see Broadus, ad loc., who compares the scourging of Jesus by Pilate, an act obviously carried out by soldiers at Pilate's behest (John 19:1).

In v 6 Matthew makes a request out of the description of the servant's illness (so Luke) in order to compensate for his omitting the Jewish elders' words to Jesus. In this direct discourse he inserts "Lord" (not in the initial request reported by Luke). This anticipates and parallels the same address in v 8, where it appears also in Luke. The stress on Jesus as κύριος typifies Matthew's theology (34,15) and ties the story more closely to the preceding, where the leper addresses Jesus in the same way (v 2; cf. 11QtgJob 14:[5], 7; [26:8], discussed by J. A. Fitzmyer in *NTS* 20 [1974] 386-89). παῖς, which means "servant, boy," replaces δοῦλος, which means "servant, slave." The replacement avoids a confusing correspondence between Jesus as Lord and the servant as a slave—but a slave to the centurion rather than to Jesus. It also works a parallel, and thus consistency, with ὁ παῖς μου in v 8 (so also Luke). Cf. v 13, where ὁ παῖς αὐτοῦ is distinctive and corresponds to ὁ παῖς μου in vv 6 and 8.

παῖς may mean "boy" (in the sense of "son") as well as "servant." Some think that Matthew switches from an alternation between δοῦλος and παῖς (so Luke) to a consistent use of παῖς in order to imply the meaning "son" rather than "servant"— this because of the centurion's affection for the boy (cf. John 4:46-53). But Matthew omits the clause that expresses that affection (Luke 7:2b). Therefore the reasons given above for his consistent use of παῖς stand firm. Notably, Matthew does not heighten the miracle by making the servant dead. He does not even retain the imminency of death for the sake of dramatic effect.

The sending of a delegation from the centurion to Jesus is out of the picture. So Matthew almost necessarily inserts "in the house," i.e., "at home," as an indication of some distance between Jesus and the place where the servant lies prostrate. οἰκία typifies Matthew's diction (5,3). The identification of the servant's malady as paralysis is absent from Luke. It compensates for the delay of the story concerning the paralytic carried by four and makes specially appropriate the thought of prostration contained in βέβληται (not in Luke). Cf. Matthew's distinctive uses of βάλλω for the prostrations of Peter's mother-in-law (v 14) and the paralytic carried by four (9:2) as well as other distinctive occurrences (12,8). The change from "was about to die" (so Luke) to "being terriby tortured" takes emphasis from the imminency of death and puts it on the severe tormenting of the servant by his paralysis, which is a malevolent force Jesus overcomes with his lordly authority. Matthew shows some fondness for words beginning with βασαν- (2,1).

8:7 (Luke 7:6) Verse 7 opens with a vivid historical present tense in λέγει (not in Luke). The word appears in this form often throughout chaps. 8–9 and typifies Matthew's style (47,11). It always has Jesus as its subject in these chapters, and it points up Matthew's emphasis on his authoritative words. Again Matthew makes a direct quotation ("I will come and heal him") out of a description ("and Jesus went with them," so Luke). None of the words in the direct quotation is paralleled in Luke even though the thought corresponds. Matthew likes the emphatic ἐγώ (12-13,3), especially for Jesus. Here, as in the Sermon on the Mount, it emphasizes

Jesus' authority. The nominative participle ἐλθών and θεραπεύσω character-ize Matthew's diction (10,10; 10,0).

Since Matthew composes the direct discourse to emphasize Jesus' authority to heal, we ought not to read the words as an astonished and indignant question meaning "Shall I a Jew contract ceremonial defilement by entering the house of you a Gentile to heal your servant?" Besides, if it were a question of coming into a Gentile's house, we should have ex-pected ἐλθών to be more than the mere participle it is, and perhaps have expected to read "into your house." But the stress falls on healing. Not till the response of the centurion does the stress fall on entry into his house. In 15:21-28 Jesus will rebuff a Gentile at first. But that rebuff hardly favors one here, for tradition supplies the rebuff in 15:21-28 (see Mark 7:24-30). It is Matthew who does so here. He wants to highlight Jesus' authority. Therefore the astonishment lies on the side of the centurion rather than Jesus, and the centurion's response arises out of that astonishment rather than from submission to the force of a negatively voiced question.

8:8-9 (Luke 7:6-8) In place of the centurion's further sending of some friends and speaking through them (note the singular of λέγων in Luke 7:6), Matthew uses the stereotyped ἀποκριθείς with ἔφη. εἶπε(ν) always appears in the phrase elsewhere in his gospel (29,6). But here the recency of λέγει in v 7 leads him to use ἔφη. "Lord" reappears, this time matched in Luke. But Matthew drops "do not trouble yourself" and, consequently, γάρ in the following clause. Thus the unworthiness of the centurion does not merely provide the reason why the Lord should not trouble himself to come to his house (so Luke). The centurion's unworthiness is the sole point—and it contrasts with Jesus' authority. To underline the contrast, Matthew moves μου away from στέγην and up to the beginning of the clause. There, ahead of the prepositional phrase to which it belongs, the centu-rion's unworthy μου gets heavy emphasis and acts as a foil to Jesus' au-thoritative ἐγώ (v 7).

Not according to the OT but according to rabbinic legislation, a Jew contracted ceremonial defilement by entering the house of a Gentile (*m. 'Ohol.* 18:7; cf. Acts 10:1–11:18). The centurion's feeling unworthy may go beyond ceremonial defile-ment in his house, however, and extend to recognition of his moral guilt and Jesus' holiness.

Because he omitted the sending of the friends, Matthew naturally drops the centurion's statement "For this reason I did not even consider myself worthy to come to you" (Luke 7:7) and skips to "but say a word." Typically, he inserts μόνον (7,0). This implies that Jesus' authority needs only a little exercise for accomplishment of the healing. "And let my servant be healed" (so Luke) becomes the confident prediction "and my servant will be healed." Thus the emphasis stays on Jesus' authoritative word, which will effect the healing.

With one significant exception, the concluding part of the centurion's statement in v 9 corresponds to Luke's version word for word. This cor-respondence includes retention of δούλῳ in the statement about the slave's carrying out orders. The παῖς is paralyzed; therefore he is unable to carry out orders and must be distinguished from the slave. The centurion refers to his being accustomed as a subordinate military officer both to obeying and to being obeyed. The governmental authority under which he stands is the same as that with which he is invested; hence, his soldiers and slave obey his word. Similarly, his servant's malady will respond in obedience to the word of Jesus, who both stands under God's authority and administers it ("for I *too* . . .").

But since Jesus is "God with us" (1:23), Matthew wants to show the immediacy and supremacy of Jesus' authority. He therefore drops "being placed [under]" and thereby suggests that the initial καί does not mean "too," but "even" ("for even I [a centurion!] am a man under authority") and, moreover, that the centurion stands under the authority of Jesus, with whom he is talking. In Matthew, then, only Jesus' authority comes in view. The centurion's following statements do not imply, as in Luke, that the centurion's authority stands beside Jesus' authority in a comparison. Rather, the centurion's speaking and being obeyed stand in subordination to the only true authority there is, that of Jesus, who said, "All authority in heaven and on earth has been given to me" (28:18). If even the word of a subordinate is obeyed, how much more effective the lordly word of Christ will be.

Since it is much easier, the reading of the Sinaitic version of the Syriac text, "a man who has authority," does not deserve serious consideration. It probably does not derive from an original Aramaic text, but results from a scribe's or a translator's difficulty with the description of the centurion as "under authority," which might seem to contradict his having soldiers under him.

8:10 (Luke 7:9) Three omissions occur at the start of v 10. Matthew drops "these things." As an introductory participle in Matthew, ἀκούσας normally lacks a direct object. Here the omission steers attention away from the centurion's words. Similarly, the omission of "him" diverts attention from the centurion himself. And the dropping of "turning" avoids notice of Jesus' physical movement. Together, these omissions allow the authoritative speaking of Jesus—"he said"—to stand out. We have already read that "many crowds followed him" (v 1, peculiar to Matthew). Therefore Matthew omits τῷ ἀκολουθοῦντι αὐτῷ ὄχλῳ (so Luke) and refers simply to τοῖς [supply ὄχλοις from v 1] ἀκολουθοῦσιν. The plural contrasts with Luke's singular and derives from v 1. Those who follow become the indirect objects of Jesus' speaking rather than of his turning (as in Luke). The tradition probably supplied ἀμήν, which Luke dropped. In the statement about faith, the reference to Israel moves far back in the clause, where it lacks emphasis. The emphatic "not even" vanishes. In its stead appears "with no one," which is characteristic of Matthew's style in the use of παρά with the dative (2,2). He is implying that Jesus could hardly expect to find such faith as the centurion's in Israel as a nation, though he might have found it among individual Israelites. The greatness of the centurion's faith lay in his believing that Jesus could heal at a distance with a mere word and would do so even though asked by a Gentile.

8:11-12 (Luke 13:28-29) But such faith as the centurion's Jesus did not find among individual Israelites, either. Therefore Matthew imports sayings concerning the entrance of Gentiles into the future kingdom and concerning the exclusion of Israelites. These sayings appear in Luke in the context of the narrow door, a topic already treated by Matthew without their inclusion (cf. 7:13-14 with Luke 13:28-29). For renewed emphasis on Jesus' authoritative words, Matthew characteristically inserts "I say to you" (27,7). Instead of making reference first to the exclusion of unbelieving Israelites (so Jesus in Luke), he reverses the order of the sayings to gain an immediate reference to the influx of believing Gentiles into the coming kingdom. The typical addition of "many" (23,1) increases emphasis on the salvation of Gentiles (cf. "Universality" in the Topical Index).

"From east and west" stays (cf. 24:27), but "and from north and south" (so Luke) drops out. Matthew then inserts "with Abraham and Isaac and Jacob" (so Luke in another position) between "will recline" and "in the kingdom of heaven." This insertion compensates for his omitting "when you see Abraham and Isaac and Jacob and all the prophets in the kingdom of God" (so Luke). The dropping of "and all the prophets" conforms to the OT, where the trio of patriarchs, without addition, is a stereotype. See 22:32. Besides, Matthew views the prophets as predictors of the kingdom more than as participants in it. The importation of this saying implies that the faith of the centurion will gain him not only the cure of his servant, but also his own entry into the kingdom.

At formal meals it had become customary to recline on couches, or pillows, with feet extended away from the table, weight concentrated on the left elbow, and right hand left free for bringing food to the mouth. Eating together connoted an almost mysterious fellowship and solidarity. That Gentiles should recline on couches to eat with the sainted Jewish patriarchs at the messianic banquet was astonishing. In constructing the saying, Jesus probably conflated phrases from Isa 49:12 and Ps 107:3, but applied them to the ingathering of Gentiles rather than of Jewish exiles (so the OT passages; see Gundry, *Use of the OT* 76-77). That he really did refer to the salvation of Gentiles we can conclude from the near impossibility of his distinguishing Jews in the Dispersion from Jews in Palestine and predicting salvation only for the Dispersion. Nobody doubted the salvation of faithful Jews in the Dispersion; therefore they would hardly have provided an example of surprising inclusion in contrast with surprising exclusion. Concerning the messianic banquet, see the comments on 5:6. The OT prophets predicted a pilgrimage of Gentiles to Mount Zion when Israel is restored (see J. Jeremias, *Jesus' Promise to the Nations* [SBT 1/24; London: SCM, 1958] 55-63). But here the salvation of the Gentiles is bound up with the rejection of Israelites and therefore results from worldwide evangelism in the present age (see esp. 28:19-20) rather than the Lord's presence in Zion during the messianic kingdom. See further W. D. Davies, *The Setting of the Sermon on the Mount* (Cambridge: Cambridge University Press, 1964) 327-32.

From the participial phrase "but you yourselves being thrown outside" (so the tradition, represented by Luke), Matthew makes a full-scale sentence to emphasize judgment on the mass of Jews who reject Jesus. These Jews he calls "the sons of the kingdom," a Semitic expression for those who belong, or by privilege should belong, to the kingdom. The same designation will appear at 13:38 in a distinctive passage. But there the sons of the kingdom are "the righteous," who "will shine like the sun in the kingdom of their Father"; i.e., they are Christians. By introducing the designation here, Matthew shows the parallel between Jews and Christians, between Israel and the church. Jews were the sons of the kingdom, their nation the chosen people. Now the sons of the kingdom are Jesus' disciples, and the chosen people the new nation called the church (see 16:18 with 21:43, both peculiar to Matthew).

To strengthen the horror of the judgment, Matthew expands the simple adverb "outside" (so Luke) to the phrase "into the outermost darkness" (so also 22:13; 25:30, both uniquely Matthean). This refers to the darkness outside the brightly lit hall where the festivities of the messianic banquet are taking place (see esp. the preceding context in Luke). Having worked backward, Matthew finally arrives at the first in the group of sayings, the one concerning weeping and grinding of teeth (Luke 13:28a). Sufficiently severe already, the saying satisfies Matthew to the extent that he adopts it without revision and will use it without parallel several times again (see 13:42, 50; 22:13; 24:51; 25:30). The later occurrences have to do with the fate of false disciples. Hence, the fate of faithless Israel will become a warning to the church in the later passages. The very ambivalence of "the sons of the kingdom," which may refer either to Israel or to the church, helps make the present statement precursive of the warnings to the church—and even itself an indirect warning to the church. Ps 112:10 provides the basis of the saying. We cannot be sure whether the grinding of teeth represents sorrow, in strictly synonymous parallelism with weeping, or anger or vexation as a complement to weeping. "There" refers to the outermost darkness, where those shut out from the messianic banquet vent their frustration.

The severity of this warning to Israel has no equal in rabbinic and apocalyptic literature. In ἐξώτερον we have a comparative in the elative sense of a superlative ("outermost"). For darkness and weeping, see quotations and references in Allen, ad loc. Luke rather than Matthew, it is usually thought, has transposed the sayings about reclining at the messianic banquet and being excluded from it, because "there" lacks a referent in Luke but has a natural referent to the outermost darkness in Matthew's order of sayings. But the adverb does have a referent in Luke, viz., the "outside" of the banquet hall in v 25. The theme of standing outside with no possibility of entry continues till it reaches a climax in v 26: there, outside the shut door, those who hear the Lord's "Away from me" will weep and grind their teeth. The repetition of "outside" at the end of v 28 makes an inclusio with the first occurrence. Then, as a contrast, we are told again of those who enter through the narrow door to enjoy the feast (see v 29 with v 24a), and an overall comment wraps up the section (v 30). The unity of Luke's passage looks original. It is Matthew who has edited heavily, as is evident not only in the features of his text already noted, but also in his usual drive for consistent parallelism: the many who come from the east and west parallel the sons of the kingdom who are thrown into outermost darkness, and the reclining with Abraham, Isaac, and Jacob in the kingdom of heaven parallels the weeping and grinding of teeth "there," i.e., in the outermost darkness. The more disjointed arrangement in Luke has the appearance of spoken words; the careful parallelism in Matthew the appearance of literary artistry with theological purpose.

8:13 (Luke 7:10) In v 13 Matthew returns to the story proper. Where Luke gives only the finding of the servant well, Matthew first gives Jesus' authoritative words that effected the healing. The Mattheanism ὕπαγε (5,6) echoes the healing use of ὕπαγε in 8:4 and anticipates the same use in 9:6 (cf. 8:32). "As you have believed" recalls attention to the centurion's faith. The whole expression, "as you have believed, let it happen to you," comes close to "according to your faith let it happen to you" in 9:29, where, as here, Matthew will insert the expression in common tradition (cf. 15:28, to which add 6:10; 26:42 for all Matthew's insertions of the form γενηθήτω). Similarly, "and [his] servant was healed at that hour" comes close to like statements in 9:22 (so Matthew alone right before a reference to faith and with a rejection, as here, of the stem ὑγι-, "well," in Mark 5:34); 15:28 (again alone, right after a reference to faith, and, as here, with a combination of γενηθήτω σοι and ὡς); and 17:18 (referring to a παῖς, as here). All these passages contain references to "that hour." Cf. Matthew's insertions of "in that hour" in 10:19; 18:1; 26:55. "Was healed" replaces "well" (so Luke) for a parallel with "will be healed" in v 8. And "[his] servant" replaces "the slave" for consistency with "my servant" in vv 6 and 8. Matthew's stating the healing in a way that matches the centurion's request highlights the effectiveness of Jesus' authoritative word.

It is not permissible to delete the miraculous element and retain only the element of faith, for Matthew subordinates faith to the motif of Jesus' authority. And without the miracle, Jesus' authority would collapse. On the possibility of a relation between the present passage and John 4:46-53, see commentaries on John. Because of Matthew's omission and the supposed unlikelihood of the centurion's sending two successive delegations to speak for him, some think that that part of Luke's version comes into the story by invention. But, as we have seen, Matthew had good reason to omit the material; and concerning the probabilities of the centurion's action we can hardly make negative psychological judgments with any more certainty than we can make positive psychological judgments. The unlikelihood of the centurion's sending two successive delegations is matched by the unlikelihood of an invention of such an awkward literary device. We have no compelling reasons, then, to think that Matthew worked with material different from what we find in Luke.

JESUS' AUTHORITY IN HEALING PETER'S MOTHER-IN-LAW, CASTING OUT DEMONS, AND HEALING ALL THE SICK IN FULFILLMENT OF PROPHECY

8:14-17 (Mark 1:29-34; Luke 4:38-41)

Matthew now returns to material paralleled in Mark as well as Luke, and in so doing moves backward to Mark 1:29-34 (see also Luke 4:38-41). Several purposes come into play in his reaching back for this material. He wants to prepare his readers for Peter's role in 14:28-31; 16:13-19; 17:24-27, to capture a reference to exorcisms for rounding out this first subsection on the authority of Jesus in his deeds, and to win a general statement about Jesus' healings as a basis for quoting an OT prophecy as fulfilled.

8:14 (Mark 1:29-30; Luke 4:38) Because of Matthew's rearrangement of materials and omission of the exorcism in the synagogue at Capernaum (Mark 1:21-28; Luke 4:31-37), Mark's reference to exit from the synagogue drops out. As in the preceding story (v 7) and often elsewhere (cf. esp. the distinctive "coming . . . and seeing" in 9:23) Matthew uses the participle ἐλθών (10,10). But where Mark writes "they," understood in context as Jesus and his disciples, Matthew writes of Jesus alone (so also Luke) and characteristically identifies him by name (80,12). Similarly, where Mark makes Simon's mother-in-law the subject of lying in bed with a fever, Matthew makes Jesus the subject of seeing her prostrate with a fever. In these ways the evangelist concentrates attention on Jesus and gives him the initiative in the exercise of his authority (cf. v 17).

A secondary emphasis falls on Simon, whom Matthew calls by his complimentary nickname "Peter" (Πέτρος—8,1; cf. esp. 16:17-19). The names of Andrew, James, and John withdraw before Peter's name (as in Luke, except that Luke does not replace Mark's "Simon" with "Peter"). Thus Matthew begins to establish a representative role for Peter.

In Matthew, the illness of the mother-in-law merits only a pair of participles. βεβλημένην (12,8) replaces Mark's κατέκειτο, and πυρέσσουσαν comes over from Mark. Like ἐλθών, βεβλημένην ties this story to the preceding, where βέβληται occurs (v 6; cf. 9:2). Matthew has mentioned only Jesus' entry into the house. Therefore the disciples' speaking to Jesus about the mother-in-law drops out. Despite Matthew's liking of Mark's προσελθών (38,6), Jesus' approaching her also disappears. In Matthew, others approach Jesus; he does not need to approach them. There are only two exceptions, 17:7 and 28:18, where Jesus has to approach his disciples because his transfiguration and resurrection have incapacitated them.

8:15 (Mark 1:31; Luke 4:39) Tersely, Matthew mentions only Jesus' touching the hand of the mother-in-law. The rest needs no inclusion. What Jesus does counts for everything in the miracle. Matthew reserves the raising of the woman till later, and then makes it a getting up (ἠγέρθη) rather than a being raised by Jesus (ἤγειρεν αὐτήν, so Mark). In its place he puts Jesus' taking the woman's hand and strengthens the action by turning a participle into a main verb. But Mark's "taking hold of" gives way to "touched." In Mark, then, Jesus seizes Peter's mother-in-law by her hand and raises her up. The fever leaves. In Matthew, Jesus merely touches her and the fever leaves. Then she gets up. Mark locates the cure in the visible raising of the woman by Jesus, Matthew in Jesus' initial touching of her, i.e., before the cure becomes noticeable. Just as in the preceding story a mere word sufficed to heal the centurion's servant (vv 8, 13), so here just a touch effects the cure of Peter's mother-in-law. Raising her as a means of healing (so Mark) becomes her getting up as a sign of healing. And her waiting on, i.e., serving food to, "them" (so Mark and Luke, referring to Jesus and his disciples) becomes her waiting on "him" (a reference to Jesus).

148

Thus the authoritative figure of Jesus dominates the story from beginning to end.

8:16 (Mark 1:32-34; Luke 4:40-41) In the sequel to the healing of Peter's mother-in-law, Mark has two synonymous references to time, "and after evening came" and "when the sun had set." This emphasis on the onset of evening stems from a contextual reference to the Sabbath: after sunset people could carry their sick to Jesus without violating the prohibition of work on the Sabbath, for Jews regarded sunset as the beginning of a new day. Luke refers to the Sabbath, but has no concern to call his Gentile readers' attention to Jewish avoidance of work. Therefore he avoids the redundancy in Mark's emphasis by dropping the first expression. Matthew drops the second expression. In his gospel there is no contextual reference to the Sabbath; hence, a twofold emphasis on sunset would have had no point.

Mark's ἔφερον changes to προσήνεγκαν. The latter is a favorite of Matthew and may connote an offering to Jesus (see the comments on 2:11; 4:24). Matthew has described three healings; so he omits the bringing of the sick and mentions only the bringing of demoniacs for exorcism. His transferring "many" from "demons" to "demoniacs" forestalls a false inference that Jesus failed to cast out some of the demons. Many demoniacs were brought. Jesus cast the spirits out of them. There were no exceptions.

The gathering of the populace at the door (so Mark) drops out (as in Luke). For the moment, the healing of the sick also drops out. Instead, Jesus' casting out "the spirits" occupies center stage. Furthermore, Matthew alone tells us that Jesus did this with a mere "word," as in the healing of the centurion's servant (see vv 8, 13 and cf. the authority of Jesus' teaching in chaps. 5–7). Where Mark has δαιμόνια πολλά in an emphatic first position, Matthew's corresponding τὰ πνεύματα occupies an unobtrusive middle position. The stress thus falls on exorcism with a word and enhances Jesus' authority. Then, despite his omission of the bringing of the sick, Matthew mentions their healing. But he drops "with various diseases" (so Mark) in anticipation of "our diseases" in the following quotation. And he replaces Mark's "many" with "all" in order to avoid any implication that some were not healed (cf. 4:24 and 12:15 with Mark 3:10). "All the sick" advances to an emphatic first position in the statement about healing. As a whole, that statement goes to last place and, as a result, becomes a general summary leading into a quotation from Isaiah. The summary and quotation displace Jesus' command that the demons keep silent about his identity (so Mark and Luke). Matthew has greater interest in the fulfillment of prophecy than in the messianic secret.

This is the only place in the NT where "spirit" occurs without a modifier for unclean spirits, i.e., demons. Mark's demons become spirits because Matthew wants to avoid demons in a clause right after one that mentions demoniacs. The intervention of two whole clauses saves Mark from such a piling up of cognates. A chiastic order of verb–object, object–verb characterizes v 16bc.

8:17 The introduction to the quotation begins with ὅπως, which Matthew reserves for fulfillment-quotations climaxing a series of items (see also 2:23; 13:35). As in 4:14 and 12:17, he names Isaiah. In contrast with the doleful quotations from Jeremiah (see 2:17-18; 27:9-10), the quotations from Isaiah all occur in summaries of Jesus' salvific work.

The present quotation comes from Isa 53:4. As in the LXX, the initial אָכֵן, "surely," is missing in translation. This lack makes Matthew's nearly total divergence from the LXX in the rest of the quotation all the more remarkable. The Septuagintal translator renders the Hebrew very loosely in order to gain a reference to sins (cf. the Targum). Matthew translates independently in order to make the quotation apply to physical maladies cured by Jesus. Cf. the distinctive νόσος here with its insertion in summaries of Jesus' healings (4:23, 24; 9:35). Matthew's intensive αὐτός, "he himself," has first position through the omission of אָכֵן. Matthew likes αὐτός (14,3). It emphasizes the figure of Jesus and corresponds to הוא, which has third position in the Hebrew text.

There is no implication that Jesus vicariously became sick. Rather, he removed sicknesses. Because it might be taken to imply that Jesus became sick, Matthew replaces the Septuagintal φέρει, "carries," with ἔλαβεν, "took" (cf. 5:40; 15:26). ἐβάστασεν also indicates removal rather than carrying (see the comments on 3:11). On the other hand, the second of the Hebrew verbs in Isaiah—viz., סְבָלָם—means "carry a load." Therefore its ambiguous parallel verb נָשָׂא probably connotes carrying rather than taking. Matthew's stopping short with the thought of removal and carefully avoiding the connotation of carrying point to his recognition that Jesus' vicarious physical suffering and death were yet to come. For now, Jesus heals with a lordly "word." See the comments on 27:57 for Matthew's applying Isaiah 53 to Jesus' passion. The healings anticipate the passion in that they begin to roll back the effects of the sins for which Jesus came to die. Some think that Isaiah spoke only figuratively in 53:4; i.e., sicknesses and pains there stand for sins. Along with forgiveness of sins, however, physical well-being was thought to characterize the messianic age (cf. Isa 29:18; 32:3-4; 35:5-6). We therefore do well to follow Matthew's literalism. Of course, Isaiah 53 goes on to the topic of sins (cf. Gundry, *Use of the OT* 230-31).

In Matthew it looks as though Jesus taught on a mountain, descended, healed a leper, entered Capernaum, healed a centurion's servant, entered Peter's house, and healed Peter's mother-in-law all on the same day—and in the evening healed others, sailed across the Sea of Galilee during the night, delivered two demoniacs the next morning, came back across in the afternoon, and so on. In fact, Matthew's failure to provide a string of chronological notices implies a lack of concern for exact chronology.

Jesus' Authority in the Demands of Discipleship
8:18-22 (Mark 4:35; Luke 9:57-62)

8:18 (Mark 4:35) The authority of Jesus in his deeds has been established. Now Matthew wants to show that that authority demands total commitment. To show this, he inserts in his collection of miracle stories some teaching of Jesus on discipleship. This teaching appears also in Luke 9:57-62, where the context deals with Jesus' starting his last journey to Jerusalem. By contrast, Matthew slips the teaching into the first part of the story about Jesus' calming a storm, which according to Mark 4 happened after he taught in parables from a boat. And Mark 2:1 says he had already returned to Capernaum, whereas in Matthew he has come to Capernaum only once. The chronology does not concern Matthew, however; his point lies in the meaning of Jesus' deeds and words.

More particularly, Matthew inserts the material on discipleship between the resolve to go to the other side of the Sea of Galilee and the actual embarkation. The "crowd" seems to refer to those who had come to Peter's house. Of greater importance, it relates to 7:28; 8:1 and comes from Mark 4:36a. Where Mark refers to the disciples' leaving the crowd (and taking Jesus with them), Matthew gives the initiative to Jesus. His seeing a crowd around himself makes him decide to cross the Sea of Galilee—not to get away from the crowd, as we will see, but to get them to follow him as disciples. The nominative participle ἰδών and the phrase ἰδών . . . ὄχλον typify Matthew's style (10-11,7; 3,0).

Notably, Matthew refers to the crowd as "around him [Jesus]" (absent from Mark) and later omits this phrase in 12:46-47 (contrast Mark 3:31-32). Though it does not contain the phrase, Luke's parallel to the later passage immediately precedes the calming of the storm (Luke 8:19-21; cf. Matthew here). We may infer, then, that Matthew draws the phrase from Mark 3:31-32, where Jesus identifies the crowd around him as his true family, those who do God's will. The crowd around Jesus are his disciples, then. Both of those who speak to Jesus in the next verses represent the crowd of disciples. In contrast with Luke, where the start of discipleship is in view, Matthew's teaching on discipleship has to do with its genuineness in those who already profess it. Such profession will become evident in the insertions "a certain [Christian] scribe" and "another of the disciples." The first evangelist has his eye on the church as a mixed body of false and genuine Christians (see *Corpus mixtum*" in the Topical Index).

To play up Jesus' authority, Matthew inserts ἐκέλευσεν, "commanded" or "gave orders." The verb occurs also in 14:9, 19, 28; 18:25; 27:58, 64, but not at all in Mark and only once in Luke. Typically, Matthew changes διέλθωμεν (Mark 4:35) to ἀπελθεῖν (14,11). The replacing of δι- with ἀπ- matches ὅπου ἐὰν ἀπέρχῃ in the next verse and thus makes the voyage a going away in discipleship.

8:19 (Luke 9:57) Where Luke refers to the last journey to Jerusalem ("and as they were going along the road"), Matthew characteristically substitutes προσελθών for the approach of a certain scribe to Jesus (38,6). See the comments on v 14 for approaching Jesus as a pointer to his majestic authority. γραμματεύς is a Mattheanism (10,2). Here it takes the place of Luke's indefinite τις. Several things favor that this scribe is to be considered a disciple, i.e., a "scribe" by Christian discipleship though not necessarily by Jewish occupational background: (1) the portrayal of the crowd, from which he comes, as disciples; (2) Matthew's special use of εἷς for emphasis (24,7); (3) Matthew's not calling the man one of "*their* scribes" (contrast 7:29); (4) the implication of the matching phrase "and *another* of his disciples" in v 21 (cf. 6:24); and (5) the distinctive use of γραμματεύς in 13:52; 23:34 for Jesus' disciples.

εἷς occasionally appears as the equivalent of τις, but at least in Matthew it carries an emphasis lacking in the indefinite pronoun.

At the beginning of the scribe's positive response to Jesus' command, Matthew inserts διδάσκαλε, "Teacher" (4,1). Though nondisciples use this address in speaking to Jesus elsewhere in Matthew (12:38; 19:16; 22:16, 24, 36), all but one of those instances fail to be peculiar to Matthew, and Jesus uses the term concerning himself a number of times (10:24, 25; 23:8 [unique]; 26:18). Furthermore, we have just noted ample evidence of the Christian profession of the scribe in this dialogue. Matthew inserts διδάσκαλε, then, to emphasize Jesus' authority as a teacher (cf. the comments on 5:1-2). In order to learn from his teacher's words and exemplary actions, the scribe promises to follow him wherever he goes. The going refers to crossing the Sea of Galilee as a symbol of discipleship. The scribe's positive response to Jesus' command therefore marks him out as a true disciple, one of the wheat, in the *corpus mixtum*. Contrastingly, the next respondent will represent tarelike false disciples.

8:20 (Luke 9:58) Luke uses εἶπεν to introduce all the statements, both of the would-be disciples and of Jesus. Matthew uses it only for the statements of the disciples (vv 19, 21) and characteristically introduces Jesus' responses with λέγει (47,11—vv 20, 22). The historical present tense implies that Jesus is speaking also to the church. Matthew and Luke agree word for word in the saying about foxes, birds, and the Son of man. But in Luke the homelessness of Jesus has to do with his leaving on the fateful and fatal journey to Jerusalem. In Matthew it has to do with his having to sleep in a boat during a storm and being repulsed on arrival at the other side of the lake. In both gospels homelessness stands for rejection by people rather than lack of lodging as such. Disciples must expect similar rejection. "Son of man," a Semitic expression for "human being," "man," refers to Jesus; otherwise the saying has no relevance. Furthermore, the expression is a title, not a general or unimposing self-designation; otherwise the saying has no punch. If Jesus took the expression to himself from Dan 7:13-14, this saying conveys the shocking truth that the manlike figure who in Daniel's vision comes to receive universal dominion—this exalted figure wrapped with clouds like God himself—first suffers rejection!

Derivation of the dominical title "Son of man" from Dan 7:13-14, where "one like a son of man" receives universal dominion, provides a basis for sayings concerning Jesus' future exaltation as the Son of man (see later comments on Jesus' identity with the exalted Son of man in the future) and gives point to those sayings that describe his earthly activity, especially his suffering and death. In the synoptics, the limitation of the title to words of Jesus argues strongly for his using it. Had the evangelists, or the early church, chosen the title themselves, it would surely have appeared also in others' statements *about* Jesus and as an address *to* him. Cf. *1 Enoch* 37–71 (probably postsynoptic, because this section of *1 Enoch* failed to show up among the fragments of the book discovered near Qumran and because both allusive and direct quotations from this section of the book are lacking in Jewish and Christian literature before the end of the first century). Also cf. 2 Esdras 13 (almost certainly post-Christian, as generally agreed). The literature on the Son of man is too voluminous to cite here, and the questions too complicated to discuss adequately.

8:21 (Luke 9:59) To "another" in the next dialogue, Matthew typically adds "of his disciples" (31,5). Again the respondent to Jesus' command already belongs to the circle of professing disciples. He addresses Jesus as "Lord." Matthew likes κύριε (34,15) and probably inserts it, as he inserted "Teacher," to stress Jesus' authority. Though the UBS adopts κύριε in Luke, there we should probably omit it with B* D syr^s *al*. Addition by copyists is more likely than deletion, especially in view of Matthew's dominance in scribal harmonizations of parallel passages; and the hypothesis that a transcriptional blunder resulted in accidental omission (see Metzger, *Textual Commentary* ad loc.) has against it the unusualness of the agreement between B* and D syr^s against most other textual witnesses.

Whether or not it is an addition by Matthew, "Lord" smacks of the same address, doubled, by the false prophets in 7:21. For though the authority of Jesus is emphasized in the address, the substance of the disciple's response to his command shows a lack of willingness to obey immediately and fully. Matthew brings out this lack clearly. Luke has the going away as a mere participle modifying the pronoun ("me, going away"). Consequently, the requested permission to do something else first deals primarily with burying the father. Matthew turns the going away into a coordinate infinitive and first object of the request ("allow me first to go away . . ."). Thus the going away to bury the father stands in sharp contrast with the going away to follow Jesus as a true disciple (vv 18-19).

8:22 (Luke 9:60) Matthew's delaying Jesus' command "Follow me" (in Luke it precedes the request to bury the father) makes this dialogue fit the pattern of the first: again the disciple responds to Jesus' initial command to cross the lake and then Jesus responds to the disciple. Furthermore, the delay makes the second disciple's response an indication of falsity in a discipleship already begun rather than an indication of hesitancy to start following Jesus. The command to "let the dead bury their own dead" may mean that the spiritually dead (cf. Luke 15:24, 32; John 5:24; Eph 2:1) should be left to bury the physically dead. Alternatively, the statement refers only to the physically dead and is laden with irony: "Let those who have been dead for some time bury those who have just died." Impossible? Yes, and in the very impossibility lies an irony that implies, "Let the business take care of itself—it is no concern of yours." In Palestinian Judaism great stress fell on the duty of children to bury their parents (see Gen 50:5-6; Tob 4:3; 6:14; Str-B 1. 487-89; *TDNT* 5. 982-83 n. 236). Some commentators try to make Jesus' demand seem less harsh by pointing to the custom of mourning for six days after the burial (which normally took place on the day of death) or by supposing that the father had not yet died. Thus the son was asking for at least a week and perhaps for an indefinite delay. But the text contains nothing of this, and all attempts to soften Jesus' imperious demand for immediate and unadulterated discipleship would have offended Matthew—and doubtless Jesus himself, who seems to be saying, "To follow me is more demanding than following Elijah, who allowed Elisha to say goodbye to his parents" (see 1 Kgs 19:19-21; cf. Deut 33:9; Mark 10:29; Matt 10:34-36; 19:29; Luke 12:51-53; 14:25-33; 18:29). Matthew stops with this hard saying. His emphasis therefore rests on the absoluteness of Jesus' authority, whereas in Luke the thought goes on to the duty of proclaiming God's kingdom.

Attempts to make "the dead" who are to "bury their own dead" a mistranslation of an Aramaic original that referred to gravediggers (so McNeile, ad loc.) or slow people (so Black, *Aramaic Approach* 207-8) empty the saying of its dramatic irony and substitute a pedestrian meaning of inferior likelihood.

The tradition includes a third dialogue, in which a would-be disciple asks for permission to say goodbye to his family at home (Luke 9:61-62). But Matthew has his wheat and tare, his true disciple and false. The third dialogue therefore vanishes.

The Authority of Jesus as Seen in a Storm
8:23-27 (Mark 4:36-41; Luke 8:22-25)

8:23 (Mark 4:36; Luke 8:22) Matthew now returns to the voyage across the Sea of Galilee. In his gospel, Jesus takes the initiative by getting in a boat (similarly Luke, but not Mark). The disciples follow. Matthew likes μαθηταί (31,5) and ἠκολούθησαν (8,0). Luke refers to the disciples, but not to their following Jesus. In Mark, on the other hand, the disciples take Jesus as he is, already in the boat. Furthermore, the disciples leave the crowd in Mark, but not in Matthew. Here the crowd consists of disciples. Matthew therefore omits their leaving the crowd and transmutes the accompaniment of other boats (so Mark) into the following of Jesus by his disciples; i.e., the crowd gets in other boats and follows Jesus *as* his disciples. Thus the voyage, called the "going away" in vv 18-19, represents discipleship as a response to Jesus' command to follow him in vv 18-22.

8:24 (Mark 4:37-38; Luke 8:23) Verse 24 begins with a typical insertion of ἰδού (34,9). Though in vv 20 and 22 Matthew diverged from Luke in preferring the historical present tense for Jesus' sayings relevant to the church, for the storm he agrees with Luke in changing Mark's historical present to an aorist. Mark's λαῖλαψ μεγάλη ἀνέμου, "a great gale of wind," becomes σεισμὸς μέγας, "a great shaking." The form of the adjective μέγας no longer matches the later μεγάλη with γαλήνη so exactly as in Mark. But Matthew wants to use σεισμός (3,0). This word normally refers to an earthquake; therefore he adds "in the sea" to clarify its use here for a storm. Other passages, too, contain σεισμός. It occurs in 24:7 for earthquakes as one of the birthpangs just before the consummation; distinctively in 27:54 for an earthquake at Jesus' crucifixion; and in 28:2, again distinctively, for an earthquake at Jesus' resurrection. Only in this last passage is σεισμός accompanied, as here in 8:24, by καὶ ἰδού, ἐγένετο, and μέγας. By contrast, the one use referring to an apocalyptic woe comes from the tradition (24:7).

In Matthew, therefore, the storm does not pose a threat to the disciples. Rather, in correspondence with 28:2 it is a sign of Jesus' majesty. The great shaking in the sea previews the majesty of Jesus in his resurrection, at which a great shaking again occurs and upon which he claims "all authority in heaven and on earth" (28:18). The similarity of Matthew's peculiar description of the storm with the phraseology of Jonah 1:4 (see esp. the Hebrew text) combines with his distinctive comparison between Jonah's experience and Jesus' rising from the dead (12:40) to confirm the symbolism of the great shaking as a preview of the risen Jesus' authority.

In order to leave emphasis solely on that symbolism, Matthew refuses to coordinate the clause concerning the beating of the waves into the boat (so Mark and, similarly, Luke). Instead, his reference to the waves goes into the subordinate clause indicating result, and in that clause Mark's two verbs ἐπέβαλλεν and γεμίζεσθαι collapse into the single infinitive καλύπτεσθαι (cf. Luke). The choice of καλύπτεσθαι results from the peculiar use of σεισμός; the upheaval of the waters veils the boat from view as it descends into troughs between waves. Matthew changes Mark's "and" introducing Jesus' sleep into a more natural "but." He also pares the narrative of Mark's details concerning the stern and the cushion and shortens ἦν . . . καθεύδων to ἐκάθευδεν (cf. Jonah 1:5). The paring has the effect of letting the emphasis stay on the great shaking as a sign of Jesus' majestic authority, and omission of the cushion avoids a seeming contradiction with Jesus' statement that the Son of man has no place to lay his head.

For the storm as a sign of divine majesty, see Exod 19:16-25; Pss 29:1-11; 107:23-32; Isa 63:19–64:2(64:1-3); Ezek 1:4-28; etc. The boat hardly represents the church if the great shaking represents divine majesty rather than persecution and other onslaughts against the church (against G. Bornkamm in *Tradition and Interpretation in Matthew* [Philadelphia: Westminster, 1963] 52-57).

8:25 (Mark 4:38; Luke 8:24) To enhance Jesus' majesty, Matthew writes προσελθόντες for the disciples' approach to Jesus (so also Luke but not Mark; cf. v 14 with comments). Again Mark's historical present ("they arouse") changes to an aorist in contrast with Matthew's using the historical present for Jesus' sayings. Mark's "and they say to him" becomes a mere participle, "saying," perhaps as a matter of style, but perhaps also to deemphasize the disciples' words in favor of Jesus' words, which Matthew will introduce with a finite verb in v 26. In all these respects Matthew and Luke agree.

Though this story began with a stress on discipleship, the stress has shifted to Jesus' majesty. Therefore Matthew replaces "Teacher," which was recently used in v 19 and is somewhat more appropriate to the motif of discipleship (so Mark), with his favorite "Lord" (κύριε—34,15; cf. Luke's ἐπιστάτα, "Master" [bis]). In Mark the disciples suggest that Jesus does not care whether they are perishing. In Matthew and Luke this suggestion disappears. But unlike Luke, Matthew substitutes "save [us]!" (cf. Peter's "Lord, save me!" during another storm in 14:30, again peculiar to Matthew; cf. also Matthew's fondness for σῴζω—5,1). It is only in the first gospel, then, that the disciples ask for a miracle. This request leads to the dropping of Mark's "that" before "we are perishing" and to the transformation of a question (". . . don't you care that we are perishing?" so Mark) into a declaration (". . . we are perishing," so Matthew and Luke). Cf. Jonah 1:6.

8:26 *(Mark 4:39-40; Luke 8:24-25)* Matthew characteristically introduces Jesus' speaking to the disciples—and through them to the church—with the historical present λέγει (47,11). Mark reverts to the aorist. In his gospel these words of Jesus come after the words of rebuke to the storm and a description of their effect. But Jesus' words to the storm hold little interest for Matthew. He refers to them with an aorist (ἐπετίμησεν, so also Mark and Luke; cf. Ps 105:9 LXX), which contrasts with the historical present for the words to the disciples; and he does not even bother to quote the words of rebuke to the storm (Luke agrees, but not Mark). Jesus' words to the disciples take first position with the historical present for the sake of emphasis. The first question in Mark 4:40, "Why are you timid?" stays. But Matthew omits the second question, "Don't you have faith yet?" because its implication that the disciples do not yet have faith offends him. He does not want any reader of his gospel to think that discipleship is possible without faith. Therefore he borrows a term from a saying of Jesus recorded in 6:30 and paralleled in Luke 12:28—viz., ὀλιγόπιστοι, "you of little faith"—and tacks it on the end of the first question as an address to the disciples. See also 14:31; 16:8; 17:20 for other insertions of the term and its cognate noun. In reducing the implication that the disciples do not yet have faith to the charge that they have but little faith, Matthew is not whitewashing the disciples (he alone will insert the term as a rebuke in later passages!) so much as protecting the concept of discipleship. Here the question carries a rebuke for failure to rest in the divine authority of Jesus. The rebuke implies that the disciples should have seen in the great shaking a sign of his majesty rather than a threat.

Matthew finally comes to the rebuke of the storm without quoting it. He replaces Mark's καί with his favorite τότε (66,17). The replacement underscores the priority of Jesus' words to the disciples over the rebuke of the storm. "Wind" changes to "winds" (cf. v 27), perhaps in reminiscence of 7:25, 27 (so Matthew alone). A reference to "the sea" stems from the otherwise omitted statement to the sea. Luke shares this omission. The coming of a great calm stays (cf. Jonah 1:15).

8:27 *(Mark 4:41; Luke 8:25)* In describing the response of the disciples, Matthew calls them "the men" (not in Mark or Luke). Thus he casts them as a foil to the divine figure of Jesus, whose majesty and authority he cannot emphasize too much. ἄνθρωπος is a favorite of his (35,17). For its use in contrast with God elsewhere in Matthew, see 6:1-18; 7:9-11; 9:8 (all unique at least in this respect); 10:32-33; 16:23; 19:26; 21:25-26. The disciples' fear (so Mark and Luke; cf. Jonah 1:16) becomes admiration (so also Luke, who conflates fear and admiration). Cf. insertions of θαυμάζω in 15:31; 21:20. For the disciples' words, Matthew and Luke again have a mere participle, "saying," instead of Mark's finite verb. Matthew drops "to one another," perhaps because he has in view an audience wider than the original disciples. τίς ("Who?") changes to ποταπός. In view of ἐθαύμασαν and the many other stresses on Jesus' majesty, ποταπός is to be taken as an exclamatory "How wonderful!", not as an interrogative "What kind of?" The obedience of the winds and sea provides the evidence of Jesus' awe-inspiring authority (cf. Yahweh's calming the sea in Pss 65:8[7]; 89:10[9]; 107:23-32).

Some think that Matthew calls the disciples "men" rather than "disciples" because of their fear and doubt concerning Jesus' nature. But Matthew omits these very elements of fear and doubt and writes, instead, about the disciples' admiration. Others think that Matthew uses "men" for those who hear the story through the preaching of the church. The awkwardness of such a reference, felt especially in the aorist tense of ἐθαύμασαν, militates against it. Both of these suggestions fail to take account of the use of "men" for contrast with divine majesty, and they fail to bring into play the dominant motif of Jesus' authority.

JESUS' AUTHORITY IN KILLING DEMONS
8:28-34 (Mark 5:1-20; Luke 8:26-39)

8:28 (Mark 5:1-5; Luke 8:26-27) As in Mark and Luke, the story of the violent demoniacs follows the calming of the storm. Matthew prunes and subordinates parts of the story to make the figure of Jesus stand out in bold relief. The independent clause concerning arrival on the other side turns into a genitive absolute, and "of the sea" falls away. The country of the Gerasenes becomes the country of the Gadarenes; i.e., Matthew identifies the region by the city of Gadara just six miles southeast of the Sea of Galilee, whereas Mark and Luke identify it by the capital city Gerasa some thirty miles southeast of the sea. The greater closeness of Gadara probably led to the change. The city from which people later came to see what had happened is not necessarily to be identified with the city by which Mark and Luke identify the inhabitants of the region, but the inference comes easily. Therefore Matthew may want to forestall a mistaken inference that people came from thirty miles away. In all of this we need to keep in mind the possibility of confusion, or deliberate association, of Gadara and Gerasa with Gergasa (modern Kursi), which is right at lakeside and has tombs and a cliff in the vicinity (see E. M. Yamauchi in *JAAR* 42 [1974] 722; J.-B. Livio in *BTS* 152 [1973] 6-16; and, on the text-critical question, Metzger, *Textual Commentary* ad loc.). Perhaps the exorcism took place near Gergasa and the synoptists variously identified the region by better-known cities. Cf. the still valuable note by Broadus, ad loc.

The region was Gentile, as evidenced by the herd of pigs, which would not be found in Jewish territory. But Matthew does not make Jesus' excursion into this region symbolic of the church's mission to Gentiles, for he omits the preaching at the end of the story. The rebuffing of Jesus by the inhabitants probably kept Matthew from playing on the motif of Gentile evangelism.

Strikingly, Matthew writes about two demoniacs rather than one man with an unclean spirit. With Mark, Luke writes of only one; but with Matthew he speaks of demons. Do Mark and Luke mention only the spokesman in a pair of demoniacs? Hardly, because according to Matthew both demoniacs spoke to Jesus (v 29). We have already noted Matthew's habit of compensating for omitted material by extracting and including elsewhere bits and pieces of that material (see "Compensation" in the Topical Index). Matthew omitted the story of the man with an unclean spirit in the synagogue at Capernaum (Mark 1:21-28; Luke 4:31-37). Here he compensates for the omission by associating that man with the demoniac on the other side of the Sea of Galilee. The similarity of the two demoniacs' responses to Jesus made the association natural (see Mark 1:24 with Mark 5:7). Cf. Matthew's adding a second blind man in 9:27-31; 20:29-34 because of the omission of the blind man in Mark 8:22-26. The compensatory doubling may have something to do with Matthew's distinctive interest in establishing every matter by two or three witnesses (18:16). The coming reference to Jesus as God's Son would benefit from a double witness (v 29).

Mark uses the singular for the demoniac till mention of the name "Legion," and then the plural. Luke has the singular only in his vv 29-30. Matthew uses the plural all the way through because, despite omission of the name "Legion," he writes of two demoniacs.

Matthew omits Jesus' getting out of the boat. Both Matthew and Luke omit Mark's "immediately." Matthew's participle "coming out" derives from Mark's genitive absolute. In Mark the participle (in the aorist and singular) refers to Jesus in relation to the boat; in Matthew the participle (in the present and plural) refers to the two demoniacs in relation to the tombs. Several items drop out: (1) the dwelling in the tombs; (2) the lengthy description of other men's inability to chain and subdue the demoniac successfully; and (3) his incessant yelling and self-lacerating. Luke shares the second and third omissions. Matthew summarizes by referring generally to the demoniacs' fierce violence and to the resultant inability of people to travel the road that went through the area. λίαν is a Mattheanism (3,1).

The insertion of "through that road" may be significant. Elsewhere in Matthew ὁδός refers prominently, though not always, to the path of discipleship (see esp. the insertions in 7:13-14; 21:32; cf. 22:16). The lack of the term in Mark's and Luke's versions of the present story and the lack of an antecedent for "that" possibly indicate a symbolic reference to discipleship, for which Jesus' authority clears away demonic opposition. Neither Mark nor Luke mentions the inability of people to pass that way. And Matthew characteristically uses ἐκεῖνος for special emphasis (26,9). If he does insert "that way" for the reason suggested, this story follows the pattern of the former in beginning on the note of discipleship and climaxing with Jesus' majestic authority.

8:29 *(Mark 5:6-10; Luke 8:28-31)* Matthew omits the demoniac's seeing Jesus from a distance, running to him, and worshiping him. For the evangelist, worship of Jesus presupposes a faith in him scarcely characteristic of demoniacs. To emphasize the identification of Jesus as God's Son, Matthew inserts ἰδού (34,9). His preference for the participle λέγοντες

(61,23) causes Mark's participle and verb to switch roles. The loudness of the demoniac's voice and the description of God as "the Most High" drop out lest they divert attention from Jesus' divine sonship.

The attempt of the demoniac to adjure Jesus in God's name not to torment him becomes a question, followed by an affirmative answer, whether Jesus has come to torment the demoniacs "before the appointed time," i.e., before the last judgment. With a different punctuation the attempt becomes in Matthew a declaration, followed by confirmation, that Jesus has so come. καιρῷ is a Mattheanism (6,1), which will occur again in 13:30 for the last judgment. At 18:34 there is a distinctive use of βασανισταῖς, which is cognate to the present βασανίσαι, in a parable that extends to the last judgment. Matthew draws "have you come?" (or "you have come") from the story of the demoniac in the synagogue at Capernaum (Mark 1:24; cf. Matthew's interest in Jesus as the Coming One—3:11). This expression confirms that he was compensating for omission of that story by bringing in its demoniac as a second demoniac here.

By exchanging the adjuration for a question or a statement concerning Jesus as the Coming One, Matthew insulates Jesus' majesty against any inference that the demoniac succeeded in the adjuration. If Jesus will allow the demons to go into the pigs rather than send them "out of the country" (so Mark) or "into the abyss" (so Luke), that will happen because of his authoritative command, not because of their adjuration. The insulation of his majesty also results in omission of the flashback to the earlier conversation Jesus had with the demoniac. In that conversation, his telling the demon to come out, his asking for the demon's name, and the demoniac's insistence in the request for permission to go into the nearby pigs might suggest that Jesus had some difficulty and needed to gain supremacy by discovering the name "Legion." (To know the name of someone—i.e., to know his character as revealed in the name—was to gain influence over or through him.) Matthew even omits the name "Legion" and the self-description of the demons as "many" to avoid the suggestion that Jesus had difficulty.

Because Matthew does not make the story symbolic of the church's mission to Gentiles, ὧδε carries only its simple meaning "here," not a pregnant meaning "here in Gentile country." On the freedom of demons to afflict people till the last judgment, see *1 Enoch* 15–16; *Jub.* 10:5-9; *T. Levi* 18:12. For βασανίζω at the last judgment, cf. Rev 9:5; 14:11; 18:7, 10, 15. With the omission of Jesus' question "What is your name?" cf. Matthew's frequent dropping of questions to avoid the implication of ignorance on Jesus' part (9:22; 14:17; 16:4; 17:11, 14, 18; 18:1; 19:4).

8:30-31 (Mark 5:11-12; Luke 8:32) Instead of recording the earlier conversation, Matthew immediately notes the herd of pigs and the request of the demons, whom he now introduces. He takes the imperfect tense of παρεκάλουν from the earlier conversation rather than adopt the aorist παρεκάλεσαν in the present parallels; yet the request lacks the earlier πολλά, "insistently" (Mark 5:10). Rather, πολλά becomes πολλῶν, "many," to describe the pigs. This change leads to the dropping of Mark's "great" from "herd." The herd was grazing within sight on a mountainside. Matthew notes their distance ("some distance from them") rather than their being within view ("there," so Mark and Luke). His doing so avoids an association between Jesus and unclean animals (cf. 15:15-20 with Mark 7:17-23 and following comments). Mark's and Luke's reference to the mountainside falls away. Matthew introduced a mountain as the place where Jesus taught (5:1). He does not want to desecrate it with pigs.

The demons' request in v 31 gains the conditional clause "If you cast us out" (not in Mark or Luke), and Mark's telic clause "in order that we may enter into them" drops out. Thus Matthew softens the request proper. Now it sounds less like a command to a Jesus struggling for supremacy and more like a plea to a dominant Jesus. Before mentioning the pigs Matthew inserts "the herd" for a parallel with the preceding verse. ἀπόστειλον replaces Mark's πέμψον and connotes the authority of Jesus. Outside the present Markan parallel πέμπω never stands for a sending by him.

8:32 (Mark 5:13; Luke 8:32-33) For even greater enhancement of Jesus' authority, "and he permitted them" (so Mark and Luke) changes to a command that is directly quoted: "and he said to them, 'Go' " (cf. vv 4, 13). Matthew likes ὑπάγετε (5,6). "The unclean spirits" (so Mark) drop out because they detract from the figure of Jesus. The prefixing of ἀπ- rather than εἰσ- to -ῆλθον makes the obedience of the demons match their sending exactly (ἀπό + στειλον). This revision highlights the effectiveness of Jesus' authoritative command.

To the rushing of the herd down the steep bank into the sea, Matthew characteristically adds "behold" (34,9) and "all" (63,25-26). "All" takes the place of Mark's "about two thousand," which Luke omits. This double emphasis on the frustration of the demons' request again enhances Jesus' authority. Matthew replaces Mark's "were drowning" with "died." Furthermore, whereas *"the herd"* rushes down in Mark, *"they"* die in Matthew. With omission of the reference to approximately two thousand pigs, Matthew's phraseology refers to the dying of the demons rather than to the drowning of the pigs. The dying of the demons consists in their going to the torments of hell when the herd plunged in the sea. Thus Jesus does indeed "torment" the demons "before the appointed time." By calling attention to his doing so, Matthew deals in a bit of realized eschatology. "Waters" avoids a second successive mention of the sea and ties this story to the similar one in 14:22-33, where the term occurs twice in specially Matthean material (vv 28-29). In Matthew it occurs in the plural only in these two passages.

The ancients commonly believed that on exorcism, demons vented their anger with some mischief (Josephus *Ant.* 8.2.5 §§46-48; Philostratus *Vit. Ap.* 4.20). But since the *demons* die, the action of the pigs that causes their death is hardly a piece of mischief intended by the demons—at least not in Matthew.

8:33 (Mark 5:14; Luke 8:34) As in Luke, "them" (the pigs) drops out of the statement regarding the flight of the herders. Omission of "the fields" leaves only the city, which Matthew likes (πόλις—18,3). The insertion of ἀπελθόντες typifies Matthew's diction (14,11) and echoes v 32. The insertion also makes εἰς τὴν πόλιν refer to the going away *"into* the city" rather than to the announcement *"in* the city" (so Mark and Luke). This shift enables Matthew more easily to insert the subject matter of the herders' announcement: "all things and the things concerning the demoniacs" (not in Mark or Luke). πάντα and, to some extent, δαιμονιζομένων belong to his preferred diction (63,25-26; 2,0). He is interested in what the herders said because it enhances Jesus' majesty.

8:34 (Mark 5:14-20; Luke 8:34-39) For a third time in the story Matthew inserts "behold" (34,9). Each insertion plays a Christological role. In v 29 it underlined Jesus' divine sonship. In v 32 it emphasized the effect of Jesus' command in the death of the demons. Here it highlights the city's meeting and seeing *Jesus*—not the former demoniac, as in Mark and Luke. The majestic figure of Jesus entirely crowds out the former demoniacs in the climax of Matthew's version. Furthermore, it is "all" the city that comes out. "All" is an emphatic and typical insertion (63,25-26). The people do not come to see what had happened (so Mark and Luke). They come to meet Jesus (cf. 25:10, also peculiar to Matthew). ὑπάντησιν often connoted the meeting of an honored visitor outside a city (see G. Milligan, *St. Paul's Epistles to the Thessalonians* [Grand Rapids: Eerdmans, 1952] 62). In that sense it contributes to Jesus' majesty here.

In Mark and Luke, then, the people come to Jesus; but they come to see, and they do see, the former demoniac sitting clothed and tamed. They become afraid. The report of the eyewitnesses follows. In Matthew the center of gravity shifts to Jesus. Matthew omits both the demoniacs and the eyewitnesses. All the city sees Jesus and beseeches him to leave their region. Such is the awe they feel in his presence. Here Matthew ends the story. In his account we read nothing about the plea of the former demoniac to go with Jesus, about Jesus' refusal, about the command to proclaim what had happened, or about the carrying out of that command. Not a single detail of the sequel is allowed to distract attention from Jesus himself.

Matthew, along with Luke, drops Mark's auxiliary ἤρξαντο. And since he has recently used ἀπελθόντες (v 33), μεταβῇ substitutes for Mark's ἀπελθεῖν. Like ἀπελθεῖν, μεταβῇ is a Mattheanism (5,1). Mark's infinitive construction turns into a clause beginning with a characteristic ὅπως (8,7).

JESUS' AUTHORITY TO FORGIVE SINS AS A MODEL OF THE DISCIPLES' AUTHORITY TO FORGIVE SINS
9:1-8 (Mark 2:1-12; 5:18a, 21; Luke 5:17-26)

Matthew has shown Jesus' authority over the law (chaps. 5–7), over diseases and demons (8:1-4, 14-17, 28-34), over men (8:18-22), and over creation (8:23-27). Now he shows Jesus' authority over sin (9:1-8). But he will go back to Jesus' authority over men (9:9-13, 14-17), over diseases (9:18-26, 27-31), and over demons (9:32-34). The mixing of materials goes against arrangement according to the objects of Jesus' authority.

9:1 (Mark 5:18a, 21; 2:1-2; Luke 5:17) Jesus is back on the west side of the Sea of Galilee. Matthew picks up material that precedes the foregoing

161

in the other synoptics. In both Mark and Luke the story follows that of the healing of the leper, with which Matthew started his series of miracle stories (8:1-4). The introduction takes shape with a piecing together of elements from Mark 5:18, toward the close of the exorcism of Legion, and from Mark 5:21, at the beginning of the raising of Jairus's daughter, and from Mark 2:1-2, at the beginning of the healing of the paralytic. Matthew omitted Mark 5:18 in 8:34 and will yet omit Mark 5:21 in 9:18. "And getting in a boat" comes from "And as he was getting in the boat" in Mark 5:18. "He crossed over" comes from "And after Jesus crossed over" in Mark 5:21. "Again . . . after several days" (so Mark 2:1) drops out, because in Matthew's rearrangement of material the return to Capernaum immediately follows the rebuff in the country of the Gadarenes.

The authority of Jesus and his disciples comes at the end of the story. Matthew wants to reach that theme as quickly as possible; so he bypasses the hearing of the report that Jesus was at home, the gathering of many at the door, and Jesus' speaking the word to them (so Mark 2:1-2). These omissions lead him to escalate Jesus' entry into Capernaum from Mark's participial phrase ("and entering . . . into Capernaum") to an independent clause ("and he came into his own city"; cf. 4:13). The replacement of "Capernaum" with πόλιν suits Matthew's diction (18,3) and interest in cities as places of ministry. The characteristically Matthean ἰδίαν (6,0) recalls Jesus' having taken up residence in Capernaum to fulfill Isa 8:23–9:1(9:1-2) (Matt 4:13-16).

9:2a (Mark 2:3-4; Luke 5:18-19) Because "came" has just been used for Jesus, Matthew omits "they [the people] come" (Mark 2:2). He is more interested in Mark's φέροντες πρὸς αὐτόν, which becomes προσέφερον αὐτῷ (cf. προσενέγκαι in Mark 2:4, omitted by Matthew). The typically Matthean insertion of ἰδού (34,9—so also Luke) and transference of πρός to the verb (9,2) may imply an offering to Jesus (cf. the comments on 2:11 and 4:24).

Instead of reading that the paralytic was being carried by four others (so Mark), we read that he was "prostrate on a bed." Thus the four others do not vie with Jesus for attention. Luke shares with Matthew the phrase "on a bed," and the Mattheanism βεβλημένον (12,8) links this story to the preceding stories concerning the centurion's servant and Peter's mother-in-law, where the word has already occurred without parallel in the same sense (see 8:6, 14). Again Matthew diverts attention from the four by leaving out all the material concerning their inability to push through the crowd, their digging through the roof, and their lowering the pallet on which the paralytic was lying. Instead, he puts προσφέρω in the imperfect tense—his only hint of their difficulty—and skips to Jesus' seeing their faith and speaking to the paralytic. But their faith cannot refer to the escapade on the roof, for Matthew has omitted that. It refers, rather, to their "offering" the paralytic to Jesus. The faith of the paralytic does not come into view.

9:2b (Mark 2:5; Luke 5:20) To introduce Jesus' words to the paralytic, Matthew uses εἶπεν (so also Luke) rather than Mark's λέγει. The result is a parallel with εἶπαν in v 3, where the present tense would not fit well, and with εἶπεν in v 4 (cf. εἰπεῖν in v 5 [bis]). Indeed, the stem εἰπ- ties together the whole story in this gospel. Matthew now inserts the greeting "Take courage." It anticipates the story of Jesus' walking on the water during a storm on Galilee (14:27). Matthew has this story in mind because only recently he recorded a similar one about Jesus' calming a storm on Galilee (8:24-27). In that one we found evidence of a forward look to the later story, where "Take courage" comes from Mark 6:50. Behind the greeting lies the intent of dispelling fear (see esp. 14:27). The insertion is appropriate to the coming exercise of Jesus' authority to forgive sins—a happy thought that is enough to encourage anyone.

The Jewish view of illnesses as direct results of particular sins (cf. John 9:2) contributed to Jesus' pronouncing the paralytic's sins forgiven. In the opinion of the onlookers, only a cure could confirm the pronouncement of forgiveness. Continuance of the illness would mean persistence of guilt. The present tense of the verb indicating forgiveness carries the connotation "at this moment." Behind the passive voice lies God's forgiveness. But Matthew takes pains to identify Jesus as God. And prior to Matthew's editing, the granting of forgiveness by the Son of man (see v 6) implies his deity (cf. the theophanic symbolism of the clouds in Dan 7:13-14). The Jews of Jesus' day expected forgiveness in the messianic age (CD 14:19; 11QMelch 4-9), but did not expect the Messiah himself to forgive sins or to be divine.

9:3 (*Mark 2:6-7; Luke 5:21*) Matthew replaces the scribes' "sitting there and reasoning in their hearts" (so Mark) with "they said within themselves," characteristically emphasized by ἰδού (34,9). "Within themselves" comes from Mark 2:8 and does not appear again in Matthew's version of the story. Thus Matthew sets up an antithetic parallel between what Jesus said to the paralytic and what certain of the scribes said within themselves. Except for "this one," Mark's "Why does this one speak thus?" drops out before "he is blaspheming." The following question concerning who is able to forgive sins also disappears. These omissions leave the charge in the form "This one is blaspheming." Alone, the charge becomes more forceful. There also results a closer parallel with Jesus' single declaration that the paralytic's sins are forgiven. Further omission of the question implying that God alone can forgive sins forestalls any inference that Jesus is not God. To the contrary, Matthew has been accentuating the deity of Jesus, who will save his people from their sins (1:21). Omission of this question also prepares for the implication that "the men" of Jesus have authority to forgive sins (v 8).

9:4 (*Mark 2:8; Luke 5:22*) Matthew, along with Luke, drops Mark's "immediately." Mark's and Luke's ἐπιγνούς becomes εἰδώς for a parallel with εἰδῆτε in v 6. We see, then, a parallel between the knowledge of Jesus and that of the scribes. This is similar to the parallel Matthew set up between their sayings. Because of the parallelism, Jesus' spirit (so Mark) drops out. It lacks a counterpart later in v 6. In sharing this omission but not the consistency of parallelism, Luke shows influence from Matthew alongside dependence on Mark. "That thus they reason within themselves" (so Mark) becomes "their thoughts" (so also Luke, except that he retains Mark's stem διαλογιζ-). In this way Matthew conforms v 2b ("and Jesus, seeing their faith, said") and v 4a ("and Jesus, knowing their thoughts, said") to each other. He wants a contrast between faith that brings an offering to Jesus and unbelief that charges Jesus with blasphemy. Also, the questions the scribes were asking themselves have been eliminated; so Matthew switches from διαλογίζονται to ἐνθυμήσεις. διαλογίζομαι and διαλογισμός connote blameworthy uncertainty in 15:19; 16:7, 8; 21:25. ἐνθύμησις and ἐνθυμέομαι, neither of which occurs in the other gospels, connote resolute thinking in 1:20; 9:4; 12:25. The first part of 12:25 provides an especially close parallel with the present passage. Thus in Matthew the scribes appear in a severer light: their thoughts as well as their charge lack any element of doubt. Correspondingly, Jesus' initial question to the scribes carries a sting that is sharper in Matthew than it is in Mark or Luke. Not only does ἐνθυμεῖσθε, "think resolutely," replace διαλογίζεσθε, "think questioningly." But also Matthew introduces the question with ἱνατί, a stronger "Why?" than Mark's and Luke's τί (cf. 27:46 with Mark 15:34), and characteristically calls the scribes' thoughts "evil things" (πονηρά—10,4) rather than write the tame "these things" (so Mark; Luke omits). In effect, Jesus' question becomes a countercharge.

9:5 (Mark 2:9; Luke 5:23) The typical insertion of γάρ (62-63,15) makes Jesus' next question a substantiation of the charge contained in "evil things." After the first εἰπεῖν, Mark's "to the paralytic" drops out (as also in Luke). The omission makes for a closer parallel with the next εἰπεῖν, which lacks an indirect object. The references to forgiveness of sins, getting up, and walking match Mark's wording exactly. But Matthew, along with Luke, omits the taking up of the pallet, probably because he prefers pairs of expressions rather than trios. Cf. v 6, where according to the probably original text Matthew reduces Mark's ἔγειρε to a participle in order to have only two main verbs. Jesus asks the question "What is easier?" from the standpoint of a skeptic who wants visible confirmation of an unobservable and therefore doubtful forgiveness.

9:6 (Mark 2:10-11; Luke 5:24) In v 6 the spotlight shines on Jesus' authority. Mark already has ἐξουσίαν in an emphatic early position. Matthew keeps it there. But along with Luke, he brings forward ἐπὶ τῆς γῆς from the end of the clause, where it tells the place of forgiveness, to a position right after ὁ υἱὸς τοῦ ἀνθρώπου, where it tells the place of the Son of man's authority. The stress thus shifts from forgiveness of sins to the figure of Jesus as the Son of man and, more particularly, to the demonstration that the Son of man, a heavenly figure in Dan 7:13-14, retains his authority on earth. Before "he says to the paralytic" Matthew adds his beloved τότε (66,17) to give a clear sense of progression. The retention of Mark's λέγει, rather than a switching to εἶπεν (as in Luke), enables him more easily to omit the redundant "I say to you." In ἐγερθείς he has made the command "Rise" into a participle in order to have only a pair of matching imperatives, "take up" and "go" (cf. Luke). The participial form typifies his style (2-3,5).

We should read ἐγερθείς with א C Θ *pl* and the Byzantine family (so the UBS) rather than ἔγειρε with B (D it) (so Aland); for, as we have just noted, the participial form characterizes Matthew's style. The old word κλίνην replaces Mark's new and colloquial χράβαττον. Similarly, Luke uses χλίνης and, because of the paralytic's picking up the bed, the diminutive χλινίδιον. Elsewhere in the synoptics, too, χράβαττον appears only in the second gospel.

9:7 (Mark 2:12; Luke 5:25) In v 7 Mark's ἠγέρθη becomes ἐγερθείς for a match with ἐγερθείς in Jesus' command (cf. Luke's ἀναστάς). But the whole reference to taking the bed, or pallet, falls away; and "he went out in the sight of all" (so Mark) becomes "he went away into his house" (so also Luke). ἀπῆλθεν is a Mattheanism (14,11) and forges a link with 8:18, 19, 21, 32, 33. "Into his house" corresponds to Jesus' command. Matthew's rewording suggests that the paralytic's getting up and going away to his house represents obedient discipleship, just as going away to the other side of the Sea of Galilee represented obedient discipleship (8:18ff.).

9:8 (Mark 2:12; Luke 5:26) Matthew begins his description of the onlookers' response to the miracle by inserting ἰδόντες, which typifies his style (10-11,7). The onlookers themselves are called "the crowds." In mentioning the crowds here, Matthew brings up Mark's reference to "all the crowd" at the beginning of the next story (Mark 2:13), but drops the adjective and compensates by making the noun plural (cf. the plural in 4:25; 5:1; 7:28; 8:1 and often in later passages). As before, these crowds are Jesus' disciples who, in contrast with the unbelieving scribes, are filled with a fear that befits the presence of deity (cf. Luke, but contrast Mark—see also 10:28; 17:6; 28:4). They also glorify God.

Matthew does not quote the crowds' expression of amazement. Instead, he returns to the theme of authority by describing God as "the one who gives such authority to men." This description does not make up the content of the crowds' glorification of God. It is Matthew's own characterization of God. We might have expected the evangelist to refer to Jesus as the recipient of such authority. But he refers to "the men." Who are they? They can hardly be different from the disciples whom Matthew strikingly called "the men" when Jesus calmed the storm (see 8:27 with comments). As there, "the men" stand in contrast with the divine Jesus. Matthew has in mind Jesus' giving the disciples authority to forgive sins (see 16:19; 18:18 [cf. John 20:23]). That such authority is given to mere men is astounding. It is confirmed by the authority Jesus gave his disciples over unclean spirits and every kind of disease and sickness (10:1). For Matthew, then, Jesus is the God whom the crowds glorify. And Jesus' forgiving and healing the paralytic is a model for Christians' declaring sins forgiven and performing miraculous cures to substantiate the forgiveness.

We should not confuse the authority of Jesus' disciples to forgive sins committed against God with their obligation to forgive those who have sinned against them.

JESUS' AUTHORITY TO EXERCISE MERCY TOWARD PUBLICANS AND SINNERS IN ACCORD WITH THE OLD TESTAMENT
9:9-13 (Mark 2:13-17; Luke 5:27-32)

9:9 (Mark 2:13-14; Luke 5:27-28) As in Mark and Luke, the call of Matthew-Levi, who represents publicans and sinners, appropriately follows Jesus' forgiving sins. Matthew omits the first verse in Mark's report. That verse speaks of Jesus' going out to the seaside again, the coming of all the crowd to him, and his teaching them. Matthew has just mentioned crowds in v 8 and will yet pick up several elements from the verse in Mark, e.g., Jesus' exit from the house where he forgave and healed the paralytic. Except for retaining Jesus' exit, Luke shares the omission with Matthew. See further the comments on 13:1.

Typically, Matthew inserts the name of Jesus (80,12) and ἐκεῖθεν (8,1), which partly compensates for his omission of Mark's introductory verse. "Levi the son of Alphaeus sitting at the tax office" (so Mark) becomes "a man sitting at the tax office." The juxtaposition of Jesus and "a man" suggests that Matthew continues to portray Jesus as the majestic God who gives great authority to men; the man at the tax office is a foil to the divine Jesus. Finally, Matthew mentions the man's name, but it is "Matthew" rather than "Levi" (cf. 10:3). Since the evangelist likes to give alternative personal names with the use of λέγω as a participle meaning "called" (10,2), we have some reason to think that he is doing so here despite his omitting the other name Levi. For Jesus' words, Mark's historical present "he says" is retained because the following call to discipleship still speaks to people. The recording of that call and of Matthew's obedience to it shows no revision.

Some suggest that the first evangelist replaced Levi with Matthew in order to gain a reference to one of the twelve apostles. But his stressing the discipleship of the crowds rather than that of the twelve and the obscurity of Matthew among the twelve tell against the suggestion. Nor does the substitution of the mother of Zebedee's sons (27:56) for Salome (Mark 15:40) provide a strong argument from analogy in favor of the suggestion; for there we do not have a switch in names (the mother remains anonymous) as we have here. And in view of the anonymity of the one to whom Jesus said "Follow me" in 8:22, just as he says to Matthew here in 9:9, it lacks cogency to argue that the evangelist felt so embarrassed by Levi's nonapostleship that he switched to the apostolic name Matthew to get a parallel with the call of the apostles Peter, Andrew, James, and John in 4:18-22. Why did he not give the disciple in 8:21-22 an apostolic name, too? Both in location and in phraseology, 4:18-22, where we read "Hither! After me!" is more distant from 9:9 than 8:21-22 is.

Perhaps "Levi" represents tribal origin (cf. Neh 11:15-22). Or "Matthew," because it means "gift of Yahweh" (the Aramaic מַתַּאי or מַתַּי is probably an abbreviation of מַתַּנְיָה—see 2 Kgs 24:17; Neh 11:17, 22; cf. 1 Chr 9:31; Neh 8:4; Acts 1:23), is a name given to Levi when he became a disciple. If so, the preconversion name is avoided because of the emphasis on discipleship (cf. the immediate introduction of "Peter" in the account of Simon's call—so 4:18 against Mark 1:16-20). Or the man bore two Levitical, Semitic names (Neh 11:15-22), neither of which was a descriptive nickname (for similar examples easily accessible, see the citations in W. L. Lane, *The Gospel According to Mark* [NICNT; Grand Rapids: Eerdmans, 1974] 100-101 n. 29; and Josephus *Ant.* 18.2.2 §35; 18.4.3 §95; 20.8.11 §196). If the latter is so, the evangelist switches from Levi to Matthew in order to gain the better-known name. On the probability that Matthew-Levi worked in the taxation of fishermen, see W. H. Wuellner, *The Meaning of "Fishers of Men"* (Philadelphia: Westminster, 1967) 43-44. Alternatively, Matthew-Levi may have worked at a customs post where he collected charges on goods that were going from the territory of Philip to that of Herod Antipas.

9:10 (Mark 2:15; Luke 5:29) Matthew now changes Mark's "and it comes to pass" to "and it came to pass," and Mark's infinitive construction becomes a genitive absolute. In Mark the coming to pass has to do with the meal, to which the presence of many publicans and sinners is coordinate; in Matthew the coming to pass has to do with the presence of many publicans and sinners, to which Jesus' reclining at meal is subordinate. Additional emphasis falls on the reclining of publicans and sinners with Jesus and his disciples in the typically Matthean insertions of ἰδού (34,9) and ἐλθόντες (10,10). The latter compensates further for the omission of Mark 2:13 and probably represents a coming for discipleship (cf. the use of ἀπέρχομαι for discipleship in 8:18, 19). But as in Luke, Mark's statement that "they were many and were following him [Jesus]" drops out because of its redundancy and apparent discrepancy with their reclining. To make the figure of Jesus stand out more prominently, Matthew omits Mark's "his," which refers to the owner of the house where the meal took place. Does "his" refer to Levi or to Jesus? Mark offers no answer. Luke makes the house Levi's. But because Matthew wrote in 4:13 that Jesus set up house in Capernaum, distinctively Matthean references to a house not otherwise qualified (as here) point to Jesus' house in Capernaum (see also 9:28; 13:1, 36; 17:25). The casting of Jesus in the role of host enhances his authority in exercising mercy on sinners.

9:11 (Mark 2:16; Luke 5:30) To match the construction of v 9, Matthew brings the participle "seeing" to the head of the sentence. "The scribes of the Pharisees" (i.e., scribes from among the Pharisees, so Mark) become simply "the Pharisees" because the previous story has already dealt with a controversy between Jesus and the scribes (see also the comments on v 14 and cf. Luke). Matthew omits "that Jesus is eating with sinners and publicans." Luke shares the omission, which saves the following question of the Pharisees from redundancy. διὰ τί replaces Mark's interrogative ὅτι for a parallel with διὰ τί in the question introducing the next segment of material (v 14). Luke shares this replacement, which is somewhat of a Mattheanism (3,0). Matthew then inserts "your teacher" in the Pharisees' question as another compensation for his omitting Mark 2:13, where we read "he began to teach." The insertion is typical (4,1) and prepares for "learn" in v 13. *"Your* teacher" from the Pharisees makes a counterpart of *"their* scribes" from Matthew (7:29). Though it is put in the mouths of the Pharisees, the designation "Teacher" enhances Jesus' authority (cf. the comments on 5:1-2 and see 17:24).

Jews despised publicans for collaboration and contact with Gentiles, for the handling of currency with pagan inscriptions and iconography, and for dishonesty. See further *TDNT* 8. 88-105. The publicans in the gospels seem to be Jewish customs officials (working under Herod Antipas in the area of Galilee) rather than Roman tax collectors. In Jewish vocabulary "sinners" referred to pagan Gentiles and to Jews careless about the fine points of the OT law as interpreted by the rabbis. Even though pagan Gentiles may not have eaten with Jesus on this occasion, to Matthew the Jewish sinners who ate with Jesus probably held promise of the later evangelization of Gentiles.

9:12-13 (Mark 2:17; Luke 5:31-32) The dropping of Mark's "to them" again highlights the figure of Jesus. Because he does not direct the following words to his disciples (and through them to the church), the historical present "he says" (so Mark) changes to "he said." Jesus' name moved to the head of the story for emphasis (see v 9); so it drops out here. In the saying about the strong, who have no need of a physician, in contrast to the ill, who do have such need, Jesus defends his eating with publicans and sinners. The figurative use of illness for sin comes from the causal relation between sin and illness (whatever the directness or indirectness of that causal relation) and makes appropriate the presence of this passage among stories of healings.

To the saying of Jesus about his not having come to call the righteous but sinners, Matthew distinctively prefixes a command to "go learn what it means, 'I want mercy and not sacrifice' " (Hos 6:6a). "Go learn" corresponds to the rabbinic formula צֵא וּלְמֹד, "go and learn." Words with the stem μαθ- belong to Matthew's favorite diction (33,8). Typically, the going reduces to a participle (πορευθέντες—8,4). Therefore the conjunction "and" of the rabbinic formula drops out. The resultant stress on learning rather than going suits Matthew's interest in discipleship, which by definition is learning. For a comparable combination, see 28:19. The same use of Hos 6:6a will occur in 12:7, where Matthew inserts the quotation in a similar story. The key word in the quotation, "mercy," plays a large role in his theology (see the comments on 5:7). The importing of Hos 6:6a indicates that for Matthew this story displays Jesus' exercise of authority through showing mercy to publicans and sinners. Such mercy fulfills the law and the prophets (cf. 5:17-20) and gives an example for disciples to follow.

The question of sacrifice does not arise in the story. Either Matthew regards sacrifice as symbolizing the Pharisees' concern about ritual contamination from eating with publicans and sinners, or he uses the quotation solely for its positive statement about mercy. Does his changing the probable reading of the LXX—viz., ἤ, which might be taken in the sense "more than"—to the literally accurate καὶ οὐ arise out of the Christian negation of offering sacrifices? The characteristic insertion of γάρ (62-63,15) in the clause following the quotation makes Jesus' coming to call sinners rather than righteous people a reason for going and learning about mercy. In view of Matthew's making Jesus host at the meal, "to call" connotes his invitation to the messianic banquet of salvation, which is anticipated in his inviting sinners to have table fellowship with him in his home (cf. 22:3-4, 8-9; Pr Man 7-8).

JESUS' AUTHORITY IN THE PRESERVATION OF FASTING
9:14-17 (Mark 2:18-22; Luke 5:33-39)

9:14 (Mark 2:18; Luke 5:33) Once again we do not have the story of a miracle or exorcism, but one in which the center of interest lies in a didactic dialogue concerning an aspect of discipleship. And again Matthew, Mark, and Luke agree in the sequence of incidents (cf. Mark 2:18-22; Luke

5:33-39). The question of fasting follows naturally the question of eating with publicans and sinners. To indicate progression, Matthew begins by replacing Mark's καί with his favorite τότε (66,17). "They come and say to him" changes to "they come to him . . . saying." Matthew's προσέρχονται is characteristic (38,6) and portrays Jesus as an authoritative figure whom others approach respectfully. Retention of the historical present tense and a typical de-escalation of the verb of speaking to a participle (61,23) add to this portrait.

Matthew mentions only the disciples of John the Baptist as approaching Jesus. Though the Pharisees shortly appear along with them in fasting, the Pharisees tend to fade out. They have already figured in vv 9-13, and Matthew wants a progression from scribes (vv 1-8) to Pharisees (vv 9-13) to John's disciples (vv 14-17). On the other hand, Mark begins by writing that John's disciples and the Pharisees were fasting. He then writes that they, apparently both John's disciples and the Pharisees, came and spoke to Jesus. Matthew regards the reference to fasting as unnecessary, since the matter will come up in the following question to Jesus. As usual, he wants to reach the dialogue as soon as possible. Mark's opening reference to the fasting by John's disciples and the Pharisees therefore drops out. Luke, too, omits this reference, but also omits the coming to Jesus. In Luke, as a result, those who speak to Jesus appear to be the Pharisees alone (see vv 30-31).

In the question to Jesus, "the disciples of John" becomes "we" in order that John's disciples may act alone in the role of Jesus' interlocutors. If accepted textually, the addition of πολλά, "much," probably alludes to the Pharisees' practice of fasting on Mondays and Thursdays. However, ℵ* B cop^sa^ms geo^B lack the word; and despite his frequent use of it as an adjective (23,1), elsewhere Matthew never uses it in the adverbial accusative.

9:15 (Mark 2:19-20; Luke 5:34-35) According to Mark, Jesus responds, "The wedding guests are not able to fast while the bridegroom is with them, are they?" For a moment Matthew delays the temporal clause "while the bridegroom is with them." With an eye on Jesus' being "taken away" in death (cf. Isa 53:8), he also puts "to mourn" in place of "to fast." This replacement produces a contrast between weddinglike joy at table fellowship with Jesus and funerallike mourning at Jesus' death. "They are not able to fast" drops out (as in Luke). And Mark's two temporal clauses beginning "while" and "as long a time as" collapse into one clause beginning "for as long as." These changes have the effect of removing any justification for failure to fast that antinomians might try to draw from the failure of Jesus' disciples to fast during his earthly ministry. The cutting away of Mark's "in that day" from "and then they will fast" has the same effect. For the omission forestalls any limitation of fasting to a brief period at the time Jesus is taken away. Rather, the entirety of the church age constitutes "the days" that "will come when the bridegroom is taken away."

Matthew also changes the wording and order of words in the temporal clause in ways that put all possible emphasis on the figure of Jesus. χρόνον is left unexpressed. The originally adverbial ὅσον becomes objective after ἐφ' (see 25:40, 45 for two further occurrences of this distinctive phrase)

169

and introduces the clause in which the bridegroom is subject rather than the clause in which "they" is the subject of "have" (so Mark). And μετ' αὐτῶν, "with them," comes forward to emphasize that Jesus is Immanuel, "God with us" (1:23).

"For as long as the bridegroom is with them" reflects the Jewish practice of extending wedding festivities for several days. The bridegroom's presence during those days represents Jesus' earthly ministry. Late Judaism did not know a comparison of the Messiah with a bridegroom. But a messianic connotation does not necessarily adhere to the present metaphor. Besides, somebody was first to make the comparison; otherwise it would not appear in the NT. Therefore we have no good reason to deny that Jesus invented the metaphor and applied it to himself. Thus also there is no need to generalize the meaning by translating "During the wedding." Cf. Isa 54:4-8; 62:4-5; Ezekiel 16; Hos 2:21-22[19-20]; *Pesiq. R.* 149a; and see H. Riesenfeld, *The Gospel Tradition* (Philadelphia: Fortress, 1970) 152-54. On the possibility of a single Aramaic word behind fasting and mourning, see *TDNT* 4. 1103 n. 41. But Matthew is working with Mark's Greek text. Therefore we may not have alternate translations in our Greek gospels, but only a line of thought from the Greek for fasting to the Aramaic, which allows for mourning as well, and back to the Greek for mourning. The obviousness of the relation between fasting and mourning makes unnecessary even this latter recourse to Aramaic.

9:16 (Mark 2:21; Luke 5:36) Matthew inserts δέ to relate the sayings about the new patch and old garment and the new wine and old wineskins to the future fasting of Jesus' disciples. Since he has taken care to defend the resumption and continuance of fasting after Jesus' being taken away, we may assume a positive relation between fasting and these sayings. Fasting is not incompatible with the law of Christ, then, for fasting belongs to the contents of that law and that law carries out the intent of the Mosaic law (cf. 6:16-18).

Matthew smooths out Mark's rough text, translated literally "No one a patch of unshrunk cloth sews on an old garment," so that it reads in his gospel, "And no one puts a patch of unshrunk cloth on an old garment." Notably, Matthew and Luke engage in a bit of wordplay by changing Mark's ἐπιράπτει to ἐπιβάλλει, which is cognate to ἐπίβλημα. The further part of Mark's rough text is translated literally "Otherwise, it [the patch] draws away the fullness [the overlapping edge of the patch] from it [from the garment], the new from the old" (see M. G. Steinhauser in *ExpTim* 87 [1976] 312-13). Again Matthew simplifies the text, so that it reads "For its fullness [that of the patch] takes away from the garment." In other words, the unshrunk patch becomes the source of rending at the first washing and shrinking of the patch. The change entails a shift in the referent of αὐτοῦ from the garment (so Mark) to the patch. Luke smooths out the roughness in Mark's text differently.

Matthew's substitution of γάρ for εἰ δὲ μή typifies his diction (62-63,15). Some think that αὐτοῦ refers forward to the garment, others that it refers back to "no one." But "his [no one's] patch" makes doubtful sense, and an anticipation of the garment is not so easy as "the fullness of the patch."

9:17 (Mark 2:22; Luke 5:37-39) In the saying on new wine and old wineskins, Matthew replaces Mark's καὶ οὐδείς with οὐδέ for a parallel with δέ in the preceding saying. The loss of "no one" leads to the third plural of the verb ("people put") instead of the third singular. Mark's "otherwise" stays, but is strengthened with "indeed" (so also Luke). The future "will burst" (so Mark and Luke) becomes the present "bursts" for a closer parallel with "takes away" in the preceding saying. And where Mark and Luke put the emphasis on the wine that bursts the wineskins, Matthew puts it on the wineskins by making them the subject of the verb, now passive (literally "are burst"), and by omitting the wine entirely at this point. The perishing of the wine and wineskins (so Mark in a single clause) becomes a second pair of clauses in Matthew: "the wine is poured out, and the wineskins perish" (similarly Luke, but with future forms of the verbs). Thus the wineskins are emphasized again by having their own independent clause, in contrast with Mark, where they appear to be tacked on the single clause as an afterthought. This emphasis on the wineskins alongside the wine will attain its purpose in the final statement about the preservation of both.

For the putting of new wine in new wineskins, Matthew characteristically supplies βάλλουσιν (12,8—cf. βλητέον in Luke). The verb comes from v 17a and makes the parallelism more apparent. Then, to gain a third pair of clauses concerning the theme, Matthew adds "and both are kept together." See 13:30 for another distinctive occurrence of ἀμφότεροι; and with συντηροῦνται cf. Matthew's liking of τηρέω (5,1). For the third time, then, emphasis falls on the wineskins as well as the wine. Their preservation links with Matthew's stress on the coming of Jesus to fulfill the law and the prophets rather than destroy them (5:17-20). Thus the resumption and continuance of fasting after the brief interlude of Jesus' ministry—a resumption and continuance sanctioned by Jesus himself—exemplifies this preservative fulfillment. Individual identifications of the old wineskins, new wine, and new wineskins spoil a simple metaphor concerning the need to preserve a good religious practice. For example, if we were to identify the new wine with the gospel and set it in contrast with the old wineskins of Judaistic forms, what could we make of the concern not to let the old wineskins of Judaistic forms perish?

JESUS' AUTHORITY OVER DEATH
AND IN THE SALVATION OF THE WOMAN WITH THE FLOW
9:18-26 (Mark 5:21-43; Luke 8:40-56)

9:18 (Mark 5:21-23; Luke 8:40-42) Matthew now returns to a passage in Mark from which he drew his introduction to the last three stories. That introduction has already put Jesus back on the west side of the Sea of Galilee (see 9:1; cf. Mark 5:21). To get a new introduction, therefore, Matthew reaches into the middle of the passage for "while he was still speaking" (Mark 5:35; so also Matt 12:46; 17:5; 26:47). He drops "still," adds "these things" and "to them" (i.e., the things Jesus said concerning sinners and fasting to his guests at the meal—9:9-17), and typically inserts ἰδού for emphasis (34,9—so also Luke; cf. v 20).

171

But the emphasis does not fall on Jairus, for Matthew omits his name entirely. Rather, it falls on his approaching and worshipping Jesus. Obviously, then, Matthew is still stressing Jesus' deity. προσελθών comes from ἔρχεται in Mark and substitutes for Mark's ἰδών. Though the UBS reads ἐλθών with C D W Θ f¹ *al* syrˢ and the Byzantine family, Matthew's diction favors προσελθών (38,6), which probably has superior external support as well. No textual doubt plagues the Mattheanism προσεκύνει (6,5), which replaces Mark's "he falls at his feet." "One of the rulers of the synagogue" becomes "a certain ruler" because the man appears as a worshipper of Jesus. Matthew can hardly relate this worshipper of Jesus to the synagogue, which in his gospel has become "theirs," that of the Jews who opposed Jesus and now oppose those who worship him.

The imperfect of προσεκύνει begins a series of imperfects that weld Matthew's story together. See verbs in vv 19, 21, 24. To gain the series, Matthew twice changes Mark's historical present (cf. vv 18 and 24 with Mark). Nowhere in the story does he take over a historical present.

To keep attention on the ruler's worshipping Jesus, Matthew omits "and he beseeches him much." Only Mark's "saying" remains. It introduces the ruler's statement. In that statement, Matthew changes Mark's "little daughter" to "daughter" for a parallel with Jesus' address to the woman with a flow (v 22) and perhaps in anticipation of his omitting the reference to her age as twelve years (cf. v 25 with Mark 5:42; but the diminutive "girl" remains in vv 24-25). Luke also changes "little daughter," but he retains, and even advances, the reference to the girl's age.

In anticipation of his omitting the last minute report of the daughter's death (Mark 5:35-36; Luke 8:49-50), Matthew changes Mark's "is at the point of death" to "has just died." Both ἄρτι and ἐτελεύτησεν are favorites of his (7,0; 2,1). Cf. his telescoping the cursing and withering of the fig tree (21:18-22). Mark's awkward ἵνα ἐλθὼν ἐπιθῆς τὰς χεῖρας αὐτῇ, which readers might mistake to mean that the girl was dying *in order that* Jesus should lay hands on her, becomes ἀλλὰ ἐλθὼν ἐπίθες τὴν χεῖρά σου ἐπ' αὐτήν, "but coming, lay your hand on her" (cf. 1QapGen 20:29). The change to the singular "hand" conforms to 8:3, 15; 9:25. The addition of "your" focuses attention on Jesus more clearly. Mark's "in order that she may be saved and live" becomes "and she will live." This changing of a purposive clause to a confident prediction enhances both the ruler's faith and Jesus' authority. The omission of a reference to salvation leaves the verb of living to stand alone as a contrast to the verb of dying.

9:19 (Mark 5:24; Luke 8:42-43) "Getting up" replaces Mark's "he went away with him" and refers to Jesus' getting up from the table (cf. v 10). Matthew likes ἐγερθείς (2-3,5). A typical addition of Jesus' name (80,12) and a subtraction of Jairus's name in the preceding verse push Jesus into the foreground and Jairus into the background. Furthermore, to insert Jesus' name Matthew changes the subject of "was following" from "a large crowd" to "Jesus." For still greater emphasis on Jesus, he brings ὁ Ἰησοῦς to the front of the clause. Mark's large crowd does not quite disappear, however, for Matthew characteristically identifies them as Jesus' "disciples" (31,5) and leaves them in last place in the clause (as in Mark). Omission of the crowd's pressing Jesus also belongs to Matthew's program of concentrating attention on Jesus.

Instead of ἠκολούθει (so Aland), the UBS reads ἠκολούθησεν with B W Θ f¹ *pl f k* and the Byzantine family. But everywhere else in this passage Matthew retains Mark's imperfect whenever he has a corresponding verb. He even changes Mark's historical present to the imperfect. Normally his use of ἀκολουθέω connotes discipleship. No such connotation attaches to Jesus' following Jairus, of course. We have already seen the reason for Matthew's giving up the usual connotation, viz., the desire to focus on Jesus.

9:20-21 (Mark 5:25-33; Luke 8:43-47) The added "behold" (34,9) parallels "behold" at the beginning of the story concerning the ruler (v 18). There it called attention to his approaching and worshipping Jesus. Here it calls attention to a woman's approaching and touching Jesus' clothing. Typically, προσ- joins Mark's ἐλθοῦσα for the connotation of reverential approach (38,6). Matthew describes the woman's ailment in the fewest possible words—"flowing twelve years" (Mark has "being with a flow of blood twelve years")—and omits Mark's description of the great suffering of the woman from many physicians, her spending all her resources, her lack of benefit, her growing worse, her hearing about Jesus, and her being in the crowd. These details all disappear in order that Jesus may stand out more prominently. To Jesus' garment Matthew adds a reference to its tassel (so also Luke). This anticipates Mark 6:56 (cf. Matt 14:36; 23:5). The addition implies Jesus' fulfillment of the law requiring such tassels (Num 15:38-39; Deut 22:12; cf. Matt 5:17-20).

Insertion of "within herself" corresponds to the distinctive "within themselves" in v 3 and compensates for the present omission of Jesus' knowing "within himself" (Mark 5:30). The favorite μόνον (7,0) takes the place of Mark's κἄν, modifies the touching ("if only I may touch") rather than Jesus' garments ("at least his garments," so Mark), makes a parallel with the centurion's statement "But only [μόνον] speak a word" (8:8), and compensates for the otherwise omitted command "Only [μόνον] believe" (Mark 5:36; Luke 8:50). Later, Matthew will insert his adverb in a similar reference to the touching of a tassel on Jesus' garment (see 14:36). Mark's "the garments" becomes singular for a parallel with the singular in the preceding verse. Just as Jesus' touch effected the cure of Peter's mother-in-law (see 8:15 in some contrast with Mark and Luke), so only a touch by this woman effects her deliverance. Only a word, only a touch—such emphases show that Jesus' authority is so great that for miraculous cures it needs but little exercise.

Because her flowing made her ritually unclean and defiling to others (see Lev 15:19-33), the woman approached Jesus from behind to sneak a touch. The tugging of the hem of Ḥanin ha-Neḥba's coat by small children to gain attention (*b. Taʿan.* 23b) hardly parallels the reaching down of a grown woman who wants to avoid attention on account of her uncleanness.

9:22 (Mark 5:34; Luke 8:48) Again Matthew omits a large amount of material: the drying up of the flow of blood, the woman's feeling healed, Jesus' knowledge that healing power had gone from him, and the whole dialogue regarding the discovery of the healed woman. The elimination of Jesus' loss to know who had touched him and of the disciples' almost ridiculing comment about the senselessness of asking who touched him when a whole crowd of people were touching him—these omissions keep Jesus' majesty intact. Instead of the omitted material, Matthew reintroduces the name of Jesus (not in Mark or Luke; cf. v 19) and inserts his turning and seeing the woman. στραφείς and ἰδών are Mattheanisms (3,2; 10-11,7) and parallel Jesus' earlier "getting up" to follow the ruler (v 19). Jesus' words to the woman gain the introductory greeting "Take courage" for a parallel with v 2 and a preparation for the gift of salvation.

Jesus' command "Go in peace" drops out. Only the statement that the woman's faith has saved her and Matthew's corresponding statement that the woman is indeed saved remain. The latter statement substitutes for Jesus' additional command "and be healed from your affliction." Along with omission of the drying up of the woman's flow, the systematic excision of specifically physical notations in the description of the cure and the retention and addition of various forms of the general verb "save" make the woman's deliverance a symbol of Jesus' saving his people from their sins (cf. 1:21). To stress the immediacy and permanence of salvation upon the exercise of faith, Matthew inserts the typically rabbinic phrase "from that hour" (not in Mark or Luke, but comparable to "immediately" in Mark 5:29; cf. Luke 8:44, 47; see Schlatter, ad loc.; Black, *Aramaic Approach* 108-12). Concerning healings, the same phrase will reappear as an insertion in 15:28; 17:18. Here it recalls the similar phrase "in that hour" inserted in the story concerning the centurion's servant (8:13).

Matthew's dominant interest does not lie in the element of faith, which comes from the tradition, but in the ability of Jesus to save a believer. Though omissions in the first gospel bring the statement concerning salvation by faith to the center of the story, the woman's action in touching Jesus' garment hardly suffers loss. To the contrary, Matthew inserts the tassel and supplies "only" (v 21). The implication in the perfect tense of σέσωκεν is that the woman was already saved by the time Jesus pronounced her so. Therefore we should not think that to avoid magic Matthew transfers the moment of salvation from the woman's touching Jesus to Jesus' speaking to her.

9:23-24 (Mark 5:35-40; Luke 8:49-53) Matthew returns to the story of the ruler and his daughter, but omits the report of her death (she has already died in v 18), the ensuing conversation, and Jesus' leaving all but Peter, James, and John (Mark 5:35-37). The narrative goes straight to the figure of Jesus, whose name is given for the third time (cf. the insertions in vv 19, 22 and throughout this gospel—80,12). Characteristically, Matthew describes him as "coming" (ἐλθών—10,10). In Mark 5:38, by contrast, "they" go into the house of the ruler. Matthew will not allow the presence of others to detract from the majesty of Jesus the Coming One (cf. the comments on 3:11). Still wanting Jesus to stand in the foreground, he reduces Mark's independent clause concerning the lamentation over the girl's death to a participial phrase and scales down the triple object "clamor and people who were weeping and wailing much" to the double object "the flute players and the clamoring crowd." (Even the poorest families hired at least two flute players and one female wailer for funerals—see *b. Ketub.* 46b; cf. Josephus *J.W.* 3.9.5 §437.)

In v 24 Mark's redundant second reference to Jesus' entrance into the ruler's house and the indirect object "to them" drop out (so also Luke). The latter omission further contributes to Jesus' solitary splendor. The Mattheanism "Depart" (ἀναχωρεῖτε—4,5) then substitutes for the question "Why are you clamoring and weeping?" (cf. Luke's transformation of the question into a command to stop weeping). As in vv 21-22, Matthew is eliminating a question that might spoil his emphasis on Jesus' deity. Instead, we read an authoritative command. See the comments on 8:29 concerning the omission of such questions throughout Matthew.

In the next clause Matthew's typical insertion of γάρ (62-63,15) makes the girl's not having died a reason for the added command that the flute players and clamoring crowd depart. This unique emphasis on their departure contributes yet again to Jesus' solitary splendor. Similarly, Matthew changes Mark's "the child" to "the girl" for a parallel with "the girl" in v 25 and puts the designation in an unemphatic position after its verb (contrast Mark). Jesus' saying that the girl has not died but sleeps, at which the hearers laugh, presupposes her being raised shortly. Her death will amount to no more than a nap (cf. Dan 12:2; John 11:11-13).

9:25-26 (Mark 5:40-43; Luke 8:54-56) Matthew changes the "all" whom Jesus expelled from the ruler's house (so Mark) to "the crowd" (see also v 23). Since they were already in the house when Jesus arrived, they probably do not represent the crowds (usually plural) whom Matthew regularly portrays as disciples, those who *follow* Jesus. Even otherwise, the expulsion of the crowd would not differ in principle from Matthew's omitting the entrance of Peter, James, and John. Mark's "throwing out" becomes "was thrown out." The voice changes from active to passive because Matthew has made Jesus order their departure already: the crowd "was thrown out" by the authoritative command "Depart." This second emphasis on the exit of the crowd yet again contributes to the solitariness of Jesus' divine might and majesty.

As in vv 19, 22, and 23, Matthew introduces Jesus' action with a participle—this time εἰσελθών—in contrast with Mark's finite and different verb εἰσπορεύεται. The participle closely parallels ἐλθών . . . εἰς in v 23 and exactly matches εἰσελθών in Mark 5:39, omitted earlier because of its redundancy. Here it is not redundant, for it refers to further entrance within the house to the place "where the child was" (so Mark). But the mention of where the child was drops out as distractive from Jesus. The narrative moves directly to his taking hold of her hand. For emphasis on this action, Matthew turns Mark's participle "taking hold" into a main verb, "he took hold," and de-emphasizes the girl by using a mere pronoun, "her" (so also Luke), instead of Mark's nominal phrase, "of the child." The Aramaic words of Jesus to the girl and the translation of those words into Greek vanish. Matthew skips to the statement that the girl got up. But for Mark's ἀνέστη he puts ἠγέρθη to compensate for the omitted command ἔγειρε and to conform to the healings in 8:15 and 9:5-7. In Matthew, then, this healing takes place as a result of Jesus' merely taking hold of the girl's hand and thus complements the healing of the woman because of her touching Jesus' garment (vv 20-21).

Details concerning the girl's walking around, her age, the great astonishment of the observers, the urgent command that no one come to know what happened, and the instruction that the girl be given something to eat all disappear. Instead, Matthew writes, "And this report went out into that whole land." In this clause he conflates Mark's conclusions to the stories of the exorcism in the synagogue at Capernaum (Mark 1:28) and of the leper's cure (Mark 1:45). The conflation makes up for previous omissions of both. So the present story ends with the fame of Jesus rather than with the girl's eating (so Mark) or a prohibition of publicity (so Luke).

THE LORDLY AUTHORITY OF JESUS IN HEALING TWO BLIND MEN
9:27-31 (20:29-34; Mark 10:46-52; Luke 18:35-43; cf. Mark 8:22-26)

In 9:27-31 Matthew presents us with his "first edition" of the story concerning Jesus' healing two blind men, which will appear again in 20:29-34. In 9:32-34 he will do the same with the story concerning Jesus' healing a deaf mute, which will appear again in 12:22-23. The stories are brought in here to fill out the serialization of Jesus' miracles in a way that will have provided examples for the listing in 11:5. These first editions concentrate on Jesus' deity. The stories also contain an emphasis on Jesus as the Son of David, however (cf. the twin themes of Jesus' Davidic sonship and divine sonship in chaps. 1-2). The importance to Matthew of both Christological themes leads him to repeat the stories in the settings where they appear in Mark.

On the possibility that in narratives of healings and exorcisms the designation "Son of David" connotes a kind of Solomon, whom the Jews had come to regard as a wise master in the art of exorcism, see D. C. Duling in *HTR* 68 (1975) 235-52. Duling argues that Matthew goes beyond the Jewish exorcistic tradition to a therapeutic Son of David. Cf. the comments on 12:22-23.

In working up a first edition of these two stories, Matthew draws the basic material from Mark and pre-Lukan tradition. A number of editorial changes take the form of assimilations to omitted material and compensations for omissions in other passages, especially in the preceding stories of miracles (chaps. 8-9). Matthew writes freely and indulges his appetite for parallelism. In this first story, "and going along from there" in v 27 matches "and going into the house" in v 28. "Two blind men followed him" in v 27 matches "the blind men approached him" in v 28. "Crying and saying" in v 27 corresponds to "and Jesus says to them" in v 28. And "Have mercy on us, Son of David" in v 27 corresponds to "Do you believe that I am able to do this?" in v 28.

Similarly in the latter part of the story, "Then he touched their eyes, saying" in v 29a matches "And Jesus sternly warned them, saying" in v 30b. "According to your faith let it happen to you" in v 29b matches "See that you let no one know" in v 30c. "And their eyes were opened" in v 30a corresponds to "But they, going out, reported about him in that whole land" in v 31. All of this parallelism leaves "They say to him, 'Yes, Lord' " as the centerpiece at the close of v 28—a fitting tribute to Jesus' lordly authority as expounded by Matthew throughout chaps. 8–9.

9:27 (20:29-31; Mark 10:46-48; Luke 18:35-39) Naturally, Mark's mentioning an entrance into Jericho falls away as unsuitable here. In writing καὶ παράγοντι ἐκεῖθεν τῷ 'Ιησοῦ, Matthew conforms Mark's καὶ ἐκπορευομένου αὐτοῦ ἀπὸ 'Ιεριχὼ to his own καὶ παράγων ὁ 'Ιησοῦς ἐκεῖθεν in 9:9. The place from which Jesus goes in the present passage is the house of the ruler. Matthew's favorite ἠκολούθησαν αὐτῷ (8,0) substitutes for accompaniment by Jesus' disciples and a large crowd in Mark. A similar replacement will occur in 20:29. But there it refers to a crowd's following Jesus (while the blind men sit alongside the road), here to the blind men's following him. Thus the blind men appear as disciples immediately in the story. In the later version they will follow Jesus after their healing.

As in 20:30 and Luke, the name of the blind man drops out. The doubling of the blind man lies behind the omission. The absence of such a doubling in Luke shows Matthew's influence; otherwise we would have expected Luke to include the name. Matthew omits the description of the blind man as begging and hearing that Jesus the Nazarene is going by, because in his version they are already following as disciples. The plea for mercy and the address to Jesus as David's son come from Mark. But Matthew omits Jesus' name because he mentioned it at the head of the verse. Omissions of the crowd's rebuke and the renewal of the plea stem again from Matthew's having made the blind men begin to follow Jesus already.

9:28 (20:32-33; Mark 10:49-51; Luke 18:40-41) "And going into the house" comes from Mark 3:20-21, a passage in Mark's parallel to the next story, which Matthew otherwise omits. The phrase contains a reference to Jesus' house in Capernaum (see 4:13 and the comments on 9:10). It also replaces Mark's reference to Jesus' standing still and prepares for the "going out" Matthew will interpolate in v 31. That the blind men are already following Jesus yet again leads to an omission, this time of Jesus' summons and their excited response. As before, the similar omission in Luke lacks Matthew's reason and therefore suggests Matthean influence. The blind men's approaching Jesus comes from Mark, links with usually distinctive occurrences of the compound verb in 8:2, 5, 19, 25; 9:14, 18, 20, and implies the majesty of the one approached (see the comments on 4:3; 8:14). "Says" replaces "answering . . . said" and matches "they say" immediately following in the verse (cf. 8:4, 7, 10, 11, 20, 22, 26; 9:6, 9 and passim throughout Matthew—47,11).

Jesus' questioning what the blind men want him to do becomes a question whether the blind men believe that he is able to do this, i.e., to have mercy on them by healing their blindness. Matthew is fond of πιστεύετε (3,3), δύναμαι (13,0), and ποιῆσαι (19,19). The motif of faith represents assimilation to 8:10, 13; 9:2, 22; and Matthew takes the matter of Jesus' ability from 8:2. As in the preceding story, however, the primary emphasis rests on Jesus' ability rather than on the blind men's faith. "They say" arises from the influence of "he says" just preceding and substitutes for Mark's "and the blind man said." The Mattheanisms ναί, κύριε (2,2; 34,15) replace "Rabboni, that I might see again" (so Mark; both 20:32 and Luke look like conflations of Mark and the present verse). Cf. especially 13:51, a uniquely Matthean verse in which the entire clause "They say to him, 'Yes' " matches the present clause except for lack of "Lord." Here the emphasis falls on Jesus' lordship.

9:29-31 (20:34; Mark 10:52; Luke 18:42-43) A characteristic τότε (66,17) stands in place of Mark's and Luke's καί and makes Jesus' touching the eyes of the blind men consequent on their confessing Jesus as Lord. Matthew interpolates Jesus' touching the blind men's eyes in order to assimilate the story to the touchings mentioned in 8:3, 15; 9:20, 21. More especially, however, the addition of touching comes from the story of the blind man in Bethsaida (Mark 8:22-26), a story omitted as such by Matthew but providing the second blind man and the element of Jesus' touch in both the present and later Matthean versions of the healing. The conflation of the two stories offers a double witness to Jesus' Davidic sonship and deity. The double witness fulfills the requirements of the OT law (Deut 19:15; see Matt 18:16, which is peculiar to the first gospel). The construction of a finite form of "touch" followed by the participle "saying" has its origin in 8:3. "According to your faith let it happen to you" comes from "Go, your faith has saved you" in Mark. But the blind men's already following Jesus causes "Go" to drop out, and heavy influence has come from the uniquely Matthean expression in 8:13: "as you have believed, let it happen to you" (cf. 9:22; 13:58). Apparently Mark's "Go" reminded Matthew of 8:13, where "Go" preceded the clause mentioning "faith."

In v 30 the statement that "the eyes" of the blind men "were opened," where the later version and its parallels have references to "seeing again," is due to Matthew's earlier replacement of the request to see again, to Jesus' having touched their eyes, and to Matthew's liking for ἠνεῴχθησαν (5,2) and ὀφθαλμοί (8,1). The expression has its roots in the OT (see 2 Kgs 6:20; Isa 35:5; 42:7) and therefore appeals to Matthew. For the third time in the story he mentions Jesus' name, which does not occur at this point in the later version, Mark, or Luke (but see vv 27, 28). Matthew wants Jesus to dominate the entire episode. The insertion of λέγων reflects Matthew's style (61,23). Jesus' stern command not to let anyone know has no match. It prepares for an emphasis on Jesus' humility (see esp. 11:29; 12:16, 17-21; 21:5) and stems from the story of the leper's healing (Mark 1:40-45). "He sternly warned them" makes up for the omission of Mark's "sternly warning him" in that story (cf. 8:4 with Mark 1:43). "See, let no one know" comes from "See, tell no one anything" in Mark 1:44. As in 8:4, μηδέν drops out. Here alone, however, the Mattheanism γινωσκέτω (8,2) substitutes for εἴπῃς. Consequently, μηδενί changes to μηδείς.

178

Since in this first edition of the story the blind men have been following Jesus from the start, Matthew dispenses with their starting to follow Jesus now (so Mark, Luke, and 20:34). Instead we read, "But they, going out, spread the news about him in that whole land." Thus, in order to link this story with the preceding, Matthew again adapts Mark's conclusions to the stories of the exorcism in the synagogue at Capernaum and of the leper's healing, and he compensates for earlier omissions (see the comments on v 26). Both the command to silence and the contrary publicity derive, then, from formerly omitted parts of Mark's version of the leper's healing.

JESUS' MARVELOUS AUTHORITY IN EXORCISING A DEMON FROM A DEAF-MUTE
9:32-34 (12:22-24; Mark 3:22; Luke 11:14-15)

To prepare for the deaf who hear in the summarizing statement at 11:5, Matthew advances the story of the deaf-mute. As in vv 27-31, freedom in writing the first edition of a story to be repeated later (12:22-24) results in an indulgence of Matthew's appetite for parallelism. "And as they were going out" in v 32 matches "And when the demon was cast out" in v 33. The following clauses concerning the bringing of the deaf-and-dumb demoniac (v 32) and his speaking (v 33) correspond. Similarly, "And the crowds marvelled, saying" in v 33b corresponds to "But the Pharisees were saying" in v 34a; and "Never has it appeared thus in Israel" in v 33c parallels "By the ruler of demons he casts out demons" in v 34b. All these parallels are antithetic.

9:32-33 (12:22-23; Luke 11:14) The initial genitive absolute harks back to the exit of the two blind men in the preceding verse (cf. the connective genitive absolute in v 18). "They brought to him . . . a demoniac" echoes "They brought to him demoniacs" in 4:24; 8:16. The phrase is peculiar to Matthew in all these passages (see also 12:22 and cf. 9:2). As usual, προσήνεγκαν may imply an offering to Jesus (see the comments on 2:11 and 4:24). The insertion of "behold" (34,9) adds emphasis.

The reference to the demon's being cast out, where the later version states a healing, comes close to Luke 11:14b ("when the demon came out"). But in the use of "cast out" it is due to parallelism with the following charge that Jesus casts out demons by the ruler of the demons. Cf. Luke 11:14a and earlier use of that verb for exorcism in Matt 7:22; 8:16, 31. Matthew describes the results of the exorcism exactly as Luke describes them (cf. Matt 9:33). As in his later version but not in Luke, Matthew quotes the crowds. But instead of asking about Jesus' Davidic sonship (so 12:23), they exclaim, "Never has it appeared thus in Israel." Every one of the major words is a Mattheanism. The exclamation compensates for earlier omission of Mark's conclusion to the story of the paralytic: "We have never seen thus" (Mark 2:12; cf. Matt 9:8).

Dumbness receives the emphasis in this story because its reversal in the gift of speech is more quickly obvious than the reversal of deafness. Nevertheless, κωφός

179

includes deafness. Thus this story does indeed supply an example of the healing of deafness listed in 11:5. The closest Matthew comes to the walking of the lame, which is listed there, is the walking of the paralytic (9:1-8). For the conjunction of blindness and deafness, as here in vv 27-34, cf. Isa 29:18; 35:5; 42:18. The Mattheanisms in the crowds' exclamation are οὐδέποτε (5,0), ἐφάνη (5,8), οὕτως (18,5), and Ἰσραήλ (5,4).

9:34 (12:24; Mark 3:22; Luke 11:15) The story closes with an abbreviation of the charge that Jesus casts out demons by the ruler of demons. Mark's recitative ὅτι and reference to Beelzebul disappear. As in 12:24, Matthew identifies Jesus' opponents as the Pharisees. Mark calls them "the scribes from Jerusalem" and Luke, "certain of them [i.e., from among the previously mentioned crowds]." Here again we see the influence of earlier passages in this series of miracles: 9:11, where "the scribes of the Pharisees" (Mark 2:16) became "the Pharisees," and 9:14, where "the disciples of the Pharisees" (Mark 2:18) became "the Pharisees." And so Matthew completes the series with a contrast between the marvelling of the crowds at Jesus' authority and the rejection of that authority by the antagonistic Pharisees.

On the omission of v 34 in the Western textual family, see Metzger, *Textual Commentary* ad loc. The way this verse fills out the parallelism that abounds everywhere in vv 27-31, 32-34 argues strongly for originality. Omission would leave the parallelism truncated.

THE WORK AND COMPASSION
OF THE LORD OF THE HARVEST
9:35-38 (Mark 6:6b, 34; Luke 8:1; 10:2)

9:35 (Mark 6:6b; Luke 8:1) As in 4:23-25, a summary of Jesus' activities with special references to the crowds and disciples rounds out a narrative section and leads to a great discourse. The first statement comes from Mark, where it occurs at the beginning of the mission of the twelve. But Matthew expands it in accord with his interests and the summary in 4:23. To "and he was going about" (so also 4:23 and Mark) he characteristically adds "Jesus" (80,12). To "the towns" mentioned by Mark he prefixes "the cities" (18,3; cf. Luke) to further his emphasis on the importance of cities in Jesus' life and ministry. His typical addition of "all" (63,25-26) adds to that emphasis and possibly corresponds to "whole" in 4:23. Jesus' activity of teaching appears also in Mark. But in word-for-word repetition of 4:23 Matthew fills it out with references to "their synagogues" (cf. the opposition of the Pharisees in the preceding verse) and Jesus' preaching "the gospel of the kingdom" and healing "every disease and every sickness." The final phrase in 4:23, "among the people," drops out because of an immediately following reference to the crowds. See further the comments on 4:23.

9:36 (Mark 6:34) In order to satisfy two further interests of his—crowds as symbolic of those to be discipled from all nations and Jesus' compassion—Matthew now imports Mark 6:34 from the first part of the feeding of the five thousand. The importation of the crowds and of Jesus' compassion on them makes the commissioning of the twelve in chap. 10 a preview of Jesus' sending the disciples to make disciples of all nations, i.e., a preview of the current mission of the church (28:16-20). In taking over Mark 6:34, Matthew characteristically makes "he saw" into the introductory participle ἰδών (10-11,7) and substitutes it for Mark's "going out." This change puts the weight of emphasis on "he felt pity." "A great crowd" becomes "the crowds," pluralized as usual, perhaps to point toward "all the nations" that must be discipled. To the picture of the crowds as sheep not having a shepherd Matthew adds "harried and huddled." Thus the already existing allusion to the OT picture of God's people as not having a shepherd (Num 27:17; 1 Kgs 22:17; 2 Chr 18:16; cf. Jer 23:1-6; Jdt 11:19) gains a further allusion to the OT picture of God's people as attacked and scattered by wild beasts (Ezek 34:5; see Gundry, *Use of the OT* 32-33).

9:37-38 *(Luke 10:2)* Mark 6:34, which Matthew has been following, closes with the statement "and he began to teach them much." But since Matthew has already mentioned Jesus' teaching (v 35) and will take up Jesus' commissioning of the disciples next (chap. 10), he moves to the tradition behind Luke 10:2, the introduction to the mission of the seventy-two. "And he was saying [or, 'began to say'] to them" becomes "Then he says to his disciples." We discover Mattheanisms in τότε (66,17), the historical present λέγει (47,11), and μαθηταῖς (31,5). The present tense of "he says" makes Jesus' following words an address to the church. For the first time Matthew distinguishes Jesus' disciples from the crowds. But he has to do so in order to prepare for the sending of the twelve in chap. 10, where he will mention the twelve disciples for the first time in his gospel. Nevertheless, the crowds do not appear in a bad light. They are the objects of Jesus' compassion and of the mission of the twelve; i.e., they symbolize those who will be discipled from all nations. The statement concerning the harvest exactly matches Luke's version (cf. John 4:35). Since Jesus will send the twelve to do the work of harvesting in chap. 10, he himself is the Lord of the harvest to whom the disciples are to pray for the thrusting out of workers. The phrase "Lord of the harvest" means one who hires workers and sends them to the field.

THE WORKERS OF THE LORD OF THE HARVEST AND THEIR AUTHORITY
10:1-4 (Mark 3:13-19; 6:7; Luke 6:12-16; 9:1; cf. Acts 1:13)

10:1 (Mark 3:13-15; 6:7; Luke 6:12-13; 9:1) In this passage Matthew utilizes materials concerning Jesus' choice of the twelve and the mission of the twelve. The first verse draws on the latter (cf. Mark 6:7; Luke 9:1). Mark's "he summons" reduces to the participle "having summoned" (as also in 15:10, 32; 18:2, 32; 20:25; cf. Luke's "having called together"). To "the twelve" (so Mark and Luke) Matthew characteristically adds "his disciples" (31,5—added to "the twelve" also in 11:1 and the probably original readings in 20:17; 26:20). But he deletes Jesus' beginning to send the twelve two by two (so Mark). Luke omits the clause, too, but does not make up for the omission as Matthew will do in v 5. Mark's "he was giving" becomes "he gave" (so also Luke) for a parallel with the aorists concerning the authority given to Jesus (see 21:33; 28:18). Thus emphasis falls exclusively on Jesus' giving his authority to the twelve in order that they might multiply themselves as disciples (cf. 28:16 with 19; and 9:8 with comments). In fact, the desire for this emphasis causes Matthew to interject chap. 10 before 11:1-6, which relates closely to chaps. 8–9.

In particular, Jesus gives the twelve disciples authority over "unclean spirits." To show the effect of that authority, Matthew switches to material concerning the choice of the twelve (Mark 3:13-19; Luke 6:12-16). But first he makes a number of omissions: that of Jesus' going up into a mountain, or the hill country (so Mark 3:13a; Luke 6:12a), because he has already used that piece of information in 5:1; that of Jesus' summoning those whom he wanted, their coming to him, and his choosing twelve of them (Mark 3:13bc-14a; Luke 6:13), because he has already written about Jesus' summoning the twelve in v 1 and because Jesus' ascending a mountain in 5:1 makes an appointment of the twelve topographically and chronologically out of place in the present passage; that of Jesus' purpose that the twelve might be with him (Mark 3:14c, omitted also in Luke), because he regards Jesus as God *with them* (1:23; 28:20); and that of Jesus' sending them to preach (καὶ ἵνα ἀποστέλλῃ αὐτοὺς κηρύσσειν, Mark 3:14d, omitted also in Luke), because he is about to use ἀποστόλων in v 2, ἀπέστειλεν in v 5, and κηρύσσετε in v 7. These omissions bring Matthew to the authority of the twelve apostles to cast out demons (Mark 3:15, omitted in Luke). The immediately preceding mention of "authority" and "unclean spirits" makes "authority" and "demons" otiose here. Yet Matthew wants to emphasize the effect of the disciples' authority; therefore he writes "so as to cast them out." To define the effect of the authority yet further, and especially in terms of Jesus' own authority, Matthew adds from his summary of Jesus' work in 9:35 "and to heal every disease and every sickness" (cf. Luke 9:1).

10:2-4 (Mark 3:16-19; Luke 6:13-16) The probably original text of Mark 3:14b (see the UBS and Metzger, *Textual Commentary* ad loc.) and the last clause in Luke 6:13 refer to Jesus' giving the name "apostles" to the twelve. Matthew calls the twelve "apostles" *on his own part*—i.e., without saying that Jesus named them "apostles"—and simply lists their *personal* names. This change stems from his omitting their appointment (when they were named "apostles") and results in a string of nominative forms following the statement "And the names of the twelve apostles are these" (contrast Mark's and Luke's accusative forms). The center of gravity shifts, then, from the appointment of the twelve to their being sent (v 5a).

In the list of names, Mark's awkwardly parenthetical "and he put the name 'Peter' on Simon" becomes "first Simon, the one called Peter." "Simon" gains the Mattheanism πρῶτος (2,5-6) and "put . . . on" changes to "the one called" for emphasis on Peter as the representative disciple. Andrew comes up from fourth place to second, alongside Simon Peter (so also Luke), and gets the addition "his brother" (so also Luke, but not Mark). Matthew likes ἀδελφός (11,8), which connotes the larger brotherhood of the church. As in Mark and Luke, the names of James the son of Zebedee and John the brother of James follow. But "the brother of James" becomes "his brother," and Mark's awkwardly parenthetical clauses regarding the nicknaming of James and John "Boanerges" drop out (as also in Luke). Matthew makes these changes in order to conform the first part of his list to the call of these four disciples in 4:18-22.

In accord with 4:18-22 Simon Peter, Andrew, James, and John have appeared as a foursome, their names all coordinated with "and." Now Matthew lists the names of the remaining apostles in pairs by putting "and" between the names in each pair and leaving it out between pairs (contrast Mark and Luke). In this way he compensates for his earlier omission of Mark's "two by two" and satisfies the OT law of two or three witnesses, to which he alone will refer in 18:16 (cf. his pairing of demoniacs in 8:28-34 and of blind men in 9:27-31; 20:29-34). In allusion to 9:9 "Matthew" gains the designation "the publican." "Matthew" comes after rather than before "Thomas" (contrast Mark and Luke), perhaps out of the feeling that an addition sits more easily with the second member of a pair. The Semitic designation of Judas as Ἰσκαριώθ (so Mark and Luke) gets the Greek suffix -της (see also 26:14 and cf. Matthew's preference for βαπτιστής in place of the corresponding participle—3:1 with comments). Concerning possible meanings of "Iscariot"—"man from Kerioth," "assassin," "redhead," etc.— see BAG, s.v.; Metzger, *Textual Commentary* ad loc.; and literature cited in those places. As Matthew has omitted Mark's disruptive clauses in this list, so also he transmutes Mark's clause concerning Judas's betrayal of Jesus into an appositional phrase similar and parallel to the foregoing appositional phrases.

We have no convincing reason to think that the nominative case of the apostles' names in Matthew is due to a catechetical list used for memorization. See the foregoing comments on Matthew's omitting the appointment of the twelve and the consequent shift from accusative to nominative. Luke shares a number of Matthew's peculiarities in the listing of the first four apostles. But he entirely lacks Matthew's reason for changing Mark, viz., conformity to the call of Peter, Andrew, James, and John in Matt 4:18-22, to which Luke 5:1-11 offers no parallels that matter here. This lack strongly suggests that Luke used Matthew. The designation ὁ Καναναῖος for the second Simon stays in its Aramaic form, apparently because it had frozen as part of his name. Its meaning most probably has to do with zeal for the Jewish law (cf. Acts 21:20; Gal 1:14; 2 Macc 4:2; 4 Macc 18:12) or with the political party whose religious zeal extended to revolution against the pagan Roman overlords (Josephus *Ant.* 18.1.1, 6 §§1-10, 23-24; *J.W.* 2.8.1 §118; 2.22.1 §§647-51; 4.3.9 §§158-61).

JESUS' COMMISSIONING THE TWELVE
TO HARVEST ISRAEL
10:5-15 (11:24; 15:24; Mark 6:7-13; Luke 9:2-5; 10:1-12;
1 Tim 5:18)

10:5-8 (15:24; Mark 6:8a; Luke 9:2; 10:8-9) In vv 5-15 Matthew conflates materials concerning the mission of the twelve (Mark 6:7-13; Luke 9:2-5) and the mission of the seventy-two (Luke 10:1-12, often regarded as a doublet of the mission of the twelve). By and large, however, the first four verses lack parallels in the other synoptics. τούτους picks up the distinctive ταῦτα at the beginning of the preceding list (v 2). "The twelve" harks back to v 1. "He sent" (cf. Luke 9:2) makes up for Matthew's omission in v 1 of "he began to send" (Mark 6:7b). The characteristic use of Jesus' name (80,12) marks the beginning of a new passage and makes Jesus the Lord of the harvest.

Now come Jesus' instructions, introduced with the phrase "commanding them" (cf. Mark 6:8a) plus a typically Matthean λέγων (61,23— cf. Luke 9:3a). The first part of the instructions (vv 5b-8) consists of an expansion of the tradition behind Luke 9:2: "and he sent them to preach the kingdom of God and to heal the sick." The expansion delineates the range and content of the disciples' preaching and details their healing activity. It also has the purpose of carrying further the correlation between Jesus' ministry and that of the disciples, to whom he gives his authority. Notably, however, the command that the disciples teach waits till Jesus has completed all his instructions to them (28:20). Here we read only of their preaching.

We see Matthew's hand first of all in the careful balancing of parallel clauses and expressions. "Do not go away into a road of Gentiles" balances "and do not go into a city of Samaritans" exactly. "But go rather to the lost sheep of the house of Israel" matches "And as you go, preach, saying, 'The kingdom of heaven has come near.' " By picking up the main verb in the preceding clause, the introductory participle πορευόμενοι indicates Matthew's relating the two clauses in parallelistic fashion. Together they form an antithesis to the opening pair of prohibitions. The commands to heal the sick and raise the dead make a couplet in which the second member marks a climax. Similarly, the command to cleanse lepers progresses to the command to cast out demons. Both lepers and demons were regarded as unclean (cf. the expression "unclean spirits" in 10:1; 12:43; and elsewhere). Finally, "freely you have received" and "freely give" form the last couplet in the series.

The diction also shows signs of composition by Matthew. He likes ὁδόν (9,2), ἐθνῶν (7,2), ἀπέλθητε (14,11), πόλιν (18,3), and πορεύεσθε (13,10). The combination of ὁδόν and ἐθνῶν echoes ὁδὸν θαλάσσης . . . Γαλιλαία τῶν ἐθνῶν in 4:14-16, a Matthean insertion. The nominative participle πορευόμενοι also suits his taste (8,4) and strikingly corresponds to πορευθέντες in Matthew's version of the great commission (28:19). We meet further favorites of his in πρόβατα (6,2), which echoes the comparison of the crowds with shepherdless sheep in 9:36, and ἀπολωλότα (8,1). "House of Israel" typifies his conforming Jesus' phraseology to the OT (see the concordance for many examples). Similarly, the comparison of Israel to lost sheep comes straight out of Jer 50(27):6 (cf. Ezek 34:6, 11-12; Matt 9:36). In 15:24 Matthew will insert a limitation of Jesus' ministry to "the lost sheep of the house of Israel." This insertion confirms his composition here (cf. also forms of the verb of sending in v 5 and 15:24).

Matthew often uses a participial form of λέγω to introduce direct discourse (61,23). The message the disciples are to preach, "The kingdom of heaven is near," matches the proclamation of Jesus in 4:17 and that of John the Baptist in 3:2. The latter came into the text by way of Matthew's insertion. In all three passages, forms of κηρύσσω and λέγω introduce the proclamation. The command to repent in the earlier passages drops out here, perhaps because of Matthew's portraying Israel as shepherdless, lost sheep more to be pitied than blamed (cf. 9:36). Matthew shows some liking for ἀσθενοῦντας (see also 25:36, 39; cf. 8:17) and δαιμόνια (see 7:22; 12:24; 17:18 for further insertions), and a definite liking for θεραπεύετε (10,0), ἐγείρετε (11,8), ἐκβάλλετε (10,1), and ἐλάβετε (21,16). δωρεάν is cognate to δῶρον, a Mattheanism (7,1), and δότε occurs often without parallel (8-9,10).

Gentile territories bounded Galilee on all sides except the southern. There, Samaria hemmed it in. Consequently, the prohibitions against departure to Gentiles and entry into any city of Samaritans initially limits the disciples to Galilee. In this way Matthew indicates that their ministry must follow the pattern of Jesus' ministry, which, he has already taken pains to show, began in Galilee (4:14-16). The correlation will be strengthened by Matthew's repeating the limitation to "the lost sheep of the house of Israel" and applying it to *Jesus'* being sent (15:24). So also the sameness of Jesus' and the disciples' message and deeds strengthens the correlation (see v 7b with 4:17; v 8 with chaps. 8–9 and Luke 10:9). "Freely you have received" refers to Jesus' giving the disciples authority to perform their deeds. That authority is the same as Jesus' authority (see 9:6, 8). Thus Matthew establishes continuity between Jesus and the apostolic church.

Matthew's composition of vv 5-8 in expanding the tradition behind Luke 9:2 rules out their origin in a Jewish Christianity opposed to evangelization of Gentiles. For Matthew himself hardly opposes such evangelization; rather, he urges it (2:1-12; 8:11-12; 10:18-19; 21:43; 24:14; 25:31-46; 28:18-20; see "Universality" in the Topical Index). Some exceptional Gentiles become believers in Jesus during his public ministry (2:1-12; 8:5-13, 28-34; 15:21-28), but a mission to Gentiles does not start till the Jewish leaders engineer his crucifixion and he rises from the dead, i.e., not till the kingdom is transferred from Israel to the church (see esp. 21:43 with 28:18-20). The limitation in the present passage belongs to an initial stage alone, then, and rests on the parallel between the ministries of Jesus and the disciples.

Some have thought that πόλιν mistranslates the Aramaic מְדִינָא, here carrying the meaning "province" instead of its other meaning "city." But Matthew's composition of these verses and interest in cities as places of ministry eliminate the need for such a hypothesis, as also for supposing an early miscopying of an original πάλιν, "again." The anarthrousness of πόλιν is due to parallelism with the anarthrous ὁδόν, which with εἰς makes an idiom meaning "to."

The limitation of ministry to Galilean Jews, despised as being among "the people of the land," who failed to observe the rabbinic traditions closely, suggests that "the lost sheep of the house of Israel" are that despised class within the nation. The contrast with Gentiles overturns the suggestion, however, and favors a general reference to the whole Jewish nation. The lostness of the nine and one-half northern tribes, which was supposed in some quarters during the NT era, may have sharpened the point of the metaphor. The regathering of the lost sheep heralds the messianic age of salvation.

On the originality of νεκροὺς ἐγείρετε in Matthew's text, see Metzger, *Textual Commentary* ad loc. The command is necessary to the arrangement in couplets. The paralleling of Jesus' and the disciples' ministries militates against a metaphorical interpretation of the command, for we can hardly think that Matthew intended his readers to take the story of Jesus' raising the deceased daughter of a certain ruler in a nonliteral way (9:18-19, 23-26).

10:9-10 (Mark 6:8-9; Luke 9:3; 10:4, 7; 1 Tim 5:18) The command to give freely fits Matthew's concern about false prophets (see 7:15-23 on their rapacity) and leads to prohibitions against taking various things. Jesus made the prohibitions for the sake of a speedy mission through Galilee: the disciples were to depend entirely on hospitality in order to accomplish their mission quickly. As the statement at the close of v 10 shows ("for the worker is worthy of his food," not in Mark, but imported from the tradition behind Luke 10:7), Matthew has an eye on the mercenary motives of false prophets in the church. But the same point appears immediately in his changing "take" (so Mark 6:8 and, similarly, Luke 9:3) to "acquire." Thus the prohibitions against taking money *for* the itinerant ministry become prohibitions against acquisition *from* the itinerant ministry. It might be thought, on the contrary, that Matthew's prohibition deals with acquiring money *prior* to the start of ministry. But the immediately preceding command to give freely (i.e., without charge or acceptance of anything more than hospitality), the lack of any indication of the way the disciples might acquire more money than they already have to take, and the conjunction "for," which makes the worthiness of the worker to receive his food a reason for the preceding—all these require that mercenary profit as a *result* of ministry is being prohibited (cf. 6:19-20). The greatness of Matthew's concern to emphasize this prohibition shows itself in the advancing of money from fourth to first place among the prohibitions (contrast Mark 6:8 and Luke 9:3, but cf. Luke 10:4) and in the tripling of the reference to money with three parallel terms arranged in climactic order: neither "gold" (so Matthew alone) nor less valuable "silver" (so also Luke 9:3) nor even "copper" (so Mark). "For your belts [in the fold of which money was carried]" applies to the whole of the prohibition and matches Mark except for a smoother ordering of words, a pluralizing, and the clarifying addition of a possessive pronoun.

The Mattheanism χρυσόν (4,1) never occurs in Mark or Luke. ἄργυρον occurs only here in the synoptic tradition. The synonymous ἀργύριον appears nine times in Matthew and only once in Mark and four times in Luke. Does ἀργύριον in Luke 9:3 therefore depend on influence from Matthew?

Matthew arranges the next four prohibited items in an ascending order of need: neither a knapsack for carrying food to eat along the way, nor two tunics for a change of undergarments or for additional warmth, nor footgear for protection of the feet, nor even a staff for warding off wild beasts and steadying oneself on dangerously steep and slippery mountain paths. This order requires Matthew to bring up the knapsack from fourth or third place to first. "For the road" now goes with "knapsack" rather than with "nothing." The two garments advance from sixth, or last, place to second. The footgear remains next to last (so also Mark; Luke omits it in 9:3 and puts it last in 10:4). The staff goes from second place to last. And Matthew leaves the bread to be supplied mentally as the contents of the knapsack.

Remarkably, though Mark's text allows a staff "only," and then goes on to allow sandals as well, Matthew allows neither. This intensification of rigor falls in line with his desire to expose false prophets, who would object to such self-sacrifice (cf. his insistence on the continuation of fasting—6:16-18; 9:14-17). Luke agrees with Matthew in the prohibitions against staff and footgear (Luke 9:3; 10:4; 22:35). Yet, in view of the *lifting* of restrictions in Luke 22:35-36, he lacks Matthew's purpose of counteracting mercenaries in the church. Therefore the agreement against Mark reflects influence from Matthew.

"For the worker [is] worthy of his food" comes from the tradition behind Luke 10:7; 1 Tim 5:18 (cf. 1 Cor 9:14). "Worker" links with 9:37-38. Indeed, it makes the mission of the twelve fulfill Jesus' concern for workers in that passage. Though he likes μισθοῦ, "reward, wages" (2,5—so Luke and 1 Timothy), Matthew switches to τροφῆς, "food" (3,0), in order to distinguish acceptance of free board in hospitable homes from the prohibited acquisition of money and goods, which μισθοῦ might seem to include. In Luke, the conjunction "for" makes the worker's worthiness of reward the reason for accepting free room and board. Because prohibitions immediately precede in Matthew, the conjunction makes the worker's free board a reason for those prohibitions. Thus the stress shifts from the positive note of supply to the negative warning against self-aggrandizement.

The notion that the prohibitions simply imply the sacredness of the mission, just as the sacredness of the Temple demanded that worshippers leave behind staff, sandals, wallet, and dust on the feet (*m. Ber.* 9:5), stumbles over the additional prohibition of two tunics in all three synoptics, the additional prohibition of bread in Mark and Luke, and the original allowance of both staff and sandals in Mark. See the comments on 5:47 concerning Matthew's dropping the prohibition of greetings along the road (Luke 10:4). With Matthew's and Luke's reversing the allowance of sandals, cf. Diogenes Laertius 6.34. For the possession of two tunics, see Luke 3:11; Josephus *Ant.* 17.5.7 §136. On the question of charity versus salary for Christian preachers, see Acts 20:33-35; 1 Cor 9:14-18; 2 Cor 11:7-21; 12:13-18; 1 Thess 2:9; 1 Tim 5:18-19; *Didache* 11–13, especially 11:6. For the dependence of Jewish scribes on work or charity rather than on salary for their scribal services, see *m. 'Abot* 1:3, 13; 4:6[?]; *m. Bek.* 4:6; cf. *m. Ned.* 4:3 (cf. Matthew's Christian scribes in 8:19; 13:52; 23:34). The attempt to harmonize the synoptics by saying that in Mark Jesus allows taking a staff and sandals already possessed and in Matthew disallows procuring a staff and sandals does not succeed. Luke uses Mark's "take" instead of Matthew's "acquire" but agrees with the absolute prohibition in Matthew (Luke 9:3; cf. 10:4). Besides, we have seen that "acquire" has to do with benefits from ministry, not with preparations for ministry. And why would Jesus let those who already had a staff and sandals use them, but prohibit those who did not from getting such necessaries? The somewhat different thought that in Matthew Jesus prohibits only the acquisition of an *extra* staff and pair of sandals also stumbles against Luke's use of "take" and the proper reference of Matthew's "acquire"; additionally, it stumbles against Jesus' use of "two" when he wants to prohibit taking more than necessary.

He says, "Do not acquire . . . two tunics," but not, "Do not acquire . . . two pairs of sandals or two staffs."

10:11 (Mark 6:10; Luke 9:4; 10:8) In vv 11-14 the instructions shift to the behavior of the twelve apostles toward the cities, towns, and households they will visit. As in Luke 9:4, Mark's "and he was saying to them" drops out as unnecessary because of the direct discourse that carries over from the preceding verses. In his first clause, Matthew substitutes a double reference to city and town in place of Mark's single reference to a house. The substitute makes the disciples' ministry parallel Jesus' ministry in that according to 9:35 Jesus ministered in "all the cities and the towns." Emphasis on the city typifies Matthew (18,3). For that emphasis he moves "and into whatever city or town" to the head of the clause. In Luke 9:4a the construction reflects Matthew's form, but the retention of "house" reflects Mark's diction. On the other hand, Luke 10:8a reads like Mark except for the substitution of Matthew's "city" (but not "or town") for "house."

Next we read a clause unique to Matthew: "ask who in it [the city or town] is worthy" (v 11b). In the gospels ἐξετάσατε occurs only here and in 2:8. ἄξιος often attracts Matthew (7,0). Here it matches the worthiness of the worker in the preceding verse. We may surmise, then, that Matthew composes the clause to play up the concept of worthiness, the worthiness of willingness to follow Jesus' teaching no matter what the demands are. For the rest, Matthew follows Mark except for adding "and," changing Mark's present tense "stay" to the aorist in agreement with 11:23; 26:38, and omitting Mark's redundant "from there" at the end. (Luke gets rid of the redundancy by coordinating the two clauses.)

More significantly, the substitution of "city or town" for "house" and the insertion of the command to ask who is worthy require that "there" refer not to any house that will provide free room and board (so Mark and Luke), but only to the residence of a worthy person, i.e., a fellow disciple. Of course, it might be assumed in Mark and Luke that only such a person would provide room and board without charge. Nevertheless, the explicitness of Matthew agrees with his emphasis on Christian brotherhood. Thus, instead of staying wherever they can find hospitality, the disciples are to stay where the proclamation of the kingdom has already found a favorable reception. In Matthew we are reading about itinerant ministry in evangelized communities rather than about itinerant ministry in unevangelized communities.

10:12-13 (Luke 10:5-6) Now Matthew makes up for his substitution of city and town for house by writing "And entering the house [sc. of a worthy person], greet it." The more original form of this saying, as betrayed by Matthew's following references to "peace" (v 13 bis), reads, "And into whatever house you enter, first say, 'Peace [be] to this house' " (Luke 10:5). But Matthew has just used "And into whatever . . . you enter" (v 11a), and he intends to subsume the concept of peace to the concept of worthiness. Therefore he uses a participial form of εἰσέρχομαι, and instead of the very words of greeting he uses the word for greeting that appears in Luke's prohibition of greetings along the road (Luke 10:4).

In v 13 the Mattheanism μέν . . . δέ (15,1) tidies up the parallelism already inherent in Luke 10:6. Also making the parallelism more explicit are the filling out of the third and fourth clauses (contrast the ellipses in Luke), and the reversal of the order of subject and prepositional phrase in the second clause (contrast Luke) to conform with the fourth clause (despite the chiastic order of the verbs). "Will rest" changes to "let [your peace] come" for linkage with the foregoing: just as the disciples come into a house, so also (under the right conditions) their peace comes on a house. Instead of Luke's ἀνακάμψει, "it will return," we read ἐπιστραφήτω, "let [your peace] return" (cf. 12:44 with Luke 11:24, and Matthew's liking στρέφω—3,2). Strikingly, the switch from the predictive future to the aorist imperative points up the authority Jesus has given the disciples (cf. 9:8; 10:1; 16:19; 18:18). They control the coming and going of peace, i.e., of divine blessing (see BAG, s.v. εἰρήνη). Just as strikingly, where Luke writes about the presence or absence of a "son of peace" (originally a Semitic expression for a recipient of messianic salvation), Matthew writes about the worthiness or unworthiness of the house. Thus he assimilates the saying more closely to the preceding context and wins renewed emphasis on the concept of worthy Christian households.

Cf. Josephus *J.W.* 2.8.4 §§124-27 on the hospitality of the Essenes to one another. Again we need to remind ourselves that worthiness in Matthew does not imply the earning of salvation (see 20:1-16), but means willingness to take up one's cross and follow Jesus in costly discipleship. Luke's ἐφ' ὑμᾶς changes to πρὸς ὑμᾶς because Matthew switched to a verb prefixed by ἐπί and because he wants to avoid redundancy. As in prophecy, so in the greeting and withdrawal of greeting the very act of speaking with divine authority triggers the accomplishment of the words. Here the simple Semitic greeting "Peace" lies at the base of the larger connotation of messianic blessing.

10:14 (Mark 6:11; Luke 9:5; 10:10-11) Since Matthew has been writing about the worthiness or unworthiness of a household, he deletes "place" from the clause "and whatever place will not receive you" (so Mark). The deletion gives him a more personal "whoever" (cf. vv 40-41; 18:5; and Luke 9:5, where "as many as" lacks the raison d'être of the similar expression in Matthew). Mark's text disjointedly switches from "place" to "they" in the next clause: "and they will not hear you." Because he has already personalized the saying, Matthew slides smoothly into the second clause with a change of the verb to the singular. This agrees with his initial "whoever." More importantly, he adds "the words." λόγους is a favorite of his (16,2), and the addition makes ὑμῶν a subjective genitive ("the words you speak") rather than the object of the verb ("hear you," as in Mark). Insertion of the disciples' words puts another emphasis on the contents of their message ("the kingdom of heaven is near," v 7b) and further contributes to the parallel and continuity between Jesus and his disciples; for Matthew frequently stresses Jesus' "words" (see the insertions in 7:26, 28; 19:1; 26:1; cf. 7:24; 13:19, 20, 21, 22 [bis], 23; 15:12; 24:35).

In writing about the disciples' departure because of others' refusal to receive them or hear their words, Matthew goes back to "house" and "city" (v 14b). Mark's "from there" becomes "from" for the sake of the added nouns. Since Matthew has been writing about the worthiness or unworthiness of a house (vv 12-13), he needed to mention only a house here. The addition of the city and the attaching of "that" to it (cf. Luke 9:5b) bring us back to his emphasis on the city as a sphere of ministry and prepare us for the judgment of "that city" in the next verse. Shaking the dust of (or from) the feet (so Matthew and Luke) probably means shaking out the dust that has been kicked up and has settled in one's clothing during the course of walking (cf. Neh 5:13; Acts 13:51; and esp. Acts 18:6, in contrast with Luke 10:11, where we read of *wiping off* dust that *clings* to the feet). To explain Mark's "dust under the feet" as dust that has settled in clothing, Matthew replaces χοῦν with a word that often connotes a cloud of dust, κονιορτόν (so also Luke). The gesture of shaking out such dust signifies a separation that results in deliverance to divine judgment. In other words, the merely ritual habit of Jews in shaking out the contaminating dust of Gentile territory has taken on a judgmental meaning—with new objects in view, i.e., unbelievers among the Jews themselves. But Matthew drops Mark's εἰς μαρτύριον αὐτοῖς, "for a witness against them," because he wants to retain the phrase for a positive witness of the gospel (see 8:4; 10:18; 24:14).

10:15 (11:24; Luke 10:12) At this point Mark 6:12-13 and Luke 9:6 summarily tell about the disciples' accomplishing their mission. Matthew omits even a cursory comment of this sort and will never make up the omission. For him, the actuality of the disciples' mission pales before Jesus' instructions, which he carries further by bringing in a judgmental saying of Jesus that appears in Luke 10:12 and will appear again in Matt 11:24. He strengthens "I say to you" by prefixing "truly." The failure of "truly" to appear in 11:24 favors that here Matthew adds to the tradition rather than that Luke subtracts from it. The lack of ὅτι, "that," gives the following threat a certain abruptness. But Luke may have added the conjunction. For emphasis, ἀνεκτότερον ἔσται advances to the head of the next statement (contrast Luke and 11:24). Characteristically, Matthew inserts γῇ (21,6). And to Sodom he adds Gomorrah in an assimilation of Jesus' words to OT phraseology (see Genesis 19 passim; Deut 29:22[23]; 32:32; Isa 1:9, 10; 13:19; etc.; cf. 2 Pet 2:6; Jude 7). "In that day" (so Luke) becomes "in the day of judgment" in order to sharpen the warning. The phrase occurs in the gospels only here and in 11:22, 24; 12:36 (but see *Pss. Sol.* 15:12; *Jub.* 4:19; 2 Pet 2:9; 3:7; 1 John 4:17).

JESUS' WARNING CONCERNING PERSECUTION IN A MISSION INCLUDING GENTILES

10:16-42 (16:24-25; 18:5; 19:29; 23:34; 24:9-10, 13-14, 31; Mark 4:22; 8:34-35, 38; 9:37, 41; 10:29-30; 13:9-13; Luke 6:40; 8:17; 9:26; 10:3; 12:2-9, 11-12, 51-53; 14:25-27; 17:33; 21:12-19; cf. John 12:25; 13:16; 15:20)

In this passage Matthew brings together various materials scattered in Mark and Luke and relates them to the persecution of the twelve disciples, who stand for all disciples of Jesus. The persecution results from their witness and furthers it. Verses 16-23 contain a description of the persecution with instructions to beware of informers, not to worry about preparing statements for court, and to flee from one city to another rather than stay suicidally in a city that poses a threat to life and limb. Reasons not to fear the persecution appear in vv 24-42. They include the solidarity in suffering of the disciples and their master (vv 24-25), the impossibility of hiding the truth (vv 26-27), the paltriness of physical martyrdom compared with eternal punishment of the whole person (v 28), the value God the Father places on Jesus' disciples (vv 29-31), the necessity of confessing Jesus before men in order to be confessed by him before God the Father (vv 32-33), the unworthiness of anyone who draws back through fear of personal abuse (vv 34-39), and the conveyance of eternal life in Christ through such costly ministry (vv 40-42).

10:16 *(Luke 10:3)* As an introduction, Matthew uses the first of Jesus' sayings in the instructions to the seventy-two. But the command "Go" drops out as part of Matthew's deleting the fulfillment of the disciples' mission in Galilee. The omission allows "behold, I send" to come first. The characteristic insertion of ἐγώ (12-13,3) focuses attention on Jesus and his authority (cf. 23:24 with Luke 11:49). The metaphor of the disciples as lambs changes to sheep (πρόβατα, a favorite word of Matthew—6,2). The figure of sheep, which has recently represented the lost and shepherdless people of Israel (9:36; 10:6), now represents Jesus' missionaries, who are threatened by the wolflike leaders of the people. Thus a certain solidarity exists between the persecuted missionaries and the harried people; both suffer from the same source.

The command to become wise as serpents (cf. Gen 3:1 LXX) and innocent as doves (cf. Rom 16:19; Phil 2:15) appears nowhere else in the gospels. Matthew's liking οὖν (35,11) and φρόνιμοι (2,4) and the parallelism of "as sheep ... as serpents ... as doves" suggest that he composes the command in the parallelistic style typical of his writing. As in 7:24, wisdom consists in obedience to Jesus' instructions; and innocence, along with obedience, contrasts with the lawlessness of the mercenary false prophets, who appear in the contexts preceding both the present verse and 7:24. But what is the implication of "therefore"? The need for wisdom and innocence does not stem from the threat of persecution by the "wolves," as though wisdom and innocence would combine to protect one from persecution. Rather, it stems from the authority of Jesus, whose ἐγώ dominates Matthew's version. Since he sends the disciples, they must go in obedience.

10:17-22 *(24:9-10, 13-14; Mark 13:9-13; Luke 12:11-12; 21:12-19)* In vv 17-22 Matthew takes a chunk out of Jesus' eschatological discourse, in particular out of Mark 13:9-13 (cf. Luke 21:12-19), and follows it so closely that in his later version of that discourse he will give only a loose summary of this section. Nevertheless, even here some revisions appear. In place of Mark's "But watch out for yourselves" Matthew writes "But beware of men." Despite his fondness for βλέπω (9,3), προσέχετε ἀπό replaces βλέπετε in another echo of the passage on false prophets that closes the Sermon on the Mount (see 7:15). προσέχω is always distinctive in Matthew (3,3). "Yourselves" could hardly follow "beware of"; therefore Mark's

191

reflexive changes to "men," a Mattheanism that anticipates and parallels vv 32-33: the disciples must beware of men (v 17) before whom they confess Jesus (vv 32-33). The statistics on ἄνθρωπος are 35,17. Mark's emphatic ὑμεῖς drops out in order to avoid diverting attention from Jesus, whose emphatic ἐγώ continues to reverberate.

The characteristic insertion of γάρ (62-63,15) makes the delivering of the disciples to courts and their being whipped in synagogues and led before governors and kings reasons for wariness. Mark's and Luke's "synagogues" becomes "their synagogues" (5,0) because of the estrangement of the church from Judaism. And "you will be beaten" becomes the more specifically judicial "they will whip you," which provides a better match for "they will give you over." Again cf. 23:34 with Luke 11:49. In both passages Matthew uses whipping to portray persecution of the disciples in terms of Jesus' suffering (see 20:19 for the whipping of Jesus; cf. 10:24-25 and Matthew's frequent correlating of Jesus and the disciples).

In taking over Mark's saying about the disciples' standing before governors and kings, Matthew looks forward to the following Markan clauses about the proclamation of the gospel to "all the nations" and the disciples' being "led" for handing over to the authorities (Mark 13:10-11). "You will be led" comes from the latter as a substitute for Mark's "you will stand." "And to the nations" comes from the former. Thus the mission that began with a limitation to Israel expands to include Gentiles. This expansion takes place because of rejection by Jewish courts and synagogues. In other words, Matthew arranges Jesus' instructions in a manner that follows the historical transference of the kingdom from Israel to the church (see 21:43). Even before the inclusion of Gentiles, the adding of δέ makes the first καί in v 18 mean "both" and prepares for transference of the kingdom by indicating a certain contrast between the foregoing witness among Jews alone and the later witness among Gentiles as well. Though Matthew has extracted the all-important reference to nations from the saying in Mark 13:10, his omitting that saying as a whole leaves it for later use in 24:14.

The drawing up of Mark's "they lead" into the preceding saying leaves "giving over" to become the main verb in Matthew's next clause: "but whenever they give you over" (v 19; cf. Mark 13:11). There results a parallel with "they will give you over" in v 17. In the subsequent command not to be anxious about how or what to speak, Mark's "beforehand" falls away. This omission leads to an exact parallel with the two prohibitions against being anxious about tomorrow that Matthew inserted in the Sermon on the Mount (6:31, 34). In agreement with the assuring tone of that passage, he changes the command to speak whatever is given in that hour into a promise: "for what you should say will be given you in that hour" (similarly Luke, but without Matthew's reason for the change). The repetition of "what" without "how" in the last part of v 19 shows that the added "how" in the first part has to do with content rather than style. Thus stress falls again on the message of the disciples (see the comments on vv 7, 14).

Emphasis on their message continues in v 20. Matthew adds "that speaks in you" to "the Spirit"; i.e., the disciples' message comes from the Spirit himself. To emphasize the point still further, Matthew shifts ὑμεῖς forward with the result of a stronger "not you . . . but the Spirit." The Spirit is described further as "of your Father" (not in Mark or Luke). The note of assurance sounds again in a reecho of the heavenly Father's provisions promised in 6:31-34. Matthew likes πατήρ (22,13).

The Father's provision of words to speak contrasts with the betrayals and conflict in families described in v 21 (cf. Mic 7:6 and Gundry, *Use of the OT* 33). Therefore Matthew changes Mark's καί to an adversative δέ. Otherwise his text corresponds with Mark's in vv 21-22. The treachery of unbelievers toward believers in their own families expands into a general hatred of believers on the part of all (v 22). In allusion to Dan 12:12-13 (see Gundry, *Use of the OT* 47; cf. Mic 7:7) Jesus promises salvation to those who hold out till the end, i.e., till the coming of the Son of man (see v 23; cf. 24:13-14, 29-31). This promise has the purpose of steeling the disciples against treachery in their families and against hatred in the world at large. Naturally, those who die for their discipleship before the end will enjoy salvation. But those disciples who survive need encouragement to stick true as a demonstration that they are genuine.

Only by overlooking v 23 could we say that Matthew removes the eschatology from Mark 13:9-13. And only by overlooking Mark 13:9b-11 (esp. the phrase "for my sake") could we say that Matthew alone relates the persecution of disciples to their Christian witness, as though in Mark persecution is just a stock apocalyptic woe, more Jewish than Christian. On local Jewish courts see *m. Sanh.* 1:1-6; and on beating and whipping see Deut 25:1-3; Acts 16:22-23; 22:19, 24; 2 Cor 11:24. It is disputable whether Mark's εἰς μαρτύριον αὐτοῖς means "for a witness to the governors and kings" or "for a witness against the accusers of the disciples," and whether Matthew's εἰς μαρτύριον αὐτοῖς καὶ τοῖς ἔθνεσιν means "for a witness to the Gentile governors and kings and to the nations in general" or "for a witness to the Jews and to the Gentiles." Matthew's positive attitude toward evangelizing Gentiles provides a firm base to translate τοῖς ἔθνεσιν "to the nations" rather than "against the nations." His coordination of αὐτοῖς then seems to require "to them" rather than "against them." And since those who haul the disciples before the authorities presumably have heard the preaching of the disciples already, the "them" to whom witness in court is directed probably refers to the governors and kings just mentioned. Though Mark does not coordinate αὐτοῖς and "the nations," his πάντα with τὰ ἔθνη probably implies that the witness begins before Gentile governors and kings and extends to all their subjects. The plurality of "governors," a term hardly applicable to Jewish authorities, favors a general reference to authorities throughout the world rather than a particular reference to the Roman governor of Judea; hence, the following βασιλεῖς probably refers to kings everywhere, not just to the Herodian princes who ruled in different parts of Palestine.

On social strife as a sign of the end, see *Jub.* 23:19; *1 Enoch* 56:7; 99:5; 100:1-2; 2 Esdr 5:9; *2 Apoc. Bar.* 70:3. At least in Matthew, "on account of my name" (cf. 19:29) probably refers to the use of Jesus' name in prophesying, exorcising demons, and performing miracles (cf. 7:22). The meaning "for me" (cf. v 18) seems too weak, and Matthew shows no interest in the name "Christian" (cf. Acts 11:26; 26:28; and esp. 1 Pet 4:16). Here, the verb θανατώσουσιν does not mean to kill or condemn to death, but to cause to be condemned to death by means of accusations.

Despite the absence of the definite article with τέλος (so also 24:13) in contrast with its presence in 24:14, the allusion to Dan 12:12-13 (cf. 11:35) favors a reference to the end of the age rather than to the end of life through martyrdom (cf. Rev 2:10) or a general meaning "continually" (cf. Luke 18:5). The absence of the article then stems from the stereotyping of εἰς τέλος (see lexicons and concordances). Possibly, but not probably, the phrase belongs to "this one will be saved." If so, it means "at the end." On survival and salvation at the end, see 2 Esdr 6:25; 9:7-8.

10:23 (23:34; 24:31) Martyrdom is not to be sought. In Mark and Luke, Jesus goes on to command flight at the sight of the abomination of desolation and then to describe the coming of the Son of man. Here in v 23 Matthew summarizes that part of the eschatological discourse and makes certain assimilations to the present context of the disciples' mission in Galilee. ὅταν occurs five times in his gospel as an insertion and five times as part of distinctive passages, besides nine common occurrences. διώκωσιν, "they persecute," echoes several insertions in the Sermon on the Mount (see 5:10, 11, 12, 44) and anticipates 23:34. We have already noted two points of contact between 23:34 and the present passage (see the comments on vv 16-17). In 23:34 we read, "and you [scribes and Pharisees] will persecute" (similarly Luke 11:49). Both passages have to do with the mission of Jesus' disciples, and in both passages Matthew adds references to movement from city to city as a result of persecution. The additions stem from his interest in cities (18,3). Here the addition links with frequent references to cities in the preceding context (9:35; 10:5, 11, 14, 15).

We do not have to consider φεύγετε a favorite of Matthew, but it does appear distinctively also in 2:13; 23:33 (cf. "Flight from persecution" in the Topical Index). ἑτέραν is a Mattheanism (5,1) and gives ταύτῃ its point. Thus Matthew strikes a balance between perseverance in discipleship and preservation of life. The balance avoids tipping into the laxity of antinomianism or the self-righteousness of obsession with martyrdom.

"For truly I say to you" typifies the style of Matthew (15,8) and his emphasis on Jesus' authoritative teaching (see further the comments on 5:18). τελέσητε is another favorite (5,2). πόλεις appears for a second time in the verse (18,3). Here it is qualified by τοῦ Ἰσραήλ, yet another Mattheanism (5,4). "The cities of Israel" comes close to "a city of the Samaritans" in v 5. Thus it appears that v 23, like vv 5-8, comes from Matthew's pen rather than from prior tradition.

For encouragement not to give up persevering and fleeing, by both of which the gospel is spread, a reference to the coming of the Son of man closes this summary of the climactic portion of the eschatological discourse (see Mark 13:26 and further references to the coming of the Son of man in Matt 16:27, 28 [distinctive]; 24:30, 44; 25:31 [distinctive]; 26:64). Since Matthew knew that Jesus did not return as the Son of man before the twelve completed their circuit of Galilee, in writing v 23 he implies a continuing mission to Israel alongside the mission to Gentiles. In other words, the taking of the kingdom from Israel (21:43) does not stall the mission to Israel. The church includes believing Jews, too. Yet persecution by the Jewish leaders (a matter that occupies Matthew very much) threatens to turn Christian evangelism completely away from Israel. To guarantee continuance of the mission to Israel, therefore, Matthew composes this saying in v 23 and then omits any reference to a carrying out of the Galilean mission by the twelve.

To finish the cities of Israel means to finish visiting them, just as to finish words or parables means to finish speaking them (cf. 7:28; 13:53; 19:1; 26:1). Since Matthew is summarizing Mark 13:24-27, this saying refers to the Son of man's coming to earth rather than his being assumed to heaven (much less going on a preaching mission). Some have thought that ταύτῃ has no antecedent, that the definite article before ἑτέραν is unskillful, and that therefore the saying was traditional and isolated. But it is these very two words that give each other point: "this city" stands over against "the next [city]." The words hardly overturn, then, the indications of Matthew's composition noted above. His composition, in turn, rules out a narrowly Jewish outlook as the matrix of the saying (see "Universality" in the Topical Index). Any view that Jesus or an early Christian prophet spoke the saying out of expectation of a very near end likewise falls to the ground. Matthew takes into account a worldwide mission to Gentiles as well as a continuing mission to Jews.

10:24-25 (Luke 6:40) As an antidote to fear, Matthew now draws a parallel between the persecution of the disciples and the suffering of Jesus. To do so, he imports and expands a saying that appears also in Luke 6:40: "A disciple is not above the teacher; but fully prepared, every [disciple] will be like his teacher." The first clause stays unchanged. But to emphasize Jesus' authority, Matthew adds "neither a slave above his master" (cf. John 13:16; 15:20; *b. Ber.* 58b). The addition agrees with Matthew's love of parallelism and fondness for κύριος as a designation of Jesus (34,15).

For further emphasis, Matthew expands the second clause of the tradition reflected in Luke by making it into another pair of lines (v 25ab). But where Jesus talks about every disciple's being like his teacher as a result of instructional preparation, Matthew writes about the sufficiency (i.e., appropriateness) of a disciple's being persecuted just as his teacher is persecuted. The highly elliptical and parallelistic "and [it is enough for] the slave [that he becomes] like his master" repeats the point. Matthew directs these statements against falsely professing Christians who exalt themselves above their persecuted Teacher and Lord by evading persecution through keeping quiet (cf. vv 26-33). Flight is the only legitimate way to escape (v 23).

To round out the parallel between Jesus and his disciples, Matthew composes a final pair of clauses in anticipation of the charge that Jesus casts out demons by Beelzebul, the ruler of the demons (12:24, 27; cf. an earlier anticipation of that passage in 9:32-34). Intensified by Matthew, the charge reads that people have called the master of the house *himself* by that Satanic epithet, and the slanderous epithet covers Jesus' disciples as well. οἰκοδεσπότην is a Mattheanism (2,4) and here derives by wordplay from Βεελζεβούλ, regarded as the Hebrew בַּעַל ("master"/-δεσπότην) + the Hebrew זְבוּל ("house"/οἰκο-; see also 12:29 with comments). πόσῳ and μᾶλλον are two further Mattheanisms (3,0; 5,1). οἰκιακούς complements οἰκοδεσπότην and occurs in the NT only here and in v 36. Cf. *TDNT* 1. 605-6.

10:26-33 (Mark 8:38; Luke 9:26; 12:2-9) We now come to a series of three prohibitions of fear paralleled with different surroundings in Luke 12:2-9. First, Jesus tells his disciples not to fear those who call him and them Beelzebul, because the truth will out (v 26). Second, he tells them not to fear those who can kill the body, because they cannot kill the soul (v 28a). Third, he tells them not to fear, because they are more valuable than many sparrows, not one of which falls apart from the Father's will (vv 29-31). The first two prohibitions lead to positive commands—to proclaim Jesus' teachings publicly (v 27) and to fear God, who can destroy both soul and body in Gehenna (v 28b). The third prohibition leads to a positive statement about Jesus' confessing those who confess him and about his denying those who deny him (vv 32-33).

10:26-27 (Luke 12:2-3) To get the first "Fear not" (cf. also Mark 4:22; Luke 8:17), Matthew draws up the prohibition from the tradition behind Luke 12:4. The importing of this first "Fear not" and the replacing of δέ with γάρ in the following clause make God's future revealing of everything covered and making known everything hidden a reason for courage in Christian witness. In Luke, on the other hand, the revelation and making known contrast with the Pharisees' hypocrisy (see Luke 12:1). The insertion of "therefore" makes the preceding solidarity of disciple and master a reason for not fearing, and the addition of "them" points back to those who hurl the epithet Beelzebul. The persecution of the disciples is nothing more than their Master suffers. Both γάρ and οὖν belong to Matthew's special vocabulary (62-63,15; 35,11).

In its warning against hypocrisy, portrayed as a cover-up, Luke's parallel continues with predictions of a future hearing in the light of as many things as the disciples have said in the dark and of a future proclamation on the housetops of what they have spoken in the back rooms; i.e., the impossibility of keeping secrets past the last judgment makes hypocrisy futile (Luke 12:3). Matthew transforms these warning predictions into commands to publicize *now* what *Jesus* has said in the hearing of the disciples (v 27). Because of this radical shift, Luke's "accordingly" drops out as inappropriate. "What" replaces "as many things as" for an exact parallel with foregoing and succeeding clauses beginning with the same pronoun (vv 26 [bis], 27b). "I say," a typically Matthean reference to Jesus' teaching (27,7), replaces "you have said," a reference to offhand speech of the disciples. "In the dark" indicates privacy. Matthew changes "will be heard" to the imperative "speak." "In the light" indicates publicity, that of the last judgment in Luke, that of Christian preaching in Matthew. "And what you hear in the ear" refers to Jesus' private instruction of the disciples, in contrast with Luke's traditional reference to what the disciples have whispered in private conversation. Thus in Matthew the proclamation on the housetops consists in preaching throughout the present age; in the tradition taken over by Luke it consists in exposure at the end. Cf. Josephus *J.W.* 2.21.5 §611.

10:28-30 (Luke 12:4-7) To avoid interrupting the series of three exhortations not to fear, Matthew deletes "but I tell you my friends" and simply writes "and." This second exhortation has to do with fear of men who kill the body. He has already used the aorist tense of the verb for fearing; here he anticipates the present tense in the tradition behind the next exhortation not to fear (contrast Luke 12:4). And since he began with "and," he now changes the traditional "and" in the middle of the saying to "but," which makes the contrast more evident. Though "after these things" occurs four times in Luke and "have" + an infinitive five times, the neat parallelism in Matthew looks like Matthew's style and does not invite change. On the other hand, it is easy to think that he omits "after these things" for the sake of parallelism. It is also easy to think that he wants to explain "not having anything more to do" (so Luke) as inability to kill the soul and therefore inserts his favorite "are able" ($\delta\upsilon\nu\acute{\alpha}\mu\epsilon\omega\nu$—13,0), repeats "kill," and adds "soul." Thus antithetic parallels develop between killing and not killing and between the body and the soul. Despite much current opinion to the contrary, Jews as well as Greeks regarded physical death as separation of the soul from the body (see, e.g., Isa 10:18; 38:10, 12, 17; Tob 3:6; Sir 38:23; Bar 2:17; *Jub.* 23:31; *1 Enoch* 9:3, 10; 22:5-7, 9-14; 51:1; 67:8-9; 71:11; 98:3; 102:4; 103:3-8; *2 Apoc. Bar.* 23:4; 30:2-5; 2 Esdr 7:75-101; *Adam and Eve* 43:1; *As. Mos.* 32:4; 42:8; *Testament of Abraham* passim; Ps.-Philo *Bib. Ant.* 32:13; *b. Ber.* 28b; *b. Sanh.* 91a; *Lev. Rab.* 24:3; *Qoh. Rab.* 3.20-21; see R. H. Gundry, *Sōma in Biblical Theology* [SNTSMS 29; Cambridge: Cambridge University Press, 1976] 87-160). But since persecutors cannot separate the soul of a disciple from God by putting it in hell, there is no need to fear them.

Again for neater parallelism, Matthew drops "but I will show you whom you should fear" (so Luke). Only $\delta\acute{\epsilon}$ remains to contrast the two commands not to fear and to fear. The aorist of the verb changes to the present to match the first member in Matthew's parallelistic construction. As elsewhere, he inserts $\mu\tilde{\alpha}\lambda\lambda o\nu$ (5,1), here in order to stress the contrast between men's inability and God's omnipotence. Again a prepositional phrase beginning "after" drops out and "having" gives way to "is able." The body and soul reappear (contrast Luke), but in chiastic order for emphasis on God's ability to destroy in hell the soul as well as the body. Despite his liking $\beta\acute{\alpha}\lambda\lambda\omega$ (12,8) and $\acute{\epsilon}\kappa\beta\acute{\alpha}\lambda\lambda\omega$ (10,1), Matthew replaces $\acute{\epsilon}\mu\beta\alpha\lambda\epsilon\tilde{\iota}\nu$ with another of his favorites, $\acute{\alpha}\pi o\lambda\acute{\epsilon}\sigma\alpha\iota$ (8,1), because its meaning "to destroy" comes closer to the preceding "to kill." And "Yes, I say to you, fear this one" vanishes lest it spoil his coupling of the commands "And do not fear . . . but do fear." In all these changes, the poetic urge for parallelism shows itself strong.

In the command not to fear those who kill the body, $\acute{\alpha}\pi\acute{o}$ may connote a shying away. If so, it disappears in the command to fear God, because there is no shying away from him in godly fear. Rather, there is reverential approach. Matthew and Luke agree in these respects. See Jas 4:12 against identifying the one to fear as the Devil. Elsewhere the NT contains no command to fear the Devil. Cf. 4 Macc 13:14-15.

Sparrows were sold for food. An assarion was one-sixteenth of a denarius. A denarius, in turn, was a day's wages for a manual laborer (cf. 20:1-16). The selling of five sparrows at a price of two assarions (so Luke) becomes the selling of two sparrows for one assarion (v 29; cf. 6:26). Perhaps Matthew narrows down the sale for a stronger emphasis on fewness in contrast with "all the hairs of your head," which, according to the next verse, are numbered (cf. his liking of δύο—19,4). According to habit he conforms "and not one of them is forgotten in the sight of God" (so Luke) to OT phraseology. His verb πεσεῖται, his phrase ἐπὶ τὴν γῆν, and his preposition ἄνευ—none of which Luke has—all derive from the LXX of Amos 3:5: "Will a bird fall on the ground apart from a fowler?" The substitution of "your Father" for "God" not only exhibits a Mattheanism (22,13), but also makes a nice contrast with the fowler in Amos 3:5 LXX. Thus the falling to the ground by the destructive design of a fowler becomes a falling to the ground—i.e., dying—in the will of the gracious Father (see BAG, s.v. ἄνευ 1; cf. m. Meg. 4:9). Considering the persecution under which Matthew writes, this saying means that Christians do not need to fear even martyrdom.

In the statement that all the hairs of the disciples' heads are numbered (v 30), Matthew advances ὑμῶν to the beginning for an emphatic a fortiori in relation to the sparrows (cf. v 31b). δέ stands in place of Luke's ἀλλά and conforms to the δέ which tied together the pair of sayings in v 28. The periphrastic perfect passive form of ἠριθμημέναι εἰσίν may be more emphatic than Luke's simple perfect passive ἠρίθμηνται. Cf. 16:19; 18:18.

10:31 (Luke 12:7) A final command not to fear follows. Typically, Matthew inserts οὖν (35,11), which makes the Father's caring for even a single sparrow and going much farther in counting all the hairs on the disciples' heads reasons enough not to fear persecutors. The final statement confirms these reasons: "you are more valuable than many sparrows." The emphatic ὑμεῖς (not in Luke but a favorite of Matthew—15,3) again brings out the a fortiori more clearly (cf. the position of ὑμῶν in v 30). "Many" may mean "all," as often in Semitic literature.

10:32-33 (Mark 8:38; Luke 9:26; 12:9) To weld together the foregoing and following sayings, Matthew deletes "and I say to you" (so Luke 12:8a). Cf. the recent omissions of the tradition behind Luke 12:4a, 5cd. To further the connection, Matthew again inserts οὖν (35,11). This makes the Father's great care for the disciples a reason for their confessing and not denying Jesus before men (vv 32-33). The addition of τις to the relative ὅς typifies Matthew's diction (23,5) and puts emphasis on the actions of confessing and denying Jesus rather than on the identity of those who perform these actions. Matthew replaces "the Son of man also" with a characteristic "I also" (κἀγώ—5,3) to emphasize Jesus and prepare for the first person possessive pronoun in the further, double replacement of "the angels of God" with "my Father in heaven" (10,2).

In v 33 the writing of another relative clause beginning with a distinctive ὅστις (23,5), the double replacement of ἐνώπιον with ἔμπροσθεν (9,4), the repetition of the active voice (cf. v 32 and contrast Luke's "will be denied"), and the repetition of κἀγώ (5,3) again demonstrate a penchant for parallelism and a desire to reemphasize the person of Jesus and the fatherhood of God. The verb of denying takes the aorist subjunctive in its first occurrence. Though we may consider the aorist subjunctive equivalent to the future indicative (cf. v 32a), Matthew may want to lessen the suggestion of denying Jesus.

The sayings in vv 32-33 probably derive from 1 Sam 2:30 (see Gundry, *Use of the OT* 77-78). The ἐν after the verb of confessing represents an Aramaism (BAG, s.v. ὁμολογέω 4). Since proclamation from the housetop as well as testimony in court appears in the preceding verses, we should probably include both in confessing Jesus before men.

10:34-36 (Luke 12:51-53) The next three verses have their parallel in Luke 12:51-53. But Luke's question "Do you suppose that I have arrived . . . ?" becomes the command "Do not think that I have come . . . ," just as in 5:17 (so Matthew alone). To secure his emphasis on Jesus as the Coming One (cf. the comments on 3:11) Matthew pushes εἰρήνην out of its emphatic position to an unobtrusive spot after its infinitive. The infinitive changes from δοῦναι to βαλεῖν, a favorite of his (12,8), which is rabbinic in style (Str-B 1. 586). This change enables him to replace "in" with "on." The resultant phrase "on the earth" parallels the same phrase in v 29, where Matthew alone had it.

For unity, parallelism, and yet greater emphasis on Jesus as the Coming One, "I did not come to bring peace" replaces "No, I say to you" (cf. earlier omissions of Luke 12:4a, 5cd, 8a). The "division" Jesus brings becomes a "sword" for conformity to Ezek 38:21: "every man's sword will be against his brother." Cf. the three occurrences of μάχαιρα in 26:52, an inserted saying peculiar to Matthew.

For yet another emphasis on Jesus as the Coming One, Matthew skips the division of a household of five into three against two and two against three, and, going immediately to the listing of father and son, mother and daughter, mother-in-law and daughter-in-law, he writes "For I came to separate" (v 35) instead of "they will be divided" (so Luke). Matthew uses διχάσαι (literally "to halve") because of its appropriateness to his noun "sword": Jesus divides families just as a sword slices in half. Though Luke's "son" is a better complement to "father" than "man" is, Matthew substitutes the latter to set up an inclusio with "man" in v 36. Furthermore, he is fond of ἄνθρωπος (35,17).

The saying about separation in a family reflects Mic 7:6 (cf. Deut 33:9). To conform the wording more closely to that OT passage, Matthew adopts only the second phrase in each of the three pairs. "Father against son," "mother against daughter," and "mother-in-law against daughter-in-law" disappear; and "man against father," "daughter against mother," and "daughter-in-law against mother-in-law" remain, as in Mic 7:6. The addition of "her" to "mother" and again to "mother-in-law" provides two further assimilations to the OT text. For parallelism, Matthew adds "his" to "father." The substitution of κατά for ἐπί makes the thought of antagonism more immediately apparent and conforms to Matthew's style (κατά + genitive—10,1). Yet another assimilation to Mic 7:6 marks v 36: "and a man's enemies [are] the members of his household" (not in Luke). By filling out the quotation in this manner, Matthew gains a link with v 25, where members of a household appeared.

10:37-38 (Luke 14:25-27) Now come three parallel sayings that appear also in Luke 14:25-27 (cf. Matt 16:24; 19:29; Mark 8:34; 10:29-30; 4QTest 14-20). They contain references to father, mother, son, and daughter and play on the theme of Jesus' upsetting family loyalties. Their similarities to the foregoing sayings brought them to Matthew's mind. In order to unify them with the foregoing, he omits the transition that appears in Luke 14:25-26a (cf. the comments on vv 28, 32, 34). Because of this omission, Jesus' emphasis on discipleship as requiring greater loyalty to him than to one's family changes to an emphasis on persecution as requiring such loyalty if one is to "endure to the end." But where Jesus speaks about the necessity of hating the members of one's immediate family, Matthew writes about the danger of loving one's close relatives above Jesus. Not only does Matthew like φιλῶν somewhat (2,1), but also his emphasis on love (see 5:43-47; 22:34-40) leads him to avoid a positive use of "hate," which always has a bad connotation in his gospel (see 5:43; 6:24; 10:22; 24:9, 10). The change from "not hating" to "loving more than" correctly interprets the comparative use of "hate" (see 6:24).

The putting of ἤ for καί between pairs of relatives stems from the change in the verbal expression and conforms to Matthew's predilection for ἤ (32,12). Furthermore, ἤ leads to a pairing of father and mother, son and daughter, where Luke's text has a string of nouns repeatedly connected by καί. The pairing of father and mother results in a parallelistic expansion of "children" to "son or daughter." Matthew is content with these two pairs; so he deletes the traditional references to wife, brothers, sisters, and one's own self.

The change in the verbal expression also leads to Matthew's "above me" (bis), which forges a link with "above the teacher . . . above his master" in v 24. To further this Christological emphasis, Matthew rewrites "is not able to be my disciple" to read "is not worthy of me" (bis). He likes ἄξιος (7,0). Here it links these sayings to those in vv 10, 11, and 13 and accentuates the risking of danger from informants in one's own family. Such risking of danger shows the genuineness—i.e., the worth—of already professed discipleship, whereas the tradition states conditions for taking up discipleship (so Luke). The putting of μου before ἄξιος echoes the Christological emphasis in ὑπὲρ ἐμέ. The repetition of these phrases in the parallel statements concerning the one who loves father or mother and concerning the one who loves son or daughter (Luke has only a single statement) increases Matthew's stress on Jesus.

Matthew inserts "and" at the start of the saying about the cross (v 38) in order to make it the third in a series along with the two in v 37. The reference to bearing one's cross in following Jesus suffers an incongruity in that Jesus will not begin to predict his crucifixion till 16:21-23 (cf. 16:24-26). But Matthew is thinking topically rather than chronologically. Though he twice added τις to ὅς in vv 32-33, here the suffix falls away for a closer parallel with the preceding substantive participles. βαστάζει yields to the Mattheanism λαμβάνει (21,16). Matthew's context makes the disciple's cross stand for persecution to the point of martyrdom. To take one's cross is to expose oneself to this possibility through open discipleship.

Ordinarily in this gospel ἔρχεται, which Luke has here, refers to Jesus as the Coming One (cf. the comments on 3:11). For discipleship, therefore, Matthew switches to ἀκολουθεῖ, a favorite of his (8,0). A third time we read "is not worthy of me." This replaces "is not able to be my disciple" and shifts emphasis from inability to become a disciple to worthy perseverance in discipleship.

10:39 (Luke 17:33) Verses 39-41 consist of three sayings. Each is a couplet of parallel lines. A nominative substantive participle stands at the head of each line. The traditional reference to hating oneself (Luke 14:26), omitted above by Matthew, suggested the tradition behind Luke 17:33 (cf. Matt 16:25; Mark 8:35; John 12:25). After the pattern of the two sayings in v 37 and the one in v 40 (cf. Luke 10:16), Matthew changes "whoever seeks to keep his soul" to a substantive participle. He also changes "seeks to keep" to "finds" (εὑρών—7,8), which contrasts better with "will lose." The stronger meaning of "he who finds" suggests that he has in mind professing disciples who have actually retrieved their lives by recanting or keeping quiet during persecution. For parallelism he again uses a substantive participle in ὁ ἀπολέσας (contrast Luke's relative clause), writes a second "his soul" (contrast Luke's "it"), and replaces "will preserve it alive" with a second use of εὑρίσκω in "will find it." Most strikingly, he disturbs his careful balancing of the two clauses by inserting "for my sake" (cf. 5:11; 10:18; 16:25). The insertion relates the saying more specifically to persecution and yet again highlights the figure of Jesus.

To lose one's soul is to lose one's life and therefore oneself. Like the Hebrew נֶפֶשׁ, ψυχήν carries all these meanings. As in v 28, an essentialist notion of the soul is not to be ruled out as Hellenistic.

10:40 (18:5; Mark 9:37; Luke 9:48; 10:16) Now Matthew conflates a saying found in Luke 10:16 at the end of Jesus' instructions to the seventy-two and a saying in Mark 9:37; Luke 9:48, which he will record more exactly in 18:5 (cf. John 12:44-45; 13:20; m. Ber. 5:5). The construction of ὁ δεχόμενος as a substantive participle derives from Luke 10:16 and from the preceding saying in Matthew (contrast 18:5 and Mark 9:37; Luke 9:48). But the choice of δεχόμενος derives from Mark 9:37 (see also 18:5; Luke 9:48; and contrast ὁ ἀκούων in Luke 10:16). The object "you" agrees with Luke 10:16 and differs from "one such child" in the other passages. But "accepts" goes back to those other passages, against "hears" in Luke 10:16. The next clause follows the same pattern, except that for the sake of a couplet Matthew omits the second clause in the tradition behind Luke 10:16 ("and he who rejects you rejects me"). The third clause, "and he who rejects me rejects him who sent me," provides the basis for the second clause in Matthew's couplet. But "accepts" again pushes out Luke's verb. "Him who sent me" occurs in all the passages except Matt 18:5. As a result of this conflation and parallelism, great emphasis falls on the authority of the disciples as representatives of Jesus and the Father who sent him (cf. v 1). Accepting the disciples means harboring those who are fleeing persecution (v 23). Because of their greater exposure to public view, apostles, prophets, and teachers of righteousness are naturally the first to suffer persecution. But even obscure ("little") disciples may need help in escaping. Who will harbor such refugees? Only their fellow disciples, for who else would dare to do so? Therefore these sayings indicate that willingness to risk danger to oneself by harboring fleeing disciples characterizes true discipleship. Only the false disciple will refuse.

10:41 The parallelism and diction in v 41, which has no counterpart in the other gospels, lead to the conclusion that Matthew has composed it after the pattern of the two preceding sayings. Like them, it begins in each of its two lines with a substantive participle; indeed, ὁ δεχόμενος (bis) comes from the immediately preceding saying, where it has already appeared twice. "Prophet" occurs three times in the first clause; "righteous" occurs three times in the second clause. Matthew has a special interest in both words (προφήτης—19,6; δίκαιος—9-10,7-6). The distinctive pairing of "prophet" and "righteous [man]" will be seen again in 13:17; 23:29. μισθόν (bis) and λήμψεται also fall inside the circle of Matthew's favorite words (2,5; 21,16). "In the name of" will occur distinctively in 18:20; 28:19 also. In the present passage it means "with faith that he is what his title implies"; i.e., it denotes acceptance of Jesus' messengers as prophets and righteous men (cf. the comments on 28:19). Because the context deals with mission, "righteous [man]" may carry not only the connotation of righteousness in conduct, but also that of righteousness as subject matter in teaching (cf. 28:19; Dan 12:3; the conjunction of teaching and doing in Matt 5:19; "the Teacher of Righteousness" in the QL passim; and Matthew's portrayal of the Christian scribe, concerning which see the comments on 8:19). The reward of a prophet and righteous man will be the gaining of God's approval in heaven (cf. 5:12; 6:1).

10:42 (Mark 9:41) Matthew now skips from Mark 9:37 to Mark 9:41. As a result, the story of the man who was exorcising demons in Jesus' name but was not following Jesus (Mark 9:38-40) drops out. Matthew's emphasis on following Jesus (see ἀκολουθέω in the Greek Index) may have caused omission of the story elsewhere in the gospel, too; but here the omission is due to the unity of 10:5b-42 as a collection of Jesus' sayings. They are not to be interrupted by narrative. Thus in v 42 Matthew changes Mark's conjunction "for," which relates to the omitted story, to "and," which makes the following saying an addition to the preceding sayings. In anticipation of 18:6, 10, 14, giving a drink to "you" becomes giving a drink to "one of these little ones" (so also Mark 9:42). Matthew then transmutes "a cup of water" to a "cup of cold [water]." The refreshingness of *cold* water heightens the notion of acceptance (cf. vv 40-41; Prov 25:25). His characteristic insertion of μόνον (9,0—perhaps to be taken with ποτήριον) performs the same service. Mark's awkward "in name, because you are Christ's" becomes "in the name of a disciple" for a parallel with the preceding "in the name of a prophet/righteous [man]" (v 41).

Typically, Matthew inserts μαθητοῦ (31,5) as a definition of "one of these little ones." Yet in the context of a question concerning greatness in the kingdom, Jesus distinguishes them from the disciples he is speaking to. He does so by telling his disciples not to despise the little ones (18:10a).

At the same time, the little ones believe in Jesus (18:6) and have angels in heaven who continually behold the face of Jesus' heavenly Father (18:10b). It thus appears that they are disciples who do not occupy positions of leadership in the church. Consequently, we have a hierarchical list descending from the apostles (v 40) through Christian prophets and teachers of righteousness (v 41) to ordinary church members (v 42). The concern of Matthew to produce this list sparked his composition of v 41; and his concern to emphasize the importance of the little ones, despite their lack of leading roles, makes him change the "you" spoken to the apostles (Mark 9:41) to "one of these little ones" (v 42). The context of mission implies that the little ones share with the apostles, prophets, and teachers of righteousness in witness, persecution, flight, and reception of hospitality from fellow disciples willing to harbor them.

The rest of v 42 follows Mark except for the inconsequential dropping of ὅτι, "that." "Truly I say to you" provides a point of contact with vv 15 and 23, where it has already appeared. "Will not lose" links with v 39, and "his reward" with v 22.

A CONCLUDING FORMULA
FOR THE SECOND "BOOK" OF JESUS' LAW
11:1

11:1 The statement in 11:1 has no parallels in the other gospels, but it matches other conclusions to Matthew's pentateuch of Jesus' discourses (see the comments on 7:28-29). As in all these conclusions, we read, "And it came to pass [that] when Jesus finished." Matthew suits the remainder of the statement to its context. διατάσσων, "ordering," explains the preceding discourse as a commission. "His twelve disciples" harks back to 10:1 and makes an inclusio. μετέβη and ἐκεῖθεν are Mattheanisms (5,1; 8,1). In 12:9; 15:29 Matthew will insert these two words together. "To teach and preach in their cities" harks back to 9:35 and contributes further to the inclusio (cf. 4:23). "Their cities" echoes "their synagogues" and "their scribes" in 4:23; 7:29; 9:35 (cf. 10:17) and implies the estrangement of Israel and the church (see the comments on 7:28-29). Most remarkably, however, Matthew writes nothing about teaching and preaching by the disciples. According to chap. 10, Jesus instructs them to preach; but in contrast with Mark and Luke, it is Jesus who proceeds to do so—and in the very cities where the disciples were to go! Such is the dominance of Matthew's Christ. The unfulfilled mission of the disciples to Israel thus remains till Christ's return (see the comments on 10:23).

THE OPPOSITION AND PERSECUTION
INCURRED BY JESUS AND HIS DISCIPLES
11:2–12:50

A narrative section that goes through 12:50 starts at 11:2. As usual, however, Matthew puts emphasis on Jesus' words even in narrative. Just as chaps. 8–9 carried out the theme of Jesus' authority prominent in the Sermon on the Mount (chaps. 5–7), so also chaps. 11–12 carry out the theme of opposition to and persecution of Jesus and his disciples prominent in the discourse on mission (chap. 10). The story about the messengers of John the Baptist (11:2-24) climaxes in the saying on suffering violence (v 12). The associated sayings about the rejection of John and Jesus by "this generation" (vv 16-19) reiterate the theme; and those concerning the unrepentant cities of Chorazin and Bethsaida (vv 20-24) give assurance that opponents will be judged. Jesus' gentleness toward his disciples, who are called "infants," provides a foil to the heavy-handed scribes and Pharisees, who are the source of Jesus' and the disciples' trouble (11:25-30). The Pharisees' criticisms of the disciples for plucking grain on the Sabbath (12:1-8) and of Jesus for healing a man with a withered hand on the Sabbath (12:9-13) climax in a plot to destroy Jesus (12:14) and in his consequent withdrawal (12:15-21). His retiring provides another foil to the murderous initiative of his opponents (12:18-21; cf. 10:23a). The charge that he casts out demons by Beelzebul (12:22-37) harks back to the similar charge in 10:25 and includes assurances of coming judgment on persecutors. The same assurance appears in Jesus' response to the demand for a sign (12:38-45). The narrative section finally closes with a more positive assurance regarding the true members of Jesus' family (12:46-50).

THE SUFFERING OF VIOLENCE BY THE KINGDOM OF HEAVEN
11:2-24 (10:15; 13:9, 43; Mark 1:2; Luke 7:18-35; 10:12-15; 16:16)

11:2-3 (Luke 7:18-22) Mark states that the disciples carried out their mission (6:13) and then describes the death of John the Baptist (6:14-29). Luke follows Mark, except that he fails to describe John's death, but only makes a passing reference to it and emphasizes the perplexity of Herod Antipas over Jesus' activity (9:6-9). Matthew, too, brings John into the story line—but in a different way, since he delays the account of John's death till 14:1-12. The material he puts here concerning John has a parallel in Luke 7:18-35. Matthew has already told his readers that Jesus had heard of John's being taken into custody (4:12). Now we read of John's hearing in prison about the works of Jesus, whom Matthew from his own standpoint calls "the Christ" (v 2).

The participle ἀκούσας is an insertion that typifies Matthew's style (10,3). δεσμωτηρίῳ, "prison," literally means "a keeping in bonds" and anticipates Mark 6:17, according to which Herod "bound" John and put him "in prison" (cf. Matt 14:3 and Matthew's liking of δε- [8,2]). The allusion to John's imprisonment puts the following in the framework of persecution, a leading motif that grows out of chap. 10. ἔργα is lacking in Luke and represents Matthew's diction (4,1). Here it refers to the deeds of Jesus as distinct from his words, or teaching. Elsewhere in Matthew words do not fall within the meaning of "works," and in 23:3 they contrast with them. Matthew will add Christ's words in vv 4-5. Throughout his gospel emphasis falls on Jesus as Χριστός (8,5), almost always with the definite article, as here, to denote "the Christ."

Concerning John's imprisonment, see the comments on 14:3. In view of Jesus' giving authority to the disciples (10:1) and identifying himself with them (10:40), some have thought that "the works of the Christ" include those of the disciples. This inference overlooks Matthew's remarkable deletion of the carrying out of the mission by the disciples.

In Luke some stress lies on John's disciples, who are mentioned twice. They tell John all the things Jesus is doing. John sends two of them to Jesus. In Matthew, stress lies on John. He appears as the subject of the sentence at the very beginning. We read nothing about his disciples' reporting Jesus' activities to him or about his summoning two of them, but only about his hearing of the Christ's works and sending a question through his disciples. But even those references merit only participles ("hearing . . . sending") in contrast with Luke's finite verbs ("they reported . . . he sent"). Matthew accentuates what John said (εἶπεν, a contrast with Luke's mere participle λέγων, which Matthew usually prefers—61,23). A typically Matthean parallel between John and Jesus comes into being by virtue of the further occurrence of εἶπεν in v 4, where Jesus is the subject (see "John the Baptist parallel Jesus" in the Topical Index).

With one exception, John's question appears the same in Matthew and Luke. σύ is emphatic; because of its position, ἕτερον is also emphatic: "Are *you* the Coming One, or should we expect *another?*" Though Matthew likes ἄλλον (14,4—so Luke), here he writes ἕτερον (5,1) to emphasize difference: ". . . or should we expect a different kind of Coming One?" (see *TDNT* 2. 702).

See the comments on 3:11 concerning Matthew's interest in Jesus as the Coming One (so also Luke). The literature of late Judaism does not know this expression as a messianic title, but cf. Ps 118:26; Isa 59:20. The NT contains several quotations of the former text (Matt 21:9; 23:39; Mark 11:10; Luke 13:35; 19:38; John 12:13). We should probably regard προσδοκῶμεν as a deliberative subjunctive, "should we expect?" rather than as an indicative, "do we expect?" John predicted that the Coming One would baptize the repentant in the Holy Spirit and would destroy the unrepentant (3:7-12; Mark 1:7-8; Luke 3:7-9, 15-18). Jesus' failure to fulfill these predictions raised a question in John's mind, a question particularly nettlesome because of John's imprisonment.

11:4-6 (Luke 7:22-23) Matthew is eager to arrive at Jesus' words; so he omits the coming of John's disciples, their repetition of John's question, and the noting of many healings "in that hour" (Luke 7:20-21). The narrative goes directly to Jesus' response (v 4). Typically, Matthew inserts Jesus' name (80,12). The insertion makes a parallel with John's name (v 2). Both are subjects of εἶπεν (bis).

In Jesus' words, πορευθέντες looks Matthean (8,4), but it has a parallel in Luke. The traditional ἃ εἴδετε καὶ ἠκούσατε (so Luke) becomes ἃ ἀκούετε καὶ βλέπετε. Matthew likes βλέπω (9,3). More importantly, he has changed the order of the verbs. Hearing comes before seeing because he wants to stress Jesus' words (cf. v 1). In Luke seeing and hearing immediately follow a statement about Jesus' performing miracles on the spot. The present tense of the verbs in Matthew contrasts with Luke's aorist and compensates for Matthew's lack of such a statement by *implying* the performance of miracles. But reversing the order of verbs keeps the stress on accompanying teaching.

The abundance of specially Lukan diction in Luke 7:20-21 indicates at least a re-writing of traditional material. Luke probably did not create material *ex nihilo*, however; for Matthew's "you hear" and "you see" imply the contents of Luke 7:20-21 and, as noted, compensate for omission.

In the listing of details, Matthew can hardly forsake the traditional order in which the things seen (healings of the blind, the lame, lepers, and deaf mutes and raisings of the dead) precede the things heard (proclamations of good news to the poor). A lone "and" already appears between the cleansing of lepers and the causing of deaf mutes to hear (so Luke). Matthew retains it and, in order to get two pairs, adds another "and" between the giving of sight to the blind and the making of lame people walk. The insertion of "and" both before the raising of dead people and before the preaching of good news to the poor gives these items individual significance. The remarkableness of raising people from the dead and the greatness of Matthew's interest in Jesus' verbal ministry led to individuation rather than to another pairing of items.

The itemizing of Jesus' miracles reflects the phraseology of Isa 35:5-6, a passage that tells what God will do in the time of salvation (cf. Isa 29:18-19). Jesus had not yet fulfilled John's prediction that the Coming One would baptize the repentant in the Holy Spirit and destroy the unrepentant. He had not conformed to popular Jewish messianism by bringing political, social, and economic deliverance or by coming in the wake of such a deliverance. His failure to do so caused disappointment. But his performing miracles was more than the Jews expected the Messiah to do. Jesus' doing miraculously what only God was predicted and expected to do should more than counterbalance the disappointment. That is the import of Jesus' answer to John. Doubtless Matthew also saw an indication of Jesus' deity in his doing what Isaiah predicted God would do.

Raising the dead does not appear in Isa 35:5-6 (or 29:18-19), but it does appear in Isa 26:19. Cleansing lepers does not appear in any of these passages or others of similar kind. This surplus shows that Jesus' deeds exceed the demands of John's question and that the stories of Jesus' miracles do not arise out of the OT texts. The preaching of good news to the poor corresponds to the work of the Lord's Servant in Isa 61:1 (cf. Luke 4:18; 11QMelch; 1QH 18:14).

Matthew takes Isaiah's expressions literally, and we may doubt that Isaiah intended them to be taken any less literally than he intended the reclaiming of the scorched land to be taken literally in his immediately following statements. See Gundry, *Use of the OT* 79-80, on the text of the allusive quotation. Concerning "the poor," see the comments on 5:3.

Jesus' final response to John's question takes the form of a beatitude on those who do not fall away: "And blessed is he who does not take offense [stumble into sin] at me" (so also Luke; cf. Matt 13:57; 26:31, 33). Take offense at what in Jesus? His failure to conform to popular messianic expectations? His unascetic behavior and association with the poor, the publicans, and sinners (v 19)? His coming death (26:31, 33)? It is hard to know what he had in mind. Perhaps his wording was deliberately general to allow for all kinds of offense taking. For Matthew, the beatitude makes John's doubt a dangerous example not to be followed by Christians who find themselves in similar straits.

11:7-8 (Luke 7:24-25) Luke's description of John's two disciples as "messengers" does not appear in the first gospel. Matthew reserves the term for John himself as the Lord's messenger (v 10). In place of Luke's ἀπελθόντων Matthew writes πορευομένων to show exactness of obedience to Jesus' command (cf. v 4, where πορευθέντες occurred). Again the insertion of Jesus' name gives prominence to him (cf. v 4). We may translate his rhetorical questions, "What did you go out into the wilderness to see? A reed. . . ?" (similarly vv 8-9). Or we may translate them, "Why did you go out into the wilderness? To see a reed. . . ?" (similarly vv 8-9). See Metzger, *Textual Commentary* ad loc. Because of "being shaken by the wind" and because of the parallel with a man clothed in soft things (v 8), κάλαμον probably does not refer collectively and literally to cane-grass growing along the banks of the Jordan River (cf. Job 40:21; Ps 68[67]:30; Isa 19:6; 35:7), but individually and figuratively to a person as frail (cf. 12:20; Isa 42:3; 3 Macc 2:22). John's earlier baptizing along the bank of the Jordan gave rise to the figure. Jesus is denying that his warning against apostasy implies instability in John, whose courageous condemnation of the illicit marriage between Herod Antipas and Herodias caused him to be imprisoned (Mark 6:14-29; Matt 14:1-12; Luke 9:7-9). Luke's phraseology, "the ones who live in splendid clothing and luxury are in palaces," typifies his style. The traditional wording, which Matthew keeps, concentrates attention entirely on softness: "in soft things . . . the soft things." Just as John's condemnation of Herod Antipas witnessed against any reedlike weakness (see 14:3-4), so the garment of camel's hair and the leather belt witnessed against his wearing soft things, in contrast with the finery worn by Herod Antipas and his courtiers (cf. a similar contrast in Josephus *J.W.* 1.24.3 §480 v.1.; *Ant.* 16.7.3 §204 v.1.).

ἀλλά has the force of the Aramaic אֶלָּא, "if not." Luke uses the Hellenistic expression "in palaces" where Matthew has "in the houses of kings."

11:9-10 (Mark 1:2; Luke 7:26-27) When they went out to see neither a weakling nor a courtier, but a prophet, the people found more than a prophet. They found the very forerunner of the Lord, in accord with Mal 3:1. For the most part, however, the OT quotation follows the text of a passage similar to Mal 3:1, viz., Exod 23:20 (see Gundry, *Use of the OT* 11-12, 225, for details). The putting forward of Malachi's text in the cloak of the text in Exodus results in a shift from "before me" (so Malachi) to "before you" (cf. Mark 1:2 and the comments on Matt 3:3). In Exod 23:20 "you" refers to the nation of Israel. Here it refers to Jesus. Thus three personages appear—God, the forerunner John sent by God, and Jesus the Coming One—instead of only two personages, God and his forerunner (so Mal 3:1). On the other hand, "will prepare" rests on the Hebrew text of Malachi and leads to a second translation of לְפָנַי, which is first translated literally πρὸ προσώπου σου, "before your face," and then idiomatically ἔμπροσθέν σου, "before you."

11:11 (Luke 7:28) The following tribute to John as the greatest among those born of women (i.e., among human beings—Job 14:1; 15:14; 25:4; Gal 4:4; 1QH 13:14; 18:12-13, 16, 23; 2 Esdr 4:6; 7:46) begins, "Truly I say to you." Either Luke omits ἀμήν or Matthew adds it. The awkward but emphatic "greater, among those born of women, than John no one is" (so Luke literally translated) becomes "there has not risen among those born of women a greater than John the baptizer." The use of ἐγήγερται in place of ἐστιν agrees with Matthew's diction (11,8) and with occurrences of ἐγείρω in 24:11, 24 for prophets' rising on the scene. Matthew's characteristic addition of τοῦ βαπτιστοῦ (5,0) marks John as a model Christian baptizer in the kingdom of heaven (cf. 28:19).

The comparative μικρότερος is often used for a superlative. But what does the surpassing greatness of the "lesser," or "least," mean? Is it that John could not enjoy the benefits of God's rule because he was imprisoned just before it started—hence the enjoyment of a greater privilege by the least member of the kingdom? But that would require an unnatural change from greatness of importance (more-than-prophetic ministry) to greatness of privilege (reception of salvific blessings). And though greatness may apply to blessings (cf. 2 Pet 1:4), it doubtfully applies here or elsewhere to a person because of the amount of blessing he has received. Rather, it regularly refers to importance or honor. Furthermore, the inclusion of Abraham, Isaac, and Jacob in the kingdom of heaven (8:11 and, with addition of "all the prophets," Luke 13:28) implies the inclusion of John, who exceeds them in greatness. Therefore, only by an unusual limitation of the kingdom to its present form could we see in Jesus' statement any reference to a dispensational juncture that works to John's disadvantage and the advantage of Jesus' disciples. Nothing in the statement suggests such a limitation.

Jesus would hardly have needed to say that the least in the future kingdom will surpass the greatest at the present time. This interpretation, too, rests on a confusion of importance and amount of blessing. And nothing in the saying suggests a limitation of the kingdom to its future form. To identify the lesser as Jesus himself because he was John's junior, yet had come to surpass John in greatness, avoids these difficulties. But it disagrees with Jesus' condemning claims to greatness. It also disagrees with his meekness and call to humility (18:1-5; 20:25-28; 23:11-12). Furthermore, John's being "greater" than anyone else up to that time seems to require our taking μικρότερος in the sense "lesser, least" rather than "younger."

In 18:4 Matthew will interpret Jesus' present statement by inserting "whoever therefore will humble himself as this child, this one is the greatest [ὁ μείζων] in the kingdom of heaven" (18:4). In the main clause of 18:4, each expression except "this one" comes out of the present passage; therefore the "whoever"-clause interprets greatness. That the least in the kingdom of heaven is greater than the greatest—i.e., than John—is more a challenge than a statement of fact, then, a challenge to humble Christian service that exposes disciples to persecution (cf. 23:11, another insertion). Cf. Matthew's emphasis on meekness in persecution (see πραΰς in the Greek Index) and warnings against overweening pride.

11:12-13 (Luke 16:16) Matthew now inserts a bit of tradition that appears also in Luke 16:16; but he puts the first clause, which concerns the lasting of the law and the prophets till John, at the end. This reversal makes for a lead into an additional statement regarding John's being the prophesied Elijah. The addition links with Matthew's emphasis on fulfilled prophecy. Delaying the initial clause leaves the motif of violence in first place. This motif shows Matthew's primary purpose in locating the material here, viz., portrayal of John as a prototype of persecuted Christians, the lowly little ones who voluntarily suffer humiliation for Jesus' sake (cf. the comments on 3:1ff. concerning John as a prototype of Christian preachers; and see 17:9-13, where Matthew portrays John and Jesus as partners in suffering). Matthew's insertion of δέ contrasts greatness in God's kingdom (v 11) with the suffering of persecution (v 12). Despite that greatness, there is persecution.

In Matthew "since then" always excludes the point of reference (see the insertions in 4:17; 16:21; 26:16). Luke has the expression here (and only here). But Matthew does not wish to exclude John from the kingdom of heaven. Therefore he changes "since then" to "from the days of John the baptizer till now." When not followed by "then," Matthew's "since" may either exclude or include the point of reference (see 1:17 for examples of both uses in the same verse), but usually it includes the point of reference (see 2:16; 9:22; 17:18; 19:4; 22:46; 25:34, all unique except for the occurrence in 19:4). Both the changing of "since then" and the evident purpose to portray John as a prototype of the persecuted show that Matthew includes the days of John the Baptist in the period of the kingdom's suffering violence. By the same tokens, his "till" is inclusive. For the doubly inclusive sense of ἀπό ... ἕως, see 20:8; 23:35; 24:21, 31; 27:45, 51. In addition, the present tense of "suffers violence" requires the present time to be included in the period of violence. Matthew likes ἄρτι (7,0). Its insertion here emphasizes the presence of persecution. Matthew models "the days of John" (not in Luke) after "the days of Herod the king" (2:1), "the days of our fathers" (23:30), and "the days of Noah" (24:37). The days of John refer, of course, to the days of his public ministry. The typically Matthean designation of him as "the baptizer" (5,0; not in Luke) again brings him in the Christian fold (see the comments on 3:1ff.) and links this saying to the preceding, where the same designation appeared (v 11).

As usual, Matthew substitutes "heaven" for "God" with "the kingdom." On the other hand, his βιάζεται, "suffers violence," looks original, since Luke's "the kingdom of God is preached as good news" is a demonstrable Lukanism. In Luke 4:43; 8:1; 16:16 Luke inserts the expression in shared material (cf. Acts 8:12). His transformation of the kingdom's suffering violence into the kingdom's being preached as good news implies that everyone presses into the kingdom as a happy result of evangelism. If the evangelism derives from Luke's editing, the conversions do, too. Thus Matthew sticks to the original sense, which fits his emphasis on persecution: "and violent [men] plunder it." In agreement with the pejorative connotation of ἁρπάζουσιν, the plundering of the kingdom represents the persecution of its members, e.g., the imprisonment of John the Baptist. In summary, the original saying read, "The law and the prophets [were] till John. Since then, the kingdom of God [here we switch from Luke's text to Matthew's] is suffering violence, and violent [men] plunder it."

Matthew now goes to work on the initial statement, which he has reserved till last (v 13). He is about to add that John is Elijah. Now it was a prophet—Malachi—who predicted that Elijah would come to unite Israel in righteousness (Mal 3:23[4:5]). Matthew therefore puts the prophets first: "the law and the prophets" becomes "the prophets and the law." But Malachi's prophecy of Elijah's coming is but one of many prophecies now being fulfilled. Characteristically, then, Matthew adds πάντες (63,25-26) to "the prophets." Out of the same desire to emphasize OT prophecy and its current fulfillment, he also changes the implied "were" to "prophesied." Words with προφη- enjoy his favor (23,6). Luke's μέχρι probably comes from the tradition, since it occurs only once in the third gospel. It may either include or exclude the point of reference. Matthew uses it inclusively wherever it occurs in his gospel (11:23; 13:30 v.1.; 28:15). Therefore, to keep John outside the period of the prophets and the law and inside the period of fulfillment, Matthew substitutes ἕως for μέχρι. Though ἕως often includes the point of reference (cf. the comments on v 12), sometimes it does not (see 13:30; 26:29, 38). Thus Matthew switches from a preposition always inclusive in his gospel to a preposition sometimes exclusive. The switch allows John to stand in the time of fulfillment rather than in the time of prophecy. The insertion of γάρ (62-63,15) makes transition from the time of the prophets and the law the reason for including John's ministry in the present period of the kingdom's persecution (v 12).

Matthew's changing ἀπὸ τότε and μέχρι says nothing about the inclusiveness or exclusiveness of these expressions in Luke or in the tradition behind Luke. For a well-balanced treatment of Luke's including John in the present period, see W. Wink, *John the Baptist in the Gospel Tradition* (NTSMS 7; Cambridge: Cambridge University Press, 1968) 51-57. It is implied, of course, that by the time Jesus made his statement, God's rule had started. What had drawn near during John's ministry (3:2) and at the outset of Jesus' ministry (4:17) had become present in "the works of the Christ" (11:2). Luke's statement that "the kingdom of God is preached as good news" appears to be impossible in Aramaic, for אתבשר would mean to receive good news rather than to be preached as good news. This impossibility confirms our estimate of Matthew's originality in the statement that the rule of heaven βιάζεται. Because of the overarching theme of persecution we ought to understand βιάζεται as passive ("suffers violence") rather than middle ("exercises its power forcefully"). The latter would require that the seizing of the kingdom by violent men refer to the forceful faith of the repentant. Yet the forcefulness of heaven's rule would eliminate any need for the repentant to beat down the gates of the kingdom in order to gain entrance. Matthew's insuring that John is kept out of the period of the prophets and the law and kept in the time of the kingdom does not imply the abolition of the prophets and the law (see 5:17-18). The prophecies now gain fulfillment, and the law is perfected (see the comments on chaps. 5–7).

11:14-15 (13:9, 43) The diction of the unique statement in v 14 shows that Matthew composes it as an interpretation of Mal 3:1 (cf. 17:13; Luke 1:17, 76-77; Sir 48:10). He has recently quoted Mal 3:1 in v 10. Its interpretation comes from Mal 3:23(4:5) and follows from John's belonging to the time of fulfillment. Matthew likes θέλετε (18,8). Besides, this verb belongs to the tradition concerning John the Baptist (see 17:12; Mark 9:13). δέξασθαι (7,0), αὐτός (14,3), μέλλων (5-6,1), and ἔρχεσθαι (31,19) come from the circle of words Matthew regularly inserts and uses in distinctive passages. Thus every term of importance—except the name Elijah, which Malachi provides—is a Mattheanism. The composition and insertion of the saying exhibit a strong desire to play on the theme of fulfillment and urge readers of the gospel to accept John as the inaugurator of the messianic time. This acceptance is to be willing, despite John's suffering, which contradicts Jewish expectation concerning Elijah redivivus. We should probably supply "him" rather than "this" or "it" after "accept" and see in the accepting of John a parallel with the accepting of Jesus' disciples in 10:14, 40-41. "Are willing" anticipates the unwillingness of the children in the marketplaces (vv 16-19). The gentle urging, "And if you are willing to accept [him]," becomes a command in v 15: "he who has ears, let him hear." The command is added in anticipation of 13:9 (so also Mark 4:9; Luke 8:8) and 13:43.

11:16-19 (Luke 7:29-35) Matthew now returns to the tradition behind Luke 7:24-35. But he saves the sayings behind Luke 7:29-30 for 21:31-32 and goes to the comparison of "this generation" with stubborn children (vv 16-17). Because he interpolated vv 12-15, the traditional οὖν (Luke 7:31) has lost its point; so it gives way to δέ for a contrast between willingness (v 14), or heedfulness (v 15), and the stubbornness of "this generation." Luke's text has "the men of this generation" in parallel with "children" who represent them. Matthew's omission of "the men" conforms to its nonappearance where "this generation" occurs elsewhere (12:39, 41, 42, 45; 16:4; 17:17; 23:36; 24:34 and parallels); and it better allows for the qualitative meaning of "this generation," viz., a certain kind of people rather than a certain period of time. Matthew omits "and what are they like?" as redundant.

In the comparison proper, "calling to" shifts from the clause beginning with ὅμοιοι to the one beginning with ἅ. The shift gives a better balance to the two clauses and enables "in the marketplaces" to follow "sitting" without disrupting a compound participial construction, as it would in Luke. More significantly, Matthew pluralizes the marketplace to match "their cities," in which Jesus has been teaching and preaching (so Matthew alone in v 1).

Luke's ἀλλήλοις, "one another," changes to a typically Matthean τοῖς ἑτέροις, "the others" (5,1). The traditional pronoun implies that two groups of children speak: the girls complain that the boys have not responded to their flute playing with a round dance (danced by men) in a game of mock-wedding; the boys complain that the girls have not responded to their singing a dirge with mourning (done professionally by women) in a game of mock-funeral. The singing of a dirge represents John's proclamation of coming judgment; the mourning represents the repentance this proclamation was designed to elicit. The flute playing stands for Jesus' preaching the good news; the dancing represents the joy of salvation brought by belief in the good news. In other words, the doleful game of mock-funeral corresponds to the severe style characteristic of John, "who neither ate bread nor drank wine," the happy game of mock-wedding to the festive style characteristic of Jesus, who came "eating and drinking" (see vv 18-19; Luke 7:33-34).

But Matthew does not care about the conflict between stubborn boys and girls, or about the correspondence between the games suggested and the differences in style between John and Jesus. In fact, he consistently assimilates those two to each other (see "John the Baptist parallel Jesus" in the Topical Index). His τοῖς ἑτέροις implies that only one group is speaking. Consequently, the *same* people have refused to respond both to John and to Jesus. In this way Matthew doubles the stubbornness of "this generation."

The adjective "like" refers to the whole of the parable rather than to the blameless children to whose overtures the other children will not respond (cf. the comments on 7:24). In Luke, as noted, both groups of children are blameworthy.

Further changes appear in Matthew. Weeping becomes beating the breast for a closer parallel with the physical activity of dancing. The perfect tense ἐλήλυθεν becomes the more usual aorist ἦλθεν. Matthew never writes the perfect of ἔρχομαι, and at 17:12 he will make the same change, again in a reference to John the Baptist (cf. Mark 9:13). Here the change results in a statement echoed in 21:32: "for John came." ὁ βαπτιστής drops out despite Matthew's liking it (5,0). He has just inserted it twice (see vv 11-12), and by omitting it here he gains a closer parallel between "John came" (v 18) and "the Son of man came" (v 19). "The Son of man" lacks an additional designation. Also for the sake of closer parallelism, Matthew drops "bread" and "wine" as the objects of John's not eating or drinking. Though meant to be supplied, those objects do not appear in the statement about the Son of man's eating and drinking. The parallelistic reasons for these omissions make us think again of Matthew's habit of correlating John and Jesus.

The addition of τε to the first μή (v 18; contrast Luke 7:33) makes for a better parallel: μήτε . . . μήτε rather than μή . . . μήτε. Again ἐλήλυθεν becomes ἦλθεν (v 19), this time for the (first) coming of the Son of man as a parallel with the coming of John (v 18). More importantly, Matthew changes "you say," which twice introduces charges of demonic possession against John and gluttony and drunkenness against Jesus, to "they say" (vv 18b, 19b). This change has the effect of distinguishing "the crowds" Jesus is addressing (see v 7; Luke 7:24) from "this generation" of stubborn "children" who reject both John and Jesus. Thus Matthew keeps "the crowds," who in his gospel represent disciples out of all nations, from being cast in the bad light of unbelief.

The charge that Jesus is a glutton and a drunkard (v 19) is couched in phraseology drawn from Deut 21:20, which has to do with the stoning of a rebellious and stubborn son (see Gundry, *Use of the OT* 80). Here the charge links up with the additional charge that Jesus is "a friend of publicans and sinners." In other words, ceremonial contamination from the publicans and sinners with whom he eats and drinks exacerbates his gluttony and drunkenness. It is easy to think that Jesus' daring to transgress the boundaries of ceremonial purity led his critics to exaggerate his festive behavior. Because of Matthew's interest in publicans (see 10:3 and the comments on 5:46), τελωνῶν advances to first position (contrast Luke).

In the saying that wisdom has been justified (i.e., vindicated), Matthew writes "by her works" (v 19) in place of "by all her children" (so Luke for those who in contrast with "this generation" of recalcitrant "children" obey the teaching of wisdom). The first evangelist likes ἔργων (4,1). "The works of wisdom" are "the works of the Christ" in v 2 (so Matthew alone). Indeed, the dropping of "all" and replacing of "children" with "works" for the sake of the parallel makes an equation of the Christ with wisdom (cf. Matthew's substituting Jesus' "I" for "the wisdom of God" in 23:34 [cf. Luke 11:49]). Thus the statement no longer alludes to the disciples' obedience, but to the miracles Jesus performs as the Christ (see the comments on v 2). Confirmation of this shift in meaning comes from Matthew's immediate importation of sayings regarding Jesus' miracles (vv 20-24) and an insertion in the very first saying of an additional reference to Jesus' miracles.

The self-designation "Son of man" here connotes authority to transgress rabbinic regulations concerning ritual purity. Both the authority of the Son of man and his "coming" derive from Dan 7:13-14. For the personification of wisdom, see Job 28; Proverbs 8–9; Sirach 24; Wisdom 7–8. For the application of wisdom to Christ, see 1 Cor 1:21, 24, 30. Though Matthew identifies wisdom with Jesus, we should hardly understand wisdom's children in Luke to be Jesus and John as envoys of wisdom. The adjective "all" is inappropriate to only a pair, and the term "children" does not represent envoys very well.

11:20 (Luke 10:12) Matthew now turns to sayings recorded also in Luke 10:12-15 after the commission of the seventy-two. But the first saying, which concerns Sodom, has appeared already in Matt 10:15 and will reappear in 11:24. Therefore Matthew composes a general statement in v 20, partly as a carry-over of the works of wisdom, partly as an introduction to the following, and partly on the pattern of the following. He begins with a characteristic τότε (66,17). "He began to reproach" echoes "he began . . . to say" in v 7 and signals the character of the subsequent sayings. "The cities" derives from "their cities," to which Jesus departed to teach and preach, in v 1 (so Matthew alone). πόλεις is a Mattheanism (18,3). "In which [cities] the miracles took place" anticipates and parallels "because if in Tyre and Sidon the miracles had taken place" in v 21. "The miracles" in v 21 are modified by "which have taken place in you" (so also Luke). Here Matthew puts πλεῖσται, "most" or, elatively, "very many of" (cf. 21:8 with Mark 11:8). This superlative form of the Mattheanism πολύς (23,1) accentuates the miracles. Further, he writes "his" to identify them with the works of the Christ, who is wisdom. "Because they did not repent" anticipates and parallels "they would have repented" in v 21.

    11:21-22 (Luke 10:13-14) The two woes against Chorazin and Bethsaida and the comparison of those cities with Tyre and Sidon have the same wording in Luke—with two small exceptions. Instead of Luke's first aorist ἐγενήθησαν we read the second aorist ἐγένοντο, which conforms to the second aorist γενόμεναι. And despite Matthew's liking καθήμενοι (8,0), it drops out in order that "in sackcloth and ashes" might modify the main verb "would have repented" rather than the participle "sitting" (as in Luke). Thus Matthew gains a more exact parallel with "in Tyre and Sidon," which modifies the main verb "happened."

OT prophets regularly condemned Tyre and Sidon as typical heathen cities (see Isaiah 23; Jer 25:22; 27:3; 47:4; Ezekiel 26–28; Joel 4:4[3:4]; Amos 1:9-10; Zech 9:2-4). On sackcloth and ashes as signs of mourning or repentance, see Esth 4:3; Isa 58:5; Jer 6:26; Dan 9:3; Jonah 3:5-6; and the concordance for further references to each item by itself.

    "Nevertheless" introduces the comparative lightness of the judgment on Tyre and Sidon (v 22). Matthew characteristically adds λέγω ὑμῖν (27,7) to compensate for his recent omission of the tradition behind Luke 10:12, which began with the expression (cf. the comments on v 20; see also v 24a). Furthermore, he expands τῇ κρίσει to the typically Matthean ἡμέρᾳ κρίσεως (4,0) to parallel the same phrase in v 24, where the corresponding Luke 10:12 has only ἐν τῇ ἡμέρᾳ ἐκείνῃ. In other words, he conflates "that day" (Luke 10:12) and "the judgment" (Luke 10:14) and uses the conflated expression in both v 22 and v 24. See also 10:15; 12:36.

    11:23-24 (10:15; Luke 10:15) In the address to Capernaum, τοῦ drops from ἕως τοῦ ᾅδου for closer correspondence with ἕως οὐρανοῦ. "You will be brought down" gives way to a favorite of Matthew, "you will go down" (καταβήσῃ—5,0). This substitution assimilates the text to Isa 14:15 LXX (see Gundry, *Use of the OT* 81).

Cf. the comments on 4:13 concerning Capernaum. We may put a question mark after ὑψωθήσῃ and translate, ". . . you will not be exalted to heaven, will you? To Hades you will go down!" Or we may eliminate the question mark and translate, ". . . lest you be exalted to heaven, you will go down to hell." See Metzger, *Textual Commentary* ad loc., on the originality of καταβιβασθήσῃ in Luke (cf. Isa 14:15 MT). In itself, "Hades" refers to the abode of the dead in general, i.e., to the netherworld in contrast with heaven, not particularly to the place of torment. The tenor of the passage implies the latter, however.

214

For a parallel with the woes against Chorazin and Bethsaida, Matthew adds to the condemnation of Capernaum "because if the miracles that have happened in you had happened in Sodom, it would have remained till today" (cf. v 21). Sodom takes the place of Tyre and Sidon and leads to the traditional mention of Sodom in the next saying. ἐγενήθησαν replaces ἐγένοντο, apparently to compensate for the reverse in v 21. Otherwise, the first of these additional clauses agrees exactly with the corresponding clause in v 21. The second added clause differs markedly, however. "Would have remained" arises out of the proverbial obliteration of Sodom and corresponds to "would have repented" in v 21. "Till today" will occur distinctively also in 28:15 and corresponds to "long ago" in v 21. Matthew likes σήμερον (4,3). His addition further stresses the miraculous works of the Christ, who is wisdom, and the guilt of Capernaum.

Matthew closes this section on the note of judgment by using the tradition behind Luke 10:12, already used in Matt 10:15 and replaced above in v 20. The insertion of "nevertheless" makes a parallel with v 22a. To the mention of Sodom, Matthew adds a characteristic γῆ (21,6), which echoes "land of Sodom" in 10:15. "It will be easier" advances in position for a better parallel with v 22b (cf. the word order in the Greek text). "In the day of judgment" represents conflation and corresponds to v 22. "Than for you" replaces "than for that city" (so Luke and Matt 10:15) for a better parallel with "than for you" in v 22. The parallelism carries an emphasis on judgment.

The saying in v 24 implies degrees of punishment ("it will be easier"). It must have startled unbelieving Jews to hear Jesus say that they will receive severer judgment than pagans.

THE GENTLENESS OF JESUS TOWARD HIS DISCIPLES
11:25-30 (Luke 10:21-22)

Matthew is still following the tradition behind Luke 10. But since he has already used the saying in Luke 10:16 (see Matt 10:40), he omits it here. And since he nowhere includes the mission of the seventy-two, he omits the material in Luke 10:17-20 concerning their return. These omissions bring him to the sayings in the tradition behind Luke 10:21-22. He uses them in vv 25-27 as a springboard to his showing in vv 28-30 exactly what disciples come to know about Jesus, viz., his gentleness, which reflects the Father's gentleness and contrasts with the overbearingness of those who oppose and persecute John, Jesus, and Jesus' disciples. In other words, the mutual knowledge of the Father and Son stands behind and feeds into a revelation to Jesus' disciples (vv 25-27), particularly into a revelation of divine gentleness (vv 28-30).

11:25-27 (Luke 10:21-22) Here the traditional "in that very hour" would have lacked its point of reference, the return of the seventy-two. So Matthew shies away from an exact indication of time and substitutes "in that season." The appearance of this phrase marks the first in a series of

215

three such appearances (see 12:1; 14:1 for further insertions). Unless it is Luke's addition, Jesus' rejoicing in the Holy Spirit drops out for lack of its occasion in the glowing report of the seventy-two. In its place we read ἀποκριθείς . . . εἶπεν. The combination is typically Matthean (29,6). Luke has only the εἶπεν.

In Jesus' words (vv 25b-27) Matthew makes few changes. The calling of God "Father" (22,13), his particular designation as the Father of Jesus (7,2), the address "Lord" (34,15), the combination of heaven and earth (6,0), and the portrayal of Jesus as God's "Son" (4,2) must have appealed to him. They all suit his theological interests and diction. So far as diction is concerned, the following words are also among his favorites: ἔκρυψας (4,2), ναί (2,2), οὕτως (18,5), ἔμπροσθεν (9,4), πάντα (63,25-26), παρεδόθη (6,3), and ἐπιγινώσκει (5,0). On the other hand, the occurrence of all these words in Luke and the un-Matthean character of the following important words forestall any thought of composition by Matthew: ἐξομολογοῦμαι, σοφῶν, συνετῶν, ἀπεκάλυψας, νηπίοις, εὐδοκία, and βούληται.

The opening thanksgiving typifies Jewish style (cf. 2 Sam 22:50; Dan 2:19-23; Sir 51:1; 1QH passim). Jesus' giving thanks has to do with the whole of the following, not just with the ignorance of the wise or the revelation to infants. The address to God as Father goes back to the Aramaic אַבָּא (see the comments on 6:9). For God as "Lord of heaven and earth," see Tob 7:18; Jdt 9:12; 1QapGen 22:16; the Tephilla (cited by Jeremias, NT Theology 1. 187-88); and on his hiding "these things" from the wise and intelligent, see Isa 29:14; 1 Cor 1:19. Divine revelation contrasts with native insight. That Jesus included in his thanksgiving the Father's hiding things from the wise should not shock us. This hiding is the dark side of grace, a foil to God's revelation to the infants. In the tradition behind Luke the hidden things refer to the falling of Satan from heaven, to the revelation of the authority given to Jesus' disciples, and, above all, to the recording of their names in heaven (Luke 10:17-20). Matthew's shifting the context makes the hidden things refer to the works of the Christ (i.e., of wisdom—vv 2, 5, 19), the significance of which escapes "this generation." ἀπ- drops from ἀπέκρυψας because of redundancy with the following ἀπό. The infants are those teachable people who are not well versed in the law and rabbinic traditions. For them the Father provides an education by divine revelation through his Son (cf. Pss 19:8[7]; 116:6; 1 Corinthians 2; many parts of the QL discussed by W. D. Davies, Christian Origins and Judaism [Philadelphia: Westminster, 1962] 119-44; and esp. the Gospel of John for passages that have given rise to designation of the present passage as the "Johannine Thunderbolt"). The "all things" which the Father "has given over" to the Son are all the items of revelation (not "all authority," as in 28:18, where we read the simple verb ἐδόθη, "has been given"). The idea approaches that of handing on tradition, but here Jesus speaks of revelation through a perfectly qualified medium.

In the description of the Son's qualification to mediate revelation from the Father, Matthew changes "knows who the Son is" to "recognizes the Son." The same thing happens in the converse statement, where Luke leaves γινώσκει to be supplied and Matthew repeats ἐπιγινώσκει to fill out the parallel and advances τὸν πατέρα for greater emphasis on God as the Father of Jesus. The changing of καί to οὐδέ (a Mattheanism—17,3) serves the same purposes. Since Matthew's verb regularly means "know" in the sense of "recognize" (see passages referred to in the comments on 7:15), there is no essential shift from the tradition that the Father and the Son know each other's identity, i.e., each other's inmost character.

Personal identity is in view. Therefore interpretation in terms of a father's teaching his son a trade and his son's learning the trade does not commend itself. The Son does not know all things. Rather, he knows the Father. All things are *given over* to the Son. Conversely, the Father does not know all things. Rather, he knows the Son. Furthermore, the Father's knowing the Son would be irrelevant—and hardly first in the couplet making up v 27bc—if Jesus is merely using the illustration of a son who learns his father's trade.

We might regard the definite article as generic because of its Aramaic origin and translate "a son . . . a father . . . a son" (v 27). Several features of the passage militate against a generic use, however: the immediately preceding address to God as "Father" (vv 25-26, bis), the preceding designation of God as "my Father" (v 27a), and the immediately following designation of Jesus as "the Son" (v 27d, where "a son" very doubtfully would fit "wants . . . to reveal"). (The definite article in Aramaic does not have to be taken as generic, of course.) Even though we were to accept a mere illustration, its application to Jesus and God requires a Johannine Christology of Jesus as the Father's unique Son. Cf. οὐδείς and εἰ μή (bis), which have no parallels in passages cited for the common simile (see John 5:19, 20a; *3 Enoch* 48C. 7; 45:1-2 MS E).

To interpret the Father's knowing the Son as the Father's choosing the Son takes account of the occasional use of "know" for "choose" in Hebrew (see, e.g., Amos 3:2) and at least allows the Father's knowing the Son and its first position to have real significance. But it necessitates an unnatural shift in the meaning of the verb. The Son's knowing the Father can hardly mean his choosing the Father. It would have to describe his living according to the Father's will. But the parallelism works against a sudden change in meaning. And "no one knows the Son, except the Father" makes an odd way of saying what would be expressed more naturally "The Father knows [i.e., chooses] the Son." If it were a matter of the Father's choosing *only* the Son, we should have read "And the Father knows [i.e., chooses] no one except the Son"—and similarly, but vice versa, in the next line. As it is, the saying does not indicate any exclusiveness concerning the Son as the *object* of knowing. But it does indicate an exclusiveness concerning the Father as the *subject* of knowing: only the Father knows the Son. Conversely, only the Son knows the Father—*not*, the Son knows only the Father.

All in all, knowledge of personal identity—knowledge that is intimate and personal identity that includes character—best fits the requirements of the text, especially the exclusiveness and reciprocal nature of the knowledge and the more-than-common usage of the term "Father" with which the passage begins.

For reviews of textual and form-critical questions and background in the history of religions, see, among others, M. J. Suggs, *Wisdom, Christology, and Law in Matthew's Gospel* (Cambridge, Mass.: Harvard, 1970) 71-108, and the polemical, older work by G. Vos, *The Self-Disclosure of Jesus* (Grand Rapids: Eerdmans, 1954) 143-61. The high Christology in these sayings constitutes an objection to their being regarded as authentic words of Jesus. But in view of his absolute use of the term "Son" in Mark 13:32; Matt 24:36—a saying very unlikely to have been put in his mouth, since it ascribes to him ignorance concerning the time of the end—the objection has the look of a Procrustean bed.

J. Jeremias has identified a number of Semitisms that favor an early date for the material and thus heighten the probability of its authenticity (*NT Theology* 1. 57-59): (1) the un-Greek οὐδείς . . . εἰ μή and οὐδέ . . . εἰ μή, which correspond to the Aramaic אִילּוּלָא . . . לָית, a paraphrase for "only" (but see the comments on 15:24); (2) the un-Greek use of ἀπεκάλυψας in the sense "you have revealed"; (3) parallelism in statements of theme (vv 25b, 27a), in elaborations of theme (vv 26cd, 27bc), and in emphatic conclusions (vv 26, 27d); (4) asyndeton at the beginning of v 27; (5) the un-Greek repetition of ἐπιγινώσκει; (6) repetition in v 27bc because of the lack of a reciprocal pronoun in Semitic languages; and (7) the resting of πάτερ and ὁ πατήρ on אַבָּא. To these we should add (8) εὐδοκία . . . ἔμπροσθέν σου, "gracious will . . . before you," a periphrastic avoidance of anthropomorphism (see, e.g., *Tg. Isa* 53:6, 10; *b. Ber.* 17a; 19a; 28b; 29b; *b. Ta'an.* 24b; cf. Matt 18:14). Though 4QFlor 10-14 applies 2 Sam 7:14 to the Messiah as a son of God, there the mutuality of knowledge that gives the present passage its special flavor is lacking.

11:28-30 Matthew caps this section with a distinctive composition that exhibits his characteristic attention to parallelism, diction typical of him, and his habit of conforming phraseology to the OT. Verse 28 and the first half of v 29 contain parallel commands, the one to go after Jesus and the other to take up his yoke. In the first command we see synthetic parallelism: going after Jesus leads to refreshment. In the second we see synonymous parallelism: learning from Jesus defines the taking of his yoke on oneself. The latter half of v 29 and the whole of v 30 express two reasons for obeying the commands. In the first we again see synthetic parallelism: Jesus' meekness and humility in heart lead to the disciples' finding refreshment. In the second we again see synonymous parallelism: the light load defines the easy yoke.

Because it is parallel with the γάρ that introduces and governs v 30, the ὅτι that introduces and governs the latter half of v 29 is to be considered causal. The self-description in v 29c echoes Jesus' call, "And learn from me," in v 29b. Therefore the self-description provides a reason for the call: "and learn from me, because I am meek and humble in heart." Similarly, "refreshment" in v 29d echoes "I will refresh" in v 28b: "and I will refresh you . . . because you will find refreshment for your souls." "My yoke" in v 30a echoes "my yoke" in v 29a: "take my yoke upon you . . . for my yoke is easy." "My burden" in v 30a echoes "burdened" in v 28a: "Come to me, all you who are weary and burdened . . . for my burden is light." To recognize this structure, we need to note not only the verbal echoes mentioned, but also the governing by ὅτι and γάρ of *both* the clauses that follow each of them. In each set of correspondences—the dependence of v 29c on v 29b, of v 29d on v 28b; and the dependence of v 30a on v 29a, of v 30b on v 28a—we see chiasm. It seems doubtful that such intricate parallels arose in the spoken word. More probably they derived from careful attention to literary detail. This kind of attention characterizes Matthew so much that we may attribute these verses to him.

We also discover a large amount of specially Matthean vocabulary in these verses:

δεῦτε (2,2); πάντες (63,25-26); κἀγώ (5,3; cf. the simple dominical ἐγώ—12-13,3); ἄρατε (2,3); μάθετε (with cognates—33,8); πραΰς (2,1—cf. Moses' meekness in Num 12:3 with "Moses parallel Jesus" in the Topical Index); καρδία (5,2); εὑρήσετε (7,8); and γάρ (62-63,15). For ἐφ᾽ ὑμᾶς see 10:13; 12:28; and especially 23:35 with Luke 11:50 for an insertion (cf. 27:25). ταπεινός occurs only here in Matthew, but its cognate verb will be inserted at 18:4. Especially impressive is Matthew's insertion of τῇ καρδίᾳ as a dative of respect (as here) in 5:8 (cf. the insertion of τῷ πνεύματι as a dative of respect in 5:3). 2 Cor 10:1 is sometimes used as evidence for the dominical origin of Matt 11:28-30; but "the meekness and gentleness of Christ" needs no source beyond the behavior of Jesus during his trial.

Matthew also makes allusive quotations of the OT, a common practice of his which accounts for most remaining words of importance. "Who are weary and burdened" (v 28a) echoes Jer 31:25: "for I have satisfied the weary soul, and every faint soul I have replenished." "And I will give you refreshment [or 'rest']" (v 28b) echoes the very same words in Exod 33:14. "And you will find refreshment [or 'rest'] for your souls" (v 29d) is a verbatim quotation of Jer 6:16 (see Gundry, *Use of the OT* 136, for special contacts with the LXX in the future tense and in the plural of "souls").

Typically Matthean diction and allusive quotation of the OT leave only "yoke," "easy," and "light" unaccounted for—hardly a significant number of words out of so many. The first of these was a well-known metaphor for obedience (see Acts 15:10; Gal 5:1; Sir 51:26; *Pss. Sol.* 7:9; 19:32; *m. 'Abot* 3:6; *2 Apoc. Bar.* 41:3; *b. Ber.* 13a; and Str-B 1. 608-10 for further references). The last of these words anticipates "heavy," which Matthew will insert in 23:4 to describe the "burdens" the scribes and Pharisees tie on men's shoulders (cf. Luke 11:46). Thus the burden Jesus puts on his disciples in chap. 11 contrasts with the burdens the scribes and Pharisees put on their followers in chap. 23. Confirmation that Matthew intends his readers to relate the two passages in this way comes from his omitting "you burden" in 23:4 (again cf. Luke 11:46); he has already used it here as a slightly loose translation of דְּאָבָה, "faint," in Jer 31:25.

But in what does the easiness of the yoke Jesus imposes and the lightness of the load consist? In an interpretation of the law less stringent than that of the scribes and Pharisees? Far from it! According to the Sermon on the Mount, Jesus teaches a more stringent law (see chaps. 5–7; cf. 23:2-3, 23). The heaviness of the burdens loaded by the scribes and Pharisees on their admirers (23:4) consists in demands that those admirers fawn on them in ways that feed their pride. "They do all their deeds to be noticed by men . . . and they love the place of honor at banquets, and the

219

chief seats in the synagogues, and respectful greetings in the market places, and being called by men, Rabbi" (23:5-7; see also 6:1-6, 16-18). Correspondingly, the lightness of the burden Jesus imposes consists in his meekness and humility in heart. These characteristics make his demands, greater though they are, much easier to bear than the lesser demands of the scribes and Pharisees, whose overweening desire for recognition makes them treat the common people as camels or donkeys to be overloaded rather than as yokefellows to share the load with. As counterparts to the scribes and Pharisees, the church leaders who lord it over "the little ones" are lurking in the shadows of Matthew's text.

Since it comes from his meekness and humility in heart, the refreshment Jesus promised does not wait for the consummation, but begins immediately on coming to him. "Learn from me" means "Learn from my words and example." This line shows that Matthew intends vv 25-27 to provide the foundation for vv 28-30. The mutual knowledge of the Father and the Son legitimizes learning from the Son. Since soul and body lie alongside each other in 10:28 (bis, so Matthew alone; cf. 6:25), "your souls" probably means "your inner selves." We should not explain the lightness of Jesus' load as his delivering people from their own efforts by going to the cross or as consisting in the love-commandment. Such explanations do not take into account the contrast between Jesus' meekness and humility in heart and the overbearing conceit of the scribes and Pharisees in their quest for public recognition.

A number of expressions similar to those in Matt 11:28-30 occur in Sir 51:23-27: "draw near to me"; "your souls"; "the yoke"; "receive instruction"; "I have labored little"; and "I have found for myself much rest." Matthew's two mentions of rest, or refreshment, and the term "your souls" go back to OT texts, however; and there is a big difference between ben Sira's finding rest *for himself* and Jesus' offering rest *to others*. Furthermore, laboring little hardly corresponds to laboring to the point of weariness; and in Matthew it is not Jesus who labors, as ben Sira labors, but those whom Jesus calls. Matthew's δεῦτε probably comes from Jesus' earlier call to discipleship (4:19), not from ben Sira's "Draw near to me." And we can hardly think that Matthew is contrasting the yoke of the law in Sirach with Jesus' yoke of the kingdom, for in his gospel the yoke of the kingdom prominently includes the yoke of the law (see chaps. 5–7). At most, therefore, the passage in Sirach exercised an indirect and vague influence on Matthew. That the passage did do that much we might deduce not only from the parallels considered above, but also from Matthew's identification of Jesus with wisdom in v 19 (but ben Sira speaks *about* wisdom, not *as* wisdom) and from the parallel between "I thank you, Father, Lord of heaven and earth" in v 25 and "I will thank you, O Lord and King" in Sir 51:1. Parallels in Sir 24:19-22; Epictetus *Discourses* 4.8.18; and *Poimandres* are too distant to merit discussion here.

THE PHARISEES' PLOT TO DESTROY JESUS
12:1-21 (Mark 2:23–3:6; Luke 6:1-11, 17-19)

Since he has just written about the rest Jesus gives (11:28-30), Matthew now brings in two stories about the issue of rest on the Sabbath. The stories appear in Mark 2:23–3:6; Luke 6:1-11. He is therefore returning to Markan material he left in 9:18. Mark's passage follows Jesus' response to the question about fasting that the disciples of John the Baptist asked. John has played an important role in Matthew 11. Therefore Mark's passage attracts Matthew not only because it deals with rest, but also because it provides a sequel to material involving John. Most of all, the climaxing of the two stories in the Pharisees' plot to destroy Jesus fits the motif of persecution that dominates 11:2–12:50.

Josephus (*Ag. Ap.* 2.2 §27) describes the Sabbath as a day of ἀνάπαυσις (cf. Matt 11:29). σάββατον alternates between singular and plural (with a singular meaning) because of early confusion of the Aramaic emphatic state singular שַׁבְּתָא with the Greek plural σάββατα (possibly helped by the idiomatic Greek plural for names of festivals).

12:1 (Mark 2:23; Luke 6:1) The first story begins with the second occurrence of "in that season" (not in Mark or Luke; but see insertions of the phrase in 11:25; 14:1). This is a general designation of time due to the switch in materials. Omission of the Semitism "and it came to pass" results in the advance of "was going along" and in its escalation from an infinitive to the main verb, "went." παρα- drops off, leaving the simple ἐπορεύθη, a favorite of Matthew (13,10; cf. the complete omission of παραπορεύομαι in 17:22; 21:19b in contrast with Mark 9:30; 11:20). The typical insertion of "Jesus" (80,12) starts a concentration on the figure of Jesus that continues throughout the story.

At this point Matthew inserts a reference to the disciples' getting hungry. This produces a parallel with the hungering of those who were with David (v 3). We may doubt that Matthew is trying to establish the disciples' innocence (v 7) by citing their hunger as an excuse; for he omits "need" (Mark 2:25), deletes the saying that the Sabbath came into being on account of man rather than vice versa (Mark 2:27), and lets the stress fall instead on Jesus' authority as the Son of man, who is greater than the Temple and Lord over the Sabbath. Thus the parallel between the disciples' hunger and the hunger of David's men implies a parallel between Jesus and David (cf. υἱὸς Δαυίδ in the Greek Index). This parallel is designed to enhance the authority of Jesus as David's greater son. At first blush, it looks inexact in that David hungered, but Jesus did not. Matthew will tell his readers later, however, that Jesus hungers in the hunger of his disciples, or "brothers" (see 25:35, 37, 42, 44, unique to this gospel). The insertion of the disciples' hunger results in the addition of a δέ that begins a series: "but his disciples" (over against Jesus, just mentioned—v 1), "but the Pharisees" (over against the disciples, v 2), "but he [Jesus]" (over against the Pharisees, v 3). Mark writes καί in all these phrases. In accord with the overarching theme of persecution, Matthew's repetition of the adversative δέ heightens the sense of conflict.

Both Matthew and Luke omit Mark's ὁδὸν ποιεῖν, perhaps because of its difficulty (does it mean simply "to journey" or quite literally "to make a path" through a field by plucking ears of grain?), perhaps to make room for "and to eat" (similarly Luke, but not Mark). By adding a reference to eating, Matthew provides another parallel between the disciples and David's

221

men (cf. v 4) and so reinforces the parallel between Jesus and David (and gives us good reason to accept the reading ἔφαγον, "they ate," in v 4 א B 481 instead of ἔφαγεν, "he ate," in the remaining textual evidence, influenced by Mark and Luke; see Metzger, *Textual Commentary* ad loc.).

12:2 *(Mark 2:24; Luke 6:2)* The Mosaic law allowed plucking grain on a journey through another man's field (Deut 23:26[25]), but the Pharisees regarded the action as reaping and therefore as work, prohibited on the Sabbath (cf. Exod 34:21; *m. Šabb.* 7:2; CD 10:14–11:18). As often, Matthew adds ἰδόντες (10-11,7). Mark's ἔλεγον changes to εἶπαν for a parallel with εἶπεν in v 3 (so also Luke). The closer parallelism (Mark follows his imperfect ἔλεγον with a present λέγει) pits the Pharisees' words against Jesus' words more clearly. This heightening of the conflict takes yet another turn in Matthew's making the Pharisees' question ("Why . . . ?" so Mark and Luke) into an accusation: "Behold, your disciples are doing what is not permissible to do on the Sabbath." The typically Matthean insertion "your disciples" (31,5) suggests an identification of Jesus with his disciples in their persecutions (cf. 25:31-46). The addition of ποιεῖν (19,19) and the transferal of "on the Sabbath" from the clause regarding the disciples' action to the clause regarding what is not permissible shift the emphasis from the disciples' action to the question of the Sabbath. Luke shares the transferal but not the addition.

12:3-4 *(Mark 2:25-26; Luke 6:3-4)* "He said" (so also Luke) replaces Mark's "he says." Matthew often uses the historical present for Jesus' teaching the disciples, but here we have a response to the Pharisees' accusation. The change of Mark's "never" (Luke has "not even") to a simple "not" more obviously implies an affirmative answer to the question whether the Pharisees have read what David did, and consequently makes their accusation of Jesus' disciples all the more sinister in motivation. The dropping of "had need" leaves only "hungered" (so also Luke). Similarly, the omission of Mark's and Luke's αὐτός helps the parallel between Jesus and David by de-emphasizing David's hunger. There is no mention of Jesus' hungering. The stress therefore falls on the hunger of those who were with David, which parallels the disciples' hunger, inserted by Matthew in v 1. Since Luke does not share this parallel, his partial agreements with Matthew against Mark show influence from Matthew.

The historically difficult reference to Abiathar the high priest disappears (so also Luke; see 1 Sam 21:2-7[1-6] for Ahimelech as the high priest David dealt with). The changing of "he [David] ate" (so Mark and Luke) to "they ate" reinforces the correspondence between Jesus' disciples and David's men and, in the interest of the parallel between Jesus and David, plays down the difference between Jesus and David in the matter of hungering and eating. Mark's and Luke's οὕς, which refers to the loaves of shewbread, changes to ὅ for a reference to the impermissible eating. This change forces the further change of ἔξεστιν to ἐξὸν ἦν and the addition of αὐτῷ, "for him [to eat]." Now φαγεῖν acts as an appositive to ὅ rather than a supplement to οὐκ ἔξεστιν, and ὅ acts as the subject of οὐκ ἐξόν rather than the object of φαγεῖν.

Matthew makes these revisions in order to insert "neither for those with him." Except for "neither" (οὐδέ—17,3), this insertion comes from v 3, underscores the parallel between David's men and Jesus' disciples yet again, and, along with the change of "he ate" to "they ate," enables Matthew to omit without loss Mark's "and he gave also to those who were with him" (omitted also in Luke). The dative in εἰ μὴ τοῖς ἱερεῦσιν μόνοις replaces Mark's and Luke's accusative and stems from parallelism with Matthew's distinctive αὐτῷ just preceding. The emphatic addition of μόνοις (cf. Luke) represents Matthew's diction (9,0). Omission of the final clause in Mark leaves the priests at the end for an uninterrupted lead into the following verse, where they are mentioned again.

In vv 3-4 we do not have a counter question, for Matthew has turned the Pharisees' preceding question into an accusing declaration. See Exod 25:30; Lev 24:5-9 on the shewbread (more literally "bread of the Presence"). According to the Midrash, the story concerning David took place on a Sabbath. But in the present passage no argument rests on that tradition. Jesus makes several inferences from the OT text: (1) that David and his men hungered; (2) that he entered the house of God (a tent); and (3) that he brought out the bread and shared it with his men. The first and third inferences seem obvious. The second probably rests on the priest's failure to see anyone with David.

12:5-6 Matthew now composes vv 5-6 as a halachic argument (one based on a definite precept in the OT law) in addition to the preceding haggadic argument (one based on inference from the OT). The preceding did not include a specific reference to profaning the Sabbath. The halachic argument does, and emphasizes that the law itself commands such profanation. "Or have you not read in the law . . . ?" (v 5a) parallels "But I say to you" (v 6a) in a manner reminiscent of Matthew's "antitheses" (5:22, 28, 32, 34, 39, 44). "That on the Sabbath the priests in the Temple profane the Sabbath and are innocent" (v 5b) parallels "that a greater than the Temple is here" (v 6b).

The opening ἤ belongs to Matthew's special vocabulary (32,12). "Have you not read. . . ?" comes from v 3b. Though ἀναγινώσκω rests on tradition in 12:3; 21:42; 22:31; 24:15, Matthew inserts it at 12:5; 19:4; 21:16, always in negative questions. νόμῳ is a favorite of his (6,0). "On the Sabbath" echoes v 1 (cf. vv 10, 11, 12), and "the priests in the Temple" comes largely from v 4. But the common word for Temple (ἱερῷ—5,0) replaces "the house of God." In the reference to profaning the Sabbath Matthew characteristically assimilates Jesus' words to OT phraseology (see Neh 13:17-18; Isa 56:2, 6; Ezek 20:13; also 1 Macc 1:43, 45; 2:34). λέγω . . . ὑμῖν, μεῖζον, and ὧδε belong to his preferred diction (27,7; 6,0; 7,1). His Christological emphasis insures that μεῖζον refers to Jesus (cf. πλεῖον, "a more than," in vv 41-42). The neuter gender of μεῖζον stresses the quality of superior greatness rather than Jesus' personal identity (cf. the neuter adjective in Luke 16:15). Parallelism, diction, and assimilation to OT phraseology show, then, that Matthew composed vv 5-6. His purpose was to argue that though the disciples profaned the Sabbath, they—like the priests who worked in the Temple on Sabbath days—were guiltless because of a higher legal consideration: if the greatness of the Temple surpasses the sanctity of the Sabbath, the superior greatness of Jesus surpasses the sanctity of the Sabbath much more.

See Lev 24:8 for the changing of shewbread on the Sabbath, and Num 28:9-10 for the doubling of the burnt offering on the Sabbath. Cf. *m. Pesaḥ*. 6:1-2; *m. 'Erub*. 10:11-15; John 7:22-23. Here Matthew uses the rabbinic kind of argument called "the light and the heavy," i.e., an argument *a fortiori*. To describe the priestly service on the Sabbath as profanation is a shocking way to say that the Temple is more important than the Sabbath. Presumably the Temple is more important because it was made for God, the Sabbath for man. Of course, the disciples' acting out of mere hunger does not compare well with the service of priests obeying God's command. But Matthew bases his argument solely on the authority of Jesus, who is God with us and whose allowance of the disciples' action suffices regardless of the na'ure or cause of that action. Notably, the text does not read that Jesus is greater than the law, but that he appeals to the law in claiming a greatness surpassing that of the Temple. There is a reflection against the Temple no more than there is a reflection against Jonah and Solomon in vv 41-42. An argument from the less to the greater requires acceptance of the less.

12:7 Matthew now inserts a quotation of Hos 6:6 as he did in 9:13. Both passages deal with the Pharisees and have a clause beginning with γάρ immediately after the quotation. Therefore the repetition of the quotation implies that the Pharisees had not learned their lesson. "But" contrasts the Pharisees' scripturally ignorant condemnation of Jesus' disciples (v 7) with his scripturally informed statement (vv 5-6). ἐγνώκειτε is a Mattheanism (8,2). κατεδικάσατε will be echoed without parallel in v 37; it belongs to a family of words dear to Matthew (18-19,10-9 for δικ-). ἀναιτίους echoes the distinctive use of that word in v 5. Matthew quotes "I want mercy, and not sacrifice" in order to show the opposition between the mercy demanded by God and the Pharisees' persecution of the innocent disciples on ritualistic grounds which, on close inspection, lack scriptural substance.

Mercy does not stand over against sacrifice as moral law over against ceremonial law. Neither does mercy have to do with God's mercy or with forgiveness of the disciples, for Matthew stresses their innocence. Rather, mercy stands over against sacrifice in contrast with persecution arising out of ritualistic considerations.

12:8 (Mark 2:27-28; Luke 6:5) Mark's "And he was saying to them" drops out in order that the final saying may follow the foregoing without interruption. For exclusive emphasis on Jesus as Lord of the Sabbath, Matthew (followed by Luke) then omits Mark's statement that the Sabbath came into being on account of man and not man on account of the Sabbath. For the same Christological emphasis in the saying on lordship over the Sabbath, "even" drops out before "of the Sabbath" (so also Luke in contrast with Mark), and the reference to the Sabbath retreats to an unobtrusive position in the middle of the clause (again Luke agrees against Mark). These revisions leave "Lord" and "the Son of man" to share honors at the two extremities of the saying. Matthew replaces Mark's ὥστε with his favorite γάϱ (62-63,15) to make the Son of man's lordship over the Sabbath a reason for not condemning his innocent ones, rather than a conclusion drawn from the saying about the purpose of the Sabbath, which Matthew has omitted.

The deletion of Mark 2:27 hardly stems from fear that that saying might encourage laxity toward the law. Such a fear would have forestalled insertions of the saying about a greater than the Temple (v 6) and the quotation advocating mercy and not sacrifice (v 7). The authority of the Son of man (cf. Dan 7:13-14) parallels the authority of David. Even in Mark "the Son of man" does not mean man in general. Though we read "man" twice in Mark's preceding verse, "and he was saying to them" at the beginning of that verse shows that Jesus is the Lord of the Sabbath in that he exercises authority as the Son of man: he does so *by making the pronouncement* about the humanitarian purpose of the Sabbath.

12:9 (Mark 3:1; Luke 6:6) The healing on a Sabbath of the man with a withered hand (vv 9-14) is narrated also in Mark 3:1-6; Luke 6:6-11; but Matthew brings in several elements from the healing on a Sabbath of a man suffering dropsy (Luke 14:1-6). These elements compensate for his omitting that story elsewhere. In both stories the Pharisees are Jesus' antagonists. Additionally, Matthew anticipates 15:14 (cf. Luke 6:39) and 18:12-14 (cf. Luke 15:1-7). The insertion of "departing from there" makes Jesus go from one place to another because of opposition just as he told his disciples to do (10:23). Matthew is fond of μεταβάς (5,1) and ἐϰεῖθεν (8,1). In 11:1; 12:9; 15:29 only he writes them together. εἰσ- falls away from Mark's εἰσῆλθεν. The deletion gets rid of a redundancy with the following εἰς, and the resultant simple form points to Jesus as the Coming One (see the comments on 3:11). Matthew deletes "again," which in Mark refers back to Jesus' entering the synagogue in Capernaum (Mark 1:21), because that passage does not appear as such in his gospel. But it does appear in Luke 4:31-32; so Luke's agreement in deleting "again" shows influence from Matthew. Typically, Matthew adds "their" to "synagogue" to indicate the estrangement of the church and the Pharisees (5,0—cf. vv 2, 14).

12:10 (Mark 3:1-2; Luke 6:6-7) In changing "and a man was there" to "and behold, a man," Matthew makes his first assimilation to the story of the man with dropsy (Luke 14:2). In the description of the man as having a withered hand, Matthew puts χεῖϱα before ἔχων, changes ἐξηϱαμμένην to ξηϱάν, and puts ξηϱάν last. These changes compensate for the coming omission of v 3 in Mark, where the second evangelist uses ξηϱάν and, according to the more difficult and preferable text of B *pc*, puts τὴν χεῖϱα before ἔχοντι and ξηϱάν last.

In the next clause ἐπηϱώτησαν, "they asked," substitutes for Mark's παϱετήϱουν, "they were watching closely." Though Matthew often rejects the verb that he uses here, he does insert it also at 16:1; 22:41. Here it links with a typical addition of λέγοντες (61,23) to make the following words a question quoted from the lips of the Pharisees rather than a mere description of what they were looking for. In Matthew, then, the Pharisees do not merely wait to see what Jesus will do. They deliberately egg him on to break the Sabbath in order that they may accuse him. Cf. the heightening of the Pharisees' guilt in vv 2-4, 14, and elsewhere, especially chap. 23. Matthew inserts "it is permissible" in order to make the question correspond to the answer, where the verb will reappear in agreement with Mark and Luke (v 12; cf. vv 2, 4). The insertion of "it is permissible" marks a second allusion to the story of the man with dropsy, for we read in Luke 14:3, "Is it permissible to heal on the Sabbath. . . ?" almost exactly as here in Matthew. The omission of Mark's "him" after "heal" both conforms to the absence of an object in Luke 14:3 (cf. Luke 6:7) and generalizes the issue: it is no longer a question concerning the healing of a particular man, it is a question concerning the legality of healing anyone on the Sabbath.

Rabbinic law allowed medical help on the Sabbath where life was immediately endangered (see *m. Yoma* 8:6; *Mek. Exod.* 22.2; 23.13). Obviously, the healing of a withered hand could wait a day. The clause beginning "in order that" depends on the clause containing "they asked."

12:11-12 (Mark 3:3-5; Luke 6:8-10) Because Matthew has made the Pharisees' watching Jesus into a question, Jesus' following question becomes a counter question in the style of a rabbinic debate. To dramatize the verbal conflict, Matthew deletes Jesus' telling the man with the withered hand to get up in the middle of the audience and juxtaposes the counter question alongside the Pharisees' question. But the counter question has no parallels in Mark's and Luke's versions of this story. Matthew draws it from the story of the man with dropsy (Luke 14:1-6) with some help from the parable of the lost sheep (18:12-14; Luke 15:1-7).

"But he" sets Jesus over against the Pharisees and contrasts with Mark's "and." "Says" becomes "said" because the audience consists of Pharisees, who do not represent the church Jesus still speaks to. Now comes Matthew's interpolation, which has the purpose of providing a foundation for the distinctive assertion of legality in v 12b. Matthew needs a figure of speech for needy people such as the man with a withered hand. The parable of the one lost sheep provides him that figure. Hence we read, "Who is the man from among you that will have one sheep . . . ?" (τίς ἔσται ἐξ ὑμῶν ἄνθρωπος ὃς ἕξει πρόβατον ἕν. . .;). This comes from the parable in its traditional form: "What man from among you, having a hundred sheep and having lost one of them. . .?" (τίς ἄνθρωπος ἐξ ὑμῶν ἔχων ἑκατὸν πρόβατα καὶ ἀπολέσας ἐξ αὐτῶν ἕν. . .; so Luke 15:4). That in his later and direct parallel to the parable of the lost sheep Matthew shies away from τίς ἄνθρωπος ἐξ ὑμῶν confirms his drawing from that parable here (see 18:12).

Matthew has his figure of speech; so he returns to the story of the man with dropsy, which closes with a son's or an ox's falling into a well and being pulled up on the Sabbath (Luke 14:5). But sheep graze in the wilderness. Therefore Matthew changes "well" to "pit," which anticipates 15:14: "both will fall [πεσοῦνται] into a pit." Luke's parallel to 15:14 reads ἐμ-, "into," at the beginning of the verb (Luke 6:39). Just as anticipation of the parable of the sheep leads Matthew to alter its original wording when he comes to that parable, so also his anticipation of the saying about falling into a pit leads him to alter the verb slightly when he comes to that saying.

This phenomenon confirms that he is indeed writing in anticipation. Instead of "Will he not immediately pull it up?" (Luke 14:5), Matthew writes "Will he not grab it and lift [it]?" (cf. 9:25 where his two verbs occurred in conjunction). Both κρατήσει and ἐγερεῖ belong to his special vocabulary (4,1; 11,8).

On the legality of rescuing animals on the Sabbath see *b. Šabb.* 128b (cf. *b. B. Meṣ.* 32b). Opinions varied. The stricter Essenes did not allow such an action under any circumstances (CD 11:13-14). At most the rabbis allowed the kind of indirect assistance that would enable an animal to extricate itself. Matthew implies direct assistance, but Jesus is not addressing rabbis. Rather, he is speaking to a general audience, who might be expected to disregard the niceties of rabbinic pilpulism. Such disregard is likely especially because the present picture is that of a poor man who has only one sheep: losing it means losing all.

In another argument *a fortiori* (cf. v 6), the exclamation following Jesus' question (v 12a) has a typically Matthean οὖν (35,11). As a whole, "Therefore how much more valuable is a man than a sheep!" echoes the tradition behind Luke 12:24: "How much more valuable you are than birds!" The parallel to Luke 12:24 in Matt 6:26 lacks "how much" and the specific mention of birds. In writing "how much" here and specifically mentioning a sheep, Matthew may be compensating for his former omissions. Cf. also 10:31 with Luke 12:7.

In Matthew, Jesus has already asked a counter question (v 11). Therefore the evangelist changes "Is it permissible . . . ?" into an application of the conclusion drawn from the counter question (v 12). His favorite ὥστε (10,0) introduces the application: "So then, it is permissible. . . ." The turning of a question into a pronouncement wreaks havoc with the detailed alternatives in Mark: ". . . to do good or to do evil, to save life or to kill?" The pronouncement will not allow evildoing or killing. "To do well" therefore summarizes and makes a positive judgment on "to heal" in the Pharisees' question (v 10). In other words, with Mark's "evil" out of the way, no need exists for its antonym "good" (ἀγαθόν); therefore Matthew chooses "well" (καλῶς), whose adjective form occurs with "do" also in 5:16; 7:17, 18, 19; 12:33. The adverb "well" emphasizes the action itself rather than the thing done; and it anticipates Mark 7:37 ("he has done all things well"), which Matthew will omit in his version of Mark 7:31-37 (Matt 15:29-31). This omission will be due to his present use of the expression.

The Pharisees' silence drops out of Matthew because Jesus' question has become a pronouncement to which they need not respond. That Luke's omission of their silence does not rest on the switch from a question to a pronouncement suggests influence from Matthew. Deletion of the silence takes away the reason for Jesus' looking around with anger and grieving over the Pharisees' hardness of heart. Matthew therefore omits these, too (so also Luke, except for inclusion of Jesus' looking around).

12:13 (Mark 3:5; Luke 6:10) To signal a shift to the man with a withered hand, Matthew inserts τότε (66,17) and adds "your" (so also Luke) to "hand." In the statement concerning restoration, "his hand" drops out.

"Healthy as the other" comes in its place. The substitute enhances the effectiveness of the miracle and draws on words well liked by Matthew: ὑγιής (2,0), ὡς (23,8), and ἄλλη (14,4).

12:14 (Mark 3:6; Luke 6:11) Matthew introduces the Pharisees' going out with "but" (cf. Luke) rather than with Mark's "and." The new conjunction sets the murderous plotting of the Pharisees against the merciful miracle of Jesus and intensifies the motif of persecution. As usual, Mark's "immediately" drops out. To heighten the Pharisees' guilt again, Matthew omits Mark's reference to the Herodians (cf. v 10). The Pharisees alone take counsel against Jesus. Perhaps they were leading the persecution of Matthew's church. (Luke, too, deletes the Herodians, but softens the plotting of the Pharisees, whom he mentioned earlier in his version.) As elsewhere, Matthew writes "they took counsel" in contrast with Mark's "they were giving counsel" (see also 22:15; 27:1, 7; 28:12).

12:15-16 (Mark 3:7-12; Luke 6:17-19) At the start of v 15 Matthew substitutes δέ for Mark's καί in order to contrast Jesus' withdrawal with the Pharisees' plot. The omission of "with his disciples" stems from the limitation of the plot to Jesus' life. Matthew characteristically adds γνούς (8,2) to point up the divine omniscience of Jesus and make his knowledge of the plot the reason for withdrawal. The substitution of ἐκεῖθεν for Mark's πρὸς τὴν θάλασσαν typifies Matthew's diction (8,1), matches the addition in v 9, and intensifies the notion of withdrawal. Thus Matthew carries forward his program of making Jesus an example of the fleeing he commanded his disciples to practice under persecution (10:23). Cf. 14:13, where the substitution of ἐκεῖθεν with ἀνεχώρησεν (as here) after news of John the Baptist's death will again make Jesus an example of flight from persecution.

By advancing ἠκολούθησαν to the head of its clause and inserting "him," Matthew emphasizes following Jesus' example. "Many" replaces "a large multitude." Both the crowd's geographical origins and Jesus' ordering a boat in order to avoid being crushed by the crowd drop out. Jesus' healing takes up only a single, summarizing clause, in contrast with Mark and Luke; and the crying out of the unclean spirits, "You are the Son of God," entirely vanishes (so also Luke). All of this happens in order that readers' attention may fasten solely on Jesus' retiring behavior under persecution. In the summary of his healing, καί replaces γάρ because the omission of his ordering a boat leaves γάρ without a point of reference (so also Luke). Because Matthew has used "many" in the preceding clause, here he substitutes "them all." Cf. the comments on 8:16.

Verse 16 opens with the third successive clause introduced by καί, a first aorist verb, and a third person pronoun. To attain this parallelism, Matthew changes Mark's ἐπετίμα to ἐπετίμησεν and drops πολλά. Mark's imperfect and adverb have both lost their point anyway because Matthew has omitted the unclean spirits' seeing Jesus, falling down, and crying out his divine sonship. This omission also changes the objects of Jesus' charge: αὐτοῖς no longer refers to the unclean spirits, but points to the people healed. In the charge not to publicize Jesus' presence, Matthew puts φανερόν before αὐτόν to emphasize further his retirement from persecutors (contrast Mark's order of words).

228

Though Matthew makes Jesus' suppression of publicity an example of retirement from persecution, Jesus' own motive poses the large question of "the messianic secret." Under the assumption that Jesus really did suppress publicity at times, we may think that he wanted to steer away from popular political messianism and avoid a premature confrontation with the authorities. The assumption of inauthenticity in the suppressions of publicity requires invention by the early church either to excuse a nonmessianism in Jesus' ministry or to play down a politically embarrassing overmessianism in it.

12:17-21 A final emphasis on Jesus' exemplary flight, which results in continuation and extension of ministry, comes in a long quotation from Isa 42:1-4. ἵνα implies that Jesus' behavior fulfills the divine intention revealed in Isaiah. As in 4:14; 8:17, Matthew mentions Isaiah's name. All three passages deal with summaries of Jesus' salvific activity. For the rest of the introductory formula, see the comments on 1:22.

Though Matthew diverges from the LXX most of the time in the quotation, he follows the LXX in writing παῖς instead of δοῦλος for עַבְדִּי, the Servant of the Lord. Because παῖς means "boy" as well as "servant," it fits better than δοῦλος the following "beloved"—and "I have chosen" too, if that verb connotes adoption of a child (BAG, s.v. αἱρετίζω). Matthew would hardly mean to contradict Jesus' being *born* as "God with us," however (see 1:18-25); and he probably draws "whom I have chosen" from Isa 44:2 as a substitute for "whom I uphold" in Isa 42:1. The substitute compensates for the loss of "my chosen one," which gives way to "my beloved one." The latter echoes the Father's statement at Jesus' baptism (3:17) and anticipates the transfiguration (17:5). In other words, these revisions underscore the Father's love for Jesus in the midst of his suffering persecution, an assurance not to be lost on the persecuted readers of Matthew's gospel.

In the next clause εὐδόκησεν, a natural but non-Septuagintal translation of רָצְתָה, again harks back to the Father's statement at Jesus' baptism (see also 17:5). Matthew's "I will put" agrees with the Targum against the MT and LXX ("I have given"). The future tense points up the predictive character of the passage, and "put" suits "on him" better than "have given" does.

Just as persecution results in witness to Gentiles (see 10:17-20), so also the Servant of the Lord "will proclaim justice to the Gentiles." Matthew's emphasis on discipling Gentiles requires that κρίσιν be taken positively as "justice" (almost "righteousness"—so also v 20; 23:23) instead of negatively as "judgment." With the Targum and again in agreement with his emphasis on discipling Gentiles, Matthew interprets יוֹצִיא as promulgation rather than self-defense (cf. Num 14:37; Deut 22:14, 19; Neh 6:19; and Isa 48:20 MT with LXX). Therefore he interprets לֹא יִצְעַק, "he will not cry out," as meaning οὐκ ἐρίσει, "he will not wrangle," and וְלֹא יִשָּׂא, "neither will he raise [his voice]," as meaning οὐδὲ κραυγάσει, "neither will he shout." Again he agrees with the Targum. And where the MT says, "neither will he make his voice heard in the out of doors," Matthew writes, "Neither will anyone hear his voice in the streets," perhaps for a contrast with his distinctive picture of hypocrites who pray standing on street corners (6:5).

229

In other words, the persecuted Jesus does not seek justice by taking his cause to the public. Neither should his persecuted disciples. Like him, they are to proclaim justice, not seek it.

The bruised reed and smoldering wick (v 20) stand for the "little ones," whom Jesus treats tenderly (cf. 9:36; 11:28-30). Matthew omits the refusal of the Lord's Servant to be disheartened or crushed (Isa 42:4a) and conflates the two clauses in Isa 42:3c ("he will faithfully put forth justice") and 4b ("till he has established justice in the earth"). Matthew's conflation reads, "till he puts forth justice successfully." Because disheartening is no longer in view, the period covered by "till" has to do with the Servant's gentle ministry rather than with courageousness. εἰς νῖκος may come from Hab 1:4 as a replacement of לָאֱמֶת, "for truth," or בָּאָרֶץ, "in the earth." On its translation "successfully" instead of a stilted "to victory," see R. A Kraft in *Septuagintal Lexicography* (ed. R. A. Kraft; SBLSCS 1; Missoula: University of Montana for the SBL, 1972) 153-56. The successful putting forth of justice refers again, not to self-defense, but to the teaching of justice (see v 35 for the use of ἐκβάλλω twice in the sense of speaking).

To emphasize the conversion of Gentiles in the final clause of the quotation (v 21), Matthew follows the LXX: "and in his name Gentiles will hope." The ἐπί of the LXX drops out. Matthew likes ὀνόματι (9,5). Here it substitutes for תוֹרָתוֹ, "his law" (1QIs^a reads the plural). Matthew also likes ἔθνη (7,2). Here it replaces אִיִּים, "islands, coastlands," which resembles גּוֹיִם, "Gentiles" (cf. Isa 41:5 MT with LXX; 1QpHab 3:2; and Gundry, *Use of the OT* 118-21). Thus Jesus' retiring from persecution and pursuing itinerant evangelism rather than defending himself exemplify his disciples' flight from place to place in a persecuted ministry that results in conversion of Gentiles.

THE PERSECUTORS' FALSE
AND UNFORGIVABLE ACCUSATION
12:22-37 (7:16-20; Mark 3:22-30; Luke 6:43-45; 11:14-23; 12:10)

Matthew skips the appointment and listing of the twelve in Mark 3:13-19 because he has used that material already in 5:1; 10:1-4. With Luke, he also omits the charge that Jesus is insane (Mark 3:20-21). Superficially, that charge would seem to fit the theme of persecution emphasized by Matthew. But for his purposes, the attempt to seize Jesus on grounds of insanity comes from the wrong source, viz., from "his own family" rather than the Jewish leaders. And even when viewed as untrue, the charge of insanity does not sit easily alongside Matthew's majestic portrait of Jesus. The evangelist goes, then, to the tradition behind Luke 11:14-23. There he finds a challenge to the resting of the Lord's Spirit on Jesus (cf. Matt 12:18-21). The first part of this tradition deals with an exorcism that Matthew has already narrated in 9:32-34 but that he now narrates a second time in order to provide an occasion for the accusation that Jesus casts out demons by Beelzebul. With the accusation, Mark's parallel (3:22-30) reappears. The frequent agreements of Matthew and Luke against Mark include a number of Mattheanisms and suggest Luke's use of Matthew.

12:22-23 (Luke 11:14) The story of the exorcism opens with a typically Matthean τότε (66,17). Much as in 9:32, we read about the bringing of a demon-possessed deaf-mute, in contrast with Luke's writing immediately about the exorcism. προσηνέχθη is a Mattheanism (9,2) and may connote an offering to Jesus (see the comments on 2:11; 4:24). For demoniacs, Matthew habitually uses the participle δαιμονιζόμενος and its cognate noun (6,0). The story of the two blind men (9:27-31) immediately precedes the first edition of the story of the deaf-mute (9:32-34), and Matthew has a special interest in τυφλός (9,0). Therefore he inserts τυφλός here for further description of the deaf-mute. Thus, just as Matthew the conflator doubled the blind men (see 9:27-31; 20:29-31), so he doubles the malady of the demoniac in a conflation of the stories of the blind men and the deaf-mute (cf. the comments on "Son of David" in v 23).

Instead of a reference to the casting or going out of the demon (so 9:33 and Luke), we read "and he healed him," an echo of a similar statement in v 15 (cf. also v 10). In this way Matthew ties together the different elements in the larger passage and satisfies his interest in the verb "heal" (10,10). The use of ἐθεράπευσεν as the main verb leads to the reduction of ἐλάλησεν (so 9:33 and Luke) to an infinitive introduced by the Mattheanism ὥστε (10,0). And alongside that infinitive Matthew puts "to see" (not in 9:33 or Luke) to carry out his conflation of the stories concerning the two blind men and the deaf-mute.

In 9:33 and Luke ἐθαύμασαν describes the crowds' marvelling at the exorcism. Here Matthew substitutes ἐξίσταντο, which comes from the charge that Jesus was insane (Mark 3:20-21). By using that verb here, Matthew not only compensates for his omitting the charge, but also changes the reference and meaning of the verb from the falsely supposed insanity of Jesus to the crowds' amazement at his healing the blind and deaf-mute. To emphasize their amazement, the evangelist characteristically adds πάντες (63,25-26—not in 9:33 or Luke).

As an introduction to the expression of all the crowds' amazement, we discover the finite verb ἔλεγον (not in Luke) instead of Matthew's beloved participle λέγοντες (as in 9:33). The stronger form enhances the following Christology of Jesus as the Son of David. The crowds' question, "This one is not the Son of David, is he?" has not the slightest parallel in 9:33 or Luke. But Jesus appears as the Son of David in the two versions of the healing of the blind men (9:27; 20:30-31). Matthew inserts the motif here to carry forward his conflation of the stories of the blind men and deaf-mute and keep his readers from forgetting Jesus' identity as the Davidic Messiah. The past portrayals of the crowds as disciples unite with the contrasting negative opinion of the Pharisees in the next verse here to give μήτι the force of a hopeful "perhaps" (cf. BAG, s.v.).

The Jews did not expect the Davidic Messiah to perform healings or exorcisms. But Matthew constructs the question from the standpoint of a Christian who believes in Jesus as both healer and Davidic Messiah. It may therefore be otiose to appeal to Jewish belief in Solomon, David's son, as a master of exorcism (cf. the comments on 9:27-31).

12:24 (Mark 3:22; Luke 11:15-16) Mark identifies those who say that Jesus casts out demons by Beelzebul as "the scribes who came down from Jerusalem," Luke as "some of them," i.e., certain ones from the crowds. As in 9:34, Matthew substitutes the Pharisees in order to cast them in the role of Jesus' persecutors (cf. vv 2, 14) and reserve the scribes for a passage where Jesus will reply in terms of the OT (v 38). Φαρισαῖοι typifies his diction (18,1). The replacement of Mark's καί with δέ (so also Luke) sharpens the contrast between the Pharisees as Jesus' persecutors and the crowds as Jesus' disciples, who represent the large number of Gentiles to be discipled later. Elimination of the scribes who came down from Jerusalem leads to the replacement of Mark's καταβάντες with the typically Matthean ἀκούσαντες (10,3). What the Pharisees said becomes a response to the hopeful question of the crowds that Jesus might be the Son of David, a question inserted only by Matthew. He has just used ἔλεγον to introduce the crowds' question; so here he uses εἶπον instead of Mark's ἔλεγον. That Luke makes the same switch though he lacks Matthew's reason (since he does not report that the crowds were saying anything) suggests Matthean influence.

Matthew and Luke again agree in omitting the recitative ὅτι in Mark (bis) and the first antagonistic statement, "He has Beelzebul." Because Mark lacks an immediately foregoing story of an exorcism, he needs that introductory charge against Jesus. Furthermore, the charge means that Jesus is himself a demoniac, and it follows naturally the immediately preceding charge that he is berserk. But in Matthew and Luke the lack of such a preceding charge deprives the charge of having Beelzebul of its antecedent; and the immediately foregoing story of an exorcism makes unnecessary the charge of having Beelzebul. Its omission enables a quick entree into the charge expressly related to exorcism, viz., that Jesus does not cast out demons except by Beelzebul, the ruler of the demons.

Matthew inserts οὗτος as a parallel to the same word in the crowds' question (v 23). The negative form (οὐκ . . . εἰ μή) differs from the positive statement, "By [Beelzebul] the ruler of the demons he casts out demons," in 9:33, Mark, and Luke; and it parallels μήτι in the crowds' question (cf. Matthew's insertions of οὐκ . . . εἰ μή in 14:17; 15:24; see also 5:13). Thus Matthew develops his contrast between the Pharisees' blasphemy and what amounts to a confession of Jesus as David's Son by the crowds. Furthermore, the two occurrences of οὗτος make a Christological emphasis by shifting the accent from the ruler of demons to Jesus. To compensate for omission of the charge "He has Beelzebul" the name "Beelzebul" makes its way into the charge that Jesus casts out demons by the ruler of the demons (contrast 9:34 and Mark). Luke shares the insertion of Beelzebul, but makes it the object of "by" with "the ruler of the demons" as its appositive. In Matthew the attributive position of "Beelzebul" gives it the force of an adjective ("the Beelzebulian ruler of the demons").

Matthew contrasts the crowds and the Pharisees also in 9:32-34; 23:1-2. Some think that he and Luke do more than Mark by identifying Beelzebul with the prince of demons (Satan). But the two lines in Mark where the terms occur are to be considered synonymously parallel.

12:25 (Mark 3:23-25; Luke 11:17) In place of Mark's "and summoning them" Matthew puts "but knowing their thoughts," a repetition from 9:4, where he inserted the same phrase in a reference to "some of the scribes" (cf. Mark here) who "said within themselves, 'This one [οὗτος; cf. Matthew here] blasphemes [cf. the blasphemies in the following verses here].'" Luke's "but he, knowing their thoughts" looks very similar to Matthew's phrase, contrasts with Mark's, and seems to show influence from Matthew, since Luke lacks the links of οὗτος and blasphemies. Mention of the Pharisees' *thoughts* probably implies that what they said in the preceding verse they said within themselves (as Matthew alone writes in 9:4), not to the crowds. Thus in Matthew they retain their pious appearance and the evangelist can later tack on dominical sayings against hypocrisy (vv 33-37). Mark's ἔλεγεν becomes εἶπεν (so also Luke) for a parallel with the preceding εἶπον. This change and the replacement of Mark's καί with δέ (so also Luke) set the Pharisees' statement and Jesus' sayings in sharper opposition. Such opposition accords with Matthew's overarching theme of conflict (see also vv 2-3). Matthew deletes "in parables" in order to save the term "parable" for introduction in chap. 13. That Luke does the same thing even though he has employed the term seven times already again suggests his use of Matthew.

Jesus' opening question, "How is Satan able to cast out Satan?" (so Mark), drops out only to appear in v 26 for the sake of a parallel with another, non-Markan question in v 27 (so also Luke). The present deletion leaves the parallelism between the clauses concerning divisions free from excess baggage and makes Jesus' words start with a forceful declaration. The change of Mark's ἐφ᾽ + the accusative to καθ᾽ + the genitive sharpens the meaning "against" and conforms to Matthew's style (10,1). Luke agrees with Mark in ἐφ᾽ + the accusative and also in putting the prepositional phrase "against itself" before the verb expressing division. Matthew's word order μερισθεῖσα καθ᾽ ἑαυτῆς reads more smoothly. The addition of πᾶσα to βασιλεία typifies Matthew's diction (63,25-26), accentuates the contrast with God's kingdom, and appears also in Luke. Mark's μερισθῇ becomes μερισθεῖσα in both Matthew and Luke (with δια- prefixed in Luke). This change results in a collapsing of the two clauses in Mark 3:24. There remains a single clause in which "is laid waste" takes the place of the entire Markan clause "that kingdom is not able to stand." The prior omission of Mark 3:23b, with its "is able," may have led to riddance of the same verb here; and perhaps "is laid waste" is meant to complement "plunder" in a later figure of speech (vv 29-30). At any rate, "is laid waste" forestalls a repetition of "stand" in the next line.

In v 25c Matthew again adds πᾶσα (63,25-26), but this time Luke agrees with Mark in lacking it. Before "house" Matthew inserts "city or" as a pointer to the cities in which Jesus ministered. Both πόλις and ἤ are Mattheanisms (18,3; 32,12). Again we find a smoother order of words and a shortening to one clause. (Luke shares the latter.) Matthew borrows his main verb from Mark, however, and changes "will not be able to stand" to "will not stand." Thus again it is not a matter of inability but, more forcefully, of the defeat itself.

The request for a sign, inserted in Luke 11:16, comes later in Matthew (v 38; Mark 8:11). Jesus may have meant "house" in the sense of a political domain or a ruling family rather than a private household. Matthew's addition of "city" makes for a progression from kingdom to city to house.

12:26 (Mark 3:26; Luke 11:18) The application of the figures begins in v 26. Instead of Mark's "rose up" Matthew puts "casts out Satan" in order to compensate for prior omission of Mark 3:23b, where the latter expression occurred. But that expression resists Mark's "against himself." Therefore Matthew transfers "against himself" to "has been divided." That Luke agrees with Matthew in the transference, but not in the reason for it (Luke does not write about Satan's casting out Satan), again suggests Matthean influence. καθ' has substituted for ἐφ' twice in v 25; so here Matthew retains Mark's ἐφ'. The deletion of Mark's "and" before "has been divided" makes that verb, with its prepositional phrase, the key of the apodosis rather than the second part of the protasis. Matthew revises the saying this way to make possible the remainder of his compensation for prior omission of Mark 3:23b. That remainder is the turning of Mark's "he is not able to stand" into the question "How then will his kingdom stand?" (cf. πῶς . . .; in Mark 3:23b). οὖν is a Mattheanism (35,11). As before, Matthew deletes δύναται. His substituting Satan's kingdom for Satan himself sets up a parallel and conflict between Satan's kingdom and God's (cf. v 28). βα-σιλεία is another Mattheanism (18,12). Mark's "but comes to [literally 'has'] an end" now drops out entirely, because it does not fit Matthew's switch from a declaration to a question. Furthermore, that switch makes somewhat of a parallel with another question following another clause beginning with καὶ εἰ (see v 27). Such parallelism characterizes Matthew's style. That Luke agrees with these typically Matthean revisions (except for his lack of οὖν) yet again points toward influence from the first gospel.

On Jewish exorcism, see Acts 19:13-16; Josephus *Ant.* 8.2.5 §§45-49; *J.W.* 7.6.3 §185; Tob 8:1-3; Justin *Dial.* 85; Irenaeus *Haer.* 2.6.2. "They will be your judges" demands a distinction between the Jews who accuse Jesus of employing Satanic power and the Jews who themselves practice exorcism. And "your sons" favors a distinction between the elder Jewish leaders (Pharisees in Matthew) and their younger followers or students. For a remarkable parallel, see again Acts 19:13-16, where Luke identifies the Jewish exorcists as the "seven sons of a certain Sceva, a Jewish chief priest."

12:27 (Luke 11:19) The "and" which opens v 27 links the following saying positively with the foregoing. "And if I cast out demons by Beelzebul, by whom do your sons cast [them] out?" implies that the followers of Jesus' accusers will convict his accusers of hypocrisy. They will do so in that his accusers do not bring charges against their own followers, who

234

practice exorcism, as well as against him. Thus we read, "On account of this they themselves will be your judges." The argument does not necessarily imply Jesus' acceptance of the exorcisms practiced by his antagonists' followers. (His next statement, which affirms the arrival of God's kingdom only recently, implies the opposite.) Rather, the argument points up the hypocritical inconsistency in his antagonists' accusation.

12:28 (Luke 11:20) Jesus now presses home the alternative that his power to exorcise demons signals the recent arrival of God's kingdom. In place of Luke's "by the finger of God" Matthew writes "by the Spirit of God." This derives from the putting of the Spirit on the Lord's Servant (v 18) and provides a more exact antithesis to "by Beelzebul" (v 27). The change pays Matthew several other dividends, too: (1) fulfillment of Isa 42:1; (2) a closer parallel with "the kingdom of God" in v 28b; (3) a lead into the blasphemy of the Holy Spirit (vv 31-32); and (4) a trinitarian allusion to the Spirit, God, and Jesus (as in 3:16; 28:19). The addition of ἐγώ (not in the Lukan text of P⁴⁵ ℵ* A W Θ f¹ pm lat and the Byzantine family) makes a parallel with ἐγώ in the preceding saying, adds a Christological emphasis, and characterizes Matthew's diction (12-13,3). Even greater emphasis falls on "the Spirit of God," however; for ἐν πνεύματι θεοῦ comes before ἐγώ, whereas ἐγώ precedes "by Beelzebul" in v 27. Instead of his usual "of heaven" with "the kingdom," Matthew retains "of God" for correspondence with the foregoing references to Satan's kingdom (v 26) and the Spirit of God (v 28a). The retention maintains the trinitarian cast of the passage.

Jesus borrowed "finger of God" from the OT (Exod 8:15[19]; Deut 9:10; cf. Ps 8:4[3]). Cf. also Exod. Rab. 10.7. Had Matthew's "Spirit of God" been original, Luke would probably have kept the phrase because of his overpowering interest in the Holy Spirit. On ἔφθασεν as indicating arrival, not just near approach, see G. E. Ladd, The Presence of the Future (Grand Rapids: Eerdmans, 1974) 138-45.

12:29-30 (Mark 3:27; Luke 11:21-23) In the figure of the strong man's house, Matthew veers from the tradition behind Luke 11:21-23 to Mark 3:27, which he picks up again after discontinuance in his two preceding verses. ἤ is a Mattheanism (32,12), which here takes the place of ἀλλ'. Characteristically, Matthew adds πῶς (6,1) and turns Mark's and Luke's declaration into a question parallel with the question beginning the same way in v 26c. Consequently, Mark's "not" drops out and his "no one" becomes an indefinite "anyone." Despite its deletion four times recently, "is able" stays. "Having entered" becomes "to enter" for a parallel with the following "to plunder." To compensate for his omitting the story of the strange exorcist (Mark 9:38-40), Matthew adds the saying in Mark 9:40: "for he who is not against us is for us." But he turns it into a statement concerning persecution, "the one who is not with me is against me," and adds a synonymous line to satisfy his desire for parallelism: "and he who does not gather with me scatters" (v 30). Luke's agreement with Matthew in the additions again suggests Matthean influence, since Luke does not omit the story of the strange exorcist (see Luke 9:49-50). "With me" (bis)

235

echoes "with him" in v 3. On κατ', especially in the context of persecution, see v 25 (bis) and 5:11; 10:35 (ter); 12:32 (bis); 27:1 (all containing Matthew's insertions of this preposition). And for συνάγων see especially 3:12; 13:30; the word is a Mattheanism (12,12). σκορπίζει occurs only here in Matthew and Luke (and never in Mark); but διασκορπισθήσονται will occur for persecution in 26:31; Mark 14:27.

Who is the strong man? What is meant by the binding of him and the plundering of his goods? And who does these things? In Mark, obviously, Satan is the strong man. Jesus first overpowers him (perhaps by resisting the temptation in the wilderness—1:12-13) and then plunders his goods by exorcising demons. Several elements in Matthew suggest, however, that just as Matthew has turned the saying concerning tolerance (in the story of the strange exorcist) into a saying concerning persecution, so also he turns this figure concerning exorcism into a figure concerning persecution; i.e., for Matthew Jesus is the strong man whose goods are his disciples. "Strong" has referred to Jesus before (3:11). "Plunder" referred to persecution in 11:12, will describe Satanic activity in 13:19, and is an insertion by Matthew in both places. Mark's ἀλλ' contrasts the inability of Satan to stand if he opposes himself and the ability of Jesus to plunder Satan's goods because of his having bound Satan. But Matthew switches to ἤ, "or," in order to indicate an *alternative* to Jesus' casting out demons by God's Spirit. That alternative is Satan's persecution because of the exorcisms. Above all, the addition of the saying in v 30 concerning persecution (see esp. the expressions "against me," "scatters") leads to the conclusions that Matthew portrays Jesus as the strong man who owns a house and that the goods in danger of being plundered are Jesus' persecuted disciples. Cf. 10:25 (a verse peculiar to this gospel) and Matthew's stress on Jesus as a houseowner in Capernaum (see the comments on 4:13; 9:10). But just as the questions beginning "How?" in vv 26 and 34 imply an impossibility, so also here. Satan cannot bind Jesus. Therefore persecutors will not prevail. Cf. 10:26-33 and the uniquely Matthean 16:18. This interpretation explains Matthew's keeping the question of ability (δύναται) after rejecting it four times earlier in this very passage. Luke's sharing some of Matthew's differences from Mark implies Matthean influence, but Luke's meaning seems to match Mark rather than Matthew.

The saying about taking spoils from a strong man may rest on the OT or a proverb stemming from the OT (see Isa 49:24-25; *Pss. Sol.* 5:4; cf. Isa 53:12). According to the original intent, "the house of the strong man" may play on the meaning of Beelzebul, "master of the house" (cf. the comments on 10:25). σκεύη refers widely to all household effects that might be plundered. With the binding of Satan as the strong man (so Jesus' meaning), cf. Rev 20:2; *As. Mos.* 10:1. Jesus' meaning rests on the presupposition that demons do the work of Satan. The saying in v 30 is addressed to the Pharisees and does not point toward those who think they can take a neutral stance concerning Christ. Rather, it exposes unbelievers as opponents or persecutors. On the gathering and scattering of God's people, cf. Isa 40:11; Ezek 34:13, 16.

12:31 (Mark 3:28) Despite his liking Mark's ἀμήν with λέγω ὑμῖν (15,8), Matthew substitutes διὰ τοῦτο. The phrase echoes its recent occurrence in v 27, belongs to his special vocabulary (4,2), and identifies the Pharisees' accusation that Jesus exorcises demons by means of Satanic power with the blasphemy of the Holy Spirit. By including the sayings not only in Mark 3:28-29 but also in the tradition behind Luke 12:10, Matthew doubles the Pharisees' guilt. In v 31 he smooths out Mark's order of words by advancing τὰ ἁμαρτήματα καὶ αἱ βλασφημίαι to a position right after πάντα at the head of the clause. This advance has the effect of making πάντα modify the nouns (thus the loss of the definite articles in Matthew); the nouns no longer act as appositives to πάντα. Matthew also switches from Mark's plural to the singular, "every sin and blasphemy," in anticipation of "blasphemy of the Spirit" in the following, parallel line. "The sons of men [i.e., human beings]" becomes "men." Matthew does not object to the descriptive use of the Semitic phrase "son(s) of . . ."; often his gospel alone has it (see 8:12; 9:15 [paralleled]; 13:38 [bis]; 23:15). Here he gets rid of it, though, because it comes too close to "the Son of man," a designation of Jesus in the next saying (v 32ab), which Mark does not have. This next saying delays Matthew's taking over the other half of Mark's passage (v 32cd; Mark 3:29). Therefore, to gain the contrast he immediately needs, Matthew composes the clause "but the blasphemy of the Spirit will not be forgiven" (v 31c). The nominal phrase comes by anticipation of Mark's reference to blaspheming the Holy Spirit; the verbal phrase simply negatives the verb in Matthew's preceding line. Thus the first evangelist gains an antithetic parallel between v 31b and v 31c.

12:32 (Mark 3:29; Luke 12:10) The saying recorded also in Luke 12:10 now enters as an interpolation. "Everyone" falls off the reference to "whoever speaks a word against the Son of man." Thus Matthew gains a closer parallel with the beginning of the next, antithetically parallel line: "but whoever. . . ." "Speak a word against" carries the sense of "blasphemy." The aorist subjunctive εἴπῃ displaces Luke's ἐρεῖ for a parallel with εἴπῃ in the next line, where the aorist subjunctive rests on Mark's βλασφημήσῃ. The substitution of κατά + the genitive for εἰς + the accusative (so Luke) sharpens the meaning "against" and conforms to Matthew's style (10,1; cf. the comments on vv 25, 30). The future tense of "will be forgiven" corresponds to the imperfect tense in Galilean Aramaic, which usually has a virtual rather than future meaning—thus, "can be forgiven." This half of the saying means that speaking against Jesus is forgivable, presumably because Jesus was not conforming to expectations (cf. 11:2-3). By contrast, the powerful workings of the Holy Spirit could hardly be mistaken, whatever their implication concerning Jesus.

The next half of the saying in Matthew (v 32cd) comes into being through conflation of Mark 3:29 and the tradition behind Luke 12:10c. "But whoever speaks [supply 'a word' from the preceding line] against the Holy Spirit" derives from Mark's "But whoever blasphemes against the Holy Spirit" (cf. Luke). As before, κατά replaces εἰς for sharpness of meaning. And speaking a word replaces blaspheming for a parallel with the preceding line. The doubling of the expression prepares for the importance

237

of men's words as a basis for final judgment (vv 36-37; cf. 5:37—both peculiar to Matthew). "It will not be forgiven him" comes from the tradition behind Luke 12:10c. This replacement of Mark's "he does not have forgiveness" gives Matthew a parallel with the preceding half of the saying (v 32b; cf. also v 31bc). Finally, Matthew paraphrases Mark's ". . . forever, but he is guilty of eternal sin" with a reference to the two ages familiar elsewhere in the NT and in late Judaism: "neither in this age nor in the coming [age]" (cf. 13:22, 39, 40, 49; 24:3; 28:20 and see *TDNT* 1. 204-7 for further references). The parallelism of the two negative phrases adds to the judgmental tone of the saying.

The possibility of forgiveness for the person who speaks against the Son of man seems to contradict the rejection of the person who denies Jesus (10:33; Mark 8:38; Luke 9:26; 12:9). But in Matthew and Mark the forgivable sin of blaspheming the Son of man is committed by one who has never professed to follow Jesus. The warnings that one who denies Jesus will be rejected have to do with professing disciples who apostatize. A serious question of contradiction arises, therefore, only in Luke, where denial of the one who denies Jesus stands alongside forgiveness of the one who speaks against the Son of man. If we read on in Luke, however, we discover that the Holy Spirit speaks through the disciples to nondisciples (Luke 12:11-12). This implies that in Luke, too, we are to distinguish between a professing disciple's unforgivable denial of Jesus (vv 8-9) and—during the church age—a non-disciple's forgivable speaking against the Son of man (vv 10-12). Peter's denial of Jesus was forgivable probably because it occurred before the mighty displays in Jesus' resurrection and exaltation and before the giving of the Spirit, and because he repented immediately rather than continued in denial till danger passed.

In Matthew Jesus addresses the Pharisees. Here, then, a distinction between Jesus' pre-Pentecostal ministry and the post-Pentecostal ministry of the apostolic church cannot yield the reason for the greater seriousness of blaspheming the Holy Spirit. The Pharisees were already blaspheming the Holy Spirit during Jesus' ministry! In shifting the tradition behind Luke 12:10 to a new context, Matthew does not alter Jesus' addressing the saying to nondisciples; but he does change those nondisciples from future recipients of the Spirit's ministry through the disciples to present recipients of the Spirit's ministry through Jesus. This change agrees with his recent substitution of the "Spirit of God" for the "finger of God" in a reference to Jesus' activity (v 28).

On the expression "speak a word against" as a Semitic (probably Aramaic) periphrasis for blasphemy in the Lukan-Matthean tradition, see Black, *Aramaic Approach* 195. Of course, נְאַץ remains as the substratum for βλασφημέω in the Mark-an-Matthean tradition.

Some think of an originally single tradition with the Aramaic phrase לְבַר אֲנָשָׁא underlying both "to the sons of men" (Mark 3:28) and "against the Son of man" (Luke 12:10). In other words, Mark correctly took the Aramaic expression as a generic singular for man and thus translated it with a collective plural; and Luke, or his predecessor, incorrectly took the Aramaic expression as a particularistic singular for Jesus as the Son of man. Matthew then included both the correct understanding in v 31 (but laundered the Semitism "sons of men") and the incorrect understanding in v 32.

Against this reconstruction, Mark's "sons of men" appear as recipients of forgiveness. Yet in the supposed counterpart, the Son of man appears as the object of blasphemy. A common origin for the two statements despite this discrepancy then demands that the Aramaic phrase referred to men as the objects of blasphemy.

But this time it is Mark who misinterprets the phrase by making men the recipients of forgiveness. Thus the saying originally had to do with the possibility of forgiveness for those who blaspheme (i.e., slander) other men and with the impossibility of forgiveness for those who blaspheme the Holy Spirit. Yet the clause "however many blasphemies they utter" (Mark 3:28c) requires that in the original saying the sons of men were the blasphemers, not the blasphemed. The very awkwardness and redundancy of the clause argue in favor of its originality. So also does its typically Semitic beginning, ὅσα (ἐάν) (see many examples in Hatch and Redpath, s.v. ὅσος, esp. examples with verbs of speaking). Hence, the discrepancy between the sons of men as receiving forgiveness for their own blasphemies and the Son of man as the object of others' blasphemies still stands. And it favors an original independence of two distinct, though similar, sayings. The differences between Mark's and Luke's contexts and between "blaspheme" and "speak a word against" support this opinion. Because the plural is common in the Aramaic for "sons of men" (see G. Vermes in Black, *Aramaic Approach* 315-19), translation of an Aramaic singular by a Greek plural seems unlikely. On the other hand, an Aramaic plural would hardly have been mistaken for "the Son of man."

12:33 (7:16-20; Mark 3:30; Luke 6:43-44) The parenthetical explanation "Because they were saying, 'He has an unclean spirit' " (Mark 3:30) drops out. Instead, Matthew appends some revised sayings already used in a warning against false prophets (7:16-20). The sayings have to do with good and bad trees and their yielding good and bad fruit. Matthew's earlier contrast between the thoughts of the Pharisees and their pious appearance (vv 24-25) leads him to append these sayings as a warning against hypocrisy. Strikingly, the verb changes twice from a third person singular indicative (ποιεῖ, so 7:17 and, similarly, Luke) to a second person plural imperative (ποιήσατε). Thus the former axiom that a good tree *produces* good fruits and a bad tree *produces* bad fruits becomes a command to *make* the tree and its fruit good or to *make* the tree and its fruit bad, i.e., to avoid hypocrisy (so also vv 34-37). The command gains emphasis from the parallelism, which includes the startling command to make the tree and its fruit *bad*! Some have understood ποιήσατε as ponite—"*regard* the tree as good . . . or *regard* the tree as bad"—so that the saying teaches consistency in making judgments about the nature of Jesus' acts and the source of his power (see BAG, s.v. ποιέω I1dβ; Black, *Aramaic Approach* 302). But the following criticism of the Pharisees' hypocrisy, a criticism that is put in terms parallel with the good and bad in the present saying, militates against that understanding. Matthew likes ἤ (32,12). With the first δένδρον he uses καλόν (so Luke) rather than ἀγαθόν ("good," so 7:17) in order to match τὸν καρπὸν αὐτοῦ καλόν. With the second καρπόν he uses σαπρόν (so Luke) instead of πονηρόν (so 7:17 in the plural) for a match with τὸ δένδρον σαπρόν. These revisions of the diction adopted in 7:17 emphasize the need for exact correspondence between appearances and reality.

Matthew introduces the statement that a tree is known by its fruit with γάρ (so also Luke) in place of ἄρα γε (as in 7:20). The new conjunction makes Jesus' judgment according to reality the reason for avoiding hypocrisy. He cannot be fooled! He knows even the words *thought* by the Pharisees (vv 24-25). Not only does Matthew's conjunction agree with Luke's against 7:20; so also do ἐκ instead of ἀπό (as in 7:20), the singular number of "fruit" (cf. the preceding lines of v 33 and contrast the plurals in 7:16-20, with one exception), and "the tree is known" instead of "you will recognize them" (so 7:20). In fact, Matthew disagrees with Luke only in replacing "each" with the definite article and in lacking "its own." The predominance of agreements with Luke against 7:16-20 is due to the shift away from the topic of false prophets (7:16-20). Recognizing false prophets in the future has become an axiom for recognizing anybody at any time.

12:34-35 (Luke 6:45) At this point Matthew delays utilizing further sayings paralleled in Luke and constructs the question in v 34a to castigate the hypocritical Pharisees as evil. "Offspring of vipers" comes from 3:7, where John the Baptist used it for the hypocrisy of the Pharisees and Sadducees. In 23:33 Matthew will insert the phrase again as an address to "the scribes and Pharisees, hypocrites." Cf. "John the Baptist parallel Jesus" in the Topical Index.

In the question "How can you, being evil, speak good things?" πῶς is a Mattheanism (6,1) and echoes vv 26c and 29c. Cf. especially 23:33, a uniquely Matthean verse where πῶς follows γεννήματα ἐχιδνῶν, as here. Matthew likes δύνασθε (13,0). Here it echoes δύναται with πῶς in v 29. "To speak" anticipates "speaks" in the next clause. And the contrast between ἀγαθά and πονηροί is characteristic of Matthew (4,1—see the comments on 5:45). The next line comes from the tradition behind Luke 6:45c. Matthew skips several intervening lines (Luke 6:44bc, 45ab) in order to get this line for a synthetic parallel with the line he has just composed. It reads, "For out of the abundance of the heart the mouth speaks" (cf. 15:18; Sir 27:6). This differs from Luke only in the putting of the subject before the verb, the presence of definite articles with "abundance" and "heart," and the omission of "his" through lack of an antecedent. The skipping of the intervening lines causes the lack.

In v 35 Matthew retrieves the two skipped lines recorded in Luke 6:45ab. "A good man out of the good treasure . . ." matches Luke exactly. But where Luke continues ". . . of his heart brings forth good," Matthew writes ". . . puts forth good things." ἐκβάλλει replaces προφέρει and belongs to his favorite vocabulary (10,1). The plural of "good things" contrasts with Luke's singular, derives from v 34a, and refers to good coins. "And an evil man out of the evil treasure . . ." again matches Luke, except for Matthew's filling in ellipses with "man" and "treasure" for a more exact parallel with the preceding line. And in the substitution of "puts forth evil things" for Luke's "brings forth evil" Matthew makes the same revisions as before, but the "bad things" refer to counterfeit coins. The context indicates that putting forth good and bad money refers to speaking different kinds of words. Cf. *T. Asher* 1:1–2:1.

12:36-37 Matthew composes the last two sayings in this section to emphasize the judgment of persecutors. Not only his predilection for the motifs of judgment and righteousness, but also the diction, parallelism, possible borrowing of OT phraseology, and lack of counterparts in the other synoptics indicate composition by him. We discover Mattheanisms in λέγω . . . ὑμῖν (27,7), πᾶν (63,25-26), ἀργόν (1,2—with its cognates under

240

ἐργ- [6,7]), and possibly in ῥῆμα (inserted four times—4:4; 12:36; 18:16; 27:14—and paralleled only in 26:75). Because of the foregoing insistence on correspondence between appearance and reality, we should take ἀργόν in its literal sense, "workless" (cf. 20:1-16). "Will speak" comes down from the preceding sayings. "They will render account concerning it in the day of judgment" presents us with further Mattheanisms in ἀποδώσουσιν (5,11), λόγον (16,2), and ἡμέρᾳ κρίσεως (4,0). Matthew makes a play on λόγον, which here means "account" and will next mean "word(s)," in harmony with the preceding context.

The final saying consists of two lines antithetically parallel to each other: "for by your words you will be justified, and by your words you will be condemned" (v 37). A third time we read ἐκ γάρ at the beginning of a line (so also vv 33c, 34b). Matthew likes γάρ (62-63,15) and words with the stem δικ-, such as δικαιωθήσῃ and καταδικασθήσῃ (18-19,10-9). Justification by words probably reflects the phraseology of Ps 51:6(4): "so that you are justified when you speak." In view of the distinctive κατεδικάσατε in v 7, we have poetic justice: hypocritical persecutors condemn the innocent disciples of Jesus, but they will themselves be condemned at the last judgment. The surprising change of the second person pronoun from plural (see v 36a) to singular brings the issue down to the individual level.

THE WICKEDNESS AND JUDGMENT OF JESUS' PERSECUTORS
12:38-45 (16:1-2, 4; Mark 8:11-12; Luke 11:16, 24-26, 29-32)

The main parallels to this passage appear in Luke. But the request for a sign and the initial part of Jesus' response (vv 38-39) will crop up again in 16:1-2a, 4ab, where they have a parallel in Mark 8:11-12 and appear in a context also paralleled in the context of Mark 8:11-12. Matthew introduces Mark's verses at the present point in order to further the motif of persecution: the Pharisees continue to hound Jesus. Both here and in chap. 16 we see conflation of the traditions and assimilation of Matthew's own two passages to each other. As can be seen from a listing of Luke's parallels, Matthew rearranges his materials. After introducing the request for a sign (v 38; cf. Luke 11:16), he skips over Jesus' response to the earlier charge of alliance with Beelzebul (Luke 11:17-26 with 14-15, much of which material has already appeared in Matt 12:22-30). This skipping has the purpose of putting Jesus' response to the request for a sign (vv 39-42; cf. Luke 11:29-32) immediately after that request. Matthew then steps back for most of the skipped material that has not already appeared in his text, viz., the sayings about the returning evil spirit (vv 43-45; cf. Luke 11:24-26). Their inclusion leaves unused only the tradition behind Luke 11:27-28, for which he compensates by adding vv 46-50. The delay of the sayings about the returning evil spirit enables him to use them as a judgment against the "evil and adulterous generation" of "scribes and Pharisees," who "seek a sign." The reappearance of some similar phrases in 16:1-4 further enables him to underline that judgment.

241

The separation of the request for a sign in Luke 11:16 from Jesus' response in Luke 11:29-32 bears the mark of originality, for an editor is more likely to have brought together the request and the response than to have separated them. Hence, we ought to regard Luke's order as the backdrop for Matthew's editing. Jesus first responded to those who charged him with exorcising by Beelzebul (Luke 11:17-28 with 15) and then responded to those who sought from him a sign from heaven (Luke 11:29-32 with 16).

12:38 (16:1; Mark 8:11; Luke 11:16) The passage opens with a typically Matthean τότε (66,17) and continues with the statement that "some of the scribes and Pharisees answered him, saying." The Pharisees appear also in 16:1 and Mark, but not in Luke, where we read a general reference to "others." The Pharisees are often mentioned in the first gospel (18,1). Despite their absence from the primary parallel in Luke, they come in from Mark as Jesus' persecutors (cf. vv 2, 14, 24). Alongside them, Matthew puts the scribes (not in 16:1, Mark, or Luke). He omitted the scribes in v 24 (cf. Mark 3:22) in order to insert them here, where Jesus' reply deals with the OT, their field of expertise. The combination "scribes and Pharisees" is a Mattheanism (9,0).

The following expressions occur in the parallels: "approaching . . . testing, they asked him" (16:1); "they went out . . . and began to argue with him" (Mark 8:11); "testing" (Luke 11:16). By substituting "they answered . . . saying" for those expressions, Matthew takes account of the fact that Jesus' opponents are already present in the preceding context (so also Luke, but not 16:1 or Mark) and makes their request for a sign an antagonistic riposte to Jesus' foregoing warning of eternal judgment (vv 25-37) instead of a test (so 16:1, Mark, and Luke). Usually he puts ἀποκρίνομαι in a participial form followed by a finite form of λέγω (29,6). Here he does the reverse (2,4). The resultant escalation of ἀποκρίνομαι emphasizes that the request is an antagonistic riposte.

In the request, Matthew characteristically inserts διδάσκαλε (4,1) to emphasize that Jesus is the Teacher. This insertion agrees with the previous insertion of the scribes, just as the lack of διδάσκαλε fits the absence of scribes in 16:1. θέλομεν does not appear in 16:1, Mark, or Luke, but belongs to Matthew's favorite diction (18,8). The addition "to see" arises out of the necessity to supplement "we want." ἀπὸ σοῦ is a conflation of ἐξ οὐρανοῦ (so Luke and, with the definite article, 16:1; cf. ἀπὸ τοῦ οὐρανοῦ in Mark) and παρ' αὐτοῦ (so Mark and Luke). The scribes and Pharisees ask for a sign not subject to interpretation as satanically aided (cf. Exod 4:8-9; Isa 7:11; 1 Cor 1:22). Elimination of οὐρανοῦ (a surrogate for God in 16:1, Mark, and Luke) leaves Jesus alone, in contrast with his being paired with Beelzebul in the preceding charge. In effect, some of the scribes and Pharisees are saying, "You deny that you cast out demons by Beelzebul. Show us that you do it by yourself. We want evidence, not assertion."

12:39 (16:2, 4; Mark 8:12; Luke 11:29) Verse 39 opens, "But he, answering, said to them" (so also 16:2a) instead of "And sighing in his spirit, he says" (so Mark) or "And as the crowds were increasing, he began to say" (so Luke). Thus Matthew sharpens the conflict by making Jesus' following words a counter reply to the reply of the scribes and Pharisees.

ἀποκριθεὶς εἶπεν is typical of Matthew's style (29,6). In several ways he also sharpens the tone of Jesus' counter reply: (1) he turns the question "Why. . . ?" (so Mark) into an accusation (so also 16:4a and Luke); (2) he collapses the two clauses "This generation is an evil generation; it seeks a sign" (so Luke) into a single clause in which the evil relates directly and immediately to seeking a sign: "An evil and adulterous generation seeks a sign" (so also 16:4a; cf. Mark); (3) he adds "adulterous" (so also 16:4a) in a characteristic assimilation of Jesus' words to OT phraseology (see Isa 57:3; Jer 3:1–4:2; 13:27; Ezekiel 23; Hosea 1–3; 5:3-4 for adultery as religious infidelity; cf. Mark 8:38; Jas 4:4); and (4) he prefixes a perfective ἐπί to ζητεῖ with the result that the meaning "seeks" is intensified to something like "insists on" (cf. the comments on 16:1). As in 16:4a, the omission of Mark's and Luke's "this" generalizes Jesus' statement. Now it can refer also to unbelievers at the time of Matthew's writing.

In agreement with the primary parallel in Luke, Matthew lacks "Truly I say to you" (so Mark). Though he likes that expression (15,8), its inclusion here would have broken up the synthetic parallelism of the clauses "An evil and adulterous generation insists on a sign, and no sign will be given it except the sign of Jonah the prophet." Matthew takes care to construct this parallelism by collapsing into one the two traditional clauses concerning the evil generation and the seeking of a sign. The second line of his couplet agrees largely with Luke. We read "and a sign will not be given" rather than the Semitic idiom "if a sign will be given," which is an oath calling down a curse on oneself if one does such and such a thing (so Mark). ση-μεῖον occurs at the beginning rather than at the end (as in Mark). "To it" takes the place of Mark's repetitive "to this generation." And an exception appears: "except the sign of Jonah" (not in Mark). Explanation of the sign of Jonah follows, with additional references to the Ninevites and the queen of the South (vv 40-42; cf. Luke 11:3-32), none of which Mark has.

We may understand some of the differences as natural variants (e.g., οὐ δοθήσεται as a de-Semitized version of εἰ δοθήσεται) and additions (e.g., πονηρά and the exception of the sign of Jonah). Nevertheless, the differences between Matthew-Luke and Mark are so many and extensive and the contexts so different (note in 16:1-4 Matthew switches to Mark's context!) that we do better to regard the passages in Matthew-Luke and Mark as reporting separate incidents. The apparent contradiction between the flat refusal to give a sign and the exception of the sign of Jonah then admits of a ready historical explanation: Jesus curtly refuses in Mark because he is responding to the antagonistic Pharisees (see Mark 8:11), but he allows the exception in Luke because he is addressing a mixed audience (see Luke 11:14-16). The Pharisees come into Matthew by way of conflation, and the scribes by way of editorial insertion.

12:40 (Luke 11:30) To the exception of the sign of Jonah, Matthew characteristically added τοῦ προφήτου (19,6) in order to stress Jesus' fulfilling the prophetic typology apparent in Jonah (v 39). This emphasis becomes more apparent in v 40, where the exceptive sign of Jonah is drawn out. καθώς yields to the Mattheanism ὥσπερ (6,3). "Jonah became a sign to the Ninevites" becomes "Jonah was in the belly of the sea monster three

243

days and three nights" for exact conformity to Jonah 2:1 LXX (which corresponds closely with the Hebrew text). Thus Matthew again assimilates Jesus' words to the OT.

To provide a parallel for his allusive quotation from the OT, Matthew then changes "so also the Son of man will be [a sign] to this generation" to "so the Son of man will be in the heart of the earth three days and three nights." καρδία and γῆς belong to Matthew's favorite vocabulary (5,2; 21,6—cf. references to the "heart" of the seas in Jonah 2:4[3] and the "earth" of the deep in the Targum). "The heart of the earth" does not refer simply to a grave, but means the realm of the dead (cf. Sir 51:5; Eph 4:9) and alludes to Jesus' death. The limitation to three days and three nights alludes to his resurrection.

Matthew's allusive quotation of Jonah 2:1(1:17) and construction of an apposite parallel to it thus interpret the sign of Jonah as the death and resurrection of Jesus the Son of man. In a veiled manner, Luke's text carries the same meaning, for the future tense of "will be" resists a reference to the person or proclamation of Jesus, who was *already* present and preaching; and a reference to the Son of man as a future figure distinct from Jesus would fail to meet the point of the request for a sign not only from heaven, but also from Jesus himself. Unless we were to suppose that Jesus weakened the sense of the term "sign," the request demands that term to be understood in the sense of a dramatic confirmation rather than of a symbolic person or a significant message. In late Judaism the deliverance of Jonah from death assumed a position of importance in the understanding of that OT book (see Josephus *Ant.* 9.10.2 §§208-14; the Jerusalem and Old Palestinian [Neofiti] Targums to Deut 30:13 [cf. Rom 10:7]; *m. Ta'an.* 2:4; *b. Sanh.* 89ab; *TDNT* 3. 407-10; Str-B 1. 644-47). Cf. the immediate references to the resurrection of the queen of the South and the Ninevites in Luke's text as well as in Matthew's. The explicitness of Matthew's references to Jesus' death and resurrection contributes to the overarching theme of persecution in chaps. 10–12. Cf. the adding of "the prophet" to Jonah's name (v 39) along with the fate of the prophets who will die at the hands of the Jewish leaders (23:29-37).

Jesus stayed in the realm of the dead parts of three twenty-four-hour periods, not three whole days and nights. But the reference to three days and three nights comes out of Jonah 2:1 rather than from the story of Jesus and causes no problem in view of the Jewish method of reckoning part of a twenty-four-hour day for the whole (see Gen 42:17-18; 1 Sam 30:1, 12-13; 2 Chr 10:5, 12; Esth 4:16–5:1; and rabbinic references in *TDNT* 2. 949-50). Here is the only reference to his death and resurrection that Jesus made in the hearing of Jewish leaders. The chief priests and Pharisees will allude to it in recalling that he said he would rise "after three days" (27:63, unique to this gospel). We see, then, another reason for the present insertion: it lays the groundwork for Matthew's exposing the inexcusability of their unbelief (see the comments on 27:62-66). It is only in 27:63 that he departs from the usual "on the third day" (so 16:21; 17:23; 20:19 in contrast with "after three days" in Mark 8:31; 9:31; 10:34). Why the μετά here, but the temporal dative (so also Luke 9:22; 18:33) where Mark has μετά? The reason is that Matthew's Jesus spoke to the Jewish leaders about staying in the realm of the dead three days and three nights. But Jesus rose on the third day. Though the peculiarity of the Jews' method of reckoning time eliminates a necessary contradiction, Matthew suits the two different ways of phrasing the matter to the audience of Pharisees on the one hand (27:63 with 12:40) and to the historical event on the other hand (16:21; 17:23; 20:19).

The veiled way Jesus alludes to his death and resurrection in Luke and the great uncertainty over the nature and extent of Q undercut the argument that the lack of a theology of the cross elsewhere in Q forestalls a reference to Jesus' death and resurrection here. Matthew's adding an applicatory clause at the end of v 45, apparently to parallel the same kind of clause in v 40b, militates against our omitting v 40 on the slender ground of its omission in Justin Martyr *Dial.* 107.1-2. Notably, Justin's foregoing and preceding uses of the phrase "on the third day" may imply that he is avoiding a felt chronological difficulty in v 40; and his immediate reference to Jesus' resurrection may imply a knowledge of v 40 and reveal his interpretation of it. Verse 40 does not make Jonah's preaching superfluous, but complements it. The breaking of the continuity between vv 39 and 41 does not argue against the originality of v 40 in the Gospel of Matthew, for he habitually interpolates material from the OT. See further Gundry, *Use of the OT* 136-37.

That Matthew knew of Jewish failure to respond in faith to the sign of Jonah does not necessitate that he regards the sign as including the parousia of the Son of man (24:30), but only that the guilt of the Jewish leaders is all the greater. Neither does the sign of Jonah have anything to do with preaching to Gentiles, for Jesus did not preach to Gentiles; nor with Jewish rejection of Jesus' message, for we read nothing about a Jewish rejection of any message from Jonah; nor with Jonah's coming from a distant land as the Son of man will come from heaven, for Jonah came to preach but the Son of man will come to gather the elect and judge the wicked. Personages may appear as signs apart from the supernatural (see, e.g., Isa 8:18; 20:3; Ezek 12:6); but, as noted above, the future tense of Luke's "will be" resists all identifications of the sign of Jonah with the person or proclamation of Jesus.

It is doubtful that Matthew stresses the length of time "three days and three nights" as distinct from the bare facts of death and resurrection; for otherwise he would probably have followed Mark's "after three days" in 16:21; 17:23; 20:19 (so Mark 8:31; 9:31; 10:34). Instead, he writes "on the third day" in apparent disagreement with 12:40. It is also doubtful that "three days" refers to an indefinitely short period of time; for מְעַט and the plural of אֶחָד (Aramaic חַד) presumably offered ways of saying "a few" instead of "three" (see, e.g., Gen 27:44; 29:20; 47:9; Job 10:20; Ps 109:8; Dan 11:20) and the passages usually listed for "three days" as an imprecise expression do not require imprecision of meaning (Josh 1:11; 2:16, 22; 1 Sam 30:12; 2 Sam 24:13; 2 Kgs 20:5, 8; 1 Chr 21:12; 2 Chr 20:25; Hos 6:2; Jonah 2:1[1:17]; 3:3).

12:41-42 (Luke 11:31-32) In Luke we next read comparisons between "this generation" and the Ninevites and queen of the South (i.e., the queen of Sheba from southern Arabia; see 1 Kgs 10:1-13). These comparisons are damaging to "this generation" and warn of its condemnation at the judgment. Matthew reverses their order; he wants to have the Ninevites

245

alongside Jonah, who was a sign to them. The greater than Jonah and Solomon is Jesus. The neuter gender of πλεῖον, "greater," does not refer to the kingdom, which is absent from the context and feminine in gender. Rather, it emphasizes quality as distinct from personal identity (cf. v 6). Luke's τῶν ἀνδρῶν does not appear in Matthew's comparison with the queen of the South. Either he drops it for a parallel with the comparison involving the Ninevites, where the expression is lacking; or Luke adds it (the noun occurs twenty-seven times in Luke, but only eight times in Matthew and four times in Mark). The difference between Matthew's "it" (i.e., "this generation") and Luke's "them" (i.e., "the men of this generation") rests on the preceding difference. Otherwise Matthew and Luke agree in wording. The emphases on Jesus' superiority and the condemnation of his persecutors at the judgment suit Matthew's purposes well.

See Black, *Aramaic Approach* 134, on the possibility that "will stand up with" reflects a Semitic forensic idiom meaning "dispute with, accuse." This possibility suffers considerable doubt, however, for the parallel expression "will rise up with" surely refers to the resurrection, especially with the temporal phrase "at the judgment," which occurs also with the expression under discussion. For "the wisdom of Solomon," see 1 Kgs 10:4, 6, 8; Josephus *Ant.* 8.6.5 §§165-73.

12:43-44 (Luke 11:24-25) For the material about the returning unclean spirit, Matthew steps backward in his source. There, the material follows a section in which Jewish exorcists are mentioned; and it illustrates their failure, indeed, their making matters worse (see Luke 11:24-26 with 14-23). Matthew's transposition makes the material a judgment against "this evil generation" (see esp. v 45d), which is made up of the scribes and Pharisees who requested a sign (vv 38-42). The unclean spirit ceases to be a demon indwelling a man and becomes, instead, a figure of the evil that characterizes the generation of scribes and Pharisees. Correspondingly, the period of the unclean spirit's absence ceases to be a period of temporary relief for a demoniac and becomes a figure of the apparent righteousness of the scribes and Pharisees; and the return of the unclean spirit with seven others worse than himself ceases to be repossession of a demoniac and comes to represent an outburst of multiplied evil on the part of the scribes and Pharisees, an outburst that will falsify their righteousness (cf. their engineering Jesus' crucifixion and—in Matthew—their bribing the Roman guards in order to suppress the truth of his resurrection; cf. also their evident persecution of the church in Matthew's day and see 26:57; 27:41, 62).

The changed use of this material leads to an adversative δέ (not in Luke), which contrasts the evil generation, represented by the demoniac, with the Ninevites and queen of the South. Those Gentiles prove better than the scribes and Pharisees! Matthew puts the unclean spirit's failure to find rest in the desert (literally "waterless places") in a finite verbal construction ("he does not find") rather than in a participle ("not finding," so Luke). The new construction allows a typical insertion of τότε (66,17) to parallel the τότε in v 45. The textual tradition in Luke 11:24 that has τότε should be regarded as unoriginal because the position of the word makes it look like the awkward result of scribal insertion from Matthew.

In the second clause of v 44 Matthew puts ἐπιστρέψω, "I will return," last so that its position may correspond with that of ἐξῆλθον, "I came out," which stands over against it in the next clause (contrast Luke's word order). The shift results in a parallel that causes some weight to fall on the unclean spirit's return and, consequently, on an outbreak of obvious evil in the actions of the self-righteous scribes and Pharisees. Matthew's addition of σχολάζοντα (probably not in Luke's original text; see Metzger, *Textual Commentary* ad loc.) sharpens the attack on the scribes and Pharisees in that they appear as "empty" rather than full of righteousness. The swept and decorated condition of the house represents the mere appearance of righteousness.

"Goes out" (ἐξέλθη) means "is cast out" and reflects Semitic avoidance of the passive of the verb *to cast out*. On demons' habitation of unpopulated places, see Isa 13:21; 34:14; Tob 8:3; Bar 4:35; Mark 5:10; Rev 18:2. The period of the unclean spirit's absence from the man hardly represents a period of purification by virtue of Jesus' ministry, for in Matthew the addressed scribes and Pharisees had not accepted that ministry and in Luke Jesus' words refer to the effect of *Jewish* exorcisms. We might take ἐλθόν, "coming," as a Semitic idiom for the protasis of a conditional sentence ("if it comes"); but we would read too much into the expression to think that Jesus was especially concerned to avoid implying the inevitability of a relapse, for we read no hints that he is warning against a half-hearted repentance that fails to bring in a new master. Luke's ὑποστρέψω occurs not at all in Matthew or Mark, but twenty-one times in Luke. Matthew's synonymous ἐπιστρέψω occurs four times each in Matthew and Mark, seven times in Luke.

12:45 (Luke 11:26) In v 45 Matthew adds "with himself" to "takes along" in order to tie this material more closely to its larger context, where μετά has occurred in vv 3, 4, 30 (bis), 41, 42. The addition produces a kind of parallel with the immediately following "seven other spirits more evil than himself." In that following phrase the advance of ἑπτά from last position produces a smoother order of words than Luke's and causes the emphasis to shift from the number "seven" to the greater wickedness of the spirits. The latter emphasis agrees with Matthew's repeated intensification of the scribes' and Pharisees' guilt. Seven, the number of totality, stresses the superiority of demonic power over Jewish exorcisms in Luke, the overwhelmingness of scribal and Pharisaical evil in Matthew. Cf. 27:64; Sir 41:3; John 5:14; 2 Pet 2:20.

After the statements concerning the return of the unclean spirit and his seven fellows and the consequently worsened condition of the possessed man, Matthew adds οὕτως ἔσται καὶ τῇ γενεᾷ ταύτῃ τῇ πονηρᾷ as a parallel to the clause beginning οὕτως ἔσται in the sayings on the sign of Jonah (see v 40). οὕτως is a Mattheanism (18,5). Just as Matthew draws οὕτως ἔσται from v 40, he draws τῇ γενεᾷ ταύτῃ τῇ πονηρᾷ from the preceding context (see esp. vv 39b, 41a, 42a). The incorporation of "evil" with "this generation" brings the "worse" spirits into association with the generation of the scribes and Pharisees who sought a sign.

THE PERSECUTED AS THE FAMILY
OF THE HEAVENLY FATHER
12:46-50 (Mark 3:31-35; Luke 8:19-21)

In this section Matthew goes back to Markan material that follows the sayings on blasphemy of the Spirit and precedes, as here, the parable of the sower. Luke's parallel appears in a context quite different from both Matthew's and Mark's contexts. This material takes the place of Luke's similar material concerning the blessedness of those who hear and observe the word of God (Luke 11:27-28, omitted by Matthew). By choosing this rather than that and by introducing it now rather than earlier (i.e., closely after the sayings about blasphemy of the Spirit [vv 31-32], as in Mark), Matthew enables himself to finish chaps. 11–12 with a contrast between Jesus' true relatives and those who persecute Jesus and his disciples. In addition, Matthew can now move into his next major section, chap. 13, without breaking stride. He will simply continue with Mark.

12:46 (Mark 3:31-32; Luke 8:19-20) The genitive absolute construction behind "While he was still speaking to the crowds" characterizes Matthew's style. "While he was yet speaking" comes from Mark 5:35 (cf. Luke 8:49) and compensates for Matthew's omitting these words (and much else, too) between 9:22 and 23. The crowds come from Mark 3:32. But there a crowd sits around Jesus and speaks to him; here Jesus is speaking to the crowds. His topic is the evil generation of scribes and Pharisees (vv 38-45). As often, Matthew puts the crowds in the plural (despite their being inside a house!). The reason is probably that they represent the many from all nations who will become disciples (28:19). This entire genitive absolute will reappear as an insertion in 17:5 (see also 26:47; Mark 14:43; Luke 22:47).

Jesus' mother and brothers stand outside (i.e., outside the house; see 13:1). Typically, Matthew inserts ἰδού (34,9). This parallels the ἰδού with which someone announces their presence to Jesus (v 47; Mark 3:32) and the distinctive ἰδού with which Jesus identifies his true relatives (v 49). Matthew conforms vv 46 and 47 to each other in further respects, too. In v 46 he omits Mark's "comes," turns Mark's participle "standing" into the finite verb "stood" (εἰστήκεισαν; see 13:2 for another distinctive pluperfect of this verb), substitutes "seeking" for Mark's "they sent to him" in order to gain a parallel with "seeking" in v 47, and replaces Mark's "calling him" with "to speak to him" for correspondence with "speaking to the crowds" in his immediately preceding genitive absolute. Mark's "And a crowd was sitting around him" drops out because Matthew has already referred to crowds in the genitive absolute and inserted "around him" in 8:18 (cf. the comments ad loc.). We now see that advancing the crowds not only provided Matthew with a transition; it also enabled him to juxtapose Jesus' mother and brothers alongside them.

The reference in 1:25 to Joseph's not having sexual intercourse with Mary till Mary had given birth to Jesus makes it natural to think of Jesus' brothers as younger half-brothers. For a lengthy discussion of various possibilities, see J. B. Lightfoot, *The Epistle of St. Paul to the Galatians* (reprinted, Grand Rapids: Zondervan, 1957) 252-91.

12:47 (Mark 3:32; Luke 8:20) At the beginning of v 47 Matthew replaces Mark's καί with δέ (so also Luke) in order to set the announcement of the one who speaks to Jesus over against Jesus' speaking to the crowds (v 46). In other words, he portrays the unnamed herald of Jesus' mother and brothers as interrupting the Lord's discourse. This herald receives the mere designation "someone," where Mark writes "they say" and Luke, "it was announced." The reason for this change will soon become apparent. The shift from Mark's "say" to "said" is due to Matthew's reserving the historical present to words (usually those of Jesus) that bear closely on the church at the time of writing. In the announcement of the presence of Jesus' mother and brothers Matthew inserts ἑστήκασιν for correspondence with εἱστήκεισαν in v 46. That Luke also has ἑστήκασιν even though he lacks Matthew's parallelistic reason for its insertion (this is Luke's first and only reference to standing) suggests Matthean influence. Again for parallelism Matthew changes "they are seeking you" to "seeking to speak to you" in conformity with v 46 ("seeking to speak to him").

On the omission of v 47 in part of the textual tradition, see Metzger, *Textual Commentary* ad loc. The omission is a result of homoeoteleuton. The hypothesis of later insertion from Mark into Matthew does not take account of the typically Matthean revisions that characterize the verse as it appears in Matthew.

12:48 (Mark 3:33; Luke 8:21) The opening of v 48, ὁ δὲ ἀποκριθεὶς εἶπεν, echoes v 39 (where Mark and Luke differ) and here has an exact parallel in Luke and a partial parallel in Mark. Matthew is fond of the two verbal forms in combination (29,6). Again Mark's "he says" becomes an aorist (as in v 47; see also v 49). And because of the previous change from Mark's "they" to "someone," "to them" becomes "to the one telling him." In Matthew, then, Jesus does not address his words concerning those who do the will of God—i.e., his disciples—to the crowd, but to the individual who has just announced the presence of Jesus' mother and brothers outside. This change derives from Matthew's equating the crowds with disciples: Jesus no longer speaks to the crowds *about* his disciples, but to the anonymous herald about the crowds *as* his disciples. This equation prompted Matthew's introduction of the anonymous herald in the first place. The wording of Jesus' question "Who is my mother, and who are my brothers?" follows that of Mark except for Matthew's filling out an ellipsis by inserting "who are" in the second clause to parallel "who is" in the first clause.

12:49 (Mark 3:34; Luke 8:21) Verse 49 opens with a participle + εἶπεν in parallel with the same construction in v 48. For his participial phrase Matthew writes "stretching out his hand toward his disciples" instead of Mark's "looking around at those sitting in a circle around him." This revision does not distinguish the disciples from the crowds mentioned in v 46. Rather, it characteristically identifies the crowds as disciples and stems from prior omission of the crowd's sitting around Jesus (see v 46 with Mark 3:32), from Matthew's liking the gesture of stretching out the hand (see 8:3; 12:13 [bis]; and, distinctively, 12:49; 14:31; 26:51), and from his fondness for μαθητής (31,5). Yet again Mark's "he says" becomes "he said," because Jesus' words are not addressed to disciples (see the comments on vv 47-48). Into the place of Mark's ἴδε goes the synonymous and more usual ἰδού (34,9) for a closer parallel with vv 46 and 47 (cf. vv 41, 42). See Rom 8:29; Col 1:18; Heb 2:11-12.

12:50 (Mark 3:35; Luke 8:21) In the explanatory identification of Jesus' true family Matthew adds τις to ὅς in order to emphasize the quality of obedience described in the following words (ὅστις—23,5). But doing "the will of God" (so Mark) becomes doing "the will of my Father in heaven." Matthew inserted this phrase in 7:21, and similar insertions occur in 6:10; 18:14; 21:31; 26:42. Each noun in the phrase belongs to his special vocabulary (θέλημα—3,1; πατρός—22,13; οὐρανοῖς—46,11), and God's fatherhood to Jesus and heavenly majesty typify Matthew's theology. The disciples' doing the will of the heavenly Father presupposes the teaching of that will by Jesus, who as the Son knows the Father (11:25-27). In the last clause Matthew replaces Mark's οὗτος, "this one," with αὐτός, "he himself" or "he and no other" (another Mattheanism—14,3). Finally, in its second occurrence μου advances to a position before ἀδελφός in order to give a Christological emphasis. So in the midst of persecution Jesus' disciples may comfort and encourage themselves that they belong to the family to which he belongs. And what family is that? Matthew's substitution of "my Father in heaven" for "God" has both given the answer and made the family complete.

FALSE DISCIPLES AS THOSE WHO LACK AND LOSE UNDERSTANDING; TRUE DISCIPLES AS THOSE WHO HAVE AND GAIN UNDERSTANDING

13:1-52

In 13:1-52 Matthew brings together seven parables for Jesus' third great discourse in the gospel. After the introductory gathering of many crowds (vv 1-2), the parable of the sower portrays the reason for Jesus' speaking in parables (vv 3-9). When the disciples from among the crowds approach Jesus with a question concerning that reason, Jesus' answer includes an explanation of the parable (vv 10-23; cf. 2 Esdr 9:26-37). As it turns out, Jesus speaks in parables because those who lack understanding—viz., false disciples—fall under the judgment of losing understanding through parabolic riddles and because those who have understanding—viz., true disciples—come into the blessedness of gaining further understanding through the insight granted by him (cf. 11:25-27; 16:17).

After the parable about parables and its interpretation, Matthew puts six more parables. In contrast with the parable of the sower, they all begin with a reference to the kingdom of heaven. The first deals with wheat and tares and emphasizes separation at the end (vv 24-30). The second and third constitute a pair dealing with a mustard tree (vv 31-32) and a huge lump of dough (v 33) and emphasizing largeness. At the close of the first three of the six there is a citation of fulfilled prophecy concerning Jesus' parabolic speech to the crowds (vv 34-35). At the beginning of the second three Jesus leaves the crowds, enters "the house," entertains the approach of his disciples, and explains to them the tares and wheat in order to portray true disciples as those who gain understanding because of their already having it (vv 36-43). Further understanding comes through a second pair of parables—those of the treasure (v 44) and pearl (vv 45-46)—both of which emphasize the necessity of selling all in order to enter the kingdom. The final parable deals with good and bad fish and makes an inclusio with the first of the six by reemphasizing separation at the end (vv 47-50). Matthew's breaking up the pair of parables concerning the wheat and tares and the good and bad fish in order to use them as a frame for the other two pairs causes the main stress to fall on the separation of true and false disciples at the last judgment (cf. 5:19-20; 7:13-27; 22:11-14).

This stress, in turn, explains the distinction between the crowds and the disciples: the crowds represent the whole mixed body of professing disciples, the false as well as the true—therefore the addressing of the parables of inclusion (the mustard tree and the huge lump of dough) to the crowds; the disciples who approach Jesus out of the crowds and receive further understanding because of prior understanding represent the true among the false (see esp. vv 2, 10-17, 24, 31, 33, 34, 36)—therefore the addressing of the parables of wholeheartedness (the treasure and the pearl) to the true disciples. The concluding picture of a disciple as a scribe who speaks what he has recently learned ("new things") as well as what he had already understood ("old things," vv 51-52) underscores the difference between the true and the false among the crowds who follow Jesus: the true had understanding prior to the parables and gain more of it through the parables, the false lacked it prior to the parables and lose it in the parables.

Old Understanding as a Human Responsibility
13:1-23

13:1-2 (Mark 4:1; Luke 8:4) Matthew continues in his source and takes the parable of the sower from Mark 4:1-20 (cf. Luke 8:4-15). "In that day" replaces Mark's "and again." Because of the omission of Mark 2:13 in 9:9-13, Jesus has not previously taught beside the sea in Matthew. Consequently, Mark's phrase is no longer appropriate. "In that day" will occur as an insertion again in 22:23 and has an OT ring concerning historic time (cf. the comments on 3:1). Typically, Matthew inserts Jesus' name for a Christological emphasis (80,12). Instead of reading that Jesus "began to teach beside the sea" (so Mark), we read that "going out of the house, Jesus was sitting beside the sea." "Going out" comes from Mark 2:13 and makes up for Matthew's omitting that verse in 9:9-13 (cf. Mark 2:13-17 and see the comments on 9:9). More importantly, it makes Jesus' action parallel to that of the sower ("behold, a sower went out") and helps identify Jesus with the sower (cf. v 3). The going out relates to Jesus' house in Capernaum (see the comments on 4:13; 9:10). Characteristically, Matthew alone contains a reference to the house (5,3). The insertion explains the prior standing "outside" on the part of Jesus' mother and brothers (12:46). "Was sitting" takes the place of Mark's reference to teaching because as yet no audience has appeared. Nevertheless, sitting—the posture of a teacher—connotes didactic authority (see the comments on 5:1). And doubling the reference to sitting by insertion here and retention in the next verse emphasizes that Jesus has such authority.

"Many crowds" gather to Jesus. Matthew along with Luke rejects Mark's superlative πλεῖστος, "very large." But not as in Luke, "crowd" becomes "crowds" for a preview of the masses who later came into the church as professing disciples. Matthew also changes Mark's "gathers" to "gathered," omits "in the sea" and "[facing] toward the sea," and substitutes "on the beach" (cf. v 48) for "on the land." "Stood" replaces Mark's "were" for an antithetic parallel with Jesus' sitting. The antithetic parallel further emphasizes his didactic authority. The same emphasis is served by omitting "in the sea": now καθῆσθαι stands at the end of the line in antithetic parallelism with εἱστήκει at the end of the next line. And the deletion of "toward the sea" in the next line stems from and parallels the deletion of "in the sea."

13:3 (Mark 4:2-3; Luke 8:4-5) Matthew has accentuated Jesus' didactic authority enough; so he replaces Mark's "he was teaching" with "he spoke" (cf. Luke's "he said"). Though Matthew's ἐλάλησεν may echo 12:46 (bis), 47, and especially 34-35 for a contrast between Jesus' speaking good things and the Pharisees' speaking bad things, probably Matthew has in mind 3 Kgdms 5:12 LXX: καὶ ἐλάλησεν Σαλωμὼν τρισχιλίας παραβολάς (cf. Sir 47:15-17). Such an allusion would follow his habit of conforming phraseology to the OT and explain the advance of πολλά from its last position in Mark's clause to a position closer to the verb and ahead of ἐν παραβολαῖς: in Mark πολλά means "much" as an adverbial accusative modifying ἐδίδασκεν, but in Matthew it corresponds roughly to the number 3,000 in the OT text and means "many things" as a direct object of ἐλάλησεν. Cf. the portrayal of Jesus as the "greater than Solomon" in 12:42. Matthew has studiously avoided the term "parable" till now. It relates to the Hebrew מָשָׁל and the Aramaic מְתַל, מַתְלָא, which carry a wide variety of meanings, such as "proverb, riddle, parable, fable, allegory." In Greek literature uninfluenced by the Semitic words, παραβολή means "comparison."

Matthew now replaces Mark's "and he was saying to them in his teaching" with a favorite participle of his, λέγων (61,23); and he omits the command "Listen." As a result, all the stress falls on the sower's going out to sow, a statement introduced, as in Mark, with Matthew's beloved ἰδού. Thus in Matthew we do not read, "You—listen," but only, "Behold, the sower went out. . . ." After the distinctive reference to Jesus' "going out" (v 1) we can hardly miss Matthew's identification of the sower with Jesus, an identification confirmed especially in the interpretation of the parable of the wheat and tares: "the one who sows the good seed is the Son of man" (v 37, unique to Matthew). Luke's making the same omissions Matthew makes but lacking ἰδού and an identification of Jesus with the sower suggests Matthean influence.

13:4 (Mark 4:4; Luke 8:5) Further slight indications of Matthew's identifying the sower with Jesus occur in v 4. Riddance of Mark's Semitism ἐγένετο makes the parable move quickly to the sower's sowing. And insertion of αὐτόν, "he," calls attention to the sower rather than allow the stress to fall entirely on the sowing, as in Mark. Luke also omits ἐγένετο and adds αὐτόν, but probably because of Matthean influence, since the insertion of "his seed" in the preceding line shows that Luke's real interest lies in the seed, not in the sower. Mark refers to the seed (without using the noun) in the singular till he comes to the seed that falls on good soil. This inconsistency looks original. Luke holds to the singular throughout. And in parallelistic fashion Matthew anticipates the final plural by writing plurals from the very start. His turning Mark's "came" into "coming" also contributes to parallelism in that now both clauses of v 4 have but one main verb apiece, each preceded by a verbal phrase.

Some think that παρὰ τὴν ὁδόν represents the ambiguous Aramaic עַל אוֹרְחָא, taken wrongly as meaning "beside the path" whereas the context requires its other meaning, "on the path," as shown by Luke's κατεπατήθη, "it was trampled down." But the Greek phrase may mean "on the edge of the path," as it appears to mean in Matt 20:30; Mark 10:46; Luke 18:35. That Luke adds κατεπατήθη without changing παρά supports this meaning. The unlikelihood that in the later passages Bartimaeus was sitting clear off the road also supports it. If then we take the meaning "on the edge of the path," the argument whether the sower sowed on the path with the intention of plowing in the seed afterward, or whether Jesus unrealistically and therefore emphatically makes the sower sow on the unplowed path after plowing, loses its point. For in the sowing near the path some seed accidentally fell on the edge of the path. Hence, we cannot tell whether plowing had preceded or was to follow. For the pros and cons of the argument, see J. Drury in *JTS* ns 24 (1973) 367-71. See Isa 28:24-25; Jer 4:3; Hos 10:11-12 for plowing before sowing, but *Jub* 11:11 for birds' devouring seed before it is plowed in.

13:5-6 (Mark 4:5-6; Luke 8:6) To conform with the plurals concerning what was sown, Matthew describes the ground having rock just beneath the surface with a plural instead of a singular. For contrast with the falling of some seed on the edge of the path, he introduces the falling of others on thin soil with δέ rather than καί. And to contrast the coming up of the plants with the rising of the sun, δέ again replaces καί. By turning Mark's dependent clause, "when the sun rose," into a stylistically characteristic genitive absolute, Matthew again makes both lines of a couplet have but one finite verb apiece, each preceded by a verbal phrase (cf. v 4).

It is disputed whether thinness of soil leads to rapid growth because heat from the sun concentrates in the thin layer. Or perhaps nourishment concentrates in the upper part of the plants because the roots lack space to grow to normal size. Or dew saturates the thin layer of soil and causes rapid growth. It is even questioned whether thinness of soil leads to rapid growth at all. Either the sower does not know that rock lies immediately below the surface of certain parts of his field, or some seed falls accidentally on those parts.

13:7 (Mark 4:7; Luke 8:7) The δέ that introduces the falling of other seeds on thorns once more differs from Mark's and Luke's καί and makes a contrast with the foregoing. "On" takes the place of Mark's "into" for a parallel with "on the rocky places" (v 5). Matthew repeats these revisions in his introduction of the other seeds that fell on good soil. Before that introduction, however, he drops "and it did not give fruit" (Mark 4:7c) in order to gain a parallel with the statements concerning what fell on the edge of the path and on rocky places. Neither of those statements has such a clause. That Luke shares this omission even though he does not usually show Matthew's concern for parallelism suggests influence from Matthew.

Cf. Jer 4:3. We cannot tell whether some seeds fall where the sower cannot detect seeds of thorns, whether some seeds accidentally fall among dried up thorns from the previous year, or whether the sower deliberately sows among such thorns with the intention of later plowing (but would he not know that seeds of old thorns produce new thorns to choke out the grain?).

13:8 (Mark 4:8; Luke 8:8) Concerning what fell on good soil, Matthew includes, as he must, the positive statement "and it was giving fruit." But he subtracts Mark's immediately following words, "coming up and growing, and it was bearing." The subtraction causes the emphasis to fall solely on the giving of fruit, a prominent metaphor in Matthew for works— here good works, obviously. And though Mark's numbers—thirtyfold, sixtyfold, a hundredfold—build up to a climax, Matthew reverses their order so as to put "a hundredfold" first as the best example. The hundredfold contrasts with the less desirable yields of sixtyfold and thirtyfold, each introduced with an adversative δέ in place of Mark's καί. The adversative highlights the decrease in desirability. Cf. Luke's retention of the hundredfold alone.

Matthew's ὅ μέν . . . ὅ δέ . . . ὅ δέ (see also v 23) is more literary than Mark's ἕν . . . καὶ ἕν . . . καὶ ἕν. See Gen 26:12; *Sib. Or.* 3:63-64 for a hundredfold yield, to be considered excellent but not fantastic. See further W. Corswant, "Agriculture," *Dictionary of Life in Bible Times* (New York: Oxford, 1960) 25; E. Linnemann, *Parables of Jesus* (London: SPCK, 1966) 115-17. In view of 28:18-20, it is doubtful that Matthew reverses Mark's order of yields to imply that the initial successes of Christian evangelism have tailed down.

13:9 (Mark 4:9; Luke 8:8) In v 9 Mark's "and he was saying" drops out as interruptive. For a third time Matthew reduces a finite verb, here in Mark's "he who has ears to hear," to something less, here the substantive participle "the one having ears" (cf. Luke). With omission of the redundant "to hear" the line has one finite verb, "let him hear," preceded by a lesser kind of verbal expression (cf. the comments on vv 4 and 6).

13:10 (Mark 4:10; Luke 8:9) In v 10 the disciples' "approaching" Jesus substitutes for his getting to be alone (cf. Mark). προσελθόντες is a Mattheanism (38,6) and implies Jesus' dignity (see the comments on 4:3; 8:14). In place of Mark's reference to "the ones around him along with the twelve," Matthew writes about "the disciples" for a characteristic emphasis on discipleship (μαθητής—31,5; cf. Luke). Since he regularly portrays the crowds as disciples, this substitute distinguishes between disciples in deed, who give fruit by virtue of understanding, and the rest, whose failure to give fruit falsifies their profession. Furthermore, according to Matthew these true disciples were not "asking" Jesus for the *meaning* of the parables (so Mark and Luke). Rather, they "spoke" to Jesus for the *reason* behind his talking in parables to the *others* ("Why do you talk in parables to them?"). Thus Matthew begins to portray true disciples as those who have and gain understanding, in contrast with false disciples, who lack and lose it. Except for διὰ τί, the substituted words all come from v 3. The plural "parables" rests on the plural in v 3 (so also Mark) and in the evangelists' arrangement of materials. Historically, the plural implies that the disciples have in mind other parables told by Jesus and that their question and Jesus' answer, though spoken later, have been advanced in order to make the parable of the sower a key to understanding the purpose of the following parables. This agrees with the implication of the disciples' approach: Jesus is no longer in the boat—yet he continues to teach the crowds, seemingly from the boat, and does not leave them till v 36.

13:11 (Mark 4:11; Luke 8:10) Mark's καί yields to δέ, which sets Jesus' response opposite the disciples' question (so also Luke). "He was saying" becomes the characteristically Matthean ἀποκριθεὶς εἶπεν (29,6). Since Matthew usually deletes the recitative ὅτι, we should translate the added ὅτι "because." Thus the foregoing question "Why . . . ?" (so Matthew alone) is answered in Jesus' words "Because to you has been given to know the mysteries of the kingdom of heaven." Matthew inserts "to know" in order to make the difference between true and false disciples a matter of understanding. γνῶναι is a favorite of his (8,2). Luke, too, has added it. Yet elsewhere in the passage he shows no concern to emphasize the necessity of understanding. This phenomenon suggests influence from Matthew. Similarly, Luke shares Matthew's "mysteries." Mark has the singular, which refers to God's rule itself, veiled in its coming but revealed to disciples. The plural refers to the parables as containing information about that rule.

In the second line of the saying Matthew deletes "the ones outside" (so Mark) from "to those," not only because the parallel "to you" lacks a corresponding "the ones inside," but also because he is not contrasting disciples as insiders and nondisciples as outsiders (cf. 12:46-50). Rather, he is contrasting true disciples with false disciples. For a parallel with the first line, "it has not been given" replaces "all things take place in parables." Thus, where Mark contrasts the gift of God's rule as a mystery and parabolic speech, Matthew identifies the parables and the mysteries of the heavenly rule. Matthew's contrast comes in the distinction between understanding and failing to understand those parabolic mysteries.

See R. E. Brown, *The Semitic Background of the Term "Mystery" in the New Testament* (Philadelphia: Fortress, 1968), on ancient Jewish literature where "mystery" means the secret plan of God revealed to his people.

13:12 (Mark 4:25; Luke 8:18; 19:26) Matthew now reaches forward in Mark's text for a saying related there to a warning to heed Jesus' teaching (Mark 4:25; cf. Luke 8:18b). He will use the saying again for eternal reward and loss at the last judgment (25:29; cf. Luke 19:26). Here the saying provides a reason for God's giving true disciples knowledge of the mysteries, or parables, and his refusal to give such knowledge to false disciples. The former already have knowledge; therefore Jesus rewards them with more knowledge in the parables. The latter do not have knowledge; therefore Jesus takes away their seeming knowledge (as professing disciples) by confusing them with parables. In both occurrences of ὅς Matthew characteristically adds τις to emphasize the qualities of having and not having knowledge (23,5). For emphasis on the furtherance of true disciples' knowledge he adds "and he will have an abundance." Cf. insertions of περισσεύω also in 5:20; 25:29. The addition was probably suggested by the preceding clause in Mark 4:24: "and it will be added to you." For sharper contrast between the have's and the have not's Matthew exchanges καί for δέ.

The saying in v 12 rests on the economic truism that the rich increase in wealth by investing their capital while the poor sink into deeper proverty because they lack capital to invest. Cf. Prov 1:5; 9:9; Str-B 1. 660-61.

13:13 (Mark 4:12; Luke 8:10) As the statements in vv 11-12 make clear, Jesus does not tell parables because people have not been able to understand and the parables will help them, but because people have refused to understand and the parables will obscure the truth judgmentally. Mark's parallel to v 13 continues a sentence begun in his parallel to v 11. The insertion in v 12 about having and not having breaks up that sentence. Hence, Matthew composes v 13a to provide a new independent clause on which the dependent clause concerning seeing and not seeing, hearing and not hearing, may rest: "On account of this I speak to them in parables." The new clause echoes v 10b, "On account of what do you speak to them in parables?" which itself was a Matthean construct drawn in its essentials from v 3a. διὰ τοῦτο typifies Matthew's diction (4,2) and probably refers forward to make the seeing and not seeing, hearing and not hearing, a reason for Jesus' parabolic speech so far as false disciples are concerned, just as the saying in v 12 emphasized the reason for Jesus' parabolic speech so far as true disciples are concerned. Though false disciples enter the picture in vv 11-12, the ellipsis in v 11c and the addition "and he will have an abundance" in v 12 focus attention on true disciples. In vv 13-15 attention shifts to false disciples.

Mark's "in order that" makes the seeing yet not perceiving, hearing yet not understanding, the divine, judgmental *purpose* behind Jesus' speaking to nondisciples in parables. Matthew's switch to "because" makes the seeing and not seeing, hearing and not hearing, Jesus' *reason* for speaking to false disciples in parables. The one is a goal to be attained, the other a fact to be considered. Thus Matthew emphasizes the responsibility and culpability of false disciples. The references to seeing and hearing come from Isa 6:9-10, but in reverse order. Mark's "and not perceive" drops out. Matthew will include it in a formal quotation of Isa 6:9-10 (vv 14-15). But here its omission leads to the moving of "not" to "see." The result is an intensification of guilt: in Mark nondisciples do not *perceive* what they see, in Matthew false disciples do not even *see* what they see! For parallelism

256

Matthew inserts "not" also with "hear." Thus again, in Mark nondisciples do not *understand* what they hear, in Matthew false disciples do not even *hear* what they hear! But Matthew's interest in understanding does not allow him to omit Mark's mention of failure to understand; therefore he brings it over as a negative expression: "neither understand." Luke's agreement with Matthew in dropping the failure to perceive suggests Matthean influence, since Luke does not compensate for the loss with a later, full quotation of Isa 6:9-10. Matthew reserves Mark's clause concerning God's determination that nondisciples should not convert and receive forgiveness for his formal quotation, where it serves to express the determination of the false disciples themselves not to convert (v 15d).

13:14-15 The introduction to the formal quotation differs radically from the introductory formulas of fulfillment elsewhere in Matthew (see passages listed in the comments on 1:22-23). Matthew puts the formula and the quotation in Jesus' mouth instead of presenting them as his own. The divine purpose is usually expressed in a statement that such and such happened "in order that" a prophetic word "might be fulfilled" (ἵνα + the subjunctive πληρωθῇ). Here we read "is completely fulfilled" (ἀναπληροῦται, the indicative), which implies human responsibility. The insertion "by them" emphasizes that responsibility, and the prefixing of the perfective ἀνα-, "completely," intensifies the guilt. The usual "what was spoken [by the Lord] through [Isaiah] the prophet" changes to "the prophecy of Isaiah" to avoid any thought of divine causation that might be mistaken as a lessening of human responsibility (cf. Josephus *Ant.* 5.6.2 §214). λέγουσα is a Mattheanism (61,23). The quotation itself agrees with the LXX even where the LXX disagrees with the Hebrew text of Isa 6:9-10. At least two of the agreements with the LXX suit Matthew's purpose to emphasize human responsibility rather than divine intent: (1) the future indicative of "you will hear" and "you will see" instead of the Hebrew imperatives "see" and "hear," and (2) the insertion of γάρ, which makes the people's obtuseness the reason for failure to understand and perceive. γάρ is another Mattheanism (62-63,15).

On the originality of this quotation in the text of Matthew, see Gundry, *Use of the OT* 116-18—also for a comparison with Acts 28:26-27 and consideration of other textual features. Possibly, Matthew takes ἀκοῇ as a "report" about Jesus (cf. 4:24).

13:16-17 (Luke 10:23-24) For a renewed and contrastive portrayal of true disciples as those who understand, Matthew now interpolates a pair of sayings that occur in Luke 10:23-24 right after the "Johannine thunderbolt" (cf. Matt 11:25-27). Since Jesus is already speaking to his disciples here (see v 10), the transitional "and turning to the disciples, he said privately" (so the tradition as represented by Luke) drops out. On the other hand, Matthew inserts both δέ and, in first position, ὑμῶν to emphasize the contrast between false disciples and true. His changing the description of the disciples' eyes as those "that see the things which you see" to a reason for the blessedness of their eyes ("because they see") antithetically parallels v 13b in its distinctively Matthean form ("because seeing they do not see") and again accentuates human responsibility. The deliberate changing of οἱ βλέποντες to ὅτι βλέπουσιν does away with the need to see different translations of the Aramaic ‎ל, though the ambiguity of the Aramaic may have provided a convenience for the change. To make the beatitude into a couplet of synonymously parallel lines, Matthew adds "and your ears, because they hear." The addition also continues the antithetic parallel with v 13, prepares for the distinctive command to hear the parable of the sower (v 18), and doubles the beatitude on true disciples.

In the introduction to the next saying, either Matthew adds ἀμήν or Luke omits it (see the comments on 5:18). Alongside the "many prophets" Matthew puts "righteous [men]" instead of Luke's "kings." Luke does not show favoritism toward his word, but words with the stem δικ- belong to Matthew's special diction (18-19,10-9). See the comments on 10:41-42 for the pairing of prophets and righteous men in Matthew and for righteous men as teachers of righteousness, not just those who live righteously. Concerning their unsatisifed desire to see the things the disciples see and to hear the things the disciples hear, Matthew exchanges "they wanted" (ἠθέλησαν) for "they desired very much" (ἐπεθύμησαν), which in 5:28 has already occurred distinctively in conjunction with seeing. The greater strength of Matthew's verb enhances the actuality of the disciples' seeing and hearing. Matthew reserves ὑμεῖς (so Luke with βλέπετε) for the unique command to hear in the next verse. The omission results in a closer parallel with the following line, where the pronoun does not occur.

For expectation of the days of the Messiah by OT saints, see 1 Pet 1:10-12; *Pss. Sol.* 17:50; 18:7; and, on targumic texts, M. McNamara, *The New Testament and the Palestinian Targum to the Pentateuch* (AnBib 27; Rome: Pontifical Biblical Institute, 1966) 240-45.

13:18 (Mark 4:13; Luke 8:11) Matthew returns to Mark and drops "and he says to them" in order to avoid interrupting Jesus' sayings. That Luke shares the omission suggests Matthew's influence, since Luke does not make such omissions so often as Matthew does. Matthew now composes a command to hear the parable of the sower. ὑμεῖς makes up for omission of the pronoun in the preceding saying and adds force to the command. "Hear" comes from the foregoing context. The typically Matthean οὖν (35,11) helps turn Mark's question into an authoritative command based on the foregoing beatitude, as though to say, "Since you are so blessed to hear, hear!"

"Parable" and "sower" come from Mark, but only Matthew puts them together as a title, "The Parable of the Sower," and so puts the center of gravity in the sower, i.e., in Jesus. Now we see why Matthew consistently used the plural of seed: it represents the further parables told by Jesus (cf. the comments on v 4). Since he has already identified Jesus as the sower (vv 3-4) and will yet do so (see v 37) and since he omits Mark's statement about the sower's sowing the word (Mark 4:14), we should take the genitive in τὴν παραβολὴν τοῦ σπείραντος as subjective ("the parable told by Jesus the Sower") as well as referential ("the parable told concerning the sower").

All of this results in elimination of Jesus' question, "Do you not understand [οἴδατε] this parable—and how will you understand [γνώσεσθε] all the parables?" (so Mark). In other words, Matthew does not allow Jesus' true disciples to lack understanding. They need explanation, to be sure (cf. v 36); but it is a gift to those who have, in order that they may have more, rather than a gift to those who have not.

13:19 (Mark 4:14-15; Luke 8:11-12) Though Matthew has omitted Mark's statement that "the sower sows the word," the "word" does not disappear entirely. Rather, it becomes "the word of [i.e., concerning] the kingdom" in "when anyone hears the word of the kingdom and does not understand." The genitive absolute construction in the Greek text typifies Matthew's style and represents a conflation of Mark's two clauses, "where the word is sown" and "and whenever they hear." The addition of "the kingdom" arises out of Matthew's special interest in that motif; and by putting references to the kingdom at the beginning of each of the six subsequent parables, Matthew identifies "the word of the kingdom" with those parables. His emphasis on hearing the word of the kingdom (we do not read about sowing the word, only about hearing it) grows out of the immediately preceding command to hear. Of even greater consequence, Matthew inserts "anyone" and "does not understand." These insertions make lack of understanding the reason for Satan's snatching away the word of the kingdom that was sown in the heart (cf. vv 13c, 14b, 15d). Thus the responsibility rests on the hearer who fails to understand, not on Satan (as in Mark and Luke). παντός and συνιέντος are favorites of Matthew (63,25-26; 5,1). Throughout his explanation of the parable we read the singular for the one who hears the word. This difference from Mark and Luke probably stems from the singular in v 12.

Verse 19 continues with the statement "the Evil One comes and snatches away what was sown in his heart." Matthew omits Mark's "immediately" and puts his favorite ὁ πονηρός (10,4) in place of the Semitic ὁ σατανᾶς. The vivid ἁρπάζει replaces αἴρει, "takes away," and elsewhere, too, seems to fall within Matthew's preferred vocabulary (3,0), especially for persecution (see the comments on 7:15 and cf. 13:21). For the place of sowing, Matthew writes "in his heart" rather than "into them." Luke also refers to the heart, but uses "their" and "away from" because his omission of "what is sown" results in attachment of the prepositional phrase to "takes away." Matthew likes καρδία (5,2), which here echoes the quotation from Isaiah in v 15. That Luke shares the term with Matthew even though he did not formally quote Isaiah suggests Matthean influence.

For his last clause concerning the first kind of hearer, Matthew goes back to Mark 4:15a, delayed till now because of the emphatic first position of the danger of hearing the word about the kingdom and not understanding it. This last clause identifies such a hearer as "the one sown along the edge of the path." Matthew adds "sown." Since he has just distinguished between what is sown and the person in whose heart it is sown, the person was "sown" in the sense that he received seed as though he were soil (so also in vv 20, 22, 23). This unique turn of phrase makes the stress fall on the person and his responsibility to hear and understand (cf. v 23).

13:20-21 (Mark 4:16-17; Luke 8:13) Mark's καί introducing the next kind of hearer yields to an adversative δέ (so also Luke). Outside the changes already mentioned, Matthew revises the explanation of the rocky ground very little. He delays οὗτος, and the delay results in an initial nominative phrase immediately picked up by οὗτος and in an elimination of Mark's οἵ. Also, δέ in v 21a contrasts not having root in oneself with the joyful receiving of the word at first. In v 21b δέ contrasts the immediate falling into sin because of persecution with the temporary period of professed discipleship. Mark and Luke have different conjunctions.

13:22 (Mark 4:18-19; Luke 8:14) Matthew conforms the explanation of the thorny ground to the preceding explanation by starting again with "But the one sown" and continuing with "this one is he who hears the word" plus a clause beginning with "and." Such close parallelism entails rejecting Mark's "and others are," changing "the ones being sown" to "the one sown" (cf. v 20 with Mark 4:16a), and shifting from "these" to "this one" and from "the ones who have heard" to "he who hears." Apparently Matthew prefers the aorist for sowing because it takes only a single action to throw a seed on the ground, and the present tense for hearing because one hears the word in an extended or repeated way.

"The cares of the age" becomes "the care of the age" to match the singular number of the other "thorn," viz., "the deceitfulness [or 'pleasure'] of wealth." Despite its omission in B ℵ* D it, perhaps out of parallel influence from Mark, τούτου is probably to be accepted as Matthew's original addition to αἰῶνος in reminiscence of his inserting "this age" in 12:32. Matthew omits Mark's third batch of thorns ("and the desires for the remaining things, entering") because the preceding had only two characteristics ("tribulation or persecution") and he has used ἐπεθύμησαν (cognate to ἐπιθυμίαι, "desires") in a good sense in v 17. Though he omitted the unfruitfulness of the thorny soil in the parable (see v 7), it stays in the explanation. His failure to make theologically substantive changes in the interpretations of those sown on rocky and thorny ground shows that his primary interest lies in the distinction between understanding and not understanding (see vv 19 and 23), not in the four distinctions original to the interpretation.

13:23 (Mark 4:20; Luke 8:15) In the explanation of the good soil Matthew again writes "But the one sown" followed by "this is he who hears the word." To emphasize that true discipleship requires understanding, the phrase "and understanding [the word]" replaces Mark's "and they accept [the word]." συνίημι is a Mattheanism (5,1). Instead of finishing the explanation by means of a clause beginning with "and," as in the last two explanations and Mark's and Luke's parallels here, Matthew shifts to a relative clause beginning with "who." This enables him to insert δή, "indeed," for emphasis on fruit bearing. For further emphasis he characteristically adds καὶ ποιεῖ (19,19). The addition amounts to an interpretation of fruit bearing as doing good works, for ποιεῖ appears with fruit to represent works also in 3:8, 10; 7:17 (bis), 18 (bis), 19; 13:26; 21:43. Context determines whether the works are good or bad. On Matthew's putting the yield of a hundredfold first for emphasis and contrasting the less desirable yields of sixtyfold and thirtyfold, see the comments on v 8.

That a hundredfold yield was not fantastic (see the comments on v 8) undercuts the view that the primary stress falls on the final victory of God's rule. The mentioning of lesser yields and the quadrupling of the kinds of soil also undercut this view. On the other hand, the tripling of the yields militates against the view that the primary stress falls on initial frustrations of God's rule. Therefore, the explanation in vv 18-23 gives a true understanding of the parable: it is up to those who hear the message of the kingdom to let that word become fruitful. Thus the bearing of fruit represents discipleship, not the harvest of the last judgment. The coming of the kingdom in word prior to its coming with coercion disagreed with contemporary Jewish views, according to which the kingdom was going to ride roughshod over all resistance.

A number of expressions in the interpretation of the parable of the sower occur only here or only once elsewhere in Jesus' teaching, but occur elsewhere in the NT. J. Jeremias infers the inauthenticity of the interpretation, i.e., its invention in the early church rather than its derivation from Jesus himself (*Parables* 77-79). The singularity of the expressions in Jesus' teaching may derive, however, from the singularity of the parable itself and therefore carry little weight concerning the authenticity or inauthenticity of the interpretation. And the use of the same expressions by others in the NT may imply a dominical source as the reason for common use in the church just as easily as it may imply ecclesiastical invention. See further C. E. B. Cranfield, *The Gospel According to Saint Mark* (Cambridge Greek Testament Commentary; Cambridge: Cambridge University Press, 1959) ad loc.

On the question of allegory, see J. Drury in *JTS* ns 24 (1973) 374-79. It is possible that the path represents failure to hear by not loving God with the heart, the rocky soil failure to hear by not loving God with the soul (i.e., by not risking one's life for the word in times of persecution), and the thorny soil failure to hear by not loving God with might (i.e., with the sacrifice of one's material wealth)—all of this after the pattern of Deut 6:4-5 (see B. Gerhardsson in *NTS* 14 [1968] 165-93).

New Understanding as a Gift from Jesus
13:24-52

This section contains six parables about the kingdom of heaven.

The Future Judgment
of False Disciples in the Kingdom
13:24-30 (and 36-43)

Matthew skips the next segment of Mark's material (Mark 4:21-25), which he has already used (Matt 5:15; 7:2; 10:26-27; 13:12), and composes "the parable of the tares of the field" (vv 24-30) and its explanation (vv 36-43). He does so by conflating the otherwise omitted parable of the seed growing by itself (Mark 4:26-29) and the parable of the sower (vv 1-23; cf. "Conflation" in the Topical Index). Some reminiscence of John the Baptist's preaching (3:12) adds a final touch. Why this conflation rather than a simple adoption, with relatively minor changes, of the parable of the seed growing by itself? The reason is that the keystones of that parable, "by itself" and "how, he does not know," do not fit Matthew's stress on human responsibility and understanding (see the comments on vv 1-23). The conflation enables him to shift from the inexplicable power of God's rule to the mixture of true and false disciples in the kingdom of heaven. The delay in the separation of true and false till the last judgment makes a prohibition against rigorism in church discipline, particularly against private judgments (cf. 5:21-22; 7:1-5). The certainty of a separation at the end makes a warning against false profession and an encouragement to true discipleship.

Mark's parable of the seed growing by itself provides the following expressions for Matthew's conflation: οὕτως, ἡ βασιλεία τοῦ θεοῦ, ὡς, ἄνθρωπος, βάλῃ τὸν σπόρον ἐπὶ τῆς γῆς, καθεύδῃ, βλαστᾷ, καρποφορεῖ, χόρτον, ὁ καρπός, ἀποστέλλει, and ὁ θερισμός. Sometimes Matthew revises these expressions slightly. All except οὕτως, ὡς, and ἀποστέλλει appear in the parable proper (vv 24-30). The exceptions occur in the explanation (vv 36-43). The sowing of seed and the harvest occur in both. Most strikingly, Matthew retains the significance of what happens during sleep and the stress on waiting for divine action. But in Mark the farmer sleeps, in Matthew the farmer's "men." In Mark growth takes place during sleep; in Matthew, the sowing of tares. And in Mark the waiting has to do with the opportune time for God to bring about his kingdom, as opposed to bringing the kingdom by political revolution or religious observance; in Matthew the waiting has to do with the opportune time for Jesus to separate the true and the false in his already existing kingdom, as opposed to rigorism in church discipline.

The following expressions come from the parable of the sower: ἄλλην (here for the parable rather than the seeds as in vv 3, 5, 7, 8), καλόν (here for seed rather than soil), σπέρμα (verbal in the parable of the sower), καρπὸν ἐποίησεν (from ἐδίδου καρπόν and καρποφορεῖ in the parable of the sower), ὁ σπείρων/-ας, and τοῦ πονηροῦ. The activity of the Evil One (i.e., the Devil) reflects the same one's activity in the parable of the sower. Both the parable of the sower and Mark's parable of the seed growing by itself speak about sowing seed and yielding fruit.

As we might expect in a passage edited by Matthew to the point of composition, an abundance of parallelism appears. In the parable proper (vv 24-30) there are antithetic parallels between the "man" and "his enemy" (also called a "man"), between sowing and "sowing on top of," between good seed, or wheat, and tares, between the enemy's coming and going away, between the slaves' approaching and going away, between slaves and owner, or master, between immediate collection of the tares and letting both wheat and tares grow together, and between collecting and binding the tares for burning and gathering the wheat into the barn. A number of these antithetic parallels reappear in the explanation (vv 36-43). There, we also read a long series of parallel statements each beginning "and the" (vv 37-39). Verse 40 has a comparative couplet, "just as . . . so"; and vv 41, 42, and 43 have couplets each characterized by synthetic parallelism. Besides all this, the diction and allusion to the OT are characteristic of Matthew.

13:24 Both ἄλλην and παραβολήν belong among his favorites (14,4;

5,2). The preceding parable of the sower suggests "another parable." Though Matthew elsewhere rejects παρέθηκεν, "put before," he uses it here to draw a parallel between Jesus, who put parables before the crowds of disciples, and Moses, who put the words of the Lord before the people of Israel and their elders (Exod 19:7; 21:1; Deut 4:44; cf 1 Tim 1:18; 2 Tim 2:2). αὐτοῖς echoes vv 3, 10, and 13, in each of which Matthew inserts it as a reference to the crowds (see also vv 31, 33, 34; cf. vv 14, 24, 28 and, for true disciples from among the crowds, vv 11 and 52). The later statement that Jesus left the crowds (v 36) will imply that the present αὐτοῖς refers to them rather than to the true disciples addressed in vv 10-23 (see also v 34). λέγων is a Mattheanism (61,23).

In the parable itself, "the kingdom of heaven" stems from Matthew's theological interests. For ὡμοιώθη as a Mattheanism in rabbinic style, see the comments on 7:24-25. The verb points to the whole of the following parable, not just to the immediately following phrase; and its aorist tense calls attention to the mixture of true and false disciples as already having come about (see also 18:23; 22:2 in contrast with the futuristic references in 7:24, 26; 25:1). Matthew's fondness for ἄνθρωπος (35,17) partly accounts for "a man who sowed" instead of "the sower" (as in vv 3, 18). But here the addition of "a man" comes mainly from the parable of the seed growing by itself (see Mark 4:26: "like a man who throws seed on the ground") and prepares for identification of the "man" with the "Son of man," i.e., with Jesus (v 37). Indeed, that it is the "man" who sows, not his "slaves," contains a Christological emphasis concerning Jesus' establishing God's kingdom. The close association of sowing with the good soil in v 23 ("the one sown on the good soil") eases the transfer of "good" from the soil to the seed. "In his field" replaces "on the ground" (Mark 4:26). The picture of a field in the parable of the sower and Matthew's general liking of ἀγρός (3,10) have united to overcome his fondness for Mark's phrase.

13:25 Matthew constructs ἐν δὲ τῷ καθεύδειν τοὺς ἀνθρώπους after the pattern of the opening phrase in the parable of the sower: καὶ ἐν τῷ σπείρειν αὐτόν (v 4; see 27:12 for a similar construction, contrasting with Mark 15:3). But the element of sleep comes from Mark's parable of the seed growing by itself; and δέ replaces καί to set up a contrast between sowing good seed and sowing tares (a poisonous plant, also called "darnels"). Notably, Matthew makes the man's "men" sleep rather than the man himself. Though we might take the definite article as generic, so that the noun means men in general, it seems better to take the definite article as having the force of a weak possessive, "his"; for not only does the noun exhibit Matthew's liking of ἄνθρωπος once again (see v 24); it also represents his special use of ἄνθρωπος for Jesus' disciples, as in the insertions at 8:27 and 9:8, and in vv 44, 45, and 52 below. Thus the men of the man who sows stand for Jesus' disciples. And just as their sleeping allows tares to be sown among the wheat, so also the sleeping of Jesus' true disciples allows the kingdom of heaven to be corrupted with the influx of false disciples. For the one who sows the tares, Matthew uses ἐχθρός (2,3), which has already appeared in two of his constructs based on OT passages (5:43; 10:36). The prefix ἐπ- at the beginning of ἐπέσπειρεν indicates a later sowing of the tares in the midst of the wheat. Matthew draws the figure of "wheat" for true disciples from the preaching of John the Baptist (see 3:12). ἀπῆλθεν is a Mattheanism (14,11).

13:26 Both the sprouting of the grass (i.e., the grasslike young blades) and the producing of fruit (i.e., the development of ears of grain) come from Mark's parable of the seed growing by itself, except that instead of -φορεῖ Matthew uses ἐποίησεν with καρπόν, as he does in 3:8, 10; 7:17 (bis), 18 (bis), 19; 21:43 (cf. 12:33; 13:23). Perhaps he wants to vary the expression because of his using καρποφορεῖ in v 23. δέ in v 26 contrasts the unknownness of the enemy's sowing tares and the later appearance of the tares. Matthew uses his favorite τότε (66,17) to start the statement of their appearance. ἐφάνη also falls within the circle of his preferred words (5,8).

13:27 The appearance of some tares would not have surprised the slaves. Their surprise therefore implies a large number due to deliberate sowing. The slaves' approaching the landowner contrasts—thus δέ—with the enemy's coming and going away; for προσελθόντες, another of Matthew's preferred words (38,6), connotes respect and here looks forward to the identification of the landowner as Jesus the lordly Son of man (see v 37 and the comments on 4:3; 8:14). The shift from "the men" (v 25) to "the slaves" adds to the connotation of humble respect. Matthew likes δοῦλοι (8,7) and οἰκοδεσπότου (2,4). The latter helps identify the man as Jesus the Son of man; for in its only previous occurrence Matthew inserted it for Jesus (10:25). κύριε further identifies him as Jesus, stems from Matthew's fondness for that Christological title (34,15), and forms a counterpart to δοῦλοι. Concerning the good seed in the field, see the comments on v 24. Matthew inserts πόθεν in v 56 and 21:25. οὖν is a Mattheanism (35,11). Even in the parable proper, then, the evidence of diction is building up massively alongside parallelism, conflation, and allusion to the OT to support composition by Matthew.

13:28 For the fourth time in this passage Matthew uses δέ to set off the following (here, the answer of the landowner) from the preceding (the questions of the slaves). ἔφη is a favorite of his (11,4). He repeats ἐχθρός (2,3—see v 25) and adds ἄνθρωπος (35,17). The latter is not a Semitic indefinite ("*some* enemy"); rather, it makes ἐχθρός a qualifier ("hostile") instead of a substantive ("an enemy," as in v 25) and sets the "hostile man" in sharp antithesis to the "man who sowed good seed." In other words, it sets the Devil in opposition to Jesus the Son of man (vv 37, 39). The slaves' response is introduced by another δέ and contains three Mattheanisms: θέλεις (18,8); οὖν (35,11—here parallel to οὖν in the slaves' first speaking to the landowner); and ἀπελθόντες (14,11). As often, Matthew uses the historical present in λέγουσιν (47,11). It stresses the immediate collection of tares being suggested. This immediate collection represents the rigorous discipline advocated by some in the church of Matthew's day.

13:29-30 The master immediately rejects the suggestion—hence another adversative δέ, followed by another historical present in φησιν. Matthew constructs his parallelism carefully in that he uses λέγω first in the aorist and then in the present to introduce the slaves' words (vv 27a and 28c), and φημί first in the aorist and then in the present to introduce the

264

landowner's words (vv 28a and 29a). μήποτε is a Mattheanism (2,4), and ἐκριζώσητε occurs as part of an insertion in 15:13. Customarily, volunteer tares were weeded out when the formation of heads of wheat did away with the similarity of the younger wheat and tares (see Jeremias, *Parables* 225 n. 76). Here, deliberate sowing resulted in so many tares that their roots were intertwined with those of the wheat. Therefore the landowner tells his slaves, "Let both grow together till the harvest. And in the season of harvest I will say to the harvesters, 'Collect the tares first and bind them in bundles so as to burn them, but gather the wheat into my barn' " (v 30). Matthew likes ἄφετε (12,5), ἕως (13,14), καιρῷ (6,1), ἐρῶ (18,9), πρῶτον (3,1), and συναγάγετε (10,10); and he inserts ἀμφότερα in 9:17. The harvest comes from Mark's parable of the seed growing by itself. Burning as a figure of judgment typifies Matthew's gospel (see the comments on 3:10). Here it derives, along with the gathering of the wheat into the barn, from John the Baptist's preaching (3:12). Characteristically, Matthew is assimilating John and Jesus (see "John the Baptist parallel Jesus" in the Topical Index).

The harvesters differ from the landowner's slaves. This piece of unrealism anticipates the later identification of the harvesters as angels, whereas the slaves represent Jesus' disciples. Usually the harvesters cut the grain just below the heads on the stalks, left the shorter tares standing uncut, and burned off the tares and the remaining stalks of the wheat plants in the open field (see W. Corswant, "Agriculture," *Dictionary of Life in Bible Times* [New York: Oxford, 1960] 24). Therefore the collecting of tares first and their being bound in bundles for burning, like wood, are further pieces of unrealism designed to emphasize the final judgment of false disciples.

The attempts of Pharisees, Essenes, and Zealots (or their precursors) to effect an immediate separation between the godly and the ungodly provide a natural setting for the parable in Jesus' ministry. But, of course, that setting obtained in Jewry beyond his lifetime and had its counterpart in the Christian church. Therefore the evidence still stands that Matthew composed this parable by conflating the parables of the sower and the seed growing by itself and by adding a bit of John the Baptist's preaching. His constructing the parable rules out extracanonical derivation of the version in *Gos. Thom.* 57.

The Magnitude of the Kingdom
13:31-33 (Mark 4:30-32; Luke 13:18-21)

13:31-32 (Mark 4:30-32; Luke 13:18-19) Matthew goes on in Mark from the parable of the seed growing by itself, which he has just conflated with the parable of the sower and a little of John the Baptist's preaching, to the parable of the mustard seed, better called the parable of the mustard tree in Matthew and Luke. "Another parable he put before them, saying" replaces Mark's "And he was saying" and echoes the introduction to the last parable exactly. See the comments on v 24. The two interrogative clauses, "How should we liken the kingdom of God, or in what parable should we put it?" (so Mark) collapse into the single declarative clause, "The kingdom of heaven is like . . . ," for a parallel with v 24b. But v 24b had an aorist verb pointing backward to the corruption of the kingdom that had taken place by the time the first gospel was written. Here, the present tense calls attention to the current magnitude of the kingdom indicated by the parable. Luke follows Mark in retaining the two clauses and the question, but may show Matthew's influence in "is like."

The comparison begins with "a mustard seed which, when it is sown on the ground, being smaller than all the seeds on the ground . . ." (so Mark). But "which" never does acquire a verb in Mark. Therefore Matthew eliminates "when," changes "is sown" to "he sowed" in correspondence with the active forms of this verb in vv 3, 4, 18, 24, and makes "which" the object of the verb. Then, to identify the subject he characteristically adds ἄνθρωπος (35,17). Finally, he makes Mark's participial phrase "being smaller" into the relative clause "which is smaller" for a parallel with the immediately preceding relative clause beginning with "which."

Despite the above changes, two features come over from Mark: (1) the masculine gender of the first relative pronoun, referring to the seed, and (2) the neuter gender of the second relative pronoun (in Mark a neuter participle) and predicate adjective, both referring to the mustard plant. Lying behind this seemingly irrational shift in genders, and therefore in antecedents, is the distinction between the sowing of a seed and the smallness of the mustard when it is still only a seed—hence the masculine for "seed" in the matter of sowing and the neuter for "mustard" in the matter of smallness. Matthew clarifies the distinction by adding λαβών—a favorite of his (3,7)—for the taking of the seed in order to sow it. The addition also makes a parallel between the man's taking a mustard seed here and the woman's taking leaven in v 33c. That Luke agrees with Matthew against Mark in writing ὃν λαβὼν ἄνθρωπος suggests Matthean influence, since Luke neither identifies the man with Jesus nor shows a special liking of λαβών.

Matthew has more than grammar in mind. As in the parable of the tares of the field (v 24; cf. vv 3, 4, 11 in the parable of the sower), "a man" refers to Jesus the sower (see v 37). And Matthew's using the indicative mood (ἔσπειρεν instead of Mark's subjunctive σπαρῇ) makes the verb refer to Jesus' establishing the kingdom in past history. Despite his fondness for Mark's "on the ground" (8,2), Matthew replaces it with "in his field" to link this parable with the one concerning the tares, where the latter phrase occurs (v 24). This link further confirms the identification of the "man" with Jesus, since in the explanation of the tares no doubt is left (v 37). As we shall see, the field represents the world (v 38). This symbolism enhances the kingdom's magnitude here in the parable of the mustard tree (v 32).

In manifold ways further emphasis falls on the magnitude of the kingdom: (1) in Matthew's substituting "it has grown" for Mark's second and redundant "it has been sown"; (2) in the replacing of καί with the typically Matthean combination μέν . . . δέ (15,1), which more strongly contrasts the smallness of the seed and the largeness of the growth; (3) in the omission of Mark's ἀναβαίνει καί and advance of μεῖζον τῶν λαχάνων, "larger than the herbs," to an emphatic first position; (4) in the taking of "all" from "the herbs" in order to transfer the grown mustard plant out of the class of herbs; (5) in the replacing of Mark's "and it forms large branches" with "and it becomes a tree"—a hyperbolic classification that recalls the large tree reaching to the sky, visible to the end of the whole earth, and representing a worldwide kingdom in Dan 4:7-24(10-27); and (6) in the extending of Mark's allusive quotation of Dan 4:9, 18(12, 21) to include the previously replaced branches. Consequently, the birds do not settle temporarily in the shade of an herb's large branches (so Mark); they build their nests in the branches of a huge tree (cf. Ezek 17:23; 31:6). The hyperbole becomes all the more evident when we consider that by spring, the time of nest building, the annual mustard plant has not yet grown large enough for birds to build their nests in its branches. The realistic reference to the settling of birds under the shade of the grown plant in the hot summertime (so Mark) has turned, unrealistically, into the nesting of birds in the branches of the plant as though the plant had both grown to a tree and had done so by springtime! (This revision implies a shift in the meaning of κατασκηνοῦν from "settle" [so Mark] to "nest" [so Matthew].) By emphasizing largeness Matthew wants to impress on his readers the magnitude of the kingdom, which includes a large number of professing disciples, true and false. Both in Jesus' intent and Matthew's understanding, the birds probably represent the nations of the world (so Daniel; cf. *Joseph and Asenath* 15).

Matthew's substitution of "it has grown" not only emphasizes largeness; it also forges a link with "to grow together" in the parable of the tares (v 30). The replacement of "are able" with "come" results in a characteristically Matthean parallel between ἐλθεῖν and κατασκηνοῦν and forges a link with the verbs of coming in the parable of the tares (vv 25 [bis], 27, 28). These second and third links between the two parables (see v 31c for the first) reinforce the identification of the man who sowed the mustard seed with Jesus, the man who also sowed the wheat (v 37). Matthew reserves γίνεται for the clause about the tree, where it replaces Mark's ποιεῖ. His doing so enables him to put ἐστίν with "larger than the herbs" for a parallel with ἐστιν in v 32a. Thus we read, "which is smaller than . . . but . . . is larger than. . . ." Mark's "on the ground" falls away from "all the seeds" because the previous replacement of "on the ground" has forestalled Mark's parallel between the two occurrences of the phrase. Luke's agreeing with Matthew against Mark in the reference to growth, in the mustard's becoming a tree, and in the extension of the quotation from Daniel all suggest influence from Matthew; for Luke does not otherwise show special interest in largeness. Rather, his omissions make the remaining features, which in Matthew's fuller form indicate largeness, represent the *process* of growth (cf. his writing Acts). Furthermore, he does not usually extend OT quotations. Throughout, he differs from Matthew by putting all the verbs in the aorist.

The mustard seed was the smallest of Palestinian seeds that could be seen with the naked eye and had become proverbial for smallness (see *m. Tohar.* 8:8; *m. Nid.* 5:2; cf. *m. Nazir* 1:5). On the other hand, the mustard plant grows to a height of 8-12 feet. Theophrastus writes of herbs that grow so large they might be compared to trees (*HP* 1.3.1-4), and the rabbi Simeon b. Halafta is reported to have said he had a mustard plant to the top of which he could climb as to the top of a fig tree (*y. Pe'a* 7.3). But OT influence governs Matthew's description of the grown mustard plant as a tree. Luke makes an adaptation to horticulture outside Palestine by writing "into his own garden" in place of Mark's general reference to the ground and Matthew's reference to a field (see Theophrastus *HP* 7.1.1-2). In Palestine, sowing mustard was allowed in fields (so Matthew), but not in gardens (see *m. Kil.* 3:2; *b. Kil.* 2.8). For birds as symbolic of Gentiles, see *1 Enoch* 90:30, 33, 37; *Midr. Ps.* 104.10 and cf. Matthew's emphasis on the salvation of Gentiles (see "Universality" in the Topical Index). The shift from the past tense of sowing to the present tense of the mustard's becoming a tree does not come by accident from a conflation of Mark and Q. It is a deliberate shift due to Jesus' past establishment of the kingdom and the present magnitude of the kingdom. See Gundry, *Use of the OT* 35, for a comparison of the Hebrew, Septuagintal, and Theodotionic texts of Dan 4:9, 18 (12, 21).

13:33 (Luke 13:20-21) The start of the parable of the leaven differs entirely from Luke's "And again he said," but echoes the way the parables of the tares and mustard tree began ("Another parable he put before them, saying," vv 24, 31). Here, however, Matthew substitutes ἐλάλησεν for παρέθηκεν . . . λέγων. The substitute links with ἐλάλησεν αὐτοῖς in v 3 and similar combinations in vv 10 and 13. More importantly, it prepares for ἐλάλησεν . . . τοῖς ὄχλοις in v 34 and by doing so shows that Matthew meant the crowds when using αὐτοῖς in the preceding introductions (vv 24, 31).

The question in Luke, "To what should I liken the kingdom of God?" drops out. Only the declaration ". . . is like leaven" remains, with "the kingdom of God" brought in as the subject from the omitted question and changed, of course, to "the kingdom of heaven." As in the opening of the parable about the mustard tree, then, riddance of the deliberative question and the collapsing of two clauses into one clause result in emphasis on the present magnitude of the kingdom. Again, the comparison deals with the entirety of the following, not with the leaven alone.

The two clauses concerning a woman's taking the leaven and hiding it in three measures of wheat flour till the whole is leavened correspond exactly to Luke. The first clause follows the pattern of the preceding parable about the mustard tree, where we also read ὁμοία ἐστιν ἡ βασιλεία τῶν οὐρανῶν, followed in order by a dative, a relative pronoun in the accusative, and a nominative participle of λαμβάνω with ἄνθρωπος (here γυνή) and an aorist verb. Three measures of flour amounted to about a bushel, give or take a little, and made the largest amount of dough a woman could knead. The bread would feed a crowd of about one hundred—enough for a festive occasion, as in Gen 18:6, where Sarah made bread from three measures of flour for the Lord and two of his angels. Is Jesus hinting at the messianic banquet?

Usually leaven symbolizes the pervasive power of evil (Exod 12:15-20; 23:18; 34:25; Lev 2:11; 6:10[17]; Matt 16:5-12; 1 Cor 5:6-8; Gal 5:9). But sometimes it is associated with what is good (Lev 7:13-14; 23:17). Here, the unusual use of leaven with a good association not only emphasizes the point of the parable—the pervasive power of the kingdom of heaven—but also, and perhaps intentionally, agrees with the inclusion of publicans and sinners in the kingdom. Oddly, the text reads that the woman "hid" the leaven in the flour, as though the large amount of flour engulfed the small amount of leaven (cf. the smallness of the mustard seed). Putting ὅλον, "[the] whole," last in the statement about the leavening of three measures accentuates the pervasiveness of the leaven and thus illustrates the magnitude of the kingdom (cf. the bigness of the mustard tree). For Matthew, this magnitude again has to do with the large number of professing disciples, true and false, throughout the world.

Since "hiding" and "the whole" stress the large amount of flour, three measures need not derive from Matthew's and Luke's embellishment with use of Gen 18:6. The absence of three measures in *Gos. Thom.* 96 results, then, from a realistic revision of the original rather than represents the original itself.

The Fulfillment of Old Testament Prophecy in the Parabolic Conundrums
13:34-35

13:34 (Mark 4:33-34) Matthew now returns to Mark, in particular, to some editorial statements following the parable of the mustard seed. A favorite expression of his, ταῦτα πάντα (7,1), takes the place of "and with many such parables." This change stems from the difference between Mark's making a closing comment about the parables and Matthew's making a comment that by no means closes the parabolic passage. Matthew likes to use πάντα for emphasis (63,25-26). Here it comes from the omitted line in Mark 4:34b and compensates somewhat for the omission. "Spoke" replaces "was speaking" for conformity with the aorist forms in vv 3 and 33 (both unique to Matthew). The characteristic insertion of "Jesus" (80,12) adds a Christological emphasis. Since Matthew omitted "parables" in the initial phrase, "the word" gives way to "in parables." The substitute echoes vv 3, 10, 13 and anticipates the coming quotation of Ps 78(77):2. Then, to mark off the parables thus far told from the following parables, which will be addressed solely to Jesus' true disciples, Matthew replaces "to them" with "to the crowds," who represent false disciples as well as true. The replacement typifies his interest in the crowds (17,1), enables him to use "to them" in his next line without redundancy, and makes an inclusio with the mention of crowds in v 2. This inclusio frames the parables addressed to them.

Matthew omits Mark's entire clause "as they were able to hear" because according to his unique wording in v 13 the crowds (except for the true disciples among them) did not hear what they heard. Furthermore, the omission carries out his penchant for parallelism by making the two lines of v 34 match each other. The omission of "but he was privately explaining all things to his own disciples" also contributes to that parallelism by leaving a couplet. Besides, Matthew wants to reserve the motif of private explanation to true disciples till after his quotation of a fulfilled OT text. The second line in Matthew's couplet reads, "and without a parable he was speaking nothing to them." The wording matches Mark except for substitutions of καί for δέ and οὐδέν for οὐκ. The first substitution reflects Matthew's normal use of δέ as an adversative and his contrary desire for synonymous parallelism here. The second satisfies the need for a direct object to parallel ταῦτα πάντα in the first line of the couplet.

13:35 Verse 35 is peculiar to the first gospel and opens with a typically Matthean formula of introduction to a fulfillment-quotation. ὅπως occurs in such formulas where the quotation gathers up a large amount of material—here, the preceding parables (see also 2:23; 8:17 with comments). For Matthew's great interest in fulfillment and frequent use of εἴρω in various forms (here, τὸ ῥηθέν) see the comments on 1:22-23 and 5:21-48. Though the quotation does not come from the prophetic section of the Hebrew OT, but from the Psalms in the section called "the Writings," Matthew puts down his usual "through the prophet" either out of sheer habit or out of a view that the whole OT is prophetic in a large sense. Or perhaps he had in mind the designation of Asaph, the author of Psalm 78(77) according to its traditional title, as a prophet in 1 Chr 25:2; 2 Chr 29:30. Asaph is not named by the evangelist, however, because the psalm does not appear in the prophetic section of the Hebrew OT. See Gundry, *Use of the OT* 119 n. 2, against the reading Ἡσαΐου. The preponderance of external evidence favors its omission (see the UBS, ad loc.). Scribal insertions of Isaiah's famous name in other passages suggest that the name is secondary here, too. It would contradict Matthew's mentioning Isaiah elsewhere only with happy, salvific prophecies; for the present quotation deals with the parables as a judgment on false disciples, who make up a large part of the crowds.

In the first of the synonymously parallel lines from Ps 78(77):2, "I will open" agrees with the LXX and MT. With its object "my mouth" the verb echoes 5:1, where Matthew inserted "opening his mouth" in a reference to Jesus' teaching. On the other hand, the plural of the phrase "in parables" agrees with the LXX, the OT Peshitta, and the Latin Vulgate against the singular of the MT. Outside Matthew the plural may have resulted from the plural of the parallel term חִידוֹת/προβλήματα in the next line. Matthew uses the plural to suit the plurality of Jesus' parables in chap. 13.

In the second line of the quotation we read ἐρεύξομαι, "I will belch forth" (a figure for verbal utterance), instead of φθέγξομαι, "I will utter" (so the LXX). Matthew's is a literal translation of אַבִּיעָה and a closer parallel to the opening of the mouth in the preceding line. For חִידוֹת, "enigmas" or "dark sayings," Matthew puts κεκρυμμένα, "hidden things," which is loose but closer to the Hebrew than προβλήματα, "problems," in the LXX. Matthew's word typifies his diction (4,2) and anticipates κεκρυμμένῳ for the treasure hidden in the field (v 44). In other words, the hidden things, or parables, *are* the hidden treasure of the kingdom. One finds and gains the kingdom by understanding the parables; but to false disciples, who are ignorant, their meaning stays hidden. Cf. 11:25; 13:52. The final phrase reads "from of old" in the MT, "from the beginning" in the LXX, and "from the foundation of the world" in Matthew. There is some doubt about the originality of Matthew's κόσμου (see the UBS), but the preponderance of external evidence favors inclusion (see Metzger, *Textual Commentary* ad loc.).

Inclusion is also favored by the full form of the expression in 25:34. In fact, the parallel between these two distinctive occurrences of the expression again suggests an identification between the kingdom and the parables: the heavenly Father rules through the word of his son Jesus.

Psalm 78(77) deals with the wonderful works of God and the repeated rebellions of his people. Remarkably, the parables to which Matthew applies Ps 78(77):2 have to do with the magnitude of God's rule, which because of its magnitude allows for antinomian "tares." The psalmist declares that he will not hide the riddle of God's wonderful works over against the rebellions of God's people any more than his ancestors have hidden them. Matthew's "things hidden from the foundation of the world" seems to contradict the openness of the tradition to which the psalmist belongs. But Matthew is not thinking about hiddenness of pronouncement. After all, he emphasizes the continuity of Jesus' teaching with the OT (see esp. 5:17-48). Rather, he thinks about hiddenness of meaning, the puzzle that God's kingdom should include the lawless. On the text of the quotation, see further Gundry, *Use of the OT* 118-19, 211.

The Future Judgment
of False Disciples in the Kingdom (continued)
13:36-43

13:36 Matthew now takes up Jesus' special ministry to the disciples, true ones, as distinct from the crowds, who are a mixed body of true and false (cf. Mark 4:34b). This unparalleled section begins with Jesus' leaving the crowds to enter his house (v 36a), the disciples' approaching with a request that he explain the parable of the tares (v 36bc), and the explanation itself (vv 37-43). τότε (66,17), ἀφείς (12,5), ὄχλους (17,1), ἦλθεν (31,19), and οἰκίαν (5,3) typify Matthew's diction. Cf. especially his insertion in 26:44: καὶ ἀφεὶς αὐτοὺς πάλιν ἀπελθών. Jesus' leaving the crowds may suggest a forsaking, or rejection, of false disciples. His going into the house makes a counterpart to his earlier departure from the house to the seaside (so Matthew alone in v 1). The definite article has the meaning "his" (see the comments on 4:13; 9:10 concerning Matthew's emphasis on Jesus' house in Capernaum and cf. *m. 'Abot* 1:4 on houses as places of instruction in the law).

In the second clause of v 36 προσῆλθον connotes Jesus' dignity (see the comments on 4:3; 8:14) and belongs to Matthew's special vocabulary (38,6). μαθηταί (31,5) and λέγοντες (61,23) also come from that vocabulary. "His disciples" distinguishes the true disciples, who approached Jesus, from the crowds, who included false disciples. In the true disciples' request, some doubt plagues the decision whether to adopt διασάφησον, "make clear" (see also 18:31), or φράσον, "explain" (see also 15:15). Fortunately, the readings are largely synonymous. The request enables Jesus to prepare the disciples to teach all that he commanded (28:20). They will not be blind leading the blind! The wheat are left out of the title, "The Parable of the Tares of the Field." This omission shows that Matthew puts his main stress on the current presence and future judgment of false disciples in the kingdom.

13:37 The opening ὁ δέ of v 37 starts a long series of that expression (with some variations of gender and number) and sets Jesus' reply opposite the disciples' request. ἀποκριθεὶς εἶπεν characterizes Matthew's style (29,6). An explanation of the parable of the tares follows. Like the parable itself, it is composed by Matthew, who is developing Jesus' demand for genuine discipleship. ὁ σπείρων links with ἀνθρώπῳ σπείραντι in v 24; but its being substantive, nominative, and present reflects the identical form in v 3 and gives evidence of the link between the two parables, indeed, of Matthew's drawing the parable of the tares partly from the parable of the sower. The identification of the sower with "the Son of man" ties in with the designation of the sower as a "man" in the parable proper (v 24) and with the saying about the sending of angels by the Son of man (v 41), a saying modelled after the traditional saying about the coming of the Son of man (24:30-31; cf. 16:27; 25:31). Matthew likes καλός (1,6), ἀγρός (3,10), ἐχθρός (2,3), and θερισμός (0,3).

13:38 In identifying the field as the world Matthew plays on one of his favorite, though subordinate, themes (κόσμος—5,2). Since the Aramaic word עָלְמָא, "age," probably did not yet mean "world" (see G. Dalman, *The Words of Jesus* [Edinburgh: T. & T. Clark, 1902] 162-79), we have evidence of Matthew's composition in Greek instead of Jesus' speaking the interpretation in Aramaic. "World" emphasizes the widespread extension of the kingdom through evangelism (cf. 5:14; 26:13; 28:19). Matthew does not mean that all the inhabitants of the world have or will become disciples. Rather, he means that throughout the world large numbers have professed discipleship (cf. the parables of the mustard tree and leaven). In τὸ δὲ καλὸν σπέρμα, οὗτοί εἰσιν οἱ υἱοὶ τῆς βασιλείας, "and the good seed—these are the sons of the kingdom," we have a *casus pendens*. This, too, favors composition by Matthew, since the construction occurs thirteen times in his gospel, but only four times in Mark and seven or eight times in Luke. Similarly, Matthew writes about the kingdom without qualification five or six times, but Mark never, Luke only once, and the rest of the NT writers never. Furthermore, βασιλεία is a Mattheanism with or without a qualifier (18,12). Just as "the sons of the kingdom" was inserted in 8:12, so here it occurs distinctively (see the comments on 8:12, esp. concerning the change of reference from Jews to Christians). The parallel identification of the tares as "the sons of the Evil One" reflects "the Evil One" in the parable of the sower, from which Matthew partly drew the parable of the tares (see v 19 for Matthew's replacing "Satan" with "the Evil One"). It also reflects his liking of πονηρός (10,4).

J. Jeremias notes that in Aramaic the Devil was never designated "the Evil One" and the word for kingdom referred to the contemporary worldly government unless otherwise qualified (*Parables* 81). These facts tend to support composition by Matthew. We might take τοῦ πονηροῦ as neuter and translate the entire expression, "the sons of evil," because the contrasting expression does not read "the sons of God," but "the sons of the kingdom." In other words, evil may be a better contrast with the kingdom than the Devil is. Cf. expressions such as "sons of light," "sons of darkness," "sons of thunder," and "son of perdition," where the genitive nouns are impersonal. Nevertheless, the identification of the sower of the tares as the Devil (v 39) rules out the neuter.

13:39 Since Matthew has just referred to Satan as the Evil One, he switches to "the Devil" in his identification of the enemy who sowed the tares. See 4:5 for an insertion of διάβολος and 25:41 for another occurrence in distinctive material. In describing the harvest as "the consummation of the age," he uses for the first time a favorite phrase that occurs in the gospels only in Matt 13:39, 40, 49; 24:3; 28:20. It is constructed from συντελεῖσθαι, "to come to consummation," in Mark 13:4 and the common eschatological term αἰών, "age" (cf. v 22; 12:32 and see further the comments on 24:3). The identification of the harvesters as angels anticipates v 41, which is based on the saying later recorded in 24:30-31.

13:40 Both ὥσπερ (6,3) and οὕτως (18,5) are favorites of Matthew. They are combined distinctively also in 12:40. οὖν (35,11) and πυρί (2,4) are further Mattheanisms. The burning of the tares is a figure of judgment on false disciples and agrees with the use of this figure elsewhere in Matthew (see the comments on v 30).

Cf. Dan 12:4; *T. Levi* 10:2; Heb 9:26. On the end as a harvest, see Jer 27:16 LXX; 51:33; Hos 6:11; Joel 4(3):13; 2 Esdr 4:28-32, 39; *2 Apoc. Bar.* 70:2; cf. Rev 14:14-20.

13:41 Verse 41 states that "the Son of man will send his angels, and they will collect out of his kingdom all the offenses [i.e., enticements to sin] and those who do lawlessness." Matthew is anticipating 24:30-31: "the Son of man . . . and he will send his angels . . . and they will gather together his chosen ones" (cf. Mark 13:26-27; Matt 16:27; 25:31). But Matthew has inverted the thought. In 24:30-31 the angels gather true disciples, "the chosen ones"; here the angels collect false disciples, the tares, those who entice others to sin by breaking Jesus' law themselves (cf. Matthew's insertion of σκάνδαλον, "offense, enticement to sin," for Peter in 16:23; 18:7 with comments ad loc.). σκάνδαλα comes from Zeph 1:3, where the prophet predicts that the Lord will remove "the offenses [or 'the ruins'] along with the wicked." But for "the wicked" Matthew substitutes "those who do lawlessness," which alludes to Ps 37(36):1 (cf. Ps 6:9[8]) and reflects his fondness for ποιοῦντας (19,19) and ἀνομίαν (3,1). This interweaving of OT phraseology typifies his style (see further Gundry, *Use of the OT* 137-38). The Mattheanism πάντα (63,25-26) adds emphasis to the warning. And the failure of the angels and the kingdom to belong to the Son of man elsewhere in the gospels except Matt 16:27-28; 24:31; 25:31 with 34, 40 (see also 20:21 and cf. 1:21; 16:18; Luke 22:29-30) confirms Matthew's composition.

13:42 Matthew continues to draw phraseology from the OT in writing that the angels will "cast" the offensive antinomians "into a furnace of fire" (see Dan 3:6; cf. 2 Esdr 7:36). Now we see why the tares were bound in bundles, like pieces of wood, rather than burned while standing in the open field. On Matthew's penchant for βαλοῦσιν, especially in references to the final judgment, see the comments on 5:25-26; and concerning fire as an especially Matthean figure for judgment, see the comments on 3:10. The clause about weeping and grinding of teeth comes from 8:12 (cf. Luke 13:28). The repetition adds force to the warning against the antinomian behavior of false disciples. The distinctive repetitions again in 13:50; 22:13; 24:51; 25:30 confirm Matthew's composition here. See the comments on 8:12 for interpretation.

13:43 The final verse in the explanation begins with the Mattheanism τότε (66,17) and continues, "the righteous will shine forth like [ἐκλάμψουσιν ὡς] the sun in the kingdom of their Father." Again Matthew follows his practice of working OT phraseology into Jesus' words. The statement comes from Dan 12:3: "and those who have understanding [οἱ συνιέντες in the LXX and Theod; cf. the frequency of συνίημι in this part of Matthew] will shine forth [ἐκλάμψουσιν in Theod] like [ὡς in the LXX and Theod] the brightness of the firmament, and they who turn the many to righteousness, like the stars for ever and ever" (cf. Judg 5:31; *1 Enoch* 39:7; 104:2). There may be a wordplay between הַמַּכְשֵׁלוֹת, "the offenses, ruins," in Zeph 1:3, quoted in v 41, and הַמַּשְׂכִּלִים, "they who turn [the many] to righteousness," in Dan 12:3, quoted here. Typically, Matthew collapses the two clauses into one by taking οἱ δίκαιοι from the second clause, taking ἐκλάμψουσιν from the first clause, and conflating the comparative phrases concerning the firmament and the stars into a single phrase concerning the sun, perhaps under the influence of "the sun of righteousness" in Mal 3:20(4:2). See 17:2, where he will again insert "like the sun." But there the phrase describes Jesus' glory, here that of true disciples. This twofold use of the phrase may imply that disciples will share Jesus' glory. οἱ δίκαιοι means "those who teach righteousness," as in Daniel and previously in the gospel (10:41; 13:17). Matthew likes δίκαιοι (9-10,7-6), βασιλεία (18,12), and πατρός (22,13). The last term occurs with "their," "your," and "our" twenty times in Matthew, but only once in Mark and three times in Luke. And except for the Lord's Prayer, only Matthew among all NT writers elsewhere construes "Father" with "kingdom"; see 26:29, where he changes "in the kingdom of God" (Mark 14:25) to "in the kingdom of my Father" (cf. 1 Cor 15:24). The kingdom of the Son of man becomes the Father's kingdom not because of any essential or temporal difference between the kingdoms, but solely for a warning emphasis on the Son of man's judgmental authority and an assuring emphasis on the Father's care of the righteous. Finally, Matthew repeats "he who has ears, let him hear" from 11:15; 13:9 (cf. 13:15, 16). Perhaps the occurrence of this command in Mark 4:23—i.e., in the middle of Mark's parabolic section—suggested its inclusion here.

The restraining of a premature separation of the tares and wheat in the parable does not come up in the interpretation. On the supposition that the parable came to Matthew from tradition, some think his greater interest in judgment crowded out the element of restraint. But we have ample evidence of his composing the parable as well as its interpretation. And the uniqueness to his gospel of 5:21-22 (cf. 7:1-5; Luke 6:37-42) makes it difficult to think that he had no interest in restraining disciplinary rigorism. Rather, the emphasis on separation at the end automatically answers the question of premature separation. Besides, there is no single word or expression—on the order of "the sower," "the field," "the good seed," "the tares," "the enemy," "the harvest," "the harvesters"—that would have made possible a natural introduction of the restraint into the parallelistic interpretation.

Since the field is the whole world, the sowing of the seed by the Son of man may include not only the historical ministry of Jesus, but also his sending the disciples to make disciples of all nations and his being with them in that activity (28:18-20). We would err to interpret "world" as the church, for Matthew is quite capable of using "church" (see 16:18; 18:17). And to equate the world with a universal kingdom of the Son of man would go too far in the other direction by overlooking that the Devil sowed the tares *later* and in the *midst* of the wheat. Therefore it remains best to regard the world as the sphere into which the Son of man brings his kingdom through the preaching of the gospel. Worldwide extent— yes; but not absolute domination of the world, at least not till the parousia. The presence of the Son of man's kingdom and the futurity of the Father's kingdom should not lead us to think of a basic chronological difference between them, for Jesus' kingdom appears as future in 20:21 and the kingdom of heaven (or of God) as present in 11:12; 12:28; 21:43.

The Necessity of Economic Self-Deprivation to True Membership in the Kingdom
13:44-46

13:44 We now meet a pair of parables that appear nowhere else in the gospels and define a true disciple as one who "sells all, whatever he has," for the kingdom of heaven. The first parable derives from Prov 2:1-9: "my son, if you will receive my sayings and treasure [cf. Matthew's θησαυρῷ; the LXX has κρύψῃς, comparable to Matthew's κεκρυμμένῳ and ἔκρυψεν] my commandments within you . . . incline [παραβαλεῖς in the LXX; cf. παραβολή throughout Matthew 13] your heart to understanding [in the LXX, σύνεσιν, cognate to συνίημι, which occurs often in this part of Matthew] . . . lift up your voice for understanding [see the preceding comment] . . . if you search for her as for hidden treasures [מַטְמֹנִים]; then you will understand [συνήσεις in the LXX] the fear of the Lord, and find [εὑρήσεις in the LXX; cf. Matthew's εὑρών] the knowledge of God . . . from his mouth [comes] . . . understanding [σύνεσις in the LXX]. He treasures up [θησαυρίζει in the LXX] sound wisdom for the upright. . . . Then you will understand righteousness and justice [in the LXX, τότε συνήσεις δικαιοσύνην καὶ κρίμα—all terms well liked by Matthew; cf. his having referred to true disciples as 'the righteous' in v 43]" (cf. Prov 8:18-21; Isa 33:6).

The allusion to the OT supports composition by Matthew, who habitually makes such allusions. The parallelistic structure of the parable, the borrowing of expressions from other parables and from elsewhere, the use of words especially dear to him, and, strikingly, the omission of the editorial introduction he has used for the first three parables of the kingdom—viz., "another parable he put before [or 'spoke to'] them [saying]"- (vv 24, 31, 33)—all add support to composition by him. The first three parables of the kingdom came from dominical tradition. We are able to include the parable of the tares because Matthew constructed it by conflating the parables of the sower and the seed growing by itself. Yet the parable of the hidden treasure—and also the parables of the costly pearl and bad fish, which share the foregoing characteristics except allusion to the OT—have no parallels. And Matthew omits his usual statement that Jesus put another parable before the audience *despite the continuance of parallelism in the opening words of the parables proper*. See the chart on the next page. The details of diction and borrowing will confirm that these last three of the six parables about the kingdom originated with Matthew himself.

Matthew favors ὁμοία (1,5), ἡ βασιλεία τῶν οὐρανῶν (25,7), κρύπτω (4,2—here κεκρυμμένῳ), and ἀγρῷ (3,10—cf. distinctive occurrences in vv 24, 27, 31, 36, 38). He also shows some favoritism to θησαυρῷ (1,4), which here reflects Prov 2:4. "In the field" echoes vv 24 and 31 (cf. v 27 and 22:5) and therefore represents the world, throughout which God's rule extends in the discipling of all nations. εὑρών both reflects Prov 2:5 and represents Matthew's favorite diction (7,8). The use of ἄνθρωπος for a disciple echoes v 25. See also 8:27; 9:8, in both of which passages Matthew inserted the word, and vv 45, 52 below. ἔκρυψεν not only comes from Prov 2:1 LXX and Matthew's special vocabulary (4,2). It also reflects v 33: just as a woman hid leaven (v 33), so a man hid the treasure he had found.

Similarly, the man's "joy" echoes the joy of those who receive the word in the parable of the sower (v 20, though with an unhappy reversal) and reflects Matthew's special interest in χαρά (3,2). ἀπὸ τῆς χαρᾶς has an emphatic position. In writing that the man "goes," Matthew uses another of his favorite words, ὑπάγει (5,6). The whole description of the man's going and selling all, whatever he has, comes from the story of the rich young ruler. In that story Mark 10:21 reads, "Go, sell whatever you have . . . and you will have treasure in heaven."

If we are to read πάντα in Matthew (see the UBS and Metzger, *Textual Commentary* ad loc.), there is an agreement with Luke 18:22. If not, there is an agreement with Mark. Notably, in Matthew's own version of the story of the rich young ruler, Mark's ὅσα ἔχεις becomes σου τὰ ὑπάρχοντα (19:21). Matthew changes the wording because he has borrowed the traditional phrase for use in the parable of the hidden treasure. On the other hand, we read πάντα ὅσα εἶχεν/ἔχει again in v 46 and 18:25, both unparalleled. Matthew likes the words πάντα ὅσα both individually (63,25-26; 5,6) and together (2,3). ἀγοράζει appears five times in passages peculiar to his gospel. The buying of the field represents true discipleship, consisting in and evidenced by economic sacrifice. The present tense of all the verbs except ἔκρυψεν probably reflects the present tense freely sprinkled throughout the immediately preceding explanation of the tares and the present tense of the key verb ἔχεις, borrowed from the story of the rich young ruler.

The frequency of invasions often led people to bury their treasures in the ground. Cf. the Copper Scroll in the QL. We are probably to understand the parable as referring to a day laborer who was plowing another man's field, discovered an old treasure buried before the present owner's lifetime or acquisition of the field, and

	Predicate	Subject	Dative noun	Relative Pronoun	Participle	Subject	Aorist Verb
13:24b	ὡμοιώθη	ἡ βασιλεία τῶν οὐρανῶν	ἀνθρώπῳ		σπείραντι. . . .		
13:31b	ὁμοία ἐστὶν	ἡ βασιλεία τῶν οὐρανῶν	κόκκῳ σινάπεως,	ὃν	λαβὼν	ἄνθρωπος	ἔσπειρεν. . . .
13:33b	ὁμοία ἐστὶν	ἡ βασιλεία τῶν οὐρανῶν	ζύμῃ,	ἣν	λαβοῦσα	γυνὴ	ἐνέκρυψεν. . . .
13:44a	ὁμοία ἐστὶν	ἡ βασιλεία τῶν οὐρανῶν	θησαυρῷ κεκρυμμένῳ. . .	ὃν	εὑρὼν	ἄνθρωπος	ἔκρυψεν. . . .
13:45a	πάλιν ὁμοία ἐστὶν	ἡ βασιλεία τῶν οὐρανῶν	ἀνθρώπῳ ἐμπόρῳ. . .		εὑρὼν. . . .		ἠγόρασεν. . . .
13:47a	πάλιν ὁμοία ἐστὶν	ἡ βασιλεία τῶν οὐρανῶν	σαγήνῃ βληθείσῃ. . .	ἣν. . . .	ἀναβιβάσαντες . . .		συνέλεξαν. . . .

did not extract the treasure but carefully covered it back up so as to purchase the field and forestall the possibility of the present owner's claiming to have buried the treasure himself (see Derrett, *Law in the NT* 3-13). The necessity of selling all to purchase the field shows the poverty of the day laborer.

13:45-46 Matthew links the parable of the costly pearl with the parable of the hidden treasure by adding "again." Concerning the other opening words, see the comments on v 44. Here the kingdom of heaven is compared to "a businessman who was seeking for good pearls." Once more, and typically, Matthew uses ἀνθρώπῳ for a man who becomes a disciple (see the comments on v 44). ἐμπόρῳ occurs only here in the NT, except for Revelation. But Matthew will insert the cognate ἐμπορία in 22:5. Moreover, he seems to draw the idea for this parable from the parable of the great supper, which stems from dominical tradition (22:1-14; Luke 14:15-24). But in that parable a man refuses because of his "business" (ἐμπορίαν, Matthew only)—and that right after someone else refuses to go to his "field" (ἀγρόν; cf. v 44 in the preceding parable here!). Thus Matthew constructs the parables in vv 44 and 45-46 as reversals of the bad example set by those who refused to sacrifice (22:5). Now, the buyer of a field and the businessman offer a good example by selling all, whatever they have, in evidence of true discipleship. We see, then, the source of purchasing a field in the preceding parable: Matthew borrows it from the parable of the great supper and, having borrowed the element of purchase here, omits it when he comes to that later parable (in contrast with Luke).

As a pearl merchant, the businessman is seeking good pearls. Matthew shows some favoritism toward ζητοῦντι (2,3), and καλούς occurs often in his gospel (1,6), especially in chap. 13. Elsewhere in the gospels "pearls" occurs only in the next verse of the present parable and in 7:6, where it stands for the kingdom and appears in a context dealing, as here, with true and false disciples. Matthew recalls that earlier passage, then, and introduces pearls as the stock in trade of the businessman (cf. Prov 3:14-15; 8:11; and esp. Job 28:17-18).

But the businessman, finding one very valuable pearl, went away, sold all that he owned, and bought that pearl. δέ, a favorite of Matthew, contrasts the finding of the one very valuable pearl with the search for merely good pearls. εὑρών echoes v 44 and preceding verses and typifies Matthew's diction (7,8). ἕνα also typifies his diction (24,7). It does not reflect the indefinite meaning "a" of the corresponding Aramaic numeral, but carries an emphatic meaning, "one, a single." πολυτίμου will occur in 26:7 as a variant reading. The simple adjective πολύς, here prefixed to τίμου, is another Mattheanism (23,1).

The participle ἀπελθών both comes from the parable of the great supper, on which Matthew is drawing (see 22:5), and links with vv 25 and 28 here in chap. 13. It occurs with distinctive frequency in Matthew (14,11). "He sold all, whatever he had" parallels v 44 (see the comments ad loc. for Mattheanisms) and will recur almost exactly in 18:25, another passage peculiar to this gospel. Matthew emphasizes the desirability of wholehearted devotion to the kingdom not only with a description of the pearl as very valuable, but also by using asyndeton ("finding . . . going away," without a connective) and putting "sold" in the perfect tense. "He bought" echoes v 44, where it came from the parable of the great supper.

Pearls were fished in the Red Sea, Persian Gulf, and Indian Ocean (*TDNT* 4. 472-73). ἐμπόρῳ marks the merchant as a wholesale dealer, a big businessman who travelled to such places, not a small-time, shop-keeping retailer (κάπηλος). Matthew's composition of this parable rules out dependence of *Gos. Thom.* 76 on an extracanonical and more reliable tradition. The writer of the version in the *Gospel of Thomas* tones down the radicalism of selling all to the mere sale of some merchandise. The merchant did not find the pearl *in* his merchandise, as is sometimes thought; otherwise he would not have had to sell his merchandise to gain the pearl.

The Future Judgment
of False Disciples in the Kingdom (concluded)
13:47-50

13:47-48 Matthew constructs the parable of the bad fish (vv 47-50) on the model of the parable of the tares and its explanation (vv 24-30, 36-43). But the present parable has a more exclusive emphasis on the judgment that awaits false disciples, and the introductory "again" links the parable with the preceding pair to make a triplet of Matthean constructs. This linkage implies that failure to give up everything for the sake of the kingdom characterizes false disciples, who face a fiery judgment. See the comments on vv 44 and 45 concerning the parallelism and diction in "the kingdom of heaven is like." The metaphor of fishing may come immediately from Jesus' taking to a boat at the start of chap. 13, and ultimately from fishing for men as a figure of evangelism (4:19). With the throwing of a dragnet into the sea cf. the throwing of a net into the sea in the account of Jesus' calling the disciples to become fishers of men (4:18). Matthew likes βάλλω (12,8). The dragnet, weighted at the bottom, was either dragged to shore between two boats or laid out by a single boat in a circuit from the shore and back again and then drawn to shore by hand. "Into the sea" parallels "in the field" in the companion parable of the tares (v 24) and symbolizes the worldwide extent of Christian evangelism (cf. v 38; 28:19; and the frequent OT portrayal of the nations of the world as a sea). Once it was cast into the sea, the dragnet "gathered from every kind [of fish]." συναγαγούσῃ comes from the parable of the tares (v 30) and represents Matthew's diction (10,10). Cf. the gathering of the crowds, a mixed body of true and false disciples, in 13:2, where only Matthew has συνήχθησαν. His favorite παντός (63,25-26) modifies γένους and accentuates the presence of false disciples in the kingdom.

The literalistic use of ἐπληρώθη (v 48) corresponds to Matthew's frequent use of the verb in a figurative sense and to his interpolating it in a literal sense in 23:32. "On the beach" comes from v 2, where Matthew inserted the phrase. καθίσαντες is a Mattheanism (3,2), which also comes from v 2. There, however, Matthew took over Mark's synonymous καθῆσθαι, and Jesus sat in a boat on the sea. Here, fishermen sit on the beach. The collection of the good stems from the parable of the tares (see vv 28, 29, 30, 40, 41 for συνέλεξαν and vv 24, 27, 37, 38 for καλά). The "containers" into which the good are put correspond to the "barn" into which the wheat was put in the parable of the tares (v 30), and the throwing out of the bad corresponds to the burning of the tares in a furnace (vv 30, 40-42). ἔξω and ἔβαλον typify Matthew's diction (3,1; 12,8), especially when used for judgment, and contrast sharply with the net's being thrown into the sea and gathering fish of every kind (v 47). Strikingly, Matthew writes the neuter σαπρά despite the masculine gender of the implied τοὺς ἰχθύας. The neuter shows that he has in mind the similar image of the good tree and bad tree (τὸ δένδρον καλόν . . . τὸ δένδρον σαπρόν—neuter). See 7:17, 18; 12:33 (bis).

13:49-50 "So it will be in the consummation of the age" comes without change from the explanation of the tares (v 40b). See earlier comments for Mattheanisms. "And the angels will come forth and separate the wicked from the midst of the righteous" also stems from the parable of the tares, but with some revisions. The coming forth of the angels corresponds to the sending of the angels by the Son of man (v 41a; cf. the angels' accompanying the Son of man at his coming in 16:27; 25:31). The appropriateness of the expressions to reapers and their inappropriateness to fishermen—who do not go out, but sit down on a beach (v 48)—put the borrowing from the parable of the tares in bold relief. The separation of the wicked from the midst of the righteous matches the collection of all the offenses and those who practice lawlessness (v 41b). Matthew's verb here in v 49—viz., ἀφοριοῦσιν—will be echoed in 25:32, where it will occur twice in a description of the last judgment. "The wicked" corresponds to "the sons of the Wicked One" (v 38) and makes use of a Mattheanism in πονηροῦ (10,4).

"From the midst" forms an antithetic parallel with the sowing of the tares "in the midst" of the wheat (v 25). Like the phrase to which it corresponds, it also shows that the wicked are to be understood as false professors of discipleship *within the kingdom* rather than as the wicked in general. For if the latter, the righteous would have been located among the wicked and separated from them (rather than vice versa), or the wicked would have been separated from the world (rather than from the midst of the righteous). τῶν δικαίων comes from Matthew's diction (9-10,7-6) and from the allusion to Dan 12:3 in v 43a. It refers to those who teach righteousness by word and example. The throwing of the wicked into a furnace of fire and the weeping and grinding of teeth (v 50) come in their entirety and without change from v 42. The figure of fire is inappropriate to fish, referred originally to tares, and makes the borrowing all the more remarkable. Thus the stress falls on the judgment of false disciples at the end. See the comments on v 42 for Mattheanisms.

The Disciple as a Knowledgeable Scribe
13:51-52

13:51 Matthew now adds a distinctive postlude to emphasize the understanding that marks true disciples (vv 51-52; cf. Sir 39:1-3). His preferred vocabulary stands out in συνήκατε (5,1) and ταῦτα πάντα (7,1). Where it occurs elsewhere in chap. 13, ταῦτα πάντα refers to the parables (vv 34, 56). The response of the true disciples, "They say to him, 'Yes,' " exhibits their understanding and echoes 9:28, where Matthew used these very words, with the addition of "Lord," in place of others found in Mark 10:51; Luke 18:41. Perhaps the recency of λέγουσιν in the parable of the tares (v 28) triggered a recollection of the earlier passage. The asyndetic use of λέγουσιν in the historical present typifies Matthew's style (21,6), and ναί is among his favorite words (2,2).

13:52 As in the explanation of the parable concerning the tares, Matthew introduces Jesus' response to the disciples with ὁ δέ (cf. vv 37, 38, 39 [ter]). The response itself opens with the typically Matthean διὰ τοῦτο (4,2), which means that because the true disciples have understood the parables, they will be the kind of scribe portrayed in the following part of the statement. For emphasis, Matthew characteristically puts πᾶς (63,25-26) with γραμματεύς. See the comments on 8:19 concerning γραμματεύς as his figure for a disciple of Jesus: just as Jesus is a new and better Moses, so his disciples are new and better scribes. One becomes a disciple, or scribe, through being instructed concerning the kingdom of heaven. μαθητευθείς occurs only in Matthew among the gospels (13:52; 27:57; 28:19), and "the kingdom of heaven" is a well-known emphasis of Matthew (25,7).

"Is like a man [who is] a housemaster" echoes the parallel openings of the preceding six parables (vv 24b, 31b, 33b, 44a, 45a, 47a), especially those in vv 24b and 45a, where Matthew has used "a man" as his designation of a disciple (see the comments on v 44 for Mattheanisms). οἰκοδεσπότῃ is another favorite (2,4) and echoes v 27, where it stands for Jesus. Here it stands for a true disciple of Jesus. Like master, like disciple (cf. 10:25)! θησαυροῦ is yet another Mattheanism (1,4). It represents the housemaster's understanding of the kingdom and comes from the parable of the hidden treasure (v 44). The "new things" represent the new understanding gained through the parables; and the "old things," the old understanding possessed prior to the parabolic teaching. The old understanding made the new understanding possible, "for whoever has, it will be given to him and he will have an abundance" (v 12). The Mattheanism ἐκβάλλει (10,1) refers to speaking, as also in 12:35 (bis; contrast the different verb in Luke 6:45). There, too, it goes with treasure and has to do with the true disciple as one who teaches righteousness by word of mouth as well as by example. Matthew likes ὅστις (23,5). Here it emphasizes the true disciple's quality of speaking out of new and old understanding of the kingdom.

The discipling of all nations (28:19) implies that Matthew's portrayal of a "discipled scribe" applies to every Christian, not just to a special class in the church. It would be wrong to separate becoming a disciple (μαθητεύομαι as a deponent) from being instructed as a disciple (μαθητεύομαι as a true passive); for in 28:19-20 both the initiatory rite of baptism and subsequent teaching define the making of disciples. Nevertheless, the figurative reference to speaking out of new and old understanding implies that emphasis rests on instruction concerning the kingdom (cf. vv 36c and 51a). The "every" with "scribe" tends away from the view that Matthew is referring to himself, or even making a play on his name (Μαθθαῖος—μαθητευθείς). The contextual reference to what the disciples have already understood of Jesus' earlier teaching and what they now come to understand through the parables stands against other identifications of the old things and new things as OT prophecies and Jesus' words, or as Jesus' teaching and the teaching of Christian prophets or of Matthew himself.

LACK OF UNDERSTANDING IN UNBELIEVING JEWS
13:53-58 (Mark 6:1-6a)

Matthew follows his practice of putting a block of narrative after each discourse of Jesus and goes on in Mark except for omitting materials previously used (Mark 4:35–5:43, used in Matt 8:23-34; 9:18-26). This narrative section encompasses 13:53–17:27. The editing of the stories displays typically Matthean motifs, especially a continuation of the contrast between understanding and lack of understanding. Thus the narrative illustrates the leading motif of the preceding discourse.

13:53 (Mark 6:1) The formula that concludes the third in Matthew's pentateuch of dominical discourses also leads to the illustrative narrative. See the comments on 7:28-29 concerning the repeated formula. "These parables" harks back to 13:1-52. To avoid redundancy with ἐλθών in the next verse, Matthew substitutes μετῆρεν (cf. 19:1) for Mark's ἐξῆλθεν. "From there" means exit from Jesus' house (cf. v 36); in Mark it means exit from the house of a synagogue ruler (cf. Mark 5:38-43). Luke 4:16-30 contains a different tradition.

13:54 (Mark 6:1-2) Mark's ἔρχεται changes to the typically Matthean participle ἐλθών (10,10), which identifies Jesus as the Coming One (see the comments on 3:11). The singular of "synagogue" implies that εἰς τὴν πατρίδα αὐτοῦ means "into his hometown" (i.e., Nazareth), not "into his home country" (i.e., Galilee). Of course, Jesus had moved his home to Capernaum (4:13), but Nazareth remained the town of his upbringing (2:23). The insertion of "their" makes the synagogue in Jesus' hometown typify synagogues of unbelieving Jews at the time Matthew was writing (see the comments on 7:28-29). Mark's "and his disciples follow him" disappears in order that the people in whose synagogue Jesus teaches may be understood as unbelieving Jews rather than as Jesus' disciples. Matthew also omits "And when the Sabbath came" (so Mark) in order to bring together "and having come into his hometown" and "he began to teach." Besides, readers would understand as a matter of course that it must have been the Sabbath if Jesus was teaching in the synagogue. The inchoative use of the imperfect tense in ἐδίδασκεν, "he began to teach," allows the omission of Mark's auxiliary verb ἤρξατο, "he began." As a result, stress falls more strongly on teaching (cf. the comments on 5:1-2).

Matthew often avoids ἄρχομαι as an auxiliary (see 9:27; 13:1, 54; 14:35; 19:27; 20:17, 24, 30; 21:12, 33; 24:4; 26:67, 71; 27:29 with Markan parallels). On Mark's usage as an Aramaism, see BAG, s.v. ἄρχω 2αβ.

The people are amazed at Jesus' teaching. Matthew characteristically introduces their amazement with ὥστε (10,0) instead of Mark's καί. But he omits "hearing" (so Mark) because it is not true even of false disciples. Much less do outsiders truly hear when they hear (see v 13, distinctive in this respect). Mark's "many" who were amazed become simply "they." "Many" distinguishes the large audience from Jesus' disciples. Since Matthew has not mentioned the disciples, he has no need to make such a distinction. Mark's participle λέγοντες is a Mattheanism (61,23), but it becomes the infinitive λέγειν for a match with ἐκπλήσσεσθαι.

Matthew deletes "these things, and what . . . ?" from the question beginning "From where?" Consequently, there is no question about the nature of Jesus' "wisdom" and "miracles." We read only a question about their source. Matthew probably has in mind the alternative answers, Satan and the Spirit of God (see 12:22-32; cf. 11:25-27). By dropping the descriptions of Jesus' wisdom as "given" and of Jesus' miracles as "happening through his hands," he enhances the authority and power of Jesus *in his own right* as "God with us" (1:23).

13:55 (Mark 6:3) "The son" shifts from "of Mary" to "of the builder." Thus the people do not ask, "Is not this the builder?" (so Mark), but, "Is not this the *son* of the builder?" Matthew is not protecting Jesus' dignity by shielding him from the occupation of building. We have read far more damaging charges in this gospel (11:19; 12:24). The reason for transferring the occupation of building from Jesus to his foster father lies in the associated transferal of Jesus' sonship from Mary to his foster father (cf. Luke 4:22). Matthew wants to remind his readers that through Joseph Jesus had a legal claim to the messianic throne of David (see the comments on chaps. 1–2 passim). With the same purpose the name of Jesus' brother "Joses" reverts to its original Hebrew form "Joseph," which recalls Jesus' foster father.

Since timber was scarce and stones were abundant in Palestine, τέκτων may mean a stonemason rather than, or more than, a carpenter. It is doubtful whether Joseph was still living.

Because Matthew has transferred Jesus' sonship from Mary to Joseph, he now rephrases the reference to Mary and, consequently, the references to Jesus' brothers. Insertion of "is called" with a second writing of "not" makes another question beginning with οὐχ. Such parallelism is characteristic of Matthew's style; and he has a penchant for using λέγω with names (10,2). Emphasis falls on the names of Jesus' mother and brothers, no longer on their family relationship to him. The reason for this shift is that his true family does not consist in his blood relatives, but in those who do the will of his Father in heaven (12:46-50). The names of Jesus' brothers Judas and Simon (so Mark) switch order in accord with the list of the apostles, where Simon stands first and Judas last (10:2-4). The switch confirms that Matthew is thinking of Jesus' true family, such as the apostles. (That the Apostle Judas apostatized does not take away the point.)

13:56 (Mark 6:3) In the question concerning Jesus' sisters, Matthew advances αἱ ἀδελφαὶ αὐτοῦ for a parallel with the position of οἱ ἀδελφοὶ αὐτοῦ in the preceding line. Mark's "here" seems redundant alongside "with us." Matthew therefore omits it and compensates with a typical insertion of "all" (63,25-26). Finally, he adds a last question: "Therefore, from where [did] this one [get] all these things?" This question reiterates the issue of God's Spirit versus Satan as the source of Jesus' wisdom and power and comes from the people's first question, especially in its Markan form: "From where [did] this one [get] these things?" Matthew characteristically inserts οὖν (35,11) and πάντα (63,25-26). The combination ταῦτα πάντα is a favorite of his (7,1). In sum, the introductory and concluding questions begin with πόθεν, and sandwiched between them are first a pair of questions beginning with οὐχ and then a pair of questions beginning with καί—all evidence of Matthew's love of parallelism.

13:57 (Mark 6:3-4) The people's taking offense at Jesus implies unbelief. In the introduction to Jesus' reply, Matthew writes δέ instead of Mark's καί for the sake of contrast. He also changes "he was saying" to "he said" (see Allen, xxi), advances Ἰησοῦς to the head of the clause for a Christological emphasis, and omits the recitative ὅτι. "And among his relatives" falls from Jesus' statement that a prophet is without honor in his hometown and in his house. Again, the deletion stems from the statement in 12:46-50 that Jesus' true relatives are those who do the will of his Father in heaven. Blood relatives therefore drop out of the picture. The omission leaves a pair of parallel phrases, "in his hometown and in his house."

13:58 (Mark 6:5-6) In the statement about Jesus' performance of miracles Matthew omits Mark's "he was not able," turns "to do" into "he did not do," replaces "a single miracle, except that laying his hands on a few sick people he healed [them]" (so Mark) with "many miracles," and omits "and he marvelled" in order to bring "on account of their unbelief" into immediate connection with Jesus' not doing many miracles there. Consequently, the emphasis shifts from Jesus' *inability* and the *fewness* of the miracles he performed in Nazareth. Instead, it falls on the hometowners' *unbelief* and Jesus' *refusal* to perform so many miracles as he usually did in a locality: "and he did not do many miracles there, because of their unbelief."

LACK OF UNDERSTANDING IN HEROD THE TETRARCH
14:1-12 (Mark 6:14-31; Luke 9:7-9)

14:1 (Mark 6:14; Luke 9:7) This story has to do with Herod Antipas's failure to recognize Jesus' true identity. Matthew begins with the last of his three insertions of "in that season" (cf. 11:25; 12:1). The imprecision of the phrase stems from his putting the story after the incident in Nazareth; in Mark the story takes place right after the mission of the twelve, which Matthew has already described (except for its carrying out) in chap. 10. Here, then, the death of John the Baptist (14:1-12) stands alongside the rejection of Jesus at Nazareth (cf. "John the Baptist parallel Jesus" in the Topical Index). Matthew drops "the king" before Herod's name and tacks on "the tetrarch" after it in order to forestall confusion of this Herod with King Herod in chap. 2. Luke agrees with Matthew in the change.

Some have supposed that the changing of Herod's designation from king to tetrarch is the correction of a loose and popular usage by means of a strictly accurate term. Perhaps so in Luke; but later, Matthew retains Mark's designation "the king" (v 9). Therefore it is better to think that Matthew has no concern for strict accuracy, but only wants to clarify at the outset the distinction between Herod Antipas and his father, King Herod the Great. As tetrarch, Herod Antipas governed Galilee and Perea (Josephus *Ant.* 17.11.4 §318).

Matthew writes that Herod the tetrarch "heard the news about Jesus" rather than "heard, for his [Jesus'] name had become public." Mark's statement means that Jesus' name had become public as a result of the mission of the twelve throughout Galilee. Since Matthew has not described an accomplishment of the mission, his statement has a more general reference and takes after the distinctive summary in 4:24: "and the news about him went out. . . ."

14:2 (Mark 6:14-16; Luke 9:7-9) Mark, followed by Luke, goes on to write what people in general were saying about Jesus, viz., that Jesus was John the Baptist raised from the dead, Elijah, or a prophet. Only after hearing these identifications does Mark's Herod settle on an identification of Jesus with John the Baptist. In Matthew, Herod immediately makes his own identification of Jesus with John the Baptist. The identifications of Jesus with Elijah and a prophet are reserved for 16:13-14. Thus Herod's lack of understanding, shown in the wrong identification of Jesus with John, stands alone for emphasis—but not quite alone. It stands in contrast with the crowd's correct recognition of John as "a prophet" (cf. v 5). "The crowd" stands for the professing church. The insertion of "to his servants" provides Herod with an audience. παισίν is a Mattheanism (5,1).

Matthew divides Mark's single line giving some people's opinion, "John the baptizer is risen from the dead," into two lines (v 2bc). The first consists of Herod's wrong identification, "This is John the Baptist." οὗτός ἐστιν typifies Matthew's style (12,0) and causes initial emphasis to fall on the error of identification rather than on the supposing of a resurrection. See the comments on 3:1 concerning the substitution of βαπτιστής for βαπτίζων. The second line consists of Herod's wrong deduction, "He has risen from the dead," and makes a couplet with the next line, "and on account of this miraculous powers are at work in him" (so also Mark, except for a slight difference in the order of words). The distinctive and emphatic αὐτός stresses the person of John and characterizes Matthew's diction (14,3). The shift from Mark's perfect tense in ἐγήγερται to the aorist tense in ἠγέρθη (so also Luke) probably stems from the desire to make John a prototype of Jesus, for the aorist is used of Jesus' resurrection and with ἀπὸ τῶν νεκρῶν (as here) also in 28:7 (cf. 27:64, both peculiar to Matthew). Not only the aorist tense, but also ἀπό, which here substitutes for Mark's ἐκ, brings these passages into association.

Cf. Luke 8:3; Acts 13:1. αἱ δυνάμεις ἐνεργοῦσιν ἐν αὐτῷ may awkwardly translate an Aramaic statement meaning "Miracles are done by him" (see G. Dalman, *The Words of Jesus* [Edinburgh: T. & T. Clark, 1902] 201), or may reflect an opinion of Herod (or of the people, in Mark) that magical powers are at work in Jesus. Cf. Acts 2–5 for a close association between the working of miracles and resurrection from the dead.

14:3-12 (Mark 6:17-31) Herod's deduction that John has risen from the dead triggers a flashback to the death of John the Baptist. Throughout this passage Matthew makes changes that reduce the amount of attention given to Herod and his associates and increase the amount of attention given to John as Jesus' prototype. Mark's emphatic αὐτός falls from the reference to Herod (v 3). Matthew has used it for John, instead (v 2). Herod's action of sending vanishes, and the seizure of John takes its place (v 3). Herod's name turns into a mere pronoun; only the name of John remains (v 4a).

The whole statement that Herodias had a grudge against John (Mark 6:19a) goes away (v 5). As a result, Herod wants to kill John but, through fear of the crowd, fails. In Mark, Herodias wants to kill John, but cannot because Herod fears him. Yet in all of this Matthew refuses to take Herod's name from Mark. Similarly, Herod's keeping John safe, being perplexed, and gladly listening to John (Mark 6:20bcd) drop out. The double reference to Herod's birthday in Mark 6:21 collapses into a single reference, and the statement concerning Herod's making a dinner for his lords and military commanders and the leading men of Galilee disappears (v 6). Mark's reference to the ones reclining with Herod at the dinner and the direct quotation of Herod's initial statement to Herodias's daughter (Mark 6:22) also disappear. Matthew retains Herod's oath to the girl, but changes it from direct to indirect discourse. The detailed description of the girl's going out, consulting her mother, and coming back (Mark 6:24-25a) and the references to Herod as "the king" and to the executioner who was commanded to bring John's head (Mark 6:27) drop out.

In the statement about beheading, Matthew replaces "him" with "John" (v 10). He puts the bringing of the head and its being given to the girl in the passive voice (v 11) instead of Mark's active. Thus the stress falls on John, or his head, rather than on the executioner. From the bringing of the head to the mother (v 11) Matthew deletes "the girl." The disciples of John do not "hear," as in Mark, but "approach," as though John had had a dignity similar to that of Jesus, whom others in Matthew constantly "approach" with reverence (38,6—see the comments on προσέρχομαι at 4:3; 8:14). And according to the probably original text of v 12, Matthew makes the disciples of John bury John himself (αὐτόν) rather than John's corpse (αὐτό, so Mark; see Metzger, *Textual Commentary* ad loc.). In all these ways Matthew exalts the person of John, Jesus' prototype, at the expense of others in the story.

Just after the identification of Herodias as the wife of Philip, Herod's brother, Matthew omits Mark's statement that Herod had married her (v 3; cf. Mark 6:17c). She still belongs to Philip, not to Herod. Therefore John's warning, "It is not lawful for you to have her" (v 4), is a prohibition of a marriage only contemplated, not a criticism of a marriage that has already taken place (as in Mark). Accordingly, Matthew shifts the desire to kill John from Herodias to Herod, who resents John's prohibition yet fears the crowd, whom John has convinced against such a marriage. Thus Herod no longer appears as John's protector who gladly listens to John (so Mark). Thus also, the statement that Herodias was unable to kill John (Mark 6:19c) drops out. Of course she was unable—she did not even belong to Herod's household! And the girl becomes "the daughter of Herodias" (v 6) instead of "his [Herod's] daughter" (so the best text of Mark 6:22a; see the UBS and Metzger, *Textual Commentary* ad loc.): since Herod has not married Herodias, her daughter does not belong to him. For the same reason his promise to the girl no longer includes the phrase "up to half of my kingdom"—too much to promise a young lady who is not even a member of the family. Still for the same reason, the girl does not go out to consult her mother (as in Mark), for her mother has no quarters of her own in Herod's fortress. The mother is only a guest in attendance at the party. There she puts forward her daughter with a preplanted request for John's head (contrast v 8 with Mark 6:24). And "I wish" drops out of the girl's request for John's head (v 8) because Matthew has transferred the desire to kill John from Herodias the mother to Herod the tetrarch (v 5).

Why does Matthew play with the details in a way that transmutes a historical report into a semihistorical short story? He wants to shift the onus of guilt from Herodias to Herod. Thus, according to Mark 6:26 Herod "became *very* sorry" (περίλυπος γενόμενος), but according to Matt 14:9 Herod became merely "sorry" (λυπηθείς, without the perfective preposition)—not because he did not want to kill John, as in Mark, but because he wanted to kill John under better circumstances (cf. v 5). "Here" substitutes for Mark's "immediately" in the girl's request for the head of John (v 8) and shows that Matthew's Herod wants to kill John away from public gaze, in contrast with Mark's Herod, who wants to buy time so as not to kill John at all. Herod's consideration of his guests suggests their hostility toward John (cf. the plural in 17:12). By adding "with [Herod]" to "reclining at meal" Matthew associates Herod with his guests in that hostility. Quite logically, then, the first evangelist revises Mark's statement that Herod "did not want to refuse her" to read that Herod "commanded [the head] to be given [her]" (v 9). And despite the participle "sending," Matthew's omitting the executioner brings Herod into closer connection with the beheading (v 10). As a result, Herod's wrong identification of Jesus links up with a heightening of Herod's crime. Guilt and lack of understanding—Matthew puts them together.

In his antagonism toward John, Herod Antipas takes after his father Herod the Great, who tried to kill Jesus (2:1-18). John, Jesus, and Jesus' disciples (represented by "the crowd") stand on one side. Herod the Great, Herod Antipas, and unbelieving Jews stand on the other side in their ignorant persecution of those who belong to the kingdom. In Mark 6:20 Herod Antipas fears John. In Matt 14:5 Herod fears the crowd. By replacing John with the crowd, Matthew calls attention to Jesus' disciples (the crowd regularly represents the professing church in Matthew) as those who understand John's true identity. The true identity appears in Matthew's changing Herod's description of John as "a righteous and holy man" (Mark 6:20) to the crowd's description of John as "a prophet" (v 5). This accords with Jesus' description of John as a prophet (11:9; in particular, Elijah the prophet according to 11:14; 17:10-13) and parallels Jesus' prophethood (see 21:11 and 46, where Matthew will twice insert prophetic Christology; cf. Luke 13:31-35).

On Herod's marriage to Herodias, a marriage compacted while he was still married to his first wife the daughter of King Aretas of Arabia, and on his killing John the Baptist, see Josephus *Ant.* 18.5.2 §§116-19. Josephus does not connect the two stories, but writes that Herod executed John for fear of John's popularity. Mark has Herod caught between Herodias's evil design against John and his own admiration of John. Fear of John's popularity and personal admiration of John do not necessarily contradict each other. Matthew's theological importation of the crowd agrees with Josephus's political analysis. Herod's marriage to Herodias went against the OT prohibition of taking the wife of one's brother (Lev 18:16; 20:21). On the historical and textual questions regarding the identity of Philip as Herod Philip of Rome or Philip the tetrarch, see F. F. Bruce, *New Testament History* (2nd ed.; London: Oliphants, 1971) 24-27; C. H. H. Scobie, *John the Baptist* (Philadelphia: Fortress, 1964) 181; Metzger, *Textual Commentary* ad loc.

14:3-5 (Mark 6:17-20) Matthew's rejection of "sending" (so Mark) leads him to advance the seizing and binding of John. To fill the vacant verbal position left toward the end of the clause, Matthew uses ἀπέθετο, "put away." ἐν φυλακῇ, "in prison," comes forward to a position in front of ἀπέθετο in order that this verb may be balanced by a prepositional phrase on both sides (contrast the imbalance in Mark's text). "He was saying" implies repeated warnings. As in v 2, Mark's recitative ὅτι drops out. According to Josephus, Herod imprisoned John in the fortress at Machaerus several miles northeast of the Dead Sea.

14:6 (Mark 6:21-22) Matthew's genitive absolute that opens v 6 comes from Mark 6:21a as to grammatical construction, from Mark 6:21b as to diction (except for γενομένοις). The reference to dancing changes from a participle in a genitive absolute (so Mark) to a finite verb in an independent clause. This change produces a couplet of lines exhibiting Matthew's fondness for parallelism. The daughter's "entering" (so Mark) turns into the prepositional phrase "in the midst." Four other occurrences of μέσος are peculiar to Matthew (see 13:25, 49; 18:20; 25:6). That the daughter does not enter favors her being at the party already and agrees with Matthew's later omission (v 8) of her going out, consulting her mother, and entering again.

14:7 (Mark 6:23) Matthew will insert ὅθεν also in 25:24, 26. Here it replaces καί. The revision of Mark's "he swore" to read "he promised with an oath" tallies with Matthew's insertions of ὅρκου also in 5:33; 26:72 and with the insertion of ὁμολογήσω in 7:23. Here the expression provides a clear backdrop to the later use of ὅρκους (v 9).

14:8 (Mark 6:24-25) Matthew puts δέ in place of Mark's καί to contrast Herod's promise to the girl with her mother's having put her forward or prompted her. Whether προβιβασθεῖσα refers to a putting forward or an earlier instruction (see BAG, s.v. προβιβάζω), its aorist tense indicates prior action, and the girl's taking John's head to her mother (v 11) implies the mother's coaching in Matthew as well as in Mark. Matthew's omitting "I wish that" necessitates changing the subjunctive δῷς to the imperative δός. φησίν is a Mattheanism (11,4).

14:9 (Mark 6:26) The replacement of Mark's περίλυπος γενόμενος with λυπηθείς accords with Matthew's liking of λυπέω in its simple form (2,1). The plural διὰ τοὺς ὅρκους refers to the words of the oath, which took the singular in v 7. Cf. Num 5:21 LXX[A,F]; 2 Macc 4:34; 7:24. Matthew likes ἐκέλευσεν (5,2). His inserting "to give" reflects "give" in the girl's request (v 8).

14:10 (Mark 6:27) The participle πέμψας replaces the synonymous ἀποστείλας. Matthew favors the former over the latter for first position in a clause (see also 2:8; 22:7, with only one exception in 2:16). Execution by beheading went against Jewish law, but agreed with Greek and Roman custom.

14:11 (Mark 6:28) The Salome mentioned by Josephus was born in A.D. 22. Identification of the dancer with Salome would stretch the meaning of τῷ κορασίῳ from "the girl" to "the young woman." But we do not know that Salome was the dancer. The replacement of Mark's second "gave" with "brought" avoids immediate repetition of "gave" and produces the alternation "was brought . . . was given . . . brought." The leaving of Mark's αὐτήν to be supplied mentally makes a closer parallel with the preceding line.

14:12 (Mark 6:29-31) The deletion of "having heard" and changing of "came" to "approaching" leaves "took" and "buried" as a couplet of parallel verbs. The dropping of Mark's "his" from "corpse" leaves the direct object at the very end of the phrase to parallel the next phrase, which Matthew reconstructs by displacing "they put it in a tomb" with "they buried him." Finally, out of the twelve disciples' announcement that they have successfully completed their mission (Mark 6:30) Matthew makes an announcement by the disciples of John that John has been executed. The initial participle ἐλθόντες shows that Matthew constructs the line as a parallel to the preceding line, which begins with the participle προσελθόντες. Both participles typify his diction (10,10; 38,6). The added clause suggests that John's disciples became Jesus' disciples. It also contributes to Matthew's assimilation of John and Jesus (see "John the Baptist parallel Jesus" in the Topical Index).

OBEDIENT UNDERSTANDING OF JESUS' COMMAND TO SERVE THE LORD'S SUPPER TO DISCIPLED NATIONS
14:13-21 (Mark 6:32-44; Luke 9:10b-17; John 6:1-13; cf. Matt 15:32-39; Mark 8:1-10)

14:13 (Mark 6:32-33; Luke 9:10b-11) In Mark and Luke Jesus withdraws with his twelve disciples in order to rest after the mission in Galilee. In Matthew, Jesus withdraws for safety from Herod Antipas, who has executed John the Baptist and deduced that Jesus is John risen from the dead. Just as John's imprisonment led to Jesus' leaving the Jordan Valley (4:12), so now John's death leads to evasive tactics in and around Galilee (note that "but hearing . . . he departed" repeats 4:12). Thus Matthew portrays Jesus as an example of fleeing persecution (see 10:23, unique to the first gospel, and "Flight from persecution" in the Topical Index).

The δέ that replaces Mark's καί draws a contrast between the coming of John's disciples and the departure of Jesus. ἀνεχώρησεν (cf. Luke's ὑπεχώρησεν) not only echoes 4:12, where it was inserted, but also replaces Mark's ἀπῆλθον, "they went away." Matthew likes Mark's verb (14,11), but it does not connote flight from danger. So he chooses another of his favorite verbs, which does. Cf. especially 12:15; 15:21, where it occurs, as here, in a distinctive combination with yet another Mattheanism, viz., ἐκεῖθεν (8,1). Similarly, ἀκούσας not only echoes 4:12, where as here it had no parallel, but it also comes from Matthew's favorite vocabulary (10,3) and refers to the preceding report concerning John's death, a report mentioned only by Matthew. For a Christological emphasis Matthew characteristically inserts the name of Jesus (80,12), even though the name has just appeared at the close of the last verse. Furthermore, the verb of departure no longer takes "they," as in Mark, but "he" (so also Luke). Only Jesus comes into view. When the disciples later approach him, therefore, they appear to approach him out of the crowds (vv 14-15). In other words, it looks as though Jesus alone had gone in the boat and the disciples had followed on foot as part of the crowds—naturally, since in Matthew the crowds represent professing disciples.

"From there" leaves the point of departure undefined. The rejection of Jesus in his hometown, the intervention of other material since that event (vv 1-12), and the phrase "in a boat" rule out Nazareth and favor Capernaum. Luke's mention of Bethsaida as the destination suggests a location of the deserted place in the vicinity of that city, which lay on the northeast shore of the Sea of Galilee. Since he does not care for the niceties of chronology, Matthew here goes on as though the foregoing story of John the Baptist's death did not mark a stepping back in time (see Allen, 159).

Matthew puts "the crowds" in place of Mark's "many" and makes them "follow" Jesus (so also Luke). ὄχλοι and ἠκολούθησαν are Mattheanisms (17,1; 8,0). According to Mark, many "recognized" the disciples and Jesus, "ran together there, and preceded them." That many preceded Jesus disagrees with Matthew's emphasis on *following* Jesus—hence the rejection of "preceded." Matthew retains "from all the cities," except for the omission of "all," and relates the phrase to the new verb "followed." Thus the emphasis falls on discipleship: the crowds followed Jesus from the cities just as large numbers of people were later discipled throughout the world (28:19). And the crowds followed because they "heard," not because they "saw them [Jesus and the disciples] going" (so Mark). Hearing assimilates the crowds to Jesus, who also hears (in Matthew only). It also portrays the crowds as those who hear with the result of discipleship (see chap. 13, where, because of the parables, hearing receives more emphasis than seeing). Thus Matthew carefully constructs the parallelism between the two clauses of v 13 in order to make a theological point.

14:14 (Mark 6:34; Luke 9:11) The first two clauses in v 14 match Mark exactly: "And going out, he saw a large crowd, and he had compassion on them." Since in Mark the crowd has preceded Jesus, "going out" refers to Jesus' getting out of the boat. But in Matthew the crowds have followed Jesus. Therefore "going out" refers to Jesus' coming forth from his deserted place of privacy (see v 13a). In Mark, Jesus' compassion leads to a comparison of the crowd with shepherdless sheep and a statement about his teaching. But Matthew used the comparison in 9:36 and devoted most of chap. 13 to parables. In 9:35, however, the healing ministry of Jesus was mentioned alongside his teaching. Therefore Matthew omits the comparison of the crowd to shepherdless sheep and exchanges the teaching for the healing: "and he healed their sick" (cf. 19:2 with Mark 10:1). Luke's similarity to Matthew in these respects, along with the agreements of Matthew and Luke against Mark noted above, suggests Matthean influence on Luke; for a comparison between the crowds and shepherdless sheep fails to appear in Luke's parallel to Matt 9:36—viz., Luke 8:1—so that he has no reason to omit the comparison here. Similarly, the lack of a reference to Jesus' healing people in Luke's parallel to Matt 9:35—again Luke 8:1—takes away the association which in Matthew triggers the substitution of healing for teaching in the present passage. Matthew inserts ἐθεράπευσεν ten times in his gospel. τοὺς ἀρρώστους appears nowhere else in it, but may compensate for omission of the term in 13:58 (cf. Mark 6:5) and 10:7 (cf. Mark 6:13 and "Compensation" in the Topical Index).

14:15 (Mark 6:35-36; Luke 9:12) Mark's parallel to v 15 opens, "And when the hour had already become late." Matthew substitutes the usual "But when evening came" (cf. 8:16; 14:15, 23; 16:2 v.1.; 20:8; 26:20; 27:57) in order to make the feeding of the five thousand an evening meal for the crowds, i.e., the Lord's Supper for the church. For the same expression sets the stage for the Last Supper (26:20; Mark 14:17) and, with the possible exception of 16:2 v.1., only in the present passage does Matthew go out of his way to insert it. Mark's participle concerning the disciples' approach to Jesus escalates to a finite verb. Consequently, ἔλεγον becomes the characteristically Matthean participle λέγοντες (61,23), and additional emphasis accrues to Jesus' dignity (cf. the comments on προσέρχομαι at 4:3; 8:14).

The disciples' reference to the desertedness of the place stays. But the additional reference to the lateness of the hour changes to "the hour has already passed away." In Mark 14:35-36 Jesus will pray "that if it is possible the hour might pass away from him. . . . Take this cup from me." Matthew will omit the reference to the hour and transfer "pass away" to the cup (26:39). He will make this change because he uses "hour" with "pass away" in the feeding of the five thousand. The change will confirm that he associates the feeding with the Lord's Supper. It is the more remarkable in that drinking from a cup does not figure in the feeding.

The addition of "the" to "hour" and the advancing of "hour" to first position after the conjunction lay stress on the hour. From Matthew's standpoint the hour has indeed already passed, the hour of Jesus' self-sacrifice. Because it has, the church may eat the Lord's Supper. First, however, the disciples suggest that Jesus dismiss "the crowds" to go away and buy "food" for themselves. The typical replacement of Mark's "them" with "the crowds" (17,1) again points to the masses in the church. And Matthew uses "food" to replace Mark's "something they may eat" because he will insert "eat" in the Words of Institution (26:26); i.e., he reserves "eat" for eating bread from the hand of Jesus (vv 20-21). Eating something bought in the nearest towns would not qualify to represent the Lord's Supper.

Matthew omits Mark's recitative ὅτι. His penchant for οὖν (35,11) favors the originality of that reading here (see the UBS for external evidence). He always rejects Mark's κύκλῳ (see Mark 3:34 with Matt 12:49; Mark 6:6 with Matt 9:35). And though he likes ἀγρός in the sense "field" (3,10), he always rejects the term when Mark uses it in the sense "hamlet" (see Mark 5:14 with Matt 8:33; Mark 6:56 with Matt 14:35). Thus here, too, Mark's "the surrounding hamlets" drops out.

14:16 (Mark 6:37-38; Luke 9:13) Though Matthew likes ἀποκριθεὶς εἶπεν (29,6), he puts Ἰησοῦς in place of ἀποκριθείς for another Christological emphasis (cf. the comments on v 13). Luke, too, drops ἀποκριθείς, but does not add Jesus' name. Matthew constructs the first line of Jesus' reply out of the common expression "have need" (see 3:14; 6:8; 9:12; 14:16; 21:3; 26:65), "not," and ἀπελθεῖν, which represents his special diction and echoes the disciples' suggestion (v 15). Jesus' assurance that the crowds need not go away reads like an invitation to eat the Lord's Supper. "You give them [something] to eat" becomes, then, a command to distribute the elements of the Lord's Supper. Jesus probably intended the feeding to anticipate the messianic banquet (cf. 26:29; see Gundry, *Use of the OT* 36, for a possible allusion to 2 Kgs 4:42).

14:17 (Mark 6:38; Luke 9:13) At this point Matthew omits the incredulous, if not sarcastic, question of the disciples whether they should go away and buy two hundred denarii worth of bread. Jesus' counter question, "How many loaves do you have?", the command "Go see," and the disciples' finding out also disappear. We might think that Matthew does not want to tarnish Jesus' authority with such talking back by the disciples, or Jesus' omniscience with a question the answer to which he should have known without asking. But more is at work here. Matthew makes the omission because Mark's material shows the disciples to be ignorant, and he wants to portray them as understanding. In Mark they mistake Jesus' command to mean that they should go away and purchase food. In Matthew they do not misunderstand, but immediately announce the amount of food available. Matthew's Jesus has already ruled out food bought in the nearest towns by saying that the crowds need not go away (v 16b). This implies that the provisions are on hand. Indeed, Matthew characteristically inserts "here" (ὧδε—7,1) in the disciples' statement that they have only five loaves and two fish. Yet the statement, which displays understanding, suffers from little faith. Good understanding does not guarantee great faith. See the comments on 8:26 concerning Matthew's warnings against little faith, which are always directed to disciples; also 14:31 (in the next story here) and 16:8 (with allusions to the feedings of the five thousand and four thousand).

Matthew reconstructs the disciples' response to Jesus for a parallel with Jesus' statement in v 16ab. "They say," "five," "and two fish"—these come over from Mark. But the initial καί changes to οἱ δέ for a parallel with ὁ δέ in v 16a. The insertion "to him" makes a parallel with "to them" in v 16a, and the insertion "We do not have [anything] here except . . ."

makes a parallel with "They do not have need . . ." in v 16b. For reasons mentioned above, Matthew draws "here" from Mark's account of the feeding of the four thousand (Mark 8:4) and then omits it in his own version of that later feeding (15:33). The addition "except" results of necessity from the insertion "we do not have." To "five" Matthew adds "loaves" from Mark 6:37-38, where "loaves" occurs twice in material he omits. Luke makes a similar addition, but compensates more fully for sharing Matthew's omission. He does so by tacking a part of the omitted material on the disciples' mention of five loaves and two fish. Matthew's concern to extract from the omitted material a reference to loaves of bread exhibits both his habit of compensating for omissions he makes and his desire to portray the feeding of the five thousand in terms of the Lord's Supper, where bread figures prominently.

Bread and fish made up the basic diet of poor people in Galilee (cf. 7:9-10; John 21:9-10, 13). Luke agrees with Matthew in having οἱ δέ where Mark does not. But οἱ δέ has no preceding parallel in Luke as a reason for its introduction. Luke's text is also similar to Matthew's "we do not have" (not in Mark). But again Luke lacks Matthew's reason, viz., parallelism with "they do not have" in v 16b. Therefore the similarities suggest Matthean influence on Luke.

14:18 To portray Jesus as the host at this "Lord's Supper," Matthew now composes and inserts Jesus' instruction that the disciples should bring the five loaves and two fish. "And he said" echoes v 16a. "Bring them here to me" anticipates 17:17; Mark 9:19 (cf. Luke 9:41). ὧδε is a Mattheanism (7,1) and echoes v 17b. The two successive, distinctive occurrences of this adverb emphasize the presence of the bread: where Christ is, the bread is.

14:19 (Mark 6:39-41; Luke 9:14-16) At the beginning of v 19 Matthew characteristically replaces Mark's ἐπέταξεν, which never occurs in the first gospel, with κελεύσας (5,2). The reduction of the verb to a participle falls in line with the participles λαβών, ἀναβλέψας, and κλάσας (for which Mark and Luke have the stronger κατέκλασεν, "he broke [the bread] in pieces"). Consequently, emphasis rests on the two verbs εὐλόγησεν, "he blessed," and ἔδωκεν, "he gave." εὐλόγησεν lacks an expressed object and means either that Jesus thanked God, or that he consecrated the bread and fish, or that he did both (see BAG, s.v.).

In Mark, Jesus orders his disciples (αὐτοῖς, "them") to make the people (πάντας, "all") recline (ἀνακλῖναι, "cause to recline"). Through scribal failure to understand the causative sense of ἀνακλῖναι and the different referents of αὐτοῖς and πάντας and also through parallel influence from Matthew, the reading ἀνακλιθῆναι slipped into Mark with the result that Jesus "ordered them all to recline" (see the UBS and Metzger, *Textual Commentary* ad loc.). The active, causative form of the infinitive is favored in Mark both by its slightly better external evidence and by Luke's κατακλίνατε αὐτούς, which presumably reflects Mark's original reading. But where Jesus orders the disciples to make all the people recline (so the original text of Mark, and Luke), Matthew switches to a deponent passive (ἀνακλιθῆναι), eliminates πάντας, and characteristically replaces αὐτοῖς

(Mark's reference to the disciples) with τοὺς ὄχλους (17,1). Thus Jesus himself commands the crowds to recline (cf. 15:35; Mark 8:6). He acts as their Lord, and they represent his larger group of disciples, indeed, the worldwide church.

By omitting the greenness of the grass and the arrangement of the people in different groups (so Mark), Matthew further concentrates attention on Jesus as the host at this Lord's Supper and also portrays the crowds as the whole, undivided church (cf. 16:18). Omission of the actual reclining (Mark 6:40) and of Mark's καί before λαβών has a staccatolike effect—"commanding . . . taking . . . looking up"—an effect that concentrates even more attention on Jesus' actions. The taking of the bread, the blessing, the breaking of the bread, and the giving of it to the disciples will reappear in the account of Jesus' instituting the Lord's Supper (26:26-29) and therefore provide Matthew with the link that leads him to picture the feeding of the five thousand as the Lord's Supper. The dropping of Mark's κατα- from κλάω conforms to the simple form that will be used in the feeding of the four thousand (15:36) and, more importantly, at the institution of the Lord's Supper (26:26). Similarly, the change of "he was giving" to "he gave" conforms to the aorist forms used to describe the institution of the Lord's Supper (26:26, 27; Mark 14:22-23; Luke 22:19).

By delaying τοὺς ἄρτους Matthew makes the bread the object of Jesus' giving rather than the object of his breaking (as in Mark). This shift allows "the loaves" as well as "gave" to be supplied in the next, elliptical clause: "and the disciples [gave the loaves] to the crowds." This clause replaces Mark's "in order that they might set [the loaves] before them." In other words, the disciples' obedience to Jesus' command, "You give them [something] to eat" (v 16c), replaces Jesus' mere intention. Furthermore, the disciples do exactly what Jesus did, i.e., give bread. The parallelism makes Jesus an exemplar. Obedience to his command and the following of his example are necessary ingredients of Christian discipleship. Again Matthew substitutes "the crowds" (so also Luke in the singular) for Mark's "them" to call to mind the masses in the church and perhaps cast the disciples as ecclesiastics who distribute bread at the Lord's Supper. The deletion of Mark's "and he divided the two fish for all" contributes to the picture of the feeding as the Lord's Supper, for fish are not a part of that supper.

14:20 (Mark 6:42-43; Luke 9:17) "And all ate and were satisfied" matches Mark word for word. But since in Mark Jesus gives the bread to the disciples "in order that" they may give it to the people, the disciples themselves do not appear to eat. Hence, "all" refers to the people as distinct from the disciples, as also in Mark 6:39. Matthew's omitting "in order that" changes the picture. Now Jesus gives bread to the disciples, they give bread to the crowds, and the "all" who eat includes the disciples along with the crowds. That is to say, the whole church eats the Lord's Supper. To point to the Lord's Supper, Matthew again omits the fish in describing the gathering of "the surplus" (so also Luke in contrast with Mark). The characteristic insertion of τὸ περισσεῦον (5,0—similarly Luke) emphasizes inexhaustibility of supply. The bread of the Lord's Supper will never run out. All nations may come and eat.

Cf. 5:6. We know that Jews in Italy carried baskets when travelling (Juvenal *Satires* 3.14; 6.542). Therefore the twelve baskets here may have belonged to the disciples. Their number corresponds to the twelve tribes of Israel. Thus the new people of God, represented by the disciples, have a full supply of the bread broken by Jesus. In view of 16:9 and John 6:12-13 we are probably to think that the disciples, not all the crowds, took up the extra fragments. Mark's text reads roughly: "and they took up broken pieces, twelve fulnesses of baskets." Matthew smooths it out to read, "And they took up the surplus of broken pieces, twelve baskets full." Perhaps "baskets full" anticipates Mark 8:19, where the same expression will occur in a question concerning the feeding of the five thousand (cf. 15:37).

14:21 *(Mark 6:44; Luke 9:14)* Mark's καί yields to δέ for a contrast between the large amount of leftovers and the large number whose eating would normally have more than exhausted the supply. Matthew switches from Mark's aorist οἱ φαγόντες to the present οἱ . . . ἐσθίοντες, perhaps to suggest repeated eating of the Lord's Supper by the church. And to stress the largeness of the church, he adds "besides women and children" (added also in 15:38) to "about five thousand men." The addition gives ἄνδρες the connotation "husbands." By the same token, γυναικῶν connotes "wives" and παιδίων refers to the "children" of these husbands and wives. Thus Matthew portrays the crowds as the church, a gathering of Christian families on the model of the Holy Family in chaps. 1–2 (see 1:16, 19 for Joseph as "husband" [ἀνήρ], 1:20, 24 for Mary as "wife" [γυνή], and 2:16 for Jesus, by implication, as "child" [παῖς; cf. also 12:18]). Cf. Matthew's portrayal of the church as a brotherhood.

In contrast with Mark, Matthew brings οἱ . . . ἐσθίοντες ahead of its verb in order to make room for his distinctive predicate nominative ἄνδρες. Whether or not he omits τοὺς ἄρτους (also to make room for ἄνδρες) depends on a textual question in Mark (see the UBS and Metzger, *Textual Commentary* ad loc.). The insertion of ὡσεί anticipates Mark's synonymous ὡς with the four thousand (Mark 8:9). Matthew changed Mark's ὡς to ὡσεί also in 3:16; 9:36. Because he uses this qualifier with the five thousand, he will omit it, or leave it to be understood, with the four thousand (15:38). That Luke 9:14 agrees with Matthew's present use of ὡσεί but has no account of the feeding of the four thousand suggests Matthean influence. Opinions about the miraculous element in these stories will differ largely according to opinions about the general question of the miraculous. But the presence of the fish militates against our thinking that the stories were spun out of the Lord's Supper, for there fish are missing.

UNDERSTANDING JESUS
AS SAVING LORD AND SON OF GOD
14:22-36 (Mark 6:45-56; John 6:16-25)

Matthew edits the story of Jesus' walking on the water in a way that emphasizes the disciples' understanding of Jesus as saving Lord and Son of God. The story includes a summary of Jesus' healings subsequent to the walking on water, comes from Mark 6:45-56, and has another parallel (on which Matthew shows no dependence) in John 6:16-25. Nothing intervenes between this story and the last in Mark.

14:22 (Mark 6:45) After feeding the five thousand Jesus immediately compelled his disciples to get in a boat and go ahead of him to the other side while he dismissed the crowds. Why? Was he trying to keep the disciples from being caught up in a messianic uprising directed against the Romans and wrongheadedly centered around himself (cf. John 6:15)? Or was he setting the stage for his appearance to the disciples during the storm? As commonly, Matthew pluralizes Mark's crowd in order to emphasize their numbers as representing the largeness of the church. After "to go ahead," he inserts "him." The addition amounts to a transfer of Mark's αὐτός from ἀπολύει, "he himself dismisses," to προάγειν, "to go ahead of him." In other words, emphasis no longer falls on Jesus' dismissing the crowd—that would not sit well with Matthew's portraying the crowds as the larger body of disciples, the professing church—but on the association of Jesus with his disciples in their journey to the other side.

Mark writes "toward Bethsaida" after "to the other side." Bethsaida causes a difficulty in that the other side turns out to be Gennesaret, a plain south of Capernaum on the west side of the Sea of Galilee, rather than Bethsaida, a town on the northeast side of the Sea of Galilee (see Mark 6:53). Mark's text may imply that after the disciples had set out from a deserted place on the western side and gone some distance toward Bethsaida, the storm blew them backward—"the wind was against them" (Mark 6:48)—so that after Jesus calmed the storm they landed finally at Gennesaret. Matthew gets rid of the difficulty by omitting Bethsaida. The omission makes it look as though the feeding of the five thousand took place on the eastern side, the storm thwarted the disciples' journey to the western side only temporarily, and they finally arrived on the western side as planned (see also the comments on v 34). Matthew will not allow confusing geography to siphon attention from the theology of the incident.

Concerning dismissal of the crowd, Mark writes ἕως with the historical present indicative: "while he himself dismisses the crowd." By adding οὐ to ἕως (the combination characterizes Matthew's diction—4,2) and by putting the verb in the aorist subjunctive, Matthew shifts to the meaning "till he dismissed the crowds." This change implies that the disciples' going ahead has its limit: Jesus will rejoin his disciples shortly. As much as possible Matthew is protecting the terms of discipleship, according to which disciples follow rather than go ahead of their teacher, and the Christology of Immanuel, according to which Jesus is always with his people (1:23; 28:20). Cf. the omission of Jesus' intention to pass by the disciples (v 25 with Mark 6:48).

Even in 26:36, ἕως οὐ with the subjunctive προσεύξωμαι means "till I have prayed," not "while I am praying." The expression means "till" also with the indicative mood (but still in the aorist tense) in 1:25, where the indicative rather than the usual subjunctive points to the actuality of Jesus' birth.

14:23 (Mark 6:46-47) To link v 23 with v 22, Matthew writes "And having dismissed the crowds" (cf. v 22b) in place of Mark's ambiguous "And having said farewell to them [the disciples? the crowd?]." Besides, he likes both ἀπολύσας (5,2) and ὄχλους (17,1). Where Mark writes that Jesus "went away into the mountain [i.e., 'the hill country']" (ἀπῆλθεν εἰς τὸ ὄρος), Matthew writes that Jesus "went up into the mountain" (ἀνέβη εἰς τὸ ὄρος), exactly as in 5:1 and much as in 15:29. Though ἀπῆλθεν belongs to his favorite vocabulary (14,11), it gives way to ἀνέβη in a revival of Jesus' portrayal as the greater Moses (see the comments on 5:1 and "Moses parallel Jesus" in the Topical Index). The insertion of κατ' ἰδίαν links with the same phrase in the preceding story (v 13), agrees with Jesus' being alone in the next clause (v 23b), and adds to the correspondence between Jesus and Moses, the lone intercessor on Mount Sinai (Exod 32:31-32; 33:12-23; 34:8-9). Matthew now draws up Mark's later statement, "and he himself [was] alone on the land," and changes it to "he was alone there" (cf. 17:8). Mark's αὐτός drops out, despite Matthew's favoring it elsewhere (14,3), because it no longer contrasts with the boat in the middle of the sea. And the Mattheanism ἐκεῖ (16,6) replaces ἐπὶ τῆς γῆς (also a Mattheanism—8,2) for emphasis on the mountain. The emphatic position of μόνος before the verb underlines the solitary majesty of the greater Moses as he prays on a new Sinai. As often, Matthew exchanges Mark's καί for δέ in order to contrast the onset of evening with the daylight hours.

14:24 (Mark 6:47-48) Another δέ (not in Mark) contrasts the distance of the boat from the land with Jesus' location on the mountain. ἤδη may substitute for Mark's πάλαι. But if the text of Mark used by Matthew did not contain πάλαι (see the UBS and Metzger, *Textual Commentary* ad loc.), Matthew may insert ἤδη, "already," to correspond with "when evening came" in the antithetically parallel line that precedes. Cf. the insertion of ἤδη in 17:12. The probably original text of Matthew reads "the boat was already getting many stades distant from the land" instead of Mark's "the boat was in the midst of the sea." Since he has just used ἦν for Jesus' being on the mountain, Matthew switches to ἀπεῖχεν. "From the land" compensates for the replacement of Mark's "on the land" in the last line. The insertion of πολλούς should cause no surprise (23,1). The typicalness of these changes militates against the less well-attested reading μέσον τῆς θαλάσσης, which looks like parallel influence from Mark in the process of copying (see the UBS and Metzger, *Textual Commentary* ad loc.).

Next in v 24 Matthew writes the participial phrase βασανιζόμενον ὑπὸ τῶν κυμάτων (literally "being tormented by the waves") to describe the boat. In Mark the participle belongs to the introduction of a new sentence: καὶ ἰδὼν αὐτοὺς βασανιζομένους ἐν τῷ ἐλαύνειν, "and seeing them straining at the oars." But a following parenthetical clause—"for the wind was against them"—awkwardly intervenes between the introduction and the main part of the sentence, which concerns Jesus' approach. Because of Matthew's attaching the participial phrase to the preceding, the clause about the contrariness of the wind no longer interrupts the sentence. And since the participle of βασανίζω no longer refers to the disciples' straining (middle voice in Mark), but to the boat's being beaten (passive voice in Matthew), Mark's ἐν τῷ ἐλαύνειν (literally "in the rowing [or 'advancing']") gives way to ὑπὸ τῶν κυμάτων. The replacement echoes the covering of the boat "by the waves" in 8:24 (contrast Mark 4:37; Luke 8:23). Again because the boat takes the place of the disciples, Mark's αὐτοῖς drops out of the statement that the wind was contrary. ἐναντίος advances ahead of its subject for emphasis.

A stade consisted of 192 meters, or just over two hundred yards. Some think that Matthew makes the boat an object of the storm's wrath out of a desire to make the boat a symbol of the persecuted church. Here, the storm does represent persecution, but Matthew hardly distinguishes between the boat as the church and the disciples as Christians in it. He is simply getting rid of an awkward parenthesis and conforming this story to the story of another storm, where in Mark as well as in Matthew the storm vents its fury on the boat.

14:25 (Mark 6:48) In v 25 Matthew begins with small stylistic changes. The addition of δέ contrasts Jesus' coming with the contrariness of the wind. It also marks the beginning of a new sentence; in Mark the sentence merely resumes after an interruption. The temporal reference to the fourth watch of the night (3:00 A.M.–6:00 A.M.) switches from a prepositional phrase with περί, "about, around," to an adverbial dative meaning "in, during." "He comes" changes to "he came." "Walking on the sea" stays. But "and he was intending to pass before them" vanishes even though Matthew likes ἤθελεν (18,8) and uses παρελθεῖν nine times. In Mark παρελθεῖν means "pass before" in the sense of a theophany, as in the LXX of Exod 33:19, 22; 3 Kgdms 19:11; Job 9:11 (with v 8). For Matthew, however, the verb always means "pass away," even in 8:28, where he inserted it for getting away from the region of the demoniacs (see also 5:18 [bis]; 24:34, 35 [bis]; 26:39, 42). Therefore he deletes it and the words associated with it as inappropriate to Immanuel, who promised to be with his disciples always (1:23; 28:20; cf. 18:20).

The Romans divided the night into four watches. The waters may represent the powers of evil and chaos. A storm introduces theophanies also in Exod 19:16; Ezek 1:4. Cf. Ps 107:28-29.

14:26 (Mark 6:49-50) To make the incident an object lesson concerning discipleship, Matthew characteristically inserts μαθηταί (31,5) in the statement that they saw Jesus walking on the sea. Mark states, "they thought that he was a ghost." The statement implies that they lacked understanding. But Matthew wants to portray the disciples as knowledgeable; so he replaces ἔδοξαν with Mark's later verb ἐταράχθησαν and adds λέγοντες (61,23). Even in his gospel the disciples speak about a ghost. But their terror grows out of little faith (cf. v 31), not out of ignorance (cf. the coming omission of Mark 6:52). To emphasize their little faith and provide a backdrop for Jesus' command to stop being afraid (v 27; cf. v 30), Matthew inserts ἀπὸ τοῦ φόβου before ἔκραξαν. He will insert the same phrase in the narrative concerning Jesus' resurrection (28:4). His habit is to use only the simple form of κράζω; so Mark's ἀν- falls off. And because he has already borrowed "were terrified," Mark's whole clause, "for all saw him and were terrified," disappears.

14:27 (Mark 6:50) For a Christological emphasis, Matthew inserts "Jesus" in Mark's statement, "And he immediately spoke with them, and says to them." The insertion suffers some text-critical uncertainty (see the UBS and Metzger, *Textual Commentary* ad loc.), but its frequency throughout Matthew (80,12) confirms the better external evidence, which favors "Jesus." The name displaces "with them, and . . ." (so Mark). In effect, then, the lordly figure of Jesus overshadows the disciples through the halving of Mark's two references to them. The change of λέγει to λέγων conforms to Matthew's usage (61,23) and makes a parallel with the distinctive λέγοντες in v 26. Jesus' words, "Take heart! It's me! Stop being afraid," read alike in Matthew and Mark. But elsewhere Matthew inserts the command to stop being afraid (4,1). This practice suggests that he wants to encourage persecuted Christians by making the storm represent persecution and Jesus' coming an assurance of his presence with persecuted disciples (see 10:26, 28, 31; 17:7; 28:5, 10).

The everyday self-identification ἐγώ εἰμι may carry overtones of the divine title I AM (Exod 3:14 and esp. John 8:58), because walking on the water, subduing the storm, and—in Matthew—the disciples' worshipping and confessing Jesus as the Son of God (v 33) have theophanic implications. Cf. the comments on Mark's παρελθεῖν.

14:28 Matthew now inserts unique material in vv 28-31. It begins, "But answering, Peter said to him, 'Lord. . . .'" We discover Mattheanisms in ἀποκριθείς . . . εἶπεν (29,6), Πέτρος (8,1), and κύριε (34,15). This recognition of the Lord shows that "if it is you" does not stem from lack of understanding, but from little faith (cf. v 31). Peter's "command me to come to you on the waters" echoes the peculiarly Matthean beginning of the story about the earlier storm (8:18: "he commanded [the disciples] to come away to the other side") and links with the same unparalleled and favorite verb of command in 14:19 (κελεύω—5,2). ". . . me to come to you" echoes v 25: "he came to them." Therefore we might have expected "on the sea," as in v 25. Instead, Matthew writes "on the waters," just as he substituted "in the waters" for Mark's "in the sea" in 8:32, which described the death of the demons. Perhaps "waters" represents the threat of death—by persecution (cf. Peter's beginning to drown in v 30 and Ps 69:15-16[14-15], which Matthew probably has in mind).

14:29 Jesus responded with a command to come; and "Peter, getting down from the boat, walked on the waters and came to Jesus." "Getting down from the boat" complements and anticipates getting up into the boat (v 32). Furthermore, καταβάς is a Mattheanism (5,0). Peter is portrayed, then, as a typical disciple, one who seeks Jesus' command and then obeys it. The obedience consists in walking on the waters and coming toward Jesus as Jesus walks on the sea and comes toward his disciples. Like master, like disciple!

14:30 The focus now shifts from Peter as a model of confessing Jesus as Lord and obeying Jesus to Peter as an example of little faith—an example not to be imitated. "But seeing the [strong] wind, he became afraid"; i.e., fear comes from preoccupation with persecution. Matthew has a certain fondness for βλέπων (except when it means "beware"—9,3). The wind harks back to v 24. And the becoming afraid echoes Matthew's insertion "from fear" in v 26. Peter's crying out when he begins to sink also echoes v 26. Cf. 4:17; 11:20 for other insertions of ἄρχομαι (3,2), and 18:6 for an insertion of καταποντίζομαι in its only other occurrence in the NT (see the comments on 18:6 for further interpretation). Ps 68:3, 16 LXX probably provides καταποντίζεσθαι. λέγων is a Mattheanism (61,23). Peter's outcry, "Lord, save me!" opens with a second typically Matthean recognition of Jesus as Lord and echoes the disciples' saying "Lord, save [us]!" during the earlier storm (8:25, an insertion; cf. 1:21 and the Book of Psalms, passim, including Psalm 68 LXX). Renewed recognition of Jesus' lordship now brings deliverance, i.e., saves from sinking under the judgment that will come on those who apostatize during persecution.

14:31 Matthew introduces Jesus' saving action with "immediately," an echo of vv 22 and 27. As often, he mentions the name of Jesus for a Christological emphasis (80,12) and writes about "stretching out the [Jesus'] hand" (so also 8:3 and, by way of insertion, 12:49; 26:51). Here we may detect an allusion to Ps 144:7-8, "Stretch out your hand from on high; rescue me and deliver me from the many waters, from the hand of aliens, whose mouths speak lies, and whose right hand is a right hand of falsehood," and perhaps Ps 18:17-18(16-17), "He reached from on high; he took me; he drew me out of many waters. He delivered me from my strong enemy and from those who hated me." Both OT texts suit Matthew's making the whole story symbolize the Lord's presence and help in persecution.

Jesus "grasped" Peter and "says to him, 'You of little faith, why did you doubt?'" We find Mattheanisms in λέγει (47,11) and ὀλιγόπιστε (3,0). ἐδίστασας occurs also in 28:17 and only in Matthew in the entire NT. It is also one of the δια-compounds which occur often in the first gospel (6,6). As a whole, Jesus' question echoes his question in the story of the earlier storm, "Why are you afraid, you of little faith?" (8:26). The several echoes of the story about the earlier storm and of the preceding part of the present story, the heavily Matthean diction, the theological motifs characteristic of Matthew, and the possible allusions to the OT make it difficult to resist the conclusion that Matthew did not draw the material in vv 28-31 from tradition, but composed it as a haggadic midrash on discipleship: confessing Jesus as Lord, obeying Jesus' command, being guilty of little faith in persecution, crying out for deliverance, and being rescued and rebuked by Jesus.

14:32-33 (Mark 6:51-52) Because of the insertion of vv 28-31, Jesus' going up into the boat becomes the going up of both Jesus and Peter. Mark's "to them" drops out to avoid confusion with Jesus and Peter, and Mark's independent clause becomes a genitive absolute, a favorite construction of Matthew. "The wind abated" (so also Mark). But where Mark writes that "they were exceedingly [and] utterly astonished within themselves," Matthew writes "But they in the boat worshiped him, saying, 'Truly you are God's Son.'" The δέ that replaces Mark's καί contrasts those in the boat with Jesus and Peter. "They in the boat" compensates for the omission of "to them" (followed by "into the boat") in the preceding verse and does not include Peter, since he has already confessed Jesus as Lord. προσεκύνησαν, "worshipped," typifies Matthew's diction (6,5), suits the following confession of Jesus as God's Son, and avoids the astonishment based on lack of understanding in Mark. Furthermore, the confession takes the place of Mark's statement "For they did not understand about the loaves, but their heart was hardened," and anticipates 27:54: "Truly this one was God's Son" (cf. Mark 15:39). In both passages we read ἀληθῶς and θεοῦ before υἱός for an emphasis on Jesus' deity. Matthew likes to stress that Jesus is God's Son (4,2). Again his favorite λέγοντες (61,23) introduces the confession.

14:34-35 (Mark 6:53-56) Matthew continues with Mark's summary of Jesus' healing after the storm. In Mark it is unclear whether "to the land" goes with "having crossed over" or with "they came." Matthew removes the prepositional phrase from the participle with the result, "And having crossed over, they came to the land, to Gennesaret." See the comments on v 22 concerning the geography of the statements in Matthew and Mark. The deletions of Mark's "and they dropped anchor" and "when they came out of the boat" gain a parallel between v 34, now consisting of an opening participle followed by a single finite verb, and v 35a, similarly constructed. The deletions also serve to move the narrative more quickly to the recognition of Jesus by the men of that place. The quicker introduction of that recognition suits Matthew's emphasis on understanding. Though paralleled here, ἐπιγνόντες is inserted by Matthew five times elsewhere and always means recognition of true identity. As usual, Mark's εὐθύς drops out. But Matthew inserts "the men of that place." ἄνδρες is a Mattheanism (4,2). τόπου links with vv 13 and 15 and occurs as an insertion three times. ἐκείνου distinguishes the place Gennesaret from the deserted place in vv 13, 15 and makes a parallel with ἐκείνην in the further part of the sentence: ". . . sent into all that surrounding region." The common ἀπέστειλαν substitutes for Mark's περιέδραμον, which occurs only here in the NT. Mark's verb shows its influence, however, in Matthew's περίχωρον; the prefix περι- is a remnant of the replaced verb.

14:36 (Mark 6:55-56) In place of Mark's "And they began to bring around sick people on their pallets," Matthew writes "And they brought to him all the sick people" (v 35b), an exact repetition of 4:24b (distinctive to this gospel—see comments ad loc.). Because they lose most of their point with the rejection of "they ran around" and "to bring around," Mark's clauses, "where they heard that he was, and wherever he was entering into towns or into cities or into fields, they put the ill in the market places," also drop out of Matthew's text. Thus the beseeching of Jesus (v 36a) immediately follows the bringing of the sick to him. The sick were beseeching Jesus "that they might only touch the tassel of his garment" (cf. 9:20). μόνον is a Mattheanism (7,0) and substitutes for Mark's κἄν, as also in 9:21 (cf. Mark 5:28). In further conformity with 9:20-21, Matthew brings ἅψωνται toward the front of the clause. Thus the emphasis falls on the act of touching rather than on the tassel of Jesus' garment.

The summary closes with the statement "And as many as touched were completely delivered." Mark's ἄν (a Greek particle that indicates repeated action when used with an augmented indicative verb—here ἥψαντο) drops out because Matthew has omitted κἄν in the previous line. His desire to divert attention from the tassel of Jesus' garment, as though that provided healing, exceeds his desire for strict parallelism; therefore he omits Mark's "it" after the verb of touching, much as he reduced emphasis on the tassel by advancing the verb in the preceding line. Finally, he changes σῴζω from imperfect to aorist because repeated action has been lost through omission of ἄν; and he strengthens the verb by adding a perfective δι-, "completely," perhaps to avoid a repetition of the simple form soon after v 30.

GRANTING UNDERSTANDING TO THE DISCIPLES CONCERNING TRUE DEFILEMENT
15:1-20 (Mark 7:1-23; Luke 6:39)

15:1-2 (Mark 7:1-5) Matthew continues in Mark without a break by taking up the question of defilement. As often, "then" pushes out Mark's "and." The gathering to Jesus, but without mention of his name (so Mark), becomes an approach to Jesus, with a characteristic insertion of his name (80,12). προσέρχονται connotes respect, implies Jesus' lordship, and typifies Matthew's diction (38,6—see the comments on 4:3; 8:14). The presence of πρός and ἐλθόντες in Mark made easy the substitution of προσέρχονται for συνάγονται. ἀπὸ Ἱεροσολύμων moves forward because Matthew has already taken up Mark's ἐλθόντες, on which the phrase depends, into προσέρχονται. He now skips several verses in Mark and picks up "the Pharisees and the scribes" (Mark 7:5) for his subject. But the definite articles drop out in accord with his usual practice (see also 23:13, 15, 23, 25, 27, 29 for no articles, and 5:20; 12:38 for one article, over against only 23:1 for two articles). Because of Mark's influence the Pharisees precede the scribes—the only time they do so in this gospel. The skipping of several verses enables Matthew to avoid the distinction between the Pharisees and the scribes implied in Mark 7:1, "the Pharisees and certain of the scribes." Thus he draws the Pharisees and the scribes together in a single front representing Judaism and opposing Jesus. Cf. v 12, where Matthew will refer to them with the one term "Pharisees," and 12:38, where he inserted "certain," but before the pair of nouns ("certain of the scribes and Pharisees").

The skipping of the Pharisees' and scribes' observation that the disciples eat with unwashed hands and of Mark's explanation concerning Jewish practice also enables Matthew to go immediately to the debate on the topic, a debate consisting almost entirely of Jesus' authoritative words. Matthew's first Jewish readers did not need the explanation, but omission of the Pharisees' and scribes' observation of the disciples leaves the debate somewhat occasionless. That does not matter to Matthew. For him Jesus' teaching needs no occasion; it carries its own weight. Pharisees and scribes start the debate (v 2). The replacement of Mark's "ask" with "saying" (λέγοντες—61,23) takes away the impression of an innocent question. In the question itself οἱ μαθηταί σου advances to a position right after the opening διὰ τί for emphasis and contrast with ὑμεῖς, which Matthew will insert in v 3. The contrast further hardens the tone of the debate. Also, Matthew writes "transgress" instead of "not walk." Thus a search for information ("Why do your disciples not walk according to the tradition of the elders. . . ?" so Mark) turns into an accusation ("Why do your disciples transgress the tradition of the elders?"). Matthew's verb occurs in the NT only here, in the next verse, and in Acts 1:25. In Mark the question continues, ". . . but eat bread with impure hands?" But Matthew stops the question with the accusation of transgression; and by putting "for" (γάρ— 62-63,15) in place of "but" (ἀλλά in Mark) he makes the following into a statement supporting the accusation. "For they do not wash their hands" has no counterpart in Mark, but it partly compensates for the skipped verses (see esp. Mark 7:2). Because of this insertion Matthew has to introduce Mark's "they eat bread" with "whenever."

The tradition of the elders, rejected by the Sadducees but highly esteemed by the Pharisees, was made up of legal comments or case decisions by rabbis past and present. The prescribed washing of hands did not have to do with physical hygiene so much as with ceremonial purity. Cf. Exod 30:17-21; Deut 21:6; 1QS 5:13-14.

15:3 (Mark 7:6a, 8-9) The accusation requires an answer. Therefore Matthew adds ἀποκριθείς to εἶπεν and gains a combination frequent in his gospel (29,6). In Mark, Jesus begins with a quotation of Isa 29:13 to show the hypocrisy that lay behind a seemingly innocent search for information. But because the Pharisees and scribes have already hurled an accusation in Matthew, the first evangelist delays the OT quotation and draws up material in Mark 7:8-13 for an immediate counter accusation. Mark's parallel to the first clause of the counter accusation reads, "Leaving the commandment of God, you grasp the tradition of men." For an antithetic parallel with the Pharisees' and scribes' accusation (v 2), Matthew makes several changes. Mark's declaration becomes a question, as in v 2. διὰ τί is inserted (as twice elsewhere) to echo v 2. "You also" is added to contrast with "your disciples" (v 2; ὑμεῖς is a Mattheanism—15,3). In the place of "leaving" we read "you transgress," an echo of the same verb in v 2. "The command of God" stays, but Matthew's advancing it along with the rest of Mark 7:8-13 sets it immediately against "the tradition of the elders" (v 2). For "commandment" (singular) as a reference to the whole OT law, see the LXX at 4 Kgdms 21:8; Pss 18:8; 118:96. "You transgress" leads Matthew to change Mark's "you grasp" to "because of." And "of men" becomes "your," as in the next and otherwise omitted Markan verse. Thus *"your* tradition" stands against *"God's* commandment" (cf. "your synagogues," "their synagogue[s]," and "their scribes" in Matthew).

15:4 (Mark 7:10) Except for "your tradition" Matthew omits Mark 7:9 not only because it is redundant, but also because it is interruptive in its editorial "And he was saying to them" and open to misunderstanding in its requiring that "well" be understood sarcastically. The omission brings him to Mark's "For Moses said," but he puts "God" in place of "Moses" in order to sharpen and reiterate the opposition between "the commandment of God" and "your tradition." The commandment "Honor father and mother" (Exod 20:12; Deut 5:16) and the legislation "Let him who speaks evil of father or mother be put to death" (Exod 21:17; Lev 20:9; Deut 27:16) come next. These read as they do in Mark except that in the commandment Matthew omits "your" (bis) for a parallel with its omission (as in Mark) in the legislation and the immediately following first saying about refusal to help father or mother. With some possible qualification the quotations also look Septuagintal, especially in having "he who speaks evil" for "whoever curses" (cf. the Hebrew and see further Gundry, *Use of the OT* 12-13).

15:5-6 *(Mark 7:11-13)* The opening of v 5 furthers the antithesis: "But you say" (so also Mark) contrasts with "For God said" (not in Mark) at the start of v 4. Just as Mark's "of men" was ousted in v 3, so a characteristically Matthean "whoever" (ὃς ἄν—14,1) replaces Mark's "If a man" before "should say to [his] father or mother." The replacement parallels the following "whatever." Before "a gift" Matthew deletes " 'Corban,' which means." Out of nine occurrences of δῶρον in Matthew (over against one in Mark and two in Luke) only this one has a parallel. Matthew uses δῶρον so often that he regards the Aramaic "Corban" and the formula of translation as unnecessary. "With reference to whatever you might be helped by me" comes from Mark without change. The statement as a whole deals with the practice of declaring something destined to be offered to God. Behind the declaration stands the purpose of retaining one's own use of the item, i.e., of avoiding the obligation to give it to meet the need of someone else, such as a parent (see esp. J. D. M. Derrett in *NTS* 16 [1970] 364-68, and J. A. Fitzmyer in *Jésus aux origines de la christologie* [ed. J. Dupont; BETL 40; Leuven: Leuven University Press, 1975] 89-90; cf. 1 Tim 5:4).

At this point Mark's sentence beginning "But you say . . ." breaks off before its completion and a new sentence begins: "You no longer allow him to do anything for [his] father or mother" (Mark 7:12). Matthew repairs the broken construction by changing "You no longer allow" to "shall not honor." The earlier clause beginning "whoever" is the subject of the new verb, which comes out of the commandment to honor father and mother. This change makes "shall not honor his father" *part* of what "you say," in contrast with Mark, where the corresponding clause begins Jesus' *comment* on what "you say." In effect, Matthew makes the Pharisees and scribes issue a commandment (". . . shall not honor . . .") contrary to God's commandment ("Honor . . ."). From their counter commandment the reference to mother drops off and "father" gains "his." The omission and the addition stem from a desire for parallelism between "his father" and "God's word" in the next line.

See the UBS and Metzger, *Textual Commentary* ad loc., on the omission of "or his mother." Besides the better quality of the external evidence for omission and the likelihood that parallel influence from preceding lines and from Mark led to the addition, Matthew's love of parallelism favors omission for the sake of a match between "his father" and "God's word."

Mark's "nullifying" dangles at the end of the preceding sentence to describe the "you" who do not allow the doing of anything for father or mother. Because he changed that "you" to "he," Matthew has to start a new clause with "and" (not in Mark) and change Mark's participle to "you have nullified." Nullifying God's word "by means of your tradition" becomes nullifying God's word "because of your tradition," as in v 3b. The rest of Mark 8:13—"which you hand on. And many such things you do"—falls away as unnecessary.

15:7-9 (Mark 7:6b-7) Matthew now returns to Mark 7:6b for the quotation of Isa 29:13. The delay of the quotation till now makes it the climax of Jesus' counter accusation. To sharpen the climax, Matthew draws up "hypocrites" from the end of the introductory formula and turns it into an opening address. To sharpen the accusation yet more, Matthew advances περὶ ὑμῶν, "concerning you," ahead of the subject Ἡσαΐας, "Isaiah." Typically, Mark's ὡς γέγραπται yields to λέγων (61,23) and the recitative ὅτι vanishes.

"Draw near to me" in Isaiah's text drops out in order that emphasis may fall on "honor," with a view to the commandment "Honor father and mother" (v 4). The quotation follows the basically Septuagintal text of Mark. According to some, Isaiah meant that the people feared the Lord mechanically, i.e., solely because their leaders told them to fear the Lord. More probably, the prophet meant that the people's fear of the Lord followed the false teachings of prophets and wise men whose message of no judgment led their hearers to hypocrisy (cf. Isa 29:10, 14). See Gundry, *Use of the OT* 14-16, for evidence that the LXX and the NT rest on a Hebrew text possibly used by Jesus himself (if he did not use the LXX).

15:10-11 (Mark 7:14-15) Matthew skips Mark 7:8-13, already used in vv 3b-6, and goes to Mark 7:14: "and having summoned the crowd again, he was saying to them, 'Hear me, all [of you], and understand.' " But "again" drops out, because Matthew has noticed the lack of an earlier summoning of the crowd. "Was saying" changes to "said." "Me" and "all" disappear, and the imperative verbs shift from aorist to present to conform with 13:13, where, though not imperative, they occurred in the present tense without an object or an accompanying "all" (cf. 13:14-17). Since commands usually appear in the aorist imperative, the present tense lends an emphasis to the crowd's ongoing hearing and understanding. This emphasis shows the crowd to be disciples. They, not the Pharisees and scribes, receive teaching on the question of impurity in eating. Though the Pharisees and scribes raised the question, they deserve only a scathing rebuke.

Jesus' teaching begins with an awkward statement in Mark 7:15a, literally translated "Nothing is outside a man, entering into him, which is able to defile him." To smooth it out, Matthew first changes "nothing" to "not" (v 11a). The change leaves the need for a new subject. He supplies one by making the participle substantive. In the process, the participle changes from εἰσπορευόμενον, "entering" (only in v 17 in Matthew), to the commoner τὸ εἰσερχόμενον, "what enters." Then Matthew changes "into him" to "into the mouth." The change specifies immediately that Jesus is talking about the eating of food. *It is, in other words, Matthew's way of*

305

advancing for emphasis Mark's editorial comment that Jesus was "cleansing all foods" (Mark 7:19). στόμα typifies Matthew's diction (8,1) and enables him to stress the importance of speech (cf. esp. 12:34). He will now contrast keeping dietary taboos (Leviticus 11) and speaking evil. Thus the cleansing of all foods does not countermand the law, but intensifies it by transmuting the dietary taboos into prohibitions against evil speech, just as the so-called antitheses in the Sermon on the Mount did not destroy the law, but fulfilled it (see the comments on 5:17-48). To strengthen the point, Matthew omits "which is able." The omission forces a change of "to defile him" to "defiles a man." The previous substitution of "mouth" has delayed the appearance of "a man" till now.

Matthew forms the second half of v 11 as an exact antithesis to the first half, with one exception for the sake of emphasis. Mark's strongly adversative ἀλλά introduces the antithesis. "The things that go out" changes to "what goes out" for a match with the singular in "what enters." "Out of the mouth," a reference to speech, replaces "out of the man" for an antithesis with "into the mouth," and Matthew moves the phrase from its attributive position in Mark to a place after the participle to conform with the preceding line. The resumptive τοῦτο, paralleled neither in the preceding line nor in Mark, typifies Matthew's style (5,0) and adds emphasis. "Defiles a man" comes down from the preceding line as a substitute for Mark's "are the things that defile."

15:12 (Mark 7:17) In v 12 Matthew typically replaces Mark's "And when" with τότε (66,17) and "he entered into a house away from the crowd" with προσελθόντες (38,6), a reminder of Jesus' dignity (see the comments on 4:3; 8:14). Together, the replacements recall "Then they [the Pharisees and scribes] approach" in v 1a, except that here it is the disciples who approach Jesus. As he omitted the possessive pronoun with father and mother in vv 4-5, Matthew now drops Mark's αὐτοῦ from οἱ μαθηταί. He also advances the noun ahead of its verb for emphasis on discipleship and changes "were asking him" to "say to him" in order to avoid the implication that the disciples lack understanding (see also the comments on vv 15-16). The historical present of this verb typifies Matthew's style (47,11) and emphasizes their speaking out of understanding.

Further to avoid a lack of understanding by the disciples, Matthew delays "the parable" and constructs a question regarding Jesus' awareness of the Pharisees' reaction: "Do you know that the Pharisees, when they heard the word, were offended?" The common verb οἶδας occurs twenty-five times in Matthew, often distinctively (7,2). Φαρισαῖοι is a Mattheanism (18,1). It identifies Jesus' main enemies in this gospel and here echoes v 1. The aorist nominative participle ἀκούσαντες typifies Matthew's style (10,3) and echoes v 10. So also τὸν λόγον echoes v 6, and ἐσκανδαλίσθησαν typifies his diction (3,1).

15:13-14 (Luke 17:6; 6:39) As an answer to the question which he has constructed, Matthew now inserts a saying that appears in Luke 6:39, to which he prefixes another saying that appears in Luke 17:6. The answer amounts to a pronouncement of judgment on the Pharisees. The word "parable" in the tradition behind Luke 6:39 provides the link between that tradition and Mark's passage, where the disciples ask about "the parable." Instead of the introduction "But he also spoke a parable to them" (Luke 6:39), Matthew characteristically writes ὁ δὲ ἀποκριθεὶς εἶπεν (29,6) in reminiscence of v 3a. But now he switches to the tradition behind Luke 17:6: "If you had faith as a mustard seed, you would say to this mulberry tree, 'Be uprooted and planted in the sea,' and it would obey you." The desire for a pronouncement against the Pharisees results, however, in a transmutation of the saying. The disciples' uprooting a tree and planting it by faith in the sea becomes God's uprooting a plant in judgment: "Every plant which my heavenly Father did not plant will be uprooted." Typically, Matthew inserts an emphatic πᾶσα (63,25-26) and, to comfort persecuted Christians, designates God as the heavenly Father (6,1). See also 13:29 for a distinctive use of ἐκριζόω. Because he has used the saying on uprooting here, Matthew will change the tree to a mountain (cf. 21:21; Mark 11:22) and "be uprooted and planted in the sea" to "move from here to there" when he comes to the saying again in 17:20. These later changes confirm his present use of the saying.

For the figure of the plant, see Isa 5:1-7; 60:21; Jer 45:4; Ezekiel 17; Ps 1:3; Wis 4:3-5; *1 Enoch* 10:16; *Jub.* 1:16; 7:34; 21:24; *Pss. Sol.* 14:2-3; 1QS 8:5; 11:8; 1QH 6:15-17; 7:10, 18-19; 8:4-27; 10:31; CD 1:7.

Perhaps to compensate for the replacement of ἀφίετε in 15:6a (cf. Mark 7:12) and certainly to indulge his fondness for ἀφίημι (12,5), Matthew inserts ἄφετε αὐτούς, "Leave them." These words reflect the church's break from the synagogue and lead to the saying recorded also in Luke 6:39: "A blind man is not able to lead a blind man, is he? Both will fall in a pit, won't they?" But in Matthew the question demanding a negative answer becomes a positive statement that blind men are indeed leaders of the blind. The switch from singular (so Luke) to plural points to the Pharisees (cf. 23:16, 24). Then, to set the stage for falling in a pit, Matthew constructs out of the last line the conditional clause "But if a blind man should lead a blind man." Finally, he turns the question demanding a positive answer into the declaration "both will fall in a pit." Thus the Pharisees' ignorance stands as a foil to the disciples' understanding.

The Pharisees, or their rabbis, seem to have taken "leader of the blind" as an honorific title (Rom 2:19). In the OT, falling in a pit became proverbial for disaster (see Isa 24:18; Jer 48:44; Ps 7:16[15]; Prov 26:27).

15:15 (Mark 7:17) Matthew has still not used Mark's reference to "the parable" (the puzzling saying about impurity). To build up to that reference, he introduces Peter as the typical disciple: "But answering, Peter said to him" (so also the insertion in 14:28, except for a small difference in the order of words). ἀποκριθεὶς . . . εἶπεν is a Mattheanism (29,6), which here links with the insertions in vv 3a and 13a. Peter's request, "Explain to us this parable," recalls a similar and uniquely Matthean request in 13:36.

307

Some text-critical doubt attaches to ταύτην (see the UBS and Metzger, *Textual Commentary* ad loc.). Cf. Acts 10:1–11:18; 15:7-11; Gal 2:11-21 for Peter's involvement in questions of purity.

15:16 (Mark 7:18) The introduction to Jesus' answer reads "But he said" instead of Mark's "And he says to them." The omission of "to them" goes against a false inference that the disciples are guilty in not understanding the parable. Peter's request for an explanation means that just as in chap. 13 those who have understanding gain more, so also here the lack of understanding does not belong to those who lack it entirely, but to those who have some and receive more. Thus Matthew writes, "Are you still without understanding?" The substitution of ἀκμήν, "still," for Mark's οὕτως, "in this way," implies that the lack is only temporary: they will now receive what they lack because they already have some understanding.

15:17 (Mark 7:18-19) The next sentence reads much as in Mark, except for some omissions and two substitutions: "Do you not comprehend that everything that enters into the mouth goes away and is cast out into a latrine?" As in v 11a (cf. Mark 7:15a), Matthew omits Mark's "from outside" and puts "the mouth" in place of "a man." Again, therefore, the issue concerning the tradition of the elders leads Matthew to transmute OT dietary taboos into prohibitions in speech. The transmutation shows itself also in the replacement of Mark's ἐκπορεύεται with the Mattheanism ἐκβάλλεται (10,1), a verb that has to do with speech in 12:35 (bis); 13:52 (both unparalleled). To match "is thrown out" Matthew also substitutes "goes away" (χωρεῖ—see also insertions in 19:11, 12 [bis]) for Mark's "enters." In accord with a similar omission in v 11a (cf. Mark 7:15b) and again for the sake of sharper argument and neater parallelism, Mark's "is not able to defile him" drops out. "Because it does not enter into his heart, but . . ." suffers the same fate. In order not to spoil the antithetic parallelism, Matthew also omits Mark's editorial "cleansing all foods" and the interruptive "And he was saying" with a recitative ὅτι. None of these omissions has avoiding an abrogation of OT food laws as its purpose, for Matthew has already spoken to that point with the use of "mouth" (see the comments on vv 10-11). His interest in the evangelism of Gentiles (see "Universality" in the Topical Index) agrees with the turning of dietary taboos into prohibitions in speech, but not with care to preserve dietary taboos as such.

15:18 (Mark 7:20) The second part of the antithesis opens with an adversative δέ. Mark's singular "what goes out" changes to the plural "the things that go out," and for a parallel with v 17 "out of a man" moves from its attributive position in Mark and changes to "out of the mouth." The plural agrees with Mark 7:15c, disagrees with the singular of the corresponding expressions in vv 11 and 17 as well as in the present parallel in Mark, and points to the following list of evils that come from the mouth. Matthew now adds "comes out of the heart" to compensate for his omitting most of Mark 7:19a, including "into the heart," in his last verse. But in Mark 7:19a Jesus denies that the heart is the destination of food. Matthew makes the heart the ultimate origin of evils. In the concluding part of the antithesis he changes "that" (ἐκεῖνο) to "even those things" (κἀκεῖνα) for agreement with the preceding plural and the following list of evils and for emphasis by means of an ascensive καί. The rest stays unchanged: "defiles a man."

15:19 (Mark 7:21-22) Mark's "from within" disappears because Matthew omitted "from outside" in vv 11 and 17 (cf. Mark 7:15, 18). After "for out of the heart" Matthew also lops off "of men" (cf. omissions of this noun in vv 11, 17). The more usual ἐξέρχονται takes the place of Mark's ἐκπορεύονται to parallel ἐξέρχεται in the preceding verse. The verb advances to a position ahead of the entire list of evils.

As in Mark, "thoughts" head the list, but Matthew deletes the definite article out of regard for its absence in the rest of the list; and, typically, he replaces "bad" with "evil" (πονηροί—10,4). Then he transposes the next two pairs of evils and adds "false witnessings" in order to conform, as usual, to the OT, particularly to the sixth through ninth commandments in the decalogue. Fornications come as an interruption justified by their closeness to adulteries (cf. 19:18). Notably, the sixth through ninth commandments in the decalogue immediately follow the commandment to honor father and mother, a main topic of discussion in the earlier part of the present passage. Matthew will give an example of "false witnessings" in his account of Jesus' trial by inserting ψευδομαρτυρία and ψευδομαρτύρων (26:59-60). The present addition of "false witnessings" from the decalogue and the passing over of "covetings," "evils," "deceit," "licentiousness," "an evil eye," "pride," and "foolishness" in favor of "blasphemy" stem from Matthew's concern to prohibit evil speech, especially untrue accusations in the betrayal of true disciples by false disciples (cf. 24:10—peculiar to this gospel). "Blasphemy" becomes "blasphemies" in agreement with the preceding nouns on the list. Thus Matthew ends up with a list of seven evils—seven to represent totality and each evil plural in number—over against Mark's seven in the plural (but somewhat different from Matthew's) followed by six in the singular.

15:20 (Mark 7:23) The totality represented by the choice of seven evils makes "all" unnecessary in the final sentence of the section. Therefore it drops off. Because "evil" was inserted in the preceding list, it is deleted here. Only "these things" remains from Mark's phrase. As in the last verse, Matthew omits "from within" and, consequently, its verb "goes forth." In their stead, he writes "are the things that defile a man." The revision then enables him to make "and defiles a man" (so Mark) into the concluding antithetic clause, "but eating with unwashed hands does not defile a man." The verb and its object reflect Mark. And eating with unwashed hands comes down from v 2b. With this inclusio the passage returns to the question about the tradition of the elders and ends with a denial of that tradition.

A GENTILE'S UNDERSTANDING OF JESUS AS LORD AND SON OF DAVID
15:21-28 (Mark 7:24-30)

15:21 (Mark 7:24) Matthew starts his version of Mark's next story—one that concerns Jesus' healing the demon-possessed daughter of a Syrophoenician Greek woman—by replacing δέ with καί. This correlates Jesus' ministry to a Gentile with the preceding intensification of dietary laws that erases the dietary demarcation between Jews and Gentiles (see the comments on vv 1-20). "Going out" replaces "getting up" and moves ahead of "from there." These changes accentuate Jesus' departure into a territory of Gentiles: "Jesus withdrew into the districts of Tyre and Sidon." ἐξελθών is a favorite of Matthew (10,4), and the insertion of "Jesus" is typical (80,12). Matthew substitutes ἀνεχώρησεν (4,5) for ἀπῆλθεν because his verb connotes withdrawal from danger (see the comments on 2:12; cf. vv 1-2) and enables him to portray Jesus as a model of fleeing persecution, so that evangelism takes place in the regions beyond (see "Flight from persecution" in the Topical Index). To forestall an inference that Jesus went up to the borders of Gentile territory but did not enter, Matthew changes the ambiguous εἰς τὰ ὅρια Τύριον, "to [or 'into'] the *boundaries* of Tyre" (so Mark), to εἰς τὰ μέρη Τύρου, "into the *districts* of Tyre" (cf. the similar distinctive phraseology in 16:13, where entrance is surely meant). ἀναχωρέω with εἰς regularly refers to withdrawal from one place into another (see 2:12, 14, 22 [followed by "the districts," as here]; 4:12—all unique to Matthew). With "going out" instead of "getting up" and "the districts" instead of "the boundaries," the verb insures that εἰς means "into" rather than "up to" (see also v 29). The concern to make the story a dominical example of ministry to Gentiles also leads Matthew to add "and Sidon" to "Tyre." The stereotyped pairing of the cities conforms to the language of the OT (see the comments on 11:21-22) and makes them typical of the whole world of Gentiles (cf. 28:19 and the comments on 4:24-25).

See J. Jeremias, *Jesus' Promise to the Nations* (SBT 1/24; London: SCM, 1958) 31-32 n. 3, 35-36, for a summary of evidence that the eastern Tyrian region was largely Jewish and an argument that Jesus did not go northwestward very far. This argument requires a falsification of Mark 7:31, however; and for Matthew "the districts of Tyre and Sidon" are literarily and theologically Gentile, whatever the historical character of their population.

15:22 (Mark 7:24-26) At this point Mark writes that Jesus entered a house and wanted no one to know of his presence, but could not hide successfully. Matthew omits all that, for it implies a lack of purpose to minister to Gentiles. On the contrary, his Jesus ministers to them by intent (though exceptionally) and thus sets an example of evangelizing them. Several changes in the following phrases emphasize these points. καί replaces ἀλλ᾽ for a positive connection between Jesus' withdrawal into the districts of Tyre and Sidon and the appearance of a Gentile with a request for mercy. The Mattheanism ἰδού (34,9) displaces εὐθύς and stresses that the woman was a Gentile. γυνή moves forward. "Canaanite" replaces "a Greek" (so Mark 7:26), conforms to OT terminology, and moves up from the later statement in Mark. "From those boundaries" substitutes for "a Syrophoenician by race" (Mark 7:26). It also compensates for Matthew's earlier elimination of "the boundaries" (v 21). Mark's phrase would have seemed redundant after "Canaanite." ἐκείνων belongs to Matthew's favorite vocabulary (26,9). Since he has made clear that Jesus entered Gentile territory, "from those boundaries" refers to the boundaries as enclosing the Gentile territory of Jesus' presence, not as separating Jesus from that territory. By the same token, the phrase describes the Canaanite woman, as the corresponding phrase in Mark 7:26 describes her, and is not to be taken as an adverbial phrase modifying "coming out," as though she was coming out of Gentile territory into Jewish territory to meet Jesus.

We meet a Mattheanism in ἐξελθοῦσα (10,4), which replaces Mark's "hearing about him," derives from ἐξελθών in v 21, and, with the latter, forms a parallel between Jesus' going out and that of the Canaanite woman. As often, the places from which the goings out started remain vague (see the concordance, s.v. ἐξέρχομαι). Was Jesus still in Gennesaret when he started (14:34; but see 15:1, 10, 12)? Did the woman come from her home, or city, or village? The answers do not matter. What the woman says, or what Matthew makes her say by drawing on the twin stories of the two blind men, does matter. It matters so much that he delays Mark's immediate reference to the woman's demon-possessed daughter in order to introduce ι plea for mercy (not in Mark) that amounts to a Christological confession of faith. In the doubled story of the blind men we read, ". . . crying out and saying, 'Have mercy on us, Son of David' " (9:27), and, "they cried out, saying, 'Lord, have mercy on us—Son of David' " (20:30). Here we read, "she was crying out, saying, 'Have mercy on me, Lord, Son of David.' " The borrowing from the other story shows itself not only in the phraseology, absent in Mark's present parallel, but also in the woman's seeking mercy for herself rather than for her daughter, as though she, like the blind men, needed healing. Matthew often stresses that Jesus is κύριος (34,15) and υἱὸς Δαυίδ (4,2).

The addressing of Jesus as the Son of David anticipates the limitation of his ministry to Israel (vv 24, 26) and the woman's agreement with that limitation (v 27); i.e., in her address the woman shows her recognition that Jesus came to Israel as the Davidic Messiah. But the prefixing of "Lord" (absent in the earlier story of the two blind men) shows that she hopes to win from Jesus an exceptional benefit in view of his universal dominion. The imperfect tense of ἔκραζεν prepares for the disciples' being annoyed by her repetition of the plea. Finally the daughter's plight comes into the picture, but as part of the woman's cry instead of the evangelist's description (as in Mark). The diminutive τὸ θυγάτριον becomes ἡ θυγάτηρ for consistency with ἡ θυγάτηρ in v 28. Mark begins with the diminutive and switches to the usual form (bis). δαιμονίζεται, "is demon possessed," takes the place of Mark's "had . . . an unclean spirit" and occurs seven times in Matthew, but only four times in Mark and once in Luke. Mark's expression appears twice elsewhere in Matthew, but ten times in Mark and six times in Luke. Characteristically, Matthew inserts κακῶς (4,0), which emphasizes the Gentiles' need of salvation and, because of its frequent use in the idiom ἔχειν κακῶς, "to be sick," agrees with his distinctive description of the exorcism as a healing (v 28).

To play up the greatness of the woman's faith (so v 28 in contrast with Mark), Matthew makes Jesus refuse to answer the woman, makes the disciples ask for her dismissal, makes Jesus tell the disciples that he was sent only to Jews, makes the woman repeat her plea, and makes Jesus say to the woman only that Gentiles ought not to receive benefits belonging to the Jews, not that the Jews receive benefits "first" (for that would imply the arrival of the Gentiles' time to receive benefits). Finally, Matthew makes the woman agree with the shortened, harsher statement rather than take advantage of the full, softer statement. At the same time he plays up the woman's faith in these ways, additional revisions keep the story from negating evangelism of Gentiles; rather, they encourage such evangelism.

15:23 At the beginning of v 23 (wholly unique) δέ contrasts Jesus' refusal to answer with the woman's request. The rest of the statement, "he did not answer her a word," rests on the stereotyped phrase ἀποκριθεὶς εἶπεν (29,6). The changes in it arise largely from introduction of the negative. λόγον is a Mattheanism (16,2). Here it links with v 12, where Matthew inserted a reference to the word Jesus spoke to the Pharisees. Even to the Pharisees! This poor woman's faith has to overcome silence.

The disciples approach. προσελθόντες and μαθηταί are further Mattheanisms (38,6; 31,5). The former implies Jesus' dignity (see the comments on 4:3; 8:14). "They were asking him, saying, 'Dismiss her, because she is crying out after us.'" λέγοντες and ἀπόλυσον are dear to Matthew (61,23; 5,2). He does not mean that the disciples wanted Jesus to get rid of the woman by granting her request, but that he should send her away without granting it; for Matthew never uses ἀπολύω with the implication of relenting. The one exception in 18:27 is only apparent. There, the granting of a request is expressed in *another* clause. "They were asking" is suggested by Mark 7:26. Its imperfect tense in Greek corresponds to Mark and parallels that of the woman's crying out in v 22. "She is crying out" comes down from v 22, where it reflected the twin stories of the two blind men. "After us" sets the scene outside, as opposed to Mark's setting the scene in a house (Mark 7:24, omitted by Matthew). It may also imply that the woman is following Jesus as a disciple, for she has confessed him as Lord and Son of David (v 22); and in its implication that Jesus is travelling with his disciples it may contribute to the picture of flight from persecution (see v 21).

15:24 To set Jesus' reply opposite the disciples' request, Matthew uses another δέ at the beginning of v 24, which only his gospel has. Indeed, vv 23-27 all begin with ὁ δέ or ἡ δέ to indicate shifts in the dialogue. ἀποκριθεὶς εἶπεν is a Mattheanism (29,6). Because it contrasts with οὐκ ἀπεκρίθη αὐτῇ λόγον, "he answered her not a word," at the start of v 23 and because the disciples' request immediately precedes, Matthew directs Jesus' answer to the disciples, not to the woman (cf. his directing Jesus' similar statement in 10:5b-6 to the disciples). Not till v 25 does the woman come close enough for Jesus to carry on a conversation with her. Here she is still following and yelling at a distance.

Jesus' answer harmonizes with the disciples' request that he send the woman away unsatisfied: "I have not been sent except to the lost sheep of the house of Israel" (which means "I have been sent only to the lost sheep of the house of Israel"). Thus the woman's faith faces the obstacles of antagonism on the disciples' part and, on God's part, a Jewish restriction on Jesus' ministry. "I have been sent" implies God as the sender and probably comes from 10:40, itself a construction of Matthew through conflation of two dominical sayings (cf. esp. Luke 10:16). "The lost sheep of the house of Israel" comes word for word from 10:6, part of Matthew's expansion of Luke 9:2. See the comments ad loc. for characteristic diction, motifs, parallelism, and allusion to the OT. The comments on 10:5b-6 dealt with the limitation of Jesus' ministry to Jews. The deliberate exceptions made for the Gentile centurion (8:5-13) and the Canaanite woman keep that limitation from becoming a valid argument against evangelizing Gentiles in the wake of Jesus' rejection by Jewish officialdom.

That Jesus' saying harmonizes with the disciples' desire to get rid of the woman need not imply that the saying is otiose unless addressed to her rather than to the disciples. For Matthew wants to range Jesus and the disciples together as obstacles which, being overcome, heighten her faith. This positive desire to play up the faith of a Gentile figures much more strongly than any negative intent to show the inexcusability of the Jews because they had the privilege of Jesus' ministry all to themselves. Therefore the arguments for seeing the saying in v 24 as addressed to the disciples hold firm.

Several arguments for Jesus' having spoken the saying need evaluation: (1) the unlikelihood that a particularistic saying should arise after the early, even pre-Pauline, establishment of the mission to Gentiles; (2) the so-called (but overestimated) divine passive of the verb; (3) the Aramaism in οὐκ . . . εἰ μή, a reflection of אֶלָּא . . . לֹא, "not . . . except," i.e., "only"; (4) the introduction of those to whom the sending is directed with εἰς (cf. the Hebrew בְּ), a construction uncharacteristic of Classical Greek and of Matthew elsewhere, but characteristic of the LXX and Semitized Greek (see Judg 19:29 v.1.; 3 Kgdms 18:20; Jer 30:8; Acts 22:21; 26:17); (5) the OT figure of sheep; and (6) the OT phrase "house of Israel," where the lack of the definite article with "house" reflects the construct state in Hebrew.

But the saying is not designed to attack the mission to Gentiles, even though its construction postdates that mission. Rather, it has the purpose of magnifying the faith of a Gentile. The divine passive rests on "him who sent me" in 10:40 (cf. Luke 10:16). The construction οὐκ (or a form of οὐδείς) . . . εἰ μή occurs often, four times as an insertion by Matthew (5:13; 11:27 [bis]; 12:3, 24, 39; 13:57; 14:17; 15:24; 16:4; 17:8; 21:19; 24:36). With one exception Matthew uses πρός after ἀποστέλλω when borrowing from the traditions (21:34, 37; 23:34, 37), and εἰς only when inserting the expression (8:31; 14:35; 15:24) or writing a distinctive passage (20:2). Here εἰς probably bears the sense "into the midst of" (cf. 10:16), which would not fit in the sole exception (27:19). The use of ἀποστέλλω εἰς in the LXX and other Semitized Greek weakens rather than strengthens the argument for a traditional saying; for it shows that Matthew might easily have used the expression without quoting a traditional saying. Finally, the use of OT language agrees perfectly with his habits.

We need to say, then, that Matthew constructs the saying out of Jesus' speaking of himself as sent by God, out of OT phraseology for Israel, and out of the historical limitation of Jesus' mission to Israel. Do the "lost sheep" consist of all Israel, or the masses within Israel? Probably the latter, since the OT distinguishes the lost sheep as the masses from the faithless shepherds as their leaders (see Jer 50:6, the source of this figure). Matthew makes the same distinction throughout his gospel. Even with it, the contrast with Gentiles (and in 10:5b-6 with Samaritans as well) remains intact.

313

15:25 (Mark 7:25-26) In v 25 Matthew rejoins Mark in writing about the woman's "coming" to Jesus. But in place of "she fell at his feet" he puts "she was worshipping him." This exalts Jesus as "God with us" (1:23), who deserves worship. προσεκύνει is a Mattheanism (6,5). Mark's statement that "the woman was a Greek, a Syrophoenician by race," drops out because Matthew used it in v 22. And since he used "they were asking" in v 23, he replaces "and she was asking him" with λέγουσα, another Mattheanism (61,23). Mark indirectly quotes the woman's request that Jesus cast a demon out of her daughter. But Matthew referred to the demonic possession of the daughter in the woman's first plea, which he constructed partly from Mark's description of the woman's plight. To avoid redundancy, therefore, he puts the supplicatory language of the OT, especially of the Psalms, in her mouth: "Lord, help me!" (see, e.g., Ps 109[108]:26 and numerous other examples to be found in Hatch and Redpath, s.v. βοηθεῖν). His liking of κύριε (34,15) unites with his habit of borrowing from the OT. That the woman asks help for herself, not directly for her daughter, agrees with v 22, where this feature of the plea reflected the story of the two blind men.

15:26 (Mark 7:27) Jesus responds, but not to the woman, for Mark's "to her" does not come into Matthew's text till v 28, the very close of the story. Omitting "to her" and substituting ὁ δὲ ἀποκριθεὶς εἶπεν (29,6) makes an exact parallel with v 24a, where Jesus spoke to the disciples. Therefore, Matthew makes Jesus speak to the disciples here also. Since she has come close (v 25a), the woman overhears. Matthew's heightening the snub to the woman does not imply a bias against Gentiles in his thinking or in any tradition he supposedly draws on. Far from it! The heightening builds up the obstacles to the woman's faith for dramatic effect in Jesus' later exclamation: "O woman, great is your faith!" (v 28b, so Matthew alone). In other words, the snubbing of a Gentile casts the faith of that Gentile in all the better light and by this means justifies a mission to Gentiles now that Jewish officialdom has rejected Jesus.

Matthew omits Mark's "Let the children first be fed full." Why does he not retain it in order to justify a mission to Gentiles after Jesus' mission to Jews? Again the reason is that he wants to play up the woman's faith by casting another obstacle in its way, here by transforming a reference to sequential priority into a flat refusal. This magnifying of the woman's faith makes a better justification of the mission to Gentiles than a "first," which narrow-minded Jewish Christians might use to argue for a delay till all Israel is saved and the rule of God takes over the earth (cf. the expectation of widespread conversions among Gentiles in the messianic kingdom, discussed by Jeremias, *Jesus' Promise to the Nations* 53, 57-62). In Matthew, only the negative statement of Jesus remains: "It is not good to take the children's bread and cast it to the dogs."

Jesus' saying sounds like a maxim, for which some extrabiblical evidence exists (see J. D. M. Derrett in *NovT* 15 [1973] 172; cf. *Tg. Neof.* Exod 22:30). If a maxim, it probably means something like "Charity begins at home" and did not contain a slurring reference to Gentiles in the diminutive κυναρίοις, "little dogs, puppies." Of course, the present application of the saying implies an identification of the little dogs with Gentiles (and of the children with Jews), but not necessarily an identification of a slurring kind. For though Jews commonly used "dogs" as an epithet for Gentiles (see Str-B 1. 724-25), the diminutive together with the portrayal of the dogs as eating from the table favors that we have to do with household pets rather than with the street-roaming scavengers referred to in the epithet. Jesus was probably speaking Greek to this woman, described in Mark as a "Greek." If not, he may have used one of the Aramaic words גּוּרָא, "puppy," or כַּלְבָּא, "dog." The latter might be capable of a diminutive form (see GKC §86 g, esp. n. 1), but the setting around a dinner table would connote household pets even for the undiminished form. This last point also militates against taking κυναρίοις as a faded diminutive, one that has lost its diminutive force. Explicit reference to the dinner table does not come till the woman's reply, to be sure, but her ability to reply with such a reference shows that the throwing of the children's bread to little dogs naturally implies a setting around the dinner table. Mark's γάρ drops out because the omission of his preceding clause leaves the conjunction meaningless. In contrast with Mark, Matthew puts βαλεῖν ahead of τοῖς κυναρίοις in order to match the similar position of λαβεῖν in the preceding phrase.

15:27 (Mark 7:28) Because Matthew shifted the address of Jesus' saying from the woman, she can no longer be said to answer Jesus. Therefore "she said" substitutes for Mark's "she answered and says to him." The substitution confirms that Matthew made Jesus speak to the disciples, not to the woman, in vv 24 and 26. Again Matthew borrows from the first story of the two blind men (9:28) by adding "Yes" (not in the probably original text of Mark—see the UBS and Metzger, Textual Commentary ad loc.). The addition is mildly Matthean (ναί—2,2) and turns the woman's clever rebuttal of Jesus' statement (so Mark) into an agreement with that statement. Matthew does not allow even the suggestion of insolence here, for he regards the woman's use of κύριε as an address in the full sense "Lord" (cf. 1:21) rather than in the weak sense "Sir." Because of the insertion of κύριε in v 22, the present occurrence of the word marks the second recognition of Jesus' lordship by the woman.

To the statement concerning the little dogs Matthew characteristically adds γάρ (62-63,15). Hence, the statement provides a reason for the woman's agreement with Jesus ("Yes, Lord, for also the little dogs . . ."). In Mark, contrastingly, the statement contains an expression of disagreement with Jesus ("Lord, even the little dogs . . ."). On the other hand, Matthew omits Mark's "under the table" in order to avoid denigration of the Gentiles. "Little dogs"—yes; but "under the table" provides too easy a handle for those who might wish to argue in favor of the Gentiles' inferiority. Similarly, Matthew adds "that fall from the table" to "the scraps." The scraps are not thrown to the dogs, then; they fall from the table. Thus there is no disparagement of the dogs. Neither is there any disagreement with the limitation of Jesus' mission to the Jews; for a falling scrap hardly upsets the task of feeding the children, especially if the expression refers to discarding pieces of bread used for wiping the hands (cf. Luke 16:21 and Jeremias, Parables 184). Matthew has a fondness for πιπτόντων (5,3). In a Semitic avoidance of the passive, "fall" is equivalent to being thrown (see Luke 10:18 with John 12:31; Rev 12:9; also John 12:24). But Matthew avoids writing that the dogs were the intended recipients. That would have disagreed with Jesus' statement.

The reference to the table not only has a theological purpose; it also compensates for omission of the table earlier in the saying. Matthew goes on to describe the table as the table "of their [the puppies'] masters," a substitute for Mark's "of the little children." But the table hardly belongs to the children. The masters (τῶν κυρίων) are grown-ups and represent Jesus, whose being addressed as κύριε has been doubled by Matthew (vv 22, 27). Thus "the children's scraps" (so Mark) become "the lords' table," a symbol of the Lord's Table (cf. 1 Cor 10:21 and Matthew's eucharistic editing of Jesus' feeding the five thousand [14:13-21]). The replacement of the children, representing Jews, with the masters, representing Jesus, further reduces the susceptibility of the story to anti-Gentile interpretation.

See J. D. M. Derrett in *NovT* 15 (1973) 169-70 on bread in the diet of dogs kept by a family. The domesticity of the scene disfavors an allusion to the messianic banquet. The reference to dogs, especially in its use of the diminutive, and the favorable way the woman alludes to their eating under the table resist our seeing an allusion to King Adoni-bezek's cutting off the thumbs and big toes of seventy other kings, forcing them to gather scraps under his table, and receiving like punishment for his cruelty (Judg 1:5-7). Except for tethered watchdogs, full-grown dogs were not kept in ancient Middle Eastern homes.

15:28 (Mark 7:29-30) "Then" replaces Mark's "and" to tighten up the story line. Matthew adds ἀποκριθείς and retains εἶπεν αὐτῇ in order to indicate that Jesus finally speaks to the woman (contrast vv 23, 24, 26). Both τότε and ἀποκριθεὶς εἶπεν represent his preferred diction (66,17; 29,6). The further characteristic insertion of "Jesus" (80,12) makes a Christological emphasis that lends added weight to the following praise of the woman's faith. Yet greater emphasis accrues to that faith, and especially to the fact that a Gentile has exercised it, from Matthew's adding "O woman," which echoes the description of the Canaanite woman in v 22a. The verb "go" in Mark's "On account of this saying, go," reminds Matthew of Jesus' saying to the Gentile centurion, "Go; as you have believed, let it happen to you" (8:13, so Matthew alone), with which is associated Jesus' comment, "I have not found such great faith with anyone in Israel" (8:10). Matthew leaves aside the command to go and substitutes praise of the woman's great faith in place of praise for her clever saying (so Mark). Her great faith contrasts with the little faith of Peter (14:31) and of the disciples (16:8)—both peculiar to Matthew—and with the lack of faith in the Jews at Nazareth (13:53-58). Matthew also takes over "Let it happen to you" from his distinctive wording in 8:13 and adds "as you wish," all in substitution for the statement in Mark, "The demon is gone out of your daughter." He likes μεγάλη (11,1), γενηθήτω (5,0), ὡς (23,8), and θέλεις (18,8). The last of these comes from the story of the blind men, which provides other material for his version of the present story (see 20:32; Mark 10:51; Luke 18:41).

Matthew makes up for his omitting the woman's daughter thus far in v 28 by writing "And her daughter was healed from that hour." The statement derives again from the peculiarly Matthean wording in 8:13 ("and the servant was healed in that hour") and takes the place of Mark's comment that the woman went away and found the little child laid on a bed and the demon gone out. Thus even the statement of healing has the purpose of emphasizing the faith of Gentiles; it is a reminder of an earlier story concerning such faith. Here that faith is seen particularly in the understanding of Jesus as Lord and Son of David, the Messiah of the Jews but also the Emperor of all.

See Black, *Aramaic Approach* 110 n. 1, on "from that hour" as rabbinic and Aramaic in style; also the comments on 9:22.

UNDERSTANDING JESUS' WILL
TO HEAL AND FEED THE GENTILES
15:29-38 (Mark 7:31–8:9a)

In vv 29-31 Matthew transforms the individual healing of a deaf-mute (Mark 7:31-37) into the healing of many sick people among many crowds. The transformation makes these verses an introduction to the feeding of the four thousand (vv 32-38; Mark 8:1-9a). As a whole, vv 29-38 display Matthew's desire to show that the disciples of Jesus understand his will to minister to the Gentiles in general, not just to the Gentile woman in the immediately preceding verses. In other words, vv 29-38 expand the theme of Jesus' ministry to Gentiles, a theme begun in vv 21-28.

15:29 (Mark 7:31) As often, Matthew omits Mark's "again," here because readers might suffer the misimpression that Jesus had entered and left the region of Tyre and Sidon on an earlier occasion. μεταβάς (5,1) replaces Mark's ἐξελθών for a parallel with ἀναβάς in the next line. Since Matthew has already mentioned Tyre and Sidon (v 21), he replaces "from the boundaries of Tyre ... through Sidon" with "from there" (ἐκεῖθεν— 8,1). Three times Matthew alone uses ἐκεῖθεν with a form of μεταβαίνω (see further comments on 12:9). His insertion of "Jesus" is typical (80,12). In the phrase "to the Sea of Galilee," παρά (literally "to the side of") replaces Mark's εἰς. Matthew is reserving εἰς for the next line.

Mark's "into the midst of the boundaries of Decapolis" becomes a full-blown clause: "and going up into a mountain, he was sitting there." This combination of a participial phrase plus a finite verbal phrase matches the construction in the first half of the verse and so displays Matthew's love of parallelism. The reference to going up into a mountain (not in Mark) revives the portrayal of Jesus as the greater Moses (see "Moses parallel Jesus" in the Topical Index). Jesus' sitting, the position of a teacher, adds to the portrait (cf. 5:1; 23:2). ἐκεῖ comes from Matthew's favorite diction (16,6). All in all, his revisions rid the text of Jesus' devious route northward from the boundaries of Tyre through Sidon and from there southeastward across the Leontes and along the east side of the Sea of Galilee to Decapolis. Thus Matthew leaves the attention focused solely on

Jesus' arrival at the Sea of Galilee, which he has already associated with the Gentiles (4:13-18). There, his Jesus takes the position of the Teacher greater than Moses *for Gentiles* (see esp. v 31b: "and they glorified the God of Israel").

15:30-31 (Mark 7:32-37) Mark does not give any teaching of Jesus on this occasion. Despite portraying him as the Teacher greater than Moses, therefore, Matthew takes up his ministry of healing (v 30). προσῆλθεν replaces Mark's φέρουσιν, comes from Matthew's favorite vocabulary (38,6), and emphasizes Jesus' dignity (see the comments on 4:3; 8:14). To supply a subject, Matthew reaches forward to Mark 8:1a, which he otherwise omits, and adopts the "large crowd" but makes it "many crowds." The bringing up of the crowd from the feeding of the four thousand unites vv 29-31 with that feeding and, along with the pluralizing, transforms the whole into a picture of the large number of Gentiles who were going to become disciples (cf. 28:19-20).

The foregoing substitution of "approached" for "bring" necessitates the insertion of "having with themselves." Mark's "deaf-and-dumb man" becomes "lame, crippled, blind, deaf-and-dumb people, and many others" (cf. 9:32-33 on the double meaning, "deaf and dumb," of κωφούς). Matthew models his list after the traditional lists in 9:32-33; 11:5; 12:22; 18:8 (cf. 21:14), and he likes ἑτέρους (5,1) and πολλούς (23,1). Not only the advancing and pluralizing of the crowds, but also the pluralizing of Jesus' healings enhances this preview of worldwide evangelism. Finally, in a further emphasis on Jesus' dignity Matthew changes "and they beseech him that he might lay [his] hand on him" (so Mark) to "and they threw them at his feet." Cf. 5:35; 22:44; 28:9 on a position at someone's feet as implying his divine lordship, and 9:36; 27:5 for distinctive occurrences of ἔρριψαν.

"And he healed them" typifies Matthew's style (see the comments on 4:24) and replaces Mark's long description of the healing of the deaf-mute (Mark 7:33-35). This replacement is due to the changing of the individual healing to a mass healing, and to Matthew's desire to gain a preview of mass evangelism among Gentiles. Possibly he felt some embarrassment over the means Jesus used to heal the deaf-mute—manipulation, saliva, sighing—as might be indicated by his conflating the gradual healing of the blind man in Bethsaida (Mark 8:22-26) with the healing of another blind man (see 9:27-31; 20:29-34)—minus the saliva in Mark 8:23. But his wanting to gain a preview of mass evangelism and eliminate a symbol of the disciples' lack of understanding (see the following) gives positive and perhaps sufficient reason for the omissions (but see Allen, 170). That Matthew has written about a deaf-and-dumb man twice already (9:32-33; 12:22-23; cf. Luke 11:14) eased the present omission. The desire to portray mass evangelism, which Jesus will later command (28:19-20), also leads Matthew to eliminate Jesus' command to secrecy and the subsequent breaking of the command in disobedience (Mark 8:36).

Because Matthew has omitted the command to secrecy and its being broken, he can immediately introduce the result of the healings with ὥστε (10,0) instead of Mark's καί. "The crowd" comes out of the long omission and compensates for it (cf. Mark 8:33). Instead of Mark's expressive ὑπερπερισσῶς ἐξεπλήσσοντο, "they were utterly amazed," Matthew writes the somewhat more usual θαυμάσαι, "marvelled" (cf. esp. his insertion of this word in 21:20).

Mark's continuation, ". . . saying, 'He has done all things well; he makes both the deaf to hear and the dumb to speak," gives way to ". . . seeing deaf-and-dumb people speaking, crippled people restored, and lame people walking and blind people seeing." Why these changes? "Seeing" (βλέποντας—9,3) replaces "saying" for a portrayal of the crowd as those who see, i.e., as disciples by virtue of their understanding (see 11:4; 13:16-17). The listing of those healed grows out of the preceding verse, but follows a different order. Perhaps Matthew intended to follow the earlier order, but the similarity in the first syllables of χωλούς and κωφούς led to the interchange of their first and last positions; and with κωφούς now at the head of the list its mate κυλλούς, also beginning with κ, naturally came next and, last, the originally first pair χωλούς and τυφλούς (but see the v.1.). The delay of "blind people" till last enables Matthew to form an inclusio between the two occurrences of "seeing"; i.e., the list begins with the crowd's seeing and ends with the blind people's seeing. This inclusio reinforces the symbolic value of seeing as understanding.

Those who saw were Gentiles, for "they glorified the God of Israel" (not in Mark). Cf. 5:16; 6:2; 9:8 for other distinctive occurrences of ἐδόξασαν, and v 24 for a phrase similar to "the God of Israel," viz., "the house of Israel" (also peculiar to Matthew). Because Mark's plurals "the deaf" and "the dumb" do not fit the singleness of the deaf-mute's healing, they probably stem from the related passages in Isa 29:18-19; 35:5-6. In its Septuagintal form the latter passage supplies Mark with μογιλάλον, "mute" (Mark 7:32). Matthew's noticing this allusion led him to change the individual healing into a mass healing in the first place, and also to add the lame and crippled (cf. Isa 35:6) and a further allusion to Isa 29:33 nearby: "they will stand in awe of the God of Israel" (cf. Pss 41[40]:14]13]; 106[105]:48; Luke 1:68; Acts 13:17 for "the God of Israel," and Matt 15:8-9 for a recent quotation of the neighboring Isa 29:13). Conceivably, Matthew means that Jews glorified their own God, as in Isaiah and the other passages cited. But the indubitably Gentile setting of the parallel phrase, "the house of Israel," establishes a Gentile setting here, too.

15:32 (Mark 8:1-3) Without interruption Matthew begins to describe the feeding of the four thousand. To unify the story with the preceding mass healing, Mark's introductory genitive absolute (translated, "in those days again, when there was a large crowd and they had nothing to eat") drops out in favor of a simple δέ. Matthew's characteristic insertion of "Jesus" (80,12) repeats the Christological emphasis in v 29 and distinguishes the subject of "said" (which replaces Mark's "says") from the immediately foregoing "God of Israel." Increased attention to Jesus comes from adding "his" to "disciples" and omitting "to them."

After summoning his disciples, Matthew's Jesus speaks for three clauses exactly as Mark's Jesus: "I feel compassion for the crowd, because already they have remained [literally 'are remaining'] with me for three days [ἡμέραι τρεῖς, a nominative absolute] and they have nothing to eat." For

319

literary and theological reasons Matthew now goes back to his habit of revising Mark. The foregoing words consisted of a main clause having Jesus as the subject and a subordinate clause having the crowd as the subject (v 32bc). To satisfy his appetite for parallelism Matthew constructs v 32de as another main clause having Jesus as the subject and another subordinate clause having the crowd as the subject. Thus Mark's "if I should send . . . away" becomes "to send . . . away." This revision necessitates the insertion of "I do not want." The new main verb is a Mattheanism (θέλω—18,8) and displaces "to their home." The subordination of Mark's main clause, "they will faint on the way," requires the insertion of "lest" (μήποτε—2,4) and a consequent change of the verb to the aorist subjunctive. Mark's additional clause, "And some of them have come from a distance," would not fit Matthew's parallelism. Besides, with Mark 8:1a it seems to imply a new crowd different from the crowd at the preceding healing. But Matthew wants to unify the passages, and he omitted Mark 8:1a to do so. Therefore Mark's additional clause falls away. Theologically, these changes result in another Christological emphasis: in Mark Jesus deliberates with the disciples; in Matthew he tells them what he has determined. Such is Matthew's authoritarian portrait of Jesus.

15:33 (Mark 8:4) Mark's statement that the disciples "answered" suits Jesus' deliberation with them, but not Matthew's expression of Jesus' authoritative will. Therefore Matthew substitutes "say" (λέγουσιν, a historical present he is fond of—47,11). And since he advanced "his" with "disciples" to v 32, he omits "his" here. Besides, it is otiose after "to him." As usual, Mark's recitative ὅτι disappears. In Mark the disciples' question implies their failure to understand that Jesus can feed the multitude: "How will anyone be able to satisfy these people with loaves here in the wilderness?" Matthew revises the question so as to imply that only the disciples are unable—for Jesus *is* able—and that they understand their responsibility to give bread to the crowd, as Jesus commanded them previously (see 14:16 and the comments on 14:19): "Where in the wilderness do we have so many loaves as to satisfy such a large crowd?" The substitution of "we" for "anyone" and the advancing of its position mark the shift. The addition of "so many" and the replacement of "these people" with "such a large crowd" again point forward to the many Gentiles who were to come into the church. Mark's "here" drops out as redundant with "in the wilderness." The more natural ἐν replaces Mark's ἐπ' in the geographical phrase (cf. 3:1, 3; 24:26). ὥστε is a Mattheanism (10,0).

15:34 (Mark 8:5) To make a parallel with "say" at the head of v 33, Matthew now substitutes "says" for Mark's "was asking" at the head of v 34. As before, the substitute typifies his style (47,11). Yet another Christological emphasis appears in his characteristic insertion of "Jesus" (80,12). "How many loaves do you have?" and the introduction to the disciples' response, "and they said," stay unchanged. But to the response itself, "Seven," Matthew adds "and a few little fish." The few little fish come from Mark 8:7, later in the story. Matthew introduces them here and, again prematurely, in v 36a in order to parallel the early mentions of fish in 14:17, 19 and especially to avoid the second course of fish in Mark's account. This de-emphasis of the fish helps portray the feeding as an anticipation of the Lord's Supper, where fish play no part (see also 14:19-20 with comments ad loc.).

15:35-36 (Mark 8:6-7) In vv 35-36a Matthew changes the ordering of the crowd to recline on the ground from a finite verb to an aorist participle, and the taking of seven loaves from an aorist participle to a finite verb. The result is parallel with the construction in v 36b, where Matthew agrees with Mark in writing first the aorist participle εὐχαριστήσας (preceded in Matthew by καί to avoid asyndeton) and then the finite verbs ἔκλασεν and ἐδίδου (cf. 14:19; 26:26-27; Mark 14:23; 1 Cor 11:24). Mark's "his" falls away from "disciples" because of the parallels in 14:19; 15:33 and the next clause in the present verse. "And the disciples to the crowds" comes verbatim from Matthew's distinctive wording in 14:19 and here replaces Mark's "in order that they might serve [the loaves]; and they served [the loaves] to the crowd." See the comments on 14:19 for interpretation. As noted above, Mark's reference to having a few small fish and Jesus' blessing them and saying to serve them (Mark 8:7) has been tucked away in vv 34, 36a in order to restrict the giving of thanks, breaking, giving, and eating to the bread—an assimilation to the Lord's Supper. Mark's whole verse therefore vanishes (cf. 14:19-20).

15:37-38 (Mark 8:8-10) To Mark's statement "And they ate and were satisfied" Matthew adds "all" in conformity with 14:20a and his frequent use of πᾶς for emphasis (63,25-26). Here the emphasis is on the large number of Gentiles who will enjoy the feast of salvation (cf. 26:27). Similarly, the second line of v 37 reads like 14:20b except for a delay of the verb and the substitution of ἑπτὰ σπυρίδας, "seven [flexible] baskets," for δώδεκα κοφίνους, "twelve [wicker] baskets"—thus, "and they took up the surplus of the fragments, seven baskets full" instead of Mark's "and they took up leftovers of fragments, seven baskets." The notion that the number seven derives from the seven deacons in Acts 6:1-6 and symbolizes the Gentile part of the church stumbles over the fact that the seven deacons were Hellenistic Jews, not Gentiles. Again, in place of Mark's "And they were about four thousand" we read almost exactly as in 14:21, "And they who were eating were four thousand husbands, besides wives and children." For interpretation of vv 37-38, see the comments on 14:20-21. The use of the substantive participle τὸ περισσεῦον instead of Mark's noun περισσεύματα may reflect 13:12 (cf. 25:29). If so, the surplus represents the "more" which those who already have will receive. Verbal forms occur without parallel in 13:12; 25:29 and in Matthew's two accounts of the feedings (14:20; 15:37), even though he uses the noun in another passage (12:34).

The disciples' incomprehension despite the earlier miracle of feeding (Mark 8:4) and the following of both feedings with a voyage on the Sea of Galilee favor the hypothesis that only one feeding took place and that it was subsequently divided in order to gain a feeding of Gentiles as well as of Jews. But the obvious similarities between the stories are balanced by differences in detail. And Matthew's editing and Luke's and John's omissions of the feeding of the four thousand probably show a tendency toward amalgamation of two incidents rather than evidence for cleavage of a single incident. Furthermore, in a completely different pericope Jesus will distinguish two feedings (Mark 8:19-20; Matt 16:9-10).

FAILURE TO UNDERSTAND THE SIGNS OF THE TIMES
15:39–16:4 (12:38-39; Mark 8:9b-13; Luke 11:16, 29; 12:54-56)

15:39 (Mark 8:9b-10) In Mark 8:9b the independent clause "And he dismissed them" rounds off the feeding of the four thousand. Matthew switches to a participial phrase dependent on what follows and thus makes an introduction to his second treatment of the demand for a sign (see also Matt 12:38-40 and cf. the aorist participial phrases followed by finite verbs in vv 35-36a, 36b). The replacement of "them" with "the crowds" (τοὺς ὄχλους— 17,1) again points to the large number of Gentiles who were flocking into the church. "Embarking" becomes "he embarked." It is natural that Mark's preceding "and immediately" drops out. But surprisingly, "with his disciples" also drops out. In Matthew, as a result, Jesus sails across the lake in lonely majesty. The disciples will catch up later (see the comments on 16:5). We read that he went "into the boundaries of Magadan," where Mark has "into the parts [i.e., region] of Dalmanutha." Though Mark's μέρη appears distinctively in Matt 2:22; 15:21; 16:13 (cf. 24:51), ὅρια here takes its place for a link with v 22 (cf. 2:16; 4:13; 8:34; 19:1). The location of Mark's Dalmanutha remains obscure. But Magadan, Matthew's substitute, remains equally obscure, unless we are to suppose that the well-known Magdala, on the western shore of the Sea of Galilee, stood in Matthew's original text. This supposition would require an early corruption; yet it has in its favor the resultant parallel between Jesus' going to the Plain of Gennesaret just after he fed the five thousand and his going to Magdala on the southern side of that plain just after he fed the four thousand. If Magdala provided the Mag- of Magadan and the Dal- and -a of Dalmanutha, the second and third of these place-names could be considered variants of the first.

    16:1 (12:38; Mark 8:11; Luke 11:16) According to Mark, "the Pharisees came out." To the Pharisees Matthew characteristically adds "and Sadducees" (5,0). The addition results in Jesus' having the same enemies John the Baptist had (3:7; see "John the Baptist parallel Jesus" in the Topical Index). The Mattheanism προσελθόντες (38,6) replaces Mark's ἐξῆλθον for an allusion to Jesus' dignity (see the comments on 4:3; 8:14). Next, Matthew omits Mark's "and" and advances "testing," located at the end of the sentence in Mark, in order to emphasize the evil design of the Pharisees and Sadducees. And for Mark's "they began to argue with him, seeking from him . . ." Matthew writes "they asked him . . . to show to them." Thus he gains a parallel between two occurrences of the prefix ἐπ- in ἐπηρώτησαν and ἐπιδεῖξαι. The prefix escalates the meaning of ἐπηρώτησαν from a simple asking to an insistent demand (cf. the comments on 12:39). The escalation again emphasizes the evil design of the Pharisees and Sadducees. See 22:19; 24:1 for other insertions of ἐπιδείκνυμι. In the phrase "from heaven" Matthew changes Mark's ἀπό to ἐκ (so also Luke). ἐκ precedes God's heaven in 3:17; 16:1; 21:25 (bis); 28:2; ἀπό precedes the heaven of the sky in 24:29 (against ἐκ in Mark 13:25). In asking for a sign from heaven the Pharisees and Sadducees demanded a sign not subject to interpretation as Satanically aided (cf. the comments on 12:38).

16:2-3 (12:39; Mark 8:12; Luke 12:54-56) Mark introduces Jesus' response with "And sighing deeply in his spirit, he says." In word-for-word assimilation to 12:39, Matthew writes "But he, answering, said." This revision agrees with his tendency to get rid of Jesus' emotions and with his fondness for ἀποκριθεὶς εἶπεν (29,6). The replacement of Mark's "And" with "But" and the insertions of "answering" and "to them" set Jesus' answer against the demand of the Pharisees and Sadducees and thus sharpen the sense of conflict. "Answering" suits "asking for."

At this point a big problem of textual criticism arises. Some external evidence favors the presence of material similar to the signs of weather in Luke 12:54-56; other external evidence favors the absence of that material (see the UBS ad loc.). The hypothesis that later scribes inserted Luke's material in Matthew's text necessitates the further hypothesis that they also revised the Palestinian signs of weather in Luke's material to agree with other signs of weather in their own land. It seems easier to think that Matthew himself made such revisions. This judgment is confirmed when we discover that Matt 16:2b-3 differs from Luke 12:54-56 in ways that typify his writing. The omission of the material may have come about, then, through parallel influence from Mark, where it is lacking, or from the strangeness of Matthew's signs of weather to scribes living where those signs did not obtain—say, in Egypt, where a red sky in the morning does not augur rain.

First, we may note some parallelism, which typifies Matthew's style. The indications of time in vv 2b and 3a, "when it becomes evening" and "early in the morning," correspond to each other. Also corresponding to each other are the statements "you say, 'Fair weather'" and "[you say], 'Today, stormy weather,'" and the supportive clauses "for the sky is red" and "for the sky is red, becoming threatening." Similarly, in v 3bc "You know how to discern the face of the sky" and "but you are not able [to discern] the signs of the times" parallel each other.

Second, differences in diction and style are often characteristic of Matthew. The genitive absolute ὀψίας γενομένης occurs twice as an insertion and once as part of unique material, besides three common appearances. Here it replaces "whenever" (with an ellipsis of "you see") in Luke 12:55. "You say" stays. Matthew's omission of the recitative ὅτι is typical. "Fair weather" substitutes for "There will be hot weather." Matthew, who likes πῦρ (2,4), γάρ (62-63,15), and οὐρανός (46,11), puts "for the sky is fiery [i.e., 'red']" in place of "And whenever [you see] the south wind blowing." "And it happens" drops out. "And early in the morning" substitutes for "whenever you see" (Luke 12:54). Matthew omits εὐθέως just as he often omits the synonymous εὐθύς in his revisions of Mark; and he leaves a second "you say" to be supplied (cf. v 2b). σήμερον is a favorite of his (4,3); so he adds it to χειμών. Thus "Today, stormy weather" replaces "a rainstorm is coming." Typically, another recitative ὅτι drops out. Again Matthew caters to his fondness for πῦρ, γάρ, and οὐρανός by writing "for the sky is fiery, becoming threatening" in place of "a cloud rising in the west." Will he omit στυγνάσας from the description of the rich man's countenance in 19:22 (cf. Mark 10:22) because he uses στυγνάζων here for weather? "And it happens thus" again drops out. Notably, Matthew has transposed the sayings in the tradition to conform to the beginning of the Jewish day in the evening: thus the red sky in the evening comes first; the red sky in the morning, second.

In the next two lines we see Matthew's style exemplified in μέν . . . δέ (15,1). Because of his predilection for ὑποκριταί (8,3—so Luke), it is hard to think he omitted it. Yet he will replace ὑπόκρισιν with πονηρίαν in 22:18 (cf. Mark 12:15). Possibly, however, Luke here inserts ὑποκριταί, for in the first verse of this same chapter he has ὑπόκρισις against Mark 8:15; Matt 16:6. From "the face of the earth and of the sky" Matthew deletes "of the earth and" because he changed the south wind, which relates to the earth, to a red sky, with the result that neither of his signs has to do with the earth. γινώσκετε, a favorite of his (8,2), stands in the place of Luke's synonymous οἴδατε. δοκιμάζειν yields to διακρίνειν, which belongs to a class of words having κρι- as their base and appearing often in the first gospel (11,0). With the insertion of τά . . . σημεῖα, which Matthew will insert also in 24:30; 26:48, the traditional "this time" becomes "the signs of the times." Matthew probably pluralizes the word for "time" to match the different kinds of weather. At first "the signs" seems to contradict "no sign . . . except the sign of Jonah" in the next verse. But the signs refer to Jesus' miracles already performed, the sign of Jonah to Jesus' resurrection yet to take place—the only sign of the irrefragable sort the Pharisees and Sadducees were demanding (see 12:40).

Finally, where Luke has "Why do you not know how to analyze?" or "Why do you not analyze. . . ?" (the textual evidence differs), Matthew uses a favorite verb of his in δύνασθε (13,0) and writes "you are not able [to discern]. . . ." Thus the traditional question becomes a declaration. By this means Matthew again heightens the guilt of the Pharisees and Sadducees. Indeed, his very insertion of this material in Mark's material serves the purpose of putting the Pharisees and Sadducees, who represent the Jewish persecutors of the church at the time of writing, in a worse light.

16:4 (12:39; Mark 8:12-13; Luke 11:29) Matthew rejoins Mark in Jesus' comment about the generation that seeks for a sign, but revises Mark's wording in accord with his former revisions (see 12:39 with comments ad loc.). The distinctive designation of Jonah as "the prophet" in 12:39 falls away here, because no reference to his preaching follows immediately, in contrast with the earlier passage. After 12:40 there is no need to explain "the sign of Jonah." The paragraph closes with Jesus' departure. Matthew puts καταλιπών in place of ἀφείς in order to gain the connotation of judgmental abandonment (see the comments on 4:13-16). Mark's "again embarking" and "to the other side" drop out. Consequently, Jesus goes away, but not by boat or to the other side. Why? Because in Matthew the disciples have yet to catch up with him (see the comments on 15:39 and 16:5). Thus, where Mark's Jesus sails with the disciples from the place

where the four thousand were fed to the districts of Dalmanutha, Matthew's
Jesus sails alone from the place where the four thousand were fed to the
boundaries of Magadan (possibly, Magdala). And in Mark Jesus sails again
with the disciples to the side opposite the districts of Dalmanutha, but in
Matthew Jesus goes from the place where he confronted the Pharisees and
Sadducees yet stays inside the boundaries of Magadan rather than go back
across the lake. Only then do the disciples come to the other side, where
Jesus still is even though he has departed from the particular spot where
his enemies confronted him. In other words, "the other side" to which the
disciples come (v 5) does not lie opposite Magadan, but opposite the place
where the four thousand were fed. It is the same other side Jesus went to
earlier, by himself.

THE DISCIPLES' GAINING UNDERSTANDING
CONCERNING THE EVIL TEACHING
OF THE PHARISEES AND SADDUCEES
16:5-12 (Mark 8:14-21; Luke 12:1)

16:5 (Mark 8:14; Luke 12:1) To bring the disciples back to Jesus, Matthew
begins a new paragraph with the distinctive phrase "And the disciples,
having come to the other side." Both ἐλθόντες (10,10) and μαθηταί (31,5)
typify his diction. "To the other side" comes from Mark 8:13, where it
refers to Jesus' travelling. Matthew transfers it to the disciples' travelling,
with the result that the other side is the other side to which Jesus has
already come (see the comments on v 4). Except for a transposition of the
infinitive and its object, Mark's "they forgot to take loaves" stays unchanged. But Matthew omits "and except for one loaf they did not have
[any loaves] with themselves in the boat." The omission stems from his
allowing Jesus alone to get in the boat in 15:39 (contrast Mark 8:10). Thus
the disciples have to come to the other side by land, and the reference to
their having but one loaf in the boat becomes impossible.

 16:6 (Mark 8:15; Luke 12:1) To set Jesus' exhortation to wariness in
contrast with the disciples' forgetfulness, Matthew introduces v 6 with δέ
instead of καί. His insertion of "Jesus" is characteristic (80,12). Mark's
διεστέλλετο occurs only once, and doubtfully, in Matthew (see 16:20 v.l.),
but five times in Mark. As usual, Matthew omits it and has to turn "saying"
into "said." For smoothness, "and" is inserted between the two verbs in
"Look out and beware of the leaven of the Pharisees and Sadducees."
προσέχετε (so also Luke) is a favorite of Matthew (3,3), especially with ἀπό
(3,2). Here it replaces Mark's βλέπετε, "watch out," which seems stylistically
too close to the immediately preceding ὁρᾶτε, "look out." Matthew retains
βλέπετε in the sense "watch out" only at 24:4. Five times he avoids it (contrast his liking it in the sense "see, look, watch"). The Sadducees take the
place of Mark's "the leaven of Herod" (possibly a reference to Herod's
beheading John the Baptist and being a threat to Jesus or, more probably,
a reference to the political opportunism of those Jews, mainly Sadducees,

who supported the Herodian family). The replacement conforms to v 1, where Matthew added the Sadducees to Mark's Pharisees.

16:7 (Mark 8:16) To set the disciples' thoughts opposite Jesus' warning, Matthew again replaces καί with δέ. The added οἱ, "they," is a counterpart to "Jesus," which Matthew inserted in the preceding verse. "Were reasoning" connotes blameworthy questioning (see the comments on 9:4). "In themselves" replaces "to one another." The substitution shifts the meaning from mutual discussion to private thinking (cf. 9:3, 21; 16:8; 21:38 with synoptic parallels and esp. 21:25 with Mark 11:31). Consequently, "knowing" in v 8 will imply divine omniscience of others' thoughts rather than overhearing a discussion (as in Mark). The insertion of λέγοντες represents Matthew's style (61,23). The verb in Mark's next clause is textually uncertain (see the UBS and Metzger, *Textual Commentary* ad loc.). If we read ἔχουσιν, ὅτι means "because." If we read ἔχομεν, ὅτι may be either recitative or causal (with ellipsis: "[it is] because"). A causal ὅτι makes Jesus' warning the source of the disciples' reasoning. A recitative ὅτι allows the same understanding, but also allows that the disciples' reasoning arose out of their forgetfulness prior to Jesus' warning. Matthew's insertion of "saying" makes ὅτι look recitative (though his deleting the recitative ὅτι elsewhere causes some doubt), and his writing -ομεν suggests that he found -ομεν rather than -ουσιν in his copy of Mark. But he changes "we have" to "we took" for a parallel with v 5. Thus "we took no loaves" (v 7) matches "they forgot to take loaves" (v 5).

16:8-9 (Mark 8:17-19) In v 8, Matthew writes "But . . . Jesus said" in place of Mark's "And . . . he says." The replacement parallels v 6a and again sets Jesus opposite the disciples and puts stress on his person. But though in v 6a Matthew retained Mark's "to them," here he omits it to make room for the insertion of another pronominal reference to the disciples, viz., "in yourselves," which he adds to Jesus' question, "Why do you reason. . . ?" The addition echoes Matthew's revision in v 7a and reemphasizes Jesus' divine ability to know the private thoughts of others. The further addition of ὀλιγόπιστοι (3,0) attributes the disciples' puzzlement to "little faith," which is corrected by further instruction, rather than to the unseeing, unhearing lack of understanding characteristic of nondisciples. The ὅτι that introduces "you have no loaves" may mean either "that" or "because."

By couching his warning in the figure of leaven, Jesus takes advantage of the disciples' forgetfulness to bring loaves of bread. But anxiety follows forgetfulness. Therefore Jesus reminds the disciples of his former miracles of feeding. His words ". . . neither do you understand? Do you have your heart hardened? Having eyes, do you not see? And having ears do you not hear?" (so Mark) drop out. Just as Matthew has reinterpreted the disciples' puzzlement by means of "little faith," so now he eliminates the kind of ignorance which in his theology cannot characterize disciples. For they *do* see and hear (13:16). All that remains is "Do you not yet comprehend? Neither do you remember. . . ?" Omission of the rest tends also to leave the stress on "not yet" and on Jesus' reminding the disciples about the five loaves and how many baskets they took, and about the seven loaves and how many baskets they took. Thus the disciples appear as those who are deficient but not lacking in understanding and who, because they already see and hear, are about to gain further understanding through Jesus' reminder and a subsequent explanation contained only in Matthew (see vv 11-12; 13:12; 15:15-20 with comments ad loc.). In v 9 the omission of Mark's "when" and "I broke for" makes "the five loaves" the direct object of "remember" rather than of "broke" (as in Mark). Both the description of the baskets as "full of fragments" and the whole line "They say to him, 'Twelve'" drop out.

16:10-11a (Mark 8:20-21) In v 10 Matthew deletes Mark's "when," "for" (εἰς), "fullnesses of fragments," and the line "And they say, 'Seven.'" On the other hand, he adds "loaves" to "the seven" in order to fill out the parallel with "the five loaves" in v 9. And the characteristic addition of οὐδέ (17,3) at the beginning of v 10 matches οὐδέ in v 9. These omissions and additions tighten up the parallel between vv 9 and 10 and shift the emphasis from the numbers of baskets taken up to the small numbers of loaves used to feed the large numbers of people. The replacement of ἤρατε twice with ἐλάβετε makes Jesus' questions apply directly to the disciples' forgetting "to take" (λαβεῖν) loaves (v 5; see also v 7). λαμβάνω is a Mattheanism (21,16).

Since Matthew has not given the disciples a chance to answer Jesus' questions—the dominical sayings have overpowered all else—the transitional "And he was saying to them" disappears. Jesus' next question, "Do you not yet understand?" gets a non-Markan introduction with "How is it that?" (πῶς, a Mattheanism—6,1). Mark's συνίετε becomes νοεῖτε for a match with v 9, where Matthew retained Mark's νοεῖτε but not συνίετε. And Mark's "not yet" becomes a simple "not," against v 9a, where Matthew took over Mark's "not yet." Here Matthew deletes "yet" because the further part of this very question and the subsequent statement (neither one present in Mark) give the disciples the further understanding that comes to those who already have the understanding which qualifies them to be disciples (see also v 12).

16:14 (Mark 8:28; Luke 9:19) After οἱ δὲ εἶπαν Matthew omits αὐτῷ the gospel of Matthew, who has constructed them out of the preceding material with the help of his favorite vocabulary. "That I did not speak to you about loaves" comes from the preceding. The next line comes verbatim from v 6, except for an added δέ for contrast between loaves and leaven: "But beware of the leaven of the Pharisees and Sadducees" (see the comments on v 6 for Mattheanisms). That Matthew does not begin with the traditional ὁρᾶτε of v 6 but with his own προσέχετε . . . ἀπό (3,2) confirms his editorial creativity here. "Then they understood" comes from his special vocabulary (τότε—66,17; συνῆκαν—5,1). Notably, he reserved συνῆκαν for positive use, for in vv 9 and 11 he avoided Mark's negative use of the verb. Cf. especially 17:13. The last clause comes from the preceding material, with the addition of "teaching": "that he did not say to beware of the leaven of loaves, but of the teaching of the Pharisees and Sadducees." "Teaching" belongs to a family of cognates well liked by Matthew (9,4—διδασκ-/διδαχ-). This teaching contrasts, of course, with Jesus' teaching. Thus where Mark closes with a negative question, "Do you not yet understand?" Matthew closes with an affirmation that the disciples did come to understand, and with an explication of what they came to understand.

According to some, the disciples mistakenly thought that Jesus was warning them not to buy bread from the Pharisees and Sadducees. Others think that Jesus warned against the אֲמִירָה (Aramaic for "speech, word") of the Pharisees and scribes, but that the disciples misunderstood him to say חֲמִירָא (Aramaic for "leaven"). Jesus' warning then loses its initial connection with the failure of the disciples to take enough bread, however; and the following criticism of the disciples' lack of understanding deals with a lapse in their memory of the miraculous feedings, not with inaccuracy of hearing. Probably the disciples were blaming one another (so Mark), or themselves (so Matthew), for failure to take enough bread. See p. 602 on Matthew's lumping together the Pharisees and Sadducees and cf. the comments on 22:23-24.

UNDERSTANDING THE SON OF MAN
TO BE THE MESSIAH AND SON OF GOD
16:13-20 (Mark 8:27-30; Luke 9:18-21; John 6:66-71; 20:22-23)

At this point in Mark we read about Jesus' restoring sight to a blind man at Bethsaida (Mark 8:22-26). But Matthew incorporated that healing in 9:27-31, where it provided both the second blind man and Jesus' touch. He will make the same incorporation in 20:29-34. Therefore the story drops out here and the narrative moves to Peter's confession of Jesus.

Some have thought that Matthew omits the healing of the blind man at Bethsaida because of embarrassment over Jesus' use of saliva and over the gradualness of the cure, because of offense at the story's symbolizing the disciples' hazy understanding of Jesus, or because of the lack of items concerning Christology, faith, and discipleship offering possibilities of editorial development. But we have ample evidence of Matthew's ability to revise material and add to it. Therefore we do better to think that he omits the story simply because he conflated it with another (9:27-31; cf. 20:29-34), just as he omitted the exorcism in the synagogue at Capernaum (Mark 1:23-28; Luke 4:33-37) because he had conflated it with the exorcism in the country of the Gadarenes (Matt 8:28-34). Luke's omitting the cure of the blind man at Bethsaida yet failing to conflate it with the similar cure at Jericho suggests Matthean influence.

16:13 (Mark 8:27; Luke 9:18) Mark's καί changes to δέ for a contrast between the teaching of the Pharisees and Sadducees on the one hand (v 12) and Peter's confession and Jesus' response on the other hand. Matthew then drops ἐξ- from Mark's ἐξῆλθεν and changes the verb to the participle ἐλθών, a favorite of his (10,10). The result is an allusion to Jesus as the Coming One (see the comments on 3:11). This concentration on the figure of Jesus leads to the deletion of Mark's "and his disciples" (cf. Luke; and Matt 15:39 with Mark 8:10). In an echo of his distinctive wording at 15:21 ("into the districts of Tyre and Sidon"), Matthew substitutes "the districts" of Caesarea Philippi for "the villages" of Caesarea Philippi.

Caesarea Philippi, built by Herod Philip and named "Caesarea" to honor the emperor and "Philippi" (literally "of Philip") to differentiate it from Caesarea on the Mediterranean coast, lay about twenty-five miles north of the Sea of Galilee. Historically, Jesus probably asked his questions (see also v 15) to correct misconceptions of his role, not to elicit a confession, or a reconfession, from his disciples. The immediately following teaching that he must be killed supports the probability of this supposition.

Despite the frequency of ὁδός in Matthew (9,2), "on the way" drops out (cf. Luke). Perhaps Matthew thought that it would overload his single clause (Mark distributes the weight between two clauses) or feared an apparent contradiction of Jesus' command that the disciples not go into any way of the Gentiles (10:5, peculiar to this gospel). Mark's ἐπ- falls from ἐπηρώτα. The same deletion will occur in 21:24 (cf. Mark 11:29). Here it may take place not only because of the parallel loss of ἐξ- at the beginning of the verse, but also because of the distinctive use in v 1 of ἐπηρώτησαν to express the Pharisees' and Sadducees' demanding a sign. "Them" drops out as redundant after mention of the disciples (see also v 8 with Mark 8:17). From Jesus' question Matthew deletes "I" (see the UBS and Metzger, *Textual Commentary* ad loc.) and brings up "the Son of man" from Mark 8:31. Thus the title "Son of man" is no longer the answer of Jesus himself to the question of his identity, and it no longer qualifies "the Christ" in terms of suffering. To the contrary, the change of the question from Jesus' identity to the Son of man's identity shifts the emphasis to the definition of "the Christ" as God's Son (see v 16).

16:14 (Mark 8:28; Luke 9:19) After οἱ δὲ εἶπαν Matthew omits αὐτῷ λέγοντες to parallel the omission of Mark's αὐτοῖς in v 13a and satisfy his habit of using λέγων/-οντες only after verbs of speaking different from εἶπον (22:1 is the sole exception). Mark's recitative ὅτι disappears, as often (but cf. the same omission in Luke and much of Mark's textual tradition here). The insertion of οἱ makes a parallel with the following ἄλλοι and ἕτεροι. ἕτεροι replaces a second ἄλλοι in Mark and comes from Matthew's preferred vocabulary (5,1). The insertion of μέν . . . δέ . . . δέ typifies Matthew's style (15,1). With the preceding revisions it finely balances the popular answers to the question of the Son of man's identity. As in Mark and Luke, John the Baptist and Elijah appear in the accusative case as subjects of the infinitive "to be," inferred from v 13b. Suddenly an anacoluthon appears in Mark: there is a shift from the accusative case to ὅτι εἷς τῶν προφητῶν, "[say] that [you are] one of the prophets" (cf. Luke). For strict parallelism, however, Matthew switches to the accusative in ἕνα τῶν προφητῶν. Before this phrase he inserts another prophet known, like John the Baptist and Elijah, for preaching judgment, viz., Jeremiah. Thus all three identifications contain parallel personal names.

Cf. 14:2; Mark 6:14-16; Luke 9:7-9. Though popular traditions circulated concerning Jeremiah (see 2 Macc 2:1-8; 15:12-16; 2 Esdr 2:18), we have no evidence that people expected him to return in the end time. On the unlikelihood that he appears here as the foremost of the prophets or that his book headed the collection of prophetic books in the OT, see J. Carmignac in *Tradition und Glaube* (*Festgabe* for

K. G. Kuhn; ed. G. Jeremias, H.-W. Kuhn, and H. Stegemann; Göttingen: Vandenhoeck & Ruprecht, 1971) 283-98.

16:15 (Mark 8:29; Luke 9:20; John 6:67) Matthew hurries toward the Christological confession by shortening "And he himself was asking them" (so Mark) to "He says to them." The historical present of λέγει with asyndeton typifies his style (21,6) and dramatizes the following question, "But you—who do you say I am?"

16:16 (Mark 8:29; Luke 9:20; John 6:68-69) In the introduction to v 16, Matthew adds δέ (so also Luke) to connect Peter's answer with Jesus' question. He also inserts "Simon" to prepare for "Simon son of Jonah" in v 17, which is unique to his gospel. Peter represents all the disciples. Both Matthew and Luke omit the definite article with his name. Because he has just used the historical present λέγει to introduce Jesus' question (v 15), Matthew here changes Mark's λέγει to εἶπεν. As in vv 8 and 13, "to him" drops out as otiose. The answer "You are the Christ" gains the apposition "the Son of the living God." This anticipates the distinctively Matthean statement that Peter received divine revelation (v 17), for according to 11:25-27 the knowledge that Jesus is the Son of God comes only by divine revelation. ὁ υἱὸς τοῦ θεοῦ characterizes Matthew's Christology (4,2) and here derives from the disciples' statement after Jesus came walking on the water to them: "Truly you are God's Son" (14:33, part of a Matthean insertion; cf. esp. 26:33; 27:40, 43, 54). Since Jesus asks what the disciples say, Matthew conflates their former statement with Peter's present statement. "Son of God" lacks the definite article in 14:33, but carries it here because of "the" with "Christ," to which "the Son" is appositive. Mark and Luke hardly omit an original "the Son of the living God" through fear of Jewish political overtones in the title (which was just coming into use for the Messiah). Elsewhere in their gospels Jesus appears very prominently as the Son of God.

Though in late Judaism "Son of God" might connote no more than the purely human Messiah adopted by God as his vicegerent (see esp. 4QFlor 10–13), the title "Immanuel . . . God with us" (1:23) and the whole account of the virgin birth demand in Matthew the stronger connotation of essential deity. The description of God as "living" reflects Matthew's practice of conforming to the phraseology of the OT, where we often read about the living God (cf. the possibility that 5:9 alludes to Hos 2:1[1:10]: "you are the sons of the living God"). The description also appears often in other ancient Jewish literature and in the rest of the NT and here prepares for the assurance that the gates of Hades—i.e., death—will not prevail against the church (v 18) and distinguishes God from the false gods worshipped by the Gentiles, whose conversion Matthew seeks (28:19). Again cf. 26:63, where "the living God" relates to "You are the Messiah, the Son of God."

16:17-19 Verses 17-19 lack any parallels. As in earlier passages peculiar to this gospel (e.g., 13:24-30, 36-43; 14:28-31), parallelistic structure, Matthew's favorite diction and theological motifs, OT phraseology, and echoes of other Matthean passages point to expansive composition by the evangelist himself and away from a special tradition known only to him. He composes the passage in order to portray Peter as a representative disciple—representative in his understanding Jesus to be the Christ and Son of the living God and in his consequent activity as a Christian scribe. To this extent Matthew reverses the main point in Mark, viz., Peter's misunderstanding of Jesus' messiahship.

Matthew's love of parallelism is on exhibit: each of the three verses contains a leading statement followed by a couplet:

(17b) Blessed are you, Simon Barjona,
      (17c) because flesh and blood has not revealed [this] to you,
      (17d) but my Father in heaven [has revealed this to you].
(18a) And I say to you that you are Peter,
      (18b) and on this rock I will build my church,
      (18c) and [the] gates of Hades will not overpower it.
(19a) I will give you the keys of the kingdom of heaven,
      (19b) and whatever you bind on earth will have been bound in heaven,
      (19c) and whatever you loose on earth will have been loosed in heaven.

Diction and theological motifs typical of Matthew appear throughout. ἀποκριθείς . . . εἶπεν and Ἰησοῦς are Mattheanisms (29,6; 80,12). "And answering, Jesus said" parallels "And answering, Simon Peter said" in v 16a. The addition "to him" (not in v 16a) prepares for the following emphasis on Peter. Matthew uses "blessed" seven times in beatitudes of his own making (5:4, 5, 7, 8, 9, 10; 16:17). Cf. paralleled occurrences in 5:3, 6, 11; 11:6; 13:16 (but with a distinctive "because," as here); 24:46. "Flesh and blood" emphasizes human weakness and appears nowhere else in the first gospel, but looks like the Jewish and rabbinic kind of phrase Matthew occasionally works into his text (see Sir 14:18 Hebrew; 1 Cor 15:50; Gal 1:16; Eph 6:12; Heb 2:14; Str-B 1. 730-31 and cf. esp. the rabbinic contrast between "this age" and "the coming age" in 12:32, a contrast lacking in Mark 3:29; Luke 12:10). The combination οὐκ . . . ἀλλ᾽ occurs also at 18:22 in contrast with Luke 17:4.

We meet further Mattheanisms in "my Father in Heaven" (9,2), which appears nowhere else in the gospels or the rest of the NT, κἀγώ (5,3), and δέ σοι λέγω (27,7; see the comments on 5:21-48). Matthew often puts ὅτι after λέγω. His predilection for "Peter" is evident (8,1). He inserts the resumptive ταύτῃ, which appears in "on this rock," three times. In the gospels "church" occurs only here and in 18:17 (bis). The "my" that goes with it corresponds to Matthew's unique attribution of the kingdom to Jesus the Son of man (see 13:41 and esp. v 28 in this very chap. 16) and to the attribution, again unique, of angels to Jesus the Son of man (13:41; 16:27; 24:31; cf. 25:41; 26:53). Furthermore, "my church" reflects Matthew's liking of "their [or 'your'] synagogue(s)" (5,0); the two expressions are counterparts.

Though κατισχύουσιν appears only here in his gospel, ἰσχύει occurs as an insertion in 5:13 and ἰσχυρόν in the possibly original text of 14:30, which belongs to a distinctive passage. Similarly, though κλεῖδας appears only here in Matthew, its cognate κλείω appears distinctively in 6:6; 25:10. A string of easily recognizable Mattheanisms dominates the rest of v 19: "the kingdom of heaven" (25,7), ὃ ἐάν (bis—14,1), the two forms of δέω (5,1), "on the earth" (bis—8,2), "in heaven" (bis—24,4), and the contrast between heaven and earth (6,0; cf. esp. 6:10; 28:18). The verb λύω appears as a theological metaphor without parallel in 5:19; 16:19 (bis); 18:18 (bis), but never as a theological metaphor in Mark or Luke.

Characteristically, Matthew introduces OT allusions and phraseology. The designation of Simon as Βαριωνά, "son of Jonah," belongs here. An Aramaism often taken as evidence for Matthew's use of early tradition, it points rather to the prophet Jonah. Apart from that prophet, we have no evidence earlier than the third century after Christ that Jonah was used as a man's name (see *TDNT* 3. 406-7). Furthermore, it was very unusual for a man to be addressed as the son of his physical father; and Matthew usually translates, replaces, or omits Hebrew and Aramaic expressions that come to him in the tradition (see 9:25 with Mark 5:41; 10:2 with Mark 3:17; 15:5 with Mark 7:11; 15:30 with Mark 7:34; 17:4 with Mark 9:5; 21:20 with Mark 11:21; 20:33 with Mark 10:51; 26:39 with Mark 14:36; cf. 1:21, 23). Yet for special purposes he will himself insert an Aramaic expression without translating it (see 23:7, 8; 26:25) or retain an untranslated Aramaic expression (see 26:49 with Mark 14:45).

But why the designation of Simon as "son of Jonah"? After the pattern of the expression "the sons of the prophets" in the OT, Matthew makes Simon a spiritual son of Jonah, who was designated "the prophet" in 12:39 (but not in Mark 8:12; Luke 11:29). He does so in order to associate Simon with "the sign of Jonah," which was mentioned not only in 12:39 but also in v 4 of the present chapter (contrast Mark 8:12). We know from the unique statement in 12:40 that for Matthew the sign of Jonah the prophet consists in Jesus' death and resurrection. The insertion of the sign of Jonah in v 4 makes "son of Jonah" a warning of death by martyrdom and a promise of resurrection. In facing these prospects Simon represents all who make up the church. Indeed, Matthew leads us from "the sign of Jonah" (v 4) through "the son of Jonah" (v 17) to the inability of "the gates of Hades"— i.e., death—to overpower "the church" (v 18) and finally to the necessities that Jesus be killed and rise and that his disciples take up their crosses and lose their lives in order to gain them (vv 21-28). These latter items explain the "sign of Jonah" in v 4 just as 12:40 explained the sign of Jonah in 12:39. "The son of Jonah" provides the clue to that explanation, which eliminates the need to repeat 12:40 after v 4. Cf. also the parallel between the demand for a sign "from heaven" (v 1) and the revelation by the Father "in heaven" (v 17). The choice of the Semitic Βαρ- instead of the Greek υἱός suits the Semitic character of the names Simon and Jonah.

"Church" had long been in use among Christians by the time Matthew wrote. It comes from the OT, whose Septuagintal version regularly has it for Israel as the Lord's people or congregation. "Gates of Hades" comes from Isa 38:10, where it stands for death (cf. Pss 9:14[13]; 107[106]:18; Job 38:17; Jonah 2:7[6]; Wis 16:13; *Pss. Sol.* 16:2; 3 Macc 5:51; 1QH 6:24;

2 Enoch 42:1). Though it has a more immediate source, the metaphor of building a people occurs in Jer 18:9; 24:6; 31:4; 42:10; cf. 1QH 6:25-29; 7:4-9; 4QpPs37 3:16; 1 Cor 3:9; Eph 2:20; 1 Pet 2:5. The notion of a foundation resistant to flood and storm from the underworld ("the gates of Hades will not overpower it" because Jesus will build his church on a rock) appears in Isa 28:15-18, where the Lord God lays in Zion a tested, costly cornerstone, firmly placed as the foundation. On it, the believer will not be disturbed by the hail and flood of Sheol. Though it also has a more immediate source, "the keys of the kingdom of heaven" may echo "the key of the house of David" in Isa 22:22 (cf. Matthew's fondness for Davidic messianism).

As he does elsewhere, Matthew borrows materials from other passages in his gospel. The Father's revealing Jesus' true identity to Simon has its origin in 11:25-27. "Reveal" and "my Father" are prominent in both passages; and both passages emphasize Jesus' identity as God's Son—a Matthean insertion in v 16!—and the necessity that the Father himself reveal this identity. Thus the implied object of "revealed" is neither unclear nor indicative of earlier tradition detached from its original context. "And on this rock I will build my church" derives in the main from 7:24, where, differently from Luke 6:48, Matthew writes "who built his house on the rock." "The keys" (τὰς κλεῖδας) of the kingdom of heaven anticipates 23:13, where the scribes and Pharisees "lock up" (κλείετε) the kingdom of heaven, and links with Matthew's portrayal of the disciples, whom Peter represents, as scribes (see the comments on 8:19 and cf. 28:19).

What does Matthew's composing vv 17-19 in the Greek language mean for our further understanding of the passage? It means first that we need not strain to equate "Jonah" in Βαριωνά with "John," the name of Simon's father according to John 1:42 (cf. John 21:15, 16, 17; *Gos. Heb.* fragment 9). Because of its similarity to "Jonah," the name "John" of Simon's father may have helped, or even suggested, Matthew's association of Simon with Jonah. Alternatively, in John 1:42 the more usual "John" replaces "Jonah," which went into the tradition from Matthew. But we are not to think of -ιωνά, "of Jonah," as an abbreviation of -ιωάν(ν)ου, "of John." The usual Palestinian abbreviation of the Hebrew name יוֹחָנָן, "John," was יוֹחַי or יוֹחָא, in contrast with the Hebrew name יוֹנָה, "Jonah." And the occurrences of Jonah for John in 4 Kgdms 25:23 LXX[B]; 1 Chr 26:3 LXX[B]; 1 Esdr 9:1 LXX[B], 23 LXX[A] stem from scribal confusion in the Greek textual tradition, as shown in 1 Esdr 9:23 LXX[B] by the reading Ἰωάνας, a hybrid in that the first α comes from Ἰωάναν, "John," and the final ς from Ἰωνᾶς, "Jonah." Therefore, the LXX provides no good evidence for Jonah as an abbreviation of John (against *TDNT* 3. 406-7).

Matthew's composition of vv 17-19 in Greek also means that we ought to overlook the Aramaic counterpart to Πέτρος—viz., כֵּיפָא—in our interpretation of the passage. Simon was called "Cephas," to be sure, and this Aramaic form of his nickname would provide a wordplay untarnished by the Greek distinction between Πέτρος (masculine) and πέτρα (feminine). Nevertheless, the two Greek words provide a wordplay that is good enough to obviate the need of an Aramaic substratum. They share the same stem.

No longer shackled by the need to suppose an Aramaic substratum, we can see that Πέτρος is not the πέτρα on which Jesus will build his church. For Matthew, Peter represents all disciples, including those who are weak and even those who apostatize, and thus the superstructure of the church, not its foundation (see the comments on 26:70; 28:7). In accord with 7:24, which Matthew quotes here, the πέτρα consists of Jesus' teaching, i.e., the law of Christ. "This rock" no longer poses the problem that "this" ill suits an address to Peter in which he is the rock. For that meaning the text would have read more naturally "on you." Instead, the demonstrative echoes 7:24; i.e., *this* rock" echoes "*these* my words." Only Matthew put the demonstrative with Jesus' words, which the rock stood for in the following parable (7:24-27). His reusing it in 16:18 points away from Peter to those same words as the foundation of the church. Consequently, we are free from the necessity of appealing to Aramaic in order to explain away the usual distinction between Πέτρος, "detached stone" (hardly a firm foundation), and πέτρα, "bedrock." The two words retain their peculiar Greek connotations, for Matthew's Jesus will build only on the firm bedrock of his law (cf. 5:19-20; 28:19), not on the loose stone Peter. Also, we no longer need to explain away the association of the church's foundation with Christ rather than with Peter in Matt 21:42 (cf. Mark 12:10; Luke 20:17; 1 Cor 3:10-17; 1 Pet 2:6-7; Eph 2:20).

The identification of "this rock" with "these my words" provides a beautifully natural lead into the portrayal of Peter as a Christian scribe who uses keys—i.e., Jesus' words—and binds and looses things—i.e., prohibits and allows various kinds of conduct and disciplines church members according to the law of Christ. Indeed, the unifying of the passage by this identification confirms the identification. It is not as a hierarch that Peter will use Jesus' words. For Peter is not the foundation, and Matthew portrays every Christian as a scribe (see the comments on 13:52). He will also stress childlikeness, littleness, and communal ministry involving the whole membership of the church in chap. 18 (cf. esp. the giving of the power of binding and loosing to all the disciples in 18:18; also the prohibition of calling any fellow disciple "Rabbi," "Father," or "Instructor" in 23:8-11, a uniquely Matthean passage). Furthermore, in 28:7 Matthew will delete "and Peter" right after "tell his disciples" (cf. Mark 16:7) because mention of the disciples does away with the need to mention Peter, their representative; and to mention him in addition to the others might imply his superiority over them—an implication abhorrent to Matthew. Rather, Peter represents *every* disciple in confessing Jesus as Messiah and Son of the living God, in having received the revelation of Jesus' identity from the Father in heaven, in belonging to the church founded on the rock (πέτρα) of Christ's law and helping make up that church as a stone (Πέτρος) fitted together with others to form a superstructure of obedient disciples, in facing the threat of death with the assurance of resurrection, and in having been commissioned as a Christian scribe. Cf. Peter's representativeness in 14:28-31 and contrast the leavenlike teaching of the Pharisees and Sadducees in v 12; see further the comments on 26:70 and 28:7.

Since Πέτρος does not occupy center stage, but plays a subordinate role as foil to the πέτρα of Jesus' words, "You are Peter" probably implies a play on the name as already given rather than a giving of the name at this time. For the latter, we should have expected the future tense, "You will be called"; and repeated earlier references to Simon as "Peter," most of them Matthew's insertions, take away the point of a name giving here. Otherwise we would have to suppose, doubtfully, that Matthew expects his readers to take all the earlier references as anachronisms. Cf. John 1:42. The substitution of "Simon, who is called Peter" (10:2) for "Simon he nicknamed Peter" (Mark 3:16; cf. Luke 6:14) means that Peter is still the representative disciple, not that Matthew delays the giving of the name till 16:18.

Matthew's composition of vv 17-19 in Greek eliminates the quest of the right Semitic word—קָהָל, עֵדָה, סוֹד, כְּנִישְׁתָּא—behind ἐκκλησίαν. No Semitic tradition stands behind these verses. Furthermore, Matthew's composing vv 17-19 and giving prominence to persecution in his gospel favor that "the gates of Hades" particularly represent death by martyrdom (cf. 1QH 6:24-29). Conversely, that those gates will not overcome the church signifies the impossibility of obliteration through persecution, not preservation from death or a going to heaven at death. Individual resurrection hovers in the background as part of the sign of Jonah, duplicated in the disciples' being raised at the end as Jesus has already been raised (cf. 16:1-4, 17, and 21-28 with 12:39-40). The "it" after "will not overcome" has "my church," not "this rock," as its antecedent; for persecution to the death does not threaten the rock of Jesus' words. Rather, persecution threatens the church built on that rock. The genitive object αὐτῆς implies the active meaning "will not overpower by assailing" for οὐ κατισχύσουσιν. This meaning fits well the thought of persecution (cf. TDNT 6. 927).

The allusion to scribal activity in the figure of keys leads us to think of the present form of the kingdom in the church. This agrees with the earthly locale of Peter's binding and loosing, with the indicative present tense in the contrastive locking up of the kingdom of heaven and failure to enter it (23:13), and with the emphasis throughout Matthew on partial realization of the kingdom now (see, e.g., 6:10b). The passives "will have been bound" and "will have been loosed" imply divine action. "In heaven" is a reverential substitute for God's name and also implies divine action. The periphrastic future perfect tense does not mean "will be . . . ," but "will have been . . ." (see J. R. Mantey in JETS 16 [1973] 129-38). Thus God will not ratify at the last judgment what Peter does in the present age, but Peter does in the present age what God has already determined. In other words, Peter has received direction from God for his scribal activity. This direction consists in Jesus' teaching. Other disciples have received the same direction, since Peter stands for them.

Finally, Matthew's composition of vv 17-19 falsifies the search for a more original setting of this material, such as the Last Supper or a post-resurrection appearance of Jesus (cf. R. H. Gundry in NovT 7 [1964] 1-9).

Matthew's composing the similar passage 14:28-31 favors his composition of 16:17-19. The similarity of phraseology in 16:17 and Gal 1:12, 15-16 might seem to support a very early date and traditional origin for 16:17-19. But only "flesh and blood" and "reveal" come into the picture. Matthew and Paul may both be using rabbinic language. It is even possible that Matthew knew Galatians, especially if he wrote in Syria. Notably, however, Paul writes about the possibility of consulting with flesh and blood *after* the revelation of Jesus Christ, but Matthew about the possibility of the revelation *itself* as coming from flesh and blood. The evaluation of 16:17-19 as editorial does not disagree, of course, with the undoubted prominence of Peter in the early church. Neither does this evaluation rule out Jesus' intention to form a messianic community.

Jesus is given the task of building, a task given to God in contemporary Jewish literature (e.g., 1QH 6:26-27; 7:8-9). Matthew's drawing the figure of building on a rock from 7:24 casts doubt on the theory that the rock here refers to the rock on which the Temple stood and which was thought to plug the opening from the underworld (for the rabbinic beliefs, see R. J. McKelvey, *The New Temple* [New York: Oxford University Press, 1969] 189-92). 7:24 pictures an ordinary private dwelling, and the present passage contains no hint of a temple. The rabbinic saying that portrays Abraham as the rock on which God built and founded the world (see Str-B 1. 733; cf. Isa 51:1) hardly demands an identification of Matthew's rock with Peter; for that saying lies at a much farther distance from 16:18 than 7:24 lies. Besides, the rabbinic notion may not even antedate Matthew. In rabbinic literature, binding and loosing usually signify interpretative decisions of prohibition and permission; but they also signify condemnation and acquittal in disciplining members of the synagogue who disobey the interpretative decisions. Here, association with the keys of the kingdom runs in the direction of scribal interpretation (see 23:13; Luke 11:52). In 18:18, binding and loosing will be associated with church discipline and forgiveness. Matthew pays special attention to forgiveness, which is implied in loosing, i.e., restoration to fellowship (see 9:8 with comments ad loc.). We need to remind ourselves that Matthew democratizes scribal authority. In John 20:21-23 discipline and forgiveness of church members turn into forgiving the sins of those who hear and believe the gospel and retaining the sins of those who hear and disbelieve it.

16:20 (Mark 8:30; Luke 9:21; John 6:70-71) In the last verse of the paragraph Matthew rejoins Mark and Luke. As often, "Then" replaces "And" for the benefit of the story line. The reading ἐπετίμησεν, "he rebuked," in B* D e syr^cur probably represents scribal assimilation to Mark. If so, Matthew disliked its negative connotation as inimical to his portraying the disciples, and especially Peter their representative, as having a true understanding of Jesus. Therefore the evangelist substitutes διεστείλατο, "he ordered," and thus compensates for having replaced the verb in v 6 (cf. Mark 8:15). He has inserted vv 17-19 since last mentioning the disciples, and Mark's "them" might seem to refer nonsensically to "the heavens" just preceding. So Matthew characteristically changes "them" to "the disciples" (31,5). In the command "that they should not speak to anyone," Mark's linear present λέγωσιν shifts to the nonlinear aorist εἴπωσιν, which prepares for the particular statement to follow in Matthew alone; i.e., the present tense suits a general speaking "concerning him" (so Mark), but the aorist better suits the particular statement "that he is the Christ" (so Matthew). Luke takes Mark's περὶ αὐτοῦ as neuter, "concerning it," and paraphrases with "this" (the matter of Jesus' messiahship). Matthew takes the same phrase as masculine, "concerning him," and paraphrases with the above quoted clause, which stems from Peter's confession (v 16). αὐτός is a Mattheanism (14,3). It substitutes for Peter's σύ and makes up for Matthew's omission of αὐτός in v 15 (cf. Mark 8:29). The designation of Jesus as "the Christ" is a favorite of Matthew (8,5) and stays unchanged. But "the Son of the living God," added in v 16, falls off as unnecessary. Thus Matthew turns a stern prohibition of publicity into a restatement of Jesus' messiahship. The restatement emphasizes, in turn, the disciples' understanding of Jesus' true identity.

UNDERSTANDING THE LORDSHIP OF JESUS FOR THE SUFFERING OF PERSECUTION
16:21-28 (Mark 8:31–9:1; Luke 9:22-27)

16:21 (Mark 8:31; Luke 9:22) The parallel in Mark 8:31-33 continues the account of Peter's confession without interruption (so also Luke 9:22-27) and turns that confession into a misunderstanding of Jesus' messiahship, a misunderstanding that elicits Jesus' rebuke and call to cross bearing. In order to let the understanding of Jesus' messiahship and divine sonship in 16:13-20 stand unimpaired, Matthew breaks the text at this point and in the following verses makes revisions that soften the rebuke of Peter. To indicate a new start, he expands Mark's "And he began" to read "From then on he began" (see the comments on 4:17 and cf. 26:16). He also introduces the formal "Jesus Christ" (not in Mark or Luke) to begin a section, as he did in 1:1, 18; and he characteristically replaces Mark's "them" with "his disciples" (31,5) despite the same insertion in v 20. The introduction of "Jesus" agrees with his practice elsewhere (80,12). The unusual addition of "Christ" makes particular reference to the identification "Christ" in vv 16, 20. And the bringing in of another reference to the disciples contributes to his ongoing emphasis on discipleship.

Matthew changes Mark's διδάσκειν in order to keep it for public teaching. Its replacement δεικνύειν describes private instruction (cf. 4:8; 8:4). The drawing of "the Son of man" up to v 13 results in its replacement by "him," a reference to "Jesus Christ." Thus Matthew's Jesus suffers, dies, and rises as the Messiah rather than as the Son of man. In the clause concerning the necessity of Jesus' suffering and so forth, Matthew inserts "to Jerusalem" in order to assimilate, by anticipation, this prediction of the passion to that in 20:17-18, where the phrase will appear twice with parallels (cf. 21:1, 10 and Jerusalem as the source of violence against the Messiah in chap. 2). This insertion demands a further insertion of ἀπελθεῖν, a favorite of Matthew (14,11).

The suffering stays unchanged. But Matthew omits "and to be rejected" because of his inserting ἀπελθεῖν and wanting two couplets of infinitive phrases: "to go away" and "to suffer," "to be killed" and "to be raised." The omission makes "from the elders and chief priests and scribes" depend on "to suffer" rather than on "to be rejected" (as in Mark and Luke). Matthew omits the definite article before "chief priests" and "scribes." The omission has the purpose of welding together the three groups that made up the Sanhedrin into a single front antagonistic to Jesus (cf. the comments on 2:3-4). That Luke, too, has only a single article for all three

337

nouns suggests influence from Matthew. Jesus' being killed remains unchanged. But Matthew grecizes Mark's ἀναστῆναι, "to rise," so that it becomes ἐγερθῆναι, "to be raised" (or, deponently, "to rise"—but cf. 1 Cor 15:12-17, esp. v 15). Mark's word reflects קוּם; Matthew's typifies his vocabulary (11,8). "After three days" changes to "on the third day" (see the comments on 12:40 for interpretation). Luke's agreement in these last two revisions of Mark again suggests Matthean influence. All in all, then, just as 4:17 marked the beginning of Jesus' public proclamation of repentance and the kingdom, so Matthew makes 16:21 mark the beginning of Jesus' private indications that he will soon die and be raised. The former relates to Galilee (4:12-16), the latter to Jerusalem.

See the UBS for the textual variants "Jesus" and "Jesus Christ." In the face of evenly divided external evidence, Matthew's use of the latter in 1:1, 18 tips the scales in favor of the same reading here. δεῖ implies divine predetermination or scriptural prophecy. If the latter, we may think of passages such as Ps 118(117):22; Isaiah 53; and Hos 6:2. See, e.g., M. Black in *ZNW* 60 (1969) 1-8. In the LXX of Lev 5:17; 4 Kgdms 4:13-14 (bis); Dan 2:28 (also Theod), δεῖ stands for Semitic verbal expressions concerning what shall be or ought to be. Almost certainly the Jews of Jesus' time did not think that the Messiah would suffer (cf. 17:23; Mark 9:32).

16:22 (Mark 8:32) "And he was stating the matter plainly" drops out. The plainness of Jesus' speech in Mark makes Peter's obtuseness inexcusable. Matthew's omission lightens the onus on Peter. (Luke omits the whole embarrassment to Peter.) In the statement that "Peter, taking him aside, began to rebuke him" (so Mark), Matthew advances αὐτόν to a more natural position after its participle and, as often, adds λέγων (61,23), which leads to the further addition "[May God be (or, 'God will be')] merciful to you, Lord! This will not happen to you." The parallelism in the further addition (esp. in the two occurrences of σοι) and Matthew's fondness for κύριε (34,15) and for the future form ἔσται (16,5) point to composition by him. Thus he turns Peter's rebuke into a confession of Jesus' lordship. The emphasis falls on the side of what Peter does understand about Jesus rather than on what he does not understand. And Peter's good motive appears in his wish (or declaration) that God will have mercy on Jesus. Because of Matthew's composition, we need not question whether the Hebrew חָלִילָה or חַס, "far be it," stands behind ἵλεως alone, or behind οὐ μὴ ἔσται σοι τοῦτο as well.

16:23 (Mark 8:33) In v 23 Matthew deletes ἐπι- from Mark's ἐπιστραφείς, which refers to Jesus' turning. The compound form always means "return" in Matthew (see 10:13; 12:44; 13:15; 24:18), but the simple form carries the desired meaning "turn" and belongs to Matthew's preferred diction (3,2). The omission of "and seeing his disciples" again relieves the severity in Mark's portrayal of Peter; for in Mark the phrase distinguishes Peter from the disciples, i.e., makes him a nondisciple at this point (he had left the position of a disciple behind Jesus in order to take Jesus aside and rebuke him). Furthermore, Mark's "he rebuked Peter and says" becomes "he said to Peter." Though the following words remain harsh, Jesus' tone softens—they are no longer a counter rebuke. To gain a couplet of parallel lines, Matthew adds "You are an offense to me" to "Get behind me, Satan."

σκάνδαλον falls within the circle of Matthew's favorite words (3,1). Its insertion makes Peter the representative disciple also in the danger of false profession (cf. his representing "little faith" in 14:31). The antinomians in the church, who urge others not to take the path of possible martyrdom, fall under the condemnation laid on Peter. A second couplet of parallel lines completes Jesus' statement to him: "because you do not set your mind on the things of God, but [you set your mind on] the things of men" (so also Mark). Thus Jesus' statements to Peter, "Blessed are you" (v 17) and "You are an offense to me," contrast with each other; and Peter's thinking human thoughts planted by Satan contrasts with the divine thoughts revealed by Jesus' Father and given expression by Peter (v 17).

Matthew's adding the definite article to Peter's name conforms to v 22. Jesus' command to get behind him may imply that Peter is standing between him and his appointed suffering, or that Peter needs to return to his proper position as a disciple following after his master, or both. Jesus calls Peter "Satan" because Satan is using Peter in an attempt to dissuade him from going the way of suffering (cf. 4:10; 1 Cor 1:23; 1QS 3:13–4:26).

16:24-25 (Mark 8:34-35; Luke 9:23-24) The saying in v 24 describes the nature of discipleship, not its preconditions. Matthew omits the summoning of the crowd along with the disciples. The omission brings the following words into close connection with the preceding. The close connection makes vv 24-28 a gaining of understanding by the disciples that counteracts Peter's failure to set his mind on the things of God. Matthew's beloved τότε (66,17) replaces Mark's καί and establishes the connection. The insertion of "Jesus" is also typical (80,12) and avoids a false inference that Peter is responding to the foregoing words of Jesus. The replacement of "to them" with "to his disciples" compensates for the omission of Mark's initial phrase, where the latter occurs. Throughout the rest of v 24 and the first part of v 25 Matthew follows Mark word for word. Taking up a cross means picking up the horizontal bar of a cross, carrying it through the streets from the place of judgment to the place of execution, and enduring the insults of people along the way. To do thus in following Jesus signifies open allegiance to Jesus the Crucified One. Such allegiance will expose one to the hostility of the world and entail the risk of losing one's life as he lost his.

In the latter half of v 25, Matthew drops "and the gospel" from Mark's "But whoever will lose his life on account of me and the gospel." "Gospel" occurs only four times in Matthew, but eight times in Mark. Here its omission concentrates attention on Jesus and makes "on account of me" correspond exactly to 5:11; 10:18, 39. Luke's agreeing with the omission despite his lacking parallels to "on account of me" in Matthew's earlier passages suggests Matthean influence. In the continuation of the statement, Matthew characteristically substitutes "will find" (εὑρήσει—7,8) for "will save." This substitute conforms to his distinctive phraseology in 10:39 and makes a better antonym to "will lose."

16:26 (Mark 8:36-37; Luke 9:25) At the beginning of the next saying Matthew changes "man" from the object (so Mark) to the subject (so also Luke) and the present active verb "profits" (so Mark) to the future passive

339

"will be profited" (so also Luke, except for retention of Mark's present tense). The first change produces a better parallel with the last clause of the verse, where "man" is the subject. The second change transforms a proverb about this present life into a warning about the last judgment (see "Last judgment" in the Topical Index). Since Mark's "to gain the whole world and to lose his life" can no longer be the subject, Matthew changes it to "if he should gain the whole world, but lose his life" (cf. Luke's switch to a compound participial phrase). The advance of the objects in Matthew emphasizes them, and the replacing of καί with δέ (so also Luke) produces a sharper contrast. In the last clause the Mattheanism ἤ (32,12) displaces Mark's γάρ (also a Mattheanism—62-63,15). Matthew makes this substitution in order to transmute Mark's reason behind the proverb about this life ("for what would a man give in exchange for his life?") into a synonymously parallel question about the last judgment—thus also the switch from Mark's aorist subjunctive δοῖ to the future indicative δώσει: "or what will a man give in exchange for his life?"

In vv 25-26 Jesus plays on ψυχή (or its Semitic equivalent), which means "soul" but here has the sense "life" in that the soul animates the body. We may paraphrase as follows: to save one's physical life by refusing discipleship through fear of persecution leads to loss of eternal life. To lose physical life by exposing oneself to persecution on account of discipleship leads to finding eternal life. Gaining the whole world amounts to nothing if one loses his physical life (so Mark with his present tense). Gaining the whole world amounts to nothing if one loses eternal life (so Matthew with his future tense). Nothing has enough value to buy back physical life (so Mark with his present tense). Nothing has enough value to buy back eternal life once that life is lost (so Matthew with his future tense). Because the parallel ἀντάλλαγμα means "something given in exchange," τὸν κόσμον means "the world of wealth" rather than "the world of people" (as objects of missionary work). With v 26, cf. Ps 49:8-10, 16(7-9, 15); 2 Apoc. Bar. 51:15.

16:27 *(Mark 8:38; Luke 9:26)* The first part of Mark's next saying, "For whoever is ashamed of me and my words in this adulterous and sinful generation," disappears because Matthew inserted "adulterous" with "generation" in 12:39; 16:4 and used a similar saying about denying Jesus in 10:33 (cf. Luke 12:9). Therefore he keeps "For" and skips to "the Son of man will also be ashamed of him when he comes in the glory of his Father with the holy angels." Mark's two clauses collapse into one (v 27a). Matthew adopts "the Son of man," but replaces "will be ashamed of him" with "is going to come." Both μέλλει and ἔρχεσθαι are Mattheanisms (5-6,1; 31,19). The emphasis thus shifts from shame to the coming of the Son of man. The description of the angels as "holy" changes to "his"—i.e., the Son of man's—for a Christological emphasis (see the comments on 13:41). This change produces a parallel between "his angels" and "his [each one's] practice" in the next clause, which Matthew borrows from Ps 62:12; Prov 24:12 for a final emphasis on the last judgment. τότε and ἀποδώσει are Mattheanisms (66,17; 5,11; see esp. 6:4, 6, 18; 12:36 for distinctive occurrences of the verb in references to the last judgment), and ἑκάστω occurs in Matthew three times out of four without parallel (16:27; 18:35; 25:15; 26:22). Though πρᾶξιν in the phrase "according to his practice" appears only here in the first gospel, it accords with Matthew's emphasis on conduct, especially right conduct as opposed to antinomianism.

Cf. *Pss. Sol.* 17:10. For judgment by Jesus, see also 7:22-23; 13:41-43; 25:31-46. For judgment by God the Father, see 6:4, 6, 18; 10:28, 32-33; 18:35. In the main, Matthew follows the text of the LXX in his allusive quotation of Ps 62(61):12; Prov 24:12. But the LXX corresponds closely to the Hebrew text; and Matthew's τὴν πρᾶξιν departs from τὰ ἔργα despite the frequency of ἔργον and cognates in the first gospel (6,7). The singular number of Matthew's expression also agrees with the collective singulars in the Hebrew text (see Gundry, *Use of the OT* 138). We may conclude, then, that Matthew translated directly from the Hebrew. Cf. Rom 2:6; 2 Tim 4:14; Rev 2:23; 20:12; *2 Clem.* 11:6.

All three of the vv 25, 26, and 27 begin with γάρ. The first gives a reason for cross bearing, viz., losing one's life by trying to save it and finding one's life by losing it for Jesus' sake. The second explains why the paradox in the first holds true: even possession of the whole world will not save a man's life at the last judgment. The last provides the reason for the second, viz., the Son of man will come and repay each person according to his deeds, not according to his possessions.

16:28 (Mark 9:1; Luke 9:27) As often, Matthew deletes the interruptive "And he was saying to them" (so Mark but not Luke, who also omits). Thus v 28 begins with the emphatic "Truly I say to you." Except for a different spelling of the perfect participle, the next two clauses match Mark exactly: "that there are some of them standing here who will not taste death." But Mark's "till they see the kingdom of God having come in power" becomes "till they see the Son of man coming in his kingdom" for a parallel with the preceding verse. The emphasis thus shifts from the kingdom to the Son of man. In Matthew he, not the kingdom, comes (cf. the comments on 3:11 concerning the Coming One and see esp. 10:23; 24:30; 25:31; but also 13:41; 19:28). As elsewhere and exclusively in Matthew, moreover, the kingdom is the Son of man's rather than God's (see the comments on 13:41 and cf. 13:41; 20:21; 25:31; Luke 22:29; 1 Cor 15:24). In quick succession the first evangelist has written about the Father of the Son of man, the angels of the Son of man, and the kingdom of the Son of man—a Christological emphasis hard to overestimate. "In power" drops out because "in" has shifted to "the kingdom." The new phrase carries the meaning "coming as king." Luke's agreement with Matthew in omitting Mark's reference to power looks like Matthean influence, since Luke does not share Matthew's reason for the omission.

What does the saying mean? In its Markan form and context it probably points to the transfiguration immediately following. At the transfiguration three of the disciples who heard the prediction saw Jesus' glory, perceived that the kingdom of God had come with power, and were terrified (see esp. Mark 9:6). But Matthew cares nothing for the chronology of the prediction, i.e., the promise that some standing there would not die till they caught the glorious sight. For him, only the parousia really counts. So he leaps over the transfiguration (a mere preview) and makes the prediction look forward to the parousia. He does so by welding the prediction to the foregoing statement about the Son of man's coming. The already noted omission of Mark's interruptive "And he was saying to them" and the assimilation of phraseology to the foregoing statement have this effect. As in the sayings about losing and gaining life (vv 25-26), Matthew switches from present experience to the last day in order to stress the final reward of those who bear their crosses—i.e., suffer persecution—in following Jesus.

"Truly I say" puts emphasis on the following words, but does not prove that the saying was detached in the tradition. The dying that Jesus talked about does not necessarily imply martyrdom in the tribulation preceding the parousia. That some standing there would not die before seeing the kingdom come in power (so Mark) at least suggests that they may die afterwards and thus requires that the event to be seen does not have to be the consummation. As noted, however, Matthew shifts to the parousia.

UNDERSTANDING JESUS AS THE NEW AND GREATER MOSES
17:1-8 (Mark 9:2-8; Luke 9:28-36)

17:1 (Mark 9:2; Luke 9:28) Matthew's repeated paralleling of Moses and Jesus, including some to be noted in this story, justifies the supposition that he looks on "the high mountain" as a new Sinai and on Jesus' going up it after six days as a repetition of Moses' going up Sinai after six days, i.e., on the seventh (Exod 24:16). Both times the cloud of divine glory covered the mountain. In Moses' immediately preceding ascent up Sinai, he took Aaron, Nadab, Abihu, and seventy elders of Israel, who saw God there (Exod 24:9-11). The seventy elders offer nothing to Matthew, but the three men Aaron, Nadab, and Abihu probably reminded him of the trio Peter, James, and John. And Joshua—i.e., "Jesus" according to the Greek form of the name—accompanied Moses (Exod 24:13, 15 LXX). Matthew omits Mark's definite article before the names of James and John. Consequently, a single definite article before Peter welds together all three names (cf. the single definite article that usually accompanies "Pharisees and Sadducees"). Characteristically, Matthew adds "his brother" (11,8) to the name John (see also 4:21; 10:2). The omission and the addition combine to emphasize Christian brotherhood. On the other hand, omission of Mark's "alone" after "by themselves" not only gets rid of a redundancy, but also keeps the adjective for exclusive application to Jesus (v 8).

In Mark the time of Jesus' prediction lies at the base of "after six days." In Matthew the phrase alludes to Exod 24:16, for Matthew has shifted the prediction from the transfiguration to the parousia and introduces other parallels between Jesus and Moses in the present passage. Of course, *some* parallels of this kind appear in the earlier tradition, e.g., in the command, "Hear him" (v 5; cf. Deut 18:15 and F. R. McCurley, Jr., in *JBL* 93 [1974] 67-81). Concerning Peter, James, and John, see also 26:37; Mark 5:37; 14:33; Luke 8:51; Gal 2:9 (but a different James); and cf. 1QS 8:1-8 (though there the three priests do not belong to the larger group of twelve lay leaders, as Peter, James, and John belong to the larger group of twelve disciples). Cf. also the three mighty men of David (2 Sam 23:8-17; 1 Chr 11:10-19). None of the evangelists identifies the mountain on which Jesus was transfigured. Hermon and Tabor are usually suggested.

17:2 (Mark 9:2-3; Luke 9:29) To Jesus' metamorphosis Matthew adds the shining of Jesus' face and then rejoins Mark in the turning white of Jesus' garments (cf. Rev 1:16; 10:1; 2 Esdr 7:97; *1 Enoch* 14:20; *2 Enoch* 1:5; *2 Apoc. Bar.* 51:3, 5, 10; Philo *Mos.* 3:2; *Bib. Ant.* 12:1). The result is a leading statement followed by a couplet (as in 16:17b-19 [ter]):

a) And he was transfigured before them;
b) and his face shone like the sun,
c) and his garments became white as the light.

The added clause b) echoes 13:43, Matthew's own composition: "then the righteous will shine forth like the sun. . . ." Here, the insertion of Jesus' face adds an allusion to Exod 34:29-30 for a further parallel between Jesus and Moses (see 2 Cor 3:7-18 for a similar comparison, including omission, as here, of the OT reference to Moses' skin; and Gundry, *Use of the OT* 82-83). We meet Mattheanisms in πρόσωπον (3,2) and ἔλαμψεν (3,0). The latter never occurs in Mark and only once in Luke.

The last clause of v 2 begins with a substitution of δέ for καί to set Jesus' face and garments opposite each other in the couplet of lines. "Like the light" replaces Mark's "shining . . . exceedingly" for a parallel with "like the sun." Is Matthew paralleling Jesus and the disciples by borrowing phraseology from two earlier passages concerning disciples (5:14, 16; 13:43)? Despite his fondness for ἐπὶ τῆς γῆς (8,2), δύναται (13,0), and οὕτως (18,5), Mark's "such as no launderer on earth is able thus to whiten them" drops out lest it spoil the couplet made by clauses b) and c) through the creation of b).

17:3 (Mark 9:4; Luke 9:31-32) Matthew characteristically adds ἰδού (34,9) and elevates Moses from a mere companion of Elijah ("Elijah with Moses," so Mark) by substituting "and" for "with" and putting Moses ahead of Elijah. These revisions add yet more emphasis to the parallel between Jesus and Moses. The omission of Mark's "and they were" before "talking with" leaves the latter a mere participle rather than part of the main verbal expression in a new clause. And despite Matthew's habit of adding Jesus' name (80,12), "with him" replaces "Jesus." In these ways the speaking of Moses and Elijah is de-emphasized in order that the command to hear Jesus (v 5) may stand out more clearly.

Cf. Luke 24:4; Acts 1:10; Rev 11:3-12. Both Moses and Elijah conversed with God on Mount Sinai, or Horeb (Exod 33:18-23; 1 Kgs 19:9-14). The portrayal of Moses as a prophet in Deut 18:15, alluded to here in v 5, and the failure of Elijah to appear among the writing prophets militate against Moses' standing for the OT law and Elijah's standing for the OT prophets.

17:4 (Mark 9:5; Luke 9:33) At the beginning of v 4 Mark's καί yields to δέ for a contrast between the preceding conversation and Peter's following words. "Says" changes to "said" for conformity with Matthew's usual ἀποκριθεὶς εἶπεν (29,6). "Rabbi" changes to "Lord" (κύριε—34,15) to emphasize Jesus' lordship (cf. esp. 16:22, where Matthew turned Peter's rebuke of Jesus into a confession of Jesus as Lord). Insertion of the respectful

343

"If you wish" magnifies the emphasis on Jesus' lordship and makes use of a Mattheanism in θέλεις (18,8). Because Peter is speaking and acting as the representative disciple, "let us make" becomes "I will make." As often, Matthew inserts ὧδε (7,1) in the statement about making three tents. The insertion forms a parallel with the first occurrence of the adverb in this verse. Some think that Peter's proposal to build tents alludes to the Festival of Tabernacles (Lev 23:42), but Matthew makes nothing of the possibility.

"For he [Peter] did not know what he should answer, for they became terrified" (Mark 9:6). Thus Mark takes Peter's suggestion as an indication of ignorance: Peter implies Elijah's and Moses' equality with Jesus. Mark attributes this ignorance to fear, because the transfiguration signifies the coming of the kingdom with power, as Jesus had predicted (Mark 9:1). For Mark that power is so awesome it is terrifying. But Matthew has referred Jesus' prediction to the parousia; hence, in his gospel the transfiguration does not signify the coming of the kingdom with power, but represents Jesus as the new Moses, yet greater than Moses in that he is the Lord. Furthermore, Matthew wants to portray disciples as those who already have understanding (according to his version, Peter has just addressed Jesus as "Lord") and gain more understanding (cf. the comments on 13:1-52). Therefore he omits Mark's whole verse concerning Peter's ignorance and the disciples' terror. As a result, Peter's remark now looks like a recognition of Jesus as the new Moses, a recognition characteristic of true disciples.

17:5 (Mark 9:6-7; Luke 9:34-35) To emphasize Peter's correct association of Jesus with Moses, Matthew inserts "While he [Peter] was still talking." He likes the genitive absolute construction (see the Greek text) and inserts this very same genitive absolute also in 9:18 (without "still") and 12:46, besides a shared occurrence in 26:47. ἔτι is a favorite of his (4,2). Mark's καὶ ἐγένετο becomes ἰδού (34,9) for a parallel with v 3. To describe the cloud Matthew adds φωτεινή as a counterpart to τὸ φῶς in v 2. The resultant parallel between the shining of Jesus' garments like the light and the lightlikeness of the cloud of God's presence implies Jesus' deity. Along with "behold," the escalation of Mark's "overshadowing" to the main verb "overshadowed" stresses the significance of the cloud as indicating divine presence, the Shekinah glory of God. We detect, then, yet a further parallel between Jesus and Moses. Moses meets "God with us" on a new cloud-covered Sinai just as he met God on the old cloud-covered Sinai (Exod 24:15-18; cf. Exod 40:34-38; Num 9:15-22; 1 Kgs 8:10-11; 2 Macc 2:8). The overshadowing cloud of divine presence made a covering superior to a tent of branches. "Them" probably refers to all six men on the mountain, not just to Jesus, Moses, and Elijah.

The middle of v 5—"And behold, a voice from heaven, saying, 'This is my beloved Son, in whom I am well pleased' "—matches Matthew's version of the baptismal pronouncement exactly (3:17). The replacement of Mark's ἐγένετο with ἰδού and the insertion of λέγουσα are typical of Matthew (34,9; 61,23). Mark and Luke do not have "in whom I am well pleased." Matthew inserts it to further the parallel with 3:17 (cf. 2 Pet 1:16-18). For interpretation see the comments on 3:17, and for allusions to the OT see Gundry, *Use of the OT* 36-37. In the present passage the words of the Father confirm Matthew's adding "the Son of the living God" to Peter's confession in 16:16. The Father's final statement, "Hear him," comes from Deut 18:15 (cf. Acts 3:22-23; 7:37). In taking over this Mosaic allusion from Mark, Matthew furthers the parallel between Jesus and Moses. Because of the parallel, the command to hear Jesus may seem to deal with his ethical teaching, not with his passion predictions. But obedience to his ethical teaching is linked with taking up one's cross according to the pattern of his passion. Especially in Matthew, ethics and discipleship go together.

17:6-7 Nothing in Mark or Luke corresponds to vv 6-7. Though he eliminated it earlier, Matthew now introduces the disciples' fear. But fear does not strike them because of the power with which the kingdom has come, as in Mark. Rather, they fear on hearing the Father's word that they should listen to Jesus the new Moses and Son of God (cf. the comments on 9:8). Evidences of composition by Matthew and emphasis on Jesus' deity abound in vv 6-7. "Having heard" echoes "Hear" in the Father's preceding command and typifies the style of Matthew (10,3 for the aorist nominative participle). He also likes μαθηταί (31,5), ἔπεσαν (5,3), πρόσωπον (3,2—here an echo of v 2), ἐφοβήθησαν (8,2), σφόδρα (5,2; cf. esp. 27:54, where Matthew will again insert "they became exceedingly afraid" to introduce the centurion's saying "Truly this one was the Son of God"), προσῆλθεν (38,6), Ἰησοῦς (80,12), ἐγέρθητε (11,8), and μὴ φοβεῖσθε (4,1). And though ἁψάμενος appears in common six times, Matthew inserted it in 8:15. Thus every important expression in vv 6-7 moves in the orbit of his preferred diction.

We also discover typically Matthean parallelism in the contrasts between hearing and touching, falling and getting up, fearing and not fearing. The theological stress rests heavily on Jesus' deity. The disciples' falling on their face serves this motif: Jesus' face shone like the sun, the disciples fall on their face in worship (see the comments on 2:11-12; 4:8-9; and cf. Dan 10:7-10, 15-17; Rev 1:17). Furthermore, falling on the face in fear before deity and being told and helped to get up recall OT phraseology, which Matthew likes to use (see also Ezek 1:28–2:2; Dan 8:17-18). Usually others approach Jesus. Here he has to approach them because fear took hold of them when they heard the affirmation of his divine sonship and the command to hear him.

17:8 (Mark 9:8; Luke 9:36) Now Matthew rejoins Mark. But in place of Mark's "And suddenly looking around" he writes "But lifting up their eyes" because his foregoing addition of the disciples' falling on their face requires something like that to make possible any seeing. See 5:38 (bis); 9:29, 30; 13:15 (bis); 20:33 for other insertions of ὀφθαλμούς. From Mark's statement that the disciples "no longer" saw anyone except Jesus alone, Matthew omits "no longer." With their faces to the ground the disciples had not been able to see *anybody* for the last little while. Before "Jesus alone" Matthew inserts "him" for emphasis: "except him, Jesus alone" (cf. the comments on 8:17). Mark's "with themselves" drops out. Thus the spotlight rests on Jesus.

Matthew and Luke agree against Mark in a number of ways. Both omit the definite article with the names James and John (v 1; Luke 9:28). Both insert Jesus' face, though Luke does not usually work for a parallel between Jesus and Moses (v 2; Luke 9:29). Both omit στίλβοντα, "shining." Luke's ἐξαστράπτων, "flashing like lightning," corresponds to Matthew's adding a comparison to light (v 2; Luke 9:29). Both Matthew and Luke omit Mark's clause concerning a launderer, insert "behold" to emphasize the appearance of Moses and Elijah, mention them in that order rather than in Mark's, and connect them with "and" instead of "with" (v 3; Luke 9:30). Both change "says" to "said" and make substitutions for "Rabbi," viz., "Lord" and "Master" (v 4; Luke 9:33). Both introduce the overshadowing by the cloud with a genitive absolute concerning Peter's talking, change the participle of overshadowing to a finite verb, and switch the pronoun after that verb from the dative case to the accusative. Both delay the fear of the disciples, though Luke not by so much, and add "saying" to the voice from the cloud (v 5; Luke 9:34). These agreements between Matthew and Luke against Mark suggest Matthean influence on Luke.

UNDERSTANDING JOHN THE BAPTIST AS ELIJAH
17:9-13 (Mark 9:9-13; Luke 9:37)

17:9 (Mark 9:9; Luke 9:37) Mark's "And as they were descending from the mountain" comes over. But Matthew changes διεστείλατο to ἐνετείλατο because the latter will apply to Moses in 19:7 (cf. Mark 10:3; Matt 28:20) and therefore serves the portrayal of Jesus as the new and greater Moses. Insertion of Jesus' name is typical of Matthew (18,12) and indicates the start of a new paragraph. The replacement of Mark's epexegetical ἵνα with the Mattheanism λέγων (61,23) makes the following a direct rather than indirect quotation. In the command not to tell the vision, "tell no one" replaces "they should relate to no one" for conformity with "they should tell no one" in 16:20, a prohibition of messianic publicity (cf. 8:4). Publicizing the vision would have counteracted the teaching that the Son of man must suffer. To emphasize the theophanic character of the transfiguration, Matthew changes the pedestrian "the things that they had seen" to "the vision." Mark's εἰ μὴ ὅταν becomes the more Matthean ἕως οὗ (4,2), and the rising of the Son of man from the dead takes the verb ἐγερθῇ instead of ἀναστῇ (see the comments on 16:21).

17:10 (Mark 9:10-11) Matthew now omits the entirety of Mark 9:10, "And they kept the matter to themselves, discussing what the rising from the dead means," lest it mar his portrayal of the disciples as understanding rather than ignorant. "They were asking" becomes "asked" and gains the expressed subject οἱ μαθηταὶ [αὐτοῦ v.1.]. The addition emphasizes discipleship, complements the insertion of Jesus' name in the preceding verse, and typifies Matthew's diction (31,5). The substitution of τί, "Why?" for Mark's interrogative ὅτι, "Why?" avoids confusion with the epexegetical ὅτι, "that," in the following clause. In the question "Why then do the scribes say that it is necessary for Elijah to come first?" οὖν is a characteristically Matthean insertion (35,11) and establishes a logical connection between the question and the foregoing allusion to the Son of man's resurrection:

346

since his resurrection implies his death, why do the scribes say that Elijah must come first? Will not the restoration Elijah brings forestall the Son of man's dying? In Mark, the disciples wonder only why Elijah had not appeared before Jesus the Son of man did.

The scribes could argue against Jesus' messiahship that according to Scripture Elijah had to come before the Messiah, yet he had not. See *TDNT* 2. 928-34 for Jewish traditions regarding Elijah's reappearance. In Matthew the disciples who ask the question can hardly include all the twelve, for οὖν ties the question to the preceding vision, which only Peter, James, and John saw.

17:11 (Mark 9:12) To introduce Jesus' reply, Matthew changes Mark's ἔφη to a typical ἀποκριθεὶς εἶπεν (29,6). "To them" drops out as unnecessary after the addition "the disciples" in v 10. Mark's participle "coming" becomes the finite verb "is coming" for a futuristic present tense (cf. 24:42, 43, 44, and contrast "came" in 11:18; 21:32 for John the Baptist's historical appearance). The shift results in an insertion of "and." The change of "restores" to "will restore" not only conforms to the LXX of Mal 3:24(4:6), but also furthers the futuristic reference begun in "is coming"; i.e., a historical reference becomes a prediction. Matthew omits Mark 9:12cd: "and how is it written about the Son of man that he should suffer much and be treated with contempt?"

In Mark, then, Jesus affirms the correctness of the scribes' saying that Elijah comes first and restores all things. Mark's Jesus goes on to raise, and leave unanswered, the question how it could be that the Son of man will suffer much and be treated with contempt after Elijah's ministry of restoration. But in Matthew the addition of οὖν makes the *disciples* raise that question. Thus they have understanding that Jesus will suffer, for their question presupposes such an understanding. And far from raising and leaving unanswered a question, Matthew's Jesus *answers* the chronological question—i.e., gives further understanding to those who already have understanding (see 13:12)—by putting Elijah's coming and restoration of all things in the future. Cf. Matthew's making the prediction in 16:28 refer to the parousia. In this way the first evangelist avoids the incongruity in Mark that Elijah restores all things yet is maltreated. Now the maltreatment lies in the past—i.e., in the fate of John the Baptist as Elijah—and the restoration of all things in the future.

See Gundry, *Use of the OT* 37, for the allusion to Mal 3:23-24(4:5-6). The way Matthew made 16:28 refer to the parousia, the way his present revisions solve interpretative problems in Mark's text, and the use of "came" in 11:18; 21:32 for John the Baptist's historical coming make it unlikely that "is coming" is an atemporal present tense and "will restore" a mere assimilation to the future tense in the LXX, both for a past coming of Elijah. Rather, Matthew seems to be distinguishing a past and a future reappearance of Elijah.

17:12 (Mark 9:13) Jesus' next saying opens with the emphatic "Yet I say to you." But Matthew changes ἀλλά to δέ in order to gain the construction μέν . . . δέ, a favorite of his (15,1). Mark's ἀλλά contrasts the Son of man with Elijah. Matthew's δέ contrasts the future coming of Elijah (v 11) and his past coming (v 12). In the clause "that Elijah has already come" (cf. 11:14), Matthew has omitted Mark's "also" before Elijah's name, changed the verb from the perfect tense to the aorist (see the comments on 11:18), and inserted "already" (cf. other insertions in 5:28; 14:24). This insertion compensates for his rejecting the perfect tense and makes even more emphatic Elijah's having reappeared in the past. The omission of "also" arises out of Matthew's immediately prior omission of the question concerning the Son of man. The identification of Elijah with John the Baptist has no more explicitness here than in Mark, but see 11:14 (peculiar to the first gospel).

Matthew now inserts "and they did not recognize him" to contrast the disciples' understanding with the scribes' ignorance (v 10) or, more probably, with the ignorance of nondisciples in general, since the scribes did not put John the Baptist to death (cf. the next two clauses). ἐπέγνωσαν is a Mattheanism (5,0). The next clause begins with ἀλλά instead of Mark's καί to compensate for the replacement of ἀλλά in the first line and to contrast the desirable recognition of Elijah (in the person and ministry of John the Baptist) and his actual rejection: "but they did with [ἐποίησαν ἐν] him whatever they wanted [ἠθέλησαν]" (cf. Eccl 8:3; Dan 8:4; 11:16, 36; 2 Macc 7:16; Sir 8:15 for this expression as indicating tyranny). ἐν appears with ποιέω also in 20:15; 21:23, 24, 27 (cf. Gen 40:14 LXX; Dan 11:7 Theod) and connotes treatment as an object, as would happen to the Son of man. In changing Mark's ἤθελον to ἠθέλησαν, Matthew conforms to the nearby aorist forms ἐπέγνωσαν and ἐποίησαν.

Mark's "just as it is written about him" gives way to "so also the Son of man is going to suffer from them." Matthew has made this revision not only because of failure to find anything in the OT about Elijah's suffering (though the allusion to the OT may cover only Elijah's coming, in accord with Mal 3:23-24[4:5-6]), but also out of a desire to further the parallel between Jesus and John the Baptist-Elijah. οὕτως is a Mattheanism both alone (18,5) and with καί (4,1). "The Son of man" comes from Mark 9:12cd and compensates for its earlier omission. μέλλει is another Mattheanism (5-6,1). In references to Jesus it is used also in 16:27; 17:22; 20:22, and in another reference to John in 11:14. Here it expresses certainty growing out of divine necessity (cf. "it is necessary" in 16:21).

17:13 Matthew closes the paragraph with a unique affirmation of the disciples' understanding: "then the disciples understood that he spoke to them concerning John the Baptist." We find Mattheanisms in τότε (66,17), συνῆκαν (5,1), μαθηταί (31,5), and βαπτιστοῦ (5,0).

THE THREAT OF LITTLE FAITH
17:14-20 (Mark 9:14-29; Luke 9:37-43a; 17:6)

In this passage Matthew strips down Mark's narrative to its bare essentials (cf. the comments on 8:28-34; 9:18-26) and at the end of the story adds a saying of Jesus concerning little faith. The stress thus falls on the threat of little faith to the disciples, whose understanding needs to be accompanied by larger faith.

17:14-16 (Mark 9:14-18; Luke 9:37-40) Mark's καὶ ἐλθόντες changes to the genitive absolute καὶ ἐλθόντων (with an unexpressed αὐτῶν). This change produces a parallel with the genitive absolutes that open paragraphs in vv 9, 22, 24. Matthew then conflates Mark's "to the disciples" with the "large crowd" in Mark's following clause. The result is "to the crowd." His regular portrayal of the crowds as disciples makes the conflation easy. Omission of the next two clauses in Mark also comes easily because the subject matter of the argument between the scribes and the disciples lacks specificity (Mark 9:14) and the crowd's amazement at seeing Jesus lacks a readily apparent reason (Mark 9:15a).

For Mark's "and running toward [him], they were greeting him" Matthew writes "a man approached him." The prefix προσ- on Mark's προστρέχοντες reminded Matthew of προσῆλθεν, which he often uses to imply Jesus' dignity (see the comments on 4:3; 8:14 and, concerning the substitution of reverent approach for friendly greeting, 5:46-47; cf. the replacement of "running toward" [Mark 10:17] with "approaching" in 19:16). "A man" not only replaces Mark's crowd, but also reflects "one from the crowd" in a clause otherwise omitted (Mark 9:17a). Matthew chooses ἄνθρωπος in accord with his fondness for the word (35,17) and as a foil to Jesus' deity.

"And he asked them, 'Why are you arguing with them?' " (Mark 9:16) vanishes because Matthew has just omitted the scribes' arguing with the disciples. But he adds "falling on his knees before him and saying" in order to portray the worship of Jesus as God. Cf. the insertion of "falling on their knees" in 27:29 and the comments on 2:11. λέγων is a Mattheanism (61,23).

In the man's words to Jesus (v 15), Matthew replaces διδάσκαλε (4,1) with κύριε (34,15) to put further emphasis on Jesus' deity. "Have mercy on my son" substitutes for "I brought my son to you." Cf. 9:27; 15:22; 20:30-31. The man's first words constitute a Christological confession and plea, then, rather than a historically descriptive statement. The advancing of μου ahead of τὸν υἱόν lends pathos to the plea for mercy ("*my* son").

Matthew now replaces "having a mute spirit" with "because he is epileptic and suffers badly." Demon possession will yet come into his version of the story (v 18), but the present replacement stresses illness, which requires healing (see the insertion "to heal" in v 16, and cf. 4:24). The verb referring to epilepsy occurs elsewhere in the NT only in 4:24, and Matthew inserts κακῶς four times. The insertion of κακῶς in 4:24, where ἔχοντας accompanies it, reflects the phraseology of Mark 1:32. In 15:22; 21:41, where Matthew inserts it quite independently, the associated verb is not a form of ἔχω. Furthermore, Matthew shows no favoritism toward ἔχω, but does insert ἔπαθον in 27:19. Here, then, we should follow the reading κακῶς πάσχει, "suffers badly," instead of κακῶς ἔχει, "is sick." Besides, copyists would have found the changing of the former to the latter easier than vice versa, because the latter is a common idiom. Cf. the UBS and Metzger, *Textual Commentary* ad loc. The pairing of verbs for the boy's epilepsy and suffering corresponds to the pairing of participles for the father's kneeling and speaking to Jesus.

Yet another compound expression follows: "for many times he falls into the fire and many times into the water." Matthew has brought up this clause from Mark 9:22a, located in a lengthy passage which he otherwise omits. Typically, καί yields to γάρ (62-63,15), which makes the clause parallel to the preceding (see the comments on 9:5). Thus v 15a gives a leading statement—i.e., the plea—and v 15bc yields a couplet of parallel lines both giving reasons for the plea ("because . . . , for . . ."; cf. the comments on 16:17b-19 [ter]; 17:2). Though Matthew likes ἔβαλεν (12,8), it and its object "him" give way to another of his favorites, πίπτει (5,3), because demon possession has not yet entered his version of the story. For fullness of parallelism he doubles "many times," adds the definite article to "fire," and changes "waters" to "water." As a whole, the clause replaces Mark's description of seizure, throwing down, foaming at the mouth, grinding of teeth, and stiffening (see J. Wilkinson in *ExpTim* 79 [1967] 39-42 for a medical analysis).

To compensate for his earlier replacement of "I brought," Matthew now replaces "I spoke" with "I brought him" (v 16). The addition of προσ-produces προσήνεγκα, a Mattheanism, which may connote an offering to Jesus (9,2; see the comments on 2:11; 4:24). The man found the disciples instead of Jesus, "and they were unable to heal him [the son]." Mark's intervening "in order that they might cast it out" disappears, again because demon possession has not yet entered Matthew's version. The deletion leaves a couplet of synthetically parallel lines. In the second line οὐκ ἠδυνήθησαν substitutes for Mark's synonymous οὐκ ἴσχυσαν. The substitute is an anticipatory assimilation to οὐκ ἠδυνήθημεν in v 19; Mark 9:28. Cf. Matthew's liking δύναμαι (13,0). He then inserts "to heal him." θεραπεῦσαι is dear to his heart (10,0) and occurred also in 4:24, the only other place in the NT where the word for epilepsy occurs.

17:17 (Mark 9:19; Luke 9:41) In the introduction to Jesus' answer Matthew characteristically inserts "Jesus" for a Christological emphasis (80,12). "Says" changes to "said," and "to them" (i.e., the disciples) drops out because the following description of those addressed by Jesus hardly fits Matthew's portrait of disciples. They may have little faith, but not an entire lack of faith. And certainly they do not deserve the epithet "perverted." The omission of "to them" thus shifts the following from the disciples to the nation of Israel: "O unbelieving and perverted generation" (cf. the use of "generation" for Israel in similar statements at 11:16; 12:39, 41, 42, 45; 16:4; 23:36; also Phil 2:15; Acts 2:40; and see P. Walters [Katz], *The Text of the Septuagint* [ed. D. W. Gooding; Cambridge: Cambridge University Press, 1973] 235, on the possibility that ὦ means "Oh!"). Matthew's insertion "and perverted" emphasizes the corruption of unbelieving Israel and comes from the description of the wilderness generation in Deut 32:5 (see Gundry, *Use of the OT* 83-84; cf. Matthew's habit of conforming Jesus' words to OT phraseology). Luke's agreement in the addition suggests Matthean influence.

In the question "How long will I be with you?" Matthew substitutes μεθ᾽ for πρός and thereby gets an allusion to Jesus' title "Immanuel," which means μεθ᾽ ἡμῶν ὁ θεός (1:23). In the command "Bring him to me," he changes πρός με to μοι, advances it to a position right after the verb for a further Christological emphasis, and characteristically adds ὧδε at the end (7,1; cf. esp. 14:18). πρός occurs sixty-three times in Mark and one hundred and sixty-five times in Luke, but only forty-one times in this gospel.

17:18 (Mark 9:20-27; Luke 9:42-43) Matthew now omits the lengthy description of the bringing of the boy to Jesus, the spirit's convulsing the boy, and the conversation between Jesus and the boy's father (Mark 9:20-24). This omission again stems from prior omission of the demonic element in the story. Perhaps Matthew also objected to the questioning of Jesus' ability ("if you are able" [bis]) and to the measure of unbelief still remaining in the final plea of the father ("I believe; help my unbelief"; cf. the deletion in v 17 of "to them" in order to avoid ascription of unbelief to the disciples). This omission brings Matthew to Jesus' rebuke of the unclean spirit as the crowd was running together (so Mark). He subtracts Jesus' seeing the crowd running together because it contradicts Jesus' coming to the crowd at the very beginning of the story (so Matthew and Luke in some contrast with Mark, where Jesus comes to the *disciples*, around whom they see a large crowd—v 14; Mark 9:14; Luke 9:37). "Jesus" comes from the subtracted clause, however; and because Matthew has omitted the demonic element, the object of Jesus' rebuke changes from the unclean spirit to "him," i.e., the boy, and the following words to "the deaf-and-dumb spirit" fall away.

Matthew goes, then, directly from the rebuke of the boy to the statement "and the demon came out from him." Finally the demonic element enters Matthew's version. As usual, however, he rejects Mark's "unclean spirit" in favor of "demon" (4,0). ἐξῆλθεν echoes Mark, and its advance to the head of the clause makes a parallel with the preceding clause (cf. also the positions of the other words in the two clauses). The insertion "from him" agrees with the usually distinctive pattern in 12:43; 15:22; 24:1, 27.

In Mark the unclean spirit cries out, convulses the boy, and leaves him seemingly dead. Jesus finally has to lift him up by the hand. In line with his earlier omissions, Matthew omits these details, too. According to his version, at the Lord's rebuke the demon exits without so much as a whimper. Omission of the convulsion and of Jesus' action leads to the replacement of "he got up [from the ground where he was lying as a result of the convulsion]" with the characteristically Matthean statement "and the boy was healed from that hour" (see the comments on 8:13). ἐθεραπεύθη comes from Matthew's special vocabulary (10,1) and echoes v 16. παῖς, another favorite of his (5,1), comes from ἐκ παιδιόθεν in Mark 9:20-24 and helps compensate for omission of that section. "From that hour" typifies Matthew's style (3,0; see the comments on 9:22). It also stresses the immediacy of the healing, contrasts with the struggle described by Mark, and thus accentuates Jesus' divine authority.

See H. C. Kee in *NTS* 14 (1968) 232-46 for the meaning "overcome"—with eschatological overtones—in exorcistic uses of ἐπιτιμάω, usually translated "rebuke." Matthew's shifting the object from the unclean spirit to the boy muddles the picture somewhat. Nevertheless, the verb connotes a successful rebuke.

17:19 (Mark 9:28; Luke 9:43) Verse 19 begins with "Then" instead of Mark's "And." The Mattheanism tightens the story line. In Mark we read that Jesus entered a house, in Matthew that the disciples approached Jesus. προσελθόντες is another Mattheanism (38,6) and highlights Jesus' dignity (see the comments on 4:3; 8:14). As often, "were questioning" becomes "said." Mark's verb appears in Matthew only eight times, but twenty-five times in Mark and seventeen times in Luke. διὰ τί (literally "on account of what?") replaces Mark's interrogative ὅτι ("why?") to anticipate the phrase beginning with διά in v 20 and conform with Matthew's tendency to insert διὰ τί where the other synoptics do not have it (3,0). Apart from this replacement, the disciples' question "Why were we unable to cast it out?" reads as it does in Mark.

17:20 (Mark 9:29; Luke 17:6) Mark's καί changes to ὁ δέ to distinguish Jesus from the disciples more definitely. Also, "he said" changes to the Mattheanism "he says" (λέγει—47,11), perhaps for current application to the church. But in Matthew Jesus' answer takes a different turn. First, there comes another Mattheanism in "On account of your little faith" (4,0 for ὀλιγοπιστ-). Next, Matthew takes "truly I say to you" from Mark 11:22-23, which will come over again at 21:21. This clause advances from its second position in Mark to an emphatic first position. Thus Jesus' word gains precedence over the disciples' faith. Matthew inserts γάρ (62-63,15) and then imports a saying recorded also in Luke 17:6 and conflates it with the saying in Mark.

In revised form the Lukan saying has already appeared in 15:13. It deals with faith, arises here by association with Jesus' saying in Mark 9:23 that all things are possible to him who believes, and helps compensate for the omission of Mark 9:20-24. The indicative mood in the clause "If you had faith as a mustard seed" (so Luke) changes to the subjunctive: "if you should have. . . ." The preceding charge of little faith casts doubt on the condition—hence the subjunctive—and implies that the disciples' little faith lacks even the size of a mustard seed! In accord with his liking forms of εἴρω (18,9), Matthew changes ἐλέγετε ἄν to ἐρεῖτε. "To this mulberry tree" becomes "to this mountain" for an anticipatory conflation with the similar saying in 21:21; Mark 11:22-23. Matthew has already used the figure of uprooting in 15:13. Here he wants to relate the saying to the Mount of Transfiguration. Besides, he likes ὄρει (6,1).

The horticultural character of the references to a mustard seed and a mulberry tree support their originally belonging together, as in Luke's form of the saying. Because of Matthew's shift from a mulberry tree to a mountain, "be uprooted and planted in the sea" no longer makes sense. Therefore he writes "move from here to there." ἔνθεν occurs in the NT only here and at Luke 16:26. But Matthew like μετάβα (5,1) and ἐκεῖ (16,6). For parallelism he repeats his verb—"and it will move"—rather than write "and it will obey you." The thought of the replaced clause and its pronoun "you" catch his attention, however, so that he adds "and nothing will be impossible to you." The verb in the addition echoes vv 16, 19. All of this takes the place of Jesus' answer according to Mark: "this kind cannot come out by anything except prayer." Thus Matthew exchanges a climactic saying about exorcism by means of prayer for a pair of climactic sayings about little faith and mountain-moving faith.

Cf. Isa 54:10; 1 Cor 13:2. Ancient people thought of mountains as pillars that support the sky and hold in position the disc of the earth over subterranean waters. The great depth of the bases of the mountains made the mountains natural symbols of stability. In this conceptual framework one could hardly think of a more hyperbolic figure of power than that of moving a mountain. The element of faith does not fit well the rabbinic description of acute interpreters of the law as uprooters of mountains (Str-B 1. 759). See the UBS and Metzger, *Textual Commentary* ad loc., concerning the text-critical omission of v 21.

A large number of agreements between Matthew and Luke against Mark suggest Matthew's influence on Luke, especially because many of these agreements exhibit traits that typify Matthew's writing. Both Matthew and Luke write a genitive absolute with (κατ)ελθόντων in the opening verse. Both make Jesus meet the crowd rather than meet just the disciples. Both omit the bulk of Mark 9:14-16. Both refer to Mark's "one from the crowd" as "a man" (ἄνθρωπος in Matthew, ἀνήρ in Luke). Both introduce the man's statement with λέγων and make the man immediately request help. Both use οὐκ ἠδυνήθησαν instead of Mark's οὐκ ἴσχυσαν. Both add "Jesus," omit "to them," and change "says" to "said" in the introduction to Jesus' response. Both add "and perverted" to the description of the unbelieving generation, and "here" to the command that the son be brought. Both omit the bulk of Mark 9:20-24. Both drop Jesus' seeing that the crowd is running together, his words to the unclean spirit, the convulsion of the boy, and the boy's being raised by Jesus. Both refer to the unclean spirit as a demon (though Luke uses Mark's expression, too). Both use a verb of healing (ἐθεραπεύθη in Matthew, ἰάσατο in Luke) and refer to the boy with παῖς.

UNDERSTANDING THE DEATH AND RESURRECTION OF JESUS
17:22-23 (Mark 9:30-32; Luke 9:43b-45)

17:22-23 (Mark 9:30-32; Luke 9:43b-45) Jesus' third prediction of his death and resurrection (cf. 16:21; 17:13) begins with a genitive absolute, translated, "But as they were gathering together in Galilee" (cf. vv 9, 14, 24). Matthew likes the genitive absolute construction and makes this one by substituting δέ for Mark's "And going out from there," replacing "they were going along [or 'began to go along']" with "were gathering together," and changing "through" to "in." By implying a shift of location, the adversative δέ compensates for omission of the more explicit "And going out from there." Though συστρεφομένων occurs in the NT only here and in Acts 28:3, the simple form στρέφω is a Mattheanism (3,2). Matthew chooses the infrequent complex form in order to make up for omission in v 18 of the crowd's running together (Mark 9:25). Therefore it does no good to ask why he writes that people come together even though they have not been dismissed since the last episode. He is merely compensating for a previous omission, as he often does. A general confluence of people results.

Mark's two lines "And he did not want anyone to know [that they were going through Galilee], for he was teaching his disciples" vanish because in Matthew the crowds as well as the twelve are disciples. Jesus does not withhold his teaching from them (cf. similar omissions in 14:25 against Mark 6:48, and in 15:21 against Mark 7:24). Why then does the going through Galilee change to a gathering in Galilee? The reason is that Matthew wants to extend the public ministry in Galilee—not till 19:1 does his Jesus leave Galilee—rather than note the closing down of that ministry with secret instruction on the way through. The Galileans sitting in darkness are still seeing a great light (4:12-17).

In the introduction to Jesus' prediction, Matthew changes "he was saying" to "he said," characteristically adds "Jesus" (80,12), and, as often, omits the recitative ὅτι. To the prediction itself he adds a beginning μέλλει. The addition typifies his diction (5-6,1), connotes the certainty of Jesus' death and resurrection (cf. "it is necessary" in 16:21), and echoes the same addition in v 12. Luke agrees with Matthew against Mark in writing μέλλει. But he has no parallel to the previous passion prediction, which the verb here echoes. Therefore we may surmise Matthean influence. Luke's further agreements with Matthew in beginning with a genitive absolute construction, omitting Mark's two lines concerning Jesus' not wanting to be discovered and his teaching the disciples, shifting the verb of speaking from imperfect to aorist, and changing "is given over" to the infinitive "to be given over" confirm Matthew's influence on Luke.

In the clause concerning Jesus' resurrection, Mark's "having been killed" drops out as redundant after "and they will kill him." "After three days" becomes "on the third day" (for interpretation see 12:40), and ἀναστήσεται changes to ἐγερθήσεται (see the comments on 16:21). "But they did not understand the saying, and feared to ask him" disappears entirely because it would spoil Matthew's portrayal of the disciples as understanding. He substitutes "And they were exceedingly grieved" (cf. v 6 and esp. 18:31; 26:22). ἐλυπήθησαν is somewhat of a Mattheanism (2,1) and σφόδρα very much one (5,2). Thus Matthew transmutes the ignorance of the disciples into sorrow—a sorrow that implies their understanding the import of Jesus' prediction.

See the UBS and Metzger, *Textual Commentary* ad loc., on the v. l. ἀναστρεφομένων. In the Aramaic behind "the Son of man" and "men" there may lie a wordplay between "the Son of man" and "the sons of men," provided "men" idiomatically represents "the sons of men." παραδίδοσθαι probably does not yet mean "to be betrayed," but "to be given over." In 26:24, 45, 46 Judas gives Jesus over to be killed. But here the correspondence of μέλλει with δεῖ in 16:21 suggests a correlation of divine and human action: *God* will give the Son of man over to the hands of *men* (cf. Isa 53:6, 12 [bis] LXX; Rom 8:32 for God's action, and Lev 26:25 for an example of deliverance into the hand—i.e., power—of an enemy). The quotation of Isa 53:4 in Matt 8:17 and the allusion to Isa 53:9 in Matt 27:57 strengthen the possibility that Matthew saw in παραδίδοσθαι an allusion to Isa 53:6, 12. Whether or not Jesus himself intended such an allusion remains disputed and depends primarily on the interpretation of Mark 10:45 (cf. Matt 20:28).

We have no good reason to think that "the hands of men" contains a reference to the Romans in contradistinction to the Jews; for though the Jewish authorities are not specified, as they are in 16:21; 20:18, neither are the Gentiles, as they are in 20:19 (see also the parallels). In fact, the juxtaposition of the Jewish authorities and Gentiles in 20:18-19 runs counter to a differentiation in the present passage.

AVOIDANCE OF CAUSING NON-CHRISTIAN JEWS TO SIN
17:24-27

This unique story of "Peter's Penny" forms a transition from the foregoing narrative section to the ecclesiological discourse following. Like the foregoing, the story has a narrative framework; like the following, it contains Jesus' teaching against leading others into sin. The diction, grammatical constructions, stylistic features, and use of OT phraseology show that Matthew himself composed the story. Mark 9:33, up to which Matthew has worked in the foregoing, suggested Jesus' entry into Capernaum and going into a house. Previously, Capernaum provided a location for tax collecting and for Jesus' teaching in his house (9:1, 9-13). Thus Matthew begins this instruction concerning taxes, "And when they went into Capernaum" (v 24), and later inserts "And when he [Peter] went into the house" (v 25). But Matthew long ago stressed Jesus' settling in a house in Capernaum (see the distinctive statement in 4:13). Furthermore, Mattheanisms appear everywhere in vv 24-27.

17:24 The opening genitive absolute typifies Matthew's style, parallels genitive absolutes in vv 9, 14, 22, and echoes 8:5: "And when he went into Capernaum." There is a string of Mattheanisms in προσῆλθον (38,6), δίδραχμα (6,6 for δια-compounds occurring in Matthew alone), λαμβάνοντες (21,16), Πέτρῳ (8,1), and διδάσκαλος (4,1). The designation of Jesus as "teacher" anticipates 22:16, located in a similar discussion of taxation. "Your" accompanies "teacher," as it does at 9:11; 23:8 and nowhere else in the NT. Perhaps Matthew is also compensating for his replacing "Teacher" in v 15 (cf. Mark 9:17) and omitting "he was teaching" in v 22 (cf. Mark 9:31). Such compensation is characteristic of his style. τελεῖ is another Mattheanism (5,2). That we have to translate it "pay" instead of "finish," as it means elsewhere in Matthew, does not spoil the point; for the evangelist would not have felt the difference in connotations so keenly as we, who use completely different verbs for the paying of taxes and the finishing of discourses.

17:25 In v 25 "He says" seems to anticipate 22:20-21 again. The historical present of λέγει typifies Matthew's diction (47,11), and the asyndeton with which he uses it typifies his style (21,6). He likes ναί (2,2), and the participle ἐλθόντα and the whole phrase "and having gone into the house" look Matthean (cf. ἐλθών/-όντες in the Greek Index and see the distinctive phraseology in 2:11; 9:28; 13:36, besides 8:14; 9:23). Further Mattheanisms appear in Jesus' name (80,12) and λέγων (61,23). προέφθασεν occurs only here in the NT but agrees with Matthew's emphasis on Jesus' deity by implying divine knowledge of the conversation between Peter and the collectors outside the house.

"What do you think . . . ?" again anticipates the pericope about paying tribute to Caesar. Matthew will insert the same question in 22:17. Furthermore, this question typifies his style (4,2) and occurs elsewhere in the NT only in John 11:56 (cf. Luke 10:36). Both inside and outside the question, δοκεῖ is a favorite of his (6,3). "Simon" echoes 16:17, another Matthean construct.

"The kings of the earth" is an OT phrase such as Matthew likes to use (see esp. Ps 2:2 because of the allusion to Ps 2:7 in v 5 here; also Pss 76:13[12]; 89:28[27]; 102:16[15]; 138:4; cf. Acts 4:26). By themselves, too, βασιλεῖς and γῆς are Mattheanisms (6,9; 21,6). So also are λαμβάνουσιν (21,16) and τέλη and its cognates (16,7). Though τέλη means "taxes" here and refers elsewhere to the eschatological "end," again Matthew would not have felt the difference in connotations so keenly as we, who use different words. κῆνσον again anticipates 22:17, 19. The contrast between "sons" and "those who belong to others" has, as is typical of Matthew's writing, an OT ring (Deut 29:21[22]; Judg 19:12; Neh 9:2); and υἱοί is another favorite of his (27,16).

17:26 In v 26 the genitive absolute εἰπόντος, which lacks an expressed pronoun, looks Matthean in that it echoes v 14, where only Matthew and Luke have a genitive absolute and only Matthew has it without the pronoun. Further Mattheanisms come forward in "Jesus" (80,12), ἔφη (11,4), ἄρα (4,1), and υἱοί again (27,16). In 7:20 Matthew inserted ἄρα and γε together, as here, and γε occurred in 6:1, another passage composed by him.

17:27 The main word in the first line of v 27 is σκανδαλίσωμεν (3,1). πορευθείς typifies his style both in its general use (13,10) and in its use as an aorist participle (8,4), often before imperative verbs. Here it relates to 22:15 in yet another indication that Matthew is drawing on Jesus' teaching about paying tribute to Caesar. Matthew likes βάλε (12,8). In 4:18; 13:47 (another of his constructs); 21:21 it occurs with "into the sea," as here except for omission of the definite article. θάλασσαν occurs as an insertion also in 4:15; 8:24; 23:15. And 14:23; 15:29 contain insertions of ἀναβάντα. πρῶτον is a Mattheanism (5,6-7). Though often matched, ἆρον appears in Matthew twice as an insertion (21:43; 24:39) and three times in unique passages (11:29; 17:27; 20:14).

In a different association but still with a literal meaning, "and opening his mouth" was inserted by Matthew in 5:2 (cf. 13:35). ἀνοίξας, στόμα, εὑρήσεις, ἐκεῖνον, and λαβών represent his favorite diction (5,2; 8,1; 7,8; 26,9; 21,16). He likes to use the last especially as an aorist nominative circumstantial participle (3,7).

Outside typically Matthean diction, use of OT phraseology, and anticipation of Jesus' teaching about payment to Caesar, what important words in vv 24-27 remain unaccounted for? Only the necessary furniture of talk about a stater, exemption, and fishing. The last might come easily from attention to Peter's occupation of fishing (4:18-19), the first two from Matthew's early occupation of tax collecting (9:9). In other words, hardly anything in the passage would lead us to think that Matthew drew on tradition. Almost everything speaks for his own composition. What purpose did he have, then? He wanted to portray Peter as a paradigm of obedient discipleship in paying the Temple tax—and this in order that Jewish Christians might not cause unbelieving Jews to reject the gospel (cf. Rom 14:1–15:3; 1 Corinthians 8–10; 1 Pet 2:16).

The local taxes and the poll tax levied by "the kings of the earth" (cf. Rom 13:7) hardly imply that Matthew is teaching Christians to pay civil taxes to the Romans as well as the religious tax for the Jewish Temple; for he brings in payers and nonpayers of civil taxes only as an analogy for the religious tax in question. The contrast between the kings' sons and those belonging to others is not a contrast between citizens and noncitizens. Citizens paid taxes, too. It is a contrast between members of royal households and all other subjects and implies that Jesus' disciples belong to God's household, but unbelieving Jews do not. This implication fits well Matthew's emphasizing the transfer of the kingdom from Israel to the church (see esp. 21:43) and therefore confirms his composition. The playing off of the church against Israel militates against putting the passage in the framework of intra-Jewish disputes over who was exempt from paying the Temple tax.

In v 27 Matthew uses ἀντί (literally "in place of") because of the redemptive nature of the tax (see Exod 30:11-16). There is no provision for the tax to be paid by the other disciples. But that lack comes from Matthew's habit of making Peter represent all disciples. By letting the passage close with Jesus' instructions Matthew shows that he is not interested in the occurrence of a miracle, but in proper Christian conduct. Recognition of his composition illegitimizes the inference of an originally nonmiraculous instruction to sell the caught fish for money to pay the tax. Ancient legends concerning owners' finding lost treasures in fish are of doubtful aid in understanding the present passage; for Matthew writes of only one coin, and the finder had not lost it.

Male Jews over nineteen years of age, including those living outside Palestine, paid an annual tax for upkeep of the Temple (see Exod 30:11-16; Neh 10:33[32]; cf. 2 Kgs 12:1-17[11:21–12:16]; 2 Chr 24:4-14; and other references cited by H. Montefiore in *NTS* 11 [1964] 60-64). The plural of "the double drachmas" generalizes the activity of the collectors. Jewish Christians would naturally have liked to avoid the Temple tax, for financial if not religious reasons. The priests were exempt because of their service in the Temple (see Derrett, *Law in the NT* 250-51). But the disciples are compared to king's sons, not to Jewish priests. After the destruction of the Temple in A.D. 70, the Romans transferred the tax to the temple of Jupiter Capitolinus in Rome (Josephus *J.W.* 7.6.6 §218; Dio Cassius 65.7; Suetonius *Dom.* 12). Matthew would hardly have implied in an argument for paying this later tax that Christians are the free sons of the god of that pagan temple! And his repeated attacks on the Pharisees argue against Jewish Christian support of the rabbinic school in Jamnia (against W. G. Thompson, *Matthew's Advice to a Divided Community* [AnBib 44; Rome: Biblical Institute Press, 1970] 67-68). Therefore Matthew must be writing before A.D. 70—and in the Syrian area of Antioch and Damascus, since only there did the stater correspond exactly to two double drachmas (B. H. Streeter, *The Four Gospels* [London: Macmillan, 1951] 504).

BROTHERHOOD IN THE CHURCH

18:1-35 (5:29-30; 16:19; Mark 9:33-37, 42-43, 45, 47; 10:15; Luke 9:46-48; 15:3-7; 17:1-4; John 20:23)

In chap. 18 we find the fourth great dominical discourse, put together by Matthew with use of scattered blocks of tradition and a large contribution from the evangelist himself. The theme of churchly brotherhood overarches the chapter and works its way into the following narrative. Commonly, the chapter is divided into two parts (vv 1-14—the worth of the "little people" in the church; vv 15-35—brotherliness in the church), or four parts (vv 1-4—true greatness in the kingdom of heaven; vv 5-14—the care of the "little people"; vv 15-20—restoration and discipline of a brother; vv 21-35—forgiveness of a brother), or five parts (as in the four-part outline but with division of vv 5-14 into vv 5-9 on the evil of causing a "little one" to sin and vv 10-14 on restoration and discipline of a brother).

We may discern subtopical shifts from time to time. But with the exception of v 21a Matthew does not signal these shifts with the conjunctions and introductory grammatical constructions that would make them clear. Rather, the subtopics flow one into another almost imperceptibly: the discourse begins with the condition of childlikeness for entrance into the kingdom of heaven (vv 1-3). Humility defines childlikeness (v 4). Acceptance of childlike disciples constitutes acceptance of Jesus himself (v 5). But causing one of these little people (i.e., childlike disciples) to sin brings judgment on oneself (vv 6-7). One also needs self-discipline to keep from sinning (vv 8-9). The heavenly Father wants straying (i.e., sinning) little people in the church not to be despised, but to be restored through personal reproof, church discipline, and prayer (vv 10-20). And a wronged brother must forgive an offending brother, repeatedly if necessary (vv 21-35). To honor Matthew's melding together of these subtopics, we will avoid partitioning the chapter.

18:1 (Mark 9:33-34; Luke 9:46) The first nine verses have parallels in Mark 9:33-50; 10:15; Luke 9:46-48; 17:1-2; 14:34-35. But Matthew has already used Mark 9:33 in constructing 17:24-27, particularly in borrowing Jesus' going home to Capernaum. Another introduction therefore becomes necessary, and it comes out of Matthew's favorite vocabulary. "In that hour" occurs as an insertion also in 8:13; 26:55 (cf. 10:19 for a largely, but not entirely, paralleled occurrence; 9:22; 15:28; 17:18 for insertions without the preposition; and 20:3, 5, 9, 12; 25:13 for occurrences of ὥρα in distinctive passages). προσῆλθον (38,6), μαθηταί (31,5), Ἰησοῦ (80,12), and λέγοντες (61,23) offer easily recognizable Mattheanisms. The chronological phrase links the following question about greatness to the preceding discussion of taxation and freedom. The verb connotes Jesus' dignity (see the comments on 4:3; 8:14). The mention of his name adds to the Christological emphasis. The mention of the disciples stresses the theme of discipleship, which will receive further definition in the ensuing discourse. We have no good reason to think that Matthew limits the disciples to the twelve, or that if he did they do not represent all Jesus' disciples. To the contrary, throughout his gospel the twelve melt into the crowds and the crowds appear as disciples. For close parallels with the introductory clause, except for the initial chronological phrase, see the distinctive phraseology in 5:1; 13:36; 24:3; 26:17 (and 14:15 for phraseology shared with Mark 6:35; Luke 9:12).

In place of Mark's indirect reference to the disciples' disputing about greatness on the way to Capernaum (Mark 9:34b), Matthew puts a direct quotation: "Who then is greatest in the kingdom of heaven?" "Who?" and "greatest" come from Mark. Matthew adds "is" for clarity. "The kingdom of heaven" typifies his diction (25,7). The reference to a kingdom provides another link, besides "in that hour," with the foregoing discussion of taxation, where Matthew portrayed the disciples as sons of a king (17:24-27).

The insertion of ἄρα completes the linkage of the foregoing passage with the present and comes from Matthew's preferred vocabulary (4,1). But what does this inferential "then" imply? Probably not that other disciples were questioning Peter's role because he was prominent in the question of the Temple tax; for Matthew, who composed the foregoing passage and inserts "then" here, portrays Peter as representative rather than dominant. In fact, Matthew does not mention a dispute about greatness, but only a question. According to Mark the disciples have disputed with one another who is the greatest. Jesus asks why they have, but they keep silent. According to Matthew, Jesus does not ask the disciples a question, and they do not keep silent. Rather, they take the initiative and themselves ask him a question. It is an innocent question, even a knowing question—just as we should expect, since Matthew stresses understanding as necessary to discipleship.

The disciples have not argued among themselves; so Jesus neither embarrasses them to silence by means of interrogation (so Mark) nor reads their thoughts (so Luke). And in their question we can detect no indication that any of them thinks himself the greatest. Hence, "Who?" remains general. The inferential "then" indicates that they have understood Jesus' foregoing words about their being sons of a king (17:24-27) and now want to know the implication of that for the question of rank in the kingdom. After all, a monarchy presupposes hierarchy rather than equality. But ought we to think of the present form of the kingdom, or of its future manifestation? Matthew knows both, but his emphasis tends to fall on the present form in the professing church. The following instructions about humility and concern for the little people in the church support our taking the question as dealing with present ecclesiastical rank. Jesus' following reference to future entry into the kingdom (v 3) makes humility in the present kingdom a condition (though not a cause) of entry into the coming kingdom. On the question of rank in the kingdom, cf. 5:19-20 with comments ad loc.; 1QSa; 1QS 2:19-25; 6:8-13.

18:2-3 (Mark 9:35-36; 10:15; Luke 9:47-48) Omission of the dispute among the disciples makes nonsense out of Jesus' calling the twelve and saying that if anyone wants to be first—in Matthew no one wants to be first—he must accept the last position of a servant (Mark 9:35). Matthew therefore omits the verse (not a great loss in view of the similar saying in 20:27) and goes to Jesus' taking a child. That Luke makes the same omission even though he includes the dispute over greatness points to Matthean influence. Despite Matthew's liking λαβών (3,7), this participle gives way to προσκαλεσάμενος because from the very beginning the child stands for a disciple and Matthew's word clearly indicates the summoning of disciples in 10:1; 15:32; 20:25 and probably carries the same overtone in 15:10; 18:32.

Since the child already cuts the figure of a disciple, Mark's reference to Jesus' hugging the child drops out as inappropriate. That Luke shares this omission but does not share Matthew's direct portrayal of the child as a disciple again favors Matthean influence. Omission of "to them" makes room for the saying in Mark 10:15, which Matthew will omit in 19:13-15 (cf. Mark 10:13-16; Luke 18:15-17) because of its use here. Mark's "Truly I say to you" leads to an interpretative expansion that emphasizes humility (cf. 11:29). In accord with the conditional sentence in 5:20 ("For truly I say to you that unless . . . , you will not enter the kingdom of heaven"), Mark's "Whoever does not accept the kingdom of God like a child" changes to "unless you turn and become like the children." Omission of Mark's reference to the kingdom leads to its inclusion in the apodosis, which matches the apodosis in 5:20 exactly. Thus we read "will not enter the kingdom of heaven" instead of Mark's "will not enter it." ἐάν is a Mattheanism both by itself (28,3) and in combination with μή (7,1). To reserve Mark's δέξηται for v 5, Matthew changes it to στραφῆτε (a favorite of his— 3,2), adds γένησθε ὡς (another Mattheanism when followed by a noun or an adjective, as here—3,1), and finishes the comparison with "the children" (drawn from Mark, but made plural to match the switch from a third singular verb to second plural verbs). The turning stands for change. Cf. John 3:3-5.

Matthew's composing "unless you turn and become like children" in Greek does away with the hypothesis that שׁוּב (Hebrew) or תּוּב (Aramaic) underlies στραφῆτε, carries the weak adverbial meaning "again," and results in the overall meaning "Unless you learn like children to say 'Abba' again." Cf. John 12:40. Verse 4 determines the meaning of Matthew's comparison with children, but not the meaning of Mark's comparison with a child's receiving the kingdom of God.

18:4 As indicated by "Therefore" (οὖν—35,11), v 4 provides a definition of turning and becoming like the children. The other synoptics lack the definition. Matthew constructs it with three building blocks: (1) a brief anticipation of the saying he will give fully in 23:12 ("whoever . . . will humble himself" [cf. Luke 14:11; 18:14b]); (2) the foregoing comparison, "like the children," changed to the singular for correspondence with the singular subject and verb and completed with "this" for particular reference to the child standing in the midst of the disciples; and (3) an echo of v 1 in "this one is the greatest in the kingdom of heaven" (cf. Luke 9:49c, which may show Matthean influence). ὅστις and οὗτός ἐστιν typify Matthew's diction (23,5; 12,0). For the first evangelist, then, humility defines childlikeness. This definition does not imply that children humble themselves, but that their small stature symbolizes humility (cf. the diminutive form of παιδίον). The humility does not stop with modesty in self-estimation, but goes on to concrete service for the benefit of others (cf. 25:31-46).

In contrast with their position in contemporary western culture, children occupied a low estate in the ancient world. "Like this child" alludes to that low estate, not to humility, let alone trustfulness or purity. Cf. 5:3, 5 and rabbinic classification of children alongside the deaf and dumb and weak-minded (Jeremias, *NT Theology* 1. 227 n. 2).

18:5 (Mark 9:37; Luke 9:48) Because of the insertion of vv 3-4, Matthew opens v 5 with "And" (not in Mark). In the Greek text he delays the reference to a child till after the verb. The delay takes away Mark's emphasis on the child and lets it fall solely on Jesus' "me" in the final phrase. Changing "one of such children" to "one such child" assimilates the saying to the singleness of the child standing in the midst of the disciples. The agreement of Luke with Matthew in these last two revisions looks like influence from Matthew. "In my name" implies accepting the little people in the church as Christ's own. "Accepts me" confirms this understanding (again cf. 25:31-46). Because their context dealt with mission, the similar statements in 10:40-41 referred to harboring refugees from persecution (cf. 10:23). Because its context deals with intramural relations in the church, the present statement refers to acceptance of little people, "average" Christians and especially youth, by ecclesiastical leaders. Disdain breeds dictatorialness and will keep the disdainer from entering the kingdom of heaven. Therefore ecclesiastical leaders must show evidence of childlike humility by accepting the church's little people. Cf. the comments on 10:42 concerning the hierarchical structure of Matthew's church.

18:6 (Mark 9:42; Luke 17:2) Because he used it in 10:40b, Matthew omits Mark 9:37b, which deals with receiving the one who sent Jesus. And to keep from interrupting the discourse with narrative, Matthew also omits Mark 9:38-41, concerning the strange exorcist. Besides, Mark 9:41 appeared in 10:42, and the independence of the exorcist might seem to subvert Matthew's ecclesiastical emphasis. These omissions bring Matthew to Mark 9:42 (cf. Rom 14:13; 1 Cor 8:9) and lead him to change "And" to "But" for a contrast between accepting little people in the church (v 5) and causing them to sin (with the possibility of their complete apostasy, v 6). If "in me" does not belong in the text of Mark used by Matthew (see the UBS and Metzger, *Textual Commentary* ad loc.), Matthew adds it for Christological emphasis. Mark's "it is good for him, rather, if . . ." becomes "it is advantageous to him that . . ." (cf. Luke 17:2). Three times in his gospel Matthew inserts συμφέρει + ἵνα and the subjunctive (see also 5:29, 30). The expression does not occur in Mark or Luke. Because a millstone would not fit around a person's neck, Mark's "be placed around" requires readers to infer the use of a rope. To avoid taxing the reader (and perhaps also to avoid repeating "around") Matthew substitutes "be hung," which he will insert also in 22:40. The description of the millstone as "pertaining to a donkey," i.e., too large to be worked by hand and therefore worked by an animal (contrast 24:41), emphasizes that there is no hope of escape. The judgment is portrayed as worse than being drowned in the depth of the sea. Throughout his gospel Matthew emphasizes judgment. Here he heightens the emphasis by changing "be cast" to "be drowned" and "into the sea" to "in the depth of the sea." καταποντισθῇ echoes 14:30 (unique to Matthew) and therefore suggests that Peter's brush with drowning symbolized the danger of eternal judgment for disciples with little faith.

18:7 (Luke 17:1) Matthew stresses judgment yet further by constructing in whole or in part (depending on whether Luke used Matthew or Matthew and Luke used a common source) a woe-saying. Matthew shows some predilection for οὐαί (4,0), κόσμῳ (5,2), and σκανδάλων (3,1). We saw an association of the world and stumbling blocks in 13:36-43, which Matthew composed. "For [it is] a necessity that influences to sin come" has a counterpart in Luke 17:1b: "It is impossible that influences to sin not come." Matthew's version takes the form of a positive statement, and he characteristically inserts γάρ (62-63,15) to make the necessity of sinful influences the reason for the woe he has just constructed. "Necessity" means eschatological inevitability. The influences to sin come from falsely professing disciples (cf. 13:24-30, 36-43), especially antinomian teachers in the church (cf. 7:13-27; 24:5, 10-11, 24).

"But woe to the man through whom the influence to sin comes" has a counterpart in Luke 17:1c: "but woe [to him] through whom they [influences to sin] come." Typically, Matthew inserts τῷ ἀνθρώπῳ (35,17—see the comments on 13:44 concerning its use for a professing disciple) and τὸ σκάνδαλον (3,1). The latter takes the singular, instead of the plural it took in the preceding two lines, to correspond with the singular number of "the man." In v 7bc, then, Matthew imports tradition found also in Luke 17:1bc and associated with the saying about the large millstone. In the tradition the woe preceded the saying about the millstone. But for contrast between accepting a seemingly unimportant disciple and causing him to sin, Matthew has followed Mark through the saying about the large millstone and now imports and doubles the woe to accentuate the seriousness of causing a seemingly unimportant disciple to sin.

See the UBS and Metzger, *Textual Commentary* ad loc., on the text-critical question in Luke 17:1c. Cf. 24:10; 26:24; 1 Cor 11:19.

In sum, influencing a little one to sin marks antinomians and contrasts with welcoming such a child in Jesus' name. Since that kind of welcoming grows out of humbling oneself like a child, the influencing of a little one to sin grows out of dictatorial pride. Thus antinomian leaders in the church will cause her little people—the masses—to stray into sin, perhaps even into apostasy. But these leaders had better watch out for their own salvation, too, for their disdaining others in the church calls in question the genuineness of their own profession of discipleship and exposes them to the danger of eternal punishment. Better to be drowned in the depths of the sea with a large millstone hung around one's neck! The first woe has to do with the judgment of those people who are led into sin, the second woe with the antinomian who leads such people into sin.

18:8-9 (5:29-30; Mark 9:43, 45, 47) Matthew returns to Mark, where there are three successive sayings about cutting off a hand and a foot and gouging out an eye that cause their owner to sin. He conflates the first two and adopts the third in order to have a pair instead of a trio (cf. 5:29-30, where he puts gouging out an eye first and cutting off a hand second and omits cutting off a foot). "And" becomes "but" for a contrast between the inevitability of sinful influences from others (v 7) and the requirement of self-discipline to avoid sin in oneself. The addition of "or your foot" to "your hand" shows conflation of the first two sayings in Mark. To avoid overstuffing the saying, which is already bloated by conflation, Matthew does not add "right," as he did in 5:29-30. Putting the compound subject ahead of the verb disagrees with the first saying in Mark but again shows influence from the second saying there. As in 5:29-30, Matthew's addition "and throw [it] away from you" occurs twice for parallelistic emphasis. In v 9 βάλε has a partial counterpart in Mark's ἔκβαλε αὐτόν, which Matthew makes a compound expression by using ἐκ- and the pronominal object in his ἔξελε αὐτόν and by adopting Mark's verb in its simple form.

Since "it is advantageous" has already substituted for "it is good" in v 6 (as also in 5:29-30), here Matthew sticks by "it is good" (so Mark). The substitution in 5:29-30 still makes itself felt, however, in that Mark's σέ, which is the subject of εἰσελθεῖν, comes up between καλόν and ἐστιν and changes to σοί, a dative of advantage agreeing with [συμφέρει] σοι in 5:29-30. The insertion of "lame" after "crippled," the putting of these adjectives after the reference to entering life (in contrast with the word order in Mark's first saying and in Matthew's next and Mark's third sayings), the insertion of "two feet" after "two hands," and the substitution of "to be cast" for "to go away" (so Mark's first saying) all reflect Mark's second saying and show Matthew's work of conflation.

At the end of v 8, Matthew omits "into hell" (so 5:30 and Mark) as redundant with the following "into the unquenchable fire" (so the first saying in Mark; cf. Matt 3:12; Luke 3:17) and as unnecessary because of its inclusion in the next saying. But "unquenchable" changes to "everlasting" in accord with his habit of attaching the latter adjective to people's fate, especially the punishment of the wicked (see 18:18; 25:41 [with "fire," as here], 46 [bis] for distinctive occurrences; also 19:16, 29; Rev 19:20; 20:10, 14-15; and Allen, ad loc., for extrabiblical references to everlasting punishment).

In v 9 Mark's "into the kingdom of God" becomes "into life" for a parallel with v 8 and a sharper contrast with the experience of hell fire. Putting the phrase ahead of "to enter" contrasts with Mark's order and may emphasize "into life." The last phrase of v 9, "into the hell of fire," follows Mark except for Matthew's adding "of fire" (a favorite motif of his—2,4). The addition results in an echo of 5:22 (peculiar to his gospel), a link with the everlasting fire mentioned at the end of the preceding saying, and a compensation for omission of the next several verses in Mark 9:48-50, where we read about the inextinguishability of the fire in hell and about being salted with fire. Matthew has already used the rest of Mark 9:48-50 (cf. the comments on Matt 5:13). But the thought of the very last statement in that passage, "Be at peace among yourselves," now leads him to borrow some non-Markan materials that lend themselves to instructions on the intramural life of the church.

For further interpretation of vv 8-9, see the comments on 5:29-30. On the Semitizing use of καλόν in the comparative sense "better," see Black, *Aramaic Approach* 117.

18:10 To introduce the non-Markan materials, Matthew builds v 10 out of his own special vocabulary and theology and a linking phrase from the preceding context. The digression into self-discipline (vv 8-9) makes the return to ecclesiastical leaders' treatment of nonleaders abrupt: v 10 begins with asyndeton. ὁρᾶτε is a Mattheanism (5,2). Three times Matthew inserts it in the imperative with a following verb modified by μή. Here the whole prohibition reads, "See [that] you do not despise one of these little people." Despising connotes both an attitude of disdainfulness and injurious acts growing out of that attitude (see 6:24; Luke 16:13; 1 Cor 11:22; 1 Tim 4:12). Though Matthew uses καταφρονέω only twice, its cognate φρόνιμος is more often distinctive (2,4). "One of these little people" comes from v 6 and ties Matthew's composition to its context.

"For I say to you" comes from dominical usage, which Matthew here, as elsewhere, multiplies to emphasize the authoritative words of Jesus (27,7). "For" makes the following a reason for not despising the little ones. The last clause refers to the little ones' angels, a theological notion that stems from the tradition reflected in Luke 15:10 and tallies with Matthew's distinctive doctrines of the angels of the Son of man (13:41; 16:27; 24:31; 25:31; 26:53) and the Devil's angels (25:41). As in these other passages, so also here the angels aid those they belong to. Matthew likes "in heaven" (24,4). Though διὰ παντός does not occur elsewhere in his gospel, πᾶς appears often (63,25-26). βλέπουσι (9,3), πρόσωπον (3,2), and τοῦ πατρός μου τοῦ ἐν οὐρανοῖς (10,2) all have a Matthean flavor.

Despite its simple use for seeing someone (as in Gen 43:3, 5; 46:30; Acts 20:25; Col 2:1), the idiom "see the face of" here connotes access to a sovereign. As often, Matthew draws the expression out of the OT (see 2 Sam 14:24; 2 Kgs 25:19; Esth 1:14; cf. Tob 12:15; Luke 1:19). The addition "always" indicates unrestricted access. It is unusual to have such access to any sovereign, therefore all the more striking to have it to God. According to R. Akiba even the angels who uphold the throne of glory cannot see God's glory (see *TDNT* 4. 651 and Schweizer, 367, with further references; cf. Exod 33:20). How greatly the heavenly Father must value the little people, then, to allow their angels an unrestricted access into his presence that other angels do not enjoy!

Cf. Gen 48:16; Ps 91:11; Daniel 10; Matt 4:6, 11; Luke 4:9-11, 13; Acts 12:15; 1 Cor 11:10; Heb 1:14; Str-B 1. 781-83; 2. 707-8; 3. 437-40.

18:12 (Luke 15:3-4) The parable of the lost coin, according to which there is joy in the presence of God's angels over one repentant sinner

(Luke 15:8-10), has suggested to Matthew the little ones' angels, who constantly behold the face of the heavenly Father (v 10). Immediately the parable of the lost sheep (Luke 15:3-7) comes to Matthew's mind (vv 12-14). The other parable in the tradition has to do with two brothers, the prodigal and his elder brother (Luke 15:11-32). Matthew reserves this parable for revision in 21:28-32, but now brings in corresponding materials concerning relations between brothers (vv 15-35). The three traditional parables form Jesus' apology for receiving sinners and eating with them. Matthew transmutes the parables into thrusts against antinomian influences to sin (vv 10-14) and against the hypocrisy of antinomians (21:28-32).

In particular, putting the parable of the lost sheep in the present discourse and certain revisions of detail make the parable apply to retention of little people in the church, who because of sinful influences from antinomian leaders might apostatize. Ironically, those leaders despise the victims of their teaching (cf. 2 Cor 11:20) and therefore do not care about the fate of strayers. For the sake of a smooth, nonnarrative transition, the Mattheanism "What seems good to you?" (4,2) stands in place of something like Luke's "And he told them this parable, saying." The question implies that the disciples will understand the parable and leads to a changing of "What man of you having. . . ?" (so Luke) to the more appropriate "If a certain man should have. . . ." "One hundred sheep" stays unchanged. But "having lost" becomes "should go astray." Despite his liking ἀπολέσας (8,1), Matthew substitutes πλανηθῇ for an allusion to the danger that false prophets in positions of ecclesiastical leadership might lead astray the church's little people (for another insertion see 24:11; cf. 7:15-27; 24:4, 5, 24). The shift from Jesus' seeking sinners to an ecclesiastical attempt to retain members means that the one sheep does not represent somebody lost (i.e., an unbeliever), but somebody in danger of becoming lost through straying (i.e., a professing disciple in danger of apostasy).

The more usual ἀφήσει (12,5) replaces καταλείπει (so Luke) because the latter always carries the connotation of judgmental abandonment in Matthew, yet Matthew does not want to imply judgment against the ninety-nine. Where Luke has "in the wilderness" Matthew has "on the mountains." Though ὄρη occurs often in Matthew (6,1), usually it takes the singular. Its present plural form, the mountainous character of Palestine, and Luke's replacing the mountains in Mark 5:5 with the wilderness (Luke 8:29) favor the originality of Matthew's phrase. πορεύεται (so Luke) takes the aorist participial form favored by Matthew, i.e., πορευθείς (8,4). This change results in adding ζητεῖ, which is distinctive several times in this gospel (2,3). "For the lost [one]" changes to "the one going astray" to echo the preceding line. οὐχί with the indicative mood of the verb implies that the audience would immediately infer an affirmative answer. Since the audience knew that a shepherd would not leave his flock unattended, we must suppose they took such care for granted. Otherwise the question would call forth a negative answer wreaking havoc with both the grammar and the theological point of the question. The hypothesis that Jesus spoke unrealistically for the sake of emphasis does not agree with the nature of the question.

Did children's tendency to get lost trigger importation of the parable concerning the lost sheep? To make sure none was missing, shepherds counted their flocks before putting them in the fold for the night. The aorist πλανηθῇ denotes beginning to stray; the present πλανώμενον, straying that goes on. Luke's reference to lostness rather than to straying is not necessarily the result of assimilation to the associated parables of the lost coin and the lost son, for the association of all three parables with one another may hinge on the common element of lostness. The position of ἐν before ἐξ αὐτῶν contrasts with Luke's order and gives a smoother reading. Cf. Ezekiel 34. See Black, *Aramaic Approach* 184, for paronomasia in the Aramaic substratum.

18:13 (Luke 15:5-7) At the beginning of v 13, "And if it happens that he finds it" replaces ". . . till he finds it? And having found [it] . . ." (so Luke). As often in Matthew, the replacement has the stylistic purpose of making a parallel with the conditional clause in the preceding sentence. It has the theological result of making the finding of the sheep unsure. The finding, which in Luke comes at the end of the question requiring an affirmative answer, drops out of the question altogether in Matthew and occurs only in a clause bedeviled by the uncertainty of ἐάν + the subjunctive. The church does not always succeed in restoring her little people who stray.

To make room for another emphasis Matthew omits the joyful laying of the found sheep on the shepherd's shoulders, the going of the shepherd to his house, and his celebration with friends and neighbors (so Luke). The omission brings Matthew to "I say to you." Either he prefixes ἀμήν, "truly," in a typical emphasis on Jesus' authority, or he retains the Semitism and Luke drops it (see the comments on 5:21-48 and cf. vv 3, 10, 18, 19). Matthew reserves "thus" for his next verse, changes "joy . . . will be" to "he rejoices," and delays "in heaven" till the next verse, where it will describe the Father. "Over one sinner who repents" becomes "over him" because of the shift from Jesus' seeking sinners to the church's seeking backsliders. Matthew also inserts μᾶλλον (5,1), retains "[more] than over [the] ninety-nine," and changes the latter's description from "righteous people who have no need of repentance" to "who have not gone astray" because he has just done away with the thought of repentance by an unbeliever and wants an antithetic parallel between church members who do not stray and the church member who does (cf. v 12).

18:14 Luke's version of the parable ends on the note of greater joy over the one repentant sinner than over ninety-nine righteous people who have no need of repentance. Matthew has shrunk that thought severely and shifted its reference from the repentant sinner to the repentant backslider; so he adds his own composition in v 14. It begins with οὕτως, a Mattheanism reserved from the tradition behind the preceding verse (18,5; cf. Luke 15:7), and continues with further Mattheanisms in θέλημα (3,1), ἔμπροσθεν (9,4), and τοῦ πατρός μου τοῦ ἐν οὐρανοῖς (10,2). The last of these echoes v 10, makes a typically Jewish circumlocution for God's name, and looks like Matthew's borrowing of OT phraseology, here in its targumic form (see, e.g., *Tg. Isa* 53:6, 10; cf. Matt 11:26; Luke 10:21). "The will *before* my Father" means "the will *of* my Father."

The second clause defines what that will is not, viz., "that one of these little people be lost." "These little people" derives from the preceding context; and finally Matthew takes over the verb of being lost, for which, up to this point, he has substituted the verb of straying. Thus his version closes with a divine imperative for bringing back the little members of the church lest their straying turn into lostness; i.e., lest their backsliding turn into apostasy.

The textual tradition divides between ὑμῶν and μου with τοῦ πατρός (see the UBS). Elsewhere in Matthew the two combinations occur often and in almost equal proportions. We might think that μου arises out of parallel influence from v 10 (so Metzger, *Textual Commentary* ad loc.). But Matthew himself loves parallelism, and v 14 contains other echoes of the preceding context. Therefore we should probably favor μου with B Θ f^{13} 33 syr[s,h] cop[sa,bo]. On concern over apostasy, see Hebrews passim; Jas 5:19-20; Jude 22-23; and the QL passim.

18:15 (Luke 17:3) Matthew now details the way strayers are to be sought (vv 15-20). He begins with a dominical saying that in Luke 17:3 immediately follows the sayings about influence to sin and a large millstone (vv 6-7 here in Matthew). "Take heed to yourselves" (so Luke) disappears, and δέ is inserted in the next, conditional clause in order that the sinning of one's brother might stand in contrast with and immediately alongside the heavenly Father's will that not one of the little people be lost (v 14). Some of the important textual tradition lacks "against you" (see the UBS and Metzger, *Textual Commentary* ad loc.). But Matthew's inserting "between you and him alone" in the next clause and expanding the section about forgiving a brother who has sinned against a brother (vv 21-35) favor the originality of "against you."

The insertion of ὕπαγε conforms to Matthew's diction (5,6) and puts the onus of responsibility on the brother sinned against: "go!" As often, Matthew assimilates Jesus' words to the OT, here by putting ἔλεγξον in place of ἐπιτίμησον (so Luke) for an allusion to Lev 19:17: "you may surely reprove [ἐλεγμῷ ἐλέγξεις in the LXX] your neighbor." The insertion "between you and him alone" arises from the prior insertion "against you." μόνου is another Mattheanism (9,0 for μον-).

At the start of the next clause Luke's καί drops out. Consequently, the clause goes with the following more than with the preceding; i.e., just as Matthew has connected the sayings in vv 14 and 15ab with a distinctive δέ, so he will connect the sayings in vv 15cd and 16 with a distinctive δέ. Here he omits καί in order to make this new connection. Luke's "if he should repent" gives way to "if he should listen to you." Matthew often stresses hearing the word as a true learner (ἀκούω—26,6; cf. the comments on 5:21-48 and his eliminating repentance in v 13 [cf. Luke 15:7]). "Forgive him" becomes the happy declaration "you have gained your brother." "Have gained" contrasts with the distinctive "be lost" in v 14 and occurs as an insertion also in 25:16, 17, 20, 22 and nowhere else in the gospels except 16:26; Mark 8:36; Luke 9:25. "Your brother" echoes v 15a and contributes to Matthew's emphasis on the brotherhood of Jesus' disciples (ἀδελφός—

11,8). The gaining of one's brother includes far more than personal reconciliation, then; it means winning back to the church a professing disciple who stands in danger of forfeiting salvation through sin against a fellow disciple.

18:16 Verses 16-20 come between sayings recorded also in Luke 17:3 and 4. They are an expansion by Matthew that has the purpose of emphasizing the need to exhaust every possibility in the effort to win back the disciple in danger of forfeiting salvation. The evangelist constructs "But if he should not listen" as an antithetic parallel to v 15c. He also wants a parallel for "Go, reprove him between you and him alone"; so he anticipates the law of two or three witnesses and writes "take along with you one or two more." Except for μετὰ σοῦ, every word in the clause belongs to his favorite diction: παράλαβε (4,6), ἔτι (4,2), ἕνα (24,7), ἤ (32,12), and δύο (19,4). As we might expect of Matthew, an allusive quotation of the OT now makes its entrance: "in order that by the mouth of two or three witnesses every fact may be established" (Deut 19:15; see Gundry, *Use of the OT* 139, for textual peculiarities; cf. Num 35:30; Deut 17:6; 2 Cor 13:1; 1 Tim 5:19; and the distinctive pairings in Matt 8:28-34; 9:27-31; 10:3-4; 20:29-34). Matthew leaves no indication that the one or two others shall have witnessed the sin committed against the one who takes them along. Therefore their going does not have the purpose of establishing the original charge (the truth of which is taken for granted) or of enabling them to act as witnesses before the church in case of a second refusal, but of strengthening the reproof with a view toward restoration.

18:17 The purpose of strengthening the reproof is confirmed by the first clause in v 17, "But if he refuses to listen to them," which follows the pattern in v 16a except for the replacement of μή with παρα- (giving the sense of refusal). In "tell the church" we see the second of Matthew's three insertions of ἐκκλησία. "But if he refuses to listen even to the church" takes after v 17a, but with the addition of "even" to emphasize the church, obviously the church in its local manifestation. The highly developed parallelism in these clauses typifies Matthew's style and confirms his composition. But more remains. "Let him be to you as a Gentile and a publican" exhibits Mattheanisms in ὥσπερ (6,3), ἐθνικός (3,0), and τελώνης (3,2). Cf. the insertion of ὡς οἱ ἐθνικοί in 6:7. As a whole, the expression carries the meaning of ostracism. Even ostracism aims at restoration: the ostracized brother may miss Christian fellowship and make things right. The command to ostracize him takes a singular address, σοι, because of the parallel with the preceding instructions. The involvement of the church in the final plea and the switch to the second person plural in v 18 show, however, that all the disciples are to join in the ostracism.

18:18 (Matt 16:19) In v 18 Matthew repeats a saying he used in 16:19 (cf. John 20:23). Here he introduces it with "Truly I say to you," which he uses much more often than the other synoptists do (15,8; see the comments on 5:21-48 and cf. vv 3, 13 in the present chapter). For emphasis, "as many things as" replaces "what." ὅσα is a Mattheanism (5,6). The verbs of binding and loosing change from singular (so 16:19) to plural to indicate that all disciples are to participate in these activities and that Peter received

368

the authority of binding and loosing as a representative disciple. The changing of ἐν τοῖς οὐρανοῖς (so 16:19) to ἐν οὐρανῷ may reflect the singular in the tradition recorded in Luke 15:7 (cf. Matt 18:14). See the comments on 16:17-19 for evidence of Matthew's composition and for interpretation. In 16:19 the association of binding and loosing with scribal keys points to didactic prohibition and permission of kinds of conduct. Here, association with the problem of a sinning disciple points to disciplinary retention of sins by means of ostracism, and to forgiveness of sins by means of restoration to fellowship.

With vv 15-18 cf. 1 Cor 5:1-13; 6:1-8; 2 Cor 2:5-11; 7:5-13; Gal 6:1; 1 Thess 5:11, 14-15; 2 Thess 3:14; 1 Tim 2:24-26; *T. Gad* 6:3-7; 1QS 5:25-6:1; CD 9:2-8; 13:9-10. Lev 19:17 deals with bringing personal hostilities into the open, Matt 18:15-18 with convincing another of his sin. But both passages deal with disrupted interpersonal relations among God's people. Matthew's favorable portrayals of Gentiles elsewhere in his gospel do not imply that their present unfavorable portrayal comes from pre-Matthean tradition. For the favorable portrayals depend on Gentiles' faith (see 8:5-13; 15:21-28); otherwise they are objects of evangelism (28:18-19), whose practices offer only negative examples (6:7, 32). See G. Strecker, *Der Weg der Gerechtigkeit* (2nd ed.; FRLANT 82; Göttingen: Vandenhoeck & Ruprecht, 1966) 253-54, against limiting v 18 to the twelve disciples.

18:19 In v 19 Matthew adds a saying that promises answers to the prayers which are to accompany loosing, the last-mentioned action. In other words, the disciples may have confidence in praying that *God* should forgive the sin of the brother who heeds reproof just as *they* have loosed, or forgiven, his sin. The saying comes from Matthew himself. πάλιν falls inside the circle of his preferred diction even though he often omits it for special reasons (8,4). It is followed by another Mattheanism, "[Truly] I say to you" (15,8), which harks back to the same expression in the preceding saying (cf. 19:23, 28 for a following "that," as here, in contrast with Mark 10:23, 29). Then there is the last in a long string of conditional clauses beginning with ἐάν (cf. vv 15a, 15c, 16a, 17a, 17c): "if two of you agree on earth concerning anything which you request." δύο comes from the law of two or three witnesses, just cited, and occurs in Matthew often (19,4). συμφωνήσουσιν is unparalleled also in 20:2, 13 and does not appear at all in Mark, only once in Luke. "On the earth" smacks of Matthew's style, especially as it stands in contrast with "in heaven" (6,0). The contrast echoes v 18. Since the agreement has to do with forgiving sin, Matthew means that the disciples duplicate the Son of man's forgiving sin "on the earth" (9:6, 8). πράγματος occurs only here in Matthew, but its modifier παντός occurs often (63,25-26) and shows that no sin committed by a brother in the church goes beyond the possibility of forgiveness. αἰτήσωνται occurs elsewhere in the first gospel twice as an insertion, eleven times in parallel, and suggests that Matthew is anticipating the saying on prayer in 21:22. He will insert γενήσεται in 21:21, and "my Father in heaven" is another obvious favorite of his (10,2). Here it echoes vv 10 and 14.

18:20 The last verse of Matthew's expansion consists almost entirely of words belonging to his special diction: οὐ (0,3), γάρ (62-63,15), συνηγμένοι

(10,10), ὄνομα (9,5), and ἐκεῖ (16,6). The use of εἰς with ὄνομα typifies his style (3,2). "Two or three" again echoes the law of two or three witnesses (v 16). Matthew likes to stress "name" in references to Jesus (see the comments on 1:21). Comparison with the saying in *m. 'Abot* 3:2 might lead us to think that Jesus' name has taken the place of the Torah, and Jesus himself the place of the Shekinah. But in Matthew's theology Jesus fulfills the law by carrying out its intent to perfection, not by replacing it (cf. Bonnard, 445-46). The interpretation of "in my name" as meaning "for the purpose of calling on my name" runs up against the use of εἰς ὄνομα at 10:41 (bis), 42 in a different way, viz., as indicating acceptance of the meaning and implications of various names (cf. the comments on 28:19 and see Exod 20:24; Mal 3:16). Here the name "Immanuel" is in view.

"I am in the midst of them" agrees with Matthew's habit of taking phraseology from the OT, where the Lord often promises to be with and in the midst of his people. The evangelist has combined the meaning of "Immanuel" in 1:23—viz., "God with us"—with "in the midst of them" in v 2 of the present chapter. The latter applied to a child. Hence, Matthew is making Jesus himself like a child, a model of humility in the midst of his disciples (cf. 11:29; 21:5). His dynamic presence provides the reason for the heavenly Father's answering their prayers. How could the Father refuse those who pray gathered in the name of his Son and blessed with the presence of his Son? Matthew writes "two or three" rather than "the church" to assure the two or three mentioned in v 16 that should their brother repent they do not need the rest of the church to pray successfully for his forgiveness. His refusal to heed the first reproof by the single brother sinned against might have seemed to require the prayers of the whole church.

18:21 (Luke 17:4) Now that he has composed vv 16-20 as an expansion of the saying in v 15 (cf. Luke 17:3), Matthew returns to his source for the saying that appears also in Luke 17:4. But he left his source so long ago that he makes a new start by bringing in Peter as the representative disciple, transforming Jesus' declaration (so Luke) into a question, and putting the question in Peter's mouth rather than in Jesus'. We meet Mattheanisms in τότε (66,17), προσελθών (38,6), and Πέτρος (8,1). The second of these points to Jesus' dignity (see the comments on 4:3; 8:14). The combination of Peter's name and the verb of speaking occurs fourteen times in Matthew, not at all in Mark, and only once in Luke.

Peter's question begins with the Mattheanism κύριε (34,15), which is a recognition of Jesus' lordship. The transformation of Jesus' declaration into a question from Peter results in ποσάκις, "how many times. . . ?" "Shall my brother sin against me and I forgive him?" comes from Jesus' declaration, with necessary changes of the aorist subjunctive to the future indicative and of the second person pronoun to the first person pronoun. Matthew imports ὁ ἀδελφός from v 15 because the long expansion in vv 16-20 and the new start require its repetition. Besides, he likes to emphasize Christian brotherhood (11,8). In v 15 "forgive" gave way to "you have gained" for restoration of a brother. Now Matthew retains "forgive" because the center of gravity has shifted from the need to restore the sinning brother to the need for the brother sinned against to exercise forgiveness. For this same reason, the returning of the brother seven times and saying "I repent" drops out. Matthew's expansion in vv 16-20 has taken care of that. Repentance is presupposed (see also the following parable). The last part of Peter's question, "till seven times?" comes from Jesus' declaration, with the addition of ἕως, which Matthew likes (13,14).

18:22 The putting of a question on Peter's lips requires an answer by Jesus. Therefore Matthew inserts "Jesus says to him." The historical present tense of λέγει with asyndeton characterizes Matthew's style (21,6). So also does the mention of Jesus' name (80,12). What Jesus says consists again of a lengthy expansion, the result of Matthew's own composition (vv 22-35). "I do not say to you, till seven times" arises from the evangelist's fondness for Jesus' λέγω σοι (27,7) and from the preceding "till seven times." In "but till seventy-seven times" the Mattheanism ἕως recurs (13,14) and, characteristically, an allusion to the OT is evident. Out of Lamech's formula of revenge (Gen 4:24) Matthew has created a formula of limitless forgiveness (cf. 6:12-15 with comments ad loc. and see Gundry, *Use of the OT* 139-40, on the texts and the translation "seventy-seven" rather than "seventy times seven").

18:23-25 Further emphasis accrues to personal forgiveness from a parable which Matthew seems to compose by adapting the parable of the two debtors told to Simon the Pharisee (or leper; Luke 7:41-43). It may be significant that the present parable is addressed to Peter, originally named Simon, and does not appear in 26:6-13 (cf. Luke 7:36-50), though admittedly its absence in Mark 14:3-9 may provide sufficient reason for its absence in 26:6-13. The following words in Luke's parable appear in one form or another, sometimes repeatedly, in the present parable and suggest that Matthew used them as foundation stones: χρεοφειλέτης, "debtor"; δανειστής, "moneylender"; ὀφείλω, "owe"; δηνάριον, "denarius"; and ἀποδίδωμι, "pay back."

The introduction to the parable consists entirely of Mattheanisms: διὰ τοῦτο (4,2), ὡμοιώθη (2,3), ἡ βασιλεία τῶν οὐρανῶν (25,7), ἀνθρώπῳ (35,17), and βασιλεῖ (6,9). The aorist tense of ὡμοιώθη implies that the settling of accounts does not portray the last judgment, but forgiveness that has already taken place (contrast 7:24, 26; 25:1). Except for διὰ τοῦτο, the introduction is matched word for word in 22:2, a Matthean insertion. Matthew often uses ἄνθρωπος at the start of parables (13:24, 45, 52; 18:23; 20:1; 21:33; 22:2), usually with an appositive noun (13:45, 52; 18:23; 20:1; 22:2). So also βασιλεύς appears unusually often in Matthew's parables (4,3; see 18:23; 22:2, 7, 11, 13; 25:34, 40), as in rabbinic parables.

The rest of the parable contains a full stock of Mattheanisms, in fact, almost nothing else.

ἠθέλησεν/ἤθελεν (18,8—vv 23, 30); συνᾶραι/συναίρειν (1,2—vv 23, 24; 25:19; and nowhere else in the NT); δοῦλος in various forms (8,7—vv 23, 26, 27, 28, 32; cf. 25:19); and ἀρξαμένου, a Mattheanism apart from its auxiliary use (3,2—v 24). The genitive absolute construction, in which ἀρξαμένου plays a role, typifies Matthew's style; and he likes to use δέ (vv 24, 25, 27, 28, 30). Further Mattheanisms come forward in προσηνέχθη (9,2—v 24); εἷς/ἕνα (24,7—vv 24, 28); several words having the stem ὀφειλ- (4,6 and no shared occurrences—vv 24, 28 [bis], 30, 32, 34); ταλάντων (v 24, thirteen times in 25:14-30 and never elsewhere in the NT); the genitive absolute construction of μὴ ἔχοντος δὲ αὐτοῦ ἀποδοῦναι (v 25); ἀποδίδωμι (5,11—vv 25 [bis], 26, 28, 29, 30, 34); ἐκέλευσεν (5,2—v 25); κύριος (34,15—vv 25, 26 v.1., 27, 31, 32, 34); πραθῆναι (v 25 and 13:46, a Matthean composition; see also 26:9 for a shared occurrence and, on the selling of people to pay their debts, 2 Kgs 4:1; Neh 5:1-13; Isa 50:1; Amos 2:6; 8:6); and γυναῖκα (10,3—v 25).

The list of Mattheanisms goes on and on: πᾶς (63,25-26—see vv 25, 26, 31, 32, 34 for various forms); ὅσα (5,6—v 25); πάντα ὅσα in combination (2,3—v 25); ὅσα ἔχει (0,3—v 25; see also 13:44, 46); πεσών (5,3—vv 26, 29); οὖν (35,11—vv 26, 29, 31); προσεκύνει (6,5—v 26); the combination πεσών . . . προσεκύνει (1,2— v 26; see also 2:11; 4:9); λέγων (61,23—vv 28, 29); ἐκεῖνος (26,9—see vv 27, 28, 32 for various forms); ἀπέλυσεν (5,2—v 27); ἀφίημι (12,5—see vv 27, 32, 35 for various forms); εὗρεν (7,8—v 28); σύνδουλος (see vv 28, 29, 31, 33 for various forms and 24:49 for an insertion that marks the only other occurrence in the gospels); δηνάρια (v 28—see also 20:2, 9, 10, 13 for distinctive occurrences, besides 22:19); κρατήσας (4,1 — v 28); παρεκάλει/-εσας (1,3—vv 29, 32); ἀπελθών (14,11— v 30); ἔβαλεν (12,8—v 30); ἕως (13,14—vv 30, 34); ἰδόντες (10-11,7—v 31); τὰ γενόμενα (v 31 [bis]—see also 27:54 for an insertion and 28:11 for an occurrence in distinctive material); ἐλυπήθησαν (2,1—v 31); σφόδρα (5,2—v 31); ἐλθόντες (10,10—v 31); διεσάφησαν (v 31—see also 13:36 v.1. for the only other occurrence in the NT); τότε (66,17—v 32); προσκαλεσάμενος (2,1—v 32 and elsewhere in Matthew only in this form); πονηρέ (10,4—v 32; cf. 25:26; Luke 19:22 for the combination with δοῦλε, as here); ἔδει in the imperfect tense (v 33—see 25:27 for an insertion, besides a paralleled instance in 23:23); ἐλεῆσαι/ἠλέησα (3,2—v 33 [bis]); ὡς (23,8—v 33); ὡς with καί (v 33—see 6:12 for an insertion and 20:14 for an occurrence in distinctive material of this combination, which appears nowhere else in the synoptics); κἀγώ (5,3—v 33); παρέδωκεν (6,3—v 34); βασανισταῖς (v 34—see 4:24; 8:6 for insertions of cognates); ἕως οὗ (4,2—v 34); οὕτως (18,5—v 35); οὕτως with καί (4,1—v 35); ὁ πατήρ μου ὁ οὐράνιος (6,1—v 35); ποιήσει (19,19—v 35); ἕκαστος (v 35—see 16:27; 26:22 for insertions, besides one common occurrence in 25:15); ἀδελφῷ (11,8—v 35); and καρδιῶν (5,2—v 35). See the Greek Index for fuller statistics.

This long list of expressions that elsewhere Matthew shows more or less special interest in leaves few other words of consequence in the parable. Of those, μακροθύμησον occurs in the gospels only in vv 26, 29; Luke 18:7. Matthew will insert σπλαγχνισθείς (v 34) in 20:34, besides three paralleled occurrences. δάνειον occurs only here in the NT (v 27). "Threw . . . into prison" (v 30) seems to echo 5:25, another passage dealing with disruption of fellowship among brothers. ὀργισθείς (v 34) appeared in distinctive material at 5:22, besides a shared occurrence in 22:7. Further evidence favoring composition by Matthew comes from the parallelism of initial participles that typifies his style (see vv 26a, 27a, 28a, 28b, 29a, 30b, 31a, 31b, 32a, 34a). The almost exact parallel between vv 26 and 29 also looks Matthean. The monetary base of the plot and the concentration of about a dozen monetary terms, some repeated several times, harmonize perfectly with composition by Matthew, a former tax collector.

We do not need to see Aramaic behind εἰ τι (v 28). As often, εἰ means "since." In good Matthean fashion "one of his fellow slaves" seems to echo "one of these little people" (vv 6, 10, 14). That σύνδουλοι occurs in the LXX only for high officials (2 Esdr 4:7, 9, 17, 23; 5:3, 6; 6:6, 13) does not require the same connotation here. δάνειον, "loan," occurs right within the parable, outweighs those distant references, and rules out taxation by governors. See A. Deissmann, *Light from the Ancient East* (New York: Doran, 1927; reprinted, Grand Rapids: Baker, 1978) 270, on imprisonment for debt among Greeks and Romans. Imprisonment prevented escape and prompted dependents to raise money for paying the debt and ransoming the debtor. Torture of the debtor gave his dependents added incentive to raise the necessary money. Here, however, the impossibility of paying back the huge sum makes the torture stand for eternal punishment.

Several features of the parable exhibit Matthew's desire to make the king represent Jesus as Lord. This desire, for example, stands behind προσηνέχθη, which refers to the first slave (v 24), contrasts with the first slave's finding his fellow slave (v 28—εὗρεν), and connotes a kind of offering (see the comments on 2:11; 4:24). Therefore to ask whether the slave was hauled out of prison, out of hiding, or out of a bed of feigned illness is to miss the theological point, which is all Matthew has in mind. Similarly, the man who is a king is designated ὁ κύριος (v 25, and possibly v 26, where the v.l. κύριε accords with Matthew's diction and with the possibility that v 29 caused scribal omission of κύριε). This designation does not primarily complement ὁ δοῦλος, for the latter does not come into the parable till later (v 26). Rather, ὁ κύριος echoes the designation of Jesus as Lord in the narrative leading up to the parable (v 21) and, indeed, throughout the gospel. Again Matthew is stressing the king's representation of Jesus as deity. Cf. the omission of κύριε in the fellow slave's plea (v 29). Yet again, the first slave's falling and prostrating himself before "the Lord" points to Jesus' deity (v 26—see the comments on 2:11 and contrast the fellow slave's falling and only beseeching the first slave, v 29). But along with these pointers to Jesus as Lord, v 35 indicates that Matthew also has in mind the heavenly Father: "so also my heavenly Father will do to you. . . ." Thus the king projects a double image of Jesus and his Father. They share rulership (cf. βασιλεία in the Greek Index for Matthew's ascribing the kingdom to both the Son of man and the Father).

Many think that the huge sum of the first slave's debt to the king implies that that slave holds the position of a governor, or satrap, that δοῦλος therefore means "servant" rather than "slave," and that the debt represents taxes which the governor has failed to collect from his territory or deliver to the king (for many details, see Jeremias, *Parables* 210-14; C. Spicq, *Dieu et l'homme selon le Nouveau Testament* [LD 29; Paris: Cerf, 1961] 54-61; Derrett, *Law in the NT* 32-47). But the hugeness of the debt—tens of thousands of talents, which because of the indefinite plural of the highest number used in reckoning cannot be calculated and therefore means "zillions"—goes far beyond the amounts of taxes collected from Roman provinces (see Josephus *Ant.* 17.11.4 §§317-20 for amounts of 600 talents collected from Judea, Idumea, and Samaria and of 200 talents from Galilee and Perea in 4 B.C.). Even more damagingly, the slave's debt is described

373

as a "loan" (δάνειον, v 27). Simply by recognizing the use of hyperbole for a debt owed by a common slave to his royal master we avoid illegitimately denying the accuracy of δάνειον. We also avoid having to read into the text that in answer to the slave's plea the king gave a loan for payment of the debt and immediately cancelled the loan.

The treatment of δάνειον as meaning "debt" in the Syriac versions establishes neither that definition for the Greek word nor the inaccuracy of the narrow Greek word for a supposed Aramaic word. In view of the abundant evidence favoring Matthew's composition of the parable, we shall have to say that the Syriac versions, helped by the repeated references to indebtedness, wrongly generalized the meaning of δάνειον. Debt—yes, but a particular kind of debt, one arising out of a loan.

Over against the largest unit of money, talents, and "zillions" of them at that, we read of one hundred denarii (about $20). In other words, a debt impossible to calculate, let alone to pay, stands opposite a debt easy to pay. The use of "all" for the first slave's debt in v 26, the omission of "all" for the second slave's debt in the almost exactly repetitive v 29, and the use of "all" with "that debt" in v 32 and again with "that was owed" in v 34 for the first slave's debt underscore the contrast. The huge debt of the first slave represents the large amount of sin against God that God has forgiven each disciple (see the comments on 6:12 concerning debt as sin). The impossibility of paying God that debt achieves fine irony in the absurdity of the command to sell the first slave, his wife, his children, and all his possessions for the sake of repayment. The command is designed to play up the king's compassionate act of forgiveness by emphasizing the hard justice of his sentence. A slave brought only about 500-2000 denarii on the market, Jewish practice did not allow sale of a wife, and children constitute a man's last possession (Jeremias, *Parables* 211). The impossibility of paying God one's debt of sin achieves even greater irony in the absurdity of the first slave's promise to pay all (v 26), as though a slave who has no money (v 25) could pay an incalculable debt by being given more time. Compassionately, however, the king does better than the first slave asks for. Like God, he does not grant more time, but forgives the entire debt.

The smallness of the fellow slave's debt implies that a disciple ought to forgive his fellow disciple all the more because God's forgiveness is expansive, and that he ought to do so "from the heart," i.e., sincerely, not merely with the lips (v 35; cf. 15:8; Isa 29:13). The parable does not teach repetition of forgiveness, which Peter asked about (v 21). But the allusion to Gen 4:24 took care of that (v 22). Here Matthew wants to emphasize that fellow disciples' forgiving one another is a condition of God's forgiving them (see esp. v 33; cf. 6:14-15; Mark 11:25). This emphasis reaches its warning height in the king's reversal of forgiveness and giving the first slave to the torturer till he pays back all that is owed—a dreadfully ironic impossibility referring to the last judgment (cf. the future tense of ποιήσει, "will do," in v 35).

At the last judgment the law of two or three witnesses will still be in effect. Hence, the other fellow servants report what has happened. Their great distress represents extreme sorrow over broken fellowship in the church, a sorrow that ought to characterize churches. Calling the unforgiving servant "wicked" exposes him as a false disciple: being forgiven by Jesus demands forgiving others as a sign that one has truly accepted forgiveness. "All that debt" emphasizes both the enormity of the sinful debt owed to God and the infinitude of his grace. He cancelled the debt in response to a mere plea. The master's anger represents divine wrath directed against false disciples. The giving of the king's debtor to "the torturers" stands for consignment to the punishment of hell. "So also my heavenly Father will do to you unless you each forgive his brother from your heart" leaves no room for misunderstanding the parable, and therefore no excuse for failure to forgive. "From your heart" shows that hypocrisy—merely mouthing "I forgive you"—has no part in the kind of forgiveness God demands. But the warning character of the parable shows that forgiving out of obedience need not kill sincerity, for a true disciple wants to obey his master.

ACCEPTING THE UNMARRIED IN THE CHURCH
19:1-12 (5:31-32; Mark 10:1-12; Luke 9:51; 16:18)

As usual, Matthew edits his narrative materials to carry out the overriding theme of the preceding discourse as far as possible. The theme of churchly brotherhood in chap. 18 therefore spills over into chaps. 19–22. In particular, we read about the need of the church to accept the unmarried (19:1-12), young people (19:13-26), Gentiles (19:27–20:16), the blind, the lame, and (again) young people (20:17–21:16), and publicans, prostitutes, and (again) Gentiles (21:17–22:46). Accepting such people in 21:17–22:46 has God's rejection of the Jewish leaders as its counterpoint.

19:1 (Mark 10:1; Luke 9:51) First, Matthew writes his formula concluding the foregoing discourse and introducing the following narrative. "And it came to pass [that] when Jesus finished these words" matches the formula in 7:28 exactly, emphasizes Jesus' words as authoritative, and lacks anything corresponding in Mark (see the comments on Matt 7:28-29). "He departed" echoes the formula in 13:53. "From Galilee" replaces Mark's "from there." The result is an antithetic parallel with "into the boundaries of Judea" in the next clause. Mark's "getting up" vanishes because Matthew has added "he departed" in this verse and omitted the complement to "getting up"—viz., "sitting down"—in 18:1-2 (cf. Mark 9:35).

To get the above-mentioned antithetic parallel, Matthew inserts "and." Mark's "he comes" changes to "he came" to correspond with "he departed." Mark's "and" before "on the other side of the Jordan" drops out. Consequently, Transjordan no longer appears as a destination reached *via* Judea (cf. Jesus' going through Samaria toward Judea according to Luke 9:51-56). Rather, Transjordan appears as part of Judea. This tallies with Matthew's distinctive collocation of "the wilderness of Judea" (3:1) and "all the region around the Jordan" despite his distinguishing the latter from "all Judea" (3:5). In other words, Matthew knows the distinction between Judea proper and the region around the Jordan, which includes Transjordan; but informally he merges the two under a wide definition of the Judean wilderness (cf. 4:25 with comments ad loc. and see the comments on 3:5-6).

See the UBS and Metzger, *Textual Commentary* ad loc., on the question whether καί belongs in Mark's text just before πέραν. If it does not, Matthew simply follows Mark. Otherwise, he omits καί. Cf. Strabo 16.2.21.

19:2 (Mark 10:1) In v 2 Mark's "come together" yields to "followed," a Mattheanism designed to portray the crowds as disciples (8,0). As a result, "to him" becomes "him" and, for a Christological emphasis, moves from the end of the clause to a position right after the verb and before the subject. Matthew likes "again" (8,4), but in Mark it depends on an earlier running of the crowd to Jesus (Mark 9:15). It drops out, then, because in 17:14 Matthew omitted that feature of the narrative. Characteristically, he adds "many" to "crowds" in order to portray evangelistic success among all nations (πολλοί—23,1; cf. 28:19). In sum, crowds come together *to* Jesus, according to Mark; in Matthew many crowds *follow* Jesus.

Because Matthew has just devoted a whole chapter to Jesus' instructions and now wants authentication of those instructions, Mark's "as he was accustomed [to do], he was teaching [or 'began to teach'] again" changes to "he healed." ἐθεράπευσεν is a Mattheanism (10,0). The same change occurred in 14:14 (cf. Mark 6:34). ἐκεῖ is another Mattheanism (16,6). Either we are to think that *all* the people who made up the many crowds needed and received healing, or we are to understand "and he healed them there" as shorthand for Jesus' healing the sick *among* the crowds (cf. 14:14).

19:3 (Mark 10:2) Comparison of v 3 with Mark 10:2 immediately runs into a text-critical problem in Mark: does προσελθόντες Φαρισαῖοι belong in Mark, at least in the manuscript used by Matthew, or not? Most of the external evidence favors inclusion (see the UBS). On the other hand, Mark's habit of using verbs in the impersonal third plural and the strong possibility of Matthean influence on copyists of Mark favor omission with D it[a,b,d,k,r1] syr[s] Origen. προσῆλθον and Φαρισαῖοι typify both Matthew's diction (38,6; 18,1) and his concern to emphasize Jesus' dignity and the role of the Pharisees as persecutors (cf. the comments on 4:3; 8:14). Perhaps, then, the first evangelist inserts "Pharisees approached him" and advances "testing him" to gain those emphases. But even though Mark's text reads προσελθόντες Φαρισαῖοι, Matthew escalates the participle to a finite verb and adds "him" for a Christological emphasis. To correspond with the participle πειράζοντες, the participial phrase καὶ λέγοντες substitutes for Mark's finite verbal phrase ἐπηρώτων αὐτόν. Matthew likes λέγοντες (61,23) and often dismisses ἐπερωτάω.

In the Pharisees' question (v 3b) we run into another text-critical problem: does ἀνθρώπῳ belong in Matthew's text or not? ℵ* B L 28 (700) eth[ro] Clement Augustine lack it. Except for some insignificant support of ἀνδρί (obviously the result of influence from Mark), the remaining external evidence favors it. Matthew's penchant for ἄνθρωπος (35,17) and the apparent echo of this word in v 10 (distinctive to the first gospel) favor inclusion (cf. Metzger, *Textual Commentary* ad loc., where the omission is attributed to Alexandrian conciseness). Acceptance of the word means that Matthew replaces Mark's "for a husband" with "for a man" in the question whether it is permissible to divorce a wife. In Matthew "wife" gains the definite article and "his." These insertions anticipate Gen 2:24, about to be quoted in v 5. For smoothness, "his wife" moves behind "to divorce" (contrast the Greek texts).

To prepare for his adding the exceptive phrase in v 9, Matthew adds "for any cause at all." This addition puts the question in the framework of the debate between the rabbinic schools dominated by Hillel and Shammai. The latter interpreted Deut 24:1 strictly as allowing divorce only on the ground of a wife's unchastity. The former interpreted Deut 24:1 loosely as allowing divorce for any reason whatever (see *m. Giṭ.* 9:10). In Mark the Pharisees ask a question they have no doubt about—it was agreed that the Mosaic law allowed divorce—but a question that might lure Jesus into a statement offensive to Herod Antipas (and perhaps contradictory to the Mosaic law at the same time). Herod Antipas had recently divorced the daughter of the Nabatean king Aretas in order to marry Herodias, who had recently left (and presumably divorced) Herod Philip in order to marry Herod Antipas (Josephus *Ant.* 18.5.1 §§109-12; cf. 15.7.10 §§259-60). And southern Transjordan (Perea) made up part of the territory ruled by Herod Antipas. In Mark, therefore, πειράζοντες connotes an attempt to lure Jesus into making a politically dangerous remark. In Matthew it connotes an attempt to test Jesus on a debatable point of OT interpretation. Putting the question in the framework of a rabbinic debate suits Matthew's portrayal of Jesus as Rabbi and Teacher (see esp. 23:8, 10). That Matthew frequently adds πᾶσαν (63,25-26) and that αἰτίαν occurs uniquely in v 10 favor Matthew's composition of the phrase.

Cf. Josephus *Ant.* 4.8.23 §253; *Life* 76 §§426-27; Philo *Spec.* 3.1-14; and the whole of the tractate *Giṭṭin* in the Mishna. It does not tell the whole truth to say that Mark's Jesus radically condemns divorce, whereas Matthew's Jesus identifies the adequate ground for divorce. True, Matthew's exceptive phrase allows formalization—according to Jewish requirement—of the break between husband and wife that has already occurred through the wife's immorality. But Matthew does not let the husband remarry. To the contrary, he adds vv 10-12 to emphasize remaining single. If προσελθόντες Φαρισαῖοι does not belong in Mark, later scribal addition under the influence of Matthew required changing Matthew's finite verb to a participle (because Mark already has a main verb in the clause) and also led to dropping Matthew's αὐτῷ as unnecessary because of the αὐτόν already present in Mark.

19:4 (Mark 10:3a, 6) From the introduction to Jesus' answer Matthew lops off "to them" (Mark 10:3a). That inconsequential omission is followed by the large omission—really, a delay—of Jesus' counter question concerning Moses' commandment, the Pharisees' answer in terms of Deut 24:1, and Jesus' putting Moses' commandment under the rubric of Jewish hardheartedness (Mark 10:3b-5; cf. vv 7-8 in Matthew). This omission, or delay, has the effect of making Jesus rather than the Pharisees give the first quotation of the law. In other words, he immediately steps forward as the one who did not come to destroy the law, but to fulfill and teach it (see esp. 5:17-48).

Jesus' answer begins, "Have you not read. . . ?" (not in Mark 10:6). Matthew inserts ἀνέγνωτε three times in his gospel, always in negative questions. As a whole, the present question implies that the Pharisees have indeed read the OT passages about to be quoted and therefore have no excuse for asking their malevolent question. Inserting the question requires changing Mark's "but" to "that." Matthew takes "of creation" from Mark's first phrase and makes it into "the Creator" to clarify that the subject of the following verb is God, not Moses (as it seems in Mark). The result is not only a grammatical clarification, but also an emphasis on the Creator's will. "From [the] beginning" probably reflects Gen 1:1 and goes with the following quotation from Gen 1:27: "male and female he made them" (so also the LXX).

Cf. the quotation of Gen 1:27 in CD 4:21. But there we read only a polemic against polygamy, as the immediately following lines show (CD 5:1-6). Not only does the issue of divorce fail to surface, but also the allowance of divorce—with no indication that it excludes permission to remarry—confronts us in CD 13:17. Asceticism among the Essenes is another matter. See the UBS and Metzger, *Textual Commentary* ad loc., on the v.l. ποιήσας for κτίσας. The agreement of Matthew and Mark with the LXX in ἐποίησεν, "made," for the Hebrew בָּרָא, "created," is notable.

19:5 (Mark 10:7-8) To underscore his presentation of Jesus as supporter of the law, Matthew introduces Jesus' second quotation of the OT with "And he said" (not in Mark). The quotation comes from Gen 2:24 (cf. Eph 5:31; 1 Cor 7:10-17). Since God is not speaking in Gen 2:24 and since Jesus is still speaking in Mark, Matthew intends his readers to understand Jesus, not the Creator, as the subject of the inserted "And he said." The first line of the quotation matches Mark almost exactly: "On account of this a man shall leave [Mark adds 'his'] father and mother." In Matthew the second line reads καὶ κολληθήσεται τῇ γυναικὶ αὐτοῦ but has no parallel in Mark's text represented by ℵ B Ψ 892* 1⁴⁸ syrˢ goth (see the UBS). Other Markan texts—among them D K W X Θ Π f¹³ 565 itᵇ,ᵈ,ff²,¹,⁽q⁾ vg syrᵖ,ʰ copˢᵃ,ᵇᵒ,ᶠᵃʸ—read in accord with the LXX: καὶ προσκολληθήσεται πρὸς τὴν γυναῖκα αὐτοῦ (note προσ- and πρός + the accusative where Matthew reads the simple form of the verb and the simple dative of the noun). Yet other texts of Mark read as the LXX except for τῇ γυναικί (so Matthew and A C L Δ f¹ 1546 1¹² itᵃ,ᵃᵘʳ,ᶜ,ᶠ,ʳ¹ in Mark). Metzger (*Textual Commentary* ad loc.) suggests that the omission in some Markan texts arose by a scribe's skipping from the καί before προσκολληθήσεται to the καί before ἔσονται. He argues that inclusion of the line seems necessary to the sense, since otherwise "the two" in Mark 10:8 could refer wrongly to the father and mother. But it did not bother Mark that the subject of "he made" in v 6 seems to be Moses rather than God. Actually, Mark (with Jesus) assumes a knowledge of the OT context. In Mark 10:4 Jesus skips the second member of a quotation from Deut 24:1 by taking only the first and third members, and Matthew fills in with a conflated reference to the second member (see the comments on v 7). Probably the same thing has happened here: Jesus quoted only the first and third lines (so Mark's original text), Matthew filled in the second line to reinforce his portrait of Jesus as teacher of the law, and some copyists of Mark filled in the second line under Matthew's influence, but with the Septuagintal or a largely Septuagintal text. The third line of the quotation reads with Mark and the LXX. See further Gundry, *Use of the OT* 16-17.

19:6 (Mark 10:8-9) Jesus' deductions from Gen 1:27; 2:24 that God intended the first pair solely for each other, that a man and his wife are no longer two, but one flesh, and that therefore a man should not separate what God has yoked together—i.e., a husband should not divorce his wife—reads as it does in Mark, except that Matthew changes μία σάρξ to σάρξ μία to conform with the order of words in the preceding quotation. Thus the Pharisees' question "for any reason" turns out to be irrelevant. There is no valid reason at all. Cf. R. le Deaut in *BTB* 4 (1974) 249-51.

19:7-8 (Mark 10:3b-5) Verses 7-8 come from Mark 10:3b-5, delayed till now for the purpose of setting up an "antithesis" between Jesus and Moses (see v 9). The antithesis follows the pattern of the well-known antitheses in chap. 5, for the most part, and consists in carrying to perfection the tendency of the Mosaic law, not in contradicting the Mosaic law or its rabbinic interpretations (cf. the comments on 5:21-48).

The historical present of λέγουσιν with asyndeton typifies Matthew's style (21,6). At this point Mark records Jesus' question, "What did Moses command you?" But because of Matthew's rearrangement of materials, a question by Jesus concerning Moses' commandment would have followed his citations and explication of Mosaic materials in Gen 1:27; 2:24 very awkwardly—indeed, nonsensically. Therefore, Matthew characteristically conflates Jesus' question (Mark 10:3b) and the Pharisees' answer (Mark 10:4b) and puts the result in the mouth of the Pharisees. The name of Moses appears in both Jesus' question and the Pharisees' answer (so Mark). τί and ἐνετείλατο come from Jesus' question in Mark. But the addition from the Pharisees' answer in Mark—viz., "to give [her] a certificate of divorce and dismiss her"—makes τί mean "Why?" rather than "What?"

As often, Matthew inserts οὖν (35,11). Here it parallels v 6b and means "In view of the statement in v 6, why . . . ?" Matthew's Pharisees are pitting their own quotation of the Mosaic law against Jesus' quotations of the Mosaic law. Here, then, the Pharisees appeal to Deuteronomy to qualify Genesis; in Mark Jesus appeals to Genesis to qualify Deuteronomy. "To give" replaces Mark's "to write." Both occur in Deut 24:1. But Matthew is conflating the clauses in Deuteronomy, "he writes her a certificate of divorce" and "he gives [it] into her hand." Mark alludes to the first clause, but skips the second. Both Matthew and Mark then allude to a third clause in Deuteronomy that mentions sending the wife away. Thus Matthew includes at least portions of all three clauses in Deuteronomy. His advancing "to give" conforms to the order of words in the OT text (contrast Mark). The technical ἀπολῦσαι (so also Mark) replaces שִׁלְּחָהּ (Hebrew) and ἐξαποστελεῖ (LXX); i.e., "divorce" replaces "send away." Possibly Matthew fills out the allusive quotation by adding "her," which is missing in Mark but corresponds to Deuteronomy and is well supported in a good part of Matthew's textual tradition (see the UBS and, further, Gundry, *Use of the OT* 37-38).

Verse 8 opens with a Mattheanism, the historical present λέγει with asyndeton (21,6; cf. v 7). This word replaces Mark's "But Jesus said." For a parallel with the preceding verse Matthew adds Moses' name. The addition induces him to insert a recitative ὅτι (which he usually omits) before the name lest careless readers take Moses as the subject of λέγει. "Permitted" replaces Mark's "wrote" much as "to give" replaced Mark's "to write" in v 7. "Permitted" comes from Mark 10:4b, which Matthew took up in v 7 with the substitution of the very different "commanded." Thus he contrasts the wrong interpretation of Moses as commanding divorce with the correct interpretation of Moses as permitting divorce. In Mark, it is Jesus who uses "commanded" for Moses' teaching on divorce; the Pharisees use "permitted." In Matthew, the reverse! Either Jesus wants the Pharisees to answer with Genesis instead of Deuteronomy, according to Mark; or, more likely, he means that Moses gave the commandment in Deuteronomy to cover the matter of divorce. Matthew reverses the verbs to avoid the wrong impression that Moses commanded divorce as such. "To divorce your wives" replaces "this commandment," which Matthew can hardly write after "permitted," and echoes "to divorce" in v 7b. Similarly, "your wives" echoes "her" in v 7b, but Matthew defines the pronoun and pluralizes it to correspond with the plural "you" in v 8.

The last clause of v 8 starts with a trio of words out of Mark 10:6: "But from [the] beginning." Matthew has already taken over Mark 10:6 (see v 4). So having used the prepositional phrase a second time, he goes his own way with "it has not been so." The perfect form γέγονεν and οὕτως are Mattheanisms (3,2; 18,5).

God's intent at creation, Jesus argues, weighs more than the later law of Moses (cf. Gal 3:17). Yet even that law testifies indirectly to God's original intent in that the later permission to divorce arose only in a set of instructions designed to check haste in divorce, the loaning of wives, and similar abuses by prohibiting resumption of the initial marriage. In fact, the second marriage of the woman "defiles" her according to Deut 24:1-4. Thus Moses' law runs in the opposite direction from divorce with remarriage. Jesus recognizes this tendency, notes the secondary nature of the allowance, identifies its reason as men's hardheartedness, extends the defilement of a second marriage by the woman to include a second marriage by the man, and demands that his disciples avoid such defilement. In all of this he does not pit God's original intent against the Mosaic provision so much as he harmonizes the Mosaic provision with God's original intent.

19:9 (5:31-32; Mark 10:10-12; Luke 16:18) Matthew now omits the statement in Mark 10:10, "And in the house again, the disciples were asking [or 'began to ask'] about this," because in his gospel "the house" means Jesus' house in Capernaum (see the comments on 4:13; 9:10)—yet Jesus has left Galilee (see v 1). The omission shifts the address of the saying in v 9 from the disciples (so Mark) to the Pharisees (as in v 8). Mark's "And he says to them" becomes "But I say to you," which typifies Matthew's diction (27,7) and conforms to the "antithesis" on divorce in 5:32. The addition of "that" (not in Mark) also conforms to 5:32. "Whoever dismisses his wife" comes from Mark and matches the allusion to Moses' teaching in 5:31. Here, of course, the clause falls on the dominical side of the antithesis.

The insertion μὴ ἐπὶ πορνείᾳ, "except for immorality," echoes the similar insertion in 5:32: παρεκτὸς λόγου πορνείας, "except for the matter of immorality." It is barely possible that we are to read the latter form of the exception here, too, with P[25vid?] B D f^1 f^{13} 33 1^{547} it[a,aur,b,c,d,e,f,ff1,ff2,g1,h,q,r1] syr[c,pal] cop[sa,bo] Origen Cyril. The change to μὴ ἐπὶ πορνείᾳ would then represent a scribal attempt to get rid of the Semitic παρεκτὸς λόγου [cf. דָּבָר in Deut 24:1] πορνείας for the sake of better Greek style. Otherwise, Matthew himself revises his earlier expression with the same purpose in mind or for simple variety of expression. See the comments on 5:32 concerning his legitimizing a kind of divorce that consists solely in the formalization of a break that has already occurred through sexual infidelity.

"And marries another [woman]" comes from Mark. "Commits adultery" also comes from Mark and contrasts with "makes her commit adultery" and with the application of "commits adultery" to the second man who marries the woman—both in 5:32. Thus the concern in 5:32 to keep the woman and a second man from committing adultery changes to a concern to keep her original husband from committing adultery with a second marriage (cf. *Herm. Man.* 4.1.4-11). Mark's final phrase ἐπ᾽ αὐτήν drops off, as it does in 5:32c and Luke 16:18, perhaps because of its ambiguity. It may well mean "with the second woman in remarriage" instead of "against the original wife." But readers of Mark's Greek text must have puzzled. The further omission of Mark's statement that the divorced woman who marries another man commits adultery (Mark 10:12) is due to the failure of the Mosaic law to give women the right to divorce their husbands. As usual, Matthew is conforming to the OT. In Jewish society of the NT era women could not divorce their husbands (cf. Josephus *Ant.* 15.7.10 §§259-60 with 18.9.6 §§353-62). The few apparent exceptions required the help of a court (whereas a man who divorced his wife did not—see Str-B 1. 318-19; Derrett, *Law in the NT* 381-83, 386-88). Jesus may have been alluding to Herodias's divorcing Herod Philip in order to marry Herod Antipas (cf. the divorcing of Costobarus by Salome, Herodias's great aunt). But those events in the Herodian family betray influence from Greco-Roman custom, according to which women might divorce their husbands.

19:10-12 Verses 10-12 come from Matthew himself as an expansive emphasis on Jesus' prohibiting divorce with remarriage. The disciples' comment that "it is not advantageous to marry" shows that they understand the law of Christ—in Matthew understanding characterizes disciples—and understand it not merely as an agreement with the strict but tolerable interpretation of the Shammaites, who allowed divorce with remarriage in cases of sexual infidelity, but as a seemingly intolerable prohibition of remarriage even though divorcing a wife for sexual infidelity is allowed. Jesus himself recognizes the seeming intolerability of his teaching: "Not all accept this saying." He is referring to nondisciples and false disciples, antinomians. By contrast, there are some—his true disciples—who can and do accept his stricture on divorce and remarriage; i.e., out of obedience to Christ's law concerning divorce they do not remarry, but live as eunuchs, lest their righteousness fail to surpass that of the scribes and Pharisees and entrance into the kingdom be denied them (cf. v 12 with 5:20).

Evidence of composition by Matthew abounds in the diction, parallelism, and echoing of earlier phrases. In v 10a λέγουσιν, a historical present with asyndeton, typifies his style (21,6) and along with αὐτῷ echoes v 7. μαθηταί is a favorite of his (31,5). "If the cause [i.e., 'case'] of a man with [his] wife is thus" (v 10b) echoes "Is it permissible for a man to dismiss his wife for any cause at all?" (v 3b). εἰ, αἰτία, ἀνθρώπου, and γυναικός come from the earlier saying. οὕτως comes from Matthew's special vocabulary (18,5), and ἀνθρώπου, too (35,17), though it echoes v 3b. In "it is not advantageous to marry," συμφέρει is a Mattheanism (4,0) and γαμῆσαι echoes v 9b.

See BAG, s.v. αἰτία on the probability that αἰτία is a Latinism when used with the meaning "case." But "cause" (v 3) easily shades into "case."

A stereotyped transition opens v 11: "But he said to them" (cf. v 9a). The first clause of Jesus' reply reads, "Not all accept this saying" (see the UBS and Metzger, *Textual Commentary* ad loc., for textual evidence for and against "this"). Elsewhere Matthew displays fondness for πάντες (63,25-26). χωροῦσιν will occur as an insertion again in the next verse (bis) and 15:17, but it occurs only once in Mark and not at all in Luke. Furthermore, it indicates an acceptance that includes mental comprehension and thus reflects Matthew's stress on the disciples' understanding. λόγον is a Mattheanism (16,2). The next line follows as an antithetic parallel—"but [all accept this word] to whom it has been given"—and echoes 13:11: "to you it has been given to know the mysteries of the kingdom of heaven." The first three lines of v 12 exhibit strict parallelism. γάρ belongs to Matthew's favorite vocabulary (62-63,15). εὐνοῦχοι (ter) and εὐνουχίσθησαν/εὐνούχισαν appear only here in the NT outside Acts 8. οἵτινες is another Mattheanism (23,5). κοιλίας was an insertion also in 12:40. μητρός often has a parallel, but occurs often as a Mattheanism, too (3,6). Matthew wrote ἐγεννήθησαν forty-three times in chaps. 1–2, and his favorites οὕτως (18,5) and ἀνθρώπων (35,17) appear a second time in this supplement (cf. v 10). "The kingdom of heaven" typifies his theology and phraseology (25,7), and ὁ δυνάμενος makes use of a well-liked verb (13,0). The construction of the last line, "Let him who is able to accept [this word] accept [it]," echoes "Let him who has ears hear," which Matthew has used repeatedly (11:15; 13:9, 43).

In composing vv 10-12 Matthew stresses that just as some men live as eunuchs because of congenital incapacity and some because of others' castration of them, so also Jesus' true disciples live as eunuchs after they have had to divorce their wives for immorality; i.e., in obedience to the law of the kingdom taught by Jesus, they do not remarry. Nothing in the context favors understanding the passage in terms of freedom from marital cares for the sake of evangelistic endeavor, or because of an eschatological crisis, or for considerations of ceremonial purity or asceticism. Rather, the interpretation adopted above allows Matthew's addition to support Jesus' prohibiting divorce with remarriage in the preceding context. We also avoid making Matthew's addition disagree with Jesus' favorable view of marriage. A disagreement would arise if we interpreted the addition as advocating an extension of premarital single life. Cf. the positive view of marriage in 10:37, where loving one's wife above Jesus drops out (cf. Luke 14:26); in 22:5, where Matthew omits the excuse that recent marriage to a wife hampers accepting the invitation to the banquet of salvation (cf. Luke 14:20); and in 22:24, where Matthew's omitting "and [if] he should leave a wife" (so Mark 12:19 and, similarly, Luke 20:28) implies that a man who dies will indeed leave a wife.

"This saying," mentioned in v 11, does not then refer to the disciples' saying in v 10—viz., "If the case of a man with [his] wife is thus, it is not advantageous to marry"—for Jesus describes "this saying" as "given" to a select group. In 13:11 the same expression applies to Jesus' teaching given to the disciples. Therefore, "this saying" refers to Jesus' teaching against divorce with remarriage; and the ability to accept the saying does not distinguish higher disciples from lower disciples, but characterizes true disciples as those to whom God gives ability to accept even this high standard, over against nondisciples and false disciples, who do not have such ability.

Understanding self-imposed eunuchism as abstinence from remarriage makes largely irrelevant the usual references to 1 Cor 7:7, 25-40; 1QSa 1:19–2:10. But cf. Ezek 44:22. Castration by others and self-imposition of eunuchism imply sexual incapacity or abstinence rather than sterility (cf. *m. Yebam.* 8:4-6).

In the larger context and because of near insistence on marriage in Jewish society, Matthew portrays the single life of Christian men who have not remarried after divorcing their immoral wives as an act of discipleship. His purpose is to urge full acceptance of such men in the Christian brotherhood (cf. Deut 23:2[1]; Isa 56:3-5).

ACCEPTING YOUNG PEOPLE IN THE CHURCH
19:13-26 (Mark 10:13-27; Luke 18:15-27)

19:13 (Mark 10:13; Luke 18:15) At the start of this new section Matthew's beloved τότε (66,17) replaces Mark's καί. "They were bringing [or 'began to bring']" changes to "were brought" for avoidance of the indefinite "they," common in Semitic languages but unusual in Greek outside "they say." Consequently, "children" becomes the subject instead of the direct object. After "in order that," Matthew changes Mark's "he might touch them" to "he might lay [his] hands on them" in anticipation of the same expression in v 15. An inclusio results. ἐπιθῇ is a Mattheanism (5,0). Again in anticipation of v 15 or, more properly, with an eye on Mark 10:16, Matthew draws up Mark's κατευλόγει, a hapax legomenon in the NT, and interpretatively substitutes καὶ προσεύξηται (3,4). Praying for the children probably casts them in the role of young disciples, the youth of the church.

God's establishment of marriage leads to Jesus' blessing children. On the Jewish practice of taking children to elders, or scribes, for blessing and prayer right after the Day of Atonement, see J. Jeremias, *Infant Baptism in the First Four Centuries* (Philadelphia: Westminster, 1960) 49. The disciples may have objected to the delay of Jesus' progress toward Jerusalem.

"But the disciples rebuked them" stays unchanged. In view of Jesus' subsequent command not to forbid the children to come, it is the children whom the disciples rebuked, not those who brought them. This is so in Matthew for the additional reason that changing "they were bringing" to "were brought" leaves the bringers of the children unmentioned.

19:14 (Mark 10:14; Luke 18:16) Despite Matthew's fondness for ἰδών (10-11,7), it falls from the beginning of v 14, perhaps because Jesus' response implies hearing what the disciples said rather than seeing what they did (cf. Luke). Matthew also deletes "was indignant and . . . to them." The deletion dulls the edge of Jesus' words and generalizes them in accord with Matthew's portraying the disciples as understanding (see esp. chaps. 13–17). In Jesus' words themselves, Matthew delays "to come to me" till the close of "Permit the children and stop forbidding them." In Mark and Luke the phrase follows "Permit the children." Matthew's order allows the phrase to modify both imperatives, which he connects by inserting "and" (as in Luke but not Mark), and makes the imperatives stand side by side in close, uninterrupted parallelism. The present tense ἔρχεσθαι, "to be coming," changes to the aorist ἐλθεῖν, "to come."

κωλύω, used here, occurs also in baptismal contexts in 3:14; Acts 8:36; 10:47; 11:17. But baptism as such does not come into the present passage.

19:15 (Mark 10:15-16; Luke 18:17) The saying about the need to receive God's kingdom as a child (Mark 10:15; Luke 18:17) drops out because of its earlier use in 18:3. And as in 18:3 (cf. Mark 9:36), Matthew deletes Mark's "hugging them" in order to cast the children as disciples old enough to understand rather than as infants or toddlers too young to have the understanding necessary for discipleship. To replace "hugging them," he advances Mark's later phrase τιθεὶς τὰς χεῖρας ἐπ᾽ αὐτά, "putting [his] hands on them," makes ἐπ᾽ a prefix, shifts the participle from present tense to aorist, and changes αὐτά to αὐτοῖς—all for parallelism with v 13. Since Mark's "he was blessing [or 'began to bless']" has appeared in revised form in v 13 and since it implies very young children rather than maturer young people, such as Matthew has in mind, he substitutes "he went from there." ἐκεῖθεν is a favorite of his (8,1). The substitute anticipates "going from" in Mark 10:17 and shows that Matthew is uniting the story of the rich man with the blessing of the children. So also in the following story the grown man of Mark and Luke turns into a youth (vv 20, 22). Thus vv 16-22 will make a bad example of youth going away from Jesus (ἀπῆλθεν, v 22), just as vv 13-15 offer a good example of youth coming to Jesus (ἐλθεῖν πρός, v 14).

19:16 (Mark 10:17; Luke 18:18) Matthew has just written "he went

384

from there"; so he omits Mark's "as he was going out to [the] road" and begins the story of the rich man with a characteristic insertion of ἰδού (34,9). This interjection often appears in the middle of Matthew's sections (cf. his uniting vv 13-15 and 16-26). Here it puts stress on the immediately following "one" to highlight the parallel between the "one" who approaches Jesus (v 16) and the "one" who is good (v 17). In both vv 16 and 17 Matthew pulls εἰς forward to gain the parallel. "Approaching" substitutes for Mark's "running to [Jesus] . . . and kneeling before him," perhaps because Matthew inserted "kneeling" in 17:14 and certainly because he is fond of προσελθών as a pointer to Jesus' dignity (38,6; see the comments on 4:3; 8:14). Cf. his rejecting "running to" in 17:14 (Mark 9:15). As usual, he displaces Mark's ἐπηρώτα with εἶπεν. αὐτόν moves ahead of the verb, changes to αὐτῷ, and consequently relates to προσελθών rather than to εἶπεν. The new syntax further emphasizes Jesus' dignity.

In the words of the one who approaches Jesus, Matthew retains "Teacher" and "what shall I do . . . ?" but changes ἀγαθέ, which modifies διδάσκαλε, to ἀγαθόν, which modifies τί. The change shifts attention from Jesus' goodness to the goodness of obeying the law, indeed, to the necessity of doing good in order to have eternal life (cf. Lev 18:5; Prov 4:2, 4). "Have" replaces "inherit." Matthew is reserving the latter for insertion in v 29. The reversal of the verb and its object produces a smoother order of words.

19:17 (Mark 10:18; Luke 18:19) In the introduction to Jesus' response, the unusual omission of Mark's "Jesus," which Matthew usually adds, may stem from embarrassment over the tendency of the following question to spoil Matthew's portrait of Jesus as the supreme teacher of the law. "Why do you ask me . . . ?" takes the place of "Why do you call me . . . ?" ἐρωτᾷς comes from Mark's parallel to the preceding verse, where Matthew replaced it. In adopting it here, he drops Mark's ἐπ- (see also 16:13; 21:24 with Mark 8:27; 11:29). The reason for the change in verbs comes to light in the further change of Mark's ἀγαθόν, "good" (a masculine adjective modifying με, "me," and relating to the address "Good Teacher"), to περὶ τοῦ ἀγαθοῦ, "concerning the good" (a neuter expression relating to the question "What good thing shall I do?").

In the next clause the deletion of Mark's "no one . . . except" enables Matthew to bring forward "one" for a parallel with v 16 and leads to the insertion of "is" and the shifting of the definite article from "God" to "good." God's name vanishes. The result is a broad hint that Jesus is the good one—Jesus rather than God or, better, Jesus *as* God (cf. Matthew's emphasis on Jesus' deity; also Ps 145:9; *m. Ber.* 9:2; Str-B 1. 809). The hint will become a proclamation in 20:15, where the employer in the distinctive parable of the workers in the vineyard says, "I am good." The calling of the employer ὁ κύριος (20:8) as well as οἰκοδεσπότη/-ου (cf. 10:25; 13:27) leaves little doubt concerning his identity as Jesus.

For further emphasis on keeping the law as doing the good, Matthew composes the sentence "But if you want to enter into life, keep the commandments." θέλεις comes from his favorite vocabulary (18,8) and occurs with εἰ five times as an insertion. "To enter into life" echoes 18:8, 9 (cf.

7:14; 25:46 for distinctive instances of the prepositional phrase alone). τήρησον is a Mattheanism (5,1) that never has a parallel in the other synoptics, does not appear at all in Luke, and occurs only once in Mark. "The commandments" comes from Mark's parallel to the next verse (Mark 10:19). Throughout vv 16-17, then, Matthew emphasizes keeping the law; and in v 17 he also protects the divine goodness of Jesus.

19:18-19 (Mark 10:19; Luke 18:20) The pirating of "the commandments" from Mark's "You know the commandments" in v 17 leads to a substitute for that clause in v 18. Matthew gains the substitute by anticipating the similar story of the lawyer in Mark 12:28-34. Thus we read "Which [commandments]?" taken from Mark 12:28 (see v 19b for another anticipation of that story and cf. "one" in v 16 with Mark 12:28). The insertion of "Teacher" in 22:36 (cf. Mark 12:28) matches v 16 in the present chapter and shows that Matthew associates the two stories. The question needs to come from Jesus' interlocutor, however; so Matthew introduces it with "He [the interlocutor] says to him [Jesus]." The historical present λέγει with asyndeton typifies Matthew's style (21,6). In this rabbinic conversation between teacher and student that Matthew is developing, the speaking must now return to Jesus. Therefore the evangelist inserts "And Jesus said." Notably, Jesus' name comes into the introduction of his quoting some OT commandments, whereas it dropped out of his asking why the interlocutor asked him concerning the good (see v 17). As ever, Matthew's Jesus teaches the law.

The definite article τό (not in Mark or Luke) sets off the quoted commandments as a kind of catechism (cf. our expression "the Pater Noster"). The first four commandments quoted come from the second table of the decalogue as those that deal most closely with conduct toward fellow men. Jesus chooses them with a view to his telling the interlocutor to sell his possessions and give to the poor. Matthew's use of the imperatival future with οὐ, instead of Mark's subjunctive of prohibition (so also Jas 2:11), conforms to 5:21 and the Hebrew and Septuagintal texts of Exod 20:13-16; Deut 5:17-20. The agreement of Luke with Mark in the subjunctive of prohibition favors that Luke's order of the commandments— "Do not commit adultery" before "Do not murder"—reflects their original order in Mark. We should then follow that reading in Mark, represented by A W Θ Φ *f*¹³ 157 *pm* lat C1 and the Byzantine family, and regard the reverse in B ℵ^corr C Δ Ψ *pc* syr^s cop^sa,bo as the result of scribal assimilation to the OT and Matthew. The text of Matthew exercised more influence on scribes than the text of Luke did. Therefore, just as Matthew conforms the commandments to their verbal form in the OT, he also conforms them to their order in the OT—but probably to their order in his Hebrew OT rather than in the LXX (see Gundry, *Use of the OT* 17-19, concerning OT text-critical complications). Desire to conform Jesus' words to the OT also leads to omission (as in Luke) of Mark's "Do not defraud," apparently an interpretation of "You shall not covet" (Exod 21:10; Deut 5:21), which may have been influenced by Lev 19:13 (cf. v 11); Deut 24:14; Sir 4:1.

In v 19 Jesus doubles back for the last commandment of the first table: "Honor [your] father and mother." Omission of Mark's σου after πατέρα follows the pattern of 15:4a, where Matthew omitted it after both πατέρα and μητέρα (cf. Mark 7:10 and Gundry, *Use of the OT* 12). In view of Jesus' using the fifth commandment in an attack on rabbinic tradition (see 15:1-9; Mark 7:1-13), he probably reserves that commandment till last in the present dialogue to emphasize its importance as a means of closing loopholes devised in the oral law. To emphasize love, Matthew adds "and you shall love your neighbor as yourself," which anticipates 22:39; Mark 12:31 (cf. Matt 5:43-47; 9:13; 12:7; Rom 13:8-10; Gal 5:14). The commandment to love neighbors is associated with commandments from the decalogue also in *T. Iss.* 5:2; *T. Dan* 5:3, but we have to reckon with the possibility of influence from the NT on those testaments (cf. CD 6:18, 20).

19:20 (*Mark 10:20; Luke 18:21*) For a parallel with v 20a, "And he said to him" changes to "says to him." The historical present of λέγει with asyndeton again typifies Matthew's style (21,6). Mark's later phrase "from my youth" supplies Matthew with a descriptive identification of Jesus' interlocutor as "the youth." Thus, in the interests of the church's accepting young people, a grown man who looks back on his youth becomes a lad still in his youth.

"Teacher" drops out, as also in Luke, perhaps because it seems redundant after v 16 and inappropriate in proximity to the youth's pained response to Jesus' demand. Since Matthew has made the grown-up a youth, "from my youth" naturally falls from the end of the statement "All these things I have kept." Matthew adds a question, which he composes by drawing up "is lacking" from the later statement in Mark, "One thing is lacking in your case," by changing "is lacking" to "I lack," and by writing before it an interrogative τί (cf. v 17) and a favorite adverb, ἔτι (4,2; cf. Luke 18:22): "In what respect do I still lack?" This inserted question stresses the young man's deficiency in surpassing righteousness (cf. 5:20).

It is hard to tell whether Matthew or later copyists of his gospel reversed the order of Mark's words ταῦτα πάντα (literally "these things all") for the sake of smoothness. We might think that because of its middle voice Mark's ἐφυλαξάμην means "I have guarded myself [from the conduct prohibited in the commandments quoted]" (cf. Acts 21:25; 2 Tim 4:15) and that Matthew and Luke switched to the active voice, ἐφύλαξα, to get the meaning "I have kept [the commandments]." But since in the LXX of the Pentateuch, from which the commandments are taken, the verb is often deponent and since the negative meaning of the reflexive understanding does not fit the last quoted command to honor father and mother, we do better to see no difference in meaning between the middle and active forms. ὑστερέω takes its object in the genitive. Therefore τί needs to be understood as an accusative of reference, "In what respect?" (so also Mark's σε, "In your case, with respect to you"). The question hardly represents a catechumen's desire for perfection. Jesus' interlocutor had not yet stepped onto the road of discipleship.

19:21 (*Mark 10:21; Luke 18:22*) Matthew omits Mark's "And . . . looking at him loved him and. . . ." Only "Jesus" and "said to him" remain. The latter changes to the typically Matthean historical present λέγει αὐτῷ with asyndeton (see the comments on v 20) or to ἔφη αὐτῷ (also typical— 6,1; see Aland for the textual variation). ἔφη αὐτῷ would compensate for the replacement of ἔφη in v 20a. Either reading results in an exclusive

387

emphasis on the rigorous command that follows. The severity of tone fits the youth's apparent refusal to obey. With other agreements between Matthew and Luke against Mark, Luke's omission of Jesus' love suggests Matthean influence.

"If you want to be perfect" replaces "One thing is lacking in your case" and takes its form under parallel influence from v 17d ("but if you want to enter into life"), which Matthew inserted. He likes θέλεις (18,8) and has already used Mark's ὑστερεῖ (see the comments on v 20). He did so in order to free himself to emphasize discipleship as perfection, as in 5:48 (contrast Luke 6:36). But since τέλειος connotes maturity as a concomitant of perfection, he also achieves a contrast between the youthfulness of Jesus' interlocutor (so Matthew alone) and the perfection of maturity demanded by Jesus. In other words, lack of perfection, or of maturity, means lack of discipleship (see v 22). τέλειος belongs to a family of Mattheanisms with the stem τελ- (16,7).

Matthew rejoins Mark in "go," but changes "sell whatever you have" to "sell your possessions," exactly as in Luke 12:33 except for the singular of the verb and pronoun and the advancing of the pronoun. Mark's "whatever you have" appeared in 13:44, a composition by Matthew; and in 6:19 (cf. Luke 12:33) he replaced the command to sell possessions with the prohibition of laying up treasures on earth. The coming references to giving to the poor and having treasure in heaven remind Matthew of 6:19, and Mark's present parallel reminds him of 13:44. Thus he compensates for his earlier replacement of the tradition behind Luke 12:33, and he avoids repeating Mark's expression. Cf. 25:14 for another insertion of τὰ ὑπάρχοντα.

That νεανίσκος has a semantic range falling within *modern* boundaries of adulthood in no way makes Matthew's designation compatible with Mark's and Luke's ἐκ νεότητός μου at the historical level; for νεότητος covers the period of being νεανίσκος (cf. 1 Tim 4:12 and many passages in extrabiblical literature, e.g., Philo *Jos.* 37, 40, 44, 50, 52, 56, 80, 85, 99, 105-6, 119, 127-29, 161, 254, 258, where νεότης applies to Joseph as νεανίσκος and νεανίας) and Matthew's dropping ἐκ νεότητός μου, inserting νεανίσκος, and adding τέλειος for a contrast with νεανίσκος show he intends to reduce the age of the rich man. Correspondingly, in Mark and Luke ἐκ νεότητός μου puts the period of having been νεανίσκος in the past. Diogenes Laertius (8.10) quotes Pythagoras as saying νεανίσκος means a young man in the second twenty years of his life; but he immediately adds that such a young man is μειράκιον, "a lad, a stripling" or, as in the Loeb translation, "not yet grown up." Philo (*Opif.* 105) quotes Hippocrates as saying νεανίσκος means a young man in his fourth heptad (i.e., 22-28 years old); but the young man is not yet an adult male (ἀνήρ). Note: In Philo *Cher.* 114 νεανίας (of which νεανίσκος is a diminutive) contrasts with τέλειος, just as in Matthew!

Perfection denotes discipleship as such, not a high level of discipleship; for in context the question has to do with attaining eternal life, and Matthew does not elsewhere distinguish two levels of true discipleship. Cf. the relinquishment of personal property in 1QS 1:12 and the use of תָּמִים in 1QS passim. Perfection does not imply complete sinlessness and full virtue as matters of fact. But it does imply observable dedication to those qualities of conduct. That Jesus did not command all his followers to sell all their possessions gives comfort only to the kind of people to whom he *would* issue that command.

19:22 (Mark 10:22; Luke 18:23) Matthew's ἀκούσας, "hearing," typifies his diction (10,3), substitutes for Mark's στυγνάσας, "becoming gloomy," and supports Matthew's preceding emphasis on Jesus' words (cf. the comments on 16:2-3). Again Luke's agreement with Matthew against Mark suggests some dependence on the first gospel. Matthew inserts "the youth" a second time for linkage with v 20. The insertion drives home the necessity that youth renounce affluence and obey Jesus' call to discipleship, just as vv 13-15 opened the church to young people. According to some of the textual evidence, including B it^(a,b,c,ff1,n) syr^(c,s,p) Diatessaron (see the UBS), Matthew adds τοῦτον to τὸν λόγον. If accepted, the addition would make a parallel with τὸν λόγον τοῦτον in v 11 v.1. Indeed, the two occurrences of the demonstrative support each other in the question of their originality. Further support comes from ταῦτα in Luke's present parallel (cf. the above-noted agreements between Matthew and Luke against Mark).

19:23 (Mark 10:23; Luke 18:24) The story ends with a conversation between Jesus and his disciples. But Matthew will divide the conversation between vv 26 and 27 in order to start a new section with v 27. As in Luke, δέ replaces Mark's καί to contrast the difficulty of a rich man's entering the kingdom with the necessity that the young man sell his possessions and give to the poor before following Jesus. Mark's "looking around" falls out, as it does every time Matthew comes across one of its six occurrences in Mark. Here the omission leaves the stress wholly on Jesus' words (cf. the comments on v 21 compared with Mark 10:21a). Mark's λέγει, not with asyndeton, changes to εἶπεν. For emphasis on Jesus' words and a parallel with vv 24a and 28b, Matthew characteristically inserts "Truly I say to you" (15,8). The insertion results in the displacement of Mark's "How" with "that," which he uses often, though not always, after "Truly I say to you." The substitution of "a rich [man]" for "they who have possessions" prepares for and parallels "a rich [man]" in the next saying. The putting of "hardly" right before "will enter" in the middle of the clause contrasts with Mark and Luke and makes the text read smoothly.

19:24 (Mark 10:24-25; Luke 18:25) Mark's "the disciples were astounded at his [Jesus'] words" drops out lest it mar Matthew's portrait of the disciples as those who have understanding. Because of this omission, Matthew also omits "Jesus . . . answering" and changes "says to them" to "I say to you" after retaining "And again." Thus a statement about Jesus' teaching becomes a part of that teaching. Omissions of the disciples' astonishment and Jesus' answering make pointless a repetition of the saying about the difficulty of entering the kingdom. Therefore Matthew also omits the rest of Mark 10:24 and goes to "It is easier for a camel to go through a needle's eye than for a rich [man] to enter the kingdom of God." According to one set of variant readings, Matthew draws up "to enter" from Mark's next clause, uses it to displace "to go through," and leaves readers to supply "to enter" in the next clause. According to another set of variant readings, Matthew follows Mark in writing "to go through" in the first clause and "to enter" in the second. In the second clause Matthew advances "to enter" (if it is original) for conformity with v 23, where a similar change in the order of words produced a smoother text. Against his usual practice, he also retains "of God" with "the kingdom," probably for variation from the parallel v 23c (see 12:28; 21:31, 43 with comments ad loc.).

Lexicons discuss the synonyms used for a needle's eye in the various gospels and different textual traditions. As the largest beast of burden in Palestine, the camel made a good figure (cf. 23:24). As the smallest opening in a familiar object, the needle's eye made an equally good figure. The same saying occurs in *b. Ber.* 55b, with the elephant substituted, and indicates something humanly impossible (cf. the Koran, *Sura* 7:38). A small gate named "the Needle's Eye" does not stand behind Jesus' saying, but probably arose out of the saying as an interpretative notion. We should also repress the urge to interpret the camel as a rope or cable and the needle's eye as a narrow gorge.

19:25 (Mark 10:26; Luke 18:26) Typically, Matthew adds ἀκούσαντες (10,3). The addition makes a parallel with v 22 and again emphasizes the words of Jesus. Luke's "they who heard" seems to show Matthew's influence. The further and characteristic addition of οἱ μαθηταί (31,5) echoes v 23 and associates discipleship with hearing Jesus' words. Mark's "were amazed" stays, but περισσῶς yields to σφόδρα, a favorite of Matthew (5,2). The adverb moves to a position after the verb for smoother reading. After "saying," Matthew omits Mark's πρὸς ἑαυτούς (which is to be accepted instead of the variant Alexandrian correction πρὸς αὐτόν). The omission allows the disciples to speak the following question to Jesus, as disciples ought to do in order to gain more understanding than they already have. In fact, Matthew can here retain the disciples' amazement without spoiling their understanding (contrast v 24 with Mark 10:24) only because the question elicited by their amazement leads to increased understanding (cf. 13:12). In the question, a typically Matthean ἄρα (4,1) replaces Mark's καί to establish a tighter logical bond with Jesus' foregoing remarks. Thus the question reads, "Who then can be saved?" and shows that the disciples have understood Jesus well enough to see an apparent contradiction between wealth as a sign of God's favor (as often in the OT) and wealth as an obstacle to entering God's kingdom (so Jesus). Matthew likes ἄρα (4,1).

19:26 (Mark 10:27; Luke 18:27) To contrast Jesus' answer with the disciples' foregoing question, Matthew supplies δέ (so also Luke, but not Mark). As in v 23a, Mark's "says" changes to "said" (so also Luke). Though Matthew retains "looking at" in disagreement with his omitting similar participles in vv 21 and 23, he moves αὐτοῖς from the participle to the main verb to emphasize Jesus' speaking. This emphasis led to the previous omissions.

Jesus' saying carries an allusion to Gen 18:14 (cf. Job 10:13 LXX; 42:2; Zech 8:6; see Gundry, *Use of the OT* 38-39, for a comparison of texts, and W. C. van Unnik in *Verborum Veritas. Festschrift für G. Stählin zum 70. Geburtstag* [ed. O. Böcher and K. Haacker; Wuppertal: Brockhaus, 1970] 32-33 for extrabiblical background). For a parallel with "all things" in the second line Matthew inserts "this thing" in the first line; and for clarity he inserts "is" in the first line and leaves the reader to supply the verb in the second line (cf. his penchant for οὗτός ἐστιν—12,0). As in Luke, Mark's "but not with God" falls away. In Matthew the deletion results in a couplet of lines consonant with the evangelist's love of parallelism:

With men this is impossible,
But with God all things [are] possible.

In the second line Matthew replaces Mark's γάρ with δέ in order to gain antithesis. "With God" moves to the beginning of the line for an exact parallel with the word order in the first line and a resultant emphasis on the contrast between weak men and God Almighty. Even the dropping of Mark's and Luke's definite article with God's name contributes to the exactitude of the parallelism in that now θεῷ as well as ἀνθρώποις is anarthrous.

The unusualness of παρά with the dative in the sense "with, for" may show slavish dependence on the LXX of Gen 18:14. But Matthew likes the construction (2,2); and πάντα, "all things," disagrees with the awkward ῥῆμα, "word," of the LXX for דָּבָר. The different understanding of דָּבָר as "thing, matter" agrees with the OT Peshitta.

ACCEPTING GENTILES IN THE CHURCH
19:27-20:16 (Mark 10:28-31; Luke 18:28-30; 22:28-30)

19:27 (Mark 10:28; Luke 18:28) To indicate a new beginning, Matthew inserts his beloved τότε (66,17). Another favorite of his, ἀποκριθείς . . . εἶπεν (29,6), replaces Mark's ἤρξατο λέγειν. "To him" and Peter's "Behold, we have left all and followed you!" stay unchanged except for a possible shift from ἠκολουθήκαμεν to ἠκολουθήσαμεν. Mark's perfect tense is ill suited to the linearity and incompleteness of the disciples' following Jesus (cf. the v.1. in Mark's text), and the aorist form matches the aorist of ἀφήκαμεν. The insertion of "What then shall we have?" echoes "Who then . . . ?" in v 25b and produces a second line, which is synthetically parallel to Peter's line about leaving all to follow Jesus. The content of the added question sets the stage both for Jesus' answer in the remainder of chap. 19 and for the distinctive parable in 20:1-16, where amount of pay figures prominently. Both ἄρα and the form ἔσται come from Matthew's special vocabulary (4,1; 16,5).

Peter seems to mean that he and his fellow disciples have made sacrifices of the sort the rich man found too costly. Jesus' initial response carries a positive tone and implies an acceptance of Peter's statement at face value (see vv 28-29). Only later does Jesus warn that the first will be last and the last, first (v 30).

19:28 (Mark 10:29; Luke 18:29; 22:28-30) To the introduction of Jesus' reply Matthew adds δέ (so also Luke) for a contrast with Peter's statement and question. Despite his liking Mark's ἔφη (6,1), he writes εἶπεν and inserts "to them" (so also Luke). The results are a parallel with v 26a and a clear indication that Jesus directs his answer to all the disciples, not to Peter alone. "To them" links with the plural of the second person pro-

391

nouns following. To "Truly I say to you" Matthew adds "that" for a parallel with his distinctive wording in v 23b.

Jesus' beginning to answer Peter's question reminds Matthew of what Jesus said at the Last Supper just after the disciples disputed over greatness and right before Jesus predicted Peter's denials and restoration (cf. Luke 22:24-34). This reminder leads him to import the tradition behind Luke 22:28-30. The emphatic "you" comes over. "But" falls away because of "that." "Are" also drops out. And "who stayed with me" (so Luke) changes to "who have followed me" in assimilation to "we have followed you" in Peter's evocative statement (v 27). The consequent parallelism accentuates the motif of discipleship and suits Matthew's fondness for ἀκολουθέω (8,0).

To make the saying exclusively futuristic, Matthew revises "in my trials" to read "in the regeneration." In view of the following context, "regeneration" probably refers to Israel's renewal when God fully establishes his kingdom on earth. Elsewhere in the NT the term occurs only at Titus 3:5, there concerning individual regeneration during the present age. The Aramaic and Hebrew languages have no equivalent, though ancient Jewish literature often exhibits the thought (see Isa 65:17; 66:22; *Tg. Onq.* Deut 32:12; *Tg. Neb.* Mic 7:14; 1QS 4:25; 1QH 13:11-12; *1 Enoch* 45:4-5; 72:1; *2 Apoc. Bar.* 32:1-4, 6; 44:12; 57:2; cf. 2 Pet 3:13; Rev 21:1-5). Matthew, however, has some fondness for the two components of the term— viz., πάλιν (8,4; cf. the comments on 15:29) and γένεσις (which helps make up the title of the first paragraph in his gospel—1:1; see also 1:18). Therefore it is easy to understand his use of παλιγγενεσία.

Matthew omits "And I grant you" in order to change "just as my Father granted me a kingdom" to "when the Son of man sits on the throne of his glory." We might ask why he rejects Jesus' kingdom in view of his introducing it elsewhere (see the comments on 13:41). But he does not reject it. He only transmutes it into the figure of a glorious throne. This figure marks a typically Matthean assimilation of parallel lines to each other (see the reference to thrones in the next line) and an equally typical assimilation of Jesus' words to OT phraseology (see 1 Sam 2:8; Isa 22:23; Jer 14:21; 17:12; cf. Wis 9:10; Sir 47:11; *1 Enoch* 9:4; 14:18-20; 45:3; 51:3; 55:4; 61:8; 62:2, 3, 5; 69:27, 29; 71:7; 108:12; *T. Levi* 5:1; *b. Ḥag.* 13a). Four out of five times in Matthew θρόνου occurs distinctively. It occurs not at all in Mark and three times in Luke, only once on Jesus' lips. There are two more distinctive occurrences of δόξης in 25:31, besides four shared occurrences. καθίσῃ is a favorite of Matthew (3,2; cf. κάθημαι—8,0). "Son of man" is common, but Matthew has a penchant for it (5,3). His whole clause parallels the unique saying at 25:31 in the use of ὅταν, ὁ υἱὸς τοῦ ἀνθρώπου, καθίσῃ/-ει, and ἐπὶ θρόνου δόξης αὐτοῦ.

The clause promising the disciples that they will eat and drink at Jesus' table in his kingdom (so Luke) drops out because of Matthew's foregoing transmutation of the kingdom into a throne. Matthew therefore goes directly to the disciples' thrones. To καθήσεσθε he adds καὶ ὑμεῖς to parallel "the Son of man" in the preceding line. The v.l. καὶ αὐτοί is also parallel, and either one of these emphatic expressions would represent Matthew's style (15,3; 14,3). To match "judging the twelve tribes of Israel," the phrase "on thrones" gains "twelve" and θρόνων becomes θρόνους, an accusative like φυλάς. The shift in cases favors that Matthew is assimilating the phrases rather than that Luke omitted "twelve" because of Judas Iscariot (see Acts 1:15-26 for Luke's concern to fill up the roll of the twelve). Matthew's word order reads more smoothly than Luke's τὰς δώδεκα φυλὰς κρίνοντες τοῦ Ἰσραήλ.

Neither in Jesus' intention nor in Matthew's does "Israel" mean the church (cf. the distinction maintained in 8:11, 12; 21:43; 22:7; 23:32-36; 27:25). Particular reference to the twelve tribes supports a distinction. But we may question whether judging the twelve tribes means assisting Jesus in sentencing them to punishment, or assisting him in governing them during his earthly reign. Jesus seems to have drawn his promise from Dan 7:9-27, where "thrones were set up, and the Ancient of Days took his seat . . . thousands upon thousands were attending him . . . one like a son of man was coming . . . and to him was given dominion, glory, and a kingdom . . . and judgment was passed in favor of the saints of the Most High, and the time arrived when the saints took possession of the kingdom . . . then the kingdom, the dominion, and the greatness of the kingdoms under the whole heaven will be given to the people of the saints of the Most High." Hence, judging means governing (cf. Luke 22:24-27 and the Son of man's lack of apostolic assistants at the great assize even in passages peculiar to Matthew, such as 13:41; 16:27b; 25:31-46). In Daniel the saints who receive dominion are Israel, their subjects the Gentiles. Jesus promises dominion to the twelve and makes Israel their subjects. Matthew's use of "regeneration" agrees with Jesus' promise by making the governing of Israel harmonize with Israel's renewal in a messianic kingdom on earth. Thus Matthew does not regard God's rejection of Israel (21:43) as permanent (cf. his insistence in 10:23 on continuing the mission to Israel—see comments ad loc.).

Though some would dispute the chronological accuracy of the placement of Luke 22:28-30 at the Last Supper, it is supported by the allusion to the messianic banquet in the Words of Institution vis-à-vis the mention of the messianic banquet in Luke 22:28-30. Peter's prominence in the following material would have provided Matthew an easy association of that tradition with his present passage, where Peter figures prominently. Luke's reference to Jesus' πειρασμοῖς, "trials," may look like the product of Luke's own interest in that motif (see Luke 4:13; 8:13 for insertions; also Acts 20:19; cf. Luke's frequent use of verbs with the stem μεν-). But the immediately foregoing considerations and the Matthean character of the differences in Matthew's version of the saying as compared with Luke's suggest that Luke draws his emphasis on trials from Jesus himself, in this very saying. The lack of an Aramaic equivalent for Matthew's alternative to "trials," viz., "regeneration," further supports this suggestion (see *TDNT* 1. 686-89 on παλιγγενεσία in Greek literature and Josephus *Ant.* 11.3.9 §66 for an application to the postexilic restoration of Israel). For κρίνω in the sense of governing, see especially Pss 2:10 LXX; 9:5, 9 LXX; 1 Macc 9:73; *Pss. Sol.* 17:28.

We need not think that Matthew means to assign the governing of one tribe to each of the twelve disciples. Collective governing easily satisfies his wording. Luke's saying lacks "twelve" with "thrones" because of the contextual reference to a betrayer among the twelve disciples. But that may have caused Jesus not to speak the number just as easily as it could have caused Luke to omit it. Introduction of the number by Matthew would have come easily for parallelistic reasons, especially since the new context mentions no betrayer. Cf. further 1 Cor 6:2; Rev 20:4; Wis 3:1, 8.

The passages 8:12; 21:43; 27:25 may seem to militate against Israel's restoration in the kingdom of the Son of man. But 10:23 calls for continuing the mission to Israel till his parousia. And Matthew puts the prediction that Jerusalem will bless Jesus when he comes in the name of the Lord (23:37-39) later than the triumphal entry (21:1-17). This position contrasts with the position in Luke 13:34-35 and points away from fulfillment at the triumphal entry (so Luke) and toward fulfillment in the conversion of Jews at the parousia (cf. Zech 12:10–13:1; Rom 11:25-27). Matt 8:12; 21:43; 27:25 refer, then, to judgment suffered by the Jewish masses, and especially by their leaders, who disbelieve the gospel and do not survive up to the parousia.

19:29 (Mark 10:29-30; Luke 18:29-30) In v 29 Matthew rejoins Mark and connects the saying to the preceding by inserting "And." Mark's "There is no one . . . except" gives way to the Mattheanism "everyone" (πᾶς— 63,25-26). Another favorite, ὅστις (23,5), replaces ὅς. "House" becomes "houses" to match the following plurals (except for "father or mother," which can hardly tolerate pluralizing) and compensates for the coming omission of "houses" in Mark 10:30. Mark's order of mother before father apparently reflects the circumstance of Joseph's having died and Mary's still living at the time Jesus spoke (cf. the complete omission of "father" in Mark's next verse). The reversal in Matthew conforms to the normal order, based on patriarchalism. Characteristically, Matthew exchanges "the gospel" (so Mark) for Jesus' "name" (ὀνόματος—5,5) as the reason for leaving houses, brothers, sisters, father, mother, children, and fields (cf. 1:21, 23). Because of revisions at the beginning of the sentence, "receive" changes to "will receive" in the promise of manifold reward. But Matthew's preoccupation with the persecutions being suffered by the church—a preoccupation evident throughout his gospel—also leads him to omit the seemingly self-contradictory "now in this season houses and brothers and sisters and mothers and children and fields, with persecutions" (so Mark). In Matthew, then, compensation lies solely in the future: "and will inherit eternal life" (see the comments on 6:33). "In the coming age" disappears because the balancing phrase "in this season" has already disappeared. The addition "will inherit" makes a parallel with "will receive" in the preceding line. It also compensates for the omission of "I may inherit" in v 16 (cf. Mark 10:17) and brings the promise to a conclusion with a verb that is appropriate to rebirth, houses, family, and fields.

Matthew's liking of πολύς (23,1) and the numerous agreements between Matthew and Luke against Mark in the preceding verses favor the v.l. πολλαπλασίονα in B L 1010 syr^pal cop^sa eth^ms Diatessaron Origen Cyril as well as in Luke. But ἑκατονταπλασίονα (so also Mark) has broader support (see the UBS and Metzger, *Textual Commentary* ad loc.). Especially in Mark, where Jesus speaks first of present reward, we must take the multiplied reward metaphorically: one's fellow disciples are a new family offering homes and estates. Multiplication of father and mother would not make literal sense. Matthew's omission of present reward leaves the nature of the multiplication somewhat obscure.

19:30 (Mark 10:31) "But many first ones will be last, and last ones, first" comes from Mark without change, except that the definite article is omitted before the second ἔσχατοι for a parallel with the first ἔσχατοι, which is anarthrous (cf. 20:16). The exception presumes the article stood in Matthew's text of Mark (cf. the variant omission). "Many" does not distinguish people inside each category, but describes the people in each category as numerous. Thus "many" is almost synonymous with "all."

20:1 Without interruption Matthew goes to the unique parable of the laborers in the vineyard (20:1-16). In fact, the Mattheanism γάρ (62-63,15) makes the parable substantiate and interpret the saying in 19:30 (cf. the comments on v 16). The equivalence of "the owner of the vineyard" (v 8) with what we will read in Jesus' parable of the wicked husbandmen (21:33-46, esp. v 40) suggests that Matthew is adapting the later parable to the saying about the first and last (19:30). The metaphor of a vineyard comes from the OT (see esp. Isa 5:1-7; Jer 12:10) and agrees with his frequent use of the OT. The financial dimensions of the parable tally with his former occupation of collecting taxes. He relishes ὁμοία and its cognates (8,8) and also "the kingdom of heaven" (25,7). "The kingdom of heaven is like" plus a dative noun occurs four out of six times in Matthew without a synoptic counterpart (13:31, 33, 44, 45, 47; 20:1). The present dative noun—viz., ἀνθρώπῳ—not only belongs to Matthew's favorite vocabulary in general (35,17), but also occurs often without a parallel at the beginning of Matthew's parables, usually with a following appositive (see the comments on 18:23-35). The present appositive, οἰκοδεσπότῃ, also belongs to Matthew's favorite vocabulary (2,4) and immediately implies sovereign authority, which will become important later in the parable. "Is like a man [who is] a master of a house" has already occurred in 13:52, another of Matthew's compositions.

The second line of v 1 begins with the Mattheanism ὅστις (23,5), subject of the common verb ἐξῆλθεν. The note of time (literally "together with the early morning," i.e., "early in the morning") consists of the adverb ἅμα used as a preposition with πρωΐ (another adverb) used as its object. Notably, Matthew used ἅμα as a preposition in its only other occurrence in his gospel—at 13:29, which was his own composition. The word does not appear in the other gospels. With the exception of 28:1, where he and Luke will rephrase Mark 16:2, Matthew omits πρωΐ only when omitting a whole passage. On the other hand, he inserted the adverb in 16:3. μισθώσασθαι occurs only here in v 7 in the entire NT, and throughout his gospel Matthew shows special liking of its cognate μισθός (2,5). ἐργάτας belongs to a family of words he likes (6,7—ἐργ-; see also vv 2, 8). "Into his vineyard" reappears without the possessive in vv 4 and 7. Its three occurrences exhibit the parallelism we have come to expect in Matthew's compositions. Another parable concerning a vineyard is peculiar to Matthew in 21:28. The twelve hours of the day are counted from sunrise, when work began.

20:2 The landowner's agreeing with the workers on a denarius for the day opens v 2. The nominative participial form of συμφωνήσας typifies Matthew's style. The word itself appeared in 18:19, another composition of his; and it will reappear below in v 13. The denarius also appeared in 18:28, yet another of his compositions, and will reappear below in vv 9, 10, 13. Matthew often inserts ἡμέραν and uses it in distinctive passages (15,9). The rest of v 2 indicates that the landowner sent the workers into his vineyard. The comments on 15:24 explain the Matthean character of ἀπέστειλεν . . . εἰς (3,1).

On a single denarius as the average daily wage of manual laborers, see Pliny 33.3; Tacitus *Ann.* 1.17; Tob 5:14; and rabbinic references in Str-B 1. 831. We might translate a denarius into twenty-five American cents, but wide differences between ancient and modern standards of living make such a translation misleading. Agreement between the employer and the employed left the employed without grounds for grumbling.

20:3 Verse 3 begins with another nominative participle that typifies Matthew's style and diction, viz., ἐξελθών (10,4). Its echoing ἐξῆλθεν in v 1 and reappearing in this same nominative participial form in vv 5 and 6 make parallelism, as usual. ὥραν is a favorite of Matthew (6,5). In 27:46 he will replace "at the ninth hour" (Mark 15:34) with "about the ninth hour," which is comparable to "about the third hour" here. The further phrases "about the sixth [hour] and ninth hour" (v 5), "about the eleventh [hour]" (v 6), and "about the eleventh hour" (v 9) exhibit the same Matthean traits and make another typical set of parallels. The remainder of v 3 indicates that the landowner "saw others standing idle in the market place." ἄλλους belongs to Matthew's preferred diction (14,4). It will reappear in v 6. Cf. 6:5; 13:2 for distinctive perfect and pluperfect forms of ἵστημι that are similar to ἑστῶτας and—again in typically Matthean parallelism—ἑστῶτας and ἑστήκατε (v 6). ἀργούς, "idle, not working," belongs to a group of cognates having the stem ἐργ-, which Matthew likes well (6,7), and will reappear in v 6 as a parallel to the present occurrence.

20:4-5 Verses 4-5 contain a number of Mattheanisms: ἐκείνοις (26,9), ὑπάγετε (5,6—see also vv 7, 14 for parallel instances), ὑμεῖς (15,3), δίκαιον (9-10,7-6), δώσω (8-9,10), ὃ ἐάν (14,1—cf. esp. 16:19; 18:18), ἀπῆλθον (14,11), πάλιν (8,4—though often omitted for contextual reasons), ἐποίησεν (19,19), and ὡσαύτως (2,2). The last two of these will appear together again at 21:36 in contrast with Mark 12:4; Luke 20:11.

20:6-7 εὗρεν also comes from Matthew's special vocabulary (7,8). The historical present λέγει/-ουσιν, twice with asyndeton, marks his style (47,11 overall, 21,6 with asyndeton—vv 6b, 7ac, 8a). Further favorites are evident in ὧδε (7,1), ὅλην (7,3), and ἡμέραν (15,9). "Day" echoes v 2, "hired" echoes v 1, and the whole of v 7d—"you also go into the vineyard"—exactly matches v 4b in accord with Matthew's taste for parallelism (see the comments on those verses for his diction).

Concerning unemployment, cf. Luke 16:3; Josephus *Ant.* 20.9.7 §§219-20. Questions whether the unemployed were really waiting for a job or only making an excuse for their idleness, whether their standing really means standing at the ready for an opportunity to work or carries only the weak meaning of being present in a sitting position, and whether the employer's hiring laborers late in the day implies desperation to get the harvest in or need not imply harvesttime at all—these and similar questions rest on overestimating the desire for realism and failing to recognize Matthew's composition, in which literary tastes and theological purposes infringe the actualities of daily life (contrast J. D. M. Derrett in *Studies in Jewish Legal History in Honour of David Daube* [ed. B. S. Jackson; London: Journal of Jewish Studies, February, 1974] 64-91).

20:8 The genitive absolute construction typifies Matthew's style, and this very genitive absolute ὀψίας . . . γενομένης is a favorite of his (2,1). The change from οἰκοδεσπότης (v 1) to κύριος picks up a term he likes to apply to Jesus (34,15). Further Mattheanisms come forward in κάλεσον (8,8), ἐργάτας (0,3 and 6,7 for cognates with ἐργ-), ἀπόδος (5,11), μισθόν (2,5), ἀρξάμενος (not auxiliary—3,2), ἕως (13,14), and πρώτων (2,5-6). Putting the last before the first grows out of 19:30 (cf. v 16); and the practice of paying workers every day comes from the OT (see Lev 19:13; Deut 24:14-15).

The singular number of "the wage" derives from the single denarius each worker was going to receive. Ordinarily, the early comers would have received their wage first and left without seeing how much the late comers received. Matthew reverses the order of payment in order to illustrate the firstness of the last and the lastness of the first, a reversal necessary to the grumbling of the early comers. It is possible to interpret ἀρξάμενος ἀπό . . . ἕως as meaning "not omitting [or 'including'] . . . and" without regard to order (cf. Jeremias, *Parables* 35-36 n. 41). But the Greek is more naturally translated "beginning from . . . to," and Matthew composes the passage to illustrate the reversal of first and last.

20:9-12 Both vv 9 and 10 begin with ἐλθόντες, which is typical of Matthew's style (10,10). The two occurrences make a parallel to his liking. Repetitions of "the first" (cf. v 8) and "a denarius apiece" add to the parallelism. ἐνόμισαν was an insertion in 5:17 and 10:34. We come across more Mattheanisms in ἔλαβον (bis) and λήμψονται (21,16) and πλεῖον (3,1; cf. Matthew's liking πολύς—23,1—and 11:20; 21:8 for the only two occurrences of πλεῖστος in Matthew, both times as insertions). The final phrase in v 10, "they also," echoes and parallels "you also" in vv 4 and 7. Again typically, v 11 opens with an aorist participle in the nominative, λαβόντες (3,7; cf. v 10). In the statement about the grumbling of the first-hired laborers, κατά + the genitive represents the evangelist's style (10,1); and οἰκοδεσπότου reappears to emphasize the sovereignty of Jesus, whom the landowner represents (cf. v 1). Matthew introduces the laborers' words in his most usual manner, i.e., with λέγοντες (61,23). "These last" comes out of 19:30. "One hour" consists of two words that appear often without parallel (μίαν—24,7; ὥραν—6,5). Matthew also likes ἐποίησαν/ἐποίησας (19,19; cf. v 5). The uncommon use of this verb in the sense of working, often explained as a Semitism (cf. Exod 36:1 LXX; Ruth 2:19; Prov 31:13), stems from his characteristic desire for a parallel with the next line, where the verb carries its usual meaning. βάρος occurs only here in the gospels, but belongs to a family of Mattheanisms (4-3,1 for βαρ-); and ἡμέρας is another favorite of Matthew (15,9; cf. vv 2, 6).

The first comers charge their employer with two injustices: failure to take account of the difference between twelve hours of work and one hour of work and failure to take account of the difference between the heat of midday and the cool of the evening. The separate mention of τὸν καύσωνα after "the burden of the day" and the usualness of the meaning "scorching east wind" for καύσων in the LXX (see Job 27:21; Jer 18:17; 28:1; Ezek 17:10; 19:12; Hos 12:2; 13:15; Jonah 4:8 for unambiguous examples and cf. Matthew's penchant for OT usage) favor that meaning rather than heat in general. The absence of a polite address shows the first comers' indignation. In contrast, the employer will politely address one of them (see v 13).

20:13-15 Again we meet a string of Mattheanisms: ἀποκριθείς . . . εἶπεν (29,6), ἑνί (24,7), and ἑταῖρε, which occurs only in Matthew in the NT, always in the vocative, and each time in a remonstrance to one who has wronged the speaker (see also 22:12; 26:50 for insertions). ἀδικῶ belongs to a family of cognates with the stem δικ-, well liked by Matthew (18-19, 10-9; cf. v 4). The question whether the first comers went from the foreman to their employer or whether the employer, overhearing their noisy remarks, came out of his house does not concern Matthew. For the sake of the story the evangelist probably means his readers to think—however unrealistically—that the employer is standing by all the time. In v 14 we read ἆρον, which, though not quite so common as in Mark and Luke, occurs distinctively five times in Matthew (2,3). Further evidence of Matthew's composition is seen in σόν (6,2), ὕπαγε (5,6; cf. v 4), θέλω (18,8), the parallel between "to this last" and 19:30; 20:8; and especially 20:12, δοῦναι (8-9,10; cf. v 4), and ὡς καί (1,2).

Typically, v 15 consists of two parallel lines. Each begins with ἤ, which appears unusually often in the first gospel (32,12). Omission of the first ἤ, with some of the textual evidence, would not damage the parallelism, and the second ἤ would remain as a Mattheanism. "Is it not permissible . . . ?" recalls Matthew's insertion "Is it permissible . . . ?" in 12:10. θέλω reappears as an echo of v 14 (18,8). Similarly, ποιῆσαι echoes vv 5, 12 (bis—19,19). ἐμοῖς will be inserted in 25:27 and has already appeared in unique material at 18:20, besides two shared instances. ὀφθαλμός and πονηρός typify Matthew's diction (8,1; 10,4). An "evil eye" stands for covetousness (cf. 6:23). "I am good" echoes 19:17 (see the comments ad loc. for interpretation).

20:16 The final verse of the parable echoes 19:30. But Matthew switches the order of the lines because of the parable and its requirement that the last be paid first in order that the first may see the landowner's generosity before they themselves receive their equal (but contractual) wage—and therefore may grumble. The addition of "the" (not in 19:30) to the first instance of "last" and to the second instance of "first" makes the adjectives refer anaphorically to the different groups of laborers in the parable. At the beginning Matthew characteristically adds οὕτως (18,5) to bring the saying as a whole into relation with the parable.

But what does Matthew mean by this parabolic interpretation of the saying about the first and the last? His importing extraneous material concerning the twelve disciples' judging the twelve tribes of Israel (see the comments on 19:28) shows that he takes Peter's statement and question (19:27) as a reference to the original Jewish disciples. Therefore the late comers in the parable represent Gentiles who have entered the church only recently from Matthew's standpoint, and the first comers represent their detractors among Jewish Christians. The parable makes the entire passage to which it belongs advocate churchly acceptance of believing Gentiles. Thus Matthew has proved true to the probable intention of Jesus, whose statement that many first will be last and the last will be first throws down all confidence in one's own sacrifices, however necessary to discipleship they may be (cf. 19:30 with 19:27-28 and parallels). Eternal life will come only to workers—i.e., disciples—but as a gift based on divine generosity, not as a wage based on precise calculation. Those who worked all day and got exactly what they deserved are merely a foil to those who got far better than they deserved, as is shown by the contrastive selection only of those who worked one hour—those in between are left out. This doctrine of divine grace invalidates anti-Gentile bias (cf. Matthew's emphasis on brotherly love).

It is wrong to grumble against generosity to others when one has himself received justice. Here the generosity provides a subsistence wage—manual laborers and their families lived a day at a time on the denarius earned the previous day—in place of a wage below subsistence. See also the comments on 6:22-23. Despite the element of work, the employer's generosity consists in grace, for the point of the full denarius lies in its being unearned for the most part (contrast *Cant. Rab.* 6.2; *Qoh. Rab.* 5.11). Is it possible that Matthew was influenced by immediate payment of those who worked on the cloisters of the Temple only one hour (Josephus *Ant.* 20.9.7 §§219-20)?

Because the grumbling centers on the amount of payment, not on the order of payment, some argue that the parable did not originally illustrate the reversal of first and last, but only divine generosity. Without the reversal in order of payment, however, the grumbling—a major feature of the parable—would never have occurred. Thus the reversal is as important as the grumbling it makes possible. And the grumbling provides opportunity for enhancing the employer's generosity and for the often overlooked criticism against comparing one's own hardships in service with the lot of others. In other words, emphasizing the employer's generosity at the expense of the reversed order of payment might allow separation of the parable from its context in Matthew, but it would require an illegitimate dismemberment of the parable itself and an oversight of the link between its negative point and Peter's comment in the prior passage. Cf. 21:28-32.

CHURCHLY ACCEPTANCE OF THE BLIND, THE LAME, AND YOUNG PEOPLE

20:17–21:16 (Mark 10:32–11:10, 15-17; Luke 18:31-43; 19:28-40, 45-46, 22:24-27; John 12:12-19)

This section begins with the ascent to Jerusalem and ends with arrival there. Jesus predicts his death and resurrection (20:17-19), answers a request for special honor by pointing to his service to others (20:20-28), and exemplifies such service by giving sight to two blind men (20:29-34) and entering Jerusalem and the Temple in order to heal the blind and lame and defend the youth who praise him there (21:1-16). Thus Matthew presents Jesus as an example to the church, which ought likewise to serve those who enter from deprived classes.

20:17 (Mark 10:32; Luke 18:31) Verse 17 immediately confronts us with a text-critical choice between καὶ ἀναβαίνων ὁ Ἰησοῦς εἰς Ἱεροσόλυμα (so most of the textual tradition, led by א C D L W Θ f^{13} 33 565 it vg syr^{c,s,h}) and μέλλων δὲ ἀναβαίνειν Ἰησοῦς εἰς Ἱεροσόλυμα (so B cop$^{sa?(bo?)}$ and, with variation in word order and addition of ὁ to Ἰησοῦς, f^1 syr^p Origen). We might think that μέλλων represents a topographical correction by a copyist in that before Jesus leaves Jericho—and he does not leave Jericho till v 29—he is only *about* to go up to Jerusalem. Yet Matthew likes μέλλω (5-6,1). Therefore it is better to see a topographical correction by Matthew himself, a correction that copyists assimilated toward Mark's text by omitting μέλλων. Later in this same verse, Matthew's undisputed omission of a phrase containing another form of μέλλω favors μέλλων here by suggesting that the later omission resulted from a present addition. The insertion of μέλλω before πίνειν in v 22 also favors μέλλων here by suggesting that Matthew wanted a parallel between two occurrences of the word. The present insertion forces the change of Mark's "they were going up" to the supplementary infinitive "to go up." Matthew delays "on the road" because the journey is only about to start. The reason for the delay confirms the originality of μέλλων (see also the comments on v 29).

Matthew reaches into Mark's next line and takes "Jesus" for his subject. Consequently, where Mark writes that "they" were going up to Jerusalem, Matthew writes with a Christological emphasis that "Jesus" was going up to Jerusalem. The statements "And Jesus was preceding them, and they were dumbfounded; and they who were following feared" (so Mark) drop out lest they mar Matthew's portrait of disciples as understanding. Since he has not yet gotten a main verb, Matthew omits Mark's "and" and changes the participle "taking along" to "took along." To "the twelve" he characteristically adds "disciples" (μαθητάς—31,5; not in Mark or Luke or some Matthean textual tradition assimilated to the other synoptics—see the UBS and Metzger, *Textual Commentary* ad loc.). This compensates for the omission of "they who were following" and makes the twelve's going with Jesus for his ministry of service represent a life of discipleship. The insertion "by themselves" makes the following statement to the disciples, whom Matthew has just cleared of dumbfoundedness, a private instruction of those who already have understanding in order that they may have more (cf. 13:12). Matthew inserts ἰδίαν six times in his gospel. Finally he indicates the start of the journey up to Jerusalem by inserting "on the road," omitted above and not present in Mark or Luke here. As in Luke, Mark's auxiliary ἤρξατο disappears. τὰ μέλλοντα αὐτῷ συμβαίνειν also disappears, because Matthew recently added μέλλων. Since Luke agrees in the omission but has nothing corresponding to the recent addition, we have evidence of Matthew's influence on him.

20:18-19 (Mark 10:33-34; Luke 18:31-34) Matthew leaves out Mark's recitative ὅτι. Otherwise, he follows Mark in Jesus' prediction, "Behold, we are going up to Jerusalem, and the Son of man will be given over to the chief priests and scribes, and they will condemn him to death and give him over to the Gentiles. . . ." One small but significant difference from Mark does appear, however, in the omission of the definite article before "scribes." This makes the chief priests and scribes a united front antagonistic to Jesus (cf. 16:21 and Luke 9:22 with Mark 8:31). In the further part of Jesus' prediction the giving him over to the Gentiles implies that they will ridicule him, spit on him, whip him, and kill him (so Mark). All the verbs in this series end with -ουσιν, "they" (i.e., the Gentiles). But Matthew, in contrast with Mark and Luke, omits the spitting as otiose after the ridiculing and reduces the finite verbs to telic articular infinitives. Thus the center of attention shifts from the action of the Gentiles to the malevolent purpose of the Jewish leaders in handing Jesus over to them. Insertions of the telic articular infinitive preceded by εἰς occur also in 26:2; 27:31 (cf. Mark 14:55) and always refer to Jesus' crucifixion. For Mark's "they will kill" Matthew substitutes "to crucify" to specify the manner of Jesus' death (cf. other insertions of σταυρόω in 23:34; 26:2). On Matthew's changing "and after three days he will arise" to "and on the third day he will be raised [or 'will rise']," see the comments on 12:40; 16:21 (cf. 17:22-23).

20:20 (Mark 10:35) The story of the request for places of honor on Jesus' right and left begins with a replacement of καί with τότε (66,17). This favorite conjunction of Matthew correlates the prediction of Jesus' passion (20:17-19) with the teaching of service to others: the former illustrates the latter (see esp. v 28). προσῆλθεν is another favorite (38,6) and replaces Mark's προσπορεύονται to connote Jesus' dignity (see the comments on 4:3; 8:14). The mother of Zebedee's sons replaces their names, James and John, lest the request mar Matthew's portrait of the disciples as understanding Jesus' teaching. Especially after his prediction of the passion, their asking for honored places would imply ignorance. μήτηρ is another Mattheanism (3,6). The plurals even in Matthew's form of Jesus' reply (vv 22-23) show that the mother is a secondary addition. Matthew inserts "with her sons" to prepare for her reference to "these my sons" (v 21). "Worshipping" replaces "saying to him" for emphasis on Jesus' deity. προσκυνοῦσα represents Matthew's diction both alone (6,5) and in combination with προσῆλθεν (4,0). Despite his liking διδάσκαλε (4,1), θέλομεν (18,8), and ποιήσῃς (19,19), he exchanges "Teacher, we wish that you would do for us whatever we ask" (so Mark) for "and asking something from him." Only the participle comes from Mark, but it modifies the mother. This exchange carries on Matthew's clearing the disciples of ignorance.

The mother of Zebedee's sons probably bore the name Salome (cf. 27:56 with Mark 15:40) and perhaps had Mary the mother of Jesus for a sister (see John 19:25). Family relationship, then, may lie behind the request. Had δύο stood in Mark's text (see the v.l. in the UBS), Matthew's fondness for the word would have kept him from omitting it (19,4; cf. v 21).

20:21 (Mark 10:36-37) In the introduction to Jesus' initial response, Mark's "to them" naturally becomes "to her." The same kind of change occurs throughout the rest of v 21, too. From the question "What do you want me to do for you?" Matthew lops off Mark's "me to do for you" because of his omitting "Teacher, we wish that you would do for us whatever we ask" from the last verse. The historical present λέγει with asyndeton replaces οἱ δὲ εἶπαν and typifies Matthew's writing (21,6). Changing "Give to us" to "Say" emphasizes the authority of Jesus' words, an important theme in Matthew, and suits the mother better than "Give to me" would have suited her.

In the clause introduced by the epexegetical ἵνα, Matthew advances καθίσωσιν to parallel the word order in v 23. From the preceding verse he also supplies "these my two sons" as subject, with δύο added (19,4; see esp. 26:37 in contrast with Mark 14:33). For a parallel with v 23, εὐωνύμων takes the place of Mark's ἀριστερῶν; both mean "left." The placement of σου after ἐκ δεξιῶν and its repetition after ἐξ εὐωνύμων contrast with Mark and contribute to the parallelistic structure. See 25:33, 41 for further distinctive occurrences of εὐωνύμων. The reference is to sitting on thrones, not to reclining at the messianic banquet. "In your glory" becomes "in your kingdom." Matthew likes to ascribe the kingdom to Jesus the Son of man (see 13:41; 16:28; 25:31, 34, 40; cf. the membership of James and John in the inner three [17:1; Mark 9:2; Luke 9:28] and Mark 9:38; Luke 9:54).

20:22 (Mark 10:38-39) To Mark's ὁ δὲ Ἰησοῦς εἶπεν Matthew characteristically prefixes ἀποκριθείς (29,6). But Mark's "to them" can hardly become "to her" without making nonsense of the following addresses, which necessarily refer to the two sons and therefore stay in the plural of the second person. Hence, "to them" simply vanishes. In the question "Are you able to drink the cup which I drink?" (so Mark), Matthew changes πίνω, "I drink," to μέλλω πίνειν, "I am about to drink." This parallels the insertion of Jesus' being "about to" go up to Jerusalem (v 17). Matthew has a penchant for μέλλω (5-6,1). For a cup as symbolic of testing, especially judgmental testing, see Isa 51:17; Jer 25:15-29; Ezek 23:31-34; Zech 12:2; Pss 11:6; 16:5; 75:9(8); Lam 4:21; Rev 14:10; 16:19; 17:4; 18:6; *Mart. Isa.* 5:13; and, even more appropriately, cf. tasting the cup of death in *Pal. Tg.* Gen 40:23; Deut 32:1. The second metaphor concerning Jesus' suffering and death—viz., baptism—drops out. The deletion will leave Matthew free to omit the metaphor again in the next verse. Besides, he paid special attention to Jesus' baptism as an exemplary act of obedience fulfilled long ago (see esp. the insertion 3:14-15). The historical present λέγουσιν with asyndeton replaces Mark's οἱ δὲ εἶπαν for a parallel with λέγει in v 21. Again it represents Matthew's style (21,6).

20:23 (Mark 10:39-40) Yet again for parallelism, the historical present λέγει with asyndeton replaces Mark's ὁ δὲ Ἰησοῦς εἶπεν. To the prediction "You will drink my cup" Matthew characteristically adds μέν for an antithetic parallel with δέ in the next line (15,1). The shortening of "which I am drinking" to "my" contributes to the parallel by providing a match for "my" in the next line. The figure of baptism again drops out for the sake of parallelism. There remains the statement "But the sitting on my right and left—this is not mine to give, but [it will be given] to them for whom it has been prepared by my Father." This wording follows Mark except for additions of "this" and "by my Father." The latter typifies Matthew's theology (7,2) and forms a striking contrast with the mother of Zebedee's sons.

James died as an early martyr ca. A.D. 44 (see Acts 12:2). Evidence for John's martyrdom in the middle of the first century is weak (see *IDB* 2. 954-55). According to better tradition, John died a natural death in old age, though he first suffered exile on Patmos (see John 21:22; Rev 1:9; Irenaeus *Haer.* 3.3.4; Eusebius *H.E.* 3.13, 31; 4.14; 5.8). Since the cup will later represent violent death (see 26:27, 39), Matthew hardly retains the cup but omits baptism out of regard for John's natural death (to say nothing about questions of date).

20:24 (Mark 10:41; Luke 22:24) In the account of the ten other disciples' indignation, Matthew follows his habit of omitting Mark's auxiliary ἤρξαντο. For allusion to the churchly brotherhood and a parallel with "these my two sons" (not in Mark—v 21), "concerning the two brothers" replaces "concerning James and John." This replacement also conforms to the replacement of the two names in v 20 and exhibits Matthew's love of ἀδελφός (11,8).

20:25 (Mark 10:42; Luke 22:25) To contrast Jesus' response with the doubtlessly jealous indignation of the ten, Matthew changes Mark's καί to δέ. Jesus' name advances for a Christological emphasis. Mark's "says" changes to "said," and "to them" drops out. The omission makes the following words apply to the whole church. From the clause concerning the rulers who are lords over the Gentiles Matthew omits Mark's "seem" (δοκοῦντες, elsewhere a favorite of his—6,3) and changes "to rule" to "rulers" for a closer parallel with "great [men]" in the following line. The "their" which modifies "great [men]" in Mark disappears from the second line because of foregoing and succeeding instances of the same pronoun.

20:26-27 (Mark 10:43-44; Luke 22:26) In v 26 δέ falls away from "It shall not be thus among you" in order that ἀλλ' may capture all the contrast at the start of the next line. In the first line the imperatival future "it shall not be" replaces Mark's "it is not," transforms a statement into a command, and makes a parallel with "shall be" in the second line. It also typifies Matthew's diction (16,5 for the particular form ἔσται) and therefore favors the textual tradition which contains it over the textual tradition which agrees with Mark (see the UBS). In the line "But whoever wants to become great among you shall be your servant," ἐν ὑμῖν moves up to a position just behind θέλῃ (so also Luke). This advance has the purpose of making a closer parallel with the first line of v 27, where Mark as well as Matthew writes the same phrase right after the same verb. In the command "And whoever wants to be first among you shall be your slave" (v 27), ὑμῶν pushes out Mark's πάντων despite Matthew's fondness for the latter (63,25-26). The change makes an exact parallel with ὑμῶν in the preceding line and interprets Jesus to be speaking of interpersonal relationships among his disciples, just as the context indicates (cf. 23:4).

20:28 (Mark 10:45; Luke 22:27) Matthew introduces the saying that "the Son of man did not come to be served, but to serve, i.e. [epexegetical καί], to give his life a ransom in substitution for many" with ὥσπερ, "Just as," instead of Mark's καὶ γάρ, "For even." The new conjunction suits Matthew's diction (6,3) and makes the service done by the Son of man more an example, less a reason (though Mark's "For even" probably implies an example *as* a reason). The example does not exclude kinds of service that fall short of giving one's life as a ransom for others. It simply points up the extreme to which service may attain—and did.

This saying seems to reflect the phraseology and thought of Isaiah 53. διακονη-θῆναι, "to serve," rests on Isa 53:11 read as עבד (so also the LXX, Targum, Peshitta, and Symmachus) rather than עבדי (so the MT) and understood as an infinitive (so also the Targum). δοῦναι, "to give," harks back to תָּשִׂים, "you will set, make" (Isa 53:10; cf. δῶτε, "you give," in the LXX), and τὴν ψυχὴν αὐτοῦ, "his soul," to נַפְשׁוֹ, "his soul" (see also Isa 53:11-12). That a second object is added to giving or taking life only in Isa 53:10 MT, the present saying, and 4 Macc 6:29 supports the correspondence of λύτρον, "ransom" (the second object here), with אָשָׁם, "guilt offering" (the second object in Isa 53:10). ἀντὶ πολλῶν, "in place of many," echoes both רַבִּים, "the many," in Isa 53:11-12 (cf. Matt 26:28; Dan 12:2, 10; QL passim; *m. 'Abot* 5:18) and the motif of substitution that runs throughout Isaiah 53 (see esp. vv 4-6, 8, 11-12). This motif accounts for the unique use of λύτρον, which connotes redemption by payment in equivalence, for אָשָׁם, a sacrificial term. The giving of life suffices to indicate the sacrificial character of the service rendered. λύτρον and ἀντί establish the substitutionary value of the sacrifice given in service. Cf. Rom 3:24; 2 Cor 5:21; Gal 1:4; 2:20; Eph 5:2, 25; Col 1:14; Titus 2:14; Heb 9:12; 1 Pet 1:18-19; 2:24; 3:18 and—for temporary, this-worldly atoning value to Israel in the deaths of the Maccabean martyrs—2 Macc 7:37-38; 4 Macc 1:11; 6:28-29; 17:21-22.

Since Isaiah's Servant serves the Lord by suffering death for other men, Jesus' emphasis on serving other men explains *what it means* to serve the Lord. It does not contradict serving him. In the QL "the many" often stands for all the elect. This usage favors that the present Semitic use of "many" for "all" has particular reference to believers. Does Luke's setting at the Last Supper, where the notion of service easily relates to waiting on tables, represent a historically separate occasion, the only historical occasion, or a shift (through Luke's associating service with waiting on tables and the Last Supper) from the only historical occasion, which Mark and Matthew represent? Acts 6:1-6 suggests the last possibility. Whatever the correct answer, Luke's well-known lack of emphasis on the atonement forestalls our doubting the authenticity of Matt 20:28b; Mark 10:45b merely because it is absent in Luke 22:27.

20:29 (9:27; Mark 10:46; Luke 18:35) Matthew's second version of Jesus' healing two blind men now comes into view. The first version emphasized their faith (9:27-31). The second version emphasizes the lordly compassion of Jesus in order to portray the healing as service to the needy. "And they come into Jericho" (so Mark) falls away, because Matthew has already indicated the start of Jesus' ascent from Jericho to Jerusalem by adding "being about to" in v 17 and putting "on the road" a little bit later in the same verse. So now the ascent continues: "And as they were going from Jericho." This wording is similar to Mark's, except that Matthew uses the plural, because in v 17 he omitted Jesus' going ahead of the disciples. The plural leads to deletion of Mark's "and his disciples." But Matthew retains Mark's reference to the crowd, changes its modifier ἱκανοῦ το πολύς (a favorite of his—23,1), and makes the large crowd "follow him [Jesus]" (not in Mark or Luke) to parallel the blind men's following Jesus in 9:27 (cf. v 34 here) and portray the large crowd as a vanguard of the many Gentiles who become disciples in the church age. ἠκολούθησεν is another Mattheanism (8,0).

20:30 (9:27; Mark 10:46-47; Luke 18:35-38) Typically, Matthew inserts καὶ ἰδού (34,9). This calls attention to the twoness of the blind men (so also 9:27). Mark and Luke write of only one (see the comments on 9:29-31 about Matthew's conflating the blind man in Bethsaida [Mark 8:22-26] with the blind man of Jericho, perhaps to get two witnesses—cf. 18:16—for Jesus' lordship and Davidic sonship). Thus "two blind [men]" replaces Mark's "the son of Timaeus—Bartimaeus—a blind beggar." Changing Mark's finite verb "was sitting" to the mere participle "sitting" makes the stress fall on the blind men's confessional cry. Mark's "And" disappears because Matthew used it at the beginning of the verse and continues the sentence rather than initiate a new one. The blind men hear that Jesus is passing by. But Matthew leaves out "the Nazarene" because he used and explained that designation in 2:23, perhaps also because the blind men are accepting Jesus, not rejecting him (cf. the comments on 2:23). (For a special reason he will retain the designation in 26:71.) παράγει replaces ἐστιν in reminiscence of 9:27. Luke's agreement with Matthew in having παρέρχεται, despite lacking Matthew's reason for changing Mark's verb, suggests Matthean influence.

Both Luke and Matthew omit the auxiliary ἤρξατο. As a result, Mark's "to yell and say" becomes "yelled, saying." λέγοντες is a Mattheanism (61,23). Text-critical questions bedevil the exact wording of the blind men's plea for mercy both here and in the next verse (see the UBS for evidence). Probably the Mattheanism κύριε (34,15) stands first and replaces Mark's Ἰησοῦ for emphasis on deity. υἱὲ Δαυίδ remains, but moves to last position for a parallel with 9:27 (contrast Mark and Luke). Copyists probably advanced this latter address to eliminate its awkward separation from κύριε and by this means assimilate Matthew's text to the texts of Mark and Luke. The choice between υἱέ and υἱός matters little. Omission of κύριε in part of the textual tradition obviously stems from parallel influence (see 9:27, Mark, and Luke).

20:31 (Mark 10:48; Luke 18:39) To set the first plea-cum-confession against the rebuke the blind men receive, Matthew puts δέ in place of Mark's καί. For a parallel with v 29, "the crowd" substitutes for Mark's "many." Matthew likes ὄχλος (17,1). The tense of the verb switches from imperfect to aorist. The attempt to silence the blind men results in their yelling all the more. "More greatly" replaces "much rather." Matthew retains the latter in 7:11 (cf. Luke 11:13); but here "rather" jars him, for louder yelling does not represent a contrast in kind. See 12:6; 18:4; 23:11, 17, 19 for other insertions of μεῖζον (6,0). The imperfect of "yell" becomes aorist to match "yelled" in v 30 and "rebuked" in v 31a. For a further parallel with that verse, Matthew characteristically adds λέγοντες (61,23). The blind men's second plea-cum-confession repeats the first with another reference to Jesus' lordship. This happens despite Mark's and Luke's lack of "Jesus," which "Lord" earlier replaced.

20:32 (9:28; Mark 10:49-51; Luke 18:40-41) "Jesus said" (so Mark) becomes "Jesus called them." Matthew's expression comes from the immediately following words in Mark, "Call him," and compensates for his omitting the remainder of Mark's verse, according to which they call the blind man with the words "Cheer up! Get up! He is calling you." Matthew's omission concentrates attention on Jesus' call; i.e., in Mark others issue the call on Jesus' behalf, but in Matthew Jesus himself calls the blind men— directly and authoritatively. Matthew's lordly Jesus dominates the landscape.

The blind man's throwing aside his garment, jumping up, and coming to Jesus disappear. As a result, the stress falls wholly on Jesus' words, which Matthew introduces with Mark's "and he said" minus the help of "answering, Jesus . . . to him." The subtraction is remarkable because of Matthew's fondness for Jesus' name (80,12) and ἀποκριθείς . . . εἶπεν (29,6). It stems from his observation that the blind men have not yet spoken conversationally to Jesus, but have only yelled. Except for pluralizing and improving the order of words, Matthew follows Mark in Jesus' question, "What do you want me to do for you?" (cf. vv 21, 22, 23).

20:33 (9:28; Mark 10:51; Luke 18:41) At the outset of v 33, the historical present λέγουσιν with asyndeton (a Mattheanism—21,6) replaces "And the blind man said" in reminiscence of 9:28. Mark's "Rabbi" gives way to another κύριε (so also Luke) for Matthew's characteristic emphasis on Jesus' deity (34,15; cf. vv 30 and 31). Similarly, Mark's "that I may see again" yields to "that our eyes may be opened" in reminiscence of 9:30.

20:34 (9:29-31; Mark 10:52; Luke 18:42-43) As usual, δέ replaces καί at the start of v 34. Matthew adds σπλαγχνισθείς in order to make the healing an act of service in line with vv 20-28 (cf. 18:27 for another distinctive occurrence of this form). "Jesus said to him" becomes "Jesus touched their eyes," a conflating allusion to the healing of the blind man in Bethsaida (Mark 8:22-23; cf. Matt 9:29). The switch from speaking to touching causes "Go, your faith has saved you" to drop out. Sight immediately returned and the blind men "followed him." The aorist tense of the verb replaces Mark's and Luke's imperfect. The deletion of "on the road" makes the climactic statement a general description of discipleship rather than a particular reference to the journey toward Jerusalem.

21:1-2 (Mark 11:1-2; Luke 19:28-30) The story of Jesus' entry into Jerusalem starts with a change of Mark's "they are nearing" to "they neared" and an insertion of "and they came." The insertion avoids the awkwardness of two successive but unappositional phrases beginning with εἰς: "to Jerusalem to Bethphage and Bethany" (so Mark; cf. Luke's different riddance of the awkwardness). Mark's reference to Bethany after Bethphage drops out, perhaps because in the approach toward Jerusalem pilgrims coming from Jericho first passed through Bethany on the eastern slope of the Mount of Olives and only then passed through Bethphage, situated on the Mount of Olives just across the Kidron Valley from Jerusalem. On the other hand, Matthew's insertion of ἦλθον indicates arrival in Bethphage rather than mere proximity to it (as in Mark and Luke). Arrival leaves the need for another village to which Jesus may send two disciples for animals. The omission of Bethany leaves that village to supply the need. Matthew retains "the Mount of Olives," however, and introduces it with εἰς, drawn from the rejected reference to Bethany, instead of πρός (so Mark and Luke). Thus εἰς τὸ ὄρος τῶν ἐλαιῶν (cf. Zech 14:4) stands in apposition to εἰς Βηθφαγή.

To the beginning of the next clause Matthew adds his beloved τότε (66,17) and, for Christological emphasis, the name of Jesus (80,12). As in Luke, "sends" changes to "sent." Mark's "two of his disciples" becomes a streamlined "two disciples." Luke retains Mark's partitive genitive, but shares Matthew's omission of the possessive pronoun. λέγων is typical of Matthew (61,23), replaces Mark's "and he says," and appears in Luke, too.

Despite his liking ὑπάγετε (5,6), Matthew substitutes πορεύεσθε (13,10) to set up a parallel with v 6. "Entering into it [viz., the village]" drops out as redundant after the preceding command "Go into the village opposite you." "Entering" occurs only once in Matthew, but eight times in Mark and five times in Luke. Matthew inserts ὄνον, "a donkey," to correspond with ὄνον in his coming quotation of Zech 9:9 (v 5) and to substitute for Mark's clause "on which no man [literally 'no one of men'] has ever sat." As it turns out, this donkey was a mother and *had* been ridden. That her colt accompanied her eliminates any need to describe him as unbroken, for after being broken a colt would be taken from the mother. To "a donkey" Matthew attaches "tied." This comes from Mark, but there it modifies "a colt" (cf. Gen 49:11). Finally the colt comes into view, minus its being tied but plus its being "with her" (not in Mark or Luke). Mark's finite verb λύσατε becomes a typically Matthean initial participle, λύσαντες (so also Luke). "Him" drops out because Matthew added the mother donkey and made her the one that is tied. Mark's φέρετε yields to ἀγάγετε (so also Luke) because the animals were not carried (the strict meaning of φέρετε) but led (so ἀγάγετε). The insertion "to me" makes a Christological emphasis.

Cf. *m. Sanh.* 2:5. See J. D. M. Derrett in *NovT* 13 (1971) 243-49 on Jesus' acting as a king in impressing the animal (cf. Num 16:15; 1 Sam 8:17) and on the possibility of his borrowing from a public pool of animals and (in Mark) promising to return the animal even though he is the true owner.

21:3 (Mark 11:3; Luke 19:31) Omission of Mark's ποιεῖτε τοῦτο changes the syntax and meaning of τί, so that it becomes indefinite (τι) and goes with the preceding: "And if anyone says anything to you" instead of "Why are you doing this?" Thus Matthew focuses attention on the following reference to Jesus' lordship: "you shall say that their Lord has need." Matthew prefers forms of εἴρω (18,9) and substitutes ἐρεῖτε (so also Luke) for εἴπατε. Since he dislikes the recitative ὅτι, we should probably understand his added ὅτι as epexegetical, "that." (Luke's addition of οὕτως as well as of ὅτι makes the latter recitative.) Though χρείαν takes an objective genitive, which would here yield "need of them," elsewhere Matthew's and Mark's genitives depending on χρείαν follow the verb ἔχω, which is preceded by χρείαν (see Matt 9:12; 26:65; Mark 2:17; 14:63). Here the genitive αὐτῶν follows ὁ κύριος and comes before both χρείαν and ἔχει; therefore it goes with ὁ κύριος, which in this story originally meant "master, owner" (with reference to Jesus' kingly prerogative of requisitioning means of transportation), but at least in Matthew has gained the overtone of "Lord."

In Mark's clause "and immediately he will send [futuristic present] him [the colt] back here," the expression πάλιν ὧδε, "back here," makes the clause part of the disciples' response, i.e., a promise that Jesus will shortly return the colt. For though ὧδε might point equally well to the place of Jesus' speaking, πάλιν requires a return to the place of the colt's origin. See the UBS and Metzger, *Textual Commentary* ad loc., on text-critical variations. Matthew omits πάλιν ὧδε despite his fondness for both adverbs (8,4; 7,1). The omission makes the clause a prediction that the disciples' questioner will send the animals. His submission to Jesus' demand underscores Jesus' lordship, which pushes out any mention of the conscientious return of the colt. The replacement of Mark's καί with δέ has already signalled the shift from a continuation of the disciples' message to Jesus' prediction of obedient response. Mark's futuristic present tense of the verb becomes a future tense, the word order is smoothed out, and, of course, Matthew pluralizes the pronoun.

21:4-5 To show the fulfillment of Jesus' prediction, Matthew now writes "And this happened" (cf. 1:22; 26:56). These words start an introduction to his quotation of Zech 9:9 (not in Mark or Luke; but see John 12:15). Thus the fulfillment of Jesus' prediction has roots in the OT. "This" does not refer to the triumphal entry, however; for the narrative has not yet reached that point and Matthew's fulfillment-quotations regularly hark backward. "This" refers, rather, to Jesus' instructing the two disciples to get the donkey and her colt. The emphasis stays, then, on Jesus' authoritative command. The introduction to the quotation continues, "in order that it might be fulfilled that was spoken [so also 1:22; 2:15; 4:14; 12:17] through the prophet, saying [so also the probably original reading in 13:35; also 1:22 and 2:15, with the addition of 'by the Lord,' and 2:17; 4:14; 8:17; 12:17; 27:9, with the addition of 'Isaiah' or 'Jeremiah']." That the essential part of the quotation comes from a minor prophet leads to omission of his name. The lack of reference to Jesus' divine sonship keeps Matthew from writing "by the Lord" (see the comments on 1:22; 2:15).

Zech 9:9 begins, "Rejoice greatly, daughter of Zion!" and goes on to announce the deliverance of Israel. But according to Matthew, God has rejected Israel (see 21:43), at least for the time being (cf. the comments on 10:23; 19:28). Furthermore, the city of Jerusalem is going to be upset rather than joyful over Jesus' entry (v 10). Therefore Matthew switches to the similar line from Isa 62:11, "Say to the daughter of Zion." The replacement of "Rejoice greatly" with "Say to" makes the following an evangelistic challenge to unconverted Israel. Zechariah's references to the king and his coming appeal to Matthew (βασιλεύς—6,9; see the comments on 3:11). Matthew's omitting Zechariah's description of the king as righteous and saving (see esp. the LXX) is surprising in view of his fondness for δίκαιος

(9-10,7-6) and σῴζω (5,1), but it stems from the present rejection of Israel. The center of gravity shifts to the king's meekness—a prominent motif in Matthew (see the comments on 5:5; 11:29)—and to the king's being mounted on a donkey (ὄνον) and a colt (πῶλον), the foal of a donkey. The evangelist has carefully prepared for this by introducing a mother donkey (ὄνον) earlier, prior to mentioning the colt (πῶλον) in Mark and Luke. It is hard to think that Matthew misunderstood Zechariah's synonymous parallelism in making its first line refer to a mother donkey; for his disagreements with the LXX show consultation of the Hebrew text; and a misunderstanding of the common Hebrew word חֲמוֹר, "male donkey," as a mother ὄνος is unlikely. Ambiguity in the gender of ὄνος, however, gave him opportunity to make a distinction. That the male colt had not been ridden (though he may have carried other kinds of burdens) opens the possibility of a historical reminiscence in the mention of two animals. For the sight of an unridden donkey colt accompanying its mother has remained common in Palestine up to modern times.

The donkey represents meekness in that a conqueror would have ridden a warhorse. Contrast *Pss. Sol.* 17:23-27, but cf. *Pss. Sol.* 17:37. Matthew agrees with the LXX, Targum, Peshitta, and Aquila in taking עָנִי, "humble" (MT), as עָנָו, "meek." Since copyists often confused י and ו, the latter probably appeared in the Hebrew text used by Matthew. On the mixture of agreements and disagreements with the Hebrew and LXX, see Gundry, *Use of the OT* 120-21. Since Matthew omits that the colt had not been ridden, the mother animal hardly comes in for emphasis on that point (against Gundry, *Use of the OT* 197-99).

21:6 (Mark 11:4-6; Luke 19:32-34) To compare the two disciples' actions with Jesus' orders, Matthew replaces Mark's καί with δέ (so also Luke). The nominative participle πορευθέντες shoves out ἀπῆλθον and typifies Matthew's diction (8,4). The substitute makes a parallel with πορεύεσθε in Jesus' instruction (v 2) and thus stresses exact obedience. Matthew's characteristic insertion of οἱ μαθηταί (31,5) makes that kind of obedience definitive of discipleship. He underlines the point even more emphatically by substituting "and doing just as Jesus ordered them" in place of a mere rehearsal of details concerning the finding and loosing of the colt, the conversation between the disciples and some bystanders, and the release of the colt to the disciples. Each of the words in the substitute comes from Mark's rehearsal of those details. The sole exception, "ordered," replaces Mark's "said" for stress on Jesus' authority. Cf. the comments on 1:24 for conformity to OT phraseology, and see 26:19 for another insertion of συνέταξεν and 27:10 for an occurrence in unique material.

21:7 (Mark 11:7; Luke 19:35) As in v 2, the verb of leading (ἤγαγον, so also Luke) replaces the verb of carrying (φέρουσιν, so Mark). Before mentioning the colt, Matthew inserts τὴν ὄνον, "the [mother] donkey," to bring the narrative in line with the foregoing quotation. Interest in the two animals results in deletion of "to Jesus" (but cf. the insertion of "to me" in v 2). Matthew goes immediately to the putting of garments on the animals. ἐπέθηκεν, which he inserts five times, takes the place of ἐπιβάλλουσιν. He adds ἐπ' after the verb for a parallel with the next line. The omission of αὐ-τῶν, "their," after τὰ ἱμάτια suggests that in Matthew the latter refers to saddle clothes rather than to people's garments (see also v 8). ἐκάθισεν gains the prefix ἐπ- for a parallel with ἐπέθηκαν in the preceding line. Addition of the prefix leads to a change of Mark's ἐπ' αὐτόν, "on him," to ἐπάνω αὐ-τῶν, "on top of them," which probably refers to the saddle garments rather than to the animals. ἐπάνω is a favorite of Matthew (7,1). It is doubtful that he intends his readers to visualize a trick rider balancing himself on two animals at the same time. Therefore we are to think that the garments were draped over both animals, just as in modern Palestine both mother donkeys and their unridden colts trotting after them have garments put across their backs (see E. F. F. Bishop, *Jesus of Palestine* [London: Lutterworth, 1955] 212). Though Jesus sat on top of the garments only on the colt, the asso-ciation of the garmented mother makes a kind of wide throne. Indeed, widening the throne to play up Jesus' royal majesty appears to underlie Matthew's importation of a second animal and his knowing breakup of the synonymous parallelism in Zech 9:9.

21:8 (Mark 11:8; Luke 19:36) The replacement of καί with δέ (so also Luke) clearly distinguishes the following actions of the very large crowd from the foregoing actions of the two disciples. Mark's "many" gives way to the even more emphatic "the very large crowd" for a predictive allusion to the numerous Gentiles that were going to enter the church. See 11:20 for another insertion of the superlative πλεῖστος. Distinctive occurrences of ὄχλος abound throughout Matthew (17,1). As in Luke, ἔστρωσαν ad-vances from its awkward later position in Mark. The strengthening of αὐ-τῶν, "their," to ἑαυτῶν, "their own," supports the suggestion that Matthew means to distinguish saddle clothes from people's garments. Otherwise, he is distinguishing the crowd's garments, spread on the road, from the two disciples' garments, draped over the animals. In an echo of 20:17, ἐν (so also Luke) replaces Mark's εἰς with the noun for "road."

In the next line Matthew advances "cutting" and changes it to "they were cutting." στιβάδας, which because of association with "out of the fields" carries its ordinary meaning of a layer of straw, grass, reeds, and the like, becomes κλάδους, "branches," a more natural and usual word than Mark's hapax legomenon. The switch from a layer of straw, grass, and reeds to branches provides a pavement more suitable to royalty and dictates a corresponding switch from fields to trees—hence, "from the trees" instead of "out of the fields." Mark leaves the spreading to be inferred. But Mat-thew supplies "they were spreading" and adds "on the road." As a result, there is a close parallel with the first line of the verse. Notably, against the aorist tense of the verb in the first line, Matthew puts the verbs of the second line in the imperfect tense, probably to indicate the linear process of cutting branches and spreading them on the road in contrast with the simple action of spreading garments on the road. Cf. 2 Kgs 9:13; John 12:13; 1 Macc 13:51; 2 Macc 10:7; *Tg. Esth II* Esth 3:8.

21:9 (Mark 11:9-10; Luke 19:37-38) For a parallel with v 8 and another allusion to the many Gentiles who were coming into the church, Matthew characteristically adds "the crowds" (17,1; cf. Luke's "the multitude of the disciples"). The description of the crowds as going before Jesus and following him matches Mark, except for the insertion of αὐτόν to make προάγοντες transitive (see also 14:22 with Mark 6:45). To "they were yelling" Matthew adds "saying" (λέγοντες—61,23). "Hosanna. . . ! Blessed [is] he who comes in the name of the Lord" comes from Ps 118:25-26. Matthew omits Mark's next line, "Blessed [is] the coming kingdom of our father David," and compensates for it by inserting "to the son of David" after "Hosanna." The insertion links this passage with 20:30-31 and changes the Jewish expectation of a Davidic kingdom to a Christian and typically Matthean confession of Jesus himself as the messianic son of David (υἱὸς Δαυίδ—4,2). We might also suspect that Matthew found objectionable the designation of David as "our father," in view of the exclusivity of divine fatherhood (see esp. 23:9). "Hosanna in the heights!" indicates matching heavenly jubilation among angels (cf. Ps 148:1).

Cf. *Did.* 10:6; see Gundry, *Use of the OT* 40-43, on the pre-NT change of Hosanna from a prayer meaning "Save now" to a shout of jubilation. Cf. "God save the king!" which, as shown by the absence of a comma after "God" and the escalation of an original period to an exclamation mark, has undergone the same evolution.

21:10 (Mark 11:11) Matthew lops off "into the Temple" at the end of Mark's clause beginning "And he entered into Jerusalem." The omitted phrase seemed awkward after "into Jerusalem" and unnecessary in view of its appearance shortly in v 12. That is to say, Matthew delays Jesus' entry into the Temple for the account of Jesus' cleansing the Temple, which moves up one day into the present passage. Mark's finite verbal construction reduces to a characteristic genitive absolute. The weight of emphasis consequently shifts to the next statement, where Matthew exchanges Mark's participial phrase "and having looked around at all things" for the full-scale clause "all the city was shaken, saying." His special vocabulary is evident in ἐσείσθη (3,0), πᾶσα (63,25-26), πόλις (18,3), and λέγουσα (61,23). "Was shaken" connotes the divine majesty of Jesus (see the comments on 8:24). Additional emphasis accrues from πᾶσα, suggested by Mark's πάντα. The question of the city, "Who is this?" (not in Mark or Luke), exhibits a Mattheanism in οὗτος + ἐστιν (12,0).

21:11 Matthew keeps on composing in v 11. δέ sets "the crowds" opposite the city of Jerusalem, just mentioned. In answer to the question asked by the shaken city, the crowds were saying, "This is the prophet Jesus, from Nazareth of Galilee." The Jewish leaders are ignorant; but the crowds know who Jesus is, and their understanding marks them as disciples representing the worldwide church to come. οὗτός ἐστιν (12,0) echoes the question and betrays the hand of Matthew, who also has special interest in crowds (17,1), prophets (19,6), Jesus' name (80,12), Nazareth (2,1), Galilee (3,2), and collocations of Nazareth and Galilee for identification of Jesus (see 2:22-23; 26:68 with 71).

Cf. 16:14; 21:46; John 1:21; 7:40; Acts 3:22; 7:37. Normally Matthew puts the crowds in a favorable light, and elsewhere he uses Nazareth and Galilee positively for Jesus' fulfillment of prophecy (see 2:23; 4:14-16). Therefore we can hardly think that the crowds' identifying Jesus as a prophet from Nazareth of Galilee represents a false messianic belief. The inclusivism of Matthew's Christology leaves room for Jesus' prophethood even though this motif lacks prominence elsewhere in the first gospel.

21:12-13 (Mark 11:15-17; Luke 19:45-46) Now Matthew skips the onset of evening, Jesus' going back to Bethany for the night, and the return to Jerusalem the next day with the cursing of the fig tree along the way (Mark 11:11b-15a) and takes up Jesus' cleansing the Temple. The cleansing moves up one day, then. Matthew advances it in order to bring Jesus' comments on servanthood, the healing of the blind men, the entry into Jerusalem, and the cleansing of the Temple to a sweeping conclusion in the added material concerning the blind, the lame, and the young people in the Temple (vv 14-16). In other words, he unites all these materials to portray Jesus as the divine servant, a model of accepting and serving the lesser members of society—"the little people"—who belong to the church.

Mark's and Luke's "having entered" becomes "entered" for an antithetic parallel with "threw out" in the next line. To emphasize the prophetic nature of the cleansing, Matthew repeats the name of Jesus, whom the crowds have just identified as a prophet with that name. Mark's "he began" drops out. Before "the sellers and buyers in the Temple" Matthew adds "all" (63,25-26) to emphasize the irresistibility of this prophet, whose deity has caused the whole city to be shaken (cf. v 10). He keeps Jesus' overturning the tables of the money changers and the seats of those who were selling doves—the main verb advances somewhat to avoid a long suspense—but we miss Mark's statements that Jesus was not allowing anyone to carry a vessel through the Temple and that he was teaching. These omissions are shared by Luke and cause emphasis to fall on the following quotations of the OT, to which the prohibition of using the Temple area as a shortcut does not relate. They also make the quotations entirely accusatory, with no trace of a didactic element.

Matthew further sharpens the tone of the accusation against unbelieving Jerusalem by making the question "Is it not written . . . ?" (so Mark) into the declaration "It is written . . ." (so also Luke), by leaving "for all the Gentiles" (so Mark) out of the quotation (so also Luke), and by changing the perfect tense πεποιήκατε (so Mark; cf. Luke's aorist) to the present tense ποιεῖτε, a change that at once contemporizes the accusation and favors a date of Matthew's writing prior to the destruction of the Temple in A.D. 70. Changing Mark's "he was saying" to "he says" contributes to this updating. The historical present λέγει is a favorite of Matthew (47,11). Though he favors the Gentiles, their mention here would have diverted attention from the accusatory point he wants to make against unbelieving Jewry: not even the Jews (let alone Gentiles) use the Temple properly for prayer. Omission of the Gentiles leaves the contrast between "house of prayer" and "den of thieves" without competition from Mark's additional contrast between "all the Gentiles" and "you." Now the "you" stands in terrifying isolation. Additionally, Matthew may omit the Gentiles because they are to become disciples and live as church members outside Palestine, not make pilgrimages to Jerusalem in order to pray in the Temple. "My house shall be called a house of prayer" comes from Isa 56:7; "but you have made it a den of robbers," from Jer 7:11. As usual, Matthew omits Mark's recitative ὅτι. Luke shares both the omission and Matthew's putting αὐτόν before the verb (contrast Mark). The series of agreements between Matthew and Luke against Mark suggests Matthean influence.

Cf. Lev 5:7; 12:8 *m. Šeqal.* 1:3. One could go directly from the Mount of Olives to the Temple without passing through any other part of Jerusalem. Some think that Jesus was acting out Zech 14:21: "and there will no longer be a merchant in the house of the Lord of hosts in that day." Perhaps so, but Jesus expressly refers to Isa 56:7 and Jer 7:11 (see Gundry, *Use of the OT* 19, for textual comparisons). The use of Isa 56:7 shows Jesus protesting the din of commerce that made difficult the praying of Gentiles in the outer court. The use of Jer 7:11 shows him protesting exorbitant rates of exchange for foreign currency and high prices for sacrifices (cf. John 2:14-15). Cf. Ezekiel 40–48; Mal 3:1-4; *Pss. Sol.* 17:33; *m. Ber.* 9:5.

21:14 Verses 14-17 are largely distinctive and exhibit Matthew's favorite diction and habit of alluding to the OT. He likes προσῆλθον (38,6), τυφλοί (9,0), χωλοί (3,0), ἱερῷ (5,0), and ἐθεράπευσεν (10,0). προσῆλθον suggests Jesus' dignity (see the comments on 4:3; 8:14). τυφλοί echoes the story in 20:29-34. "In the Temple" echoes v 12. There is an evident allusion to 2 Sam 5:8, according to which the saying "The blind or the lame shall not come into the house [the LXX adds 'of the Lord']" arose out of David's statement that he hates "the lame and the blind." Since the statement has to do with David's entering Jerusalem in conquest and since Matthew has just written about the acclamation of Jesus as "the son of David" (v 9—so the first gospel alone), his mind naturally turned to the OT passage. But David was using "the lame and the blind" as a figurative epithet for the Jebusites. By healing the blind and the lame right within the Temple, Jesus denies the Jews' false deduction from David's statement (cf. 1QSa 2:19-25; 1QM 7:4-5; 4QD^b/CD 15:15-17; *m. Ḥag.* 1:1). In this way Matthew combines royal messianism (Jesus as son of David) with prophetic messianism (Jesus as miracle worker).

21:15 Verse 15 opens with the Mattheanism ἰδόντες (10-11,7). "The chief priests and the scribes" appeared distinctively in 2:4 (see the comments ad loc. for historical explanation). Here the phrase comes from the next verse in Mark, viz., Mark 11:18. τὰ θαυμάσια is hapax in the NT but makes a typically Matthean allusion to the OT, where it often appears in the LXX with ποιέω, as in the present verse. Matthew inserts its cognate θαυμάζω in 15:31; 21:20, and we may surmise that θαυμαστή in 21:42 triggered his use of the Septuagintalism. Further examples of Matthew's favorite diction are ἐποίησεν (19,19), παῖδας (5,1; cf. the use of its diminutive form for disciples in 18:1-14), κράζοντας (5,0), ἱερῷ (5,1), and λέγοντας (61,23). "Yelling" echoes v 9, and "in the Temple" echoes vv 12 and 14. Similarly, "Hosanna to the son of David!" echoes v 9 with its allusion to Ps 118:25 and its Davidic Christology. "Became indignant" may echo 20:24

(cf. 26:8). The indignation of the chief priests and scribes helps Matthew intensify the guilt of unbelieving Jews (cf. the comments on v 13).

21:16 (Luke 19:39-40) In v 16 Matthew seems to revise some traditional material that appears in Luke 19:39-44 (esp. vv 39-40) just *before* Jesus' entry into Jerusalem; i.e., the future crying out of the stones of Jerusalem (so the tradition recorded by Luke) is incorporated by Matthew and transmuted into the present crying out of the children, who represent the church's little people, especially young people. In fact, we can now see that Matthew probably got his children (τέκνα in Luke 19:44) and their crying out (forms of κράζω in both gospels) from the tradition. "And some of the Pharisees from the crowd" (so Luke) drops out because Matthew has just referred to the chief priests and the scribes (v 15) and because he regularly portrays the crowd as disciples. "Teacher, rebuke your disciples" becomes "Do you hear what these are saying?" because Matthew has shifted from disciples to children. ἀκούεις is a Mattheanism (26,6).

In the introduction to the reply, Jesus' name appears, as often in the first gospel (80,12). The historical present λέγει typifies Matthew's style (47,11). Thus "But Jesus says to them" substitutes for "And answering, he said" (so Luke). This substitution takes place despite Matthew's fondness for the traditional expression (29,6) and despite his having changed the request of Jesus' opponents to a question inviting an answer. The reason lies in Matthew's turning the following reply into a counter question consisting not so much of Jesus' words—hence the replacement of another Mattheanism, λέγω ὑμῖν (27,7—so Luke)—as in a quotation of the OT, such as he likes to insert. The replacement begins with ναί (2,2) and continues with οὐδέποτε ἀνέγνωτε ... (3,0). Alone, too, οὐδέποτε is a favorite of Matthew (5,0). "Have you never read ... ?" implies that the chief priests and scribes *had* read the passage about to be quoted. Therefore their unscriptural indignation stands condemned all the more.

The quotation comes from Ps 8:3(2). It is introduced with a recitative ὅτι, which Matthew usually omits because he tends to think that the verb for "read" needs a recitative ὅτι (see also 12:5; 19:4, the very passages where he inserts that verb) in a way the verb for "say, speak" does not. "Out of [the] mouth of infants and sucklings you have prepared praise for yourself" shows dependence on the LXX in κατηρτίσω, "you have prepared ... for yourself," for יִסַּדְתָּ, "you have established," and in αἶνον, "praise," for עֹז, "strength" (see Gundry, *Use of the OT* 121-22). Infants and sucklings do not quite correspond to the children in Matthew. The children are young people old enough to visit the Temple and shout an acclamation. But Matthew can hardly change the OT text radically enough to avoid the discrepancy. The essential element of youthful praise leads him to regard the discrepancy as not fatal, if he recognized it at all. But how does he come to think of Ps 8:3 in the first place? "Blessed is he who comes in the name of the Lord" (v 9) derives from Ps 118:26 and reminds him of Psalm 8, which begins, "O Lord, our Lord, how majestic is your name in all the earth!" and goes on to speak of youngsters, whom Matthew already has gotten from the tradition. The coincidences of the Lord's name and the youngsters prove an irresistible magnet drawing the evangelist to his quotation.

THE CHURCH'S ACCEPTANCE OF PUBLICANS, PROSTITUTES, AND GENTILES AS SUPPORTED BY GOD'S REJECTION OF THE JEWISH LEADERS
21:17–22:46 (Mark 11:11b-14, 20–12:12; Luke 21:37; 20:1-8; 7:29-30; 20:9-19)

In this section Matthew justifies the church's acceptance of publicans, prostitutes, Gentiles—in general, those whom the Jewish leaders despised—by stressing God's rejection of those leaders.

THE WITHERING OF THE FIG TREE
21:17-22 (Mark 11:11b-14, 20-26)

21:17 (Mark 11:11) Matthew drew the chief priests and scribes from Mark 11:18 (v 15; cf. also Matt 7:28) and is about to extract a locative phrase from Mark 11:19; so he skips the rest of the material in those verses in order to take up the story of the fig tree. In fact, the reference to evening in Mark 11:19 turns his thoughts to that story, which begins with a similar reference. "When the hour was already late" (so Mark 11:11) changes to "And abandoning them." Matthew inserted καταλείπω with the connotation of abandonment also in 4:13; 16:4, besides only one shared occurrence. "Them" refers to the chief priests and scribes (v 15). Thus Matthew immediately sounds the note of judgment on the Jewish leaders associated with Jerusalem. Also, he retains "he [Jesus] went out to Bethany" (Mark 11:11), draws "outside the city" from Mark 11:19 (cf. the anticipation of Mark 11:18 in Matt 21:15), and slips the phrase between the verb and the reference to Bethany to make the same judgmental point (cf. esp. 10:14, where his insertion—with "house" added—appeared in a symbolic pronouncement of judgment on a city). "And he lodged there" replaces "with the disciples," makes v 17 a couplet of lines in accord with Matthew's love of parallelism, and concentrates attention on Jesus. ἐκεῖ is a Mattheanism (16,6). Because of crowding during festivals, especially the Passover, many pilgrims had to find lodging outside Jerusalem (cf. Luke 21:37).

21:18 (Mark 11:12) To contrast Jesus' leaving Jerusalem and lodging overnight in Bethany with his return in the morning, Matthew changes καί to δέ. "In the morning" comes up from the observation of the withered fig tree the *second* day after Jesus' entering Jerusalem (Mark 11:20) and replaces "on the next day" in the story of Jesus' cursing the fig tree the *first* day after entering Jerusalem (Mark 11:12). In this way Matthew begins to bring together the curse and its accomplishment in a single day. Both the antedating of the accomplishment and the consequent welding together of the two parts make the incident serve more dramatically its purpose of symbolizing God's rejection of the Jewish leaders in Jerusalem, whom the fig tree represents in Matthew. Instead of writing that "they [Jesus and his disciples] went from Bethany," Matthew writes about the "returning" of Jesus—again the disciples drop out—"into the city." This phrase not only makes a nice stylistic contrast with v 17a; it also relates the following incident, concerning the fig tree, to Jerusalem rather than to Bethany—for the symbolic purpose just mentioned. πόλιν is a Mattheanism (18,3). Jesus' hungering comes from Mark.

21:19 (Mark 11:13-14, 20) Matthew takes "And seeing a fig tree" from Mark and inserts "one" (μίαν, a favorite of his—24,7) to single out the fig tree as representing Jerusalem, or the Jewish leaders there. This purpose becomes clearer in his characteristic change of Mark's "at a distance" to "on [or 'by'] the road." ὁδοῦ is another favorite (9,2). The road goes to Jerusalem, of course, and has appeared four times recently in that sense (20:17, 30; 21:8 [bis]). Its reappearing here further links the fig tree with the city of the Jewish leaders. "Having leaves" naturally falls away, because locating the fig tree by the road rather than at a distance (away from the road, it would seem in Mark) precludes a profitless side trip at the sight of leaves on the tree. For Jesus' approach, Matthew takes "he came" and "to it" from Mark, but skips the intervening words "if perhaps he would find anything on it." The omission implies that Jesus expected to find fruit on the tree. This expectation does not rest on horticulture, however, but on the demand of God, whom Jesus represents, to find the fruit of faith and good works on the tree of Jerusalem. In other words, Matthew makes his omission at the symbolic level to eliminate any uncertainty over what God expected of the Jewish leaders. The omission leaves Mark's "coming" redundant. Therefore it, too, disappears, and Matthew continues with Mark's statement that Jesus "found nothing except leaves." To this Matthew adds "on it" in compensation for omitting Mark's clause concerning the uncertainty of finding something to eat "on it." He also adds "only" (μόνον, a Mattheanism—7,0) to intensify the guilt of figless Jerusalem. The omission of "for it was not the season of figs" takes away any excuse from the Jewish leaders represented.

To replace εἶπεν with the emphatic historical present λέγει (47,11), Matthew deletes ἀποκριθείς even though he likes Mark's combination (29,6). This revision shows the strength of his desire to emphasize Jesus' following words to the fig tree: "No longer will fruit come from you—forever!" ἐκ σοῦ advances from its third position in Mark to second and so stresses the implied address to Jerusalem. εἰς τὸν αἰῶνα goes from second position to fifth and last. The result is a more balanced emphasis with μηκέτι at the beginning: "no longer ... forever." Mark's "may no one eat fruit" becomes "fruit will no longer come." Thus, with the Jewish leaders in mind, a mere wish turns into a terrifying prediction of judgment.

Because of Matthew's compressing the story of the fig tree into one day, the intervening story of Jesus' cleansing the Temple drops out. That story has already appeared in Matthew. Hence, there is no need for listening, passing by the next morning, and recollecting what Jesus said the previous day. Those items drop out, too. "And immediately the fig tree withered" replaces "And ... they saw the fig tree withered from the roots up" (Mark 11:20). The coming forward of Mark's participle (ἐξηραμμένην) to become the main verb (ἐξηράνθη) and the replacement of "from the roots up," which implies a gradual process, with "immediately" emphasize the suddenness of the event. The withering itself takes place at once, not just the disciples' seeing what happened. The judgment represented by the withering stands in the forefront of Matthew's text.

Cf. Jer 8:13; 11:16; Ezekiel 17; Hos 9:10; Joel 1:7; Mic 7:1-6; Nah 3:12. Since according to Mark the season for figs had not yet arrived, Jesus must have hoped to find green winter figs which, not having ripened before the tree lost its leaves in the autumn, had stayed on the branches through the winter and were ripening with the leafing of the tree in the spring (see W. Corswant, *Dictionary of Life in Bible Times* [New York: Oxford, 1960] 118). Cf. *Tg. Ps.-J.* Gen 1:3 on the addition of immediacy to heighten the effect.

21:20 (Mark 11:21) The typically Matthean participle ἰδόντες (10-11,7) replaces Mark's ἀναμνησθείς. "The disciples" replaces "Peter." Matthew likes both μαθηταί (31,5) and Πέτρος (8,1), but in Mark only Peter recalls on the next day what Jesus had said the preceding day. In Matthew everything happens on the same day with all the disciples watching—Peter has no chance to exhibit the superiority of his memory over that of his fellows. The immediacy of the miracle makes the disciples "marvel" (ἐθαύμασαν, not in Mark, where the miracle lacks immediacy; cf. another insertion of this verb in 15:31). Consequently, Mark's "says" reduces, as often, to "saying" (61,23). Peter's statement, "Rabbi, look, the fig tree that you cursed has withered" (so Mark), changes to a question that both provides occasion for an answer by Jesus (vv 21-22) and reemphasizes the suddenness of the miracle: "How is it that the fig tree withered suddenly?" Except for the Mattheanism πῶς (6,1), every word in the question comes from the account of the withering in v 19. The amazing suddenness of the miracle stresses the dire threat of judgment on the Jewish leaders based in Jerusalem.

21:21 (Mark 11:22-23) In v 21 δέ replaces Mark's καί to set off Jesus' answer from the disciples' question, and "says" gives way to "said." As in 17:20, where the saying about mountain-moving faith has already appeared, "Truly I say to you" advances from second position (so Mark) to the emphatic first position. Thus Jesus' word gains precedence over the disciples' faith. Again in reminiscence of 17:20, the command "Have faith in God" (so Mark) becomes part of a conditional clause beginning "if you have faith" and continuing with "and do not doubt," which is brought up from a later clause in Mark. By making the possession of faith conditional and advancing not doubting to a position alongside faith, Matthew shows his concern over the threat of apostasy (see esp. 18:6-18).

"Not only will you do what was done to the fig tree" is unique to the first gospel. Basically, Matthew constructs it by taking the fig tree from the context and using two of his favorite words, μόνον (7,0) and ποιήσετε (19,19). The new line links the saying about the disciples' faith with Jesus' causing the fig tree to wither. In this way Matthew makes Jesus a paradigm in the exercise of faith. The new line also leads to an insertion of ἀλλὰ καί, "but even," for a parallel between the mountain about to be mentioned and the fig tree just mentioned. The καί merges with Mark's ἄν to produce κἄν, "even if." Its ascensive force draws forward τῷ ὄρει τούτῳ, "to this mountain" (which *follows* the verb in Mark), as a mind-boggling example of difficulty. Mark's third singular "whoever says" changes to the second plural "you say" for parallelism. "Be lifted up and thrown in the sea" matches Mark exactly, but earlier borrowing of not doubting leads Matthew to omit most of the following in Mark: "and does not doubt in his heart, but believes that what he says comes to pass, it will be for him." He does, however, construct "it will come to pass" from "comes to pass" and the future tense of "it will be." Cf. "no longer . . . will come" in v 19.

Cf. John 14:12; Jas 1:6. We ought not to contrast the opposition of faith and doubt with the small amount of faith in 17:20. Not doubting replaces the earlier reference to a mustard seed merely because of the present parallel in Mark. "Little faith" (17:20) and "doubt" (21:21) are synonymous. "This mountain" so naturally relates to the Mount of Olives that the saying seems to belong historically to the context where it now appears. Probably the cursing and withering of the fig tree led to removing a mountain via reminiscence of removing a sycamine tree (Luke 17:6). Throwing a whole mountain in the sea does not agree with splitting the Mount of Olives and moving its western half toward the Mediterranean Sea (so the prophecy about the day of the Lord in Zech 14:4). Therefore the saying has to do with faith as part of discipleship, not with bringing the day of the Lord by dint of faith.

   21:22 (Mark 11:24-25) Despite his fondness for διὰ τοῦτο (4,2) and λέγω ὑμῖν (27,7), Matthew does not take over these expressions from Mark lest he interrupt the parallel between the foregoing saying about moving a mountain and the following saying about prayer: "And you will receive all things whatever that you, believing, may ask for in prayer." Insertion of "And" signals the parallel. "All things whatever that" comes from Mark. But where Mark has the present tense indicative verbs, "you pray for and ask for," Matthew writes ἄν with the aorist subjunctive αἰτήσητε, "you may ask for," and puts the element of prayer in the prepositional phrase "in prayer." Mark's imperative "believe" turns into the participle "believing." And Matthew constructs "you will receive" from "that you have received" (so Mark's "prophetic aorist") and the future tense in Mark's "and it will be for you." Thus the saying becomes closely parallel with the preceding in its construction—ἄν, the aorist subjunctive, a single verb of speaking, a climactic future indicative made of two Markan verbs, all with the result that a command supported by a promise (so Mark) changes to a promise alone. Subtraction of the command to faith leaves only a reassuring promise that will counteract doubt. The remaining verse in Mark 11:25 drops out because of its use in Matt 5:23-24; 6:5-7, 14-15.

JESUS' AUTHORITY
AND THE PARABLE OF THE TWO SONS
21:23-32 (Mark 11:27-33; Luke 20:1-8)

21:23 (Mark 11:27-28; Luke 20:1-2) The account of the debate over Jesus' authority opens "And when he went into the Temple." From the first line in Mark 11:27 Matthew has taken "And they went." But "again into Jerusalem" has dropped out because he compressed the incident concerning the fig tree into one day. From Mark's second line, "And while he was walking around in the Temple," Matthew has taken the reference to the Temple, the genitive absolute construction, and the singular pronoun referring to Jesus. Mark's ἔρχονται πρὸς αὐτόν becomes προσῆλθον αὐτῷ. Matthew's compound verb typifies his diction (38,6) and connotes Jesus' dignity (see the comments on 4:3; 8:14). Characteristically, Matthew adds διδάσκοντι (3,3) to compensate for his omission of Jesus' "walking around" and to emphasize Jesus' role as teacher of the law (cf. Luke 20:1). Consequently, the following question deals with Jesus' authority to teach, whereas in Mark it deals with his authority to cleanse the Temple.

Mark identifies those who come to Jesus as "the chief priests and the scribes and the elders." Matthew adds "of the people" to "the elders" (cf. Luke's reference to "the people" as the recipients of Jesus' teaching, and the comments on 2:3-4). See 26:3, 47; 27:1 for other occurrences of the entire phrase, always the result of Matthew's editing. The scribes drop out, because Scripture does not figure in the subsequent part of the episode. They will drop out also in those passages just listed, where Matthew will write of the chief priests and elders of the people without mentioning the scribes. On the other hand, he will retain the scribes in 26:57; 27:41, where allusions to the OT come into subsequent parts of the passages. In view of 27:25, the reference to the people does not distance them from the elders and therefore from responsibility in the opposition to Jesus. On the contrary! For Mark's "And they were saying to him," Matthew puts his favorite λέγοντες (61,23; cf. Luke's "and they spoke, saying," which looks like a conflation of Mark and Matthew). The first question, "By what authority do you do these things?" matches Mark exactly. But to get *two* questions as a contrast with the *one* question of Jesus later on, Matthew changes "or" (part of a single question in Mark and Luke) to "And" at the start of the second question: "And who gave you this authority?" As in Luke, Mark's "that you should do these things" drops out. It is repetitive of the first question and would have spoiled the couplet of parallel lines and tended to make readers think of Jesus' deeds rather than teaching, which Matthew has just interpolated.

21:24 (Mark 11:29; Luke 20:3) Because of the interrogative nature of the preceding, Matthew naturally and characteristically inserts ἀποκριθείς to go with εἶπεν (29,6). Luke agrees with this insertion and also with the deletion of ἐπ- from ἐπερωτήσω (see the comments on 17:19). The insertion of κἀγώ, which probably does not belong in the original text of Mark, emphasizes the person of Jesus and typifies Matthew's diction (5,3). Mark's "one" may reflect a Semitic indefinite, meaning "a" (cf. Black, *Aramaic Approach* 104-6); but in Matthew the "one word [i.e., 'question']" of Jesus contrasts the singularity of his question with the duality of the Jewish leaders' questions. It was Matthew who made two questions out of one. Because he added ἀποκριθείς at the beginning of this verse, Mark's "and answer me" changes to "which, if you tell me" (similarly Luke). In the clause "And I will tell you by what authority I do these things," Matthew inserts a Christologically emphatic ἐγώ, which produces κἀγώ (5,3). This matches κἀγώ in the first clause of Jesus' question. In fact, to avoid Mark's awkward parataxis, Matthew revises the whole of Jesus' question in a chiastic fashion:

    a ἐρωτήσω
      b ὑμᾶς
        c κἀγώ
          d λόγον ἕνα,
          d' ὃν ἐὰν εἴπητέ μοι
        c' κἀγώ
      b' ὑμῖν
    a' ἐρῶ ἐν ποίᾳ ἐξουσίᾳ ταῦτα ποιῶ.

21:25 (Mark 11:30-31; Luke 20:4-5) "The baptism of John" gains the additional words "where was it from?" (not in Mark or Luke). Matthew has some liking for πόθεν (2,1), and "was" comes from the next set of words, "was it from heaven [i.e., God] or from men?" (so Mark and Luke). Matthew adopts the latter except for "was," which he leaves to be supplied from its earlier use. As a result, Jesus' question takes the form of a couplet. To avoid spoiling the parallelism Matthew omits the second instance of "Answer me." Luke's making the same omission even though he is not protecting parallelism suggests influence from Matthew. Jesus mentions John's baptism because the Father inaugurated his messianic ministry at his baptism by John. Thus the question of his authority was intimately related to the question of John's authority.

As also in Luke, οἱ δέ replaces Mark's καί for a contrast between Jesus and the chief priests and elders of the people, who begin to reason about his question. Mark's and Luke's "with one another" implies discussion. Matthew's "in themselves" implies private thinking. That Jesus apparently knows their thoughts shows his omniscience as God (see the comments on 9:3; 16:7). To "he will say" Matthew adds "to us" for a parallel with "the crowd" in the matching clause below. Since Luke and a good part of the textual tradition in Mark lack οὖν, Matthew may bear responsibility for that word; it is one of his favorites (35,11).

21:26 (Mark 11:32; Luke 20:6) For a parallel with v 25, Matthew changes Mark's ἀλλά to δέ and adds ἐάν. Luke agrees with these revisions. "*They* feared" shifts to "*we* fear" (similarly Luke). This shift makes the line part of the chief priests' and elders' reasoning rather than an editorial comment by the evangelist. That the Jewish leaders admit to themselves their policy of political expedience intensifies their guilt—viz., "that he really was a prophet"—the last clause in their reasoning according to Mark, advances into the preceding clause in the form of the phrase "as a prophet," defining the way all the people regarded John. Matthew' reducing the last clause to a phrase gives an unspoiled parallel between "If we say" and "But if we say," between "from heaven" and "from men," between "he will say to us" and "we fear the crowd," and between "Why then did you not believe him?" and "For all regard John as a prophet" (vv 25-26). The change of Mark's "they regarded" to "they regard" (similarly Luke) again incorporates an editorial comment by Mark into the reasoning of the Jewish leaders—for the sake of parallelism. These revisions also rid the text of Mark's broken constructions.

21:27 (Mark 11:33; Luke 20:7-8) In the introduction to the evasive answer "We do not know," Mark's "they say" becomes "they said." Similarly, the introduction to the response "And Jesus says to them" (so Mark) changes to "He said to them—also [or 'even'] he." ἔφη with asyndeton is a Mattheanism (6,1) and gives a feeling of abruptness. The moving of Mark's opening καί toward the end of the clause shifts its meaning from "and" to "also" or "even." The intensive αὐτός typifies Matthew's diction (14,3). The resultant phrase καὶ αὐτός echoes Matthew's insertion κἀγώ in v 24 (bis).

21:28-32 (Luke 7:29-30) The parable of the two sons is unique to Matthew and starts a series of three parables in the gospel (see also vv 33-46 and 22:1-14). Not even the second and third parables, though they are paralleled, appear side by side in Mark or Luke. Each of the three deals with the Jewish leaders' rejection of Jesus. The plural number of "parables" in Mark 12:1 combined with Mark's providing only one parable on the occasion and led Matthew to gather three parables together.

The parallelism that typifies Matthew's style is evident in the parable of the two sons. "And approaching the first, he said, 'Son, go work today in the vineyard' " (v 28c) corresponds to "And approaching the other, he said likewise" (v 30a). "And answering, he [the son] said" appears both in v 29a and in v 30b. "I will not" (v 29b) antithetically parallels "I will, Sir" (v 30c). "But changing his mind, he later went away [to work]" (v 29c) contrasts with "and he did not go away [to work]" (v 30d). "Who of the two did the will of the father?" (v 31a) echoes "But what do you think? A man had two sons" (v 28ab). "They say, 'The first' " (v 31b) matches "Jesus says to them, 'Truly I say to you that the publicans and the prostitutes go into the kingdom of God before you' " (v 31c). "For John came to you in [the] way of righteousness, and you did not believe him" (v 32ab) antithetically parallels "but the publicans and the prostitutes believed him, and you, seeing, did not even change your minds later so as to believe him" (v 32cd).

The foregoing sketch of parallelistic structure rests on a text-critical judgment in favor of the reading supported by ℵ* C K W and others (see the UBS). This reading has in its favor the probability that the asking of the other son depends on the initial refusal of the first son. Furthermore, with this reading the first son turns out to be last and the other, or last, son turns out to be first in accord with Jesus' statement to this effect and with Matthew's special interest in it (see 19:30 and 20:1-16). Some support for the reading comes also from Matthew's fondness for ἑτέρῳ (5,1), as opposed to the un-Matthean δευτέρῳ. The latter goes with the variant reading, which may have arisen out of later application of the parable to Jews and Gentiles. That application demanded a reversal in the order of the sons to agree with the historical order of Jewish disobedience followed by Gentiles' repentance. See further Metzger, *Textual Commentary* ad loc. Adoption

421

of a different reading would require some rearrangement, but would not destroy the parallelistic structure of the parable.

Alongside highly literary parallelism, Matthew's special diction abounds:

τί δὲ ὑμῖν δοκεῖ; (4,2); ἄνθρωπος (35,17; see the comments on 13:24 concerning its general frequency in Matthew, and on 18:23-35 concerning Matthew's special use of it in parables); δύο (bis—19,4; almost always concerning pairs of people, here concerning τέκνα; cf. other unparalleled occurrences of τέκνα in 2:18; 18:25; 27:25); προσελθών (bis—38,6); πρώτῳ/-ος (2,5-6); ὕπαγε (5,6—esp. as an imperative); σήμερον (4,3); ἐργάζου (6,7 for ἐργ-); ἀποκριθεὶς εἶπεν (bis—29,6); θέλω (18,8); ὕστερον (3,3); μεταμεληθείς/-θητε (bis; see 27:3 for its only other occurrence in the gospels); ἀπῆλθεν (bis—14,11); ἑτέρῳ (5,1); ὡσαύτως (2,2); ἐγώ (12-13,3); κύριε (34,15—"Sir, Lord," which sounds obsequious in an address to one's father); ἐποίησεν (19,19); θέλημα (3,1—always concerning the will of the Father); πατρός (22,13); the historical present λέγουσιν/-ει with asyndeton (21,6); ἀμὴν λέγω ὑμῖν (15,8—followed by an epexegetical ὅτι, "that," as also in 18:13; 19:23, 28); τελῶναι (bis—3,2; cf. Luke 7:29); πόρναι (bis—matched with publicans in the gospels only in vv 31 and 32; cf. Matthew's insertions of πορνεία in 5:32; 19:9); προάγουσιν + an accusative of person (see 2:9; 14:22 in contrast with Mark 6:45; 21:9 in contrast with Mark 11:9); βασιλείαν (18,12); γάρ (62-63,15); ὁδῷ (9,2); δικαιοσύνης (5,2; cf. Matthew's inserting the doctrine of two ways in 7:13-14 and organizing the remainder of the Sermon on the Mount under that doctrine); three forms of πιστεύω (3,3); the nominative plural ὑμεῖς (15,3); the nominative participle ἰδόντες (10-11,7; see esp. 27:3 for another distinctive combination of ἰδών with μεταμεληθείς); οὐδέ (17,3); and τοῦ + an infinitive (1,3). Furthermore, the publicans' and prostitutes' entering the kingdom of God looks like the uniquely Matthean formulae in 5:20; 7:21; 19:17.

Apparently Matthew composed this parable (1) as a counterpart to the parable of the prodigal son and his elder brother (Luke 15:11-32; see the comments on Matt 18:12), (2) in reminiscence of the distinctive parable of the laborers in the vineyard (20:1-16), and (3) with reference to John the Baptist in the debate over Jesus' authority (21:23-27). Since the Jewish leaders who challenged that authority totally lacked faith, προάγουσιν surely indicates their exclusive displacement, not merely their later entrance into the kingdom. The expression gives us an example of meiosis. The present tense of the verb probably implies entrance into the current form of the kingdom (cf. Luke 16:16). In v 32 the parable finally leads up to a wholesale revision of the tradition behind Luke 7:29-30, which Matthew replaced with 11:12-14 (cf. Luke 16:16) in a discussion about John the Baptist (see 11:7-19 together with Luke 7:24-35). All in all, behind Matthew's composition and editing lies the purpose of highlighting the Jewish leaders' guilt.

We may detect echoes of 20:1-16 at a number of points: the use of the root ἐργ- for the motif of work; the locale of the work in a vineyard; the use of ὑπάγω in the command to go to the vineyard; the use of ἀπέρχομαι in describing the going and not going; the division of the parable into chronological stages; the summarizing use of ὡσαύτως to qualify the action of getting workers into the vineyard; the identification of the owner with κύριος; the lack of a polite address on the part of the rebellious; and the reversal of first and last. The reminiscence of 20:1-16 also anticipates the immediately following parable of the vineyard in 21:33-46. Believing and not believing John the Baptist stem from the people's regarding John as a prophet and the chief priests' and elders' unbelief in John, just mentioned in vv 25-26. Thus assimilation to the preceding context leads Matthew to replace being baptized by John and not being baptized by John (so Luke 7:29-30) with believing and not believing John (v 32). "For John came" (v 32) echoes 11:18 exactly (contrast the somewhat different wording in Luke 7:33). πρὸς ὑμᾶς harks back to προσελθὼν τῷ πρώτῳ/ἑτέρῳ in the parable proper. The contextual address to the chief priests and elders of the people determines the change of the third person plural (so Luke 7:29-30) to the second person plural. The several uses of ὁδός since the beginning of Jesus' ascent to Jerusalem (see 20:17, 30; 21:8 [bis], 19) combine with ἐδικαίωσαν, "they acknowledged [God's] righteousness" (Luke 7:29), to make Matthew write ἐν ὁδῷ δικαιοσύνης, which corresponds and refers to his portrayal of the Baptist as a preacher of righteousness (see the comments on 3:1ff.). "The way of righteousness" appears also in Prov 8:20; 12:28; 16:31; 2 Pet 2:21; *Jub.* 23:26; 25:15; *1 Enoch* 92:3; 99:10; *Barn.* 1:4; 5:4 (slightly different phrases appear elsewhere). Typically, then, Matthew is borrowing a widely used expression from the OT. The borrowing will be confirmed by his inserting in v 41 a further allusion to Ps 1:3, which concerns the way of the righteous (see Ps 1:6). The publicans come from Luke 7:29-30, but we read "the harlots" instead of the associated phrase "all the people." Probably the latter phrase owes something to Luke's redaction and rests on the crowd in the tradition (see Luke 7:24 and cf. the concordance, s.v. λαός with Aland's synopsis). Matthew's previous and distinctive association of the people with the antagonistic elders (v 23) would have forestalled a favorable reference to the people here. The rejection of God's will in Luke 7:30 matches the behavior of the chief priests and the elders, who are represented by the disobedient son, remarkably well (though the term βουλήν, "will," may come from Luke's hand).

We might ask why Matthew writes about "the kingdom *of God*," instead of his usual "the kingdom of heaven," if he bears responsibility for composing the parable and its interpretation. The answer lies in the contextual need for the personal emphasis in God's name. Just as in 12:28 the contextual references to Satan's kingdom and God's Spirit called for retention of "God" with "kingdom," so also here the contextual figure of the father, whose vineyard represents the kingdom, calls for use of the divine name (cf. the v.l. in 6:33 with 6:32). Compositional use of "the kingdom of God," then, poses no greater problem than retention of "the kingdom of God" in traditional material. In other ways, too, Matthew shows he is not limited to "the kingdom of heaven." He writes of the Father's kingdom (6:10; 13:43; 26:29), the kingdom of the Son of man (13:41; 16:28; cf. 20:21), and the kingdom without qualification but in association with the gospel, righteousness, Jews ("sons of the kingdom"), the Word, and the disciples (4:23; 6:33 v.l.; 8:12; 9:35; 13:19, 38; 24:14; 25:34), as well as of God's kingdom (6:33 v.l.; 12:28; 19:24; 21:31, 43). Often these expressions are peculiar to his gospel. Therefore, it should not surprise us that in his own composition he uses "the kingdom of God" instead of "the kingdom of heaven."

In summary, then, Matthew composes the parable as an illustration of the dominical saying we find in Luke 7:29-30. Earlier, he reserved that saying for inclusion in the present passage. Both his composing the parable and his reserving the saying have the purpose of emphasizing the Jewish leaders' guilt. Like the first son, the publicans and prostitutes repented at the preaching of John the Baptist after exhibiting carelessness toward the law. Like the other son, the Jewish leaders refused John's message despite their claimed allegiance to the law. The last line of v 32 goes beyond the parable in noting that the Jewish leaders added guilt upon guilt by failing to change their minds even when given a second chance—probably a reference to Jesus' ministry, in response to which they might have reversed their refusal to believe John. This progression beyond the parable assimilates the ministries of Jesus and John both in the shifting of believing publicans and prostitutes from Jesus to John and in the making of Jesus' ministry a renewal of the opportunity granted in John's ministry. Indeed, putting John "on the way of righteousness" has already brought him alongside Jesus the Teacher of Righteousness (see esp. 5:17-48). That such assimilation typifies Matthew's theology sets the seal to composition by him. Though the two groups of Jews did not change their responses to John the Baptist, his ministry occasioned their change of behavior toward God. John preached the demand of God, whom the father represents.

THE TRANSFERAL OF GOD'S KINGDOM
FROM THE JEWISH LEADERS TO THE CHURCH
AS TAUGHT THROUGH THE PARABLE
OF THE TENANT FARMERS
21:33-46 (Mark 12:1-12; Luke 20:9-19)

21:33 (Mark 12:1; Luke 20:9) Now Matthew moves to another parable concerning a vineyard, the parable of the tenant farmers. Emphasis falls on the guilt of the wicked tenants, who stand for the chief priests and elders of the people (v 23). "Hear another parable" replaces Mark's "And he began to speak to them in parables," echoes the distinctive introduction to the interpretation of the sower (see 13:18 in contrast with Mark 4:13; Luke 8:11), and consists of three words dear to Matthew: ἄλλην (14,4), παραβολήν (5,2), and ἀκούσατε (26,6). This replacement comes from his having made Jesus start speaking in parables earlier (see 21:28) and stresses the necessity of hearing Jesus' teaching. The combination ἄλλην παραβολήν is unique to Matthew also in 13:24, 31, 33, in the last two passages by way of insertion, as here.

Matthew subordinates the action of planting a vineyard to the lordship of the man who, representing God, does the planting. "A man" comes from Mark. Matthew supplies "was" and "landowner." οἰκοδεσπότης is a favorite of his (2,4), especially in parables and especially with ἄνθρωπος in parables (see 13:27, 52; 20:1, 11; 21:33). Now he inserts ὅστις (another favorite— 23,5) and takes ἐφύτευσεν ἀμπελῶνα from Mark, where the latter two words appear in reverse order. Matthew conforms their order to Isa 5:2, allusively quoted here and throughout the next three clauses (see Gundry, *Use of the OT* 43-44). The advance of ἄνθρωπος to first position links with its first position in the parable of the two sons (see v 28 and the comments on 18:23-35). By showing that he is still thinking of the parable in 20:1-16, the conjunction of "man" and "landowner" confirms Matthew's using that parable as a primary source in composing the immediately foregoing parable here, viz., the parable of the two sons (21:28-32).

"And he put a fence around it" comes from Mark except for the adding of "it" to fill Mark's ellipsis (cf. 27:28, 48) and the reversing of Mark's order of verb–direct object to conform to the LXX. The expression rests on a deduction that gathering out stones (so the Hebrew text of Isa 5:2) led to building a stone fence. Again to conform Jesus' words more closely to the OT, Matthew inserts "in it" in the clause about digging a winepress. Mark's "vat" (ὑπολήνιον) becomes a "winepress" (ληνόν). This change indicates that Matthew takes יֶקֶב, "vat," as metonymy for a whole winepress.

See K. R. Snodgrass in *NTS* 20 (1974) 142-44 against taking *Gos. Thom.* 65 as original. The fence protected the vineyard against wild beasts and other intruders (cf. Ps 80:13-14[12-13]). The tower served as a shelter for watchmen (cf. 2 Chr 26:10; Isa 1:8). See Jeremias, *Parables* 74-76; Derrett, *Law in the NT* 286-312, for discussions of background that go far to make the parable look realistic in its details. But contrary to the idea that rebelliousness of Galilean peasants against foreign landlords underlies the parable and possibly gives the parable its point, see M. I. Rostovzeff, *The Social and Economic History of the Roman Empire* (2nd ed.; Oxford: Clarendon, 1957) 1. 269-73.

21:34 (Mark 12:2; Luke 20:10) At the beginning of v 34 Matthew adds a unique clause that emphasizes the fruits of the vineyard, because they symbolize righteousness: "but when the season of fruits drew near." "When . . . drew near" comes from 21:1, where it referred to Jesus' drawing near Jerusalem. Thus Matthew applies the parable to the Jewish leaders residing there. ἤγγισεν occurs four times in his gospel as an insertion. "Season" comes up from Mark's next clause. The addition "of the fruits" suits Matthew's interest in the figure of fruits for good works (καρπῶν—5,1; see esp. further distinctive occurrences in the interpretation of the parable— vv 41, 43). Matthew pluralizes Mark's "a slave," so that it reads "his slaves" in accord with the plurality of slaves who appear in other parables unique to this gospel (see 13:27-28; 18:23; cf. 22:3, 4, 6, 8, 10; 25:14-30) and perhaps in allusion to the early prophets in the Hebrew OT. The pluralization prepares for multiplying the initial treatment meted out by the tenant farmers in the next verse. The addition of "his" renews emphasis on the authority of the owner, who represents God (see again the passages just cited). Mark's "at the season" falls away because of its prior use, and the slaves and tenant farmers switch order for the sake of smoothness (cf. Mark and Luke). Mark's "in order that he might receive from the tenant farmers [some] of the fruits of the vineyard" becomes "to receive his fruits." This implies that all the fruits belong to the landowner (cf. the distinctive last clause of v 41), whereas in Mark they belong to the vineyard and only some of them are supposed to go to the owner. The theological symbolism of God's demanding the totality of people's lives has swallowed up economic realism, which requires rental payment of only part of the crop.

21:35 (Mark 12:3; Luke 20:10) Verse 35 begins with Mark's "And taking" and a substitution of "his slaves" (an echo of v 34) for "him." But Matthew inserts "the tenant farmers" to compensate for his omitting the tenant farmers in the preceding verse. Luke's agreeing with the insertion but lacking Matthew's reason for it suggests Matthean influence (not common dependence on Q). The insertion identifies the subject of the following parallel verbs, which Matthew ties together with one of his favorite constructions, μέν . . . δέ . . . δέ (15,1—here preceded each time by ὅν for the meaning "one . . . another . . . another"). The construction comes up from Mark's last two expressions concerning the farmers' treatment of the slaves. "They beat" corresponds to Mark. But "and they sent him away empty" disappears. In its stead, Matthew advances "they killed" from its later position in Mark and adds "they stoned" in anticipation of 22:37 (cf. Luke 13:34), which deals with Jerusalem's killing and stoning the prophets. Thus the introduction of these last two verbs interprets the slaves as prophets, identifies the tenant farmers as the Jewish leaders in Jerusalem, and intensifies their guilt by making them do the worst—i.e., kill and stone the prophets as well as beat them—from the very start. In fact, except for the initial beating, Mark's weaker verbs concerning the striking of the servants on the head and dishonoring them drop out.

Stoning follows killing because stoning carries connotations of execution on grounds of religious apostasy (the tenant farmers treated the servants as false prophets) and therefore implies disgrace as well as death. Cf. Exod 19:13; Lev 20:2, 27; 24:14, 16, 23; Num 15:35-36; Deut 13:11(10); 17:5; 21:21; 22:21, 24; 2 Chr 24:20-21 (with Matt 23:35); m. Sanh. 7:4; 9:3.

21:36 (Mark 12:4-5; Luke 20:11-13) Matthew skips Mark's initial καί, goes to "Again he sent," deletes "to them" as unnecessary (so also Luke), and pluralizes "another slave" to read "other slaves" in accord with the pluralization in v 34. The addition of πλείονας τῶν πρώτων, "more than the first," derives from Mark's πολλοὺς ἄλλους, "many others." Matthew uses the comparative to intensify the Jewish leaders' guilt and perhaps to allude to the latter prophets in the Hebrew OT as more numerous than the former prophets (cf. Jer 7:25-26). Both πλείονας and πρώτων are Mattheanisms (3,1; 2,5-6). Because he advanced the killing of the slaves to the first stage, Matthew now summarizes with the statement "and they did to them likewise," which replaces striking on the head, dishonoring, sending away, beating, and killing. Matthew has predilections for ἐποίησαν (19,19) and ὡσαύτως (2,2). The latter is always unparalleled and appears only in parables.

21:37 (Mark 12:6; Luke 20:13) Mark's "He still had one, a beloved son" drops out to permit the starting of v 37 with "And last." This expression is an echo of and link with the preceding parable of the two sons (see vv 29, 32). ὕστερον is a Mattheanism (3,3), and δέ is extremely frequent in Matthew. Mark's "he sent" stays. But Matthew skips over "him last," picks up "to them" and supplies "the son" from Mark's preceding, omitted clause. Then he replaces "beloved" with "his" for a parallel with the distinctive phrase "his slaves" in vv 34 and 35. λέγων comes over; but the recitative ὅτι vanishes, as also in Luke. "They will respect my son" remains.

Jesus' consciousness of unique divine sonship—a consciousness that pervades the gospel tradition—supports his meaning himself in the figure of the son. Doubtless the audience's understanding did not measure up to Jesus' self-understanding. Cf. 4QFlor 1:11.

21:38 (Mark 12:7; Luke 20:14) As in Matthew's summary of Mark 12:4-5 (see v 36), so also in v 38 Mark's "those" disappears. That Luke shares Matthew's omission here despite his earlier adoption of the demonstrative suggests Matthean influence. Matthew inserts "seeing the son" to link this parable with the parable of the two sons (cf. ἰδόντες, a Mattheanism—10-11,7—in v 32). The insertion also accentuates the farmers'— i.e., the Jewish leaders'—guilt. Luke's sharing ἰδόντες again suggests Matthean influence. εἶπον comes forward and πρὸς ἑαυτούς, "to one another," changes to ἐν ἑαυτοῖς, "in themselves," to parallel the inner reasoning of the chief priests and elders of the people in v 25 (so Matthew alone). In this way Matthew yet again applies the parable to the Jewish leaders in Jerusalem. Once more and as usual, Mark's recitative ὅτι disappears (so also Luke). "And the inheritance will be ours" changes to "and let us possess his inheritance" for a parallel between two hortatory subjunctives. The addition of "his" to "inheritance" harks back to "him" in the first line of the couplet and emphasizes the tenant farmers' guilt by renewing attention to their knowing the true heir of the vineyard.

"Heir" indicates that the tenant farmers thought the owner had died and the son was coming to claim the vineyard as his inheritance. In killing him, they thought they would avoid a legal battle in court and gain the vineyard for themselves by right of possession.

21:39 (Mark 12:8; Luke 20:15) The action of the tenant farmers begins with "And taking." Matthew supplies the participle with an object by advancing Mark's "him," which will have to be supplied with the main verbs. He retains the killing and casting of the son outside the vineyard, but reverses their order. Thus Jerusalem again comes into the interpretation of the parable in that the taking of Jesus outside Jerusalem to be crucified replaces the killing of the son inside the vineyard and the subsequent indignity of throwing his corpse outside to lie unburied (so Mark; see John 19:17, 20; Heb 13:12-13; and Matthew's inserting "going out" at 27:32 in contrast with Mark 15:21; Luke 23:26). That Luke agrees with the reversed order though he will not indicate that Jesus died outside Jerusalem suggests Matthean influence.

21:40 (Mark 12:9; Luke 20:15) Matthew now inserts v 40a for an allusion to the parousia as fulfilling the judgmental aspect of the parable. He advances ἐλεύσεται, "will come," from a later clause in Mark and introduces it with ὅταν οὖν, "When therefore," which changes the verbal form to ἔλθῃ, "comes." οὖν originates in Mark's parallel to Matthew's next line, and ὅταν introduces the parousia in 19:28 (as an insertion) and 25:31 (as part of a unique passage). "The owner ['Lord'] of the vineyard" again comes from Mark's parallel to the next line (cf. 20:8). The next line reads, "What will he do to those tenant farmers?" as in Mark except for deletion of the advanced terms. Matthew adds "to those tenant farmers" from the next line in Mark 12:9b except that "those" comes from Mark's preceding context and compensates for an earlier omission. The addition pinpoints the guilt of the tenant farmers—i.e., the Jewish leaders in Jerusalem—and highlights their judgment: the general question "What then will the owner of the vineyard do?" (so Mark) has become a damningly particular "What will he do *to those tenant farmers?*"

21:41 (Mark 12:9; Luke 20:16) Again Matthew inserts a line: "They say to him." The historical present λέγουσιν with asyndeton characterizes his style (21,6). The construction echoes v 31 and forges another link between this parable and the preceding parable of the two sons. In Mark it is Jesus who says, "He will come and destroy the tenant farmers and give the vineyard to others." The insertion of "They say to him" makes Matthew's version of the judgmental statement a dramatic self-sentencing by the chief priests and elders of the people (cf. v 31). He has already used "he will come"; so it falls away. "Those tenant farmers" in the preceding verse leads here to the simple pronoun "them." To intensify the guilt and judgment, however, Matthew adds—in first position for special emphasis— κακοὺς κακῶς (literally "bad ones badly"; see 24:48 for another insertion of the adjective and 4:24; 15:22; 17:15 for three more insertions of the adverb; see also Lohmeyer-Schmauch, ad loc., on this common Greek wordplay). "And he will give the vineyard to others" becomes "and the vineyard he will lease to other tenant farmers." For a parallel with v 33 the verb gains the prefix ἐκ- and goes from active voice to deponent middle, and γεωργοῖς is added. τὸν ἀμπελῶνα moves to the front to balance the addition of γεωργοῖς at the end.

Matthew inserts a relative clause to emphasize fruit bearing, i.e., doing righteousness (cf. the comments on v 34). Typically, the clause consists of an allusion to the OT, in particular Ps 1:3: "that gives its fruit in its season." The psalm speaks of the two ways, the way of the righteous and the way of the wicked. That Matthew alone quotes it confirms his composition of v 32, which also contained an allusion to the OT doctrine of two ways. Here the allusion reads, "who will give back to him the fruits in their seasons." οἵτινες echoes v 33, where Matthew inserted it, and suits his taste for the word (23,5). ἀποδώσουσιν also belongs to his favorite vocabulary (5,11; see esp. 20:8). "To him" intrudes into the allusion to indicate that the fruits belong to the landowner (cf. the distinctive "his" with "fruits" in v 34). Matthew pluralizes the "fruit" in the psalm to conform to the preceding plurals (v 34 [bis]). Similarly, the singular of "season" in the psalm becomes plural in Matthew—but not as an assimilation to v 34. There we read the singular. Here Matthew pluralizes the word to indicate the prolongation and regularity of fruit bearing by the church.

21:42 (Mark 12:10-11; Luke 20:17) The dialogue switches back to Jesus with the insertion of "Jesus says to them," which echoes v 31 and further links this parable and the parable of the two sons. Luke's having a similar clause suggests Matthean influence. We can recognize Matthew's hand in the historical present of λέγει with asyndeton (21,6) and in Jesus' name (80,12). Mark's "Have you not read even this Scripture . . . ?" becomes "Have you never read in the Scriptures . . . ?" οὐδέ, "not even," escalates to οὐδέποτε, "never" (5,0—literally "not even at any time"). ἀνέγνωτε advances; consequently, οὐδέποτε introduces the reading rather than the Scripture (see v 16, unique to Matthew). The direct object in the singular ("this Scripture") changes to a prepositional phrase with a plural ("in the Scriptures"; cf. 22:29; 26:54, 56). Matthew makes these revisions to intensify the guilt of the chief priests and elders of the people. Now their general reading of the OT, not just their reading of a particular passage, stands against them. A quotation of Ps 118:22 follows. It agrees entirely with Mark (see Gundry, *Use of the OT* 20, for points of special dependence on the LXX) and deals with the stone that the builders rejected but that the Lord amazingly made the head of the corner. The parable concludes with this quotation probably for a play on the Hebrew words בֵּן, "son" (cf. the son in the parable), and אֶבֶן, "stone" (see M. Black in *NTS* 18 [1971] 12-14).

If Jesus predicted his resurrection as well as his death, we need not think that v 42 was added later to give the parable a happy ending that figuratively alludes to his exaltation. The likelihood of a play on בֵּן and אֶבֶן and the prominence of similar quotations in Acts 4:11; Rom 9:33; 1 Pet 2:6-8 support originality. "The head of the corner" probably means a capstone, for a cornerstone in the foundation would have to be used in the very first stage of building—and that necessity seems not to allow for initial rejection. On the change of metaphors from farming to building, cf. Jer 1:10; 1QS 8:5; 1 Cor 3:9; Col 2:7.

21:43 Verse 43 is unique. Characteristically, Matthew composes it after the pattern of OT passages—viz., 1 Sam 15:28; Dan 2:44; 7:27—and as a verdict against the chief priests and elders of the people in favor of the church. διὰ τοῦτο and λέγω ὑμῖν typify his diction (4,2; 27,7) and appeared together in distinctive material at 6:25 and as an insertion in 12:31. They also make the verse an interpretation of the foregoing parable and emphasize the authority of Jesus' words. The next two lines form a couplet in antithetic parallel: "that the kingdom of God will be taken from you and will be given to a nation producing its fruits [i.e., the fruits of the kingdom]." Though often shared, ἀρθήσεται twice comes into Matthew as an insertion and appears in distinctive passages another three times. Matthew writes about God's kingdom instead of his more usual kingdom of heaven to establish yet another link with the parable of the two sons. As in v 31, the use of God's name is determined by the contextual need for the personal term: "the kingdom of God" interprets the vineyard of "the man, landowner, master." For similar contrastive uses of the verbs of taking and giving, see 13:12; 25:28-29. Matthew often inserts δοθήσεται and uses it in materials peculiar to his gospel (8-9,10). ἔθνει typifies his interests (7,2). Usually it occurs in the plural for the nations to be discipled. Here it comes from Dan 2:44, also alluded to in the next verse (see esp. the version of Theodotion), and refers to the church in a collective singular. Daniel predicts that the kingdom will *not* be passed on to another people, or nation; Matthew writes that it *will* be transferred. Elsewhere the evangelist shows special interest in ποιοῦντι and καρπούς, both separately (19,19; 5,1) and together (2,1). Here the figure renews his emphasis on good works (cf. vv 34, 41).

The discrepancy that in the parable fruits were produced but not given to the owner, whereas here it is implied that fruits were not even produced under the tenancy of the Jewish leaders, confirms Matthew's composition of this verse. He has heightened the guilt of the Jewish leaders at the cost of a discrepancy with the parable. Yet another discrepancy arises out of his composing v 43: in Mark, Luke, and Isaiah the vineyard represents the nation of the Jews, but Matthew's transferring the kingdom of God from their leaders to the nation that produces the fruits of that kingdom means that the vineyard now represents God's kingdom. Thus the church does not take the place of Israel as a whole, but of the Jewish leaders. The believing Jewish crowds melt into the throngs of believing Gentiles to form the new group of tenant farmers. Matthew's democratizing the custodianship of the kingdom fits his stressing the importance of little people in the church (10:40-42; 18:1-14). The chronology of the transfer remains ambiguous. On the one hand, the taking of the kingdom from the Jewish leaders and the fruit bearing of the church refer to the past and present. On the other hand, Matthew's distinctive allusion to Jesus' parousia ("Therefore when the owner ['Lord'] of the vineyard comes," v 40) and the use of Daniel's figures for the last judgment (v 44) point to the future. Matthew contents himself, then, with a combination of the already and not yet.

The passive verbs imply divine action. For Matthew's use of "the kingdom of God" see the comments on v 31. In ranging the Pharisees alongside the chief priests, Matthew favors theological concerns over technical description of the Sanhedrin, which consisted of chief priests, scribes, and elders. Not only have the elders disappeared, but also the Pharisees do not really substitute for the scribes, since some chief priests belonged to the Pharisaical sect and some scribes belonged to the Sadducean sect.

21:44 (Luke 20:18) Verse 44 does not appear in D 33 it[b,d,e,ff1,2,r1] syr[s] Diatessaron[v] Irenaeus[gr,lat] Origen Eusebius. Some textual critics therefore suspect an interpolation from Luke 20:18. But slight differences between Matthew's and Luke's forms of the saying favor its originality in Matthew.

Interpolation from Luke would probably have resulted in a text identical with Luke's. Furthermore, special agreements between Matthew and Luke in Markan materials crop up repeatedly; and allusion to the OT, such as v 44 contains, typifies Matthew's style. Verse 44 would have fit better right after v 42 because of the common reference to a stone in the two verses. But the awkwardness of v 44 after v 43 does not argue for clumsy interpolation of v 44. Rather, it confirms the composition of v 43 by Matthew in that his eagerness to write about transfer of the kingdom as the "marvelous" interpretation of v 42 resulted in an awkward delay of v 44. And the allusion to Dan 2:44 in v 43 leads to a further allusion to Dan 2:44 in v 44. The awkwardness in the delay of v 44 probably caused omission in the Western text (see further the UBS; Metzger, *Textual Commentary* ad loc.; and Gundry, *Use of the OT* 84-85). That Luke has nothing corresponding to v 43 despite his having a parallel to v 44, which extends the allusion to Dan 2:44, suggests Matthean influence in which part but not all of the allusion to Daniel comes across.

The first line of v 44 alludes to Isa 8:14-15, in particular to the stone of stumbling on which people fall and are broken. "And" (not in Luke) introduces a new saying after the interpolation of v 43. Matthew lacks "everyone," perhaps an addition by Luke, since Luke often adds it and Matthew's similar fondness for it (63,25-26) would probably have prevented omission. "He who falls on this stone will be broken in pieces" is matched in Luke except for "that" instead of "this." "But him on whom it will fall it will crush" (so also Luke) harks back to Dan 2:44, where the stone of God's heavenly kingdom comes tumbling down a mountain to strike the feet of the image representing worldly kingdoms and crush them to powder (see Gundry, *Use of the OT* 84-85, for textual comparisons). As a whole, v 44 adds an emphasis on the judgment of the Jewish leaders, an emphasis missing in Mark.

21:45-46 (Mark 12:12; Luke 20:19) Matthew now advances the Jewish leaders' perceiving the point of the parable. The advance highlights their guilt. It also results in a substitution of καί for γάρ because the latter has lost its base. The insertion of ἀκούσαντες typifies Matthew's style (10,3) and indicates the fulfillment of v 33, where Matthew alone wrote, "Hear another parable." "The chief priests and the Pharisees" (not in Mark or Luke) reidentifies the Jewish leaders as the guilty party. Thus in vv 15, 23, and 45 the chief priests have appeared successively with the scribes, the elders of the people, and the Pharisees. Matthew arraigns them all! ἀρχιερεῖς and Φαρισαῖοι are Mattheanisms (1,5; 18,1). "His parables" comes from Mark. But Matthew has pluralized Mark's singular to include the unique parable of the two sons (21:28-32) alongside the parable of the tenant farmers and thus gain a double indictment of the Jewish leaders. The insertion of "having heard" makes "his parables" the object of that participle rather than the object of "he spoke," as in Mark. "At them" (πρὸς αὐτούς) becomes the stronger "concerning them" (περὶ αὐτῶν) in a clear, condemnatory application of the preceding parables to the Jewish leaders. Replacement of "he spoke" with the historical present "he speaks" (λέγει, a Mattheanism—47,11) intensifies the emphasis.

Matthew avoids Mark's parataxis by reducing the finite verb "they were seeking" to the participle "seeking" and omitting the following "and." As often, "the crowd" becomes "the crowds" to suggest the largeness of the number that were to be discipled from all nations. Since Mark's explanatory statement, "For they [the Jewish leaders] knew that he spoke the parable at them," has already appeared in revised form, Matthew here substitutes a clause that harks back to the crowds' calling Jesus a prophet at his entry into Jerusalem: "since they held him for a prophet" (cf. v 11). The form of this clause stems largely from v 26c: "for all hold John as a prophet." Thus Matthew draws a parallel between Jesus and John the Baptist (cf. "John the Baptist parallel Jesus" in the Topical Index). Though revised in v 26c, Mark's imperfect εἶχον stays here. Matthew delays "And leaving him, they went away" in order to make room for the insertion of a third parable directed against the Jewish leaders.

THE SHARED CONDEMNATION OF JERUSALEM'S LEADERS AND FALSELY PROFESSING DISCIPLES IN THE PARABLE OF THE WEDDING FEAST
22:1-14 (Luke 14:15-24)

22:1-2 (Luke 14:15-16) To get a third parable condemning the Jewish leaders in Jerusalem, Matthew inserts a parable absent from Mark but present also in Luke 14:15-24. The first of the three parables centered on the ministry of John the Baptist (21:28-32). The second climaxed with the mission of Jesus the Son (21:33-44). This third looks forward to the mission of the church. From the standpoint of an assumption that Matthew found the present parable in a setting and form similar to Luke's, his revisions accord with his manner as seen in other passages. Someone's pronouncing blessed anybody who eats bread in the kingdom of God (so Luke) drops out. This omission makes the following parable a condemnation of the Jewish leaders rather than a reply to the overly enthusiastic pronouncer of the beatitude. καί contrasts with Luke's adversative δέ and sets the parable alongside the preceding two. The addition of ἀποκριθείς to εἶπεν typifies Matthew's style (29,6) and turns the parable into a response to the chief priests' and Pharisees' understanding that Jesus spoke the last parable about them and trying to seize him, but not doing so for fear of the crowds (21:45). The insertion of "Jesus" makes a Christological emphasis characteristic of Matthew (80,12). πάλιν, "again," ties the parable to the preceding two. As often, it is peculiar to Matthew (8,4—though it often drops out for contextual reasons). The addition "in parables," a stereotyped phrase in Matthew (5,0), again links the parable to the preceding two and may have been suggested by the omitted material leading up to the parable (see Luke 14:7). "To him" becomes "to them" for the sake of an address to the chief priests and Pharisees (21:45-46). As often Matthew adds λέγων (61,23).

"Parables" is a plural of category that might be translated "parabolically," but it refers in context particularly to the three parables in 21:28–22:14. Since vv 11-14

432

will come from Matthew himself, we have no reason to think of the plural as indicating that he conflated two traditional parables (vv 1-10 and 11-14). For the same reason, and also because v 7 will come from Matthew in dependence on Isaiah 5, the hypothesis that Jesus drew his parable from Zeph 1:1-16 and related verses concerning a holy war falls to the ground. Besides, Luke lacks military features; and Matthew writes of a wedding feast, to which the blitzkrieg is related only as a consequence of the refused invitation, not as a primary purpose. Nor is it good to think that Jesus used the rabbinic parable concerning a publican who arranged a midday banquet (ἄριστον) for some city councillors, was snubbed by them because of his occupation, and invited poor people to avoid wasting food (see Str-B 1. 880). For neither Luke nor Matthew identifies the man in Jesus' parable as a publican or the first invited guests as city councillors, and ἄριστον is a result of Matthew's editing (v 4). Also, Jesus' parable centers on the guests, not on the host. The unrealistic features of the parable—the concert with which the first invited ones reject the invitation, the mistreatment and murder of the slaves who bring the invitation, the repetition of the invitation, the king's sending an army to his own city, the burning of his own city, the carrying out of the military operation the afternoon of the day of the wedding feast with only a few hours' delay in the feast, and the bringing in of guests formerly deemed unsuitable—point up the message of the parable. A number of these unrealistic features are due to Matthew, not Jesus. Cf. *Gos. Thom.* 64.

In place of "A certain man" (so Luke), Matthew writes "The kingdom of heaven has been likened to a man, a king." This matches the distinctive statement in 18:23 verbatim. Except for its very last word, it also echoes 13:24 (likewise unique to the first gospel). ὡμοιώθη is a Mattheanism (2,3; see the comments on 7:24-25 for rabbinic background) and takes the aorist tense for a historical reference to the Jewish leaders' rejection of the kingdom. "The kingdom of heaven" is another Mattheanism (25,7). It was suggested by the beatitude on anybody "who eats bread in the kingdom of God" (Luke 14:15) and compensates for earlier omission of that beatitude. ἀνθρώπῳ comes from the tradition behind Luke and appears often in Matthew (35,17), especially at the start of parables with an appositive (see the comments on 18:23-35). The appositive βασιλεῖ replaces τις, emphasizes God's sovereignty, derives from the preceding parable (in which only Matthew interpreted the vineyard of the ἄνθρωπος [21:33] as the kingdom [21:43]), and typifies Matthew's diction (6,9), especially in parables (again see the comments on 18:23-35). The comparison has to do with the whole parable, not with the king alone, who represents God the Father. In 25:31-46 the king will represent Jesus the Son of man; but the alternation should not surprise us, since Matthew writes of the kingdom as belonging to both (see βασιλεία in the Greek Index).

The Mattheanism ὅστις (23,5) echoes the preceding parable, where it occurred as an insertion and referred, as here, to ἄνθρωπος (21:33). We read the aorist ἐποίησεν instead of Luke's imperfect ἐποίει. The change of δεῖπνον μέγα, "a big [late] dinner" (so Luke), to γάμους, "a wedding feast," shows influence from Jesus' "parabolic" teaching that leads up to the parable proper (Luke 14:7-14), particularly from Jesus' instructions concerning proper conduct "when you are called by someone to a wedding feast [εἰς γάμους]" (Luke 14:8). In this way Matthew compensates for his omission of that teaching. The insertion "for his son" not only represents Matthew's special diction (υἱῷ—27,16), but also reflects the prominence of sons in the preceding two parables in Matthew and links the present parable to the preceding. Since the son in the second parable represents Jesus (21:37, 38), his reappearance renews a Christological emphasis.

The messianic banquet was not ordinarily portrayed as a wedding feast, but see Rev 19:7, 9. γάμος often occurs in an idiomatic plural because of the duration of festivities.

22:3 (Luke 14:17) For the moment, Matthew skips "and he invited many" (so Luke), adopts "and he sent," and pluralizes "his slave" to agree with "he sent his slaves" in 21:34, where the plural appears only in his version (so also 21:35, 36). This assimilation to the preceding parable, where an allusion to the OT prophets seems obvious, favors an allusion to the OT prophets here, too (cf. Prov 9:1-6). That the time for the eschatological feast of salvation had not yet arrived in OT times shows the extent to which Matthew has imposed on the parable a reference to the OT prophets, whose predictions he often cites as fulfilled. Originally, the parable referred only to God's call through Jesus to the feast of salvation. "To invite" comes from "and he invited many" (so Luke) and makes up for an earlier omission. "The invited ones" anticipates vv 4 and 8 and replaces "many" for a parallel with the later verses (cf. Luke 14:7-8). Hence, the perfect tense of τοὺς κεκλημένους need not imply an earlier invitation. Besides, what invitation earlier than the ministry of the OT prophets could Matthew have in mind? Because he substituted "a wedding feast" for "a big dinner" in v 2, here he takes "to the wedding feast" from the material originally preceding the parable (Luke 14:8) and puts it in place of "at the hour of the dinner." He composes "and they did not want to go" (not in Luke) in reminiscence of 21:29: "I do not want [to go]." Thus a link is forged with the first as well as the second of the three parables. ἤθελον is a Mattheanism (18,8). See also the comments on 13:44-45 and cf. 2 Chr 30:10.

22:4 (Luke 14:17) Verse 4 begins, "Again he sent other slaves," exactly as in 21:36 against Mark 12:4; Luke 20:11 (cf. v 3 in the present chapter). So the doubling of the invitation to the first invited guests links with the two sendings of slaves in the parable of the tenant farmers. The insertion of λέγων reflects Matthew's style (61,23) and turns the infinitive "to say" into the imperative "Say." The command "Come, because [all things] are now ready" changes to the exclamation "Behold, I have readied my meal!" Matthew likes to insert ἰδού for emphasis (34,9). The shift to ἄριστον corresponds to the use of that term alongside δεῖπνον in the omitted material introducing the parable (Luke 14:12). Since ἄριστον refers to a meal early in the day, it will allow Matthew to insert a quick military attack on those who refuse the invitation (v 7). Presumably this attack takes place during the afternoon. By then the meal is delayed till evening, as evident in the mention of darkness (v 13, so Matthew alone). The perfect tense of ἡτοίμακα, "I have readied," carries the same force as Luke's ἤδη, "now," with ἕτοιμα, "ready."

For further emphasis, Matthew composes a couplet of lines that exhibit his fondness for parallelism, OT phraseology, echoes of the preceding context, and certain expressions: "my oxen and my fatlings [are] slaughtered, and all things [are] ready." The combination of oxen and fatlings recalls 2 Sam 6:13; 1 Kgs 1:9; and the association of fatlings and slaughter recalls the parable of the prodigal son (Luke 15:23, 27, 30), which seems to have given Matthew the two sons in the first of his present trio of parables (see the comments on 21:28). "And all things [are] ready" echoes "[all things] are ready" (so Luke), which Matthew revised earlier in v 4. Here he supplies πάντα, a favorite of his (63,25-26) that is implied but not stated in Luke. The verse closes with another, matching exclamation: "Hither to the wedding feast!" (not in Luke). δεῦτε is another favorite (2,2) and may echo the parable of the tenant farmers (see 21:38). εἰς τοὺς γάμους certainly echoes v 3, where it distinguished Matthew from Luke. Cf. Rev 19:17.

22:5-6 (Luke 14:18-21) οἱ δέ contrasts with Luke's καί and sets the response of the invited in opposition to the foregoing invitation. By summarizing "And they all began at once to make excuses" with "paying no attention," Matthew heightens the guilt of the Jewish leaders represented. They did not even bother to give excuses. Rather, "they went away" (ἀπῆλθον, a Mattheanism—14,11). This verb reflects "going out" (ἐξελθών) in the first excuse (so Luke), but also represents another assimilation to the parable of the two sons (21:29, 30; see also 13:46 and the comments on 13:44-46 for other changes due there to anticipation of the present parable). Matthew now summarizes the actions of the invited in typically parallelistic fashion: μέν . . . δέ . . . δέ (15,1). This construction yet again shows assimilation to the preceding parable of the tenant farmers (see 21:35 for Matthew's inserting the construction in the threefold treatment of the slaves).

"One [went away] to his own field" replaces the explanation of the first that he has bought a field and needs to go see it and the polite request to be excused (so Luke). In Matthew, the field has apparently belonged to its present owner for a long time. He neither offers an explanation nor makes a polite request, but brusquely turns his back to go about his normal work in the field. In this way Matthew again intensifies the guilt of the Jewish leaders represented. ἴδιον appeals to him (6,0). Here it indicates longtime ownership in contrast with recent purchase (cf. Luke's ἠγόρασα, borrowed by Matthew in 13:44).

"Another [went away] to his business" replaces the explanation concerning the purchase of five yoke of oxen that need to be tested and the polite request to be excused (so Luke). The original extenuating circumstance has again changed to the normal round of daily affairs. No explanation, no request—greater guilt. ἐμπορίαν occurs nowhere else in the NT, and its cognate ἐμπόρῳ was peculiar to Matthew in 13:45.

"The rest, seizing his slaves, mistreated and killed [them]" replaces the explanation offered by a single individual that he cannot come because he has married a wife (so Luke; see Deut 24:5; cf. Deut 20:7). This shift again intensifies guilt. λοιποί will occur as an insertion also in 27:49, as part of unique material in 25:11, and with a synoptic parallel only in 26:45. By echoing 21:46, κρατήσαντες forges another link between this parable and the preceding (cf. Matthew's liking the word—4,1). "His slaves" echoes vv 3 and 4 (see also 21:34, 35, 36 in the preceding parable). "Mistreated and killed" summarizes and echoes 21:35 (cf. Josephus *Ant.* 9.13.2 §265). Though the three who make excuses in the traditional form of the parable seem to represent the "many" who are invited, Matthew's pluralizing the last individual to make an excuse agrees both with the size of a royal wedding feast and with the city-wide destruction to come. It also agrees with the plurality of the murderous tenant farmers in the preceding parable. Since in Matthew the king's slaves have been murdered, the slave's reporting the excuses to his master naturally falls away.

Cf. 2 Sam 10:4; Josephus *Ant.* 9.13.2 §§263-66. Refusal of a king's invitation amounted to rebellion.

22:7 (*Luke 14:21*) For contrast, δέ stands where Luke has τότε, which Matthew usually favors. In conformity with v 2 "the king" replaces "the head of the household" (ὁ οἰκοδεσπότης—so Luke). The replacement is a Mattheanism (6,9) and not only reemphasizes God's sovereignty, but also prepares for military action. Escalation of the participle "becoming angry" to the finite verb "became angry" accentuates the divine wrath portrayed. For further emphasis, Matthew composes a couplet of lines: "and sending his armies, he destroyed those murderers and burned their city." The parallelistic structure agrees with Matthew's style. The aorist nominative participle πέμψας does, too (3,1). ἀπώλεσεν is a favorite of his (8,1) and echoes 21:41. φονεῖς occurs only here in the gospels, but Matthew inserted its cognate φονεύω twice in 5:21. In 23:31, 35 he will insert it twice again for the murder of the prophets, as here. ἐκείνους and πόλιν belong to his favorite vocabulary (26,9; 18,3). The latter reflects the tradition behind Luke 14:21 (see esp. 21:10, 17, 18 for recent insertions referring to Jerusalem, home of the antagonistic Jewish leaders). "Their city" does not imply a city different from the one where the king resided (cf. 5:35), but points to the separation of the church and Judaism. This separation is typical of Matthew's theology (cf. "their [or 'your'] synagogue" [5,0], "their scribes" [7:29], and "their cities" [11:1]).

The burning of the city illustrates Matthew's habit of alluding to the OT. Here the allusion is to Isa 5:24-25, part of a passage an earlier portion of which underlay the parable concerning the tenant farmers (21:33; cf. Isa 5:1-7). We know that Matthew was thinking about the OT passage, for he brought that parable closer to the text of Isaiah. The prophet's parable leads to a threat against Jerusalem that climaxes in "fire" and "flame . . . for they have rejected the law of the Lord of hosts [cf. Matthew's preoccupation with the law]. . . . On this account the anger [cf. the king's anger in Matt 22:7a] has burned against his people . . . and their corpses [cf. the destruction of the murderers in Matt 22:7b] were like refuse in the middle of the streets [cf. 'the outlets of the streets' in Matt 22:9]." We have no need, then, to suppose that Matthew is retrospecting the destruction of Jerusalem in A.D. 70. If he were, his distinctive "then" at the beginning of vv 8-9 would clearly imply that the mission to Gentiles represented in those later verses did not begin till A.D. 70 or shortly afterward. But that implication would disagree with his own theology of evangelism in 28:19-20, where Jesus sends out the disciples to make disciples of all nations right after his resurrection. Therefore, 22:7 does not point backward to A.D. 70, but is a dramatic figure of judgment drawn from Isaiah's prediction of a past destruction of Jerusalem, a judgment consisting in God's rejection of the Jewish leaders resident in that city. Matthew is merely following his habit of borrowing from the OT and showing his interest in the motif of judgment and his concern with cities. Jesus' prediction of Jerusalem's destruction according to the tradition taken over in chap. 24 may have triggered Matthew's present insertion (cf. pp. 599-600).

Cf. *Exod. Rab.* 18.10. The reading καὶ ἀκούσας ὁ βασιλεὺς ἐκεῖνος (so C W Δ [D Θ *f*[13]] 0138 *pm* the Byzantine family and Irenaeus) deserves some consideration because of Matthew's liking ἀκούσας (10,3) and ἐκεῖνος (26,9). "Then" at the beginning of v 8 rules out our thinking that the destruction of the city did not necessarily take place at once. That the king would hardly have invited people from a city different from his own excludes an implication of distance in πέμψας. The plural τὰ στρατεύματα may refer to a bodyguard, as in Luke 23:11; 4 Macc 5:1; *Mek. Exod.* 15:2.

22:8 (Luke 14:21) Matthew inserts his beloved τότε (66,17) in the introduction to the king's next statement and writes, as often, the historical present λέγει (47,11) where Luke has εἶπεν. The singular "to his slave" (so Luke) becomes plural, "to his slaves," in conformity with Matthew's pluralizing the slaves in vv 3, 4, 6 and 21:34, 35, 36. Since the slaves mentioned earlier in the parable have suffered death, we must think of further slaves here. If the first two contingents of slaves represent the OT prophets (perhaps the former and the latter), as they do in 21:34-36, and if the destruction of the murderers and burning of their city symbolize God's rejecting the Jewish leaders in Jerusalem, this third sending of slaves stands for the mission of the church to all nations beginning right after Jesus' resurrection. To reemphasize the guilt of the Jewish leaders, Matthew constructs a couplet of lines in the parallelistic fashion typical of his style: "The wedding feast is ready, but the invited ones were not worthy." μέν . . . δέ is a Mattheanism (15,1) and echoes v 5, where he inserted it. The readiness of the wedding feast echoes v 4. But for correspondence with τὸ ἄριστον in v 4, ὁ . . . γάμος takes the singular instead of the idiomatic plural used till now. οἱ κεκλημένοι echoes vv 3 and 4. And ἄξιοι, here negated, belongs to Matthew's special vocabulary (7,0; see esp. 10:13, 37 [bis], 38 for insertions of unworthiness in common material dealing with evangelism and conversion; cf. Acts 13:46). The unworthiness of the Jewish leaders consisted in their refusal to produce evidence of repentance by law-abiding discipleship (cf. vv 11-14 and Matthew's excoriation of the scribes and Pharisees for failure to keep the law—e.g., in 5:20 and chap. 23).

22:9 (Luke 14:21-22) In the commission proper, πορεύεσθε, a favorite of Matthew (13,10; see esp. 28:19 in the great commission), stands in place of ἔξελθε (so Luke). "Quickly" drops out, because Matthew's earlier shift from an evening meal to a mid-morning or noontime feast (vv 3-4) leaves more time than exists in the original form of the parable, where the first sending of a slave does not occur till "the hour of the evening meal" (Luke 14:17). The insertion of οὖν typifies Matthew's diction (35,11) and makes the Jewish leaders' unworthiness the reason for inviting all nations and thus recalls attention to the Jewish leaders' guilt. "To the outlets of the streets" (i.e., to the places where the streets of the city pierce through the walls and turn into country roads) replaces "into the streets and lanes of the city" because in Matthew the city has gone up in smoke (v 7). People will be found only in the country. They represent all nations (cf. 28:19-20 and Luke 14:23). "As many as you find" is made up of Mattheanisms—ὅσους (5,6), ἐάν (28,3), and εὕρητε (7,8)—and replaces "the poor and crippled and blind and lame." Luke's list is sometimes thought to be the result of assimilation to the saying in Luke 14:13, but the similarity is better taken as an indication that Luke has preserved the original setting and wording of the parable. The poor, crippled, blind, and lame begged along the streets and lanes of the city. Matthew has thrown the city to the flames and can no longer write of such beggars; so he generalizes concerning the people the slaves might find along the country roads. With his usual concern for parallelism, he replaces "bring in here" with "call [i.e., invite] to the wedding feast," which echoes an almost identical insertion in v 3. Since two summons have already gone out in Matthew and the city lies in ashes, the statement of the slave that the master's command has been followed and "yet there is room" (so Luke) vanishes.

22:10 (Luke 14:23) Matthew omits "And the master said to the slave" and turns the master's command "Go out into the roads and hedges and compel [people] to come in so that my house may be filled" into a description of obedience: "and going out into the roads, those slaves gathered together all whom they found, both evil and good, and the wedding hall was filled with diners." ἐξελθόντες corresponds to Luke's ἔξελθε, but its taking a nominative participial form at the beginning of a clause is typical of Matthew's style (10,4). He pluralizes the slave to conform with the preceding context. ἐκεῖνοι (not in Luke) is a favorite of his (26,9). "Into the roads" matches Luke, but "and hedges" drops out. "Compel to come in" gives way to "they gathered together," which portrays the gathered converts from all nations as the true synagogue (cf. the comments on 2:4). συνήγαγον is another favorite of Matthew (10,10). "All whom they found" is not in Luke. Apart from the substitution of "all" for "as many as," it comes from v 9, where Matthew inserted it. The additional insertion of "both evil and good" stems from Matthew's diction (4,1 for the combination of πονηρούς and ἀγαθούς). It points to the mixture of true and false—i.e., obedient and disobedient—disciples in the church and sets the stage for the further addition of vv 11-14 (cf. 13:24-30, 36-43, 47-50). That the evil are mentioned before the good hints that Matthew's concern focuses on the problem of false disciples.

The substitution of "and" for "in order that" makes a couplet of lines that accords with Matthew's taste for parallelism. ἐπλήσθη, "was filled," stands in place of Luke's γεμισθῇ, "may be filled" (see also 27:48 with Mark

15:36). "My house" yields to "the wedding hall" in reminiscence of vv 2, 3, 4, 8, 9. Matthew's singular stems from the singular of the replaced "house" (contrast the plurals elsewhere except v 8). Since a wedding hall, or feast, implies eating, Matthew adds "with people reclining at meal [i.e., diners]" (cf. other insertions in v 11 and 9:10; 26:7).

The variant reading νυμφών, "wedding hall," probably represents a scribal attempt to get rid of an unusual use of γάμος for a wedding hall rather than for a wedding feast, as in the preceding context. In Matthew the filling of the hall cannot have the purpose of keeping the originally invited guests from coming late, for they have been destroyed (v 7). We may doubt such a purpose even in Luke, however, because it necessitates deletion of Luke 14:20 (recent marriage hardly constituted a plea to be allowed late arrival), whereas "all" in Luke 14:18 requires at least three excuses. Besides, Luke's παραιτεῖσθαι, "to excuse themselves," normally implies release rather than delay. Luke 14:24 simply emphasizes forfeiture, not the exclusion of latecomers.

22:11 (Luke 14:24) The emphatic statement that not a single one of those men originally invited will taste the dinner (so Luke) drops out in favor of vv 11-14, which are unique (cf. *b. Šabb.* 153a). Apparently Matthew composes these verses to warn against false discipleship. Initial nominative participles such as εἰσελθών typify his style. "Entering" is an antithetic parallel to "going out" at the start of v 10 (cf. the adversative δέ). "The king" echoes vv 2 and 7 (both unique in this respect) and reflects Matthew's frequent use of βασιλεύς (6,9). θεάσασθαι occurs as an insertion also in 23:5 and as part of distinctive material in 6:1. It implies divine inspection of professing disciples at the last judgment. "The diners" echoes a similar addition in v 10. Further Mattheanisms are evident in ἐκεῖ (16,6), ἄνθρωπον (35,17), and ἔνδυμα (6,0). γάμου echoes vv 2, 3, 4, 8, 9, 10 and is singular because of the singular in the preceding verse. The missing wedding garment is probably a newly washed garment (cf. Zech 3:3-5; Rev 3:4, 5, 18; 19:8; 22:14; *1 Enoch* 62:15-16; *m. Ta'an.* 4:8) and symbolizes neither eschatological joy nor works meriting salvation, but evidential works of righteousness.

See Jeremias, *Parables* 187, on the host's allowing guests to eat by themselves and appearing during the meal. Matthew departed from the realistic features of daily life early in the parable (see the comments on v 1) and does not bother himself with the question of how the country folk could have washed their garments. After all, the slaves went out and "gathered" them, apparently in such a way as to allow no interval between their being invited and their coming. Perhaps we are meant to infer that the king made available a clean and appropriate garment for each guest (cf. 2 Kgs 25:29; Esth 6:8-9; Rev 19:8; Josephus *J.W.* 2.8.5 §§128-31). Cf. Isa 61:10 with Isa 61:8 and the rabbinic parable in *b. Šabb.* 153a; *Midr. Prov.* 16.11; *Midr. Qoh.* 9.8.

22:12 The historical present in "And he says to him" typifies Matthew's style (47,11) and echoes the insertion of λέγει in v 8. ἑταῖρε, "Friend," is always distinctive (2,1) and occurs also in 20:13; 26:50 for false disciples.

πῶς comes from Matthew's preferred vocabulary (6,1). "Did you come in here" comes from the previously replaced material appearing in Luke 14:21-22 and compensates for the earlier replacement. "Not having a wedding garment" echoes v 11. The question deals with right of entrance, not means of entrance. "And he was silenced" dramatically indicates the false disciple's lack of excuse. Later in this chapter Matthew will insert Jesus' silencing the Sadducees (see v 34).

22:13 The introduction to the king's instructions begins with two Mattheanisms, τότε (66,17) and βασιλεύς (6,9). The latter echoes vv 2, 7, and 11. Earlier in the parable some of the slaves represented disciples engaged in evangelism (vv 8-10). Still earlier in the first gospel it is angels who gather false disciples out of the kingdom and throw them into a fiery furnace (13:41-42, 49-50). Therefore Matthew now switches from slaves (we might have expected τοῖς δούλοις) to servants (τοῖς διακόνοις). The servants are distinct from the slaves and represent the same angels that do the judgmental work in the parables of the tares and bad fish, both of which are peculiar to Matthew. Cf. the unparalleled use of διάκονος also in 23:11 and of the cognate διακονέω in 25:44. Just as in the parable of the tares angels bind (δήσατε) the tares and throw (βαλοῦσιν) them into the fiery furnace (13:30, 42), so also here the servants are told to bind (δήσαντες) the man without a wedding garment and throw him out (ἐκβάλετε) into the outermost darkness. Matthew likes δέω and its cognates (8,2). Its nominative participial form and first position are typical of his style. "Feet and hands" emphasizes the severity of the judgment. Cf. *1 Enoch* 10:4. Matthew also likes πόδας (4,1) and ἐκβάλετε (10,1). Here the latter accompanies "into the outermost darkness," as in 8:12; 25:30, where Matthew twice inserts the entire expression (see the comments on 8:11-12). The next clause forms the second line of a couplet in accord with his love of parallelism: "Weeping and gnashing of teeth will be there." This statement occurs in 8:12; 13:42, 50; 22:13; 24:51; 25:30. Only in 8:12 does it have a synoptic parallel. All of this accentuates the horror of the punishment awaiting false disciples.

22:14 Why will there be weeping and gnashing of teeth in the outermost darkness? The Mattheanism γάρ (62-63,15) shows that v 14 supplies an answer: "for many are called, but few are chosen." Therefore we are to think of the "many" as the "all," "both evil and good," whom the slaves "gathered together"; i.e., the "many" represent the masses in the church. By the same token, we are to think of the "few" as the minority in professing Christendom who manifest the genuineness of their discipleship with works of righteousness (so 21:31, 43—both unique to Matthew—in the first two of the present trio of parables). The proportions seem topsy-turvy, since only one wedding guest was thrown out into the darkness of night, whereas the rest of the guests remained in the lighted wedding hall. But Matthew could hardly have emptied the wedding hall of most of the king's guests without ruining the festivities. His turning the proportions upside down only shows the pervasiveness of false profession in the church and the strength of his concern with the problem. πολλοί (23,1), ὀλίγοι (1,2; cf. 4,0 for ὀλιγοπιστ-), and the parallelistic structure of the two clauses bear Matthew's stamp. Therefore we may attribute the composition of v 14 as well as of vv 11-13 to him. "Called" echoes vv 3 (bis), 4, 8, 9; and "chosen" anticipates its use for those whom the Son of man will take as his own at the parousia (24:22, 24, 31). As a whole, v 14 is more parenetic than predestinarian.

The center of gravity in the notion of election had shifted from God's choice of the whole nation of Israel (so the OT) to that of the righteous remnant in the nation (so Wis 3:9; 4:15; *1 Enoch* passim, esp. 5:1-9; *Apoc. Abr.* 29; see *TDNT* 4. 145-72). Matthew reflects the latter use in referring to true disciples. His concern with the large number of false disciples and the fewness of true disciples makes this saying only superficially similar to 2 Esdr 8:1, 3, 55; 9:15; *2 Apoc. Bar.* 44:15, where the thought deals with the fewness of the saved and the large number of the lost in the world at large. Matthew's composing the saying in Greek militates against a treatment of "called" and "chosen" as synonyms resting on the same Aramaic word and standing in dialectical tension.

THE EVIL OF THE PHARISEES IN TESTING JESUS ON THE ISSUE OF PAYING TAXES TO CAESAR
22:15-22 (Mark 12:13-17; Luke 20:20-26)

22:15 In the first gospel this incident begins with a distinctive clause that emphasizes the evil of the Pharisees. Mattheanisms abound in τότε (66,17), πορευθέντες (8,4), Φαρισαῖοι (18,1), and συμβούλιον ἔλαβον (3,2). Together, the last two expressions echo 12:14. "The Pharisees" anticipates Mark 12:13a. For his next clause Matthew brings up "in order that they might catch him as to a statement" from Mark 12:13b. The advance shows his purpose of accentuating the evil of the Pharisees. ἵνα yields to ὅπως, another Mattheanism (8,7). παγιδεύσωσιν, which is frequent in the LXX, replaces ἀγρεύσωσιν, which is infrequent in the LXX. Mark's dative of reference λόγῳ becomes the prepositional phrase ἐν λόγῳ, "in a statement."

22:16 (Mark 12:13-14; Luke 20:20-21) Now Matthew takes up Mark 12:13a by writing "And they send" in agreement with Mark, and αὐτῷ for Mark's synonymous πρὸς αὐτόν. Because the Pharisees have been mentioned already, "their disciples" replaces "some of the Pharisees." The replacement makes the Pharisees the subject of "send," in contrast with Mark, where the chief priests and elders send some of the Pharisees (see Mark 11:27 with Mark 12:13). In 9:14 Matthew did the reverse; i.e., he exchanged "the disciples of the Pharisees" in Mark 2:18 for "the Pharisees." Opposite as they are, both revisions cast the Pharisees in a worse light, in 9:14 by putting them over against Jesus' disciples, here by making them the instigators, not merely the agents, of his testing. Now that the Pharisees are sending their disciples instead of being sent by the chief priests and elders, Mark's "and" before "the Herodians" changes to "with." For the Pharisees could hardly send the Herodians; but they could send their own disciples along with the Herodians, who go of their own accord.

Matthew now skips Mark's ἵνα-clause, which he took over in v 15, and summarizes "And coming, they say to him" with λέγοντας (61,23). The flattering "Teacher, we know that you are truthful" matches Mark verbatim. But for emphasis on Jesus' teaching the two ways, especially God's way, Matthew advances "but on the basis of truth you teach the way of God" (so Mark; cf. Matt 7:13-27; 21:32). Within this clause τὴν ὁδὸν τοῦ θεοῦ advances to the front to increase the emphasis, and ἐπ', "on the basis of," changes to ἐν, "in." In Matthew the clause forms the second line of a couplet in which there is a play on "truthful" and "in truth" (cf. 1QapGen 2:5). Advancing the clause leaves Mark's remaining two clauses as another couplet of parallel lines: "and you court nobody's favor, for you do not show partiality to any man."

22:17 (*Mark 12:14; Luke 20:22*) To stress the importance of Jesus' words, Matthew makes the Pharisees ask Jesus to tell them what he thinks: "Tell us therefore what seems right to you" (not in Mark or Luke). οὖν is frequent in Matthew (35,11) and sets the request on the foundation of Jesus' true and impartial teaching of God's way (v 16). τί σοι δοκεῖ represents Matthew's distinctive style (4,2). "Is it permissible [i.e., harmonious with divine will] to give a tax to Caesar or not?" reads alike in Matthew and Mark. But Matthew omits "Should we give or should we not give?" perhaps to leave a couplet of lines in accord with his taste for parallelism. His earlier addition of the request that Jesus say what he thinks has made the deliberative question excessive. Luke agrees with Matthew in the omission despite his having no request that Jesus say what he thinks. On the other hand, Luke may not be reflecting Matthew, but getting rid of a seemingly redundant question, just as he omits one of the references to Jesus' impartiality.

The Herodians were supporters of Herod Antipas, son of Herod the Great, and had come to Jerusalem from the territories ruled by Antipas (Galilee and Perea) to celebrate the Passover. Since Antipas held his power under Roman authority, the Herodians naturally favored payment of the tax to Rome. Though paying, the Pharisees shared the common Jewish resentment of the tax. Therefore the Pharisees and the Herodians personify the two horns of a dilemma: (1) if Jesus favors paying the tax, the Pharisees can destroy his popularity; (2) if Jesus opposes paying the tax, the Herodians can haul him to the Roman authorities under the charge of seditious teaching (cf. *b. Pesah.* 112b). Jesus gives wide berth to the second horn and will avoid the first by embarrassing the Pharisees with their own practice of paying the tax. Though Matthew omitted the Herodians in 12:14 (cf. Mark 3:6), they remain here because of their representing the second horn of the dilemma. The tax resembled a poll tax and may have been one, but we do not know its frequency or amount. Jews hated the tax all the more because the Romans insisted on payment with coins bearing the image of the head of the emperor and inscribed with his divine and other cultic claims, all in violation of the first two commandments of the decalogue.

22:18 (*Mark 12:15; Luke 20:23*) In the account of Jesus' response Matthew substitutes γνούς (8,2) for Mark's synonymous εἰδώς and, as usual, puts his nominative participle at the very beginning of the sentence. The insertion of "Jesus" tallies with his regular practice (80,12) and, with the omission of Mark's "to them" at the end of the clause, concentrates attention on Jesus the authoritative teacher. πονηρίαν, "evil," replaces ὑπόκρισιν, "hypocrisy," and recalls Matthew's penchant for πονηρός (10,4). As a matter of style, he puts αὐτῶν after its noun (contrast Mark and Luke); and to Jesus' question, "Why do you test me?" he adds the address ὑποκριταί, "hypocrites" (8,3). The addition not only compensates for the preceding replacement of hypocrisy, but also doubles the wickedness of the Pharisees.

22:19 (Mark 12:15-16; Luke 20:24) Jesus follows his question with the command "Show me the coin for the tax." ἐπιδείξατε, "show," takes the place of Mark's φέρετε, "bring," to avoid redundancy in the next line. Matthew likes his verb (3,0), which never occurs in Mark and appears only once in Luke. Nevertheless, Luke's simple δείξατε seems to show Matthean influence. Again Matthew wants to avoid redundancy in the next line; so he reserves Mark's "a denarius" and replaces it with "the coin for the tax" (cf. v 17 and 17:25). To gain a couplet of parallel lines, he omits "in order that I may see [it]" and goes to "And they brought him a denarius." Mark's ἤνεγκαν acquires προσ- to suit Matthew's diction (9,2) and connote an offering to Jesus (see the comments on 2:11; 4:24). The reservation of "a denarius" for this line, where Mark lacks an expressed object, makes for a closer parallel with Matthew's preceding line.

22:20-21 (Mark 12:16-17; Luke 20:24-26) "And he says to them, 'Whose image and inscription [is] this?'" matches Mark exactly. Matthew changes "And they said to him" to the historical present λέγουσιν αὐτῷ with asyndeton, a favorite device of his for emphasis (21,6). Similarly, the introduction to Jesus' response changes from "And Jesus said to them" to "Then he says to them." The result is a string of three historical present forms of λέγω in vv 20a, 21a, and 21b. "Give back" comes to the head of the clause in order that "the things of Caesar to Caesar" may fall at the end for a closer parallel with the following elliptical clause, "and [give back] the things of God to God." The simple δοῦναι, "to give," in the question put to Jesus (v 17) has gained the prefix ἀπο-, "back," to indicate that payment of the tax is as obligatory as payment of a debt, for it *is* a debt. The insertion of οὖν, "therefore," typifies Matthew's diction (35,11), is similar to and possibly reflected in Luke's τοίνυν, "hence," and makes Jesus' answer depend on the stamp of Caesar's likeness on the coin. Perhaps there is a suggestion that the divine image in which God created man makes it obligatory to give oneself to God in obedience to his commands.

See Prov 8:15; Dan 2:21, 37-38; Wis 6:1-11; Rom 13:1-7; 1 Pet 2:13-17 on the positive view of the state under God. Cf. Heb 5:1 with "the things of God," a reference to sacrifices and other dues, but possibly also a reference to human beings themselves.

22:22 (Mark 12:17; Luke 20:26) To the description of the questioners' reaction, Matthew characteristically adds "hearing" (ἀκούσαντες— 10,3) for stress on Jesus' authoritative pronouncement. The prefix ἐξ- vanishes from Mark's ἐξεθαύμαζον. The result is the far more usual simple form of the verb. Its imperfect tense changes to aorist (cf. Luke's aorist participle of the simple form). Mark's "at him" also falls away, for elsewhere in Matthew the verb never takes such a phrase. Finally, Matthew adds "and leaving him, they went away" from Mark 12:12b, which he has reserved till now as a fitting conclusion to Jesus' besting the Pharisees in argument (cf. 21:46).

THE CULPABLE ERROR OF THE SADDUCEES IN DENYING THE RESURRECTION
22:23-33 (Mark 12:18-27; Luke 20:27-40)

22:23-24 (Mark 12:18-19; Luke 20:27-28) "On that day" replaces Mark's "And." Matthew's phrase connotes historic time (see similar insertions in 3:1 and esp. 13:1). Changing ἔρχονται Σαδδουκαῖοι πρὸς αὐτόν το προσῆλθον αὐτῷ Σαδδουκαῖοι puts stress on Jesus' dignity by the adding of προσ- to the verb (38,6—so also Luke; see the comments on 4:3; 8:14). The delay of Σαδδουκαῖοι till last makes it easier to change "who say" to "saying" (cf. Luke). This revision does not show ignorance of Sadducean theology (as though Matthew thought that only these Sadducees denied the resurrection or that the Sadducees denied it only on this occasion but allowed or affirmed it at other times). Rather, the change reflects his style (λέγοντες is a Mattheanism—61,23), represents the strong preference in Hellenistic Greek for direct discourse (cf. BDF §§396, 397[5]; Matt 26:1-2 with Mark 14:1), and turns an academic description of the Sadducees' theology (so Mark and Luke) into a vivid account of what they said to Jesus in accordance with their theology (see the UBS and Metzger, *Textual Commentary* ad loc., on the v.1. and cf. Acts 23:8; Josephus *J.W.* 2.8.11-14 §§154-66; *Ant.* 18.1.3-5 §§12-22). In the denial of the resurrection Matthew puts ἀνάστασιν after μὴ εἶναι, for which it is the subject (contrast the word order in Mark and Luke). This placement corresponds to his placement of the subject of the main verb. "They were asking [or, 'began to ask']" changes to "they asked" (so also Luke).

In the first clause of the Sadducees' question, "Teacher, Moses wrote to us," Matthew changes the verb to "said" and omits the indirect object in order to draw a parallel between Moses' speaking and Jesus' speaking (cf. v 29 and "Moses parallel Jesus" in the Topical Index). What Moses said comes from the law of levirate marriage in Deut 25:5 and Gen 38:8 (cf. the allusion to Genesis 38 in Matt 1:3). As usual, Mark's recitative ὅτι drops out (so also Luke). "Someone's brother" changes to "someone" for closer conformity to Deut 25:5: "If . . . one of them [brothers who dwell together] dies." "And should leave behind a wife" (so Mark) drops out for the same reason (cf. the comments on 19:10-12). "And should not leave a child" becomes "not having children." The change from not leaving to not having conforms yet again to Deut 25:5: "and have no child" (cf. Num 27:4-11 for understanding בֵּן in Deuteronomy as a child of either sex; see further Gundry, *Use of the OT* 45 n. 1). "Children" rests on understanding the singular in Mark and Deuteronomy as collective. Matthew omits Mark's ἵνα, which is awkward after ὅτι, and replaces "should take" with "shall marry as next of kin" in an allusion to Gen 38:8. "His" is added to "wife" for a parallel with "his brother." Matthew continues with the imperatival future instead of Mark's aorist subjunctive ἐξαναστήσῃ. The result is ἀναστήσει in the command ". . . shall raise up seed for his brother." Gen 38:8 provides the whole line. Omission of ἐξ- conforms to the LXX and sharpens the wordplay on ἀνάστασιν (v 23) and ἀναστήσει.

22:25 (Mark 12:20; Luke 20:29) By advancing ἦσαν Matthew allows ἑπτὰ ἀδελφοί to stand at the end, where the following enumeration picks up the seven brothers more easily. The insertion of δέ avoids asyndeton and contrasts the quoted law with the supposedly impossible situation described below. The further insertion "with us" makes an actual case out of one that might be only theoretical, and it reflects Matthew's habit of using παρά with the dative (2,2). In anticipation of v 30 "took a wife" becomes "[after] marrying." Luke retains Mark's wording, but agrees with Matthew's switch to a participial construction and the consequent loss of "and." Mark's participle ἀποθνῄσκων becomes the finite verb ἐτελεύτησεν, which with its cognates represents Matthew's favorite diction (16,7). Thus for a better contrast with resurrection the stress falls on dying rather than on marrying. Again Luke agrees with Mark in diction, but with Matthew in grammatical construction. Matthew has to insert "and." Then he changes "he did not leave" to "not having" for a parallel with v 24b. The insertion "he left his wife to his brother" provides a complement to v 24c: "his brother shall marry his wife as next of kin."

22:26-27 (Mark 12:21-22; Luke 20:30-32) Rather than repeat details of the second brother's marrying the woman, dying, and not leaving seed (so Mark), Matthew reaches down for Mark's ὡσαύτως concerning the third brother, substitutes the synonymous ὁμοίως (as also in 26:35 over against Mark 14:31; cf. Matthew's liking ὅμοιος—1,5), and brings it up to apply to the second brother as well as the third. There is further summarizing in the substitution of "through the seven" for "and the seven left no seed." ἕως is a Mattheanism (13,14). These summarizations make for a quicker approach to Jesus' words, where Matthew's main interest lies. Mark's ἔσχατον never occurs as an adverb in the first gospel; here it yields to a synonymous favorite of Matthew, ὕστερον (3,3; so also Luke). The insertion of δέ avoids Mark's asyndeton and leads to the omission of καί, "also," before ἡ γυνή, which Matthew puts after the verb (contrast Mark and Luke).

22:28 (Mark 12:23; Luke 20:33) The Sadducees now attempt a reductio ad absurdum. If we read "when they rise" after "in the resurrection" in Mark, Matthew replaces the pleonastic clause with "therefore" (so also Luke in a different position). If the clause did not appear in Matthew's text of Mark, the conjunction is simply added. Either way, it belongs to his special vocabulary (35,11) and makes the Sadducees' question grow out of the story of the woman. See the UBS and Metzger, *Textual Commentary* ad loc., on the textual question in Mark. To correspond with v 26, the interrogative "whose of them?" changes to "whose of the seven?" Because of this change, "all" replaces "the seven" in the further statement that "the seven had her." πάντες echoes v 27 and comes from Matthew's preferred diction (63,25-26). Mark's "as a wife" falls off as redundant.

22:29 (Mark 12:24; Luke 20:34) Because the preceding is inter-rogative, Matthew slips ἀποκριθείς into the introduction to Jesus' reply and changes Mark's ἔφη to the synonymous εἶπεν (so also Luke) for his frequent combination ἀποκριθείς . . . εἶπεν (29,6). The addition of δέ (cf. Luke's καί) avoids asyndeton, and the predicate takes a natural position at the end of the clause. To intensify the guilt of the ignorant Sadducees, Matthew changes Mark's question, "Are you not deceived on account of this—your not knowing the Scriptures nor the power of God?" to the flat declaration "You are deceived, not knowing the Scriptures nor the power of God." The omission of "not . . . on account of this" accomplishes the switch.

22:30 (Mark 12:25; Luke 20:35-36) For a parallel with v 28, "in the resurrection" replaces Mark's "when people rise from the dead." Matthew singularizes "in the heavens" to match the singular of "in the resurrection" and delays εἰσιν till the end of the line to conform to the position of the preceding verbs. Thus he tidies up the parallelism. This saying shows God's power to change life at the resurrection, so that marriage is eliminated. Presumably immortality will make procreation needless. That the Saddu-cees denied the existence of angels lends sarcasm to Jesus' comparing the absence of marriage in the society of the resurrected with the absence of marriage among angels.

22:31 (Mark 12:26; Luke 20:37) Now Jesus identifies a Scripture which the Sadducees did not understand even though they had read it. For smoothness and correspondence with preceding occurrences of the noun for resurrection, "But concerning the resurrection of the dead" replaces "But concerning the dead, that they rise." The identification of the OT passage as "in the book of Moses at the thornbush" disappears. Conse-quently, Moses' authority fades before the higher authority expressed in "what was spoken to you by God, saying," which takes the place of "how God spoke to him, saying" (cf. Matt 1:22; 2:15). See the comments on 5:21-48 concerning τὸ ῥηθέν as a Mattheanism. The replacement of "to him [Moses]" with "to you [Sadducees]" intensifies the guilt of the Sadducees.

22:32 (Mark 12:26-27; Luke 20:37-38) The quotation itself comes from Exod 3:6: "I am the God of Abraham and the God of Isaac and the God of Jacob." Matthew's "am" (not in Mark; Exod 3:6 MT; or Acts 7:32) agrees with the LXX and clarifies the argument that God would not and does not identify himself as *presently* the God of those who have died without hope of resurrection. For him to do so would amount to a confes-sion of powerlessness (cf. v 29b). In the deduction that "he is not the God of dead people, but of living people," the insertion of "the" before "God" arises out of Matthew's desire for a closer parallel with "the God" in the first line. See the UBS and Metzger, *Textual Commentary* ad loc., on the variant omission of "the," an omission probably reflecting the other syn-optics. In accord with biblical anthropology, Jesus assumes that hope of future life includes physical life to fulfill God's intent for man at creation. Mark's "You are much deceived" drops out as redundant after v 29 and as spoiling what Matthew considered the climax in Jesus' appeal to the OT (so also Luke).

Cf. Isa 26:19; Dan 12:2. Jesus may have appealed to the Pentateuch because the Sadducees held it in higher esteem than the rest of the OT. In fact, it is hard to think that they could have denied the resurrection and the existence of angels without rejecting the authority of the rest of the OT altogether; for those doctrines are clearly taught there (on the resurrection see Dan 12:1-2; cf. Isa 26:19; Ezek 37:1-14; Job 19:25-27; and passim for angels besides the angel of the Lord, who can be regarded as a manifestation of God).

22:33 (*Luke 20:39-40*) To emphasize Jesus' authority as teacher of the law, Matthew adds the statement "And hearing, the crowds were amazed at his teaching" (cf. Luke). ἀκούσαντες is a Mattheanism (10,3) and echoes recent insertions in 21:33, 45; 22:22. Except for a slightly different order of words, the rest of the statement echoes 7:28. The plural of "the crowds" typifies Matthew's style (17,1) and symbolizes the masses of Gentiles coming into the church. For διδαχῇ cf. both 7:28, another insertion in 16:12, and cognates (9,4). Luke 20:39-40 seems to have been added under influence from Matthew. But Luke conformed the addition to Mark 12:34 (cf. Luke 10:28).

THE GATHERING OF THE PHARISEES AGAINST THE MESSIAH IN THE QUESTION ABOUT THE GREAT COMMANDMENT
22:34-40 (Mark 12:28-34; Luke 10:25-28)

22:34 Matthew starts by inserting a statement that contrasts the Pharisees' antagonistic response to Jesus' putting down the Sadducees and the favorable response of the crowds, whom he portrayed as disciples (v 33). As a result, the Pharisees appear in an extremely bad light. The opening phrase contains two Mattheanisms in οἱ ... Φαρισαῖοι) (18,1) and ἀκούσαντες (10,3; cf. 21:45; 22:15). Matthew inserts the former. The latter was suggested by Mark 12:28. As a whole, the phrase triplicates Matthew's insertions in 12:24; 15:12. "That he had silenced the Sadducees" reflects v 12, where "silenced" helped make up Matthew's addition to the parable of the great supper, and vv 23-33. "Gathered together to the same place" is a typically Matthean quotation of the OT, in particular of Ps 2:2 (see Gundry, *Use of the OT* 141, on its Septuagintal form; cf. 26:3-4; Acts 4:26; and the comments on 2:4). In Mark, one of the scribes comes, hears the discussion with the Sadducees, and asks a question about the first commandment. In Matthew, the Pharisees have already heard of Jesus' silencing the Sadducees and gather together first. Only then does one of them ask a question. Thus Matthew revises the tradition in order to gain an allusion to Ps 2:2. In that psalm it is the heathen who gather against the Lord's anointed. But Matthew has made the crowds represent converts from heathenism (v 33); so now he applies the psalm to a segment of the Jewish leadership, the Pharisees.

Matthew does not imply that the Pharisees delight in Jesus' routing the Sadducees. Rather, the two groups cooperate against Jesus. On the connotation of coalition in ἐπὶ τὸ αὐτό, see M. Wilcox, *The Semitisms of Acts* (Oxford: Clarendon, 1965) 93-100.

22:35-36 (Mark 12:28; Luke 10:25) Matthew rejoins Mark and draws "asked" from its later position to substitute for "approaching." He habitually uses the latter to connote respectful approach to Jesus as Lord (προσέρχομαι—38,6). But that does not fit the antagonism of the Pharisees in gathering against Jesus. "One of the scribes" changes to "one from among them, a lawyer" because Matthew imported the Pharisees into the preceding verse. εἷς ἐκ shows Matthew's Semitic heritage (אֶחָד מִן). "Lawyer" is text-critically suspect; it may have resulted from scribal assimilation to Luke 10:25. On the other hand, the relative weakness of the support for omission (f¹ itᵉ syrˢ arm geo Origenᵍʳ,ˡᵃᵗ), Matthew's liking the cognate "law" (νόμος—6,0), and the reasonableness of our supposing that he wanted a substitute for Mark's reference to the scribes favor that the omission of "lawyer" represents Mark's influence on copyists of Matthew. Since Matthew has already written that the Pharisees heard about Jesus' silencing the Sadducees, he now omits Mark's statements that one of the scribes "heard them [Jesus and the Sadducees] arguing and saw that Jesus answered them [the Sadducees] well." This omission occurs also in Luke 10:25-28 and therefore supports "lawyer" as another such agreement in the original of Matthew's text. Yet again, Matthew and Luke largely agree in the substitution of "testing" for Mark's "asked," which Matthew advanced earlier. Since Luke has neither imported the Pharisees nor advanced "asked," he lacks Matthew's reasons for making the present changes. Hence, influence from Matthew seems likely. Notably, Matthew has turned a mere argument in which Jesus answered the Sadducees "well" into a full-fledged victory: "he silenced the Sadducees." "Testing" echoes 4:1, 3; 16:1; 19:3 and therefore casts the Pharisaic lawyer in a Satanic role.

To the testing question, Matthew adds "Teacher," which echoes vv 16 and 24, emphasizes Jesus' didactic authority, and again agrees with Luke against Mark. The term is a Mattheanism (4,1; see 5:1-2 for its positive use on the lips of Jesus' opponents and 23:8 for Jesus' claiming the title in a passage unique to Matthew). Mark's "is" falls out between "What?" and "the first commandment of all." Omission of the copula again shows Matthew's Semitic heritage. "Great" was suggested by "greater" in Mark 12:31 and replaces "first." Matthew likes μεγάλη (11,1), but he likes πρώτη, too (2,5-6). Apparently he wants to interpret "first" as meaning "great." "In the law" replaces "of all" and accentuates the law as the revelation of God's will. It also reflects Matthew's special diction (νόμος—6,0), echoes "lawyer" in v 34, and marks yet another agreement with Luke, who uses the phrase in a slightly later position and in Jesus' mouth.

22:37 (Mark 12:29-30; Luke 10:26-27) In both Matthew and Luke the addition of "Teacher" in the preceding verse leads to the substitution of "And he" for Mark's "Jesus." Similarly, "said" (ἔφη; cf. Luke's εἶπεν) replaces "answered." These revisions and the insertion "to him" (αὐτῷ; cf. Luke's πρὸς αὐτόν) focus attention on the Pharisaical tempter, who in Matthew and Luke immediately receives from Jesus the OT commandment "You shall love the Lord your God with all your heart and with all your soul [Luke here adds 'and with all your strength'] and with all your mind" (Deut 6:5). Matthew and Luke achieve the immediacy of the command by omitting "The first is, 'Hear, Israel, the Lord our God is one Lord' " (so Mark; cf. Deut 6:4). As a Jewish Christian writing to Jewish Christians Matthew can take monotheism for granted. He is more interested in trinitarianism (see esp. 28:19) and concerned to attack antinomianism; so he goes as quickly as possible to the commandment. Matthew and Luke omit "and" at the start of the commandment (see Mark and Deuteronomy), since the Shema no longer precedes it. ἐν replaces ἐξ (so Mark and the LXX) for closer conformity with the Hebrew בְּ. Luke begins with ἐξ but immediately switches to ἐν. The switch suggests conflation of Mark and Matthew. "Heart" and "soul" agree with Mark, Luke, and Deuteronomy. "Mind" agrees with Mark and (in a later position) Luke, but not with Deuteronomy. Sometimes it is interpreted as a variant translation alongside "heart" for the Hebrew לְבָב (cf. the LXX[BF] Pap. 963), but because of its later position it probably results from reading the third Hebrew "tone" as מַדְּעֲךָ, "your mind." If so, "your strength" (so Mark and Luke) represents a second reading of the third Hebrew "tone" as מְאֹדֶךָ, "your strength" (so the MT). But Matthew omits the reference to strength in order to maintain the triplicity of the "tones." Luke inverts the order of the two readings. See further Gundry, *Use of the OT* 22-24.

22:38 For renewed emphasis on the law, Matthew composes the statement "This is the great and first commandment" (not in Mark or Luke). "This" comes from Mark's parallel to Matthew's next verse. "Great" and "commandment" echo v 36. Matthew often inserts μεγάλη (11,1). πρώτη makes up for its replacements in vv 36-37, exhibits Matthew's special interest in the word (2,5-6), and sets the stage for δευτέρα in the next clause.

22:39 (Mark 12:31; Luke 10:27) Matthew substitutes "similar to it" for Mark's "this" because he anticipated "this" in the preceding verse. ὁμοία belongs to his favorite vocabulary (1,5; with cognates—8,8). The substitute enables him to interpret the second commandment as equal to the first in importance. "Second" refers, then, to order in quotation, not to order of importance (cf. Matthew's inserting this commandment in 5:43; 19:19b). The second commandment comes from Lev 19:18: "you shall love your neighbor as yourself" (so also Mark).

Perhaps under Christian influence, the commandments to love God and neighbor appear together in *T. Dan* 5:3; *T. Iss.* 5:2 (cf. Rom 13:8, 10; Gal 5:14; Philo *Spec.* 2.63; *Sipre Lev.* 19.18). μεγάλη may carry the superlative meaning, "greatest," as is possible in Koine Greek. The greatest commandment forms part of the Shema, the credo par excellence of Judaism (Deut 6:4-9; 11:13-21; Num 15:37-41). Perhaps reading the Hebrew text so as to get "mind" shows Hellenistic influence. With the second commandment, cf. 7:12; 9:13; 12:7; 23:23. "As yourself" only makes a point of comparison with normal self-interest. It is not meant to teach self-love as obligatory or desirable. In Lev 19:18 "neighbor" means "fellow Israelite" and possibly includes resident aliens. Cf. 1 John 4:21; *b. Šabb.* 31a.

22:40 (Mark 12:31-34; Luke 10:28) Mark's statement "There is no other commandment greater than these" now undergoes radical revision. "On these two commandments" replaces "no other commandment greater

449

than these." The replacement emphasizes the pairing of the second commandment alongside rather than below the first. We meet a Mattheanism in δυσίν (19,4). "There is" yields to "The whole of the law and the prophets hang." Obviously, emphasis falls on the authority of the OT and Jesus' teaching of it. Matthew favors ὅλος (6,0), νόμος (6,0), προφῆται (19,6), and the combination of the last two (4,0; cf. the comments on 5:17). κρέμαται was an insertion also in 18:6. Here its singular number shows that Matthew adds "and the prophets" as an afterthought. This inference is confirmed by the position of the phrase, which dangles at the end. We need not dispute whether "hang" means that all the other commandments can be deduced from these two or whether these commandments summarize all the others, for what summarizes the others also provides a starting point for deduction (cf. *m. Ḥag.* 1:8; *b. Ber.* 63a). Either way, love for God and neighbor must permeate obedience to all the other commandments. At this point Matthew cuts the story short in order to leave the stress on obedience to the whole, not just part, of the law and the prophets (see 5:17-18, 19-20). He also wants to leave the Pharisees in a bad light. Thus the scribe's complimenting Jesus on his answer and Jesus' favorable response fall away (so also Luke, who goes to the parable of the Good Samaritan).

THE BESTING OF THE PHARISEES BY THE SON OF GOD
22:41-46 (Mark 12:35-37a; Luke 20:41-44)

22:41-42 (Mark 12:35; Luke 20:41) To reemphasize the Pharisees' antagonism in terms of heathen opposition to God's Son (see v 34 with comments ad loc. and Ps 2:2 with 7), Matthew provides the story of Jesus' asking about the Christ's sonship with a unique introduction: "But while the Pharisees were gathered together." συνηγμένων is a Mattheanism (10,10), which echoes v 34 and Ps 2:2 and makes the Pharisees represent the antagonistic synagogue of Matthew's day. Mark's καί gives way to δέ (so also Luke) for a contrast between Jesus' being questioned in the foregoing and Jesus' doing the questioning in the following. Insertion of the Pharisees echoes 21:45; 22:15, 34, sets the stage for a rabbinic dialogue (in Mark Jesus speaks to people in general), and exhibits Matthew's special interest in the Pharisees (18,1). In reminiscence of v 35 "asked" replaces Mark's "answering." Both here and there the verb comes right after a mention of the Pharisees' gathering together. Thus Matthew is renewing his criticism of the Pharisees. The verb also compensates for the omission of Mark 12:34, where "to ask" closes the question of the great commandment and requires the insertion of "them" (cf. Luke's "to them"). Since Matthew portrayed Jesus as Teacher in the preceding story (see v 36), he omits "teaching in the Temple." Besides, in the present story Jesus does not teach so much as he asks a question that none of the Pharisees can answer. Luke shares the omission. Characteristically, Matthew changes "was saying" to "saying" (λέγων—61,23).

Mark's "How is it that the scribes say . . . ?" becomes "What seems right to you . . . ?" which typifies Matthew's style (τί ὑμῖν δοκεῖ . . .;—4,2). The replacement echoes 21:28; 22:17 and stems from the importation of Pharisees. In Mark, then, Jesus questions the people about the scribes (most of whom belonged to the Pharisaical sect). But in Matthew, Jesus questions the Pharisees themselves and therefore speaks a direct "you." "Concerning the Christ" substitutes for "that the Christ." The new phrase enables Matthew to stop the question here and satisfy his desire for parallelism by constructing a second question, "Whose son is he?" which replaces "is the son of David." Matthew turns Jesus' monologue (so Mark and Luke) into a rabbinic dialogue and, as often, writes the historical present "they say to him" with asyndeton (21,6). This is absent in the other synoptics. Thus "David's" comes from the lips of the Pharisees, just as Jesus forced his opponents to answer him in 21:31, 41 (so Matthew alone) and 22:20. That Davidic sonship no longer appears in Jesus' question but in a scripturally correct answer suggests that Matthew is protecting Jesus' later question from being misunderstood as a denial of Davidic sonship. At the same time, that Matthew's Jesus did not even suggest Davidic sonship widens the door for divine sonship as well.

See J. A. Fitzmyer, *Essays on the Semitic Background of the New Testament* (London: Chapman, 1971) 115-21, for a convenient, brief survey of Davidic and Davidic messianic traditions in the OT and other literature of late Judaism. See especially *Pss. Sol.* 17:21(23).

22:43-44 (*Mark 12:36; Luke 20:42-43*) The typically Matthean insertion of another "he says to them" with asyndeton (21,6; cf. v 42) turns the dialogue back to Jesus. The further insertion of "How . . . ?" compensates for the omission of this word in v 42 and turns Jesus' declaration into a question. Thus, with the question in v 45, Matthew again gets the parallelism of two questions put to the Pharisees by Jesus (see the comments on v 42). The yet further insertion of οὖν (cf. Luke's γάρ) shows Matthew's fondness for the word (35,11), makes the question ride on the Pharisees' answer ("David's"), and implies the correctness of that answer. The insertions "How . . . ?" and "therefore" push out Mark's "himself." Mark's ἐν τῷ πνεύματι τῷ ἁγίῳ loses the first τῷ and τῷ ἁγίῳ. The resultant anarthrous phrase "in Spirit" seems to reflect apocalyptic usage (see Rev 1:10; 4:2; 17:3; 21:10; cf. Ezek 11:24; 37:1; Luke 2:27). Its advancing from a position right after "said" (so Mark) to a position right after "David" suggests a shift in meaning from David's *speaking* by the Holy Spirit to David's *being* in the Spirit—i.e., in a visionary state—at the time of speaking. In this way Matthew accentuates the prophetic character of the following quotation from Ps 110:1. Mark's "said" gives way to "calls him 'Lord,' saying." καλεῖ is a favorite (8,8). It shows Matthew's special interest in names and titles (cf. the comments on 1:21) and emphasizes the implication of deity in κύριον, another Mattheanism (34,15). Characteristically, he adds λέγων (61,23). The quotation itself reads exactly as it does in Mark: "The Lord said to my Lord, 'Sit at my right hand till I put your enemies underneath your feet' " (cf. Luke 20:43; Acts 2:34; 1 Cor 15:25-26; Heb 1:13; 2:8; 10:13; and see

D. M. Hay, *Glory at the Right Hand: Psalm 110 in Early Christianity* [SBLMS 18; Nashville: Abingdon, 1973] 27-33, for various views, including the messianic, of Psalm 110 in late Judaism).

22:45 (Mark 12:37; Luke 20:44) In Mark, Jesus begins his deduction from Ps 110:1 by saying, "David himself calls him 'Lord.' " To gain a parallel with v 43b Matthew writes "If then David calls him 'Lord.' " Both οὖν and καλεῖ reveal his hand (35,11; 8,8) and reemphasize the implication of deity. For a further parallel with v 43b Matthew omits καί and replaces Mark's πόθεν with his favorite πῶς (6,1; so also Luke). πῶς may mean "How is it that?" or "In what way?" If the latter, Matthew is suggesting in vv 43 and 45 that the Christ is *in a way* both David's Lord and David's son. υἱός, which occupies last position in Mark, moves ahead of αὐτοῦ ἐστιν for smoothness and emphasis on sonship.

In rabbinic questions dealing with an antinomy, usually the answer was that both sides are true (Jeremias, *NT Theology* 1. 259). It therefore seems probable that Jesus implies both the Davidic descent of the Christ and the Christ's lordship over David (cf. the combinations of Davidic descent and nonmetaphysical divine sonship in 2 Samuel 7). The double truth of Davidic descent and lordship over David does not require a chronological distinction between sonship during earthly life and later lordship, though, of course, manifestation of lordship awaited the future. Even a distinction between genealogical descent from David (undenied by Jesus) and similarity to David in military conquests (denied) need not be made. A denial of Davidic descent would almost surely have drawn fire (cf. R. E. Brown, *The Birth of the Messiah* [Garden City, N.Y.: Doubleday, 1977] 505-12).

22:46 (Mark 12:34b; Luke 20:40) In accord with his having changed the foregoing from a dominical monologue to a rabbinic dialogue, Matthew adds v 46. It comes from Mark 12:34b, which he has reserved till now to mark Jesus' victory over his antagonists in debate. To "And no one" the evangelist adds "was able to answer him a word." The addition stresses the overpowering authority of Jesus' words. ἐδύνατο, ἀποκριθῆναι, and λόγον come from Matthew's favorite vocabulary (13,0; 31,10; 16,2).

The above additions enable Matthew to divide Mark's single clause into two parallel clauses. The second begins with an insertion of οὐδέ, another Mattheanism (17,3). Matthew delays "any more," changes "was daring" to "dared," substitutes "anyone" for "no one" because of the latter's appearance in his first line, and adds "from that day" to echo the inserted "on that day" in v 23 (see the comments ad loc. and cf. the comments on 9:22). Finally, "to question him" comes from Mark with inversion of word order; and "any more" makes its appearance, but with the infinitive "to question" rather than the main verb "dared." That Jesus overpowers his opponents in debate exhibits his lordship. He is God's Son as well as David's. Cf. the way Matthew's stress on Jesus' Davidic lineage culminated in the identification of Jesus as "God with us" (chap. 1; see also chap. 2 for Matthew's double emphasis on Davidic and divine sonship).

THE REJECTION OF FALSELY PROFESSING JEWISH CHRISTIAN LEADERS AS PORTRAYED IN THE REJECTION OF ISRAEL'S LEADERS
23:1–25:46

Chapters 23–25 make up Jesus' fifth great discourse in Matthew. It balances the first one—i.e., the Sermon on the Mount—in its length, in its association with a mountain (24:3), in Jesus' taking the seated position of a teacher (24:3; cf. 23:2), in the contrast between woes (here) and beatitudes (in the Sermon on the Mount), and in the closing judgmental scenes, each of which includes the addressing of Jesus as "Lord" by the condemned (7:22-23; 25:44-46). In their immediate context chaps. 23–25 carry on and sharpen the minatory portrait of Israel's leaders already begun. Those leaders stand not only for Jewish officials who were persecuting the church at the time of Matthew's writing, but also, it appears, for antinomian ecclesiastics—"loophole lawyers" coming from the Pharisaical sect—who were exercising great influence in the church. The earlier rejection of the Jewish leaders serves as a warning to Pharisaical scribes in the church, about whose Christian profession Matthew entertains much suspicion.

Prohibition of Honorific Titles in the Church
23:1-12 (Mark 12:37b-40; Luke 20:45-47; 11:46; 14:11; 18:14b)

23:1-2 (Mark 12:37-38; Luke 20:45-46) Without interruption Mark continues, "And the large crowd was listening to him gladly." To signify a break and the beginning of Jesus' fifth discourse, Matthew replaces "And" with "Then" (66,17) and "the large crowd" with "Jesus" (80,12). But "the large crowd" does not disappear; it becomes "to the crowds." The pluralization compensates for the loss of "large." Matthew adds "and to his disciples" in order to portray Jesus' audience as the church. The disciples represent the original Jewish Christians; the crowds, the larger body of Gentile converts. μαθηταῖς is a Mattheanism (31,5). "Were listening" is replaced by "spoke . . . saying." Matthew likes both ἐλάλησεν (13,1) and λέγων (61,23). In the synoptics the verb occurs without a dative of indirect object twenty-six, twenty-one, and thirty-one times, respectively, but with a dative of indirect object (as here) thirteen, four, and seven times. The participle replaces Mark's statement "And in his teaching he was saying." Luke writes "And while all the people were listening." This reflects Mark, but Luke's main clause, "he said to his disciples," seems to reflect Matthew, especially in the mention of disciples.

"Watch out for the scribes" (so Mark) gives way to the wholesale criticism of the scribes and Pharisees that occupies the rest of the chapter in Matthew. The criticism begins in vv 2-3 with a composition of Matthew that introduces and expands the traditional saying of Jesus in v 4 (cf. Luke 11:46). "On the seat of Moses" does not exhibit Matthew's favorite diction. But it does reflect his very strong interest in the Mosaic law and the Jewish synagogue; for "the seat of Moses" probably means a stone seat on the platform of synagogues next to the ark containing the scrolls of the OT. Teachers sat on this seat to expound the law (see I. Renov in *IEJ* 5 [1955] 262-67). ἐκάθισαν and οἱ γραμματεῖς καὶ οἱ Φαρισαῖοι are Mattheanisms (3,2; 9,0). "The scribes" comes from Mark's replaced warning against the scribes, and "the Pharisees" echoes 21:45; 22:15, 34, 41. The scribes were teachers, and not all of them were Pharisees. The Pharisees were a theological sect, and most of them did not teach. But it does not matter to Matthew that he is mixing classes. He only wants to excoriate Jesus' theological antagonists; so he tosses together their most prominent representatives (the scribes) and their most prominent sect (the Pharisees). Some of the criticisms can apply only to the scribes (vv 2-4, 7b [cf. 8-12], 13, 16-22, 24). Other criticisms might apply also to nonscribal Pharisees (vv 5-7a, 15, 23, 25, 26-39). But by pairing the scribes and Pharisees repeatedly, Matthew leaves the impression that he is writing only about scribes who belong to the 'Pharisaical sect (cf. the parallel between "blind guides" [v 24]—a reference to scribes [cf. v 16]—and "blind Pharisee" [v 26]). The aorist tense of ἐκάθισαν probably means "have taken a seat and thus are sitting," as in Mark 16:19; Heb 1:3; 8:1; 10:12; Rev 3:21 (cf. the Semitic stative perfect).

Cf. *m. 'Abot* 1:1; *b. Roš Haš.* 25a. Sitting on someone's throne means replacing a former king (see the OT passim). Sitting in Moses' seat means rehearsing the Mosaic law. Since replacing and rehearsing run in opposite directions, the verbal similarity between sitting on so-and-so's throne and sitting on Moses' seat is insignificant and misleading. This is the only place where Matthew puts the definite article with both "scribes" and "Pharisees." The following criticism of Pharisaical leniency undercuts the notion that only the Shammaites come under criticism for too great strictness.

23:3 Matthew keeps on composing. οὖν is a favorite of his (35,11) and makes the sitting of the scribes and Pharisees on Moses' seat the basis for the command in v 3. We meet further favorites in πάντα ... ὅσα (2,3), ποιήσατε/-εῖτε (19,19), τηρεῖτε (5,1), ἔργα (4,1), and γάρ (62-63,15). Cf. 28:20 for another distinctive collocation of πάντα ὅσα and τηρεῖν. The antithesis between "do and keep all things whatever they say to you" and "do not according to their works" typifies Matthew's love of parallelism and his emphasis on consistency between words and actions. "For they say [things] and do not do [them]" looks like a pluralized comment on the actions of the ultimately disobedient son in 21:28-32, another composition by Matthew (cf. Rom 2:13). "Say" and "do" echo the preceding line.

Since this command deals with what the scribes and the Pharisees say when they sit in Moses' seat—i.e., when they rehearse the OT law—we need not suppose that the first half of the command needs to be understood as sarcastic, or that the first half is merely a foil to the second half, where the real meaning lies, or that Matthew has taken from the Jewish Christian tradition a legalistic saying disagreeable with his following statements and with 16:11-12, or that he is making a tactical attempt to avoid a complete break between the church and the synagogue. Matthew was neither a dim-witted tailor who, contrary to Deut 22:11, sewed together a literary garment of wool and linen without knowing the difference between his materials, nor a modern churchman who saw contradictions in the traditions that came to him but deliberately included everything so that ecumenicity might swallow up theology, lumps and all. So long as sitting in Moses' seat qualifies the speaking of the scribes and Pharisees, "all things whatever" does not include their interpretative traditions, but emphasizes the totality of the law. "Therefore" establishes the qualification. They *do* keep their traditions. But they do *not* practice what they speak while sitting on Moses' seat. Hence their traditions are not in view. Though elsewhere Matthew is concerned to criticize the scribes' and Pharisees' interpretations of the law, here he is concerned to stress the necessity of keeping the law itself. As usual, his eye is on antinomians in the church.

23:4 (Luke 11:46) Matthew's composition has led up to the tradition behind Luke 11:46. It is appropriate to the present context that in the tradition Jesus is eating at the house of a Pharisee. "And he said" (so Luke) drops out. It would have interrupted the discourse in Matthew. "And woe to you lawyers" also fails to appear, because in Matthew Jesus is still speaking to the crowds and his disciples. Only later will he address the scribes (vv 13-39). δέ stands in place of Luke's causal ὅτι and carries on the contrast between saying and doing. "They tie up" replaces "you burden . . . with" and avoids a cognate accusative in "burdens." It also reflects the anticipatory use of "burdened" in 11:28 and represents a family of words well liked by Matthew (see δε- in the Greek Index—8,2). He will insert "heavy" again in v 23 (cf. the insertions of cognates in 13:15; 20:12). Here "heavy" either substitutes for "hard to bear" (so Luke) or adds emphasis if "hard to bear" is original to Matthew's text (see the UBS and Metzger, *Textual Commentary* ad loc., on καὶ δυσβάστακτα in Matthew). Thus far Luke's "men" has not come over. Matthew now builds on it by adding "and they put [the heavy burdens] on men's shoulders." He likes to insert ἐπιτιθέασιν (5,0).

In the next line καί (so Luke) gives way to δέ to stress the antithesis. Luke's αὐτοί appears also in Matthew; but because the person of the verb has changed, it means "themselves" rather than "yourselves." We read "with their finger" instead of Luke's "with one of your fingers." In view of Matthew's liking "one" (ἑνί—24,7), a Lukan insertion that required a pluralizing of "finger" seems more likely than omission of "one" by Matthew. "You do not touch" becomes "they are not willing to remove." θέλουσιν comes from Matthew's preferred diction (18,8; see esp. 21:29; 22:3, 37, where θέλω has recently appeared with the negative in references to the Jewish leaders in Jerusalem). Some have thought that κινῆσαι refers to adjusting an imbalanced load. But it probably means "remove," as in Num 14:44; Prov 17:13 LXX; Rev 2:5; 6:14. To avoid redundancy, "them" replaces "the burdens." Contrast Gal 6:2.

Matthew's Jesus has already said and will yet say that the scribes and Pharisees teach too lax an interpretation of the law (15:1-20; 23:16-22; cf. 5:19-20; 16:5-12, esp. 11b-12). These statements confirm that in v 3 "all things whatever they say" referred to God's law, which they quote while sitting in the seat of Moses yet fail to keep in their daily conduct, not to their scribal traditions, which they do keep and in so doing void God's law. By the same token, in Matthew the heavy burdens are not to be identified with scribal traditions or interpretations of the law (as probably in Luke and Jesus' intent). Rather, they signify overbearing attempts to win adulation—to be noticed by men, gain the place of honor at banquets and the chief seats in synagogues, receive greetings in the marketplace, and be called "my Great One" (the meaning of "Rabbi"). The immediately following verses clearly define the heavy burdens as consisting in these attempts. And Matthew's expansion in 11:28-30 confirms this definition by identifying the lightness of Jesus' burden, not with any laxity in Jesus' teaching (much to the contrary, see 5:17-48!), but with his meekness and humility, which contrast sharply with the scribes' and Pharisees' overweening desire for recognition. The similarity of phraseology in "my burden is light" (11:30) and "they tie up heavy burdens" (23:4) shows that the contrast is deliberate.

23:5 (Mark 12:38; Luke 20:46) To introduce the next bit of traditional material, Matthew composes a leading statement after the pattern of an earlier leading statement he composed: "But all their works they do in order to be noticed by men" (cf. 6:1: "But beware that you not do your righteousness before men in order to be seen by them"). "But" contrasts the desire for recognition with the foregoing refusal to remove from other men the burden of playing sycophant. "All" heightens the guilt in that not a single work escapes condemnation. "Their works" echoes v 3 and reflects Matthew's penchant for words with the root ἐργ- (6,7). Also representing his favorite diction are πάντα (63,25-26), ποιοῦσιν (19,19), πρός + an articular infinitive (3,2), θεαθῆναι (2,1), and ἀνθρώποις (35,17).

The evangelist now returns to Mark, takes aim at "who delight to walk around in long robes," and turns the phrase into the compound clause "for they broaden their phylacteries and lengthen [their] tassels." The revision makes the matter one of religious ostentation, as in 6:1-6, 16-18, and exhibits his style in the parallelistic structure of the compound clause and in the allusions to the OT (see Exod 13:9, 16; Deut 6:8; 11:18 on phylacteries; and Num 15:38; Deut 22:12 and the comments on 9:20-21 concerning the tassels). He likes γάρ (62-63,15); and μεγαλύνουσιν is cognate to μέγας, another favorite of his (11,1).

Cf. *As. Mos.* 7:3-10; *T. Asher* 2:5-10. The phylacteries were worn as amulets (the proper meaning of φυλακτήρια). Matthew's penchant for bringing in the OT makes it likely he is applying the term "amulets" to the traditional Jewish *tephillin*, which were inscribed with texts from Deuteronomy 5–6, 10–11, and Exodus 12–13 (and Deut 32:14-20, 32-33 in 4Qphyl N). The *tephillin* discovered at Qumran and Murabba'at and, probably, the Nash Papyrus show some variation in the verses copied from Deuteronomy 5–6, 10–11, and Exodus 12–13. These chapters provided the verses because of statements in the chapters that the Israelites should bind the words of the Lord on their hands and wear them as frontals on their foreheads. Broadening the amulets may imply their being made of metal foil (a difference from those discovered at Qumran and Murabba'at and the Nash Papyrus) and means beating them out into unusually large dimensions for the sake of ostentatious display (see Justin Martyr *Dial.* 46.5 and a forthcoming article by R. Kotansky, who notes the large number of amuletic metal plates, Jewish as well as pagan, in antiquity). On the other hand see J. H. Tigay in *HTR* 72 (1979) 45-52 with photographs on 53. Concerning tassels, see Num 15:37-41 and S. Bertman in *BA* 24 (1961) 119-29.

23:6-7 (Mark 12:39; Luke 20:46; cf. Luke 11:43) Mark's καί changes to δέ. This shift indicates that vv 6-7 do not continue the list of works done for men's recognition, but contrast striving for adulation (vv 6-7) with the ostensible piety of broadening phylacteries and lengthening tassels (v 5). Matthew takes up Mark's next three items in reverse order. The reversal puts greetings in the marketplace in third position, where they lead naturally into Matthew's addition of loving to be called "Rabbi," an addition that leads in turn to the unique prohibitions against being called "Rabbi," against calling any earthly leader "Father," and against being called "Instructor." For his governing verb Matthew inserts φιλοῦσιν (2,1). Luke's use of the same verb, but in participial form and in connection with greetings in marketplaces, suggests Matthean influence (cf. also Luke 11:43). Matthew's adding the definite article to "first couches" and his singularizing the expression intensify the accusation: in Matthew the scribes and Pharisees are not satisfied at banquets unless they occupy the one most honorable spot beside the host (cf. John 13:23-25; Luke 16:22; Jas 2:2-3). Matthew cannot truly singularize the "first seats" in the synagogues, however; for they consisted of a bench facing the rest of the congregation and occupied by a number of men (the singular in Luke 11:43 is collective) and "greetings" can hardly go into the singular here. Therefore, for the sake of parallelism he simply adds the definite article to these expressions. "And to be called by men, 'Rabbi' " (not in Mark or Luke) heaps more guilt on the scribes and Pharisees, reflects the increasingly technical use of the term "Rabbi" for teachers (as distinct from an earlier, general meaning "Sir") at the time of writing, and displays Matthew's special vocabulary in καλεῖσθαι (8,8), ἀνθρώπων (35,17—here an echo of v 5), and ῥαββί (3,0). "To be called" differs in its infinitive form from the nouns with which it is parallel. But in this respect Matthew is following Mark, who began with an infinitive object ("to walk around") and continues with nominal objects.

23:8 Matthew applies the criticism of the scribes and Pharisees to the life of the church by making Jesus switch from describing them to instructing the disciples. δέ makes the instruction antithetic to the description. The emphatic ὑμεῖς is a favorite of Matthew (15,3) and marks the switch. "Do not be called, 'Rabbi' " turns the last item of description inside out, again displays Matthew's diction (see the comments on v 7), and implies striving for scribal honor in the church, possibly by converted scribes belonging to the Pharisees. γάρ is a Mattheanism (62-63,15) and introduces a rationale for the prohibition, viz., "one is your teacher, but all you are brothers." This rationale shows Matthew's love of parallelism and of the words εἷς (24,7), διδάσκαλος (4,1), πάντες (63,25-26), ὑμεῖς (15,3), and ἀδελφοί (11,8). διδάσκαλος reflects the special application of "Rabbi" to teachers. Its use in three previous insertions (8:10; 9:11; 12:38) and in one passage peculiar to the first gospel (17:24)—not to list a number of shared occurrences— points to Jesus as the referent (cf. v 10). The contrast between "one" and "all" is striking. "Brothers" carries the connotation of religious brotherhood, as often in Matthew, and emphasizes equality of subjection to Jesus' didactic authority. We might have expected "disciples" as a contrast with

457

"teacher." But "brothers" leads more naturally into the immediately following prohibition against a titular use of "Father."

Cf. Matthew's emphasis on meekness (πραΰς—2,1). His characterizing disciples as scribes (see the comments on 8:19; 13:52) does not disagree with his prohibiting acceptance of the corresponding title as a token of honor. Therefore we have no reason to think that he is drawing on a traditional saying in which God, rather than Jesus, takes the role of teacher. The assertion that "Rabbi" escalated from the meaning "Sir" to the meaning "Teacher" only after the Council of Jamnia began to meet in the period following A.D. 70 rests on failure to take account of Matthew's fusing the title with his portrait of Jesus as teacher. This fusion does not necessarily depend on developments in rabbinic circles. Besides, our knowledge of the rabbinic milieu prior to A.D. 70 lacks precision and detail. Of course, "Rabbi" might still mean "Sir" even in interpretative questions. But the interpretative nature of the questions exhibits the beginning of a special connotation before the Council of Jamnia. The parallel between v 8b and v 8c requires us to take ἐστε as indicative, "you are," rather than imperative, "be"; for the matching ἐστιν presents us with an unambiguous indicative, "is."

23:9 Matthew composes the prohibition "And do not call [anyone] on earth your father, for one is your heavenly Father" as a parallel to the preceding prohibition. Though the verb καλέσητε echoes vv 7-8 and belongs to his special vocabulary (8,8), its active voice differs from the passive that appears in vv 7-8, 10. The explanation for this seeming inconcinnity lies in Matthew's using "Rabbi" for teachers inside the church and "Father" for Jewish teachers outside the church. Use of the latter title for past and present Jewish teachers makes the active prohibition sensible and implies that this part of the prohibition deals with appeals to authorities outside the church, appeals Matthew will not tolerate.

"On earth" is a Mattheanism (8,2). It does not mean that the evangelist is thinking of living old men in general. The context deals with didactic leaders. Therefore the phrase contrasts the early limitation of even the most honored Jewish teachers with the absolute authority of the heavenly Father. Matthew has a penchant for contrasting heaven and earth (6,0). The parallel between the two lines in v 9, and particularly between "your heavenly Father" in the second line and "your father on earth" in the first line, favors that ὑμῶν in the first line goes with πατήρ rather than with μή (which would yield "Do not call any [one] of you 'Father' on earth"). Confirmation of this comes from Matthew's habit of attaching genitive pronouns to πατήρ throughout his gospel (see the comments on 13:43). Here he advances πατέρα to the head of the clause, away from ὑμῶν, to make obvious the link between "brothers" at the close of the preceding verse and "Father" at the opening of the present verse. The Mattheanisms εἷς (24,7) and γάρ (62-63,15) echo v 8. In fact, the words "for one is your . . ." repeat the first words of v 8b exactly. The word for father provides another Mattheanism whether used alone (22,13) or with "heavenly" (6,1).

On the use of "father" for honored figures, both past and present, see BAG, s.v. πατήρ 2. The prohibition has nothing to do with addressing one's physical father as such. Jesus taught God's fatherhood. But it also represents a strong interest of Matthew and therefore agrees with the many other indications that he composed vv 7b-10 as an expansion of Jesus' teaching; i.e., the stress on God's fatherhood does not provide solid or sufficient support for seeing a traditional saying behind v 9.

23:10 Matthew now wants to bring in humble service as true greatness among disciples. Christ himself sets the example. Therefore Matthew returns to the prohibition in v 8, restates it in a slightly different but parallel form, and makes explicit the formerly implicit reference to Jesus as the messianic teacher. This open identification of Christ forms a bridge to the following sayings on service and humility that the reference to the heavenly Father at the close of v 9 could not provide. And restating the prohibition makes it very emphatic. Matthew omits ὑμεῖς (so v 8), but takes "Neither be called" and then substitutes "Instructors" for the earlier "Rabbi." "Because" replaces "for," and "your instructor is one" parallels "one is your teacher." The change in word order allows addition of "the Christ" (not in v 8). Matthew is fond of χριστός (8,5). Sometimes it is suggested that the use of the Hebrew מוֹרֶה for the Teacher of Righteousness in the QL shows that καθηγητής means more than διδάσκαλος. But Matthew's composing this saying in Greek and his penchant for parallelism undermine the suggestion.

23:11 The statement concerning service derives from the traditional saying in 20:26. The initial clause in 20:26, "But whoever wants to become great among you," shortens to "But the greatest of you"; i.e., "whoever wants to become" drops out, because in the present context there is no longer a request to sit on the right and left of Jesus in his kingdom. μείζων echoes 18:4 and usually occurs in Matthew as an insertion (6,0). "Shall be your servant" comes without revision from 20:26 (cf. Mark 9:35; Luke 9:48b).

23:12 (Luke 14:11) Matthew has just recalled 18:4 in his use of μείζων. Now he takes ὅστις from that same verse and works it into the tradition behind Luke 14:11, where Jesus is again eating in the house of a Pharisee (cf. the comments on v 4). The pronoun is a favorite of his (23,5) and substitutes for Luke's πᾶς. δέ replaces ὅτι to indicate a second contrast with the prohibited acceptance of honorific titles (see v 11 for the first contrast). "The one exalting himself" changes to "will exalt himself" because of Matthew's replacing "everyone" with "whoever." Similarly, in the second line "the one humbling himself" becomes "whoever will humble himself" in reminiscence of 18:4. The passive voice of "will be humbled" and "will be exalted" implies divine action. The future tense probably points to the last judgment. Possibly Jesus was alluding to Ezek 21:31b(26b). Cf. Prov 15:33; 29:23; Jas 4:6; 1 Pet 5:5.

WARNINGS AGAINST HYPOCRISY
23:13–24:2 (Mark 12:37b-40; 13:1-2; Luke 6:39; 11:39-42, 44, 47-52; 13:34-35; 20:47; 21:5-6)

23:13 (Luke 11:52) Now we meet a series of seven woes pronounced against the scribes and Pharisees and built on the four woes in the tradition behind Luke 11:42, 44, 47, 52. A meal at a Pharisee's house provides the setting for the traditional woes (see the comments on v 4). For his first woe, Matthew selects the final, climactic one in the tradition. His inserting δέ makes a contrast with the exaltation of the one who humbles himself (v 12b). The identification of the addressees as "lawyers" (so Luke) comes over as a synonymous nominative of address, "scribes," with "and Pharisees" added. The addition is an assimilation to v 2 (see the comments ad loc. on the meaning and thoroughly Matthean character of the whole phrase). The further addition of "hypocrites"—another Mattheanism (8,3)—forges a link with the motif of pretense in vv 3-7 (cf. Luke 12:1). That Matthew is willing to shift from Jesus' addressing the crowds and the disciples (v 1) to an addressing of the scribes and Pharisees shows the strength of his attack on them (cf. 1QH 4:6-20; *b. Ber.* 14b; *b. Soṭa* 22b). τὴν κλεῖδα in the tradition suggested the cognate κλείετε, which Matthew uses to replace ἤρατε (see 6:6; 25:10 for other distinctive occurrences of κλείω). The present tense of his verb contrasts with the aorist of Luke and contemporizes the woe. "The kingdom of heaven" is a Mattheanism (25,7). Here it substitutes for "the key of knowledge" and exhibits the lingering influence of 18:4 (cf. the comments on v 12). Typically, Matthew adds "before men" (ἔμπροσθεν τῶν ἀνθρώπων—3,1). The addition gives another echo of 6:1, a composition of his that recently influenced v 5a.

Instead of αὐτοί (so Luke) Matthew writes ὑμεῖς, a favorite of his (15,3). The characteristic insertion of γάρ (62-63,15) avoids asyndeton and makes the line to which it belongs an explanation of the preceding line. Changing "you have not entered" to "you do not enter" again contemporizes the woe. "Neither do you allow those who are entering to enter" stands where Luke writes "and you hindered those who were entering." Because Luke likes ἐκωλύσατε just as Matthew likes ἀφίετε (12,5), it is hard to tell which of the two evangelists may have the original. But Luke's καί looks like Semitic parataxis. Furthermore, Matthew's οὐδέ typifies his diction (17,3), and there is a third contemporization in the present tense of his version. Therefore we should probably regard Luke's wording as original and Matthew's as editorial. Matthew's repeated use of the present tense indicates that he has in mind the present sphere of the kingdom, i.e., the church. Contrastingly, in Luke Jesus refers to the lawyers' hindering activity in the past, i.e., during the preaching of the kingdom up to the time of the saying. All in all, then, Luke's Jesus portrays an already locked door, to which the lawyers have a key—a door which they do not enter and a key which they take away in order that others may not enter. Matthew's Jesus portrays an open door, which the scribes and Pharisees are not entering but are locking in the face of those who would enter.

23:15 The saying about the scribes' devouring widows' houses, praying a long time for the sake of appearance, and facing all the greater judgment for such actions (Mark 12:40; Luke 20:47) drops out (see the UBS and Metzger, *Textual Commentary* on Matt 23:13). Matthew criticized religious ostentation long ago (6:5-6). Also, the omission enables him to juxtapose the disallowing of people to enter the kingdom and the making of a proselyte a twofold son of hell. (Or if Mark 12:40 and Luke 20:47 should be regarded as parallels coming right after Matt 23:7a, Matthew omitted the saying there in order to go directly from greetings in the marketplaces to the address "Rabbi"; and, again, 6:5-6 has already covered religious ostentation.)

In constructing the second woe (not in Luke), Matthew repeats "Woe to you, scribes and Pharisees, hypocrites, because . . ." (see v 13 with comments ad loc.). "You go about" echoes 4:23 (where Matthew inserted the verb in common material) and 9:35. In those two passages it refers to itineration for the purpose of converting people, as it does here. "The sea and the dry [land]" seems to come from Jonah 1:9, located in another passage dealing with preaching and, as here, with Gentiles as those to be converted (cf. Gen 1:10; Hag 2:6; 1 Macc 8:23, 32). If so, Matthew is indulging his habit of using OT phraseology. Both ποιῆσαι and ἕνα belong to his special vocabulary (19,19; 24,7). προσήλυτον occurs only here in the gospels, but tallies with Matthew's well-known interest in the conversion of Gentiles. "And when he becomes [a proselyte], you make him twice as much a son of hell as yourselves" contains Mattheanisms in ποιεῖτε (19,19), υἱόν with a descriptive genitive besides τοῦ ἀνθρώπου (2,2; see the comments on 12:31), διπλότερον (6,6 for compounds with δια-), γεέννης (3,0), the motif of judgment (see "Last judgment" in the Topical Index), and the intensification of the scribes' and Pharisees' guilt (here by means of διπλότερον, "twice as much"). "Son of hell" means "destined for hell." The reference to "judgment" in Mark 12:40, which Matthew omitted, may have given rise to his second woe.

Cf. Josephus *Ant.* 20.2.4 §§38-48 (but the failure of the journey from Galilee to Adiabene to meet the requirements of Matthew's expression "You go about *the sea and the dry land*" rules out a particular reference to the historical incident described by Josephus). We should not think of converts to Pharisaism from among the Jews, for the term "proselyte" connotes Gentiles. Emphasis does not fall on any difficulty that the scribes and Pharisees may have had in making a proselyte, but on the irony that the enormity of their efforts has doubly disastrous results. When examined closely, the real and supposed Semitisms that might seem to favor use of a traditional saying turn out to favor composition by Matthew. The paratactic καί suits his penchant for parallelism. The shift from ὅτι, "because" or "that" (v 15), to οἱ, "who" (v 16), does not reflect an ambiguous Aramaic יד, "that" or "who," but simply serves to introduce the Mattheanism λέγοντες, "say" (61,23). Along with the rest of the phrase in which it occurs the Semitic "Woe" echoes the tradition taken over in v 13. "Sea and dry land" exhibits Matthew's typical use of OT and rabbinic phraseology. ἕνα represents another Mattheanism, not an indefinite Aramaic דח, and "a son of . . ." also typifies Matthew's style (see the foregoing comments).

23:16 The third woe also lacks a synoptic parallel and begins, "Woe to you." But "blind guides" substitutes for "scribes and Pharisees, hypocrites" (cf. vv 13, 15). The substitute echoes 15:14, where Matthew revised the tradition behind Luke 6:39. The new epithet also harmonizes with the immediately foregoing and following references to misleading proselytization and teaching. The following reference necessitates the addition of "who say." The teaching itself is expressed in antithetically parallel lines:

> Whoever swears by the Temple, it [the oath] is nothing;
> but whoever swears by the gold of the Temple is obligated.

Probable Mattheanisms are ὁμόσῃ (bis—1,10), ναῷ/-οῦ (bis—5,1), χρυσῷ (4,1), and ὀφείλει (4,6 with cognates).

Cf. Rom 2:19; Josephus *J.W.* 5.5.3-6 §§201-27; 6.8.3 §§387-91; *Ant.* 14.7.1 §§105-9. As in 5:34, the use of ἐν after ὁμόσῃ, which usually takes an accusative, may reflect the Semitic use of בְּ after נִשְׁבַּע. Rabbinic literature does not contain evidence of the precise distinctions described by Matthew here and in the following verses; but that literature contains notoriously little material from the first three-quarters of the first century. Cf. CD 16:6-13.

23:17-22 The words listed as probably Matthean in v 16 reappear in vv 17-22. To them we should add μωροί (3,3-4), τυφλοί (bis—9,0), γάρ (bis—62-63,15), μείζων/-ον (bis—6,0; cf. esp. the insertion at 12:6 in shared material having to do with the sanctuary), θυσιαστηρίῳ/-ον (ter—5,0), δώρῳ/ -ον (ter—7,1), ἐπάνω (ter—7,1), οὖν (35,11), πᾶσι (63,25-26), and καθημένῳ (8,0). Furthermore, ἁγιάσας/-ζον (bis) is cognate to the Mattheanism ἅγιος (4,4); and κατοικοῦντι was peculiar to Matthew in 2:23; 4:13, too. So the diction of vv 17-22 as well as that of v 16 consists almost entirely of words in which Matthew shows more or less special interest.

The parallelism in these verses also betrays Matthew's hand. As in v 16, so also in v 18 two clauses beginning "whoever swears by" and "but whoever swears by," and ending "it is nothing" and "is obligated," provide an example of antithetic parallelism. Verses 17 and 19 exhibit synonymous parallelism:

> Fools and blind, for what is greater, the
>   gold or the Temple that sanctifies the gold? (v 17).
> Blind, for what is greater, the gift or the
>   altar that sanctifies the gift? (v 19).

Verses 21-23 offer more synonymous parallelism:

> Therefore he who swears by the altar swears
>   by it and by all things on it.
> And he who swears by the Temple swears
>   by it and by the one inhabiting it.
> And he who swears by heaven swears
>   by the throne of God and by the one sitting on it.

The order of topics in vv 16-21 falls into a chiastic pattern:

> the Temple and its gold;
>   the altar and the gift on it;
>   the altar and all things on it;
> the Temple and its inhabitant.

462

It is part of Matthew's style to allude often to the OT. In v 19 we have an allusion to the law of sanctification dealing with the altar (Exod 29:37; see Gundry, *Use of the OT* 141-42, on agreement and disagreement with various textual and interpretative traditions). In v 22 "he who swears by heaven" and "by the throne of God" recall 5:34 (peculiar to Matthew). The latter phrase represents another allusion to the OT (see Isa 66:1). Throughout these verses Matthew attacks the teaching of the scribes and Pharisees as too lax. Such attacks are typical of his redaction elsewhere, too. The address "Fools" does not contradict the prohibition in 5:22; for here Jesus is addressing the scribes and Pharisees. There he was prohibiting use of the epithet in addressing a "brother," i.e., a fellow disciple. Though commonly regarded as the result of influence from v 17, the words μωροί καί before τυφλοί in v 19 have strong external support (including B C K W f¹³ 33 565 itᶜˑᶠ syrᵖˑʰ copˢᵃˑᵇᵒ—see further the UBS) and agree with Matthew's penchant for close parallelism. On the other hand, he sometimes abbreviates (cf. the comments on vv 25-26).

Behind the Pharisaical scribal teaching on oaths lies the rationale that a creditor cannot place a lien on the Temple or the altar. The Temple and the altar provide no surety, therefore, and make oaths taken in their name meaningless. But a creditor might well claim the gold dedicated by his debtor to the Temple or the gift offered by his debtor on the altar. Jesus' charging the scribes and the Pharisees with hypocrisy in making these distinctions has nothing to do with approval or disapproval of oaths as such. In other words, the charge of hypocrisy in oaths does not contradict the total prohibition of oaths in 5:33-37.

23:23 (Luke 11:42) For the fourth woe Matthew returns to the tradition concerning what Jesus said while eating at the house of a Pharisee, in particular the tradition behind Luke 11:42, which reads, "But woe to you, the Pharisees, because you tithe mint and rue and every herb, and pass by justice and love for God. But it was necessary to do these things and not to neglect those things." At the beginning ἀλλά drops out, because in Matthew the woe forms a parallel, not a contrast, with other woes. Matthew turns the dative appositive τοῖς Φαρισαίοις (so Luke) into an anarthrous nominative of address and expands the expression to conform with the preceding woes: "scribes and Pharisees, hypocrites" (see the comments on v 13). The reference to tithing mint matches Luke. But "dill and cummin" stands where Luke has "rue and every herb." The Mishna contradicts the tithing of every herb and specifically exempts rue from the tithe (*m. Šeb.* 9:1). At this point, therefore, Luke's version of the woe looks like an adaptation, and Matthew's looks original.

Instead of παρέρχεσθε, "you pass by," Matthew has ἀφήκατε, "you have left." The aorist tense of his verb agrees better with the imperfect tense of ἔδει, "it was necessary," in the next line; and ἀφήκατε is a favorite of his (12,5). Matthew now inserts "the weightier things of the law." Both βαρύτερα and νόμου belong to his special vocabulary (2,0; 6,0). With an obvious difference, the phrase as a whole echoes the "heavy burdens" in v 4. "Justice" comes from the traditional woe, but "mercy" reflects the adjoining saying in the tradition (see "merciful deed, alms," in Luke 11:41) and replaces "love for God." The failure of Luke's phrase to appear anywhere else in Luke-Acts, the frequency of ἔλεος and cognates in Matthew (7,5), and Matthew's making neighborly love equal in importance to loving God (see the comments on 22:39) favor that Matthew turns loving God into showing mercy to people as the way to love God. The insertion "and faith" typifies his diction. For although he borrows πίστιν six times, he inserted it in 15:28, too; and the cognate πιστεύω occurs three times as an insertion and three times as part of passages peculiar to his gospel, besides five common occurrences. Elsewhere in Matthew neither πίστιν nor πιστεύω connotes faithfulness. Therefore "faith" is the correct translation here. Since faith is directed toward God, Matthew's insertion compensates for his replacing love for God with mercy to men. The last line matches Luke except for the replacement of παρεῖναι, "to leave, neglect," with the synonymous Mattheanism ἀφεῖναι (12,5—v.1. ἀφιέναι). Thus ἀφήκατε and ἀφεῖναι have the same prefix in Matthew just as παρέρχεσθε and παρεῖναι have the same prefix in Luke.

"Weightier" means "more important," not "more difficult." Matthew sees no contradiction between strict observance of tithing and the law of love or mercy. The traditional character of this saying suggests that Jesus, too, saw no such contradiction. On tithing of agricultural produce, see Lev 27:30; Deut 14:22-29; m. Dem. 2:1; M. Maʿaś. 2:1. Cf. Ps 101:1; Prov 14:22; Jer 5:1; Mic 6:8; Zech 7:9 with the ethical qualities emphasized by Jesus.

23:24 The insertion of this saying emphasizes the fourth woe. "Blind guides" harks back to v 16 (see the comments ad loc.). "Who filter out a gnat but swallow a camel" exhibits the parallelism and rabbinic language to be expected in compositions by Matthew (see Str-B 1. 934 on the straining of wine through a cloth or a fine wicker basket and on the contrast between a flea and a camel, the smallest and largest animals seen in daily life). The rabbinic practice of filtering wine had the purpose of avoiding unclean insects. Furthermore, the implication that camels are not supposed to be eaten exhibits Matthew's habit of alluding to the OT (see Lev 11:4).

"Gnat" may refer to the larva of a gnat. In Aramaic "gnat" and "camel" produce a wordplay between קַלְמָא and גְּמְלָא. The wordplay does not demand, however, that as a whole this saying existed first in Aramaic. It was easy for Matthew to draw into his Greek composition a contrast that originated in an Aramaic milieu.

23:25 (Luke 11:39) Since he has taken over the tradition behind Luke 11:42, for his fifth woe Matthew steps back to the tradition behind Luke 11:39-41 (cf. Rom 2:28-29). "And the Lord said to him" disappears, however; it would have interrupted the discourse in Matthew. "Woe to you, scribes and Pharisees, hypocrites" echoes vv 13, 15, 23 (see the comments on v 13) and replaces "Now you Pharisees" (so Luke). The insertion of a woe emphasizes judgment, the addition of the epithet "hypocrites" points up Pharisaical pretense, and the inclusion of scribes alongside Pharisees brings into focus Pharisaical scribes as distinct from other Pharisees and Jews. The insertion of ὅτι and advance of καθαρίζετε to a position just following ὅτι (contrast the last position of the verb in Luke) represent assimilation to vv 13, 15, and 23. "The outside of the cup" stays unchanged, but "and of the dish" replaces "and of the platter."

Matthew's omission of τό makes ἔσωθεν an adverb, "inwardly," instead of a substantive, "the inside" (so Luke). As a result, the singular "is full," having "the inside of you" as its subject (so Luke), changes to the plural "are full," having "the cup and the dish" as its implied subject. The insertion of ἐξ before ἁρπαγῆς may have the purpose of balancing ἔσωθεν. ἀκρασίας, "of self-indulgence," replaces πονηρίας, "of evil." Since Matthew likes the latter (cf. 22:18 and πονηρός—10,4) but uses the former only here, it is difficult to think he changed an original πονηρίας. In Luke, then, we read about niggardliness in contrast with generosity; in Matthew, about greedy self-indulgence in contrast with moral purity. The two nouns for greediness and self-indulgence disfavor a literal meaning concerning the ritual purity of a cup and a dish and favor a metaphorical use for disobedience to God's moral law (see vv 27-28; Luke 11:44; cf. *As. Mos.* 7:4-10).

23:26 (Luke 11:40-41) "Fools" changes to "Blind Pharisee." The substituted words echo vv 2 and 16, respectively (see the comments ad loc.). Matthew singularizes the Pharisees, however, in order to correlate them with "the outside of the cup and dish" (singular). Thus it is clearer that they are the referent of the metaphor. The singularizing and the adding of "Blind" lead to omission of the scribes. The accusatory nature of Matthew's context leads to a further omission of the didactic question "Did not he who made the outside make also the inside?" Consequently, the following πλήν, "nevertheless" or perhaps "therefore" (so Luke), also drops out (though the Lukanism πλήν may depend on a synonym in the tradition). Matthew assimilates this saying to the preceding by replacing "Give [as] charity" with "cleanse" (see 10:8 for another insertion of καθάρισον and 5:8; 27:59 for insertions of its cognate adjective). The replacement shifts the reference from charitable giving to inward purity. The earlier substitution of mercy for love toward God allows this shift (cf. v 23). Luke does not have πρῶτον, but it represents Matthew's favorite diction (3,1) and its insertion accentuates the priority of inner righteousness (cf. chaps 5–6). "The inside of the cup" replaces "the contents" for an antithetic parallel with "the outside of the cup" in v 25. Possibly, Matthew's replacement includes "and of the dish" (not present in Luke but supported by an impressive array of textual traditions in Matthew; see the UBS and Metzger, *Textual Commentary* ad loc.). If so, the parallel with v 25 goes on to include the additional phrase. If not, Matthew apocopates the full expression of v 25 just as he apocopated the address by leaving off the scribes mentioned in v 25.

According to Luke, Jesus balances his command to give the contents of one's tableware as charity with an abrogation of the dietary laws: "and behold all things are clean for you." In other words, the Pharisees ought to stop keeping the dietary laws, which they have corrupted by their inward greed and evil, and concentrate rather on charity. Matthew avoids abrogating the dietary laws and emphasizes moral purity as portrayed in the

465

figure of the cup: "in order that also the outside of it may become clean."
In other words, only cleansing the heart will produce an observable conduct
that is truly pure because of consistency with the inward state (cf. 5:21-30;
6:1-18; 7:17-18; 12:33-35; 15:7-9). To gain a more exact counterpart to τὸ
ἐντός, Matthew shifts slightly from τὸ ἔξωθεν (v 25) to τὸ ἐκτός.

Cf. Sir 19:26. The impersonal "its" with "outside" does not imply that Matthew's
version of the sayings concerns ritual purity as such, either partly or wholly; for
although he might have written "your," the metaphorical use of the cup for the
blind Pharisee is already plain enough from the preceding references to greed and
self-indulgence. Consequently, we have no reason to think that Luke missed or
obscured a ritual point. Jesus simply makes a ritual practice figurative of an ethical
point. Matthew's habit of assimilating sayings to each other for the sake of parallelism obviates the need to think that in Luke the Aramaic זַכִּי/דְּכִי was mistakenly
read as "give alms" rather than "cleanse," its intended meaning. Matthew's καθάρισον
is an assimilation to καθαρίζετε in v 25 (see comments ad loc.). If the Aramaic
verb comes into the picture at all, it does so as a wordplay on the part of Jesus
himself (but see the caveats in C. F. D. Moule, *An Idiom Book of New Testament Greek*
[2nd ed.; Cambridge: Cambridge University Press, 1959] 186).

23:27 (Luke 11:44) For the sixth woe, Matthew skips material already
used (see vv 6-7 and 23 with Luke 11:42-43) and goes to the tradition
behind Luke 11:44. "Woe to you" gains the usual address, "scribes and
Pharisees, hypocrites" (not in Luke; see the comments on v 13).
παρομοιάζετε, "you are similar to," replaces ἐστὲ ὡς, "you are like." Though
Matthew's verb occurs only here in the NT, his fondness for παραβολή
(5,2), ὁμοιόω (2,3), and ὅμοιος (1,5)—especially in conjunction—suggests
a conflation of those words here. τάφοις, "graves," ousts τὰ μνημεῖα, "tombs."
The latter appears often enough in the first gospel, but Matthew likes the
former (4,2). It does not occur in the other synoptics (or the rest of the
NT except for Rom 3:13), and it clearly implies the presence of corruption
within—Matthew's emphasis throughout the passage—whereas Luke's term
refers primarily to a monument. κεκονιαμένοις stands in place of τὰ ἄδηλα,
"unseen." Since Matthew's point lies in the hiding, not in the advertising,
of inward corruption, the substitute refers to decorative plastering, as in
Prov 21:9 LXX. Such plastering symbolizes the Pharisees' hypocrisy. Matthew's adding "and you adorn the tombs of the righteous" to v 29 will
confirm this understanding. Thus there is no allusion to whitewashing tombs
annually to keep people from accidentally brushing against them and con-
tracting ceremonial impurity (cf. *m. Šeqal.* 1:1; *b. Moʿed Qaṭ.* 1a, 5a; Num
6:6; 19:16; John 11:55; 18:28).

In the original form of the saying Jesus makes a figure out of con-
tracting ceremonial impurity from graves that have lost their last coat of
lime (so Luke). Correspondingly, Jesus' statement "and the men who walk
over [the tombs] do not know [it]" gives way to Matthew's composition
"which outwardly appear beautiful, but inwardly are full of dead people's
bones and of all uncleanness." The antithetic parallelism typifies Matthew's
style and shifts the center of gravity from the unsuspecting men to the
graves. His delineating the ugly contents of the graves accentuates the

hypocrisy of the scribes and Pharisees, whom the graves represent. οἵτινες is a Mattheanism (23,5). ἔξωθεν comes from v 25. μέν . . . δέ occurs with extraordinary frequency in the first gospel (15,1). Matthew likes φαίνονται (5,8), especially in criticisms of religious pretense (cf. 6:5, 16, 18). ἔσωθεν comes in to contrast with ἔξωθεν (cf. a similar insertion in 7:25). γέμουσιν echoes v 25. So also the compound reference to dead people's bones and all uncleanness reflects the compound reference to rapacity and self-indulgence in v 25. The words themselves stem from the contextual references to graves and matters of purity versus impurity. πάσης represents Matthew's favorite diction (63,25-26) and intensifies the wickedness of the scribes and Pharisees.

23:28 Matthew composes v 28 as an interpretation of the preceding figure. In particular, the two lines of v 28 exhibit his fondness for parallelism and follow the pattern and distinctive basic wording of v 27cd. οὕτως καί and ὑμεῖς are favorites of his (4,1; 15,3). ἔξωθεν and the Mattheanisms μέν . . . δέ (15,1) and φαίνεσθε (5,8) echo v 27. There, Matthew omitted "men" (cf. Luke 11:44). To compensate, he writes "to men" here (cf. his liking ἄνθρωπος—35,17—and esp. his using it with φανῶσιν for religious ostentation in 6:5). δίκαιοι represents a favorite theme of his (9-10,7-6). ἔσωθεν also comes from v 27. But for variety ἐστε μεστοί substitutes for γέμουσιν or, as it would have been here, γέμετε. "Of hypocrisy" echoes the repeated addressing of the scribes and Pharisees as "hypocrites" and interprets the figure of "dead people's bones" (v 27). "Of lawlessness" interprets the figure of "all uncleanness" (v 27). Both hypocrisy and lawlessness represent special concerns of the evangelist (9,3 for ὑποκρι-; 3,1 for ἀνομία).

23:29 (Luke 11:47) Now Matthew skips a lawyer's reply and the already used woe concerning burdens (cf. v 4) and takes up the tradition behind Luke 11:47-48. As usual, "Woe to you" gains the addition "scribes and Pharisees, hypocrites" (see the comments on v 13). "The graves" again replaces "the tombs" and implies inward corruption as a figure of hypocrisy (cf. v 27). For further emphasis, Matthew composes the parallel line "and you adorn the tombs of the righteous." κοσμεῖτε will recur in 25:7 as part of a passage unique to Matthew (see also 12:44; Luke 11:25). Its occurrence in Luke 21:5 contrasts with Mark 13:1; Matt 24:1 and therefore shows that Luke would probably have written it here, too, had it appeared in the tradition. "The tombs" comes from the tradition behind the preceding line and makes up for Matthew's substituting "the graves" in that line. "Of the righteous" parallels "of the prophets," implies teachers of righteousness as opposed to teachers of lawlessness, and comes from Matthew's preferred vocabulary (δίκαιος—9-10,7-6). Cf. 1 Macc 13:27-30; Josephus *Ant.* 18.4.6 §108; 20.4.3 §95; *J.W.* 4.9.7 §§531-32; 5.12.2 §§506-7; Acts 2:29.

23:30 (Luke 11:47) Matthew now turns the historical statement "and your fathers killed them [the prophets]" into a present claim by the scribes and Pharisees that had they been living in olden times they would not have participated in the murder of the prophets: "and you say, 'If we had been in the days of our fathers, we would not have been partners with them in the blood of the prophets.'" This change stems from Matthew's desire to emphasize disagreement between saying and doing as the essence of hypocrisy. The two occurrences of ἤμεθα and the two prepositional phrases beginning with ἐν and followed by a dependent genitive balance each other in a parallelistic fashion typical of his style. ἡμέραις is a Mattheanism (15,9). "Of our fathers" derives from "your fathers" in the tradition. αἵματι is another Mattheanism (4,3) and anticipates v 35. τῶν προφητῶν recalls v 29, represents Matthew's special diction (19,6), and makes a third instance of his interjecting the combination of prophets and righteous men in shared materials originally lacking it (see 10:41 and 13:17 with comments ad loc.). Cf. Exod 20:5.

23:31 *(Luke 11:48)* Matthew likes ὥστε (10,0), which appears in place of Luke's ἄρα. The substitution of μαρτυρεῖτε, "you bear witness," for μάρτυρές ἐστε, "you are witnesses," better enables him to insert ἑαυτοῖς, "against yourselves." The insertion emphasizes the scribes' and Pharisees' self-incrimination (cf. 21:31, 41; 22:42, all of which contain Matthean revisions to this effect; see also 22:21). Matthew delays "and you agree with the works of your fathers"; it is redundant and paratactic at this point. "Because they themselves killed them" becomes "that you are sons of the ones who murdered the prophets." This revision marks a shift in focus from the fathers to the scribes and Pharisees. The shift strengthens the accusation against those Jewish leaders. The contextual references to "fathers" suggest "sons" (not in Luke). υἱοί is a favorite word of Matthew (27,16). "The ones who murdered" replaces "they killed" and stresses their breaking the commandment against murder (5:21; 19:18). "The prophets" substitutes for "them" and echoes vv 29 and 30. Both φονευσάντων and προφῆτας are further Mattheanisms (4,0; 19,6). Together, the revisions in the clause beginning with ὅτι do not stress the principle "like father, like son" so much as the taking on of liability for national guilt. Building and adorning tombs does not show repudiation of the fathers' murderous activities; it amounts to admission of solidarity with the murderers.

Though building the tombs of prophets may look like repudiation of their murder, in Oriental thought it could carry an implication of shared guilt (see J. D. M. Derrett in *SE* IV/1 [TU 102; Berlin: Akademie-Verlag, 1968] 187-90). The suggestion that Matthew's υἱοί and Luke's οἰκοδομεῖτε go back to a single, ambiguous בני (see Black, *Aramaic Approach* 12-13) stumbles over the occurrence of the two Greek words in lines that do not correspond to each other.

23:32 *(Luke 11:48)* The ironic command "And you, fill up the measure of your fathers" replaces the statement "but you build [the tombs of the prophets]." καί ousts δέ because Matthew does not want a contrast. ὑμεῖς appears also in Luke. The rest of Matthew's replacement comes from the recently omitted clause "and you agree with the works of your fathers" (so Luke). "Fill up" substitutes for "you agree with." Matthew likes πληρώσατε (9,6). Its meaning leads to the further substitution of "the measure" for "the works" despite his fondness for ἔργοις (4,1). By putting the ironic command to fill up the measure of the fathers in place of the already mentioned building of tombs, Matthew indicates that the scribes and Pharisees were going to do more than build tombs: they were going to murder Jesus and his followers just as their fathers had murdered the prophets. Filling up the fathers' measure does not refer to building tombs, then, but to repeating the fathers' murderous deeds. In composing the ironic command, Matthew imitates prophetic style in the OT (see, e.g., Isa 8:9-10; Jer 7:21; Amos 4:4; Nah 3:14-15).

Cf. Gen 15:16; Dan 8:23; 2 Macc 6:14; 1 Thess 2:16. The meaning of πληρώσατε in the ironic command to "fill up" the fathers' measure comes close to fulfillment of ancient prophecy. Therefore we are justified in regarding the verb as the result of editing by Matthew, who exhibits strong interest in fulfillment of prophecy.

23:33 The unique question in v 33 has the purposes of intensifying the guilt of the scribes and Pharisees and emphasizing the inevitability of their judgment. "Snakes" was inserted also in 10:16 (besides one shared occurrence in 7:10). Here it doubles the charge contained in the traditional epithet "offspring of vipers." The latter comes from the preaching of John the Baptist (3:7). For a second time Matthew has put the epithet in Jesus' mouth in order to assimilate the ministries of Jesus and John (see 12:34 and "John the Baptist parallel Jesus" in the Topical Index). And for a third time Matthew has made the phrase apply to the Pharisees, whereas in its only other occurrence it refers to crowds of people in general (Luke 3:7). πῶς is a Mattheanism in its interrogative use, "How?" (6,1). Here it substitutes for "who?" (3:7), implies the impossibility of escape, and leads to the omission of "has warned you" (3:7). Because of the omission, "to flee" (so 3:7) becomes "will you flee" (φύγητε). "The coming wrath" (3:7) changes to "the judgment of Gehenna." The new phrase contains Mattheanisms in κρίσεως (8,0) and γεέννης (3,0). The latter echoes v 15, where it is part of Matthew's composition about the fate of proselytes made by the scribes and Pharisees. Thus vv 13 and 15 indicate that the proselytes and those who proselytized them will share the same terrifying fate.

23:34 (Luke 11:49) The insertion of v 33 shifts the referent of "On account of this" from the building of the prophets' tombs (which Matthew turned into an ironic command anyhow—see v 32) to the fearful prospect of judgment in hell (v 33). In order to make Jesus rather than "the wisdom of God" the sender of the prophets and others, Matthew omits "also the wisdom of God said" (cf. 9:38–10:5 with comments ad loc. on similar revisions). The omission does not identify Jesus with divine wisdom; for divine wisdom does not merge with Jesus, but with Christian "sages" (σοφούς; see a similar insertion in 11:25). Typically, Matthew identifies these sages as "scribes" (γραμματεῖς—10,2; see the comments on v 8 concerning his characterizing Jesus' disciples as scribes but prohibiting their acceptance of the corresponding title). The Christ was wisdom in 11:2, 19. Here his disciples are wise ones, sages. Like master, like disciples. "Sages and scribes" replaces "apostles," which is to be considered original because of Luke's using the definite article with it everywhere else (with the understandable exception of Luke 6:13) and because of the probability that Jesus played on the sending of the prophets in Jer 7:25-26; 25:4-7; 26:4-6; 29:18-19; 35:15; 44:4-5 (cf. their persecution in Jer 15:15; 17:18; 20:11; 1 Kgs 19:10, 14 and the use of ἀπόστολος in 3 Kgdms 14:6 LXX). Before these substitutions, Matthew inserts his favorites ἰδού (34,9) and ἐγώ (12-13,3) for Christological emphasis. "I will send" becomes "I am sending" in accord with the shift from prediction by the wisdom of God to the activity of Jesus during his ministry. Changing εἰς αὐτούς, "to them," into πρὸς ὑμᾶς, "to you," agrees with the shift from a quotation of divine wisdom to Jesus' addressing the scribes and Pharisees. Thus a prediction by the wisdom of God concerning a future sending that may have already occurred by Matthew's time turns into a description by Jesus of a current sending (see also 28:18-20).

The initial καί of the second clause in Luke 11:49 disappears because Matthew will characteristically add another, parallel clause beginning with that conjunction. As above, the third person changes to the second in the switch from "they will kill" to "you will kill." To heighten the guilt of the scribes and Pharisees, Matthew adds "and you will crucify" (see 20:19; 26:2 for other insertions of the verb and cf. Matthew's drawing a parallel between disciple and master in 10:24-25, where he expands a traditional saying). Since the Jewish leaders handed Jesus over to the Romans for crucifixion and since the Jews neither practiced crucifixion nor had the power of capital punishment, Matthew probably meant σταυρώσετε in the causative sense, "you will cause to be crucified [by the Romans]" (cf. Acts 2:36; 4:10). "And they will persecute" (so Luke) provides a nucleus for his composing the next clause: "and [some] of them you will whip in your synagogues and will persecute from city to city." "[Some] of them" comes from the preceding clause, and "you will whip in your synagogues" from 10:17, where Matthew inserted the same phrase (in the third person) in traditional material (cf. m. Sanh. 1:2; m. Mak. 3:4; m. Ḥul. 12:4). The added clause also makes a parallel between the fate of disciples and that of Jesus (see 20:19, where whipping and crucifixion go together, as here). "From city to city" echoes 10:23, another of Matthew's compositions, and exhibits his love of cities (18,3). As the disciples will flee from city to city (10:23), the scribes and Pharisees will pursue them from city to city.

23:35 (Luke 11:50-51) In the saying about the blood of the martyrs, ἵνα yields to the Mattheanism ὅπως (8,7). Luke's version of the saying includes the Semitic expression "may be required, sought out" (cf. Gen 42:22; Deut 32:43; 2 Sam 4:11; 2 Kgs 9:7; 2 Chr 24:22; Pss 9:13[12]; 79:10; Ezek 3:18; 33:6, 8). Matthew substitutes the equivalent expression "may come on you" (cf. Lev 20:9; Deut 21:8-9; 22:8; 2 Sam 1:16; 14:9; Jer 26:15; 51:35; Jonah 1:14; Acts 18:6). His distinctive use of the latter expression in 27:25, Luke's using it in Acts 5:28; 18:6, and Matthew's inserting the related idiom "let your peace come on it" in 10:13 argue for the originality of Luke's expression here. Matthew makes the substitution for the sake of its more pointed accusation, contained in the phrase "on you," which replaces "from this generation." His advancing "on you" from last position before the appositive (where Luke's "from this generation" is located) to first position after the verb confirms the accusatory emphasis. He also advances "of all," which modifies "the prophets" in Luke, to a position right after "on you," where it becomes "all" and modifies "blood." "The prophets" changes to "righteous," which also modifies "blood." δίκαιον is a Mattheanism (9-10,7-6), and "righteous blood" is a characteristically Matthean assimilation to OT phraseology, in particular to Lam 4:13 LXX, where "righteous blood" represents "blood of the righteous" in the Hebrew text. Cf. also the insertion "of the righteous" in v 29. The present participle

470

ἐκχυννόμενον, "being shed," stands in place of the perfect participle τὸ ἐκκεχυμένον, "that was shed," and conforms to the present participle τῶν ἐκχεόντων, "who are shedding," in Lam 4:13 LXX. "On the earth" replaces "from [the] foundation of [the] world," represents another Mattheanism (8,2), and echoes the story of Abel, where emphasis is put on the earth which received his blood (Gen 4:10-11).

"From the blood of Abel" gains "the righteous one." Matthew's addition reflects his similar insertion in the first part of the saying (see the comments in the foregoing paragraph) and anticipates his distinctive description of Jesus as "that righteous [man]" (27:19). Thus the line that began with the righteous Abel will reach its climax in the righteous Jesus. "To the blood of Zechariah" matches Luke and starts an allusion to 2 Chr 24:20-22. The insertion "son of Barachiah" disagrees with the Chronicler's designation of Zechariah as "the son of Jehoiada." Matthew's quoting Zech 11:12-13 in relation to "innocent blood," "the price of blood," and "the field of blood" in 27:3-10 suggests that the description of Zechariah as the son of Barachiah rests on Zech 1:1. Of course, Zechariah the preexilic martyr and Zechariah the postexilic minor prophet differ in historical identity. But Matthew conflates them for the literary-theological purpose of correlating the betrayal of Jesus' innocent blood, which fulfilled the prediction by Zechariah the son of Barachiah, with the shedding of the righteous blood of OT martyrs, which culminated in the murder of Zechariah the son of Jehoiada.

"Whom you murdered" replaces "who perished" for closer conformity to 2 Chr 24:22 (וַיַּהַרְג, "and he murdered") and the distinctive phraseology in v 31. The replacement also sharpens the accusatory tone in that the plural "you," where Luke has a participle modifying Zechariah, points straight at the scribes and Pharisees. They participated with their ancestors in the bygone murder. The gap between generations has disappeared: "the sons of those who murdered the prophets" (v 31) have themselves become murderers. Furthermore, ἐφονεύσατε is a Mattheanism (4,0) and portrays the scribes and Pharisees as breaking the law against murder (cited in 5:21 [bis]; 19:18). After all, Matthew had already described them as "full of . . . lawlessness" (v 28, so his gospel alone). "Between the Temple and the altar" replaces "between the altar and the house." We might have expected Matthew to retain "of the house" because it agrees with "the court of the house of the Lord" in Chronicles. But he is looking ahead to v 38, where he will write *your* house" (so also Luke). The house no longer belongs to the Lord; therefore Matthew calls it the Temple and puts it in the forefront, in contrast with Luke's order of words, to prepare for the discussion of its destruction. ναοῦ is a favorite of Matthew (5,1).

Cf. Num 35:33-34; Isa 26:21; Ezek 24:7-8; Joel 4(3):19; Job 16:18; *y. Ta'an.* 4.69a; and, on the targumic descriptions of Abel as righteous, R. le Déaut in *Bib* 42 (1961) 30-36, along with Heb 11:4 (cf. 12:24); 1 John 3:12. It is doubtful that Matthew would have balked at the putting of Abel among the prophets (so Luke; cf. Gen 20:7; Ps 105:15; Matt 13:35 with the heading of Psalm 78). As noted above, the real reasons for the revision are Matthew's liking δίκαιον and wanting an allusion to Lam 4:13 LXX. See further McNeile's commentary, ad loc., and Gundry, *Use of the OT* 86-88, especially against a reference to the Zechariah Josephus mentions in his description of the Jewish war of A.D. 66-73 (*J.W.* 4.5.4 §§334-44). We may add that Luke's original ἐκζητηθῇ echoes the dying words of Zechariah according to 2 Chr 24:22 ("may the Lord see and require [it]") and therefore shows that Jesus had this OT martyr in mind. Whether or not the separation of Ezra-Nehemiah from Chronicles had already occurred (see R. L. Harris in *JETS* 14 [1971] 173-74), Jesus' statement implies that the murder of Zechariah marks the last martyrdom in the OT canon (though not in the OT period—see Jer 26:23; cf. S. Z. Leiman, *The Canonization of the Hebrew Scripture* [Hamden, Conn.: Archon, 1976], on the closing of the three-part Hebrew canon in the second century B.C.). The possibility that Matthew's reference to Barachiah goes back to Isa 8:2 LXX with an understanding of "witnesses" as "martyrs" stumbles against the agreement of the LXX with the Hebrew on the sense "witnesses."

23:36 (Luke 11:51) In the introduction to the dire prediction concerning "this generation," Matthew writes the Semitic ἀμήν, "truly," where Luke translates with ναί, "yes." ἐκζητηθήσεται ἀπό, "it will be required of," yields to ἥξει . . . ἐπί, "will come on," for a parallel with ἔλθῃ ἐφ᾽, "may come on" (v 35; cf. ἐκζητηθῇ in Luke 11:50 and see Matt 24:14 for another insertion of ἥξει). In place of the understood subject "the blood of all the prophets" Matthew characteristically supplies ταῦτα πάντα, "all these things" (7,1). This heightens the guilt of the scribes and Pharisees and anticipates his inserting the same phrase in 24:8, 33, 34 for the events of the tribulation. Thus chap. 23 bonds together with chaps. 24–25. Retribution for all the righteous blood of the OT martyrs will take the form of the tribulational events yet to be described as fulfilling the forecast concerning "this generation." By context "this generation" means the scribes and Pharisees ("lawyers" in Luke). Matthew's next verse narrows the reference further to the scribes and Pharisees in Jerusalem. But his involving them in the bygone murder of an OT prophet (v 35) shows that he does not take "this generation" in a sense chronologically limited to Jesus' contemporaries, but in a qualitative sense concerning the "unbelieving and perverted" in the whole of Israel's history (see 11:16; 12:39, 41, 42, 45; 16:4; 17:17 and synoptic parallels for the same qualitative emphasis in pre-Matthean tradition; cf. 24:34; Mark 13:30; Luke 21:32). Hence, we read, "in order that on you may come . . . you murdered [for a centuries-old incident] . . . will come on this generation." In other words, if the "you" who constitute "this generation" includes those who murdered Zechariah in OT times, "this generation" can hardly bear the chronological limitation usually imposed on it. Cf. Exod 20:5; 34:7; Num 14:18; Deut 5:9.

23:37 (Luke 13:34) Matthew now imports Jesus' lament over Jerusalem. According to Luke, Jesus spoke it in the territory of Herod Antipas on his way to Jerusalem. In Matthew, Jesus laments over Jerusalem within the city itself: "Jerusalem, Jerusalem, who kills the prophets and stones those sent to her, how often I have wanted to gather your children together the way a hen gathers her chicks together under [her] wings, and you were unwilling!" Matthew's text reads as Luke's with three exceptions of no consequence: (1) Matthew writes a second aorist infinitive instead of a first aorist infinitive; (2) he fills an ellipsis with "gathers together"; and (3) "her chicks" stands where Luke has "her own brood." Because of prior changes in v 34, however, "the prophets" includes Christian prophets. Only OT prophets were originally in view (so Luke).

See Lev 20:27; Deut 17:5, 7; *m. Sanh.* 7:4 on the stoning of sorcerers, idolaters, and the like (cf. the comments on Matt 21:35). "How often!" agrees with the inherently likely indications in the Gospel of John that Jesus often ministered in Jerusalem during the pilgrim festivals. Are Jerusalem's children only the people or leaders who reside in Jerusalem? Or are they all the Jews, because Jerusalem is their religious capital? Matthew's concentrating on the Jewish leaders based in Jerusalem suggests the former. The ironic hyperbole in Luke 13:33 favors that Jesus meant to be understood the same way. ὄρνις may refer to any kind of mother bird. For the figure of speech, see Deut 32:11; Ruth 2:12; Pss 17:8; 36:8(7); 57:2(1); 61:5(4); 63:8(7); 91:4; Isa 31:5; *Lev. Rab.* 25:5. Jesus wanted to save Jerusalem from judgment (cf. 24:1-2; Mark 13:1-2; Luke 21:5-6). He wanted to even under the view that he was quoting another saying of divine wisdom. Several data go against that view, however: (1) the wide separation in Luke of the quotation of divine wisdom (Luke 11:49) from the lament over Jerusalem (Luke 13:34-35); (2) Matthew's taking sayings from diverse contexts and collocating them throughout chap. 23; (3) the narrow but distinct separation of the quotation of divine wisdom (v 34) from the lament over Jerusalem (v 37); and (4) the improbability that divine wisdom would have been portrayed as looking forward to the sending of prophets in one breath and looking backward to an already completed mission of the prophets in the next breath. Only a low estimate of Jesus' messianic and divine self-consciousness and a Procrustean application of that estimate would prevent our accepting the lament over Jerusalem as dominical.

23:38 (Luke 13:35) To the exclamation "Behold, your house is being left to you" Matthew adds "desolate" (not in Luke and part of Matthew's textual tradition apparently influenced by Luke and by the seeming superfluity of the addition; see the UBS and Metzger, *Textual Commentary* ad loc.). The words shared with Luke allude to Jer 12:7: "I have left my house." The editorial addition alludes further to Jer 22:5: "this house will become a desolation." In Jer 12:7 the house belongs to the Lord and may refer to the Temple, to the promised land, or to the covenant people; but because of God's having forsaken it, Jesus makes the house belong to the unbelieving Jerusalemites. Thus he identifies it with their city, the people residing there, or the Temple located there (see Str-B 1. 943-44 against the Temple). Jer 22:5 deals with the house of the king of Judah. The conflation of these two passages exhibits Matthew's interest in the OT and therefore favors the originality of "desolate" in his text and doubles the stress on judgment. As will appear in v 39 and 24:1, 3, he identifies "your house" as the Temple and makes its desolation start with Jesus' deserting it.

23:39 (Luke 13:35) The replacement of δέ with the Mattheanism γάρ (62-63,15)—or the addition of γάρ (see the v.l. in Luke)—makes clear that the saying in v 39 explains the desolation in terms of Jesus' absence (cf. Ezek 8:6; 11:22-25; *1 Enoch* 89:56; *2 Apoc. Bar.* 8:2). The advance of με, "me," emphasizes this point. The insertion "from now on," which Matthew will insert again in 26:29, 64, accentuates the judgmental symbolism of Jesus' leaving the Temple. Matthew writes a simple "till you say" instead of the awkward "till it will come when you say." "Blessed [is] he who comes in the name of the Lord" stays unchanged, matches 21:9, and echoes Ps 118:26. Unless Luke sharply distinguishes disciples making a pilgrimage to Jerusalem and nondisciples permanently residing there (but the presence of antagonistic Pharisees in the crowd around Jesus in Luke 19:39 and the lumping of Judeans with pilgrims from the Dispersion, the latter even being called "dwellers in Jerusalem," in Acts 2:5-11, 14 stand against such a distinction), the prediction in Luke reaches fulfillment at the triumphal entry (Luke 19:37-38). By delaying the prediction till after the triumphal entry (cf. 21:9), Matthew makes it refer to Jesus' parousia as the Son of man (see chaps. 24–25). This reference not only helps unify chaps. 23 and 24–25 (here we see the purpose behind Matthew's inserting vv 37-39); it also implies a conversion of Israel at the parousia (see the comments on 19:28 and cf. Zech 12:10–13:1; Rom 11:25-27). Therefore, casting out "the sons of the kingdom" (8:11-12) has to do with unbelieving Jews from Jesus' lifetime up to but not including those who will convert at the parousia; and the transferal of the kingdom to a fruit-bearing nation (21:43) does not rule out a return of the kingdom to Israel at the parousia (again see 19:28). The limitation of the woes to the scribes and Pharisees (vv 13-36) forestalls a contradiction between the woes and the implied conversion of Israel. Jerusalem, crowded with pilgrims from all parts of Jewry, represents Israel.

24:1 (Mark 13:1; Luke 21:5) Just as the transition in 13:34-36 united the two parts of the parabolic discourse on the kingdom, so also the transition in 24:1-3 unites rather than divides. Unification can be seen in the omission of the story about the widow's mites (Mark 12:41-44; Luke 21:1-4). The omission welds together the indictment of the scribes and Pharisees (chap. 23) and the sermon on the parousia (chaps. 24–25) in a single discourse dealing with the history of the kingdom. This history stretches from the final phase of Jesus' conflict with the Jewish religious leaders, who represent antinomian leaders in the church, to the last judgment. The first two verses of chap. 24 relate to the end of chap. 23 by giving further indication of the way "your house will be left to you desolate" (23:38).

The nominative participle ἐξελθών is a Mattheanism (10,4) and stems from the prefix of Mark's ἐκπορευομένου and the substantive participle ὁ ἐρχόμενος in Matthew's preceding verse. It thus provides a counterpoint: 23:39 specifies a future coming; 24:1 specifies a present coming out. The replacement of Mark's "he" with "Jesus" follows Matthew's practice (80,12) and emphasizes that Jesus' departure constitutes the Temple's being forsaken (23:38-39). To avoid repeating ἐκ, Matthew substitutes ἀπό. Rejection of Mark's genitive absolute construction necessitates adding a finite verb, viz., ἐπορεύετο, which comes from Mark's previously replaced ἐκπορευομένου and increases emphasis on Jesus' departure as an abandonment of the Temple. The addition of the finite verb requires the further addition of "and." "His disciples approached" is typical of Matthew's writing (see, e.g., 5:1; 13:36). προσῆλθον is dear to him (38,6). It replaces Mark's "says to him" and connotes Jesus' dignity (see the comments on 4:3; 8:14). "His disciples" replaces "one of his disciples." This change makes Jesus' reply an address to all the disciples, who represent the whole church, and finds somewhat of a match in Luke's "certain ones." "To show him the buildings of the Temple" replaces the exclamation of the lone disciple in Mark, "Teacher, see what wonderful stones and what wonderful buildings!" Matthew makes the substitution in order not to interrupt Jesus' discourse unnecessarily with anyone else's speaking. ἐπιδεῖξαι is a Mattheanism (3,0). "The buildings" comes from the exclamation of the disciple in Mark. And "of the Temple" echoes the first line of the verse. Cf. Josephus *Ant.* 15.11.3 §§391-402; *J.W.* 5.5.1-6 §§184-226.

24:2 *(Mark 13:2; Luke 21:5-6)* To contrast Jesus' reply with the disciples' pointing out the buildings of the Temple, Matthew writes δέ instead of Mark's καί. "Jesus" drops out because of its insertion in the preceding verse. The addition of ἀποκριθείς to εἶπεν makes a favorite combination (29,6). Because Matthew pluralized Jesus' address in the preceding verse, Mark's "to him" becomes "to them." For the same reason "Do you [singular] see . . . ?" changes to "Do you [plural] see . . . ?" (cf. Luke's plural). The insertion of οὐ makes a typically Matthean parallel to the negatives in the succeeding part of the verse and implies an affirmative answer. "All these things" comes from Mark 13:3, replaces "these large buildings" (Mark 13:2), and finds fairly close correspondence in Luke's "these things which." It also represents Matthew's favorite diction (ταῦτα πάντα—7,1) and an assimilation to 23:36 (see also 24:8, 33, 34). Taken together, the implied affirmative answer and the replacement indicate that the disciples understand all that Jesus has been saying about the abandonment of the Temple. That abandonment, rather than the buildings of the Temple as such, is the focus of Matthew's attention. Cf. the comments on chaps. 13–17 passim concerning his portraying the disciples as understanding. Typically, he adds "Truly I say to you" (15,8). This lends emphasis to the effect of Jesus' abandoning the Temple: "a stone will not be left here on a stone, which will not be torn down." οὐ καταλυθήσεται avoids the harshness of Mark's οὐ μή with an aorist subjunctive in each of the two clauses.

Cf. Hag 2:15. Though the Temple was razed along with the rest of Jerusalem in A.D. 70 (Josephus *J.W.* 7.1.1 §1), we might have expected a *vaticinium ex eventu* to mention the burning of the Temple. That it is not mentioned argues in favor of a genuine prediction by Jesus. Such a prediction is favored also by the absence of other striking features of the first Jewish revolt—viz., cannibalism, pestilence, and internecine conflict—and the absence of any notation concerning the fulfillment of the prophecy (contrast Acts 11:28). Cf. Mic 3:12; Jer 26:18; Mark 14:58; 15:29; Matt 26:61; 27:40; John 2:19-20; Josephus *J.W.* 6.5.3 §§288-309.

THE PERSECUTION OF DISCIPLES, THE RISE OF ECCLESIASTICAL ANTINOMIANISM, AND THE WORLDWIDE PROCLAMATION OF THE KINGDOM AS NONESCHATOLOGICAL CHARACTERISTICS OF THE CHURCH AGE

24:3-14

Though Matthew takes over Markan material concerning international upheaval and natural disasters, his revisions and expansions show that his main interest lies in the persecution of disciples, the rise of antinomianism in the church, and the worldwide proclamation of the kingdom as general characteristics of the present age that do not signal the onset of the end. The prefixing of chap. 23, which is largely unique to Matthew and warns Christians not to falsify their profession by aping the lawless ways of the scribes and Pharisees, shows that the eschatology in 24:3-14, and indeed throughout the rest of chaps. 24–25, has the purpose of motivating Christians to live by Jesus' law.

24:3 (Mark 13:3-4; Luke 21:7) To contrast Jesus' earlier "going" (v 1) with his "sitting" on the Mount of Olives, Matthew changes καί to δέ. Mark's εἰς, literally "into," becomes ἐπί, "on," which is more natural with "sitting" (cf. 27:19). "Opposite the Temple" vanishes because Jesus has now forsaken the Temple and no longer relates to it (see the comments on 23:37–24:2). "Approached" replaces "were asking," comes from Matthew's special vocabulary (38,6), implies Jesus' dignity (see the comments on 4:3; 8:14), and echoes v 1. There is another echo of v 1 in the substitution of "the disciples" for the names of Peter, James, John, and Andrew (cf. Luke's omission of those names). μαθηταί, too, is a Mattheanism (31,5). It generalizes the discourse: the disciples represent the church in receiving Jesus' instruction (cf. v 1). Matthew compensates for replacing ἐπηρώτα by adding λέγοντες, another favorite (61,23).

The first part of the disciples' request, "Tell us, when these things will be," stays unchanged. But its second part, "and what [will be] the sign when all these things are going to be consummated" (so Mark), turns into a twofold reference to Jesus' coming and the consummation of the age: "and what [will be] the sign of your coming and of [the] consummation of the age?" Because a single definite article modifies the twofold reference, the sign deals with the coming and consummation considered as a unit. By making the disciples ask about Jesus' coming and the consummation of the age—in Mark they ask only about the destruction of the Temple—Matthew tailors their request to the burden of Jesus' response, where the time of Jerusalem's destruction remains unidentified and emphasis falls instead on the Son of man's coming after the tribulation. This tailoring of the request to the response has the purpose of portraying the disciples as already having some understanding about Jesus' coming and the consummation of the age and as gaining further understanding (again cf. the comments on chaps. 13–17 for Matthew's distinctive emphasis on the disciples' understanding). Adding "of your coming" to "the sign" prepares for inserting "the sign of the Son of man in heaven" in Matthew's later description of the parousia (v 30). σῆς belongs to his favorite diction (6,2). παρουσίας occurs as an insertion in vv 3, 27, 37, 39 and appears nowhere else in the gospels. In accord with its use for visits of dignitaries (see BAG, s.v.) it connotes the publicness of the Son of man's coming—a point greatly emphasized by Matthew. The phrase "of the consummation of the age" is built on Mark's infinitive "to be consummated" and occurs five times in Matthew without parallel, but elsewhere in the NT only at Heb 9:26. It may derive in part from Dan 12:4, 13 LXX (cf. the comments on 13:39).

With "the consummation of the age," cf. 1QpHab 7:1-2; *1 Enoch* 16:1; *T. Levi* 10:2; *As. Mos.* 1:18; *2 Apoc. Bar.* 13:3; 27:15; 29:8; 30:3; 54:21; 56:2; 59:8; 82:2; 83:7, 22. Matthew's concentrating on the sign of the parousia and the consummation of the age reduces attention to the destruction of the Temple, but does not imply a date of writing after that destruction, as though the event had come and gone without Jesus' expected return. We have seen that Matthew is simply tailoring the disciples' request to the contents of Jesus' reply in order to portray the disciples as having understanding.

24:4-5 (Mark 13:5; Luke 21:8) At the start of v 4 Matthew replaces Mark's δέ, which he customarily uses in the adversative sense, with καί. This reversal of his normal procedure links the disciples' understanding, as shown in their request, with Jesus' reply, which furthers their understanding. Mark's ἤρξατο λέγειν changes to the Mattheanism ἀποκριθείς . . . εἶπεν (29,6). The change brings out the responsive character of the following instruction. Matthew adds "For" to "many will come in my name, saying. . . ." He likes γάρ (62-63,15). Its addition makes the prediction concerning deceivers the ground for warning against them. Luke shares γάρ with Matthew. He also shares Matthew's omission of Mark's recitative ὅτι before the deceivers' self-identification. "In my name" shows that their self-identification consists in a claim to be Jesus himself, returned, not merely a representative of Jesus or a rival with superior claims. This claim is made clear by Matthew's unique and characteristic addition, "the Christ" (8,5), which anticipates vv 23-24 and echoes 23:10. The latter passage, "Your instructor is one, the Christ," shows that those who claim Jesus' messiahship will be false teachers—of antinomianism, as it turns out (see v 12). Cf. Mark 14:62; John 8:58.

The lack of evidence that anyone claimed messiahship between Jesus and Bar-Kokhba a hundred years later militates against our seeing the discourse as a *vaticinium ex eventu* concerning the first Jewish revolt (A.D. 66-73). False prophets figured in that revolt (Josephus *J.W.* 6.5.2 §§285-87; 7.11.1 §§437-39; *Ant.* 20.5.1 §97); but one did not have to claim messiahship to be a false prophet. Cf. Acts 5:36; 8:9; 21:38.

24:6 (Mark 13:7; Luke 21:9) To the hearing of wars and rumors of wars, Matthew adds "you are going [to hear . . .]." The addition suits his penchant for μέλλω (5-6,1), makes up for omission of the word in v 3 (cf. Mark 13:4), and emphasizes certainty of fulfillment. The further addition of "See" to "[that] you not be disturbed" strengthens the command and exhibits another Mattheanism (ὁράω—5,2). The insertion of γάρ also betrays Matthew's hand (62-63,15). He made the same insertion in v 5; Luke shares it here. Thus the necessity of the events is made the basis of the command not to fear; for the events, dire though they be, belong to God's plan and purpose. Matthew's final insertion, "is," fills in what the other synoptists leave to be implied.

Jesus seems to have drawn phraseology from Dan 11:44 ("but rumors from the East and from the North will disturb him"); 2:28 ("what shall be [ἃ δεῖ γενέσθαι,

477

'what must take place,' in the LXX and Theodotion] at the end of days"; cf. Rev 1:1; 4:1; 22:6); and 11:27 ("for the end is still [to come] at the appointed time"). See Gundry, *Use of the OT* 46.

24:7 (Mark 13:8; Luke 21:10-11) The prediction that international conflict will precede the end stays unedited. Matthew's inserting καί at the start of the second line avoids Mark's asyndeton and makes the second line parallel to the first as another prediction giving reason why the end is not yet (cf. Luke's insertion of τε). The advancing of "famines" and the omission of Mark's second "there will be" produce a single second clause that makes a couplet with the first line. The putting of famines before earthquakes may indicate that famines result from the ravages of the warfare just mentioned (cf. Rev 6:3-6).

Jesus' phraseology reflects 2 Chr 15:6 ("and nation was crushed by nation, and city by city") and Isa 19:2 ("city against city, kingdom against kingdom"). See Gundry, *Use of the OT* 46-47, on the mixture of Hebrew and Septuagintal textual traditions. Cf. *Sib. Or.* 3:538, 635-44; 2 Esdr 13:29-31; *b. Sanh.* 97a; *Gen. Rab.* 42. 4.

24:8 (Mark 13:8; Luke 21:11) Matthew inserts δέ to avoid asyndeton (cf. Luke's τε). The insertion contrasts the wide extent of the foregoing horrors with the astonishing prediction that they will introduce worse horrors. The point is intensified by the advance of ταῦτα, "these things," and the addition of πάντα, "all" (63,25-26). The result, πάντα . . . ταῦτα, parallels 23:36; 24:2, 33, 34 and represents a favorite combination of Matthew (7,1).

For the travail that closes the present age, see 1QH 3; *1 Enoch* 99:1-100:6; *Jub.* 23:16-25; 2 Esdr 5:1-13; 6:17-24; 15:1-16:78; *2 Apoc. Bar.* 27:1-15; 48:31-41; 70:1-10; *b. Sanh.* 98ab; *b. Šabb.* 118a; *b. Ketub.* 111a; *Mek.* 50b. The lack of some of the main themes in Jewish apocalyptic—a holy war, vengeance, the destruction of Rome, the gathering of the Dispersion (but cf. v 31; Mark 13:27), renewal of Jerusalem in an ideal kingdom (but see 19:28; Luke 22:28-30), and Jewish rule over the Gentiles—favors the dominical origin of this discourse. The Book of Revelation makes up some of these lacks.

24:9 (Mark 13:9-13; Luke 21:12-17) The two clauses "Then they will give you over to tribulation, and they will kill you" typify Matthew's parallelistic style and summarize the material in Mark 13:9-13a, already detailed in Matt 10:17-22. "They will give you over" comes from the first of Mark's section, "and you will be hated by all on account of my name" from the end. Typically, Matthew begins his summary with τότε (66,17). "To tribulation" anticipates the tradition behind vv 21, 29 (cf. 13:21). "They will kill you" echoes the killing of God's messengers in 10:28; 21:35; 22:6; 23:34, 37. Matthew adds "the nations" to "you will be hated by all." The addition implies universal evangelism (see also v 14 and 28:19) and exhibits a Mattheanism in ἐθνῶν (7,2). Cf. the insertion "and to the nations" in 10:18.

Cf. Dan 12:1: "and there will be a time of tribulation." The persecution of Jesus' disciples comes on top of the ravages of war. In Mark the persecution begins in Jewish courts and synagogues and ends in the tribunals of governors and kings— Gentiles. This progression suggests that in summarizing, Matthew means unbelieving Jews as those that will give the disciples over to tribulation and kill them (or cause them to be killed by Gentile overlords). The plain inclusion of Gentiles by the insertion "and to the nations" completes the summary along Markan lines.

24:10 Persecution from without (v 9) leads to treachery inside the church (v 10), deception of many disciples by false prophets (v 11), and a lawlessness characterized by loss of mutual love (v 12). Matthew composes vv 10-12 as an expansion of Jesus' teaching against "causing someone else to stumble [i.e., sin]." The evangelist has expanded this motif elsewhere by multiplying the occurrences of σκανδαλίζω and σκάνδαλον (6,2). Throughout, we see a logical progression: persecution by outsiders causes many in the church to avoid persecution by betraying fellow disciples to the persecutors; and through failure to condemn this woeful loss of brotherly love, easygoing false prophets exacerbate the problem of treachery in the brotherhood. The first clause contains Mattheanisms in τότε (66,17; cf. v 9) and πολλοί (23,1; cf. vv 5, 11, 12) as well as σκανδαλισθήσονται. Matthew's special diction coincides with his practice of borrowing phraseology from the OT, in particular from Dan 11:41: "and many will be caused to stumble" (see Gundry, *Use of the OT* 142). "And they will give one another over" comes from Mark 13:12, part of the Markan passage just summarized (cf. Matt 10:21), and parallels "they will give you over" in v 9. Notably, treachery in families (Mark 13:12) changes to treachery in the church. The parallel clause "and they will hate one another" echoes v 9c (cf. Mark 13:13a). But again notably, being hated by all the nations has its match in professing disciples' hating one another. The parallelism typifies Matthew's style. As a whole, v 10 says that persecution will influence many church members to betray one another. Mutual hatred will result.

24:11 Matthew's warning "And many false prophets will rise, and they will deceive many" exhibits his parallelistic style again. πολλοί and πολλούς are Mattheanisms (23,1; cf. vv 5, 10, 12). Matthew inserted "false prophets" also in 7:15 (cf. v 24 below and his liking ψευδ- [6,0] and προφη- [23,6]). πλανήσουσιν echoes v 5 and is another favorite of his (4,0; see 27:63, 64 for distinctive occurrences of cognates). False prophets' rising and deceiving people in the church anticipates Mark 13:22 (Matt 24:24).

24:12 Again Matthew borrows OT phraseology. "And because lawlessness is increased" comes from Dan 12:4. ἀδικίας, "unrighteousness," in Dan 12:4 LXX apparently rests on reading רָעָה, "evil," instead of דַּעַת, "knowledge." The two Hebrew nouns look alike when written in Hebrew characters. Matthew, too, appears to read רָעָה; but he translates it with ἀνομίαν (3,1) to counter antinomian teaching in the church. "Is increased" agrees with Theodotion's passive against "will increase" in the Hebrew text and the LXX. Matthew goes on to say that "the love of the many will become cold." ἀγάπη links with his emphasis on loving neighbors (5:43-48; 19:19; 22:39), and πολλῶν (23,1) relates to vv 5, 10, 11. Since some will stick true and preach the gospel (vv 13-14), "the many" cannot carry the

Semitic meaning "all." Hence, it means "the majority." Cf. 2 Thess 2:1-12; Rev 3:15-16; 2 Esdr 5:2, 10; *1 Enoch* 91:7.

24:13 (Mark 13:13; Luke 21:18) "But he who endures to [the] end— this one will be saved" matches 10:22 and Mark 13:13 exactly. That Matthew delays this promise till after his mention of lawlessness shows that for him endurance to the end includes resisting the temptation to escape persecution by taking the antinomian way. For further interpretation, see the comments on 10:17-22.

24:14 (Mark 13:10) Matthew now steps back to Mark 13:10 for a saying from the Markan passage summarized in v 9 and omitted between 10:18 and 19 because it was inappropriate to the mission of the twelve in Galilee. "Will be proclaimed" replaces "must be proclaimed" to correspond with the string of future verbs beginning in v 5. It also advances to the front of its clause and loses the adverb "first" in anticipation of "and then," which will make the adverb unnecessary. The addition of "this" to "the gospel" strengthens the reference and identifies the gospel with the message of the book Matthew is writing (cf. 26:13). The further addition "of the kingdom" displays a special interest of his (βασιλεία—18,12), gives assurance of divine sovereignty in the face of hardships, and emphasizes the authority under which Jesus' disciples are to live. "Gospel of the kingdom" occurs only in Matt 4:23; 9:35; 24:14, each time as an insertion. "In the whole world for a witness" (not in Mark) stresses the universality of the proclamation (cf. 28:18-20). ὅλη belongs to Matthew's favorite vocabulary (7,3), and εἰς μαρτύριον echoes 10:18. πᾶσιν τοῖς ἔθνεσιν replaces Mark's synonymous εἰς πάντα τὰ ἔθνη and echoes 10:18 in the dative construction. Matthew composes the second line, "and then the end will come," to bring out more clearly the meaning of Mark's "first" (just omitted) and relate that meaning to the earlier statement "but the end is not yet" (v 6d). "And then" echoes vv 9 and 10. Matthew inserted ἥξει in 23:36, too (cf. 8:11; 24:50). And τέλος falls inside the circle of words he prefers (3,1). By implication the statement emphasizes the necessity of carrying out the great commission (28:18-20). This emphasis is due to the antinomians' withdrawal from the evangelistic enterprise. To escape persecution not only have they stopped living according to Christ's law before the world, but they have also stopped preaching the gospel to the world.

Cf. Dan 11:35. See the comments on 10:18 for the positive meaning "to all the nations" rather than the negative meaning "against all the nations," and on 10:23 for continuance of the mission to Israel, so that "all the nations" probably includes the Jews, or at least does not rule them out because of the mission to Gentiles (cf. Luke 24:47 and note the distinctive use of ἔθνος for the whole church—Jewish as well as Gentile—in Matt 21:43; see also the comments on 28:19). It is sometimes argued against the originality of εὐαγγέλιον—and possibly against the authenticity of the whole saying—that when used absolutely the corresponding Semitic noun bears an exclusively secular sense even though the cognate Semitic verb has a religious sense. This argument fails in several ways: (1) by overestimating the significance of the modern distinction between the religious and the secular in a question about ancient culture (cf. the political aspects of Isa 61:1-9); (2) by overestimating the significance of the distinction between absolute and qualified uses

480

of the Semitic noun; (3) by underestimating Jesus' use of the Semitic verb as favoring his use of the noun as well (cf. Matt 11:5; Luke 4:18; 7:22; cf. Isa 61:1); and (4) by ignoring the religious use of εὐαγγέλιον in the Hellenistic world and the Hellenization of Palestine.

The objection that Jesus could not have foreseen the evangelization of Gentiles or the time that was to take place presumes what needs to be proved. The further objection that dispute would not have arisen in the early church over evangelizing Gentiles had Jesus taught such evangelism overlooks the nature of the dispute. It did not have to do with the evangelization itself, but with the status of the Gentiles who were converted. We might move the period from the end of Mark 13:9 to the close of the phrase καὶ εἰς πάντα τὰ ἔθνη in Mark 13:10 in order to get rid of the mission to Gentiles. But doing so would create an extremely awkward parallel between αὐτοῖς and εἰς πάντα τὰ ἔθνη and a misleading impression that εἰς μαρτύριον and πάντα τὰ ἔθνη are parallel. Furthermore, the usual punctuation produces typically Markan parataxis and avoids a very harsh asyndeton. It is better, then, to accept that Jesus projected his disciples' mission to the nations.

THE ABOMINATION OF DESOLATION AS AN ESCHATOLOGICAL SIGN AND THE COMING OF THE SON OF MAN AS A PUBLIC EVENT

24:15-31 (Mark 13:14-27; Luke 17:23-24, 31, 37b; 21:20-27)

24:15 (Mark 13:14; Luke 21:20) The preceding paragraph detailed the noneschatological characteristics of the church age and closed with the statement that the end will come only after the universal preaching of the gospel of the kingdom. The replacement of Mark's δέ with οὖν (35,11) makes those characteristics, which because of their generality have no value in determining the nearness of the end, a base on which to erect a very specific sign that the end has drawn near. That sign is the abomination of desolation, which is an idol or a pagan altar that causes worshippers of the true God to stay away from the place of sacrifice (see Dan 9:27; 11:31; 12:11; cf. 1 Macc 1:54, 59; 6:7; 2 Thess 2:3-4; Rev 13:14-15). To the seeing of the abomination of desolation Matthew adds "the thing spoken through Daniel the prophet" (cf. 4QFlor 2:3-4). See the comments on 5:21-48 for τὸ ῥηθέν as a Mattheanism, especially in conjunction with a prophet, as here. Matthew's special interest in prophets and prophecy is well known (23,6). The addition makes the command "Let the reader understand" refer to the reader of Daniel. There are numerous allusions to Daniel in this discourse, and the allusion to Daniel in the abomination of desolation is obvious. Therefore Jesus probably intended such a reference; and we may discount the likelihood of an original reference to the reader of Mark's gospel or of an underlying source for the apocalyptic discourse. The very command that the reader understand derives from Dan 12:9-10, just before Daniel's final mention of the abomination of desolation: "And he said, 'Go, Daniel, for [these] words are concealed up till the end time. . . . and none of the wicked will understand, but those who have insight will understand'" (cf. 1QS 3:13; 9:18).

Prior to the command that the reader understand, however, Matthew makes two revisions, the change of Mark's masculine participle ἑστηκότα to the neuter participle ἑστός and the replacement of Mark's "where it should not" with "in the holy place." The first revision makes "standing" agree with its noun "abomination." (Mark's ungrammatical masculine participle reflects the masculine participles in Daniel's Hebrew text [see Gundry, *Use of the OT* 47-49] and interprets the neuter noun βδέλυγμα as the image of a person [again cf. 2 Thess 2:3-4; Rev 13:14-15].) The second revision turns the vague reference in Mark into a specific indication of a place of worship. Matthew is fond of τόπος (3,0) and ἁγίῳ (4,4; cf. ἁγιάζω— 2,0). Because of his attention to Daniel, "the holy place" almost certainly means the Temple, where the abomination of desolation takes the place of Mosaic sacrifices (Dan 9:27; cf. Dan 8:13; 1 Macc 2:7; Acts 6:13; 21:28).

Cf. Josephus *Ant.* 18.3.1 §§55-59; 18.8.2-9 §§261-309; *J.W.* 2.9.2 §§169-71; 6.6.1 §316. It has been suggested that once the term "desolation" was separated from its context in Daniel its meaning shifted from "desertion" (by the pious) to "destruction" (as in A.D. 70). This suggestion suffers from the immediately following command to flee, for destruction would have made it too late to flee. In Matthew, the addition of a reference to Daniel, where worship in the Temple is in view, further militates against the suggestion. The same objections stand against our seeing in the exhortation to understand a hidden allusion to some abomination in the church. Similarly, the mention of Daniel and the participle "standing" make it difficult to think of the barbarous acts of the Zealots in the Temple (cf. Josephus *J.W.* 4.3.1-4.6.3 §§121-388). All things considered, a reference to the image of some evil, deified figure such as the Antichrist seems best. Though "the holy place" means the land of Israel in 2 Macc 2:18, Matthew's reference to Daniel favors the Temple. In 13:35 Matthew cited a psalm as written by a prophet. Therefore the placement of Daniel among the prophets in the LXX need not underlie Matthew's designation of Daniel as a prophet. Not even in the LXX does the Book of Psalms appear among the prophets. Prediction, not arrangement of books, determines Matthew's designation. In the Hebrew OT, of course, Daniel appears among the writings.

24:16-18 (Mark 13:14-16; Luke 21:21-22; 17:31) The command "Then let those in Judea flee into the mountains" stays undisturbed. Jesus may have modelled this command after Gen 19:17. It hardly reflects *ex eventu* the flight of Christians from Jerusalem to Pella when the first Jewish revolt broke out (A.D. 66—Eusebius *H.E.* 3.5.3), for Pella was not situated in the mountains, but at the base of low-lying foothills in the Transjordan valley about seventeen miles south of the Sea of Galilee. Furthermore, refugees from Judea would reach it by travelling up the Jordan valley. To Judeans, flight to the mountains could hardly mean anything but flight into the rugged Judean wilderness, whose cave-filled mountains were a traditional hideout (cf. Ezek 7:16; 1 Macc 2:28; Josephus *J.W.* 5.10.1 §§420-23). We are dealing, then, not with flight from a military attack, but with flight from a persecution signalled by a religious abomination.

The probably original text of Mark 13:15 begins with δέ. If so, Matthew deletes the conjunction from the command that the person on the roof not come down to take things out of his house. The deletion makes the command an explication of the preceding command to flee. Luke's version occurs in a different context, lacks the prohibition "neither let him enter" (so Mark), and contains a reference to "his goods" (Luke 17:31). Similarly, Matthew omits "neither let him enter" and replaces Mark's τι, "anything," with τά, "the things [or an implied 'goods']." It looks as though Matthew has conflated the two forms of the saying. In the command concerning the person in the field, ἐν replaces Mark's εἰς for "in," and Mark's and Luke's εἰς τά, "to the things," drops out before ὀπίσω, "behind." Matthew's turning the prepositional phrase into a simple adverb meaning "back" makes the command somewhat more parallel to the preceding. The two prohibitions deal with a leisured man spending time on a roof and a laborer working in a field. The leisured man will be tempted to take household articles unnecessary but dear to a person of means. The laborer will be tempted to take at least his cloak, a necessity for warmth at night.

Again cf. 1 Macc 2:28. The flat roofs of houses provided a place for conversation, sleeping, and other activities (see, e.g., Acts 10:9, 20). We might think that Jesus does not prohibit coming down to flee, but only coming down to take things out of the house. But in view of the leaping from roof to roof in Josephus *Ant.* 13.5.3 §140, Jesus may well have meant that his disciples should not come down at all, but avoid the clogged streets by leaping from roof to roof for as hasty a getaway as possible.

   24:19-20 (Mark 13:17-18; Luke 21:23) The woe to pregnant women and nursing mothers because of their special difficulties in fleeing and taking refuge in the wilderness stays unchanged. To the command to pray "that it not happen during winter"—i.e., during the rainy season of flooded wadis and muddy roads that would hamper flight—Matthew adds "your flight." The addition stems from "let those in Judea flee" (v 16) and Matthew's liking φεύγω (2,1; see esp. 2:13; 10:23 for fleeing persecution). Matthew also adds "neither on a Sabbath." μηδέ belongs to his preferred diction (7,1), and similar insertions of the Sabbath occurred in 12:5 (bis). That flight is to take place even on the Sabbath, if necessary, shows that he does not regard the Sabbath as prohibitive from the standpoint of Christian discipleship. Rather, he has in mind hindrances to flight because of rabbinic restrictions, suspension of services to travellers, and especially inability to purchase supplies and the danger of being identified as a Christian—and therefore exposed the greater to persecution—through travelling on the Sabbath.

Cf. 1 Macc 2:31-38. Rabbinic tradition severely limited journeying on the Sabbath (cf. Acts 1:12). Though the rabbis allowed flight from mortal danger on the Sabbath (see *TDNT* 7. 14), Jesus envisions a state of affairs in which only his disciples will recognize the mortal danger. Thus conditions of the Sabbath as observed by others who lack this recognition would hamper the disciples' flight. The command to pray rules out Matthew's meaning that the possible necessity of fleeing on the Sabbath shows the seriousness of the catastrophe. For that meaning we would have merely a command to flee even on the Sabbath.

24:21 (Mark 13:19; Luke 21:23-24) Typically, Matthew adds τότε (66,17) to the prediction of tribulation. His reservation of "those days" for v 22 turns "tribulation" from an awkward predicate nominative (so Mark) into the subject and necessitates changing the verb from plural to singular. The result comes somewhat closer to Dan 12:1: "there will be a time of tribulation" (Dan 12:1). For emphasis Matthew adds "great" to "tribulation" (cf. 1 Macc 9:27; Rev 7:14). μεγάλη is a favorite of his (11,1). Luke's agreement in the addition and in the preceding revision suggests Matthean influence. The omission of Mark's τοιαύτη, "such as," after οἵα οὐ γέγονεν, "such as has not happened," not only gets rid of a redundancy, but also matches Dan 12:1. After "from [the] beginning" Matthew substitutes "of [the] world" for Mark's "of creation." Matthew's phrase will appear again in 25:34 as part of a unique passage. Cf. his omitting "of creation" after "from [the] beginning" in 19:4 (Mark 10:6). κόσμου is a Mattheanism (5,2). The dropping of Mark's redundant clause "which God created" furthers the conformity to Dan 12:1. οὐδ' replaces καί and represents Matthew's special diction (17,3). See Gundry, *Use of the OT* 49-50, and cf. Exod 9:18; 10:14; 11:6; Jer 30:7; Joel 2:2; *As. Mos.* 8:1; 1QM 1:9-14.

24:22 (Mark 13:20) Because he likes to use κύριος for Jesus, Matthew omits it from Mark's statement about the shortening of the tribulational days. There, "Lord" means God the Father, not Jesus. "Those days" comes from Mark 13:19 and compensates for the omission in v 21. δέ replaces ἀλλά at the start of the second clause. Matthew omits "whom he chose" because it is redundant after the phrase "on account of the chosen ones." "He has shortened" becomes "will be shortened." The future tense interprets the preceding "had been shortened" as having a future reference (like the Hebrew "prophetic perfect"). The passive voice matches the preceding passive of the verb. "The days" again changes to "those days."

Cf. *1 Enoch* 80:2; *2 Apoc. Bar.* 20:1-2; 83:1. Since Daniel's seventieth week forms the backdrop, the shortening apparently means that that period of time will not run its full course. Is it divine concern for the safety of the elect or divine pleasure in their presence on earth that prompts the shortening?

24:23 (Mark 13:21; Luke 17:23) Matthew drops "And" as unnecessary before "if anyone says to you." His beloved ἰδού (34,9) takes the place of Mark's ἴδε. Luke shares Matthew's word. After "here [is] the Messiah" Matthew characteristically inserts ἤ (32,12—so also Luke). Mark's second ἴδε drops out entirely, and a second "here" replaces Mark's "there" for a parallel with the first "here." Matthew likes ὧδε (7,1), though he likes ἐκεῖ, too (16,6). The present imperative μὴ πιστεύετε, "do not ever believe [him]" (so Mark), changes to the aorist subjunctive μὴ πιστεύσητε, "do not believe [him]."

τότε does not mean "after the shortening of those days," but "during those days." The τις who speaks is not the false messiah, but a prophet of the false messiah (see v 24).

24:24 (Mark 13:22) Jesus predicts that false messiahs and false prophets will rise and give signs and wonders. Matthew's changing "And" to "For" makes the prediction a basis for the foregoing warning not to believe any false prophet of a false messiah. γάρ is a Mattheanism (62-63,15). To heighten the deceptiveness, Matthew adds "great" to "signs." μεγάλα is another favorite of his (11,1). Mark's telic πρός changes to ὥστε, yet another favorite (10,0). The articular present infinitive τὸ ἀποπλανᾶν, "to be deceiving," becomes the anarthrous aorist infinitive πλανῆσαι, "to deceive." Matthew likes the simple form (4,0). "If possible" is not strong enough for him; so he increases emphasis on the danger of apostasy by inserting an ascensive καί, "even," before τοὺς ἐκλεκτούς, "the chosen ones."

Cf. 7:21-23 and see Gundry, *Use of the OT* 50-51, on Jesus' allusion to Deut 13:2-4(1-3), especially according to *Tgs. Neofiti 1* and *Pseudo-Jonathan.*

24:25 (Mark 13:23) Though Matthew likes βλέπω (9,3), its use in the sense "watch out" does not characterize his diction. Therefore "But you—watch out!" vanishes. The omission relates "Behold, I have told you beforehand" immediately to the foregoing prediction of false messiahs and false prophets. The addition ἰδού emphasizes Jesus' authoritative word, represents Matthew's preferred vocabulary (34,9), and makes the second link in a chain of distinctive occurrences of ἰδού (see vv 23, 25, and 26 [bis]). The omission of "all things" narrows Mark's reference to all the tribulational events down to the single threat of false messiahs and false prophets. Thus Matthew shows his concern to counteract antinomianism.

24:26 Matthew is still not satisfied that he has put enough emphasis on the danger of deception; so he composes v 26 after the pattern of v 23 (cf. his expanding the same theme in vv 10-12). οὖν represents his favorite vocabulary (35,11) and makes the following prohibitions grow out of Jesus' telling the disciples beforehand (v 25). "If they should say to you" comes from v 23, but the verb has become plural to match the intervening false prophets who will proclaim false messiahs. "Behold" likewise comes from v 23, as well as from Matthew's special diction (34,9). "He is in the desert" replaces the "here" of v 23. Jewish expectation that messianic salvation will begin in the desert and earlier passages such as 3:1, 3; 4:1; 11:7; 14:13, 15 may have suggested the phrase. "Do not go out" probably echoes 11:7-9, for there Jesus spoke of going out into the wilderness to see John the Baptist. The parallel between "Behold, he is in the desert" and "Behold, he [is] in the storerooms" typifies Matthew's style. Again typically, "do not believe" parallels "do not go out" and comes verbatim from v 23. "In the storerooms" corresponds to the second "here" in v 23, recalls Matthew's distinctive use of "storeroom" in 6:6, and contrasts hideouts in the city with the wilderness.

Antinomianism in the church is seldom brazen. Those who teach it usually offer a theological justification: the claim to have had direct and recent communications with Christ, so that no attention needs to be paid to his traditional teaching, which the new communications outdate. In Matthew's time these communications were said to have taken place in the isolation of the desert and the secrecy of hideouts in the city, where public authentication that Christ had returned and communicated to these teachers was lacking. How convenient! But little people in the church are easily taken in by teachers who enhance their authority with claims to private communications from Christ. So Matthew has emphasized that the church has not even entered the great tribulation—let alone has that tribulation ended with the return of Christ—and he will now play up the publicity of Christ's return. Begone with clandestine meetings and false revelations!

On the significance of the desert, cf. 1 Macc 2:29-30; Josephus *Ant.* 20.5.1 §97; 20.8.6, 10 §§168, 188; *J.W.* 2.13.4 §259; 6.6.3 §351; and for discussion see W. R. Farmer, *Maccabees, Zealots, and Josephus* (New York: Columbia, 1956) 114-22; *TDNT* 2. 658-59.

24:27 (Luke 17:24) In v 23 we noted some agreement between Matthew and Luke 17:23 against Mark 13:21. But Matthew continued with Mark for the next two sayings (vv 24-25) and went his own way in the third (v 26). Now he inserts two sayings that appear in Luke 17 but not in Mark 13. The first has to do with the simile of lightning and begins, "For just as the lightning comes out from [the] east and shines as far as [the] west" (cf. *2 Apoc. Bar.* 53:1-12). ἐξέρχεται, "comes out," stands in place of Luke's ἀστράπτουσα, "flashing," and conforms to the use of ἔρχομαι throughout chaps. 24-25. Its finite form contrasts with Luke's participle and, with the help of an inserted "and," produces a parallelistic structure typical of Matthew's style. Because of the prefix ἐξ- in ἐξέρχεται, ἀπό replaces ἐκ to avoid redundancy. Similarly, εἰς becomes ἕως, a favorite of Matthew (13,14). Where Luke has "one part under the sky" and "another part of the sky," Matthew has "[the] east" and "[the] west" for an antithetic parallel in reminiscence of 8:11. ἀνατολῶν appeared in 2:1, 2, 9 as part of special material. Though Matthew likes λάμπει (3,0), it yields to the synonym φαίνεται, which he favors even more (5,8). From the remainder of the saying "so also the Son of man will be in his day" Matthew lops off "in his day" and compensates by inserting "the coming" (ἡ παρουσία—4,0). This marks the second such insertion (cf. v 3) and the first appearance of the full phrase "the coming of the Son of man," which will be inserted again in vv 37 and 39. Thus the vague reference to the day of the Son of man, apparently modelled after "the day of the Lord" in the OT, turns into a specific reference to the coming of the Son of man.

24:28 (Luke 17:37) After the simile of lightning in Luke 17 there are warnings of judgment, comparisons to Noah's flood and the destruction of Sodom, sayings about the taking of one and the leaving of another, and the disciples' question "Where, Lord?" Then comes the saying "Where the body [is], there also the vultures will be gathered together." The preceding context determines that the saying be taken as a figure of judgment on the wicked when the Son of man has his day. The body stands for the wicked, the vultures for judgment, and the saying means that wherever the wicked are, the judgment will strike. They cannot escape; only the righteous will. But Matthew skips the judgmental verses intervening between the metaphors of lightning and vultures. Consequently, the metaphor of vultures loses its judgmental meaning. The saying now signifies the unmistakable visibility of the Son of man's coming. People will see the event as easily as vultures see a carcass or as easily as vultures are seen when circling over a carcass. Matthew's emphasis on visibility stands against antinomian claims that Christ has returned in secret (v 26). The words ἐὰν ᾖ, "-ever is," fill in what Luke leaves to be supplied. Matthew's πτῶμα, "corpse," may stem from special attention to Job 39:30, the source of the saying (see Gundry, *Use of the OT* 88-89, for detailed textual comparisons), or from a Hellenistic proverb concerning vultures and a πτῶμα (see A. Ehrhardt, *The Framework of the New Testament Stories* [Cambridge, Mass.: Harvard, 1964] 53-58). Or Luke may have chosen the more refined word σῶμα, "body," often used for a corpse. Luke's "also" does not appear in Matthew. And Luke's ἐπι- falls away from συναχθήσονται, which is one of Matthew's favorites (10,10). The putting of οἱ ἀετοί last in its line contrasts with Luke's order of words and produces an exact parallel with the first line.

Some have thought that οἱ ἀετοί refers to the eagles of the Roman legions swooping down on Jerusalem during the first Jewish revolt (A.D. 66-73); but the context in Luke has nothing about the destruction of Jerusalem, and Matthew focuses attention on the Son of man's coming rather than on the destruction of the city.

24:29 (Mark 13:24-25; Luke 21:25-26) Matthew returns to Mark and replaces ἀλλά with δέ (cf. v 22 with Mark 13:20 for the same substitution). Mark's "in those days" yields to "immediately" (εὐθέως—11,0). In compensation Matthew replaces Mark's "that" in the phrase "after that tribulation" with "of those days." These changes not only make for a single, smoothly flowing phrase; the initial εὐθέως also adds immediacy to the visibility of the Son of man's coming. The emphasis on immediacy lends weight to coming exhortations to watch, exhortations that Matthew will greatly expand. The darkening of the sun, the failure of the moon to give its light, the falling of the stars from the sky, and the shaking of the heavenly powers come over from Mark with little change. The expressions echo Isa 13:10; 34:4 (see Gundry, *Use of the OT* 51-52, for textual comparisons). Matthew uses the simple future πεσοῦνται in place of Mark's periphrastic future ἔσονται . . . πίπτοντες, and ἀπό for Mark's ἐκ. For conformity to Isa 34:4, "of heaven" replaces "the ones in heaven." That Luke agrees in this last revision despite lacking Matthew's degree of concern to assimilate Jesus' phraseology to the OT suggests Matthean influence.

The idea of stars falling comes from the comparison to leaves of vines and fig trees just following in Isa 34:4. That comparison, in turn, may have suggested the parable of the budding fig tree (vv 32-35). Jesus' replacing Isaiah's verb "melt, rot" with the verb "shake" may represent yet another extension of the metaphor of a fig tree. The falling of the stars refers to a shower of meteorites, and the shaking of the heavenly powers to God's displacing "the spiritual forces of wickedness in the heavenly places" (Eph 6:12). Cf. Ezek 32:7-8; Joel 2:10, 31; 4(3):15; Hag 2:6, 21; Rev 6:12-13; *1 Enoch* 80:4; *2 Esdr* 5:4; *As. Mos.* 10:5.

24:30 (Mark 13:26; Luke 21:27) To gain yet further emphasis on the universal visibility of the Son of man's coming, Matthew inserts references to the appearance of the sign of the Son of man in heaven and the mourning of all the tribes of the earth. "Will appear" stresses visibility, echoes v 27, and translates a favorite of Matthew, φανήσεται (5,8). We may detect an echo of v 3 in "the sign"; but here Matthew substitutes "of the Son of man" for "of your coming and the end of the age" (so v 3). This substitute anticipates the description of the Son of man's coming (v 30b; cf. 16:1; Mark 8:11; Luke 11:16). Similarly, "in heaven [i.e., 'the sky']" anticipates the heaven, or sky, that provides the clouds on which the Son of man comes. The phrase also sets up a contrast between heaven, where the sign of the Son of man will appear, and earth, where all the tribes will mourn. This contrast typifies Matthew's composition (6,0). All in all, the echoes of vv 3 and 27 and the anticipations of later phrases show that the sign of the Son of man is his own appearance when he comes, not some kind of standard or ensign waved ahead of him. Thus the sign of Jesus' coming (so Matthew alone in v 3) and the sign of the Son of man (so Matthew alone here in v 30) are equivalent. Both emphasize unmistakable visibility in the sky, as opposed to hiddenness in the desert or backrooms (cf. 26:64). The Son of man himself will be the standard or ensign so manifest that no room is left for doubt (cf. the meaning "standard, ensign" in association with a trumpet, as here [see v 31], in Isa 18:3; Jer 4:21; 6:1; 51:27; 1QM 2:15–4:17; *Shemoneh Esreh* 10).

For parallelism, Matthew starts the second clause of v 30 with another "and then." The allusion to Zech 12:10, 14 in "all the tribes of the earth [or 'land,' τῆς γῆς] will mourn" exhibits Matthew's habit of borrowing OT phraseology (cf. Rev 1:7). Zechariah's words serve his emphasis on the wide visibility of the Son of man's coming. Zechariah means that the families of Israel will mourn over their having pierced the Pierced One. We might think that Matthew's concern about false messiahs favors a similar limitation to the tribes in the land of Israel. But the dominant stress on wide visibility points to all the tribes of the earth. κόψονται, "will mourn," makes a fine wordplay with ὄψονται, "will see," which introduces Jesus' allusion to Dan 7:13: "the Son of man coming on the clouds of the sky." "On" agrees with the LXX and Peshitta against Mark's and Luke's "in" and against "with" in the Hebrew, Theodotion, and Rev 1:7. Matthew's adding "of the sky" extends the allusion to Dan 7:13 and revives the contrast between heaven and earth. In the final phrase he delays πολλῆς till after μετὰ δυνάμεως καὶ δόξης (so also Luke). The delay changes the probable meaning in Mark, "with a large army [cf. 2 Chr 24:24; Ezek 38:15 LXX] and glory," to the meaning "with power and great glory." In other words, the shift stresses the Son of man's glory instead of the heavenly host.

See Gundry, *Use of the OT* 52-54, on the texts of the quotations from Zech 12:10, 14; Dan 7:13-14. Matthew's context rather than Isa 11:10, 12 is the source of "the sign of the Son of man," though Matthew may have seen a happy similarity between his phrase and Isaiah's phraseology (cf. also Isa 49:22; 1QM 3:13–4:17). The context in Matthew favors a mourning of despair; the context in Zechariah favors a mourning of regret, perhaps of repentance. But the point of Matthew's allusion lies in the wide extent of the mourning—over against private manifestations in deserts and backrooms—not in the reason for mourning. See Gundry, *Use of the OT* 232-33, against the view that in Dan 7:13 and Jesus' saying the Son of man ascends to heaven rather than descends from heaven. Further, the disciples' sitting on thrones and judging the twelve tribes of Israel in the regeneration (19:28) or in Jesus' kingdom (Luke 22:30) forestall a reference to ascent soon after the crucifixion. For the sitting on thrones and judging the tribes of Israel presuppose the consummation on earth (cf. Matt 25:31-32). The absence of a coming in Luke 22:69 speaks against descent no more than it speaks against ascent. Jesus turned Daniel's descriptive phrase "one like a son of man"—i.e., someone who looked like a human being—into a title, "the Son of man."

24:31 (Mark 13:27) Matthew exalts the Son of man by identifying the angels he will send (they make up the "large army" in Mark) as "his," the Son of man's. See also 13:41; 16:27 and cf. 25:41; 26:53 for this Mattheanism, which depends on identifying Jesus with the Son of man and with God (1:23), whom the angels serve. Mark's "then" drops out after "and" because Matthew used the two words together twice in the preceding saying. With a characteristic allusion to the OT, in particular Isa 27:13, he adds "with a great trumpet" (cf. his liking μεγάλης—11,1). Thus Christ's return will be plainly audible as well as unmistakably visible. No whispered revelations in backrooms or deserts, such as antinomian teachers were claiming. Since the angels now belong to the Son of man, they do his work; hence, "he will gather his chosen ones" changes to "they will gather his chosen ones." As in Mark, the chosen ones come "from the four winds." But the combination of Deut 13:18 (=Jer 12:12) and 30:4 in the mongrel expression "from the limit of earth to the limit of the sky" (so Mark) becomes an allusion to Deut 30:4 alone in the pure expression "from the limits of the sky to its limits" (i.e., from one horizon to its opposite, whichever direction one looks).

See Gundry, *Use of the OT* 54-55, on the allusions to Isa 27:13; Zech 2:10 LXX; Deut 30:4. The plural ἄκρων (bis) contrasts with Mark's singular and agrees with Deut 30:4 according to the Peshitta and *Tgs. Onqelos, Neofiti 1*, and *Pseudo-Jonathan*. Mark's reference to the limit of the earth and the limit of the sky combines two expressions concerning universal scope: (1) from the limit of the earth to the limit of the earth and (2) from the limit of the sky to the limit of the sky. Both refer to the horizon, where earth and sky meet. Cf. Exod 19:16; Isa 43:6; Ezek 37:9; Zech 9:14; 1 Cor 15:52; 1 Thess 4:16; 2 Thess 2:1; Rev 11:15-19; *Pss. Sol.* 11:1; 2 Esdr 6:23; *Shemoneh Esreh* 10. In 13:41 the angels of the Son of man collect antinomians from among professing disciples for judgment. Here they graciously gather the chosen ones.

THE NEARNESS OF THE SON OF MAN

24:32-35

24:32-33 (Mark 13:28-29; Luke 21:29-31) The parable of the fig tree stays largely undisturbed by Matthew. In turning around Mark's words ἀπαλὸς γένηται, "becomes tender," and reversing the order of ἐκφύῃ τὰ φύλλα, "puts forth leaves," he subtly transfers the emphasis from tenderness to leaves, which can be seen easily. This shift furthers his emphasis on the visibility of the parousia: just as that event will be unmistakable, so also the events signalling it will be apparent. Mark's "is" falls out of the statement about the nearness of summer, but needs to be supplied. "Happening" disappears from the clause about seeing "these things." This latter omission and the typically Matthean addition of "all" to "these things" (7,1; cf. vv 2, 8) indicate that disciples need to see the precursive events, not in the process of fulfillment, but in the completion of their fulfillment before concluding that the Son of man "is near, at the door." As in the preceding section, Matthew is counteracting premature announcements by false messiahs and their false prophets. The addition of "all" also conforms to v 34; Mark 13:30.

Most Palestinian trees, being evergreen, keep their leaves throughout the winter. The almond tree loses its leaves in the wintertime and sprouts early in the spring. The fig tree, however, loses its leaves in wintertime but does not sprout till late in the spring. Therefore its budding signifies the approach of summer. We might suppose an underlying wordplay between קַיִץ, "summer," and קֵץ, "end," as in Amos 8:2. But "at the door" favors a reference to the Son of man rather than to "the end" as the subject in v 33b. Cf. Jas 5:9; Rev 3:20. We should not assign the parable to an originally different context (where the reference could shift to the crisis in Jesus' public ministry), for "at the door" then becomes awkward. Such awkwardness caused Luke to omit the phrase when he added "the kingdom of God" as subject. (Luke paraphrases throughout the parable without seeming to follow another or more reliable tradition.)

24:34-35 (Mark 13:30-31; Luke 21:32-33) Jesus' assurances that "this generation will not pass away till all these things happen" and that "heaven and earth will pass away," but not his words, stay almost entirely unchanged. Instead of μέχρις οὗ Matthew writes his favorite ἕως (13,14; so also Luke). Otherwise, the first evangelist merely reverses the order of ταῦτα πάντα and changes the future indicative παρελεύσονται with οὐ μή to the more usual and synonymous aorist subjunctive παρέλθωσιν with οὐ μή. Cf. Isa 40:8.

The saying in v 34 rests on Dan 12:7 (see Gundry, *Use of the OT* 55-56). We have to distinguish between Jesus' meaning, as evident in Mark, and Matthew's meaning. So far as Jesus' meaning is concerned, it might be thought that "this generation" refers to whatever generation happens to see "all these things" which precede and signal the coming of the Son of man. Thus the possibility of a distant generation is opened up and Jesus is kept from declaring his generation to be the last. But the combination of "you" and "this" in Mark 13:29-30 (note esp. the emphatic ὑμεῖς in v 29) makes a reference to Jesus' contemporaries much more natural. We might therefore restrict "these things . . . all these things" to the destruction of the Temple, which, occurring in A.D. 70, did fall within the lifetime of Jesus' contemporaries. Support for this restriction comes from the appearance of "these things . . . all these things" in the question of the disciples, who, so far as we can tell from the text, had in mind only the destruction of the Temple, which Jesus had just predicted, not the eschatological woes or the coming of the Son of man (v 4; cf. vv 1-3). But in the surrounding context Jesus makes "these things . . . all these things" signal the near coming of the Son of man; yet that event did not occur soon after A.D. 70, and has not occurred to this day. The emphasis on visibility and universality in vv 24-27 contrasts with false reports of a secret coming in vv 21-23 and rules out the positing of a spiritual coming shortly after A.D. 70. So either Jesus made a mistake—a very serious one, since he staked his truthfulness and reliability on the prediction. (The possibility of God's lengthening the period of grace [cf. Luke 13:6-9] is not enough to counterbalance the emphasis in "Truly I say to you," the strong negation of the future in οὐ μή with an aorist subjunctive, and "Heaven and earth will pass away, but my words will not pass away.") Or we are to expect a second fulfillment of "these things . . . all these things" shortly before the coming of the Son of man, the second fulfillment making the necessary connection with that coming, the first fulfillment in A.D. 70 having fallen within the lifetime of Jesus' contemporaries. Double fulfillment of biblical prophecy is a common phenomenon (an example from this passage: Jesus' predicting a further "abomination of desolation" after the one Antiochus Epiphanes perpetrated in 168 B.C., to say nothing in detail about messianic prophecies that received initial fulfillments in the near future of OT history and further fulfillments in Jesus). The difficulty remains that "you" who will see the destruction of the Temple and who will then know that the Son of man is near, at the door, seem to be Peter, James, John, and Andrew (v 3) rather than other disciples living at the time of a much later, second fulfillment. But this difficulty is part of the ambiguity necessary to the phenomenon of double fulfillment, which is to be accepted as a fact rather than objected to on literary grounds.

So far as Matthew's meaning is concerned, his insertion of "immediately" in v 29 strengthens the alternatives of a mistaken prediction and a double fulfillment by disallowing the lengthy interval of nearly two thousand years between the destruction of the Temple (taken as a single fulfillment) and the present time. And his strengthening the already existing stress on the visibility of the parousia further rules out the positing of a spiritual coming shortly after A.D. 70. Matthew seemingly shifts direction, however, by dwelling on the qualitative rather than chronological sense of γενεά. His descriptions of "this generation" (Mark 8:12) as "evil and adulterous" were unique (12:39; 16:4; cf. Luke 12:29). Therefore he may intend "this generation" to be understood as meaning "this kind." The emphasis would then fall on the perversity of the scribes, Pharisees, and Sadducees (see the contexts of 12:39; 16:4), and the chronological extent of the generation would remain open. After all, in 23:35-36 "this generation" included not only Jesus' contemporaries, but also those who had killed Zechariah the OT prophet several hundred years earlier. Otherwise, Matthew could hardly have quoted Jesus as telling his listeners, ". . . you murdered [Zechariah]." Presumably "this generation" included such murderers all the way back to Abel. With a qualitative emphasis, the saying in Matthew's present passage means that unbelieving Jews must feel the pinch of the messianic woes. That will cure them! Cf. chap. 23 (esp. vv 37-39); 2 Cor 11:26; and BAG, s.v. γένος 3.

THE UNCERTAINTY CONCERNING THE EXACT TIME OF THE SON OF MAN'S COMING
24:36-44 (Mark 13:32, 35; Luke 12:39-40; 17:26-36)

24:36 (Mark 13:32) Though precursive events, especially the abomination of desolation, will signal the general nearness of the parousia, the shortening of "those days" leaves the exact time of the parousia indeterminate (cf. v 22; Mark 13:20). Therefore we read that "no one knows about that day or hour" (so Mark). Matthew makes these alternatives into a single specification of time by replacing "or" with "and" and dropping Mark's τῆς before ὥρας. The essential reference to exact time remains, however. "The angels in heaven" changes to "the angels of heaven" after the pattern of "the kingdom of heaven," which is peculiar to the first gospel. Matthew's penchant for οὐδέ (17,3) and υἱός (27,16), the prominence of Jesus' divine sonship in his theology, and the preponderance of the external text-critical evidence favor retention of "nor the Son" (see further the UBS and Metzger, *Textual Commentary* ad loc.). The addition of "alone" accentuates the ignorance of all but the Father concerning the exact time of the Son's coming. Matthew likes μόνος (9,0).

This saying seems to rest on Dan 12:13 LXX (cf. Zech 14:7; *Pss. Sol.* 17:23; *2 Apoc. Bar.* 21:8; 1QM 1:4-13). It is very doubtful that early Christians would have made it up to excuse the delay in Jesus' return. Bold assertion of the Son's ignorance exceeds any easily conceivable daring on their part. They would hardly have put such ignorance in the framework of Jesus' relation to the Father as Son, a relation that exacerbates the problem. Less problematic ways of excusing the delay in the parousia existed. And modern students of the NT tend to exaggerate early Christians' concern over that delay and minimize Jesus' intimations of a delay. These objections militate not only against later invention of the saying as a whole, but also against later addition of the phrase "nor the Son." Theologically, we may say that just as Jesus did not exercise his omnipotence except to further the kingdom (cf. his refusal to make stones into bread), so he did not exercise his omniscience except to further the kingdom. To have known and made known the exact time of his coming would have damaged the work of the kingdom by encouraging carelessness during the interim. What Jesus could have done because he was divine did not predetermine what he did do as also a man. The incarnation did not destroy divine potencies, but it did limit actualities.

24:37 (Luke 17:26) Matthew reserves Mark 13:33-37 for v 42; 25:6, 13-15 and incorporates the tradition behind Luke 17:26-36. This incorporation broadens the base of the following commands to watch for the Son of man's coming. δέ stands in place of Luke's καί and contrasts the Father's knowledge and others' uncertainty. The surprise with which Noah's flood came on people who were routinely eating and drinking, marrying wives and giving daughters in marriage, illustrates that uncertainty. Alternatively, if we accept the variant reading γάρ as an insertion typical of Matthew (62-63,15), the surprise of Noah's flood substantiates the ignorance mentioned in the preceding verse. Where Luke writes an un-Matthean καθώς), Matthew writes a favorite ὥσπερ (6,3). He also omits "it happened." Consequently, the prepositional phrase "in the days of Noah" becomes the subject "the days of Noah." "Also in the days of the Son of man" similarly becomes the subject "the coming of the Son of man" (see the comments on vv 3, 27 concerning this distinctive phrase). The new parallelism features the parousia. Matthew is still emphasizing the publicity of the event in contrast with the private comings of false messiahs.

It would be a mistake to think that the parallel Luke 17:20-37 rules out premonitory signs in favor of utter unexpectedness. The negation of observable signs deals only with the already present kingdom of God (Luke 17:20-21). Because of its futurity, the manifestation of the Son of man (Luke 17:22-37) does not fall within the negation. Furthermore, the exhortations in Luke 17:22-37 to flee posthaste imply that the Son of man's appearance will have recognizable antecedents (in the messianic woes). Otherwise the chance to flee will have passed.

24:38 (Luke 17:27) Unless we are to think of an omission by Luke, it looks as though Matthew composed the first part of v 38 largely on the model of the preceding saying as it read before his revisions. γάρ typifies his diction (62-63,15) and makes the following words substantiate the foregoing. ὡς is another Mattheanism (23,8) and comes from ὥσπερ or καθώς in the preceding saying. "In the days before the flood" echoes the traditional form of the preceding saying ("in the days of Noah" according to Luke) and anticipates "the flood" in the next one. Instead of Luke's simple imperfect for eating, drinking, marrying, and giving in marriage, Matthew uses the periphrastic imperfect; and the inelegant τρώγοντες, "munching" (i.e., eating audibly), stands where Luke has ἤσθιον, "they were eating." These two differences may represent Luke's polishing of the tradition. Matthew pairs the verbs by supplying "and" between eating and drinking and between marrying and giving in marriage. The pairing illustrates his penchant for parallelism. "Till the day that Noah entered the ark" stays unchanged and rests on Gen 7:7.

24:39 (Luke 17:27-34) In the next clause Matthew inserts "they did not understand" to contrast the ignorance of the antediluvians, who represent nondisciples and false disciples, with the understanding of true disciples. The latter will be watching for the parousia. They will have recognized the signals, and they already know that the shortening of the tribulation makes the exact time incalculable and their own alertness necessary. The insertion requires the further addition of ἕως, a favorite of Matthew (13,14) along with ἔγνωσαν (8,2). The remaining traditional words, "the flood came and destroyed them" (so Luke), come into Matthew with the exchange of "destroyed" for "took away." The new verb anticipates similar expressions in vv 40-41. Matthew's ἅπαντας is stronger than Luke's πάντας. Cf. Nah 1:8; Dan 9:26; Wis 10:4; 3 Macc 2:4; 2 Pet 2:5-7; *Jub.* 5:1-32; *T. Naph.* 3:5; *1 Enoch* 10:2; 54:7–55:2; 65:1-12; 83:1–84:6; 106:1-19; Josephus *Ant.* 1.2.3 §§70-71; Philo *Mos.* 2.263. Matthew will repeat "the coming of the Son of man"; so he omits the largely redundant comparisons to regular life in the days of Lot and the unexpected destruction of Sodom's inhabitants and goes to the statement "It will be the same on the day that the Son of man is revealed" (so Luke). Instead of "the same" (κατὰ τὰ αὐτά) we read the Mattheanism "so" (οὕτως—18,5). "Also the coming of the Son of man" is another Mattheanism (3,0) and replaces "on the day that the Son of man is revealed." Yet again, then, Matthew stresses publicity in contrast with the private comings of false messiahs (cf. the use of παρουσία for the auspicious occasion of an emperor's visit—BAG, s.v. παρουσία 2b). The warnings not to turn back (Luke 17:31) drop out because they occurred in vv 17-18. Prior omission of the comparison with the days of Lot results

493

here in omission of the command to remember Lot's wife (Luke 17:32). The saying about losing and preserving one's life (Luke 17:33) vanishes because of its appearance in 10:39 (cf. 16:25). "I say to you" (Luke 17:43a) also vanishes. Though Matthew likes it (27,7), the other omissions would have made it interruptive; i.e., he wants to bring the taking of one and the leaving of one alongside the parousia.

24:40-41 (Luke 17:34-35) Matthew's beloved τότε (66,17) replaces "on that night" to introduce the saying about taking and leaving. "In the field" substitutes for "on one bed" and partly compensates for the preceding omission of a long section, where we read about "the one in the field" (Luke 17:31). We now see why Matthew had to get rid of "night" in the tradition: men do not work in the field at night. For closer parallelism, a second "one" appears each time in place of Luke's "other" (bis). As a result, the definite articles with these words disappear. Instead of Luke's future tense for taking and leaving, Matthew has the futuristic present (cf. vv 42-44; and 4:5, 8 with Luke 4:5, 9). The gathering of the chosen ones by angels (v 31; Mark 13:27) implies that in the tradition the taking has to do with salvation and the leaving with judgment rather than vice versa (cf. the similar use of παραλαμβάνω in John 14:3). But Matthew's parallelistic insertion of ἦρεν in v 39, where judgment is in view, makes the taking judgmental in his gospel. Hence, being left means being spared from instead of exposed to judgment. There is an ellipsis of the second "will be" in Matthew, and "at the same place" yields to "in the mill" for a match with Matthew's earlier replacement "in the field." Similarly, καί replaces δέ in the last line as well as in the second. Throughout these sayings emphasis does not lie on the separation of people in proximity so much as on the occurrence of the separation during the round of daily activities—and therefore unexpectedly unless one is watching.

24:42 (Mark 13:35) Matthew returns to Mark, but skips Mark 13:33-34 for the time being (see the comments on 25:13-15) and writes, "Watch, therefore, because you do not know on what day your Lord is coming" (cf. Mark 13:35; b. Sanh. 97a). Despite his liking Mark's γάρ (62-63,15), the conjunction changes to ὅτι for a parallel with the similar exhortation about to appear in v 44, where ὅτι is traditional. So also Mark's "when" becomes "what day" for a parallel with "what watch" (v 43; cf. Luke 12:39) and with the "day" on which "the Lord . . . will come" (v 50; cf. Luke 12:46 and Matthew's fondness for ἡμέρα—15,9). Insertion of "day" in the present verse sets the stage for the traditional but imported reference to the "hour" of the Son of man's coming (v 44). The combination of day and hour will echo 24:36, anticipate 25:13, exhibit the care with which Matthew structures his parallels, and reemphasize uncertainty concerning the exact time of the parousia. "Your Lord" replaces "lord [i.e., 'master'] of the house" because Mark's "of the house" relates to the man who left his house and went away on a journey in the preceding verse. Matthew will take up that tradition in 25:14-15. Meanwhile, he gains a direct reference to Jesus' lordship. Similarly, Mark's temporal notations, "whether in the evening or at midnight or at cockcrowing or in the early morning," await incorporation (with radical surgery) in 25:6.

494

24:43 (Luke 12:39) Now Matthew begins to import the tradition behind Luke 12:39-46. Instead of Luke's τοῦτο, "this," he writes a more emphatic and characteristic ἐκεῖνο, "that" (26,9). φυλακῇ, "watch," comes from the preceding saying in the tradition (cf. Luke 12:38). It replaces ὥρα, "hour," and compensates for Matthew's omitting the names of the four night watches in v 42. To summarize the tradition behind Luke 12:37-38, Matthew inserts "he would have watched," which echoes the command to watch in his own v 42. εἴασεν, "let," answers to Luke's synonymous ἀφῆκεν.

Cf. 1 Thess 5:2, 4; 2 Pet 3:10; Rev 3:3; 16:15. διορυχθῆναι refers to a thief's digging through the mud-brick wall of a house in order to break in (see BAG, s.v. διορύσσω). "Had known" and "would have watched" may imply a recent burglary known to Jesus and his audience. Though the figure of a thief's breaking in looks ominous, we need not reassign it to the tribulation rather than to the parousia and shift the address from Jesus' disciples to the crowds; for the disciples needed to be warned against a false profession that shows itself in failure to watch for the Son of man's coming.

24:44 (Luke 12:40) Typically, Matthew introduces "on account of this" (διὰ τοῦτο—4,2) in order to base the exhortation to readiness on uncertainty concerning exact time. Otherwise he differs from Luke only in delaying ὥρα slightly. The cutting short of the tribulation (v 22; Mark 13:20) provides the reason why Jesus stressed uncertainty even though he indicated that certain events will signal the nearness of the Son of man.

MALTREATMENT OF FELLOW DISCIPLES AS A CHARACTERISTIC OF FALSE DISCIPLESHIP WHICH WILL DRAW JUDGMENT AT THE LORD'S COMING
24:45-51 (Luke 12:39-46)

Matthew continues with the tradition behind Luke 12:39-46 and begins to define what it means to watch for the coming of the Son of man. Watching consists in an expectancy that causes the true disciple to treat his fellow disciples well. Failure to watch consists in abusive treatment of fellow disciples and marks one as a false disciple (cf. chap. 18). For Matthew this definition carries a special warning to ecclesiastical leaders, who are supposed to show love to the little people in the church. If they do not, those leaders will suffer for false discipleship the same judgment that falls on the Jewish leaders, the hypocritical scribes and Pharisees.

24:45 (Luke 12:41-42) To avoid a narrative interruption of Jesus' discourse, Matthew omits Peter's question and the introduction to Jesus' reply (Luke 12:41-42b). In the clause "Who then is the faithful and wise slave . . . ?" δοῦλος, "slave," differs from Luke's οἰκονόμος, "manager," which for a couple of reasons appears to come from Luke's editing: (1) δοῦλος will occur throughout the rest of the parable even in Luke; and (2) Luke has a penchant for οἰκονόμος and cognates, which occur eight times in his gospel but never in the others (cf. eleven occurrences in the correspondence of Paul, Luke's friend). Jesus continues, "whom the master has appointed over his household slaves to give them food at the proper time." The aorist tense of κατέστησεν contrasts with Luke's future tense and looks like a historicizing reference to ecclesiastical leaders already ensconced in positions of authority. Because of the repeated mention of slaves throughout the parable and because of the attraction Luke the physician would have felt to θεραπείας, which means "healing" as well as "service" (cf. Luke 12:42; Rev 22:2 for the only other occurrences of the word in the NT), Matthew's οἰκετείας, "household slaves," looks closer to the original. "To give them food at the proper time" comes from Ps 104:27. αὐτοῖς corresponds to the LXX (but not to the Hebrew text—see Gundry, *Use of the OT* 89) and does not appear in Luke, where the substitution of θεραπείας for οἰκετείας takes away its referent. Matthew's τὴν τροφήν, "food," differs from Luke's τὸ σιτομέτριον, "the food ration," and corresponds to the LXX (cf. the comments on 3:4). The putting of τὴν τροφήν before ἐν καιρῷ matches both the Hebrew text and the LXX, but contrasts with Luke's word order. It is hard to tell whether Luke has strayed from the OT or Matthew has drawn closer. The insertion of the dictum "For the worker is worthy of his food" in 10:10 suggests that both the present passage and the one in chap. 10 deal with tensions in the church of Matthew's time and place, tensions between settled ecclesiastics and Christian refugees dependent on hospitality and therefore, to a large degree, on the good will of the ecclesiastics. Matthew uses Jesus' teaching to take the side of the inhospitably treated refugees, who are persecuted because they refuse to compromise the way of righteousness.

24:46-47 (*Luke 12:43-44*) The blessing pronounced on that slave whom his master will find so doing—i.e., giving food to the household slaves at the proper time—reads identically in Matthew and Luke except for an insignificant difference in the order of the last two words. Also, Matthew keeps the transliteration ἀμήν, but Luke translates with ἀληθῶς in "Truly I say to you" (cf. Luke 9:27; 21:3). The two evangelists report the promise of appointment over all the master's possessions in exactly the same words.

24:48-51 (*Luke 12:45-46*) To accentuate the evil character of the inhospitable ecclesiastics, Matthew inserts κακός, "bad," in the clause "But if that bad slave should say in his heart." The adjective occurred as an insertion also in 21:41. It has a parallel only once (cf. Matthew's four insertions of κακῶς, "badly"). In the statement of the bad slave's thought, "My master is lingering," μου precedes ὁ κύριος in Matthew but follows it in Luke; and Matthew lacks the supplementary infinitive ἔρχεσθαι, "to come." For "the male and female slaves," who suffer beating, Matthew substitutes "his fellow slaves." See 18:28, 29, 31, 33 for other distinctive occurrences of "fellow slaves." This substitute brings out the need for Christian brotherhood based on mutual love and humility. Instead of the Lukanism τε, Matthew writes δέ, which contrasts the beating of the fellow slaves by the bad slave and his eating and drinking with drunkards. Matthew's turning the infinitives "to eat" and "to drink" into finite verbs makes a new line parallel to the preceding. Consequently, greater emphasis falls on the eating and drinking. Furthermore, the infinitive "to get drunk" (so Luke; cf. 1 Thess

5:7) becomes the prepositional phrase "with drunkards" for a parallel with the inserted "fellow slaves." The drunkards are absent from the original form of the parable and consist in those false disciples who follow the antinomian ways of the settled ecclesiastics. Thus Matthew strengthens the charge against the ecclesiastics: they should be sharing their resources with their fellow slaves, Christian refugees dependent on hospitality; instead, they squander those resources with people in the church who like to carouse with them.

The warning that "the master of that slave will come on a day that he does not expect and at an hour that he does not know and will cut him in two" reads just as it does in Luke. But in the warning "and he will assign him a place with the unfaithful [or 'unbelievers']" (so Luke) Matthew substitutes "the hypocrites" for "the unfaithful." The substitute suits his special interest in the condemnation of hypocrisy (9,3) and forges a link with the polemic against Pharisees in chap. 23. This link implies that the unbelieving scribes and Pharisees and the dissolute ecclesiastics not only share hypocrisy, but also will share judgment. Matthew characteristically underlines judgment by adding the clause "In that place there will be weeping and gnashing of teeth" (see the comments on 8:11-12).

Since the bad slave lives on to share the fate of hypocrites, some have supposed that διχοτομήσει does not mean "will cut in two," but "will separate [from the company of the elect]" (cf. 18:17; Ps 37:9, 22; 1QS 2:16-17; 6:24-25; 7:1-2, 16; 8:21-24), or that we are dealing with a mistranslation of an Aramaic expression which was taken to mean "he will divide him," but which Jesus intended to mean "he will apportion to him" (see Jeremias, *Parables* 57 n. 31). But both suppositions overlook that the bad slave continues to exist only in a punitive afterlife. The cutting in two of his present body simply represents an extremely severe punishment that appropriately launches him into that kind of afterlife. For such dismemberment, see references in BAG, s.v. διχοτομέω, and 2 Sam 12:31; 1 Chr 20:3; Amos 1:3 LXX; Heb 11:37; Herodotus 7.39; Suetonius *Caligula* 27.

WATCHING AS DOING GOOD WORKS
IN OBEDIENCE TO JESUS' TEACHING
25:1-13

25:1 To define watching as doing good works, over against antinomian failure to obey Jesus' teaching of righteousness, Matthew composes the parable of the ten virgins with the help of Mark 13:33-37 and the traditions behind Luke 12:35-38; 13:25-28. His special vocabulary is evident in τότε (66,17), ὁμοιωθήσεται (2,3), and "the kingdom of heaven" (25,7). The combination of the last two plus a dative occurred in 13:24; 18:23; 22:2. As distinctively in 7:24, 26, the future tense of "will be likened" alludes to the last judgment (see v 12 with comments ad loc.). The virgins derive from the setting of a wedding, which derives in turn from the tradition behind Luke 12:36. Their number, ten, is taken from the number of slaves in the next parable (vv 14-30; Luke 19:11-27), a number that Matthew will omit in that parable because of his incorporating it in the present one.

Matthew's preferred diction is evident again in αἵτινες (23,5) and λαβοῦσαι (3,7). "Their torches" (τὰς λαμπάδας ἑαυτῶν) comes from the tradition behind Luke 12:35: "let your loins be girded and [your] lamps [οἱ λύχνοι] burning." But in Matthew's new setting the indoor lamps have become torches for use outdoors in a dance before the wedding. λαμπάς ordinarily means "torch," and a lamp would not stay lighted in a breeze, would not provide enough light outdoors, and would not need an extra supply of oil. Torches resist a breeze, give a bright light, burn only about fifteen minutes, and then need to have the rags that are wrapped around the end of the stick soaked again in oil (see J. Jeremias in *Soli Deo Gloria* [New Testament Studies in Honor of William Childs Robinson; ed. J. McDowell Richards; Richmond: John Knox, 1968] 83-87). Matthew's noun appears several times below, but nowhere else in the synoptics; and elsewhere he inserts the cognate verb λάμπω three times over against only one occurrence in the other synoptics. ἑαυτῶν appears also in Luke 12:36, though in a different connection. Matthew inserted the entire expression "went out to meet" in 8:34 (cf. the insertion of "met" in 28:9; see also 1 Thess 4:16-17). In view of his penchant for OT phraseology, perhaps the phrase came to him from the LXX (Judg 11:34; 1 Chr 14:8 A; Prov 7:15 B; Jdt 2:6 ℵ; 1 Macc 9:39 ℵ). "The bridegroom" stems from the mention of a wedding in the tradition underlying Luke 12:35-36. There, however, a master comes home from a wedding with the expectation that his slaves will be waiting for him with lamps burning. Here, a bridegroom comes to his wedding with the expectation that some virgins will have torches ready for a dance as part of the festivities. The virgins' going out to meet him anticipates v 6. They hardly go out twice; therefore the waiting in vv 2-5 chronologically precedes the going out in v 1.

At whose home—the bride's, the bridegroom's, or that of the parents of the bridegroom—does the wedding take place? Most naturally, the virgins would be waiting for the bridegroom with the bride at her home (cf. Jdt 14:10-18; Tob 6:13; 8:19). But the answer does not matter, for the bride makes no appearance in the parable. The virgins represent the church, consisting of professing disciples. Introduction of the bride would have confused the symbolism with an otiose figure easily mistaken for the church (cf. esp. 2 Cor 11:2). See the UBS and Metzger, *Textual Commentary* ad loc., on the bride's presence in part of the textual tradition. Her addition was occasioned by the practice of celebrating weddings usually at the home of the groom or his parents. It seemed that the groom was returning from fetching his bride. On the comparison of Jesus to a bridegroom, see Mark 2:19-20 and Matt 9:15-16 with comments ad loc. For ancient Jewish wedding customs so far as they are known, and especially on the nocturnal setting in the present passage, see Jeremias, *Parables* 171-75.

25:2-4 The statement that five of the virgins were foolish and five wise exhibits parallelism, which typifies Matthew's style. δέ contrasts the division into two groups of five each with the preceding lump sum of ten. The division into contrastive groups follows the pattern in surrounding traditional material: taking one versus leaving one (24:40-41); the faithful and wise slave versus the bad slave (24:45-51); and the good and faithful slaves versus the evil and slothful slave (25:14-30). μωραί, "foolish," and φρόνιμοι, "wise," echo 7:24, 26, where Matthew inserted them. They represent his special designations for nonmembers and members of the kingdom (see the comments on 5:21-22; 7:24, 26 and cf. *b. Šabb.* 152b, 153a). The foolish *profess* membership in the kingdom, of course. Again we discover typically Matthean parallelism in the statements "For the foolish, taking their torches, did not take oil with themselves; but the wise took oil in flasks with their own torches." γάρ makes the couplet an explanation of the division into foolish and wise and belongs to Matthew's favorite vocabulary (62-63,15). Jesus' exhortation that disciples keep their lamps burning (Luke 12:35-36) prompted Matthew to distinguish between taking and not taking oil. Since "wise" in 7:24, 26 describes the man who obeys Jesus' teaching and "foolish" describes the man who does not, these adjectives bear the same meanings here. Hence, taking enough oil to keep the torches burning stands for good works in obedience to Jesus' teaching (cf. *Num. Rab.* 23.15-16). We may recall that in 5:14-16 Matthew alone stated that lamplight represents "good works." The failure to take enough oil represents disobedience to Jesus' teaching, i.e., lawlessness (see 7:23 and the allusion to that verse in v 12 below). As in chaps. 5–7 good works contrast with the hypocrisy of the scribes and Pharisees. Good works glorify the Father; hypocrisy has self-glorification as its object.

25:5-6 Yet again we see Matthew's penchant for parallelism: "But while the bridegroom was delaying, they all became drowsy and fell asleep" matches "But at midnight a shout came, 'Behold, the bridegroom! Come out to meet him.'" The first δέ contrasts the implied expectation of an immediate arrival with the going to sleep because of delay. The second δέ contrasts the delay with the late arrival. The genitive absolute construction in χρονίζοντος . . . τοῦ νυμφίου characterizes Matthew's style. χρονίζοντος comes from the traditional saying in 24:48. "They all became drowsy and fell asleep" and "at midnight" were suggested to Matthew by phrases in Mark 13:35-36, phrases thus far unused by him: "whether in the evening or *at midnight* or during the cockcrowing or early in the morning—lest coming suddenly he find you *sleeping*" (cf. 13:25, another composition of his). The particular form γέγονεν and ἰδού are Mattheanisms (3,2; 34,9). "The bridegroom" (bis) and "Come out to meet him" echo v 1 (see the comments ad loc.).

Matthew is concerned with unpreparedness because of the delay in Jesus' coming, not with the delay itself. The foolish virgins are not foolish because they do not take enough oil to keep their torches burning continuously during the delay, i.e., because they fail to take account of the possibility of delay. The torches are not yet burning and will not be set alight till the bridegroom's approach (v 7). They will burn about fifteen minutes and go out, not while the virgins are sleeping, but in the interval between the announcement of the bridegroom's coming and his actual arrival (cf. vv 8-10). The foolish virgins are foolish, then, in that they do not take enough oil for the procession and dance, which will take place when the bridegroom arrives. Perhaps bargaining about presents for relatives of the bride—a bargaining that shows her family's reluctance to give her up and hence compliments the bridegroom's choice—causes the delay. But that possibility plays no part in the meaning of the parable.

25:7 Several Mattheanisms occur in the statement that the virgins got up and put their torches in order: τότε (66,17), ἠγέρθησαν (11,8), πᾶσαι (63,25-26), ἐκεῖναι (26,9), and ἐκόσμησαν (1,1; cf. Matthew's liking the cognate κόσμος—5,2). "Their torches" echoes vv 1, 3, and 4.

ἐκόσμησαν includes checking the rags wrapped around the end of the stick, dipping them in oil, and setting them aflame (for the first time—see the note on vv 5-6). Some think that the virgins' sleeping and rising symbolize death and resurrection during the delay in Jesus' coming. But in the passages where Matthew uses ἐγείρω for resurrection, the context makes that meaning very clear (9:25; 10:8; 16:21; 17:9). On the other hand, the same verb refers to getting up from sleep in his version of the nativity story (1:24; 2:14, 20, 21). We should have to understand "became drowsy" as the process leading to death if "fell asleep" symbolizes dying itself. But such an understanding seems farfetched. Furthermore, if falling asleep stands for dying, why the need for watchful preparedness because the exact time of Jesus' coming cannot be known (cf. v 13)?

25:8-9 In the request of the foolish virgins and the reply of the wise we have still another example of antithetic parallelism. The designations "foolish" and "wise" stem, of course, from v 2 and ultimately from 7:24, 26. δότε is a Mattheanism in the request that the wise give some of their oil (8-9,10). The further part of the request, "because our torches are going out," again reflects Jesus' exhortation that the disciples keep their lamps burning in expectation of his coming (Luke 12:35-36; cf. the comments on v 3). The going out of the torches represents conduct that is not righteous enough to demonstrate the reality of Christian profession (cf. 5:20). The combination of the finite verb "answered" (ἀπεκρίθησαν) and the participle "saying" (λέγουσαι) typifies Matthew's style (2,4; cf. his liking the reverse combination—29,6). He inserted the finite verb in 15:23. The first part of the reply may be translated "Lest there not be enough for us and you" or "Perhaps there will not be enough for us and you." Mattheanisms are evident in μήποτε (2,4), ἀρκέσῃ (2,1 with its cognate adjective), πορεύεσθε (13,10), and μᾶλλον (5,1). The last two words carry on the reply—"Go rather . . ."—and occurred together in 10:6, another composition of Matthew. Similarly, πωλοῦντας and ἀγοράσατε occurred together in 13:44 (yet another of his compositions) as well as in 21:12 (traditional). The latter word occurs five times in passages peculiar to this gospel, besides two shared occurrences.

The reading οὐ μή would yield the meaning "Certainly there would not be enough for us and you" (see the UBS). Though good works (represented by the oil) cannot be transferred, the conversation between the foolish virgins and the wise merely sets the stage for refusing entrance to the foolish when they return from going to purchase more oil. The wise virgins rightly refuse, for otherwise all the torches would go out without possibility of replenishment before the procession and dance are completed.

500

25:10 Again we meet a typically Matthean construction in the genitive absolute ἀπερχομένων δὲ αὐτῶν, "But as they were going away" (cf. v 5). Furthermore, ἀπερχομένων falls in the circle of words favored by Matthew (14,11). "To buy" echoes v 9. Since Matthew does not indicate whether the foolish virgins were able to buy more oil in the middle of the night, the warning grows out of their deficient preparation prior to the bridegroom's coming. Throughout chaps. 24–25 ἦλθεν occurs for Jesus' coming. Concerning the bridegroom, see the comments on vv 1, 5, and 6. The description of the wise virgins as "the prepared" comes from the traditional exhortation in 24:44. "Entered" comes from 7:21, where Matthew inserted it in shared material leading to the rejection stated in 7:23 (and echoed in v 12 here) and then to the parable of the wise and foolish builders, which is the source of the descriptions of the virgins as foolish and wise. "With him" is a counterpart to Matthew's distinctive designations of Jesus as "with us" (1:23) and "with you" (28:20). "Into the wedding" corresponds to "from the wedding" in the tradition behind Luke 12:35-36. But departure from a wedding has become entrance into a wedding in order to make the messianic banquet a wedding feast, as in 22:1-14, where Matthew turned a supper (so Luke 14:15-24) into a wedding feast. "And the door was shut" comes from the tradition reflected in Luke 13:25 ("and [the master of the house] shut the door") and omitted in Matt 7:22. Thus Matthew makes up for his prior omission and begins to reuse the tradition concerning the Lord's rejection of false disciples.

25:11 The plea of the foolish virgins on their return represents the attempt of false disciples to gain entrance into the kingdom at the last judgment. The introduction to the plea begins with the Mattheanism ὕστερον (3,3) and the conjunction δέ, which contrasts the shutting of the door with the attempt to gain entrance. ἔρχονται complements ἀπερχομένων in the preceding verse. The description of the foolish virgins as αἱ λοιπαί exhibits an adjective that appeals somewhat to Matthew (elsewhere he inserts it twice) and sounds a doleful, warning note of being left out. λέγουσαι both suits his style (61,23) and reflects λέγοντες in the tradition underlying Luke 13:25. The participle did not appear in 7:22, which also depended on this tradition. Its use here makes up for that omission (cf. v 10). Similarly, in the plea "Lord, lord, open to us" Matthew draws on the same tradition. But he doubles κύριε, which occurs only once in Luke 13:25, just as he did in 7:22; and he retains "open to us," which he replaced in 7:22. Such compensation and doubling typify his style and emphasis on Jesus' lordship.

25:12 We discover a Mattheanism in ἀποκριθεὶς εἶπεν (29,6), which differs from 7:23 but agrees with Luke 13:25 except for εἶπεν versus ἐρεῖ. Another of Matthew's favorite expressions, "Truly I say to you" (15,8), expands "to you" in the tradition (see Luke 13:27 and cf. "to them" in Matt 7:23). Perhaps "Truly I say to you" in the tradition Matthew drew on earlier (see Luke 12:37) suggested this expansion. "I do not know you" matches the wording in Luke 13:25, differs from the wording in Matt 7:23, and suggests that the virgins were maidservants in the bride's paternal house. As in 7:23, "from where you are" (so Luke) drops out.

25:13 "Watch therefore" comes from 24:42 (cf. Mark 13:35). "Because you do not know the day or the hour" represents Matthew's conflation of the clause "because you do not know what day your Lord is coming" (24:42) and the day and hour of the coming in 24:36, 50. Ignorance concerning the exact time should lead, then, to watching right up to the end. Otherwise, intensified persecution during the tribulation may tempt professing disciples into antinomianism as a way of escape. Succumbing will cause them to be caught without the necessary good works. The command to watch in Mark 13:37 does not come over, because it implies that not all the disciples are present (cf. Mark 13:3-4), whereas according to Matt 24:3-4 all the disciples are present.

It would be wrong to think that the exhortation to watch contradicts the sleeping of the wise as well as the foolish virgins. For by the time the bridegroom arrived all had awakened. And more to the point, Matthew wants to teach that watching means preparedness through doing good works. The bridegroom's delay, the drowsiness and sleep of the virgins, and their being roused at midnight do not contradict the exhortation to watch, then, but illustrate ignorance concerning the exact time of Jesus' coming.

Once More, Watching as Doing Good Works
25:14-30 (Mark 13:34; Luke 19:11-27)

25:14 (Mark 13:34; Luke 19:12-13) Matthew now switches back to the exhortation to watch in Mark 13:34, but expands it with the parable recorded also in Luke 19:11-27 after the story of Zacchaeus in Jericho. The expansion once more defines watching as doing good works (cf. 25:1-13). Because of the new setting, the narrative introduction in Luke 19:11-12a does not appear in Matthew. A characteristic insertion of γάρ (62-63,15) makes the parable a further basis for the exhortation to watch in v 13. In place of Mark's ὡς Matthew puts ὥσπερ, a favorite of his (6,3). He follows Mark in not describing "a man" as "a certain noble" (so Luke). ἀποδημῶν, "going away on a journey," replaces both Mark's ἀπόδημος, "away on a journey," and Luke's ἐπορεύθη εἰς χώραν μακράν, "went into a distant country." The replacement enables Matthew to start the parable at its chronological beginning without having to backtrack, as Mark and Luke do. Mark's phrase "having left his house" drops out because Matthew has already inserted the notion of a household in 24:45. And the largely traditional phrase "to receive a kingdom for himself and return" (so Luke) does not appear because Matthew omitted the narrative introduction mentioning the expectation that God's kingdom was going to appear immediately, an expectation that elicited the parable. (Word-statistics suggest that Luke added "and return," καὶ ὑποστρέψαι.)

"He called" stems from "having called" in the tradition behind Luke. Escalation of the participle to a finite verb results in a typically Matthean couplet of parallel lines and in the loss of Luke's δέ. "Ten" (so Luke) gives way to "the" because Matthew pirated the number for his parable of the ten virgins (25:1). ἰδίους, a favorite of his (6,0), stands in place of Luke's synonymous ἑαυτοῦ. καί comes from Mark, but Matthew exchanges "having given authority to his slaves" for the tradition behind Luke. παρέδωκεν replaces Luke's ἔδωκεν. Matthew likes the compound verb (6,3). Using it here avoids redundancy with the simple form in the next verse. "To them" matches Luke. But "his possessions" substitutes for "ten minas" (so Luke). The substitution is due to prior loss of the number ten concerning the slaves and provides a link with 24:47. Cf. the insertion of "his possessions" in 19:21.

Since travellers might journey at night (see 2:9-11; Luke 11:5-8), there is no reason to suppose that without thinking about the closing of city gates at night Mark clumsily changed (and shortened) a parable about a master who goes to a wedding in his own city and returns at night (so Luke 12:35-38) to one about a master who takes a journey of some distance and returns at night.

25:15 (Mark 13:34; Luke 19:13-14) To compensate for the disappearance of the ten minas, Matthew composes the statement "And to one he gave five talents, and to another, two, and to another, one." μέν . . . δέ . . . δέ characterizes his parallelistic style (15,1). See especially 13:23; 21:35; 22:5 for insertions of this combination with a series of relative pronouns, as here. "He gave" comes from the tradition behind the preceding clause (cf. Luke). Talents had much more value than minas, which were worth about $20 each. In fact, talents were the largest of all denominations and varied from $300 to $1700 each, or from 50 to 80 pounds each in weight. The substitution of talents for minas echoes Matthew's parabolic composition in 18:24 and strengthens the slaves' obligation; indeed, it shows the necessity of righteous conduct surpassing that of the scribes and Pharisees (5:20). "Five" reflects the preceding parable of the five foolish and five wise virgins (25:1-13). Matthew likes "two" and "one" (δύο—19,4; ἕν—24,7). Possibly the five loaves and two fish lay in the back of his mind. He returns to Mark in the phrase "to each according to his own ability." But "according to his own ability" has replaced "his work" (so Mark) because of the varying numbers of talents. As an ex-publican Matthew takes an interest in financial figures. ἰδίαν and δύναμιν belong to his special vocabulary (6,0; 4,0). Though the noun elsewhere means "miracle," the cognate verb δύναμαι, which carries the sense of ability that is required here by the noun, also belongs to Matthew's special vocabulary (13,0). "According to his own ability" also substitutes for the master's command in Luke: "Do business [with this] till I come [back]." Because of the distribution of money, the command in Mark that the doorkeeper watch drops out as otiose. From this point onward Mark offers no parallel. The citizens' hating the man and sending an embassy after him to say they do not want him to reign over them (so Luke) also drop out. Earlier omission of the man's purpose to receive a kingdom has made all that meaningless (see v 14). Matthew now inserts "and he went away on the journey" for a parallel with v 15a. The expression comes from v 14a.

25:16-18 To tell what the slaves did with the talents committed to them Matthew composes vv 16-18 in the parallelistic style that typifies his writing. The composition begins with two Mattheanisms, εὐθέως (11,0) and πορευθείς (8,4; see the UBS and Metzger, *Textual Commentary* ad loc., on the text-critical question). In the phrase "the one who received five talents" λαβών comes from a favorite verb of Matthew (21,16). ἠργάσατο, "worked," belongs to a group of cognates he likes (6,7). It also anticipates προσηργάσατο, "worked for, made more," in the tradition underlying Luke 19:16. Matthew's advancing the verb for working shows the point of his version of the parable, viz., good works as a definition of watchfulness. ἐκέρδησεν, "he gained," occurs five times as an insertion in his gospel, including four such occurrences in this parable, and only once in common. ἄλλα, "other," also suits his fancy (14,4) and occurs five times in the present parable. The five talents initially entrusted to the first slave plus the five talents more add up to ten, exactly the number of minas made by the single mina of the first slave in the traditional form of the parable (so Luke). The similar statement about the gaining of two more talents by the slave who received two begins with ὡσαύτως, another Mattheanism (2,2).

The description of the last slave's action (v 18) follows the pattern of that slave's later words as recorded in Luke 19:20: ". . . behold your mina, which I have kept put away in a handkerchief." But Matthew makes changes that reflect his parabolic composition about the treasure hidden in the field (13:44). Luke's ἀποκειμένην, "put away," yields to ἔκρυψεν, "hid" (see 13:44; cf. the insertion of joy in v 21 with 13:44). "He who received one [talent]" echoes v 16 and displays Mattheanisms in ἕν (24,7) and λαβών (21,16). Other Mattheanisms are evident in ἀπελθών (14,11), γῆν (21,6), ἔκρυψεν (4,2), and κυρίου (34,15). The last of these means "master," but carries the overtone "Lord." "The money" anticipates the tradition behind Luke 19:15. "In a handkerchief" (so Luke 19:20) disappears because of Matthew's switch from a mina to a talent, which is much too large to be contained in a handkerchief (cf. the comments on v 15). Hence, the slave must dig a hole in the ground for safekeeping. The address "Master" (so Luke 19:20) becomes the description "of his master" because Matthew will turn part of the last slave's speech into a third person description of his slothfulness. The pairing of "dug" and "hid" shows Matthew's love of parallelism.

25:19 (Luke 19:15) Again we see Matthew's love of parallelism in his pairing "comes" and "settles." "But after much delay" replaces "And it came about [that] when" (so Luke) and compensates for Matthew's initial omission of Jesus' telling this parable to counteract the notion that the kingdom was going to appear immediately. The substitution of δέ for καί pits the master's coming and settling accounts against the last slave's slothfulness. χρόνον echoes the cognate verb in 24:48; 25:5. Thus, by means of references to the delay in Jesus' coming, Matthew welds together all three parables in the successive passages 24:45-51; 25:1-13; and 25:14-30. πολύν comes from his favorite vocabulary (23,1) and corresponds to the long distance travelled by the master in the traditional form of the parable (Luke 19:12). "Comes" replaces "he returned after receiving the kingdom" (so Luke) because Matthew omitted the master's going to receive a kingdom. Furthermore, he wants conformity to the use of "come" throughout chaps. 24–25. The verb repeatedly applies to Jesus' coming (see the concordance, s.v. ἔρχομαι). ὁ κύριος echoes the preceding context and suits Matthew's preference for the noun in references to Jesus (34,15). "Of those slaves" stems from "these slaves" in the next clause of the tradition (so Luke). But "those" replaces "these" in reminiscence of v 7, where "those" modified "virgins." This linkage of the two parables owes something to Matthew's fondness for ἐκεῖνος (26,9). "And he settles accounts with them" points to the last judgment and follows almost exactly the wording in 18:23-24, part of another parabolic composition by the first evangelist. It also replaces the tradition reflected in Luke 19:15bc: "and he ordered that these slaves, to whom he had given the money, be called in order that he might know what each one gained by trading." Matthew has already drawn somewhat on this tradition.

25:20 (Luke 19:16) Again we see evidence of Matthew's hand in the close parallel between vv 20-21, 22-23, and, mutatis mutandis, 24-29. καί stands in place of Luke's δέ because Matthew habitually uses δέ for contrast, yet the parable continues with the settling of accounts. Instead of παρεγένετο, a Lukanism, we read προσελθών, a Mattheanism connoting the dignity of Jesus, whom the master represents (38,6; cf. the comments on 4:3; 8:14). The change from finite verb to participle allows the insertion of προσήνεγκεν, another Mattheanism and one that connotes an offering to Jesus (9,2; see the comments on 2:11; 4:24). "He who received five talents" comes from v 16, where Matthew inserted it, and replaces "the first" (so Luke). The replacement is due to Matthew's changing the equal distribution of money to an unequal distribution (v 15). "Five other talents" likewise comes from the insertion in v 16 (see the comments ad loc. for Mattheanisms). In "saying" and "Master" Matthew returns to the tradition. But "your mina" becomes "you gave five talents over to me." παρέδωκας echoes Matthew's replacement in v 14, and the five talents echo his insertion of v 15. Matthew now adds ἴδε, "see," as he will also in vv 22, 25; 26:65. And because of the insertion of v 16, "has made ten minas more" yields to "I have gained five other talents." All of this constitutes an appeal to good works as demonstrating the reality of professed discipleship.

25:21 (Luke 19:17) In the introduction to the master's reply, ἔφη with asyndeton substitutes for καὶ εἶπεν and typifies Matthew's style (6,1). His insertion of ὁ κύριος αὐτοῦ is also typical (34,15). This designation echoes and parallels similar insertions in vv 18 and 19 and reemphasizes the lordship of Jesus, whom the master represents. In the reply, Luke's γε does not appear. Probably Luke added it, since it occurs eight times in his gospel, but only four times in Matthew and not at all in Mark. For the sake of an emphatic pair of adjectives, Matthew anticipates "faithful" later in the clause by adding "and faithful" after "good slaves." This doubling underlines the need for faithfulness during persecution, which makes persistence in good works difficult and therefore all the more commendable. Luke's "because" does not appear. Consequently, Matthew has two independent clauses. "Over a few things" replaces "in a very little thing" for a closer antithetic parallel with "over many things" in the next clause. Matthew is fond of ὀλίγα (1,2) and compounds beginning with ὀλιγο- (4,0). Five talents, having a mean worth of about $5,000, was a very large sum of money in those days (cf. the comments on v 15). To call such a sum "a few things" is ironic and emphatic. Therefore ὀλίγα not only exposes Matthew's editing, but also accentuates the obligation of disciples to do good works: surpassing righteousness is but a small requirement. Both Matthew's ἦς and Luke's ἐγένου mean "you were." The earlier insertion of πιστέ pushes πιστός to the end of Matthew's clause (contrast Luke's word order).

Matthew puts "over many things" first in its clause for a closer parallel with the preceding clause (again contrast Luke's order). The phrase replaces "over ten cities." Matthew's preposition is ἐπί; Luke's, ἐπάνω. Since Matthew likes ἐπάνω (7,1), it probably comes from Luke; otherwise Matthew would surely have adopted it from the tradition. Since he eliminated the nobleman's getting a kingdom, the reference to cities vanishes. Matthew's unkingly man has no cities to give. Despite the frequency of "cities" in Matthew, then, that term yields to "many things" for a parallel with "a few things." Matthew's liking πολλῶν facilitated the shift (23,1). Luke's ἴσθι ἐξουσίαν ἔχων, "have authority," gives way to σε καταστήσω, "I will appoint you." The new expression links with the parable of the slave (see esp. 24:45, 47 and cf. the comments on v 14). Matthew composes "Enter into the joy of your master" as a link with the parable of the ten virgins, especially v 10: "and the ones who were prepared entered with him into the wedding." In the two statements, we find correspondences between the command to enter and the description of entry, between joy and the festivity of the wedding, and between the description of the joy as the master's and the bridegroom's arrival as the occasion of festivity. The association between vv 10 and 21d rests largely on Matthew's knowledge that the Semitic words for "joy," שִׂמְחָה (Hebrew) and חֶדְוְתָא (Aramaic), also mean "festival," including "wedding feast" (see G. Dalman, *The Words of Jesus* [Edinburgh: T. & T. Clark, 1902] 117-18, and Str-B 1. 972-73 for references). The first evangelist likes χαράν (cf. esp. 13:44, yet another of his compositions). τοῦ κυρίου σου echoes vv 18, 19, 20, 21a and typifies his emphasis on Jesus' lordship (34,15).

25:22-23 (Luke 19:18-19) The insertion of δέ contrasts the preceding five talents plus five more with the following two talents plus two more and changes the meaning of καί from "and" (so Luke) to "also." The entire expression, "But also he [who had received] two talents, approaching, said," echoes v 20 in shortened form and replaces "And the second came, saying" (see the comments on v 20 for Matthean diction and motifs). With a necessary change in number and similar revisions of the tradition underlying Luke, the words of the slave who received two talents parallel the words of the slave who received five talents. The same kind of parallelism is apparent in the master's happy reply (see the comments on vv 20-21 for interpretation).

25:24 (Luke 19:20-21) "And the other came, saying" (so Luke) gives way to the statement "But also he who had received one talent, approaching, said." The latter accords with Matthew's revisions in v 22a. Naturally, the number has changed from two to one. Matthew draws from v 20a to fill the ellipsis of λαβών that he allowed in v 22a. But here he uses the more emphatic perfect participle, εἰληφώς. Thus the responsibility of the slave gets greater emphasis. "Behold, your mina, which I have kept put away in a handkerchief!" drops out because Matthew used it in v 18 and will reuse it in v 25. This omission results in the further omission of γάρ, which no longer has anything to depend on, and in the bringing forward of the master's character and activity. The master represents Jesus, who deserves a position of first prominence in the slave's words. "I knew" replaces "I feared." Matthew wants a parallel with "you knew," coming up in v 26 (cf. esp. 7:23; 25:12). The replacement causes the following ὅτι to shift from the meaning "because" (so Luke) to the meaning "that."

The slave's description of the master as αὐστηρός, "strict, exacting" (so Luke), changes to σκληρός, "harsh." Substitution of the stronger term and its advance by exchange of positions with ἄνθρωπος (cf. Luke's word order) accentuate Jesus' demand that his disciples do good works. Matthew makes the very excuse of the slothful slave contribute to this emphasis. In the original form of the parable, the slave first refers to his master's habit of taking what he did not deposit, i.e., of misappropriating money that did not belong to him (so Luke). This reference follows naturally from the banking practices that support the parable. Only then does an agricultural metaphor, "you reap what you did not sow," come into view. But for closer parallelism Matthew turns the banking terminology into another agricultural metaphor: "gathering from where you did not scatter." Since gathering, συνάγων, follows reaping (i.e., cutting the grain—θερίζων), Matthew puts the phrase with θερίζων first (contrast Luke). The finite verbs become participles to avoid asyndeton, as in Luke's parallel to the next verse, where Matthew reverts to finite verbs without asyndeton. We might think that his ὅπου, "where," and ὅθεν, "from where," and Luke's ὅ, "that which" (bis), represent variant translations of an Aramaic דִּי. But Matthew inserts both of his words twice elsewhere, and Luke uses the relative pronoun 182 times, as compared with 122 occurrences in Matthew and 85 in Mark. Therefore we are probably dealing with stylistic variations in the Greek tradition. Even so, Semitic thinking may underlie Matthew's diction.

"Gathering from where you did not scatter" may derive from the traditional saying in 12:30: "he who does not gather with me scatters" (cf. Luke 11:23). συνάγων replaces αἴρεις. Luke shows no preference for αἴρεις, Matthew shows no dislike of it, and συνάγων is unusually frequent in Matthew (10,10). Therefore αἴρεις is original and συνάγων editorial. But something more than a desire for closer parallelism in compatible agricultural metaphors underlies Matthew's choice of συνάγων, a choice that has led to a chain reaction of other revisions. That is the desire to portray the master's activity in terms that symbolize Jesus' gathering his disciples into a true synagogue from their scattering through persecution (cf. 26:31). συνάγω means gathering winnowed grain into a barn in 3:12; 6:26 (an insertion); 13:30 (part of a parable composed by Matthew; cf. Luke 12:17-18) and carries the same meaning here. διεσκόρπισας refers to the scattering of grain in winnowing, just as the Aramaic verb דְּרִי means both "scatter" and "winnow" (cf. Matthew's thinking Semitically in his use of ὅπου, ὅθεν, and—in v 24—χαράν).

25:25 Because he omitted the slave's reference to having kept the money in a handkerchief, Matthew now composes v 25. "Becoming afraid" comes from the tradition behind the foregoing verse, where he replaced "I was afraid" (Luke 19:21) with "I knew." "Going away, I hid your talent in the earth" echoes his insertion of v 18 (see the comments ad loc.). "See" also echoes his insertions in vv 20 and 22. "You have what is yours" is Jewish commercial language that disclaims responsibility (see *m. B. Qam.* 9:2; 10:5; *m. B. Meṣ.* 6:3). Also, Matthew likes the possessive adjective σόν (6,2). The slave in Matthew excuses his failure by putting blame on his master's harshness. In effect, he says that it would have done him no good to work with the talent because his master would have reaped and gathered in that part of the profits which rightfully belonged to the slave (see Derrett, *Law in the NT* 18-24, concerning the sharing of profits with slaves).

25:26 *(Luke 19:22)* Matthew's inserting δέ contrasts the master's reply with the slave's excuse. The Mattheanism ἀποκριθείς . . . εἶπεν αὐτῷ (29,6) is stronger than Luke's λέγει αὐτῷ and Matthew's ἔφη in vv 21, 23. It emphasizes the following pronouncement of judgment on this representative of disciples who falsify their profession by failing to do good works. As in vv 21 and 23, Matthew inserts "his master" to underline Jesus' lordship. The omission of "out of your mouth I judge you" leaves the emphasis solely on "evil slave," to which Matthew adds "and slothful." The addition contrasts the failure of false disciples to do good works with "worked," which Matthew inserted in v 16 to interpret the industriousness of the first two slaves as symbolizing good works. "I am an exacting man" drops out. Matthew might have taken it over, presumably with a change of "exacting" to "harsh" to conform with v 24. But he does not. Why? Perhaps he remembers his own composition concerning Jesus' gentleness (11:28-30) and draws back from allowing the master, who represents Jesus, to repeat "harsh" in describing himself. Harsh? Yes, so far as his demanding good works is concerned. But not doubly harsh so as to call in question the graciousness of his invitation to the weary and heavy laden. The omission requires escalation of the following participles (so Luke) to main verbs. The remainder of the self-description, "I reap where I did not sow and gather from where I did not scatter," follows the lines of v 24 (see the comments ad loc.).

The portrait of the master as taking what does not belong to him should bother us no more than the comparison of Jesus' coming to that of "a thief in the night" bothers us. The point of the comparison does not have to do with thievery, but with unexpectedness. So also here, the portrait has to do with the forcefulness of Jesus' demand for good works, not with the ethics of taking what belongs to others. But the last slave makes his master's forcefulness an excuse for his failure. Strikingly, the master accepts the severe portrait of his character and activity. His acceptance supports the authenticity of the parable. Early Christians would hardly have made up such a description of Jesus, even in a parable.

25:27 *(Luke 19:23)* For emphasis on the obligation to do good works, the question "And why did you not give . . . ?" (so Luke) becomes the strong declaration "It was necessary, therefore, that you deposit." Matthew likes οὖν (35,11), which replaces the interrogative διὰ τί. His omission of καί produces an asyndeton that adds vigor to the emphasis, and βαλεῖν (12,8) is more vigorous than Luke's ἔδωκας. The pluralizing of "money," despite the singular in v 18, agrees with the pluralizing of "on a table" (i.e., "in a bank"), so that it becomes "with the bankers." The slave had buried the coins of the talent collectively; he might have deposited them distributively.

Matthew likes to put ἐλθών as close to the beginning as possible (10,10); so he writes καὶ ἐλθὼν ἐγώ instead of Luke's κἀγὼ ἐλθών. ἐκομισάμην ἄν, "I would have received back," stands in place of Luke's ἄν . . . ἔπραξα, "I would have collected." But since the former verb occurs nowhere else in Matthew and the latter appears six times in Luke and thirteen times in Acts, but not at all in Matthew or Mark, Luke's verb looks editorial. τὸ ἐμόν, "what is mine" (1,2), replaces αὐτό, "it" (i.e., the money), for a parallel with τὸ σόν, "what is yours," which Matthew inserted in v 25. Unlike Luke, Matthew delays σὺν τόκῳ, "with interest," till the end of the clause to let the emphasis at the beginning rest entirely on the master, who represents Jesus the Coming One (cf. the comments on 3:11). As a whole, this verse means that the slave should at least have deposited the money in savings accounts that would have drawn interest from bankers' investments. Such a minimal action would have entailed no risk of the capital (see *m. B. Meṣ.* 3:11). Though the returns would have been low, especially in the slave's share, the master would have gained at least something.

25:28-29 (Luke 19:24-26) For reception of added reward Jesus singles out the slave with the best record. Thus that slave becomes an example to be followed. Typically, Matthew omits a narrative interruption by deleting "And he [the master] said to those present." The insertion of οὖν (35,11) makes the slothfulness of the slave the reason for the command to take away the talent from him and give it to the one who had ten talents (so also Luke, except for Matthew's substitution of talents for minas and an insignificant difference in word order). Again to avoid a narrative interruption and also to bring the two clauses containing "to him who has" alongside each other, and perhaps to keep from any implication that the master's— i.e., Jesus'—authority might be challenged, Matthew omits the protest "And they said to him, 'Master, he has ten minas.'" (Omission of the protest in the so-called Western text of Luke arises out of parallel influence from Matthew, for influence of this kind runs rife in the Western text— see the UBS for the text-critical evidence.) The following "I say to you" has to go, too, in order to bring together the clauses having "to him who has." Consequently, ὅτι changes to γάρ, a Mattheanism (62-63,15). The new conjunction expressly makes the following principle the reason for the foregoing command. In the statement of the principle, Matthew puts παντί after τῷ . . . ἔχοντι rather than vice versa (as in Luke) to gain a closer parallel with the next line. He adds "and he will have an abundance" after "it will be given," just as he did in an earlier statement of the principle (13:12; cf. Mark 4:25; Luke 8:18b; see the comments on 13:12). For a closer parallel with τῷ γὰρ ἔχοντι, the preposition ἀπό falls away from ἀπὸ δὲ τοῦ μὴ ἔχοντος, "from him who does not have." The omission makes τοῦ . . . μὴ ἔχοντος a genitive of possession, "what belongs to him who does not have," and leads to the addition of ἀπ᾽ αὐτοῦ, "from him," after καὶ ὃ ἔχει ἀρθήσεται, "even what he has will be taken away." The addition carries a certain pathetic emphasis and balances τῷ . . . ἔχοντι, "to him who has," at the start of the saying.

Since the slaves share their master's resources, we need not ask how the first slave can be called the one who has ten talents after he has already brought them to the master. Having and not having refer to good works and lack of good works; having an abundance and suffering the loss of the little that one has refer to reward and punishment. To say more is to run the risk of overinterpretation.

25:30 (Luke 19:27) Matthew entirely ignores the traditional ending of the parable, "But bring here these enemies of mine who did not want me to rule over them, and slaughter them in front of me." This omission is due to his earlier omission of the citizens' hating the man and sending an embassy after him to express the wish that he not be given rule over them. The first line of Matthew's substitute begins, "And the useless servant." It looks as though Matthew draws on the otherwise unparalleled tradition behind Luke 17:7-10, takes the humility of disciples' saying "We are useless servants" (Luke 17:10) after doing works of obedience, and transforms those humble words into the Lord's word of judgment for lack of good works! The continuation "Throw [him] out into the outermost darkness; in that place there will be weeping and gnashing of teeth" follows exactly the addition in 22:13 (see also 8:12; 13:42, 50; 24:51 with comments ad loc. for interpretation). Thus the parable closes on a threatening note concerning the punishment Jesus will mete out to disciples who falsify their profession by failing to do good works.

The Jesus who spoke of weeping and gnashing of teeth in the punishment of the wicked hereafter (see Luke 13:28 as well as the Matthean passages listed above) might well have portrayed the judge at the last judgment as a king who commands the slaughter of his enemies in front of him, despite modern sentiment to the contrary. In view of 13:41, 49; 25:31, we are probably meant to understand the angels as taking away the talent from the slothful slave, giving it to the slave with ten talents, and casting the slothful slave into the outermost darkness (cf. 24:31; Mark 13:27). So far as the parable as a whole is concerned, many find Luke's version highly edited, but the foregoing investigation shows that everything falls in place according to the known style of Matthew when we assume that he conflates Mark 13:34 and a tradition preserved without much revision in Luke 19:11-27. Therefore we have little evidence for reaching back to a parabolic point more original than the one occasioned by the wrong expectation of an immediate appearance of God's kingdom (so Luke). It lacks conviction to argue for Luke's fusing two different parables by saying that an additional reward for the first slave is meaningless after his appointment over ten cities. Such parabolic inconcinnities often carry an emphatic point by design. The much greater modesty of the amounts of money in Luke and the difficulty that though ten slaves receive a mina each, only three are called to account at the end, speak for a comparative lack of editing by Luke. Because of the responsibility loaded on the slaves, we might better call them "servants" (cf. their expecting a share of the profits). The talents do not refer to natural abilities; they symbolize opportunities to do good works.

510

The Criterion of Neighborly Love
at the Last Judgment
with Particular Reference to Demonstrating
True Discipleship Through Doing Charity
to the Persecuted Messengers of Jesus
25:31-46

25:31a Matthew himself is responsible for the description of the judgment of the sheep and goats. He takes from Jesus' sayings already used in 16:27 and 19:28 and goes on in his typical fashion with OT phraseology borrowed from Zech 14:5 and Dan 12:2. These materials are utilized according to the pattern of the parables of separation, also composed by him (13:24-30, 36-43, 47-50). His characteristic diction and parallelistic style appear everywhere in the passage. δέ sets the section off from the preceding. Mark 8:38, used with some revision in 16:27, provides "when the Son of man comes in his glory," except that Matthew brings in "the Son of man" from Mark's preceding clause, as he did also in 16:27, and changes "of his Father" (so Mark and 16:27) to "his" (cf. Luke 9:26). Thus the Father's glory becomes that of the Son of man. In the remainder of this section the Son of man's role as judge of the entire human race caps this high Christology. "And all the angels with him" comes from Zech 14:5. "And" has no counterpart in the MT, but agrees with the Targum, LXX, Peshitta, and Vulgate. In agreement with 16:27; Mark 8:38; Luke 9:26, "angels" interprets the "holy ones" in Zechariah's text (cf. 1 Thess 3:13). Matthew's "with him" agrees with the Targum, LXX, Peshitta, and Vulgate against "with you" in the MT (see Gundry, *Use of the OT* 142). Notably, the Son of man does not come with angels, as in 16:27; Mark 8:38; Luke 9:26; rather, they come with him, as in Zech 14:5, where the Lord God is subject (cf. Matt 13:39, 41, 49; 24:31).

25:31b-32a The following couplet of lines exhibits Matthew's parallelistic style. In v 31b τότε is a Mattheanism (66,17). The remainder, "he will sit on the throne of his glory," comes verbatim from Matthew's distinctive version of Jesus' saying in 19:28 and furthers the high Christology of the present passage (see the comments on 19:28). The first line of v 32 consists almost entirely of Mattheanisms: συναχθήσονται (10,10), ἔμπροσθεν (9,4), πάντα (63,25-26), ἔθνη (7,2), and the combination πάντα τὰ ἔθνη (1,2). Furthermore, these expressions make an evident and typically Matthean allusion to the OT, in particular to Joel 4(3):2, 11-12.

We can hardly restrict "all the nations" to professing disciples among all the nations. Such a restriction would violate Matthew's use of the expression elsewhere. But we can hardly suppose that he implies at least a formal conversion of all the nations—i.e., of everybody in the world—by the time the Son of man comes. Such a supposition would violate his indications that persecution lasts right up to the end, indeed, increases just before the end (10:22-23; 24:9, 30; cf. 10:14-15, 35-36; 22:5-7). We should therefore take this account as describing the judgment of all humanity. Thus the δέ in v 31a contrasts this general judgment with the foregoing parables dealing with true and false disciples in the church.

We may think of a divine passive in συναχθήσονται, "will be gathered," only with the understanding that angels carry out the divine will (cf. 13:41, 49; 24:31; 25:31).

25:32b-33 In the separation and the standing on the Son of man's right hand and left, Matthew treats us to another couplet of parallel lines. The verb "separate" echoes the parable of the good and bad fish caught in the same net and then separated (13:49). ὥσπερ belongs to Matthew's favorite vocabulary (6,3; see esp. the insertion in 25:14 at the start of the last section). The figure of the shepherd comes from Jesus' teaching (9:36; 26:31; John 10), perhaps with some encouragement from Ezekiel 34. The figure of sheep for God's people, though dominical, holds special appeal to Matthew (πρόβατον—6,2). Further Mattheanisms are evident in στήσει (4,6), μέν . . . δέ (15,1), and εὐωνύμων (1,2). Cf. 20:21, 23; 27:38 for traditional combinations of the right hand and left, which may have suggested the present figure to Matthew.

The shift from the neuter πάντα τὰ ἔθνη, "all the nations," to the masculine αὐτούς, "them," implies individual rather than national judgment (cf. 28:19-20). Palestinian shepherds commonly herded mixed flocks of sheep and goats, but separated the sheep and goats in the evening because sheep prefer the open air at night and goats need the warmth of shelter. The greater value of sheep and their white color suit them to stand for the saved. Because most people are right-handed, the right hand often symbolizes favor. Angels performed the separation in 13:41-43, 49-50. Here the Son of man himself does it. But the parables of separation in chap. 13 dealt with the separation of false disciples from true. The present account of the last judgment deals with separation of the righteous from the wicked in the whole human race. Therefore we have neither a contradiction nor a piece of evidence for use of pre-Matthean tradition.

25:34 In introducing the pronouncement to the sheep, Matthew uses several of his favorite terms: τότε (66,17), ἐρεῖ (18,9), and βασιλεύς (6,9). He especially likes to portray Jesus as king (cf. his distinctive ascription of the kingdom to the Son of man on the ground that since Jesus is God as well as the Son of man, he is the king in the kingdom of heaven just as much as the Father is—1:23; 13:41; 16:28; 20:21). That the Son of man will pronounce the blessing of his Father on the sheep shows the Father's association with him in ruling the kingdom. The pronouncement begins with a couplet of parallel lines and moves to its close with another. The first couplet reads, "Come, you blessed of my Father, inherit the kingdom prepared for you from the foundation of the world." Matthew likes δεῦτε (2,2), πατρός (22,13), and κληρονομήσατε (2,1). ἡτοιμασμένην echoes 20:23, where it occurred, as here, in the perfect tense, in conjunction with positions on Jesus' right and left, and in conjunction with Jesus' "kingdom" and "Father" (both inserted by Matthew). See also the distinctive perfect tense of ἡτοίμακα in 22:4. "For you" corresponds to "for whom" in 20:23 (cf. 5:3, 10; 19:14; 21:43 for the belonging of the kingdom to disciples). βασιλείαν holds an attraction to Matthew (18,12). And "from the foundation of the world" echoes 13:35, where he inserted a quotation of Ps 78:2. That quotation related to parables concerning the kingdom (cf. the mention of the kingdom here and the present allusions to the parables of separation in chap. 13). The inheritance of the sheep consists in the kingdom and is equivalent to eternal life (see v 46). Eternal life is portrayed as an inheritance to indicate that Jesus' disciples will be compensated for the dispossessions they suffered in their persecutions. Eternal life is portrayed as a kingdom to indicate that they will be compensated for their disfranchisement through persecution. The preparation of the kingdom ever since the creation of the world shows that persecuted disciples need not despair: their reward already exists, reserved for them. They suffer for a present reality, not for an uncertain hope.

The king cannot represent God the Father, for the king refers to God as his Father. Though the blessedness of the sheep comes from the Father, the Son pronounces the sentence of blessedness. Therefore Jesus the Son, not God the Father, is acting as the royal judge. Cf. the comments on 18:23; 20:2.

25:35-36 The γάρ introducing the reason for the favorable sentence just pronounced typifies Matthew's diction (62-63,15). At this point he begins to paraphrase Isa 58:7, which reads, "Is it not to share your bread with the hungry, and bring the homeless poor into the house; when you see the naked, to cover him; and not to hide yourself from your own flesh?" This verse belongs to a passage about fasting (see the comments on 4:2 concerning Matthew's special interest in fasting). To the distribution of food to the hungry Matthew adds the giving of drink to the thirsty. This addition produces parallelism and an allusion to the hospitality given by genuine Christians to a fellow disciple who is fleeing persecution (cf. 10:42). In Matthew's hands the unsheltered poor becomes an unsheltered stranger, again referring to a Christian refugee, whose nakedness comes over from Isaiah to indicate his poverty. Helping one's own relatives (so Isaiah) turns into visiting a disciple who has fallen sick and suffered imprisonment because of his labors as a witness of Jesus. With all of this cf. 10:9-14.

Parallelism prevails throughout Matthew's targum of Isa 58:7. Couplets of lines describe giving food to the hungry and drink to the thirsty, providing shelter for the stranger and clothing for the naked, and visiting the sick and the imprisoned. ἐδώκατε is a Mattheanism (8-9,10). See 14:16 on its combination with φαγεῖν. In 5:6 Matthew inserted a combination of hungering and thirsting, as here. ἐποτίσατε echoes 10:42 (cf. v 40 below). ξένος was distinctive in 27:7 (cf. vv 38, 43, 44 below). συνηγάγετε belongs to Matthew's favorite diction (10,10), and he inserted περιβάλετε in 6:31 (cf. vv 38, 43 below). φυλακή appeared once in a parable composed by Matthew (18:30) and once in an insertion (24:43).

Cf. T. Jos. 1:5-7 (probably influenced by the NT) and Gundry, Use of the OT 142-43. On the meaning "receive as a guest" for συνηγάγετε, see BAG, s.v. συνάγω 5. Besides Isa 58:7, see also Ezek 18:7; Tob 4:16; 2 Esdr 2:20; Sir 7:35; 2 Enoch 9. The interpretation of Matt 25:31-46 in terms of general humanitarianism rests on an oversight of Matthew's drawing Isa 58:7 through the grid of the discourse on Christian mission (chap. 10; cf. 2 Cor 11:23-27; 2 Tim 1:16-17; 4:13). That there will be heathen who never encountered a messenger of the gospel does not concern Matthew, if it even crosses his mind. He is interested only in evidence of genuine discipleship where the gospel has been preached, and he assumes that the gospel will have gone to all nations (cf. 24:14; 28:19). Therefore it is not convincing to argue for the humanitarian interpretation from the need for a universal norm such as neighborly love.

25:37-39 The introduction to the response of the sheep complements v 34a and includes the Mattheanisms τότε (66,17), ἀποκριθήσονται . . . λέγοντες (2,4; cf. the reversal of verb and participle—29,6), and δίκαιοι (9-10,7-6). The last of these identifies the sheep not only as those characterized by the surpassing righteousness Jesus demands in his disciples' conduct (see esp. 5:17-48; 28:20), but also as teachers of righteousness (see the comments on 10:41). In accord with Matthew's Christology κύριε emphasizes Jesus' lordship (34,15). Except for a shift from the verb "gave" with the supplementary infinitive "to eat" (so v 35) to ἐθρέψαμεν, "we fed" (cf. 6:26), the phraseology of vv 37-39 echoes Matthew's paraphrase of Isa 58:7 (vv 35-36) and again exhibits his parallelistic style. Indeed, his putting "But when . . . ?" between the first and second couplets and between the second and third couplets (vv 38a and 39a), and "or" between the lines of each couplet, confirms our having seen pairs of lines in vv 35-36. ἤ is a Mattheanism (32,12).

25:40 The introduction to the king's response contains further Mattheanisms in ὁ βασιλεύς (6,9) and ἀποκριθείς . . . ἐρεῖ (29,6), which echo v 37a in ἀποκριθείς and v 34a in ὁ βασιλεὺς ἐρεῖ plus a dative. The list of Mattheanisms goes on: ἀμὴν λέγω ὑμῖν (15,8), ἐφ' ὅσον (see 9:15 for an insertion of this phrase), ὅσον considered by itself (5,6), ἐποιήσατε (bis—19,19), ἑνί (24,7), ἀδελφῶν (11,8), and ἐλαχίστων (2,3). "To one of these littlest brothers of mine" echoes Matthew's insertion of "one of these little ones" in 10:42. That insertion dealt with giving a drink of cold water in the name of a disciple to one who comes preaching the gospel and fleeing persecution (cf. 18:6, 10, 14). The king's identifying himself with the littlest of his brothers rests on 10:40: "he who receives you receives me." Therefore, though Jesus' brothers include all those who do the will of his Father (12:48-50), "one of these littlest brothers of mine" refers to those who carried the gospel from place to place as they fled from persecution (cf. 10:23; and 23:8; 28:10 with 28:16-20). To show the hospitality of faith to such a disciple is to demonstrate the genuineness of one's own discipleship.

"These littlest brothers" can hardly denote an elite corps of Christian preachers in the church; for all those who do the will of the Father belong to the brotherhood (12:48-50) and "the little ones" refers especially to obscure people in the church, who are easily despised and prone to stray but whose low position ecclesiastical leaders must themselves assume (18:1-14). Furthermore, all true disciples bear witness. "One" does not reflect a Semitic indefinite pronoun. On the contrary, it lends emphasis, as elsewhere in Matthew's distinctive uses of the word. The escalation of "little" (10:42; 18:6, 10, 14) to "littlest" furthers the emphasis. Accordingly, even the littlest brother in the church represents Christ. "These" seems at first to distinguish the littlest brothers from the righteous. But the statement invites the righteous to look at their fellows; i.e., the demonstrative simply points to the large group not only in which each of the righteous stands, but also in which each will find the church's little people, through whom he ministered to Christ himself. See "Immanuel" in the Topical Index on Matthew's stressing Jesus' presence with the disciples; and cf. Acts 16:30-34.

25:41 "Then he will say also to those on [the] left" echoes v 34a. But Matthew omits "the king" as unnecessary to repeat (esp. after v 40), adds "also" to introduce the second group, substitutes "left" for "right" to distinguish the second group, and omits "his" as needless (cf. 20:23; Mark 10:40). See the comments on v 34a for Mattheanisms, and cf. vv 31b, 37a. πορεύεσθε, "Go," is a favorite of Matthew (13,10) and ominously contrasts with δεῦτε, "Come," in the favorable sentence pronounced to the righteous (v 34b). "From me" contrasts starkly with the king's identifying himself with the righteous and stems from the condemnatory sentence "Depart from me" in 7:23, a passage recently recalled in 25:10-12 (cf. Luke 13:27). "You who are accursed" takes the place of "you who work lawlessness" (7:23; cf. Luke 13:27) and contrasts with "you who are blessed" (v 34). "Into the eternal fire" echoes 18:8, where the same phrase appeared in the middle of a discussion of the little ones, a discussion just reflected in the king's explanation to the righteous (v 40). Cf. 3:10; 7:19 and Matthew's penchant for πῦρ (2,4). ἡτοιμασμένον, "prepared," echoes v 34b (see the comments ad loc.). "For the Devil" makes another allusion to the parables of separation, in particular the parable of the tares, which Matthew composed (see 13:39). The added mention of the Devil's angels represents another Mattheanism in that these angels contrast with the angels of the Son of man in the parable of the tares (13:41) and elsewhere in Matthew— always uniquely (see the comments on 18:10). The kingdom is prepared for the righteous (v 34), the eternal fire for the Devil and his angels (v 41). The righteous inherit the kingdom (v 34); the accursed depart into what was not prepared for them. Both the diction and the contrasts color the verdict with sadness and horror. Cf. Rev 19:20; 20:10, 14-15; *1 Enoch* 10:13.

25:42-44 Matthew puts the reason for the condemnation (vv 42-43) in parallel lines drawn from vv 35-36, but negated (see the earlier comments for interpretation and identification of Mattheanisms). The introduction to the response of the accursed (v 44) follows the pattern of v 37a (again see the earlier comments). But Matthew omits "to him" and substitutes "they also" for "the righteous." The response follows the pattern of vv 37b-38, shortened by detailing only the needs and summarizing the ways of meeting those needs: "and we did not serve you" (cf. the distinctive occurrences of διάκονος, "servant," in 22:13; 23:11). Again for the sake of condensation, Matthew neither repeats "When?" as he did in vv 37-38, nor pairs the expressions by alternating "or" and "but," as in vv 37-38. Rather, he uses only his favorite ἤ, "or" (32,12), as he races toward the end of the passage.

The confession "Lord" has nothing in the previous lifetime to back it up. The accursed do not claim evidence of discipleship, as the false prophets did in 7:22, but only express their ignorance that they have ever faced the king and failed to meet his needs.

25:45 The introduction to the king's final statements begins with τότε (66,17) and ἀποκριθήσεται ... λέγων (see the comments on v 40a). The further and emphatic Mattheanism "Truly I say to you" (15,8) echoes v 40b. "Insofar as you did not do [it] to one of these littlest [of my brothers], neither did you do [it] to me" reflects v 40cd, with additions of "not" and "neither" and an ellipsis of the king's brothers. See the earlier comments for Mattheanisms and interpretation.

25:46 Because of "these" and "the righteous," the king no longer seems to be speaking in the final verse of the discourse. We should have expected him to use "you" in a continued address to the accursed. The two lines of the verse display typically Matthean parallelism, here of the antithetic kind (cf. John 5:29). Moreover, Matthew is characteristically borrowing OT phraseology, that of Dan 12:2. But he transposes the order of phrases in Daniel to bring the going away into eternal punishment next to the foregoing sentence of condemnation. ἀπελεύσονται belongs to his favorite diction (14,11). "Into eternal punishment" echoes v 41, with the substitution of κόλασιν from Dan 12:2 in place of τὸ πῦρ, "the fire." See Gundry, *Use of the OT* 143, concerning the derivation of κόλασιν from κολάζω, "prune off," equivalent to חָרַף, from which Daniel's לַחֲרָפוֹת, "to reproach," comes. δέ signals the antithesis. οἱ δίκαιοι reflects the next verse in Daniel, echoes v 37 in the present passage, and represents Matthew's special vocabulary (9-10,7-6). "Into eternal life" comes from Dan 12:2 (cf. Matt 19:16, 29).

We might have expected Matthew to write βληθήσονται, "will be thrown"; but the switch from πῦρ, with which he regularly uses that verb (see 3:10; 7:19; 13:42, 50; 18:8 [bis]), to κόλασιν leads him to a verb that will double for eternal punishment and eternal life—viz., ἀπελεύσονται. The parallel between eternal punishment and eternal life forestalls any weakening of the former. Though αἰώνιον may hyperbolically describe things which by nature last a long time but not forever, the lack of need to make such a qualification in the present passage leaves us with the meaning "everlasting." It would be a mistake to exclude the chronological sense of the term from its larger qualitative meaning, for the latter includes the former. The comments on vv 31-46 have shown that Matthean use of the OT and dominical tradition accounts for the data of the passage much more satisfactorily than dependence on *1 Enoch* 90:20-27 or, generally, on the Parables of Enoch.

THE DISCIPLES' UNDERSTANDING THAT JESUS MUST BE CRUCIFIED
26:1-5 (Mark 14:1-2; Luke 22:1-2)

26:1 The first verse of chap. 26 is unparalleled and presents us with the last occurrence of the formula that closes each of Jesus' five discourses in Matthew. The opening words, "And it came to pass [that] when Jesus finished," exactly match those in 7:28; 11:1; 13:53; 19:1. "These words" echoes 7:28; 19:1. But here Matthew inserts his characteristic and emphatic "all" (πάντας—63,25-26) and omits any new setting forth in further ministry. The insertion and omission indicate that chaps. 23-25 form Jesus' final discourse (cf. 28:20). "All" may reflect Deut 32:45 and carry forward Matthew's portrayal of Jesus as the greater Moses (see "Moses parallel Jesus" in the Topical Index). The addition "he said to his disciples" helps transform the following words (v 2) from a mere editorial note of time (so Mark and Luke) into another prediction by Jesus concerning his crucifixion. The transformation effects a portrait of Jesus as the Teacher. The verb for speaking and τοῖς μαθηταῖς (αὐτοῦ) occur together as an insertion in 9:37; 26:1, 26, besides four shared instances. And by itself μαθηταῖς represents Matthew's special interest in discipleship (31,5).

See the comments on 7:28-29 concerning the Matthean character of the formula that ends Jesus' discourses. The added "all" hardly makes Jesus' "words" cover all five dominical discourses in Matthew. "These" limits the "words" to chaps. 23-25, and the agreement of the initial words of the formula with those in its preceding four occurrences disfavors a blanket meaning.

26:2 (Mark 14:1; Luke 22:1) The transformation of the temporal note into a directly quoted prediction of the passion causes Mark's δέ to disappear. Matthew adds "You know that," however, in order to revive his portrayal of the disciples as those who understand (see esp. chaps. 13-17 passim). οἴδατε is a favorite of his (7,2; cf. his fondness for γινώσκω—8,2). "After two days" advances to a position ahead of "the Passover," and "the Unleavened Bread" disappears. In this way Matthew gets rid of a redundancy. He also gains a more accurate statement, for strictly speaking only the Passover followed after two days. The week-long Festival of Unleavened Bread did not begin till the day after Passover (see Lev 23:5-6; Num 28:16-17). γίνεται substitutes for Mark's ἦν. The substitute echoes ἐγένετο in the preceding verse and suits the change from an editorial note to a direct quotation. Matthew now inserts "and the Son of man is being given over to be crucified." This insertion makes the disciples know not only the date of the Passover (a matter of course), but also the event of Jesus' crucifixion, because they have understood his earlier predictions of the passion, particularly those in 17:22-23 and 20:18-19, from which Matthew takes the phraseology of the present insertion. Typically, the insertion also exhibits parallelism. Both the coming of the Passover and the giving over of Jesus to be crucified are expressed with the futuristic present tense. Matthew likes παραδίδοται (6,3) and σταυρωθῆναι (3,0). The latter echoes the insertion in 20:18-19 and highlights the disciples' knowledge by indicating that they know even the mode of Jesus' execution. And just as advancing "the Son of man" in 16:13 made that title blanket the following passage, so also the present insertion of the title makes the passion fulfill Jesus' predictions concerning the fate of the Son of man. Matthew's entire account of the passion becomes the record of a fulfillment.

26:3 (Mark 14:1; Luke 22:2) To begin his description of the Sanhedrin's plot against Jesus, Matthew characteristically replaces Mark's καί with τότε (66,17). Though τότε might mean "at the time Jesus was speaking about his crucifixion," it probably means "right after Jesus spoke about his crucifixion" and implies that the Sanhedrin's plot began to fulfill (and perhaps was effected by) the prediction. For an allusion to Ps 31:14(13) "gathered together" takes the place of "were seeking" (cf. John 11:47 and see Gundry, *Use of the OT* 56). Not only does the new verb illustrate Matthew's habit of borrowing OT phraseology (see also v 4); it also belongs to his favorite vocabulary (10,10; see esp. 22:34, 41; 26:57; 27:17, 27, 62 for distinctive references to the gathering together of Jesus' enemies; cf. Ps 2:2; Acts 4:25-26). Matthew keeps "the chief priests," but drops "the scribes" in favor of "the elders of the people." The dropping of the scribes agrees with the lack of scriptural, theological discussion in this meeting of the Sanhedrin. Substituting the elders of the people enables Matthew to distinguish the Jewish masses from their leaders. The distinction further enables him to concentrate the blame for Jesus' crucifixion on the leaders, who are persecuting the church at the time of Matthew's writing, and excuse the masses as deceived by their leaders. As much as possible, then, Matthew protects his earlier portrayal of the crowds who followed Jesus as symbolizing the many Gentiles who were to become disciples; and he avoids offending the Jewish masses, whom he wants to make into Christian disciples (cf. the comments on 10:23). "The elders of the people" occurs in 21:23; 26:3, 47; 27:1, always as an insertion. In all but the present passage Matthew takes the elders from Mark. As here, however, the people come from Matthew himself (cf. 2:4 with comments ad loc.). The replacement of "were seeking" with "gathered together" leads Matthew to insert "into the court [or 'palace'] of the high priest" as an indication of the place of meeting. This insertion anticipates Mark 14:54, 66. The further insertion, "who was called Caiaphas," contains a Mattheanism in λεγομένου in the sense "called" (10,2) and forms somewhat of a parallel with v 14. Matthew will insert "Caiaphas" also in v 57 (cf. Luke 3:2; John 11:49; 18:13, 14, 24, 28).

The chief priests and elders of the people were based in Jerusalem and come to the fore in the passion narrative. Up to this point, the far-flung scribes and Pharisees have occupied center stage as Jesus' antagonists.

26:4 (Mark 14:1; Luke 22:2) The insertion καὶ συνεβουλεύσαντο, "and they planned together," revives and extends the allusion to Ps 31:14(13) and, with v 3, makes a typically Matthean couplet of parallel lines. The prefix συν-, "together," does not appear in the LXX of Ps 31(30):14, but stems from the parallel with συνήχθησαν in the first line of the couplet. The added reference to planning already contains the idea of πῶς, "how," at the beginning of the next clause in Mark. By substituting a telic ἵνα, Matthew spotlights the malevolent purpose of the Jewish leaders. The insertion of Caiaphas at the close of the preceding verse almost necessitates the replacement of "him" with "Jesus" to avoid confusion. But Matthew likes to mention Jesus' name (80,12). The remainder of the verse, δόλῳ κρατήσωσιν καὶ ἀποκτείνωσιν, "[in order that] they might seize [Jesus] with stealth and kill [him]," comes from Exod 21:14. Matthew omits Mark's ἐν before δόλῳ for closer conformity to the LXX and escalates the participle "seizing" to a finite verb, adds καί, and has a pair of parallel verbs, "seize and kill," as a result. This revision stresses the treachery of the Jewish leaders.

26:5 (Mark 14:2; Luke 22:2) Mark's γάρ changes to δέ for a contrast between the resolve to seize and kill Jesus and the resolve to avoid an uproar among the people (cf. the reference to "stealth" in the preceding verse). The contrast emphasizes the treachery of the Jewish leaders yet again. μήποτε yields to ἵνα μή for an antithetic parallel with ἵνα lacking the negative at the end of the preceding verse. Again, the antithesis highlights the treachery. See 5:29, 30; 7:1 for other insertions of ἵνα μή. γένηται substitutes for Mark's ἔσται and follows its subject (contrast Mark's word order) in reflection of a similar change and word order in v 2. "Of the people" becomes "among the people" for a parallel with "in the festal assembly." Both "among" and "in" go back to ἐν.

Presumably Jesus would have left Jerusalem with the other pilgrims from Galilee right after the festival, and those pilgrims had already flocked into Jerusalem. Therefore μὴ ἐν τῇ ἑορτῇ needs to be translated "not in the festal assembly." So the Sanhedrin did not resolve to seize Jesus before or after the festival considered as a period of time, but resolved to seize him apart from the festival considered as an assembly of people—yet during the festal period (cf. Luke 22:6; John 7:10-11).

JUDAS'S BARGAIN TO BETRAY JESUS AS A RESULT OF JESUS' DEFENDING THE LARGE EXPENDITURE FOR HIS ANOINTING
26:6-16 (Mark 14:3-11; Luke 7:36-50; 22:3-6; John 12:1-8; 13:2, 27)

26:6 (Mark 14:3; Luke 7:36; John 12:1-2) Matthew follows Mark 14:3-9. Discussion of the great differences in Luke 7:36-50 belongs in commentaries on Mark and Luke. John 12:1-8 offers little, if anything, for elucidation of Matthew's text. Matthew begins his account of Jesus' anointing by changing Mark's καί to δέ. The change establishes a contrast between the preceding plot of the Sanhedrin against Jesus' life and the following "good work" performed on Jesus by an unnamed woman (v 10; see John 12:2-3 for her identification as Mary the sister of Lazarus and Martha). As often, Matthew substitutes Jesus' name for Mark's αὐτοῦ (80,12). He also advances the name to the head of the sentence for a Christological emphasis (cf. 2:1). Mark's ὄντος changes to γενομένου in reflection of similar revisions in vv 2 and 5. The references to Bethany and the house of Simon the leper stay unchanged except for omission of Mark's definite article with "house."

26:7 (Mark 14:3; Luke 7:37; John 12:3) To emphasize Jesus' dignity, ἦλθεν moves forward and characteristically gains the prefix προσ- (38,6; see the comments on 4:3; 8:14). These changes lead to the insertion of "him" and the delay of Mark's "as he was reclining [at a meal]." Matthew keeps "a woman having an alabaster [flask] of perfume," but omits νάρδου πιστικῆς, "of pure [or pistachio] spikenard," and substitutes βαρυτίμου, "very expensive," or πολυτίμου, "very valuable," for Mark's πολυτελοῦς, "very costly." The substitute shows that Matthew is interested only in the costliness of

519

the perfume (cf. his having been a publican). We should probably favor the reading βαρυτίμου as original. It is supported by B W *f*¹ *f*¹³ *pm* as well as the Byzantine family, and by Matthew's having inserted βαρύς in 23:4, 23. The simple adjective appears nowhere else in the gospels and the compound adjective nowhere else in the NT. βαρυτίμου literally means "of heavy price" and contrasts with the cheap τιμήν of thirty pieces of silver that the Sanhedrin paid Judas for Jesus (v 15; 27:3-10, the latter an insertion by Matthew). The omission of "breaking the alabaster [flask]" and addition of "and" avoid Mark's asyndeton and make the two clauses of v 7 parallel in structure. After κατέχεεν Matthew drops αὐτοῦ in anticipation of adding αὐτοῦ ἀνακειμένου. He also inserts ἐπί before τῆς κεφαλῆς in partial imitation of Septuagintal style, and finally takes up Mark's earlier genitive absolute κατακειμένου αὐτοῦ, but reverses the word order and substitutes ἀνα- for κατα-. Mark's verbal form never occurs in Matthew (though it appears four times in Mark and three in Luke), but Matthew inserted his also in 9:10; 22:10, 11.

Matthew's liking πολύς (23,1) and distinctive use of πολυτίμου in 13:46 favor the originality of πολυτίμου in the present passage. But the considerations adduced above favor βαρυτίμου over πολυτίμου, which may have arisen from scribal reminiscence of 13:46 as well as from Mark's parallel πολυτελοῦς. καταχέω usually takes a genitive object. As here, however, ἐπί follows it in Job 41:15 LXX. In the LXX we usually read ἐπιχέω, often followed by ἐπί and an accusative. Possibly, Matthew's ἐπί reflects Septuagintal usage and the following genitive represents Mark's influence.

26:8 (Mark 14:4; Luke 7:39; John 12:4) To introduce the indignation of some present, Matthew adds the nominative participle ἰδόντες (10-11,7) and characteristically identifies Mark's indefinite "some" as "the disciples" (31,5). The identification makes Jesus' subsequent statement a furthering of the disciples' knowledge (cf. 13:12 and the comments on v 2). Mark's periphrastic ἦσαν . . . ἀγανακτοῦντες becomes the synonymous ἠγανάκτησαν. "To one another" drops out, and the Mattheanism λέγοντες (61,23) comes in, probably for the sake of an implication that the disciples spoke silently within themselves, not aloud to one another. Such an implication would give point to Matthew's insertion of "knowing" in v 10; indeed, that insertion will confirm our estimate of the reason for the change here. "Why did this waste of the perfume take place?" (so Mark) shortens to "Why this waste?"

26:9 (Mark 14:5; Luke 7:39; John 12:5-6) "The perfume" drops out. "For over three hundred denarii" shortens to "for much." πολλοῦ is a Mattheanism (23,1) and perhaps a compensation for the replacement of Mark's πολυτελοῦς in v 7. The definite article disappears from "the poor" (cf. John 13:29). These abbreviations and the further omission of Mark's statement "And they were scolding her" reduce attention to the disciples' misstatement and shield Matthew's favorable portrayal of them as knowledgeable. The omission of their scolding the woman also links with Matthew's making their complaint a silent speaking within themselves.

26:10 (Mark 14:6; Luke 7:40-44; John 12:7) The limitation to silent speaking has the purpose of enhancing Jesus' deity by representing him as capable of hearing their inwardly spoken thoughts (see the comments on 9:35; 16:7-8). Thus Matthew inserts γνούς, "knowing" (8,2). The result is a parallel between the disciples' knowledgeability (v 2, unique in this respect) and that of Jesus. Like master, like disciples. To the statement that Jesus spoke, Matthew adds "to them" to insure that the following words are taken as a teaching of the disciples, a furthering of their knowledge (cf. the comments on v 8). "Leave her alone" falls away to avoid a misimpression that the disciples should have nothing to do with her. She, too, belongs to the church (cf. Matthew's emphasis on community in chap. 18). In Jesus' question why they are causing her trouble, Matthew delays αὐτῇ to balance the words on either side of the verb and emphasize κόπους. He then replaces αὐτῇ with its referent, "the woman" (see v 7), and adds γάρ to the next clause. The addition is typical (62-63,15) and makes that clause a justification of the preceding question and a parallel to the statements in vv 11 and 12, which also have γάρ. In other words, for three reasons the disciples should not cause the woman trouble: (1) the nobility of her deed; (2) the constancy of having the poor with them versus Jesus' impending departure; and (3) the nature of the anointing as a preparation for burial. In contrast with Mark but in conformity to many other passages in Matthew, καλόν follows its noun ἔργον (see 3:10; 7:17, 18, 19; 13:8), perhaps for emphasis on the noun (cf. Matthew's fondness for ἐργ-: 6,7). Mark's "in me" becomes "to me" (cf. BDF, 1 n. 2, §§205-6, 218).

26:11 (Mark 14:7-8; John 12:8) After the statement "For the poor you have with you always," Matthew omits "and whenever you wish, you can do well to them." The omission brings the next clause, "but you do not always have me," into the immediate proximity of having the poor always and thus effects an antithetic parallel. The omission also forestalls a wrong deduction that doing well to the poor is a matter of desire rather than obligation (cf. 6:1-4). The further omission of "What she had [we would say 'could'] she did" also contributes to the antithetic parallel. See Gundry, Use of the OT 56, concerning a loose quotation of Deut 15:11 in the first part of this verse.

26:12 (Mark 14:8; Luke 7:44-46; John 12:7) Matthew again inserts γάρ (62-63,15; see the comments on v 10). Jesus does not say whether the woman intended her action to have the significance that he attributes to it, i.e., an anointing of his body for burial. "This [woman] . . . [by] putting" replaces "she anticipated" because the preceding omission of "What she had she did" deprived Mark's present expression of its base. βαλοῦσα belongs to Matthew's favorite diction (12,8). In view of the contrast between the price of the perfume and the price of Jesus' betrayal (see the comments on v 7), perhaps βαλοῦσα contrasts with Judas's throwing the thirty pieces of silver into the treasury (27:6, unique to Matthew). The participle requires Matthew to change μυρίσαι, "to anoint," to τὸ μύρον τοῦτο, "this perfume." The demonstrative pronouns modifying the woman (understood) and the perfume parallel each other. Since "my body" has lost the infinitive it depended on, it changes to "on my body," which parallels "on "his head" in v 7 (so Matthew alone). In fact, we might wonder whether not only the omission of Mark 14:8a but also the desire for this parallel prompted the changes at the very beginning of the present verse. Mark's εἰς τὸν ἐνταφιασμόν, "for the preparation for burial," becomes πρὸς τὸ ἐνταφιάσαι με, "in order to prepare me for burial," to allow the addition of ἐποίησεν from Mark 14:8a. This addition compensates for the earlier omission of Mark 14:8a. πρός + an articular infinitive typifies Matthew's style (3,2).

26:13 (Mark 14:9; Luke 7:47-50) Mark's continuative δέ drops out because Matthew ordinarily uses that conjunction in an adversative sense and no contrast follows here. "Truly I say to you, wherever the gospel is proclaimed in the whole world, also what this [woman] has done will be mentioned in memory of her" (so Mark) remains unchanged, with three exceptions: (1) the insertion of "this" to identify "the gospel" with "this gospel of the kingdom" mentioned in 24:14 and explicated throughout Matthew (cf. the demonstrative pronouns in vv 12 [bis] and 13c); (2) the merely stylistic substitution of ἐν ὅλῳ τῷ κόσμῳ for Mark's εἰς ὅλον τὸν κόσμον (cf. the comments on v 10); and (3) the advancing of λαληθήσεται ahead of its subject to parallel the order of verb and subject in the preceding clause.

Does "this" point to Jesus' death as implied by the reference to burial in v 12? Probably not, for the similarity of the phraseology in 24:14 favors Matthew's having the earlier saying in mind. Denial that Jesus foresaw a worldwide mission for his disciples will lead to omitting "in the whole world" or interpreting the saying without respect to the church. According to such an interpretation, angels will proclaim divine triumph at the end of the age (cf. Rev 14:6-13) and God will remember the woman at the last judgment (rather than those who hear the gospel, including this story, remember her when they hear the disciples preach). But see the comments on 24:14; 28:19-20 concerning the possibility of Jesus' foreseeing—indeed, inaugurating—a worldwide mission.

26:14 (Mark 14:10; Luke 22:3) The replacement of καί with Matthew's beloved τότε (66,17) relates Judas's striking a bargain to betray Jesus to the preceding anointing of Jesus. In other words, Jesus' authoritative interpretation of his anointing now starts to be worked out. The advance of Mark's ἀπῆλθεν and its change to πορευθείς typify Matthew's style (8,4). "One of the twelve" comes forward to stress Judas's treachery. In contrast with Mark, Matthew identifies Judas, first as one of the twelve, only then by name (cf. Matthew's concern with Christians' betraying one another in persecution—24:10, an insertion). To ὁ, delayed till now, Matthew characteristically adds λεγόμενος in the sense "called" (10,2); this addition makes a parallel with a similar insertion in v 3 concerning the high priest Caiaphas. Judas Iscariot and Caiaphas, the treacherous disciple and the persecuting high priest, stand together. Because Matthew substituted "going" for "went away," he adds "said" for a needed finite verb.

Matthew stresses the fulfillment of Jesus' prediction, not Judas's motives, which remain obscure. Disappointment in Jesus' failure to satisfy political expectations of the Messiah, jealousy, avarice, and loss of face (cf. John 12:4-8) are possible motives. On the term "Iscariot," see the literature cited in the comments on 10:2-4.

26:15 (Mark 14:10-11; Luke 22:4-5) The addition of "said" makes the following a direct quotation instead of an editorially descriptive narrative such as we read in Mark and Luke. Matthew composes "What do you want to give me . . . ?" (not in Mark or Luke) for a parallel with the following line. But he not only wants to satisfy his desire for parallelism; he also wants to set the stage for giving thirty pieces of silver to Judas (not in Mark or Luke) by making Judas ask for money, as Judas does *not* in Mark or Luke. The ascription of greed to Judas intensifies his guilt and casts in a bad light church members who follow his example of betrayal. θέλετε belongs to Matthew's favorite diction (18,8) and compensates for his earlier omission of Mark 14:7b, where θέλετε occurred. δοῦναι comes from Mark 14:11, where Matthew will replace it in favor of an allusion to the OT. Cf. 20:14, also a Matthean composition, for another combination of θέλω and δίδωμι. "And I" represents a Mattheanism (κἀγώ—5,3) and replaces Mark's "in order that" because of the change to direct quotation and as part of the parallel between this and the preceding, inserted line. Consequently, "he might give [him] over" becomes "I will give [him] over," and "to them" becomes "to you." Putting "to you" ahead of the verb and "him" after the verb contrasts with Mark's word order and stems from Matthew's desire to match more nearly the position of "to me" in his preceding, parallel line.

In order to move as quickly as possible to his distinctive OT allusion, Matthew omits "hearing, they rejoiced and. . . ." "They weighed out" replaces "they promised to give" for an allusion to Zech 11:12 (cf. Matt 27:9-10, unparalleled). "To him" stays and the allusion to Zech 11:12 revives in the substitution of "thirty pieces of silver" (cf. Exod 21:32) for Mark's "money" (see Gundry, *Use of the OT* 143-44). Not only does Matthew gain a particular sum of money in fulfillment of Zechariah's prophecy; but also Judas gets the money on the spot (cf. his throwing it back in 27:5—so Matthew alone). In Mark he gets only a promise (cf. Luke).

26:16 (Mark 14:11; Luke 22:6) Matthew inserts ἀπὸ τότε, "from then on" (see the comments on 11:12-13). Just as in 4:17 this phrase indicated the beginning of Jesus' Galilean ministry and in 16:21 indicated the beginning of his teaching the disciples about the coming passion and resurrection, so here it indicates the beginning of the passion-cum-resurrection itself. As in Luke, εὐκαιρίαν, "favorable opportunity," replaces πῶς . . . εὐκαίρως, "how . . . conveniently." This substitute enables Matthew to smooth out Mark's slightly awkward construction with "in order that he might give him over" (cf. Luke's telic articular infinitive) instead of "he might give him over."

THE PREPARATION OF THE PASSOVER AND THE OBSERVANCE OF THE LORD'S SUPPER AS OBEDIENCE TO JESUS' COMMANDS
26:17-29 (Mark 14:12-25; Luke 22:7-23; John 6:51-59; 13:1, 21-30; 1 Cor 11:23-26)

26:17 (Mark 14:12; Luke 22:7) Matthew leaves Mark's "day" to be understood and omits "when they were sacrificing the Passover." The latter omission probably stems from awareness that his Jewish reading audience did not need the explanation. προσῆλθον replaces λέγουσιν to emphasize Jesus' dignity (38,6; see the comments on 4:3; 8:14). "His" no longer modifies "the disciples" because replacing "to him" with "Jesus" (80,12) makes obvious whose disciples are in view. The replacement spotlights Jesus as the lordly figure approached. Matthew's putting the subject before the indirect object contrasts with Mark and makes for a smoother word order. The addition of λέγοντες characterizes his style (61,23) and compensates for the earlier substitution of προσῆλθον for λέγουσιν. Mark's ἀπελθόντες vanishes. Though Matthew likes it (14,11), here it is unnecessary (cf. a similar omission in v 14) and detracts from the point he wants to stress, viz., the preparation of the Passover in obedience to Jesus' command (cf. esp. v 19). Jesus' dominance comes out also in Matthew's changing "in order that you may eat the Passover" to "for you, to eat the Passover." σοι goes with the main verb ἑτοιμάσωμεν. Thus in Matthew the emphasis does not fall on preparation for eating (so Mark), but on preparation for Jesus.

Because Exod 12:18 prescribes eating only unleavened bread at the Passover meal on the evening of Nisan 14, the Jews exceeded the command in Exod 12:15; Lev 23:6; Num 28:17 to remove all leaven on Nisan 15 (the first day of the Feast of Unleavened Bread) by removing it during the daytime of Nisan 14 (see *m. Pesah.* 1:1-4). This exceeding of the OT command apparently gave rise to an improper calling of Nisan 14 (the day of Passover) the first day of the Feast of Unleavened Bread (see Josephus *Ant.* 17.9.3 §213; 18.2.2 §29; 20.5.3 §§106-9; *J.W.* 5.3.1 §§98-99; cf. the alternation of the Feast of Unleavened Bread and the Passover in *J.W.* 6.9.3 §§420, 422 and contrast *Ant.* 3.10.5 §§248-49). When combined with the Passover, the Feast of Unleavened Bread lasts for eight days according to Josephus *Ant.* 2.15.1 §317 (though J. Jeremias [*Eucharistic Words* 17-18] thinks of the eighth day as added to the end of the Feast of Unleavened Bread and supposes an error of translation in the calling of Passover the first day of Unleavened Bread). See also Str-B 1. 987-88; *TDNT* 2. 902. In Matthew as well as Mark the disciples prepare the Passover on the first day of Unleavened Bread. Hence, Matthew's omitting the reference to sacrificing hardly has the purpose of distinguishing the preparation of the Passover before sunset on Nisan 14 from the eating of the Passover after sunset when, strictly speaking, the first day of Unleavened Bread began. Cf. Josephus *J.W.* 6.9.3 §§420, 422. As in Mark, the Last Supper is a Passover meal. Discussion of the date and character of the Last Supper belongs in commentaries on Mark and John.

26:18 (Mark 14:13-14; Luke 22:8-11) In keeping with the omission of "going away" in the preceding verse, "And he sends two of his disciples" drops out here. As a result, Matthew has the disciples in general, not just two of them, go prepare the Passover in obedience to Jesus' command (cf. v 19). In this way he magnifies obedience as a sine qua non of discipleship. ὁ δέ sets off Jesus' answer more clearly than Mark's καί does. "He said" (cf. Luke) replaces Mark's historical present "he says." The omission of "to them" generalizes the following command in accord with Matthew's including the disciples in general. The command to go into the city stays undisturbed. But "to so-and-so" replaces "and there will meet you a man carrying a jar of water. Follow him, and wherever he enters. . . ." As is typical of Matthew's practice, the replacement reflects OT phraseology (see Ruth 4:1; 1 Sam 21:3[2]; 2 Kgs 6:8). Omission of Mark's vivid details concerning the man, the jar of water, and his entering the city keeps attention on the disciples' obedience to Jesus' command, avoids a following of anyone but Jesus on the part of the disciples, and makes "so-and-so" not the man with a jar of water but "the master of the house." Matthew's καί comes from the first clause of Mark 14:14, otherwise omitted. "To him" replaces "to the master of the house" because the large, foregoing omission has obliterated Mark's distinction between a slave (the man with the jar of water) and his master. The replacement also avoids the rivalling of Jesus, the primary authoritative figure in Matthew, by the master of the house. As often, Matthew omits Mark's recitative ὅτι. Luke agrees with the omission.

"The teacher says" comes from Mark without revision. But prior omission of Mark's reference to the master of the house leads to replacing "Where is my guest room . . . ?" with "My time is near." Matthew likes καιρός (6,1), and 24:32-33 may have suggested ἐγγύς ἐστιν. The statement stresses Jesus' divine foreknowledge. "Where I may eat the Passover" becomes "With you [σε—singular] I am celebrating the Passover." Thus Jesus' polite question (so Mark and Luke) becomes an authoritative pronouncement, and the Passover meal comes to include the unnamed owner of the premises as one with whom Jesus will celebrate the Passover. By this means Matthew shows that Jesus instituted the Lord's Supper during the Passover for the church at large, represented by the unnamed person, not just for the twelve. ποιῶ is a Mattheanism (19,19) and often appears with the Passover in the LXX (Exod 12:48; Num 9:4, 6, 10, 13, 14; Deut 16:1; Josh 5:10; 4 Kgdms 23:21; 1 Esdr 1:6; 2 Esdr 6:19).

Cf. Jesus' using "my hour" in John and Judas's seeking εὐκαιρίαν, "opportunity" (v 16). Matthew's use of καιρός elsewhere hinders our seeing a specially eschatological meaning here, even though the concept of nearness appears often in eschatological passages (see, e.g., Isa 13:6; Zeph 1:7; Rev 1:3; 22:10). All three synoptists imply that Jesus had previously made arrangements.

26:19 (Mark 14:15-16; Luke 22:12-13) Because Matthew omitted Mark's references to a houseowner and a guest room, "And he will show to you an upstairs room—large, furnished, ready" disappears. Because Matthew included all the disciples in the preparation and inserted "With you" to include "so-and-so" in the celebration, "and there prepare for us" also disappears (cf. Luke's omitting "for us" despite his lacking Matthew's reasons). These omissions cause all the emphasis to fall on the following statement concerning the disciples' obedience. "Did" represents a Mattheanism (ἐποίησαν—19,19) and replaces "went out and went into the city and found. . . ." After the pattern of the distinctive expressions in 1:24; 21:6; 27:10, "as Jesus commanded them" takes the place of "just as he said to them." Thus enormous emphasis falls on the disciples' exact obedience to Jesus' command rather than on the confirmation of Jesus' words about a man with a jar of water. We now see clearly that from the very start Matthew omitted that man in order to emphasize obedience. "And they prepared the Passover" fits the emphasis and therefore comes into Matthew without change.

26:20 (Mark 14:17; Luke 22:14) For a contrast between preparation and dining δέ replaces καί. Matthew reaches into Mark's next verse to get "he was reclining at meal" as a substitute for "he comes." Since the coming of the disciples does not appear in Matthew, neither does the coming of Jesus. In view of Matthew's inserting "disciples" with "twelve" in 10:1; 11:1; 20:17, perhaps we should here favor the text-critical addition of "disciples" (31,5) after "with the twelve." The omission in part of the textual tradition should then be regarded as due to Mark's influence (but see the UBS for strong evidence favoring the originality of the omission).

26:21 (Mark 14:18) Because "reclining at meal" was anticipated in v 20, Matthew takes from Mark only "and while they were eating." Jesus' name drops out because of its recent insertion in v 19. Mark's allusion to Ps 41:10(9), "he who eats with me," drops out despite Matthew's fondness for OT allusions. Perhaps this happens because of his unhappiness with the regrettable participation of false disciples, such as Judas, in the Lord's Supper (cf. his wrestling with the problem of the mixed church in 13:24-30, 36-43, 47-50). Or Matthew may consider the allusion to Ps 41:10 redundant in view of v 23; Mark 14:20.

26:22 (Mark 14:19) The addition of καί avoids Mark's asyndeton. "To be sorrowful" advances, turns into the participle "being sorrowful," and gains the Mattheanism σφόδρα, "exceedingly" (5,2). The resultant phrase echoes "And they became exceedingly sorrowful," which Matthew inserted after Jesus' second prediction of the passion (17:23). Also, stressing the disciples' sorrow over the announcement that one of them will betray Jesus puts them in a good light. The substitution of εἷς ἕκαστος, "each one," for Mark's εἷς κατὰ εἷς, "one by one," is a stylistic improvement (see P. Walters [Katz], *The Text of the Septuagint* [ed. D. W. Gooding; Cambridge: Cambridge University Press, 1973] 310). The insertion of εἰμι fills out Mark's ellipsis in the question "I'm not the one, am I?" (cf. 14:27). Characteristically, Matthew adds κύριε to emphasize Jesus' authority and deity (34,15).

26:23 (Mark 14:20; Luke 22:21) The preceding question makes Matthew's insertion of "answering" appropriate. The combination ἀποκριθεὶς εἶπεν typifies his style (29,6). "To them" falls out in a generalizing omission reminiscent of v 18. Mark's "one of the twelve" also drops out, perhaps because it seems redundant after v 21c, but more probably because Matthew does not want to give a handle to those who would take an easygoing view of false profession in the church (cf. the comments on the omission of Mark 14:18d in v 21). Perhaps something of the same desire lies behind the turning of Mark's present participle ὁ ἐμβαπτόμενος, "he who dips," which might be taken as iterative and therefore conducive to laxity, into the aorist participle ὁ ἐμβάψας, "he who dipped." The further change of the participle from middle voice, "for himself," to active voice requires the addition of τὴν χεῖρα, "the [his] hand" (cf. Luke). The substitution of "in" for Mark's "into" may stem from Matthew's reasoning that one dips into the sauce in a dish, but not into the dish itself, or from a desire to conform the preposition to the participial prefix ἐμ-, "in." Adding "this one will betray me" fills out the sentence, comes from v 21, and reemphasizes the treachery of betrayal in Christian ranks (see 24:10).

Does Matthew's addition of τὴν χεῖρα imply a violation of protocol through refusal to wait for the Messiah to dip first? Cf. 1QSa 2:11-22. Reference to the common bowl aggravates the element of deceitfulness and heightens the pathos of betrayal by a supposed friend.

26:24 (Mark 14:21; Luke 22:22) The immediately preceding addition eliminates the need for Mark's "because," which therefore disappears. Its disappearance makes v 24 a parallelistic restatement instead of a reason for v 23. The Son of man's going, the reference to Scripture, and the pronouncement of woe on the betrayer stay unchanged except for the addition of ἤν, "would have been," in the last clause. Cf. 1 Enoch 38:2; b. Ḥag. 11b.

26:25 Again to highlight the danger of false profession and the treachery of those who betray their fellow disciples to persecutors, Matthew composes the whole of v 25. δέ sets the following question of Judas opposite the preceding pronouncements of Jesus. ἀποκριθείς . . . εἶπεν exhibits Matthew's style (29,6) and echoes the insertion in v 23. "Judas, who betrayed . . ." comes from 10:4; 26:46, 48; 27:3 (see esp. 10:4 for the participle, as here, in contrast with the finite verb in Mark 3:19). "Him" follows as a matter of course. "I'm not the one, am I?" comes from v 22, where only Matthew expressed the verb. "Rabbi" suits his diction (3,0), portrays Jesus as teacher (see esp. 23:8 with comments), and anticipates Judas's addressing Jesus as Rabbi in the Garden of Gethsemane (26:49). The historical present λέγει with asyndeton characterizes Matthew's style (21,6). He will insert "You said [it]" again in 26:64 (cf. 27:11). The present insertion heightens the guilt of Judas by implying that he already knows the affirmative answer to his own question, which therefore lacks sincerity. Woe to the hypocrite!

In view of 23:8, we ought not to think that Matthew rejects "Rabbi" as a Christological title by putting it on the lips of Judas and his like. G. Dalman (The Words of Jesus [Edinburgh: T. & T. Clark, 1902] 309-10) and I. Abrahams (Studies in Pharisaism and the Gospels [1924; reprinted, New York: Ktav, 1967] 2. 1-3) favor the use of אָמַרְתָּ, "you said [it]," as a qualified affirmative. Since the corresponding Greek expression is Matthew's insertion and can hardly bear a negative meaning in context or in the light of 23:8, doubts concerning the meaning of the Aramaic expression need not trouble us here.

26:26 (Mark 14:22; Luke 22:19) Mark's καί changes to δέ to contrast Jesus' conversation with Judas and the Words of Institution. In the reference to taking bread and blessing it, Matthew characteristically inserts "Jesus" (80,12). The mention of that name brings Jesus back to center stage after the insertion of Judas's name (v 25). The insertion "and" pairs "taking" and "blessing." "Broke" stays, but Matthew reduces "he gave" to the participle "giving" to gain a parallel with the introduction to the words over the cup (v 27a). There, only one finite verb appears among participles. The reduction leaves all the emphasis on Jesus' command, introduced by "he said." Mark's "to them" becomes "to the disciples." The substitute stems from Matthew's interest in discipleship (μαθητής—31,5) and may contrast with the betrayer Judas, inserted in v 25. To the command "Take," Matthew adds "eat" in order to complement "Drink" in the words over the cup, where he will turn a description of what the disciples did into a command by Jesus that his disciples drink (cf. the comments on 14:15).

Cf. v 21 and Exod 16:15. See G. J. Bahr in *NovT* 12 (1970) 181-202 for a discussion of the Passover liturgy and a collocation of primary sources concerning it. Though Jewish blessings of this sort had God as their object—hence the meaning "praise" for "bless"—here the bread is the expressed object of "taking" and the implied object of "he broke" and "giving." Therefore εὐλογήσας refers to invoking God's blessing on the bread, i.e., asking him to make the bread a means of blessing to those who eat it. This understanding is confirmed by Luke 9:16; 1 Cor 10:16.

26:27-28 (Mark 14:23-24; Luke 22:20) As in v 26, Matthew inserts "and" between participial phrases—here between "taking a cup" and "giving thanks"—in order to pair them. λέγων is a favorite of his (61,23). Its insertion causes the following description in Mark, "and they all drank from it," to turn into Jesus' command, "Drink from it, all of you." (Luke and Paul [1 Cor 11:25] also have λέγων, but at this point they lack a reference to drinking.) Thus Matthew lays huge emphasis on Christians' obligation to eat and drink the Lord's Supper in obedience to Jesus' commands. Even the Lord's Supper becomes part of the law of Christ.

The insertion of λέγων leads to omission of Mark's "And he said to them." Consequently, Jesus' words continue without interruption. Matthew adds γάρ (62-63,15) to give the command to drink, which is unique to his gospel, a reason. In the description of Jesus' blood as "being poured out concerning many," ὑπέρ gives way to περί. Matthew's preposition reflects sacrificial terminology in the LXX. There, περί often occurs with ἁμαρτίας, "sin" (cf. Rom 8:3; Gal 1:4 v.1.; Heb 5:3; 10:8, 18; 1 Pet 3:18; 1 John 2:2; 4:10). The advance of περὶ πολλῶν to the attributive position leaves room to add "for remission of sins" from Mark 1:4. In 3:2 Matthew omitted the phrase. Thus he transfers forgiveness from John's baptism of repentance to Jesus' sacrifice. The benefit of that sacrifice comes on those who obey Jesus' commands, such as the one to eat and drink the Lord's Supper (cf. 1:21 with comments; Eph 1:7; Col 1:14). Perhaps the promise of forgiveness in Jeremiah's prophecy concerning a new covenant (Jer 31:34) prompted the shift (cf. the use of Jer 31:15 in Matt 2:18).

See the comments on 20:22 for references concerning the cup as symbolic of death and judgment. Cf. *m. Pes.* 10:6, and see Gundry, *Use of the OT* 57-59, on allusions to Exod 24:8 in the blood of the covenant, to Isa 53:12 in the pouring out and "many," and to Jer 31:34 in the forgiveness of sins. See Isa 53:12, too, for the last item. "Many" echoes 20:28 and means "the elect" (see also Dan 11:33; 12:2; and 1QS passim). Pouring out blood connotes violent death (see Matt 23:35; Luke 11:50-51; Acts 22:20; Rom 3:15 [= Isa 59:7]; Rev 16:6), which alone can have the value of a sacrifice (cf. Heb 9:22). The present participle ἐκχυννόμενον probably rests on an Aramaic participle used for the future. Despite his stressing obedience to Jesus' commands, Matthew bases forgiveness on the pouring out of Jesus' blood. Therefore obedience is evidential of true discipleship, not meritorious of forgiveness.

26:29 (Mark 14:25; Luke 22:18) Matthew is partial to ἀμήν (15,8), but here it yields to δέ for a contrast between the disciples' drinking and Jesus' not drinking. Mark's ὅτι vanishes (cf. part of Luke's textual tradition). "From now on" rests on the Mattheanism ἀπ' ἄρτι (3,0; cf. Luke's synonymous ἀπὸ τοῦ νῦν) and replaces οὐκέτι, "no longer," which occurs only twice in Matthew, but seven times in Mark and four in Luke. Matthew's phrase always refers to the church age. Delaying the phrase till after πίω balances οὐ μή before the verb (so also Luke). In reminiscence of v 26 and especially v 28, Matthew inserts "this" before "the fruit of the vine." Similarly, in reminiscence of Immanuel, "God with us" (1:23), he adds "with you" after "that day when I drink it new" (see "Immanuel" in the Topical Index and the comments on v 36). "The kingdom of God" becomes "the kingdom of my Father" in a typically Matthean emphasis on God's fatherhood and Jesus' divine sonship. The presence of Jesus with his disciples here and now insures his presence with them in the coming kingdom.

Cf. Isa 32:12 LXX; Hab 3:17 LXX; *m. Ber.* 6:1. We do not know whether Jesus drank on this occasion. Speculations that he was going to abstain from wine because he thought the end so near that the next meal with his disciples would be the messianic banquet, or because he wanted to intercede for Israel on account of the nation's rejection of him, do not have the probability of the simplest explanation: he refused to feast because of sorrow over his imminent separation from the disciples (cf. Matthew's inserting "with you"). "In the kingdom" needs to be understood in the temporal and dynamic sense, "when the rule is established." See the comments on 5:6 concerning the messianic banquet.

PETER AS AN EXAMPLE OF PRAYERLESSNESS THAT WILL LEAD TO DENIAL OF JESUS IN TIME OF PERSECUTION
26:30-46 (Mark 14:26-42; Luke 22:31-34, 39-46; John 12:27; 13:36-38; 14:31; 16:32; 18:1)

26:30-32 (Mark 14:26-28; Luke 22:39) Mark's references to the singing of the Hallel (Psalms 113–118)—a custom at the Passover meal—and to Jesus' and his disciples' going to the Mount of Olives remain undisturbed. Typically, Matthew substitutes τότε (66,17) for καί and drops the recitative ὅτι from the introduction to Jesus' statement. In that statement, the addition of ὑμεῖς typifies Matthew's style (15,3) and emphasizes the dire nature of Jesus' prediction that all the disciples will be led to sin. The further addition "in me" echoes 11:6; 13:57, anticipates 26:33, and provides a Christological reason for the persecution that will lead the disciples to sin. The still further addition "during this night" anticipates Mark 14:30, where the subject matter deals with Peter's denials of Jesus. By importing the phrase here, Matthew makes those denials a paradigm of all the disciples' being led to sin in their forsaking Jesus at his arrest. In other words, Peter warningly represents weakness under persecution.

The Mattheanism γάρ replaces Mark's ὅτι with "it is written." In Jesus'

529

quotation of Zech 13:7 (cf. Matt 26:56; John 16:32) Matthew keeps the smiting of the shepherd unchanged, but advances διασκορπισθήσονται to start both lines of the quotation with a verb. He also adds "of the flock" after "the sheep" in agreement with LXX^A. Though suspected of being conformed to Matthew's text, Codex Alexandrinus probably represents an early reading known and used by Matthew; for in all likelihood a scribal conforming of LXX^A to Matthew would have included changing the aorist imperative πάταξον (so LXX^A) to the future indicative πατάξω (so Matthew in agreement with Mark). Possibly Matthew followed the textual tradition represented by LXX^A in order to gain a parallel between τὸν ποιμένα, "the shepherd," and τῆς ποίμνης, "of the flock." Furthermore, he may have wanted a figurative allusion to the church (cf. 16:18; 18:17; Ezek 34:31; see further J. de Waard, *A Comparative Study of the Old Testament Text in the Dead Sea Scrolls and the New Testament* [STDJ 4; Leiden: Brill, 1965] 37ff.; Gundry, *Use of the OT* 25-28). Insignificantly, Mark's ἀλλά yields to δέ in Jesus' statement that he will precede the disciples to Galilee after his resurrection.

By changing the imperative "Smite" in the MT and LXX to "I will smite," Jesus suggests that God's action lies at the base of his passion (cf. "it is necessary" in the first prediction of the passion—Mark 8:31; Matt 16:21; Luke 9:22). In Mark 14:28; 16:7, seeing Jesus does not refer to the parousia in accord with Mark 14:62 (so that Matthew might be viewed as turning the parousia into a resurrection appearance); for if προάξω means *leading* the disciples to Galilee, they would hardly see him coming on the clouds of heaven. He would be on the road in front of them! Neither would they see him coming on the clouds if προάξω means *precede*, because he would have arrived in Galilee ahead of them. See the comments on 28:7 for the meaning "precede." Since Mark 14:28; 16:7 cannot refer to a still awaited parousia, the failure of Mark's short text to describe a fulfillment of the prediction that Jesus would precede the disciples to Galilee becomes so serious that we need to suppose a truncation of Mark's original ending. Here higher criticism comes to the aid of textual criticism. But Matthew knew Mark's original ending (see the comments on 28:9-20 and W. G. Kümmel, *Promise and Fulfilment* [2nd ed.; SBT 1/23; London: SCM, 1961] 77-79).

26:33 (Mark 14:29; Luke 22:33) Matthew replaces ἔφη with ἀπο-κριθείς . . . εἶπεν (29,6). His omitting "even" in the reference to all the disciples' falling into sin tones down the contrast between Peter and the other disciples in favor of Peter's representing them. The insertion "in you" echoes and parallels the insertion "in me" in v 31. The replacement of ἀλλ' οὐκ, "but not," with οὐδέποτε, "never," exhibits a favorite word of Matthew (5,0) and emphasizes Peter's false confidence. The addition σκανδαλισθήσομαι fills the ellipsis in Mark and makes the parallelism more obvious.

26:34 (Mark 14:30; Luke 22:34; John 13:38) In the introduction to Jesus' answer, ἔφη αὐτῷ with asyndeton replaces καὶ λέγει. Matthew's expression is typical of his style (6,1). He omits Mark's σύ to tone down as much as possible the distinction between Peter and the other disciples and make Peter represent them (see the comments on v 33 and cf. Matthew's insertion of the second person plural pronoun in v 31). The needless and awkward "today" drops out before "this night," to which Matthew prefixes a temporal ἐν, "during" (so also v 31). In anticipation of Mark 14:72 ἤ drops out of Mark's expression πρὶν ἤ δὶς ἀλέκτορα φωνῆσαι, "before [the] rooster crows twice." The omitted word is unnecessary, for πρίν by itself means "before." As in Luke and John (and a part of Mark's textual tradition probably influenced by the other gospels), Mark's "twice" also drops out, because Mark will not indicate when the rooster crowed the first time, but only imply the first crowing. Here and in v 74, then, Matthew mentions only the more important crowing after the third denial. Perhaps Luke and John show influence from Matthew in their similar omissions. The reversal of Mark's and Luke's με ἀπαρνήσῃ, "me you will deny," makes for smoothness and shows up in John, too.

26:35 (Mark 14:31) Typically, the historical present λέγει with asyndeton (21,6) replaces Mark's "But he was saying" and parallels the asyndetic ἔφη in v 34 (so Matthew alone). The omission of "vehemently" avoids any implication that Peter showed disrespect to Jesus. Matthew inserts Peter's name (8,1) to bring him forward as the representative disciple. Especially with forms of λέγω, as here, the insertion typifies Matthew's writing (see the comments on 18:21). The addition "to him" follows naturally after "says" and links with the address to Jesus in the subsequent quotation.

"If" becomes "even if" to compensate for omitting "even" from Peter's similar statement in v 33. There the word would have set Peter opposite the other disciples, against Matthew's giving Peter a representative role. Here the word does not set Peter opposite them, but stresses his false confidence and martyrdom as a possible consequence of true discipleship (cf. the comments on v 33). In his statement that he will die with Jesus, if necessary, σοί advances ahead of the verbal form it depends on. This advance establishes a parallel with the next line, where σε will precede its verb, and requires shifting σύν from the beginning of συναποθανεῖν (so Mark) to a position ahead of σοί. Mark's δέ drops out because Matthew's normal use of it as an adversative does not fit the lack of contrast, indeed, the positive comparison. ὡσαύτως, "in the same way," yields to ὁμοίως, "similarly," perhaps for a nice distinction between sameness and similarity. Typically, Matthew inserts "the disciples" to stress Peter's representing disciples in general (31,5). "Were saying" changes to "said."

26:36 (Mark 14:32; Luke 22:39-40) By replacing καί with his favorite τότε (66,17), Matthew relates the disciples' prayerlessness, especially Peter's, to the foregoing prediction of falling into sin. The one fulfills the other. "They come" changes to "comes" (cf. Luke) in conjunction with Matthew's characteristic insertion of "Jesus" (80,12). Before that insertion there is another, viz., "with them," which recalls Matthew's portrait of Jesus as Immanuel, "God with us" (1:23; cf. 26:29). In the identification of Gethsemane, the replacing of Mark's "the name of which [was]" with λεγόμενον, "called," typifies Matthew's diction (10,2). The insertion of "Jesus" makes αὐτοῦ, "his," fall away from "the disciples."

The word αὐτοῦ reappears in its adverbial sense "here" and substitutes for Mark's synonymous ὧδε in the command to sit. Despite Matthew's fondness for ὧδε (7,1), he wants to compensate for omitting "his" and gain an allusion to Gen 22:5: "Sit here [αὐτοῦ in the LXX] . . . and I and the lad will go yonder." In accord with his usual practice Matthew adds ἄν or οὗ (the textual tradition is divided) to Mark's ἕως. With the subjunctive this expression means "till" in the sense "as long as." ἀπελθών is a Mattheanism (14,11). Matthew's inserting it prepares for the following and anticipates v 42 (cf. Luke 22:41). The meaning "going away" makes natural the further insertion of "there" (ἐκεῖ—16,6).

26:37 (Mark 14:33) The reduction of "he takes along" to "taking along" shows Matthew's fondness for introductory nominative participles. It also lets the emphasis fall on Jesus' sorrow and distress. The substitution of "the two sons of Zebedee" for "James and John with him" makes Peter, the only one named, stand out as the representative disciple. "To be sorrowful" replaces "to be alarmed" for a parallel with "very sorrowful" in the next verse. Matthew shows some liking of λυπεῖσθαι (2,1).

26:38 (Mark 14:34) As in v 36 and elsewhere many times, "Then" replaces "and" in the introduction to Jesus' expression of sorrow. To the command "Stay here and keep awake" Matthew adds "with me" as a counterpart to Jesus as "God with us" in vv 29 and 36. Furthermore, the addition makes Jesus' staying awake to pray an example to be followed.

See Gundry, *Use of the OT* 59, concerning Jesus' probable allusions to Pss 42:6(5), 12(11); 43:5; Jonah 4:9 (cf. Num 11:14-15; Judg 16:16; 3 Kgdms 19:4; Sir 37:2; 51:6). The comparable OT passages suggest that because of his sadness Jesus wanted to die peacefully in Gethsemane. Alternatively, his sadness had almost reached the point of killing him (cf. his asking that the cup pass away from him). Some think that the command to watch has eschatological overtones and that Jesus believed the period of final tribulation to be starting with his passion. If we allow for his inaugurating the disciples' worldwide mission, however (see the comments on 24:14; 28:19-20), the command to watch deals solely with his passion and may reflect the Jews' regarding the Passover celebration as ended when sleep overpowered the celebrants. It may also imply Jesus' hoping that God would intervene during the celebration (cf. the alarm, distress, and prayers of Jesus and Jewish hopes of redemption at the time of the Passover). Did Jesus fear that the disciples were killing the chance of divine intervention by ending the celebration through going to sleep? See *m. Pesaḥ.* 10:8; *b. Pesaḥ.* 120b; D. Daube, *The New Testament and Rabbinic Judaism* (London: Athlone, 1956) 332-35; D. E. H. Whiteley in *SE* 1 (1959) 111-12.

26:39 (Mark 14:35-36; Luke 22:41-42) Mark's imperfect tense ἔπιπτεν, "he was falling [or 'began to fall']," becomes the aorist ἔπεσεν, "he fell." Despite Matthew's liking the phrase "on the ground" (8,2), it changes to "on his face," which reflects OT language (Gen 17:3, 17; Num 14:5; 16:4; etc.), recalls the same insertion in 17:6, and better suits "praying." Again Matthew gets rid of Mark's imperfect tense, this time by changing προσηύχετο, "he was praying [or 'began to pray']," to προσευχόμενος, "praying," and ἔλεγεν, "he was saying," to his favorite λέγων (61,23—so also Luke). "That, if possible, the hour might pass away from him" (so Mark) drops out and leaves προσευχόμενος and λέγων as parallel participles. The omission of Jesus' hour is due to Matthew's inserting "the hour has already passed away" in 14:15 (see the comments ad loc.). That Luke agrees with the omission despite not having Matthew's reason for it suggests influence from Matthew.

The Aramaic ἀββά, "Father," drops out as unnecessary before its Greek translation (so also Luke). Mark's arthrous nominative of address ὁ πατήρ becomes the more proper anarthrous vocative πάτερ (so also Luke), to which Matthew adds μου. "My Father" on the lips of Jesus typifies Matthew's emphasis on Jesus' divine sonship (7,2). Matthew has delayed "if it is possible" (Mark 14:35), but now brings it in to replace "all things [are] possible for you." That Luke also has a conditional clause at this point again suggests Matthean influence. "Let [this cup] pass away" replaces Mark's and Luke's "take away," once more to compensate for omission of the last clause in Mark 14:35. Even the shifting of ἀπ' ἐμοῦ to a position in front of τὸ ποτήριον τοῦτο is due to Matthew's conflating the latter halves of Mark 14:35 and 36. Mark's ἀλλ' yields to πλήν (cf. the insertion of πλήν in 11:24 to avoid ἀλλά in two successive clauses). Yet again Luke agrees with Matthew against Mark. Twice the Mattheanism ὡς (23,8) replaces Mark's colloquial τί.

Unless the synoptics offer us a collocation of prayers and sayings spoken by Jesus on various occasions (cf. John 12:27; 14:30-31; 18:11; and other Johannine passages concerning Jesus' hour), Peter, James, and John presumably sat close enough to hear what he prayed before they dozed off repeatedly. It is easier to think so than it is to think that early Christians invented the story or—if the rest of the story is historically true—that they invented the prayer in the story by constructing it with the help of the Lord's Prayer. Jesus' prayer in Gethsemane violates the pietistic serenity we should expect early Christians to have attributed to Jesus. This consideration also militates against the view that the synoptics offer a collocation of prayers and sayings spoken earlier, for in the Johannine passages mentioned above we do not discover the depth of despair that causes the synoptic Jesus to ask his Father to remove the cup, if possible. In the OT the cup is a figure of suffering punishment (Pss 11:6; 75:9[8]; Isa 51:17, 22; Jer 25:15; 49:12; 51:7; Ezek 23:31-34; Hab 2:15-16; Zech 12:2; cf. Rev 14:10; 16:19; 17:4; 18:6). Jesus' use of the figure therefore suggests a vicarious suffering of punishment. Was Jesus shrinking, then, not from death as such, but from the sacrificial kind of death he had predicted for himself? Even so, we dare not tone down his shrinking. Cf. the comments on 19:26 concerning possibility with God. Matthew could hardly have expected his readers to take πλήν in the asseverative sense "indeed" rather than in its usual adversative sense "nevertheless." The asseverative sense would be awkward here and is doubtful elsewhere. Therefore the explanation given above stands firm.

26:40 (Mark 14:37; Luke 22:45-46) Matthew adds "to the disciples" to "And he comes" for a complement to his making Jesus go away from the disciples in v 36. The addition also exhibits his special interest in μαθητάς (31,5) and helps make the present story emphasize that constant prayer is necessary to true discipleship. Yet again Luke agrees with Matthew. Since Peter's sleeping is obvious, Matthew's Jesus does not ask, "Simon, are you sleeping?" That question gives way to the Mattheanism οὕτως (18,5) in the question "So you were able to keep awake with me one hour, weren't you?" Mark's singular "you" has become plural despite the specification of Peter as the addressee. Thus Matthew conforms to the third person plurals earlier in the verse and the second person plurals in v 41 and makes Peter represent all disciples. "With me" is an insertion that parallels an identical insertion in v 38 (see the comments ad loc. for interpretation).

26:41 (Mark 14:38; Luke 22:46) The command to keep awake for prayer comes over from Mark without change. In the clause "lest you go into [i.e., succumb to] testing" Matthew prefixes a second εἰς τὸ ἔλθητε in order to conform Jesus' prayer more exactly to the prayer he taught his disciples (cf. καὶ μὴ εἰσενέγκῃς ἡμᾶς εἰς πειρασμόν, "and do not bring us into testing," a Matthean insertion in the Lord's Prayer—6:13). In this way Matthew establishes a parallel in which Jesus exemplifies his own law of prayer. The statement about the readiness of the spirit to pray and the weakness of the flesh in falling asleep reads as it does in Mark.

See Gundry, Use of the OT 59-60, on a probable allusion to Ps 51:14(12). In both the psalm and the present text we should think of the human spirit rather than God's Spirit (see R. H. Gundry, Sōma in Biblical Theology [NTSMS 29; Cambridge: Cambridge University Press, 1976] 110-11).

26:42 (Mark 14:39) Mark's "And" drops out as unnecessary before "again." Matthew inserts "a second time" because of his earlier insertion of "going away" (v 36), which anticipated "going away" in the present verse. Since he is about to quote Jesus' second prayer rather than stop with a summarizing reference to it, "the same statement" disappears after "he prayed." His favorite λέγων (61,23) then replaces Mark's εἰπών. In the first clause of the second prayer, "My Father, if it is not possible [that] this [cup] pass away," Matthew conflates the first two clauses of the first prayer, including the features peculiar to his version (see the comments on v 39).

The earlier adjective δυνατόν, "possible," turns into the verb δύναται, "is possible." Matthew prefers the verb (13,0). "Not" is added to prepare for the insertion "unless I drink it." ἐὰν μή is a Mattheanism (7,1; see also the comments on 18:2-3). "Drink" echoes Jesus' usage in 20:22, 23; 26:27, 29 (bis). "Let your will come to pass" reflects the thought of the last two clauses in Jesus' first prayer (v 39), but takes its phraseology from the Lord's Prayer in Matthew's version (cf. the insertion of 6:10b as a link with Jesus' teaching the law). The particular form γενηθήτω and the noun θέλημα belong to Matthew's special diction (5,0; 3,1). Again, then, he makes Jesus an example of prayer and obedience to God's will.

26:43 (Mark 14:40) In contrast with Mark's word order, "coming" moves forward, perhaps to parallel the position of "he comes" in v 40, perhaps to shift "again" from "coming" to "he found" and stress Jesus' finding the disciples asleep, perhaps to hint that Jesus is the Coming One (see the comments on 3:11-12). These possibilities are compatible with each other. In the explanation that the disciples' eyes were heavy, Matthew changes καταβαρυνόμενοι, "being weighted down," to βεβαρημένοι, "weighted," for stylistic improvement. Mark's statement that "they did not know what they might answer him" drops out because it is inimical to Matthew's portrayal of disciples as knowledgeable and understanding (see esp. chaps. 13–17).

26:44 At best Mark only implies a third prayer by Jesus (see Mark

14:41), but Matthew composes a direct description. Behind the composition lies the purpose of reemphasizing Jesus' example in keeping awake to pray. Such prayer results in not going into a test, i.e., not wilting under persecution by failing to do God's will because of the cost. Jesus' three prayers are antithetically parallel to Peter's three denials of Jesus, which will result from failure to keep awake in prayer. ἀφείς, "leaving," belongs to Matthew's special diction (12,5). Its redundancy with "going away" serves to stress Jesus' displeasure with sleepy prayerlessness. "Again going away he prayed a third time" comes from v 42 with the necessary change of "a second time" to "a third time" and a delaying of this phrase till the end of the clause to insure that readers construe the phrase with "prayed" rather than, or at least more than, with "going away." The need for prayer dominates Matthew's editing. See further the comments on v 42. "Speaking the same statement" comes from Mark's reference to Jesus' second prayer (Mark 14:39), compensates for Matthew's omitting the phrase in v 42, and stresses Jesus' example of submitting to the Father's will (see Matthew's distinctive wording in v 42). The redundancy of a second "again" in the present verse not only illustrates Matthew's fondness for πάλιν (8,4), but also adds more weight to the emphasis on Jesus' example of staying awake and praying.

26:45-46 (Mark 14:41-42) By omitting Mark's ἀπέχει, "he [Judas] is receiving his pay in full," and inserting καί in the last clause, Matthew gains three parallel clauses, each having a pair of verbs connected with καί. We will see that he has further reasons for these revisions. As often, τότε replaces Mark's καί; and "to the disciples" replaces "the third time" after "he comes" because Matthew inserted "the third time" in the preceding verse and wants a parallel with "he comes to the disciples" in v 40. This reference to the disciples typifies his diction (31,5) and reminds Christian readers that the story is a warning to them.

The words καθεύδετε τὸ λοιπὸν καὶ ἀναπαύεσθε come over from Mark without change (except for the omission of τό in a v.1.). Since Mark's ἀπέχει implies the uselessness of further prayer now that Judas is receiving his pay in full, καθεύδετε and ἀναπαύεσθε need to be taken as imperative in Mark: "Sleep on and rest." The command to get up and go then marks a transition due to Judas's approach. Despite Matthew's liking ἀπέχει (1,3), he omits it here because according to v 15 Judas received his money at the striking of the bargain—in contrast with a mere promise or agreement (so Mark and Luke) and in contrast with the present tense of Mark's ἀπέχει. The earlier payment in Matthew robs the praying of its point in Mark, viz., that God might prevent, if possible, the payment to Judas that would result in betrayal. The center of gravity moves to Jesus' request that God's will be done (see esp. Matthew's insertion in v 42d). The loss of ἀπέχει shifts the meaning of καθεύδετε and ἀναπαύεσθε from a command to sleep on and rest because of the uselessness of further prayer (so Mark) to a rebuking question or accusation in the indicative mood: "Are you sleeping on and resting?" or "You are sleeping on and resting!" (cf. Mark 14:37). Matthew's concern to emphasize staying awake for prayer makes him resist a command to sleep rather than pray. In his gospel, then, the following command to get up and go not only relates to Judas's approach, as in Mark, but also rises out of disgust with the disciples' sleepy prayerlessness.

"Behold" comes to the head of the next sentence, where it emphasizes the whole, not just the Son of man's betrayal (as in Mark). This advance and the replacement of Mark's "has come" with "is near" set up a parallel between "Behold, the hour is near" and "Behold, the one giving me over is near" (cf. v 46b). In Matthew, then, the hour is near, but it arrives only when Judas comes (contrast Mark). The advance of "Behold" leads to the insertion of "and" where Mark has "Behold." παραδίδοται and ὁ υἱὸς τοῦ ἀνθρώπου switch places in Matthew for conformity to 17:22; 20:18; 26:2 (an insertion), 24. In the announcement "Behold, the one giving me over is near," ἤγγικεν comes from its last position in Mark to second position. This advance completes the parallel between vv 45c and 46b (cf. the order of words in 3:2; 4:17; 10:7).

Mark's ἀπέχει occurs often in the papyri for full receipt of payment. The frequency of this usage and its obviousness in the context of the Sanhedrin's promise to give Judas money invalidate other suggestions. The present tense implies that Judas receives his pay as he fulfills his part of the bargain, not before. "Sinners" may refer to Gentiles, ungodly Jews, or both. It is possible that Jesus turned this epithet, which legalistic Jews applied to Gentiles and careless fellow Jews, against those who so used it. See BAG, s.v. ἁμαρτωλός. The hortatory ἄγωμεν, "let us go," may carry the connotation of setting out to meet an advancing enemy (see C. H. Dodd, *The Interpretation of the Fourth Gospel* [Cambridge: Cambridge University Press, 1960] 406-7).

JESUS' DEATH AS A FULFILLMENT OF OLD TESTAMENT PROPHECY
26:47-56 (Mark 14:43-52; Luke 22:47-53; John 18:2-12)

26:47 (Mark 14:53; Luke 22:47) As often, Mark's εὐθύς vanishes and Matthew inserts "Behold" (34,9—so also Luke, but with a different referent). "Behold" recalls vv 45 and 46. Mark's definite article disappears from before Judas's name (see also 10:4; 26:14, 25; 27:3), and the name and its appositive "one of the twelve" advance to a position right after "Behold." Together, the insertion of "Behold" and the advance of the references to Judas heighten the emphasis on his treachery, which foreshadows the treachery of false disciples who betray their fellow disciples in the persecuted church of Matthew's environment (see esp. 24:10, an insertion). παραγίνεται becomes ἦλθεν in anticipation of Mark 14:45. To the description of the crowd accompanying Judas with swords and clubs Matthew adds a favorite adjective of his, πολύς (23,1). This addition not only furthers the emphasis on Judas's treachery, but also implies the large number of betrayers in Matthew's church. παρά changes to ἀπό before the identification of the groups making up the Sanhedrin. After the chief priests, Mark's "and the scribes" vanishes because no scriptural, theological discussion takes place during Jesus' arrest. The omission of Mark's definite article before "elders" welds together the chief priests and elders more closely. The addition "of the people" describes the elders and typifies Matthew's usage (4,0; see further the comments on v 3).

26:48 (Mark 14:44) For yet another emphasis on Judas's treachery and foreshadowing betrayers in Matthew's church, ὁ παραδιδοὺς αὐτόν comes to the head of the sentence. The advance also eliminates the awkwardness of Mark's σύσσημον, "signal," in juxtaposition with αὐτόν, "him." In keeping with Matthew's disuse of the pluperfect tense (excepting ᾔδειν and εἰστήκειν), the aorist ἔδωκεν, "gave," replaces the pluperfect δεδώκει, "had given." Consequently, a signal arranged prior to the arrival in Gethsemane (so Mark) changes to a signal arranged on arrival in Gethsemane. αὐτοῖς advances to a position right after the verb. σημεῖον replaces Mark's σύσσημον, which is hapax in the NT. Since Matthew later retains the leading away of Jesus (v 57), the omission of Mark's "and lead him away securely" has a stylistic reason, viz., Matthew's characteristic desire to have a couplet of lines: "Whomever I kiss is the one. Seize him."

Though the moon shone during Passover (except when clouds covered it, of course), the nighttime, the presence of the eleven, and the possibility of a melee dictated the need of Judas's identifying Jesus in an ostensibly peaceful way. The additional suggestion that other pilgrims were bivouacking in Gethsemane rests on an oversight of the need and plan to arrest Jesus in the absence of a crowd of sympathetic pilgrims (see vv 4-5).

26:49 (Mark 14:45; Luke 22:47) Mark's ἐλθών may seem otiose with προσελθών; but it is not really so, because the former relates to Gethsemane and the latter to Jesus. Nevertheless, ἐλθών drops out on account of its advance to v 47. The omission lets all the emphasis fall on προσελθών, a Mattheanism here shared with Mark (38,6). The word connotes Jesus' dignity (see the comments on 4:3; 8:14). εὐθύς changes to εὐθέως (11,0). As often, Jesus' name replaces "him" (80,12). Matthew wants no emphasis accruing to Judas's hypocritical greeting from the historical present "says"; so he switches to "said." Before "Rabbi," he inserts "Hail!" in anticipation of 27:29; Mark 15:18. Both χαῖρε and its cognate χαρά are favorites of his (2,1; 3,2). The insertion shows the falsity of Judas's discipleship: he is on the side of those who will mock Jesus with a "Hail!" in 27:29. The prefix κατ- before -εφίλησεν apparently implies a kiss on the hand or foot rather than on the face. Cf. Xenophon *Mem.* 2.6.33.

26:50 (Mark 14:46; Luke 22:48-49) The introduction "But Jesus said to him" lacks a parallel in Mark but has an exact parallel in Luke (except for Luke's omitting the definite article with Jesus' name). Again, ἑταῖρε, ἐφ' ὃ πάρει, "Friend, [do] what you are here for" or "Friend, on what an errand you are here!" lacks a parallel in Mark but has a parallel in Luke. ἑταῖρε occurs three times in Matthew (2,1), only in Matthew in the entire NT, and always for false disciples (see the comments on 22:12). Here it replaces "Judas" (so Luke) to identify Judas as a false disciple. Jesus' question, "Are you betraying the Son of man with a kiss?" (so Luke), becomes an ironic command for emphasis on Jesus' authoritative word, or a horrified exclamation to stress the treachery of Judas and similar betrayers in the church.

537

Matthew rejoins Mark, substitutes τότε (66,17) for δέ, and inserts his favorite προσελθόντες for a second allusion to Jesus' dignity (cf. v 49). After "they laid [their] hands on," the pronoun "him" changes to "on Jesus." The naming of Jesus typifies Matthew's Christological emphasis (80,12); and ἐπί, which is redundant after the prefix ἐπ-, probably makes for a parallel with ἐφ' in Jesus' statement according to Matthew's version.

In conjunction with τι or δι' the relative pronoun ὅ, "what," suits a question, "Why?" But it does not in conjunction with ἐφ'. For a command, cf. John 13:27; for an exclamation, Menander *Epit.* 1.46. See N. Turner, *Grammatical Insights into the New Testament* (Edinburgh: T. & T. Clark, 1966) 69-71, on the possibility of Matthew's thinking of the Aramaic עַל מָא and avoiding the interrogative by using ὅ rather than τι.

26:51 (Mark 14:47; Luke 22:50) A continuative καί replaces δέ because Matthew's normal adversative use of the latter would not fit here: the unnamed disciple's swordplay does not contrast with Judas's betrayal as good to bad, but parallels the betrayal as evil to evil. Typically, Matthew inserts ἰδού (34,9). The insertion establishes a correspondence between the violent disciple and Judas the betrayer, also introduced by an inserted ἰδού just before εἷς with a partitive genitive (cf. v 47). In this way Matthew shows that violent response to persecution is no better than betraying others to persecutors (cf. 5:5, 38-48). Mark's classical εἷς . . . τις, "a certain one," changes to the simpler and more popular εἷς (see BDF §247[2]). "With Jesus" replaces Mark's "standing by" and echoes insertions in vv 38 and 40 (see v 38 for interpretation). This replacement insures an identification of the swordsman as a disciple (cf. the obscurity in Mark, the similar clarification in Luke, and the naming of Peter in John 18:10-11).

The insertion ἐκτείνας τὴν χεῖρα, "stretching out [his] hand," typifies Matthew's style (3,0 for the whole phrase) and makes for parallelism in the two clauses of v 51: each clause consists of a participial phrase plus a finite verbal phrase. Also for the sake of this parallelism, Mark's participle σπασάμενος, "drawing," turns into the finite verb ἀπέσπασεν, "drew out." The addition of ἀπ- prepares for Matthew's complementary insertion of the command to return the sword to its place (ἀπόστρεψον—v 52b). The switch from Mark's middle voice to the active agrees better with the direct object "sword," to which Matthew adds "his." At the beginning of his next clause Matthew adds "and." Then the finite verb ἔπαισεν, "struck," changes to the participle πατάξας, "smiting," and Mark's "and" before "severed" drops out—all for the sake of the parallelistic structure noted above. The change in diction from ἔπαισεν to πατάξας reflects v 31 and implies that only God's smiting of Jesus is legitimate (cf. the common use of πατάσσω with a sword in the LXX). The change of ὠτάριον to ὠτίον (cf. Luke 22:51) has no significance: both words mean "ear" (cf. Luke's οὖς).

26:52 (Luke 22:51) As in the first part of the preceding verse, Matthew shows contact with a tradition preserved also in Luke but lacking in Mark. His beloved τότε (66,17) replaces Luke's δέ. The historical present λέγει is often favored by Matthew (47,11) and stands here in place of Luke's ἀποκριθείς . . . εἶπεν, favored by Matthew in other passages (29,6). Before Jesus' name Matthew's text has "to him" (not in Luke). For Luke's ἐᾶτε ἕως τούτου, "No more of this!" or literally "Let unto this," Matthew substitutes ἀπόστρεψον τὴν μαχαιράν σου εἰς τὸν τόπον αὐτῆς, "Return your sword to its place." This substitute prepares for his expansion in the next line. The expansion, in turn, puts forward Jesus' teaching against retaliation (5:38-42). It also puts forward Jesus himself as an example of that teaching. The returning of the sword to its place complements the drawing out of the sword in v 51, where only Matthew had ἀπ-, "out." Cf. the insertions of ἀποστραφῇς in 5:42 and τόπον in 14:35; 24:15 as well as here. Except for Matthew's characteristic addition of γάρ (62-63,15), "for all who take a sword will perish by means of a sword" comes from *Tg. Isa* 50:11 and exhibits Matthew's habit of conforming Jesus' words to the OT (see H. Kosmala in *NovT* 4 [1960] 3-5; Gundry, *Use of the OT* 144). John 18:11 seems to show Matthean influence.

26:53-54 Matthew composes the next two sayings: "Or do you think that I am not able to beseech my Father, and he will now put at my disposal more than twelve legions of angels? How then would the Scriptures be fulfilled that thus it must happen?" Mattheanisms abound: ἤ (32,12), δοκεῖς (6,3), δύναμαι (13,0), παρακαλέσαι (1,3), τὸν πατέρα μου (7,2), ἄρτι (7,0), πλείω (3,1), "angels" that belong to Jesus the Son of man (3,1), πῶς (6,1), οὖν (35,11), πληρωθῶσιν (9,6), and οὕτως (18,5). Among the evangelists, Matthew alone uses πῶς with οὖν (see the insertions in 12:26; 22:43; 26:54). The possibility that one angelic legion (six thousand) might protect each of the eleven disciples plus Jesus suggested the number twelve (see the peculiarly Matthean reference to guardian angels in 18:10; cf. also 2:13; 4:6). Thus the legion of demons Matthew omitted in 8:28-34 (cf. Mark 5:1-20; Luke 8:26-39) turns into twelve legions of angels to enhance Jesus' majesty. The fulfillment of the Scriptures anticipates Mark 14:49. So also "it must happen" prepares for "But this whole thing happened" in v 56 (distinctive in this respect); but the phraseology itself more exactly mirrors 24:6 (cf. Rev 1:1). The insertion "for the forgiveness of sins" in 26:28 showed that forgiveness rests on Jesus' self-sacrifice; the present insertion shows that he sacrifices himself to fulfill the OT obediently (see 5:17-18). Though he can gain the assistance of angelic warriors, he will not go against God's will revealed in Scripture.

26:55 (Mark 14:48-49; Luke 22:52-53) The insertion "In that hour" represents Matthew's special diction (3,0) and links with v 45, "Behold, the hour has drawn near," which contrasted with "The hour has come" (Mark 14:41). No longer is the hour merely near. With the arrest, Matthew finally sees Jesus inside the hour. Because Jesus has been speaking to only one of his disciples, whereas he is now going to speak to the crowds, Mark's "answering" drops out. The simple "he said" takes the position of the omitted participle (so also Luke). The replacement of "to them" with a typically Matthean "to the crowds" (17,1) echoes v 47 (cf. the comments on vv 3, 47). In Jesus' statement that they did not seize him when he was teaching daily in the Temple, Matthew substitutes "I was sitting" for Mark's "I was with you." He is portraying Jesus as the one legitimate rabbi, who sits in Moses' seat (cf. 23:8 with 23:2, both of which were insertions by Matthew). The verb comes later than it does in Mark; Matthew wants it to stand beside "teaching." Since rabbis sat to teach, this shift in the word order appropriately stems from the change of "I was" to "I was sitting."

We might punctuate the first clause of Jesus' statement as an indignant declaration rather than a question. It is hard to determine whether ληστήν means "bandit" or "revolutionary" (see BAG, s.v.) and whether daily teaching in the Temple refers to the past week alone or to earlier teaching such as the fourth evangelist recounts.

26:56 (Mark 14:49-52; Luke 22:53) As often, Matthew favors δέ, which replaces ἀλλ'. The insertion "this whole thing happened" fills Mark's gap before the ἵνα-clause and derives from the distinctive formula Matthew uses to introduce quotations of fulfilled OT passages (see esp. 1:22 with comments ad loc.; cf. 21:4). It also echoes v 54, another insertion of his, and accentuates the actuality of the fulfillment. Both ὅλον and the particular form γέγονεν come from his favorite vocabulary (7,3; 3,2). To "the Scriptures" he adds "of the prophets." Prophets appear often in his gospel (19,6), especially in the formula of fulfillment. In particular, the addition "of the prophets" flashes back to 2:23: both that passage and this deal with rejection of Jesus the Nazarene. As a whole, the first sentence in v 56 looks back on the events that will guarantee Jesus' death in fulfillment of Scripture.

Again καί gives way to τότε (66,17). The insertion οἱ μαθηταί (31,5) typifies Matthew's diction and links the disciples' flight with Jesus' prediction in vv 31-35 (see esp. the same insertion in v 35). πάντες moves forward to join οἱ μαθηταί (cf. v 35). As in Luke, Mark's "signature" concerning the young man who fled away naked vanishes as irrelevant to Matthew's purposes.

JESUS' EXAMPLE OF NONRETALIATION AND REFUSAL TO TAKE AN OATH
26:57-68 (Mark 14:53-65; Luke 22:54-71; John 18:13-24)

26:57 (Mark 14:53; Luke 22:54) For a contrast between the disciples' leaving Jesus and the crowds' seizing him, δέ replaces καί. Luke, too, has δέ, but with the meaning "and" instead of "but." From vv 4, 48, 50, 55, Matthew adds "they who seized" (not in Mark; but cf. Luke's "taking"). The addition differentiates those who led Jesus away and the disciples, who fled. The advance of Jesus' name makes it the immediate object of "seized" rather than of "led away" (as in Mark). The insertion of "Caiaphas" echoes v 3. Mark's second "and" yields to a stylistically better "where" (cf. Matthew's inserting the Sanhedrin's place of meeting in v 3). "The scribes" remains, and even advances, because theological issues are coming up regarding Jesus' messiahship and divine sonship (contrast v 47). Despite retention of the chief priests in v 59, here "all the chief priests and . . ." drops out as unnecessary after the mention of Caiaphas the high priest. Also, Matthew wants to highlight the scribes and have a pair rather than a triplet of expressions. Thus he keeps and advances "the elders" ahead of the verb, which changes from "come together" (so Mark's historical present) to "came together."

See F. M. Young in *NTS* 19 (1973) 331-33 on Jewish persecution as a historical fact, though such persecution was exaggerated in early Christian literature. Because of Matthew's dependence on Mark, discussions of possible illegalities in Jesus' trial and the Sanhedrin's right or lack of right to pass and inflict capital sentence belong in commentaries on the other gospels and in special studies.

26:58 *(Mark 14:54; Luke 22:54-55)* Mark's καί yields to δέ for a contrast between leading Jesus away and Peter's following him at a distance. (In Luke δέ contrasts Jesus' being led into the high priest's house and Peter's staying outside because of his distance from Jesus.) ἠκολούθησεν αὐτῷ comes forward (cf. Luke), perhaps merely for smoothness in word order, perhaps also for emphasis on Peter's discipleship rather than on the distance at which he followed. Furthermore, the tense of the verb changes from aorist to imperfect to indicate linear action: "was following" (so also Luke). "As far as" comes from Mark's "as far as the inside," and "the courtyard [or 'palace'] of the high priest" from Mark's "into the courtyard of the high priest." Thus Matthew conflates Mark's cumbersome pair of phrases. He compensates for this abbreviation by adding "entering inside." Both εἰσ- and ἔσω derive from the foregoing omissions. ἐκάθητο replaces Mark's periphrastic ἦν συγκαθήμενος. συγ-, "together," has dropped off as unnecessary because of the following μετά, "with." Matthew replaces "and warming himself [facing] toward the light [of the fire]" with "to see the end." The replacement correlates the outcome of the trial in Jesus' death and resurrection with the eschatological end, i.e., with his parousia as the Son of man (cf. 10:22; 24:6, 13, 14 and Matthew's wholesale importation of eschatology in 27:51-53).

26:59 *(Mark 14:55)* Mark's mention of the chief priests and whole Sanhedrin comes over with only one change, the delay of ὅλον, perhaps to avoid readers' wrongly separating the Sanhedrin from the chief priests. After "were seeking," Matthew advances "testimony" and characteristically prefixes "false" (6,0 for words with ψευδ-). The prefix anticipates Mark 14:56 and, with the advance, heightens the guilt of the chief priests and the whole Sanhedrin. In violation of the law (see 15:19; 19:18), they are seeking false testimony instead of true. In Mark, contrastingly, they seek true testimony instead of false. ὅπως plus the subjunctive replaces Mark's telic εἰς plus an articular infinitive. Matthew likes his conjunction (8,7) and possibly means it to be a stronger and therefore more damning indication of the Sanhedrin's desire to kill Jesus. The putting of αὐτόν (i.e., Jesus) before θανατώσωσιν, "they might kill," contrasts with the word order in Mark and intensifies the guilt by emphasizing the person against whom they seek false testimony.

26:60 *(Mark 14:55-57)* Mark's "they were not finding" becomes "they did not find." Then a typically Matthean genitive absolute, translated "though many false witnesses approached," replaces "for many were testifying falsely."

Mark's "against him" disappears. The seeking of *false* testimony "so that they might kill him" has made "against him" otiose. Furthermore, it has made the falsity of the testimony something in spite of which the authorities did not find what they wanted rather than a reason for their failing to find what they wanted (so Mark with γάρ). According to Matthew false testimony *is* what they wanted. "And the testimonies were not in agreement" also disappears, because in Matthew the Sanhedrin does not face the problem of discovering true testimony, but the problem of finding false testimony serious enough to excuse putting Jesus to death. Cf. Matthew's doubling the element of blasphemy in v 65.

Mark's καί gives way to δέ for a contrast between not finding and finding. ὕστερον and προσελθόντες come from Matthew's favorite vocabulary (3,3; 38,6). The latter replaces ἀναστάντες for linkage with the foregoing genitive absolute, where προσελθόντων occurred. Perhaps Matthew wants his readers to understand a respectful approach to Jesus rather than to the Sanhedrin, which had seventy-one members (cf. the comments on 4:3; 8:14). δύο substitutes for Mark's τινες, typifies Matthew's diction (19,4), and points to the establishment of truth by the testimony of two or three witnesses, a law Matthew has shown special interest in (see esp. 18:16, an insertion; cf. Deut 17:6-7; 19:15). Mark says that the Sanhedrin sought true testimony and found false, Matthew that they sought false testimony and found true. To stress his point he puts "two" right beside "said" in contrast with the earlier position of Mark's corresponding "certain ones."

With the two witnesses, cf. the two demoniacs in 9:28-34, the two blind men in 9:27-31 and again in 20:29-34, and the pairing of the twelve in 10:2-4. The distinctive ὕστερον does not distinguish between the following true witnesses and the preceding false witnesses as such, but between false witnesses with testimony insufficient to excuse Jesus' execution and true witnesses with testimony wickedly distorted by the Sanhedrin to excuse Jesus' execution.

26:61 (Mark 14:58-59) "Said" replaces "were testifying falsely against him" because in Matthew the two witnesses speak the truth! As often, Mark's recitative ὅτι vanishes. "This one said" replaces "We have heard him saying" because Matthew is not interested in what they falsely claimed to hear (so Mark), but in what Jesus really did say according to their true testimony. ἔφη is a Mattheanism (11,4). Again Mark's recitative ὅτι drops out.

As in v 53, Matthew inserts one of his favorite verbs, δύναμαι (13,0), to emphasize Jesus' power as the Son of God. Because of this insertion, Mark's ἐγώ falls out and "will destroy" and "will build" become infinitives. Matthew changes the derogatory "this handmade Temple" to the complimentary "the Temple of God" and omits "another [Temple] not handmade." The omission obliterates the distinction between two Temples and makes the new Temple a rebuilt one, not a brand new Temple. "Of God" has the effect of identifying the one remaining Temple with Jesus himself in that Matthew's substituting "of God" here links up with his substituting "of God" for "of the Blessed One" in v 63 (cf. Mark 14:61). In other words,

542

he is setting up a parallel between God's Temple and Son for the purpose of identifying the two. This identification is confirmed by his special interest in the three days of Jesus' death, burial, and resurrection (see his insertions 12:40 and 27:62-66 and cf. the three days in which Jesus will build the Temple). Though the Sanhedrin sought false testimony, they got true testimony concerning Jesus as God's Temple and concerning Jesus' ability to destroy and rebuild that Temple or, in Johannine terms, to lay down his life and take it again (John 10:18). Further confirmation will come from Matthew's replacing "he expired" (Mark 15:37; Luke 23:46) with "he let [his] spirit go," which implies voluntariness (27:50). Because he has presented the testimony of the two witnesses as true, "and not even thus was their testimony in agreement" disappears (cf. the earlier omission of Mark 14:56b). Besides, in Matthew the Sanhedrin are not bothered by inconsistencies. They seek false testimony in the first place. That they regarded the true testimony as damaging to Jesus and blasphemous against God heightens their guilt.

Matthew is not merely toning down a saying hostile to the Jewish Temple, but is identifying the Temple of God with the Son of God. Cf. John 2:19-22; Acts 6:14. Because of its falsity, the testimony in Mark leaves us uncertain about the meaning Jesus intended.

26:62 (Mark 14:60) Mark's unnecessary phrase "in the midst" drops from the reference to the high priest's standing up. εἶπεν replaces Mark's ἐπηρώτησεν, which Matthew dislikes (see the comments on 17:19), and causes the loss of λέγων, which Matthew does like (61,23). "To him" substitutes for "Jesus" because the omission of Mark 14:59 has reduced the need to mention Jesus' name (cf. the comments on v 63, however). οὐδέν comes forward to displace οὐκ in the high priest's question "Do you answer nothing?" which is followed by the further question "What [is it that] these are testifying against you?" (so also Mark). It is possible that we should construe the two clauses of the high priest's question together by taking τι as an accusative of general reference: "Do you answer nothing with respect to what these are testifying against you?" (cf. 27:13 with Mark 15:4; also Isa 53:7; Ps 38:14-16[13-15]).

26:63 (Mark 14:61; Luke 22:67, 70) By inserting "Jesus" Matthew makes up for his displacing Jesus' name in the preceding verse. "He was not answering anything" drops out as redundant after "But Jesus kept silent." Besides, because he portrays Jesus as the Teacher of the law, Matthew is more interested in what Jesus does say than in what he does not say. "Again" also drops out. "Said to him" replaces "was asking him and says to him" for a parallel with the similar replacement in v 62a (see the comments ad loc.). These revisions have the effect of drawing close together the preceding questions about Jesus' ability to destroy God's Temple and build it in three days and the following adjuration concerning Jesus' being the Messiah, God's Son. This tightening confirms our earlier estimate of Matthew's intent to identify the Temple of God as the Son of God (see the comments on v 61).

To compensate for omitting the high priest's "asking" Jesus and especially to set the stage for a portrayal of Jesus as exemplifying his law against oaths (5:33-37, peculiar to the first gospel), Matthew inserts "I put you under oath by the living God that you tell us" (cf. Luke's later "tell us," perhaps the result of Matthew's influence). By the same token, Matthew portrays the high priest as violating that law in putting Jesus under oath. This latter portrayal heaps more guilt on the Jewish leadership. ἐξορκίζω occurs only here in the NT, but it reflects usage in conjunction with the divine name in Gen 24:3 LXX; 3 Kgdms 22:16 LXX (cf. Matthew's interest in ὀμνύω, "take an oath"—1,10). κατά + the genitive typifies Matthew's style (10,1). "The living God" matches Matthew's identical insertion in 16:16 (see the comments ad loc. on its OT flavor). Both insertions have to do with Jesus as the Messiah and Son of God. Thus Matthew's composition is confirmed. The adjuration dictates an addition of "if" before "you are the Messiah, the Son of God." "Of God" appears also in Luke 22:70 and replaces "of the Blessed One," a reverential substitute for the divine name. Again see 16:16, where Matthew added "the Son of God" to "the Christ" (cf. his general interest in Jesus as υἱὸς τοῦ θεοῦ—4,2).

We should not think that Matthew portrays the high priest as an exorcist by attributing to him the use of ἐξορκίζω; for in Mark 5:7 the *demoniac* adjures Jesus, and in Acts 19:13 the exorcist adjures the demon to come out, but here the high priest adjures Jesus to talk. Though the high priest would not have implied the Son's deity in his own use of "the Son of the Blessed One," he might have suspected the higher meaning in a claim to divine sonship by Jesus.

26:64 (Mark 14:62; Luke 22:67-69) For emphasis, "Jesus says" replaces "And Jesus said." λέγει with asyndeton is a Mattheanism (21,6). Matthew inserts αὐτῷ, "to him," in anticipation of σύ, "you," which he will insert in Jesus' answer (v 63b). "I am" yields to "You said [it]." This replacement echoes an identical insertion in v 25, anticipates the traditional use of the same expression (but in the present tense) in 27:11, and makes Jesus exemplify his own prohibition of oath taking. He does not accept the adjuration, but merely agrees with the answer implicit in the terms of the high priest's question (again see 5:33-37, a passage peculiar to Matthew). Furthermore, this replacement heightens the guilt of the high priest by implying that he himself knew the answer to be affirmative, indeed, by implying that the high priest himself, rather than Jesus, blasphemed when he used God's name in an unlawful adjuration (so Matthew alone in v 63; cf. v 65). The shift from "tell us [plural]" (v 63) to "You [singular] said [it]" (v 64) signals the latter implication. The plural ὑμεῖς λέγετε, "you say," in Luke 22:70 shows agreement with Matthew except for number. The frequency of agreements between Matthew and Luke against Mark, including two such agreements in v 63, favors Matthean influence rather than independent editing of Mark by Luke. So also does Luke's lack of Matthew's reasons for the revision, reasons associated with the uniquely Matthean insertion of an adjuration.

For contrast with the foregoing insertion "You said [it]," Matthew inserts "Nevertheless I say to you," an expression that occurred in 11:22, 24 (the second time as an insertion; see also 18:7; 26:39 for πλήν alone and the comments on 5:21-48 for Matthew's liking λέγω ὑμῖν—27,7). The contrast does not imply a denial by Jesus of the high priest's terms "the Christ, the Son of God" (which Matthew likes—8,5; 4,2), or even a correction by Jesus of the high priest's understanding of those terms. For "You said [it]" does not issue a qualified yes, much less a no, but stoutly affirms that the questioner himself knows the affirmative answer as obvious (see the comments on 26:25). The contrast arises out of Jesus' refusal to answer under oath: he avoided the adjuration with "You said [it]"; now his own words will be spoken with a magisterial authority that owes nothing to an oath. The switch from the singular σύ to the plural ὑμῖν directs the following statement to the whole Sanhedrin and, ultimately, to the unbelieving Jewish leaders at the time Matthew wrote.

The Mattheanism ἀπ' ἄρτι (3,0) replaces Mark's καί. Luke's ἀπὸ τοῦ νῦν agrees in thought with Matthew but conforms to the usual wording in Luke-Acts (Luke 1:48; 5:10; 12:52; 22:18, 69; Acts 18:6). The very meaning of ἀπ' ἄρτι, "from now on," and the indubitable and distinctive use of the phrase in 23:39; 26:29 for the church age demand a similar use here. In Mark, Jesus refers to a single, literal seeing of the Son of man at the last day: heaven will open and the Son of man will be seen sitting at the right hand of the Power; still in full view he will get up and come with the clouds of heaven. Matthew's allusion to the church age, which dates from Jesus' time onward, doubles the reference: first there is a mental seeing of the Son of man sitting at God's right hand, a seeing that will begin immediately as a result of the events described in 27:51b-53 and the report of the guards, related in 28:11-15 (both passages being peculiar to Matthew); then a literal seeing of the Son of man coming on the clouds of heaven, a seeing that awaits the parousia (see BAG, s.v. ὁράω 1a and c). The mental seeing does not demand or imply conversion; rather, it increases the guilt of the Jewish leaders by showing that their unbelief goes against what they know to be true. Here we have Matthew's reason for inserting ἀπ' ἄρτι: the desire to excoriate the Jewish leaders. This desire shows itself repeatedly. καθήμενον comes forward for correspondence with the position of its mate ἐρχόμενον and for conformity with the word order in Ps 110:1. The agreement of Luke with Matthew's order, despite Luke's lacking the allusion to Dan 7:13 ("and coming . . ."), again indicates Matthean influence. Mark's "with the clouds" changes to "on the clouds," as in 24:30 (see the comments ad loc.).

Cf. John 18:37. ἀπ' ἄρτι hardly means "after this"—i.e., "at a later time"—with the possibility of a more or less lengthy interval. The phrase goes in the opposite direction and means "from now [on]." Furthermore, it modifies "you will see," not the exalted state of the Son of man. Jesus switches from "the Christ, the Son of the Blessed" to "the Son of man" in order to indicate a reversal of roles. "The Son of man" connotes judgmental authority (see Dan 7:13-14); at the parousia he will judge, not be judged (as now). On "the Power" as a reverential substitute for God's name, see the references listed and discussed by G. Dalman, *The Words of Jesus* (Edinburgh: T. & T. Clark, 1902) 201, and cf. the explanatory combination "of the Power of God" in Luke 22:69. See Gundry, *Use of the OT* 60-61, on the texts of the allusions to Zech 12:10; Ps 110:1; Dan 7:13; and ibid. 232-33 for the meaning of descent rather than ascent in both Dan 7:13 and Jesus' uses of that passage (cf. 24:30 and note [1] the lack in Dan 7:9 of any suggestion that the scene has shifted from the terrestrial sphere of the preceding part of the vision; [2] the setting of thrones, which does not need to be done in heaven, where God normally sits enthroned; [3] the coming of the Ancient of Days, a movement hardly needed for or appropriate to a God who dwells in heaven, but needed for and appropriate to his appearance in an earthly scene; [4] the parallel of the coming of the manlike figure; and [5] the regularity with which clouds are associated with divine appearances on earth).

26:65 (Mark 14:63-64; Luke 22:7) Mark's δέ gives way to τότε (66,17) because the following material grows out of the foregoing rather than contrasts with it in a way that would suit Matthew's habit of using δέ adversatively. "Tearing" becomes "tore" to allow the shift from "says" to the Mattheanism "saying" (λέγων—61,23). Matthew exchanges τοὺς χιτῶνας αὐτοῦ—properly, "his inner clothing," but probably meant generally as "his clothing"—for τὰ ἱμάτια αὐτοῦ, "his outer clothing," because the high priest would naturally tear his outer clothing (cf. 5:40). The distinctive "He has blasphemed" anticipates the later declaration that the Sanhedrin has heard blasphemy. Matthew's doubling the motif by means of this addition increases the high priest's guilt. The insertions of ἴδε, "See," and νῦν, "just now," accentuate the statement "You have heard blasphemy!" and thus heighten the high priest's guilt again. ἴδε is often omitted or replaced by Matthew, but was inserted also in 25:20, 22, 25; νῦν will be inserted once more in 27:43. Mark's genitive τῆς βλασφημίας becomes the accusative τὴν βλασφημίαν because Matthew reserves the genitive after ἀκούω for people who are heard (see 17:5; 18:15) and the accusative after ἀκούω for things that are heard (as here and in other passages too numerous to list).

Cf. 2 Kgs 18:37; Acts 14:14; and especially *m. Sanh.* 7:5. The prohibition in Lev 21:10 that a high priest not tear his clothes deals only with mourning the dead. Jesus' supposed blasphemy did not consist in his claim to messiahship (other messianic claimants were not judged blasphemers), but in his claim to deity. That claim does not consist alone in the expression "Son of God," which might connote divine ordination—to kingship, for example—without divine nature (see 2 Sam 7:13-14). Rather, it consists in Jesus' modifying the expression—here by associating it with sitting beside God and coming with the theophanic symbol of clouds—so as to connote divine nature as well as divine ordination.

26:66 (Mark 14:64) Mark's φαίνεται is a favorite of Matthew (5,8). Nevertheless, it changes to δοκεῖ (6,3) to produce the characteristically Matthean question τί ὑμῖν δοκεῖ; "What does it seem to you?" (4,2; see further the comments on 17:25). In Matthew φαίνω always denotes visible appearance, but here in Mark it denotes logical appearance. Therefore Matthew did not find the change difficult to make. He reserves "all" for insertion in 27:1. ἀποκριθέντες εἶπαν typifies his style (29,6) and displaces Mark's κατέκριναν αὐτόν. Matthew is reserving κατέκριναν for distinctive use in 27:3. These reservations show his desire to make clear that the Sanhedrin's formal condemnation of Jesus did not come till after dawn.

"He is deserving of death" matches Mark, with two exceptions: (1) the advance of θανάτου in order to highlight the Sanhedrin's guilt again and (2) the necessary change of "to be" to "is" on account of Matthew's shift to direct discourse.

26:67-68 (Mark 14:65; Luke 22:63-65) As often, τότε overpowers καί; and Mark's auxiliary ἤρξαντο, "began," vanishes. The omission of Mark's indefinite τινες, "certain ones," heightens the guilt of the Jewish leaders: most of them, not just some of them, spit in Jesus' face. "In his face" replaces "on him" and comes from Mark's next phrase, "and to cover his face," which Matthew otherwise omits. Thus in his first line Matthew conflates Mark's first two expressions for an allusion to Isa 50:6, where the suffering Servant of the Lord says, "I did not hide my face from shame and spitting" (see Gundry, *Use of the OT* 61). Furthermore, spitting in Jesus' face, as distinct from spitting on Jesus' clothes, heightens the Sanhedrin's guilt yet again.

Matthew's inserting οἱ δέ, "but some," differentiates those who slap Jesus from those who spit in his face and hit him with their fists. Only those who slap him challenge him to prophesy. Mark writes nothing about a challenge that he prophesy *who hit him* (though readers of Mark might deduce that correctly). Matthew has omitted the covering of Jesus' face. Therefore the challenge that Jesus prophesy who struck him with an open hand (so Matthew alone) has nothing to do with his not being able to point out his assailants because of a blindfold (contrast Luke 22:64). On the contrary, they apparently challenge Jesus to tell their names as he looks on. Matthew brings up Mark's ῥαπίσμασιν, "with slaps," in the form of the verb ἐρράπισαν, "slapped," to make Jesus exemplify his own law of non-retaliation in 5:39, where only Matthew has a form of the verb (contrast Luke 6:29). He is also making room in v 68b to explain the kind of prophecy Jesus' assailants had in mind (cf. Luke 22:64). Moreover, the insult of slapping Jesus now comes from members of the Sanhedrin rather than from their servants (as in Mark). Thus the guilt of the Jewish leaders is heightened again. λέγοντες represents Matthew's preferred style (61,23) and replaces καὶ λέγειν αὐτῷ. Luke agrees with Matthew, though the setting differs. The command to prophesy gains the indirect object "to us" (not in Mark or Luke). By adding the address "Christ," Matthew shows his liking of that term (8,5), makes even the assailants of Jesus acknowledge his messiahship, and through that acknowledgment heightens their guilt in rejecting him. "Who is the one who struck you?" replaces καὶ οἱ ὑπηρέται ῥαπίσμασιν αὐτὸν ἔλαβον, translated literally "and the servants received him with slaps" (a Latinism). The replacement is due to Matthew's advance of the slapping. Again Luke agrees with Matthew; but because Luke's setting differs radically, probably we should not think of Matthean influence, but of Matthew's conflating two historical traditions—the Markan and the pre-Lukan.

See D. L. Miller in *JBL* 90 (1971) 309-13 on the game of blind man's buff played with Jesus. Perhaps Jesus' prophecy in v 64 prompted the Sanhedrin's challenge that he prophesy again. Cf. *Pss. Sol.* 17:37-51 on the prophetic discernment expected of the Messiah; also *b. Sanh.* 93b.

THE NEGATIVE EXAMPLE OF PETER'S DENIALS
AS A CONTINUATION OF THE WARNING
AGAINST PRAYERLESSNESS
26:69-75 (Mark 14:66-72; Luke 22:56-62; John 18:15-18, 25-27)

26:69 (Mark 14:66-67; Luke 22:56) The debilitating effect of prayerlessness on discipleship shows up especially in the disowning of Jesus during persecution. Therefore in this passage Matthew completes the warning he started in vv 30-46. δέ replaces καί for a contrast between Jesus' patient endurance of persecution, just described, and Peter's cracking under pressure in the subsequent narrative. By turning Mark's genitive absolute into an independent clause, Matthew gains a couplet of lines: "Peter was sitting . . . and a maid approached. . . ." The replacement of Mark's ὄντος with ἐκάθητο exhibits a Mattheanism (8,0) and echoes v 58 exactly (cf. the sitting of the maid in Luke and contrast Mark 14:54). To balance "inside" (from a standpoint without the courtyard) in v 58, Matthew puts "outside" (from a standpoint within the palace) in place of Mark's "below." ἔξω is another Mattheanism (3,1).

Matthew replaces Mark's ἔρχεται with his favorite προσῆλθεν (38,6), which leads to the addition of αὐτῷ. A maid would naturally approach a man with respect. "One of the maids" becomes "one maid," and "of the high priest" drops off. Matthew emphasizes, then, that just one female slave made Peter stumble into a denial of Jesus. Beware of prayerlessness, for it will make you as weak as that! The maid's seeing Peter warming himself and her staring at him also disappear. These vivid details do not interest Matthew, who restricts himself to items, usually sayings, that convey a message. Only Mark's λέγει stays, but in the participial form λέγουσα (61,23). In the maid's statement, ἦσθα advances for a smoother order of words. Matthew reserves "the Nazarene" for v 71 and substitutes "the Galilean" (cf. the comments on v 73). The result is a distinctive parallel between the phrases "with Jesus the Galilean" and, in v 71, "with Jesus the Nazarene." This parallel echoes the association of Galilee and Nazareth in 2:22-23, where Matthew portrayed Jesus as the despised Branch. He puts Jesus' name before the designation according to place—a more natural order than the reverse in Mark.

That the rebel Judas was called "the Galilean" (Acts 5:37) does not demand that "Galilean" meant "rebel, revolutionary." Judas may have been called "the Galilean" simply because he came from Galilee. Besides, "Galilean" here originates from Matthew, who hardly uses it in a revolutionary sense. Does καὶ σύ mean "Even you," "You as well as those who fled," or "You as well as the disciple who influenced the maid to let Peter in the door" (John 18:15-16)?

26:70 (Mark 14:68; Luke 22:57) Matthew inserts "before all" to recall 10:33 as a warning not to follow Peter's dangerous example. ἔμπροσθεν is a Mattheanism (9,4). The link with 10:33, according to which Jesus will deny before his heavenly Father anyone who denies Jesus before men, shows that Peter is forfeiting his salvation. Naturally, then, his name will disappear from the story of Jesus' resurrection (cf. 28:7 with Mark 16:7). This disappearance will confirm that he was not the rock Jesus was going to build his church on (see the comments on 16:17-19). Instead, Peter represents a whole range of possibilities in discipleship: reception of special revelation (16:17-19); Christian witness (10:1-2); little faith (14:28-31); apostasy in persecution and consequent loss of salvation (the present passage). Matthew omits "nor do I understand" as redundant. Therefore Mark's first οὔτε gives way to οὐκ. Luke agrees with Matthew in having "I do not know" alone. Mark's σύ disappears as unneeded and perhaps as falsely emphatic.

26:71 (Mark 14:68-69; Luke 22:58) To set off the next denial, δέ replaces καί. This sharper division agrees with Matthew's interest in the threefoldness of Peter's denials vis-à-vis the threefoldness of Peter's falling asleep in Gethsemane: one denial for each failure to pray (cf. the comments on 26:30-46). ἐξελθόντα replaces Mark's ἐξῆλθεν and exhibits Matthew's tendency to put participles at the heads of sentences (though ἐξελθόντα is accusative rather than the usual nominative). Mark's ἔξω drops out as awkward and redundant, not because of ἐξελθόντα (see v 75), but because of the insertion of ἔξω in v 69. Indeed, Matthew replaces προαύλιον, "forecourt," with πυλῶνα, "gateway," because in v 69 he put Peter outside rather than below, in the courtyard. To go out any farther in Matthew's account Peter has to enter the gateway. If the clause "and a rooster crowed" appeared in Mark (see the UBS), Matthew omits it because he omitted "twice" in v 34 (cf. Mark 14:30).

Mark's καί disappears because Matthew changes ἐξῆλθεν to a participle. Now he changes the participle ἰδοῦσα to the finite verb εἶδεν and advances it because of a feeling that the sentence has gone on long enough without a main verb. The change of ἡ παιδίσκη, "the maid," to ἄλλη, "another [maid]," entails a division of Mark's single maid into two successive maids. Matthew likes ἄλλη (14,4) and wants two witnesses of Peter's denials in accord with the law of two or three witnesses (see the comments on v 60 and 18:16). The passage 28:1-8 shows that Matthew regards the testimony of women as valid. A second challenger appears in Luke, too, but he is male. Matthew's insertion "and" makes a couplet of verbs out of "saw" and "says." The latter reflects Mark 14:67 and replaces "began to say." Mark's "again" drops out because Matthew created another maid rather than narrate the reappearance of the original one. τοῖς ἐκεῖ, "to those there," substitutes for Mark's τοῖς παρεστῶσιν, "to those present." Matthew prefers ἐκεῖ (16,6) over παρεστῶσιν, which he regularly avoids in the sense "be present" and uses only in 26:53 in the sense "put at one's disposal." Furthermore, ἐκεῖ fits the new location and different accuser. As usual, Mark's recitative ὅτι vanishes. "With Jesus the Nazarene" replaces "of them" to forge a link with 2:23 (cf. the comments on 21:11) and echo vv 18, 20, 23, 29, 36, 38 (see the comments ad loc.), 40, 51 (cf. John 18:26). The replacement forces a change of Mark's ἐστιν to ἦν, because Peter was not with Jesus at the moment. The verb comes forward to a position right after οὗτος, its usual position with this pronoun in Matthew. Ναζωραίου derives from Mark's earlier and synonymous Ναζαρηνοῦ, replaced in v 69.

26:72 (Mark 14:70; Luke 22:58) Because Matthew normally uses δέ as an adversative, the present lack of contrast dictates that he switch from Mark's continuative δέ to καί. "He was denying" changes to "he denied." Matthew often avoids Mark's use of the imperfect tense. The insertion "with an oath" anticipates v 74; Mark 14:71. The resultant doubling of the oath stresses that Peter is a bad example of oath taking and highlights the contrastive example set by Matthew's Jesus, who refused to answer under oath (vv 63-64). Matthew likes to insert ὅρκου (3,0). For emphasis, he inserts the recitative ὅτι; and he paints Peter's apostasy in darker warning colors by offering a direct quotation: "I do not know the man" (not in Mark; cf. the contemptuous use of "the man" in Plutarch *Mor.* 870C). Luke, too, quotes Peter, but differently: "Man, I am not!" This looks like a revision of Matthew. For the sake of parallelism, Matthew has repeated "I do not know" from v 70 and anticipated the very same words of Peter in v 74; Mark 14:71 (cf. 10:32, 33; 25:12). The emphasis on Peter's not knowing indicates apostasy, for in Matthew true discipleship requires knowledge (see esp. chaps. 13–17 passim).

26:73 (Mark 14:70; Luke 22:59) Matthew's δέ replaces καί to make the third denial stand out more distinctly and contrast the little time between the second and third denials with the apparently longer interval between the first two. The greater distinctness of each denial (cf. δέ in v 71, too) clarifies the correspondence with Peter's three failures to watch and pray in Gethsemane: each failure brought a denial. Mark's "again" drops out because the following challenge to Peter does not come from either of the first two maids, but from a group of men (cf. the omission of "again" in v 71 for a similar reason). Matthew inserts his favorite προσελθόντες (38,6) for a parallel with the same insertion in v 69. οἱ παρεστῶτες loses the prefix παρ-, "by," so that the men are simply standing (see the comments on v 71). The imperfect ἔλεγον gives way to the aorist εἶπον. Matthew inserts καὶ σύ, "you also," for a parallelistic emphasis drawn from v 69. He is fond of σύ (6,4). "Your speech makes you obvious" replaces "you are a Galilean" because of his recent insertion of "the Galilean" in v 69. The replacement not only explains why Peter's association with Jesus was obvious, but also keeps Jesus as the preeminent Galilean (see 2:22-23 and cf. 4:14-16). ποιεῖ belongs to Matthew's special vocabulary (19,19).

26:74 (Mark 14:71-72; Luke 22:60) The Mattheanism τότε replaces ὁ δέ. Mark's nonauxiliary ἤρξατο stays. The cursing, oath taking, and claim not to know the man Jesus come from Mark with only a few changes: (1) the exchange of Mark's perfective ἀνα- for the possibly stronger κατα-, "against," with -θεματίζειν, "to curse"; (2) the shift in spelling from ὀμνύναι to ὀμνύειν; and (3) the dropping of "this" in order that "the man" may parallel "the man" in v 72, where the expression distinguished Matthew. The exchange of ἀνα- for κατα- may echo the distinctive use of κατά with ἐξορκίζω in v 63 (cf. also κατηραμένοι in 25:41, part of a Matthean composition). Matthew omits "about whom you speak" because he cannot find any preceding statement by the men concerning Jesus. Mark's εὐθύς becomes εὐθέως (11,0), unless we are to follow the reading εὐθύς in the Matthean text of B L Θ. As in Luke, "a second time" disappears because of the omission of "twice" in v 34. John 18:27b matches the final clause in v 74 exactly.

Elsewhere καταθεματίζειν is transitive and not reflexive; therefore "Jesus" is probably implied as its object here, though omitted out of reverence (see H. Merkel in *The Trial of Jesus* [Cambridge Studies in Honour of C. F. D. Moule; ed. E. Bammel; SBT 2/13; London: SCM, 1970] 66-71).

26:75 (Mark 14:72; Luke 22:61-62) Mark's unnecessary prefix ἀν- falls away from the verb for Peter's remembering. The accusative τὸ ῥῆμα becomes the genitive τοῦ ῥήματος—a purely stylistic change (so also Luke). "Spoken by Jesus" replaces "how Jesus said to him," which is somewhat awkward after "the word." Matthew likes to use forms of εἴρω, such as εἰρη- κότος (18,9). In the repetition of Jesus' prediction, "twice" drops out, as also in Luke; and the order of Mark's με ἀπαρνήσῃ is reversed. Both of these changes conform to v 34 (see the comments ad loc. for interpretation). ἐξελθὼν ἔξω, "going outside," replaces Mark's difficult ἐπιβαλών, "putting [his cloak] over [his head]," "thinking about [it]," or perhaps something like our colloquial "pushing on" in the sense of movement, which would harmonize with Matthew's revision. The nominative participle ἐξελθών typifies his style (10,4). Perhaps, then, Luke's agreement with him shows his influence. ἔξω is a Mattheanism (3,1). In view of Matthew's making Peter go out into the gateway earlier (v 71), this further exit means that Peter went completely outside (cf. the comments on v 69). The aorist ἔκλαυσεν replaces Mark's imperfect ἔκλαιεν. Again Luke agrees with Matthew against Mark. The addition "bitterly" intensifies the warning: bitterness awaits those who, like Peter, crack under persecution because they failed to keep awake and pray. Yet again Luke agrees with Matthew against Mark.

THE MALICE OF JEWISH OFFICIALDOM
27:1-2 (Mark 15:1; Luke 22:66; 23:1; John 18:28)

27:1 (Mark 15:1) In this short section Matthew emphasizes the malice of Jesus' persecutors. They are the Jewish leaders, who also persecute Matthew's church. The replacement of Mark's καί with δέ contrasts the preceding night and the new morning. εὐθύς disappears, and in place of the simple adverb πρωΐ, "in the morning," Matthew writes πρωΐας . . . γενομένης, "when morning came." He likes the genitive absolute construction. Mark's ποιήσαντες, "making," after συμβούλιον, "a plan," becomes ἔλαβον, "they took," which Matthew always uses with συμβούλιον (3,2). The latter is translated "counsel" with its new verb. "All" has been reserved from Mark 14:64 (cf. Matt 26:66) and now makes its appearance with "the chief priests and the elders." Its addition clearly identifies this part of the session, rather than the earlier, as the occasion of Jesus' formal condemnation by the Sanhedrin (see also the comments on 26:66 and 27:3). Mark's "with" yields to "and," the usual connective in combinations of Jewish leaders. To "the elders" Matthew adds "of the people" (4,0; see the comments on 26:3 for

551

interpretation). The scribes drop out because there is no scriptural, theological discussion in what follows. "And the whole Sanhedrin" also drops out because it might seem to imply yet another group, whereas Mark apparently intends it to summarize the preceding list: "*even* the whole Sanhedrin." Matthew's inserting "against Jesus" shows his fondness for κατά + the genitive (10,1). It also echoes 26:59, makes up for the omission of "against him" in 26:60-61 (cf. Mark 14:56-57), and stresses the Jewish leaders' malice. To stress that malice even more, Matthew adds "so as to kill him." ὥστε is a favorite of his (10,10). The rest of the phrase comes from Mark 14:55, which Matthew revised somewhat in 26:59.

Mark's aorist participle ποιήσαντες does not necessarily indicate prior action and therefore eliminate a morning session of the Sanhedrin. In fact, it almost certainly does not indicate prior action, for that would contradict his adverbs εὐθὺς πρωΐ, "immediately in the morning," which by position modify ποιήσαντες—and perhaps δήσαντες, "binding," and ἀπήνεγκαν, "they took away," as well (v 2). Hence, Matthew does not create a morning session. He emphasizes its significance.

27:2 (Mark 14:1; Luke 23:1) The insertion "And" starts a new clause where Mark has not yet reached the verb of his first clause. Because Jesus' name appeared in v 1, a pronoun replaces it here. ἀπήγαγον, "they [led] him away," replaces ἀπήνεγκαν, "they took [him] away," for a parallel with 26:57 (cf. 27:31). Matthew's verb occurred as an insertion also in 7:13, 14 and seems to be reflected in Luke's ἤγαγον. To the statement that they gave Jesus over to Pilate is added "the governor" (τῷ ἡγεμόνι, a Mattheanism—7,2; see the comments on 2:5-6 for interpretation). The addition makes Jesus a model for his disciples, who "will be led before governors" (10:18), and prepares for following substitutions of "the governor" for Pilate's name. "Pilate" will fade out to concentrate attention on Jesus.

Concerning Pilate, see Josephus *Ant.* 18.3.1-2 §§55-62; 18.6.5 §177; *J.W.* 2.9.2-4 §§169-77; Philo *Legat.* 38; Tacitus *Ann.* 15.44. Tacitus calls Pilate a "procurator," the usual meaning of ἡγεμών. A recently discovered Palestinian inscription calls Pilate only a "prefect." Did he gain promotion? Or does ἡγεμών carry an informal meaning such as "governor"? On the apparent contrast between Pilate's cruel inflexibility and capitulation to Jewish pressure during Jesus' trial, see H. W. Hoehner in *New Dimensions in New Testament Study* (ed. R. N. Longenecker and M. C. Tenney; Grand Rapids: Zondervan, 1974) 115-26, especially 121-25. Pilate was probably staying at Herod's old palace rather than in the Tower of Antonia (see Josephus *Ant.* 20.5.3 §§105-12; *J.W.* 2.15.5 §§325-29).

THE DREADFUL END OF JUDAS:
AN EXAMPLE THAT WARNS AGAINST TREACHERY
IN THE CHURCH DURING PERSECUTION
27:3-10 (Acts 1:15-20)

The story of Judas's end shows the fulfillment of Jesus' dire prophecy in 26:24; Mark 14:21; Luke 22:22. More especially, however, Matthew inserts the story to complement the warning example of Peter's denials with that of Judas's death. Both have unhappy endings: bitter weeping and suicide. Both relate to problems caused by persecution: professing Christians who renounce Jesus to avoid persecution and professing Christians who betray others in the church to persecutors in order to save their own necks. Both carry the same point: do not do it—you will be sorry!

Because of Matthew's special diction, parallelism, heavy use of OT phraseology, and the absence of parallels in the other gospels, we might have thought that the story of Judas's end is a wholesale creation by Matthew himself. But the very different version of Judas's end in Acts 1:15-20, one with signs of an early date (see esp. the Aramaic in Acts 1:19), favors that Matthew is working with historical tradition. His revisions, however, show how creatively he works with material at his disposal. We have already seen evidence of such creativity in his use of Mark and the tradition shared only with Luke. But his revisions in the present story are especially striking and do not suffer any disadvantage from modern differences of opinion on the synoptic problem. They also support a similarly creative use of tradition in passages such as chaps. 1–2.

Here we may note several major revisions before examining the text in detail. According to Acts, Judas purchases a field with the price of betrayal. The purchase takes place prior to his death, and there is no remorse. Matthew makes Judas remorsefully return the price of betrayal for the sake of a point about treachery: "Do not betray your fellow Christian—you will regret it if you do." It is the chief priests and scribes, not Judas, who purchase a field. They do so only after Judas has committed suicide. All of this happens in fulfillment of OT prophecy, a favorite theme of Matthew. In Acts, Judas does not commit suicide; he merely has an accident. In Matthew, Judas commits suicide as a warning example of the hopeless remorse suffered by those who falsify their profession of discipleship through betraying their fellow disciples to persecutors. In Acts, Judas falls and bursts and his bowels gush out on the field he has purchased. In Matthew, Judas hangs himself in an unidentified location, initially because the purchase of the field comes after his death and is made by the chief priests and scribes, and then because Matthew sees a chance to relate his suicide to that of David's friend Ahithophel, who hanged himself (2 Sam 17:23). Consequently, Matthew has to change Judas's blood (so the implication of the ecbatic ὥστε in Acts 1:19) to Jesus' blood. Typically, he makes the best of this necessary change by using an OT expression, "innocent blood," to stress Jesus' innocence. Also as a consequence, Matthew can no longer present the field as a field of Judas's blood; hence, he again makes the best of necessity by turning the field of blood, where Judas died (but we do not read that he was buried there), into the potter's field, where aliens were buried. This revision conforms to the OT, which Matthew characteristically quotes as fulfilled.

27:3 Both τότε and the nominative participle ἰδών typify Matthean composition (66,17; 10-11,7). "Judas, who betrayed him" echoes 10:4; 26:25 (an insertion), 46, 48 and alludes to the problem of betrayal in the persecuted church. "That he [Jesus] was condemned" comes from Mark 14:64 and compensates for the omission in 26:66. Matthew probably means that

553

Jesus' condemnation became apparent to Judas in the transferal of Jesus to Pilate. μεταμεληθείς occurred distinctively in 21:29, 32 and here points to the remorse felt by church members who betray their fellows. ἔστρεψεν belongs to Matthew's special vocabulary (3,2). "The thirty pieces of silver" echoes a similar insertion in 26:15 and anticipates the coming quotation of Zech 11:12-13. The return of the money warns that ultimately there will be no reward in betraying one's fellow disciples. "To the chief priests and elders" echoes v 1 (cf. Jer 19:1).

27:4 Matthew's hand is evident in λέγων (61,23) and παραδούς (6,3). The latter comes after the confession "I have sinned," echoes the designation of Judas in v 3, and reemphasizes that betrayal will bring remorse to the betrayer. αἷμα ἀθῷον, "innocent blood," comes from the OT, where it occurs often (fifteen times in the LXX). In particular, it reflects Jer 19:4 (cf. Deut 27:25) and stresses the dastardly character of Judas's deed and of corresponding betrayals in the church. The two words of the expression will be inserted again, but not together, in v 24. αἷμα is especially frequent in the first gospel (4,3).

It is typical of Matthew's style that the answer of the chief priests and elders appears in a couplet of parallel lines: "What [is that] to us?" and "You shall see" (an imperatival future meaning "You see to that yourself— it is your affair!"). The latter will reappear as an insertion, again in relation to innocence and blood, in v 24, where the context will pluralize it. σύ is a Mattheanism (6,4). Out of the curt reply of the chief priests and elders Matthew is making the point, "You will hardly win the friendship of persecutors by betraying your fellow disciples to them."

See the UBS and Metzger, *Textual Commentary* ad loc., on the text-critical possibility of "righteous blood," which would also reflect OT usage and Matthew's fondness for δίκαιον (9-10,7-6). The apparent inconsistency between the chief priests' and elders' going away to Pilate (v 2) and their presence in the Temple (v 4) arises because the present story is being inserted in Markan material. If Matthew thought about the problem at all, he probably intended τότε at the beginning of v 3 to mean "during the time of the Sanhedrin's morning session, which ended in the taking of Jesus to Pilate." The expression "What is that to us? You see to it" accentuates the responsibility of Judas for his act rather than indicate an acceptance of responsibility by the Sanhedrin.

27:5 In v 5 we again meet the parallelism that typifies Matthew's compositions. Each of the two lines starts with καί, continues with a participle, and closes with a verb. As a whole, the verse luridly describes the fate a betrayer might expect. ῥίψας was an insertion in 9:36; 15:30. Its nominative participial form reflects Matthew's style. "The pieces of silver" echoes v 3; 26:15 and anticipates v 9. There will be further distinctive occurrences of ἀργύρια in 28:12, 15. An ex-publican such as Matthew would have had an interest in money. The entire expression "And having thrown the pieces of silver into the Temple" reflects Zech 11:13: "So I took the thirty [pieces] of silver and threw them to the potter in the house of the Lord" (cf. v 9). The LXX has εἰς, as Matthew does, before "the house of the Lord." Where Zechariah speaks of "the house of the Lord," however, Matthew uses his favorite ναόν (5,1). ἀνεχώρησεν and ἀπελθών also come from his special vocabulary (4,5; 14,11). ἀπήγξατο, "he hanged himself," is hapax in the NT and alludes to Ahithophel's suicide by hanging (2 Sam 17:23). The allusion not only exemplifies Matthew's habit of borrowing OT phraseology. It also agrees with his interest in Jesus as the son of David (4,2), for Ahithophel was a friend of David. As Ahithophel turned against David, Judas turned against Jesus.

See Metzger, *Textual Commentary* ad loc., on the variant readings "into the Temple" and "in the Temple." The question whether τὸν ναόν means the inner sanctuary (the proper definition, which would raise possibilities of Judas's breaking into an area forbidden to all but priests or throwing the money into a forbidden area) or the Temple in general (a loose usage, which would obviate the need to make the foregoing suggestions) arises out of failure to take account of Matthew's editing. Acts 1:15-20 says nothing about the Temple. Matthew does not draw it from historical tradition; it comes from Zech 11:13. We do not know how he thought of τὸν ναόν, unless he intended the throwing of the money into the treasury to define what Judas had already done rather than what the chief priests and elders might have done. The difference between Ahithophel's hanging himself because his advice was not taken and Judas's hanging himself because his bargain was carried through does not bother Matthew. His use of the OT tolerates such differences. Wis 4:18-19 bears a certain resemblance to Acts 1:18; but the realistic details in the latter passage make it doubtful that the former provided the foundation for a fabricated superstructure. Though swelling and bursting as a result of putrefaction may have been a traditional motif (so P. Benoit, *Jesus and the Gospel* [New York: Herder, 1973] 1. 194), the same thing can hardly be said for falling headlong and bursting open.

27:6-7 Verses 6-7 again present us with Matthew's beloved parallelism. Each verse has δέ at the beginning. Each continues with a participial phrase. Each closes with a finite verbal phrase (including a direct quotation in v 6). The first δέ contrasts the chief priests' decision not to put the pieces of silver in the treasury (cf. Deut 23:19[18]) with Judas's action of throwing them into the Temple. Matthew singles out the chief priests at the expense of the elders, who were also mentioned in v 3, because the chief priests had charge of the Temple and Judas had struck his bargain with them alone (26:14; Mark 14:10). Especially as a nominative participle, λαβόντες represents Matthew's diction (3,7). "The pieces of silver" echoes 26:15 and vv 3 and 5 in the present chapter. ἔξεστιν occurred as an insertion in 12:10 and as part of unique material in 20:15 (with οὐκ, as here), besides six shared occurrences. βαλεῖν appears in Matthew often (12,8; see esp. 25:27, where it was inserted with money as its object).

Matthew probably gets εἰς τὸν κορβανᾶν, "into the treasury," by reading אֶל־הָאוֹצָר in Zech 11:13 (cf. Josephus *J.W.* 2.9.4 §175). His phrase compensates for the omission of κορβᾶν in 15:5 (cf. Mark 7:11 and the omission of Mark 12:41-44 at the end of chap. 23). That the chief priests object to putting the money in the treasury sets them against Zechariah's prophecy. But if Judas's throwing the money into the Temple means putting it in the treasury, the prophecy was fulfilled before they withdrew it. Or if it did not go into the treasury at all, the prophecy is fulfilled nevertheless in the sense provided by reading אֶל־הַיּוֹצֵר, "to the potter" (see v 10). One way or another the prophetic Scriptures must reach fulfillment; they cannot be frustrated (see 26:54, a Matthean insertion, and the comments on 1:22-23). The chief priests' refusal to allow the money in the treasury reemphasizes the dastardliness of Judas's betraying Jesus. Again Matthew is discouraging betrayals in the church. ἐπεί was an insertion in 21:46 and part of a unique passage in 18:32, but appears only once each in Mark and Luke. τιμή, "price," anticipates the quotation from Zechariah in v 9 (cf. μισθοῦ, "wages," in Acts 1:18). αἵματος echoes v 4 and represents Matthew's preferred diction (4,3). Naturally, he will not have the chief priests speaking of the blood as "innocent" (as Judas does in v 4). But just as the expression "innocent blood" highlighted Judas's treachery and, by implication, the treachery of betrayals in the church, so also the expression "price of blood" highlights the same treacheries.

The second δέ contrasts the decision not to allow the money in the treasury with the use of the money for purchasing a field. "Taking counsel" echoes v 1 and typifies Matthew's phraseology (3,2). ἠγόρασαν, "they bought," appears five times in Matthew without parallel, besides two common occurrences (cf. ἐκτήσατο, "acquired," in Acts 1:18). The verb had ἀγρόν, "field," as its object also in 13:44, one of Matthew's compositions. The use of ἐξ with money in payment corresponds to his distinctive usage in 20:2. "The field of the potter" combines the potter mentioned in Zech 11:13; Jer 19:1, 11 and the field in the historical tradition of Judas's death (Acts 1:18-19), though Matthew uses ἀγρόν, as in 13:44, instead of Luke's χωρίον (cf. also the valley just outside the Potsherd Gate in Jer 19:1). "For burial" comes from and alludes to Jer 19:11. But where Jeremiah spoke about the burial of Judeans, Matthew writes τοῖς ξένοις, "for aliens." Perhaps the evangelist had that in his historical tradition even though it does not appear in Acts. But because it does not appear in Acts and ξένος appeared four times in 25:31-46, a composition of his, we should probably think of his transforming the burial of Judeans into the burial of aliens. Jer 19:4 helped Matthew do this, for there the Lord calls the valley outside the Potsherd Gate "an alien place" because of its profanation with heathen sacrifices. This transformation has the purpose, again, of highlighting the dastardliness of Judas's betrayal: the field was fit only for a graveyard, and that only for aliens! Neither Matthew nor Luke indicates that Judas was buried in the field; in fact, Matthew's "for aliens" implies the opposite.

The Jewish use of ill-gotten gain for public benefit (see J. Jeremias, *Jerusalem in the Time of Jesus* [London: SCM, 1969] 138-40) does not favor the historical rather than editorial character of Matthew's account at this point. Acts 1:18-19 stands in the way. The Jewish custom rather shows how easily Matthew could change the tradition.

27:8 "Therefore that field was called" reflects Jer 19:6: "Therefore . . . this place will be called." Matthew likes ἐκεῖνος (26,9). "Field of blood" comes from the historical tradition, " 'Hakeldama,' that is, 'Field of Blood' " (Acts 1:19), and recalls Jer 19:6, "the Valley of Slaughter." The switch from

Judas's blood, spilled out as a result of disembowelment upon falling, to Jesus' blood, declared "innocent" in v 4, reemphasizes the treachery of Judas and like betrayers in the persecuted church. "To this day" typifies Matthew's OT style (see the concordance for many examples of this expression in the OT) and contains two Mattheanisms, ἕως (13,14) and σήμερον (4,3; cf. the distinctive μέχρι τῆς σήμερον in 11:23; 28:15).

27:9-10 Matthew climaxes the story with an indication of fulfilled prophecy. The introductory formula, "Then was fulfilled what was spoken through Jeremiah the prophet, saying," matches 2:17 exactly. The employment of "Then" (τότε) instead of the more usual "in order that" (ἵνα or ὅπως—1:22; 2:15, 23; 4:14; 8:17; 12:17; 13:35; 21:4) stems from the dastardly character of the fulfilling event, hardly to be attributed to divine purpose in a direct sense (see also 2:17-18). The main words of the introduction form a chain of Mattheanisms. The naming of Jeremiah but not Zechariah not only follows a Jewish practice in composite quotations and makes mention of the prophet to whose writing a reader's mind might not be drawn because of the subtlety of the allusion (in contrast with the obviousness of the other side of the quotation—see esp. 2 Chr 36:21 with Lev 26:34-35 and Jer 25:12; 29:10). It also reflects Matthew's using Jeremiah as a prophet of woe in 2:17-18. By naming the prophet of woe Matthew closes the story on a note of warning to all church members who might be tempted to betray their fellow Christians—and on a note of doom concerning those who have succumbed to that temptation.

"And I [or 'we'] took the thirty pieces of silver" comes from Zech 11:13b. We might understand ἔλαβον to mean "I took," in accord with Zechariah, or "they [the chief priests] took," in accord with Matthew's preceding context. The use of μοι, "me," in the clause added at the close and as part of the quotation cancels the argument from Matthew's preceding context, however, and tips the scales in favor of the meaning "I took." Later, then, we should read ἔδωκα, "I gave," instead of ἔδωκαν, "they gave" (see the UBS for external text-critical evidence). The latter reading arose out of the preceding context. Matthew intends "I" and "me" to refer collectively to the chief priests, those who unconsciously fulfilled the prophecy. This reference marks a startling switch from the "I" of the prophet, Zechariah himself.

"The price of the one who was priced, whom [some] from the sons of Israel priced" comes from Zech 11:13a. The substantive participle τοῦ τετιμημένου goes back to הַיֹּקֶר read as הַיְקָר or הַיָּקָר (so the Peshitta) rather than as הַיֹּקֶר, "the price." Matthew takes Zechariah's מֵעֲלֵיהֶם, "from them" in the sense "by them," partitively, "[some] from," and expands "them" to "[the] sons of Israel." The latter phrase occurs often in the targums. Matthew uses it to distinguish the guilty Jewish leaders from the crowds, whom he has regularly portrayed as disciples, and as a foretaste of the many converts to come from all nations. This understanding forces the change of Zechariah's אֲשֶׁר, "at which," to the personal ὅν, "whom," and Zechariah's יָקַרְתִּי, "I was priced," to the third person middle ἐτιμήσαντο, "they priced [for themselves]."

There was a field in the historical tradition concerning Judas's death.

Jeremiah also contributed to Matthew's making the field a potter's field. His contribution is the reason Matthew mentions him in the formula introducing the OT quotation. But as such the words "and I gave them [the thirty pieces of silver] for the field of the potter" correspond roughly to Zechariah's statement "and I threw them to the potter." Matthew's revisions conform to the narrative in v 7 and to the necessity of a less forceful verb for payment in purchase. ἔδωκα is a favorite of his (8-9,10).

The clause καθὰ συνέταξέν μοι κύριος, "as the Lord commanded me," appears in neither Zechariah nor Jeremiah, but corresponds to καθὰ συνέταξεν κύριος τῷ Μωϋσῇ, "as the Lord commanded Moses," in the LXX at Exod 40:25; Num 8:3, 22; 9:5; 27:11; 31:31; etc. Matthew assimilates Moses' name to "I" and "me" in the present context and in the otherwise unquoted clause in Zech 11:13a: "the Lord said to me." Elsewhere συνέταξεν occurs twice as a Matthean insertion, but not at all in Mark. Why did Matthew's mind go from Zechariah to the pentateuchal statements regarding the Lord's commanding Moses? Probably the mention of a furnace in Zech 11:13 LXX reminded Matthew of the ashes of the furnace mentioned in the account of the sixth Egyptian plague (Exod 9:1-12). At the close of that account comes the phrase καθὰ συνέταξεν κύριος. The phrase refers to the Lord's determining Pharaoh's hardening of heart; but with the help of Zech 11:13a it apparently reminded Matthew of similarly worded statements about the Lord's commanding Moses.

See further Gundry, *Use of the OT* 122-27, especially against commonly affirmed allusions to Jer 18:1-12; 32:6-15. The wide separation and lack of connection between Jeremiah's visiting a potter and buying a field militate against Matthew's referring to them. Similarly, a reference to Jer 2:34-35 seems unlikely, despite phraseological and conceptual similarities, because there we read a false declaration of innocence by the guilty, but in Matthew we read about the true innocence of Jesus' blood. Besides, the topic of innocence arises in Matthew long before the OT quotation, and in Jer 2:34-35 the topics crucial to Matthew—a field, a potter, and burial—do not appear. Though we might wish for somewhat closer phraseological similarities between Matthew and Jeremiah 19, that passage offers Matthew's most probable source. The present comments correct some points in the earlier discussion cited above.

Though Matthew has increased the guilt of the Jewish leaders, he has not conversely reduced Judas's guilt. What we might mistake for reduction really amounts to a warning that the sweet relief from persecution obtained by betraying fellow Christians quickly turns sour. Judas's remorse leads to suicide, not to repentance and restoration.

THE MEEKNESS OF JESUS
27:11-14 (Mark 15:2-5; Luke 23:2-5; John 18:29-38)

27:11 (Mark 15:2; Luke 23:2-3) Because he inserted the story of Judas's end, Matthew has to compose the first clause of v 11 as a means of return to the story of Jesus' trial. δέ contrasts the two stories. The name of Jesus reintroduces him into the narrative. "Stood" seems to reflect Mark 13:9 and compensate for Matthew's having exchanged this verb in 24:18. Here and in Mark 13:9 we read of standing before governors. Matthew likes both ἔμπροσθεν (9,4) and ἡγεμόνος (7,2). The latter echoes v 2 (see the comments on v 2 and 2:5-6).

In rejoining Mark, Matthew may change the imperfect ἐπηρώτα to the aorist ἐπηρώτησεν, but part of the textual tradition in Mark reads the aorist. For a parallel with the first line, "the governor" replaces "Pilate." The elimination of Pilate's name focuses attention on Jesus. The addition of λέγων (so also Luke) corresponds to Matthew's style (61,23).

To increase the Christological emphasis Matthew adds Jesus' name again. The addition is typical (80,12). ἔφη appears also in Luke and replaces Mark's λέγει. Matthew likes both verbs (11,4; 47,11), but substitutes the one for the other as part of his omitting ἀποκριθείς, another of his favorites (29,6). This initially baffling revision of the verbal construction teams up with the omission of Mark's αὐτῷ, "to him [Pilate]," and with the above-mentioned suppression of Pilate's name and double insertion of Jesus' name to exhibit the dominance of Jesus: in a sense he does not answer anybody, but speaks in solitary majesty. Luke's ὁ δὲ ἀποκριθεὶς αὐτῷ ἔφη looks like a conflation of Matthew and Mark. σὺ λέγεις, "You're saying [it]," reads the same in all three synoptics and John 18:37. By himself Matthew prefers the aorist in the expression and uses the expression in a way that implies the questioner's already existing knowledge of an affirmative answer (see 26:25, 64). Not so in the present historical tradition, however; for had Pilate understood a clear affirmative, he would not have hesitated to condemn Jesus for sedition. But since Matthew's Pilate will turn out to be a convert, the expression may retain its usual Matthean flavor even here.

27:12 (Mark 15:3) The replacement of Mark's "they were accusing him" with "when he was being accused" allows Matthew to add "he answered nothing." This addition stems from the later question, "Do you not answer anything?" in Mark 15:4. Matthew advances Jesus' lack of response to emphasize the law of meekness (5:5, 38-48). Mark's "much" drops out; but Matthew adds the elders to the chief priests (cf. 26:3, 47, 57; 27:1, 3).

27:13 (Mark 15:4) As often, τότε replaces δέ. Matthew almost has to retain Pilate's name to avoid confusion, but he delays it to reduce attention to Pilate and increase attention to Jesus as an example of meekness. The historical present λέγει is a Mattheanism (47,11). Here it substitutes for ἐπηρώτα . . . λέγων, "was asking . . . saying," to prepare for the coming shift from not answering (so Mark) to not hearing (so Matthew). This replacement of Mark's second ἐπηρώτα (Matthew adopted the first in v 11) leads to the omission of πάλιν, "again." Because Matthew took "Do you not answer anything?" into v 12, it now changes to "Do you not hear . . . ?" ἀκούεις is another Mattheanism (26,6). "See" drops out in order that "how many things they testify against you" may be attached to "Do you not hear . . . ?" Thus Matthew has a single question instead of a pair. Though he likes pairs for the sake of parallelism, without the present continuation his switch from answering to hearing would have made the first question sound like one concerning physical deafness. Mark's "accuse" turns into "testify against" for an echo of 26:62 (cf. 26:65). This echo is a reminder of Jesus' earlier example of meekness.

27:14 (Mark 15:5) Mark's δέ changes to καί because Matthew does not want a contrast between Pilate's questioning and Jesus' refusal to answer so much as he wants a continuation of emphasis on Jesus' meekness. For this emphasis he advances οὐκ ἀπεκρίθη, "he did not answer." οὐκ replaces οὐκέτι, "still not," which occurs only twice in Matthew, but seven times in Mark and four in Luke. The addition of "him [Pilate]" forms a parallel with v 13a. Mark's "nothing" becomes "to not even one thing [or 'word']." This expansion lays even heavier stress on Jesus' meekness. Both οὐδέ and ἕν belong to Matthew's special diction (17,3; 24,7). In his quotation of the law of two or three witnesses (18:16), ῥῆμα referred to an accusation, as it does here. Again Pilate's name gives way to "the governor" to keep attention on Jesus (see the comments on v 2). For a final emphasis on Jesus' meekness, Matthew adds "exceedingly" to the governor's marvelling. λίαν is a favorite of the evangelist (3,1).

THE ACKNOWLEDGMENT OF JESUS AS RIGHTEOUS BY THE GENTILES PILATE AND HIS WIFE
27:15-26 (Mark 15:6-15; Luke 23:17-25; John 18:39-40; 19:16a)

27:15 (Mark 15:6) After adopting "But each feast" from Mark, Matthew changes the customary imperfect ἀπέλυεν, "he was [in the habit of] releasing," to the easier εἰώθει . . . ἀπολύειν, "was accustomed to release," and inserts "the governor" to clarify the subject and start a new section (see the comments on v 2 for ἡγεμών). ἕνα moves forward a step to emphasize the "one" as a counterpart to "the crowd." "To them" becomes "to the crowd," which comes up from Mark 15:8. "Whom they were [in the habit of] requesting" describes the prisoner in Mark. Matthew switches the verb to "wanted" (ἤθελον, a favorite of his—18,8). The result is a parallel with vv 17 and 21 and an emphasis on the coming free choice of Barabbas.

Cf. John 18:39. Apart from Matthew, Mark, and John, we have no evidence for the releasing of a prisoner each Passover. But cf. Josephus *Ant.* 20.9.3 §§208-10; Livy 5.13.

27:16 (Mark 15:7) Probably δέ means "And" or "Now" in Mark and "But" in Matthew. The contrast in Matthew consists in the kind of prisoner the crowd ordinarily wanted versus the kind of prisoner Barabbas was, viz., ἐπίσημον, which Matthew substitutes for "with the rebels . . . who had committed murder during the rebellion." Therefore ἐπίσημον carries its bad sense "notorious" rather than its good sense "notable." In order to heighten the Sanhedrin's guilt, Matthew wants to highlight the undesirability of Barabbas, not his association with Jewish patriotism. A freedom fighter *would* be the kind of prisoner the Jews usually wanted. "They had" replaces "was bound" because of the parallelistic repetition of "prisoner" from v 15; i.e., "prisoner" makes "was bound" unnecessary. The addition of τότε alongside δέ is remarkable, but represents Matthew's preferred diction (66,17), indicates present imprisonment, and thus makes up for Matthew's losing the force of the perfect participle δεδεμένος. Mark's ὁ drops out because of the added δέσμιον, which now governs λεγόμενον. Naturally, the switch from ἦν to εἶχον causes words associated with Barabbas to go from nominative to accusative. As will be confirmed below, Matthew adds "Jesus" (so Θ f[1] 700* syr[s,pal mss] arm geo[2] Origen mss[according to Peter-Laodicea]) to dramatize the choice between the "notorious prisoner called 'Jesus Barabbas' " and "Jesus the one called 'Christ.' " The dramatization heightens the guilt of the Jewish leaders in persuading the crowds to ask for Barabbas (v 20).

Unless the "they" in εἶχον is indefinite, the Romans are in view. Reverence for Jesus of Nazareth gave copyists reason to omit "Jesus" before "Barabbas"; but unless they thought as deeply as Matthew, they had no discernible reason to insert "Jesus" before "Barabbas." There is also the possibility of a purely accidental omission of "Jesus" before "Barabbas" in v 17 (see Metzger, *Textual Commentary* ad loc.), an accidental omission that worked backward to v 16. That Mark has ὁ λεγόμενος before Βαραββᾶς does not hint at another name, such as Ἰησοῦς, because Mark needs the phrase simply to introduce Barabbas as distinct from the other rebels.

27:17 (Mark 15:8-9) Mark's καί gives way to οὖν (35,11), which makes the following a consequence of the above-mentioned custom and of Barabbas's imprisonment. A typically Matthean genitive absolute construction takes the place of Mark's participle. "Going up, the crowd began to ask [him to do] just as he was [in the habit of] doing for them" (so Mark) changes to a simple "when they gathered together." Matthew is alluding to the unbelieving synagogue of his own day as a source of persecution. συνηγμένων comes from his preferred diction (10,10). In Mark the crowd asks Pilate to follow the custom. Matthew's revisions make Pilate appear to take initiative for Jesus' release. Surely the crowd would not want that notorious prisoner Jesus Barabbas! Here we see Matthew's first move to Christianize Pilate. Other moves will follow.

Because of its advance to v 15, "the crowd" becomes "they." Matthew's genitive absolute forces out δέ. The substitution of gathering for going up and asking leads to the replacement of Mark's "answered . . . saying" with a simple "said." The delay of Pilate's name till the end of the clause carries on the de-emphasis of Pilate to give Jesus the limelight. Before "do you want me to release for you," Matthew inserts "Whom?" to prepare for his replacing "the king of the Jews" with "Jesus the 'Barabbas' [Aramaic for 'son of Abba'] or Jesus the one called 'Christ' " (see the note on v 16 concerning the text-critical question). Again, the choice dramatizes the guilt of the Sanhedrin and, by implication, of the Jewish leaders in Matthew's day for influencing their people to reject Jesus. λεγόμενον is a Mattheanism (10,2) and recalls 1:16 as well as parallels λεγόμενον before Ἰησοῦν Βαραββᾶν (v 16). Here the participle does not mean "so-called," for it comes editorially from the believer Matthew, not historically from Pilate, and therefore must not bear its bad sense before "Christ." Furthermore, its parallel in v 16 can hardly mean "so-called," and Matthew will go on to

561

finish his portrait of Pilate as a Christian, a portrait in which a sneering "so-called Christ" would not fit on the governor's lips. Rather, Pilate *confesses* Jesus as the Christ. "Christ" is a Mattheanism (8,5) and corresponds to "king of the Jews" in Mark. It also distinguishes this Jesus from Jesus the "Barabbas," echoes 26:63, 68 (where it broke into traditional material), and emphasizes the messiahship of Jesus of Nazareth. As a whole, "Jesus the one called 'Christ' " will reappear as an insertion in v 22.

27:18 (Mark 15:10) Despite his liking Mark's ἐγίνωσκεν (8,2), Matthew uses the synonym ᾔδει in reminiscence of 26:2, 70, 72, 74 (cf. 27:65; 28:5 as well as the much earlier distinctive occurrences in 6:8; 9:4; 15:12; 25:12). As usual, Mark's pluperfect becomes aorist in the shift from παραδεδώκεισαν αὐτόν, "had given him over," to παρέδωκαν αὐτόν, "gave him over." Matthew omits "the chief priests" for a parallel with v 2, where παρέδωκαν took its subject, "the chief priests and elders of the people," from the context (v 1; cf. the same expression in v 20 of the present context). The chief priests and elders envied Jesus' revived, growing influence over the people (cf. the triumphal entry and John 11:45-53; 12:9-11).

27:19 Matthew inserts the snippet containing the statement of Pilate's wife in order to portray Jesus as the model of righteous conduct and prepare for Pilate's following her advice (v 24). Thus, in a preview of wholesale conversion among all the nations, Pilate's wife and Pilate himself become Gentile disciples of Jesus (see "Universality" in the Topical Index and esp. 28:19-20). The Christianizing of Pilate and his wife makes them a foil to the Jewish leaders, whose guilt stands out all the more. δέ contrasts the giving over of Jesus with the attempt of Pilate's wife to save him.

Again Matthew begins with a genitive absolute (cf. v 17). Its participle καθημένου comes from one of his favorite verbs (8,0). δέ contrasts Jesus' being given over with the attempt of Pilate's wife to save him. The rest of the verse is peppered with Mattheanisms: ἀπέστειλεν (4,4); γυνή (10,3); λέγουσα (61,23); δικαίῳ (9-10,7-6; cf. the variant readings in vv 4, 24); ἐκείνῳ (26,9); γάρ (62-63,15); πολλά (23,1); σήμερον (4,3); and κατ' ὄναρ (1,5). As a variant reading ἔπαθον was an insertion in 17:15. The combination of πολλά with ἔπαθον occurred also in 16:21 (cf. Mark 8:31) and may compensate for omissions and revisions in 9:20 (cf. Mark 5:26); 17:12 (cf. Mark 9:12). The demonstrative "that" adds weight to the declaration that Jesus is righteous, which in terms of Matthew's theology is tantamount to a Christian confession. See the comments on 1:20-21 for Matthew's use of dreams as indicators of divine initiative (cf. Valerius Maximus 1.7.2; Dio Cassius 44.17).

27:20 (Mark 15:11) To "the chief priests" Matthew adds "and the elders" (4,2) for a parallel with 26:3, 47, 57; 27:1, 3, 12. The addition has the effect of expanding the attention given to the Jewish leaders responsible for persuading the crowd to ask for Barabbas's release and Jesus' execution. ἀνέσεισαν, "stirred up," changes to ἔπεισαν, "persuaded," which will occur as an insertion also in 27:43 and as part of distinctive material in 28:14. The new verb lightens the crowd's burden of guilt by making them victims of evil persuasion. As often, Matthew pluralizes the crowd. Mark's "rather" drops out in anticipation of an addition that will emphasize the alternative far more than μᾶλλον does. Matthew omitted αἰτεῖσθε in v 17 (cf. Mark 15:8). Here he compensates by substituting αἰτήσωνται for ἀπολύσῃ αὐτοῖς. The substitute shifts the blame from Pilate ("he should release for them," so Mark) to the crowds ("they should ask"). This shift adds to the Christianization of Pilate and would mar Matthew's portraying the crowds as disciples except that they are misled and thus symbolize the masses in the church who are led into sin by antinomian leaders (cf. the apostasy of Peter). The crowds come from Mark. When Matthew writes independently concerning Jewish responsibility, he switches to "the people" (v 25).

In contrast with Mark's word order, Barabbas's name waits till the end of its clause for the sake of chiasm with the next, parallel clause, which Matthew will insert. The chiasm allows Barabbas and Jesus to stand side by side in the text for yet another dramatization of the alternative (see the comments on vv 16-17). The inserted, antithetic clause reads, "but [that] they should destroy Jesus"—another damning indictment. Matthew's diction is evident in Jesus' name (80,12) and ἀπολέσωσιν (8,1; see esp. 2:13; 12:14, where it concerns the destroying of Jesus).

27:21 (Mark 15:12; Luke 23:18-19; John 18:40) For stylistic reasons Mark's ἀποκριθείς comes forward. Again "the governor" replaces Pilate's name (see the comments on vv 2, 14). Matthew inserts "said to them" to introduce non-Markan tradition. Luke and John preserve this tradition more fully, and Matthew conforms it to the preceding. The addition heightens Jewish guilt. "Whom do you want . . . me to release for you?" comes verbatim from v 17. Matthew inserts "of the two" to summarize his insertion, "Jesus the 'Barabbas' or Jesus the one called 'Christ,'" in v 17. δύο is a favorite of his (19,4). He never seems to tire of reiterating the choice between Barabbas and Jesus in order to stress Jewish guilt in the choice of Barabbas. That choice is noted succinctly: "But they said, 'Barabbas'"—a trenchant reduction of the tradition preserved in Luke and John.

27:22 (Mark 15:12-13; Luke 23:20-21) The historical present λέγει with asyndeton is a Mattheanism (21,6). Here it replaces Mark's imperfect ἔλεγεν. Pilate's name stems from the earlier part of Mark 15:12, where Matthew replaced it with "the governor." We may prefer the reading without θέλετε in Mark, not only because of its brevity and the better quality of the external evidence favoring it (‭א‬ B C W Δ Ψ f¹ f¹³ 33 *al*), but also because of the unlikelihood that Matthew omits θέλετε (18,8). Or we may accept the longer reading in Mark, regard the shorter as scribal assimilation to Matthew, and say that Matthew omitted the verb because of his immediately preceding insertion of it (v 21b). "Jesus, the one called 'Christ'" takes the place of "him whom you call 'the King of the Jews'" for a parallel with v 17 (see the comments ad loc.). "They say" replaces "And they yelled" to match the similar revision in the first clause of the present verse. Matthew reserves the historical present of λέγω for sayings he wants to emphasize. Here the emphasis falls on Jewish guilt, which increases with the typically Matthean addition of "all" (πάντες—63,25-26). "Again" falls out because of Matthew's observation that the crowd has not yet shouted "Crucify him!" That shout changes to "Let him be crucified!" The switch from active voice to passive alleviates Pilate of blame in order that the Jews may have it all and Pilate be propelled by Matthew into Christian faith.

The text-critical question regarding ὃν λέγετε in Mark (see the UBS and Metzger, *Textual Commentary* ad loc.) does not materially alter the picture in Matthew.

27:23 (Mark 15:14; Luke 23:22-23) Because of its insertion in the preceding verse, "Pilate" drops out here. ἔφη, often preferred by Matthew (11,4), replaces ἔλεγεν and provides some variation after three forms of λέγω in v 22. The omission of "to them" generalizes the following words, so that they become a question to the whole world: "Why? What bad thing has he done?" Matthew switches the order of Mark's ἐποίησεν κακόν to bring κακόν closer to τί, with which it goes. Typically, he adds λέγοντες to the crowds' yelling (61,23). Atypically, he turns Mark's aorist into the imperfect to stress that they repeatedly yelled for Jesus' crucifixion. The repetition puts Jesus' persecutors in a worse light. "Crucify him!" again changes to "Let him be crucified!" (see v 22).

27:24 (Mark 15:15) "But Pilate" comes from Mark. ἰδών is a Mattheanism (10-11,7). "Seeing that he in no way succeeds [or 'that nothing succeeds']" starts an insertion that takes the place of "wanting to satisfy the crowd"; i.e., Matthew changes Pilate's wanting to satisfy the crowd to Pilate's pinning the blame on the Jewish people. By contrast, Pilate himself appears in a rosy light: he follows his wife's advice not to cooperate in the condemnation of "that righteous one" (v 19, a Matthean insertion). By obeying the OT law of hand washing and, probably, by calling Jesus "this righteous one," he joins his wife in the vanguard of the many Gentiles who have flocked into the church by the time Matthew writes. "But rather an uproar takes place" is antithetic to the preceding. Such parallelism typifies Matthew's style. μᾶλλον comes from his special vocabulary (5,1), and θόρυβος γίνεται reflects the tradition in 26:5.

The nominative participle λαβών is another favorite of Matthew (3,7). He follows his custom of drawing on the OT by taking "water" from Deut 21:4 and "washed [his] hands" from Deut 21:6. The passage in Deuteronomy deals with freedom from the guilt of "innocent blood" (Deut 21:8-9; cf. Matt 27:4). ἀπέναντι, "over against," appears where we might have expected ἔμπροσθεν, "before" (9,4), and demarcates Pilate from "the crowd," who under the influence of the chief priests and elders ask for Barabbas instead of Jesus. This demarcation provides another indication of Pilate's discipleship. He not only keeps the law in accord with Jesus' teaching in Matthew; he also stands on Jesus' side opposite those who are clamoring for the crucifixion. "The crowd" comes from Mark and echoes 26:47, 55; 27:15, 20. λέγων characterizes Matthew's style (61,23).

"Innocent" echoes v 4, a Matthean composition containing the only other occurrence of the adjective in the NT. There Judas is guilty of Jesus' innocent blood. Here Pilate is innocent of Jesus' blood. Moreover, Pilate's declaration of innocence rests on Deut 21:8-9. Matthew means to say that as a law-abiding citizen of the kingdom of heaven Pilate really is innocent. The reference to blood in the phrase ἀπὸ τοῦ αἵματος also goes back to Deut

21:8-9, and it echoes Matt 27:4, 6, 8. As a whole, this declaration of innocence looks remarkably similar to Sus 46 (Theodotion; cf. Pss 26:6; 73:13 and see further Gundry, *Use of the OT* 144, and esp. S. van Tilborg, *The Jewish Leaders in Matthew* [Leiden: Brill, 1972] 92).

We should probably accept the reading τοῦ δικαίου τούτου in ℵ K L W Π f^1 f^{13} 33 565 etc. it^{c,ff1,g1,l,q} vg syr^h co$^{sa mss,bo}$ etc., which is also supported by A Δ 064 1230 it^{aur,f,h} syr^{p,pal} etc. in the order τοῦ δικαίου τούτου. This reading is usually thought to reflect the parallel scribal variant δίκαιον in v 4 and to have arisen from a desire to separate clearly τούτου from the preceding ἀπὸ τοῦ αἵματος, i.e., avoid the understanding "from this blood." But Greek manuscripts that have τοῦ δικαίου here do not have δίκαιον in v 4. Also, Matthew has a penchant for δίκαιος (9-10,7-6). There is a general editorial correlation between this passage and v 19. And some copyists might well have omitted τοῦ δικαίου because it seemed awkward in front of τούτου (so that other copyists put it after τούτου). Yet the awkward order corresponds to the order in v 19, which Matthew composed and inserted. All these considerations favor that Pilate does confess Jesus as "this righteous one," just as Pilate's wife confessed Jesus as "that righteous one."

"You see [to it]" echoes v 4, a Matthean composition, where the expression occurred in the singular and, as here, in association with innocence and blood. In the present passage the expression heaps blame on the Jews. Matthew likes ὑμεῖς (15,3). The parallel with v 4 rules out understanding ὄψεσθε as a predictive future referring to the events of A.D. 70. Rather, we have an imperatival future (so certainly v 4).

27:25 Matthew's favorite vocabulary is evident in ἀποκριθείς . . . εἶπεν (29,6) and πᾶς (63,25-26). "The people" comes from 26:5, where it is associated with "uproar" (cf. the preceding verse here). Though λαός does not appear in Matthew nearly so often as it does in Luke, Matthew inserts it eight times and includes it in unique material four times, besides two common occurrences. "His blood [be] on us and on our children" echoes 23:35, an insertion by Matthew (see the comments ad loc. and cf. 23:37; Isa 1:15-16; Jer 26:15; Acts 5:28; 18:6; 20:26). τέκνα occurs in distinctive passages four times elsewhere in this gospel. Matthew's composition of v 25 implies the transferal of the kingdom from the Jewish people to the church.

To take v 25 as historical would require us to think that the people were claiming innocence. Composition by Matthew makes their words an acknowledgment of guilt.

27:26 (Mark 15:15; Luke 23:24-25) For transition back to Markan material Matthew inserts his beloved τότε (66,17). Pilate's wanting to satisfy the crowd drops out as disagreeable with Matthew's Christianization of Pilate. But Matthew can hardly avoid Pilate's releasing Barabbas to them. For a contrast between Barabbas and Jesus, δέ replaces Mark's καί and τόν . . . Ἰησοῦν φραγελλώσας, "having scourged Jesus," comes forward. On scourging as a Roman preliminary to crucifixion, see Josephus *J.W.* 2.14.9 §§306, 308; 5.11.1 §449; Livy 22.13; Cicero *Against Verres* 5.62 §162. The handing over for crucifixion remains unchanged.

JESUS AS THE MODEL
OF A PERSECUTED RIGHTEOUS PERSON
27:27-50 (Mark 15:16-37; Luke 23:26, 33-46; John 19:2-3, 16b-30)

27:27 (Mark 15:16) Because there will be no contrast with the preceding, τότε replaces δέ. The characteristic insertion "of the governor" (7,2) identifies whose soldiers take Jesus to the praetorium, the governor's official residence (see the note to v 2). The lack of any previous mention of the soldiers makes Matthew feel the need of such an identification. παραλαβόντες comes from his preferred diction (4,6), complements παρέδωκεν in v 26, replaces Mark's ἀπήγαγον, and results in the loss of καί before συγκαλοῦσιν (cf. 4:5 with Luke 4:9). The switch from verb to participle starts a string of five successive clauses consisting of a participial phrase plus a finite verbal phrase (vv 27, 28, 29a, 29b, 30). Matthew's parallelistic style is on display. The name of Jesus replaces "him," as it often does for a Christological emphasis (80,12). Instead of "inside the palace [or 'courtyard'], which is the praetorium" (so Mark), Matthew writes "into the praetorium" so as not to cause confusion with the courtyard or palace of Caiaphas the high priest in 26:3, 58, 69.

"Gathered together" replaces "call together," typifies Matthew's diction (συνήγαγον—10,10), and parallels a similar insertion in 26:3, where the chief priests and elders of the people "gathered together into the palace of the high priest called Caiaphas." Inserting "against him" heightens the element of persecution. Throughout the remainder of the passion, Matthew will stress the persecution of Jesus to encourage those who are suffering persecution at the time of writing. Mark's reference to "the whole cohort" stays. A cohort usually consisted of 500-600 soldiers, but the present circumstances suggest loose usage for a smaller number.

27:28 (Mark 15:17) "Having stripped" replaces "they dress." The substitute again heightens the element of persecution by playing up the indignity done to Jesus. "A purple garment" becomes "a scarlet cloak"; i.e., a truly royal robe becomes an ordinary soldier's mantle (cf. BAG, s.v. πορφύρα and χλαμύς; *TDNT* 3. 813). Yet again the indignity is heightened. Mark's καί disappears because of Matthew's initial participle. This disappearance makes "they put around" refer to the scarlet cloak rather than to the crown of thorns (as in Mark). An aorist tense replaces Mark's historical present.

See the UBS and Metzger, *Textual Commentary* ad loc., on the v.l. ἐνδύσαντες, "having clothed," which goes against Matthew's desire to heighten the indignities done to Jesus.

27:29 (Mark 15:17-18) For parallelism, Matthew adds καί (see the comments on v 27). As a matter of style, "thorny" drops out in front of "crown" and reappears as the prepositional phrase "of thorns" right after "crown." Because "they put around" shifted its reference (see v 28), Matthew must now add "they put . . . on his head." ἐπέθηκαν parallels περιέθηκαν and belongs to his special vocabulary (5,0). In 26:7 he alone wrote ἐπί with τῆς κεφαλῆς, as here. His inserting "and a reed in his right hand" increases the indignity done to Jesus. The reed anticipates Mark 15:19, where the soldiers will hit Jesus on the head with a reed. But only in Matthew does Jesus hold a reed as part of the mockery. δεξιᾷ is a Mattheanism (4,3).

In another heightening of indignity, "kneeling in front of him, they mocked him" replaces "they began to greet him." The replacement may also hint that in kneeling the soldiers did what they should before God's Son. A mere greeting would not have sufficed (see 17:14 in contrast with Mark 9:15; cf. the comments on 5:46-47). γονυπετήσαντες anticipates τίθεντες τὰ γόνατα in Mark 15:19 (cf. also Matt 17:14). ἔμπροσθεν is a Mattheanism (9,4). ἐνέπαιξαν anticipates v 31; Mark 15:20. Typically, Matthew adds λέγοντες (61,23). "Hello! King of the Jews!" stays unchanged.

Cf. John 19:2. See H. St. J. Hart in *JTS* ns 3 (1952) 66-75 on the possibility that the spikes of the thorns turned outward in a mocking imitation of the radiate crowns of the period, rather than inward for the infliction of pain. With the mocking of Jesus as king, cf. Philo *In Flacc.* 6 §§36-39; V. A. Tcherikover and A. Fuks, eds., *Corpus Papyrorum Judaicarum* 2 (Cambridge, Mass.: Harvard, 1950) nos. 154, 158; Plutarch *Pomp.* 24.

27:30 (Mark 15:19) In order to make a parallel with 26:67, Matthew reverses the Markan order of hitting and spitting. And for the sake of parallel structure in the immediate context (see the comments on v 27) he turns the verb ἐνέπτυον, "they were spitting," into the participle ἐμπτύσαντες. Mark's αὐτῷ changes to εἰς αὐτόν in reminiscence of εἰς τὸ πρόσωπον αὐτοῦ in 26:67, where only Matthew had εἰς (see the comments on 26:67). Since Jesus is holding a reed only in Matthew (see v 29), the soldiers' hitting him with it requires adding the transition "they took the reed." ἔλαβον is a common verb, but extraordinarily frequent in Matthew (21,16). After καὶ ἔτυπτον Matthew inserts εἰς to go with τὴν κεφαλὴν αὐτοῦ. The insertion makes a parallel with εἰς αὐτόν and leads to the transfer of αὐτοῦ from its Markan position before τὴν κεφαλήν. "And bending [their] knees, they were worshipping him" disappears, partly because Matthew has already used the item of kneeling (v 29) and partly because the mockery offends his use of προσκυνέω for genuine worship.

27:31 (Mark 15:20; Luke 23:26) Mark's statements about the ridiculing, stripping, and reclothing of Jesus come over with two substitutions: (1) χλαμύδα, "cloak," for πορφύραν, "purple garment," and (2) αὐτοῦ, "his," for τὰ ἴδια, "his own." The first substitution is an assimilation to v 28 (see the comments ad loc.); the latter is doubtful, for in Mark B C Δ Ψ *pc* read αὐτοῦ and Matthew's fondness for ἴδια (6,0) would probably have led him to retain it if he had seen it in his copy of Mark. ἀπήγαγον, "they led [him] away," replaces ἐξάγουσιν, "they lead [him] out," for a parallel with 26:57; 27:2 and in compensation for replacing ἀπήγαγον in v 27 (cf. Mark 15:16). Luke agrees with Matthew's aorist against Mark's historical present. The change from ἐξ- to ἀπ- will allow Matthew to use ἐξ- for an exit from Jerusalem in the next verse. For the present, Jesus departs only from the palace. Instead of Mark's ἵνα-clause, "in order that they might crucify him,"

Matthew writes εἰς with an articular infinitive, "for the purpose of crucifying [him]." This phrase echoes 20:19 and especially 26:2, where only Matthew had the infinitive construction.

27:32 (Mark 15:21; Luke 23:26) δέ replaces καί in order to contrast the soldiers' leading Jesus away to crucify him and their requisitioning Simon of Cyrene to carry Jesus' cross. As a nominative participle ἐξερχόμενοι is favored by Matthew (10,4). ἐρχόμενον ἀπ', slightly later in Mark, prompted its insertion here as a pointer to Jesus' death outside Jerusalem (see 21:39 with comments ad loc.). Since the soldiers have already led him away from the palace (v 31), the participle refers to exit from the city. The insertion of "they found" helps make two clauses out of Mark's awkwardly long first clause. εὗρον is a Mattheanism (7,8). ἄνθρωπον, "a man," replaces παράγοντά τινα, "a certain one passing by." Since Matthew not only likes this noun (35,17) but also uses it sometimes for disciples (see the comments on 13:44), he may be portraying Simon as a model of Jesus' cross-carrying disciples. "Cyrenian" comes forward (cf. Acts 6:9). Because of his concern with the great commission (28:19-20), Matthew is interested in geographical regions (cf. "Cyrenian man" with "Canaanite woman" in 15:22, which differs from Mark 7:25-26). The inserted ὀνόματι typifies Matthew's diction (9,5). "Coming from a field [or 'the country']" disappears because earlier in this verse he turned Simon's coming from the country to Jerusalem into an exit from Jerusalem by those who were leading Jesus to crucifixion. The further designation of Simon as "the father of Alexander and Rufus" drops out as meaningless to Matthew's audience, who did not know those men as Mark's audience apparently did. Luke agrees with Matthew's omission. The starting of a new sentence where Mark continues without break requires the insertion of "This one." Finally, in this more natural spot, Matthew takes up Mark's ἀγγαρεύουσιν, "they requisition," but changes it to the aorist.

27:33 (Mark 15:22; Luke 23:33) Because Mark's φέρουσιν, "they bring," probably meant "bear, carry" to Matthew (with the possible exception of 17:17), it changes to ἐλθόντες, "going" (cf. Luke). This nominative participle typifies his style (10,10). Naturally, αὐτόν drops out (so also Luke). Matthew's participle starts another series of parallel clauses, each consisting of a participial phrase plus a finite verbal phrase (vv 33-34a, 34b, 35, 36; cf. the comments on v 27). εἰς replaces Mark's ἐπί for motion toward "a place." Mark's τόν disappears, and τόπον moves forward. Matthew inserts λεγόμενον, which is a favorite of his (10,2); and the phrase closes with Mark's reference to Golgotha. μεθερμηνευόμενος, "translated," yields to λεγόμενος, "called, means," for a parallel with λεγόμενον, which Matthew has just inserted. The advance of κρανίου τόπος, "Place of a Skull," adds a note of foreboding.

Matthew probably read μεθερμηνευόμενος rather than μεθερμηνευόμενον in Mark, since he himself writes λεγόμενος rather than λεγόμενον at the end of the verse and would have found the other easier because of its agreement in gender with ὅ. The ending -ος makes the participle modify τόπος rather than the relative pronoun. Did Golgotha get its name for its shape, its use as a place of execution, the discovery of a skull there once upon a time, or some other reason?

27:34 (Mark 15:23) Matthew omits καί because of the foregoing participial construction and changes the conative imperfect ἐδίδουν, "they were trying to give," to the aorist ἔδωκαν, "they gave," for conformity to Ps 69:22(68:21) LXX. He inserts "to drink" and changes "myrrhed wine" to "wine mixed with gall" in further assimilations to Ps 69:22(68:21) LXX (see Gundry, *Use of the OT* 144-45, 202). Myrrhed wine was a delicacy (see *TDNT* 7. 458-59). Matthew's exchanging it for wine mixed with gall adds to the indignities done to Jesus. For a transition from giving drink to tasting, Mark's awkward "but who" yields to "and tasting." Thus Matthew gains both an introductory participle and an opportunity to give a reason for Jesus' refusing the drink, viz., the bitter taste of the gall, mentioned only by Matthew in dependence on the OT. In Mark, Jesus does not taste the wine, but refuses it altogether. Mark's "he did not take [it]" becomes "he did not want to drink [it]" to satisfy Matthew's penchant for ἠθέλησεν (18,8) and make a parallel with "to drink" in the preceding clause.

Myrrhed wine was used as a painkiller externally, but not internally (see G. W. van Beek in *The Biblical Archaeologist Reader II* [Garden City, N.Y.: Doubleday, 1964] 116-17). Since Roman soldiers appear to have offered the wine (see the context), we ought not to think of the philanthropic practice of Jewish women explained in *b. Sanh.* 43a (cf. Prov 31:6-7). The similarity between the Aramaic מוּרָא/מוֹר, "myrrh," and the Hebrew מְרֹרָה, "gall," may have helped Matthew's shift.

27:35 (Mark 15:24; Luke 23:33-34) The changing of καί to δέ produces a contrast between the soldiers' failure to make Jesus drink the galled wine and their parting Jesus' garments, about which Jesus does nothing because he is hanging on the cross. For parallelism, the verb "crucify" becomes the participle "having crucified" (see the comments on v 33). Astonishingly, then, the stress in Matthew does not fall on the crucifixion at all, but moves to the parting of Jesus' garments in keeping with Ps 22:19. This OT allusion is already evident in Mark. The making of Mark's historical present διαμερίζονται into the aorist διεμερίσαντο agrees with Matthew's practice of avoiding the historical present (except for λέγω) and conforms to the LXX and the Peshitta against the imperfect of the Hebrew text. As in Luke, Mark's ἐπ' αὐτὰ τίς τί ἄρῃ, "over them [as to] who should take what," falls off as otiose after βάλλοντες κλῆρον, "casting lots."

Executioners customarily took their victims' personal possessions. On the method of crucifixion, see J. A. Fitzmyer in *CBQ* 40 (1978) 493-513.

27:36 (Mark 15:25) To multiply the indignities done to Jesus, Matthew inserts "and sitting down, they were guarding him there." Almost every word of the insertion is a favorite of his: καθήμενοι (8,0), ἐτήρουν (5,1), and ἐκεῖ (16,6). Mark's noting the third hour (9:00 A.M.) drops out as irrelevant to the motif of persecution, and his restating the crucifixion drops out as redundant. In view of the lengthy continuation of the passion account, Matthew's inserting v 36 hardly has the purpose of forestalling the belief that Jesus was removed from the cross before he died.

27:37 (Mark 15:26; Luke 23:38; John 19:19) On a condemned man's way to execution it was customary for a tablet with a statement of his crime to be carried before him, or hung around his neck, and then for the tablet to be attached to the cross. The substitution of "they put" for "an inscription was inscribed" and the addition "over his head" make a parallel with Matthew's revision in v 29. He likes ἐπέθηκαν (5,0), and his switching from ἐπί, "on" (v 29), to ἐπάνω, "over," suits the present passage as well as displays his predilection for ἐπάνω (7,1). He inserts another favorite in "This is . . ." (12,0), which changes the accusation from an insulting joke to a Christian confession, a proclamation of Jesus' kingship (cf. the comments on 3:17). Luke seems to conflate Mark and Matthew by putting οὗτος at the end without ἐστιν. The further insertion of "Jesus" (so also John) adds Christological emphasis in a manner typical of Matthew (80,12).

27:38 (Mark 15:27; Luke 23:33; John 19:18) τότε forces out καί. For smoothness Matthew reverses "with him" and "they crucify" (so Mark in that order). The active voice of "crucify" turns into the passive to conform to the passives in 26:2; 27:22, 23, 26, 44; 28:5 (though the active also appears in 20:19; 23:34; 27:31, 35). In 26:2 Matthew inserted the passive, and in 27:22, 23 he changed the traditional active to a passive. Mark's "his" drops out as needless because of the earlier phrase "with him."

Cf. Isa 53:12. λῃσταί may mean "revolutionaries" as well as "robbers." But since Matthew wants to heighten the indignities done to Jesus, he probably means criminal robbers rather than patriotic revolutionaries. Cf. the comments on vv 16, 44.

27:39-40 (Mark 15:29-30; Luke 23:35) Mark's καί becomes δέ for a contrast with being crucified. Otherwise, the passing by, blaspheming of Jesus, shaking of heads, and speaking are described in words identical with Mark's. In the direct quotation, however, "Ha!" drops out; and "if you are [the] Son of God" is inserted, exactly as in 4:3, 6. Characteristically, Matthew is emphasizing Jesus' divine sonship (υἱὸς θεοῦ—4,2). Especially cf. 26:63-64, where he alone put the question of Jesus' sonship in a conditional clause, as here, and wrote "the Son of God" instead of "the Son of the Blessed One" (see also vv 43 and 54 below). The advance of ἐν τρισὶν ἡμέραις stresses the three days (cf. 12:40) and conforms to the word order in 26:61.

See Gundry, Use of the OT 62-63, on allusions to Lam 2:15 in the passersby (cf. Lam 1:12) and to Lam 2:15; Ps 22:8(7) in the shaking of heads (cf. Ps 109:25).

In the last line of v 40 we face a text-critical question: Should we read καί or not? See the UBS for external evidence. Retention puts the conditional clause with the preceding: ". . . save yourself if you are the Son of God, and come down from the cross." Omission allows, but does not require, the preceding and following clauses to go together: ". . . save yourself. If you are the Son of God, come down from the cross," or ". . . save yourself if you are the Son of God. [Asyndeton] Come down from the cross." Since the conditional clause reflects the similar conditional clause in 26:63, where Matthew goes his own way in attaching it to the preceding (see also 27:43, an insertion of his), we should favor the same syntax here and accept καί as Matthew's insertion to avoid asyndeton. Mark's participle καταβάς changes to the imperative κατάβηθι in order that a parallel may develop between "save yourself" and "come down from the cross." Cf. Wis 2:6-20.

27:41-42 (Mark 15:31-32; Luke 23:35) As in Luke, "to one another" drops out of the statement that the chief priests were mocking along with the scribes. The third person in the following direct quotation makes it plain enough that they were not addressing Jesus any longer. Matthew uses ἀλλήλους only three times, Mark five times, Luke eleven. In view of Luke's favoring the term, he probably omitted it here because of Matthew's influence. To the chief priests and scribes mentioned by Mark, Matthew adds "and elders" to conform to the regular appearance of the elders in the passion narrative (see the comments on 26:3).

"He saved others, himself he cannot save" stays unaltered. Surprisingly at first, "the Christ" vanishes. Matthew likes the title (8,5), but can well afford to omit it since he inserted it several times in the preceding context (26:68; 27:17, 22). He omits it here in order to add "he is" alongside "king of Israel." Mark's definite article drops out before the latter term to show that it is a predicate nominative. We do not read a slurring allusion, then, but a clear declaration that Jesus is king of Israel. Thus Matthew makes even the worst enemies of Jesus proclaim his kingship.

"Let him now come down from the cross" reads as it does in Mark. Then Matthew substitutes "and" for "in order that" and correspondingly changes the following verb to the indicative mood in order to weld together the continuous line "Let him now come down from the cross and we will believe on him." The result is a couplet consisting of this line and the preceding "He is king of Israel." This couplet corresponds to the couplet that challenges Jesus to save himself and come down from the cross. Mark's "we may see" vanishes to give Matthew a pair of verbs in "let him come down" and "we will believe." Adding "on him" provides a structural counterpart to the phrase concluding the first line of the couplet, "from the cross." It also stresses that the proper object of faith is Jesus, God's Son (cf. 18:6 with Mark 9:42).

Matthew does not omit "the Christ" to keep the title from profanation on the lips of the Jewish leaders, for elsewhere he does not hesitate to use them to Jesus' advantage. In the immediate context, for example, they use "the king of Israel" and "the Son of God," hardly terms that Matthew is willing to throw away.

27:43 Typically, Matthew borrows from the OT and puts a further statement on the lips of Jesus' enemies in order to subpoena them as witnesses to his divine sonship. Matthew has prepared for this subpoena by inserting "if you are [the] Son of God" in v 40. With the exception of "now," which is inserted for a parallel with v 42, the words "He has put his trust on God; let him deliver [him] now if he wants him" come from Ps 22:9(21:8) (cf. Wis 2:6-20; 5:4-5 and see Gundry, *Use of the* OT 145-46, on the mixture of textual traditions and novelties in the quotation). "Now" not only parallels v 42, but also substitutes for a redundant "Let him rescue him" in the psalm. "Let him save him" (so the LXX) disappears because of references to salvation in vv 40 and 42. Matthew's use of εἰ, "if," for the Hebrew כִּי, properly translated ὅτι, "because," in the LXX, shows parallelistic influence from v 40. It also interprets the irony of the OT text and implies the speakers' unbelief.

"For he said" provides a transition to Jesus' self-identification. γάρ is a Mattheanism (62-63,15) and makes that self-identification justify the foregoing challenge. Atypically, Matthew introduces the self-identification with a recitative ὅτι. The rarity of his using this turn of phrase lays stress on the direct quotation, "I am [the] Son of God." See the comments on v 40. Does εἰμι compensate for the replacement of ἐγώ εἰμι in 26:64 (cf. Mark 14:62)? The first position of θεοῦ strongly emphasizes Jesus' deity (cf. the comments on v 54). The Jewish leaders' mocking the divine sonship of Jesus here and in v 40 stands in striking contrast with the Gentile centurion's confession of Jesus' divine sonship (v 54).

27:44 (Mark 15:32; Luke 23:39) Matthew inserts δ' to allow the placement of καί, which means "and" in Mark, just before "the robbers," where it means "also" or "even." "The robbers" is another insertion and comes from the tradition recorded in v 38. Matthew puts "the robbers" ahead of "the ones crucified with him" to heap more indignity on Jesus: even the robbers ridicule him. "Crucified" represents Matthew's present participle, which replaces Mark's perfect. The insertion "in the same way" makes the robbers' insults identical in content with the Jewish leaders' insults; both have to do with Jesus' self-identification, "I am [the] Son of God."

27:45 (Mark 15:33; Luke 23:44-45) The exchange of καί for δέ sets up a contrast between the preceding mockery of Jesus and the darkness at noon, which signals God's displeasure (see Amos 8:9-10). Despite his liking the genitive absolute construction, Matthew replaces Mark's γενομένης ὥρας ἕκτης, "when the sixth hour came," with ἀπό . . . ἕκτης ὥρας, "from [the] sixth hour." The replacement parallels and complements "till [the] ninth hour [i.e., 3:00 P.M.]." Perhaps for chiasm, he also reverses ὥρας ἕκτης but keeps the order of ὥρας ἐνάτης. πᾶσαν is a favorite of his (63,25-26). Here it replaces ὅλην, another of his favorites (7,3). This revision is an assimilation to Exod 10:22 and may have the purpose of extending darkness "over the whole land" (so Mark and Luke; cf. this meaning and the distinctive use of ὅλος with γῆ in 9:26, 31) to darkness "over all the earth" (cf. 24:30).

Astronomically, a natural eclipse would not have occurred during the Passover, a time of the full moon. Some think of a heavy dust storm, however; others of supernatural darkness, and yet others of eschatological or apocalyptic language without historical substance (cf., e.g., Mark 13:24; Matt 24:29; Luke 21:25). γῆν is ambiguous. Does it mean "earth," as would be suggested by an eschatological or apocalyptic frame of reference, or "land [of Judea or Palestine]," as would be suggested by a well-timed natural phenomenon? With one possible exception, the lack of eschatological or apocalyptic features in the immediate context of Mark suggests the meaning "land [of Palestine]." The one possible exception—viz., the tearing of the veil of the Temple from top to bottom—is so Jewish that it, too, favors the narrow meaning. The abundance of eschatological or apocalyptic features in Matthew (see vv 51-54) may favor the wide meaning "earth." But again the features are very Jewish.

27:46 (Mark 15:34) The replacement of καί with δέ sets off Jesus' cry from the preceding darkness. The adverbial dative τῇ ἐνάτῃ ὥρᾳ, "at the ninth hour," gives way to περί . . . τὴν ἐνάτην ὥραν, "around the ninth hour," which typifies Matthew's composition (see 20:3, 5, 6, 9). Unless we are to omit ἀν- with B L W 69 700 al, its addition to ἐβόησεν intensifies the cry of Jesus, whose suffering previews the persecution of the church. To introduce Jesus' cry, Matthew adds λέγων (61,23). His transliteration ἠλὶ ἠλί represents Hebrew, whereas Mark's transliteration ἐλωΐ ἐλωΐ represents Aramaic (see Metzger, Textual Commentary ad loc., and, for a caveat, J. A. Fitzmyer in NTS 20 [1974] 393-94). Both mean "My God," as the following translation indicates. Matthew's revision has the purpose of conforming to the Hebrew text of Ps 22:2(1) and providing better auditory and visual bases for confusion of the divine name with Ἠλίαν, "Elijah" (see vv 47 and 49). The textual variations from λεμὰ σαβαχθάνι have no value for us here. τουτ᾽ ἔστιν, "that is," replaces ὅ ἐστιν μεθερμηνευόμενον, "which is translated," much as in v 33 (cf. Mark 15:22). Instead of the nominative ὁ θεός μου (so Mark and the LXX bis) Matthew twice writes the vocative θεέ μου to conform to the vocative πάτερ in Jesus' prayers at Gethsemane (26:39, 42 in contrast with Mark 14:36). Matthew's ἱνατί, "why?" agrees with the LXX and replaces Mark's εἰς τί much as it replaced τί in 9:4 (cf. Mark 2:8). The reversal of order of ἐγκατέλιπές με, "forsaken me" (so Mark and the LXX), brings the pronoun forward to increase the pathos.

See Gundry, Use of the OT 63-66, on the text-critical questions in the OT quotation and the many modern conjectures concerning them.

27:47 (Mark 15:35) δέ replaces καί to contrast Jesus' cry with the bystanders' misunderstanding. The insertion of "there" sharpens the picture. ἐκεῖ is a favorite of Matthew (16,6). As usual, he rejects the prefix in παρεστώτων or παρεστηκότων (the textual tradition varies in Mark, where Codex Vaticanus even agrees with Matthew), and in reminiscence of v 43 he inserts a recitative ὅτι (see the comments on v 43). Mark's ἴδε, "See!" drops out because of the emphasis already lent by the recitative ὅτι. Matthew often rejects ἴδε, though he also inserts it four times. The addition of "This one" to "[he] is calling Elijah" transfers attention from Elijah to Jesus.

27:48 (Mark 15:36) Mark's δέ, which usually means "but" in Matthew, yields to καί because of the lack of contrast. The insertion of εὐθέως, "immediately," typifies Matthew's diction (10,0) and emphasizes the kindliness of the following action. This emphasis implies that Christians ought to help their persecuted brothers and sisters (see the comments on 27:55-61). "One of them" replaces Mark's indefinite "someone" to prepare for a contrast with "the rest," inserted by Matthew in v 49 (see also 10:29; 18:12; 22:35 [an insertion]; 26:21 for occurrences of Matthew's phrase). "Sponge" comes forward to become the object of an inserted "and taking." The insertion shows Matthew's fondness for λαβών as a nominative participle

(3,7). It also exhibits his parallelistic style in that the participle contributes to a string of four participles, which also include "running . . . and filling [the sponge] with wine vinegar and putting [it] around a reed" (so also Mark except for Matthew's inserting τε and καί and substituting πλήσας—cf. its insertion in 22:10—in place of Mark's synonymous γεμίσας). Cf. Ps 69:22(21).

27:49 (Mark 15:36) Despite his liking Mark's λέγων (61,23), Matthew expands it to οἱ δὲ λοιποὶ ἔλεγον, "But the rest were saying." In Mark, somebody tries on behalf of all the bystanders to prolong Jesus' life with a little refreshment. They want to see whether Elijah will come. Matthew's expansion transforms this effort into the bystanders' frustrating the attempt by one of their number to ease Jesus' suffering. In Mark the one acts and speaks on behalf of the others. In Matthew the one does not act and speak on behalf of the others, but meets their resistance. *They* speak, and in their mouths the once positive words become negative. The one's wanting to prolong Jesus' life on their behalf turns into their wanting to hasten Jesus' extremity. A hopeful thinking that more time will better the chance of Elijah's coming to help turns into a cynical thinking that less time will bring a quicker answer to the question of Elijah's coming. Thus Matthew heightens the indignity. There is some evidence that he likes λοιποί (2,1). Instead of εἶπαν we should probably read ἔλεγον as a parallel to ἔλεγον in v 47. The parallelism would typify Matthew's style. The plural of the verb, as opposed to the singular of Mark's corresponding λέγων, and the switching of ἄφετε, "Let" in the plural, to ἄφες, "Let" in the singular, grow out of the revisions noted above. The telic future participle σώσων, "to save," replaces Mark's telic infinitive καθελεῖν, "to take down," and represents Matthew's diction (5,1). It also echoes vv 40 and 42 and intensifies the mockery of the one who was expected to save others (cf. 1:21).

It is not a matter of whether wine vinegar prolonged, or was thought to prolong, life in a medicinal fashion. (It does not.) Rather, it is a matter of simple refreshment to keep Jesus going a little while longer. ἄφες/-ετε followed by a verb in the first person plural subjunctive means "let us. . . ." The futuristic present ἔρχεται, "is coming," may reflect Aramaic use of the participle for the future. Because Elijah went to heaven without dying (2 Kgs 2:11), Jews believed that he would come to save the righteous in their times of distress (Str-B 4/2. 769-71). Elijah's failure to help Jesus did not improve unbelieving Jewish opinion about Jesus. See the UBS and Metzger, *Textual Commentary* ad loc., concerning the text-critical question involving John 19:34.

27:50 (Mark 15:37; Luke 23:46) Concerning Jesus' last cry, Matthew inserts "again" to recall the earlier cry (v 46). Though he sometimes omits πάλιν for contextual reasons, it is often distinctive in his gospel (8,4). He likes κράξας, "shouting" (5,0), which replaces Mark's less natural ἀφείς, "letting go," and reflects Ps 22:3(2), 6(5), 25(24) (cf. the use of Ps 22:2[1] in v 46). ἀφῆκεν τὸ πνεῦμα, "he let go [his] spirit," substitutes for ἐξέπνευσεν, "he expired." Matthew's verb comes from Mark's ἀφείς and compensates for its replacement. His noun comes from the stem of Mark's ἐξέπνευσεν.

This revision has the purpose and result of making Jesus, who is a majestic and authoritative figure throughout the first gospel, die of his own accord. He does not die with a last gasp, but by an act of the will (cf. John 19:30 and the comments on Matt 26:61—also Gen 35:18 LXX; Ps 104:30; Eccl 12:7; Ezek 37:1-10; Sir 38:23; Wis 16:14).

ENCOURAGEMENT TO THE PERSECUTED: THE CIRCUMSTANCES OF JESUS' DEATH AS ESCHATOLOGICAL PROOF THAT HE IS GOD'S SON

27:51-54 (Mark 15:38-39; Luke 23:45, 47-48)

27:51 (Mark 15:33; Luke 23:45) For a special emphasis that subsequent expansion confirms, Matthew inserts "Behold" (34,9). Mark's statement that the veil of the Temple was torn stays undisturbed till Matthew reverses "in two" and "from top to bottom." His putting "from top to bottom" first stresses that the event is a miraculous vindication of Jesus. Since he has been portraying Jesus' passion as a paradigm of Christians' persecution, this vindication has the value of encouraging the persecuted to hold fast: their vindication will come, too (cf. the similar content and purpose of apocalyptic literature).

Cf. Josephus, *J.W.* 6.5.3-4 §§288-315; *b. Yoma* 39b; *y. Yoma* 43c, 61. καταπέτασμα refers either to the inner curtain dividing the holy place from the holy of holies in the Temple or to the outer curtain at the front of the holy place (see BAG, s.v., whose certainty in favoring the inner curtain is not justified). If the outer curtain is meant, we might think of a sign of judgment visible to the general public, perhaps in the form of a sirocco wind tearing the outer curtain as well as bringing the darkness. Since the evangelists do not make the rending symbolize an end to the Jewish cult or an opening of the way to God, but present it only as a supernatural portent of Jesus' deity (cf. "from top to bottom"—i.e., done by God rather than man—and the centurion's confession), the kind of theologizing we read in Heb 6:19; 9:12, 24; 10:19-22 does not lie at the base of the event as its source, but rests on top of the event as its later interpretation. The connection between the destruction of the Temple and its being rebuilt on the one hand and Jesus' death and resurrection on the other hand raises the possibility that the tearing of the veil originally represented Jesus' death. But "from top to bottom" would then imply that God killed Jesus (contrast "I [Jesus] will destroy this Temple . . ." [Mark 14:58; similarly Matt 26:61] and "Destroy this Temple" [spoken to the Jews—John 2:19]).

The rest of v 51 and the whole of vv 52-53 are an insertion by Matthew. In it he adds to the tearing of the veil several more supernatural events. Because these events focus on the resurrection of the saints and of Jesus the crucified, they sound the note of eschatological vindication for persecuted disciples. In short, this preview of the end guarantees the hope of those who suffer in the way of righteousness.

The parallelism in the insertion typifies Matthew's compositions. It is evident especially in the first aorist passive verbs with which each of the first four lines ends. The earthquake is a prelude to the opening of tombs and resurrection of past saints, who, of course, are Israelites. Typically, Matthew draws the earthquake from the OT, in particular from Ezek 37:7, 12-13, where an earthquake occurs, graves are opened, and the people of Israel come up out of their graves. γῆ and ἐσείσθη represent his diction (21,6; 3,0) and point to Jesus' deity (see the comments on 8:24; 28:2). Probably the splitting of the rocks does not come from 1 Kgs 19:11, for there it is wind that splits them and an earthquake occurs only afterwards. Rather, the rocks derive from Matthew's own interest in πέτρα (3,0; cf. Πέτρος—8,1) and especially from his anticipating the rock of Jesus' tomb in v 60. ἐσχίσθησαν echoes ἐσχίσθη, part of Mark's tradition concerning the veil.

27:52 Similarly, "and the tombs [μνημεῖα] were opened" comes from Ezek 37:12-13: "I will open your graves [μνήματα, 'tombs,' in the LXX]." Matthew's using μνημεῖα for Ezekiel's plural of קֶבֶר anticipates μνημείῳ, the tomb in which Jesus was buried (v 60; cf. 28:8 and the use of μνημεῖον for קֶבֶר a dozen times in the LXX). Matthew likes ἀνεῴχθησαν (5,2). The statement "and many bodies of the saints that had fallen asleep were raised" recalls Dan 12:2 and contains a string of Mattheanisms in πολλά (23,1), σώματα (5,0), ἁγίων (4,4), and ἠγέρθησαν (11,8). Thus Matthew uses his favorite diction to express what he reads in Ezek 37:12-13: "Behold [cf. Matthew's ἰδού in v 51] . . . I will cause you to come up [cf. Matthew's ἠγέρθησαν] out of your graves . . . when I have caused you to come up out of your graves." Since Ezekiel and Daniel do not restrict the resurrection to a few select saints, Matthew probably describes the resurrection of all the OT saints. In Semitic speech, "many" often meant "all." The euphemism of sleep for death was common in both non-Christian and Christian vocabulary (see BAG, s.v. κοιμάω 2).

27:53 As a nominative participle ἐξελθόντες comes from Matthew's preferred diction (10,4). "Out of the tombs" echoes v 52. With the phrase μετὰ τὴν ἔγερσιν αὐτοῦ, "after his [Jesus'] resurrection," we may compare the use of μετά with Jesus' resurrection in 26:32; 27:63 (the latter being unparalleled). ἔγερσιν (hapax in the NT) reflects Matthew's interest in the cognate verb, just used. In all the temporal uses of μετά elsewhere in the first gospel, including distinctive occurrences, the preposition and its accusative object precede the verb qualified (1:12; 17:1; 24:29; 25:19; 26:2, 32, 73; 27:62, 63). Hence, Matthew probably means that the resurrected saints entered Jerusalem only after Jesus' resurrection. It is unclear whether they also came out of their tombs only after Jesus' resurrection, or came out earlier but stayed in the countryside till Jesus had risen. The doctrine that he is "the first-born from the dead" (Col 1:18; Rev 1:5) and "the first fruits of those who are asleep" (1 Cor 15:20) favors the former view because a delayed exit from the realm of death would seem less liable to contradict that doctrine. Thus Matthew probably means that the saints stayed in their tombs for several days even though their bodies had been raised to life. Then they came out and "entered into the holy city and appeared to many." Matthew inserted "the holy city" also in 4:5. The expression occurs nowhere else in the gospels, consists of two words that

Matthew likes individually—ἁγίαν (4,4) and πόλιν (18,3)—and probably suggests τῶν . . . ἁγίων to produce a parallel between "the holy people" and "the holy city" into which they enter. ἐνεφανίσθησαν connotes juridical appearance for the purpose of testimony (see Acts 23:15, 22; 24:1; 25:2, 15; Heb 9:24; and BAG, s.v. ἐμφανίζω 2) and occurs only here in the synoptics; but the simple φαίνω belongs to Matthew's favorite diction (5,8). "To many" represents another Mattheanism (πολλοῖς—23,1). The many raised bodies correspond to the many to whom they appear. Since the only other reference to "the holy city" occurred in 4:5, the resurrection and testimony of the saints provide the miraculous demonstration of divine sonship that Jesus refused to give at the Devil's behest.

Cf. Zech 14:4; Rev 11:17-19; and the panel concerning Ezekiel in the synagogue at Dura Europos. On that panel the split mountain and crumbling house signify an earthquake. The ten men garbed in white represent OT saints who have been raised from the dead and come out of their tombs, opened by the earthquake. The patently striking similarities between the panel and Matthew's present insertion show the ease with which he could have developed this expansion. He does not want to show that the end has come, or begun, with Jesus' death and resurrection. To the contrary, see 24:6, 8, 13, and especially his insertion at the close of 24:14. He only wants to show a preview of the end. This preview has the purpose of encouraging the persecuted. Matthew's concern with persecution is evident throughout his version of the passion. The many literary indications of his composing the insertion call in question the use of earlier tradition, such as that associated with Jesus' descent into hell (1 Pet 3:19). See D. Senior in CBQ 38 (1976) 314-18 against the view that Gos. Pet. 28-49 independently draws from such a tradition.

27:54 (Mark 15:39; Luke 23:47-48) Matthew rejoins Mark but delays "seeing." κεντυρίων, "centurion," which occurs three times in Mark but never in Matthew, gives way to the synonymous ἑκατόνταρχος, which occurred in 8:5, 8, 13. The added phrase, "and the ones with him who were guarding Jesus," echoes Matthew's similar addition in v 36 and replaces Mark's description of the centurion as "the one who stood opposite him [Jesus]." Luke agrees with Matthew in the omission, but not in the addition. Matthew has predilections for τηροῦντες (5,1) and Jesus' name (80,12).

Now Matthew takes up Mark's earlier ἰδών, "seeing," and pluralizes it because of his adding the ones who were guarding Jesus under the centurion's command. The insertion of "the earthquake" makes a reference back to the earthquake inserted in v 51 (cf. the insertion in 8:24, too). The substantive participle τὰ γενόμενα, "the things that happened," represents Matthew's special diction (1,3) and summarizes the results of the earthquake, viz., the splitting of the rocks and the opening of the tombs. Luke 23:47 has τὸ γενόμενον, "what happened," singular because of the lack of Matthew's added events. But the singular turns into Matthew's plural form in Luke 23:48. The failure of the plural to have the antecedents which justify it in Matthew—a failure pointed up by the initial singular—shows Matthean influence on Luke. The whole phrase, "seeing the earthquake and the things that happened," replaces "that thus he expired" and agrees with Matthew's replacement of "expired" in v 50 (cf. Mark 15:37).

"Became exceedingly afraid" echoes Matthew's identical insertion in 17:6. That it refers there to several disciples at the transfiguration suggests that here it implies the centurion's and soldiers' conversions, for such fear characterizes disciples in the awesome presence of Jesus (see also the comments on 9:8). Both ἐφοβήθησαν and σφόδρα represent Matthew's special vocabulary (8,2; 5,2). Mark's εἶπε gives way to the Mattheanism λέγοντες (61,23). Luke's agreements with Matthew's participial form and Mark's singular number point to conflation. The confession of the single centurion in Mark becomes, in Matthew, the godly fear and confession of the centurion and his soldiers as well—the vanguard of the Gentiles who will flock into the church. The raising of Jewish saints and the conversion of Gentiles typify the Jewish-cum-Gentile ecclesiology of Matthew. He retains "Truly," omits Mark's "man," delays "this," and puts "God's" before "Son" in contrast with Mark's word order (but in conformity to the identical change in v 40; see also 14:33)—all to lay as much emphasis as possible on Jesus' deity. Thus the supernatural phenomena that preview the end and offer assurance to those who follow Jesus into suffering also give dramatic evidence of his awesome majesty. Because he is God's Son, the persecuted may well put their confidence in him.

We might assume that historically the centurion meant "a son of God" in a pagan sense and that the evangelists intended their readers to take the designation in the Christian sense, "the Son of God." The absence of the definite article before "Son" allows but does not demand an indefinite meaning.

CHRISTIAN MINISTRY
TO PERSECUTED FELLOW CHRISTIANS
27:55-61 (Mark 15:40-47; Luke 23:49-56; John 19:24b-27, 38-42)

27:55 (Mark 15:40-41; Luke 23:49) Matthew edits the tradition concerning Jesus' burial in a way that encourages Christians to care tenderly for their persecuted fellows. ἐκεῖ is a favorite of his (16,6) and replaces καί for a parallel with identical insertions in vv 36 and 47. "Many" comes up from Mark 15:41 to modify "women." The whole clause, "who followed Jesus from Galilee to minister to him," also represents an advance of the material in Mark 15:41. By advancing this material Matthew stresses the women's exemplary ministry to Jesus, the persecuted teacher of righteousness. Mark's simple αἵ yields to the emphatic αἵτινες, a Mattheanism (23,5). The aorist, translated "followed," substitutes for the imperfect, translated "were following." The advance of this verb within its clause accentuates discipleship and helping the persecuted as characteristic of true discipleship. Typically, "Jesus" substitutes for "him" and provides a Christological emphasis (80,12). "From Galilee" replaces "when he was in Galilee" to echo Matthew's identical insertion in 19:1 and a similar insertion in 21:11, and possibly to parallel "from afar" in the preceding clause.

The omission of Mark's καί allows the changing of his imperfect verb διηκόνουν, "were ministering," to the participle διακονοῦσαι, "ministering."

Thus the women's helping Jesus during his successes in Galilee (so Mark) becomes a helping of Jesus on his trail to the cross, i.e., an example of Christian ministry to the persecuted. In 25:44, part of a composition by Matthew, διακονέω described such ministry. Luke agrees with Matthew in advancing the material about the women and writing "from Galilee." But he writes nothing about the women's ministry, just as Mark does not till his next verse, to which Luke, like Matthew, has no parallel besides what has been advanced. It therefore appears that Luke has conflated Mark and Matthew.

The women's watching with concern has no proper parallel in the aloofness mentioned in Ps 38:12(11), sometimes cited here. We do not know whether fear, unwillingness to associate with the mockers around Jesus, feminine hesitancy in a culture dominated by males, or a combination of these reasons caused them to stay at a distance. Since their ministry to Jesus consisted in financial assistance (Luke 8:1-3), they must have been widows in control of their own property.

27:56 (Mark 15:40-41) The supplying of "was" fills Mark's ellipsis and provides a parallel to "were" in v 55a. Mark's "both" before "Mary Magdalene" drops out as unneeded. From the identification of the second Mary as "the mother of James the small [presumably meaning 'short' or 'younger'] and of Joses," Matthew omits "the small" because the following reference to the sons of Zebedee (James and John) will distinguish the present James well enough. The listing of James first, his later designation "the Just" (Hegesippus; Origen *Cels.* 1.47; Eusebius *H.E.* 2.23.1-25), and his leadership in Jewish Christianity (see, e.g., Acts 15:13-21; 21:18; Gal 1:19; 2:9, 12; and the whole Epistle of James) also may have contributed to omission of "the small." Adding the definite article before James's name somewhat compensates for the omission. The name of Joses yields to "Joseph" in conformity to 13:55, where Matthew made the very same change and Mary is indubitably the mother of Jesus. In both Mark and Matthew, but especially in Matthew because of the identical revisions, the parallel between the two passages favors a reference to Mary the mother of Jesus. See the comments on 13:55. Salome's name gives way to "the mother of the sons of Zebedee," an exact repetition of Matthew's insertion in 20:20. The obscurity of Salome, the prominence of the sons of Zebedee, and the desire for a parallel with the immediately preceding description of Mary as a mother (whose prominence will not allow the loss of her name) combine to influence Matthew's revision. See also 26:37 with Mark 14:33 for another insertion of the sons of Zebedee. Matthew has already used the first part of Mark 15:41 and "many" from the second part. Since nothing more in that verse will further his aim, he skips it.

27:57 (Mark 15:42-43; Luke 23:50-51) δέ replaces καί for a contrast between daytime and evening. "Already" falls from the statement that "evening had come" because the further omission of "since it was Preparation, i.e., Friday" would have made readers think of evening past sunset. Yet in accord with Deut 21:22-23 Jews removed corpses of the hanged and crucified before sunset (see Josephus, *J.W.* 4.5.2 §317). Therefore Mark indicates that despite its being evening already, it was still Friday, i.e., prior to sunset in Jewish reckoning. Matthew saves Mark's reference to the Preparation for a later, special use (see 27:62) and avoids a misimpression by omitting "already." Mark takes so long to reach his main verb that Matthew changes "coming" to "came."

Since Matthew has a penchant for OT phraseology and inserted a quotation of Isa 53:4 in 8:17, probably "a rich man" replaces "a prominent councilman" for an allusion to Isa 53:9: "His grave was assigned [to be] . . . with a rich [man] in his death." Dissociated from the council, Joseph is now free to be made a full-fledged Christian disciple. The advance of his new designation results in its becoming the subject instead of an appositive (as in Mark) and puts some emphasis on the allusion to Isa 53:9. Matthew is fond of ἄνθρωπος (35,17). See the comments on 13:44 concerning his occasional use of the term for disciples, a use which suggests the portrayal of a man who shows his discipleship by ministering to the persecuted, now martyred Jesus (cf. the comments on v 32). Matthew adds τοὔνομα, "as to name," in reminiscence of the synonymous dative of reference ὀνόματι inserted in v 32, where we read similar and distinctive phraseology concerning Simon the Cyrenian. ὄνομα is a Mattheanism (9,5).

Matthew's portrayal of Joseph as a disciple now comes out clearly in his replacing "who also himself was waiting for the kingdom of God" with "who also himself had become a disciple of Jesus." Both ἐμαθητεύθη and Jesus' name typify Matthew's diction (1,2; 80,12; cf. 33,8 for cognates with μαθ-). That he would allow himself to dispose of a reference to the kingdom, one of his main themes, shows the strength of his desire to associate discipleship with ministry to the persecuted.

Cf. John 19:38. Modern doubts about the text-critical originality of "a rich man" in Isa 53:9 do not affect the probability that Matthew read the text that way. Furthermore, since wickedness and wealth often go together in the OT, the phrases "with the wicked" and "with a rich man" make a better parallel in Isa 53:9 than is sometimes recognized. That the rich man Joseph of Arimathea was not also a wicked man did not bother Matthew. His use of the OT easily surmounts such obstacles.

27:58 *(Mark 15:43-45; Luke 23:52)* The resumptive οὗτος, "This one," typifies Matthew's style (5,0) and stems from his earlier breaking up of Mark's awkwardly long sentence. "Daring" disappears because προσελθών connotes a respectful approach (see the comments on 4:3; 8:14). The latter word comes from Matthew's favorite diction (38,6), replaces "he entered," and takes its participial form from the omitted "daring." Other changes follow as a matter of course, but Matthew keeps "the body of Jesus." Despite the decay that set in, the Romans usually left victims of crucifixion on their crosses for some time. Pilate's wondering whether Jesus was already dead and finding out from the centurion that he was (so Mark) drop out as not furthering Matthew's theme of ministry to the persecuted and as competing with the following story about a false report of theft. The possibility of theft, not the actuality of death, is the question among the Jewish readers of Matthew. Despite his lacking some of Matthew's reasons for these revisions of Mark, Luke shares all of them—surely a remarkable indication of Matthean influence.

The next sentence begins with τότε (66,17). Pilate's name comes from the omitted portion in Mark that concerns the actuality of Jesus' death. "Pilate commanded [it] to be given back" replaces "he granted the corpse to Joseph." The new wording echoes the distinctive phraseology in 14:9 and thus carries on Matthew's parallel beween John the Baptist and Jesus. Here Matthew adds "back" (not in 14:9) in order to indicate a return of the corpse to a disciple, to whom it rightfully belonged. The evangelist's hand is evident in ἐκέλευσεν (5,2) and ἀποδοθῆναι (5,11).

27:59 (Mark 15:46; Luke 23:53; John 19:40-41) "Buying linen" drops out. It is unnecessary in view of the following reference to linen and overfull with the next participial phrase. Luke shares the omission. Mark's καθελών yields to a favorite participle of Matthew, λαβών (3,7). Instead of "him," he writes "the body" for a link with the preceding verse. σῶμα is another favorite of his (5,0). Because of the loss of Joseph's name at the close of that verse, "Joseph" enters here. ἐνετύλιξεν, "wrapped," substitutes for the synonymous ἐνείλησεν. Luke agrees with the substitution. "It" (i.e., the body) fills a Markan ellipsis. Again Luke agrees with Matthew. If original, the ἐν added before σινδόνι in B D Θ pc represents an assimilation to ἐνετύλιξεν. Mark's anaphoric definite article modifying σινδόνι vanishes because Matthew has not mentioned the linen before. Yet again Luke agrees with Matthew. To enhance Joseph's ministry to Jesus and Jesus' dignity, Matthew adds "clean" to describe the linen. Four times in his gospel he inserts words based on καθαρ-.

27:60 (Mark 15:46; Luke 23:53-54; John 19:41-42) "It" replaces "him" for conformity to the distinctive "body" and "it" in the preceding verse. Again to enhance Jesus' dignity and Joseph's ministry to him, Matthew adds "his" and "new" to "tomb." In a periphrastic way Luke agrees with the newness of the tomb. The cultic purity of the linen and tomb displays the care with which Matthew's Joseph handles the corpse of the model Sufferer. Furthermore, only Matthew makes the tomb in which Jesus was buried Joseph's tomb. His doing so clinches the fulfillment of Isaiah's prophecy that the suffering Servant of the Lord will be assigned a grave with a rich man in his death (see the comments on v 57).

"He hewed" substitutes for "was hewn" in agreement with Matthew's having made the tomb belong to Joseph. In another enhancement of Joseph's sacrificial service, then, Matthew makes Joseph himself hew out the tomb, which he gives up to Jesus. Replacing "out of" with "in" clarifies the location of the tomb and Jesus' corpse inside the rock. This clarification brings the place of Jesus' burial into close association with the tombs in the rocks which were split open at Jesus' death (so Matthew alone in vv 51-52). The addition of "the" to "rock" furthers that association by making an anaphoric reference to the rock tombs in vv 51-52. This correlation of Jesus' death and burial with that of "the saints" (a term that in v 52 must refer to the godly people of the OT, but by Matthew's time had gained a Christian connotation, too) aids the application of Joseph's burying Jesus to the ministry of Christians toward their fellows under persecution.

Cf. Isa 22:16. Tombs hewn out of rock had recesses and shelves on which wrapped corpses were laid.

"He rolled" becomes "having rolled." This change arises partly from Matthew's habit of starting sentences with nominative participles and partly out of parallel influence from v 59, but mainly out of his intent to add a main verb at the end for a reason we have yet to see. Typically, he describes the stone as "large" (μέγαν—11,1). This insertion anticipates Mark 16:4 (which Matthew will otherwise omit), shows why the stone has to be rolled away by the angel of the Lord (so Matthew alone in 28:2), and further enhances the exemplary care and effort shown by Joseph. The switch from ἐπὶ τὴν θύραν, "to the entrance," to the synonymous τῇ θύρᾳ is merely stylistic. But the addition of ἀπῆλθεν, "he went away," prepares for the further addition of a guard at the tomb (so Matthew alone in vv 62-66 and 28:4, 11-15). The verb is a Mattheanism (14,11).

27:61 (Mark 15:47; Luke 23:55) The addition ἦν . . . ἐκεῖ, "was there," echoes and parallels v 55, where, as often, Matthew inserted ἐκεῖ (16,6; see also the distinctive phraseology in vv 36 and 47). The omission of Mark's anaphoric definite article before Mary Magdalene's name represents an assimilation to v 59. Because "James" is missing alongside "Joses" in Mark, "other" takes the place of "the [mother] of Joses" in describing the second "Mary" (see v 56; Mark 15:40). Matthew likes ἄλλη (14,4). He might have added James (and changed the name of Joses to Joseph, as in v 56 and 13:55), but he finds it simpler to abbreviate with a favorite adjective. The participle "sitting" replaces Mark's verb "were watching," which Matthew reserves till 28:1 for a special purpose. The replacement echoes similar insertions in vv 19 and 36 and shows his fondness for καθήμεναι (8,0). "Over against the grave" substitutes for "where he was placed." The preceding change necessitated some such substitution; and ἀπέναντι provides a parallel with v 24, where Matthew inserted the preposition. τάφου comes from his special vocabulary (4,2). In Mark the women merely observe the location of Jesus' burial. In Matthew they sit opposite the grave in vigil. Their vigil, too, exemplifies the care and concern for the persecuted that true discipleship requires.

THE CONTRAST BETWEEN THE JEWISH LEADERS' DECEITFULNESS AND JESUS' TRUTHFULNESS
27:62-66

Matthew inserts vv 62-66, a unique report of the setting of a guard at Jesus' tomb, to prepare for a second insertion in 28:11-15, which tells about the bribed circulation of a false report that the disciples stole Jesus' body. These two insertions contrast the deceitfulness of the Jewish leaders and the truthfulness of Jesus in predicting his resurrection after three days. Such truthfulness gives encouragement to his persecuted followers. They may trust his word and hope for like vindication.

27:62 δέ contrasts the women's vigil at Jesus' tomb with the chief priests' and Pharisees' request for a guard at the tomb. How different the two concerns! "On the next [day]" puts the time on the Sabbath. But Matthew describes the Sabbath with the circumlocution "which is after the Preparation [i.e., Friday]." ἥτις is to his liking (23,5). The failure of the word "Sabbath" to appear forestalls our thinking that he is portraying the chief priests and Pharisees as breaking the Sabbath by going to Pilate. Rather, he is compensating for omitting the reference to Preparation in v 57 (cf. Mark 15:42). But why did he make that omission? It now appears that he saved the day of Preparation till now to use it in a description of the Sabbath that points up the succession of days beginning with the day of Jesus' crucifixion: the Preparation, the day after the Preparation, and "the evening of the Sabbath as the day was developing into the first day of the week" (28:1). The careful highlighting of this succession (see also vv 63b and 64a) points to Jesus' prediction that he will rise after three days, in particular to the only such prediction heard by Jewish leaders. That is the one in 12:40, which Matthew inserted. In view of the resurrection, then, great stress falls on the truthfulness of Jesus' prediction in contrast with the deceitfulness of the Jewish leaders.

Matthew describes the gathering together of the Jewish leaders with συνήχθησαν (10,10). This verb connotes the unbelieving synagogue of his day (see the comments on 2:3-4). "The chief priests and the scribes" echoes his distinctive wording in 21:45. But since he has in mind Jesus' prediction in 12:40, we need to compare the mention of the scribes and Pharisees in 12:38. In the present passage the chief priests replace the scribes because of the chief priests' dominance throughout the passion narrative (see the note to 26:3). Besides, the scribes did not belong to the Markan tradition behind 12:38 (see Mark 8:11); and no scriptural, theological discussion arises here in vv 62-66. Matthew does bring the Pharisees from 12:38 into the present verse, however. This is their only appearance in his passion narrative, and it stems from their having heard Jesus' only public prediction of his resurrection after three days, the one in 12:40. Cf. Matthew's general interest in the Pharisees (18,1).

27:63 To introduce the request of the chief priests and Pharisees, Matthew employs his usual λέγοντες (61,23). κύριε also typifies his diction (34,15). To be sure, it normally refers to Jesus, but Matthew makes them address Pilate as "Lord" and, shortly, describe Jesus as a deceiver in order to show that they do not speak the truth. ἐμνήσθημεν occurred as an insertion in 5:23 (see also 26:75 with Mark 14:72; Luke 22:61). Further Mattheanisms are evident in ἐκεῖνος (26,9; cf. esp. v 19), πλάνος (6,2 with cognates included), ἔτι (4,2), and ζῶν (2,1). We might have expected "In three days," as in v 40, or "On the third day," as in 16:21; 17:23; 20:19. Instead, "After three days" summarily paraphrases 12:40, according to which "the Son of man will be three days and three nights in the heart of the earth." The other expressions all occurred in private communications to the disciples. So Matthew switches to Mark's "after three days," which he always rejected before, in order to indicate a particular reference to the only prediction of Jesus' resurrection heard by the Jewish leaders (cf. Mark 8:31; 9:31; 10:34; see also the comments on 12:40). ἐγείρομαι, "I am being

583

raised," is a futuristic present and represents Matthew's special diction (11,8).

27:64 Further Mattheanisms come forward in κέλευσον (5,2), οὖν (35,11), and τάφον (4,2). κέλευσον echoes a recent insertion in v 58 for a command by Pilate, as here. ἀσφαλισθῆναι, "to secure," grows out of the circumstances of the story and occurs in the gospels only in vv 64, 65, 66. The reference to the third day echoes v 63 (and ultimately 12:40), and ἕως is another favorite of Matthew (13,14). "After three days" requires the inclusive sense, "up to and including," and an assumption by the chief priests and Pharisees that Jesus was not implying an indefinite gap between the third day and the time of his resurrection. Otherwise, the securing of the grave "till the third day" would not suffice. It remains possible, too, that the third day in the request for a guard means the third day from the time of the request (Saturday) rather than from the time of the crucifixion (Sunday). Cf. the comments on 11:12-13.

The remainder of v 64 offers a series of Mattheanisms: μήποτε (2,4), ἐλθόντες (10,10), μαθηταί (31,5), κλέψωσιν (2,2), λαῷ (8,4), ἠγέρθη (11,8), νεκρῶν (4,1), the particular form ἔσται (16,5), ἐσχάτη (0,6), πλάνη (6,2 with cognates included), and πρώτης (2,5-6). ἠγέρθη ἀπὸ τῶν νεκρῶν, "He has been raised from the dead," exactly matches the distinctive wording in 14:2; 28:7. John the Baptist is the subject in 14:2. The present repetition therefore carries on Matthew's correlation of John and Jesus (see "John the Baptist parallel Jesus" in the Topical Index and cf. 17:19). "And the last deception will be worse than the first" echoes Jesus' saying in 12:45, with the Mattheanisms ἔσται and πλάνη added. The first deception apparently has to do with Jesus' messiahship and divine sonship.

27:65 ἔφη with asyndeton typifies Matthew's style (6,1). Pilate's name echoes v 62. We should not understand ἔχετε κουστωδίαν as indicative, "You have a guard [i.e., your own Temple guard—so use them]"; for then the possibility of needing to persuade the governor concerning the guards would never arise (cf. 28:14). Rather, we should understand the imperative, "Have a guard." In the NT κουστωδίαν occurs only at 27:65, 66; 28:11. ὑπάγετε is a Mattheanism (5,6), especially as a second person imperative. "Secure [it]" echoes v 64. "As [well as] you know [how]" shows that Pilate, whom Matthew has Christianized (see esp. v 24), does not believe the guard will succeed. ὡς and οἴδατε belong to Matthew's favorite vocabulary (23,8; 7,2).

27:66 The nominative participle πορευθέντες represents the evangelist's diction (8,4). "They secured" echoes vv 64, 65. The Mattheanism τάφον reappears (4,2). "Sealing" occurs only here in the synoptics and comes from Dan 6:18(17). Borrowing from the OT is typical of Matthew. "Stone" echoes v 60, and "with a guard" mirrors v 65.

The comparison of Luke's and Matthew's versions of Judas's death (see the comments on 27:3-10) should have taught us neither to underestimate Matthew's creativity in the use of tradition nor to deduce that an abundance of his distinctive traits in a passage lacking a synoptic parallel necessarily implies wholesale invention by him. Our estimate of the likelihood or unlikelihood of the Jewish authorities' going to Pilate and then to the tomb and securing the tomb on a Sabbath that was also a feast day depends on earlier estimates of the seriousness with which they took Jesus' case and of their ability to find legal loopholes (cf. the Sanhedrin's condemning Jesus on the ground of blasphemy, which may well have taken precedence over a question of keeping the Sabbath). Would the soldiers have consented to spread a story that they had failed at guard duty? The penalty of death for such a failure suggests that they would not have done so. But if the corpse was nowhere to be found, they had nothing to lose by cooperating with the Jewish leadership; for the emptiness of the tomb and their inability to produce the corpse would have shown their failure at guard duty anyway. At this point, then, our estimate of the likelihood or unlikelihood of the soldiers' consenting to spread the rumor of theft depends on an earlier estimate of the evidence for an empty tomb. At the very least—i.e., even though we suppose complete invention of the story by Matthew—the insertion of vv 62-66 presupposes Jewish admission that Jesus' grave was empty. Otherwise, the story lacks a reason for being.

THE RESURRECTION OF JESUS AS A DEMONSTRATION OF HIS DEITY AND TRUTHFULNESS
28:1-10 (Mark 16:1-8; Luke 24:1-12; John 20:1-13)

28:1 (Mark 16:1-3; Luke 24:1-2; John 20:1) The exchange of καί for δέ makes a contrast between the securing of the tomb and the following account of Jesus' resurrection. Mark's singular τοῦ σαββάτου, "the Sabbath," becomes the plural σαββάτων (cf. the unique plural in 12:5). The plural conforms to the closely following plural of the same noun, this time in agreement with Mark. Mark's genitive absolute means "when the Sabbath was over." Matthew changes διαγενόμενου to ὀψέ and gets the meaning "on the evening after [the] Sabbath" or, if he is using ὀψέ as an improper preposition, "after the Sabbath" (BAG, s.v.). Because Sunday morning would be after the Sabbath, some take the prepositional meaning and think that Matthew agrees with the reference to Sunday morning in Mark 16:2. But the Sabbath ended at sundown, a whole night intervened before Sunday morning, and ὀψέ would hardly have been used in a prepositional phrase referring to Sunday morning when its adverbial meaning is just the opposite, viz., "in the evening." Therefore whether ὀψέ is an adverb or a preposition, Matthew is pointing to Saturday evening, as Mark 16:1 seems to do, not to Sunday morning. In the next phrase, then, ἐπιφωσκούσῃ refers to the onset of evening (as it undoubtedly does in Luke 23:54) rather than to the dawn (as it usually does).

Mark 16:2 goes on to indicate that after purchasing the spices on Saturday evening, the women came to the tomb early the next morning. Matthew obliterates this temporal shift. For the time being the names of Mary Magdalene, Mary the mother of James, and Salome drop out, and their buying spices and intending to anoint Jesus vanish permanently. Furthermore, Mark's καὶ λίαν πρωΐ τῇ μιᾷ τῶν σαββάτων, "And exceedingly early on the first [day] of the week," becomes τῇ ἐπιφωσκούσῃ εἰς μίαν σαββάτων, "as [the day] was developing into the first [day] of [the] week." Since the first day of the week started at sunset on Saturday, the women come and discover the empty tomb at the time initially indicated, viz., Saturday evening. Matthew's advancing their discovery of the empty tomb from early Sunday morning to Saturday evening is confirmed by his omitting "when the sun had risen" at the close of Mark 16:2. In Matthew, then, the resurrection occurs right after the setting of the guard, which was unique to this gospel. Matthew makes the answering demonstration of Jesus' truthfulness and deity all the more impressive by making it immediate.

The rumor that the disciples stole Jesus' body during the night (v 13) does not contradict this understanding of Matthew; for nighttime is dictated by the false charge of theft and bears no necessary correlation to what Matthew wants to say from his own standpoint. Some have thought he writes on the presupposition of a solar calendar and reckons days from sunrise to sunrise rather than from sunset to sunset. This would keep him in agreement with the other evangelists on a time in the early morning. But such an understanding fails to take account of ὀψέ as connoting evening, not morning. It also fails to take account of Matthew's obliterating Mark's λίαν πρωΐ in favor of the more ambiguous τῇ ἐπιφωσκούσῃ, which can mean evening twilight as well as morning twilight. (The possibility of an unusual transmutation of twilight at dawn to evening twilight is proved by Luke 23:54 whether Luke is writing independently or under Matthean influence.) Finally, it fails to take account of Matthew's omitting Mark's reference to sunrise.

The aorist singular ἦλθεν replaces Mark's present plural ἔρχονται. The names of the two Marys finally cross over from Mark. But "the other" replaces "the [mother] of James," and Matthew omits "and Salome" to assimilate the phrase as a whole to 27:61 and parallel the omission of Salome in 27:56 (cf. Mark 15:40 and see the comments on 27:56, 61). "To look at the grave" compensates for losing "they bought spices in order that they might come and anoint him" (so Mark). Matthew's infinitive comes from "they were looking at" in Mark 15:47, for which he substituted another word (27:61). Thus the women's coming to anoint Jesus' corpse changes into their coming to gaze at the tomb, i.e., continue their vigil (cf. the comments on v 61). This change grows out of Matthew's inserting the setting of a guard at the tomb and the sealing of its stone. The concern has switched from the state of Jesus' corpse to the state of the tomb. Since the Jewish authorities had taken precautions to make the tomb secure, the resurrection of Jesus again looks all the more impressive in Matthew. The women's wondering who will roll back the stone and finding it already rolled away (Mark 16:3-4) drops out because inserting the sealing of the stone and the guarding of the tomb makes their question senseless. Nobody would dare unseal the stone and roll it away for them. Because of the guard, nobody could. (The women need not have known about the sealing and the guard, of course; but Matthew writes from his own standpoint.) Matthew replaces "to the tomb" with "the grave" to echo 27:61, 64, 66 and satisfy his liking of τάφον (4,2).

28:2 (Mark 16:5; Luke 24:3-4) The insertion "And behold, an earthquake took place" mirrors the unique statement in 8:24. But here Matthew adds "great" from Mark 16:4, where it modifies "the stone" (cf. Matt 27:60). The Mattheanism ἰδού (34,9), the theophanic signal of an earthquake (also a Mattheanism—3,0; cf. the comments on 8:24; 21:10; 27:51-54), and the shifting of largeness from the stone to the earthquake all have the purpose of playing up Jesus' majestic deity, displayed in his resurrection. With the same purpose in mind Matthew inserts another clause: "for the angel of the Lord, having descended from heaven and approached, rolled away the stone." We see more Mattheanisms in γάρ (62-63,15) and "the angel of the Lord" (2,4). As in 1:20, 24; 2:13, 19, the angel of the Lord accompanies an emphasis on Jesus' deity and not only appears, but also goes on to explain the event and give instructions. Here the angel of the Lord replaces the young man later mentioned by Mark. Matthew likes καταβάς (5,0) and οὐρανοῦ (46,11). When preceded by ἀπό, the latter refers to the sky; when preceded by ἐκ, as here, to the heaven of God's abode (see the comments on 16:1). Not only the mention of the angel of the Lord, then, but also his descent from the highest heaven points to Jesus' deity. In the same vein, προσελθών betrays Matthew's hand (38,6) and connotes Jesus' deity (see the comments on 4:3; 8:14). The rolling away of the stone derives from the women's question in Mark 16:3. But only Matthew indicates that the angel of the Lord rolled it away. (In fact, Mark and the other evangelists never do say who rolled it away.) Since the earthquake in 27:51-54 split open the rock tombs at the moment of the saints' resurrection, we are probably meant to understand that Jesus' resurrection occurs with the present earthquake and that the angel's rolling away the stone has the purpose of letting him out of the tomb (though he remains unobserved for the time being). The women's entering the tomb drops out because the actions of the angel of the Lord are still in the process of happening before their eyes. In other words, according to Mark the women find the tomb open, enter it, and see a young man inside; according to Matthew, however, they feel a great earthquake and see the angel of the Lord descend from heaven, approach the grave, roll away the stone, and sit on it outside. Thus, "entering into the tomb, they saw a young man" disappears; and "he was sitting on it" substitutes for "sitting on the right [side of the interior of the tomb]." Matthew likes ἐπάνω (7,1).

   28:3 (Mark 16:5; Luke 24:4) The unique clause, "But his face [or 'appearance'—see BAG, s.v. εἰδέα] was like lightning," enhances the angel's role as a pointer to Jesus' deity and alludes to the OT, in particular to Dan 10:6: "his face was like lightning." Such allusions typify Matthew's style. He uses ὡς, a favorite of his (23,8), instead of the synonymous ὡσεί, which appears in the LXX and Theodotion. δέ contrasts the welcomed actions of the angel with his dreadful appearance. The addition of καί, followed by a switch from Mark's participial construction to an implied ἦν with another ὡς, signals the second line of a characteristically Matthean parallel. The changing of Mark's στολήν, "robe," to τὸ ἔνδυμα αὐτοῦ, "his garment," starts an allusion to Dan 7:9 and exemplifies Matthew's frequent insertion of ἔνδυμα (6,0). λευκὸν ὡς χιών completes the allusive quotation of Dan 7:9; but because of Mark's "white robe," Daniel's "like white snow" becomes "white like snow." That Daniel's phrase appears in a description of the Ancient of Days enhances the connotation of deity that Matthew wants to associate with Jesus by means of the angel. Luke's phrase ἐν ἐσθῆτι ἀστραπτούσῃ, "in flashing clothes," looks like a conflation of the lightning-like face in Matthew and the white robe in Mark.

28:4 (Mark 16:5; Luke 24:5) For a contrast between the angel's impressive appearance and the guards' weakness, Mark's καί yields to δέ (so also Luke). The insertion of ἀπό . . . τοῦ φόβου αὐτοῦ, "because of fear of him," draws out the contrast (cf. Dan 10:7). The words ἀπό . . . τοῦ φόβου were inserted in Markan material and pointed to Jesus' deity also in 14:26 (cf. Matthew's fondness for φοβέομαι—8,2). Essentially, Luke's ἔμφοβων, "frightened," agrees with Matthew against Mark. Further Mattheanisms are evident in ἐσείσθησαν, "quaked, were shaken" (3,0), and οἱ τηροῦντες, "those who were keeping guard" (5,1). The former replaces Mark's ἐξεθαμβήθησαν and connotes Jesus' deity (see the comments on 9:8; cf. Isa 28:7 LXX; Hab 3:14 LXX; *1 Enoch* 1:2-7). The latter stems from Matthew's inserting the setting of a guard in 27:54. Thus the alarm of the *women* (so Mark) turns into the quaking of the *guards* because of a demonstration that the divine Jesus, represented by his angel, frustrated the design of his opponents to prevent a theft of his corpse—a theft now seen to be unneeded because he really did rise—and falsified their calling him "that deceiver" for predicting his resurrection (27:63). Matthew's inserting "and they [the guards] became like dead [men]" (cf. Luke; Rev 1:17) sharpens his point. Yet again we notice the Mattheanism ὡς (23,8; cf. v 3). In an ironic reversal, Jesus is alive and the guards seem dead. Cf. Dan 10:8-9.

28:5 (Mark 16:6; Luke 24:5) Matthew adopts Mark's δέ, which contrasts the fear of the guards with the command to the women not to fear. But Mark's λέγει gives way to ἀποκριθείς . . . εἶπεν, a Mattheanism (29,6). "The angel" (not in Mark) comes from the insertion in v 2, and the substitution of "the women" for "them" stems from Matthew's need to reintroduce the women after inserting the guards in the preceding verse. For assimilation to v 4, "Do not be afraid" replaces "Do not be alarmed." Matthew is fond of φοβεῖσθε (8,2), especially with μή (4,1). Typically, he adds an emphatic ὑμεῖς (15,3) to mark off the women from the guards. The further addition "for I know that . . ." adds a note of authority and assurance (cf. the similar distinctive wording in 6:8, 32). Matthew likes οἶδα (7,2) and γάρ (62-63,15). His omitting "the Nazarene" makes a cleaner contrast between Jesus as the one who was crucified and the announcement that he has been raised (cf. 20:30 with Mark 10:47). The putting of τὸν ἐσταυρωμένον, "the crucified," before ζητεῖτε, "you are searching for," emphasizes the contrast and differs from Mark.

28:6 (Mark 16:6; Luke 24:6) Matthew reverses the order of "He has been raised" and "he is not here" (so Mark) to allow the insertion of γάρ, a favorite of his (62-63,15). The insertion, in turn, makes Jesus' being raised the ground of the statement "He is not here." Thus Matthew exchanges Mark's chronological order for a logical order. If we assume the incorrectness of the omission in D and much of the Old Latin, Luke agrees with Matthew in reversing the order of Mark's clauses, but puts ἀλλά instead of γάρ with ἠγέρθη. Matthew now reaches forward to Mark 16:7d for "just as he said to you," from which he lops off "to you" because of his changing the address from the disciples (so Mark 16:7d) to the women, who had not heard Jesus predict his resurrection. The advance of the clause stresses the resurrection as a fulfillment of Jesus' word, a confirmation of his truthfulness, which contrasts with the Jewish authorities' deceitfulness, about to be described. The advance also changes the referent from Jesus' saying that he will precede the disciples to Galilee after his resurrection (so Mark; cf. Mark 14:28; Matt 26:32) to his earlier predictions of the passion and resurrection (16:21; 17:22-23; 20:18-19). Out of these revisions comes parallelistic structure such as Matthew loves:

Leading clause: "Do not be afraid"
  Substantiating clause with γάρ: "for I know"
    Epexegetical clause: "that you are searching for Jesus the crucified."
Leading clause: "He is not here"
  Substantiating clause with γάρ: "for he has been raised"
  Epexegetical clause: "just as he said."

Matthew characteristically inserts "Come!" (δεῦτε—2,2) because the presence of the guard and the frightful appearance of the angel have caused the women to remain outside and not approach close enough even for a look into the empty tomb. In Matthew, moreover, the angel is sitting outside the tomb on the stone that once closed its mouth. Therefore the invitation to see the place where Jesus has been lying does not mean that the women should enter the tomb to see, but only that they should come to its mouth, where the angel sits, and peer in. Because of the exclamatory δεῦτε, Mark's exclamatory ἴδε, "See!" changes to the truly imperative ἴδετε. Consequently, the nominative ὁ τόπος becomes the accusative τὸν τόπον. Matthew changes "they put him" to "he was lying" because, strictly speaking, "they" did not put Jesus there—only Joseph did (see 27:60; Mark 15:46; Luke 23:53). Mark 15:46 shows the indefiniteness of "they" here in Mark 16:6.

28:7 (Mark 16:7; Luke 24:6-8) Because of the harmonious continuation that follows, καί replaces ἀλλά. To prepare for the element of joy, which he will insert in v 8, Matthew inserts "quickly" (cf. the same insertion in 5:25). He reserves Mark's ὑπάγετε for v 10 and here substitutes πορευθεῖσαι, a favorite of his (8,4). "Say to his disciples" stays unchanged. "And to Peter" drops out, however, not because no special appearance to Peter follows (Jesus' words do not imply such an appearance), but because Matthew's Peter has apostatized (see the comments on 26:70). Mark's recitative ὅτι is kept for emphasis.

By adding "He has been raised from the dead" (not in Mark; but cf. Luke), Matthew reemphasizes the resurrection. The addition is the first line of a couplet and so exhibits his parallelistic style; it also duplicates part of 27:64 (see the comments ad loc. for evidence of his composition). There the Jewish authorities tried to forestall the false rumor, "He has been raised from the dead." Inserting these very words as a *true* message highlights the reliability of Jesus' predicting his resurrection. The added καί introduces the second, parallel line. The inserted ἰδού typifies Matthew's diction (34,9) and stresses the announcement "he is preceding you into Galilee" (cf. 26:32; Mark 14:28). "There you will see him" shows that προάγει means "precedes" rather than "leads." The substitution of another ἰδού for Mark's καθώς provides a parallel to the foregoing ἰδού and stems from Matthew's having advanced καθὼς εἶπεν to v 6. That advance leads also to the substitution of "I have said" for "he said."

28:8 (Mark 16:8; Luke 24:9) The change of ἐξ- to ἀπ- in front of -ελθοῦσαι not only reflects Matthew's liking ἀπέρχομαι (14,11), but also arises out of the fact that whereas in Mark 16:5 the women were *in* the tomb and now go *out*, in Matthew they did *not* go in (but were only invited to peer in—v 6) and therefore now go *away*, just as Joseph "went *away*" (ἀπῆλθεν, Matthew's insertion in 27:60). The insertion of "quickly" heightens the element of joy about to be added and corresponds to an identical insertion in v 7. The omission of "they fled" continues the change from speechless terror (so Mark) to communicative joy (cf. Luke). Similarly, "for trembling and astonishment had gripped them" gives way to Matthew's happier phrase, "with fear and great joy." "Fear" substitutes for "trembling" and derives from the last clause in Mark 16:8: "for they were afraid" (cf. the comments on v 4). Because it is milder than trembling, fear allows the switch from astonishment to great joy, from speechlessness to quick announcement (cf. the comments on 2:10 concerning the "great joy" of the magi). These revisions prepare not only for the women's announcement in vv 8-10, but also for the great commission in vv 19-20. Both χαρᾶς and μεγάλης are Mattheanisms (3,2; 11,1).

Matthew now omits καί because of his previous omission of εἶχεν. He replaces "they said nothing to anyone" with "they ran to announce [these things] to his disciples." "Ran" links with the insertions of "quickly" in v 7 and the first part of the present verse. ἀπαγγεῖλαι, which replaces Mark's εἶπαν, anticipates the allusion to Ps 22:23(22) in v 10 and comes from Matthew's favorite vocabulary (3,2; cf. the association of ἀπήγγειλαν with ἀπελθόντες in 8:33, where the former has a parallel but the latter does not). The reference to Jesus' disciples reflects v 7. "For they were afraid" drops out as already used in the phrase "with fear." Luke agrees with Matthew both in general and in some particulars. For example, he uses ἀπήγγειλαν despite not having a later allusion to Ps 22:23(22), and he omits Mark's statement "For they were afraid," despite not having advanced the element of fear. Such agreements point to Matthew's influence.

28:9-20 From this point on we lack a reliable text of Mark (see the UBS and Metzger, *Textual Commentary* ad loc.). Some have thought that Mark ended at 16:8. But something seems required to jolt the women out of their speechlessness. If not, the women fail to tell the disciples and Peter that they will see Jesus in Galilee and Mark closes on a note of disobedience (cf. Mark 16:7). It does no good to say that the women have not yet had a chance to tell the disciples and Peter, for according to Mark 16:8 the women failed even to start carrying out their commission. Fleeing and telling nothing to anyone hardly mean starting out to tell the disciples and Peter. Moreover, in Matt 28:9-10 Jesus' command that the women go tell the disciples to meet him in Galilee is wholly unnecessary, since the women, though fearful, have great joy and are already running to tell the disciples to meet him in Galilee (vv 7-8). The repetitiousness of vv 9-10 does not indicate Matthean dittography, then, but dependence on now lost Markan material that had its raison d'être only in Mark, where the women are struck dumb with terror and need a second command, this time by Jesus himself, to effect their report. Apropos Matt 28:16-20, Mark must have originally included Jesus' appearing to the disciples in Galilee and giving them the great commission there; for otherwise the seeing of Jesus in Galilee never takes place, despite two advance notices of it (Mark 14:28; 16:7; Matt 26:32; 28:7). See further the note on 26:32. We may legitimately assume, then, that in vv 9-10 and 16-20 Matthew edits Markan material no longer available to us and that vv 11-15 represent an inserted continuation of the story started in 27:62-66, also an insertion.

28:9 The exclamation ἰδού adds emphasis and reflects Matthew's diction (34,9). ὑπήντησεν occurs elsewhere in Matthew only at 8:28, but Matthew uses its cognate ὑπάντησις once as an insertion and once as part of distinctive material. λέγων is an obvious favorite of his (61,23). The Greek greeting χαίρετε, "Rejoice," echoes the insertion of χαρᾶς, "joy," in v 8 and again exhibits Matthew's diction (5,3 for the two cognates). δέ contrasts the actions of the women with Jesus' action. προσελθοῦσαι connotes Jesus' dignity and adds to the list of Mattheanisms (38,6). The list continues with κράτησαν (4,1), πόδας (4,1), and προσεκύνησαν (6,5). Especially with προσελθοῦσαι, the last of these emphasizes Jesus' deity. Matthew inserts the combination of approaching and worshipping four times in his gospel.

28:10 The list of Mattheanisms grows longer with τότε (66,17), the emphatic historical present λέγει (47,11), the name of Jesus (80,12), and μὴ φοβεῖσθε (4,1). The command not to be afraid echoes the replacement in v 5 and obliterates the element of fear mentioned in v 8. Now joy suffers no admixture of fear. So it will be when the persecuted disciples of Jesus see him again. So it can now be by faith. ὑπάγετε (5,6) compensates for Matthew's substituting πορευθεῖσαι instead of ὑπάγετε in v 7 (cf. Mark 16:7). ἀπαγγείλατε τοῖς ἀδελφοῖς μου, "announce [these things] to my brothers," typifies Matthew's habit of borrowing OT phraseology (see Ps 22:23[22]; cf. John 20:7; Heb 2:12). This command also brings into view his portrayal of the church as a brotherhood (ἀδελφός—11,8). He likes ἀπέλθωσιν (14,11). "Into Galilee" echoes 26:32; 28:7. "And there they will see me" mirrors v 7. Matthew inserted κἀκεῖ also in 5:23; 10:11 (cf. ἐκεῖ by itself—16,6).

See especially G. W. Trompf in *NTS* 18 (1972) 308-30. Since Matthew portrays the church as a brotherhood, the brothers of Jesus hardly mean his half brothers.

THE CONTRAST BETWEEN THE DECEITFULNESS OF THE JEWISH LEADERS AND THE TRUTHFULNESS OF JESUS (CONTINUED)
28:11-15

28:11 Verses 11-15 complete the story begun and inserted in 27:62-66. δέ contrasts the bribing of the guards with the actuality of Jesus' resurrection.

The genitive absolute construction of the opening phrase typifies Matthew's style. πορευομένων typifies his diction (13,10) and echoes a similar insertion concerning the women in v 7. As often, he uses ἰδού for emphasis (34,9). "Some of the guard" reflects 27:65-66. The nominative participle ἐλθόντες again represents Matthew's style (10,10). "Into the city" echoes his insertion at 27:53 and exhibits his special interest in cities (18,3). ἀπήγγειλαν echoes vv 8 and 10. Just as the women went to tell the disciples about Jesus' resurrection, so some of the guard go to tell the chief priests, who therefore have no excuse for their unbelief. They now know from unprejudiced witnesses that the sign of Jonah has been given (see 12:40, distinctive of the first gospel and spoken to Jewish leaders). Thus Matthew heightens their guilt. Only in his gospel do we read about guards at the tomb who observe what happens. "To the chief priests" echoes 27:62; but the Pharisees, also mentioned in 27:62, drop out, just as in 27:3 both the chief priests and the elders were mentioned, but several verses later only the chief priests (27:6). In the latter passages Matthew leaves the reader to supply the second member of the pair recently mentioned. He likes the expression τὰ γενόμενα (1,3), which here gets the modifier ἅπαντα (see 6:32 for his inserting it in traditional material; cf. his liking πᾶς—63,25-26). The guards reported to the chief priests, not because they belonged to the Temple guard, but because Pilate had put them at the disposal of the chief priests. If they had belonged to the Temple guard, they would not have needed to fear Pilate's response.

28:12 συναχθέντες, "having gathered together," connotes the unbelieving synagogue and comes from Matthew's favorite vocabulary (10,10; see the comments on 2:3-4). "With the elders" makes a parallel with 27:1, where he alone wrote that the chief priests and the elders of the people "took counsel," as they do here. Significantly, the Markan parallel to 27:1 read μετά and lacked Matthew's phrase "of the people" (see Mark 15:1). Thus the present verse conforms not only to 27:1, but also to its Markan parallel to compensate for former revisions. Matthew pays special attention to the elders (4,2). See the comments on 27:1 for συμβούλιον . . . λαβόντες (3,2). Six times Matthew uses ἀργύρια, "money, pieces of silver," in his stories about Judas's suicide and the guards. The distinctiveness of these occurrences suggests the interests of a publican, such as Matthew had been. In the distinctive occurrences and 25:27 (against Luke 19:23); 26:15 (against Mark 14:11; Luke 22:5), the noun takes the plural. The bribery of the soldiers exposes the Jewish leaders' lack of honesty. The large size of the sum it took to silence the awestruck, convinced soldiers argues for the truth of Jesus' resurrection and the falsity of the rumor about to be concocted by the chief priests and elders and circulated by the soldiers.

28:13-14 After indicating that the Jewish leaders gave much money to the soldiers, Matthew characteristically introduces their statement to the guards with λέγοντες (61,23). The statement displays favorites of his in μαθηταί (31,5), νυκτός (4,3), ἐλθόντες (10,10), ἔκλεψαν (2,2), ἀκουσθῇ (26,6), ἡγεμόνος (7,2), πείσομεν (2,1), and ποιήσομεν (19,19). "Coming . . . his disciples stole him" echoes 27:64. The genitive absolute construction in ἡμῶν κοιμωμένων, "while we were sleeping," typifies his style. See 27:52 for sleep as part of an insertion. In the NT, ἀμερίμνους occurs only here and in 1 Cor 7:32, but Matthew inserted its cognate μεριμνάω in 6:31, 34 (bis). πείσομεν, "we will persuade," may connote pacification or bribery (see BAG, s.v.). Philo writes that Pilate took bribes (*Legat.* §38; cf. Acts 24:26).

28:15 The promise to satisfy the governor and keep the soldiers out of trouble if he hears a report that the tomb is empty and the disciples are proclaiming Jesus' resurrection brings to a climax Matthew's picture of the deception perpetrated by the chief priests and elders. "But the ones who took the money" duplicates almost exactly a similar phrase in 27:6, part of a distinctive passage. δέ contrasts the possibility of trouble with Pilate and the soldiers' carrying out the instructions despite that possibility. λαβόντες, ἀργύρια, and ἐποίησαν are Mattheanisms (3,7; 0,6; 19,19) and echo vv 12, 14. ὡς and ἐδιδάχθησαν also represent Matthew's diction (23,8; 3,3). The striking use of the verb "teach" pits the Jewish leaders' deceitful instruction against Jesus' trustworthy teaching. The contrast is reinforced by the expression ὁ λόγος οὗτος, "this report." Cf. the insertion of τοῦτον with τὸν λόγον in 19:22 and many other unique occurrences of λόγος (16,2). Matthew mentions the wide circulation of the false rumor among the Jews not only to help explain the unbelief of most of them, but also to bring them out of their unbelief by an exposé of the fraud it rested on. In the phrase παρὰ Ἰουδαίοις, "among the Jews," we have his typical use of παρά + the dative (2,2). μέχρι τῆς σήμερον, "till the present," matches his insertion in 11:23 (cf. 27:8 and the general frequency of σήμερον in Matthew—4,3). The text-critical evidence for an added ἡμέρας, "day," wavers. On the one hand, the echo of 11:23 favors omission with ℵ A W Γ Δ *f*¹ *f*¹³ *pl* and the Byzantine family. On the other hand, Matthew's liking ἡμέρας (15,9) favors inclusion. Cf. Justin *Dial.* 108.

THE MISSION TO ALL THE NATIONS AND RELATED MATTHEAN THEMES
28:16-20

Verses 16-20 have no extant parallel (but see the comments on vv 9-20 concerning Matthew's use of a Markan ending now lost), and they offer a compendium of important Matthean themes: Jesus as the greater Moses, the deity of Jesus, the authority of his commands, the trinitarian associations of baptism, the danger of doubt among disciples, the teaching ministry of disciples, discipleship as keeping Jesus' law, the presence of Jesus with his disciples, and the directing of Christian hope to the consummation. Paramount among these themes, however, is the mission to all the nations.

28:16 δέ contrasts the false report that the disciples stole Jesus' body with the truth of Jesus' appearance to the eleven disciples (cf. Luke 24:9; Acts 1:26). Matthew's adding "disciples," which does not appear elsewhere with "eleven," typifies his diction (31,5). ἐπορεύθησαν, "went," likewise comes from the stock of his favorite words (13,10). "Into Galilee" reflects 26:32; 28:7, 10. The reference to the mountain again displays an interest of Matthew (ὄρος—6,1) and begins to renew his portrayal of Jesus as the greater Moses. Both the Mosaic law and that of Jesus were issued from a mountain. In fact, despite the lack of a mountain in v 10, εἰς τὸ ὄρος repeats what Matthew inserted at the start of the Sermon on the Mount (5:1). "Where Jesus appointed them" implies Jesus' authority, prepares for even stronger emphases on that theme, and contains characteristically Matthean uses of the adverbial οὗ (0,3) and the name "Jesus" (80,12).

The return to Galilee arises out of simple obedience to Jesus' command (26:32; 28:7, 10; Mark 14:28; 16:7), not out of a specially Matthean desire to establish continuity between Jesus' Galilean mission and the disciples' mission to all nations everywhere. We might well attribute that desire to the risen Jesus himself. And we do better to associate the mountain in the present verse with the mountain of the law (5:1) than with the mountain of Jesus' third temptation (4:8-9); for Jesus issued his commands, to which he refers in the present passage (v 20), from the former mountain; but the universal authority he claims here in v 18 is lacking in Matt 4:8-9, and no mountain is mentioned in Luke 4:5-6, where Satan offered such authority.

28:17 Typically, Matthew writes the nominative participle ἰδόντες (10-11,7), which harks back to vv 7 and 10, and προσεκύνησαν, "they worshipped," which implies Jesus' deity (6,5; cf. esp. v 9). As in Matthew's unique phraseology at 26:67, οἱ δέ means "but some" (in contrast with the generality of a larger group, here "the eleven") rather than "but they" (which would create a needless contradiction between worship and doubt or an uncharacteristic meaning "and" for δέ; cf. the comments on 26:67). ἐδίστασαν was part of an insertion in 14:31 (the location of its only other occurrence in the NT) and belongs to a family of words well liked by Matthew (6,6 for compounds with δια-). "Doubted" exposes the little faith of some disciples (see the comments on 14:31). Notably, in Matthew neither the appearance of Jesus removes doubt—on the contrary, it occasions doubt (contrast the inauthentic Mark 16:14)—nor does proof of Jesus' corporeality remove doubt, as in Luke 24:36-43; John 20:24-29. Rather, it is Jesus' word that quiets all doubt even though that word does not take up the question of doubt. We could hardly ask for better evidence of the authority of Jesus' teaching in Matthew's theology.

Seeing Jesus risen hardly measures up to seeing him at the parousia, as though Matthew (and perhaps Mark before him) portrays this incident as the parousia; for the parousia follows the tribulation, the age of the church, and the carrying out of the great commission and includes a coming on clouds with power and great glory (see chap. 24 and cf. the note on 26:32).

28:18 προσελθών comes from Matthew's special diction (38,6). But here, as in the insertion at 17:6-7, it is Jesus who approaches—and for the same reason, viz., that his disciples lie prostrate before him. Here, they worship at the very sight of him, before he comes close. Far from divesting the term of its usual connotation of Jesus' dignity, then, this transferal from the worshippers to the one worshipped intensifies that connotation.

594

Matthew's style is evident in the naming of Jesus (80,12), ἐλάλησεν (13,1), and λέγων (61,23).

It is commonly thought that Matthew draws ἐδόθη μοι . . . ἐξουσία, "authority has been given to me," from Dan 7:14 (see esp. the LXX; cf. his fondness for ἐδόθη [8-9,10] and the insertion of ἐξουσία in 9:8). The addition of πᾶσα, "all," then represents his favorite diction (63,25-26), heightens the thought of Jesus' authority, and possibly reflects Dan 4:14 LXX. But in the present passage we do not discover a forward reference to the parousia in accord with other allusions to Dan 7:13-14. Therefore it is better to say that Matthew takes "All authority has been given to me" from the tradition behind Luke 4:6b, "to you I will give all this authority," which he omitted in Matt 4:9. Its use here compensates for its omission there. Matthew inserted "in heaven and on earth" also in 6:10. The phrase adds heavenly authority to the earthly authority offered by the Devil. Matthew has a penchant for pairing heaven and earth (6,0), likes to use ἐπὶ τῆς γῆς (8,2), and has a general liking for οὐρανός (46,11) and γῆ (21,6). Emphasis does not fall on Jesus' resurrection, then, or even on his exaltation to heaven, let alone his coming as the Son of man to judge and rule the world. It rests, rather, on the universal authority delegated to him (by God, it is naturally understood in this context, not by the Devil, as in Luke 4:6). This emphasis lays the foundation of the command to make disciples of all nations. The church dare not disobey in view of the universal authority of the commander. The passages 7:29; 9:8; 11:27; 21:23 show that Jesus had this authority before his resurrection. That he did was the reason for Matthew's omission in 4:9. Hence, the present passage confirms that such authority stood behind Jesus' earlier commands, which the disciples are to teach new converts (v 20).

28:19 Every word in the first part of v 19—"Going, therefore, make disciples of all the nations"—comes from Matthew's special vocabulary: πορευθέντες (8,4), οὖν (35,11), μαθητεύσατε (1,2; with cognates—33,8), πάντα (63,25-26), ἔθνη (7,2), and the combination πάντα τὰ ἔθνη (1,2). The presence of the same combination in Luke 24:47 suggests either Matthean influence on Luke or dominical tradition or a bit of both. The recent mention of the Jews in v 15 and the contrastive earlier commission not to depart into the way of Gentiles or enter any city of Samaritans, but to go rather to Israel (10:5-6, an insertion by Matthew), suggest that the expression may mean "all the Gentiles" rather than "all the nations." On the other hand, in 25:32 it helps describe the general judgment and hardly excludes Israel, especially since the "brothers" of the judge must include everybody who does God's will (cf. 12:46-50). To include Gentiles as well as Jews, therefore, the present commission expands the earlier commission (cf. Matthew's bringing Gentile women into the genealogy of Jesus, the descendant of Abraham, through whose seed God promised that all the nations of the earth should be blessed [Gen 22:18; cf. Gen 12:3]). Such an expansion not only provides enough contrast with v 15 and 10:5-6. It also agrees with Matthew's insistence that the mission to Israel be prolonged to the parousia (see the comments on 10:23; 23:34). Furthermore, "to this day" in v 15 may indicate continuing contact with Jews in an attempt to win them; for it sounds as though Christians hear the rumor concerning a theft of Jesus' corpse from the Jews they are trying to win (cf. Matthew's use of fulfillment-quotations, the genealogy in chap. 1, the Jewish tone of the whole nativity story, the portrayals of Jesus as the greater Moses and Son of David—all indications of evangelistic appeal to Jews). The use of μαθητεύσατε, "make disciples [i.e., learners]," puts evangelism in terms of learning the law of Jesus (cf. v 20).

For those who enter the school of Christ, baptism is the rite of initiation. Matthew describes this baptism as "into the name of the Father and of the Son and of the Holy Spirit." εἰς τὸ ὄνομα is a favorite phrase of his (3,2) and occurs nowhere else in the synoptics. Further Mattheanisms include πατρός (22,13), υἱοῦ (27,16), and ἁγίου πνεύματος (0,3). Matthew edited the story of Jesus' baptism so as to emphasize the Trinity (see the comments on 3:16-17; cf. 12:28); yet only Jesus' name is associated with baptism in Acts 2:38; 8:16; 10:48; 19:5; 1 Cor 1:13, 15 (cf. Rom 6:3; 1 Cor 6:11; 10:1-4). Therefore Matthew seems to be responsible for the present formula. But the formula does not imply utterance of the trinitarian phrase at the time of baptism. Instead, "in the name of" means "with fundamental reference to" and distinguishes Christian baptism, demanding allegiance to the triune God, from John's baptism, requiring only repentance.

Luke 24:44-53; John 20:21; Acts 1:8; and the unlikelihood that evangelizing Gentiles would have become prominent in the early church, especially in view of the Jewish limitation of Jesus' ministry, support the basic authenticity of the great commission. The Jewish limitation of Jesus' ministry, the Jewishness of the first disciples, the temptation to avoid persecution from unbelieving Jews by remaining a Jewish sect, and the initial concentration on Jerusalem and Judea (cf. Acts 1:8) made the recipients of the great commission somewhat tardy in carrying it out. But they did not oppose the conversion of Gentiles. Even the Judaizing party objected only to failure to require that converts from among the Gentiles be treated as proselytes who came into Judaism, i.e., be accepted into the church on condition of circumcision and observance of the Mosaic law, including its other ceremonial features. The requirement of baptism hardly limits πάντα τὰ ἔθνη to Gentiles; for John had baptized Jews, and even Jesus submitted to baptism—in Matthew he insisted on it! Nor does calling Jesus' blood on themselves and their children (27:25) exclude the Jews as objects of the great commission, for the similar and distinctively Matthean statement in 23:35 stands right alongside one of Matthew's indications that the mission to Israel should continue (see the comments on 23:34). The blood of Jesus will come on the Jews in the events of the tribulation and the parousia (see chap. 24, with care not to confuse the persecution of the church with the distress of Israel). See further J. P. Meier in *CBQ* 39 (1977) 94-102. If we were to restrict πάντα τὰ ἔθνη to Gentiles, this commission would supplement, not replace, the continuing mission to Israel.

See *m. Nid.* 5:6 and L. Hartman in *NTS* 20 (1974) 432-40 for εἰς τὸ ὄνομα as resting on the Semitic idiom לְשֵׁם (Hebrew) and לְשׁוּם (Aramaic) instead of the Greek banking usage for transferal to someone's account. The short, nontrinitarian text discussed by F. C. Conybeare in *ZNW* 2 (1901) 275-88 does not have enough support to merit our consideration (see B. J. Hubbard, *The Matthean Redaction of a Primitive Apostolic Commissioning: An Exegesis of Matthew 28:16-20* [SBLDS 19; Missoula: Scholars Press, 1974] 151-75). With the long, trinitarian text, cf. 1 Cor

12:4-6; 2 Cor 1:21-22; 13:13(14); Gal 4:6; Eph 1:3-14; 4:4-6; 1 Pet 1:2, 3ff.; *Did.* 7:1-13; Justin *1 Apol.* 61.

28:20 In the parallelistic style typical of Matthew, the participial phrases "teaching them" and "baptizing them" match each other (cf. 4:23; 9:35 for this structure). See especially 5:19 and the comments on 5:1-2 concerning the importance of teaching in Matthew. As Jesus taught, so the disciples are to teach in making other disciples. This teaching contrasts sharply with the deceptive teaching spawned by the chief priests and elders and circulated by the guards (v 15). Since learning includes doing, Matthew goes on to write, "to keep all [literally 'all things whatever'] I have commanded you." As a whole, this expression typifies Matthew's habit of borrowing OT phraseology (see, e.g., Exod 7:2; Deut 1:3; 30:8; Josh 1:7; Jer 1:7). Furthermore, τηρεῖν is a Mattheanism (5,1; see esp. the insertions in 19:17 and 23:3). So also are πάντα and ὅσα both as a pair (2,3) and individually (63,25-26; 5,6). Matthew inserted ἐνετειλάμην at 17:9. In the LXX of the Pentateuch the verb often introduces divine commands given through Moses (cf. Matt 19:7 and "Moses parallel Jesus" in the Topical Index). Thus Matthew delivers his final, emphatic blow against antinomianism.

The emphatic ἰδού and ἐγώ characterize Matthew's style (34,9; 12-13,3). "I am with you" recalls "Immanuel . . . 'God with us' " (1:23; cf. *m. 'Abot* 3:2, 6, esp. because the similarity between the Matthean and mishnaic passages includes the matter of law, or commands, as well as divine presence). The presence of Jesus "with" his disciples when they go to make disciples, as distinct from his presence "in the midst of" his disciples when they gather together (18:20), recalls similarly expressed promises of protection in the OT (Gen 26:24; 28:15; Exod 3:12; Josh 1:5, 9; Judg 6:12, 16; 2 Sam 7:3; Isa 41:10; 43:5; Hag 1:13; cf. Matt 28:10). In other words, Jesus assures his disciples the way Yahweh assured his people in the OT. Despite the distinction between 18:20 and the present passage, Jesus' presence is associated with his name in both passages. Matthew's favorite diction is evident in πάσας (63,25-26), ἡμέρας (15,9), ἕως (13,14), and τῆς συντελείας τοῦ αἰῶνος (1,4). His putting ἡμέρας with συντελείας reflects Dan 12:13 (see esp. the LXX and Theodotion). Thus Matthew closes his gospel—characteristically and appropriately—with an assimilation of Jesus' words to God's Word in the OT.

Jesus does not promise that the teaching of his commands will mediate his presence to those who obey, but that his presence will be with those who go and make disciples by baptizing and teaching. 2 Chr 36:22-23 offers comparisons with Matt 28:18-20. So far as form is concerned, however, a commission follows an assurance of divine presence in 2 Chronicles. The reverse is true in Matthew. So far as content is concerned, the assurances of divine presence look alike; but there are striking differences between Cyrus's being a pagan emperor and Jesus' being the ever present God, between Cyrus's being commanded and Jesus' issuing commands, and between going to Jerusalem to rebuild the Temple and going to all the nations to make disciples. The dissimilarities in form and content militate against positing a relation between the two passages.

597

Some Higher-Critical Conclusions

THE LITERARY FORM OF MATTHEW

The commentary proper has left us in a good position to draw some higher-critical conclusions about Matthew. The overall question of the literary genre "gospel" has not reached a resolution. It is even debatable whether we should speak of such a genre. Limitation of space prevents a full-scale discussion of the topic here. But we can note that taken alone the first gospel defies easy classification, just as the four gospels taken together resist it.

Since the discovery of the QL, it has become common to say that the distinctive features of Matthew show it to be a Christian counterpart to the Manual of Discipline, i.e., a book of church order (cf. the *Didache*). But this description requires an overlooking of distinctive features besides the rules of the kingdom. For example, Matthew emphasizes proof from prophecy in his well-known string of fulfillment-quotations (see the comments on 1:22-23) and takes large amounts of narrative from Mark. To be sure, he edits Mark's material in ways that stress Jesus' words. But a book of church order should have little, if any, narrative. Furthermore, Matthew often adds narrative to what he takes from Mark (see not only chaps. 1–2; 4:3-11; 8:5-13; 27:3-10, which have corresponding passages in Luke-Acts, but also unique narratives in 14:28-31; 21:14-16; 27:19, 51b-54, 62-66; 28:11-15). Like the other gospels, then, Matthew remains a literary anomaly testifying to Jesus' impact (for a review, see Gundry, "Recent Investigations" 97-114).

THE DATE OF MATTHEW

The Roman destruction of Jerusalem and the Temple in A.D. 70 forms a natural boundary between the possibilities of an early date and a late one for the writing of Matthew. Unless we are to think of pre-Matthean tradition, the apparent allusions to Matthew in the letters of Ignatius and the *Didache* prohibit a date later than ca. A.D. 100. But for some, Matthew's describing the destruction of a city by a king's army (22:7, an insertion) reflects the destruction of Jerusalem and therefore requires a date after

A.D. 70. Throughout the rest of the parable in which the description occurs, however, the king represents God. A reference back to the destruction of Jerusalem would imply an identification of the king with the Caesar in Rome, or at least a double image in which the Caesar acts unwittingly in God's stead (cf. Eusebius *H.E.* 3.5.3; Sulpicius Severus *Chron.* 2.30, though this view seems absent in earlier Christian writings). But the association of Caesar with God requires so much daring, especially since it cannot extend to any other actions of the king in the parable, that we may begin to doubt it. The absence from Matthew 24 of many striking features of the Jewish revolt—cannibalism, pestilence, internecine conflict, and the burning of the Temple—encourages such doubt.

More seriously, if Matthew is alluding to past events in A.D. 70, his "then" at the start of 22:8-9 clearly implies that the mission to Gentiles, which is represented in those later verses, did not begin till A.D. 70 or shortly afterward. But that disagrees with his theology of evangelism in 28:19-20, where Jesus sends out his disciples to make further disciples of Gentiles right after his resurrection. As we have seen in the commentary on 22:7, the burning of the city derives from Isa 5:24-25, not from the destruction of Jerusalem in A.D. 70. We do not even need to suppose that Matthew uses a fixed general description of punitive expeditions (so K. H. Rengstorf in *Judentum, Urchristentum, Kirche: Festschrift für Joachim Jeremias* [ed. W. Eltester: BZNW 26; Berlin: Töpelmann, 1960] 106-29).

But other arguments are put forward in favor of a late date. The rejection of the Jewish nation as indicated in 21:43 (so Matthew alone; cf. 8:12; Luke 13:28); the distant and usually peculiar way the first evangelist writes about "their synagogues" (4:23; 9:35; 10:17; 12:9; 13:54; cf. 23:34); the unique references to the "church" (16:18; 18:17 [bis]) and the other "nation" that will receive the kingdom (21:43); Matthew's special interest in the life of the church (see esp. chap. 18); the development of a high Christology up to the point of a distinctive trinitarian formula (28:19); the use of ῥαββί in its late sense "Teacher" rather than in its early sense "Sir" (23:7-8); the supposed legendary character of at least parts of the nativity story (chaps. 1–2), of Peter's walking on the water (14:28-31), of the dream of Pilate's wife (27:19), of the resurrection of saints (27:51-53), and of the story about the guard at the tomb (27:62-66; 28:11-15); and Matthew's use of Mark—all of these are thought to support a late date, probably the 80s or 90s. More exactly, Matthew's preoccupation with the Pharisees is thought to reflect their rise to dominance at Jamnia, their claim to represent the true Israel, and their reading Jewish Christians out of the synagogue with the Benediction against Heretics, usually dated ca. A.D. 85.

The undisputed persecution of the church by Paul when he was a Pharisee and his anti-Pharisaical theology after becoming a Christian show, however, that conflict between Pharisaism and Christianity need not point to a post-Jamnian date. Intense conflict of that sort marked the earliest history of the church (see esp. Phil 3:5-6; but also Acts 8:3; 9:1-2, 13-14, 21; 22:3-5, 19; 26:9-11; 1 Cor 15:9; Gal 1:13; 1 Thess. 2:13-16; 1 Tim 1:13). The Essenes isolated themselves. The Sadducees lived above the masses and centered in Jerusalem. But the Pharisees had long exercised widespread influence in Jewish society. Given that influence and their theological concerns, they became the Christians' chief antagonists from the start. Josephus clearly states that in Judaism the Pharisees enjoyed dominance before A.D. 70 (*J.W.* 2.8.14 §162; *Ant.* 18.1.3 §15). His statements are not to be discounted on the ground that he wanted to convince the Romans that the Pharisees should govern the Jewish community under the Roman aegis. Exaggerating the Pharisees' influence prior to the revolt would hardly commend them to the Romans. We may well suspect, then, that both the importance of Jamnia and our knowledge of what happened there have been exaggerated. Even W. D. Davies makes some telling admissions in this direction (*The Setting of the Sermon on the Mount* [Cambridge: Cambridge University Press, 1964] 292 n. 2; see further G. Stemberger in *Kairos* 19 [1977] 14-21). At the very least, anti-Pharisaism in Matthew easily fits into the pre-Jamnian period.

Against the other points raised in favor of a late date, divine rejection of the Jewish nation except for a remnant of grace appears already in Pauline literature (see Romans 9–11). Furthermore, the unique statement in Matt 10:23 (see the commentary proper on its redactional character) indicates that the mission to Israel must continue till the Son of man comes. Matthew may not only insist on continuing the mission to Israel. He may also expect the final conversion of Israel, as Paul does; for in contrast with Luke 22:28-30 the saying in Matt 19:28 mentions a regeneration in the context of the Son of man's future rule and speaks about the disciples' sharing that rule by judging—easily taken in the sense of governing—the twelve tribes of Israel (see further the comments on 19:28; cf. Rom 11:25-27).

By the time Jerusalem was destroyed, the church had long since become a counterpart to the synagogue. According to traditions recorded in Acts, Christian missionaries and their converts regularly suffered expulsion from synagogues before the Benediction against Heretics, largely because of Jewish resentment over Christians' poaching Gentile proselytes and God-fearers who attended the synagogues. Matthew's emphasis on evangelizing Gentiles fits this picture (see esp. 28:19-20). The use of ἐκκλησία had started early in the Christian movement (again see the undisputed Pauline epistles). We find trinitarian references in NT books certainly dating from a time before A.D. 70 (see 1 Cor 12:4-6; 2 Cor 13:14), to say nothing in detail about a generally high Christology during that period. The paucity of rabbinic materials from that same period deflates the argument that ῥαββί did not mean "Teacher" till shortly after A.D. 70. Furthermore, Matthew's fusing the title with his portrait of Jesus as a teacher of the law (cf. esp. 5:2 with Luke 6:20) does not have to depend on semantic developments in rabbinic circles (see further the comments on 23:8). And whatever the character or origin of Matthew's distinctive materials, nothing forestalls our dating them before A.D. 70.

By general consent, we have less evidence for dating Mark than we have for Matthew. From the standpoint of method, therefore, dating Matthew should help determine the date of Mark more than vice versa. Besides, the attempt to make Mark's theology of the cross reflect the Neronic persecution and counteract the Christology of Jesus as God's Son (i.e., a divine man) probably needs turning upside down. Mark emphasizes the numinous element in Jesus' life, death, and resurrection. This emphasis calls for an estimate of the theology of the cross as traditional and the Christology of Jesus as God's Son as an apologetic attempt to counteract popular ridicule concerning the disgraceful manner of Jesus' death (see Gundry, "Recent Investigations" 109). Such ridicule arose immediately (cf. esp. Acts 2:22-24; 1 Cor 1:18-25). If then the other reasons adduced for dating Matthew late lack cogency, Matthew's use of Mark hardly strengthens the argument for a late date. We may simply have to date Mark somewhat earlier than Matthew in the period before A.D. 70. Furthermore, the lack of cogency in data supposedly favoring a date after A.D. 70 leaves us no reason to assign other data, which indicate a date before A.D. 70, to an earlier stage of the tradition incorporated by Matthew.

We now turn to those other data, which look surprisingly ample and crop up in those very parts of Matthew that distinguish it from the other gospels. Mark and Luke mention the Sadducees only once each, but Matthew both retains that reference (22:23) and inserts yet another half-dozen references to them (3:7; 16:1, 6, 11, 12; 22:34). The Sadducees lost influence after A.D. 70. A large proportion of them perished in the destruction of Jerusalem. Matthew's special interest in them does not make good sense, then, outside the supposition of a date before A.D. 70. His failure to distinguish the Sadducees sharply from the Pharisees (but note that he does not pair them in the highly edited chap. 23) has no bearing on the date of the gospel, for he cares mainly for their shared opposition to Jesus (cf. his lumping together "Herod the king . . . and all Jerusalem with him" against Jesus in 2:3). This concern, not ignorance of differences between them, suffices to explain the blurring of distinctions. And care for their shared opposition to Jesus could have characterized the evangelist's writing before A.D. 70 as easily as after A.D. 70. Afterward, he had no reason to mention the Sadducees at all—apart from historicization. But the attempt to see in Matthew's Sadducees a historicizing device stumbles against the infrequency of their mention, which contrasts with the many mentions of the Pharisees. If Matthew wanted to make his narrative seem more historical by inserting the Sadducees, why did he not bring them into the picture more often, especially in his version of Jesus' last week in Jerusalem, where the Sadducees held court? As it is, the predominance of the Pharisees and the occasional presence of the Sadducees correspond to what we should expect in a gospel slanted toward Jews and dating from the period before A.D. 70.

Similarly, Matthew's preoccupation with Jerusalem as the center of the Jewish leaders antagonistic to Jesus and his disciples—a preoccupation that pervades Matthew's accounts of the nativity and the week of Jesus' passion and resurrection—favors a date before A.D. 70. For after that date, Jerusalem no longer provided the geographical base of power in Jewish society. Matthew's preoccupation with Jerusalem first shows up in 2:1-12, where opposition to the infant Messiah comes from Jerusalem. In 16:21 he alone specifies Jerusalem as the place of Jesus' coming passion. In 21:10b he adds that "all the city was shaken" when Jesus entered. In 21:17 he adds "outside the city." In the next verse a reference to Jerusalem replaces the reference to Bethany in Mark 11:12. As a result, the cursing and withering of the fig tree signify divine judgment on Jerusalem. The distinctive and already discussed 22:7 belongs here, too. Matthew puts Jesus' lament over Jerusalem, spoken in the territory of Herod Antipas according to Luke 13:34-35, right within Jerusalem (23:37-39). The risen saints appear in the holy city according to the unique passage 27:51b-53. And according to another unique passage, the guards go from the tomb into the city to report what happened at Jesus' resurrection (28:11-15). See further the commentary proper on these passages.

Yet again, Matthew inserts the Sabbath day alongside winter as a time undesirable for flight from Jerusalem (24:20; contrast Mark 13:18). This insertion lacks purpose if the destruction of Jerusalem and previous flight of the Christians to Pella had already taken place. And if he wrote after A.D. 70, we should have expected him to conform the time of the flight from Jerusalem to the historical reality of the flight to Pella *before* the Romans defiled the sanctuary (Eusebius *H.E.* 3.5.3) rather than retain a command to flee only *after* the abomination of desolation (24:15-16). His stress on exact obedience (see the comments on 1:24-25) strengthens our unfulfilled expectation.

Furthermore, the insertion of εὐθέως, "immediately," in the statement that celestial portents and the coming of the Son of man will take place "immediately after the tribulation of those days" (24:29) shows that Matthew allows no gap between the period during which the disciples flee from Jerusalem and the end of the age. After the destruction of Jerusalem, Matthew would have needed to create a gap in accord with the Son of man's delay instead of eliminate even the possibility of a gap and thus aggravate the problem of delay. The regularity with which he usually omits Mark's synonymous εὐθύς makes this point doubly forceful; and his heightening Mark's stress on the visibility of Jesus' return (see the comments on chap. 24 passim) closes the door against a spiritualizing explanation for Jesus' failure to return immediately after the destruction of Jerusalem.

In 24:3, then, Matthew does not concentrate on the sign of the parousia and the consummation of the age and de-emphasize the destruction of the Temple because that destruction has come and gone without the expected return of Jesus. To the contrary, by omitting the story of the widow's mites and juxtaposing the abandonment of Jerusalem's "house" (23:38-39) and Jesus' prediction that not one stone of the Temple will remain on another (24:1-2), he has just emphasized the coming destruction of the Temple. This emphasis frees him in 24:3 to tailor the disciples' request to the contents of Jesus' reply and thus portray the disciples as having understanding, a leading theme in his gospel. Notably, he brings in nothing from A.D. 70 to make Jesus' answer correspond better to the disciples' question regarding the destruction of the Temple. This lack of assimilation to the historical event—if it really has happened by the time he writes—does not tally with his letting the crucifixion of Jesus cause a shift from the verb "kill" to the verb "crucify" in two of the passion predictions (cf. 20:19; 26:2 with Mark 10:34; 14:1; Luke 18:33; 22:1). To say that in 24:15 he makes the abomination of desolation allude to the Roman threat against the church everywhere late in the first century is to overlook his inserting the phrase "in the holy place," which surely specifies the Temple, especially in view of the similar Mattheanism "the holy city" (cf. 4:6; 27:53).

We have seen that in 21:14-16 Matthew turns the crying out of the tumbled-down stones of Jerusalem (Luke 19:39-40) into the crying out of children in praise of Jesus. It is hard to think that the evangelist made such a change after A.D. 70. For then the debris of the city would have offered dramatic proof of God's displeasure with Jerusalem and the Jewish leaders there.

And why should Matt 5:23-24, almost entirely peculiar to the first gospel, speak of offering "a gift at the altar" if the altar was no longer standing at the time Matthew wrote? The verses bristle with Mattheanisms in the references to the altar, a gift, a brother, in ἐὰν οὖν, the verb for bringing an offering, the preposition ἔμπροσθεν, the verbs for remembering, leaving, and going, and the words κἀκεῖ, ἐκεῖ, πρῶτον, τότε, and ἐλθών (see further the commentary proper). The more Matthean the passage, the more incongruous a date of writing after A.D. 70.

Both Mark and Luke use past tenses in Jesus' charge that the Jews have made the Temple a den of robbers. But Matthew uses the present tense and even stresses it with a preceding, vivid historical present in λέγει, "he says" (contrast 21:13 with Mark 11:17; Luke 19:46). Why does he make such revisions if the Temple is no longer standing and the traffic no longer going on? Even though he may be fixing on the continuing result implied by Mark's perfect tense (πεποιήκατε, "you have made"), his switch to the present tense is odd for anyone writing after A.D. 70. For the present tense indicates action in progress. We might suppose that he takes the temporal standpoint of Jesus. But that supposition would require that he writes like a modern historian interested in verisimilitude. By now we have surely learned that he writes as an ancient churchman concerned to adapt Jesus' words and deeds to the situation current at the time of writing.

Again, why the completely unparalleled paragraph on swearing by the Temple and items associated with it (23:16-22) if Matthew wrote after the destruction of the Temple? Who could swear by it, its gold, and its altar then? Only before A.D. 70 could inclusion of such material have a very sharp point. In fact, the passage is characterized by careful parallelism, an allusion to the OT, and an attack on the teaching of the scribes and Pharisees as too lax—all traits of Matthew's composition. Furthermore, we find his favorite vocabulary in the references to swearing, gold, the Temple, being obligated, fools, the blind, comparative greatness, the altar, a gift, sitting, holiness, and inhabiting, and in the words "for," "on," "therefore," and "all" (see the commentary ad loc.). Why the composition of such material after A.D. 70? Even the supposition that Jewish sacrifices continued at an altar on the site of the destroyed Temple (cf. K. W. Clark in *NTS* 6 [1960] 269-80) does not meet the requirements of a Temple still standing complete with adornment of gold (against Clark's position see W. D. Davies, *The Setting of the Sermon on the Mount* [Cambridge: Cambridge University Press, 1964] 260 n. 1; cf. also A. Guttmann in *HUCA* 38 [1967] 137-40; E. Schürer, *The History of the Jewish People in the Age of Jesus Christ (175 B.C.–A.D. 135)* [new English version revised and edited by G. Vermes and F. Millar; Edinburgh: T. & T. Clark, 1973] 1. 521-23). To say that Matthew expects the rebuilding of the Temple in the church age (cf. rabbinic expectation) we should have to forget his interest in Jesus' abandoning the Temple, to which rebuilding would run counter.

Matthew's concern to evangelize Jews as well as Gentiles tends toward an early date. For the longer the majority of Jews resisted the gospel, the more Christian evangelism shifted from the Jewish sphere. Of course, Matthew stresses the conversion of Gentiles, but not at the expense of the mission to Jews. He himself appeals to Jews by tracing Jesus' genealogy to Abraham, often citing OT passages as fulfilled, portraying Jesus as the Davidic Messiah, emphasizing Jesus' affirmation and teaching of the law, and insisting that the Christian witness to Israel shall not end "before the Son of man comes." For this last point see 10:23. There, Matthew anticipates and summarizes that part of the Olivet Discourse which deals with flight from the abomination of desolation (Mark 13:14), just as the two preceding verses come from Mark 13:12-13. In so doing he makes certain assimilations to the present context of the disciples' mission throughout Galilee and uses his favorite diction (see the commentary proper). His knowing that Jesus did not return as the Son of man before the twelve completed their circuit of Galilee implies a continuing mission to Israel alongside the mission to Gentiles. Matthew composes the saying in 10:23 and then omits any reference to a carrying out of the Galilean mission by the twelve disciples to show that the task of Jewish evangelism remains for the church right up to the parousia. Just as Paul is concerned to keep Jewish and Gentile Christians together in the period before A.D. 70 (see Rom 15:25-31), so Matthew wants to keep the church from losing interest in the conversion of Jews and prevent a retreat into Judaism by Jewish Christians suffering persecution from the leaders in Jewish society (cf. the Epistle to the Hebrews).

The Jewish leaders, especially the Pharisees, come under heavy criticism in Matthew. They have passed the point of redemption. But the common people in Jewish society, the crowds, fare better because Matthew is trying to win them. His efforts to do so are patent. He alone says that Jesus was sent "only to the lost sheep of the house of Israel" (15:24). The distinctive phrase "to this day" in the stories of Judas's suicide (27:8) and the guard at Jesus' tomb (28:15) shows that the Jewish mission is still going on at the time Matthew writes. In fact, the whole story of the guard at the tomb, which is unique to his gospel, has the purpose of showing the Jewish common people that their leaders have deceived them (27:62-66; 28:11-15). So believe in Jesus instead of falling under the spell of those hypocritical liars! And since we are thinking about evangelism, here is the place to note that in 28:19 baptism comes before teaching, not the other way around as in later times, but already in *Did.* 7:1. Matthew's order favors an early date.

Furthermore, Matthew turns the dietary taboos of the OT into prohibitions in speech rather than follow the bald abrogation of dietary taboos in Mark 7:1-23 (see the comments on 15:1-20). According to Luke 11:39-41, Jesus balanced his command to give the contents of one's tableware as charity with an abrogation of the dietary laws: "and behold all things are clean for you." But again Matthew avoids a bald abrogation of the dietary taboos by turning them into a demand for moral purity, portrayed in the figure of a cup: "in order that also the outside of it may become clean" (23:25-26). Only cleansing the heart will produce an observable conduct that is truly pure because of consistency with the inward state (cf. 5:21-30; 6:1-18; 7:17-18; 12:33-35; 15:7-9).

The distinctive passage 17:24-27 teaches that Jewish Christians should not contribute to their fellow Jews' rejection of the gospel by refusing to pay the Temple tax. This exhortation not only shows Matthew's concern to win Jews. It specifically favors a date of writing before A.D. 70; for after the destruction of God's Temple in Jerusalem the Romans shifted the tax to the Temple of Jupiter Capitolinus in Rome (Josephus *J.W.* 7.6.6 §218; Dio Cassius 65.7; Suetonius *Dom.* 12), and *m. Šeqal.* 8:8 says that the laws concerning "the Shekel dues . . . apply only such time as the Temple stands." Surely Matthew does not include this passage to support upkeep of a pagan temple, for then the argument implies that the disciples are sons of a pagan god! Nor can we suppose that Matthew is urging Jewish Christians to support the school of Pharisaical rabbis that formed in Jamnia during the aftermath of the Jewish rebellion, for he excoriates the Pharisees throughout his gospel. The argument from 17:24-27 for an early date gains further cogency from the evidence that Matthew himself composed the passage (see the commentary proper on the diction, grammatical and stylistic constructions, and use of OT phraseology).

Jewish terms, such as "the tradition of the elders" (15:2), "phylacteries" (23:5), and "whitewashed tombs" (23:27), go unexplained. Matthew's intended audience, being Jews, will understand them readily. For other Jewish characteristics besides those that are evangelistic, see E. L. Abel in *NTS* 17 (1971) 143-44; M. D. Goulder, *Midrash and Lection in Matthew* (London: SPCK, 1974) 21-27 et passim. Goulder provides a good antidote to the wrongly exclusive emphasis on Matthew's Hellenistic features by G. Strecker (*Der Weg der Gerechtigkeit* [2nd ed.; FRLANT 82; Göttingen: Vandenhoeck & Ruprecht, 1966]).

How much earlier than A.D. 70 did Matthew write his gospel? To answer this question we might start with the great attention he pays to the persecution of Jesus' disciples. Primarily, this persecution comes from Jewish rather than Roman sources (see esp. 23:34 with Luke 11:49). Since the primary source of persecution tended to shift to the Roman side from shortly before A.D. 70 onward, we have another pointer toward an early date for the writing of Matthew. But the argument is capable of greater precision. Since the Jewish authorities handed Jesus over to the Romans for crucifixion and since the Jews neither practiced crucifixion nor possessed the power of capital punishment, in 23:34 Matthew probably means σταυρώσετε, which he inserts, to be taken in the sense "you will cause to be crucified [by the Romans]" (cf. Acts 2:36; 4:10). There are several reasons which, taken together, suggest that his mentioning the crucifixion of Christians at Jewish instigation reflects the Neronian persecution beginning in A.D. 64 or 65. Though we will reject them in the end, they are worth mentioning:

(1) Matthew's inserting σταυρόω in 20:19; 26:2 to reflect the manner of Jesus' death.

(2) Nero's crucifixion of Christians to help divert from himself blame for the great fire of Rome (Tacitus *Ann.* 15.44; cf. Suetonius *Ner.* 16; Tertullian *Praescrip.* 36; Eusebius *H.E.* 2.25; 3.1.2; Sulpicius Severus *Chron.* 2.29).

(3) The statement by Clement of Rome concerning fratricidal struggles that "the greatest and most righteous pillars of the church"—i.e., Peter and Paul—were killed "through jealousy and envy," apparently including that of non-Christian Jews, since Clement's delineation of Peter's and Paul's sufferings covers those known from the NT to have come from unbelieving Jewish as well as Gentile sources (1 Clement 4–5).

(4) The sameness of the charges brought against the Roman Christians and the charges brought earlier against the Roman Jews (Tacitus *Ann.* 15.44).

(5) The avenue of influence on Nero had by the Jews in no less a person than Nero's wife Poppaea Sabina, whom Josephus describes as a worshipper of God and one who pled with her husband on behalf of the Jewish leaders in Jerusalem (*Ant.* 20.8.11 §§189-96).

(6) The consequent probability that non-Christian Jews succeeded in shifting to Christians blame that earlier would have fallen on them (see further W. H. C. Fremd, *Martyrdom and Persecution in the Early Church* [New York: New York University Press, 1967] 121-26, and, for a contrary view, D. R. A. Hare, *The Theme of Jewish Persecution of Christians in the Gospel according to St. Matthew* [SNTSMS 6; Cambridge: Cambridge University Press, 1967] 70-74).

Since we have no evidence that Christians were crucified before A.D. 64 or 65, reflection of the Neronian persecution would provide a terminus a quo for the writing of Matthew. Thus we might date Matthew after A.D. 64 or 65, but before A.D. 70 to allow for indications of writing before the destruction of Jerusalem and the Temple and, in view of the later irrelevance of the command to pray against having to flee on the Sabbath (24:20), before the Christians' flight from Jerusalem some time prior to the destruction. Matthew writes, then, in A.D. 65-67.

Locating Matthew in the Neronian persecution would make the evangelist's theological emphases come alive. Persecution always sharpens the problems of a mixed church; therefore Matthew attends to them. They include betrayals by false disciples seeking to please the persecuting authorities; relaxation of standards of behavior in order to escape identification as Christians; secrecy in profession of faith; church discipline and reclamation of those who have backslidden under pressure of persecution; inhospitality toward itinerants fleeing for their lives and posing the possibility of suffering for those who dare to help them; and little faith, or doubt, in the midst of danger. Matthew's sustained attack on Jewish leaders grows out of their instigating the persecution. His portraying Jesus and the Father in majestic colors has the purpose of counterbalancing the downtrodden condition of the church. Attention to God's fatherhood brings comfort to the persecuted. Emphasis on the final judgment of persecutors and false disciples inspires hope of vindication.

The association of Matthew's gospel with a current persecution instigated by Jewish leaders rings true. Surely his intensifying the theme of persecution reflects something going on at the time of writing, not a past experience. But we should probably reject the identification with Nero's persecution, despite the arguments listed above. That persecution was limited to Rome and its environs. Yet the provenance of Matthew lies far to the east, probably in Syria (see the next subsection). Furthermore, in none of our primary sources concerning the Neronian persecution does Jewish influence on Nero come in the picture. Not even Clement attributes to the Jews the jealousy and envy that resulted in the deaths of Peter and Paul. He may be referring to jealousy and envy in the church (cf. Phil 1:15-17) rather than to antipathy between non-Christian and Christian Jews. And Matthew's penchant for paralleling disciples with Jesus explains the crucifixion of disciples in 23:24 well enough; like master, like disciples—there is no need to resort to Nero's crucifixion of Christians.

Throughout the commentary proper we have noticed evidence of Matthean influence on Luke. Therefore if Matthew writes in A.D. 65-67 in response to the Neronian persecution, Luke-Acts must be written later. But if so, Luke does not write up to the events so far as they have taken place. For Paul landed in his Roman prison ca. A.D. 61, the two whole years he spent there brought him to ca. A.D. 63, and he had not yet even come to trial (Acts 28:30-31). Luke's stopping the story of Paul without telling the outcome of the trial is most naturally explained by a date of writing at the end of the two years. If Paul has suffered condemnation and martyrdom already, Luke would hardly dare use him and his freedom to preach as an apologetic device for defending the legality of the Christian religion. What happened to Paul would ruin the argument. In fact, if Paul is known to have died at the hands of Nero, the great amount of space devoted to Paul's labors undermines Luke's purpose. And it is hardly conceivable that Luke would fail to play up Paul's martyrdom in order to win admiration for the gospel, as he does in the story of Stephen's martyrdom, if the great apostle has already died in Rome. (In Acts 20:23-24 we read only about "bonds and afflictions" and at most about the possibility of martyrdom in risking life to finish a course of ministry; and in 21:13 the possibility of martyrdom has to do with Jerusalem, not Rome.) Similarly, Luke's failure to mention some of the most striking features in the fall of Jerusalem— viz., internecine warfare among the defenders, cannibalism, fire, and, above all, the destruction of the Temple—points to a date before A.D. 70 for Luke-Acts (see further R. H. Gundry, A Survey of the New Testament [Grand Rapids: Zondervan, 1970] 96-97, 219). If then we are to recognize Matthean influence on Luke and date Luke-Acts ca. A.D. 63, Matthew must write his gospel some time before—and Mark yet earlier. Nero's persecution comes too late. For lack of data we cannot pinpoint the particular

Jewish persecution during which Matthew wrote (but see 1 Thess 2:13-16 and Eusebius *H.E.* 2.23.1-25; 3.5.2 for such persecution in the early 50s and early 60s; cf. Acts passim).

Cf. J. A. T. Robinson, *Redating the New Testament* (Philadelphia: Westminster, 1976) 107-17, on early traditions that put the writing of Mark (though Robinson would have it Markan traditions and a proto-Mark) before A.D. 62. The arguments for dating 1 Thess 2:13-16 after A.D. 70 (see B. Pearson in *HTR* 64 [1971] 79-94) take insufficient account of Paul's self-confessed persecution of the church and the re-alized eschatology of wrath in Rom 1:18-32.

THE PROVENANCE OF MATTHEW

There is no way to distinguish between the place of origin and the desti-nation of Matthew's gospel; so we may treat them together. In 4:24 "Syria" replaces "Tyre and Sidon" (Mark 3:8; Luke 6:17). This difference suggests that Matthew writes at some place in Syria besides Tyre and Sidon. We learn from the distinctive passage 17:24-27 that the coin called a stater equals two double drachmas, as only in Damascus and Antioch in Syria (see B. H. Streeter, *The Four Gospels* [London: Macmillan, 1951] 504). Jewish Christians from Palestine started the church in Antioch, and evan-gelism of Gentiles flowered there according to Acts 11:19-21 et passim. The Jewish-cum-Gentile character of Matthew fits Luke's description of the church in Antioch. Unless we unnecessarily conjecture that Ignatius draws on another, unknown source, he alludes to the Gospel of Matthew as early as the beginning of the second century (*Smyrn.* 1:1). His being bishop of the church in Antioch confirms the other evidence favoring An-tioch as our best guess concerning the place of origin and destination of the first gospel. This provenance facilitates Matthean influence on Luke (see Eusebius *H.E.* 3.4.6; Acts 11:28 D for Luke's association with Antioch; cf. the prominence of Peter in Matthew with Peter's presence in Antioch according to Gal 2:11-21).

THE AUTHORSHIP OF MATTHEW

Nowhere does the Gospel of Matthew identify its author by name. Yet by the second quarter of the second century the book was circulating under the title KATA MAΘΘAION, "According to Matthew," and the preposition KATA was understood as pointing to the author. It is even possible that the book never circulated without that title, for we have no positive evi-dence to the contrary.

    The church father Papias cites a tradition that "Matthew arranged [συνετάξατο] the oracles [τὰ λόγια] in Hebrew 'dialect' [διαλέκτῳ], and each interpreted [ἡρμήνευσεν] them as he was able." A great deal of controversy has raged around this statement, relayed to us by Eusebius (*H.E.* 3.39.16). For reasons yet to be mentioned, some scholars reject the possibility that the Apostle Matthew could have written the gospel bearing his name; and since they recognize that the cited tradition ascribes the first gospel to the Apostle Matthew, in their opinion the statement merits no trust whatever. Nonetheless, even with the concession that Papias and other fathers of the church made historical mistakes, the persistent and unrivalled character of this particular tradition calls for a higher estimate of its worth.

A higher estimate is favored also by the early date of Papias's writing and the even earlier date of the tradition (and his acquisition of it) which he passed on. Modern handbooks usually put the date of his writing at ca. A.D. 135. Early though it is, this date is not early enough. The only hard evidence in its favor comes in a statement of Philip of Side, who makes Papias refer to the reign of Hadrian (117-138; see the citation in Aland, 531). But we have good reasons to distrust Philip's statement. He is notoriously unreliable and wrote approximately a century later than Eusebius did (Philip—ca. 430; Eusebius—ca. 324). Hence, if Eusebius leads us to an earlier date for Papias's writing, we should probably prefer the earlier. In fact, Eusebius does lead us to an earlier date by saying that Papias became famous during the time of Polycarp and Ignatius, with whom he associates Clement of Rome (H.E. 3.36.1-2; 3.38.1-5). Polycarp did not die till the middle of the second century; but Ignatius died ca. 107 and Clement, ca. 100. Eusebius's discussion of Papias's writings comes right at this point, i.e., before Trajan's persecution, which started ca. 110 and which Eusebius does not describe till Book 4 of his *Ecclesiastical History*, whereas the fragments of Papias appear in Book 3.

Comparison of Philip's statement with Eusebius's favors that Philip depended on Eusebius but garbled the information he got. Eusebius mentions a Christian writer named Quadratus, who addressed an apology to Hadrian, the very emperor during whose reign Philip puts Papias's writings. The claim of Quadratus that some of the people Jesus healed and raised from the dead have lived up to his own day sounds something like the claim of Papias to have gotten information about the Lord's commands "from the living and abiding voice" of the elders and other disciples of the Lord (see Eusebius H.E. 3.39.1-4 with 4.3.1-2). More strikingly, however, when Philip quotes Papias, the phraseology sounds more like Eusebius's quotations of Quadratus than of Papias; in other words, it looks as though Philip transferred what Quadratus wrote over to Papias. Thus, just as Eusebius associates Quadratus with Hadrian's reign and quotes Quadratus as referring to people raised from the dead by Jesus and still living, so Philip associates Papias with Hadrian's reign and writes that Papias referred to people raised from the dead by Jesus and still living. Furthermore, there appears to have been another Quadratus, who was a prophet, not an apologist. Eusebius discusses him in association with Jesus' original disciples and their immediate successors (H.E. 3.37.1). Philip probably confuses Quadratus the apologist with Quadratus the prophet. It was easy for him to do so, because he found Eusebius's similar discussion of Papias bounded by references to the name "Quadratus." A final cause of Philip's mixing up Papias's writings with an apology by a Quadratus is Eusebius's associating this Quadratus with the daughters of Philip the evangelist (H.E. 3.37.1) just as Eusebius also associates Papias with them (*H.E.* 3.39.9). Poor Philip fell into a trap.

In summary, then, a number of considerations unite to disfavor a date ca. 135 in accordance with Philip of Side and to favor a date before Trajan's persecution (i.e., before ca. 110) for Papias's report concerning Mark and Matthew: (1) the late date of Philip of Side; (2) his generally acknowledged unreliability; (3) the ease with which he might have confused Papias's writing with the apology by Quadratus; (4) the earlier date and greater reliability of Eusebius, who had in his hands the writings of both Papias and Quadratus; (5) Eusebius's associating Papias with Ignatius and, through Ignatius, with Clement of Rome; and (6) Eusebius's discussing the fragments of Papias prior to his description of Trajan's persecution.

Now by his own testimony Papias is not surmising. He is passing on an earlier report by a certain elder. Properly speaking, the tradition does not go back merely to Papias, as most discussions leave the impression it does, but behind Papias to an elder. If Papias writes before ca. 110, then, the tradition he passes on reaches back to the beginning of the second century or the end of the first century. We can say even more. It is usually thought that Papias stands twice removed from the apostles, whom he calls "the Lord's disciples"; i.e., he is separated from them both by supposedly nonapostolic elders and by those who heard such elders and told him what they had heard. But certain data in the text indicate that he claims to have listened often to those who had themselves heard some of the disciples speak; in other words, Papias stands only once removed from these original and closest disciples of Jesus, including Matthew, whom he names along with six others of the twelve (Eusebius *H.E.* 3.39.3-4). We have, then, only three links, not four, in the chain of tradition: (1) the apostles; (2) those who heard the apostles; and (3) Papias. What are the data supporting this view?

First, Papias equates "the words of the elders" with "what Andrew or Peter or Philip or Thomas or James or John or Matthew or any other of the Lord's disciples had said." Why this equation? There are two possible, but mutually exclusive, reasons. One is that the elders are identical with the original disciples of Jesus, i.e., with the apostles. Another is that the elders are different from them but faithfully handed down their teaching. Against the view which sees a distinction, the passage Eusebius quotes from Papias contains no apparent indication that Papias means to distinguish the elders from the disciples. The listing of the apostolic names under the designation "the Lord's disciples" certainly does not imply such a distinction, for Papias immediately identifies John "the elder" as one of "the Lord's disciples." Here he is using the two designations as synonyms. Their interchange so far as John is concerned points to their being synonymous so far as Andrew, Peter, Philip, Thomas, James, Matthew, and other disciples, too, are concerned.

Second, taking the two designations as synonymous conforms to the natural understanding of Papias's text. For if they are not synonymous, Papias jumps backward from second-generation elders to first-generation disciples without any warning only to turn around and use "elder" and

611

"Lord's disciple" for one and the same man. This use of "elder" and "Lord's disciple" for John shows that we are not to regard the repeated τί as an accusative of general reference (the accusative of "last resort") meaning "the words of the elders *concerning* what Andrew or Peter . . . had said," but as an appositive: "the words of the elders, *i.e.*, what Andrew or Peter . . . had said." This use also shows that the expressions do not stand in apposition to each other because later elders repeated what earlier disciples had said; rather, what the Lord's disciples had said is identical with the words of the elders because the elders *were* the disciples Andrew, Peter, and the rest.

Third, though Eusebius distinguishes between John the disciple and John the elder for a tendentious reason yet to be exposed, the truth slips out in *H.E.* 3.39.7, where he writes that Papias "confesses that he had received the words of the apostles from those who had followed them." Here we find only one generation between the apostles and Papias. Thus, in a lapse, Eusebius himself implies that Papias used both the terms "elders" and "Lord's disciples" to mean "apostles."

Fourth, Papias emphasizes the elders' truthfulness in repeating the commandments given by the Lord. A supposedly earlier generation of disciples do not step in as obvious go-betweens to pass the commandments from Jesus to the elders. If Papias were distinguishing later elders from original disciples, we would have expected him to say outright that the elders got the Lord's commandments from the disciples. We might also have expected some emphasis on the truthfulness of the disciples as well as on that of the elders. The absence of such items means that we have no good reason to think that the elders differed from the disciples. On the other hand, Papias implies that he has not heard the elders; it is others who have heard them: "but if ever anyone came who had followed the elders, I inquired about the words of the elders." So it is easy to think that he did not hear the elders simply because they were the apostles and all of them except John had already died.

An elder named John was still speaking. Since "elder" is being used as a synonym for "Lord's disciple" and "apostle," the Elder John is none other than the Apostle John; and Papias heard others who had heard his voice. To be sure, Eusebius distinguishes between the Apostle John and the Elder John (*H.E.* 3.39.6). But the distinction is tendentious. Eusebius does not like the Book of Revelation—the millenarianism that Papias, Irenaeus, and others have drawn from it seems crassly materialistic to him (*H.E.* 3.39.12-13)—so he wants to belittle the book by making it unapostolic, i.e., written by an elder named John as opposed to the apostle named John. Papias, however, not only pins the designation "the elders" on the apostles who had spoken in past times; he also repeats the term "elder" with John, yet not with Aristion. Why? The reason is that although Aristion was one of Jesus' original disciples, he was not an elder, i.e., not an apostle. Like John, however, Aristion was still speaking because he was still living. Papias did not mention him earlier because not till after all the apostles except John had died did what Aristion had to say attain great significance. Why go to Aristion when most of the apostles are still available? But after they have died, the fact that Aristion was an original disciple thrusts him into prominence despite his not having been an apostle. Thus it appears that Papias repeats John's name because John is the last surviving elder and therefore is one whose current statements Papias has been hearing by first-hand report. Since Papias uses the present tense concerning the elder's speaking and since the Apostle John, who is the elder, died at least by the end of the first century or the first few years of the second, Papias must have acquired this tradition before that time.

Some regard the change from the aorist εἶπεν, "said" or "had said," to the present λέγουσιν, "say" or "were saying," as awkward if the same John is in view. But, we may ask, how else could it be expressed in Greek that somebody has spoken and is still speaking? In English the perfect tense may indicate past action that continues in the present, as when a laborer says, "I have been working at this job for twenty years." But in Greek the perfect tense indicates action completed in the past; and Greek offers no other tense that covers both past and present action. Even in English we often juxtapose the past and present tenses, as in statements beginning, "He was, and is . . . ."

Papias delivers the statements about Mark and Matthew, not as his own, but as those of "the elder," apparently "the Elder John," since he has just designated John by that title (Eusebius *H.E.* 3.39.15-16). The phrase "as I said" in the statement concerning Mark may be a brief intrusion by Papias into the elder's words, or may be the elder's own words in a reference to his immediately preceding identification of Mark as Peter's interpreter. Prior to the phrase there is no indication that Papias has stopped quoting the elder and started giving his own comments. Moreover, the verb Eusebius uses to introduce Papias's account, "sets out" (ἐκτέθειται), and the one he uses to refer back to it, "are related" (ἱστόρηται, which has the connotation of narrating what one has learned by inquiry), appear to make Papias responsible only for relaying information from the elder, not for interpreting it as well. What we have, then, is a quotation by Papias from the elder clear to the end of the paragraph in Eusebius *H.E.* 3.39.15.

A slight disjunction exists at the beginning of the next paragraph: "These things, then, are related by Papias concerning Mark; but concerning Matthew these things were said." Eusebius, however, is merely making an editorial transition. Consequently, Papias's quoting the elder not only extends throughout the statement concerning Mark, but also carries over to the one concerning Matthew. That no need was felt in the statement concerning Matthew to redescribe "the oracles" as "the Lord's" (as in the statement concerning Mark) confirms the original continuity in Papias's quotation from the elder, which Eusebius takes over. This is also confirmed by Eusebius's εἴρηται, "were said." If Eusebius meant to distinguish Papias as the speaker concerning Matthew from the elder quoted by Papias concerning Mark, instead of εἴρηται he would almost certainly have written φησί, ". . . he [Papias] said." For this is the word he uses three times in the preceding context for Papias's speaking (Eusebius *H.E.* 3.39.2, 7, 12). Furthermore, the perfect tense of εἴρηται suits especially well a speaking on the elder's part prior to the time of Papias's writing. A final confirmation of original continuity in Papias's quotation from the elder lies in οὖν at the beginning of the statement concerning Matthew, for this word links that statement to the one about Mark by nicely introducing the contrast between Matthew's orderliness and the previously mentioned disorderliness of Mark.

When recognized as referring back to the statement about Mark, οὖν contains an immensely important implication for synoptic studies. The word normally carries the inferential meaning "therefore." Nothing in the present context indicates that the unseen hand of divine providence is under consideration. Rather, Matthew's reason for writing is in view. So the elder—i.e., the Apostle John—is saying that Matthew wrote his gospel for the precise purpose of bringing order out of the chaos in Mark. Thus we have astonishingly early external evidence that Mark wrote first and that Matthew knew Mark's gospel and wrote his own in view of it. (This evidence would be only slightly less impressive if the statement with οὖν comes originally from Papias rather than from the elder; later patristic reversal of the order of writing was probably due to the emerging canonical order, which, in turn, depended on Matthew's greater suitability to liturgical reading—perhaps also on its beginning with a genealogy forming a link with the OT; cf. Clement of Alexandria's dating both Matthew and Luke before Mark expressly because of Jesus' genealogies in the first two—Eusebius H.E. 6.14.5.)

Papias does not give any further or different identification of "the elder" who spoke concerning Mark. This fact suggests that in quoting Papias, Eusebius is following the order of a text which flows directly, not only from the section on Mark to that on Matthew, but also from the section where Papias identifies "the elder" as John to the section on Mark. If not, why the lack of further or different identification? If such an identification appeared in a different preceding context unknown to us but known to Eusebius because he had in his possession all Papias's "Exposition of the Lord's Oracles," Eusebius would surely have indicated a shift from the Elder John, who has just occupied his attention, to another elder. Since the Elder John seems to be none other than one of the Lord's disciples—i.e., the Apostle John—both the statements about Mark and Matthew come from an apostolic source. (At the very least, they come from the generation before Papias's; and that is still so early it falls within or right at the close of the apostolic period.)

In the 180s Irenaeus designated Papias "the hearer of John" (Haer. 5.33.4; quoted by Eusebius H.E. 3.39.1). From his own standpoint, Eusebius can accept this designation (H.E. 3.39.7) only because he distinguishes between the Apostle John and the Elder John (H.E. 3.39.5-6); otherwise, he could not heap scorn on Papias as a nonhearer of any apostle and on the Book of Revelation as an unapostolic document (H.E. 3.39.2, 8-14). But how should we evaluate his affirmation that Papias heard the Elder John? Papias himself does not say so in the statement Eusebius quotes. That Papias often quotes the Elder John by name presents us with a non sequitur; for Eusebius quotes Papias as saying he got the traditions of the elders by listening to *others* who had heard the elders and were still hearing the Elder John (and Aristion). Nowhere in the quotation does Papias claim to have heard any of them himself. Nevertheless, Irenaeus's designation and Eusebius's agreement with it suggest that Eusebius found in parts of Papias's "Exposition of the Lord's Oracles" no longer available to us indications that Papias did hear John. His hearing John could only strengthen the case for taking his quotation of the elder's statements about Mark and Matthew very seriously.

On the other hand, we need not take seriously Eusebius's inferring a distinction between the Apostle John and an Elder John from the story of two Ephesian tombs (as μνήματα is usually understood), both identified as John's. We might think that rival burial sites came into existence (cf. the ancient rivalry between the *Memoria Apostolorum ad Catacumbas* and the monuments on the Vatican hill and the Ostian way for the burial sites of Peter and Paul; also the modern rivalry between the Garden Tomb and the Church of the Holy Sepulchre as the place of Jesus' burial) and that the rival sites led to a distinguishing of persons in the story Eusebius appeals to. Or it is possible that a second tomb may have belonged to a later Christian named John but quite unrelated to anyone Papias had in mind; for V. Schultze noted the frequency of ancient Christian graves in honor of elders who had NT names, such as John, Paul, Stephen, etc. (*Altchristliche Städte und Landschaften. II. Kleinasien* [Gütersloh: Bertelsmann, 1926] 1. 120). Better yet, T. Zahn noted that μνήματα may mean a memorial or monument of any kind, not only a burial site, and was able to cite church tradition to the effect that the two memorials in Ephesus both related to the Apostle John, one being the house where he had lived and a church had met, the other being the place he was buried (*Acta Joannis* [Erlangen: Deichert, 1880] CLIV-CLXXII; also Schultze, op. cit. 2. 106 n. 4).

We need to keep in mind that Eusebius had an axe to grind concerning the Book of Revelation. He speaks vaguely concerning "the story of the ones who have said" and makes no claim that these storytellers linked the supposedly different men named John to Papias's text (*H.E.* 3.39.6). Finally and most damagingly, he quotes Dionysius of Alexandria as saying in the mid-third century, "But I think that there was a certain other [John] of those who came to be in Asia, since they say that there also came to be two memorials in Ephesus and that each is called John's" (*H.E.* 7.25.16). Dionysius's οἶμαι, "I think," is remarkably weak. And the vague "they say" anticipates Eusebius's expression, "the ones who have said." In fact, almost all Eusebius's phraseology echoes that of Dionysius exactly:

...τῶν ἐν ᾿Ασίᾳ γενομένων, ἐπεὶ καὶ δύο φασὶν
ἐν ᾿Εφέσῳ γενέσθαι μνήματα καὶ ἑκάτερον ᾿Ιωάννου
λέγεσθαι (Dionysius).
...τῶν δύο κατὰ τὴν ᾿Ασίαν ὁμωνυμίᾳ κεχρῆσθαι εἰρηκότων δύο τε
ἐν ᾿Εφέσῳ γενέσθαι μνήματα καὶ ἑκάτερον ᾿Ιωάννου ἔτι νῦν
λέγεσθαι (Eusebius).

To debunk the Book of Revelation, then, Eusebius apparently turns Dionysius's cautious inference, "I think there was another John," into a confident assertion, "there were two Johns." He then adds ἔτι νῦν, "still now," to strengthen the argument from two memorials and uses Dionysius's statement as a whole to distinguish an Elder John from the Apostle John in Papias's statement. But Dionysius himself would not have recognized this use of his statement; for in his own context he has just identified the elder who wrote 2-3 John with the Apostle John, and he has made no mention of the tradition passed on by Papias. In all likelihood, then, Eusebius gains the dubious honor of being first to make a false distinction between the Apostle John and the Elder John. Since the distinction is not only false, but also rests on an unnecessary inference from two memorials, the argument is doubly weak. Papias means to ascribe his information concerning Mark and Matthew to one and the same John, who was a disciple and elder, i.e., the famous apostle. For further discussion see E. Gutwenger in *ZKT* 69 (1947) 385-416.

If Papias were setting Mark as an authoritative gospel over against Luke, which was captured and truncated by Marcion (so R. P. Martin, *Mark: Evangelist and Theologian* [Grand Rapids: Zondervan, 1972] 80-83), we would have expected a comparison between Mark and Luke. As it is, we have a comparison between Mark and Matthew. To be sure, there are some similarities between the statement of Papias's elder concerning Mark and certain terms in Luke 1:1-4, viz., ἀνατάξασθαι, παρέδοσαν, παρηκολουθηκότι, ἀκριβῶς, and καθεξῆς; but there is no reason why the elder could not have known the Gospel of Luke and been influenced by the terminology of its prologue when making a defense of Mark over against Matthew, as he does. Apart from the possibility of such influence, any statement concerning the way tradition was written down is likely to contain the terms common to Luke 1:1-4 and Papias's elder. The elder's saying that Mark did not leave out anything he had heard from Peter may defend Mark against the attractions of Matthew's greater fullness as easily as it might argue for Mark against Marcion's truncated Luke. Indeed, since the elder compares Mark with Matthew, his purpose may be to save Mark from being eclipsed by Matthew. Matthew gained greater favor in the early church, but the elder achieved his purpose (if such it was) to the extent that the canonization of Mark saved it from total eclipse. Against the insinuation that Papias has put his own words in the elder's mouth stand Papias's preoccupation with and devotion to "the living and abiding voice" of oral tradition and his emphasizing that he "learned well and remembered well" the things that came from the elders (Eusebius *H.E.* 3.39.3). The possibility that Papias and Marcion confronted each other face-to-face (cf. the Anti-Marcionite Prologue to John) need not have anything to do with the date of the elder's comparing Mark and Matthew; for the date of such a confrontation would remain uncertain and the elder's statement is better understood against the rising popularity of Matthew than against Marcion's truncating of Luke.

Those who for reasons such as the foregoing feel compelled to take seriously the elder's statement quoted by Papias understand it in different ways. If considerations that go against authorship of the first gospel by the Apostle Matthew seem strong to them, they interpret the statement in a way that avoids authorship by this apostle. Some suggest that he drew up a collection of Hebrew OT passages to be used as proof texts showing fulfillment through Christ, that the unknown, later author of the gospel incorporated some or all of these proof texts (see 1:22-23; 2:15, 17-18, 23; 4:14-16; 8:17; 12:18-21; 13:14-15, 35; 21:4-5; 27:9-10; cf. 2:5-6), and that this incorporation led to a transfer of Matthew's name from the earlier collection to the gospel.

But the unlikelihood of such a transfer from what became a few bits and pieces in the gospel to the whole of the gospel militates against this hypothesis. Furthermore, if Papias's elder was referring to OT passages collected before their incorporation in the gospel and therefore before the transfer of Matthew's name, the parallel between Matthew and Mark in his statement breaks down; for Mark wrote a gospel, not anything comparable to a collection of OT proof texts. But if the elder was referring to our Greek Gospel of Matthew after the collection had been incorporated and after Matthew's name had been transferred, why the need for each person to translate as he was able? Under this hypothesis, the OT passages had already been translated into Greek, which is the language of the gospel and which nearly everybody knew.

Others suggest that the Apostle Matthew compiled a collection of Jesus' sayings (usually designated Q) no longer extant, that the unknown, later author of the first gospel incorporated it (as Luke also did in his gospel), and that a transfer of Matthew's name took place. We may cast doubt on the likelihood that Matthew's name was transferred at a stage so early that people who knew the apostles were still living. Again, if the elder quoted by Papias was referring to Q, the parallel with the Gospel of Mark, which is a different kind of book, breaks down. But if he was referring to our Greek Gospel of Matthew after the incorporation of Q and after the transfer of the apostle's name, why (again) the need for translation? Furthermore, the term λόγοι, "sayings," would have described Q better than the elder's term did. That term is λόγια, "oracles." Some of these objections spoil the similar suggestion that behind the elder's statement lies a loose body of materials concerning Jesus' deeds as well as sayings, stemming from the Apostle Matthew, taken up by the later, unknown author of the gospel, and giving to the gospel Matthew's name by transfer.

More traditionally and conservatively, some have thought that Papias's elder refers to a gospel written by the Apostle Matthew in the Aramaic language (the usual interpretation of Ἑβραΐδι διαλέκτῳ, literally "a Hebrew dialect"; thus, possibly but not necessarily, Irenaeus *Haer.* 3.1.1, cited by Eusebius *H.E.* 5.8.2; and, certainly, Pantaenus, cited by Eusebius *H.E.* 5.10.3; and Origen, cited by Eusebius *H.E.* 6.25.3-4). This view has the advantages of agreeing with the early ascription "According to Matthew" and treating "the oracles" in terms of Matthew's gospel book just as the elder uses "the Lord's oracles" for Mark's gospel book; i.e., the literary parallel between Mark and Matthew is preserved, whereas it is damaged in the preceding hypotheses.

We might account for the loss of an Aramaic Gospel of Matthew by noting the limited appeal of the Aramaic language and the dominance of Greek in the Hellenistic world. But our present Gospel of Matthew does not bear the marks of translation from Aramaic to Greek; and Matthew often shows familiarity with the LXX. Once in a while this Greek form of the OT seems necessary to his meaning where the Hebrew text differs (see, e.g., 12:21; 13:14-15). Besides, it is the currently prevalent and well-substantiated opinion that our Greek Matthew shows many signs of drawing in large part on the Gospel of Mark, also written in Greek. Therefore, those who believe in an Aramaic Gospel of Matthew usually say that because people had difficulty translating it, Matthew wrote another gospel as well, viz., the Greek gospel we now have, not translated from the earlier Aramaic gospel but probably incorporating materials from it. Or such scholars qualify their belief in the words of Papias's elder by saying that he spoke accurately in ascribing a gospel to Matthew, but erred in confusing that gospel, which is really our Greek Gospel of Matthew, with some other and perhaps similar Hebrew or Aramaic document, such as the Gospel according to the Hebrews, which was not written by Matthew. Against such an explanation, since Papias is not giving his own opinion but relating a tradition derived from the elder in an earlier Christian generation, the supposed confusion seems improbable. Possibilities of confusion decrease the closer we approach the time of writing. It is especially hard to think that one of the twelve apostles, John himself, fell into such an error.

Now it is extremely odd that Papias's elder should have talked about a collection of OT passages fulfilled by Jesus, or a collection of Jesus' sayings, or a loose body of materials concerning Jesus' deeds and sayings, or an Aramaic gospel, yet not about our Greek gospel, the only one of these to survive, let alone achieve canonicity. Or if the elder also talked about our Greek gospel, but somewhere else, it is extremely odd that Papias and then Eusebius do not quote what he said about it rather than what he said about a collection of OT passages, a collection of Jesus' sayings, or one of the other possibilities. This oddity arises out of the high degree of interest we should expect to have been shown toward the only one of the documents (if we assume the existence of the hypothesized ones) treasured enough to become canonical. Also, Eusebius, Papias, and the elder himself, whom they quote, are making a comparison between what Matthew wrote and the Gospel of Mark. Since the latter was written in Greek and quickly canonized, our Greek Gospel of Matthew provides by far the best comparison.

In his statement quoted by Papias, the elder shows concern over Mark's style, particularly over the disorderly way the single points concerning Jesus' ministry appear in the Gospel of Mark. This concern favors a similar frame of reference in the statement about Matthew, whose writing, by contrast, exhibits orderliness (a description especially damaging to the hypothesis that the elder refers to a loose body of Matthean materials). This contrast comes out clearly in the elder's parallelistic use of the verb συνετάξατο, "arranged," to describe what Matthew *did* do with the Lord's oracles, and of the cognate noun σύνταξιν, "arrangement," to describe what Mark, following Peter, did *not* do with the Lord's oracles. Thus far, the contrast has to do with the structuring of materials, not with their linguistic form. This structural contrast is supported by the technical rhetorical meaning of χρείας, which the elder uses properly for Mark's loose, anecdotal style. Furthermore, the elder says nothing at all about the linguistic form of Mark, which he ought to mention if it is his intention to introduce, by way of contrast, a different linguistic form in Matthew. Apparently Matthew does not have a linguistic form different from Mark's Greek.

But what of Matthew's "Hebrew dialect," which "each person interpreted as he was able"? The elder's and Papias's own earlier usage gives us guidance. In *H.E.* 3.39.3 Eusebius mentions that Papias describes his "Exposition of the Lord's Oracles" as "the interpretations" (ταῖς ἑρμηνείαις). Out of context an interpretation may be either a translation or an explanation. But here the associated word "Exposition" (ἐξηγήσεως) in the title shows that "the interpretations" can hardly be taken in the sense "the translations"; to the contrary, "the explanations." Furthermore, the elder quoted by Papias calls Mark an "interpreter" (ἑρμηνευτής) of Peter (Eusebius *H.E.* 3.39.15). But the context says nothing about Mark's translating for Peter. Rather, we are told that Mark remembered and recorded what Peter had said. By the same token, when the elder compares Matthew with Mark and says that each person "interpreted" (ἡρμήνευσεν) Matthew, we should think of explanation rather than translation. The phrase "as he [each person] was able" refers, then, to expository rather than linguistic ability. Moreover, the phrase does not imply a greater difficulty in comparison with Mark. Just the opposite! Matthew's orderly arrangement of the Lord's oracles makes them easier to understand than those in Mark, where disorder prevails. (The elder excuses Mark's disorder, however.)

It might be thought that the last clause in Eusebius *H.E.* 3.39.16 means that each of the two evangelists Mark and Matthew interpreted the dominical oracles as he was able. But the μέν . . . δέ construction in the sentence as a whole sets up a comparison between Matthew's Hebrew style and each person's exposition of the dominical oracles written in that style. Hence, ἕκαστος means "each reader of Matthew." The exposition may have to do with private understanding rather than public dissemination.

"A Hebrew dialect," then, does not imply that Matthew wrote in the Aramaic language. In other connections we should expect the conjunction of "Hebrew" and "dialect" to form a linguistic reference. But the stylistic contrast between Mark and Matthew cancels such an expectation here. And the lack of a definite article in Ἑβραΐδι διαλέκτῳ facilitates (though it does not prove) a different reference, since διάλεκτος always has the definite article in its six occurrences for languages in Acts, including three for the Hebrew or Aramaic language (1:19; 2:6, 8; 21:40; 22:2; 26:14). Besides, the generality of each person's interpreting as he was able fits better the exercise of reading and understanding a gospel written in the lingua franca, Greek; for comparatively few people had the knowledge of Aramaic that would have enabled them to translate an Aramaic gospel into Greek or whatever other language was native to them. διάλεκτος commonly carried a stylistic meaning, especially when referring to debate (cf. the English word "dialectic"). In describing Matthew, then, "a Hebrew dialect" means a Hebrew way of presenting Jesus' messiahship. Immediately we think of all those Jewish features of Matthew—the stress on Jesus as the Son of David and Messiah, the tracing of his genealogy back to Abraham, the frequent and unique citations of OT passages as fulfilled by Jesus, and so on—that capture a large amount of attention in modern introductions to this gospel. To these traditionally recognized features must now be added Matthew's midrashic style.

What understandings have we reached? (1) That Papias wrote his book containing information about Mark and Matthew before A.D. 110. (2) That Philip of Side does not provide good support for a later date. (3) That the fragments from Papias scattered in Eusebius *H.E.* 3.39.1-16 formed a continuous text in Papias's book. (4) That Papias quotes the elder concerning Matthew as well as concerning Mark. (5) That the elder makes Matthew write after Mark and in view of Mark. (6) That the contrast between Mark and Matthew has to do with literary style, not with linguistic form. (7) That Matthew's literary artistry made his gospel easier to understand than Mark's gospel was. (8) That Eusebius misuses a statement by Dionysius of Alexandria in order to distinguish the Elder John from the Apostle John. (9) That the elder who passed on this information was the Apostle John. (10) That John the elder and apostle ascribes the first gospel to the Apostle Matthew, just as he makes the Apostle Peter the source of Mark's material. Cf. J. Kürzinger in *BZ* ns 4 (1960) 19-38; 21 (1977) 245-64, especially on the technical rhetorical connotations of the elder's key terms; and A. F. J. Klijn and G. J. Reinink, *Patristic Evidence for Jewish-Christian Sects* (NovTSup 36; Leiden: Brill, 1973) 46-50, on the confusion and contradictions in Jerome's statements about a Hebrew or Aramaic Gospel of Matthew.

In favor of this ascription we may ask, Why did an apostle so comparatively lacking in prominence as Matthew enter the picture if he did not actually write the gospel ascribed to him? The mere shift from "Levi" (Mark 2:13-17; Luke 5:27-32) to "Matthew" (Matt 9:9-13) seems insufficient to have generated the ascription. Since Christian apocryphal books tended to gain the names of apostles prominent in the NT, we should have expected a more prominent name.

The special interest devoted to money in the unique passages 17:24-27; 18:23-35; 20:1-16; 27:3-10; 28:11-15 (see also the comments on 25:15; 26:7) lends some internal support to the ascription of our gospel to the Apostle Matthew, for he had been a tax collector in Galilee and was known also as Levi. Further support of this kind comes from three insertions of tax collectors, including a description of Matthew (10:3), and two references to tax collectors in distinctive passages, besides three shared references. Both the Hellenization of Palestine, especially of "Galilee of the Gentiles," and the necessity of dealing with Gentiles as well as Jews in the work of collecting taxes harmonize with this ascription; for the first gospel displays a combination of Jewish and Hellenistic features. Furthermore, the substitution of Gadara for Gerasa (8:28; cf. Mark 5:1; Luke 8:26) may show familiarity with the region around Galilee, since Gadara was both smaller, less well known, and closer to the lake than Gerasa. Such familiarity agrees with authorship by Matthew, a Galilean. The change in 1:15

of Ματθάτ (Luke 3:24) to Ματθάν, the base of Μαθθαῖος, points in the same direction (cf. 9:9 with Mark 2:14; Luke 5:27).

But how can we believe that Matthew, an apostle, used the gospel of a nonapostle, Mark? The elder quoted by Papias as saying that Matthew wrote our gospel also indicates that Mark wrote down the reminiscences of Peter concerning Jesus' ministry (Eusebius *H.E.* 3.39.15). According to extremely early tradition, then, the Gospel of Mark is essentially apostolic. Therefore we should put the question as follows: Is it too hard to think that one apostle took material that came from a fellow apostle? Of course not—especially since the apostle borrowed from was none else than the foremost among the twelve. Furthermore, Matthew did not merely copy the Petrine tradition set forth by Mark. He used it in ways we are just now coming to appreciate for their originality. Most important of all, doubt that he would have used the Gospel of Mark rests on modern antipathy toward literary borrowing. Moderns regard such borrowing as plagiarism or, at best, unworthy dependency. Ancients did not share this antipathy. On the contrary, they strongly believed in literary borrowing as a way of preserving tradition.

The implication that we are to take the elder's words about the Petrine background of Mark just as seriously as his words about the apostolic authorship of Matthew raises questions about Mark which cannot be discussed here, but which ought not to be dismissed with hasty negatives: May signs of ecclesiastical adaptation of the Jesus-tradition in Mark be due to Peter's preaching in the very manner described by Papias's elder? May geographical and chronological disorganization in Mark and indications of pre-Markan summaries and collections of material be attributed to such preaching rather than to non-Palestinians, non-eyewitnesses, nonapostolic editors prior to Mark? May the use of Greek as the language of Mark's gospel and of the LXX in a number of its OT quotations tie in with growing scholarly recognition that Palestinian Jews of the NT era used Greek as well as Aramaic (and Hebrew)? Prima facie, such Markan characteristics seem to suit Peter's anecdotal preaching, for which we have the word of Papias's elder, quite as well as they would suit the activity of shadowy figures who owe their existence to what may be—if the elder's words are very early, probably apostolic, and therefore trustworthy—gratuitous hypotheses (cf. the exhortation of a classicist, George Kennedy, that NT scholars give more credence to external testimony such as that of Papias's elder—though Eusebius is probably right in taking Mark's "memorandum" [ὑπόμνημα] as a finished gospel [cf. Eusebius *H.E.* 2.15.1 with 6.14.6; also cf. the use of ὑπομνήματα for the finished gospels of Matthew and John in 3.24.5] and Kennedy wrong in taking Mark's memorandum as a preliminary set of notes [in *The Relationships Among the Gospels* (ed. W. O. Walker, Jr.; Trinity University Monograph Series in Religion 5; San Antonio: Trinity, 1978) 125-92]).

We might ask another question concerning the first gospel: Would the Apostle Matthew, an eyewitness, have edited Mark and other materials so extensively as the author of the first gospel did? Even under the supposition of unhistorical writing at a number of points, authorship by an eyewitness is far from inconceivable. Plato not only rehearsed the teachings of Socrates, but also used Socrates as a vehicle of Platonic thought growing out of those teachings. We should therefore broaden our horizons with respect to the authorial possibilities immediate disciples took advantage of when they presented and developed the thought of their masters—and that right within the lifetime of others who had heard their masters. There is a difference between Plato and Matthew, to be sure. The one belonged to classical Greek culture, the other to Jewish culture. But Matthew's Jewish culture had been Hellenized. What cultural difference there was makes it easier to think that an immediate disciple of Jesus did what has been done in the Gospel of Matthew. For if even an exacting Greek philosopher could purvey as his master's teachings his own highly advanced development of them, how much more might a midrashically, haggadically oriented Jew do something similar (cf. the development by R. Jonathan of a parable told by his teacher R. Ḥama b. R. Hanina [*Gen. Rab.* 9.4] and the teaching of R. Joshua of Sichnin in the name of R. Levi [*Gen. Rab.* 16.3], both cited by Goulder, *Midrash and Lection* 53, 64). In the Jewish sphere we find the freedom of midrash and haggadah alongside careful memorization and passing on of both the written law and the oral law.

Opinions differ concerning the degree to which Plato put his own development of Socratic thought in the mouth of Socrates. It is generally agreed, however, that he did so fairly extensively at least in the later dialogues. For a survey, see A. R. Lacey in *The Philosophy of Socrates* (ed. G. Vlastos; Garden City, N.Y.: Doubleday, 1971) 22-49.

Finally, standing in the shadows is the question of miracles. For even under a wide interpretation of authorial possibilities, we would find it hard to make a clean escape from the miraculous element in apostolic material. The proximity to Jesus is too great. Apart from entering a philosophical discussion inappropriate to a commentary, there remains only the observation that refusal to accept the possibility of miracles may force a cavalier treatment of historical and literary data. Treated more naturally, these data may favor the miraculous in Jesus' life and therefore call in question a rigidly antisupernaturalistic presupposition. Obviously, we should require extraordinarily good evidence for accepting the miraculous; otherwise the distinction between the miraculous and the nonmiraculous loses its significance. But apostolic materials would provide just that—extraordinarily good evidence for the miraculous in Jesus' life.

A Theological Postscript

Clearly, Matthew treats us to history mixed with elements that cannot be called historical in a modern sense. All history writing entails more or less editing of materials. But Matthew's editing often goes beyond the bounds we nowadays want a historian to respect. It does not stop at selecting certain data and dressing them up with considerable interpretation (let alone reporting in the relatively bare style found on the front page of a modern newspaper). Matthew's subtractions, additions, and revisions of order and phraseology often show changes in substance; i.e., they represent developments of the dominical tradition that result in different meanings and departures from the actuality of events. Though reticent, no less a champion of the Bible than N. B. Stonehouse found it necessary to admit as much in the story of the rich young ruler (*Origins of the Synoptic Gospels* [Grand Rapids: Eerdmans, 1963] 108-12; cf. M. Silva in *WTJ* 40 [1977-78] 77-88, 281-303). Consequently, the question of biblical authority arises—and this in the very center of Christian faith, viz., the life and teaching of Jesus.

The conservative wing of Protestantism emphasizes biblical authority. This emphasis carries a rejection of higher-critical assumptions and results judged destructive of that authority. Furthermore, it tends toward minimizing the human manner in which the biblical writers went about their work and leads to depreciation of postcanonical ecclesiastical tradition and, through that depreciation, to overlooking the development of tradition right within the NT canon.

Liberal Protestantism pays much attention to the historical setting of the Bible, the cultural influences playing on the biblical authors, and the literary conventions according to which ancient authors wrote. This attention links up with modern bias against supernaturalism. As a result, the human characteristics of the Bible devour its authority as God's Word, and theology dances to the ever-shifting tunes piped by the panjandrums of worldly culture.

Attempts to rescue the Bible from such servility have abounded. We may think of the replacement of an infallible Bible with a normative Bible, the rejection of inerrancy in favor of an infallibility subject to error, the substitution of an existentially inspiring Bible for a propositionally inspired Bible, and the redefinition of inspiration by distinguishing the evocative

623

function of language from the informative and choosing the evocative at the expense of the informative. The biblical theology movement avoided the question of scriptural inspiration. In the salvation-history school of thought, biblical history smothered biblical teaching. In the Pannenberg circle, universal history replaces biblical teaching as the lodestar. Process theologians plot trajectories through and from the Bible to the present day in a way that leaves the Bible little more than a point of historical origin for beliefs indebted mainly to modern humanism. And in theological semiotics the deep structures of human psychology displace both biblical history and biblical doctrine.

None of these and similar semantical and theological "emperor's new clothes" successfully hides the nakedness of the liberal Protestant Bible. Stripped of divine authority, that Bible does not belong on a pulpit, but in an archeological museum along with other artifacts that tell us about the history of religions. The fundamental refusal to equate the Bible as such with God's Word lies at the bottom of this embarrassing state of affairs. Put another way, disaccreditation of the biblical canon has led to searchings for a new canon contained, or at least represented, in the Bible; but because the biblical canon has suffered disaccreditation, nothing better than sentiment seems to center the search there. Why not go elsewhere ostensibly as well as in fact?

Because they appreciate the development of tradition in the church, Roman Catholics have thought themselves able to uphold biblical authority even in the face of higher-critical demonstrations that the Bible has many human traits. For them, these traits help make up ecclesiastical tradition, which has authority both inside and outside the Bible. Then, however, biblical authority starts dissolving in the ocean of ecclesiastical tradition, especially in its postcanonical developments. This tradition depends, moreover, on an authority increasingly difficult to maintain, that of the institutional church. In effect, refusing to draw the boundary of authority at the limits of the biblical canon dilutes the very idea of a biblical canon. Thus it was only a matter of time before the orthodox Roman Catholic view of biblical inspiration fell prey to historical-critical study, complete with the same attempts at rehabilitation that liberal Protestants had futilely put forward. The traditionalism that prolonged the orthodox view proved to be a Trojan horse.

Conservative Protestants have maintained the equation between the Bible and God's Word. That equation makes room for the kind of biblical authority which provides a firm base for historic Christianity. But the human phenomena of the scriptural text have seemed to cast a dark shadow over the equation. What of the tendentious patterns of diction, style, and theology in the Gospel of Matthew? These patterns attain greatest visibility in, but are by no means limited to, a number of outright discrepancies with the other synoptics. At least they are discrepancies so long as we presume biblical writers were always intending to write history when they used the narrative mode. As we have seen, Matthew's taking away the disciples' misunderstanding at the feeding of the five thousand (14:16-17; contrast Mark 6:37-38) is part of a thoroughgoing program that pervades his gospel.

Not allowing the disciples to take even a staff and sandals (10:9-10; so also Luke 9:3; 10:4), where in Mark 6:8-9 Jesus allows both, links up with increased rigorism throughout Matthew. Making the chief priests and elders sentence themselves at the close of the parable of the tenant farmers (21:41), where in Mark 12:9; Luke 20:16 Jesus pronounces the sentence, provides but one instance among many of Matthew's intensifying the Jewish leaders' guilt. And so on and on. We are not dealing with a few scattered difficulties. We are dealing with a vast network of tendentious changes. Taking a different view of the synoptic problem (e.g., that Mark and Luke used Matthew) offers no escape; for then the tendencies merely run in another direction (Mark blackballed the disciples, relaxed Jesus' rigorism, and so on). Whatever synoptic theory we adopt—and even though we remain agnostic on the synoptic problem—somebody was making drastic changes.

Conservative Protestants respond to such phenomena in several ways. Sometimes they simply sidestep the details of the text. But to do so is inexcusable. Belief in verbal plenary inspiration demands close attention to those details. A more sophisticated avoidance of the details makes appeal to the looseness of informal language. The Bible is not meant to be put under a microscope, as though it were a carefully worded contract or constitution to be pored over by lawyers and judges. No, by and large the Bible represents the language of the home, the shop, the street. So goes the argument. But for this argument to work where it is most needed, biblical language would have to be so loose as to be—much to the dismay of those who take this out—indistinguishable from ancient Jewish midrash and haggadah in distance from historical actualities, in liberties taken with historical data. And many of the tendentious patterns do not depend on textual subtleties, but on obvious meanings. Furthermore, taking refuge in the generalities of the text limits the practical benefits that might be reaped from the doctrine of verbal plenary inspiration; the richness of the biblical message suffers from preoccupation with avoiding problems in the text. What starts from a desire to preserve a high view of Scripture ends in a shrinkage of its value.

Conservative Protestants also plead for holding problems in suspension till adequate solutions are found. Up to a point this plea has some legitimacy, for we all know of higher-critical problems once thought damaging to a high view of scriptural inspiration that have long since reached well-recognized solutions. There remain, however, a large number of data that will not float in suspension. They drop to the bottom, like millstones. The number of these data is hardly decreasing. It is probably increasing; for, despite a historical solution now and then, increasingly sophisticated methods of literary analysis, coupled with new discoveries of comparative materials, turn up more and more evidence of editorial liberty in what was naively thought to be purely historical narrative. To try holding such data in suspension amounts to denying the clarity of Scripture; for many of them rest, not on ambiguities or arguments from silence, but on the plain, explicit wording of the text. According to Matt 8:26, for instance, the disciples had little faith when the storm raged on the Sea of Galilee; according to Mark 4:39-40; Luke 8:24-25, they had no faith. These statements are unambiguous. To pretend they are not—by suggesting, say, that no faith means not enough faith or that different kinds of faith are in view—is to open the door to somersaulting exegesis which could with equal legitimacy deny the clarity of scriptural statements expressing primary doctrines. Jesus' view of Scripture—a mainstay of those who argue for a high view of scriptural inspiration—is expressed in terms no clearer than those that tell of the disciples' little faith in Matthew and no faith in Mark and Luke. There are, of course, obscurities in Scripture. But the tendentious patterns in Matthew are not among them. Either we recognize them or we obfuscate the text arbitrarily—and by doing so betray our own tendentiousness and forfeit our right to rest Christian theology on the clear teaching of Scripture. It is true, of course, that redaction-critical judgments are subjective and sometimes vary from one critic to another. But they are no more subjective than harmonizations, which also vary from one harmonizer to another. And there are plenty of tendentious patterns generally agreed on by those with eyes to see—plenty to establish the point that denying them is tantamount to denying the clarity of Scripture. (Here, clarity of Scripture refers to the plain meaning of its words, not as in Reformation theology to the unmistakability of its salvific message.)

Yet again, conservative Protestants bend over backward for harmonizations. Differences are attributed to alternative translations from Aramaic or Hebrew originals into the present Greek text of the gospels; to paraphrases as distinct from direct quotations; to complementary relationships in which one evangelist reports some parts and another evangelist other parts of the same story, sermon, or saying; to Jesus' own repetitions of sayings and deeds; and to topical rather than chronological arrangements. Other things being equal, these methods of harmonization have some validity when used with discretion. But other things are not always equal; for the patterns of the differences in traditional materials used by Matthew, correlating as they do with the distinctive interests seen in his editorial passages, point to deliberate changes. And sometimes the differences are so acute that suggested harmonizations look pathetic, as in the views (all actually put forward) that Peter denied Jesus not just three times, but four, six, and even eight times. Bending over backward for harmonizations results in falling flat on the ground. Furthermore, harmonizations often become so complicated that they are not only unbelievable, but also (and again) damaging to the clarity of Scripture. They actually subvert scriptural authority by implicitly denying the plain meaning of the text.

Inability to provide natural harmonizations finally causes some conservative Protestants to retreat into a principial silence. Here, belief in the infallibility and inerrancy of the Bible resists even a discussion of the textual phenomena. But what principle governs this view of biblical infallibility and inerrancy? Is it that embroidering history with unhistorical elements à la midrash and haggadah would be inappropriate to God's Word, though proverbs and parables, apocalyptic and erotic poetry are not? Who are we to make such a judgment? And what reason would we have for it? Would it be anything more than lack of appreciation for a literary genre that we think strangely ancient or personally unappealing? If a presumption does not make good sense of certain phenomena, yet we insulate that presumption from being informed by those phenomena, what is to keep us from becoming candidates for membership in the Flat Earth Society? If the principles we bring to the text ride roughshod over a significant number of its characteristics, the text might as well not exist—it is those principles, not the text, which determine our beliefs.

We need, then, to avoid the mistakes and capitalize on the insights of conservative Protestants, liberal Protestants, and Roman Catholics. The equation of the Bible with God's Word must stay, the straining to resolve all historical difficulties in the Bible must go. Attention to the historical milieu in which the Bible took shape must continue, subordination of the Bible to other canons of truth must stop. Appreciation of development in tradition must increase, the authority of tradition must evaporate beyond the limits of the biblical canon.

The last point needs expansion. Neither the oral and literary prehistory of the Bible nor later interpretations and additions bind us. Of course, many early traditions were adopted in the Bible. In that they were, inspiration imbues them with authority, i.e., with authority in the use to which the inspired writers put them (which may differ from their use outside the Bible). Apart from inscripturation, however, they have no more authority than interpretative traditions growing out of the canon. We must respect the boundaries of the canon at both ends.

Let us suppose that we could identify several layers of meaning in a book of the Bible and that those layers of meaning correspond to different stages, stretching from the original tradition through successive redactions to the form that was canonized. Thus we would be dealing, not with the intended meaning of one writer or speaker, but with the intended meanings of several. Or would we? It was neither the originally spare tradition nor any of the intermediate redactions that impressed themselves on God's people as canonical. To the extent the final author or redactor (and whatever assistants or amanuenses he may have had) not only added a new layer of meaning but also deliberately and positively incorporated meanings intended at earlier stages into the form of the book finally canonized, those earlier meanings lived on in the intention of the final author or redactor and thus gained recognition as inspired. This recognition implies, of course, that the Holy Spirit guided the process from beginning to end, from the formation of the original tradition through the successive stages of redaction. It also implies, however, that the Holy Spirit may have seen to the reversal or elimination of earlier layers of meaning; thus they were not incorporated in a deliberate and positive manner into the form that finally attained canonicity. It is obvious that when more than one stage of biblical tradition gained recognition as canonical (e.g., Samuel-Kings and Chronicles, the synoptics, and a number of smaller units taken from one book into another), each stage came to have its own weight of authority.

The upshot of our discussion is that the Gospel of Matthew does not have to give us unmixed history, not even unmixed history of a highly interpreted sort. The data of the text understood against the backdrop of ancient literary genres, not a presumption that narrative style in the Bible always implies the writing of history, should govern our understanding of authorial intent. Combinations of Matthew's favorite vocabulary (as shown by comparative word-statistics), style (especially the tight parallelism characteristic of his writing as opposed to the loose parallelism characteristic of extemporaneous speech), theological emphases, and habit of conforming traditional phraseology to the OT—combinations of these features where he differs from and even disagrees, at the historical level, with Mark and Luke signal his redactional activity. We have also seen that at numerous points these features exhibit such a high degree of editorial liberty that the adjectives "midrashic" and "haggadic" become appropriate.

There are differences between the Gospel of Matthew and midrash and haggadah in ancient Jewish literature. For one, those who produced midrash and haggadah were embroidering the OT. Matthew was not. Or was he? In a way, we may regard his gospel as a wholesale embroidering of the OT with the story of Jesus. Nevertheless, Mark and the further tradition shared with Luke remain Matthew's primary sources. But he treated these sources, which, like the OT, were written and venerated, in much the same way the OT was treated by those who produced midrash and haggadah. Of course, experts on such Jewish literature debate the exact definitions of "midrash" and "haggadah" and the applicability of these terms to particular pieces of literature. Semantics aside, it is enough to note that the liberty Matthew takes with his sources is often comparable with the liberty taken with the OT in Jubilees, the Genesis Apocryphon, the Testaments of the Twelve Patriarchs, 1 Enoch, the Targums, and the Midrashim and Haggadoth in rabbinic literature. In his *Antiquities* Josephus takes similar liberties, or includes materials in which they have been taken. We call him a historian, but doing so requires us to make a considerable distinction between what we mean by a historian in the modern sense (roughly the sense conservatives have assumed for Matthew) and what we mean by a historian at those points where the *Antiquities* hardly reflects the actualities of past events. Cf. the note on 2:22-23.

In principle, what we have discovered concerning Matthew might be true of Mark and Luke, too. In fact, however, there is not enough evidence to hold that Mark and Luke took so much liberty with historical data that their gospels merit the descriptions "midrashic" and "haggadic." Luke states a historical purpose along lines that run closer to modern history writing than to ancient Jewish midrash and haggadah (Luke 1:1-4). (Recent attempts to denude Luke's prologue of its historical emphasis do not pass muster—see I. H. Marshall, *Luke: Historian and Theologian* [Grand Rapids: Zondervan, 1971] 37-41; idem, *The Gospel of Luke* [The New International Greek Testament Commentary; Grand Rapids: Eerdmans, 1978] 39-44, and other literature cited there.) Mark's gospel is relatively artless; and if it represents Peter's anecdotes concerning Jesus' ministry, as Papias's elder says it does, we have added reason to separate it from midrash and haggadah (see pp. 609-21 on the very early date and reliability of this tradition). We may put it this way: Jesus was so extraordinary that he evoked both efforts to recall his life as it was and efforts to amplify it. Evangelistic and pastoral purposes lay behind both kinds of effort. Amplification, no less than recollection, shows high regard for the historical Jesus. For what T. W. Manson said concerning the liberties NT writers often took when quoting the OT applies mutatis mutandis to the liberties Matthew took with dominical traditions: "Odd as it may seem to us, the freedom with which they handled the Biblical text is a direct result of the supreme importance which they attached to it" (*JTS* 46 [1945] 135-36).

None of this should occasion alarm. Elsewhere in Scripture and in other literature we live comfortably with differences of intent. "Every literary form has its own proper kind of truth" (Hummelauer, quoted by B. Vawter, *Biblical Inspiration* [Philadelphia: Westminster, 1972] 122). We do not read the Psalms as we read the Proverbs, or Jesus' parables as we read the Acts of the Apostles. Even language that seems historical at first ("Behold, a sower went out to sow; and it came to pass . . ."—Mark 4:3-4; "A certain man was going down from Jerusalem to Jericho"—Luke 10:30; "Now there was a certain rich man . . . and a certain poor man named Lazarus"—Luke 16:19-20) may, on close inspection, look unhistorical and be accepted as such by the majority of the most historically minded readers. If, then, Matthew writes that Jesus said or did something Jesus did not say or do in the way described—this supported by adequate exegetical and comparative data—we have to say that Matthew did not write entirely reportorial history. Comparison with midrashic and haggadic literature of his era suggests he did not intend to do so.

One extreme breeds another, however; so it is easy to understand why radical historical reductionism has caused a recoil into conservative historical positivism, i.e., a system of orthodox belief based solely on the positive data of historical experience. Such an empiricism, blended as it is with a fixation on history, tends to exclude literary possibilities that would diminish even slightly the amount of history contained in the Bible. But nobody has the right to insist that Scripture conform to standards of writing he happens to feel comfortable with and rule out those he does not. Otherwise, we would have to excuse those who allegorize the Song of Solomon because its literal meaning makes them too fidgety. What Matthew wrote bears the stamp of inspiration in the meaning he intended—be it historical, unhistorical, or a mixture of the two—not in any meaning he did not intend, for then we could attach to the text whatever meaning we want and claim divine inspiration for it.

A number of questions may attend our determination of authorial intent. Did Matthew have more than one intent in writing a passage? What are the boundaries of the passage characterized by his intent? How high a level of consciousness is required for authorial intent? Answers do not always come easily. But they do come, and the difficulty of these and similar questions poses far less a hermeneutical problem than the difficulty of discovering meanings unintended by an author and therefore wholly unfalsifiable. Though God intended more than the authors of the OT had in their minds, apart from the NT we would not have known that he did so. To find further meanings in either the OT or the NT would require us to have the kind of inspiration the NT authors had in interpreting the OT. But the closing of the canon implies that we have only illumination for interpreting scriptural truth, not inspiration for adding to it, much less changing it. Such illumination enables us to keep discovering applications of Scripture that would surprise the biblical authors. But these applications do not carry the weight of canonical authority; they do not become canonical themselves.

See E. D. Hirsch, Jr., *Validity in Interpretation* (New Haven: Yale, 1967), against misuse of the so-called intentional fallacy (pp. 10-14) and for the importance of what an author means (passim; idem, *The Aims of Interpretation* [Chicago: University of Chicago, 1976] 1-92; cf. S. T. Logan, Jr., in *WTJ* 36 [1974] 334-60).

Both the doctrinaire antisupernaturalism of extreme historical reductionists and the literary insensitivity of conservative historical positivists lack openness to the data of Scripture and lead to cavalier treatments of those scriptural data that do not fit the prescribed scheme. When the data call for accepting the supernatural, doctrinaire antisupernaturalism must fall. By the same token, certain parts of the Bible, such as Jesus' parables, show that it conveys truth apart from history as well as through history. Jesus' speaking the parables is historical; at least ordinarily, however, the contents of the parables are unhistorical—yet they convey truth. A mixture of history and nonhistory should not put us off, then. If each can convey truth separately, there is no presumptive reason to think they cannot convey truth together, provided their mixture was a recognized and accepted mode of communication. Ancient midrash and haggadah show that it was. Modern historical novels, drama, cinema, and preaching show that it still is. Hence, "Jesus said" or "Jesus did" need not always mean that in history Jesus said or did what follows, but sometimes may mean that in the account at least partly constructed by Matthew himself Jesus said or did what follows (cf. the description of the gospels as "dramatic history" by the literary critic R. M. Frye, though he probably errs in homogenizing the gospels under this rubric—see *Jesus and Man's Hope* [ed. D. G. Miller and D. Y. Hadidian; Pittsburgh: Pittsburgh Theological Seminary, 1971] 206-14, 219 n. 36).

Let us sample a modern mixture of history and nonhistory, a biographical novel. Among the many biographical novels that have been written, we might select Irving Stone's treatment of Michelangelo, *The Agony and the Ecstasy*. It may not be the best of its genre, but it is typical. Its genre is modern rather than ancient (though *biographical* novels have closer antecedents in ancient literature than other kinds of novels do), and its temporal distance from Michelangelo is greater than that of Matthew from Jesus (though other biographical novels have appeared very soon after the lifetimes of their subjects). But these differences do not affect the points of the analogy. *The Agony and the Ecstasy* is not strictly historical, for Stone has inserted conversations and incidents of his own construction. We do not accuse Stone of telling untruths, however. As a whole, the biography rests on a massive amount of historical research and conveys much historical information. But to give an impression of Michelangelo's character, life, and significance, Stone took accepted and understood literary liberties. Even so historically minded a biographical novelist as Catherine Drinker Bowen admits she "often embellished" her sources, and did so despite writing about her subject within ten years of his death (*Yankee from Olympus: Justice Holmes and His Family* [Boston: Little, Brown and Company, 1944] 433—Holmes died in 1935). The analogy does not imply close correspondence between the degrees of liberty taken by Matthew and authors such as Stone and Bowen (who differ among themselves in this respect). Much less does it require that their works, like Matthew's, be considered infallible and inerrant in terms of their literary genre. But it does illustrate both that history mixed with nonhistory is still an accepted mode of communication and that unhistorical embellishment can carry its own kind of truth alongside historical truth.

Closer to home, present-day preachers and writers regularly embellish the biblical text with unhistorical elements that often go beyond what the text says, overstep the boundaries of paraphrase, and even belie the biblical data in order to make certain theological points. Among many available examples we may consider some remarks of R. C. Sproul in a volume defending the inerrancy of the Bible (*Can We Trust the Bible?* [ed. E. D. Radmacher; Wheaton: Tyndale, 1979] 116-23). To strengthen a contrastive parallel with Christ, but contrary to Gen 3:2-3, Sproul includes Adam with Eve in answering the serpent. To relate the story of the Fall to modern denials of the law of noncontradiction, he imagines Adam's thinking dialectically and uses the phrase "says Adam" to indicate a lengthy direct quotation of his thoughts. The biblical text attributes nothing of the sort to Adam. The little in Sproul's imaginative reconstruction that does reflect the biblical text ("It [the tree of knowledge] looks sweet; it's delightful") he attributes to Adam; but the Bible ascribes it to Eve and does not tell us that she *said* anything (Gen 3:6). To stress the importance of God's word, Sproul makes Jesus answer Satan, "There is nothing I would like better than a piece of bread. . . . you've forgotten that it is my duty to live by every word that proceeds from the mouth of God." But do we really know how much Jesus wanted a piece of bread? And had Satan actually forgotten Jesus' duty? Yet again, Sproul makes Satan refer to Jesus' passion ("your humiliation . . . the *via dolorosa*"). The biblical text offers no such reference; and we might question whether Satan did, in fact, know so much at the time of Jesus' temptation. Whatever the answer, Sproul is certainly backdating the theology of the cross in a haggadic, midrashic fashion. To make the temptation yet more beguiling, he adds "ever so slightly" to Satan's inviting Jesus to "genuflect"—a clear contradiction of the biblical text, which speaks of "falling down" in the posture of "worship" (προσκυνέω, "prostrate oneself," hardly a slight bending of the knees). Not satisfied, however, Sproul goes so far as to limit Satan's temptation to "*one* knee, that's all" (italics added) and attributes to him foreknowledge of Jesus' Sermon on the Mount. And so on and on. But the pinnacle is reached when, in the midst of his own extensive midrash, Sproul rules the possibility of midrash out of the Bible by putting "*midrashic* tradition and the like" on Satan's lips as part of the temptation of Jesus.

Well, if midrash is devilish, is satanically antithetical to divine truth, why do we all, Sproul included, practice the technique? Not because we devalue the Bible or disregard historical truth in it (in fact, those who hold the Bible in highest regard and insist on full historicity are usually those who practice the technique with the most abandon). On the contrary, we do so out of deep conviction that the Bible should speak to us today even at some cost to historical accuracy! Are we to deny Matthew the privilege of speaking to people of his day in a way we relish using (and our audiences relish hearing and reading)? Our lack of divine inspiration hardly excuses a looser standard than we find in Matthew; if anything, it would demand a stricter standard for us. But we are following normal procedure, accepted and well understood as not designed to be taken as strictly historical or strictly exegetical; and in this respect it hardly falls behind Matthew's procedure, which looks positively restrained alongside the nearly contemporary 1QapGen. Nor, to take a different example from the NT era, does it fall behind what we find in *Jub.* 3:15-29. There, the author follows his legalistic bent by importing into the story of the Fall "the first week of the first jubilee"; making Eve cover her shame with fig leaves *before* she gives the forbidden fruit to Adam; omitting God's search for Adam and Eve and the conversation after he has found them; going immediately to the curse, which highlights the broken commandment; and having Adam offer an incense offering immediately after expulsion from the garden. Given correct theology, the normality of such procedure means that Sproul should not be faulted for his haggadic, midrashic flourishes (except at the point where he implicitly denies their legitimacy); nor should Matthew.

It does not necessarily matter whether an author or speaker announces the genre he is using. Stone does, but Sproul does not, nor did ancient midrashists (or, for that matter, Stone in another biographical novel, *Clarence Darrow for the Defense*). Sometimes Jesus announced he was telling a parable, sometimes he left it to be inferred. Usually we leave aside the formality of such announcements and let our audience recognize genre from the style and contents of what we say vis-à-vis shared knowledge and traditions of communication (cf. Hirsch, *Validity in Interpretation* 78-102, 262-64). The charge of deception will not stick unless there is a deliberate attempt to lead astray through oversubtle use of a genre or unless an honest use is so clumsy that it results in undesigned misunderstanding.

It might be argued that biblical clarity demands that Matthew identify the unhistorical elements in his gospel. But the argument presumes it was always important for a biblical writer to distinguish between history and nonhistory. This presumption betrays a modern preoccupation with historical-critical concerns. Whether the distinction was always important to make is one of the points in question. If it was not always important, if the all-or-nothing approach to biblical history is misguided, if there is enough solid history to tolerate the interjection of unhistorical elements, failure to identify the latter does not mean the Bible is unclear. Clarity has to be measured according to the message the author is trying to get across, not according to what we want him to say, which would vary from one person to another.

The use of the OT in the NT should have prepared us for some inspired license in the use of dominical materials. Matthew converts historical statements about the Exodus and the Babylonian Exile into messianic prophecies (Hos 11:1; Jer 31:15; cf. Matt 2:15, 18) and negates what Micah affirmed about the smallness of Bethlehem (Mic 5:1; cf. Matt 2:16, which shows signs of Matthew's assimilation to the context of his gospel, as opposed to a verbatim report of the chief priests' and scribes' quotation of Mic 5:1). Paul uses statements concerning the restoration of Israel, who had been God's people, for the calling of Gentiles, who had never been God's people (Rom 9:25-26; cf. Hos 2:1[1:10]; 2:25[2:23]). Many similar examples could be cited. If NT writers go so far in the transformation of OT texts, what is there to keep us from accepting Matthew's shifting the meaning of Jesus' words and altering the particulars of Jesus' deeds? The Chronicler's treatment of the tradition in Samuel-Kings provides a canonical prototype of this practice; indeed, it represents the beginnings of midrashic and haggadic style.

One evangelist may disagree with another, then, both at the level of reporting and in the interpretation of an event or a saying. But so long as we understand that Matthew is neither making a historical mistake nor trying to correct the tradition, it need not damage scriptural authority to admit, say, that the lost sheep represents an unbeliever in Luke 15:1-7 but a backslider in Matt 18:12-14 (an interpretative difference) or that Matt 21:18-22 disagrees with Mark 11:12-25 concerning the day the fig tree was seen to be withered (a factual difference). In such places Matthew is not writing as a historian; he is writing as a midrashist and haggadist who bends and shapes his materials to make certain points.

We must remind ourselves that taking Matthew's intent to be solely historical is as much a critical judgment (conscious or unconscious) as taking it to be a mixture of the historical and unhistorical. Both positions require justification. It is not as though the solely historical may be assumed true unless proved false. The question is, which position has the better justification? The textual phenomena argue strongly for a mixture.

That we have only lately recovered the dichromatic intent of Matthew is due to the modernity of historical criticism. Neither oversubtlety nor clumsiness on his part has deceived people into thinking he wrote simply as a historian. Their lack of acquaintance with midrash and haggadah has done so (though we may doubt his theological purposes suffered very much damage from the misunderstanding). Ever since people began to read the Bible with historical-critical sensitivity, however, the difficulty of taking all the gospels as history has been felt keenly and increasingly. The early church saw differences among the gospels (see H. Merkel, *Die Widersprüche zwischen den Evangelien. Ihre polemische und apologetische Behandlung in der Alten Kirche bis zu Augustin* [Tübingen: Mohr, 1971]; H. K. McArthur, *The Quest Through the Centuries* [Philadelphia: Fortress, 1966] 11-13). But these differences were treated as isolated problems of harmonization. Not till the advent of historical criticism in the last two hundred years or so has it become clear that the differences often fall into tendentious patterns.

Apart from what they regarded as isolated problems of harmonization, earlier generations of Christians did not have the question of historicity on their minds. Therefore their unthinking presumptions hardly call in question the tendentious patterns—and with them the not-entirely-historical intent—that were lost sight of early. These patterns surface only when historical-critical questions are asked, just as many other features of Scripture come into view only in response to appropriate questions. It was not so long ago, for example, that the poetic form of most OT prophetic literature was recognized. Yet no one argues against its poetic form from the recency of this recognition. Earlier unawareness was not due to obscurity in the text, but to a cultural shift (the de-Semitizing of Christianity) and subsequent failure to ask questions that would have recovered what was obvious in the text. The Song of Solomon gives another canonical example of centuries of misunderstanding. Yet few scholars even among conservative evangelicals would go back to the allegorical interpretation even though not doing so implies that nearly everybody was wrong for two thousand years. Inside and outside the Bible we often fail to see the obvious till someone points it out.

Papias's elder referred to Matthew's Hebrew style (see pp. 619-20). This reference may show an early awareness of midrashic and haggadic characteristics in the first gospel. Apart from this evidence, a tunnel period intervenes between Matthew and early Christian literature containing the kinds of references that enable us to know how Matthew was understood. By the end of the period—nearly a hundred years later when Justin Martyr called the gospels "memoirs" (1 Apol. 66)—Christians had long since cut loose from the synagogue, where midrash and haggadah were at home (cf. the Benediction against Heretics, inserted into the liturgy of the synagogue ca. A.D. 85 and effectively keeping Jewish Christians from worshiping in synagogues); and the church consisted largely of Gentile believers. We should not expect such Christians to have recognized or appreciated these Jewish features, then; and their failure to do so means nothing so far as Matthew's intent is concerned. They sharply distinguished their beliefs from pagan mythology, of course; but we should not see in that distinction even an implicit denial of midrash and haggadah, for midrash and haggadah were designed to enliven and contemporize historical and scriptural traditions, not to impugn their trustworthiness.

But did Matthew's original audience understand his intent? We must first say that Matthew's intent, not the impression left on the mind of readers, remains the center of gravity even for the first century. Knowing how the original audience took Matthew would aid, but not determine, our understanding of authorial intent; other considerations, in particular the phenomena of the text itself and the literary conventions of the time and place, would still carry more weight. Nonetheless, the presumption is that Matthew's original audience did understand his intent. Saying so does not necessarily imply they made careful comparisons between Matthew's gospel and Mark and Q in the manner of a modern redaction critic. They may have done so, but they did not have to. Matthew's emphases are evident without such comparisons. Redactional analysis merely helps us see these emphases; and we need help because of centuries-long melding of the gospels in sermons, liturgies, hymns, harmonies, and even in their being grouped together in the NT. Matthew's first readers did not work under this handicap.

But were they able not only to recognize Matthew's emphases, but also to distinguish the historical and the unhistorical in his gospel? If so, how? If not, did he not deceive them—either consciously (because he wanted to make points lacking the support of the historical Jesus) or unconsciously (because he overestimated his readers' powers of perception and his own powers of communication)? At least in their implications these questions are probably anachronistic. They seem to read back current historical-critical demands into the minds of a first-century author and his readers. What if Matthew's readers were no more insistent on unmixed history than he was? No deception, conscious or unconscious, would attach to his mixture. Since his readers were first-century Jews who were used to midrash and haggadah, the burden of proof rests on those who would argue that if Matthew wrote midrashically and haggadically he deceived his readers by not measuring up to their historical expectations.

Though the possibility is not at all necessary to save Matthew from the charge of deception, early Christians may well have been able to compare his gospel with the tradition, may actually have done so, and thus may have distinguished clearly between history and embroidery. Surely they knew the traditions about Jesus at least in their oral form, perhaps also in written forms such as those Luke refers to in his prologue (Luke 1:1-4). It is even realistic to suppose that among the latter were Mark and so-called Q. After all, if these written traditions were available to Matthew for use in his gospel, the likelihood is they were known also to the Christians around him. Private copies were doubtless scarce, but if the Bereans were able to compare Paul's message with the OT "daily" (Acts 17:11), there is no reason to think Matthew's readers were unable to compare his gospel with his sources. They would have recognized many of its distinctive features as embroidery. When writing, he would have known they were going to recognize them as such. There would have been no intent to deceive, probably not even a chance of deception.

We may compare the Chronicler's treatment of the traditions in Samuel-Kings. For example, he gives us not only the David and Solomon of history, but also the messianic king of his expectation—victorious, receiving tribute from the nations and the universal, total, and instantaneous support of God's people, and nearly faultless (the sin with Bathsheba is passed over and the census is blamed on Satan, so that David's guilt is secondary; and Solomon is similarly idealized). The Chronicler is hardly trying to pull the wool over anyone's eyes, for he often relies on his readers' knowledge of the earlier accounts. So it seems with Matthew.

We are not to "second-guess" Matthew, i.e., to point to subsequent misunderstandings as evidence that midrashic and haggadic style cannot have characterized the first gospel without calling in question the foresight of the apostle and the Spirit who inspired him. How many other parts of the Bible, too, have suffered misunderstanding—sometimes widely and long! We can be sure that whatever literary genres might have gone into the Bible, people somewhere, sometime would have misunderstood them. Our task is not to criticize, but to understand the modes of communication used in Scripture, correct ourselves where we have erred, and develop appreciation of those modes unfamiliar to our usual ways of understanding it (though, ironically, we may already have some appreciation of those modes, or like ones, outside Scripture).

Appeal to different intentions among the evangelists puts us in a better position to maintain the unity of the NT. For now what we would have to call a discrepancy under the presumption that Matthew always wrote historically can be explained literarily. Another evangelist may intend to pass on a piece of theologically significant history; Matthew may intend to play with that history for the sake of an unhistorical theological point. Whether historical or unhistorical, the theological points may have a unity that surmounts any difference in other respects. For example, the reclaiming of a backslider (so Matthew's presentation of the parable of the lost sheep) complements the conversion of an unbeliever (so Luke's and doubtless Jesus' presentation of the same parable).

It may seem paradoxical at first, but apostolic authorship of Matthew and midrashic and haggadic style go well together. This assertion not only means that just as Plato put his own thoughts into Socrates' mouth in the later *Dialogues* even though he was an immediate disciple of Socrates and wrote during the lifetime of others who had known him, so also the Apostle Matthew put his thoughts into Jesus' life and teaching even though he was an immediate disciple and wrote during the lifetime of others who had known him (cf. pp. 621-22). What is more, there is a certain theological advantage in combining apostolic authorship with midrashic and haggadic style. Some have thought that ancient midrashists and haggadists embroidered the biblical tradition because they thought, for one reason or another, "This is the way it must have happened." Most of the time they were mistaken in thinking so. Now we might question whether ancient midrashists and haggadists really were self-deceived. Did they take liberties under a delusion or, like modern preachers, quite deliberately? The Apostle Matthew accompanied Jesus and knew that things did not always happen as he described them. So unless we attribute to him an unusually poor memory or an attempt to deceive his readers concerning historical actualities—and neither of these is likely in view of his writing when others could easily have falsified his presentation—he did not write under a delusion when he wrote midrashically and haggadically. He would no more have denied the historicity of the data behind his embellishments than Sproul would deny the historicity of the biblical stories he changes around for homiletical reasons. The same thing, of course, might easily be said of a subapostolic evangelist.

Are we then providing for the Christian faith a haven secure in the principle of authorial intent from every threat of historical criticism? The appeal to authorial intent does pose the danger of theological romanticism. Theoretically, we might conclude upon a literary study of the Bible that the writing of history formed no part of authorial intent and remain ourselves fully committed to biblical inspiration. This possibility does not imply that we have gone astray in appealing to authorial intent, however; it simply means that Christianity needs more planks in its platform than the doctrine of verbal plenary inspiration. Historical matters of Christology and soteriology and a good deal else must help make up the platform.

The danger of theological romanticism also leads to questions of definition. If Matthew's gospel contains midrash and haggadah, what does it mean to call it inspired, authoritative, infallible, inerrant? If we protect the Bible by regarding historical difficulties as inspired midrash and haggadah rather than as errors, does not inspiration fail to guarantee historicity? Does not inspiration lose its value? By itself, inspiration does fail to guarantee historicity. But we have taken nothing from the doctrine of inspiration. We have only revised our understanding of what certain passages in the Bible were meant to say. What does inspiration mean for a passage of biblical poetry, a parable, an exhortation? How could the message of such biblical materials be falsified? Certainly not by the historical-critical method, for they were not written as history. Likewise, Matthew's midrash and haggadah were inspired as such, not as history, so that historical-critical recognition of their unhistoricity takes nothing away from what they were intended to be.

But our line of questioning has not reached its end. What would count for an error if an apparent one can always be attributed to midrashic and haggadic style? First, it needs to be stressed again that we do not call Matthew midrashic and haggadic merely because problems of harmonization crop up here and there—to do so would be too convenient—but because free revisions and additions pervade the gospel and fall into tendentious patterns. More fundamentally, since by definition midrash and haggadah include unhistorical embroidery, their message—like that of biblical poetry, parables, exhortations, and theological statements the truth of which is not contingent on a historical incident ("God is spirit," "To obey is better than sacrifice," etc.)—could be falsified only by means different from historical criticism. Let us say that Matthew designs a piece of midrash or haggadah to make the point that Christian discipleship requires knowing the mysteries of the kingdom. That point must be consistent with what Matthew says elsewhere in his gospel and with what is said elsewhere in the Bible. If elsewhere it is denied that knowing the mysteries is requisite to discipleship, one or the other statement is wrong and a high view of inspiration crashes down. But in and of itself the question whether midrash and haggadah are to be found in Matthew is a question of hermeneutics, not a question of biblical authority.

Classifying elements of Matthew as midrash and haggadah narrows the historical base of Christian faith, but not nearly so much that the Christian faith is threatened with collapse. That historical base extends throughout the NT; and even though some other parts of the NT were found to be midrashic and haggadic, too, we should not be so nervous as to think that everything has to be historical else all is lost. Such thinking would be like "building a fence around the law," i.e., like adding regulations to avoid even coming close to breaking the law. As we all know, however, playing safe has as many perils as being careless. This truism applies to historical judgments as much as to moral legislation.

How much in the text of the gospels conforms to modern canons of history writing and how much does not will remain a matter of dispute. We will have to live with ambiguities, and these ambiguities will help leave room for the persuasive work of the Holy Spirit, without which no true faith is born. Nevertheless, the necessity of discovering and rediscovering the historical foundations of the Christian faith remains, for historic Christianity demands a genuinely historical base with respect to the events out of which grew the major tenets of the faith (see Luke 1:1-4; John 1:14; 2 Pet 1:16-18; 1 John 1:1-3). If our assessments of authorial intent do not measure up to that demand, we are in theological trouble. Had midrash and haggadah so reduced the historical element that neither in Matthew nor elsewhere could we feel confident of adequate knowledge concerning the historical Jesus, our faith would lack historical grounding. For this reason alarms need to be sounded in docetic quarters of Christendom. Thankfully, reasons too numerous to detail here save us from such uncertainty. Therefore we can fearlessly appreciate the positive contributions made by Matthew even in those parts of his work where he takes liberties with historical data. See F. F. Bruce, *The New Testament Documents: Are They Reliable?* (5th ed.; Grand Rapids: Eerdmans, 1960); Gundry, *Use of the OT* 189-93; idem, "Recent Investigations" 97-114; H. Riesenfeld in *Studien zum Neuen Testament und seiner Umwelt* (ed. A. Fuchs; Linz: A. Fuchs, 1976) 9-25; I. H. Marshall, *I Believe in the Historical Jesus* (Grand Rapids: Eerdmans, 1977); and B. Gerhardsson, *The Origins of the Gospel Traditions* (Philadelphia: Fortress, 1979) for representative arguments favoring historicity.

At this point a caveat needs to be issued. What the biblical authors intended to say should exercise a magisterial role over our interpretation of the Christian faith. It would be dishonest to use their literary habits as critical tools for ridding the Scripture of items unpalatable to our tastes or supposedly unacceptable to "modern man." Therefore, though disagreements over the originally intended meaning of the biblical text merit exegetical discussion, rejection of that meaning calls for theological warfare. Otherwise we stand in danger of losing the faith altogether. (That it does not deserve to be lost is properly discussed by the Christian apologist.)

How then should we go about discovering what biblical authors intended to say? Just as in the study of other literature, our demands of the text ought to vary according to the diverse intentions evident in its several parts. We require logic of a textbook in philosophy, accuracy and editorial responsibility in a book of history, and so on. But we do not demand scientific precision in a fairy tale or prosaic accuracy in poetry. We do not even demand that a historical novel be entirely historical. The most ardent proponents of biblical infallibility and inerrancy recognize parables as unhistorical and proverbs as sententious sayings each containing a truth but not necessarily the whole truth (for taken as exceptionless statements they would often contradict each other as well as observable facts). Our identification of the kind of literature an author intended to write governs the criteria by which we judge the truthfulness as well as the meaning of his work.

Furthermore, our identification of the kind of literature an author intended to write should depend on the data of his text studied in their historical setting. Of course, we cannot approach the data or their historical setting without some presumptions. But our presumptions need to be held with a tentativeness that keeps them subject to correction from otherwise awkward data, just as the data need interpretation according to presumptions. In this way alone can we avoid the pitfalls of hermeneutical solipsism on the one side and of mere chronicling on the other (cf. R. S. Crane, *The Languages of Criticism and the Structure of Poetry* [Toronto: University of Toronto, 1953] 174-80).

The historical setting of a biblical book includes materials outside the Bible as well as other books within the Bible. To try forestalling a correlation between Matthew and extrabiblical midrash and haggadah by denying the legitimacy of extrabiblical comparisons, then, is unacceptable. After all, the Bible exists in the form of human languages. And our understanding of those languages depends partly on comparisons with extrabiblical materials in those same and cognate languages. How else do we know the meanings of words and grammatical constructions (micro-grammar)? Similarly, our understanding of literary genres within the Bible is enriched and refined through comparison with literary genres outside the Bible (macro-grammar). The Bible was not given in a hermetically sealed capsule.

Apart from the doctrine of inspiration, it will not do to deduce an unhistorical intent on the part of a biblical author just because his text looks unhistorical; for he might be making mistakes despite his intent to write history. The freedom with which an author treats materials available to him and the measurement of this freedom by the literary conventions of the time must enter our determinations of his intent. The first gospel repeatedly offers data leading to the conclusion that to make certain didactic and hortatory points Matthew edited historical traditions in unhistorical ways and in accord with midrashic and haggadic practices to which he and his first readers were accustomed. Because he intended not only to pass on historical information but also to elaborate on its significance by embellishing it, the judgment "unhistorical" concerning this or that element in his gospel ought not to carry negative overtones.

In sum, if we do not enlarge the room given to differences of literary genre and, consequently, of intended meaning, scriptural inspiration, authority, infallibility, or inerrancy—call it what we will—cannot survive the "close reading" of the biblical text now going on. The old method of harmonizing what we can and holding the rest in suspension has seen its day, like worn-out scientific theories that no longer explain newly discovered phenomena well enough. In Matthew we have a document that does not match even a selective report of Jesus' words and deeds. Comparison with the other gospels, especially with Mark and Luke, and examination of Matthew's style and theology show that he materially altered and embellished historical traditions and that he did so deliberately and often. To admit this does not undermine a high view of Scripture so long as we properly measure the first gospel according to authorial intent. Matthew's intent was to tell the story of Jesus with alterations and embellishments suited to the needs of the church and the world at the time the gospel was written. We would feel uneasy to learn that he edited his materials so freely that they are historically unrecognizable. And continuing freedom to edit in his manner would lead to the wild growth of the apocryphal gospels and all kinds of open-ended speculation. But the canonizing of those writings that come from Matthew and his NT cohorts implies the sufficiency of Scripture, blocks the way to further editing of the materials in any authoritative manner, and makes the postapostolic task of Christian theology expository and applicative rather than creative. It takes only a comparison of Matthew with the other gospels to discover that even where Matthew spins out the tradition he is developing dominical motifs. The verbal plenary inspiration of Scripture implies the full authority of his editing, whatever the liberties he took, just as the closing of the canon blocked authoritative editing subsequent to the NT. We are not to think, in other words, that materials attributable to Jesus himself possess more authority than materials attributable to Matthew. The Spirit of Christ directed the editing, so that its results, along with the historical data, constitute God's Word. This view enables us to take the phenomena of the scriptural text more seriously. To do less is to undermine the authority of the Bible unwittingly—and despite the best of intentions to support it.

Editorial transformations in Scripture imply that systematic theologians should concern themselves with variety as well as with commonality in the expression of the Christian faith, that they should use the variety in Scripture to guide and guard, prompt and limit their own contemporary expressions, and that they should pay close attention to the historical circumstances which evoked various scriptural expressions in order to determine what sorts of expressions are appropriate to present historical circumstances. All Scripture is God's Word and God's Word is entirely true, but not all of it is equally applicable all the time and every place. Only by building theological systems can we speak effectively in a given setting. Only by reminding ourselves that the theological systems we build are no less historically conditioned than the Scripture on which they rest do we avoid the error of canonizing them as though they consisted of timeless truth abstracted from Scripture.

Indexes

GREEK INDEX

For discussion of the following word-statistics, see the very first section of this commentary. Below, the first figure represents the number of Matthean insertions in paralleled material, the second the number of occurrences in passages peculiar to Matthew, and the third the number of occurrences shared with one or both of the other two synoptics, Mark and Luke. The figures in parentheses represent, in order, the total numbers of occurrences in Matthew, Mark, and Luke. Note the listing of special forms as well as initial lexical forms.

ἄγγελος 4,9,7(20,6,25)
  ἄγγελος κυρίου 2(including an anaphoric reference in 28:5),
    4,0(6,0,2)
  ἄγγελοι belonging to the Son of
    man 3,1,0(3,0,0)
ἁγιάζω 2,0,1(3,0,1)
ἅγιος 4,4,2(10,7,20)
  ἅγιον πνεῦμα/πνεῦμα
    ἅγιον 0,3,2(5,4,13)
ἀγοράζω 0,5,2(7,5,5)
ἀγρός 3,10,4(17,9,9)
ἀδελφός 11,8,20(39,20,24)
ἀδικέω. See διχ-.
ἄδικος. See διχ-.
αἷμα 4,3,4(11,3,8)
αἴρω 2,3,14(19,20,20)
  See also συναίρω.
αἰτέω 2,1,11(14,9,11)
αἰων- 2,7,5(14,7,11)
  αἰών 1,4,3(8,4,7)
  αἰώνιος 1,3,2(6,3,4)
ἀκολουθέω 8,0,17(25,18,17)
ἀκούω 26,6,31(63,44,65)
  ἀκούσας/-σαντες 10,3,8(21,10,9)
  See also the comments on 5:21-48

concerning the hearing of authoritative teaching.
ἄλλος 14,4,11(29,22,11)
ἁμαρτία 2,1,4(7,6,11)
ἀμὴν (γὰρ) λέγω ὑμῖν/
  σοι 15,8,8(31,13,6)
  See the comments on 5:18 for a refinement of these statistics. Cf.
    λέγω ὑμῖν/σοι.
ἀμφότεροι 1,1,1(3,0,5)
ἀναβαίνω 2,1,6(9,9,9)
ἀναγινώσκω 3,0,4(7,4,3)
ἀναίτιος 2,0,0(2,0,0)
ἀνάκειμαι 4,0,1(5,2,2)
ἀνατέλλω 2,0,1(3,2,1)
ἀνατολή 1,3,1(5,0,2)
ἀναχωρέω 4,5,1(10,1,0)
ἀνήρ 4,2,2(8,4,27)
ἄνθρωπος 35,17,61(113,56,95)
ἀνοίγω 5,2,4(11,1,7)
ἀνομία 3,1,0(4,0,0)
  See also νόμος.
ἄξιος 7,0,2(9,0,8)
ἀπαγγέλλω 3,2,3(8,5,11)
ἀπ' ἄρτι 3,0,0(3,0,0)
ἀπέρχομαι 14,11,10(35,23,19)

641

δεῦτε   2,2,2(6,3,0)
δέχομαι   7,0,3(10,6,16)
δηνάριον   0,5,1(6,3,3)
δια- (compounds occurring in Matthew alone)   6,6,0(12,0,0)
  διακωλύω   1,0,0(1,0,0)
  διαλλάσσομαι   1,0,0(1,0,0)
  διασαφέω   0,2,0(2,0,0)
  δίδραχμον   0,2,0(2,0,0)
  διετής   0,1,0(1,0,0)
  διπλόος   1,0,0(1,0,0)
  διστάζω   1,1,0(2,0,0)
  διϋλίζω   1,0,0(1,0,0)
  διχάζω   1,0,0(1,0,0)
διάβολος   1,2,3(6,0,5)
διακονέω   0,1,5(6,5,8)
διακρίνω. See κρι-.
διαλογιζ-   0,0,4(4,8,12)
  διαλογίζομαι   0,0,3(3,7,6)
  διαλογισμός   0,0,1(1,1,6)
διὰ τί   3,0,4(7,3,5)
διὰ τοῦτο   4,2,4(10,3,4)
διδασκ-/διδαχ-   9,4,16(29,34,35)
  διδάσκαλος   4,1,7(12,12,17)
  διδάσκω   3,3,8(14,17,17)
  διδαχή   2,0,1(3,5,1)
δίδωμι   8-9,10,38-37(56,39,60)
δικ-   18-19,10-9,2(30,2,22)
  ἀδικέω   0,1,0(1,0,1)
  ἄδικος   1,0,0(1,0,4)
  δίκαιος   9-10,7-6,1(17,2,11)
  δικαιοσύνη   5,2,0(7,0,1)
  δικαιόω   1,0,1(2,0,5)
  καταδικάζω   2,0,0(2,0,1)
διώκω   5,0,1(6,0,3)
δοκέω   6,3,1(10,2,10)
δοξ-   3,3,5(11,4,22)
  δόξα   1,2,4(7,3,13)
  δοξάζω   2,1,1(4,1,9)
δοῦλος   8,7,15(30,5,26)
δύναμαι   13,0,14(27,33,26)
δύναμις   4,0,8(12,10,15)
  δυνάμεις, "miracles"   3,0,4(7,2,2)
δύο   19,4,17(40,19,28)
δώδεκα   3,1,9(13,15,12)
  δώδεκα μαθηταί   1-3,1,0(2-4,0,0)
δῶρον   7,1,1(9,1,2)

ἐάν   28,3,26(67,35,29)
  ἐὰν μή   7,1,2(10,6,3)
  ἐὰν/εἰ οὖν   4,0,0(4,0,0)
ἐγγίζω   4,0,3(7,3,18)

ἐγείρω   11,8,17(36,19,18)
  ἐγερθείς   2-3,5,1(8-9,0,1)
ἐγώ   12-13,3,14-13(29,16,22)
  Cf. κἀγώ.
ἐγὼ δὲ λέγω ὑμῖν   6,0,0(6,0,0)
  The synoptics also have this expression once each with οὐδέ in place of δέ, and Luke has it once again with καί in place of δέ.
ἐθνικός   3,0,0(3,0,0)
ἔθνος   7,2,6(15,6,13)
  See also πάντα τὰ ἔθνη, and "Universality" in the Topical Index.
εἰ (apart from εἰ μή, εἰ οὐ, εἴπερ, and εἴ τις)   18,1,23(42,13,31)
εἴρω   18,9,3(30,2,19)
εἷς, μία, ἕν   24,7,34(65,37,44)
εἰσέρχομαι τὴν
  βασιλείαν   5,0,2(7,5,2)
  All Matthew's insertions are accompanied by a negative; Mark and Luke each have only one negative expression.
εἰς τό + an infinitive   3,0,0(3,1,1)
εἰς (τὸ) ὄνομα. See ὄνομα.
εἰς τὸ σκότος τὸ
  ἐξώτερον   3,0,0(3,0,0)
ἕκαστος   2,1,1(4,1,5)
ἐκβάλλω   10,1,17(28,18,20)
  ἐκβάλλω + references to demons, spirits, and Satan   4,0,9(13,10,9)
ἐκεῖ   16,6,6(28,11,16)
ἐκεῖθεν   8,1,3(12,5,3)
ἐκείνη ὥρα   6,0,1(7,1,1)
ἐκεῖνος   26,9,19(54,23,33)
ἐκκλησία   3,0,0(3,0,0)
ἐκτείνας τὴν χεῖρα   3,0,1(4,1,1)
ἐλάχιστος   2,3,0(5,0,4)
ἐλεε-   7,5,3(15,3,12)
  ἐλεέω   3,2,3(8,3,4)
  ἐλεημοσύνη   0,3,0(3,0,2)
  ἐλεήμων   1,0,0(1,0,0)
  ἔλεος   3,0,0(3,0,6)
ἐλθών/-όντες (and other genders of the nominative participle, used circumstantially)   10,10,8(28,16,12)
ἐμός   1,2,2(5,2,3)
ἐμπαίζω   1,1,3(5,3,5)
ἔμπροσθεν   9,4,5(18,2,10)
  ἔμπροσθεν τῶν
    ἀνθρώπων   3,1,1(5,0,1)
ἔνδυμα   6,0,1(7,0,1)

643

ἐν ἑαυτοῖς 4,0,2(6,4,2)
ἐν ἐκείνη τῇ ὥρα/ἐν τῇ ὥρα
  ἐκείνη 3,0,1(4,1,1)
ἐνθυμε- 3,1,0(4,0,0)
  ἐνθυμέομαι 1,1,0(2,0,0)
  ἐνθύμησις 2,0,0(2,0,0)
ἐντέλλομαι 1,1,2(4,2,1)
ἐξαιρέω 2,0,0(2,0,0)
ἐξέρχομαι in the nominative
  participle 10,4,4(18,9,11)
ἔξεστι 1,2,6(9,6,5)
ἐξετάζω 1,1,0(2,0,0)
ἐξουσία 1,1,8(10,10,16)
ἔξω 3,1,5(9,10,9)
ἐπάνω 7,1,0(8,1,5)
ἐπεί 1,2,0(3,1,1)
ἐπερωτάω 3,0,5(8,25,17)
ἐπιγινώσκω 5,0,1(6,4,7)
ἐπιδείκνυμι 3,0,0(3,0,1)
ἐπὶ (τῆς) γῆς 8,2,1(11,10,5)
ἐπιτίθημι 5,0,2(7,8,5)
ἐργ- 6,7,6(19,3,8)
  ἀργός 1,2,0(3,0,0)
  ἐργάζομαι 1,1,2(4,1,1)
  ἐργασία 0,0,0(0,0,1)
  ἐργάτης 0,3,3(6,0,4)
  ἔργον 4,1,1(6,2,2)
ἔρχομαι 31,19,60(110,86,100)
ἔσται 16,5,16(37,7,33)
ἔσχατος 0,6,4(10,5,6)
ἔσωθεν 3,0,1(4,2,3)
ἑταῖρος 2,1,0(3,0,0)
ἕτερος 5,1,3(9,1,33)
ἔτι 4,2,2(8,5,16)
(ἔτι) αὐτοῦ λαλοῦντος. See λαλέω.
εὐαγγέλιον τῆς
  βασιλείας 3,0,0(3,0,0)
εὐθέως 11(including seven substitutions for εὐθύς),0,0(11,0,6)
εὐθύς (adverb) 0,0,7(7,42,1)
εὑρίσκω 7,8,12(27,11,45)
εὐώνυμος 1,2,2(5,2,0)
ἐχθρός 2,3,2(7,1,8)
ἔχω χρείαν 3,0,3(6,4,6)
ἕως 13,14,21(48,15,28)
  ἕως as a
    conjunction 6,5,9(20,5,15)
  ἕως as a
    preposition 7,9,12(28,10,13)
  ἕως οὗ/ὅτου 4,2,1(7,0,7)

ζητέω 2,3,9(14,10,25)

ἤ 32,12,16(60,33,45)
ἡγεμών 7,2,1(10,1,2)
ἤδη 3,0,4(7,8,10)
ἥκω 2,0,2(4,0,5)
ἡμέρα 15,9,21(45,27,83)
  ἡμέρα κρίσεως 4,0,0(4,0,0)
Ἠσαΐας 5,0,1(6,2,2)

θάλασσα 3,2,11(16,19,3)
θαυμάζω 2,0,5(7,4,12)
θεάομαι 2,1,1(4,0,3)
θελ- 21,9,18(48,25,32)
  θέλημα 3,1,2(6,1,4)
  θέλω 18,8,16(42,24,28)
    θέλω with εἰ
    preceding 5,0,1(6,2,1)
θεραπεύω 10,0,6(16,5,14)
θεριζ- 0,5,6(11,1,6)
  θερίζω 0,0,3(3,0,3)
  θερισμός 0,3,3(6,1,3)
  θεριστής 0,2,0(2,0,0)
θησαυρ- 3,4,4(11,1,5)
  θησαυρίζω 2,0,0(2,0,1)
  θησαυρός 1,4,4(9,1,4)
θρόνος 2,2,1(5,0,3)
θυσιαστήριον 5,0,1(6,0,2)

ἴδε 4,0,0(4,9,0)
ἴδιος 6,0,4(10,8,6)
ἰδού 34,9,19(62,7,57)
ἰδών/-όντες (nominative
  participle) 10-11,7,8(25-26,18-20,
  31-32)
  ἰδὼν ὄχλον/τοὺς
  ὄχλους 3,0,0(3,0,0)
ἱερόν, "Temple" 5,0,6(11,9,14)
Ἱεροσόλυμα 2,2,7(11,10,4)
Ἱερουσαλήμ 0,0,2(2,0,27)
Ἰησοῦς 80,12,58(150,81,89)
ἴσθι 1,1,0(2,1,1)
Ἰσραήλ 5,4,3(12,2,12)
ἵστημι 4,6,11(21,9,26)
ἰσχύω 1,0,3(4,4,8)

κἀγώ 5,3,1(9,0,6)
  See also ἐγώ.
καθαρ- 4,0,6(10,5,10)
  καθαρίζω 2,0,5(7,4,7)
  καθαρισμός 0,0,0(0,1,2)
  καθαρός 2,0,1(3,0,1)
κάθημαι 8,0,11(19,11,13)
καθίζω 3,2,3(8,8,7)

TOPICAL INDEX

INDEX OF MODERN AUTHORS